FEDERAL INCOME TAXATION OF CORPORATIONS AND SHAREHOLDERS

SEVENTH EDITION

JAMES S. EUSTICE

Gerald L. Wallace Professor of Taxation, New York University

2007 CUMULATIVE SUPPLEMENT
TO STUDENT EDITION

D1551202

WARREN, GORHAM & LAMONT
OF RIA

This publication is designed to provide accurate and authoritative information
in regard to the subject matter covered. It is sold with the understanding that
neither the author(s) nor the publisher is engaged in rendering legal, accounting, or other professional service. If legal advice or other expert assistance is
required, the services of a competent professional should be sought.

In response to IRS Circular 230 requirements, Thomson-RIA advises that any
discussions of federal tax issues in its publications and products, or in third-
party publications and products on its platforms, are not intended to be used
and may not in fact be used to avoid any penalties under the Internal Revenue Code, or to promote, market, or recommend any transaction or subject
addressed therein.

FEDERAL INCOME TAXATION OF CORPORATIONS AND SHAREHOLDERS

SEVENTH EDITION

Revised Chapter 5 (replacing Chapter 5 in the main
volume of the student edition)

2007 ABRIDGED EDITION
FOR STUDENT USE ONLY

WARREN, GORHAM & LAMONT
OF RIA

How to Use
This Student Edition

Chapter 5 of *Federal Income Taxation of Corporations and Shareholders*, Seventh Edition, has been completely revised and is included in this student supplement in its entirety, printed on gray pages. Chapter 5 in the main volume of your student edition is out of date and should no longer be consulted.

The supplement begins on the white pages that follow the revised Chapter 5.

CHAPTER **5**

The Corporation Income Tax

¶ 5.01 CORPORATE TAX RATES

[1] In General

Section 11(b) levies an income tax on a corporation's taxable income at the following rates, effective for taxable years beginning on or after January 1, 1993:

Taxable Income	Rate
Up to $50,000	15%
Over $50,000 but not over $75,000	25
Over $75,000 but not over $10,000,000	34
Over $10,000,000	35

The rate advantages of the first two brackets, however, are phased out by a surtax of 5 percent (which reaches a maximum of $11,750) on taxable income between $100,000 and $335,000, and the advantage of the 34 percent rate is similarly phased out by a surtax of 3 percent (which reaches a maximum of $100,000) on taxable income between $15,000,000 and $18,333,333.[1] As a re-

---

[1] See IRC § 11(b) (if a corporation's taxable income exceeds $100,000, the amount of tax is increased by the lesser of 5 percent of the excess or $11,750 (5 percent of $235,000); if the corporation's taxable income exceeds $15,000,000, the amount of the tax is increased by the lesser of 3 percent or $100,000 (3 percent of $3,333,333). Thus, § 11(b) now contains a "double bubble."

sult of these phaseouts, the marginal rates rise from 15 percent to 39 percent and then decline to 35 percent, as follows:

Taxable Income	Rate
Up to $50,000	15%
Over $50,000 but not over $75,000	25
Over $75,000 but not over $100,000	34
Over $100,000 but not over $335,000	39
Over $335,000 but not over $10,000,000	34
Over $10,000,000 but not over $15,000,000	35
Over $15,000,000 but not over $18,333,333	38
Over $18,333,333	35

A "qualified personal service corporation," however, is taxed at the flat 35 percent rate on all of its taxable income.[2]

The top corporate rate of 35 percent, like its 34 percent predecessor under the Tax Reform Act of 1986, breaks with tradition in being the lowest top corporate rate in at least fifty years prior to 1987. Unlike the original 1986 Code rate regime, however, the current top corporate rate is lower than the top personal rate (39.6 percent), which for most of the fifty years prior to 1987 had been at least twenty-two, and sometimes as much as forty-nine, percentage points higher than the corporate rate.[3] Of course, the effective rate paid by a corporation on its *economic* income may be substantially less than these nominal rates that are applied to *taxable* income. This divergence led to adoption of the alternative minimum tax (AMT).[4]

A corporation computes its taxable base in much the same manner as any other taxpayer; that is, § 63(a) defines "taxable income" as gross income (under § 61) less the deductions allowed by Chapter 1 of the income tax subtitle of the Internal Revenue Code (the Code). Among the topics discussed in

---

[2] Section 11(b)(2) defines "qualified personal service corporation" by reference to § 448(d)(2), which limits the term to corporations that perform one of eight specific types of services and are substantially owned by employees performing those services or their partnerships or corporations, by retirees, or by heirs. See Regs. § 1.448-1T(e).

[3] For a history of the corporate rates, see Eustice, Kuntz, Lewis & Deering, The Tax Reform Act of 1986: Analysis and Commentary ¶ 2.02 (Warren, Gorham & Lamont 1987). The top individual rate subsequently was lowered to 35 percent by 2003 legislation.

[4] See infra ¶ 5.01[3], 5.08. For computations of the effective tax rates on corporations and discussions of the conceptual difficulties in making such computations, see Bittker, "Effective Tax Rates: Fact or Fancy?" 122 U. Pa. L. Rev. 780 (1974); U.S. Treasury Dep't, Effective Tax Rates Paid by United States Corporations in 1972 (1978); Kaplan, "Effective Corporate Tax Rates," 2 J. Corp. Tax'n 187 (1975); Clowery, Outslay & Wheeler, "The Debate on Computing Corporate Effective Tax Rates—An Accounting View," 30 Tax Notes 991 (1986).

The Securities and Exchange Commission (SEC) indirectly requires reporting corporations to compute their effective rates by requiring a reconciliation between the amount of reported total income tax and the amount computed by multiplying book income before tax by the applicable statutory tax rate. SEC Accounting Reg. SX-4-08.

this chapter are the differences between an individual's gross income and a corporation's gross income; the differences in deductions; certain special deductions and related issues that are unique to the corporate-shareholder relationship; the corporation's method of accounting and taxable-year requirements; the corporate alternative minimum tax; and certain distinctions between large and small corporations.

[2] Corporate Capital Gains

Before 1987, corporations, like individuals, were subject to lower rates on their long-term capital gains; but the Tax Reform Act of 1986 eliminated this rate differential for taxable years beginning on or after July 1, 1987. Section 1201(a), however, provides that if the regular corporate income tax rate ever exceeds 35 percent, then a corporation's net capital gains shall be taxed at 35 percent.[5] While Congress could, of course, raise this firewall if it were to raise the corporate tax rate (a tactic employed in 1993), the existence of § 1201(a) may give at least some comfort to advocates of a capital gain preference.

In keeping with § 1201(a) and the substantial preference for individual capital gains that returned to the Code in 1993,[6] the rest of the statutory framework relating to corporate capital gains and losses remains in the Code.[7] Thus, § 1211(a) continues to restrict the deduction of corporate capital losses to capital gains, § 1212(a) treats corporate capital loss carrybacks and carryovers differently than ordinary operating loss carrybacks and carryovers, and so forth.

---

[5] Section 1201(a) also applies if the rates under § 511, § 831(a), or § 831(b) exceed 35 percent. Cf. US v. Foster Lumber Co., 429 US 32 (1976) (dealing with problems created by the predecessor of this provision when net operating losses were carried back to the year in which the corporation received capital gains).

[6] IRC § 1(h) (28 percent for net capital gains as compared with 39.6 percent for ordinary income, at 1993 rates).

Proposed legislation, HR 1215, would have restored the pre–1986 Tax Reform Act rule of § 1202, allowing a 50 percent deduction for capital gains; this legislation passed as HR 2491, the Revenue Reconciliation Act of 1995, but was vetoed by President Clinton. But the Taxpayer Relief Act of 1997, Pub. L. No. 105-34, 105th Cong., 1st Sess., § 311, restored a significant capital gain rate preference for individuals, though not for corporations. Subsequent legislation (especially in 2003) has lowered the top capital gain rate to 15 percent in § 1(h).

[7] See Conf. Comm. Rep. No. 841, 99th Cong., 2d Sess. II-106 (1986), stating that the current statutory structure for capital gains "is retained in the Code to facilitate reinstatement of a capital gains rate differential if there is a future tax rate increase." This retention was either coldly realistic or prescient.

[3] Alternative Minimum Tax

Section 55 imposes a tentative tax of 20 percent on the corporation's alternative minimum taxable income (AMTI) (computed after a $40,000 exemption and subject to certain other conditions and qualifications), which is payable if and to the extent that it exceeds the corporation's regular tax. The relationship of the alternative minimum tax to the regular corporate income tax and the base on which it is imposed are examined in detail later in this chapter.[8]

[4] Specialized Corporate Taxes

Corporations are subject to various special tax rates, and also to penalty taxes if (1) they accumulate income beyond the reasonable needs of the business in order to avoid shareholder taxes;[9] (2) they are classified as personal holding companies or as foreign personal holding companies;[10] or (3) they are foreign corporations and derive investment income from sources within the United States.[11] The penalty taxes on unreasonable accumulations and personal holding companies are imposed in addition to the regular § 11 tax, although the regular corporate tax reduces the taxable base on which these taxes are computed. The tax imposed on investment income received by foreign corporations, however, is in lieu of the regular § 11 corporate tax.

Section 59A imposes an "environmental tax," also known as the superfund tax, as a surtax on top of the regular corporate tax liability. The tax falls only on relatively profitable large corporations, since it equals 0.12 percent of the excess of "modified alternative minimum taxable income" over $2 million. The tax was scheduled for sunset after 1995, but given the burgeoning number of contaminated sites needing cleanup, this tax could shine on after the sun goes down (the sun set in 1996 and it hasn't risen yet, but a new dawn has been proposed in the Treasury's 1998 and 1999 lists of revenue raisers). Darkness still prevails as of 2005.

---

[8] See infra ¶ 5.08.

[9] IRC § 531, discussed at ¶¶ 7.01–7.09.

[10] See IRC § 541 (personal holding companies), discussed at ¶¶ 7.20–7.24; IRC § 551 (foreign personal holding companies), discussed at ¶ 15.41. But the 2003 tax act lowered the § 531 and § 541 rates to 15 percent (the same as for dividends), and 2004 legislation repealed the foreign personal holding company provisions.

[11] IRC § 881, discussed at ¶ 15.03. For the taxation of foreign corporations engaged in a U.S. trade or business, see IRC §§ 882 and 884, discussed at ¶ 15.04.

[5] Planning Implications of Current Rate Regime

The rate inversion effected by the Tax Reform Act of 1986 (under which the top corporate rate exceeded the top individual rate between 1986 and 1993, contrary to prior custom), coupled with the repeal of the rate differential for long-term capital gains (and the 1997 reinstatement of a significant preference for capital gains of individuals), has had far-reaching planning implications for existing corporations and their shareholders. Foremost among these implications was increased pressure to ameliorate the higher corporate tax by extracting funds from the corporation on a tax-deductible basis, thus exacerbating the thin-capitalization and reasonable compensation issues, as well as problems resulting from the leasing or licensing of property by shareholders to their corporations on non-arm's-length terms for excessive rents or royalties.[12]

Avoidance of the corporate tax altogether by electing subchapter S has been the simplest and most effective escape route, but a subchapter S election is not always available (e.g., because the corporation has outstanding preferred stock, too many shareholders, or impermissible shareholders, such as another corporation, a partnership, or a discretionary trust).[13] If available, however, a subchapter S election eliminates not only the § 11 tax but also the possibility of the accumulated earnings and personal holding company penalty taxes. In addition, S corporations are not subject to the corporate alternative minimum tax, as discussed later in this chapter. Thus, eligible existing corporations that did not make the S election under the special rules applicable through 1988[14] should still seriously consider making the election.

More costly than a subchapter S election would be a conversion of the corporation to a partnership or limited liability company that is taxed as a partnership, since both the liquidating corporation and its shareholders are taxable on any appreciation in their assets or stock.[15] If, however, the corporation's basis for its assets or the shareholder's basis in its stock, or both, are high, avoidance of the corporate tax on its future income stream may be worth the tax cost of liquidating.

Planning for a new business entity, of course, offers more flexibility than planning for an existing corporation. Thus, the partnership and the limited liability company should be explored before adopting the corporate form. If the corporate form is to be used, the S election must be considered by every cor-

---

[12] For the thin-capitalization issue, see   4.01. For excessive compensation, rent, and royalties, see   8.05[3] and 8.05[5]. For the allocation of gross income, deductions, and other items under § 482 if the Internal Revenue Service (the Service) finds this action necessary to clearly reflect income, see   13.20.

[13] See Chapter 6 for discussion of subchapter S.

[14] See Eustice & Kuntz, Federal Income Taxation of S Corporations   7.06[4][k] (Warren, Gorham & Lamont, 4th ed. 2001).

[15] See Chapter 10.

poration that can fit, or can be made to fit, its mold. Between 1986 and 1993, only the well-advised would voluntarily join the ranks of C corporations, which, in the main, have been largely populated by widely held companies. The Revenue Reconciliation Act of 1993, however, reestablished the historic practice of a maximum individual rate higher than the maximum corporate rate (but lowered to 35 percent in 2003), and it also reintroduced a significant individual capital gains rate preference (which was increased again in 1997 and 2003). Thus, it can once again be advantageous to retain or create a C corporation, as compared with using pass-through entities, for the purpose of compounding earnings taxed at the lower maximum corporate rate and later realizing the corporate appreciation through stock sales. Careful analysis, however, must be made in each case, taking into consideration the expected dividends, compensation, and other payouts to shareholders, recognition of appreciation in possible corporate assets, and the likelihood of dispositions of the entire business or of all or most of the corporate stock.

In addition to these options, a C corporation can remove future income from the two-tier regime by paying dividends, the price being the second tier of taxation on the distributed corporate earnings when received by its shareholders (but now only at a 15 percent rate). Further pressure to pay dividends will be exerted by the accumulated earnings and personal holding company penalty taxes, whose rates were the same as the top individual rate—39.6 percent, but which were lowered to 15 percent in 2003 (the same rate applicable to dividends).

The 1993 reintroduction of a significant capital gains preference for individuals (and subsequent expansion of that preference) will also have important ramifications in a variety of specialized areas, as explained later in this book, including the treatment of collapsible corporations, "section 306 stock," market discount, integrated liquidation-reincorporations, and stock redemptions.[16] In all of these situations, the statutory imposition of ordinary income status on the proceeds of transactions involving stock that otherwise would generate capital gains will ordinarily be disadvantageous, especially if the taxpayer has offsetting capital losses. If the loss of capital gain status also entails a loss of the right to offset the taxpayer's stock basis against the amount received (as under § 302, which treats the entire amount paid by a corporation in redemption of stock as a dividend) or the right to report gain on the installment method under § 453, the penalty will be a matter of even greater concern unless the stock

---

[16] See generally ¶¶ 10.60 (collapsible corporations; but § 341 was repealed in 2003), 8.60 ("section 306 stock"), 4.44 (market discount), 10.08 (liquidation-reincorporations), and 9.01 (stock redemptions). For the corporate versus pass-through comparison under pre-1993 law, see Faber, "Capital Gains vs. Dividends in Corporate Transactions: Is the Battle Still Worth Fighting?" 64 Taxes 865 (1986); Bogdanski, "Using Corporations for Tax Savings—A Reappraisal," 14 J. Corp. Tax'n 160 (1987).

basis is trivial in amount or acceleration of income is either a matter of indifference or a desired goal.

¶ 5.02 CORPORATE TAXABLE INCOME

Corporations, like individuals, are taxed on their "taxable income," which § 63(a) defines as "gross income minus the deductions allowed by this chapter."[17] In defining "gross income," § 61(a) does not explicitly distinguish between corporations and individuals, but there are some differences between them with respect to particular items, as explained later; and there are also important differences between them in the tax treatment of deductions, as discussed later. There are also differences in tax collection procedures between corporations and other taxpayers, which are beyond the scope of this book.[18]

Although § 61(a) defines "gross income" in the same way for corporations and for individuals, some items listed in § 61(a) are rarely or never received by corporations (e.g., alimony and income in respect of a decedent). While a few statutory exclusions from gross income apply by their terms only to corporations (e.g., § 118, relating to contributions to capital), many other statutory exclusions involve items that, by their nature, could not be received by corporations, such as combat pay, Social Security benefits, and employee fringe benefits.[19] Such an item might be collected by a corporation following an assignment by the individual originally entitled to receive it; but the item's tax status almost certainly would be transformed in the process—that is, an amount that would constitute a scholarship in the hands of a student might be characterized as a contribution to capital or a repayment of a loan in the hands of the assignee-corporation, depending on the reason for the assignment.

---

[17] Section 63(a) treats the standard deduction specially, but this does not affect corporations, since the standard deduction is confined to individuals.

[18] See, for example, IRC §§ 6621(c) (increase in interest rate for large corporate underpayments), 6672 (100 percent penalty for nonpayment of employment taxes). See generally Saltzman, IRS Practice and Procedure (Warren, Gorham & Lamont, 2d ed. 1991).

[19] A few specific inclusionary sections apply only to corporations or only to individuals. For example, § 78 (gross-up in computing derivative foreign tax credits) applies only to certain domestic corporations, and § 80 (recovery of a previously deducted worthless-security loss from foreign government expropriation) applies only to domestic corporations.

Section 74(b), relating to tax-exempt prizes and awards, may have been intended to apply only to individuals, but it does not explicitly exclude corporations. The use of the word "his" in § 74(b)(1) should not in itself exclude corporations, since "his" is used in other sections (e.g., §§ 75 and 1221) that clearly apply to corporations in order to avoid the more cumbersome form "his, hers, or its."

¶ 5.03 CORPORATE DEDUCTIONS

The Code allows individuals to take a number of deductions that are not allowed to corporations, including the standard deduction, the deduction for personal exemptions, and the additional itemized deductions for such items as medical expenses, alimony, moving expenses, and retirement savings, which are set out in Part VII of subchapter B (§§ 211 through 220). The Code applies a 2 percent floor on miscellaneous itemized deductions only to individuals.[20] The other principal differences between corporations and individuals vis-à-vis deductions are set out in the following paragraphs.[21] As will be seen, some statutory provisions do not distinguish between individuals and corporations as such, but instead draw a line separating individuals and closely held corporations from other corporations in order to prevent restrictions aimed primarily at individuals from being sidestepped by a transfer of the restricted activities to a closely held corporation.

[1] Deductibility of Business Expenses and Losses

Sections 162(a) and 167 explicitly permit taxpayers, including corporations, to deduct business expenses or depreciation only if incurred in a trade or business or in connection with property held to produce income. No such requirements explicitly apply to other deductions that are allowed to corporations, although individuals generally are allowed such deductions only if the deductions have a business or profit connection, as described later. The reason for this difference is not that the Code authorizes corporations to deduct items that have no business rationale; to the contrary, it seems that all corporate deductions require a business connection. But the Code, in effect, presumes that all corporate transactions arise in the corporation's trade or business, with the important exception of transactions serving the interests of the corporation's shareholders, rather than its own interests.[22] Another way of putting the point is that transactions not serving the corporation's business purpose are, ipso facto, not "true" corporate transactions.

Thus, perhaps even charitable contributions might be deducted by a corporation as business expenses were it not for § 162(b), which regulates all corporate charitable gifts to the limits of § 170. Furthermore, § 165(a) provides that any loss sustained during the taxable year, if not compensated for by in-

---

[20] IRC § 67.

[21] For restrictions on deductions for certain transactions between related parties (e.g., a sale of property by a corporation to its controlling shareholder or vice versa), see infra ¶ 5.04.

[22] See Regs. § 301.7701-2(a)(1) (an objective to carry on business is a characteristic of associations).

surance or otherwise, may be deducted. In the case of an individual, however, § 165(c) goes on to restrict the breadth of § 165(a) by allowing the deduction only if the loss was incurred in a trade or business, a transaction entered into for profit, or a casualty. These restrictions are not applicable to corporations, presumably on the theory that all corporate losses arise in trade or business. Likewise, in the case of bad debts, § 166(d) confines a taxpayer other than a corporation to a capital loss on nonbusiness debts. A corporation, however, may deduct wholly or partially worthless debts under § 166(a) against ordinary income, presumably on the theory that a corporation will have no nonbusiness bad debts.[23] The exclusion of nonbusiness deductions of taxpayers other than corporations from net operating losses seems to be based on the same assumption.[24]

Furthermore, the same regime exists with respect to investment expenses. Section 212 was enacted in 1942 to permit the deduction of nonbusiness expenses paid or incurred for the production of income or for the management, conservation, or maintenance of property held for the production of income, and was enlarged in 1954 to embrace expenses incurred in the determination, collection, or refund of taxes. Section 212 is restricted to individuals, however, presumably on the theory that § 162(a) covers the same ground for corporations that §§ 162(a) and 212 in combination cover for other taxpayers.[25] Thus, if a corporation engaged in manufacturing holds some securities as an incidental investment, the cost of a safe-deposit box, investment advice, bookkeeping, and so forth incurred with respect to the securities would be deductible under § 162(a) as trade or business expenses, even though an individual proprietor holding such securities would have to resort to § 212 as authority for deducting such expenses.

Similarly, whereas § 163(a) provides generally for an interest deduction, §§ 163(d) and 163(h), which are applicable only to individuals, limit that deduction as to investment and personal interest. Section 183, which limits the deductibility of so-called hobby losses, applies only to S corporations and individuals.

The conclusion suggested by the rules discussed previously is that implicit in § 165(a) as to losses, in § 166(a) as to bad debts, and in § 163(a) as

---

[23] But see Regs. § 1.166-9(a) (which seems to allow the deduction of losses by all guarantors only if made in the course of a trade or business).

[24] IRC § 172(d)(4).

[25] During the 1942 hearings on § 212, a taxpayer representative recommended enlargement of § 212 to include corporations. See Hearings on Revenue Act of 1942 Before the Senate Finance Comm., 77th Cong., 2d Sess. 1733 (1942). The recommendation was not adopted, probably because it was thought to be unnecessary. At any rate, it has been generally assumed since 1942 that a corporation can deduct under § 162(a) any expenses that could be deducted under § 212 by an individual proprietor or partnership. See generally Bittker & Lokken, Federal Taxation of Income, Estate and Gifts   20.5.1 (Warren, Gorham & Lamont, 3d ed. 1999) (hereinafter Bittker & Lokken, 3d ed.).

to interest expense is the limitation that is explicit in §§ 162(a) and 167(a) (as to depreciation): To be deductible, the expense or loss must have been incurred in a trade or business, or at least in a transaction entered into for profit. Assuming the Code concomitantly presumes that all corporate transactions arise in a corporate trade or business or in a transaction entered into for profit, and thus that all deductions satisfy any implicit or explicit requirement of a business connection, the result is not an automatic deduction of expenditures incurred in such transactions.

First, §§ 63, 161, and 263 require that expenditures be capitalized unless a specific deduction is allowed, and other more specific limitations, such as § 274, may also apply. Second, while the transaction generally might grow out of the corporate trade or business, its true character might differ from its form; for example, salary paid by a corporation may be a disguised payment for a capital asset and thus not be currently deductible by the corporation. Third, and most important, even if neither of the foregoing limitations applies, the expenditure may be nondeductible because it violates the presumption stated earlier that all corporate transactions are in connection with a corporate trade or business or for the corporation's profit-seeking activity. Such a violation can ordinarily occur only when the expenditure is an overt or disguised dividend, that is, a distribution with respect to stock or a payment to the shareholder in his capacity as such and not as a corporate creditor, vendor, employee, and so forth. It is, of course, the disguised dividend area that creates the greatest potential for dispute.[26] A disguised dividend has been referred to as a payment reflecting a "noncorporate motive."[27] Courts sometimes overlook the centrality of the disguised dividend issue in their quest for a transaction's corporate trade or business connection.[28] Since it appears that a noncorporate motive can arise

---

[26] See Black Dome Corp., P-H TC Memo. ¶ 46,130 (1946) (corporate payments to maintain country estate were not deductible); Savarona Ship Corp., P-H TC Memo. ¶ 42,596 (1942) (same for yacht); International Trading Co. v. CIR, 275 F2d 578 (7th Cir. 1960) (deduction denied for expenses of summer residence in excess of shareholder's reasonable rental payments); Greenspon v. CIR, 229 F2d 947 (8th Cir. 1956) (corporate expenditures to maintain "unique horticultural showplace" at sole shareholder's farm determined not to be corporate business expenses and hence taxable as constructive dividends); Royal Cotton Mill Co., 29 TC 761, 788 (1958) (acq.) (factual issue whether litigation expenses paid by corporation were for its benefit or shareholders' benefit); PAL Int'l Corp., TC Memo. 1993-53 (disallowing loss deduction for "theft" by shareholder-employee; loss held to be neither compensatory nor a theft).

Disguised dividends from the shareholder's standpoint are discussed at ¶ 8.05. But the pain of these dividends has been sharply reduced (to 15 percent) as a result of the 2003 legislation in § 1(h)(11); see ¶ 8.06[2].

[27] Anthony Yelencsics, 74 TC 1513, 1531 (1980) (acq.) (corporate guaranty of shareholder's debt).

[28] See Haverhill Shoe Novelty Co., 15 TC 517 (1950) (payment for shareholder's daughter's wedding reception characterized as a nondeductible "gift"); Gibson Prods. Co., 8 TC 654 (1947) (acq.) (payment for president's airplane use was not deductible to extent

only in connection with a transaction with or for the benefit of a shareholder, publicly held corporations can pay millions annually to their executives without the Internal Revenue Service (the Service) questioning the trade or business connection (or raising a reasonable compensation issue) under § 162(a), even though more modest salary payments to shareholder-employees are closely scrutinized.[29]

Thus, while a corporation generally can deduct a "personal" expense paid on behalf of an employee, such as the cost of the employee's vacation,[30] the Service can determine that such a payment on behalf of a shareholder-employee is in the nature of a dividend, and the burden will be on the corporation to prove that it was intended as additional salary. Personal benefits found to be in the nature of a dividend to the shareholder might simply be the satisfaction of the shareholder's urge to engage in a certain activity or to control a certain asset, if there is no substantial business-oriented reason to pursue the activity or to own the asset.[31] If the transaction does not directly or indirectly benefit a shareholder in his capacity as such, however, related deductions that are otherwise available presumably would be allowed.[32]

Because the statutory language in some cases seems to flatly allow a deduction, as in the case of bad debts, the courts sometimes appear to allow a deduction almost reflexively without question. For example, an early opinion of the Board of Tax Appeals allowed a corporation to deduct an uncollectible loan made to the son-in-law of the principal shareholder, stating that "it is not

---

use was not on company business; that he was a major, if not sole, shareholder can be inferred, but was not stated by the court); Mountain Paper Prods. Corp. v. US, 287 F2d 957 (2d Cir. 1961) (payment to another corporation owned by same person who owned the taxpayer was held not deductible, because payment was "extraordinary").

[29] See   2.07, 8.05[3]. See, for example, Sheldon P. Barr, PC, TC Memo. 1992-522 (salary deduction denied as unreasonable because attorney-shareholder failed to prove that he performed legal services for corporate clients). But see IRC § 162(m), added by the Revenue Reconciliation Act of 1993, restricting the deductibility of excessive compensation to key executives of publicly held corporations; putative ceiling on deductibility is $1 million, but an important exception for performance-based compensation is allowed by § 162(m)(4)(C).

[30] See Rev. Rul. 57-130, 1957-1 CB 108.

[31] See, e.g., Fred W. Amend Co., 55 TC 320 (1970) (retention of a Christian Science practitioner for the benefit of shareholder-employee was held a dividend), aff'd, 454 F2d 399 (7th Cir. 1971). But see Tempel Smith, TC Memo. 1979-324 (corporate ownership of Lipizzaner horses found as a matter of fact to have predominant corporate motivation); Henry J. Knott, 67 TC 681 (1977) (acq.) (charitable contribution by closely held corporation not a disguised dividend to shareholder who obviously was the only breathing person with charitable intent).

[32] See International Trading Co. v. CIR, 484 F2d 707 (7th Cir. 1973) (§ 165(a) did not limit deductibility of corporation's loss on sale to unrelated party of property, even though expense deductions had been disallowed in part because the property had been maintained for shareholder use).

proper for this Board to go into the question of the motive of petitioner's officers in making the...loan...nor into the question of whether or not such loan was an ultra vires act."[33] Although the Service acquiesced in the decision,[34] it would be perilous to assume that such a transaction could never be regarded as a dividend in cases where the related borrower was known not to be creditworthy or where there never was any intent to collect the note. Similarly, if a corporation were found to have provided real estate for a shareholder's personal use, the corporation should not be able to deduct property taxes paid thereon.

The foregoing discussion also generally applies to S corporations as well as C corporations. The character of an item of income or deduction is determined at the S corporation level, and the item then passes through to the shareholders.[35] The S corporation generally enjoys the presumption discussed previously that all of its activities are business related. The principal exception is that § 183, which denies deductions for so-called hobby losses, applies to individuals and S corporations but not to C corporations. Consequently, the issue with respect to a corporation's conduct of activities that may benefit its shareholders directly will often be examined in the context of § 183, rather than, or in addition to, the constructive dividend context.[36] Of course, once deductions pass through to an S corporation's shareholders, the deductions are subject to those limitations that apply to individuals, such as limitations on the deductibility of investment interest, charitable contributions, and passive activity losses.

[2] Charitable Contributions

The deduction for charitable contributions is computed differently for corporations than for other taxpayers. Under the general rule of § 170(a)(1), the contribution must be paid within the taxable year, regardless of the taxpayer's method of accounting, but corporations on the accrual method may elect under § 170(a)(2) to treat a contribution as paid during the taxable year if it is authorized by the board of directors during the year and paid within the first two and one-half months of the following taxable year.

---

[33] Cooper-Brannan Naval Stores Co., 9 BTA 105 (1927) (acq.). Cf. Federated Graphics Cos., TC Memo. 1992-347 (citing *Cooper-Brannan* for the quoted point, but case did not involve a related borrower).

[34] VII-1 CB 7 (1928).

[35] IRC § 1366(b). See ¶ 6.06.

[36] See Gary L. Schlafer, TC Memo. 1990-66 (S corporation's expenses for auto racing disallowed under § 183 and also denied as advertising expenses of auto sales business because they were "personal recreation expenses" of owner-employee).

While the ceiling on the deduction for charitable contributions is, in the case of individuals, 30 percent of adjusted gross income (increased to 50 percent for certain contributions), the ceiling for corporations is 10 percent of taxable income (computed with certain adjustments).[37] Corporations may carry forward contributions in excess of this amount for five years, subject to application of the 10 percent ceiling to the total of carryover and current contributions for each later year during the carryforward period.[38]

Other rules applicable only to corporations define the charitable contribution and the amount of the deduction.[39] The Service attempted at one time to treat charitable contributions by closely held corporations as constructive dividends to the controlling shareholders who desired to assist their favorite charities, but this effort was rebuffed by the courts and seems to have been abandoned by the Service.[40]

[3] Limitation on Capital Losses

A corporation may deduct its capital losses only to the extent of capital gains; it does not enjoy the privilege granted to other taxpayers of applying the excess against a limited amount of ordinary income.[41] Individuals can carry unused capital losses forward for an unlimited period, while a corporation's net capital losses may be deducted during a carryback period of three years and a carryforward period of five years, with exceptions for foreign expropriation losses, S corporations, and a few other specialized categories.[42]

Like other taxpayers, a corporation enjoys ordinary loss treatment if it has a net loss from sales of noncapital assets, such as inventory and other property held for sale to customers in the ordinary course of a trade or business.[43] Thus,

---

[37] IRC §§ 170(b)(1) (individuals), 170(b)(2) (corporations).

[38] IRC § 170(d)(2). See also IRC § 162(b) (denying deduction as business expense for excess charitable contributions).

[39] See IRC §§ 170(c)(2) (limiting deductions for certain corporate donations for use outside the United States), 170(e)(3) (modifying the limit on deductions for certain ordinary income property).

[40] See Henry J. Knott, 67 TC 681 (1977) (acq.); Rev. Rul. 79-9, 1979-1 CB 125 (shareholders or their families must receive property or an economic benefit as a result of the corporation's charitable contribution in order to recharacterize it as a dividend). Cf. C.F. Mueller Co. v. CIR, 479 F2d 678 (3d Cir. 1973) (donation to parent, which was itself a charity, was held to be a dividend). See also   8.05[8].

[41] IRC §§ 1211(a), 1211(b).

[42] IRC § 1212(a). Note that this section defines "corporate net capital loss" as a short-term capital loss in the year to which it is carried. Thus, the loss cannot be carried beyond the limited period to other years by increasing the corporation's "net capital loss," which term excludes short-term capital losses of corporations. IRC § 1222(10).

[43] IRC § 1221(1).

a distinction between a corporation's trade or business motives and its investment motives becomes important for this purpose. Under the rule of *Arkansas Best*, most investment losses are now held to be capital unless the asset is a proxy for inventory.[44] Although a holding company was held to be engaged in a trade or business for this purpose in a 1984 case, the decision was severely undermined by the subsequent decision in *Arkansas Best*.[45]

[4] Net Operating Losses

Corporations, like other business taxpayers, are allowed a deduction against the current year's income for net operating losses of prior or subsequent years.[46] As discussed previously,[47] since corporations are ordinarily presumed to be engaged exclusively in trade or business, they may increase their net operating losses by all deductions otherwise allowed, whereas individuals must exclude nonbusiness deductions in computing this loss.[48] Furthermore, a corporation may generate a net operating loss that fully reflects its current dividends-received deduction even though that deduction would be limited in the year when the dividend was received to 80 percent (or 70 percent, depending on stock ownership of the payor) of the corporation's taxable income before the dividends-received and net operating loss deductions.[49]

As discussed elsewhere in this book, a corporation's ability to use net operating losses may be restricted after certain changes in its stock ownership,

---

[44] Arkansas Best Corp. v. CIR, 485 US 212 (1988); see Azar Nut Co., 94 TC 455 (1990) (loss on corporate resale of home required to be purchased from terminated employee held capital loss per *Arkansas Best*), aff'd, 931 F2d 314 (5th Cir. 1991); but see Circle K Corp. v. US, 23 Cl. Ct. 665, 68 AFTR2d 5462 (1991) (loss on sale of supplier's stock held to be ordinary even under *Arkansas Best* because sufficiently inventory-related); but contra Cenex, Inc. v. US, 38 Fed. Cl. 331 (1997), aff'd, 1998-2 USTC ¶ 50,781 (Fed. Cir. 1998); Federal Nat'l Mortgage Ass'n, 100 TC 541 (1993) (various business-related hedging transactions held ordinary losses).

[45] Campbell Taggart, Inc. v. US, 744 F2d 442 (5th Cir. 1984) (extensive analysis of "trade or business" concept as applied to holding and investment companies).

[46] IRC § 172(a).

A proposal in the Clinton budget bills of 1996, 1997, and 1998 would have changed the § 172 period to a one-year carryback and a twenty-year carryforward; and the Taxpayer Relief Act of 1997, Pub. L. No. 105-34, 105th Cong., 1st Sess., § 1082, reduced the carryback to two years and increased the carryover to twenty years (effective in 1998).

[47] See supra ¶ 5.03[1].

[48] IRC § 172(d)(4). Other modifications applicable only to individuals appear in §§ 172(d)(2) and 172(d)(3).

[49] IRC §§ 172(d)(5), 246(b)(2). See infra ¶ 5.05[7][b] for dividends-received deductions.

while an S corporation's net operating losses pass through to its shareholders under the general conduit regime.[50]

[5] Certain Shareholder Taxes Paid by Corporation

Section 164(e) permits a corporation to deduct taxes levied on a shareholder because of his interest as a shareholder, if the corporation pays the tax and is not reimbursed by the shareholder. The taxes for which this deduction was enacted are imposed by some states on the capital stock of banks and some other corporations.[51] Since this provision effectively transfers the § 164 deduction for taxes paid from shareholders to their corporation, the regulations appropriately refuse to treat the payment as a constructive dividend includible in the shareholders' income.[52] If a corporation pays any taxes for which a shareholder is liable, however, the payment almost certainly will be treated as a nondeductible dividend.[53]

[6] At-Risk and Passive Loss Rules

Section 465, which limits the current deductibility of losses incurred in various business activities to the amount the taxpayer has at risk (as defined), applies to all business and income-producing activities.[54] Although aimed primarily at individuals, § 465 applies to C corporations meeting the stock ownership requirements of § 542(a)(2) (i.e., a corporation more than 50 percent in value of whose stock is owned directly, indirectly, or constructively by not more than five individuals).[55] Section 465 does not apply to S corporations, but an S corporation's tax shelter losses are passed through to its shareholders, who are subject to § 465 as individuals.

---

[50] See generally Chapter 14, Part C; for S corporations, see   6.06.

[51] See General Motors Corp. v. US, 283 F2d 699 (Ct. Cl. 1960); Rev. Rul. 92, 1953-1 CB 39; Hillsboro Nat'l Bank v. CIR, 460 US 370 (1983) (no tax benefit income to corporation on recovery by shareholders of state intangibles taxes previously deducted by corporation under § 164(e)).

[52] Regs. § 1.164-7.

[53] Cf. Virginia Nat'l Bank v. CIR, 450 F2d 1155 (4th Cir. 1971) (payment by corporation to exempt shareholder to equalize its treatment with taxable shareholders for whom corporation had paid a § 164(e) tax was held to be a nondeductible dividend), cert. denied, 405 US 1065 (1972); Rev. Rul. 73-42, 1973-1 CB 142 (same).

[54] In the case of real estate, which is subject to this limitation only if placed in service after 1986, the taxpayer's at-risk investment includes nonrecourse financing meeting the conditions of § 465(b)(6)(B).

[55] IRC § 465(a)(1)(B). For discussion of § 542(a)(2), see   7.23.

Section 469 imposes restrictions on the current deduction of so-called passive activity losses incurred by individuals, corporations meeting the stock ownership rules of § 542(a)(2), and personal service corporations.[56] As with § 465, § 469 applies to shareholders of S corporations in their individual capacities.[57] Proposed legislation in the Treasury's fiscal year 2000 budget plan would extend the passive loss principles of § 469 to all leases of tax-exempt use property.[58]

[7] Percentage Cutbacks in Corporate Tax Preferences

Section 291 imposes specified percentage limits on certain otherwise allowable corporate tax preferences, both deductions and exclusions. This provision was enacted in 1982 because, according to the Senate Finance Committee, "there is increasing concern about the equity of the tax system, and cutting back corporate tax preferences is a valid response to that concern."[59] The nature and severity of the cutbacks mandated by § 291 vary, but the affected items are (1) certain § 1250 property (primarily, real property subject to accelerated depreciation), which is treated as if it were § 1245 property for recapture purposes; (2) percentage depletion on iron ore and coal; (3) the interest expenses related to exempt state and local bond interest income of financial institutions;[60] (4) the exempt foreign sales income of certain closely held foreign and possessions corporations; (5) amortization of pollution control facilities; and (6) intangible drilling costs and mineral exploration and development costs.

---

[56] "Personal service corporation" is defined by § 269A(b)(1), as modified by § 469(j)(2). See generally August, "How Do the Passive Activity Loss Rules Apply to C and S Corporations?" 5 J. Partnership Tax'n 218 (1988).

[57] See Eustice & Kuntz, Federal Income Taxation of S Corporations 7.08[12] (Warren, Gorham & Lamont, 3d ed. 1993).

[58] See Sheppard, "Lease In, Lease Out: Safe Harbor Leasing Revisited," 81 Tax Notes 1167 (Dec. 7, 1998) (description of lease-in, lease-out (LILO) transactions that would be hit by this proposal); see also Rev. Rul. 99-14, 1999-13 IRB 3 (generalized attack on LILO transactions under current law); Cozart, "Disputing Rev. Rul. 99-14: Pre-Tax Profit, Defeasance, and Circular Leases," 83 Tax Notes 557 (Apr. 26, 1997). For general discussion of corporate tax shelters, and Treasury's response thereto, see infra 5.10. This proposal ultimately passed in the American Jobs Creation Act of 2004 (2004 Jobs Act) (including "SILO", or sale-in, sale-out transactions, as well). American Jobs Creation Act of 2004, §§ 847, 848, Pub. L. No. 108-357 (Oct. 22, 2004).

[59] S. Fin. Comm. Rep. No. 494, 97th Cong., 2d Sess. 119 (1982).

[60] See also IRC § 265(b).

[8] Other Corporate Deduction Rules

Sections 243 through 246 permit corporations to deduct certain dividends received from other corporations. Of these provisions, the most important is § 243, providing for a deduction of 70 percent or more of dividends received from domestic taxable corporations. These deductions are discussed later in this chapter, along with § 248, which permits a corporation to amortize its organizational expenditures over a period of sixty months or more.[61]

Other statutory remedies for tax shelters and similar tax avoidance arrangements that apply not only to individuals but also to some corporations, and other deduction rules that apply specifically to corporations, include the following:

1. Section 464, which requires farming syndicates to capitalize certain otherwise deductible expenditures for feed, seed, and other supplies and which defines "syndicate" to include partnerships and certain S corporations.

2. Section 183, which relates to hobbies and other activities not engaged in for profit and which applies to S corporations as well as to individuals.

3. Section 280A, which relates to home offices and which also applies to both individuals and S corporations.

4. Section 267, which denies or defers deductions for payments to related parties.[62]

5. Section 311(a), which denies a loss deduction upon a corporation's distribution of depreciated property to shareholders.[63]

6. Section 249, which limits deductions of bond premium on a repurchase by the issuing corporation.[64]

7. Section 269, which empowers the Treasury to deny or otherwise limit corporate deductions in certain abusive cases.[65]

8. Section 279, which denies deductions for certain interest on debt incurred to acquire another corporation.[66]

9. Section 280G, which denies deductions for certain "golden parachute payments."[67]

---

[61] See generally infra ¶¶ 5.05, 5.06[1].

[62] See infra ¶ 5.04[2].

[63] See ¶ 8.21.

[64] See ¶ 4.60[2].

[65] See ¶ 14.41.

[66] See ¶ 4.26.

[67] See infra ¶ 5.04[7].

10. Section 280H, which applies to personal service corporations electing fiscal years.[68]
11. Section 162(m), which disallows a deduction by certain publicly held corporations for certain compensation in excess of $1 million paid to any one of a limited number of top employees.[69]

[9] Corporate Tax Benefits From "Tax Shelter Transactions" Denied

The Treasury's fiscal year 2000 budget plan proposed a comprehensive package of legislation aimed at various types of corporate tax shelter transactions which, if fully enacted as proposed, would provide the Service with a formidable arsenal for combatting these schemes.[70] Few if any well-advised corporate taxpayers would willingly try to engage in these ventures under this regime (which would become "risky business" with a prohibitive downside). After a long struggle, some, but by no means all, of these proposals were enacted in the American Jobs Creation Act of 2004 (2004 Jobs Act).[71]

---

[68] See infra   5.07[1].

[69] Proposed regulations under § 162(m) were issued on December 20, 1993, as Prop. Regs. § 1.162-27 (the key provisions of which are in Prop. Regs. § 1.162-27(e), the exception for performance-based compensation). Additional regulations under § 162(m) were proposed on December 1, 1994, amending and clarifying the 1993 proposed regulations and adding more examples. These regulations became final in TD 8650 on December 20, 1995.

See generally Ginsburg & Levin, Mergers, Acquisitions and Leveraged Buyouts 1317 (Panel 1999); Levin, Javaras & Welke, "Code Section 162(m)—New $1 Million Deduction Limitation on Executive Compensation," 61 Tax Notes 95 (Oct. 4, 1993); Levin, Javaras & Welke, "Code Section 162(m)—$1 Million Deduction Limit on Executive Compensation," 63 Tax Notes 723 (May 9, 1994); Villasana, "Executive Compensation: An Analysis of Section 162(m)," 72 Taxes 481 (1994); Note, "Rethinking Section 162(m)'s Limitation on the Deduction of Executive Corporation: A Review of the Commentary," 15 Va. Tax Rev. 371 (1995); Sollee, "Ensuring Deductions for Performance-Based Compensations in Excess of $1 Million," 84 J. Tax'n 360 (1996); Nelson, Executive Compensation Deduction Limits Revisted, 106 Tax Notes 304 (Jan. 17, 2005).

A Senate floor amendment to the 1995 budget bill extended the § 162(m) cap limit to *all* employees of *all* corporations, but this provision was dropped from the final conference bill (which in turn was vetoed on December 6, 1995).

[70] See infra   5.10.

[71] See infra   5.10[8][d].

[10] Deduction Relating to Income Attributable to Domestic Production Activities: § 199

The 2004 Jobs Act[72] created a new special deduction in § 199 to assuage U.S. businesses loss of the repealed export subsidy benefits of the extraterritorial income exclusion.[73] In general, a deduction is allowed in an amount equal to 9 percent[74] of the *lesser* of (1) "qualified production activities income"[75] of the taxpayer for the taxable year or (2) taxable income for the year.[76] This deduction is one of the centerpieces of the 2004 legislation, but has spawned much confusion and uncertainty as to its proper scope and application.[77] Further discussion of this provision is in Chapter 15.[78]

¶ 5.04 SPECIAL DEDUCTION PROBLEMS ARISING FROM CORPORATE-SHAREHOLDER RELATIONSHIP

The relationship between corporations and their shareholders often generates questions about the deductibility of expenditures incurred by both, as well as

---

[72] American Jobs Creation Act of 2004, § 102, Pub. L. No. 108-357 (effective beginning in 2005, though on a phased-in basis; it is not fully effective until 2010).

[73] See ¶ 15.23[4]; for guidance, Notice 2005-14, 2005-7 IRB 498 (Feb. 14, 2005). Proposed regulations under § 199, were issued on October 20, 2005.

[74] But not until 2010; the percentage for 2005–2006 is 3 percent; for 2007–2009 it is 6 percent.

[75] Defined as the tax base in § 199(c), the key part of the section.

[76] The deduction is further limited by § 199(b) to 50 percent of W-2 wages paid during the taxable year.

[77] Much guidance will be needed from the Service, and quickly. See Stratton, 105 Tax Notes 1172 (Nov. 29, 2004); Atkinson, "Assembling the Pieces of the Manufacturing Deduction," Daily Tax Rep. (BNA) No. 215, at J-1 (Nov. 8, 2004). For such comprehensive guidance, see Notice 2005-14, 2005-7 IRB (Feb. 14, 2005); see also proposed regulations under § 199 issed on October 20, 2005 (the preamble is half as long as the regulations. Taxpayers are allowed to "cherry-pick" here (using either the notice or the proposed regulations until the latter become final).

[78] See ¶ 15.23[5]. For comments, see Cummings & Hanson, "American Jobs Creation Act: New Section 199 Domestic Production Deduction," 16 J. Int'l Tax'n 14 (Apr. 2005); Deloitte Tax LLP, "Producing Results: An Analysis of the New Production Activities Deduction," 106 Tax Notes 965 (Feb. 21, 2005); Conjura et al., "The Domestic Manufacturing Deduction: Treasury and IRS Fill in Some Gaps," 102 J. Tax'n 198 (Apr. 2005); Kehl, "Alternatives for Allocation of Costs Under Internal Revenue Code Section 199," Daily Tax Rep. (BNA) No. 23, at J-1 (Feb. 4, 2005); Benko & Rohrs, "Domestic Production Deduction Overview of the Interim Guidance," 106 Tax Notes 569 (Jan. 31, 2005); Reistein, "What's in It for You? Determining Who Has Benefits and Burdens of Ownership for New Code Section 199 Deduction," Daily Tax Rep. (BNA) No. 75, at J-1 (Apr. 20, 2005).

the deductibility of losses incurred in their dealings with each other. The corporation's right to deduct expenditures it incurs in dealings with shareholders is governed in large part by § 162 (ordinary and necessary business expenses), whereas the individual shareholder's right to deduct corporate-connected outlays can be governed by either §§ 162 or 212 (investment expenses); but in either case, account must also be taken of §§ 262 and 263(a)(1), denying deductions for personal expenses and capital expenditures respectively. The application of these statutory provisions depends so heavily on principles growing out of noncorporate contexts that a full discussion of this topic is beyond the scope of this book; but mention may be made of a few areas of special interest.

[1] Shareholder's Payment of Corporate Expenses

Shareholders of closely held corporations often pay corporate expenses from their own pockets. If the payments are made with an understanding that they will be reimbursed, the payment will be a nondeductible loan and the reimbursement will not be included in the shareholder's income.[79] If the shareholder is also an employee of the corporation and is reimbursed for expenses incurred in the corporation's business, and the expenses qualify for deduction by the corporation, the employee may exclude both the payment and the reimbursement from his return.[80] If the shareholder-employee is not reimbursed, he may deduct the payment only if it is made in his own trade or business of being an employee.[81]

Outside of these cases, the Supreme Court held in *Deputy v. Du Pont* that a shareholder's payment of his corporation's business expense does not qualify for deduction under § 162(a) by the shareholder, because, even if the shareholder's stock investments were a business, it was not ordinary or necessary for that business to pay the expenses of another business.[82] Because the *Du*

---

[79] See Rev. Rul. 84-138, 1984-2 CB 123.

[80] Regs. § 1.62-2.

[81] Regs. § 1.162-1(a). See Rev. Rul. 57-502, 1957-2 CB 118; Tom C. Connally, TC Memo. 1961-312 (business meals not deductible where no effort was made to demonstrate that they were part of taxpayer's own business); Kleithermes v. US, 27 Fed. Cl. 111, 92-2 USTC 50,584 (1992) (uncompensated officer-shareholder could not deduct expenses incurred on behalf of corporation, because he was not engaged in a trade or business); Bittker & Lokken, 3d ed. 20.1.4.

[82] Deputy v. Du Pont, 308 US 488 (1940). See also CIR v. Groetzinger, 480 US 23 (1987) (discussing history of "trade or business" definition and holding a gambler to be engaged in a trade or business); Walton O. Hewitt, 47 TC 483 (1967) (sole shareholder denied deduction for payments to others who were selling newly issued stock for the corporation); Frank A. Leamy, 85 TC 798, 809 (1985); Bert B. Rand, 35 TC 956 (1961) (ordinary-and-necessary requirement of § 212).

Pont opinion held that the payment was not ordinary when made by a share-holder, it is unlikely that a shareholder could claim a deduction under § 212, which, like § 162(a), has an ordinary-and-necessary requirement.[83]

If, however, the shareholder is also an employee and can show that the payment was made to protect his job (which is his trade or business), then a § 162(a) deduction may be allowed.[84] Otherwise, the shareholder's payment of his corporation's expense should be treated as a contribution to capital, for which the corporation may be allowed a deduction as if it had paid that amount with its own funds.[85] For example, when a person acquires all of the shares of a corporation from a retiring shareholder and also pays him for a covenant not to compete with the acquired corporation, the payment for the covenant is a contribution to capital.[86] A similar issue arises in connection with a shareholder's loss on payment of the corporation's debt, as discussed in Chapter 4.[87]

The same principles apply to payments by a corporate parent of its sub-sidiary's expenses, with minor variations.[88] The parent may be able to deduct its own expenses for the general monitoring of its investment in the subsidiary,

---

The personal liability of the shareholder for corporate debts does not change the re-sult. See James E. Stewart, TC Memo. 1992-211, aff'd, 986 F2d 1429 (10th Cir. 1993) (denying shareholder deduction for corporate debts paid while corporate charter was sus-pended; fact that corporation was still recognized by state law as entity prevented deduc-tion).

[83] See Fischer v. US, 490 F2d 218 (7th Cir. 1973) (bargain element in sale of stock by corporate officer to convertible bondholders to settle their claim against corporation held not deductible by seller; it was neither his expense nor an ordinary expense deducti-ble under § 212).

[84] See, for example, James O. Gould, 64 TC 132 (1975) (purpose of payment was to protect shareholder-employee's employment with another corporation).

[85] See Bautzer v. US, 36 AFTR2d 75-5868 (Ct. Cl. 1975) (shareholder expense for benefit of corporation held nondeductible under § 212; expense treated as contribution to capital); Joe Richard Aidoo, TC Memo. 1993-28 (shareholder's payment of corporate ex-penses increased his stock basis). See also Rev. Rul. 84-68, 1984-1 CB 31 (parent corpo-ration's payment of bonuses to subsidiary's employees treated as contribution to capital; subsidiary allowed to claim deduction); Regs. § 1.83-6(d) (same for payments in-kind); Thomas A. Safstrom, TC Memo. 1992-587 (shareholders paid corporation's research ex-penses; as between the two, shareholders were not entitled to § 174 deduction). See also ¶ 3.13 (contributions to capital).

But see IRC § 176 (deduction allowed for payment of foreign affiliate's Federal Un-employment Tax Act taxes).

[86] See Johanna Miller, TC Memo. 1993-55 (shareholder could not deduct cost of cov-enant not to compete); see also Edwin E. Markwardt, 64 TC 989 (1975) (denied loss de-duction to shareholder when covenant breached).

[87] See ¶ 4.22[3].

[88] See ¶ 13.23[5][b]. But see Square D Co., 121 TC 168 (2003) (subsidiary payments of fees incurred by parent and assumed by subsidiary were deductible because expenses were incurred for benefit of the subsidiary).

but not its expenses for supervision of its day-to-day activities.[89] Furthermore, a parent corporation may be able to show, more readily than an individual shareholder, that a payment for the benefit of a subsidiary or other affiliate was actually made for the parent's own business benefit.[90]

[2] Related-Party Transactions

Section 267(a)(1) provides that losses from sales or exchanges of property, directly or indirectly, between certain related persons may not be deducted except in the case of a loss recognized by a corporation under § 336 upon distributing its assets to shareholders in a complete liquidation.[91] Section 267(b) specifies the tainted relationships, which include (1) an individual and a corporation if the individual owns directly or indirectly[92] more than 50 percent in value of its outstanding stock; (2) a fiduciary of a trust and a corporation if the trust or a grantor thereof owns directly or indirectly more than 50 percent in value of the corporation's outstanding stock; (3) a corporation and a partnership if the same persons own more than 50 percent in value of the corporation's stock and more than 50 percent of the capital or profits interest in the partnership; and (4) an S corporation and another corporation (whether an S or a C corporation) if the same persons own more than 50 percent in value of the stock of both. In all these situations, the ownership of stock is determined by reference to the constructive ownership rules of § 267(c).[93]

---

[89] See Columbian Rope Co., 42 TC 800, 814 (1964) (acq.).

[90] See Fishing Tackle Prods. Co., 27 TC 638 (1957) (acq. in result) (parent could deduct payments to subsidiary to reimburse latter's net operating losses where it was sole source of supply of item needed in parent's business); Rev. Rul. 73-226, 1973-1 CB 62 (parent's payments to creditors of insolvent subsidiary deductible under § 162 because they were necessary to protect parent's goodwill and reputation); Newark Morning Ledger Co. v. US, 539 F2d 929 (3d Cir. 1976) (corporation owning 87 percent of another corporation was allowed to deduct expenses of bringing derivative action because the action benefited both parent and subsidiary's business; origin of the claim was diversion of parent's corporate assets).

[91] See generally   10.05 concerning liquidations. See also Cochran, "The Infield Fly Rule and the Internal Revenue Code: An Even Further Aside," 29 Wm. & Mary L. Rev. 567 (1988); Keller, "At a Loss: A Half Century of Confusion in the Tax Treatment of Transfers of Depreciated Property Between Related Taxpayers," 44 Tax Law. 445 (1991).

[92] See Robert Boehm, 28 TC 407 (1957), aff'd per curiam, 255 F2d 684 (2d Cir. 1958) (ownership found indirect by step transaction analysis).

[93] See also W.A. Drake, Inc., 3 TC 33 (1944), aff'd, 145 F2d 365 (10th Cir. 1944) (applying § 267 when shareholder drops below 50 percent stock ownership as a result of the sale); Homes Beautiful, Inc., P-H TC Memo.   47,166 (1947) (corporate sale to three shareholders treated as sale to partnership so that attribution applied despite lack of formal partnership). Cf. Hallbrett Realty Corp., 15 TC 157 (1950) (mere co-ownership not a partnership).

In addition, losses from the sale or exchange of property (except certain sales of inventory in the ordinary course of business) between two members of the same "controlled group" of corporations, as defined by § 267(f), are deferred, rather than disallowed, until the losses are realized by a sale or other transfer of the property outside the controlled group.[94] For this purpose, the "controlled group" definition of § 1563 is used with modifications, the principal one being a reduction of the stock ownership line from 80 percent to more than 50 percent.

Taxpayers subject to the related-party loss rules of § 267(a)(1) are also subject to the matching rules of § 267(a)(2) if an expense or item of interest owed by a party on the accrual method of accounting to the related party is not includible in the latter's gross income until it is paid if the related party is on the cash method.[95] The deduction is deferred until the item is includible in the payee's gross income (ordinarily, as a result of payment); but it is not disallowed, no matter how long the delay in payment. While § 267(a)(3) appears to extend the matching rule to any amounts payable to unrelated foreign persons, the Secretary has exercised his regulatory authority to limit application of the subsection to amounts payable to foreign persons that are related under § 267(b) and whose income will not be taxable by the United States, because it is not effectively connected with a U.S. trade or business but is composed of interest or certain other payments with respect to which withholding of tax is required upon payment by §§ 871(a) and 881(a).[96]

Another rule, found in § 163(j), defers a corporation's deduction for so-called excess interest paid to a related tax-exempt (or reduced-rate) person, as discussed elsewhere in this book.[97] Other rules limiting tax benefits from vari-

---

But see Turner Broad. Sys., Inc., 111 TC 315 (1998) (time for testing § 267(f) relationship is immediately *after* the loss transaction, which affinity was ended here as the result of another corporation's simultaneous acquisition of the loss-seller corporation; asset buyer's attempt to plan "into" § 267 treatment rejected); for earlier description of this transaction, see Sheppard, "The Affirmative Use of Anti-Abuse Rules," 73 Tax Notes 18 (Oct. 7, 1996).

[94] See generally Gardner, "Disallowed or Deferred Losses, Expenses and Interest: Related Party Transactions and IRC Section 267," 44 NYU Inst. on Fed. Tax'n ch. 29 (1986); ¶ 13.23[5][d]. For § 267(f) generally, see Turner Broad. Sys., Inc., 111 TC 315 (1998), supra note 93; see also UnionBanCal Corp., 113 TC 309 (1999), for history of § 267(f) and 1984 temporary regulations (held valid, and taxpayer not entitled to retroactive benefit of prospective 1995 regulations; *Union BanCal* was affirmed, 305 F3d 976 (9th Cir. 2002)).

[95] The operational language of § 267(a)(2) embraces any payment that is deductible by one party and includible in the related recipient's gross income; by virtue of § 7806(b) the heading's reference to expenses and interest should not limit the section's scope. See generally ¶ 13.23[6][b].

[96] See Notice 89-84, 1989-2 CB 402; Regs. § 1.267(a)-3; ¶¶ 15.03, 15.04 (taxation of foreign corporations).

[97] See ¶¶ 4.04[8], 13.23[8], 15.04[4].

ous transactions between related parties that can apply in the corporation-shareholder context include (1) § 453(g) (denying installment sale treatment on the sale of depreciable property to a controlled entity); (2) § 482 (allocation of income and deductions among related taxpayers); (3) § 304 (stock sales treated as redemptions); (4) § 336(d) (denying a corporation's recognition of loss on its distribution of property to related persons in liquidation); and (5) § 1239 (ordinary gain on sale of depreciable property between related parties).

[3] Shareholder Stock Acquisition Costs and Selling Expenses

Expenses incurred by a shareholder in connection with the acquisition of stock in a corporation ordinarily constitute nondeductible capital expenditures to be added to the basis of the acquired stock (as the buyer's comparable costs of acquiring any other type of property would be),[98] whether the acquisition is a negotiated purchase from the corporation or an existing shareholder or the result of a hostile takeover by using the tender offer route. The Supreme Court in the *Woodward* and *Hilton Hotels* cases reemphasized the capital character of costs originating in the acquisition process by denying deductibility for the acquirer's legal expenses incurred in stock appraisal litigation brought by dissenting shareholders to determine the value of their stock.[99] These two decisions render suspect many authorities that predate 1970. Indeed, under current

---

[98] IRC § 1016 (adjusted basis for all items properly chargeable to capital account); Regs. §§ 1.263(a)-2(a), 1.263(a)-2(c), 1.263(a)-2(e) (commissions paid on purchasing securities), 1.212-1(k), 1.212-1(n); Dwight Williamson, 17 BTA 1112 (1929). See generally Nickell v. CIR, 831 F2d 1265 (6th Cir. 1987) (litigation among shareholders over ownership of stock; costs relating to recovery or retention of title to stock held to be nondeductible capital expenditures, but costs to recover dividends were deductible under § 212(2)); Mitchell v. CIR, 73 F3d 628 (6th Cir. 1996) (restitution payment made to keep stock obtained in violation of federal banking regulations held capital).

[99] Woodward v. CIR, 397 US 572 (1970) (shareholders who voted for charter change were required by state law to buy shares of dissenters; held, cost of appraisal litigation originated in acquisition process; no justification for applying the "uncertain and difficult" test for deciding whether litigation expenses were incurred for "primary purpose of defending or protecting property"). See also US v. Hilton Hotels Corp., 397 US 580 (1970) (same result when merging corporation was required to buy dissenter's shares; for stock redemptions, see infra 5.04[6]). See also Estate of McGlothlin v. CIR, 370 F2d 729 (5th Cir. 1967) (guaranty by shareholder in connection with merger treated as cost of stock acquired); Locke v. CIR, 568 F2d 663 (9th Cir. 1978) (buyer's expenses of defending Rule 10(b)-5 suit for fraud in purchase of stock held nondeductible capital expenditures, not related to taxpayer's position as corporate officer); Rev. Rul. 80-119, 1980-1 CB 40 (same); McKeague v. US, 12 Cl. Ct. 671 (1987) (allocation between shareholder's deductible business expenses and nondeductible capital expenditures to obtain forced buyout under origin-of-the-claim test), aff'd, 852 F2d 1294 (Fed. Cir. 1988).

See generally Schenk, "*Arrowsmith* and Its Progeny: Tax Characterization by Reference to Past Events," 33 Rutgers L. Rev. 317 (1981).

law even expenses preparatory to hostile or friendly takeovers and expenses arising under a general program of acquisitions must be capitalized.[100]

Similar capital treatment is imposed on expenses incurred by shareholders upon the disposition of their stock, which are either added to the stock basis before computing the seller's gain or loss or deducted from the sale proceeds and thus reduce the shareholder's gain or increase his loss.[101]

Costs related to stock acquisition and disposition, however, may be deductible under special circumstances. Post-sale expenditures incurred in collecting income from the sales proceeds, rather than collecting the sale proceeds

---

[100] See Rev. Rul. 73-580, 1973-2 CB 86 (expenses of in-house corporate acquisition department must be capitalized, including compensation of legal, accounting, and internal audit staffs; deduction of some part allowed later if acquisition abandoned). See also Ellis Banking Corp. v. CIR, 688 F2d 1376 (11th Cir. 1982) (fees for investigation by accountants of potential target corporation held part of the cost of acquisition of the stock). But see IRC § 195, allowing amortization of business start-up expenses and accompanying S. Rep. No. 1036, 96th Cong., 2d Sess. 11–14 (1980) (amortization of expenses incurred in investigating the acquisition of a new trade or business where same amounts paid in connection with an existing business would have been deductible; rule applies to stock acquisition where corporation is to be liquidated or is to become a member of acquirer's consolidated group).

See also Dana Corp. v. US, 38 Fed. Cl. 356, 80 AFTR2d 5412 (1997) (corporation's payment of annual retainer held a deductible § 162 expense even though credited against acquisition-related fees in some, but not all, of the eight-year period; fact of crediting did not turn retainer into a capital expenditure); But *Dana* was reversed on appeal, and that portion of the annual retainer credited against acquisition costs was required to be capitalized; Dana Corp. v. US, 174 F3d 1344, 1999-1 USTC ¶ 50,411 (Fed. Cir. 1999). See Raby & Raby, "Direct vs. Absorption Allocation of Takeover Costs," 83 Tax Notes 537 (Apr. 26, 1999); Hillsborough Holdings Corp. v. US, 2000-1 USTC ¶ 50,420 (Bankr. Fla. Ct. 2000) (professional fees and costs in connection with leveraged buyout acquisition held nondeductible capital costs); American Stores Co., 114 TC 458 (2000) (legal expenses of resisting state anti-trust challenge to taxpayer's acquisition of target held capital acquisition costs per *INDOPCO* et al.); but compare PNC Bancorp. v. CIR, 212 F3d 822, 2000-1 USTC ¶ 50,483 (3d Cir. 2000) (loan origination fees currently deductible as ordinary § 162 expenses); David Lychuk, 116 TC 324 (2001) (employees' salaries part of acquisition process because directly related to acquisition of assets; but overhead costs were not and hence could be currently expensed; multiple concurring opinions and dissents; distinguished *Wells Fargo* and declined to follow *PNC Bancorp.*).

[101] Regs. §§ 1.263(a)-2(e), 15A.453-1(b)(2)(v); see Woodward v. CIR, 397 US 572 (1970) (legal, brokerage, accounting, and similar expenses of asset disposition); William Wagner, 78 TC 910 (1982) (seller's expenses of defending a Rule 10(b)-5 fraud action were not deductible under § 212 and should have been added to the basis of the stock sold); Third Nat'l Bank in Nashville v. US, 427 F2d 343 (6th Cir. 1970) (dissenters' cost of selling their stock); Helgerson v. US, 426 F2d 1293 (8th Cir. 1970) (expenses of litigation to enforce sales agreement); Rev. Rul. 79-2, 1979-1 CB 98 (shareholders' expenses of preparing for public secondary offering must offset sales proceeds because the expenses produce an intangible asset, separate from the stock; but if offering is abandoned, costs are deductible as a loss). But see Petschek v. US, 335 F2d 734 (3d Cir. 1964) (deduction allowed for expenses of pursuing claim for expropriation of foreign corporation's stock).

themselves, may be deductible.[102] Expenses for tax advice in connection with the sale may be deductible, although such a deduction by an individual is subject to the 2 percent floor on miscellaneous itemized deductions.[103] Sometimes litigation expenses related to a sale are deductible if shown to have their origin in the protection of the taxpayer's job or assets, for example, rather than relating to the sale transaction.[104] Of course, expenses relating to holding and conserving stock are deductible.[105]

While the costs of effecting a successful stock acquisition are capital expenditures that must be added to the basis of the acquired property, expenses of unsuccessful bids or aborted acquisitions apparently are deductible in the year when it becomes clear that the acquisition will not occur, either as business or investment expenses under §§ 162 and 212 or as business or investment losses under § 165.[106] Capitalization is not appropriate in this situation,

---

[102] See CIR v. Doering, 335 F2d 738 (2d Cir. 1964) (allowing deduction of expenses in collecting claims received on corporate liquidation). Contrast Estate of Meade v. CIR, 489 F2d 161 (5th Cir.) (shareholder expense of collecting open liquidation claim held to be capital expenditure; expense was attributable to disposition of stock for assets of liquidating corporation), cert. denied, 419 US 882 (1974); Estate of Baier v. CIR, 533 F2d 117 (3d Cir. 1976) (legal fees in collecting sale proceeds were capital expenses).

[103] See IRC § 212(3); Sharples v. US, 533 F2d 550 (Ct. Cl. 1976) (court rejected Service's argument that § 263 controlled as to individual taxpayer); IRC § 67 (2 percent floor).

[104] See Mitchell v. US, 408 F2d 435 (Ct. Cl. 1969) (principal shareholder-officer's expenses in defense of suit for alleged fraud in shareholder's sale of stock; expenses deductible as expenses of carrying on business as corporate officer; but note that *Mitchell* predated *Woodward* and *Hilton Hotels*). Contrast Locke v. CIR, 568 F2d 663 (9th Cir. 1978) (buyer's expenses of defending Rule 10(b)-5 suit for fraud in purchase of stock held nondeductible capital expenditures, not related to taxpayer's position as corporate officer); William Wagner, 78 TC 910 (1982) (stock seller's expenses of defending Rule 10(b)-5 action not deductible under § 212 and should have been added to basis of stock sold); James C. Bradford, Jr., 70 TC 584 (1978) (disgorged profits were capital expenditures of broker-dealers who used insider information); Brown v. US, 526 F2d 135 (6th Cir. 1975) (seller's derivative action costs held to reduce sale gain; no allocation to conserving value of stock allowed). See infra   5.04[8] for discussion of defendants' repayment of short-swing profits. See generally Berry Petroleum Co., 104 TC 584 (1995) (litigation costs had origin in merger acquisition and thus were held capital costs), aff'd per curiam, 1998-1 USTC   50,398 (9th Cir. 1998).

[105] See Allied Chem. Corp. v. US, 305 F2d 433 (Ct. Cl. 1962) (stockholder's expenses of opposing SEC proceedings to dissolve corporation deductible as § 162 business expenses). See also IRC § 212(2).

[106] See Rev. Rul. 67-125, 1967-1 CB 31; Johan Domenie, TC Memo. 1975-94 (costs of abandoned business-acquisition plan deductible § 165 losses); Rev. Rul. 73-580, 1973-2 CB 86 (costs of abandoned acquisition plans deductible); In re Federated Dep't Stores, Inc., 76 AFTR2d 95-7897 (SD Ohio 1994) (break-up fee paid to white knight to consummate merger with taxpayer held deductible; thus, corporate heart-balm payments are allowable as § 162 expenses or § 165 abandonment losses); A.E. Staley Mfg. Co. v. CIR, 119 F3d 482, 1997-2 USTC   50,521 (7th Cir. 1997) (costs attributable to abandonment

since the preliminary activities did not culminate in the acquisition of a specific property interest by the offerer-taxpayer or in the creation of long-term benefit.

Costs incurred to investigate the creation or acquisition of a business can be amortized under § 195 (so-called start-up costs); but costs incurred to acquire a specific business are nondeductible capital expenditures under § 263 according to a 1999 revenue ruling.[107]

[4] Expenses of Proxy Fights and Resisting Tender Offers

If the acquisition or disposition of stock is not the origin of the expense, several decisions have allowed insurgent shareholders to deduct the expense of soliciting proxies from their fellow shareholders for the purpose of altering the business policies of the incumbent management in order to increase their dividend income or the value of their stock.[108] Similarly, expenses incurred by a corporation in resisting insurgent shareholders have been held deductible, at

---

of plans in hostile takeover defense currently deductible); David Lychuk, 116 TC 374 (2001) (allowed § 165 ordinary loss for costs attributable to rejected applications).

[107] Rev. Rul. 99-23, 1999-20 IRB 3, holding that expenses of a general search for, or investigation of, an active business to determine *whether* to enter, and *which* business to enter or acquire, are amortizable under § 195. But costs of acquiring a specific business are capital costs under § 263. Thus costs incurred in the search for a mate (i.e., "dating") are § 195 items, but "wedding" costs are § 263 capital costs. Gamino, "The Answer to the Riddle? Rev. Rul. 99-23 and Start-Up Expenditures," 83 Tax Notes 1929 (June 28, 1999). See also Wells Fargo & Co. v. CIR, 224 F3d 874, 2000-2 USTC ¶ 50,697 (8th Cir. 2000) (some preliminary merger investigation costs held deductible under § 162); David Lychuk, 116 TC 374 (2001) (extensive discussion and multiple concurring and dissenting opinions; *Wells Fargo* distinguished and declined to follow *PNC Bancorp*). See comment in 15 J. Tax'n Fin. Insts. No. 50 (Sept. 2001); Carrington, "Capitalization After *INDOPCO* and Into the New Millenium," 93 Tax Notes 813 (Nov. 5, 2001) (extensive collection of post-*INDOPCO* authorities); Bittker, McMahon & Zelnak, "Capitalization of Benefits Beyond the Tax Year," 97 Tax Notes 257 (Oct. 14, 2002).

[108] See Graham v. CIR, 326 F2d 878 (4th Cir. 1964) (deduction allowed for cost of settling suit arising from proxy fight); Surasky v. US, 325 F2d 191 (5th Cir. 1963) (contribution to fund used to solicit proxies was deductible); Rev. Rul. 64-236, 1964-2 CB 64 (agreeing to follow *Graham* and *Surasky* but only to extent expenses are proximately related to production of income or conservation of income-producing property); Alleghany Corp., 28 TC 298 (1957) (acq.) (controlling corporate shareholder's expenses in defending against proxy fight and other threats to its ownership in bankruptcy reorganization of corporation were held deductible); Jean Nidetch, TC Memo. 1978-313 (deduction allowed for costs of preparing for anticipated proxy contest to change corporate policies). But see Dyer v. CIR, 352 F2d 948 (8th Cir. 1965) (expenses of shareholder crusading for particular point of view; nondeductible because they were not reasonably related to dividend income or stock value); J. Raymond Dyer, 36 TC 456 (1961) (acq.) (same taxpayer, same result for earlier year). See also McKeague v. US, 87-2 USTC ¶ 9401 (Cl. Ct. 1987) (expenses of enforcing proxies deductible), aff'd, 852 F2d 1294 (Fed. Cir. 1988).

least where the management believed in good faith that resistance was in the best interests of all shareholders.[109] One case even permitted a corporate business expense deduction for reimbursement of the proxy expenses of both the winning and the losing shareholder groups.[110]

An analogous issue arises in connection with expenses paid by the corporation in resisting a hostile tender offer. Such expenses probably should be deductible on the same basis as the cost of defending a proxy fight—that is, the expenses are incurred primarily to protect the business rather than to acquire property and are primarily related to questions of corporate policy. While ownership of the corporation might be viewed as a matter of indifference to the entity itself, a hostile acquirer in fact almost always wants to change the board of directors and in many cases the management, and it may also want to break up the assets and businesses of the corporation, which the current board may properly view as inimical to the corporation and the current shareholders.[111]

The deduction issues in this area have become confused, however, because of the variety of ways in which an initially hostile takeover attempt can play out and because of the Supreme Court's 1992 decision in *INDOPCO, Inc.*[112] This decision, which is further discussed later in this chapter,[113] required

---

[109] Locke Mfg. Cos. v. US, 237 F. Supp. 80 (D. Conn. 1964); Rev. Rul. 67-1, 1967-1 CB 28 (accord with *Locke*, and analogous to shareholder expenses, if expenses related primarily to questions of corporate policy rather than for benefit of particular individuals or officers); Dolese v. US, 605 F2d 1146 (10th Cir. 1979) (expense deductible to extent it related to preservation of corporation's business, but not deductible to extent it was personal to divorce proceedings between husband and wife shareholders; proxy fight analogy applied), cert. denied, 445 US 961 (1980).

[110] Central Foundry Co., 49 TC 234 (1967) (acq.).

[111] Cf. Welch v. Helvering, 290 US 111 (1933) (under § 162, deduction should be allowed for costs of defending a lawsuit that could affect the safety of business). For the business judgment rule, which constrains the responses of corporate boards of directors to takeover bids, see Lipton & Steinberger, Takeovers and Freezeouts § 5A.01 (Law Journal Seminars Press 1999).

See A.E. Staley Mfg. Co. v. CIR, 119 F3d 482, 1997-2 USTC ¶ 50,521 (7th Cir. 1997) (costs of defending against hostile takeover bid currently deductible under § 162, and costs attributable to abandoned plans deductible under § 165).

[112] INDOPCO, Inc. v. CIR, 503 US 79, 112 S. Ct. 1039 (1992). See generally Faber, "*INDOPCO*: The Unsolved Riddle," 47 Tax Law. 607 (1994); Adams & Hinderliter, "*INDOPCO, Inc. v. Commissioner*: Impact Beyond Friendly Takeovers," 55 Tax Notes 93 (Apr. 6, 1992); Lee, "Doping Out the Capitalization Rules After INDOPCO," 57 Tax Notes 669 (Nov. 2, 1992); Note, "Deductibility of Takeover and Non-Takeover Expenses in the Wake of *INDOPCO, Inc. v. Commissioner*," 45 Tax Law. 815 (1992).

[113] See infra ¶ 5.06[2][d]. Carrington, "Capitalization After *INDOPCO* and Into the New Millenium," 93 Tax Notes 813 (Nov. 5, 2001) (extensive collection of post-*INDOPCO* authorities). Bittker, McMahon & Zelenak, "Capitalization of Benefits Beyond the Tax Year," 97 Tax Notes 257 (Oct. 14, 2002). Lee, "Transaction Costs Relating to the Acquisition or Enhancement of Intangible Property: A Populist, Political, But Practical Perspective," 22 Va. Tax Rev. 273 (Fall 2002).

a target corporation to capitalize its costs incurred in a friendly takeover, reasoning that since significant future corporate benefits were obtained as a result of the reorganization, its failure to create a separate and distinct asset for the corporation did not alter the need to capitalize the costs. Applying this rationale of *INDOPCO, Inc.*, it could be argued that a corporation's successful efforts to block a hostile takeover do not create any new benefit that the corporation did not already possess, and that its expenses should be deductible as ordinary and necessary business expenses.[114] Where an initially hostile

---

The long-awaited intangibles capitalization regulations were finally released on December 18, 2002, Prop. Regs. § 1.263(a)-4. The preamble is must reading here and is nearly as long as the regulations. The proposals are remarkably liberal; see especially Regs. § 1.263(a)4(e) and the seventeen examples in Regs. § 1.263(a)-4(e)(7). The key concept of the new regulations reverses *INDOPCO*'s presumption of capitalization and replaces it with a presumption of deductibility if an item of expense is not specifically listed as a capital expenditure.

See Hamilton, "Treasury Turns *INDOPCO* on Its Head," 97 Tax Notes 1508 (Dec. 23, 2002); Sheppard, "Bringing the Separate Asset Test Back From the Dead," 97 Tax Notes 1655 (Dec. 30, 2002); Bambino & Nugent, "The Proposed INDOPCO Regulations: A Primer," 99 Tax Notes 259 (Apr. 14, 2003); Hardesty, "The New Proposed Regulations on Capitalization of Intangibles," 98 J. Tax'n 86 (Feb. 2003); Willens, "Deal Community Should Be Pleased With Proposed Rules Addressing Costs Associated With Capital Transactions," Daily Tax Rep. (BNA) No. 32, at J-1 (Feb. 18, 2003); Johnson, "Destroying Tax Base: The Proposed *INDOPCO* Capitalization Regulations," 99 Tax Notes 1381 (June 2, 2003).

The intangibles regulations were adopted as final regulations by TD 9107, issuing Regs. §§ 1.263(a)-4 and 1.263(a)-5 (effective Dec. 31, 2003). For comment, see Sheppard, "More Giveaways in Final Intangibles Regulations," 102 Tax Notes 12 (Jan. 5, 2003). New Regs. § 1.263(a)-5 deals with the merger and acquisition transaction cost rules of proposed Regs. § 1.263(a)-4(e), but the change in location did not alter the substantive liberality of these provisions.

See Melone, "Final Intangible Asset Regulations Make Significant Changes to the Proposed Rules," 31 Corp. Tax'n 15 (May/June 2004) (generally for the better); Blasi & Lee, "New Capitalization Rules: Their Sweeping Effect on Financial Institutions," 17 J. Tax'n Fin. Insts. 19 (May 6, 2004); Maydew, "New Code Sec. 263 Capitalization Regulations Provide Guidance," 82 Taxes 50 (Aug. 2004); Altizer & Bryant, "An Analysis of the Final Sec. 263(a) Regulations on Capitalization of Intangible Assets," 82 Taxes 39 (July 2004); Yale, "The Final INDOPCO Regulations," 105 Tax Notes 435 (Oct. 25, 2004) (special supplement, a very thorough analysis).

[114] But see TAM 9144042 (Service recognizes no distinction between hostile and friendly takeovers; taxpayer has burden of showing that expenditures will not create significant long-term benefits in order to take current deduction); A.E. Staley Mfg. Co., 105 TC 166 (so holds); but *Staley* was reversed, 119 F3d 482, 80 AFTR2d 5060 (7th Cir. 1997) (most defense costs held to be deductible under §§ 162 and 165).

For the expenses of unsuccessfully defending against a hostile takeover, see In re Federated Dep't Stores, Inc., 69 AFTR2d 92-731 (Bankr. SD Ohio 1992) (merger break-up fee paid as corporate heart-balm to jilted white knight was deductible as ordinary § 162 expense or § 165 abandonment loss; no long-term benefits created); *Federated* was affirmed by the district court; In re Federated Dep't Stores, Inc., 171 BR 603, 1994-2 USTC   50,430 (SD Ohio 1994). For comments, see Friedrich, "Break-Up Fees Paid to

tender offer turns friendly when the offering price is raised, or where the target finds a suitable white knight with which to mate, the rationale of *INDOPCO, Inc.*, may require the target's expenses to be capitalized.[115] But where no take-over materializes, advisory fees should be deductible as ordinary business advice expenses and one case so holds.[116]

Unsuccessful White Knight Held Deductible as Ordinary Business Expenses or as Abandonment Loss," 22 J. Corp. Tax'n 193 (1995). The *Federated* view was followed in A.E. Staley Mfg. Co. v. CIR, 119 F3d 482, 80 AFTR2d 5060 (7th Cir. 1997).

[115] See Victory Mkts., Inc., 99 TC 648 (1992) (tender offer was initially unwanted, but resulting takeover was not hostile; expenses must be capitalized because takeover was expected to produce long-term benefits to the corporation, as shown by recommendation of target's directors to shareholders); see also A.E. Staley Mfg. Co., 105 TC 166 (1995) (target's costs of defending against hostile takeover that ultimately succeeded held nondeductible capital expense per *INDOPCO* and *Victory Mkts.*—hostility not a distinction— origin of fees was a change in ownership and costs incurred in connection with a change of corporate ownership are nondeductible; five dissents thought costs were deductible per *Federated*). See Raby, "'Friendly' Is Not the Issue With Takeovers," 68 Tax Notes 1613 (Sept. 25, 1995); Lipton, "Divided Tax Court Applies *INDOPCO* to Hostile Takeovers," 84 J. Tax'n 21 (1996). See also Norwest Corp., 112 TC 89 (1999) (target's indirect costs related to its eventual acquisition also held nondeductible under *INDOPCO*; acquisition not hostile here either). Fitzgerald, *"Norwest Corp.*: Can You Bank on Deductibility of Compensation Expense and Legal Costs Incurred Incident to an Acquisition?" 78 Taxes 51 (Mar. 2000); American Stores Co., 114 TC 458 (2000) (costs of resisting state antitrust challenge to acquisition nondeductible per *INDOPCO* et al.). But *Norwest* was reversed sub nom. Wells Fargo & Co. v. CIR, 224 F3d 874, 2000-2 USTC ¶ 50,697 (8th Cir. 2000); comment in 88 Tax Notes 1303 (Sept. 11, 2000). In *Wells Fargo* salaries of target's officers deductible in full; legal and investigation expenses before "final decision to merge" also deductible (but legal expenses after decision date not). See Prusieki, "*Wells Fargo*: Right Result, But Not a Jurisprudential Masterpiece," 88 Tax Notes 1541 (Sept. 18, 2000); Sheppard, "What Part of 'Capitalize' Don't You Understand?" 88 Tax Notes 1435 (Sept. 18, 2000); Faber, "Setting the Record Straight on INDOPCO," 88 Tax Notes 1675 (Sept. 25, 2000); Raby & Raby, "INDOPCO Starts to Lose Its Starch," 88 Tax Notes 1637 (Sept. 25, 2000); Giannattasio & Blank, "*Wells Fargo* (The *Norwest* Reversal)—Is It Just the Eye of the Storm?" 89 Tax Notes 1433 (Dec. 11, 2000), republished in 90 Tax Notes 107 (Jan. 1, 2001) to correct footnotes; Levy et al., "*Wells Fargo* Provides Guidance on Acquisition Costs," 14 J. Tax'n Fin. Insts. No. 3, at 40 (Jan. 2001).

The Tax Court's decision in *Staley* was reversed, however, 119 F3d 482, 1997-2 USTC ¶ 50,521 (7th Cir. 1997) (most defense costs held to be deductible under §§ 162 and 165). See comment by Sheppard, "Will There Ever Be Another Friendly Takeover?" 76 Tax Notes 461 (July 28, 1997) (no); Lipton, "The Treatment of Defense Costs in a Hostile Takeover After the CA-7 Opinion in *Staley*," 87 J. Tax'n 176 (1997). See also Metrocorp, Inc., 116 TC 211 (2001) (Swift, concurring, noted Eighth, Seventh, and Third Circuits' rejection of Tax Court's expansive application of *INDOPCO*; fees here produced no significant future benefits and thus were currently deductible).

[116] Pope & Talbot, Inc., RIA TC Memo. ¶ 97,116 (1997) (investment banking fees for advice on potential hostile takeovers (which did not occur) held deductible).

[5] Derivative Suits, Indemnity Agreements, and Other Corporate-Shareholder Disputes

Payments by a corporation or its officers and directors to resist or settle claims arising in shareholder derivative suits for breach of a fiduciary duty in the conduct of the corporation's business affairs have usually been held deductible as ordinary and necessary outgrowths of the trade or business of the corporation, officer, or director.[117] Courts apparently treat expenses for the defense or settlement of such suits as ordinary and necessary costs of doing business in corporate form. Since the corporation usually pays the entire cost of defending these suits under the court decree, settlement agreement, or indemnification bylaw, the issue of deductibility typically involves only the corporate payor, although occasionally payments are also made by directors and officers or shareholder-plaintiffs.[118] The fact that the suit is settled or even that the corporation loses is generally no bar to a deduction. Deductions have been allowed for corporate reimbursement of both the shareholder-plaintiff's and the director-defendant's litigation expenses in a derivative action if the suit challenged the conduct of the corporation's business affairs.

Deductibility for derivative suit expenses, however, is not automatic. If the suit relates to the recovery or defense of title to specific property, the litigation expenses may have to be capitalized by the corporation as costs incurred in defending or perfecting its title to the property.[119] But an allocation between capital and noncapital expenditures may be appropriate if the taxpayer claiming the deduction can prove the relationship of the litigation expenses to the various elements of the suit; thus, there is a premium on accurate record

---

[117] See Larchfield Corp. v. US, 373 F2d 159 (2d Cir. 1966) (expenses of corporation as neutral party in derivative suit were deductible; reimbursement of defendant-directors' liabilities under indemnification bylaw was deductible; reimbursement of plaintiffs' costs was deductible except to extent attributable to recovery of specific property), and cases cited therein; Ingalls Iron Works v. Patterson, 1 AFTR2d 785 (ND Ala. 1958) (corporation's reimbursement of shareholders' expenses in derivative suit was deductible); B.T. Harris Corp., 30 TC 635 (1958) (acq.) (shareholder's expenses that were paid as court costs by taxpayer were deductible).

[118] See Hochschild v. CIR, 161 F2d 817 (2d Cir. 1947) (director's legal fees in successful defense suit alleging breach of corporate opportunity doctrine were deductible; but since suit involved return of stock, application of later-developed origin-of-the-claim test might have produced different result); Graham v. CIR, 326 F2d 878 (4th Cir. 1964) (payment by director in settlement of suit alleging waste of corporate assets was deductible); Ingalls v. Patterson, 158 F. Supp. 627 (ND Ala. 1958) (plaintiff who did not deduct expenses may exclude reimbursement by corporation).

[119] See Larchfield Corp. v. US, 373 F2d 159 (2d Cir. 1966); Iowa S. Util. Co. v. CIR, 333 F2d 382 (8th Cir.), cert. denied, 379 US 946 (1964) (corporation could not deduct cost of recovering property as result of derivative action); Pennroad Corp., 2 TC 1087 (1954) (acq.) (same), aff'd, 228 F2d 329 (3d Cir. 1955).

keeping.[120] Allocation, however, may be contrary to the origin-of-the-claim test of *Woodward* and *Hilton Hotels*.[121]

It is commonplace in many corporations for key executives and directors to seek protection against liability for the improper conduct of their business duties by indemnity agreements, reimbursement bylaws, or business liability insurance. Direct payments of such liabilities to third parties by the corporation are deductible, absent an agreement that the employee reimburse the corporation.[122] The Service has ruled that premiums paid by a corporation for group liability insurance indemnifying the corporation's officers for the expenses of defending lawsuits alleging misconduct in the officers' official capacities were deductible § 162 expenses of the corporation and did not constitute gross income to the officers.[123]

The litigation expenditures of shareholder-plaintiffs may be either deductible expenses under § 162 or § 212 or capital outlays to be added to the basis of their stock under §§ 263(a)(1) and 1016(a)(1) (or partly one and partly the other), depending on the nature of their claims and the outcome of the suit.[124]

---

[120] Larchfield Corp. v. US, 373 F2d 159 (2d Cir. 1966). See also Regs. § 1.212-1(k) (directing allocation of attorney fees between those capitalizable and those deductible in suit to quiet title and to collect income).

[121] See supra ¶ 5.04[3] (discussing Supreme Court's opinions in *Hilton Hotels* and *Woodward*); Brown v. US, 526 F2d 135 (6th Cir. 1975) (plaintiff in derivative action not allowed to allocate expenses between stock sale and conserving value of stock; expenses held to be entirely capital); Berry Petroleum Co., 104 TC 584 (1995) (costs of fighting class action suit for breach of fiduciary duty in connection with merger not currently deductible because origin of claim was the merger), aff'd per curiam, 1998-1 USTC ¶ 50,398 (9th Cir. 1998).

[122] See Larchfield Corp. v. US, 373 F2d 159 (2d Cir. 1966) (payment to a defendant-director pursuant to an indemnity bylaw held deductible as compensatory fringe benefit, even though director could not have deducted all payments individually if he had paid them); Rev. Rul. 78-210, 1978-1 CB 39 (self-insured professional medical association). Note, however, that if the corporation pays the expense of an employee and has a right of reimbursement from that employee, the corporation has merely made a loan to the employee that it cannot deduct unless it proves to be uncollectible. Cf. Peter J. Webbe, TC Memo. 1987-426, aff'd, 902 F2d 688 (8th Cir. 1990).

[123] Rev. Rul. 69-491, 1969-2 CB 22. See also Rev. Rul. 76-277, 1976-2 CB 41 (deductible if paid by officer). For treatment of such payments as a nontaxable fringe benefit of employment, see IRC § 132(d).

[124] See Newark Morning Ledger Co. v. US, 539 F2d 929 (3d Cir. 1976) (parent corporation's legal fees in litigation against its subsidiary alleging diversion of earnings and of corporate business opportunity were held deductible); Brown v. US, 526 F2d 135 (6th Cir. 1975) (shareholder's derivative suit had origin in buyout offer from other shareholder; hence, litigation expenses were nondeductible capital costs under *Woodward* and *Hilton Hotels*, even though suit resulted in increased price for stock and larger future income flow); Galewitz v. CIR, 411 F2d 1374 (2d Cir.), cert. denied, 396 US 906 (1969) (not a derivative suit; legal expenses of shareholder in defending groundless suit challenging right to hold stock; nondeductible expense of defending title to stock); supra ¶ 5.04[3] (costs incurred in buying or selling stock must be capitalized).

Shareholders, of course, may sue their corporations outside the derivative action context. One such case involved a veritable cornucopia of claims, all the costs of which were held to be deductible: seeking access to corporate books; to force the corporation to hold board meetings; to enforce a recapitalization agreement affecting the shareholder's control; to force dividends; to prevent improper issuance of stock options; to obtain admission of the shareholder's counsel at board meetings; and to enforce proxies.[125] On the other hand, where the suit's origin is an effort to force the corporation to purchase the shareholder's stock, the court may look past the immediate aim of the suit and require capitalization.[126]

[6] Corporate Expenses of Redeeming Stock

The corporate takeover movement of the early 1980s led Congress in 1986 to enact § 162(k), which disallows otherwise allowable deductions for "any amount paid or incurred by a corporation in connection with the redemption of its stock."[127] While aimed at the deduction of so-called greenmail payments to

---

[125] McKeague v. US, 60 AFTR2d 87-5267 (Cl. Ct. 1987). But see Rev. Rul. 56-111, 1956-1 CB 513 (shareholder's expenses of merely attending a shareholders' meeting are not deductible absent some showing of need in connection with investment activities; this ruling may account for the small number of annual meetings of U.S. corporations in places like Monte Carlo), declared obsolete by Rev. Rul. 69-227, 1969-1 CB 315 (because ruling concerned the excise tax).

[126] Ralph Neely, 85 TC 934, 953–955 (1985) (suit to obtain corporate financial information relevant to buyout of taxpayer's shares).

[127] The corporation's right to deduct amounts paid to reacquire its stock was extremely doubtful even before the enactment of § 162(k), although some hopes had been built on a 1966 decision allowing a deduction for amounts paid to purchase stock of a 50 percent dissenting shareholder in order to settle a lawsuit. Five Star Mfg. Co. v. CIR, 355 F2d 724 (5th Cir. 1966). That decision was substantially undermined, however, by the Supreme Court's later decision in US v. Hilton Hotels Corp., 397 US 580 (1970) (merging corporation required to buy dissenters' shares; survivor could not deduct appraisal expenses), and still later, the Court of Appeals for the Fifth Circuit itself confined the Five Star decision to expenditures "made to save the corporation from dire and threatening consequences." Jim Walter Corp. v. US, 498 F2d 631, 639 (5th Cir. 1974).

See also Stokely–Van Camp, Inc. v. US, 66 AFTR2d 90-5918 (Cl. Ct. 1990) (no § 162 deduction for redemption payment, and also no § 167 amortization deduction), aff'd, 974 F3d 1319, 70 AFTR2d 5649 (Fed. Cir. 1992); Frederick Weisman Co., 97 TC 563 (1991) (Tax Court, in reviewed opinion, rejects Five Star as no longer viable, even on identical facts); Lane Bryant, Inc. v. US, 35 F3d 1570 (Fed. Cir. 1994) (same as Stokely–Van Camp); US v. Houston Pipeline Co., 37 F3d 224, 74 AFTR2d 94-6793 (5th Cir. 1994) (Five Star distinguished and redemption premium nondeductible because there was no threat to corporate existence). But see Wrangler Apparel Corp. v. US, 931 F. Supp. 420, 1996-2 USTC   50,364 (DNC 1996) (no § 162 deduction, but maybe § 167 amortization if part of price paid for stand-still agreement); Rogers v. US, 58 F. Supp. 2d 1235, 2000-1 USTC   50,237 (D. Kan. 1999), aff'd, 281 F3d 1108, 2002-1 USTC   50,240

redeem shares held by corporate raiders, this section appears to apply to all stock redemption transactions regardless of color.[128]

Section 162(k) flatly disallows any deductions for the amounts paid for the stock, for expenses connected with its redemption (e.g., legal, brokerage, and accounting fees),[129] and payments under so-called standstill agreements by which the redeemed shareholder agrees not to purchase any additional shares, whether the amounts are paid by the corporation or by a shareholder or other related party.[130] On the other hand, § 162(k) explicitly exempts (1) interest, if otherwise deductible under § 163; (2) dividends deductible under § 561, relating to dividends paid in computing the accumulated earnings tax and in certain other circumstances;[131] and (3) expenses incurred by mutual funds all of whose stock is redeemable on the shareholder's demand. A transaction characterized for tax purposes as a redemption can occur in the form of a cash merger that

---

(10th Cir. 2002); (alleged "loan" held in substances to be de facto redemption of stock and payments thus not deductible); comment by Raby & Raby, "Getting Deductions From Stock Redemptions," 86 Tax Notes 1601 (Mar. 13, 2000). See also Custom Chrome, Inc. v. CIR, 217 F3d 1117, 2000-2 USTC ¶ 50,566 (9th Cir. 2000) (§ 162(k) applied by means of step doctrine, and also incurred understatement penalty).

[128] For discussion of greenmail generally, see ¶ 9.25. See also US v. Kroy (Europe) Ltd., 70 AFTR2d 92-6092 (D. Ariz. 1992) (reversing refusal of bankruptcy court to apply § 162(k) to amortization of loan fees, which refusal had been based on view that § 162(k) was aimed only at greenmail payments); but Kroy was reversed on appeal, 27 F3d 367 (9th Cir. 1994) (loan fees were incident to a separate transaction, even though loan proceeds were used to redeem stock); contra Fort Howard Corp., 103 TC 345 (1994) (reviewed, two dissents; § 162(k) interpreted broadly and loan fee deduction denied); but allowed in later opinion, 107 TC 187 (1996) (because of retroactive change in § 162(k)(2) in 1996). See also TAM 9342005; Ludtke & Moll, "Loan Fees, LBOs, and the 'Plain Meaning' of Section 162(k): The Ninth Circuit Considers United States v. Kroy (Europe) Ltd.," 61 Tax Notes 1605 (Dec. 27, 1993); Raby, "Financial Consulting Fees and Other Costs of Stock Redemptions," 64 Tax Notes 1733 (Sept. 26, 1994); Booth & Bailine, "Kroy: 'Bungling' Ninth Circuit Still Got It Right," 65 Tax Notes 631 (Oct. 31, 1994).

But Fort Howard result changed by 1996 legislation, and amortization of fees allowed by supplemental opinion, 107 TC 187 (1996); Akselrod & Bernstein, "Are Expenses in Obtaining LBO Loans Deductible?" 20 J. Corp. Tax'n 295 (1993). (Yes, see infra ¶ 5.04[6]). Square D Co., 121 TC 168 (2003) (loan fees and related legal costs amortizable over term of loan).

[129] See Rev. Rul. 67-125, 1967-1 CB 31 (under prior law, a corporation could not deduct legal fees for tax advice relative to a stock redemption); IRC § 317(b) for a definition of "redemption of stock" (which apparently would include a partial liquidation). (See ¶ 10.07[3]).

[130] See HR Conf. Rep. No. 841, 99th Cong., 2d Sess. II-168, II-169 (1986). See Ludtke & Moll, "Loan Fees, LBOs, and the 'Plain Meaning' of Section 162(k): The Ninth Circuit Considers United States v. Kroy (Europe) Ltd.," 61 Tax Notes 1605 (Dec. 27, 1993).

[131] For discussion of § 561, see ¶ 7.09.

is carried out with a transitory corporation formed by an acquirer.[132] Both § 162(k) and other capitalization principles should clearly apply to deny a deduction for expenses related to such a transaction.[133]

Expenses of a stock redemption transaction that may result in a corporate deduction are loan fees and similar costs that are directly related to borrowing the funds used to redeem the shares. Historically, such expenses that are incurred for services and are not themselves interest have been held to be amortizable over the life of the loan.[134] The Service has contested the amortization of such loan fees under § 162(k).[135] Of course, loan fees that are interest because they are for the use of the borrowed funds are deductible as interest or as original issue discount.[136]

Moreover, being confined to payments "in connection with the redemption of [the corporation's] stock," § 162(k) leaves room for the deduction of payments, if otherwise allowable, that occur "in a transaction that has no nexus with the redemption other than being proximate in time or arising out of the same general circumstances." Thus, a lump-sum payment to a departing employee may be split between a nondeductible payment for the employee's stock and a deductible payment in discharge of the corporation's obligations under an employment contract.[137]

A provision contained in the 1996 Small Business Act[138] amended § 162(k) retroactively (to 1986) as follows: (1) the holding of *Kroy* (as described by the Ninth Circuit) is codified (i.e., amortizable loan costs are not disallowed by § 162(k)) but (2) coverage of § 162(k) is broadened to include acquisitions of any related corporation stock (with a very low threshold).[139]

---

[132] See Rev. Rul. 78-250, 1978-1 CB 83 (redemption where cash came from target). Cf. Rev. Rul. 73-427, 1973-2 CB 301 (stock purchase where cash came from acquirer).

[133] Cf. INDOPCO, Inc. v. CIR, 503 US 79, 112 S. Ct. 1039 (1992) (cash-out merger in which acquirer supplied the cash; predated § 162(k), and Court pointed to substantial future benefits in requiring capitalization). For an example, see TAM 9342005 (reverse cash merger using transitory subsidiary was held in substance to be § 302 stock redemption and § 162(k) applied).

[134] See, e.g., Rev. Rul. 70-360, 1970-2 CB 103; Rev. Rul. 70-359, 1970-2 CB 103; infra 5.04[9].

[135] See supra note 128.

[136] See IRC § 162(k)(2)(A)(i).

[137] HR Conf. Rep. No. 841, 99th Cong., 2d Sess. II-168 (1986).

[138] Pub. L. No. 104-188, 104th Cong., 2d Sess., § 1704(p) (the 1996 Small Business Job Protection Act). See Fort Howard Corp., 107 TC 187 (1996) (allowing the amortization deduction because of this change); Square D Co., 121 TC 168 (2003) (same); Raby & Raby, "IRS Tries to Stretch in Connection With the Reacquistion of Its Stock," 102 Tax Notes 1369 (Mar. 15, 2004).

[139] The relationship line of § 465(b)(3)(C) would be used (i.e., § 267(b), with a 10 percent test in lieu of 50 percent test). For comment, see Sheppard, 73 Tax Notes 1269 (Dec. 11, 1996).

[7] Golden Parachute Payments

The corporate takeover movement that led Congress to enact § 162(k) in 1986 was also the impetus for the enactment in 1984 of § 280G. Specifically, Congress was concerned that contracts between a corporation and its employees providing golden parachutes upon a takeover of the company could (1) discourage takeover activity; (2) encourage management to favor a takeover; or (3) siphon off corporate value that should go to the shareholders.[140] Therefore, § 280G disallows any deduction for certain payments to a "disqualified individual" (whether or not incident to termination of the individual's employment) if the payment (1) is contingent on a change in the ownership or effective control of a corporation or in the ownership of a substantial portion of a corporation's assets,[141] provided the present value of the payment exceeds three times a defined base amount, or (2) is paid pursuant to an agreement violating any generally enforced securities laws or regulations. Any payment pursuant to an agreement or amendment thereof entered into within one year before a change of ownership or control is presumed to be contingent on the change unless the contrary is established by clear and convincing evidence.

---

[140] See generally Staff of Joint Comm. on Taxation, General Explanation of the Revenue Provisions of the Deficit Reduction Act of 1984, at 199–207 (1984). Proposed regulations under § 280G were issued on May 5, 1989, as Prop. Regs. § 1.280G-1, in question-and-answer format. See Rocap, "Golden Parachute Proposed Regulations Clarify Many Issues," 71 J. Tax'n 204 (1989); McKinney, "Golden Parachutes: An Analysis With Comments on the Proposed Regulations," 68 Taxes 242 (1990). Prop. Regs. § 1.280G-1 reissued on Feb. 20, 2002, to revise and replace the 1989 proposed regulations (the new proposals keep the same structure as the 1989 regulations, but revise, clarify, and materially liberalize the former version in several respects). Also, Rev. Proc. 2002-13, 2002-8 IRB 549 (issued a safe harbor for valuing compensatory options); expanded by Rev. Proc. 2002-45, 2002-27 IRB 40. See generally Ginsburg & Levin, Mergers, Acquisitions and Leveraged Buyouts ¶ 1318 (Panel 1999); Hevener, "Golden Parachutes: Exemptions for Some People and Some Deals But Bigger 'Excess Parachutes,'" 96 J. Tax'n 261 (May 2002).

These proposals were adopted without material change as final Regs. § 1.280G-1 by TD 9083 on Aug. 4, 2003 (effective Jan. 1, 2004). The Service also issued Rev. Proc. 2003-68, 2003-34 IRB 398 (methods for valuing stock options). See Hevener, "Golden Parachutes: Final Regs. Increase Penalties for Many Post-2003 Changes in Control," 99 J. Tax'n 156 (Sept. 2003); Raby & Raby, "Tax Tarnish on the Golden Parachute," 101 Tax Notes 243 (Oct. 13, 2003); Rizzi, "New Case Heightens Impact of Golden Parachute Rules on Corporate M&A Practice," 31 J. Corp. Tax'n 19 (Jan. 2004).

See generally Rocap, Levin & Ginsburg, "Revisiting Golden Parachutes," 102 Tax Notes 237 (Jan. 12, 2004).

Although nondeductible for regular tax purposes, parachute payments ought to reduce earnings and profits (see ¶ 8.03).

[141] The proposed regulations define "substantial portion of the corporation's assets" as one third of the assets for purposes of triggering an asset ownership change. Prop. Regs. § 1.280G-1, Q&A 29. The 2002 proposals provide likewise, as do the final regulations.

The term "disqualified individual" includes an officer, shareholder, or highly compensated individual (including a personal service corporation or similar entity), as well as any employee, independent contractor, or other person who performs personal services for the corporation and is specified in regulations.[142] A disqualified individual's "base amount" is defined by reference to the individual's average annual taxable compensation for a five-year base period preceding the change of control or ownership. The parachute payments that are compared with three times the base amount to determine the excess parachute payments are net of an allowance for amounts established as reasonable compensation for personal services that were rendered before the change (if not already compensated for) or that are to be rendered after the change.[143] The definition of "base amount" not only determines whether § 280G will apply but also determines the amount of the deduction limitation, since only payments in excess of the portion of the base amount allocable to the payment are nondeductible.

While many compensation agreements will be presumed to be subject to § 280G because they were made or modified within one year before the change in ownership, others must be shown to be contingent on the change. For this purpose, the proposed regulations adopt a but-for test, with variations.[144] They also undertake to define the crucial "change in ownership" transaction that was left undefined by the statute. Generally, "change in ownership" means the acquisition of more than 50 percent of the corporate stock (tested by

---

[142] IRC § 280G(c). See Prop. Regs. § 1.280G-1 (question 19), which defines "highly-compensated individual" as an individual in the smaller of the group of the top one percent or top 250 employees in terms of compensation (individuals earning less than $75,000 are per se not highly compensated). Question 18 of Prop. Regs. § 1.280G-1 defines "officer group" as the greater of three in number or 10 percent of the total number of employees (but not more than 50); question 17 defines "shareholder" as the owner of stock valued at at least the lesser of $1 million or one percent of the total fair market value of the corporation's stock. Fees to brokers, attorneys, and investment bankers incident to the control change, however, are not parachute payments (question 19).

The 2002 proposals raise the threshold in question 19 to $90,000, and drop the $1 million alternative in question 17; adopted by the final regulations.

[143] IRC §§ 280G(b)(3), 280G(b)(4), 280G(d)(1), 280G(d)(2). Query, would the effect of an *Oswald* payback agreement (see　8.05[2]) reduce the parachute payment to an acceptable limit? Square D Co., 121 TC 168 (2003) (but reasonable compensation test for § 280G different from § 162 test; court applied multi-factor analysis and compensation held to be unreasonable). See Raby & Raby comment, supra note 140; Rizzi, supra note 140.

[144] Prop. Regs. § 1.280G-1, Q&As 22–26. The new proposals retain the basic rule of question 22, but modify and clarify the rules in question 23 and question 24; the final regulations adopted these proposals. Square D Co., 121 TC 168 (2003), supra note 143, was hit by the but-for test. See also Ronald Yokum v. US, 2005-2 USTC　50,470 (Fed. Cl. 2005); comment by Raby & Raby, "Asset Transfer to Joint Venture Incurs Golden Parachute Tax," 110 Tax Notes 99 (Jan. 9, 2006).

vote or value) by one person or by a group of persons acting in concert.[145] A change in effective control is presumed to occur when one person or a group acting in concert acquires 20 percent or more of the total voting power or when a majority of the board is replaced during a twelve-month period against the wishes of a majority of the old board.[146]

While the impetus for § 280G was the much-criticized use of golden parachutes to cushion the departure of the management of publicly traded corporations following a hostile takeover or to deter the takeover itself by increasing its cost, § 280G applies whether a change in ownership or control is friendly or hostile and whether the corporation is closely held or publicly traded. There are, however, two important exceptions to the section's coverage, both added in 1986: Section 280G does not apply to (1) a "small business corporation," defined by § 1361(b) as a corporation that is eligible to elect S corporation status[147] or (2) a corporation whose stock is not readily tradable (on an established securities market or otherwise), provided the parachute payment is approved by the owners of more than 75 percent of the corporation's voting stock after adequate disclosure of all material facts.[148] The provision is also inapplicable if the acquirer strikes a deal to buy off an employee after the change of ownership or the change of effective control.[149]

Even with these exceptions, § 280G can raise questions about the deductibility of payments in a variety of unexpected circumstances, such as unreasonably large payments under a contract not to compete, entered into upon a sale of a family corporation that does not qualify for the exemption for S corporations (e.g., because it has two classes of stock) and that does not meet the shareholder approval exemption (e.g., because the transfer was authorized by the dominant shareholder-employee, who has customarily made all business and financial decisions but who owns less than 75 percent of the stock). In situations like these, the corporation's principal protection may prove to be the threefold cushion of § 280G(b)(2)(A)(ii), which allows a substantial margin for error in fixing the amount to be paid under a bona fide contract not to com-

---

[145] Prop. Regs. § 1.280G-1, Q&A 27. The 2002 proposals are the same. See Rev. Rul. 2005-39, 2005-27 IRB 1 (July 5, 2005) (effect of § 83(b) election in determining ownership or control; treat as outstanding stock); comment by Raby & Raby, 107 Tax Notes 1665 (June 27, 2005).

[146] Prop. Regs. § 1.280G-1, Q&A 28. The 2002 proposals modify and ease the presumption rules of question 28 (group acting in concert), and the final regulations retain these revisions. But the final regulations adopt a "one change only rule" for purposes of these tests.

[147] IRC § 280G(b)(5)(A)(i). For discussion of § 1361(b), see ¶ 6.02. The final regulations clarify that this exception applies even though no election is made.

[148] IRC § 280G(b)(5)(A)(ii). The 2002 proposals significantly modify and clarify the shareholder approval rules of question 7. The final regulations eased up a bit more here; e.g., the shareholder pool test period is doubled to six months, Q&A 7(b)(2).

[149] Prop. Regs. § 1.280G-1, Q&A 23; the final regulations continue this rule.

pete, separation agreement, or post-retirement consulting arrangement. Even that margin, however, can be sliced thin when, for example, untaxed fringe benefits are excluded from the base amount but included as parachute payments.[150]

In their zeal to penalize genuine golden parachutes, the drafters of § 280G may well have been simultaneously over-inclusive and under-inclusive; over-inclusive by raising problems for run-of-the-mill sales of closely held corporations and under-inclusive by defining the crucial term "parachute payment" as a "payment in the nature of compensation," thus opening the door to the argument that *real* golden parachutes are justified handouts of corporate assets, not objectionable because they are *non*compensatory. Presumably, however, the courts will rescue § 280G from this construction by ruling that excessive payments to departing corporate managers are in the nature of compensation if they *purport* to be compensatory.

Unfortunately, a disallowance of the corporation's deductions under § 280G increases the loss suffered by the preexisting shareholder group. That group bears the ultimate burden of both the golden parachute payments and the additional corporate tax attributable to § 280G, even if the shareholders sell out, because the well-advised buyer of stock will discount the value of the corporation by this dual burden on the corporation. As if recognizing that § 280G penalizes the wrong party to the perceived abuse, Congress enacted § 4999 as a companion provision, imposing a 20 percent excise tax on the recipient of a golden parachute payment. Canny insiders will require the corporation to reimburse them if they bail out and are caught by this tax, however, and these reimbursements will be additional parachute payments, creating a pyramid effect. On the other hand, corporations may attempt to write caps into parachute agreements to avoid excess payments or may attempt to characterize such excess amounts as loans.

The Service issued a generally helpful ruling in August 2004[151] dealing with the impact of the golden parachute rules in the context of various bankruptcy scenarios.

---

[150] See Prop. Regs. § 1.280G-1, A 34(c). See also John N. Balch, 100 TC 331 (1993), aff'd sub nom. Cline v. CIR, 34 F3d 480 (7th Cir. 1994). Query, could the parachute payments be reduced back to the safe harbor line by an employee payback agreement in his contract? IRC §§ 280G(b)(3), 280G(b)(4), 280G(d)(1), 280G(d)(2). Query, would the effect of an *Oswald* payback agreement (see   8.05[2]) reduce the parachute payment to an acceptable limit? See also 2002 Prop. Regs. § 1.280G-1, A 34(c); adopted by the final regulations.

[151] Rev. Rul. 2004-87, 2004-32 IRB 154 (Aug. 9, 2004).

[8] Securities Law Violations; Fraud

The tax implications of fines, penalties, civil damages, and legal expenses incurred by corporate officers, directors, shareholders, attorneys, accountants, and underwriters in criminal prosecutions and civil suits for violations of the federal securities laws are beyond the scope of this book; but comments on certain aspects of this area are in order at this point.[152] The Supreme Court held in 1966 that legal expenses incurred in the unsuccessful defense of a criminal prosecution arising out of the taxpayer's business activities were deductible as business expenses and did not run afoul of the judge-made frustration-of-public-policy doctrine, under which a mixed bag of deductions had been disallowed.[153] This conclusion was codified by §§ 162(c), 162(f), and 162(g), which, in effect, eliminated the ad hoc frustration-of-public-policy doctrine by explicitly disallowing deductions for—but only for—fines, penalties, bribes, and certain other payments.[154]

Thus, while fines and penalties paid for violations of securities and other laws cannot be deducted under § 162(f), legal expenses incurred by the corporation or its officers in defending against either criminal or civil charges generally are deductible. When the fraud involves the purchase or sale of stock, however, the expenses may have to be capitalized because they have their origin in the stock transaction.[155] Moreover, premiums paid for business liability insurance policies indemnifying corporate officers and directors (or attorneys, accountants, underwriters, and so forth) for expenses and liabilities incurred in connection with alleged securities law violations are deductible under § 162(a).[156]

If a corporate insider repays so-called short-swing profits under § 16(b) of the Securities Exchange Act of 1934, a deduction is allowable, but in line with *Arrowsmith v. CIR*, it constitutes a capital loss rather than a deduction from

---

[152] See generally Gideon, Lawsuits and Settlements (Little, Brown Tax Practice Series 1995).

[153] CIR v. Tellier, 383 US 687 (1966) (securities law fraud prosecution). See also Rev. Rul. 68-662, 1968-2 CB 69 (tax fraud prosecution).

[154] See Regs. § 1.162-1(a). See generally Bittker & Lokken, 3d ed.   20.3.3–20.3.5.

[155] See William Wagner, 78 TC 910 (1982) (fraud action defense costs added to basis of stock sold); Rev. Rul. 80-119, 1980-1 CB 40 (legal expenses and out-of-court settlement payments by shareholder-director accused of violating § 10(b) of Securities Exchange Act of 1934 held nondeductible capital expenditures attributable to acquisition of shareholder's stock); Mitchell v. US, 408 F2d 435 (Ct. Cl. 1969) (contra; pre-*Woodward*); supra   5.04[3].

[156] Rev. Rul. 69-491, 1969-2 CB 22. See also Rev. Rul. 76-277, 1976-2 CB 41 (business liability insurance premiums deductible by corporate executives from adjusted gross income rather than from gross income). See supra   5.04[5].

ordinary income if, as would generally be true, the insider's profit qualified as capital gain.[157]

While a corporation cannot deduct statutory penalties, including civil penalties and the trebled portion of anti-trust damages related to a criminal violation, it can deduct the damages themselves, including ordinary fraud damages, as business expenses.[158] Similarly, corporate officers can deduct damages paid by them for acts committed in the course of their individual trade or business.[159] If the corporation committed fraud in the issuance of its own shares, however, it cannot deduct the expense of settling the suit because it did not recognize gain upon issuance of the shares under § 1032.[160]

[9] Stock and Debt Issuance and Shareholder Relations Expenses

Expenditures incurred by a corporation in issuing or reselling its own stock (whether upon initial organization or pursuant to a stock dividend, recapitalization, acquisitive reorganization, public offering, or private placement) are capital outlays that can be neither amortized nor deducted when the stock is ultimately retired or the corporation is liquidated.[161] These costs reduce the

---

[157] See Arrowsmith v. CIR, 344 US 6 (1952); Brown v. CIR, 529 F2d 609 (10th Cir. 1976), and cases cited therein. But see Joseph A. Barrett, 96 TC 713 (1991) (§ 1341 credit relief allowed for insider repayment; legal expenses not deductible, because their origin was in purchase and sale of options) (nonacq.).

[158] See Rev. Rul. 80-211, 1980-2 CB 57 (punitive fraud damages deductible).

[159] See C.A. Ostrom, 77 TC 608 (1981) (fraud damages deductible by 10 percent shareholder and president of closely held corporation who induced plaintiff to buy stock from corporation).

[160] Missouri Pac. Corp. v. US, 84-1 USTC ¶ 9474 (Cl. Ct. 1984).

[161] See generally McCrory Corp. v. US, 651 F2d 828 (2d Cir. 1981) (contrasting organizational and reorganizational expenses, which can be deducted when the corporation dissolves, and the expenses of acquiring a subsidiary, which can be deducted when the subsidiary is disposed of, with stock issuance expenses, which are never deductible); Pacific Coast Biscuit Co., 32 BTA 39 (1935) (acq.) (no deduction for cost of retiring stock and reissuing new stock); Van Keuren, 28 BTA 480 (1933); General Bancshares Corp. v. CIR, 326 F2d 712 (8th Cir.), cert. denied, 379 US 832 (1964) (nondeductible stock dividend expense); Surety Fin. Co. of Tacoma v. CIR, 77 F2d 221 (9th Cir. 1935) (cited by Senate report to 1954 Code as showing that expenses of issuing stock were never amortizable, even by a corporation of limited life; S. Rep. No. 1622, 83d Cong., 2d Sess. (1954) (discussion of § 248)); Regs. § 1.248-1(b)(3) (excluding issuing and selling costs from amortization under § 248); Rev. Rul. 67-125, 1967-1 CB 31 (no deduction for legal fees for tax advice relative to stock split, unless not consummated); ¶ 10.07[2] (liquidations).

See also Skaggs Cos., 59 TC 201 (1972) (fee paid to investment banking group to ensure that taxpayer would not have to redeem preferred stock during pendency of attempts to force conversion of preferred stock into common stock; held not § 162 business expense, not deductible retirement premium, and not amortizable cost; rather, fee was nondeductible cost related to stock issuance); Quality Brands, Inc., 67 TC 167 (1976)

capital proceeds (if any) received by the corporation for its stock.[162] The cost of registering stock with the Securities and Exchange Commission (SEC), either at or after original issuance, is a similarly nondeductible capital structure cost, as is the cost of listing the stock on a stock exchange.[163] Subsequent stock-related or shareholder-related expenses that do not relate to the stock issuance, however, should be deductible under § 162.[164]

While the costs of equity financing are nondeductible capital items, the cost of issuing debt can be amortized over the term of the indebtedness, and loan fees that are treated as interest can be deducted as such, thus adding yet another tax incentive for the use of debt instead of equity in the corporate capital structure.[165]

(costs of corporate name change held nondeductible capital expenditures); Walton Hewett, 47 TC 483 (1967) (shareholder's payment of corporation's expenses of issuing stock to public held nondeductible as not related to business of shareholder).

But see Rev. Rul. 73-463, 1973-2 CB 34 (right of shareholders of open-end mutual fund to demand redemption makes company's capital-raising efforts after its initial stock offering a part of day-to-day operations; hence, expenses after ninety-day initial stock-offering period are deductible; same for expenses during and after ninety-day period starting with post-effective statements relating to additional shares). See also IRC § 162(k), discussed supra 5.04[6].

For the deductibility of organizational, reorganization, and similar expenses upon dissolution, see supra 5.04[4] (tender offers), infra 5.06 (organization, reorganization, and liquidation).

[162] See S. Rep. No. 1622, 83d Cong., 2d Sess. (1954) (detailed discussion of § 248 of 1954 Code). But cf. Sun Microsystems, Inc., RIA TC Memo. 93,467 (1993) (warrants issued as incentive to buy taxpayer's products reduced gross sales proceeds to the extent of bargain element upon exercise; held to be a sales discount or allowance; *INDOPCO* not applicable, because future benefit was only incidental); accord Convergent Techs., Inc., RIA TC Memo. 95,320 (1995).

[163] See Rev. Rul. 69-330, 1969-1 CB 51 (registration); Dome Mines Ltd., 20 BTA 377 (1930) (listing on exchange); Davis v. CIR, 151 F2d 441 (8th Cir. 1945), cert. denied, 327 US 783 (1946) (shareholder's registration expenses for secondary public offering); Consumers Water Co. v. US, 369 F. Supp. 939 (D. Me. 1974) (stock registration costs held nondeductible capital expenditures; extensive discussion); Affiliated Capital Corp., 88 TC 1157 (1987) (cost of updating registration not deductible).

[164] Annual fees for maintaining stock exchange listings were held deductible in Chesapeake Corp. of Va., 17 TC 668 (1951) (acq.) (reasoning that even if item is a capital outlay, value is exhausted within one year). See also Affiliated Capital Corp., 88 TC 1157 (1987) (maintaining public trading is an accommodation to shareholders; *Chesapeake* distinguishable from case involving initial registration of stock). The Service also allowed deductions for stock transfer fees paid to the corporation's registrar and transfer agent in Rev. Rul. 69-615, 1969-2 CB 26. Other corporate housekeeping expenses (e.g., annual reports, shareholder relations, and proxy solicitation costs) should similarly be deductible under § 162.

[165] See, e.g., Union Pac. RR Co. v. CIR, 69 F2d 67 (2d Cir.), aff'd, 293 US 282 (1934); Denver & R.G.W.R.R., 32 TC 43 (1959) (acq.), aff'd on other issues, 279 F2d 368 (10th Cir. 1960), and cases cited therein (cost of authenticating, printing, and listing); Rev. Rul. 70-353, 1970-2 CB 39 (bond issue discount deductibility); Rev. Rul. 70-359,

[10] Abandonment of Transaction for Which Expenses Were Capitalized

The discussion in the preceding paragraphs assumed that the transaction whose expenses had to be capitalized (whether an issue of stock, a redemption, and so forth) occurred as planned. If, however, the transaction is called off and the plan is abandoned, there is good authority for allowing a deduction at that time for these preliminary capitalized costs.[166] The line separating abandonment from mere deferral, however, is easier to announce than to draw.[167]

1970-2 CB 103; Rev. Rul. 70-360, 1970-2 CB 103 (method of amortizing bond issue expenses); Rev. Rul. 59 387, 1959 2 CB 56 (expenses of recapitalization that are allocable to new debentures are amortizable over their term); Duncan Indus., Inc., 73 TC 266 (1979) (stock issue discount held deductible on facts as amortizable loan origination fee because stock issue tied into loan transaction); Chicago, M., S.P. & Pac. RR v. US, 404 F2d 960 (Ct. Cl. 1968) (amortization stops when bonds are exchanged for stock); Rev. Rul. 86-67, 1986-1 CB 238 (unamortized loan costs deductible in year debtor's existence terminates); Square D Co., 121 TC 168 (2003) (loan commitment fees and related legal costs of incurring loan to finance acquisition held amortizable debt costs).

[166] See Rev. Rul. 67-125, 1967-1 CB 31 (redemption called off); Sibley, Lindsay & Curr Co., 15 TC 106 (1950) (acq.) (merger and refinancing called off); Rev. Rul. 73-580, 1973-2 CB 86 (corporate-mergers-and-acquisitions-department expenses related to abandoned acquisitions); Rev. Rul. 79-2, 1979-1 CB 98 (shareholder expenses of abandoned public stock offering); In re Federated Dep't Stores, Inc., 69 AFTR2d 92-731 (Bankr. SD Ohio 1992) (expenses of failed merger deductible as either § 162 business expenses or § 165 losses); Federated was affirmed by the district court in In re Federated Dep't Stores, Inc., 171 BR 603, 1994-2 USTC ¶ 50,430 (SD Ohio 1994); see also A.E. Staley Mfg. Co. v. CIR, 119 F3d 482, 80 AFTR2d 5060 (7th Cir. 1997) (costs attributable to abandoned takeover defense plans deductible under § 165); Freidrich, "Break-Up Fees Paid to Unsuccessful White Knight Held Deductible as Ordinary Business Expenses or as Abandonment Loss," 22 J. Corp. Tax'n 193 (1995); David Lychuk, 116 TC 374 (2001) (costs attributable to rejected applications allowed as § 165 ordinary loss).

If several capital adjustment plans are considered that are separate and distinct rather than merely alternative routes for the same transaction, the Sibley case, supra, permits the costs attributable to the abandoned plans to be deducted, but deduction will be denied where the taxpayer is unable to prove that the services rendered and the fees paid were divisible.

[167] Arthur T. Galt, 19 TC 892 (1953), aff'd on other issues, 216 F2d 41 (7th Cir. 1954) (refusing to find that two prospective leases were separable); see also El Paso Co. v. US, 694 F2d 703 (Fed. Cir. 1982) ("[t]emporary dormancy does not amount to abandonment").

¶ 5.05 DIVIDENDS-RECEIVED DEDUCTION AND RELATED PROBLEMS

Dividends received by a corporate taxpayer ordinarily qualify for the dividends-received deduction provided by § 243 (either 70 percent, 80 percent, or 100 percent of dividends received from a domestic corporation subject to federal income taxes), § 244 (at 2005 rates, about 48 percent of dividends received on certain preferred stock of public utilities), or § 245 (70 percent, 80 percent, or 100 percent of a specified portion of dividends received from certain foreign corporations), all subject to the limitations imposed by § 246. These deductions (complemented by the consolidated return rules) function somewhat imperfectly to tax corporate income only once until it is finally distributed to noncorporate shareholders.[168] The deductions cause corporate investors to favor holding corporate equity (and sometimes to accept a lower rate of return on relatively secure equity, as compared with debt), and they tend to counterbalance the usual preference of corporations for issuing debt when they need to raise capital.

Of these provisions, § 243(a)(1) is of principal importance. By permitting the corporate taxpayer to deduct 70 percent of dividends received from other corporations, § 243 reduces to 10.5 percent the effective maximum tax rate on dividends received by a corporation on portfolio stock; that is, the normal top corporate tax rate of 35 percent (2005) is imposed on only 30 percent of the dividends received. If the corporation's taxable income is below $15 million (the start of the top rate bracket), the effective tax rate on dividends received can range from a low of 4.5 percent (15 percent of 30 percent of dividends received) to 10.2 percent (34 percent of 30 percent of dividends received).[169] The tax benefit of this deduction is of course greater if the dividends qualify for the 80 percent or 100 percent deduction.

---

[168] From 1917 to 1935, corporations were not taxed on dividends received from other corporations in order to prevent the multiple taxation of corporate earnings as the earnings passed from one corporation to another, possibly within the same chain of beneficial ownership. The law was revised in 1935, however, to exempt only 85 percent of the dividends received in order to discourage the use of multiple entities for tax avoidance and as part of the New Deal program that pressed for the simplification of elaborate corporate structures. The 85 percent benchmark, adopted in 1935, was controlling until 1986, when it was lowered to 80 percent. It was further lowered to 70 percent in 1987 in the case of "portfolio dividends."

See generally Lynch, "Taxing Major Corporate Distributions (Not Involving Changes in Control)," 71 Taxes 811 (Dec. 1993); Schaffer, "The Income Tax on Intercorporate Dividends," 33 Tax Law. 161 (1979); Francis, "The Tax on Intercorporate Dividends: Current Problems and Proposed Reforms," 64 Taxes 427 (1986); Mundstock, "Taxation of Intercorporate Dividends Under an Unintegrated Regime," 44 Tax L. Rev. 1 (1988).

[169] For the effect of the alternative minimum tax on the tax cost of receiving dividends, see infra   5.08[6].

[1] Dividends From Domestic Corporations

Section 243(a)(1) provides generally that 70 percent of the amount received as dividends from a domestic corporation that is subject to federal income taxation may be deducted.[170] If, however, the shareholder owns 20 percent of the stock by vote and value (or more), it is entitled to an 80 percent deduction.[171] The requirement that the paying corporation be subject to income taxation reflects the fact that the purpose of the deduction is to mitigate the multiple taxation of corporate earnings. In harmony with this principle, dividends paid by mutual savings banks and domestic building and loan associations (loosely referred to as interest) and by real estate investment trusts do not qualify for the deduction, and certain dividends received from regulated investment companies also receive special treatment.[172]

[2] "Qualifying Dividends" of Affiliated Groups

Section 243(a)(3) permits a 100 percent deduction for certain intercorporate dividends received from a member of the same "affiliated group." This term has the same meaning as for determining whether corporations can file consolidated returns, with certain minor modifications.[173] Thus, complete tax immunity for dividends is ordinarily feasible for an affiliated group, whether or not it elects to file a consolidated return. Indeed, a basis increase similar to those in consolidated returns can be obtained by contributing the deducted dividend back to the paying corporation.

　　To qualify for the 100 percent deduction, the common parent of the group must file an election to which all members consent (a wholly owned subsidiary is deemed to consent).[174] Qualifying dividends must be paid from earnings and profits accumulated during the period of affiliation; indeed, both corporations must have been members of the affiliated group for each day of the year in or-

---

[170] In the case of a small business investment company (see ¶ 1.06[4]), under § 243(a)(2) the deduction is 100 percent of the dividends received, and the limit of § 246(b)(1) is inapplicable.

[171] IRC § 253(c). Ownership for this purpose apparently must be *direct*. In applying the 20 percent test, pure preferred stock as described in § 1504(a)(4) is ignored. This rule benefits corporate owners of other qualified stock that can still qualify for the deduction, but prevents the holder of such stock from acquiring it to obtain the increased deduction. See IRC § 243(c)(2). Treasury proposals (in 1997, 1998, and 1999) would deny the deduction to holders of "debt-like" preferred stock as defined in § 351(g); see ¶ 3.05[4]; but this proposal was not adopted.

[172] IRC § 243(d).

[173] IRC § 243(b)(2). See ¶ 13.41[2] for definition of "affiliated group"; for consolidated returns generally, see Chapter 13, Part C.

[174] See Regs. § 1.243-4(c). See also Regs. § 1.243-5 (discussing various effects of election).

der for the earnings of the year to count.[175] Thus, a corporation cannot buy into the deduction, although the regulation's last-in, first-out tracking rule for earnings and profits is favorable to the newcomer.[176]

[3] Dividends on Public Utility Preferred Stock

In increasingly rare instances, § 247 allows public utility corporations to deduct a portion of dividends paid by them on preferred stock issued before October 1, 1942, or issued thereafter to refund debt or preferred stock issued before that date. At the 35 percent rate (for 2005), fourteen thirty-fifths (40 percent) of the dividend paid is deductible by the paying corporation. To counterbalance the utility's right to deduct certain dividends paid by it under § 247, § 244 allows the recipient corporation to take only about 48 percent of the dividend into account in computing its dividends-received deduction, in lieu of the normal deduction under § 243.

[4] Dividends From Certain Foreign Corporations

[a] Doing Business in the United States

Dividends paid by a 10 percent owned foreign corporation qualify for the dividends-received deduction under § 245 if (1) the paying corporation is not a foreign personal holding company or a passive foreign investment company;[177] (2) it is subject to federal income taxation; and (3) at least 10 percent (by voting power and value) of its stock is owned by the recipient corporation. If the dividends qualify under these tests, the 70 percent or 80 percent deduction of § 243 is applied to a portion of the dividends, determined by reference to the ratio of the payor's post-1986 undistributed earnings from sources within the United States to its total post-1986 undistributed earnings. By virtue of these complex limitations, the deduction embraces dividends paid by a foreign corporation only to the extent that, roughly speaking, they reflect income that has been subjected to U.S. taxation. Thus, if 60 percent of a 20 percent owned foreign corporation's earnings are from business sources within the United States,

---

[175] IRC § 243(b)(1)(B)(i). See Rev. Rul. 85-144, 1985-2 CB 86, and Rev. Rul. 84-154, 1984-2 CB 61 (qualification of newly organized holding company for the 100 percent deduction).

[176] Regs. § 1.243-4.

[177] See   15.41, 15.44; see also Naporano v. US, 834 F. Supp. 694 (DNJ 1993) (S corporation shareholder not entitled to claim § 245 deduction). But 2004 legislation repealed the foreign personal holding company provisions (effective 2005), so its dividends can now qualify.

60 percent of its dividends will be eligible in the hands of a recipient corporation for the 70 percent or 80 percent deduction.

The 100 percent deduction of § 243(a)(3) for qualifying dividends cannot apply, because a foreign corporation cannot be a member of an affiliated group.[178] If, however, the foreign corporation is wholly owned by U.S. corporate shareholders and if all of its gross income is effectively connected with a U.S. business, the dividends qualify for a 100 percent deduction; in this situation, the foreign subsidiary is treated as the economic equivalent of a U.S. enterprise.[179]

[b] Doing Business Abroad: The Deemed Paid Foreign Tax Credit

While intercorporate dividends between domestic corporations are substantially relieved from double taxation by the deduction mechanism of § 243, relief from international double taxation is generally accomplished by means of the foreign tax credit rules of §§ 901 through 906. One of these provisions, the so-called deemed paid foreign tax credit of § 902, allows a domestic parent corporation that owns 10 percent or more of a foreign corporation and receives a dividend therefrom to elect to claim a so-called derivative foreign tax credit for taxes paid by the foreign corporation.[180]

[5] Deductions by Foreign Corporations

A foreign corporation not engaged in trade or business in the United States is taxed on dividends received from U.S. corporations, but is not allowed the 70 percent or 80 percent dividends-received deduction or, for that matter, any other deductions.[181] Foreign corporations with a domestic business situs, however, are allowed to deduct items that are effectively connected with the U.S. business, including dividends received if they constitute U.S. business income.[182]

[6] Definition and Amount of "Dividend"

Although §§ 43 through 245 do not say so explicitly, dividends should not qualify for the dividends-received deduction unless they are includible in the recipient's gross income. For this reason, stock dividends that are excluded

---

[178] See supra ¶ 5.05[2]; IRC § 1504(b)(3).

[179] See IRC § 245(b).

[180] These provisions are considered in greater detail at ¶ 15.21[2].

[181] See IRC §§ 881, 882(c).

[182] These matters are considered at ¶¶ 15.03, 15.04.

from gross income under § 305 should not give rise to a dividends-received deduction.[183]

More difficult issues, however, are whether an includible amount qualifies as a "dividend," as opposed to capital gain or some other type of nondividend income and, if it is a dividend, what is its amount. As discussed later in this book, § 316 defines the term "dividend" for purposes of the entire income tax subtitle, including §§ 243 through 245, as a distribution of property by a corporation to its shareholders from its accumulated or current earnings and profits.[184] Section 301 prescribes the treatment of property distributions by corporations to their shareholders, whether such amounts are treated as dividends or as a return of stock basis. In so doing, § 301 defines "amount of the distribution" to be the fair market value of property or the amount of cash received and requires that the resulting dividend portion of that distribution be included as such in gross income. Thus, the rules of §§ 301 and 316 for determining the amount of the distribution and the dividend component thereof control not only the shareholder's taxable portion of the distribution but also the correlative amount of a corporate shareholder's dividends-received deduction.[185] Furthermore, the taxable recipient of a dividend is the owner of the stock on the dividend record date, even though another person owns the stock on the later ex-dividend date.[186]

Nondividend distributions from a corporation that clearly should not be entitled to the dividends-received deduction include (1) distributions in excess of earnings and profits; (2) redemption proceeds that are treated as received in a sale or exchange of the stock under § 302(a);[187] (3) liquidation proceeds;[188] and (4) receipts that are not received by a shareholder with respect to his stock but are received in some other capacity.[189] Reorganization boot dividends,

---

[183] For § 305, see 8.41. Furthermore, the sale of stock rights by a shareholder who did not take the rights into income upon receipt usually produces capital gain under § 1234 and not a dividend, so the dividends-received deduction should not apply to the sales proceeds.

[184] See 8.02.

[185] See Regs. § 1.243-1(a)(3).

[186] See Rev. Rul. 82-11, 1982-1 CB 51. Cf. Silco, Inc. v. US, 779 F2d 282 (5th Cir. 1986) (prior rule).

[187] See Chapter 9 for redemptions. See also Fostoria Glass Co. v. Yoke, 45 F. Supp. 962 (ND W. Va. 1942) (when redemption was treated as dividend, dividends-received credit under 1939 Code allowed).

[188] IRC § 331(b) (§ 301 not applicable to proceeds of complete liquidation).

[189] See Liston Zander Credit Co. v. US, 276 F2d 417 (5th Cir. 1960) (alleged dividends were refunds of insurance premiums, not eligible for § 243 deduction). See also US v. Georgia RR & Banking Co., 348 F2d 278 (5th Cir. 1965) (§ 243 deduction belongs to beneficial owner of stock on which dividends were paid, in this case the "lessee" of the stock, not its "lessor"), cert. denied, 382 US 973 (1966).

however, have been held by the courts to qualify for the § 243 dividends-received deduction, and the Service agrees.[190]

Corporate shareholders about to sell stock in a controlled corporation often arrange to receive a dividend shortly before the stock sale for the purpose of stripping value out of the stock at a lower overall tax cost (because of the dividends-received deduction) than would be imposed if they sold the stock and were taxed on their capital gain. Generally, this ploy will work if the proper formalities are observed; that is, if the dividend is actually paid from the controlled corporation's assets rather than from the assets of the acquiring party, a matter discussed later in this book.[191] Similar threshold distributions made in close proximity to the corporation's liquidation also receive close scrutiny as to their true character: ordinary dividends or liquidating distributions.[192]

Of course, if the distribution is not made with respect to "stock," but is paid instead as a return on a "debt," no dividends-received deduction is allowed, since the corporate investor is receiving interest rather than dividend income. Thus, corporations desiring to raise capital from corporate investors often strive to provide their investors with debt-like paper with a sufficient equity flavor to qualify payments thereon for the dividends-received deduction.[193]

---

[190] See ¶ 12.44[2][b].

[191] See ¶¶ 8.07[2] and 9.06, discussing these so-called bootstrap acquisitions.

[192] See Roberts Gage Coal Co., 2 TC 488 (1943) (acq.) (nominal regular dividend held to be liquidating distribution).

For a related problem under the deemed paid foreign tax credit provision of § 902, see Assoc. Tel. & Tel. Co. v. US, 306 F2d 824 (2d Cir. 1962), cert. denied, 371 US 950 (1963) (distribution in complete liquidation not a dividend under § 902); Fowler Hosiery Co. v. CIR, 301 F2d 394 (7th Cir. 1962) (same for partial liquidation).

[193] For debt versus equity generally, see Chapter 4. See also Rev. Rul. 90-27, 1990-1 CB 50 (floating-rate, money-market preferred stock was held to be equity); IRC § 1503(f) (denying "special purpose subsidiary" the ability to share in group's net operating losses to the extent that subsidiary's income is used to pay dividends on "pure preferred" stock held by nongroup members, discussed in ¶ 13.46[3]).

Legislation enacted in 1990 and 1993 restricted various tax benefits of certain debt-like preferred stock, but not its continued qualification for the § 243 deduction. Thus, § 305(c) conforms the treatment of preferred stock redemption premiums to the original issue discount rules applicable to debt. See ¶¶ 8.41[2][e], 8.41[3]; ¶ 4.25[3] ("disqualified stock" under repealed stock-for-debt exception); ¶ 4.43 (stripped preferred stock).

The Clinton 1996 and 1997 revenue bills proposed to treat certain debt-like preferred stock as "boot" for purposes of §§ 351 and 356 (see ¶¶ 3.05[4], 12.41[5]); presumably such instruments would continue to constitute "stock" for purposes of the § 243 deduction. But broad regulation authority was granted to prescribe treatment under "other" Code provisions and it seemed unlikely that regulations would designate dividend payments on this type of preferred stock as "interest," at least with respect to the corporate payor. The debt-like preferred boot proposal was enacted in the 1997 Tax Act (but the Conference report states that "stock" status generally continues for other purposes unless and until prospective regulations hold otherwise).

[7] Overall Restrictions on Deductions

Although there are technically three separate dividends-received deductions (§ 243, for dividends paid by domestic corporations in the amount of 70 percent, 80 percent, or 100 percent of the dividend; § 244, for certain preferred dividends paid by public utilities; and § 245, for dividends paid by certain foreign corporations), they are aggregated in large part by § 246 for the purpose of imposing the limitations explained in the following text.[194]

[a] Certain Distributing Corporations Excluded

Section 246(a) provides that the dividends-received deductions of §§ 243 through 245 do not apply to dividends paid by corporations that are exempt from tax under § 501 (charitable corporations, federal instrumentalities,[195] mutual telephone companies, and so forth) or § 521 (farmers' cooperative associations).[196] These corporations are disqualified because their earnings are wholly or partially tax-exempt; when another corporation receives their earnings in the form of dividends, the earnings will be taxed for the first time at the corporate level.

[b] Ceiling on Aggregate Deduction

Unless the taxpayer corporation has incurred a net operating loss in the taxable year (computed under the usual rules of § 172, without any ceiling on the dividends-received deduction), a limit is applied to the aggregate of its 70 and 80 percent deductions plus most of its other deductions under §§ 244 and 245.[197] This limitation is computed first by recomputing taxable income without regard to net operating loss carryovers, capital loss carrybacks, and the dividends-received deductions subject to this process, with certain other adjust-

---

Subsequent proposals, however, would totally deny the dividends-received deduction for dividends paid on debt-like preferred stock, but they were not included in the final 1997 legislation. Denial of the dividends-deceived deduction for dividends on debt-like preferred stock was proposed again in 1998, and has returned once again in the Treasury's February 1999 revenue raising provisions (effective on date of enactment); but this proposal has not been adopted (as of January 2006), nor does it now appear likely to be.

[194] See generally Scanlan & Gardner, "The Dividends-Received Deduction: The Limitations of Section 246," 18 J. Corp. Tax'n 341 (1992).

[195] Section 246(a)(2) contains a special rule for Federal Home Loan Board dividends. See also Rev. Rul. 56-510, 1956-2 CB 168 (dividends paid by Federal National Mortgage Association qualify; although exempt, it makes payments to Treasury in lieu of taxes).

[196] In the case of payor corporations that are exempt under §§ 501 and 521, the disqualification of § 246(a) is operative if the forbidden status exists either during the year of the distribution or in the preceding year.

[197] See Regs. § 1.246-2(b).

ments.[198] Second, 80 percent of the recomputed taxable income is compared with the normally allowed 80 percent deduction with respect to dividends from 20 percent owned corporations, and the lesser amount is allowed as the actual deduction with respect to those dividends for the year.[199] Third, 70 percent of the recomputed taxable income is compared with the normally allowed deduction with respect to all other dividends subject to the rule (principally, portfolio dividends from less than 20 percent owned corporations, with respect to which a 70 percent deduction normally is allowed), and the lesser amount is allowed as the actual deduction with respect to those dividends for the year.[200]

[c] Brief Holding Periods

Before 1958, the dividends-received deduction held out to the corporate taxpayer the possibility of buying stock just before a dividend became payable and selling it immediately thereafter in order to deduct the loss on the sale (presumably equal to the amount of the dividend, assuming no interim market fluctuations), while paying income tax on only 15 percent (under then applicable law) of this amount.[201] A similar manipulative device was the maintenance of both long and short positions in the stock over the dividend payment date in order to deduct the amount of the dividend paid to the lender of the short stock from ordinary income while reporting only 15 percent of the dividend received on the long stock.[202] To close these loopholes, Congress enacted § 246(c) in 1958[203] and strengthened it in 1984.[204] Section 246(c) denies any deduction under §§ 243 through 245 if the stock is not held for more than

---

[198] IRC § 246(b)(1). See supra ¶ 5.03[4]. For the interrelationship of the limitation with other rules, see Rev. Rul. 56-151, 1956-1 CB 382 (prior alternative tax on capital gains); Lastarmco, Inc. v. CIR, 737 F2d 1440 (5th Cir. 1984) (§ 613A); Rev. Rul. 79-347, 1979-2 CB 122 (related ruling).

[199] IRC § 246(b)(3)(A).

[200] IRC § 246(b)(3)(B).

[201] See Rev. Rul. 82-11, 1982-1 CB 51 (corporation that purchases stock after record and before ex-dividend date is not entitled to the dividends-received deduction). Cf. Silco, Inc. v. US, 779 F2d 282 (5th Cir. 1986) (prior law). See also Reg. § 1.1502-13(f)(2)(iv)(A) (dividend on subsidiary's stock sold ex-dividend relates back to pre-sale date in consolidated return context).

[202] Regs. § 1.246-3(c)(3) (discussing long and short positions).

[203] See S. Rep. No. 1983, 85th Cong., 2d Sess. 28–29, 139–140 (1958). See also ¶ 8.07[2], discussing bootstrap acquisitions of stock.

[204] Section 263(h), enacted in 1984, also requires payments in lieu of dividends on stock sold short to be capitalized unless the short sale is held open for at least forty-six days (more than one year in the case of extraordinary dividends), thus reversing the holding in Rev. Rul. 62-42, 1962-1 CB 133. See also IRC § 7701(f), also enacted in 1984, authorizing regulations to prevent the use of related parties to avoid provisions that deal with the linking of borrowing to investment or diminishing risks (as of 2005, no regulations have been issued here).

forty-five days (ninety days in the case of certain preferred stock), the holding period being tolled if the taxpayer substantially diminished its risk of loss from holding the stock.[205] The deduction is also denied if the taxpayer maintained a short position in substantially similar or related stock or securities, or was subject to a similar obligation with respect to the dividend.[206] Proposed legislation in the Clinton 1996 and 1997 budget bills would extend the § 246(c) holding period to include both pre- and post-dividend terms, and this proposal was adopted in the 1997 Tax Act.[207]

[d] Debt-Financed Portfolio Stock Dividends

Section 246A deals with the tax rate arbitrage effects created by the use of leveraged portfolio stock, under which interest on debt incurred to finance the investment was fully deductible while the associated dividend income on the acquired stock was taxed at a low effective rate because of the dividends-received deduction. Section 246A reduces the recipient corporation's § 243 deduction to the extent of the debt-financed percentage of the stock. Thus, if half

---

[205] IRC §§ 246(c)(1)(A), 246(c)(2), 246(c)(3), 246(c)(4). See Rev. Rul. 80-238, 1980-2 CB 96 (writing call option on stock held by corporate shareholder did not shorten holding period for § 246(c) purposes); Progressive Corp. v. US, 970 F2d 188 (6th Cir. 1992) (application of § 246(c) to various put and call option transactions); Rev. Rul. 90-27, 1990-1 CB 50 (floating-rate preferred stock held to be equity and reset provisions do not violate § 246(c) so as to deny dividends-received deductions). But see Rev. Rul. 94-28, 1994-1 CB 86 (mandatory redemption right equivalent to an option for § 246(c)(4) limit).

Regulations proposed in 1993 embodied an expansive view of transactions that diminish the taxpayer's risk of loss. Prop. Regs. § 1.246-5. See Sheppard, "Dividends Received Deduction Regulations: A Good Start," 59 Tax Notes 1447 (June 14, 1993). See also Willens, "Dividend-Stripping Proposed Regulations Broaden the Scope of Risk Diminution," 79 J. Tax'n 138 (1993); Friedrich, "Proposed Regulations Reduce Holding Period for Purposes of Dividends-Received Deduction Where Risk of Loss Is Diminished," 20 J. Corp. Tax'n 400 (1994); Lynch, "Taxing Major Corporate Distributions (Not Involving Changes in Control)," 71 Taxes 811, 823 (Dec. 1993).

The proposed regulations became final as Regs. § 1.246-5 in TD 8590 on March 17, 1995, and generally adopted the expansive view of the "substantially similar or related property" and "diminished risk of loss" concepts, although their scope was contracted somewhat (Examples 3, 6, and 8 of the proposed regulations were deleted and a mechanical safe harbor of sorts was adopted, subject to the inevitable anti-abuse exception). See generally Ferguson, Goodman & Biller, "The Latest Stock Hedging Regulations," 67 Tax Notes 1795 (June 26, 1995) (extensive analysis of "substantially similar or related property" concept).

[206] IRC § 246(c)(1)(B). See Duke Energy Corp. v. US, 49 F. Supp. 2d 837 (WDNC 1999) (securities not substantially similar here).

[207] This proposal was reintroduced on February 6, 1997, as part of the fiscal 1998 budget bill (although this time with a prospective effective date, for stock *issued* after date of enactment), and it passed in Pub. L. No. 105-34, 105th Cong., 1st Sess., § 1015 (effective thirty days after the date of enactment, which was August 5, 1997).

of the stock basis is debt-financed, half of the § 243 deduction can be denied; the reduction, however, cannot exceed the amount of deductible interest.[208]

This provision does not apply, however, if the taxpayer acquired at least 50 percent of the stock (or owned at least 20 percent, and five or fewer corporate shareholders owned at least 50 percent of the paying corporation); nor does it apply if the taxpayer is entitled to the 100 percent dividends-received deduction.[209]

The Treasury has proposed to tighten § 246A by adopting a new and far looser "linkage" test:[210] that is, the new limitation would be the sum of (1) the percentage of stock directly financed by debt and (2) the percentage indirectly financed by debt determined by using a pro rata allocation concept.

[8] Basis Reduction for Extraordinary Dividends: § 1059

If corporation P buys stock in corporation T, the purchase price will presumably reflect the value of any potential dividends inherent in the stock. If T pays a dividend shortly thereafter, P's dividend income will be reduced by the 70 percent or 80 percent dividends-received deduction (or possibly even the 100 percent deduction if T becomes part of P's affiliated group and the dividend is

---

[208] See McKenna & Chudy, "Tax Leveraged Investments: Section 246A, Section 7701(f), and Other Recent Developments," 13 J. Corp. Tax'n 3 (1986). The linkage between borrowing and investment is tighter under § 246A than under § 265(a)(2), a similar provision restricting the interest deduction, since the latter provision applies only if the debt is incurred or maintained to purchase or carry the tax-exempt obligations while the former requires *direct* attribution (but see proposals to loosen that linkage, infra). See also IRC §§ 7701(f) (regulations authorized to prevent avoidance of this section through use of intermediaries), 246A(f) (regulations authorized to reduce interest deduction in lieu of § 243 deduction). For examples of the linkage required by § 246A, see Rev. Rul. 88-66, 1988-2 CB 35 (failure to sell portfolio stock investment; but temporary investment of loan proceeds in stock was linked, despite ultimate purpose to use funds for construction; intra-group borrowing not covered by § 246A). See also H. Enters. Int'l, Inc., 105 TC 71 (1995) (subsidiary's borrowings for use of loan proceeds by parent to purchase stock and tax-exempts raised a question of fact as to linkage for purposes of §§ 246A and 265(2); thus, motion for summary judgment denied; not exempt from these sections merely because of separate entity structure); for decision on the merits (for the government), see RIA TC Memo. 98,097 (1998); *H. Enters.* was affirmed per curiam, 1999-2 USTC 50,723 (8th Cir. 1999).

But the taxpayer prevailed in OBH, Inc. v. US, 2005-2 USTC 50,627 (DC Neb. 2005). For comments on OBH, see Willens, Viewpoint, Daily Tax Rep. (BNA) No. 211, J1- (Nov. 2, 2005); Cummings, "IRS Tries to Apply DRD Limits to the King (Warren Buffett)-And Fails," 109 Tax Notes 1191 (Nov. 28, 2005); Leeds, "Berkshire Hathaway Successfully Litigates DRD Controversy," 109 Tax Notes 1345 (Dec. 5, 2005).

[209] See IRC §§ 246A(b)(1), 246A(c)(2).

[210] Effective on date of enactment. But this proposal has not (as of July 2005) been adopted.

paid from earnings for a full year of affiliation), and the market value of the T stock should drop by approximately the amount of the dividend; however, P's basis in the T stock (at least prior to 1984) would be undiminished, permitting P to sell the T stock and, assuming no interim market fluctuations, to claim a capital loss equal to the decline in value when the stock goes ex-dividend.

These results not only appear to be too good to be true, but they are too good to be true. There are various mechanisms for dealing with this scenario in the context of affiliated corporations filing consolidated returns, as will be discussed later in this book.[211] In the unconsolidated context, the statutory mechanism is § 1059[212] (first enacted in 1984 and later modified in 1986 and 1997), which does not reduce the dividends-received deduction itself but instead imposes a special basis reduction rule that requires a corporate shareholder to reduce its basis for stock owned by it to the extent of the nontaxed portion of any "extraordinary dividend." The latter is a dividend equaling or exceeding a prescribed "threshold percentage" (5 percent for preferred stock and 10 percent for other stock) of the underlying stock basis, unless the stock was held for more than two years before the "dividend announcement date" or satisfies certain other conditions.[213]

> **EXAMPLE:** If corporation P purchased common stock of target T, which then distributed a dividend equal to or greater than 10 percent of P's basis for its T stock, P would reduce the basis of the T stock (but not below zero) by the amount of its § 243 deduction unless the transaction satisfied one of § 1059's exceptions. On a later sale or exchange of the stock, P's gain or loss would be computed by reference to its stock basis as reduced by § 1059. If the amount of the dividends-received deduction is not fully absorbed by the stock's basis, the remainder was (between 1986 and 1997) treated as gain at the time of a later stock sale; this deferral rule re-

---

[211] See Chapter 13 generally and ¶¶ 13.43[5][c] and 13.43[8] specifically for investment basis adjustment rules and rules denying losses on the sale of stock in subsidiaries. All dividends between members of an affiliated group during a consolidated return year are eliminated in determining the group's taxable income because consolidated taxable income is computed by aggregating the separate taxable income of the group members without the dividends-received deduction and then using a consolidated dividends-received deduction that excludes intercompany dividends. See Regs. § 1.1502-13(f)(2)(ii) (1995). See also Regs. §§ 1.1502-12(n), 1.1502-26(b).

[212] The 1986 legislative history made clear that § 1059 did not apply to dividends between affiliated group members filing consolidated returns, except as provided in future regulations. See HR Conf. Rep. No. 841, 99th Cong., 2d Sess. 166 (1986) (also noting that the § 1059 basis will not apply in computing earnings and profits on the later sale of the stock (see ¶ 8.03)). The legislative history regarding various 1988 technical corrections amendments, however, indicates that § 1059 can apply to consolidated groups, presumably by regulation. See S. Rep. No. 445, 100th Cong., 2d Sess. 50–51 (1988).

[213] IRC § 1059(c). But see IRC § 1059(e) for certain per se extraordinary dividends (a list that has been expanded several times since the initial enactment of this provision).

sulted in the creation of a negative basis for the stock, but was changed in 1997 to an immediate gain recognition rule.[214]

Because its consequences are so significant, it is important to understand some significant limitations on the application of § 1059. Obviously, § 1059 applies only to corporate shareholders who enjoy a dividends-received deduction, and (until regulations are issued to the contrary) it does not apply to dividends from an affiliated group member with which the recipient files a consolidated return.[215] It also does not apply to dividends announced more than two years after the stock acquisition, using a broad definition of "announcement,"[216] or to stock held during the entire period of the payor's existence, provided the payor corporation's earnings and profits have not been augmented by earnings and profits of other corporations (e.g., through mergers) with which the shareholder did not have the same historic relationship.[217] Section 1059 does not apply to qualifying dividends that are eligible for the 100 percent dividends-received deduction, except to the extent attributable to earnings accumulated prior to the time of affiliation, or to gain on the payor's property that accrued before the payor became a member of the affiliated group.[218] It also does not apply to certain preferred stock dividends if the taxpayer holds the stock for more than five years.[219]

---

[214] The initial 1984 version of § 1059 taxed any excess amount currently as gain from the sale of stock; the 1986 amendment switched to a deferred gain rule, triggered by a later sale of the stock. HR 2491, § 11301, proposed to return to the 1984 rule and require current taxability in place of a negative basis rule. Although HR 2491 was vetoed in 1995, the Clinton 1996 and 1997 budget bills had an identical rule, and all versions contained a May 3, 1995, effective date. The Clinton 1998 budget bill included the same provision (and the same effective date), and, as expected, it finally passed in HR 2014, § 1011 (with the May 3, 1995, effective date).

[215] But see S. Rep. No. 445, 100th Cong., 2d Sess. 50–51 (1988) (indicating that § 1059 can apply to consolidated groups).

[216] IRC § 1059(d)(5) (the earliest date on which the corporation declares, announces, or agrees to the amount or payment of the dividend). Furthermore, the holding period can be tolled by the rules of §§ 246(c)(3) and 246(c)(4), substituting two years for forty-five days. IRC § 1059(d)(3). Apparently, all preferred dividends attributable to the first two years are agreed to in amount by the terms of the preferred stock. See S. Rep. No. 445, 100th Cong., 2d Sess. 47–49 (1988).

[217] IRC § 1059(d)(6). But see Regs. § 1.1059(e)-1(a) (§ 1059(e)(1) trumps § 1059(d)(6) in overlap case), adopted in TD 8724 on July 16, 1997.

[218] IRC § 1059(e)(2). While earnings that accrued prior to the time of affiliation are not eligible for the 100 percent dividends-received deduction in any event, this rule apparently is aimed at tiered-up dividends from subsidiaries' earnings during earlier years. See S. Rep. No. 445, 100th Cong., 2d Sess. 50 (1988). Prop. Regs. § 1.1059(e)-1(a) (June 18, 1996) (§ 1059(e)(2) exception); final regulations issued on July 16, 1997, in TD 8724, are the same.

[219] IRC § 1059(e)(3).

Certain dividends, however, are automatically deemed to be extraordinary: (1) redemptions that either are treated as partial liquidations or that are non–pro rata but nevertheless are treated as dividends, regardless of the holding period of the stock,[220] and (2) dividends on so-called self-liquidating preferred stock, that is, stock that has a declining dividend rate or a redemption price less than its issue price or stock that is otherwise structured so as to enable corporate shareholders to reduce tax through a combination of dividends-received deductions and loss on the sale of the stock.[221] Moreover, regulations proposed in 1996 and adopted in 1997[222] provide (prospectively) that § 1059(e)(1) trumps any of the exceptions to § 1059. Finally, proposed legislation would expand the per se basis reduction rules of § 1059(e)(1) (once again) to include all dividends not subject to current U.S. tax, including a proportional part of dividends subject to reduced treaty rates.[223] The Treasury's proposed dividend exclusion[224] would also extend the § 1059 basis reduction rules

---

[220] IRC § 1059(e)(1). Legislation proposed in May 1995 would have dropped the basis reduction rule of § 1059(e)(1) and replaced it with per se § 302(a) sale treatment for these transactions; see ¶ 9.03[4]. But the 1997 Tax Act retained § 1059(e)(1) and expanded it to cover dividends created by option attribution under § 318, reorganization boot dividends, and dividends created by § 304; this legislation also returned to the 1984 rule requiring current gain if the adjustment exceeds basis. Moreover, the last sentence of § 1059(e)(1)(A) provides that *only* the basis of the stock redeemed can be counted in computing recognized gain under § 1059(a). The general effective date of these amendments is May 3, 1995 (except for the § 304 per se rule, which is June 9, 1997). Stewart, Randall & Gardner, "Extraordinary Dividends After TRA '97," 25 J. Corp. Tax'n 259 (1998); Friedel, "The Labyrinth of Sections 304 and 1059—New Fictions Create Real Questions," 89 J. Tax'n 79 (1998); Friedel, "Virtual Stock Sales Under Section 304: Wrestling With the Aftermath of TRA '97," 89 J. Tax'n 154 (1998).

The Treasury proposed (in February 1999) to expand the per se basis reduction scope of § 1059(e)(1) again to include all dividends not subject to current U.S. tax (including a proportional part of dividends subject to reduced treaty rates). But see Notice 2001-45, 2001-22 IRB 129 (attacking offshore Seagram-type basis shifting shelters under current law general principles); Sheppard, "Dissecting the Basis Shifting Transaction," 92 Tax Notes 870 (Aug. 13, 2000). Prop. Regs. § 1.302-5, issued on October 16, 2002, respond to Notice 2001-45, and stop the basis-shifting transactions in the case of redemptions taxable as a dividend; see ¶¶ 9.09[4][d], 9.22[2].

[221] IRC §§ 1059(f), 1059(g) (effective for stock issued after July 10, 1989).

[222] Prop. Regs. § 1.1059(e)-1(a) (June 18, 1996); the proposed regulations also provided that § 356(a)(2) reorganization boot dividends were subject to the § 1059(e)(1) rules (a result now codified in § 1059(e)(1)(B) as amended in 1997); these regulations became final in TD 8724 on July 16, 1997, without change.

[223] This proposal is part of the Treasury's corporate tax shelter package (infra ¶ 5.10), and would be effective on the date of first committee action. It would also apply § 1059 to noncorporate shareholders in this situation. For description of the transactions targeted by this proposal, see Sheppard, "Attention Kmart Shoppers: Tax Shelters in Aisle Six," 80 Tax Notes 1402 (Sept. 21, 1998).

[224] See ¶¶ 1.08[4], 8.06.

to tax-exempt dividends and basis step-up allocations to all shareholders, corporate and individual.[225]

The normal rules for identifying an extraordinary dividend require a comparison of the amount of the dividend with the underlying stock's adjusted basis. However, since dividends obviously can be segmented, one rule aggregates all dividends received within an 85-day period, while another rule treats as extraordinary all dividends with ex-dividend dates during the same 365 consecutive days if their total exceeds 20 percent of the stock's basis.[226] Finally, the shareholder has the option to show the fair market value of its stock in the payor corporation as of the day before the ex-dividend date, and to use that amount, rather than its adjusted stock basis, in calculating the 5 percent or 10 percent thresholds.[227]

[9] Proposed Dividend Exclusion: Effect on § 243 Dividends-Received Deduction

The Treasury's proposed exclusion for dividends paid from previously taxed income[228] would apply to corporate shareholders as well as individuals. Thus qualified dividends would be exempt at the corporate level as well and would increase its excludable distribution amount (and hence will remain excludable when redistributed by the recipient corporation).[229] The current 100 percent dividends-received deduction for 80 percent owned corporations would be retained, but the 80 and 70 percent deductions would be phased out under a transition rule.[230] But this proposal failed to pass.

---

[225] HR 2 and S. 2, § 202(c)(6), amended in § 1059 and § 1059(g) (Feb. 27, 2003). For the treatment of § 1059 dividends in the final version, see § 1(h)(11)(D)(ii).

[226] IRC § 1059(c)(3).

[227] IRC § 1059(c)(4). See Rev. Proc. 87-33, 1987-2 CB 402; Rev. Rul. 88-49, 1988-1 CB 297.

[228] See 1.08[4], 8.06; these excluded dividends would not qualify for the § 243 deduction under proposed § 246(f).

[229] Prop. IRC §§ 116, 281, 282.

[230] HR 2, § 202(c)(2)(B), adding § 243(f). The Thomas alternative dividend relief proposal (taxing dividends at the same rates as capital gains) applies only to noncorporate shareholders (and thus would have no effect on § 243). This was the version ultimately adopted in the final 2003 legislation.

¶ 5.06 ORGANIZATIONAL, REORGANIZATION, AND LIQUIDATION EXPENDITURES

[1] Organizational Expenses

[a] Section 248 Election

Before 1954, a corporation's organizational expenditures, such as legal fees for drafting the charter, bylaws, and stock certificates, could not be deducted when paid or incurred, but were treated as investments to be deducted as a loss upon dissolution or, in the unusual case of a corporation of limited duration, to be amortized over the life specified in the corporation's charter.[231] For the stated purpose of conforming "tax accounting more closely with general business accounting for these costs," § 248 was enacted in 1954 to permit the corporation to elect to amortize its organizational expenditures over a period of sixty months or more from the month in which the corporation begins business.[232] The regulations state that the date a corporation begins business is a question of fact and that ordinarily it is the date when the corporation "starts the business operation for which it was organized," not the date when it comes into existence.[233]

The term "organizational expenditures" is defined by § 248(b) to mean any expenditure that is (1) incident to the creation of the corporation; (2) chargeable to capital account; and (3) of a character that, if expended incident to the creation of a corporation having a limited life, would be amortizable over such life. Thus, § 248(b) applies to the same expenses that were capitalized under pre-1954 law.

The regulations list as examples of expenditures that qualify under § 248:

legal services incident to the organization of the corporation, such as drafting the corporate charter, bylaws, minutes of organizational meetings, terms of original stock certificates, and the like; necessary accounting services; expenses of temporary directors and of organizational meetings of directors or stockholders; and fees paid to the State of incorporation.[234]

---

[231] See infra ¶ 5.06[1][b].

[232] S. Rep. No. 1622, 83d Cong., 2d Sess. 37 (1954). See Rev. Rul. 67-15, 1967-1 CB 71 (corporation can deduct § 248 amortization, even though expenditure was capitalized on its books).

[233] Regs. § 1.248-1(a)(3) (acquisition of operating assets necessary to the type of business contemplated may constitute beginning business). See C.E. McManus III, TC Memo. 1987-457 (corporate business never began), aff'd, 865 F2d 255 (4th Cir. 1988).

[234] Regs. § 1.248-1(b)(2).

The regulations go on to exclude expenditures connected with issuing or selling stock, such as commissions, professional fees, and printing costs. This exclusion of the expense of raising capital is in harmony with authority ruling that such expenses are the equivalent of selling the stock at a discount and that they do not create an asset that is exhausted over the life of the corporation.[235] The regulations also exclude from § 248 similar expenses of selling debt securities, but these costs may be amortized over the term of the loan.[236] The regulations state that expenditures connected with the transfer of assets to a corporation do not qualify for amortization under § 248; no examples are given, but the reference presumably is to the cost of title searches, recordation, transportation, and so forth, which would be added to the basis of the assets themselves, to be depreciated over their useful life or offset against the proceeds when the assets are sold.[237] Finally, the regulations state that expenditures connected with a corporation's reorganization, unless "directly incident to the creation of a corporation," do not qualify under § 248, echoing a statement in the Senate report on the 1954 Code.[238] Some reorganizations include the creation of a new corporation (e.g., some consolidations and transfers to controlled corporations), and this part of the expenses can be amortized under § 248.[239]

Expenses incurred in amending the corporation's charter, although similar to organizational expenses, cannot satisfy the requirements of § 248(b)(1), since they are usually incurred after the enterprise has gotten underway.[240] Exclusion from § 248, however, should not bar a deduction when the corporation liquidates, as long as the expenditure did not relate to issuing stock. Further-

---

[235] Regs. § 1.248-1(b)(3)(i). See Surety Fin. Co. of Tacoma v. CIR, 77 F2d 221 (9th Cir. 1935) (endorsed by S. Rep. No. 1622, 83d Cong., 2d Sess. (1954)). (See also supra 5.04[9].)

[236] See supra   5.04[9].

[237] See Warsaw Photographic Assocs., Inc., 84 TC 21, 47 (1985) (Issue III.B of opinion required capitalization of asset acquisition costs).

[238] S. Rep. No. 1622, 83d Cong., 2d Sess. (1954).

[239] See generally Reef Corp., TC Memo. 1965-72, aff'd on other issues, 368 F2d 125 (5th Cir. 1966) (organizational expenses of creating a new corporation in the context of a Type D reorganization amortizable under § 248); Rev. Rul. 70-241, 1970-1 CB 84 (organizational expenses of new corporation created incident to a Type F reorganization amortizable under § 248); Deering Milliken, Inc., 59 TC 469 (1973) (taxpayer formed by consolidation of several existing corporations; legal fees and related expenses incurred in connection with appraisal proceeding by dissenting shareholders not deductible organization expenses under § 248, because not functionally related to creation of new corporation, per *Woodward* and *Hilton Hotels*). For the *Woodward* and *Hilton Hotels* cases, see supra   5.04[3].

[240] See, e.g., Borg & Beck Co., 24 BTA 995 (1931) (acq.). But see Rev. Rul. 63-259, 1963-2 CB 95 (expenses of renewing charter amortizable under § 248). See also US v. General Bancshares Corp., 388 F2d 184 (8th Cir. 1968) (expense of changing corporation's name was a nondeductible capital expenditure).

more, organizational expenses must be distinguished from business start-up expenses, which must be capitalized and may be amortized over sixty months under § 195.[241]

Organizational costs incurred by the shareholders (as opposed to costs incurred by the new corporation) do not qualify for amortization under § 248 by the shareholder, but ordinarily must be capitalized as part of the transferors' stock basis under the *Woodward* and *Hilton Hotels* principle that costs originating in the stock acquisition process constitute capital expenditures.[242] However, such expenses for the benefit of the corporation might be includible in the amortizable organizational expenditures of the corporation on the theory that the shareholder paid the expenses as a contribution to the corporation's capital, implying that in effect the corporation itself made these expenditures.[243]

The corporation must make the election to amortize organizational expenditures under § 248 on a timely filed tax return for the taxable year in which it begins business.[244] The election must specify an amortization period of sixty months or longer that must commence with the month in which the taxpayer begins business, which may not be altered, and over which the expenditures are to be deducted ratably.[245] The regulations state that an election "shall apply" to all the corporation's organizational expenditures, thus prohibiting a partial election, but that only expenditures incurred before the end of the taxable year in which business begins will qualify.[246] This statement leaves ambiguous the status of subsequently incurred organizational expenditures.[247] The Treasury's position might be that such expenditures are not only outside

---

[241] For discussion of § 195, see generally Javaras et al., Start-Up Expenses (Little Brown Tax Practice Series 1995). See Rev. Rul. 99-23, 1999-20 IRB 3 (investigation costs amortizable under § 195; but acquisition costs are capital under § 263).

[242] See supra ¶¶ 5.04[1] (discussing contributions to capital, which is how such payments may be characterized if made by a shareholder), 5.04[3].

Individual incorporator's expenses for tax advice in connection with the corporate organization may, however, be deductible under § 212(3). See Kaufmann v. US, 227 F. Supp. 807 (WD Mo. 1963) (cost of getting tax ruling on a merger deductible by shareholder), appeal dismissed, 328 F2d 619 (8th Cir. 1964).

[243] See supra ¶ 5.04[1].

[244] See IRC § 248(c); Regs. § 1.248-1(c).

[245] Regs. § 1.248-1(a)(1). See Bay Sound Transp. Co. v. US, 20 AFTR2d 5418 (SD Tex. 1967), aff'd in part and rev'd in part on other issues, 410 F2d 505 (5th Cir.) (filing return that erroneously claimed full current deduction for organizational expenses constituted binding failure to elect under § 248), cert. denied, 396 US 928 (1969); Warsaw Photographic Assocs., Inc., 84 TC 21 (1985) (same; action not close enough to raise an issue of "substantial compliance").

[246] Regs. § 1.248-1(a)(2).

[247] Cf. Farmers Grain Mktg. Terminal, 434 F. Supp. 368 (ND Miss. 1977) (later billed amount can be added to amortizable amount in later year of five-year period), aff'd without opinion, 609 F2d 1006 (5th Cir. 1980).

§ 248 but are also disqualified for deduction upon dissolution, although this position seems unreasonably formalistic.

If a corporation that elects under § 248 is dissolved before its organizational expenditures have been fully amortized, the corporation should be entitled to deduct the balance at that time, but § 248 is silent on this point.[248] A deduction could be defended on the ground that the unamortized expenses represent an investment in the corporate shell, which is in effect abandoned as worthless upon its liquidation.

When a corporation with unamortized § 248 organizational expenses undergoes a reorganization that does not terminate its corporate existence (e.g., a recapitalization or the acquisition of all of its stock solely in exchange for the voting stock of the acquiring corporation in a Type B reorganization), the corporation's deferred organizational expense account is unaffected.[249] Matters are less clear, however, if the taxpayer corporation is acquired by another corporation in a Type A reorganization (merger or consolidation) or a Type C reorganization (where assets are transferred to the acquiring corporation in exchange for its stock) or if the taxpayer corporation reincorporates into another corporate shell (in certain nondivisive Type D or Type F reorganizations) or if a subsidiary liquidates into its parent under § 332. It is likely, but not certain, that the transferor corporation's unamortized organizational expense account passes over to the acquiring corporation by virtue of §§ 381(a)(2) and 381(c)(4) and continues to be amortized by its successor. The Service has allowed this treatment in the case of a Type F reorganization (reincorporation into another shell).[250]

Under pre-1954 Code case law, deductibility of the transferor corporation's capitalized organizational expenses depended on whether its legal existence terminated or survived in the reorganization (or subsidiary liquidation); deduction was permitted if the taxpayer dissolved, but was denied if the merger resulted in continued corporate existence.[251] The vitality of these deci-

---

[248] See　10.07[2]. Cf. IRC § 195(b)(2) (unamortized business start-up expenses deductible when business is disposed of); infra　5.06[2][h], 5.06[3] (ultimate deduction of reorganization expenses).

[249] See Chapter 12 for reorganizations generally.

[250] See Regs. § 1.381(c)(4)-1(a)(1)(ii), which provides that an acquiring corporation in a § 381 transaction takes into account the acquired corporation's dollar balances that, because of the acquired corporation's method of accounting, were not required or permitted to be deducted in full prior to the acquisition; Rev. Rul. 70-241, 1970-1 CB 84 (unamortized § 248 expenses carried over to successor corporation in a Type F reorganization). See also　14.23.

[251] See Citizens Trust Co., 20 BTA 392 (1930) (merger preserved identity; no deduction); Motion Picture Capital Corp. v. CIR, 80 F2d 872 (2d Cir. 1936) (same); Koppers Co. v. US, 278 F2d 946 (Ct. Cl. 1960) (§ 332 liquidation of controlled subsidiary; deduction allowed); Bryant Heater Co. v. CIR, 231 F2d 938 (6th Cir. 1956) (same). Cf. Dragon Cement Co. v. US, 144 F. Supp. 188 (D. Me. 1956) (deduction for original expense al-

sions after the enactment of § 381 is unclear, as discussed in the following paragraph. Furthermore, § 381 has no impact on transactions outside its scope.

[b] No § 248 Election

If the corporation does not make an election, it may deduct organizational expenditures only upon dissolution (except for a corporation of limited life, which may amortize the expenses over that life) under the judicial rules that were developed before the enactment of § 248.[252] If a corporation that did not make a § 248 election (e.g., its organization predated 1954) later reorganizes, there is authority under the 1954 Code that the corporation's ability to deduct the expenses at that time depends on whether it liquidates in the reorganization.[253] If § 381 applies to the transaction, however, it seems that the carryover rule described previously should apply.

[2] Expenses of Reorganization

[a] General Rule

The well-established rule in the area of reorganization expenses is that amounts incurred to effectuate a corporate "reorganization"—in the broad sense of a rearrangement resulting in a restructuring of the corporate entity, enterprise, or its debt or equity structure, even if not a technical "reorganization" as defined by § 368(a)[254]—are not currently deductible as business ex-

---

lowed upon merger under unusual facts requiring identical expenses to be paid again), vacated on other issues, 244 F2d 513 (1st Cir. 1957).

[252] See Shellabarger Grain Prods. Co. v. CIR, 146 F2d 177, 185 (7th Cir. 1944); Liquidating Co., 33 BTA 1173 (1936) (nonacq.) (deduction allowed in year franchise became worthless, and corporation could not be revived); Hershey Mfg. Co. v. CIR, 43 F2d 298 (10th Cir. 1930); Koppers Co. v. US, 278 F2d 946 (Ct. Cl. 1960); Hollywood Baseball Ass'n, 42 TC 234 (1964) (acq.), aff'd, 352 F2d 350 (9th Cir. 1965), vacated on other issues, 383 US 824 (1966); Kingsford Co., 41 TC 646 (1964) (acq.) (liquidation in Type C reorganization). See also infra ¶ 5.06[3] and ¶ 10.07[2].

[253] See Kingsford Co., 41 TC 646 (1964) (acq.) (1957 Type C reorganization and liquidation; deduction allowed); Vulcan Materials Co. v. US, 446 F2d 690 (5th Cir.), cert. denied, 404 US 942 (1971) (deduction denied for previously capitalized reorganization and reorganization expenses upon a 1957 statutory merger of the taxpayer into another corporation following *Citizens Trust* (supra note 251) and distinguishing *Kingsford* as a true dissolution); Canal-Randolph Corp. v. US, 568 F2d 28 (7th Cir. 1977) (court denied deduction of 1939 organizational expenses upon a 1964 merger because the merged corporation's rights continued under state law).

[254] See Chapter 12 for discussion of § 368. For examples of other restructurings to which the rule applies, see Bilar Tool & Dye Corp. v. CIR, 530 F2d 708 (6th Cir. 1976) (§ 355 division of corporation into two parts; creation of new subsidiary was a § 368(a)

penses under § 162 by the person incurring such costs.[255] If, as is usual, the reorganization is a transaction with respect to which any portion of the gain or loss is not recognized under §§ 351 through 368, the related professional fees and transaction costs are specifically excluded by § 197(e)(8) from the intangibles amortization regime enacted in 1993.

The rule is easier to state than its reasons. In *INDOPCO, Inc.*,[256] the Supreme Court seemed most concerned with making clear that capitalization is not limited to expenses of creating or enhancing a separate and distinct asset. Rather, the Court stated that while the presence of an "incidental future benefit" may not in itself warrant capitalization, the production of significant benefits that extend beyond the tax year on the facts of that case did require capitalization, even though no distinct asset was created or enhanced. *INDOPCO, Inc.*, involved an advisory fee a public company paid to an investment banker in connection with its friendly takeover by a much larger public company. The opinion listed the following long-term benefits to the smaller company: (1) the acquirer's resources became available to the smaller company; (2) synergy was created between the two companies' products; (3) the shareholder relations expenses of a public company were shed; and (4) authorized but unissued shares were reduced. Apparently desiring to place its decision in the line of prior authorities requiring capitalization, the *INDOPCO*

---

reorganization, but distribution of subsidiary's stock was not); General Bancshares Corp. v. CIR, 326 F2d 712 (8th Cir.) (stock dividends), cert. denied, 379 US 832 (1964); In re Placid Oil Co., 69 AFTR2d 92-623 (Bankr. ND Tex. 1990) (debtor's Chapter 11 bankruptcy expenses are capital even though not a technical § 368 tax-law reorganization; but expenses of day-to-day bankruptcy administration are deductible), aff'd, 69 AFTR2d 92-639 (ND Tex. 1991), rev'd and remanded, 988 F2d 554 (5th Cir. 1993) (must be allocated to deductible, amortizable, and nonamortizable categories); Rev. Rul. 77-204, 1977-1 CB 40 (same).

[255] INDOPCO, Inc. v. CIR, 503 US 79 (1992) (quoting this book), and cases cited therein. See generally Adams & Hinderliter, "*INDOPCO, Inc. v. Commissioner*: Impact Beyond Friendly Takeovers," 55 Tax Notes 93 (Apr. 6, 1992); Lee, "Doping Out the Capitalization Rules After INDOPCO," 57 Tax Notes 669 (Nov. 2, 1992). See also Rev. Rul. 73-580, 1973-2 CB 86 (expenses of in-house merger and acquisition staff must be capitalized; costs of abandoned acquisition plans deductible in year of abandonment). But compare In re Federated Dep't Stores, Inc., 92-1 USTC   50,097 (Bankr. SD Ohio 1992) (expenses of attempting to arrange unsuccessful mergers deductible either as § 162 ordinary and necessary business expenses or § 165 abandonment losses); *Federated* was affirmed, 171 BR 603, 1994-2 USTC   50,430 (SD Ohio 1994); supra   5.04[4] (expenses of resisting tender offers). See Faber, "*INDOPCO*: The Unsolved Riddle," 47 Tax Law. 607 (1994); Silverman & Weinstein, "*INDOPCO* and the Tax Treatment of Reorganization Expenses," 75 Tax Notes 243 (Apr. 14, 1997); Salem & Clair, "Emerging Post-*INDOPCO* Issues: Rationale and Strategies," 78 Tax Notes 1419 (Mar. 16, 1998). But see new Regs. § 1.263(a)-5 (Dec. 2003), which materially contracted the scope of *INDOPCO*, supra note 113.

[256] INDOPCO, Inc. v. CIR, 503 US 79 (1992). But see Regs. § 1.263(a)-5 (Dec. 2003), supra note 113.

opinion cited both (1) cases that relied on the requirements of § 162(a) that the expenses must be "ordinary and necessary" and must be incurred "in carrying on any trade or business" and (2) cases that focused on the corporation's operations and whether the expenses resulted in significant benefits lasting for a period beyond the current year.

The opinion placed greater weight on the latter ground, which evidently made it appropriate for the Court to list the long-term "benefits" that inured to the acquired corporation as a result of the reorganization.[257] Perhaps if there is sufficient business purpose to effect a change in the structure of a corporation, the expense should be presumed to be for a future benefit of more than incidental value and hence should be capitalized.[258] Moreover, it appears that corporate directors who recommend acceptance of a takeover proposal almost necessarily thereby supply the Service with evidence that they expect long-term benefits to the corporation.[259]

[b] Potential Exceptions

Like all general rules, the rule that the expenses of corporate reorganizations must be capitalized is subject to important exceptions, which mirror the complexity and variety of the problems encountered in the tax-free-reorganization area generally. In the final analysis, deductibility of a particular expense turns on the mix of such factors as (1) the nature of the expense; (2) the relationship and proximity of the expense to the reorganization transaction; (3) the person who incurred the expense (transferor corporation, transferee corporation, or shareholders and security holders of the reorganizing companies);[260] (4)

---

[257] Although some of those benefits were as inconsequential as the elimination of authorized but unissued preferred shares and the reduction of the total number of common shares, it is conceivable that there may arise a new defensive ploy of taxpayers attacking both the value and the business purpose of their own reorganizations in order to avoid the capitalization results dictated by *INDOPCO.* Such an effort, however, could backfire by causing loss of tax-free reorganization status if the business purpose for the transaction is only an "incidental future benefit" and the actual purpose, as revealed by the dispute over expense deductions, is tax avoidance. See   12.61[1].

[258] But see infra   5.06[2][e], discussing cases that allowed deduction of the expenses of compulsory corporate divestures on the ground that the transactions did not benefit the corporation.

[259] See Victory Mkts., Inc., 99 TC 648 (1992) (initially unwanted tender offer was not hostile, because board entertained it; fact that acquirer would cause target to incur debt to pay off cost of leveraged buyout could not be considered as detrimental to the target, because it was the norm; board's press releases stated that takeover would strengthen target). But Reg. § 1.263(a)-5 (Dec. 2003) have substantially contracted the scope of *INDOPCO,* supra note 113.

[260] See infra   5.06[2][c], 5.06[2][d], 5.06[2][i]. See also TAM 9326001 for an extensive analysis of authorities in connection with allowing a deduction for the target's compensation expenses that were capitalized for book purposes by the acquiring consoli-

the form and structure of the particular transaction (i.e., merger, consolidation, stock-for-stock exchange, stock-for-assets exchange, transfer of assets to a controlled corporation, reincorporation, recapitalization, corporate division, or bankruptcy reorganization);[261] (5) the ability of the taxpayer to identify with reasonable exactitude the functional steps in the reorganization proceedings to which the costs relate and the parties for whose benefit they were incurred;[262] and (6) whether the transaction is actually consummated.[263]

The diverse expenses that can arise in effecting a reorganization include preliminary investigation and negotiation expenses;[264] costs of preparing legal documents required to effect the reorganization; finder's fees; appraisal expenses; legal and accounting fees for preparation of SEC registration statements;[265] fees for audit and preparation of financial statements; costs of proxy statements and the solicitation of shareholders;[266] costs of shareholders' meetings; costs of amending the terms of existing indentures, mortgages, and loan agreements; costs of amending the corporate charter; expenses in selling or disposing of unwanted assets;[267] expenses incident to the transfer of assets; legal research bearing on corporate law, tax law,[268] or other legal problems presented by the reorganization plan; costs of obtaining a tax ruling;[269] costs of listing the issued securities on an exchange;[270] charges by transfer agents; and court costs and other litigation expenses arising out of the reorganization.[271] In addition to costs directly associated with the reorganization transaction itself,

---

dated group. See also Reg. § 1.263(a)-5 (Dec. 2003), which have materially expanded the deductibility potential; supra note 113.

[261] See infra ¶¶ 5.06[2][c], 5.06[2][d], 5.06[2][e], 5.06[2][f], 5.06[2][g].

[262] See infra ¶ 5.06[2][b]. See generally In re Placid Oil Co., 988 F2d 554 (5th Cir. 1993).

[263] See supra ¶ 5.04[10].

[264] See Ellis Banking Corp. v. CIR, 688 F2d 1376 (11th Cir. 1982) (fees for investigation by accountants of potential target corporation held part of stock acquisition cost), cert. denied, 463 US 1207 (1983). This same treatment would also cover the usually much larger fees of investment bankers.

[265] See supra ¶ 5.05[9].

[266] See supra ¶ 5.04[5].

[267] See supra ¶ 5.04[3].

[268] See Rev. Rul. 67-125, 1967-1 CB 31 (legal fees in securing advice on tax consequences prior to consummation of merger, stock split, and redemption must be capitalized).

[269] See El Paso Co. v. US, 694 F2d 703 (Fed. Cir. 1982) (cost of obtaining ruling on spin-off must be capitalized).

[270] See supra ¶ 5.04[9].

[271] See supra ¶¶ 5.04[5], 5.04[8].

collateral expenses may be incurred in organizing new corporations[272] and/or in liquidating corporate parties to the reorganization.[273] The latter amounts, if sufficiently identifiable, may stand on a different footing from the pure reorganization expense items. Moreover, expenses incurred by the corporation for the direct benefit of a shareholder would be nondeductible as dividends.[274]

If any of these costs are to be deductible, accurate records of who sustained them and the proceedings to which they relate are essential. A failure to allocate costs contemporaneously will not foreclose a later allocation by the courts, but the chances of losing on burden-of-proof ground are increased by lack of attention to itemization, especially since these expenses are difficult to apportion under the best of circumstances.[275]

[c] Acquirer's Expenditures

In acquisitive reorganizations (whether the form is an acquisition of assets or stock and whether the corporate fusion is by merger, consolidation, or practical merger in a Type C reorganization), the expenses of the acquiring corporation are the most vulnerable to capital expenditure classification. The Supreme Court decisions in *Woodward* and *Hilton Hotels* holding that costs originating in the acquisition process (whether the transaction is taxable or tax-free) must be treated as nondeductible capital items are probably conclusive of the capitalization question;[276] but some of the expenses may be deductible or

---

[272] See supra   5.06[1] for treatment of organizational expenses; Rev. Rul. 70-241, 1970-1 CB 84 (organizational expenses of corporation created in Type F reorganization were amortizable under § 248).

[273] See infra   5.06[3].

[274] See   8.05 (constructive dividends). Cf. Nat. Starch & Chem. Corp., 93 TC 67 (1989) (court did not reach government's assertion of constructive dividend, since court held the payments nondeductible on other ground), aff'd, 918 F2d 426 (3d Cir. 1990), aff'd sub nom. INDOPCO, Inc. v. CIR, 112 S. Ct. 1039 (1992).

[275] Compare Sibley, Lindsay & Curr Co., 15 TC 106 (1950) (acq.) (investment banker's lump-sum fee allocated one third to each of three plans, only one of which was carried out; two thirds of fee ruled deductible because plans were not alternatives) with Arthur T. Galt, 19 TC 892 (1953), aff'd in part and rev'd in part, 216 F2d 41 (7th Cir. 1954) (allocation of attorney fees not proven). See also Mills Estate, Inc. v. CIR, 206 F2d 244 (2d Cir. 1953) (Tax Court applied the *Cohan* rule to allocate half of expenses to capital reorganization and half to deductible expense of distributing cash, but appellate court viewed entire proceeding as a single capital transaction); A.E. Staley Mfg. Co. v. CIR, 119 F3d 482, 1997-2 USTC   50,521 (7th Cir. 1997) (court noted taxpayer should have avoided paying a flat fee to investment bankers and instead provided for an itemized breakout, although taxpayer succeeded in getting deductions for most of its costs in an unsuccessful defense against a hostile takeover bid).

[276] See supra   5.04[3], discussing stock acquisition expenses. See generally Berry Petroleum Co., 104 TC 584 (1995), aff'd per curiam, 1998-1 USTC   50,398 (class action defense litigation costs had origin in merger acquisition and hence were capital).

amortizable. For example, if a new subsidiary is created to act as the acquiring vehicle, its nativity expenses may qualify as amortizable organizational expenses under § 248.[277] If two corporations consolidate to form a new corporation, the costs attributable to the newly created corporation may also be amortizable under § 248.[278] A parent's expenses of setting up a new subsidiary or of transferring the acquired assets to a new or existing subsidiary should be added to the parent's basis for its stock in the subsidiary.[279] If the proposed acquisition is abandoned, however, the Service agrees with decisions allowing the potential suitor to deduct its preliminary costs as an abandonment loss under § 165, and one case allowed a deduction for the cost of reorganization plans that the parties discarded, even though another plan was in fact consummated.[280]

Some of the costs of the acquiring corporation (or of a subsidiary, if that is the vehicle utilized) may be attributable to the issuance of the acquirer's own stock and thus are never deductible or amortizable.[281] Indeed, one case concluded that an acquisitive reorganization is necessarily a capital-raising transaction in part, the costs of which are never deductible.[282] The other part of the transaction would be the acquisition of stock or assets, and the burden would be on the taxpayer to prove the amount allocable to each part.[283] The issue will arise when the acquired assets or the stock is later disposed of or, in the case of depreciable assets, they are gradually written off. In the case of an asset acquisition, if an allocation of the expenses among the assets is not feasible, or is otherwise limited by provisions such as § 1060, the costs presumably should be capitalized as a separate asset on the books of the acquiring company (e.g., goodwill, which under § 197, enacted in 1993, can now be written off over fifteen years).

---

[277] See Regs. § 1.248-1(b)(4); supra ¶ 5.06[1].

[278] Regs. § 1.248-1(b)(4). See also Rev. Rul. 70-241, 1970-1 CB 84 (organizational expenses of corporation created pursuant to Type F reorganization were held amortizable under § 248).

[279] See also IRC § 195 (election of corporation to amortize its own start-up, investigation, and pre-opening costs of new business over five years).

[280] See supra ¶ 5.04[10]. See also McCrory Corp. v. US, 651 F2d 828 (2d Cir. 1981) (costs attributable to asset acquisition by means of merger should be added to asset basis and deductible on later disposition of acquired assets; costs attributable to stock issued by acquiring corporation are never deductible).

[281] See supra ¶ 5.04[9].

[282] See McCrory Corp. v. US, 651 F2d 828 (2d Cir. 1981) (costs attributable to asset acquisition by means of merger should be added to asset basis and deductible on later disposition of acquired assets; costs attributable to stock issued by acquiring corporation are never deductible).

[283] See McCrory Corp. v. US, 651 F2d 828 (2d Cir. 1981). For taxable acquisition allocations, see IRC § 1060; ¶ 10.40.

[d] Target's Expenditures

The *acquired* corporation's reorganization expenses in an acquisitive reorganization transaction likewise are generally not deductible currently under *INDOPCO, Inc.*, which involved a target taxpayer.[284] The subsequent tax fate of these capitalized expenses, however, is unclear. Do they pass over to the acquiring corporation by means of the carryover-basis rules of § 362(b) or the tax attribute carryover rules of § 381? Do they represent part of the target's cost of acquiring the transferee's stock (under *Woodward* and *Hilton Hotels*) to be added to the target's transitory § 358 basis for the acquired stock (in which case, the expenses will have precious little significance, since that basis disappears when the target distributes the stock to its shareholders in another tax-free exchange)?[285] Do they evaporate into thin air? If, as is normally required, the transferor corporation liquidates as part of the reorganization plan, can the liquidation and dissolution expenses be severed from the reorganization expense category and deducted as such?

The few authorities that have focused on these problems are not illuminating. Most likely, the transferor's capitalized reorganization costs should carry over as an asset or corporate attribute to the acquiring corporation.[286] In a case like *INDOPCO* (a transitory subsidiary reverse cash merger), where the

---

[284] See supra   5.06[2][a]. See also A.E. Staley Mfg. Co., 105 TC 166 (1995) (costs of waging unsuccessful defense to hostile tender offer held nondeductible capital expense per *INDOPCO*); see comments by Raby in 68 Tax Notes 1613 (Sept. 25, 1995); Lipton, "Divided Tax Court Applies *INDOPCO* to Hostile Takeovers," 84 J. Tax'n 21 (1996). But see Pope & Talbot, Inc., RIA TC Memo.   97,116 (1997) (investment banking fees for advice as to potential hostile takeovers—which did not occur—held deductible). See Silverman & Weinstein, "*INDOPCO* and the Tax Treatment of Reorganization Expenses," 75 Tax Notes 243 (Apr. 14, 1997). See also Norwest Corp., 112 TC 89 (1999) (target's indirect costs of investigating proposed acquisition also required to be capitalized under *INDOPCO*; not a hostile acquisition here either); Fitzgerald, "*Norwest Corp*: Can You Bank on the Deductibility of Compensation Expense and Legal Costs Incurred Incident to an Acquisition?" 78 Taxes 51 (Mar. 2000). But *Norwest* was reversed sub nom. Wells Fargo & Co. v. CIR, 224 F3d 874, 2000-2 USTC   50,697 (8th Cir. 2000); Eighth Circuit allowed current deduction for indirect merger expenses (target officers' salaries) and also for legal and investigation expenses before final merger decision day (though not after that date). For comments on *Wells Fargo*, see supra note 115 (first paragraph). For new capitalization regulations adopted in Reg. § 1.263(a)-5 (2003), see supra note 113, which materially contracted the scope of *INDOPCO*.

Also, *Staley* was reversed, 119 F3d 482, 80 AFTR2d 5060 (7th Cir. 1997) (costs deductible under §§ 162 and 165); Lipton, "The Treatment of Defense Costs in a Hostile Takeover After the CA-7 Opinion in *Staley*," 87 J. Tax'n 176 (1997). Note, "Investment Banking Fees Incurred by the Target During a Hostile Tender Offer Are Deductible: *A.E. Staley Manufacturing Co. v. Commissioner*," 51 Tax Law. 433 (1998). See also Metrocorp, Inc., 116 TC 211 (2001) (Swift, concurring, noted numerous reversals of Tax Court decisions).

[285] See   12.42[4].

[286] See supra   5.06[1][a], discussing an analogous issue for organizational expenses.

Supreme Court held that no distinct asset of the target was created or enhanced by the merger,[287] it appears that the target must capitalize the reorganization expense as a separate intangible asset (with an undefined label, presumably to be supplied by the accounting profession).

If the transferor corporation liquidates in a practical merger Type C reorganization, the Tax Court has permitted its liquidation expenses and capitalized organizational expenses to be deducted.[288] If, however, dissolution of the transferor occurs pursuant to a statutory merger or consolidation (a Type A reorganization), the courts so far have denied deduction for the transferor's liquidation expenses and capitalized organizational expenses on the ground that the transferor corporation's existence continues and carries over into the successor corporation.[289] The line between an existence-terminating liquidation and a continuity-preserving reorganization is at best highly technical and in any event of doubtful relevance. The acquired corporation ought to be able to deduct its liquidation and dissolution expenses whether the acquisition is cast in the form of a Type C or a Type A reorganization, but the courts have shown few signs of abandoning their emphasis on formalities in this area.[290]

---

[287] INDOPCO, Inc. v. CIR, 503 US 79 (1992). See also In re Federated Dep't Stores, Inc., 171 BR 603, 1994-2 USTC ¶ 50,430 (SD Ohio 1994) (fees paid to white knights in failed merger attempts were deductible under either § 162 or § 165; INDOPCO not applicable because no benefit created here, either long- or short-term); Faber, "INDOPCO: The Unsolved Riddle," 47 Tax Law. 607 (1994); Lipton & Brenneman, "Expenses Related to Failed Merger Defense Held to Be Deductible Despite INDOPCO," 82 J. Tax'n 26 (1995). See also Freidrich, "Break-Up Fees Paid to Unsuccessful White Knight Held Deductible as Ordinary Business Expenses or as Abandonment Loss," 22 J. Corp. Tax'n 193 (1995); Silverman & Weinstein, "INDOPCO and the Tax Treatment of Reorganization Expenses," 75 Tax Notes 243 (Apr. 14, 1997); A.E. Staley Mfg. Co. v. CIR, 119 F3d 482, 80 AFTR2d 5060 (7th Cir. 1997) (followed approach of Federated in allowing deductions for hostile takeover defense costs). See also Wells Fargo & Co. v. CIR, 224 F3d 874 (8th Cir. 2000), see supra note 270 (indirect merger expenses currently deductible). See also Metrocorp, Inc., 116 TC 211 (2001) (especially concurring opinion by Judge Swift), which noted the three circuit court reversals of the Tax Court's expansive application of INDOPCO—fees here produced no significant future benefits and thus should be currently deductible). But Wells Fargo was distinguished in United Dairy Farmers, Inc. v. US, 267 F3d 510 (6th Cir. 2001) (fees paid for outside advice on reorganization designed to allow corporation to make an S election held capital because paid to outsiders and directly related to the reorganization). For new liberalized capitalization rules in Regs. § 1.263(a)-5, adopted in December 2003, see supra note 113.

[288] Kingsford Co., 41 TC 646 (1964) (acq.). See supra ¶ 5.06[1][b].

[289] See supra ¶¶ 5.06[1][a], 5.06[1][b].

[290] See supra ¶ 5.06[1][b].

[e] Divisive Transactions

Expenses of divisive reorganizations are generally nondeductible under the principles discussed previously.[291] Corporate divisions or separations may (but need not) involve both the creation of a new corporation and the distribution of its stock. In such cases, the new corporation's organizational expenses are nondeductible, although amortizable, under the rules of § 248 as previously discussed;[292] and any remaining expenses (attributable to the stock distribution) are subject to the general capitalization rule.

But several decisions involving a forced divestiture of a subsidiary (because of a court ruling or change of law or regulations) have allowed the transferor distributing corporation to deduct the expense of effectuating a divisive reorganization where the costs were not incident to the issuance of its own stock or the creation of a new corporate entity.[293] These decisions rested on the theory that the taxpayer corporations did not acquire a capital asset, change their capital structure as a result of the transaction, or achieve a corporate benefit; instead, they merely preserved or protected existing assets and rights or contracted the scope of their activities. As one court stated, the dominant aspect of the plan of divestment was in the nature of a partial liquidation, and the technical reorganization of the taxpayer's corporate structure was merely incidental to liquidation. The court tested the deductibility of the expenses by reference to the effects of the transaction at the corporate rather than shareholder level; expenses incurred by the parent in organizing the controlled corporation would, however, be nondeductible capital expenditures to be added to the parent's basis for its stock in the newly created subsidiary.[294] These cases can be viewed as forerunners of the Supreme Court's approach in

---

[291] E.I. du Pont & Co. v. US, 432 F2d 1052 (3d Cir. 1970) (non–pro rata split-off, with taxpayer continuing to own the corporate shell; capital per *Woodward* and *Hilton Hotels*); Bilar Tool & Die Corp. v. CIR, 530 F2d 708 (6th Cir. 1976) (expenses of non–pro rata split-off held nondeductible capital structure adjustment costs because two viable corporations were saved from one corporation that was "going down the drain"). For discussion of § 355 (divisive transactions) generally, see Chapter 11; see also supra 5.06[2][a].

[292] See supra 5.06[1].

[293] US v. General Bancshares Corp., 388 F2d 184 (8th Cir. 1968) (spin-off); US v. Transamerica Corp., 392 F2d 522 (9th Cir. 1968) (spin-off); El Paso Co. v. US, 694 F2d 703 (Fed. Cir. 1982) (nonorganizational expenses of forced divestiture proceedings incurred by parent corporation were attributable to successful plan, and abandoned plans are generally deductible § 162 expenses; transaction was in substance a partial liquidation because of contraction effects; no continuing benefit for taxpayer or its subsidiaries). Cf. E.I. du Pont & Co. v. US, 432 F2d 1052 (3d Cir. 1970) (forced divestiture held to benefit corporation so that expenses were not deductible).

[294] US v. General Bancshares Corp., 388 F2d 184 (8th Cir. 1968); El Paso Co. v. US, 694 F2d 703 (Fed. Cir. 1982) (costs of organization of subsidiary and of tax ruling were nondeductible capital items).

INDOPCO, Inc., where the touchstone for capitalization was the creation of a future benefit, even if no separate asset is enhanced or acquired, and perhaps the cases even suggest that there is no per se rule for capitalizing all reorganization expenses regardless of the functional nature of those expenses.

If the corporate division takes the form of a split-up (whereby assets are transferred to two or more controlled corporations and the transferor corporation then liquidates) rather than a spin-off or split-off,[295] part of the expenses presumably would be deductible as liquidation expenses rather than capitalized as reorganization expenses.

[f] Recapitalizations

Expenses of recapitalizing a corporation generally are capital expenditures for the acquisition of an intangible capital asset (i.e., the altered corporate structure) and hence are not currently deductible.[296] This leaves open the possibility of a loss deduction on eventual liquidation of the corporation, but the possibility that at least some of these costs may be allocated to the issuance of new stock and hence permanently disallowed under the stock issue expense cases should not be overlooked.[297]

The cost of effecting a recapitalization exchange of debt securities, as opposed to an exchange of equity instruments, presumably is amortizable over the life of the new securities, since these costs have a definite and limited useful life.[298]

---

[295] For the terms "split-up," "spin-off," and "split-off," see ¶ 11.01[1][e].

[296] See, e.g., Mills Estate, Inc. v. CIR, 206 F2d 244 (2d Cir. 1953) (characterizing redemption that was a partial liquidation accompanied by reissuance of the remaining shares as a recapitalization); Gravois Planing Mill Co. v. CIR, 299 F2d 199 (8th Cir. 1962) (stating the rule but finding that the partial liquidation involved was not a recapitalization); Farmers Union Corp. v. CIR, 300 F2d 197 (9th Cir.), cert. denied, 371 US 861 (1962) (expenses of partial liquidation not deductible); Fishing Tackle Prods. Co., 27 TC 638 (1957) (acq.) (expenses must be capitalized even if purpose of recapitalization is to permit stock to be issued to employees); Jim Walter Corp. v. US, 498 F2d 631 (5th Cir. 1974) (payments to cancel warrants in connection with public issue of stock; held not deductible); Rev. Rul. 59-387, 1959-2 CB 56 (underwriter's fees); Rev. Rul. 77-204, 1977-1 CB 40 (bankruptcy reorganization expenses were nondeductible § 263 capital expenditures; but bankruptcy liquidation expenses were deductible, and expenses of operating business during bankruptcy were deductible whether proceeding is reorganization or liquidation).

[297] See supra ¶ 5.04[9] (expenses of issuing stock are never deductible).

[298] See Rev. Rul. 59-387, 1959-2 CB 56; supra ¶ 5.04[9]. See also ¶ 12.27[4][c], discussing the difficulties of distinguishing between currently deductible retirement premium and amortizable issue discount (or currently taxable retirement discount and deferrable issue premium) when the principal amounts of the old and new securities differ at the time of the exchange; IRC § 249, denying a deduction for retirement premium attributable to the conversion feature of convertible securities, discussed at ¶ 4.60; Rev. Rul. 74-210,

[g] Bankruptcy Reorganizations

The expenses of a corporate debtor in effecting a bankruptcy reorganization are capitalized under § 263, even if the reorganization does not qualify under § 368.[299] The debtor may, however, deduct its day-to-day operating expenses while in bankruptcy, as well as expenses incurred in a liquidation if the reorganization effort fails.[300]

[h] Ultimate Deduction of Capitalized Reorganization Expenses

The issue of the ultimate deductibility of capitalized reorganization expenses is analogous to the question of the ultimate deductibility of capitalized organizational expenses previously discussed.[301] To the extent that capitalized reorganization expenses were incurred pursuant to the issuance of the taxpayer's own stock and the raising of its equity capital, they are never deductible.[302] But to the extent such expenses are required to be allocated to various acquired assets, they are deductible either through depreciation deductions or as basis offsets upon the disposition of the assets. Any remaining expenses that were required to be capitalized as separate intangible assets are deductible when the corporation liquidates.[303] However, efforts to deduct reorganization expenses before the taxpayer's final liquidation, upon an event such as recapitalization that eliminated the stock previously created, have failed, and properly so.[304]

When the target liquidates in a Type C reorganization or merges, its capitalized expenses attributable to the reorganization presumably should carry over to the acquirer rather than be currently deductible as liquidation expenses. The deductibility of the target's organizational expenses is discussed earlier.[305]

1974-1 CB 48 (premium to retire convertible debt deductible to extent not disallowed by § 249).

[299] See Rev. Rul. 77-204, 1977-1 CB 40; In re Placid Oil Co., 69 AFTR2d 92-628 (Bankr. ND Tex. 1990), aff'd, 92-1 USTC ⁋ 50,051 (ND Tex. 1991), but rev'd and remanded, 988 F2d 554 (5th Cir. 1993) (lower court must allocate between deductible, amortizable, and nonamortizable categories).

[300] See Rev. Rul. 77-204, 1977-1 CB 40.

[301] See supra ¶ 5.06[1][a], 5.06[1][b].

[302] See supra ¶ 5.04[9].

[303] See infra ¶ 5.06[3], ¶ 10.07.

[304] See U.S. Gypsum v. US, 304 F. Supp. 627 (ND Ill. 1969), aff'd and rev'd on other grounds, 452 F2d 445 (7th Cir. 1971).

[305] See supra ¶ 5.06[1], 5.06[2][d].

[i] Shareholder Expenses

Expenses incurred by shareholders pursuant to a reorganization or recapitalization of their corporation ordinarily constitute nondeductible capital expenditures to be added to the basis of the stock or securities distributed to them in the reorganization transaction, whether the expenses were for the benefit of the shareholders or the corporation.[306] Where the value of a shareholder's stock is threatened, however, as in a bankruptcy reorganization, the shareholder's expenses may be deductible as being incurred to protect his investment.[307] In one decision, a shareholder was permitted to deduct expenses incurred in obtaining a tax ruling from the Service on a proposed reorganization, but not the cost of determining the tax basis of new stock received in the reorganization; the court treated the latter amount as a capital expenditure.[308] Furthermore, some courts have held expenses of forced divestitures to be deductible, as discussed earlier.[309]

When the shareholder pays the corporation's expenses, and the payments are treated as contributions to the corporation's capital, it seems that the corporation should be able to treat the contributed amount as if it had paid the expenses itself, deducting them if otherwise deductible.[310]

[3] Liquidation Expenses and Unamortized Deferred Deductions

A corporation generally may deduct the costs connected with its liquidation under § 162, except expenses relating to the sale of its assets, which amounts must be charged against the proceeds of the sale, as discussed below.[311] Unamortized organizational and reorganization expenses, stock redemption expenses, and other similarly capitalized costs (excluding any expenses of issuing stock)

---

[306] See Rev. Rul. 67-411, 1967-2 CB 124 (corporate expenses in Type C reorganization assessed to shareholders pro rata; ruled capital expenditures to be added to the basis of stock received in the reorganization); Regs. § 1.263(a)-(2)(f) (assessed reorganization expenses are capital contributions); Edwards v. US, 25 AFTR2d 70-526 (WD Pa. 1970); Estate of McGlothlin v. CIR, 370 F2d 729 (5th Cir. 1967) (shareholder expenses related to merger must be capitalized); Third Nat'l Bank in Nashville v. US, 427 F2d 343 (6th Cir. 1970) (dissenting shareholder's legal fees in appraisal proceeding held nondeductible).

[307] See Alleghany Corp., 28 TC 298 (1957) (acq.).

[308] Kaufmann v. US, 227 F. Supp. 807 (WD Mo. 1963). See also Sharples v. US, 533 F2d 550 (Ct. Cl. 1976) (holding that § 212(3) allows deduction for expenses of tax advice regardless of relation to capital transaction).

[309] See supra ¶ 5.06[2][e].

[310] See ¶ 3.13[3] and supra ¶ 5.04[1].

[311] See Rev. Rul. 77-204, 1977-1 CB 40. See generally ¶ 10.07[3]. See also Gerli & Co., 73 TC 1019 (1980) (attorney fees of parent for obtaining § 367 ruling on liquidation of foreign subsidiary under § 332 held capital expenditure), rev'd on other grounds, 668 F2d 691 (2d Cir. 1982).

can also be deducted upon the corporation's liquidation, although possibly not if the liquidation occurs as part of a tax-free reorganization, as noted earlier and further discussed in Chapter 10.[312]

[4] Special Problems in Corporate Asset Acquisitions With Assumed Liabilities: Current Expense Versus Capital Cost Treatment

As noted previously, property acquisition costs generally are not currently deductible by the acquiring party but instead must be capitalized as part of the cost basis of the acquired stock or properties.[313] Liabilities of the acquired party that are taken over by the buyer likewise are generally subject to this rule of capitalization, including expense-type obligations that would otherwise ordinarily be deductible.[314] Like all seemingly well-settled principles of taxation, however, problems and ambiguities can arise, depending on the type of liability assumed, the extent to which the liability is a past, present, or future obligation, the form of the acquisition (i.e., stock or assets, taxable or tax-free), and the details of the parties' business bargain.[315]

Thus, assumed potential or contingent liabilities should generally not be treated as part of the purchase price and should be capitalized or deducted only when actually accrued or paid by the acquiring party (although the line between accrued and potential liabilities is not always a bright one). Assumed expense liabilities in the context of a § 351 incorporation are given special treatment by § 357(c),[316] and liabilities assumed in a tax-free reorganization likewise operate under a special statutory regime, as explained throughout this book where the issues arise.[317]

---

[312] See supra　5.04[9], 5.06[1], 5.06[2][d], 5.06[2][h], and　10.07[2].

[313] See supra　5.04[3].

[314] See, e.g., Crane v. CIR, 331 US 1 (1947).

[315] See Lynch, "Transferring Assets Subject to Contingent Liabilities in Business Restructuring Transactions," 67 Taxes 1061 (Dec. 1989); Crane, "Accounting for Assumed Liabilities Not Yet Accrued by the Seller: Is a Buyer's Deduction Really Costless?" 48 Tax Notes 225 (July 9, 1990); Soukup, "A Response," 43 Tax Notes 637 (July 30, 1990); New York State Bar Ass'n, Tax Section, "Report on the Federal Income Tax Treatment of Contingent Liabilities in Taxable Asset Acquisitions," 49 Tax Notes 883 (Nov. 19, 1990); Sheppard, "Cognitive Dissonance on Contingent Liabilities in Asset Acquisitions," 78 Tax Notes 142 (Jan. 12, 1998) (review of articles).

[316] See　3.06[4], 3.06[7].

[317] See　12.65 and 14.23[4] for reorganization expenses; see also　4.40, 4.60, 10.07, 10.40, 10.43[2][c].

¶ 5.07 THE CORPORATION'S TAXABLE YEAR AND METHOD OF ACCOUNTING

Under §§ 441 and 446, a corporation, like any other taxpayer, must report its income on a taxable-year basis and use a method of accounting that clearly reflects its income. Subject to several important limitations, a newly organized corporation is free to adopt either the calendar year or a fiscal year (i.e., one ending on the last day of any month other than December) as its taxable year, but it must use an accrual method of accounting unless it qualifies to elect to use the cash method. These choices are made during the first year of the corporate taxpayer's existence and are binding thereafter unless the Service consents to a change or forces the taxpayer to change its accounting method in order to reflect income clearly.

[1] Taxable Year

A C corporation can adopt either a calendar year or any fiscal year for tax purposes, provided it keeps its books on that basis,[318] unless it is a personal service corporation.[319] A "personal service corporation" is a corporation whose principal activity is the performance of personal services by shareholder-employees who own more than 10 percent of the value of its stock.[320] Such a corporation must use the calendar year unless it establishes to the Service's satisfaction that it has an acceptable business purpose (other than deferral of income to shareholders) for using a fiscal year.[321] Similarly, an S corporation must use the calendar year unless it can satisfy the Service that its natural business year is a fiscal year.[322]

Even if the "required taxable year" of a personal service corporation or an S corporation under the foregoing rules is the calendar year, a new corporation may nevertheless adopt a fiscal year ending on September 30, October 31, or November 30.[323] The price of this election, however, is a minimum payment of

---

[318] Regs. § 1.441-1T(b)(2) (new taxpayer may adopt any taxable year satisfying § 441). For change of the annual accounting period, see IRC § 442 and regulations thereunder; Rev. Proc. 92-13, 1992-1 CB 665 (procedure for approval of corporate changes).

[319] IRC § 441(i). Regs. § 1.441-4T(d)(1)(i) limits the application of § 441(i) to personal service corporations that are C corporations.

[320] IRC § 441(i); Regs. § 1.441-4T(d). See Rev. Rul. 91-30, 1991-1 CB 61 (veterinary corporation was subject to § 441(i)); Rev. Rul. 92-65, 1992-2 CB 94 (limiting Rev. Rul. 91-30 to application to taxable years beginning after May 13, 1991).

[321] IRC § 441(i)(1); Regs. § 1.441-4T(c); Rev. Proc. 87-32, 1987-2 CB 396; Rev. Rul. 87-57, 1987-2 CB 117.

[322] IRC § 1378.

[323] IRC § 444. See Regs. §§ 1.444-1T, 1.444-2T, 1.444-3T.

tax in the case of an S corporation[324] and minimum distributions by a personal service corporation,[325] both designed to eliminate the benefits of tax deferral.

[2] Method of Accounting

Section 448 mandates the use of an accrual method of accounting for all C corporations subject to its provisions and for any "tax shelter," a broadly defined term that can include S corporations.[326] Certain corporations engaged in the farming business[327] and qualified personal service corporations, however, are exempted from this provision (if they are not tax shelters), as are corporations whose average annual gross receipts for the three-year period preceding the taxable year do not exceed $5 million.[328] "Qualified personal service corporation" is defined as a corporation substantially all of whose activities involve the performance of services in the fields of health, law, engineering, accounting, architecture, actuarial science, performing arts, or consulting, and substantially all of whose stock is held by its employees (active or retired), their estates, or their heirs (but only for the two-year period after death).[329] If an accrual method is required, the corporation may accrue its receivables on the basis of collection experience unless interest is payable on such amounts or penalties are imposed for late payment.[330]

The matching rules of § 267(a)(2) were expanded in 1986 to cover all shareholder-employees of a personal service corporation regardless of the amount of stock ownership.[331] In effect, this provision places the accrual-method payor corporation on the cash-basis method of accounting with respect to payments to its cash-method employee-shareholders, thus deferring deductions until the item is includible in the payee's gross income.

---

[324] IRC § 7519. See Regs. §§ 1.7519-1T, 1.7519-2T, 1.7519-3T.

[325] IRC § 280H. See Regs. § 1.280H-1T; see also IRC § 444(b)(3) for grandfather clause for certain corporations using a fiscal year in 1986.

[326] IRC §§ 448(a)(3), 448(d)(3), 461(i)(3); Regs. § 1.448-1T(b)(3).

[327] But see IRC § 447 (requiring certain large-scale farming corporations to use an accrual method of accounting).

[328] IRC §§ 448(b), 448(c).

[329] IRC § 448(d)(2). Special rules in § 448(d)(4) exclude stock held by § 401 plans and disregard community property laws in determining qualified owners. See also Rev. Rul. 91-30, 1991-1 CB 61; Rev. Rul. 92-65, 1992-2 CB 94 (veterinary corporation is a qualified personal service corporation).

[330] IRC § 448(d)(5).

[331] See supra ¶ 5.04[2].

¶ 5.08　CORPORATE ALTERNATIVE MINIMUM TAX

[1] Introductory

A centerpiece of the corporate tax provisions of the Tax Reform Act of 1986 was the repeal of a prior add-on corporate minimum tax and the enactment of a comprehensive alternative minimum tax with a broader base, a higher rate, and greater complexity than its predecessor.[332] According to the Senate Finance Committee, the AMT was designed to "serve one overriding objective: to ensure that no taxpayer with substantial economic income can avoid significant tax liability by using exclusions, deductions, and credits because, however worthy their goals, these provisions become counterproductive when taxpayers use them to avoid virtually all tax liability."[333] Measured on this standard, the pre-1987 corporate add-on tax and its counterpart for individuals were found wanting.

In brief outline,[334] the corporate AMT imposed by § 55 has the following features:

1. A tentative minimum tax is computed by (a) applying a 20 percent rate to the corporation's alternative minimum taxable income to the extent that it exceeds an exemption of $40,000 (which phases out at $310,000 of AMTI), and (b) reducing the resulting sum by the alternative minimum foreign tax credit.[335]
2. If the corporation's tentative minimum tax exceeds its "regular tax" for the taxable year—defined as the normal income tax, excluding such special levies as the accumulated earnings tax, the personal holding company tax, and so forth (which means, in effect, that these

---

[332] For prior law, see generally Khokhar, Alternative Minimum Tax, Tax Mgmt. Portfolio (BNA) No. 288-4th (1989) (covering both pre-1986 and post-1986 rules).

[333] Senate Finance Comm. Rep. No. 313, 99th Cong., 2d Sess. 518–519 (1986).

[334] For more detailed analysis, see Lathrope, Alternative Minimum Tax (Warren, Gorham & Lamont 1994); Abbin, Corrick, Levy & Hriszko, Corporate Alternative Minimum Tax (Aspen Law & Business 1996); Khokhar, Alternative Minimum Tax, Tax Mgmt. Portfolio (BNA) No. 288-4th (1989); Eustice, Kuntz, Lewis & Deering, The Tax Reform Act of 1986: Analysis and Commentary ¶ 3.05 (Warren, Gorham & Lamont 1987).

Proposed legislation, HR 1215, § 331, however, would phase out the corporate AMT, repealing it completely after the year 2000 (see infra ¶ 5.08[7]). See Stone & Chaze, "The Alternative Minimum Tax Separate System: How Far Does It Go?" 68 Tax Notes 2011 (July 10, 1995). The 1997 tax bill eased, but did not repeal, the corporate AMT, however (see infra ¶ 5.08[7]).

[335] See IRC § 59(a) (which includes an adjustment of the foreign tax credit to the AMT system). The 1997 Tax Act adopted a simplified § 904(a) limitation election in § 59(a)(4) (using regular foreign taxable income as the numerator and AMTI as the denominator).

extra taxes accumulate on top of AMT)—the *excess* amount (less a limited allowance for business tax credits)[336] is the AMT due.

3. Section 55(b)(2) defines "AMTI," on which the tentative minimum tax is based, as the taxpayer's taxable income (i.e., the base on which the regular tax is imposed), adjusted as provided by §§ 56 and 58, and increased by the tax preferences listed in § 57. These modifications of taxable income are examined below.

4. The AMT sometimes has the effect of a down payment on the regular tax because AMTI includes some income items that are deferred for regular tax purposes (e.g., gains on installment sales) and disallows some accelerated deductions (e.g., the excess of accelerated over straight-line depreciation). Recognizing that the taxpayer's regular tax liability will eventually reflect these timing differences, § 53 protects the taxpayer against double counting by allowing the AMT allocable to such items to be credited against the taxpayer's regular tax in the appropriate later years by means of a minimum tax credit. The taxpayer's minum tax credit can be carried forward indefinitely (until used), but no carryback is allowed.[337]

5. Even when no AMT is owed, the AMTI is the base for the superfund tax, which will be due if modified AMTI exceeds $2 million.[338]

As items 1 and 2 indicate, if a corporation's tentative minimum tax for a given year is $1.2 million and its regular tax is $1 million, it must pay $1.2 million to the Treasury. This leads to the unwarranted conclusion that the taxpayer must pay *either* the AMT *or* the regular tax, whichever is greater, an error that is fostered by the fact that the minimum tax bears the label "alternative." Despite this label, the AMT is not a true alternative to the regular tax; in the preceding example, the AMT is $200,000, not $1.2 million, as the taxpayer will eventually discover when computing its credits under § 53, which cannot exceed $200,000. Thus, the AMT is as much an add-on tax as its statutory predecessor, since the taxpayer pays either the regular tax or *both* the regular tax *and* the misnamed "alternative tax," not merely the alternative tax (unless the regular tax happens to be zero). On the other hand, AMTI, the *base* on which the AMT is imposed, deserves the "alternative" label, since it diverges in many important ways from the taxable income base on which the regular tax is imposed. Furthermore, as described below, the adjustment of preliminarily determined AMTI by adjusted current earnings (ACE), as defined

---

[336] See IRC § 38(c)(2).

[337] For a special adjustment in computing the MTC for certain pre-1990 minimum tax items, see § 53; see also Grossman, "RRA '89 Eases Corporate Alternative Minimum Tax Somewhat," 72 J. Tax'n 140 (1990).

[338] See supra ¶ 5.01[4].

by § 56(g), involves a second truly alternative tax base within the AMT regime.

[2] Alternative Minimum Taxable Income: § 57 Tax Preferences

In converting a corporation's taxable income to AMTI, the simplest adjustment is the addition of the tax preferences listed in § 57 (i.e., certain intangible drilling costs, tax-exempt interest on certain private activity bonds, excess deductions by financial institutions for bad-debt reserves, and accelerated depreciation on pre-1987 property). These add-backs are computed after taking into account the percentage reductions already imposed by § 291 on the amounts deducted in computing taxable income.[339]

The tax preference adjustments in computing AMTI involve a few complexities, but they are relatively straightforward. From here on, however, the process is heavy lifting all the way.

[3] Alternative Minimum Taxable Income: §§ 56 and 58 Adjustments (Other Than for Book Income or Adjusted Current Earnings)

Continuing the process of converting taxable income into AMTI, § 56 mandates a series of adjustments that (1) stretch out the corporation's deductions for depreciation on personal and real property placed in service after 1986, as well as for mining exploration and development costs and pollution control facilities; (2) require income from long-term contracts to be computed under the percentage-of-completion method prescribed by § 460; and (3) recompute net operating losses to reflect AMTI and limit the deductible portion to 90 percent of AMTI.[340] Section 58 requires personal service corporations and some other closely held corporations to make various additional adjustments for certain farm and passive activity losses in computing their AMTI.[341]

---

[339] IRC § 59(f). For § 291, see supra   5.03[7]. For an example of some technical complexities in computing the depletion preference of § 57(a)(1), see Hill v. US, 506 US 546, 113 S. Ct. 941 (1993) (adjusted basis excludes undepreciated cost of tangible improvements to the mineral property).

[340] See Stout & Weiss, "Alternative Tax NOLs After the Tax Reform Act of 1986," 68 J. Tax'n 48 (1988).

[341] Losses from farming and passive activities are also limited in computing taxable income for regular tax purposes, but § 58 imposes somewhat more severe limits for AMTI purposes. For example, farm losses are disallowed by § 58(a)(1)(A) on an activity-by-activity basis, without any offset of losses from one activity against income from another. For the passive activity loss limitations, see supra   5.03[6].

Because these § 56 adjustments affect the basis of property and/or have other ongoing consequences, AMTI is best regarded as a parallel taxable base that should be computed for every taxable year even if the taxpayer incurs no actual AMT liability for a particular year or a series of consecutive years. Moreover, the timing differences between taxable income and AMTI in computing depreciation and amortization can have surprising consequences upon disposition of the underlying property. For example, if property with an original cost of $1 million qualifies for depreciation deductions of $600,000 in computing taxable income but for only $250,000 of AMTI deductions, the property's basis will be $400,000 for the regular tax and $750,000 for the AMT; and if the property is sold for $500,000, the sale will generate a gain of $100,000 for regular tax purposes but a loss of $250,000 for AMT purposes. Furthermore, a separate adjusted basis history may be required for the corporation's "adjusted current earnings," as defined by § 56(g), described as follows, since ACE uses yet another depreciation method for property placed in service before January 1, 1994.[342]

[4] Alternative Minimum Taxable Income: § 56(f) Adjustment for Book Income (1987 Through 1989)

The most dramatic, novel, and intricate adjustment required to transmute taxable income into AMTI was the adjustment for the corporation's book income under § 56(f).[343] The book income adjustment, which was a creature of the Tax Reform Act of 1986, was explained as follows by the Senate Finance Committee:

> The minimum tax cannot successfully address concerns of both real and apparent fairness unless there is certainty that whenever a company publicly reports substantial earnings (either pursuant to public reporting requirements, or through voluntary disclosure for substantial nontax reasons), that company will pay some tax (unless it has sufficient net operating losses to offset its income for the year).
>
> Thus, the committee believes that it is important to provide that the alternative minimum taxable income of a corporation will be increased when book income for the year exceeds alternative minimum taxable income. Such a provision will increase both the real and the perceived fair-

---

[342] See infra ¶ 5.08[5].

[343] See Brown & Wiesner, "The Corporate Alternative Minimum Tax: Some Questions and Answers on the Book Income Adjustment," 40 Tax Executive 7 (1987); Feinberg & Robinson, "The Corporate Alternative Minimum Tax—Working With BURP, While Waiting for ACE," 15 J. Corp. Tax'n 3 (1988); Karliniky & Hickey, "Corporate Alternative Minimum Tax Book-Tax Adjustment," 40 S. Cal. Tax. Inst. ch. 3 (1988); Leder, "Giving Rise to BURPs (and Other Preferences) Under the New Corporate Alternative Tax: Selected Aspects," 40 Tax Law. 557 (1987).

ness of the tax system, eliminate the highly publicized instances in which corporations with substantial book income have paid no tax, and further broaden the minimum tax base to approach economic income more closely.[344]

The real-and-perceived-fairness issue that troubled the committee arises because book income often reflects items that are included neither in the corporation's taxable income nor in its AMTI, even after AMTI is increased for the tax preferences and other adjustments summarized earlier. The committee did not supply a list of the offending items, and an exhaustive list would be difficult to compile; but it was concerned presumably about items such as tax-exempt interest, unrecognized gains on exchanges, and accrued income earned by cash-basis taxpayers, that swell a corporation's reported book income without generating any current regular tax liability.

Despite the committee's reference to both real and perceived fairness, it is hard to escape the conclusion that the book income remedy (which was repealed in 1989) was concerned solely with perceptions, since the adjustment depends on what the corporation reports, not on the underlying naked facts. For example, assume that (1) the 1988 financial history and operations of corporations A and B were identical in every respect; (2) both A and B had taxable income and AMTI (before the book income adjustment) of zero; (3) both A and B received \$500,000 of tax-exempt interest and were advised of a potential tort claim of \$1 million; (4) A reported zero book income because it created a contingency reserve of \$500,000 for the tort liability that offset its \$500,000 of tax-exempt interest; and (5) B reported book income of \$500,000 because it chose not to set up a reserve for the contingent tort liability. On these facts, A incurred no AMT liability, while B did, solely because of the difference in their reported book income. Of course, B's financial report may have created a public perception of unfairness—no tax liability despite financial prosperity—that was not created by A's financial report. If the book income adjustment was a response to this perception rather than to reality, then, and only then, could the 1987 to 1989 difference in tax treatment between A and B be defended.

The starting point in computing the book income adjustment was the net income or loss reported on the taxpayer's "applicable financial statement," a term that was defined by § 56(f)(3)(A) in a hierarchical fashion as (1) a statement required to be filed with the SEC; (2) a certified audited income statement to be used for credit, shareholder, or any other substantial nontax purpose; (3) an income statement required to be filed with a federal, state, or local government or agency thereof; or (4) an income statement to be used for credit, shareholder, or any other substantial nontax purpose. If the corporation

---

[344] Senate Finance Comm. Rep. No. 313, 99th Cong., 2d Sess. 520 (footnote omitted) (1986).

had more than one financial statement, the highest on this list was controlling; if the corporation had no statement (or had only a class (4) statement and elected accordingly), its net income or loss was treated as equal to its current earnings and profits without diminution for distributions. The Senate Finance Committee's report stated that it did not intend "to establish the Secretary of the Treasury as an arbiter of acceptable accounting principles" and that the taxpayer's choice of a "reasonable" accounting method would be controlling unless it resulted in the omission or duplication of items of income or expense.[345]

A series of adjustments was then mandated to determine the corporation's "adjusted net book income," a pre-tax amount, and 50 percent of the excess of this amount over AMTI (with minor changes) was added to AMTI. The excess of adjusted net book income over AMTI was informally termed BURP, the acronym for "business untaxed reported profit."[346] Since the rate on AMTI (after the $40,000 exemption) was 20 percent, the effective rate on the corporation's BURP was 10 percent. This suggests that Congress viewed the book income "preference" as only half as unfair as the other preferences and adjustments included in AMTI.

[5] Alternative Minimum Taxable Income: Adjusted Current Earnings (1990 and Thereafter)

The BURP adjustment described previously was replaced for taxable years beginning after 1989 by an adjustment based on the corporation's ACE, defined by § 56(g) as a hybrid concept with features resembling both traditional earnings and profits and taxable income.[347]

Under ACE, AMTI (as computed before the ACE adjustment and the alternative tax net operating loss deduction, an amount that might be labeled "interim AMTI") must be increased by 75 percent of the excess (if any) of a

---

[345] Senate Finance Comm. Rep. No. 313, 99th Cong., 2d Sess. 534 (1986). See also Regs. § 1.56-1 (regulations for determining applicable financial statement); CSX Corp. v. US, 78 AFTR2d 96-5475 (D. Va. 1996) (Regs. § 1.56-1(d) held invalid because it denied an adjustment mandated by § 56(f)(2)(J) for omitted item), rev'd, 124 F3d 643 (4th Cir. 1997) (regulation valid).

[346] Professor Michael Graetz has been credited with the original suggestion that Congress could deal with the perception of unfairness created by high-reported, low-taxed corporate income by taxing the otherwise untaxed portion of book income, thus confirming the maxim: "When Big Mike burps, Wall Street trembles."

[347] For earnings and profits, see ¶ 8.03. Recognizing that the ACE adjustment will require novel computations and records, the Treasury was directed to conduct a study of the operation and effect of §§ 56(f) (BURP) and 56(g) (ACE). Pub. L. No. 99-514, § 702, 100 Stat. 2345 (1986) (this "study" has not seen the light of day as of July 2005; nor is it likely to as respects the now departed book income preference).

corporation's ACE over its interim AMTI.[348] The reason for using a 75 percent adjustment for ACE as compared with the 50 percent adjustment previously used for BURP is unclear, since both BURP and ACE are pre-tax amounts. The Conference report sheds no light on this matter, but perhaps Congress viewed ACE as only three fourths as unfair as other preferences, but more unfair than BURP by half. Unlike the BURP adjustment, the ACE adjustment can reduce AMTI; subject to the limit set out in § 56(g)(2)(B), if AMTI (computed as explained previously) exceeds ACE, AMTI is reduced by 75 percent of the excess.[349] Thus, interim AMTI computed before the ACE adjustment can be thought of as a way station to the ultimate AMTI, with the ACE adjustment to interim AMTI as an add-on.

The computation of ACE starts with adjustment of interim AMTI under § 56(g)(4) to include most additions to earnings and profits that are not taxable income items (but not, e.g., cancellation-of-debt income excluded by § 108), to deny most deductions that are denied for earnings and profits but not for taxable income (e.g., the § 243 70 percent deduction, but not the 80 percent and 100 percent dividends-received deductions, if such dividends are paid from income that was subject to tax), and to make certain other adjustments (including the elimination of the installment method, with some exceptions).[350] However, ACE is a pre-tax figure, so that § 11 taxes and any other tax (e.g., § 531 taxes and § 541 taxes) will not reduce ACE, although they do reduce regular earnings and profits. Nondeductible expenses and dividends paid also do not reduce ACE, even though they reduce regular earnings and profits.[351] Thus, ACE is not a true earnings and profits account but instead is a hybrid version based on both earnings and profits and taxable-income concepts.

In stressing the fact that ACE is designed to be a broad-based alternative taxing regime, the preamble to the ACE regulations noted that ACE is generally broader than AMTI (the starting point for its computation) and also that ACE is intended to be "at least as broad as pre-tax net book income as mea-

---

[348] See generally Rosenthal, "Changes Sought in AMT Adjusted Current Earnings Preference," 40 Tax Notes 118 (July 11, 1988); Starr & Solether, "The Corporate AMT: Is Adjusted Current Earnings an Ace in the Hole?" 42 Tax Notes 1489 (Mar. 20, 1989); Duxbury & Grafmeyer, "The Minimum Tax and Adjusted Current Earnings," 40 Tax Notes 195 (July 11, 1988); Gramlich, Pearson & Solether, "The New Current Earnings Component of the Corporate Alternative Minimum Tax Base," 17 J. Tax'n 251 (1990); Feinberg, "Adjusted Current Earnings—The Future Is Now," 18 J. Corp. Tax'n 91 (1991).

[349] IRC § 56(g)(2); Regs. § 1.56(g)-1(a)(2).

[350] Section 56(g)(4) also requires an adjustment for property placed in service during the period 1990–1993, establishing a fourth depreciation regime (in computing regular tax, earnings and profits, regular AMTI, and ACE).

[351] See Regs. § 1.56(g)-1(a)(6)(iii).

sured for financial accounting purposes."[352] In keeping with this theme, items permanently excluded from AMTI, but included for current earnings and profits purposes, go into the ACE base (e.g., tax-exempt interest, life insurance proceeds, tax benefit exclusions),[353] while deduction items must be deductible for purposes of both AMTI and earnings and profits (e.g., "excess" capital losses and charitable contributions, bribes, fines, penalties, disallowed travel and entertainment expenses, and golden parachute payments) in order to be deductible for ACE.[354] The timing rules for ACE computations are generally those applicable for AMTI rather than for earnings and profits purposes.[355]

Specialized issues dealt with by the ACE regulations include:

1. Income from installment sales can be deferred in computing ACE only to the extent that the § 453 obligations are subject to the interest rules of § 453A.[356]

2. Upon a § 382 change of ownership, a § 338-type step-down of basis is imposed.[357]

3. The ACE adjustment is computed on a consolidated basis if an affiliated group files a consolidated return.[358]

4. An ACE adjustment is generally not required when appreciated or encumbered property is distributed as a dividend, since § 311(b) ordina-

---

[352] See TD 8307; TD 8340; Regs. § 1.56(g)-1. See Starr & Green, "Proposed Regulations Provide Some Clarification in Computing the ACE Adjustment," 73 J. Tax'n 150 (1990).

[353] See Regs. § 1.56(g)-1(c)(6) for a partial list of exempt items that are includible in earning and profits and hence in ACE. Temporary earnings and profits deferrals under the § 312(n) rules, however, are not currently included in ACE. Regs. § 1.56(g)-1(e).

[354] For nondeductible earnings and profits items (which are never deductible for this purpose), see Regs. § 1.56(g)-1(d). For nondeductible AMTI items, see Regs. § 1.56(g)-1(e); Snap-Drape, Inc. v. CIR, 98 F3d 194 (5th Cir. 1996) (deductible dividends paid to an employee stock ownership plan *not* deductible for ACE computation; Regs. § 1.56(g)-1(d)(3)(iii)(E), so providing, valid even though applied retroactively—not unreasonable even though a change in "settled law"); accord Schuler Indus., Inc. v. US, 109 F3d 753, 79 AFTR2d 97-1430 (Fed. Cir. 1997).

[355] See Regs. §§ 1.56(g)-1(c)(1), 1.56(g)-1(d)(1).

[356] Regs. § 1.56(g)-1(f)(4).

[357] IRC § 56(g)(4)(G); Regs. § 1.56(g)-1(k). See ¶¶ 10.42, 14.43, 14.44. However, Regs. § 1.56(g)-1(k)(2) notes that while the ACE basis rules generally apply in this case, the initial determination of whether the corporation is a "loss corporation" (i.e., whether it has built-in losses and, thus, is subject to the § 382 ownership change rules) is made by reference to regular tax basis rules (at least, as the preamble notes, if no abuse cases arise under this rule).

[358] Regs. § 1.56(g)-1(n); note that application of ACE to foreign corporations is reserved.

rily requires recognition of the corporation's gain and hence the distribution does not result in the exclusion of income from AMTI.[359]

5. ACE does not embrace tax-exempt lessee improvements or non-shareholder capital contributions to the corporation's capital.[360]

[6] Examples

In the following examples, assume that corporation T has regular § 63 taxable income of $400, tax preferences (after § 291 cutbacks) of $100, and ACE of $900. On these facts (and disregarding the $40,000 exemption of § 55(d)(2), which is assumed to have phased out), T's § 11 regular tax liability would be $136 (a flat 34 percent of $400), and T's § 55 tentative AMT liability would be $160 (20 percent of the $800 AMTI base, figured as $400 taxable income, plus $100 of preferences, plus the special $300 ACE preference of § 56(g), which is 75 percent of the $400 excess of the $900 ACE over the $500 AMTI as computed without the ACE adjustment). Thus, T's total tax consists of $136 of regular tax and $24 of AMT.[361] Each of the following examples is an alternative to the foregoing basic facts.

EXAMPLE 1: T derives another $100 of § 103 tax-exempt state general obligation bond interest. AMTI increases by $75 (75 percent of the increase in ACE), and an additional AMT liability of $15 arises under § 55. If the bonds are private activity bonds, the interest is a preference in full in its own right under § 57(a)(5)(A), resulting in an increase in AMT of $20. The ACE preference is unchanged at $300, since the AMTI threshold was raised by the same amount as the ACE figure; therefore, the excess is still $400.

EXAMPLE 2: T receives a $100 dividend from its wholly owned but unconsolidated subsidiary, S, that qualifies for the 100 percent dividends-received deduction. Neither T's ACE nor T's AMT is increased.

Alternatively, if the dividend qualified only for the 70 percent dividends-received deduction, the regular taxable income and interim AMTI would increase by $30, to $430, the ACE preference would increase by $52.50 (75 percent of $70), and the AMT would increase by $10.50 (20 percent of $52.50). Thus, the effective tax rate on the portfolio dividend

---

[359] Regs. § 1.56(g)-1(q). See   8.21. The regulations also clarify the treatment of encumbered property in Regs. § 1.56(g)-1(q)(2), Ex. (2).

[360] Regs. § 1.59(g)-1(c)(7).

[361] The § 55(a) tax is the excess of tentative minimum tax (in this case, the $160 tax under § 55(b) on AMTI) over the regular tax under § 11(b) (in this case, $136). As a practical matter, however, T's tax liability is simply the greater of the two taxes (except for purposes of the § 53 credit, which uses the excess figure).

in the AMT regime is 16.5 percent (i.e., 20 percent of the $30 included dividend amount and 15 percent of the $70 amount that is included in ACE).[362]

EXAMPLE 3: *T* sells nondepreciable real property for a capital gain of $400 that is deferred under both § 453 and the interim AMTI calculation, but that cannot be deferred for ACE purposes. The ACE preference is increased by $300 because ACE now exceeds interim AMTI by $800, instead of $400 (i.e., because the threshold did not go up along with the increase in book income). Thus, final AMT increases by $60.

EXAMPLE 4: *T* realizes a gain of $500 on the liquidation of a wholly owned subsidiary. The gain is not recognized for tax purposes. No additional income results under the ACE rules in this case, because gains realized in nonrecognition transactions are excluded by § 312(f)(1) from earnings and profits and from ACE.

EXAMPLE 5: *T* receives $200 of prepaid income that it defers for book purposes until earned in the following year. *T* is taxable in the year of receipt on this income, resulting in an increase in regular tax of $68 and thereby moving *T* out of AMT for that year (i.e., 34 percent of $600 regular taxable income is more than 20 percent of $1,000 of AMTI). Since earnings and profits timing rules generally follow taxable income rather than financial income principles, the ACE does not increase.[363]

EXAMPLE 6: *T* has a net operating loss carryover deduction of $700 (which eliminated the $400 regular taxable income and, hence, eliminated regular tax liability). However, the alternative net operating loss deduction of § 56(d) can offset only 90 percent of AMTI, which amount is now only $800 as in the basic facts, computed without the special AMT net operating loss deduction. As a result, $80 of AMTI still exists after the limited deduction under § 56(d) for the net operating loss. *T* thus has an AMT liability of $16. A similar result would occur if *T* had foreign tax credits, which are limited by § 59(a) to 90 percent of gross AMT liability (resulting in a 2 percent bottom-line AMT regardless of the size of *T*'s net operating loss deductions or foreign tax credits).

---

[362] IRC § 56(g)(4)(C)(ii). If the Clinton proposal to lower the dividends-received deduction from 70 percent to 50 percent is ever enacted, the effective tax rate on portfolio dividends in both the regular tax and ACE regimes would be 17.5 percent (i.e., 20 percent of $50, or $10, plus 15 percent of $50, or $7.50); but this proposal did not pass in the 1997 tax bill, and has not been reproposed since.

[363] See ¶¶ 8.03, 8.04.

[7] Phaseout (and Eventual Repeal) of Corporate Alterative Minimum Tax?

Proposed legislation[364] would have totally repealed the corporate AMT for years after 2000, and also would have phased out various adjustments over a shorter period,[365] some as early as 1996.[366] Whether the necessary revenues could be found to replace this provision is another matter, and reality eventually rescued the AMT despite corporate America's fervent wish for its demise.[367] The final version of this legislation was more modest in scope, being content merely to modify the depreciation rules and provide for the allowance of long-term unused credits against the minimum tax.[368]

The Treasury's simplification proposals offer a less drastic approach: Small corporations (defined as those with average gross receipts of less than $5 million over the prior three-year period) would be removed from the AMT regime. This proposal would not help everyone, but it would relieve large numbers of corporations from the AMT system.[369] The 1997 tax bill picked up on this proposal and included it in the final legislation.[370] In addition, the de-

---

[364] HR 1215, § 331(a), which was approved by the House Ways and Means Committee on March 14, 1995, and passed the House in April 1995 (but went no further).

[365] For example, bill § 331(b) would end the general accelerated depreciation preference on March 14, 1995, while the long-term contract, pollution control facilities, installment sales, depletion, intangible drilling, bad-debt reserves, and tax-exempt interest preferences all would end after 1995.

[366] For example, various items included in computing the ACE preference would end after 1995 (greatly shrinking its scope), and the limitations of § 56(d)(1) (on the net operating loss deduction) and § 59(a) (on the foreign tax credit) likewise would end after 1995.

[367] There is unlikely to be sufficient revenue to fund the repeal of the corporate AMT, which is a significant revenue raiser, despite its universal loathing in the business world. In short, corporate taxpayers should not hold their breath on this one. See generally Joint Comm. on Tax'n, "Present Law and Issues Relating to the Corporate and Individual Alternative Minimum Tax (AMT)" (JCX-22-95) (May 2, 1995), Daily Tax Rep. (BNA) No. 85, at L-1 (May 3, 1995).

[368] HR 2491, §§ 11031 and 11032. However, this legislation was vetoed by President Clinton on Dec. 6, 1995. Pending legislation, HR 2488 and S. 1429, have returned to this scene; the House bill would gradually repeal the corporate AMT (by the year 2008); the Senate version is far more modest, merely easing up on the ATM in several ways. Neither version, however, has much chance of eventual passage (certainly the House bill has virtually none). The final legislation, HR 2488, § 301, adapted the more modest Senate version (effective after the year 2004), but this legislation was slated for a near certain veto, which occurred on September 23, 1999.

[369] The Treasury's simplification package was released on April 14, 1997, in summary form (no legislative language was provided), but a more detailed explanation was issued on April 16, 1997, reprinted in Daily Tax Rep. (BNA) No. 74, at L-1 (Apr. 17, 1997).

[370] Pub. L. No. 105-34, 105th Cong., 1st Sess., § 401, adding new § 55(e) ("smallness" for the first year after 1996 is $5 million of gross receipts; thereafter, the figure is

preciation adjustment was removed from the AMT preference regime, and this amendment applies to all corporations regardless of size.[371]

The Joint Committee Staff study of the federal tax system and recommendations for simplification, released in April 2001,[372] proposed repeal of both the corporate and individual AMT provisions which, if ever adopted, would be a major step for simplification; but nothing has come of this proposal as of July 2005 (and budgetary constraints have doomed it for the foreseeable future).

¶ 5.09 CORPORATE SIZE: "SMALL" VERSUS "BIG" BUSINESS

[1] In General

The Code has long distinguished between large and small corporations, not as a systematic policy but on an ad hoc basis in response to specific problems.[373] It is clear, however, that the corporate tax regime is multifaceted, with an impact that can vary dramatically depending on the size of the corporate enterprise.

"Size," however, is defined in different ways for this purpose. Thus, effective tax rates are determined by annual income levels; the progressive effects of the lower § 11(b) rates begin to phase out at $100,000 of taxable income and disappear at $335,000, and the highest rate of 35 percent is reserved for the truly large corporation with taxable income in excess of $10 million.[374] Some other tax benefits (or burdens) depend on the corporation's value, its annual gross receipts, or the character of its activities, while others depend on the number of the corporation's shareholders or the degree of concentration of shareholder ownership. Still other Code provisions depend on whether the corporation's stock is publicly traded.

$7.5 million in computing the three-year-period average figure). This amendment is effective for 1998.

[371] Pub. L. No. 105-34, 105th Cong., 1st Sess., § 402, amending §§ 56(a)(1) and 57(a)(6), effective for property placed in service in 1998. The AMT is dying slowly, but dying hard.

[372] This proposal is in Vol. II, Pt. 3, § I, of the staff study, released on April 25, 2001, and reprinted in Daily Tax Rep. (BNA) (special supplement) (Apr. 2001).

[373] For the taxation of closely held corporations, see Ness & Vogel, Taxation of the Closely Held Corporation (Warren, Gorham & Lamont, 5th ed. 1991).

[374] See supra　5.01[1].

Many of these matters are considered elsewhere in this work: subchapter S small business corporations having a limited number of shareholders;[375] losses on § 1244 small business stock;[376] the penalty taxes of §§ 531 and 541 (unreasonable accumulations and personal holding companies, respectively);[377] foreign personal holding companies and controlled foreign corporations;[378] affiliated corporations;[379] and redemptions under § 303 to pay death taxes.[380] Various other instances where the Code distinguishes in some significant manner between the tax consequences applicable to small, closely held corporations and those applicable to large, publicly traded companies are noted here.

[2] Tax Rates

Perhaps the most evident tax distinction is based on the size of the corporation's taxable income. Section 11(b), discussed earlier in this chapter, taxes income of less profitable companies at progressive rates up to $75,000 of taxable income, switches over to a flat 34 percent tax regime when taxable income reaches the $335,000 level, and holds that rate steady over a broad income range until $10 million of taxable income is reached.[381] Moreover, as noted previously, the $40,000 exemption from the corporate AMT phases out when AMTI reaches $310,000. If the corporation is able to make an S election, eligibility for which is limited to corporations with a limited number and restricted type of shareholders (generally, U.S. individuals only), corporate tax liability can be eliminated altogether. While denominated as a small business corporation, however, an S corporation has no size limitations save the number of its shareholders (increased to seventy-five in 1996); thus, the corporation can be large economically but qualify for S status benefits if its shareholder family is sufficiently concentrated and acceptably constituted.

---

[375] See Chapter 6. This line was raised to 75 by the 1996 Small Business Tax Act, and increased to 100 in 2004 legislation.

[376] See ¶ 4.24.

[377] See Chapter 7. Although § 531 clearly applies to publicly owned corporations (since 1984), in practice it continues to be a problem principally for closely held corporations; § 541 specifically requires concentrated stock ownership in individual shareholders. But 2003 legislation reduced both of these rates to 15 percent, materially reducing their significance.

[378] See Chapter 15, Parts C and D. But 2004 legislation repealed the § 551 foreign personal holding company provisions (effective in 2005).

[379] See Chapter 13.

[380] See ¶ 9.08.

[381] See supra ¶ 5.01[1]. There are now two phaseout bubbles in § 11(b)(1) as well, one for small corporations (between $100,000 and $335,000 of taxable income) and one for the giants (between $15 million and $18,333,333).

Proposed legislation would impose constructive liquidation treatment on conversion of a large "C" corporation to "S" status;[382] but the Treasury has also proposed legislation (which passed in 1997) to allow "small" corporations to avoid the AMT regime,[383] and permit the tax-free conversion of an S corporation to partnership status if the corporation has no built-in gain.[384]

The penalty tax provisions of § 541 likewise focus on concentrated shareholder ownership (characterized by five or fewer individuals owning more than 50 percent of the corporation's stock, determined pursuant to complex ownership attribution rules), but are triggered only if the corporation's activities are also essentially passive in character. Until 1984, there was some authority to the effect that publicly held corporations were immune from the accumulated earnings tax of § 531, but § 532(c) now specifically includes publicly held corporations as § 531 candidates, although as a practical matter, the penalty seems to be a problem primarily for closely held corporations.[385]

Finally, the low-bracket rate benefits of § 11(b) are restricted if the corporation is a "member of an affiliated corporate group" as defined by §§ 1561 through 1563[386] and are denied completely for personal service corporations.[387]

[3] Accounting Methods and Taxable Year

As noted previously, S corporations and personal service corporations must use the calendar year, subject to certain exceptions.[388] Conversely, S corporations and most personal service corporations generally are exempted from the mandatory accrual accounting method rules of § 448,[389] as are C corporations whose average annual gross receipts for the three-year period prior to the taxable year do not exceed $5 million. Similarly, farming corporations are exempted from the mandatory accrual-method rules of § 447 if they are family-controlled or have annual gross receipts of $1 million or less. Likewise, the capitalization rules of § 263A do not apply to retailers whose average annual gross receipts for the three-year period preceding the taxable year are $10 mil-

---

[382] See   6.07[4] (largeness here is $5 million of stock value).

[383] See supra   5.08[7] ("smallness" here is less than $5 million of gross receipts over the prior three-year period).

[384] There is no size limitation for this proposal (save the absence of corporate-level gain, or an election to recognize that gain).

[385] See   7.02. Both rates (§§ 531, 541) were lowered to 15 percent by 2003 legislation.

[386] See   13.02.

[387] IRC § 11(b)(2). See   2.07; Rev. Rul. 91-30, 1991-1 CB 61; Rev. Rul. 92-65, 1992-2 CB 94 (veterinary corporation was personal service corporation).

[388] See supra   5.07[1].

[389] See supra   5.07[2].

lion or less.[390] A similar exception to the restrictive long-term contract rules of § 460 is provided in cases where average annual gross receipts do not exceed $10 million.[391]

The at-risk rules of § 465 apply only to closely held C corporations that meet a concentrated stock ownership test (ownership of more than 50 percent by five or fewer individuals, including stock owned by attribution pursuant to § 544).[392] Moreover, the passive activity loss limitation rules of § 469 apply only to closely held C corporations (using the § 542(a)(2) "personal holding company" definition) and to personal service corporations described in § 269A(b)(1);[393] but the § 469 limitations apply more leniently to closely held regular C corporations than to personal service corporations, since the latter are treated as individuals for purposes of these provisions.[394]

Finally, § 474 provides a simplified dollar-value, last-in, first-out inventory method for certain "small businesses," defined as those whose average annual gross receipts for a three-year period do not exceed $5 million.[395]

[4] Other Special Provisions

Certain closely held corporations are exempted from the golden parachute rules of § 280G,[396] that is, corporations that would be entitled to elect subchapter S or corporations whose shares are not publicly traded. As to a corporation whose shares are not publicly traded, exemption is granted only if more than 75 percent of its shareholders approve the golden parachute payment upon full disclosure of all material facts.[397]

Shareholders of publicly traded corporations cannot use § 453 to defer gain on the sale of the corporation's publicly traded stock or debt securities.[398] Furthermore, the installment sale method is not available if readily tradable debt is received.[399] Moreover, the original issue discount rules of §§ 1273 and 1274 operate differently, depending on whether the debt instruments (or the property for which such instruments are issued) are publicly traded.[400]

---

[390] IRC § 263A(b)(2)(B).

[391] IRC § 460(e).

[392] IRC §§ 465(a)(1)(B), 542(a)(2).

[393] See ¶ 2.07.

[394] IRC § 469(a)(2).

[395] IRC § 474(c).

[396] See supra ¶ 5.04[7].

[397] IRC § 280G(b)(5).

[398] IRC § 453(k)(2).

[399] IRC § 453(f)(4)(B).

[400] See ¶ 4.42[2].

[5] Public Trading

In practice, the C corporation regime must be used by publicly traded active businesses. Such businesses cannot be S corporations, because of their many shareholders; they cannot be partnerships, because of the rule treating publicly traded partnerships as corporations;[401] and they cannot be limited liability companies for the same reason.[402] The limitation of § 162(m) on the deductibility of compensation to an employee in excess of $1 million also is limited to certain publicly traded corporations.[403]

¶ 5.10 CORPORATE TAX SHELTERS

[1] General Background

The Tax Reform Act of 1986 finally put an end to the proliferation of tax shelter promotions targeted for high-income individuals (principally by enactment of the passive activity limitations in § 469 and, to a lesser extent, the minimum tax regime of § 55). A decade later, however, a new version of the tax shelter industry has returned to the scene in force, this time with corporate America assuming the principal tax sheltered investor role formerly played by doctors, dentists, and other high-income investors. Most of these deals have in-

---

[401] See   2.04[4].

[402] See   2.05[2]. Thus, publicly traded partnerships are prevented from entering the elective status regime under the check-the-box regulations; see   2.02[3]. But the Treasury's "simplification" proposal of April 14, 1997, would allow an S corporation to elect into partnership status (if otherwise available) on a tax-free basis if the corporation had no built-in gain (or elected to recognize that gain); for detailed description of this proposal (issued on April 16, 1997) see Daily Tax Rep. (BNA) No. 74, at L-1 (Apr. 17, 1997). This proposal was not included in the 1997 Tax Act, however.

[403] Proposed regulations were issued under § 162(m) on December 20, 1993, as Prop. Regs. § 1.162-27 (the key provisions of which are in Prop. Regs. § 1.162-27(e), the exception for "performance-based" compensation). Additional regulations under § 162(m) were proposed on December 1, 1994, amending and clarifying the 1993 proposals and adding further examples. These regulations became final in TD 8650 on December 20, 1995.

See generally Ginsburg & Levin, Mergers, Acquisitions and Leveraged Buyouts 1317 (Panel 1999); Levin, Javaras & Welke, "Code Section 162(m)—$1 Million Deduction Limit on Executive Compensation," 63 Tax Notes 723 (May 9, 1994); Henderson, "Executive Compensation: New Section 162(m) Limits Excessive Remuneration," 21 J. Corp. Tax'n 195 (1994); Villasana, "Executive Compensation: An Analysis of Section 162(m)," 72 Taxes 481 (1994).A Senate floor amendment to the 1995 budget bill extended § 162(m) limits to *all* employees of *all* corporations, but this provision did not survive in the final legislation (which, in any event, was vetoed).

volved pre-packaged transaction formats aggressively marketed by tax shelter promoters, frequently with attendant confidentiality agreements, and designed to generate current artificial loss deductions for the corporate investor with little or no economic risk.[404] Large sums are involved here, and the threat to the integrity of the corporate tax base was no small matter.[405]

The Service tried its best to cope with this surge in financial engineering, issuing notices of proposed regulations to shut down what it considered abusive manipulations of the tax system,[406] and challenging others in litigation (the

---

[404] For a description of these transactions, see Glicklich & Leitner, "'Loss Importation'—Opportunities and Limitations," 82 Tax Notes 1051 (Feb. 15, 1999); Sheppard, "Business Revenue Raisers: Cleaning Up and Necessary Fixes," 82 Tax Notes 760 (Feb. 8, 1999); Bankman, "The New Market in Corporate Tax Shelters," 84 Tax Notes 1775 (June 21, 1999).

[405] See generally Holden, "Dealing With the Aggressive Corporate Tax Shelter Problem," 82 Tax Notes 707 (Feb. 1, 1999); Sheppard, "What Should We Do About Corporate Tax Shelters?" 81 Tax Notes 1431 (Dec. 14, 1998); Johnson, "Corporate Tax Shelters, 1997 and 1998," 80 Tax Notes 1603 (Sept. 28, 1998); Lorence, "The Demonization of Structured Finance Transactions," 10 J. Int'l Tax'n 17 (Jan. 1999). See also Kleinbard, "Corporate Tax Shelters and Corporate Tax Management," 51 Tax Executive 231 (May/June 1999); Trier, "Beyond the Smell Test: The Role of Anti-Avoidance Rules in Addressing Corporate Tax Shelters," 78 Taxes 62 (Mar. 2000); Ferguson, "How Will a Court Rule?" 53 Tax Law. 721 (2000); Hariton, "Tax Benefits, Tax Administration and Legislative Intent," 53 Tax Law. 579 (2000); Symposium, "Business Purpose Economic Substance, and Corporate Tax Shelters," 54 SMU L. Rev. 3 (2001); Lavoie, "Deputizing the Gunslingers: Co-Opting the Tax Bar Into Dissuading Corporate Tax Shelters," 21 Va. Tax Rev. 43 (2001); "Symposium on Corporate Tax Shelters, Part I," 55 Tax L. Rev. No. 2 (Winter 2002); Part II, 55 Tax L. Rev. No. 3 (Spring 2002); Hariton, "Kafka and the Tax Shelter," 57 Tax L. Rev. 1 (Fall 2003). More currently, Pollack & Soled, "Professionals Behaving Badly," 105 Tax Notes 201 (Oct. 11, 2004) (the same day as Congress passed the 2004 anti-shelter legislation infra ¶ 5.10[8][d]); Lipton, "Reliance on Tax Opinions: The World Changes Due to Long Term Capital Holdings and the AJCA," 101 J. Tax'n 344 (Dec. 2004).

[406] See, e.g., Notice 97-21, 1997-1 CB 407; Prop. Regs. § 1.7701(l)-3 (1999) (step-down preferred stock, see ¶ 4.03[8]); Notice 95-53, 1995-2 CB 334; Prop. Regs. § 1.7701(l)-2 (1996) (lease stripping transactions); see also Rev. Rul. 99-14, 1999-13 IRB 3 (LILO leasing deals attack). See also Notice 99-59, 1999-52 IRB 761 (rejecting the "BOSS" transaction); for comments, see Sheppard, "Another Corporate Tax Shelter, Another Tax Court Decision," 85 Tax Notes 1229 (Dec. 1999); Lurie, "I Know Crane and BOSS Isn't Crane," 86 Tax Notes 1932 (Mar. 27, 2000); see also Notice 2000-44, 2000-36 IRB 255 (same for variations of "BOSS" transaction). Rev. Rul. 2000-12, 2000-11 IRB 744 (debt straddle transaction rejected); Notice 2000-60, 2000-49 IRB 568 (stock compensation corporate tax shelters rejected); Notice 2000-61, 2000-49 IRB 569 (same for Guam-based grantor trusts); Notice 2001-16, 2001-9 IRB 730 (conduit intermediary shelter); Notice 2001-17, 2001-9 IRB 730 (contingent debt assumption shelter); Notice 2001-45, 2001-33 IRB 129 (offshore basis shift transactions). See Sheppard, "Should We Have Tax Shelter Legislation," 89 Tax Notes 955 (Nov. 13, 2000). This blacklisting process has continued during 2002, 2003, and 2004 for suspicious transactions. For the updated "black list," see Notice 2003-76, 2003-49 IRB 1181; Notice 2004-67, 2004-41 IRB 600 (Sept. 24, 2004).

most famous example being the "Colgate" transaction, in which the Service was victorious in the Tax Court, though somewhat less so on appeal).[407] It became increasingly clear, however, that something more radical needed to be done to stem the spread of these transactions. The former Treasury's fiscal year 2000 budget plan[408] responded massively to the corporate tax shelter problem with a multi-pronged package of legislative proposals, which, if enacted

---

[407] ACM P'ship v. CIR, RIA TC Memo.   97,115, aff'd in part, 157 F3d 231 (3d Cir. 1998), cert. denied, 119 S. Ct. 1251 (1999); for comments on the ACM litigation, see 12.61[1]. See also Saba P'ship, RIA TC Memo.   99,359 (1999) (same transaction, and same result); comment by Sheppard, 85 Tax Notes 1229 (Dec. 6, 1999). ASA Investerings v. CIR, 201 F3d 505 (DC Cir.), cert. denied (Oct. 2, 2000) (held sham partnership rather than sham transactions). But *Saba Partnership* was vacated and remanded for reconsideration in light of the *ASA Investerings* holding of sham partnership, 273 F3d 1135 (DC Cir. 2001). But the taxpayer prevailed in an *ACM* clone deal in Boca Investerings P'ship v. US, 167 F. Supp. 2d 298, 2001-2 USTC   50,690 (DDC 2001) (transaction found not to be a sham; had economic substance and adequate business purpose; taxpayer seemed to have made a better factual case here; but a different judicial lens clearly evident here; court also found a valid partnership and investors held true partners). Sheppard, "Corporate Tax Shelters: Getting Away From the Script," 93 Tax Notes 460 (Oct. 22, 2001); Klieforth & Goldman, "A Contingent Payment Installment Sale Upheld—Why Did This Transaction Pass Muster?" 96 J. Tax'n 114 (Feb. 2002). But *Boca* was reversed, 314 F3d 625 (DC Cir.) (partnership ignored as sham because no business purpose for existence in the deal), cert. denied, (Oct. 6, 2003); Shepard, "No Partnership in Boca Investerings Tax Shelter," 98 Tax Notes 300 (Jan. 21, 2003).

For two excellent articles on the long-standing doctrine of form versus substance, and the more recent (variant) doctrine of economic substance (as applied in the *ACM* case), see Steinberg, "Form, Substance and Directionality in Subchapter C," 52 Tax Law. 457 (1999); Hariton, "Sorting Out the Tangle of Economic Substance," 52 Tax Law. 235 (1999); Sheppard, "Borrowing Economic Substance," 91 Tax Notes 1831 (June 11, 2001); Sheppard, "Drafting Economic Substance," 92 Tax Notes 1258 (Sept. 3, 2001); McMahon, "Economic Substance, Purposive Activity, and Corporate Tax Shelters," 94 Tax Notes 1017 (Feb. 25, 2002); Sheppard Drafting Economic Substance, Part 3, 106 Tax Notes 1012 (Feb. 28, 2005).

[408] Reprinted in Daily Tax Rep. (BNA) No. 21, at L-32 (Feb. 2, 1999). For comments, see New York State Bar Ass'n, Tax Section, "Comments on the Administration's Corporate Tax Shelter Proposals," 83 Tax Notes 777 (May 10, 1999); Sheppard, "Is There Constructive Thinking About Tax Shelters?" Tax Notes 782 (May 10, 1999); Tucker, "ABA Offers Comments on Corporate Tax Shelter Problem," 83 Tax Notes 919 (May 10, 1999); also comments by AICPA and TEI at 83 Tax Notes 1241, 1245 (May 24, 1999); Kies, "A Critical Look at the Administration's 'Corporate Tax Shelter' Proposals," 83 Tax Notes 1463 (June 7, 1999); contra Bankman, "The New Market in Corporate Tax Shelters," supra note 404; Stratton, "Treasury Responds to Critics of Corporate Tax Shelter Proposals," 84 Tax Notes 17 (July 5, 1999); Johnson, "The Anti–Skunk Works Corporate Tax Shelter Act of 1999," 84 Tax Notes 443 (July 19, 1999) (a proposed legislative attack); contra (in part) Jensen, "Skunk Works Bill Has Some Stinky Provisions," 84 Tax Notes 633 (July 26, 1999).

For the Treasury's White Paper study and the Joint Committee Staff's study of corporate tax shelters, see infra   5.10[6][b] and 5.10[6][c]. Trier, supra note 405; Kleinbard, supra note 405.

intact, should rid the landscape of these transactions for all but the most daring or incurably optimistic investors. While not exactly retroactive, there is a very early effective date for all of these provisions (date of the first committee action).[409]

As will be seen subsequently, not much happened with respect to those proposals during the years 1999 to 2003; moreover, the current Treasury's enthusiasm on these issues was suspect at best. But they finally seem to have joined the anti-shelter brigades, though not with the avidity of their predecessors.[410]

[2] General Definitions: "Corporate Tax Shelter," "Tax Avoidance Transaction," and "Tax-Indifferent Parties": *Former Treasury Proposals*

[a] "Corporate Tax Shelter"

The transactional scope of this term is a broad one, encompassing any entity, plan, or arrangement in which a corporate participant attempts to obtain a tax benefit in a tax avoidance transaction. "Tax benefits" include reduction, exclusion, avoidance, or deferral of tax (or increase in a tax refund). The term would not include tax benefits "clearly contemplated" by the applicable provision, however, though the line between acceptable tax planning and an improper tax-driven investment will be a challenging one to determine.

Possible examples of acceptable planning (drawn from § 269 and § 482 litigation)[411] may include the following: (1) availability of alternative methods to obtain the tax benefit in question; (2) status electivity provided by statute or regulation (e.g., filing consolidated returns, electing subchapter S, electing noncorporate status under the check-the-box regulation regime and the like); (3) utilizing "tax incentive" provisions (e.g., accelerated depreciation, and the various tax "preferences" dealt with by the minimum tax regime); and (4) substantive Code provisions providing for nonrecognition and derivative basis results for certain statutorily prescribed transactions (e.g., corporate organizations, re-

---

[409] Presumably this means the date that will be set when first adopted by the first committee (Ways and Means or Senate Finance) that acts favorably on a particular proposal. Treasury resubmitted a slightly modified version of this package in its February 2000 budget proposals. For regulations attack, see infra ¶ 5.10[7]. For Senate Finance Committee proposed draft legislation, see infra ¶ 5.10[8][a]; see infra note 410.

[410] For the current Treasury's March 20, 2002, anti-shelter proposals, see infra ¶ 5.10[8][b]. For an incisive "overview" of current shelter developments during 2000–2003, see Lurie, "Woe Unto You Guys in the Tax Shelter Business," 99 Tax Notes 1411 (June 2, 2003).

[411] See ¶¶ 14.41[2][b], 14.41[5]; see also § 482, at ¶ 13.20[4].

organizations, and subsidiary liquidations).[412] On balance, however, it is clear that very little room for maneuver will exist to avoid classification as a corporate tax shelter.[413]

[b] "Tax Avoidance Transactions"

The other key element for finding a prohibited corporate tax shelter is existence of a "tax avoidance transaction," defined broadly as one where the reasonably expected present value of the pre-tax profit potential is insignificant in relation to the present value of expected net tax benefits.[414] Also covered would be cases involving elimination (or significant reduction) of tax on "economic income." Presumably this latter situation includes cases where taxable income from the transactions is expected to be absorbed by "tax-indifferent parties" (e.g., tax-exempts, foreign persons, loss corporations, and the like).

Several features of this proposed definition are evident. First, state-of-mind or bad purpose tax avoidance motives are *not* part of the definition (unlike other anti-abuse provisions, which require either the principal purpose, a purpose, or a significant purpose to avoid tax).[415] Although purporting to be an objective result-oriented test, numerous ambiguities are present—what is a "significant" level of potential economic profit when compared to the expected tax benefits; what is a "significant reduction" of tax on economic income; in applying present value principles to the profit potential–tax benefit comparison, what discount rate is applied; finally, what are clearly sanctioned tax benefits that can be pursued without risk of tax shelter classification? Obviously, extensive regulation guidance will be necessary to flesh out these questions.

Certain "badges" of tax avoidance have been noted by Treasury officials, among them the following: (1) the income stream from property is separated from the associated deductions thereon, resulting in a mismatching of timing, and, or location as to those items; (2) a tax-indifferent third party is a participant in the transaction (typically to absorb the bulk of the taxable income flow); (3) there is little or no economic risk to the respective parties; (4) the transaction has been marketed in a "pre-packaged" format; and (5) the old reli-

---

[412] For § 351, see Chapter 3; for § 332, see   10.20; for § 368, see Chapter 12.

[413] For "badges" of a tax shelter transaction, see Tax Notes comment, "Treasury Official Outlines New Approach to Tax Shelters," 81 Tax Notes 538 (Nov. 2, 1998); infra   5.10[2][b]. See Hariton, "How to Define 'Corporate Tax Shelter,'" 84 Tax Notes 883 (Aug. 9, 1999), for a sensible measured approach to this task.

[414] For a paradigm example of this case, see the *ACM Partnership* transaction, supra note 407.

[415] E.g., IRC § 269, see   14.41; the partnership anti-abuse regulations, Regs. § 1.701-2; see generally   14.40 for a partial list of these anti-abuse regulations, which now appear throughout this work.

able business purpose requirement that the transaction bore little or no relationship to the taxpayer's business activities save reduction of its tax liabilities.

What is clear, however, is that the former Treasury intended both the definitions of a corporate tax shelter and a tax avoidance transaction to have a broad scope, and one whose principal impact would be a powerful in terrorem effect due in no small part to its very vagueness.[416]

[c] "Tax-Indifferent Parties"

A frequent player in the corporate tax shelter game is a tax-indifferent party, whose primary role in the transaction is to absorb the adverse tax consequences (for a negotiated fee), while the tax benefits flow to the fully taxable parties. Such entities are defined as foreign persons, Native American tribes, tax-exempt organizations, and domestic corporations with expiring net operating losses or credit carryovers (which will be treated as expiring if the carryover is more than three years old—a pretty young age for net operating losses, which now have a twenty-year term). The presence of such persons neutralizes the normal adverse interests that would be present were the parties instead dealing at arm's length, thus rendering suspect the economic reality of allocations directed in their favor.

Several of the former Treasury's anti-shelter proposals aimed to raise the taxable stakes for these entities, not the least of which would be to convert their former tax "indifference" into a much more attentive mode.

[3] General Rules: Penalty Enhancement, Excise Taxes, and Deduction Denial

[a] Substantial Understatement Penalty: § 6662

The § 6662 penalty for substantial understatement in a tax shelter transaction would be doubled, from 20 percent to 40 percent, for any item attributable to the tax shelter deficiency. More significantly, the reasonable cause exception of § 6664(c) would be eliminated. Taxpayers could reduce the penalty to 20 percent if they disclose the transaction to the Service within thirty days of closing, verify such disclosures on their tax return, and file disclosure statements with their return for all years to which the transaction relates. In effect, the § 6662 penalty would become a no-fault strict liability of at least 20 percent if the taxpayer loses its case (even where the full disclosure route is

---

[416] A classic example of a provision that is difficult to "plan around" due to its lack of bright lines is § 269, see ¶ 14.41 (the proposed major expansion of this provision, infra ¶ 5.10[4][a], will make it even more "terrifying"); other examples are § 482 (¶ 13.20), and § 385 (¶ 4.02[8][a]).

adopted); absent such disclosure, a per se 40 percent penalty would apply unless the taxpayer ultimately prevails in court.[417]

[b] Transaction Advice Fees: Deduction Denial and Excise Tax on the Advisor

Fees paid for tax and investment advice in connection with a corporate tax shelter transaction would be subjected to a double-whammy; disallowance of any tax deduction for the corporate payor of the fee, and a 25 percent excise tax on the recipient. Promoters, investment bankers, and other professional advisors in these transactions obviously are going to be less than thrilled with this proposal.[418]

[c] Excise Tax on Rescission Rights and Tax Benefit Guarantees

In another innovative proposal, a 25 percent excise tax would be imposed on tax benefit protection payments made by the corporate investor in a tax shelter transaction. The measure of the tax would be the maximum amount the taxpayer could receive under the arrangement if the expected tax benefits were denied. Thus, the tax benefit insurance payoff maximum would be subject to this excise tax even though ultimate collections under these clauses was a lesser sum. It is also unlikely that these taxes would be deductible under § 162 in view of their penal character.[419]

---

[417] For easing of the strict liability feature, see infra　5.10[6][b]. But Senate Finance Committee Staff revised tax shelter legislation (Oct. 5, 2000) provides for a per se strict liability penalty for "highly abusive" shelters, see infra　5.10[8][a], in proposed § 6662A (described as "abusive tax shelter devices"). A third version of this legislation (Aug. 3, 2001), however, dropped the strict liability feature and focuses exclusively on return disclosure, registration, and list maintenance as the touchstone for penalty impositions. The fourth version, released in May and revised in July 2002, however, returned to strict liability for failure to disclose a "listed transaction" and also tightened up materially on numerous other aspects of the anti-shelter legislation. This version passed the Finance Committee in further revised (and toughened) form on June 18, 2002, as S. 2498; it has been included in various Senate legislative proposals during 2002 and 2003, see infra　5.10[8][a].

Ways and Means Chair Thomas introduced HR 5095, Part I (July 2002); this bill likewise opts for a strict liability penalty for failure to disclose a listed or reportable transaction, see infra　5.10[8][c].

[418] But the Treasury's White Paper, see infra　5.10[6][b], drops the deduction denial proposal.

[419] The Treasury's White Paper, however, also dropped this proposal.

[4] General Anti-Abuse Provisions

[a] Expanded Scope of § 269

The relatively narrow scope of the § 269 anti-avoidance rule[420] would be vastly expanded to allow the Service to disallow any deduction, credit, exclusion, or other allowance obtained in a tax avoidance transaction. In effect, § 269 would be turned into a general anti-abuse rule applicable to any transaction that constituted a tax avoidance transaction. As noted throughout this work, anti-abuse rules are a standard element in virtually every recent regulation; proposed § 269 would serve to give a statutory foundation for these rules, at least where the tax avoidance transaction test is activated. This provision is probably all that is really needed to rid the system of any but the most benign of tax motivated transactions. As noted in Chapter 14, it would make § 269 one of the most powerful tools available to the Service for attacking tax-driven transactions, largely surpassing in scope even the already formidable limitations of § 382.

But omnibus legislation introduced in July 2002 by Ways and Means Chairman Thomas proposed to codify the economic substance doctrine (similar to an earlier proposal by Representative Doggett).[421] But this proposal was

---

[420] See ¶ 14.41. For criticism of this proposal, see Kleinbard, "Corporate Tax Shelters and Corporate Tax Management," 51 Tax Executive 231 (May/June 1999); see also Trier, "Beyond the Smell Test: The Role of Anti-Avoidance Rules in Addressing Corporate Tax Shelters," 78 Taxes 62 (Mar. 2000); New York State Bar Ass'n, Tax Section, "Report on Treasury's Proposal to Codify the Economic Substance Doctrine," 88 Tax Notes 937 (Aug. 14, 2000); Canellos, "A Tax Practitioner's Perspective on Substance, Form, and Business Purpose in Structuring Business Transactions and in Tax Shelters," 54 SMU L. Rev. 47 (2001). For an embrace of it, see Sheppard, "News Analysis—Corporate Tax Shelters: A Snowball's Chance of Pre-Tax Profit," 88 Tax Notes 728 (Aug. 7, 2000); Weisbach, "The Failure of Disclosure as an Approach to Shelters," 54 SMU L. Rev. 73 (2001); Sheppard, "Borrowing Economic Substance," 91 Tax Notes 1831 (June 11, 2001); Sheppard, "Drafting Economic Substance," 92 Tax Notes 1258 (Sept. 3, 2000). But the final 2004 Jobs Act did not adopt it, see infra ¶ 5.10[8][d].

[421] HR 5095, § 101, adding new § 7701(m). See Joint Comm. Staff Technical Explanation, reported at Daily Tax Rep. No. (BNA) 140, at 2-6 (July 22, 2002). See infra ¶ 5.10[8][c]. Comment by Hariton, "Economic Substance Complaint No. 1: Too Vague and Too Broad," 96 Tax Notes 1893 (Sept. 30, 2002); Treasury also opposes this proposal. Similar legislation is contained in the Senate charity bill HR 476, § 701, which passed the Senate on April 9, 2003 (but is not effective until Feb. 16, 2004). But this proposal moved to the Senate's general tax reduction bill, which passed the Senate on May 15, 2003 (and is effective May 8, 2003). It did not survive the final legislation, however. Chairman Thomas's second bill, HR 2896 (July 25, 2003) dropped the codification proposal, and so did the Senate version of pending shelter legislation; but current Senate anti-shelter legislation has revived this proposal. But it did not make the final 2004 Jobs Act legislation.

See generally McMahon, "Beyond a GAAR: Retrofitting the Code to Rein in 21st Century Tax Shelters," 98 Tax Notes 1721 (Mar. 17, 2003); New York State Bar Ass'n,

dropped in later versions of the Thomas bill (though it was still contained in pending Senate versions). It did not survive in the final 2004 legislation, however.

[b] Transaction Form Consistency and Anti-Hybrid Rules

This proposal would expand several existing consistency rules (e.g., in §§ 385(c) and 1060)[422] to preclude a corporate taxpayer from arguing against its chosen form where a tax-indifferent party has a direct or indirect interest in the transaction, and thus the normal adverse interests do not exist to ensure arm's-length dealing. For this purpose, the "form" of the transaction would include various "hybrid" situations where transactions or entities are classified differently under U.S. and foreign law or regulations.[423] The consistency rule would not apply, however, if the taxpayer discloses its inconsistent position on a timely filed original return for the transaction year, or if regulations provide that the substance of the transaction more clearly reflects income of the taxpayer, or to other transactions prescribed by such regulations.[424]

The principal function of this proposal seems aimed at giving the Service an early warning notice for likely audit in cases where the potential for less than arm's-length results is present—that is, a "red flag" requirement for the Service to check the facts as well as the form of the offending transaction.

[c] Tax Income Allocated to Tax-Indifferent Parties

Another proposal of far broader scope would get the attention of "tax-indifferent parties" who participate in a corporate tax shelter by renting their tax favored status for a fee, and whose principal function is to absorb most of the taxable earnings from the shelter. This proposal would neutralize the tax favored status of these entities by fully taxing all income allocated to such par-

---

Tax Section, "Economic Substance Codification," 99 Tax Notes 1829 (June 23, 2003); Hyde & Kohl, "The Shelter Problem Is Too Serious Not to Change the Law," 100 Tax Notes 119 (July 7, 2003); Keyes & Light, "Developments in the Economic Substance Doctrine," 20 J. Tax'n Investments 284 (Summer 2003); Bennett, "Dow Chemical: The Formula for Economic Substance," 81 Taxes 13 (Aug. 2003); Keinan, "The Profit Motive Requirement Under the Economic Substance Doctrine," 21 J. Tax'n Investments 81 (Fall 2003); Hariton, "Kafka and the Tax Shelter," 57 Tax L. Rev. 1 (Fall 2003).

[422] See ¶¶ 4.02[8][b], 10.40[1]. See Harris, "Should There Be a 'Form Consistency' Rule?" 78 Taxes 88 (Mar. 2000).

[423] For current controversy over "hybrids," see Notice 98-11, 1998-1 CB 433, and Notice 98-35, 1998-27 IRB 35, discussed at ¶¶ 15.01[4], 15.03[7], and 15.61[4]. See also Notice 98-5, 1998-1 CB 334, at ¶ 15.21[1][d].

[424] The consistency rule of § 385(c) likewise can be escaped by disclosure, but that of § 1060 presumably cannot. But inconsistency would be a tax shelter "indicator" under the Treasury White Paper revision to its February 1999 proposals, see infra ¶ 5.10[6][b].

ties regardless of their tax-exempt status, net operating loss carryover allowances, or treaty protection.[425] All non-tax favored participants also would be jointly and severally liable for the tax owed by the tax-indifferent party. If enacted, it is unlikely that any such tax favored entities would ever again want to participate in these transactions (or be invited to do so by the other participants).[426]

[5] Targeted Anti-Abuse Proposals

[a] In General

As if the above proposals were not enough to stamp out excessive corporate tax maneuverings, numerous other substantive reform proposals were added to the pile (several of which have been previously submitted). It should be emphasized that all of the Treasury's anti-shelter proposals are cumulative in their application, and also are in addition to such traditional doctrines as business purpose, sham transactions, step transactions, assignment of income, economic substance, and clear reflection of income.[427]

[b] Attribute Imports: "Fresh-Start" at the Border

Tax attributes generated while the taxpayer is not subject to current U.S. taxation can be "imported" into the United States through either a change in the taxpayer's status (by repatriation or acquisition), or by a relocation of the asset's situs into the United States. Inbound transfers of unfavorable tax attributes tend to be purged offshore by the taxpayer before becoming subject to U.S. tax jurisdiction, but favorable tax attributes (e.g., high basis assets, and potential tax deductions or credits) are sought to be preserved for eventual use in determining U.S. tax liability. The Treasury asked for regulatory authority to deal with tax loss attribute import transactions in 1998[428] and has renewed this request once again in its 2000 fiscal budget plan. In 2000, however, the

---

[425] In the case of tax-exempt organizations, their allocated income will be subject to unrelated business income tax (UBIT); for domestic corporations with net operating losses, tax on their income would be computed without benefit of any carryovers; tax on a foreign person's allocated share of income would first be determined without regard to any exclusion (or treaty) as deemed U.S.-source effectively connected income (see 15.02[3]), but if such person properly claims treaty protection the tax otherwise due would be collected from the other taxable participants in the shelter.

[426] But the Treasury's White Paper has modified this proposal, see infra 5.10[6][b].

[427] See 1.05[2], 1.05[3]. The Treasury's White Paper did not discuss these specific proposals.

[428] See 15.80[7][e], 15.81[3][g].

Treasury requested legislation that would deal far more broadly with this area than the prior request, covering both favorable and unfavorable tax attributes.

The main thrust of the proposal is to provide a fresh-start at the border by eliminating all foreign generated tax attributes and marking-to-market asset bases when an entity or asset becomes "relevant" for U.S. purposes. The details of this proposal are considered elsewhere in this work;[429] suffice it to say it looks like it will be a very complicated regime (based heavily on the analogous attribute transfer limitation principles in §§ 338, 381, 382, 384, and 367),[430] although the proposal most closely resembles a mandatory § 338 election.[431]

[c] Offshore § 302 Basis Shifts: Seagram-DuPont Abroad

Despite the 1997 legislative crackdown on domestic basis shifting transactions by way of intentionally created dividend equivalent stock redemptions (exemplified by the widely publicized Seagram-DuPont transaction),[432] the same transaction could be used abroad by foreign shareholders (who are not subject to the basis reduction rule of § 1059).[433] The Treasury's budget plan for the fiscal year 2000 would remedy this defect by extending § 1059 treatment to include the amount of any dividend not subject to current U.S. tax (if subject to treaty rate reduction, basis would be reduced by the proportional amount of the treaty rate reduction).[434]

---

[429] See ¶¶ 14.47[6], 15.85[7]; see also Glicklich & Leitner, "'Loss Importation' — Opportunities and Limitations," 82 Tax Notes 1051 (Feb. 15, 1999); Sheppard, "Business Revenue Raisers: Cleaning Up and Necessary Fixes," 82 Tax Notes 760 (Feb. 8, 1999). But this proposal moved from the corporate tax shelter venue to the "international" proposals in Treasury's February 2000 budget plan (but has not as yet been acted on). But see the 2004 Jobs Act and new § 362(e); ¶ 15.85[7][e] (blocking loss imports).

[430] See ¶ 10.42 for § 338; Chapter 14, Part B, and ¶¶ 14.42–14.45 for §§ 381, 382, 384; Chapter 15, Part E for § 367.

[431] See ¶ 10.42.

[432] See ¶ 9.03[4].

[433] See supra ¶ 5.05[8] for § 1059; Sheppard, "Attention K Mart Shoppers: Tax Shelters in Aisle Six," 80 Tax Notes 1402 (Sept. 21, 1998) (description of the offshore version of Seagram-DuPont).

[434] But see Notice 2001-45, 2001-33 IRB 129 (transaction attacked under current general tax law principles with penalty warnings; added to the "black list" of tainted transactions); Sheppard, "Dissecting the Basis Shifting Transaction," 92 Tax Notes 870 (Aug. 13, 2001); Leatherman, "Should Notice 2001-45 Apply to Basis Shifts Within a Consolidated Group?" 15 J. Tax'n Fin. Insts. 9 (Mar. 2002). For a specific attack on these basis-shifting transactions, see Prop. Regs. § 1.302-5 (Oct. 16, 2002); Willens, "IRS Clamps Down on Basis-Shifting Tax Shelter Schemes With a New Approach That Defers Loss," 98 J. Tax'n 71 (Feb. 2003).

Regulations proposed on October 16, 2002, responded to Notice 2001-45 transactions by preventing basis shifts in the case of redemptions taxable as a dividend.[435]

[d] Section 357 Basis Step-Up

Legislation preventing an artificial basis inflation under § 357(c) was introduced several times in 1998, returned again in 1999 (it was also included in the Treasury's budget plan proposals), and finally passed.[436] But the Treasury's plan would also tighten the tax avoidance rule of § 357(b), and it would also require a basis reduction for assumed contingent liabilities (if deductible by the corporate transferee).[437]

[e] Other Proposals

Other portions of the former Treasury's budget plan would

1. Require a corporation that enters into a forward contract to issue its own stock to report a portion of the deferred payment as interest;[438]
2. Modify the treatment of employee stock ownership plans (ESOPs) as S corporation shareholders;[439]
3. Apply the § 469 passive loss limitations to leases involving tax-exempt use property;[440] and

---

[435] Prop. Regs. §§ 1.302-5, 1.304-2(a), 1.304-2(c); see   9.09[4][d], 9.22[2].

[436] See   3.06[4][f], 3.11[7]. It passed in June 1999.

[437] See   3.06[3], 3.06[7]. This proposal was included in the 1999 tax bill, but that legislation was vetoed (although the return of this proposal seems highly likely). This proposal finally passed on December 21, 2000, HR 5662, § 309, adding § 358(h) (stock-basis step-down to fair market value), effective October 19, 1999. But see Notice 2001-17, 2001-9 IRB 730 (broad attack on contingent liability shelters with penalty warning); but contra Black & Decker Corp. v. US, 2004-2 USTC   50,359 (D. Md. 2004), and Black & Decker Corp. II, 340 F. Supp. 2d 621, 2004-2 USTC   50,390 (D. Md. 2004); so also is Coltec Indus., Inc. v. US, 62 Fed. Cl. 716, 2004-2 USTC   50,402 (Fed. Cl. 2004). But Black & Decker v. US, 436 F3d 431 (4th Cir. 2006), was remanded for trial on the "sham" issue. For regulations under § 358(h), see Regs. § 1.358-7, adopted by TD 9207 (May 26, 2005).

On appeal, the basic transaction in Black & Decker survived the government's summary judgement attack, but the taxpayer's summary judgement victory was reversed, and the case was remanded for trial on the "sham" issue. Black & Decker Corp. v. US, (4th Cir. 2006).

[438] See   3.12[1].

[439] See   6.02[2]. A 1997 Act amendment freeing the ESOP shareholder of an S corporation from UBIT would be repealed.

[440] See supra   5.03[6].

4. Tighten § 267(a)(3) to prevent mismatching of income and deductions in transactions with related foreign persons.[441]

While it is unlikely that *all* of the proposals noted herein will pass in the form proposed by the former Treasury, it is highly likely that *some* of them will; depending on which proposals survive in the final legislation, it is clear that the corporate tax shelter world will be a different, and far more dangerous one in which to operate, and that simplification in the world of subchapter C will take another heavy hit. The 2004 Jobs Act did contain major anti-shelter provisions,[442] but not nearly as rigorous and wide-ranging as the former Treasury proposals.

[6] Subsequent Developments: Treasury White Paper and Joint Committee Staff Study

[a] In General

On July 1, 1999, the former Treasury published its White Paper on corporate tax shelters spelling out in far greater detail the reasoning underlying its February 1999 budget proposals, and refining its proposals in light of those comments.[443] Shortly thereafter, on July 22, 1999, the Joint Committee Staff released its study of the penalty provisions and corporate tax shelters (derived independently from the Treasury White Paper), which includes numerous legislative recommendations as well, many of which echo Treasury's proposals (but several of which are new).[444] This latter study is in two volumes; Volume I contains the Joint Committee Staff study, and Volume II contains summaries (and reprints) of various comments submitted to the staff.

Both of these documents should provide a powerful impetus for legislative action, especially the latter (since Congress is far less likely to ignore the urging of one of its own committees). Moreover, legislation introduced in June

---

[441] See ¶¶ 13.23[6][b], 15.03[2].

[442] See infra ¶ 5.10[8][d].

[443] Treasury White Paper, "The Problem of Corporate Tax Shelters: Discussion, Analysis, and Legislative Proposals," published in Daily Tax Rep. (BNA) Vol. 99, No. 127 (July 2, 1999). Several of the February 1999 proposals were not mentioned in the White Paper (most notably the attribute border purge). For comments, see Sheppard, "Slow and Steady Progress on Corporate Tax Shelters," 84 Tax Notes 191 (July 12, 1999).

[444] Joint Comm. on Tax'n, Study of Present-Law Penalty and Interest Provisions as Required by Section 3801 of the Internal Revenue Service Restructuring and Reform Act of 1998 (Including Provisions Relating to Corporate Tax Shelters) (JCS-3-99) (July 22, 1999), published in Tax Analysts' Highlights and Documents, Vol. 54, No. 17 (July 26, 1999).

1999 by Representative Doggett (and several other members) is specifically targeted to eliminate abusive corporate tax shelters and reflects many of the Treasury's February 1999 budget proposals, and in turn was clearly reflected in the Treasury's July 1999 White Paper.[445]

[b] Treasury White Paper

The White Paper is nothing if not exhaustive (167 pages and over 500 footnotes). Consisting of an executive summary (21 pages), six parts, and three appendixes, be prepared for a serious read. Those less fascinated by a sustained reading project can confine their efforts to the executive dummary; the core of the report however is Part V, which consists of an analysis of the administration's legislative proposals, and Appendix C, a detailed discussion of the Treasury's revised definition of "tax avoidance transactions" (the key to invocation of the proposed new anti-shelter regime).

The White Paper scaled back the February 1999 budget proposals somewhat, adopting a more tightly focused approach than that of the Treasury's initial anti-shelter model (which offered sixteen specific provisions), some quite broad, others narrowly targeted to specific transactions.[446] Also of interest was the Treasury's omission of one major substantive provision contained in the February 1999 budget package—the proposal to purge foreign-generated tax attributes at the border when those attributes first become "relevant" for U.S. tax purposes.[447]

Other significant modifications from the February 1999 budget proposals include the following:

1. The Treasury withdrew its proposals for nondeductibility of advisor fees, and for an excise tax on various types of tax indemnities and rescission (or back-out) rights.[448]
2. The White Paper also suggested modification of the strict liability penalty if adequate disclosure, certification, and due diligence is made

---

[445] HR 2255, The Abusive Tax Shelter Shutdown Act of 1999 (June 17, 1999). See Hariton, "How to Define 'Corporate Tax Shelter,'" 84 Tax Notes 883 (Aug. 9, 1999). For the final anti-shelter legislation enacted in 2004, see infra   5.10[8][d] (which focused solely on disclosure and penalty enhancements).

[446] The White Paper does not discuss these latter targeted proposals that amounted to ten of the sixteen proposals (e.g., tax-free § 332 liquidation of U.S. subsidiaries, ESOPs as shareholders of S corporations, expansion of §§ 357(b), 267(a)(3), offshore basis shifts, and "LILO" disallowance).

[447] See supra   5.10[3][b]. Presumably this proposal was not strictly a tax shelter, since it could also give favorable results to taxpayers. This proposal was moved to the "international" section of Treasury's February 2000 budget plan, a more neutral venue. For the 2004 Jobs Act version of this proposal, see § 362(e), discussed at   15.85[7][e].

[448] See supra   5.10[3][b], 5.10[3][c].

by the taxpayer and a tougher reasonable cause standard is satisfied.[449]

3. The White Paper revised the definition of a "tax avoidance transaction" by focusing on the economic substance standard (which concept would be codified).[450]

4. Enhanced disclosure requirements would be imposed based on various tax shelter characteristics or "indicators" (proposed "filters," or badges of bad activity, that will trigger the required reporting regime).[451]

5. The excise tax on advisor and promoter fees would apply only to a "facilitator" (i.e., an enabler's fees would be taxable, but those who just say "no" would not be taxable).[452]

Despite the above pull-backs and other minor modifications, the White Paper retained the core of the February 1999 budget proposals, focusing on four general lines of attack on corporate tax shelters: (1) increasing disclosure; (2) toughening the underpayment penalty; (3) disallowing tax benefits; and (4) providing "incentives" for other participants (promoters, advisors, and tax-indifferent parties) to "straighten up and fly right."

1. **Increase Disclosure.** As noted above, the Treasury modified its February disclosure proposal by limiting reporting to cases where a combination of tax shelter characteristics are present (described as

---

[449] See supra ¶ 5.10[3][a]. For temporary (now final) disclosure regulations, see infra ¶ 5.10[6][g]; for Senate Finance Committee draft legislation, see infra ¶ 5.10[8][a]. The Senate Finance Committee proposal was revised in a new draft released on October 2000 (it contained a per se strict liability penalty for "highly abusive" shelters (both corporate and noncorporate)). But the Senate Finance Committee Staff's third version (Aug. 3, 2001) dropped the strict liability feature and focused exclusively on disclosure. The Treasury's anti-shelter proposal (Mar. 20, 2002) would apply a strict liability penalty for non-disclosure, see infra ¶ 5.10[8][b]. So does the Finance Committee's fourth and final version (July 2002) as well as the Ways and Means Chairman Thomas's July 2002 proposal, HR 5095, see infra ¶ 5.10[8][c]. So does the final 2004 Jobs Act, see infra ¶ 5.10[8][d].

[450] See supra ¶ 5.10[2][b]; see Illustration C of the White Paper. See also Hariton, "How to Define 'Corporate Tax Shelter,'" 84 Tax Notes 883 (Aug. 9, 1999).

[451] See White Paper, pt. VA 3. Examples of these indicators are: book-tax difference in excess of a certain amount; a rescission agreement or tax benefits indemnity guaranty; involvement of a tax-indifferent party; large advisor fees or contingent fees; a confidentiality agreement; offering to multiple parties and a difference between the form of the transaction and how it is reported. For temporary (now final) regulations, see infra ¶ 5.10[7][b]; for Senate Finance Committee draft legislation, see infra ¶ 5.10[8][a] (which legislation is now in its fourth incarnation). For Ways and Means Chair Thomas's proposal, see infra ¶ 5.10[8][c]. For the final 2004 legislation, see infra ¶ 5.10[8][d].

[452] See White Paper, pt. VD 3, and supra ¶ 5.10[3][b].

"filters" in the White Paper).[453] Moreover, the disclosure requirement would be a dual one—a short-form notice statement to the Service, filed contemporaneously with the offer to a corporation (the early warning signal), and a more detailed filing with the corporate participant's return (and signed by an officer with knowledge of the transaction, who would be personally liable for its accuracy).[454] Disclosure also would be required where the taxpayer treats the transaction differently from its form (but only if the tax benefits exceed a threshold amount, such as $1 million).[455]

2. **Tighten Penalties.** The White Paper also modified the budget proposal by backing away from strict liability for the underpayment penalty; instead, the penalty could be avoided if adequate disclosure is made, due diligence has occurred, and a heightened standard of due diligence is met.[456] The White Paper proposed penalty structure thus would involve a multi-level analysis based on the interplay between the adequacy of disclosure and the strength of the taxpayer's position (strict liability for *some* penalty, the current 20 percent figure, could only be avoided if adequate disclosure exists, and the taxpayer has a reasonable belief that it has a "strong" probability of success on the merits).[457]

3. **Disallow Tax Benefits.** Probably the most important substantive part of the White Paper, however, is its decision to codify the economic substance doctrine as the touchstone for defining a "tax avoidance

---

[453] See supra note 449. The stated list of "filters" is not exhaustive, but apparently more than one filter would be required (though how many more is not "disclosed" by the White Paper).

[454] The authors have yet to meet such a person, although it is conceivable that he or she may exist. Failure to file either notice would attract penalties (if both are not filed, a larger penalty would ensue). See the slightly less rigorous rule of Regs. § 1.6011-4T, which became final in March 2003, infra   5.10[7][b]. The May 2000 Senate Finance Committee's draft legislation adopted this attest rule, see infra   5.10[8][a]; but the revised October 2000 version dropped it (and so does the revised August 2001 version). But the fourth version (July 2002) expects that implementing regulations will require the corporate disclosure form to be verified under penalties of perjury.

[455] The "threshold" suggestion is a modification of the budget proposal; also changed was elimination of the requirement of a tax-indifferent participant.

[456] See supra   5.10[3][a]; White Paper, at 93–95.
But the Senate Finance Committee's revised draft legislation of October 5, 2000, included a strict liability penalty for highly abusive shelters, see infra   5.10[8][a], with *no* escapes (unless taxpayer prevails on the merits). But a later draft version (Aug. 3, 2001) dropped the strict liability penalty and focused exclusively on disclosure as its touchstone, but its July 2002 version reverted to a strict liability penalty.

[457] The White Paper, at 94, n. 349, lists numerous conditions and requirements for an acceptable tax opinion that can meet this heightened reasonable cause standard (and what will cause such an opinion to be "unreliable").

transaction."[458] This approach, based primarily on *Gregory* and *Knetsch*, and most recently applied in the *ACM* case,[459] compares the present values of expected pre-tax profits with expected tax benefits; if the former is insignificant when compared to the latter, the transaction in question will not be sustained. In other words, tax benefits unsupported by any realistic and significant economic profit potential will not be sustained.

Codification of this proposal as a statutory general anti-abuse rule (presumably to be located in § 7701, rather than § 269), and providing that it be self-executing (rather than discretionary with the Service) are the two principal modifications of the February 1999 budget proposals. But the White Paper also proposed to extend this disallowance provision to noncorporate participants as well as corporations (similar to the proposal in HR 2255), thus broadening its scope considerably in this respect.[460]

Fans of precision, however, are not going to be happy with this provision despite its alleged "objectivity." The proposed two-part definition of acceptable "economic substance" for a transaction ((1) reasonable expectation of significant pre-tax profits in relation to expected tax benefits, using present value principles, and (2) in the case of a "financing" transaction, deductions claimed by the taxpayer must be reasonably commensurate to the counterparty's economic return) is at best a highly general guide subject to a wide range of possible interpretations.[461] One can only shudder at the eventual regulation project that tries to grapple with this proposal should it ever be enacted. On the other hand, the very vagueness of the provision could easily be its strongest virtue, deterring all but the foolish or fearless adventurer from attempting to test its application. Moreover, the provision would largely swallow much of what is now covered by § 269 (and possibly also § 382),[462] since there are virtually no transactional limits, other than obtaining a tax benefit, to its potential application.

But impatience with several dubious court decisions, coupled with the corporate scandals of 2002, has sparked new interest in the codification propo-

---

[458] This modification was inspired by, and essentially adopts, the position in HR 2255, The Abusive Tax Shelter Shutdown Act of 1999, introduced on June 17, 1999.

[459] See ¶ 12.61[1], and infra ¶ 5.10[6][e]; Hariton, "Sorting Out the Tangle of Economic Substance," 52 Tax Law. 235 (1999).

[460] The White Paper presumably does not adopt (at least specifically) the treatment of *Cottage Savings*–type, built-in losses that have been economically borne by the taxpayer (which losses would still be allowable under HR 2255).

[461] See, e.g., Jensen, "Skunk Works Bill Contains Some Stinky Provisions," 84 Tax Notes 633 (July 26, 1999).

[462] Not having to deal with those provisions with the intensity presently required may also be considered a plus by some.

sal; both the Senate[463] and the chairman of Ways and Means[464] have legislative codifications of the economic substance doctrine (in what would be § 7701(m)). But the final 2004 Job Acts did not adopt it.

One thing is clear, however: If the proposed disallowance rule eventually becomes law, the corporate tax shelter (or for that matter, any tax shelter) as the Treasury has come to know and loath it will become a thing of the past.

4. **Other Participants (Promoters, Advisors, and Tax-Indifferent Parties).** The last leg of the White Paper's anti-shelter package deals with the other participants in a tax shelter transaction and is intended to provide for significant downside risks to such persons if the transaction fails to pass muster.[465] The White Paper proposes to modify these financial "disincentives" in the following ways:[466]

   a. The penalty excise tax on advisor fees would apply only to advice that encourages participation, not to those who counsel against it.
   b. The White Paper suggests that the excise tax could instead be converted into (and subsumed by) the promoter penalty system.
   c. Denial of deductibility for fees was dropped, as was the proposed excise tax on tax indemnity benefits.
   d. Taxability of tax-indifferent parties would be modified somewhat.[467]

The White Paper seems to reflect a view that the combined new disclosure, penalty, and disallowance proposals considered above were starting to approach overkill even for the despised tax shelter players. Even as modified,

---

[463] HR 476 (the Senate's charity bill or CARE), § 701 (effective Feb. 16, 2004) (passed the Senate on Apr. 9, 2003, see infra 5.10[8][a]; the Senate proposal moved into the Senate's general tax relief bill, S. 2, in May 2003, and passed on May 15, 2003 (effective May 8, 2003), but it did not survive the final 2003 legislation.

[464] HR 5095, § 101 (introduced in July 2002), see infra 5.10[8][c]. But later versions of the House bill have dropped it, and so did the final 2004 Jobs Act legislation.

[465] Thus, income allocated to a tax-indifferent party would be taxed, excise taxes would be imposed on fees and tax indemnity benefits, and fees paid to promoters and advisors would not be deductible.

[466] The report labels these provisions as "incentives"—they are incentives only in the sense that they strongly motivate the intended targets *not* to participate.

[467] Thus, due process procedures would be added; only those trading on their tax favored status would be covered, and joint and several liability for tax would run only between the tax-indifferent party and the corporate participant. In addition, foreign participants would be covered only if they have a nexus to the United States.

however, there would still be significant downside risks to all the participants in the shelter should the revised proposals be enacted.[468]

[c] Joint Committee Staff Study

The Joint Committee Staff study primarily focused on the penalty and interest provisions (as mandated by the Service's 1998 reform legislation), but also included a substantial section devoted exclusively to corporate tax shelters, together with numerous legislative and administrative recommendations designed to curb these transactions (and their participants).[469] The Joint Committee's specific responses propose that a meaningful penalty structure be established to discourage corporate participation in tax shelter transactions, and that enhanced disclosure and registration requirements also be adopted. In addition, the report proposes numerous enhancements to standards of practice before the Service with respect to corporate tax shelters,[470] and also heightened enforcement against promoters and advisors of these transactions.[471] All in all, its a surprisingly tough package of proposals that, considering its source, stands a substantial likelihood of adoption, if not in toto, then at least in some readily recognizable form.[472]

1. **Definition of "Tax Shelter."** The Joint Committee definition of a "corporate tax shelter" for purposes of the substantial underestimation penalty takes a different approach from the Treasury's proposal (and also from that of HR 2255); thus, if one or more objective "tax shelter indicators" are present, then a significant tax avoidance purpose

---

[468] The Joint Committee Staff proposals, see infra ¶ 5.10[6][c], are considerably more onerous than the Treasury's, although the staff's general approach is exclusively penalty-based.

[469] Part VIII, Vol. I, of the study contains the corporate tax shelter material; the staff's specific recommendations are in Parts C and D of that section. For comments, see Sheppard, "Joint Committee Penalty Study Stuck in Same Old Rut," 84 Tax Notes 657 (Aug. 2, 1999).

[470] Including a substantial revision and toughening of Circular 230; for which see infra ¶ 5.10[7][c] (Dec. 2004).

[471] Including injunctions against promoters of abusive shelters.

[472] For draft legislation proposed by the Senate Finance Committee, which strongly resembled these proposals, see infra ¶ 5.10[8][a]. The subsequent draft version (Aug. 3, 2001), however, was far milder than the Joint Committee Staff proposals. Treasury's March 2002 anti-shelter proposals likewise are closely modeled on these proposals (including a strict liability penalty for nondisclosure), see infra ¶ 5.10[8][b]. The fourth version of the Senate Finance Committee legislation (July 2002), however, was the toughest of all versions (even, in many respects, those proposed by the Joint Committee Staff).

will be deemed to exist.[473] Those indicators would consist of the following characteristics: the reasonably expected pre-tax profit is insignificant relative to expected net tax benefits (also the Treasury definition); the presence of a tax-indifferent party whose role is to absorb the unfavorable tax burden; a tax indemnity or similar agreement for the benefit of the corporate participant; a permanent difference between book and tax reporting; and, the taxpayer incurs little if any economic risk.[474]

2. **Enhanced Penalty.** If the enterprise is found to constitute a corporate tax shelter under these tests, then the penalty rate would be doubled (to 40 percent), and could not be waived by the Service (i.e., it is automatic).[475] But if the revised and strengthened disclosure requirements are met (infra), and the taxpayer reasonably believes there is at least a 75 percent chance of success (a new and very high standard), then all of the penalty would be abated; it could be reduced to the regular penalty level (20 percent) if disclosure requirements are met, and the taxpayer has substantial authority to support its position. If a corporation incurs a penalty under the tax shelter provision, it must also disclose that fact to its shareholders (in effect requiring public "shame" for corporate "shams").

3. **Other Participants: Penalties, Registration, and Sanctions.** Parties who participate in the creation, implementation, or reporting of a tax shelter that results in a penalty for the corporate participant would face a significant array of unpleasant consequences under the staff's proposals. Thus, the return preparer standard for disclosed positions taken on a return (or claim for refund) would be raised (to substantial authority), and the penalty thereunder raised by a substantial amount; undisclosed positions must also meet a higher standard ("more likely than not") for success.[476] Similarly, the penalty for aiders and abettors (i.e., advisors) would be increased, as would the scope of that provision.[477] Finally, the current tax shelter registration requirements would be modified and strengthened as would the promoter injunction rules,

---

[473] Even in the absence of an indicator, a tax shelter could be found if a significant tax avoidance effect exists; that is, the present-law tax shelter definition continues to apply.

[474] The report contains extensive discussion of each of these indicators (the usual suspects), at § 2(a)(i)(C), of its specific recommendation in Section D. See also Hariton, "How to Define 'Corporate Tax Shelter,'" 84 Tax Notes 883 (Aug. 9, 1999).

[475] Thus precluding use by the Service as an audit leverage tactic.

[476] The standards under present law are "reasonable basis" (disclosed positions) and "substantial authority" (undisclosed positions).

[477] The principal target here is the less than sterling tax opinion (one that a reasonable tax practitioner would refuse to render). Renderers of "junk-tax opinions" would suffer the additional shame of publication of their name.

and rules governing professional conduct of practice in Circular 230. As to the latter, authority to impose monetary sanctions would be provided (by statute), and would cover any individual who issues a tax shelter opinion or is required to register a corporate tax shelter. Moreover, publication of the name of any practitioner who receives a letter of reprimand would be required, and automatic referral would be made to the Director of Practice, who would be required to notify state licensing authorities upon the imposition of any suspension from practice, letter of reprimand, or monetary sanction imposed on the practitioner (and the underlying basis for the disciplinary action).

All told, the above proposed schedule of penalties, fines, and disciplinary sanctions should definitely encourage the tax shelter promoters and advisors to clean up their act. Failure to do so will result in significant monetary and professional pain under the proposed Joint Committee recommendations.

[d] Conclusion

If all, or even some, of the changes proposed by the Treasury (in HR 2255) or the Joint Committee Staff had become law, the world of corporate tax shelters would become a very different (and a decidedly dangerous) place. That is, of course, the very clearly articulated intent of all three proposals. As discussed subsequently, most (though by no means all) courts, the Service, and the Senate Finance Committee have all moved aggressively on a variety of fronts (in decisions, regulations, and proposed legislation) against these transactions. The final 2004 Jobs Act contained a significant package of anti-shelter rules (but focused only on augmented penalties and disclosure provisions).

[e] Case Law Developments: Post–*ACM Partnership* Decisions ("Old Wine in New Bottles")

Whatever the eventual outcome on the legislative front, the Service has enjoyed a remarkable run of litigation victories since *ACM Partnership* in attacking various forms of tax shelter transactions.[478] These decisions share a common theme in their invocation of "economic substance" and "business pur-

---

[478] For a "clone" of *ACM*, with similar results, see Saba P'ship, RIA TC Memo. 99,359 (1999). The government scored a huge victory in the widely followed *Long-Term Capital Holdings* (*LTCH*) litigation (with major penalties), 330 F. Supp. 2d 122, 2004-2 USTC 50,351 (D. Conn. 2004). See Sheppard, "LTM Case: What They Won't Do for Money, Part 2," 104 Tax Notes 1006 (Sept. 6, 2004); Leeds & Rubinger, "When Common Sense Failed: Tax Planning After Long Term Capital," 105 Tax Notes 237 (Oct. 11, 2004); Lipton, "Reliance on Tax Opinions: The World Changes After Long Term Capital and the AJCA," 101 J. Tax'n 344 (Dec. 2004); Warren, "Understanding Long Term Capital," 106 Tax Notes 681 (Feb. 1, 2005). Long Term Capitol lost its appeal on

pose" principles (or, more accurately, the lack thereof) in striking down a wide variety of tax-driven transactions as "shams," citing *ACM Partnership*. But the Service's initial string of litigation victories has been snapped in several other decisions, though they rebounded spectacularly in the *Long-Term Capital* case.[479]

---

the penalty issue, which was affirmed by the Second Circuit in an unpublished opinion on September 27, 2005 (decision entered five days after oral argument).

   But contra to *Long-Term Capital Holdings* is TIFD III-E, Inc. v. US, 342 F. Supp. 2d 94, 2004 USTC ¶ 50,401 (D. Conn. 2004) (the Castle-Harbour–GE lease stripping transaction). For comment, see Sheppard, "Bury Your Tax Shelter in a Business," 106 Tax Notes 20 (Jan. 3, 2005); Lipton, "Lessons From Castle Harbour: The Service Loses a Significant Tax Shelter Case," 102 J. Tax'n 32 (Jan. 2005). See also ASA Investerings v. CIR, 201 F3d 505 (DDC Cir. 2000) (sham partnership), cert. denied, Oct. 2, 2000. *Saba Partnership* was remanded for reconsideration of sham partnership issue in light of the *ASA Investerings* decision, 275 F3d 1135 (DC Cir. 2001). But see Boca Investerings P'ship v. US, 167 F. Supp. 2d 298, 2001-2 USTC ¶ 50,690 (DDC 2001) (taxpayer prevailed in an *ACM* clone deal; not a sham; held valid partnership, economic substance present, and adequate business purpose); but reversed, infra note 478; comment by Sheppard, 93 Tax Notes 460 (Oct. 22, 2001). See generally Carlson & Lenahan, "The Importance of Taxpayer Credibility in Resolving Tax Disputes," 87 Tax Notes 1263 (May 29, 2000); Trier, "Beyond the Smell Test: The Role of Substantive Anti-Avoidance Rules in Addressing Corporate Tax Shelters," 78 Taxes 62 (Mar. 2000); Bryant, "Courts Join IRS in Keeping Up Attack on Corporate Tax Shelters," 17 J. Tax'n Investments 289 (2000); Cook et al., "Tax Court Stretches Concept of Sham in *Winn-Dixie* and *UPS* Cases—Part I," 14 J. Tax'n Fin. Insts. 34 (Sept. 2000); Cook et al., "Tax Court Stretches Concept of Sham in *Winn-Dixie* and *UPS* Insurance Cases—Part II," 14 J. Tax'n Fin. Insts. 15 (Nov. 2000); Ferguson, "What Will a Court Do?" 53 Tax Law. 721 (2000): McMahon, "Economic Substance, Purposive Activity, and Corporate Tax Shelters," 94 Tax Notes 1017 (Feb. 25, 2002); Hariton, "The *Compaq* Case, Notice 98-5 and Tax Shelters: Theory Is All Wrong," 94 Tax Notes 501 (Jan. 28, 2002); Shaviro & Weisbach, "The Fifth Circuit Got It Wrong in *Compaq v. Commissioner*," 94 Tax Notes 511 (Jan. 28, 2002); Hariton, "Kafka and the Tax Shelter," 57 Tax L. Rev. 1 (Fall 2003).

   But the Service won big again in Santa Monica Pictures, RIA TC Memo. 2005-104 (2005); comment by Leeds, "The Pendulum Swings Back," 107 Tax Notes 1669 (June 27, 2005).

   [479] E.g., Boca Investerings P'ship v. US, 167 F. Supp. 2d 298, 2001-2 USTC ¶ 50,690 (DDC 2001) (*ACM*-type clone, but taxpayer victorious), rev'd, 314 F3d 625 (DC Cir. 2003), cert. denied, (Oct. 6, 2003); UPS, Inc. v. CIR, 254 F3d 1014 (11th Cir. 2001) (Tax Court reversed; transaction not a sham); IES Indus., Inc. v. US, 253 F3d 350 (8th Cir. 2001) (transactions had economic substance and adequate business purpose); Compaq Computer Corp. v. CIR, 277 F3d 778, 2002-1 USTC ¶ 50,144 (5th Cir. 2001) (good enough business purpose and transaction had economic substance); Sheppard, "Should Riskless Profit Equal Economic Substance?" 94 Tax Notes 153 (Jan. 14, 2002); Klieforth & Goldman, "A Contingent Payment Installment Sale Upheld—Why Did This Transaction Pass Muster?" 96 J. Tax'n 114 (Feb. 2002) (good fortune helped); McMahon, supra note 477; Hariton, id., Shaviro & Weisbach, id.; Sheppard, "No Partnership in Boca Tax Shelter," 98 Tax Notes 300 (Jan. 21, 2003). Compare Long-Term Capital Holdings v. US, 330 F. Supp. 2d 122, 2004-2 USTC ¶ 50,351 (D. Conn. 2004). See also Black & Decker Corp. II, 340 F. Supp. 2d 621, 2004-2 USTC ¶ 50,390 (D. Md. 2004), but remanded for new trial on the "sham" issue. Black & Decker v. US, 436 F3d 431 (4th Cir.

Thus, in the *UPS* case,[480] involving the use of an offshore captive insurance affiliate, the court disregarded the taxpayer's attempt to deflect its stream of insurance fees into that affiliate as a transparent transactional "sham" and an impermissible assignment of income (and, for good measure, imposed the negligence penalty). Similarly, in the *Compaq Computer* case,[481] the court denied claimed foreign tax credit benefits from a pre-packaged "dividend dumping foreign tax credit strip" transaction as a sham totally lacking in economic substance, and motivated entirely by tax considerations, again citing *ACM*, and again applying the negligence penalty. Although the transaction involved in *Compaq* is now (since 1997) blocked by § 901(k), the court was unimpressed by this prospective legislative fix, holding that "a transaction does not avoid economic substance scrutiny because (it) predates a statute targeting the specific abuse."[482]

2006); Coltec Indus., Inc. v. US, 62 Fed. Cl. 716, 2004-2 USTC 50,402 (Fed. Cl. 2004) (contingent liability assumption shelter; taxpayer wins after full trial). Also, contra to the *LTCH* decision is TIFD III, Inc. v. US, 342 F. Supp. 2d 94, 2004-2 USTC 50,401 (D. Conn. 2004) (the Castle-Harbour–GE lease stripping case); had enough business purpose to survive sham assertion despite a tax avoidance purpose as well). For comment, see Sheppard, supra note 477. See also Lipton, "New Tax Shelter Decisions Present Problems for the IRS," 102 J. Tax'n 211 (Apr. 2005); Burke, "Castle Harbour, Economic Substance and the Overall-Tax-Effect Test," 107 Tax Notes 1163 (May 30, 2005).

For comment on *LTCH*, see Sheppard, supra note 477; Leeds & Rubinger, supra note 477; Lipton, supra note 477; Warren, supra note 477.

[480] UPS, Inc., RIA TC Memo. 99,268; comment by DeHoff, "Tax Court Slams Insurance Sham: Industry Weighs Impact of UPS," 85 Tax Notes 19 (Oct. 4, 1999); see 1.05[2]. See Cook et al., supra note 477. But *UPS* was reversed on appeal, 254 F3d 1014, 2001-2 USTC 50,475 (11th Cir. 2001) (transactions had economic substances and enough (barely) business purpose to neutralize tax planning motives; one dissent who still thought transaction was a sham; but remanded to Tax Court on the § 482 issue). Sheppard, "Why the IRS Should Argue the Statue First," 92 Tax Notes 465 (July 23, 2001); Kingson, "The Confusion Over Tax Ownership," 93 Tax Notes 409 (Oct. 15, 2001); Lupi-Sher, "Corporate Tax Shelters Regain Vitality?" 92 Tax Notes 11 (July 2, 2001); Wexler, "Notes on the Economic Substances and Business Purposes Doctrines," 92 Tax Notes 127 (July 2, 2001); Lorence, "Corporate Tax Shelters—A Never-Ending Series," 12 J. Int'l Tax'n 10 (Oct. 2001).

[481] Compaq Computer Corp., 113 TC 214 (1999); cf. Hariton, "How to Define 'Corporate Tax Shelter,'" 84 Tax Notes 883 (Aug. 9, 1999); see IRC § 901(k), discussed at 15.21[1][c]; see also Notice 98-5, 1998-1 CB 334, discussed at 15.21[1][d]. But contra is IES Indus., Inc. v. US, 253 F3d 350 (8th Cir. 2001) (court found transactions had economic substance and taxpayer had sufficient business purposes; same deal as *Compaq*, but taxpayer did a bit more due diligence here). See Lupi-Sher, "Corporate Tax Shelters Regain Vitality?" 92 Tax Notes 11 (July 2, 2001). *Compaq* was reversed on appeal to the Fifth Circuit, however, 277 F3d 778, 2002-1 USTC 50,144 (Dec. 28, 2001), which held for the taxpayer.

[482] For a prediction of judicial approval for these transactions, which ultimately proved not to be overly optimistic, see Hariton, "Sorting Out the Tangle of Economic Substance," 52 Tax Law. 235, 272 (1999). For comments, see Raby & Raby, 85 Tax Notes 211 (Oct. 11, 1999); Sheppard, "News Analysis," 85 Tax Notes 569 (Nov. 1,

Finally, the third decision in the post-*ACM* trilogy, *Winn-Dixie*,[483] struck down the widely used leveraged corporate owned life insurance (COLI) transaction (repealed by Congress in 1996) as lacking economic substance and business purpose (other than tax reduction), and therefore as a sham for tax purposes, again citing *ACM* (but this time no penalty was asserted by the Service). The court again noted that legislative repeal of a targeted abuse (in 1996) does not thereby bless sham transactions.[484] Moreover, *Winn-Dixie*'s

---

1999); Yin, "Letters," 85 Tax Notes 815 (1999); Teitelbaum, 85 Tax Notes 816 (Nov. 8, 1999). Kingson, "The Confusion Over Tax Ownership," 93 Tax Notes 409 (Oct. 15, 2001); Teitlebaum, *Compaq Computer & IES Inds.*—The Empire Strikes Back," 86 Tax Notes 829 (Feb. 7, 2000); Shaviro, "Economic Substance, Corporate Tax Shelters and the *Compaq* Case," 88 Tax Notes 221 (July 10, 2000); Lorence, "Corporate Tax Shelters—A Never-Ending Series," 12 J. Int'l Tax'n 10 (Oct. 2001).

For comments on the Fifth Circuit's reversal of *Compaq*, see McMahon, "Economic Substance, Purposive Activity, and Corporate Tax Shelters," 94 Tax Notes 1017 (Feb. 25, 2002); Hariton, The *Compaq* Case, "Notice 98-5 and Tax Shelters: The Theory Is All Wrong," 94 Tax Notes 501 (Jan. 28, 2002); Shaviro & Weisbach, "The Fifth Circuit Got It Wrong in *Compaq v. Commissioner*," 94 Tax Notes 511 (Jan. 28, 2002).

[483] Winn-Dixie Stores, Inc., 113 TC 254 (1999), aff'd per curiam, 254 F3d 1313, 2001-2 USTC ¶ 50,495 (11th Cir. 2001), cert. denied, (Apr. 15, 2002). See also IRS v. CM Holdings, Inc., 2000-2 USTC ¶ 50,791 (D. Del. 2000) (similar case, similar results, but this time with an accuracy penalty added; although there were nice words for the lawyers, but not a happy result), aff'd, 301 F3d 96, 2002-2 USTC ¶ 50,596 (3d Cir. 2002); American Elec. Power, Inc. v. US, 136 F. Supp. 2d 762, 2001-1 USTC ¶ 50,232 (DC Ohio 2001) (deductions denied; a sham transaction; but at least no penalty assertion, though additional taxes will be considerable here); comment by Lupi-Sher, "Three Strikes, You're Out—The COLI Wars," 90 Tax Notes 1462 (Mar. 12, 2001); Lorence, "Corporate Tax Shelters—A Never-Ending Series," 12 J. Int'l Tax'n 10 (Oct. 2001).

But taxpayers finally won a COLI case in Dow Chem. Corp. v. US, 250 F. Supp. 2d 748, 2003-1 USTC ¶ 50,346 (DC Mich. 2003) (found economic substance for taxpayer's plans so interest deductions allowed); comment by Almeras, "Dow Chemical Scores First Victory in COLI Wars," 99 Tax Notes 10 (Apr. 7, 2003); Sheppard, "Finding Economic Substance in COLI," 99 Tax Notes 320 (Apr. 21, 2003). But they lost again on the appeal in American Elec. Power, 326 F3d 737, 2003-1 USTC ¶ 50,416 (6th Cir. 2003) (and this is the circuit court to which *Dow Chemical* is appealable, so that lower court's decision looks to be on shaky ground). Bennett, "*Dow Chemical*: The Formula for Economic Substance," 81 Taxes 13 (Aug. 2003). Dow Chem. Co. v. US, 2003-2 USTC ¶ 50,681 (DC Mich. 2003) (court reaffirmed its previous decision despite Sixth Circuit opinion in *American Electric Power* and also reversed its holding of a factual sham in the first opinion and vacated that portion of the opinion). But Dow Chemical was reversed by the Sixth Circuit (Jan. 23, 2006) (one dissent); thus the government is one hundred percent in COLI litigation.

[484] Very large sums are involved in these deals, which have been popular with major corporations since 1987. For comment, see DeHoff, "Service Scores in COLI Wars ...," 85 Tax Notes 714 (Nov. 8, 1999); Sheppard, "Whistling Dixie About Corporate Tax Shelters," 85 Tax Notes 569 (Nov. 11, 1999); Cook et al., supra note 477. The Tax Court decision in *Winn-Dixie* was affirmed per curiam, 254 F3d 1313, 2001-2 USTC ¶ 50,495 (11th Cir. 2001), and *CM Holdings* was affirmed by the Third Circuit, 2002-2 USTC ¶ 50,791 (3d Cir. 2002).

"plan" was a "conservative" version of these transactions, unhappy news indeed for those who opted into the more aggressive version.

In a related vein, *The Limited* decision[485] did not expressly involve a "tax shelter transaction" (although the taxpayer was attempting, unsuccessfully initially it turned out, to shelter itself from the imputed dividend rule of § 956), but the court nevertheless found that the taxpayer's business purpose claims for its corporate structure were dubious at best, and clearly subordinate to the tax reduction motives. Relying heavily on the "spirit" of the subpart F provisions, and eschewing a "literal" application thereof, the court concluded that the taxpayer was subject to § 956 (in spirit if not literally so, and in a clash between the "letter and the spirit" of a code provision, "spiritualism" triumphs). *The Limited* opinion has been criticized,[486] primarily because the statutory labyrinth of subpart F is tough enough to decipher "literally," let alone divine "spiritually."[487] One is prompted to recall the timeless wisdom embodied in a famous comment by Louis Eisenstein (a highly regarded tax practitioner and author) that "I'm always literal, unless I can do better being spiritual."

The clear message of at least some of the above decisions, however, is that transactions heavily freighted with tax motives will be closely scrutinized and, if found to fall on the wrong side of the "tax planning" versus "tax avoidance" line (i.e., as lacking economic substance or a credible business purpose aside from reducing taxes), they will be treated harshly by some courts as well as the Service. Thus, *ACM Partnership* seems to be well on track to powerfully revitalizing this old, but much applied, principle of the tax law (stemming back to that fountainhead decision in *Gregory v. Helvering*, and "refreshed" by the *Knetsch* and *Goldstein* decisions discussed in Chapter 12), and a principle that corporate America disregards at its peril. One salutary feature of these cases, however, may give aid and comfort to those arguing that the Service has more than enough weapons to deal with corporate tax shelters,

---

But taxpayers finally won one in *Dow Chemical Corp.*, supra note 482; though *Dow Chemical* is appealable to the Sixth Circuit, which subsequently found for the government in the *American Electric Power* case on April 28, 2003), supra note 482. But in *Dow Chemical II*, supra note 482, the court concluded that *American Electric Power* did not change its conclusion; in fact the taxpayer did even better the second time around, since the judge reversed its holding of factual sham and vacated that portion of the prior opinion. But Dow was reversed on January 23, 2006, by the Sixth Circuit (one dissent)

[485] The Limited, Inc., 113 TC 169 (1999); see 15.62[4][a]. But *The Limited* decision was reversed, 286 F3d 324 (6th Cir. 2002) (held, taxpayer was in "banking" business).

[486] See, e.g., Raby & Raby, "Getting at Foreign Earnings Without Paying U.S. Tax," 84 Tax Notes 1763 (Sept. 27, 1999).

[487] See, e.g., Coltec Indus., Inc. v. US, 62 Fed. Cl. 94 (Fed. Cl. 2005); comment by Lipton, supra note 478; Notice 98-11, 1998-1 CB 433, and the ensuing struggle to discover the "purpose" of these rules described at 15.61[4].

and that the legislative proposals considered in this section are not needed to add to that arsenal. But the Service has not batted 1,000 in the courts, and if history is any guide, it is unlikely to do so as several apellate and district court decisions have illustrated.[488]

[f] Tax Shelter Hearings

The Ways and Means Committee hearings on corporate tax shelters on November 10, 1999,[489] held few surprises; the usual suspects reiterated the usual responses. Most agreed, though with varying emphasis, that there is a problem[490] and something must be done about it, but what that "something" should be produced little in the way of a consensus. Thus, the Treasury continued to urge adoption of its February 1999 budget proposals (as revised by its July 1999 White Paper), Representative Doggett urged adoption of HR 2255, and the Joint Committee Staff testimony rejected part of the former (the substantive law amendment elements) and focused exclusively on its recommen-

---

[488] See, e.g., Salina P'ship LP, RIA TC Memo. ¶ 2000-352 (income acceleration deal survived sham attack; taxpayer had valid business purpose for transactions and also had real losses in addition to created gain). Comment by Sheppard, "Economic Substance Abuse," 89 Tax Notes 1095 (Nov. 27, 2000). See also Compaq Computer Corp. v. CIR, 277 F3d 778, 2002-1 USTC ¶ 50,144 (5th Cir. 2001) (Tax Court reversed and held for taxpayer on all issues); UPS, Inc. v. CIR, 254 F3d 1014, 2001-2 USTC ¶ 50,475 (11th Cir. 2001); IES Indus., Inc. v. US, 253 F3d 350 (8th Cir. 2001). An even bigger surprise was the initial taxpayer victory in an *ACM* clone deal, Boca Investering P'ship v. US, 167 F. Supp. 2d 298, 2001-2 USTC ¶ 50,690 (DDC 2001) (total victory on all points). See articles supra note 478; but *Boca* was reversed, 314 F3d 625 (DC Cir. 2003) (partnership ignored as sham because no business purpose for its existence), cert. denied, (Oct. 6, 2003). But they are batting nearly 500, see, e.g., Long-Term Capital Holdings v. US, 330 F. Supp. 2d 122, 2004-2 USTC ¶ 50,351 (D. Conn. 2004) (lease strip deal a sham; major penalties applied as well); Long Term Capitol was affirmed without opinion by the Second Circuit on September 27, 2005; compare Black & Decker Corp. II, 340 F. Supp. 2d 621, 2004-2 USTC ¶ 50,390 (D. Md. 2004). On appeal, the transaction was held to be technically correct, but the case was remanded for the new trial on the "sham" issue. Black & Decker v. US, 436 F3d 431 (4th Cir. 2006). For comments on *LTCH*, see Sheppard, Leeds & Rubinger, Lipton, and Warrent, supra note 477.

But contra to *LTCH* is TIFD III-E, Inc. v. US, 342 F. Supp. 2d 94, 2004-2 USTC ¶ 50,401 (D. Conn. 2004) (the Castle-Harbour–GE lease stripping case, which had enough business purpose to survive sham assertion even though tax avoidance purpose as well). For comment, see Sheppard, "Bury Your Tax Shelter in a Business," 106 Tax Notes 20 (Jan. 3, 2005); Lipton, "Lessons From Castle Harbour ...," 102 J. Tax'n 32 (Jan. 2005).

[489] For reports (and list of documents), see 85 Tax Notes 836 (Nov. 15, 1999) (which also has a bibliography of prior coverage); Daily Tax Rep. (BNA) No. 218, at G-12 (Nov. 11, 1999).

[490] Amazingly, some argued that everything is just fine the way it is. They shall remain nameless.

dations for an enhanced penalty regime, as explicated in its July 1999 study.[491] The committee chairman, however, appeared reluctant to embrace any of the above.

The principal position of note seemed to be that of the Joint Committee Staff and its now specific aversion to tinkering with the substantive tax law rules. The staff testimony argued current Code provisions (e.g., §§ 269, 482, 446, and 7701(l)), together with the common law doctrines of business purpose, sham transactions, economic substance, substance over form, and step transactions, were more than adequate to deal with the tax shelter problem[492] *if* some significant downside risk is added to the calculus; that is, an enhanced penalty regime (together with disclosure, due diligence, and registration requirements).

As Congress's creature, the views of the Joint Committee Staff carry special weight; if anything is going to be done here, it will more likely reflect the staff's recommendations than those of the Treasury (or those of the minority party).[493] It is by no means clear, however, that anything is going to be done; certainly not in this millennium, and little legislative results occurred until passage of the Jobs Act in 2004.[494]

The Senate Finance Committee hearings on March 8 and 9, 2000, generally reprised those held by Ways and Means, with the former Treasury again urging adoption of its legislative package, the Joint Committee Staff continuing its aversion to substantive legislation, and committee Chairman Roth urging caution (although this time around admitting that *some* legislation is probably needed here).[495] It is difficult to believe that some could still testify

---

[491] See supra　5.10[6][c]. Appendix II to the Joint Committee testimony contains a revised update of its July 1999 study (with a useful analysis of the *ACM, UPS, Compaq*, and *Winn-Dixie* cases); it can be found in Tax Analysts' Highlights and Documents, Vol. 56, No. 29, at 1777 (Nov. 12, 1999).

[492] Witness the decisions noted supra　5.10[6][e], which the staff study explicated at length (and with admirable lucidity).

[493] E.g., HR 2255, sponsored by Rep. Doggett and others; after the next election, however, likelihood of its adoption could increase considerably.

[494] Chairman Archer's enthusiasm for any legislative action appears to be under total control. For general comment on these proceedings, see Sullivan, "One Shelter at a Time?" 85 Tax Notes 1226 (Dec. 6, 1999); Wilkins, "What Will Congress Do About Corporate Tax Shelters?" 1 Bus. Ent. No. 6, at 24 (1999). For proposed legislation by the Senate Finance Committee, see infra　5.10[8][a]; for the Ways and Means Chair's proposal, see infra　5.10[8][a]. For the final legislative results in the Jobs Act of 2004, see infra　5.10[8][d] (which closely tracts the Joint Committee Staff model).

[495] For a report on these hearings, see Donmoyer, "Rich Man, Poor Man: Penalties, Interest, and Shelters," 86 Tax Notes 1519 (Mar. 13, 2000). The Treasury and Joint Committee submissions are collected in Daily Tax Rep. (BNA) No. 47 (special supplement) (Mar. 9, 2000). See also testimony of Tax Executives Institute, printed in 86 Tax Notes 1783 (Mar. 20, 2000); and also report at 37 Tax Notes 477 (Apr. 24, 2000), "Roth, Moynihan Writing 'Best of Antishelter Bill.'"

that there is not a serious problem here, though some did. The glacial pace that Congress is moving to address the shelter problem—if it is moving at all—is also surprising. One would think that Joint Committee testimony alone (even disregarding the Treasury's input) would be enough to provoke a prompt legislative response, but apparently that is not the case (so far at least), but major anti-shelter legislation finally passed in the 2004 Jobs Act.[496]

[7] Administrative Response: Regulations on Disclosure, Registration, and List Maintenance

[a] In General

Perhaps because of Congress's perceived hesitancy to act with dispatch, or because Congress rarely does anything significant at a pace resembling "speed," the former Treasury jumped the gun on the Finance Committee hearings, by releasing a salvo of temporary and proposed regulations (plus an "announcement," a "notice," and a "ruling") on February 28, 2000.[497] The Treasury attempted to halt (or at least slow) the spread of corporate tax shel-

---

[496] But for recently proposed legislation by the Senate Finance Committee, see infra ¶ 5.10[8][a] (which was then in its third draft version as of August 3, 2001, the latter being the most benign). But the fourth version, the Tax Shelter Transparency Act (S. 2498), of this proposal (and by far the toughest) was released on May 20, 2002, passed the Finance Committee on June 18, 2002, and was incorporated in the Finance Committee's charity bill on July 2002, HR 10, Title VI A; see Daily Tax Rep. Special Supplement (BNA) Vol. 2, No. 138 (July 18, 2002), for Senate Finance Committee Report (S. Rep. No. 211, 107th Cong.). The current version included in HR 476, Title VII, the Senate charity bill, passed the Senate on April 9, 2003. It subsequently moved into S. 2, which passed on May 15, 2003 (and was effective May 8, 2003) (but did not survive in the final legislation).

For the final legislative anti-shelter provisions, see infra ¶ 5.10[8][d] (modeled largely on the Joint Committee proposals).

[497] Ann. 2000-12, 2000-12 IRB 835 (overview of the Treasury's anti-shelter strategy); TD 8875, issuing Regs. § 301.6112-1T (requiring promoters of corporate tax shelters to maintain lists of corporate investors); TD 8876, issuing Regs. § 301.6111-2T (requiring the promoters of large confidential corporate tax shelters to register with the Service, as required by the 1997 amendments in § 6111(d)); TD 8877, issuing Regs. § 1.6011-4T (tax return disclosure reporting requirements for corporate investors, the most important of the three regulations); Notice 2000-15, 2000-12 IRB 826 (a list of the "tax avoidance transactions" that will trigger the new reporting and disclosure regime, updated by Notice 2001-51, 2001-34 IRB 190), updated again by Notice 2003-76, 2003-49 IRB 1181, and then again by Notice 2004-67, 2004-41 IRB (Oct. 12, 2004). Finally, Rev. Rul. 2000-12, 2000-11 IRB 744 (closed down yet another shelter deal—the debt straddle). See infra ¶ 5.10[7][b].

The temporary disclosure and registration regulations were modified by TD 8896, issued on August 11, 2000, which clarified various provisions and slightly narrowed (very slightly) some of the provisions, but expanded the scope of the investor list maintenance

ters by administrative fiat. The central theme of these pronouncements is disclosure; corporate taxpayers that want to play the tax shelter lottery will have to make their participation known and accept the consequences of that transparency and participation if they turn out to be wrong.[498]

The Bush administration Treasury finally roused itself to the tax shelter problem by proposing a series of anti-shelter initiatives on March 20, 2002, grounded principally on broadened disclosure (with enhanced penalties, including strict liability penalties for inadequate disclosure).[499] Strict liability penalties were also contained in the revised July 2002 Senate Finance Committee's fourth version of its proposal (the July 2002 model). Ways and Means Chair Thomas's proposal, also released in July 2002, likewise contained strict liability penalties and also codified the economic substance doctrine; but a later version, released in July 2003, dropped this provision. Thus, both tax committees as well as the Treasury have proposed strict liability penalties, though in slightly differing versions.[500] The final 2004 tax legislation adopted on October 22, 2004, contained a significant package of augmented penalties, including strict liability (but no substantive amendments), and no codification of the economic substance doctrine.

---

regulations. They were modified again (and narrowed further) by TD 8961 (Aug. 8, 2001).

The disclosure regulations of § 1.6011-4T were amended by TD 9000 on June 14, 2002, but this time the regulations were tightened (expanded to include noncorporate taxpayers; gave an example of indirect participation; defined "substantially similar" transactions). These regulations are to be interpreted broadly in favor of disclosure. See Sheppard, "Drafting Economic Substance," 92 Tax Notes 1258 (Sept. 3, 2001). Yet another revision occurred in October 2002 by TD 9017 (further broadening and toughening the disclosure rules); they became final in TD 9046 on Mar. 4, 2003, which, however, narrowed the scope and focus of the regulations and made other clarifying changes.

[498] See infra   5.10[7][b]. See also infra   5.10[8][a] for proposed draft legislation by the Senate Finance Committee Staff dealing with large corporate tax shelters, which was revised by a later draft version issued on October 5, 2000 (adopting a per se strict liability penalty for "highly abusive" shelters, and also dropping the "large" threshold). The third version of this legislation, released on August 3, 2001, dropped the strict liability penalty and focused exclusively on disclosure as its touchstone. The fourth version, however, proposed significantly stronger medicine, supra note 495, including strict liability penalties. For the Ways and Means Committee Chair's proposal (which also contains strict liability penalties), see infra   5.10[8][c]. Chairman Thomas's proposal also would codify the economic substance doctrine (à la Rep. Doggett's proposals); but his later version dropped this provision. For the final 2004 legislation, see infra   5.10[8][d].

[499] See infra   5.10[8][b]. See also Joint Comm. on Taxation, Background and Present Law Relating to Tax Shelters (JCX-19-02), March 19, 2002, Prepared for Finance Committee Hearing March 21, 2002, reported in Daily Tax Rep. (BNA) No. 54, at L-34 (Mar. 20, 2002), and in Tax Analysts' Highlights and Documents, Vol. 64, No. 54, at 3587 (Mar. 20, 2002); but his later version dropped this provision.

[500] For the Finance Committee's latest July 2002 version, see infra   5.10[8][a]; for the Treasury's version, see infra   5.10[8][b]; for Chairman Thomas's bill, see infra   5.10[8][c]. For the final 2004 legislation, see infra   5.10[8][d].

[b] New Regulations: Registration, Disclosure, and Investor List Maintenance

As noted previously, Treasury promulgated a multi-pronged regulatory regime on February 28, 2000, centered principally on disclosure by promoters and organizers of, and corporate participants in, corporate tax shelters (and the tax shelter disclosure regulations were modified by additional regulations on August 11, 2000, and further narrowed again by regulations issued on August 3, 2001).[501] The disclosure regulations were amended again on June 14, 2002, but this time they were significantly tightened.[502] This regime, in turn, is triggered by the list of various "tax avoidance transactions" described in Notice 2000-15 (and updated by Notice 2004-67). These so-called listed transactions, initially consisting of ten tainted transactions, are expandable by the Service (and have been expanding) as new tax avoidance transactions are identified.[503] Scarcely four months later, expanded disclosure and list maintenance tempo-

---

[501] See supra note 496. For comments, see Bergin et al., "Treasury Turns Up the Spotlight on Abusive Corporate Tax Shelters," 86 Tax Notes 1333 (Mar. 6, 2000); Sheppard, "Corporate Tax Shelter Disclosure: But Will It Work?" 86 Tax Notes 1337 (Mar. 6, 2000); Cryan et al., "A Guide to the New Corporate Tax Shelter Regulations," 87 Tax Notes 107 (Apr. 3, 2000); Gideon & Bowers, "The New Tax Shelter Disclosure Rules," 92 J. Tax'n 261 (May 2000); Stratton, "Disclosure Regs.: Overbroad, Burdensome,…and Effective?" 87 Tax Notes 1311 (June 5, 2000); Stratton, "Corporate Tax Shelter Reg. Hearing Crowded, But Quiet," 87 Tax Notes 1691 (June 26, 2000); Edwards & Stretch, "New Regulations Explain Disclosure Requirements for Corporate Tax Shelters," 14 J. Tax'n Fin. Insts. 12 (Sept. 2000); New York State Bar Ass'n, Tax Section, "Comments on the New Tax Shelter Regulations," 89 Tax Notes 1447 (Dec. 11, 2000); Mendelson & Jones, "Corporate Tax Shelter Regulations: How Do We Comply?" 27 J. Corp. Tax'n 292 (Oct. 2000).

[502] TD 9000, June 14, 2002, amending Regs. § 1.6011-4T. The Service also provided in Announcement 2002-63, 2002-27 IRB 72, that it may request tax accrual work papers in audits of abusive tax shelters. See Stratton, "The Service's Tough Shelter Talk Turns to Action," 96 Tax Notes 183 (July 8, 2002).

[503] Notice 2000-15, 2000-12 IRB 826. The initial hit list included Notice 95-53 (lease-strips), Notice 98-5 (foreign tax credits strips), *ACM Partnership* and *ASA Investerings*–type transactions, Rev. Rul. 99-14 (LILO deals), Notice 99-59 (the "BOSS" transactions), Notice 2000-44 (son-of-BOSS transactions), fast-pay referred stock deals, and the latest entrant, Rev. Rul. 2000-12 (debt straddles). Subsequent additions include Notice 2000-60 (stock compensation shelters), and Notice 2000-61 (Guam-based grantor trusts), Notice 2001-16 (intermediaries), Notice 2001-17 (contingent liabilities), and Notice 2001-45 (basis shifts). See supra note 391.
Notice 2000-15 also incorporated Treasury's proposed legislative definition of "tax avoidance transactions," that is, one in which the net present value of the reasonably expected economic profit is insubstantial in comparison to the net present value of expected tax benefits. Notice 2001-15 was updated by Notice 2001-51, 2001-34 IRB 190 (but it omits the "tax shelter" definition). A later updated black list is Notice 2003-76, 2003-49 IRB 1181 (Nov. 10, 2003), and Notice 2004-67, 2004-41 IRB 800 (Sept. 24, 2004); revised again by Notice 2004-67, 2004-41 IRB (Oct. 10, 2004).

rary regulations were revised and broadened yet again.[504] The new October 2002 regulations were the most far reaching of the various disclosure regions and would clearly result in many more disclosures than their predecessors (as is their express intention). Finally, proposed regulations issued on December 31, 2002, and adopted a year later on December 29, 2003, will deny penalty protection for taxpayers who fail to disclose reportable transactions.[505] The disclosure, registration, and list maintenance rules became final on March 4, 2003.[506]

---

[504] TD 9017, October 22, 2002, issuing Regs. § 1.6011-4T (disclosure), effective January 1, 2003; TD 9018, October 22, 2002, issuing Regs. § 301.6112-1T (list maintenance requirements), also effective January 1, 2003.

See Nijenhuis et al., "The New Disclosure and Listing Regulations for Tax Shelters," 97 Tax Notes 943 (Nov. 18, 2002); Friedrich, "Second Bite: The Treasury Tries Again on Tax Shelter Disclosures and Investor Lists," 30 J. Corp. Tax'n 3 (Jan. 2003); Leeds, "Focusing the Crosshairs: IRS Revises the Shelter Disclosure and Listing Rules," 97 Tax Notes 937 (Nov. 18, 2002); Lipton, "New Tax Shelter Disclosure and Listing Regulations Promise Headaches for Everyone," 98 J. Tax'n 5 (Jan. 2003); Darrow & Balsam, "New Tax Shelter Disclosure and List Maintenance Regulations Cover Broad Array of Transactions and Investments," 16 J. Tax'n Fin. Insts. 5 (Jan. 2003); Rojas & Stratton, "Tax Shelter Regulations Too Burdensome, Practitioners Tell Government," 97 Tax Notes 1509 (Dec. 23, 2002) (Service intends them to cast a wide, wide net and that they do especially the list maintenance rules).

[505] Prop. Regs. §§ 1.6662-3(a), 1.6662-3(b)(2), 1.6662-3(c)(1), 1.6664-4(c) (also effective Jan. 1, 2003). They were adopted as final regulations by TD 9109 on December 29, 2003.

[506] TD 9046 (Mar. 4 2003), issuing Regs. §§ 1.6011-4 (disclosure), 301.6111-2 (registration), and 301.6112-1 (list maintenance). The final regulations narrowed the scope of disclosure and list maintenance in several significant respects and also made other clarifying changes. In addition, a separate revenue procedure exempted various nonabusive losses from the reporting requirements. Rev. Proc. 2003-24, 2003-11 IRB 599, and Rev. Proc. 2003-25, 2003-11 IRB 601, did the same for some thirty items of book-tax difference that do not have to be taken into account in determining the book-tax differences factor. For the many common loss transactions that will not qualify for this relief, see Braithwaite et al., "Section 165 Losses: Top 12 Unexpected Disclosures," 103 Tax Notes 331 (Apr. 19, 2004).

For comment on the new regulations (generally favorable at last), see Leeds, "The Tax Shelter Disclosure, Registration and Listing Rules for 2003 and Beyond," 98 Tax Notes 2025 (Mar. 31, 2003); Lipton, "Final Corporate Tax Shelter Disclosure and List Maintenance Regulations Impose Burdens on Everyone," 98 J. Tax'n 133 (Mar. 2003); Rosenthal & Falstrom, "Me, A Material Adviser? What Now?" 98 Tax Notes 1749 (Mar. 17, 2003); Doering, "The Final Disclosure and List Maintenance Tax Shelter Regulations," 81 Taxes 31 (May 2003); "Final Reportable Transaction Rules Indicate Treasury Listened to Some Comments, But Much Complexity Remains," 16 J. Tax'n Fin. Insts. 37 (May 2003); Wheeler & Lane, "Potentially Abusive Tax Shelter List Rules Finalized," 16 J. Tax'n Fin. Insts. 44 (May 2003); Spencer, "Tax Disclosure Boilerplate and the Confidentiality Conundrum," 101 Tax Notes 1203 (Dec. 8, 2003); Lewis & Pearson, "The Confidential Transaction Tax Shelter Regulations," 31 Corp. Tax'n 15 (May 2004); Rizzi, "Tax Shelters Invade: Corporate Tax Shelters and the Anti-Shelter Crusade," 31 Corp. Tax'n 22 (July 2004).

Of the three regulation disclosure regimes, the corporate tax shelter registration provisions of temporary regulations issued under § 6111(d) (requiring tax shelter promoters and "organizers" to register various "listed" confidential corporate shelters with the Service, and also submit any written offering materials with the registration form) seemingly are the most limited in scope, being confined by the statute to "confidential" transactions. The temporary regulations, however, were anything but narrow; rather they were about as broad in their coverage as even the most fervent opponent of these transactions could hope for. (But revised regulations, issued on August 2, 2001, narrowed the scope of these regulations significantly.) Thus, the number and type of covered transactions was expansive (and exceptions thereto tightly limited):[507] not only were the per se listed tainted transactions of Notice 2000-15 included here, but so too were any transactions lacking in "economic substance" (i.e., ones that violated the Treasury's proposed legislative codification of that doctrine),[508] or those in which tax benefits were an important part of the transaction and were expected to be offered to more than one participant.[509] Moreover, "confidentiality" also was defined broadly (and was presumed to exist unless explicitly

---

[507] Regs. § 301.6111-2T(b)(5) exempts only those transactions that would elicit a "will opinion," or that the Service explicitly exempts by published guidance or in a private ruling issued under Regs. § 301.6111-2T(b)(6). In short, it must be more likely than not that the Service will *not* challenge the transaction.

Revised regulations issued by TD 8961 on August 2, 2001, narrowed the scope of reportable transactions of redesignated Regs. § 301.6111-2T(b)(3), redesignated Regs. § 301.6111-2T(b)(4), and also dropped the economic substance test of former Regs. § 301.6111-2T(b)(3). The revised regulations also dropped the "long-standing" language and clarified that there is no minimum period for which the generally accepted understanding must exist under revised Regs. § 301.6111-2T(b)(3)(ii). The revised regulations also clarified the excepted transactions standard in redesignated Regs. § 301.6111-2T(b)(4)(i) as imposing the same standard on the Service's position as is applicable to taxpayers under Regs. § 1.6662-3(b)(3) (no reasonable basis for Service to deny the claimed tax benefits). Sheppard, "Drafting Economic Substance," Tax Notes 1258 (Sept. 3, 2001); Cryan et al., "A Guide to the New Corporate Tax Shelter Regulations," 92 Tax Notes 1449 (Sept. 10, 2001).

The final regulations issued in March 2003 generally retained the above rules in redesignated Regs. §§ 301.6111-2(b)(4)(i) (no reasonable basis for Service denial), 301.6111-2(b)(4)(ii) (published Service guidance), 301.6111-2(b)(4)(iii) (private ruling), and 301.6111-2(b)(3) (generally accepted understanding of customary commercial practices).

[508] Regs. § 301.6111-2T(b)(3) (lack of meaningful profit potential, or borrowing transactions in which value of the potential deductions significantly exceeds pre-tax value of the expected return).

But revised regulations issued on August 2, 2001, in TD 8961 dropped the economic substance test of Regs. § 301.6111-2T(b)(3) (as redundant and inappropriate in some cases), and the final 2003 regulations did not revive it.

[509] Regs. § 301.6111-2T(b)(4) provides an exception here for "ordinary business transactions" in a form consistent with "customary commercial practice," now in final Regs. § 301.6111-2(b)(3).

waived in writing by the promoter).[510] Similarly, the definition of a "tax shelter promoter" was equally expansive.[511] Since this is a regime that few will willingly seek to enter, these regulations should exert a powerful deterrent to the marketing of these deals. Although modified in August 2000, and narrowed slightly (very slightly) on a prospective basis, their coverage continued to be expansive. Even the revised regulations issued in August 2001, while again narrowing the scope of the registration regulations (again on a prospective basis), continued to cast a broadly inclusive net.

The tax return disclosure regime for corporate participants in a designated tax shelter transaction in Regs. § 1.6011-4T, like the promoter registration regulations under § 6111(d), was also expansively drawn, although failure to disclose a reportable transaction here would have a negative impact under the penalty provisions if the corporate taxpayer lost on the merits.[512] Thus, "report-

---

Revised Regs. § 301.6111-2(b)(3)(ii) clarified this exception by dropping the "longstanding" language and further clarifying what constitutes a generally accepted tax treatment; final Regs. § 301.6111-2(b)(3)(i).

[510] But new regulations issued December 29, 2003, in TD 9108, amended Regs. § 1.6011-4(b)(3) to significantly scale back the circumstances under which a confidential tax transaction will have to be disclosed (to the vast relief of practitioners). See infra note 510. For proposed legislation to delete the confidentiality requirement, see infra ¶ 5.10[8][a].

The most recent version of this draft legislation (Aug. 3, 2001), however, does not contain this proposal.

[511] Regs. § 301.6111-2T(f); also Regs. § 301.6111-2T(g) includes as required registrants those who discuss the transactions where the promoters are foreign persons (unless they say no, in writing, or get written confirmation that the foreign promoter has registered); final Regs. §§ 301.6111-2(f), 301.6111-2(g).

[512] This will be the touchstone for penalty impositions under the Senate Finance Committee's latest legislative draft (issued on August 3, 2001), see infra ¶ 5.10[8][a]. The regulations warn that a "more likely than not" opinion is not necessarily a protection here, see TD 8877 explanation, pt. 1. The August 2000 modifications of TD 8896 clarified, and slightly narrowed, the scope of these regulations as to the document retention rules of Regs. § 1.6011-4T(e).

The disclosure regulations were narrowed again (more broadly this time) by TD 8961, issued on August 2, 2001. The revised regulations dropped the foreign law inconsistency "filter," dropped the "long-standing" language from the customary commercial practice exception in Regs. § 1.6011-4T(b)(3)(ii)(B), and clarified that no reasonable basis for the Service to deny the tax benefits exception of Regs. § 1.6011-4T(b)(3)(ii)(C) imposes the same standards on Service positions as those applicable to taxpayers under Regs. § 1.6662-3(b)(3) (there is no reasonable basis for the Service to deny the tax treatment).

The disclosure regulations of § 1.6011-4T were amended once again on June 14, 2002, by TD 9000, but this time they were materially tightened by (1) expanding the disclosure universe to include all taxpayers; (2) defining substantially similar transactions (a provision to be interpreted broadly); and (3) dropping the "projected tax effect" test for disclosure (which will result in more disclosure).

Finally, Regs. § 1.6011-4T was materially broadened yet again by TD 9017, October 22, 2002; supra note 502. This latest version of the disclosure regulations is the most expansive yet, and will result in far more disclosures (as is their intended goal). Moreover,

able transactions" included not only the per se listed transactions of Notice 2000-15[513] but also any other "large shelter"[514] that had two out of six listed tax shelter "characteristics" (similar to the Treasury's legislative proposal).[515] Conversely, exceptions to disclosure were narrowly drawn here (i.e., an ordinary and customary business transaction that would be done without regard to taxes, or one that had gained long-standing "respectability" (e.g., a leveraged leasing business), or one where the taxpayer had obtained a "will" opinion).[516] The final 2003 regulations contain very few exceptions to reporting where one of the six listed reporting events apply.

---

proposed regulations under § 1.6664-4(c) (issued Dec. 31, 2002) will deny penalty protection if taxpayers fail to follow the disclosure rules of Regs. § 1.6011-4T. The final 2003 disclosure Regs. § 1.6011-4 were narrowed in several respects, however, see supra note 505, but they are still by no means a love pat. The principal relaxations occurred in the loss trigger factor in Rev. Proc. 2003-24, 2003-11 IRB 599, and the book-tax difference factor in Rev. Proc. 2003-25, 2003-11 IRB 601. For comments, see supra note 504. But revised regulations issued on December 29, 2003, amended Regs. § 1.6011-4(b)(3) to sharply scale back the circumstances where a confidential tax transaction will have to be disclosed (to the vast relief of practitioners). See Udrys, Reeder & Church, "The Revised Confidentiality Filter," 102 Tax Notes 1372 (Mar. 15, 2004).

[513] Regs. § 1.6011-4T(b)(2); but only if the expected tax benefits exceed $1 million for a single year (or $2 million for multiple years), Regs. § 1.6011-4T(b)(4). But the projected tax effect test of Regs. § 1.6011-4T(b)(4)(i) was dropped by the June 2002 amendment as resulting in inadequate disclosure. Final Regs. § 1.6011-4(b)(2) dropped the dollar threshold (though such thresholds do apply under the loss factor of Regs. § 1.6011-2(b)(5)(i)).

[514] Having projected tax benefits in excess of $5 million for a single year, or $10 million over multiple years. Later regulations (including the final 2003 regulations) drop these threshold limits.

[515] These "badges" of a tax shelter were: confidentiality, tax indemnity protections, promoter fees in excess of $100,000, tax-book disparity, participation of a tax-indifferent party, and cross-border tax arbitrage (e.g., hybrids—a new addition to the shelter indicator list), Regs. § 1.6011-4T(b)(3)(i).

Revised regulations issued by TD 8961 on August 2, 2001, drop this latter tax shelter indicator however. The final 2003 regulations require reporting if only one of the six listed factors exists.

[516] Regs. § 1.6011-4T(b)(3)(ii) (published Service acceptance to disclosure also will suffice here); see, e.g., Notice 2000-18, 2000-9 IRB 731; final Regs. § 1.6011-4(b)(8).

Revised regulations issued on August 2, 2001, in TD 8961, drop the "long-standing" language and clarify that the same standards apply to Service denials as would apply to taxpayers under Regs. § 1.6662-3(b)(3) (i.e., reasonable basis for the Service to deny the asserted tax treatment). The final 2003 regulations do not contain such an exception (and a tax opinion is irrelevant under the disclosure rules).

The disclosure regulations of Regs. § 1.6011-4T were revised again on June 14, 2002, by TD 9000, this time, however, they were materially tightened, infra note 516. But the final 2003 regulations pulled back in several respects and are more narrowly focused, infra note 520.

The disclosure regulations of § 1.6011-4T were revised once again in 2002, this time, however, they were materially tightened.[517] Yet another revision of the disclosure regulations was effected in October 2002,[518] in which these provisions again were materially expanded and toughened.[519] Finally, proposed regulations issued on December 31, 2002, and adopted on December 29, 2003, deny penalty protection for taxpayers that fail to follow this disclosure regime.[520] The disclosure regulations of § 1.6011-4 were adopted in final form on March 4, 2003, but this time the several revisions to the temporary regulations narrowed their scope somewhat and attempted to strike a better balance between over and under reporting.[521]

---

[517] TD 9000, June 2002. The principal changes in the 2002 revisions were (1) including all taxpayers in the disclosure regime; (2) providing an example of indirect participation (e.g., the lease stripping transaction of Notice 95-53); (3) defining substantially similar transactions, with two examples (a provision to be broadly interpreted in favor of disclosure); and (4) dropping the "projected tax effect" test of Regs. § 1.6011-4T(b)(4)(i) as resulting in inadequate disclosure.

Also Announcement 2002-63, 2002-27 IRB 72, provided that the Service may request tax accrual work papers in audits of abusive shelter cases; see Stratton, supra note 501.

[518] TD 9017, Oct. 22, 2002, issuing revised Regs. § 1.6011-4T (effective Jan. 1, 2003); supra note 501.

[519] The latest version requires disclosure reporting in six specific categories of transactions: (1) listed transactions (same); (2) confidential transactions; (3) transactions with contractual protection; (4) transactions generating losses exceeding specified thresholds (i.e., $10 million for corporate taxpayers in one year or $20 million over multiple years, $5 million in one year for partnerships and S corporations, or $10 million over multiple years); (5) transactions with a significant book-tax differential; and (6) transactions generating a tax credit exceeding $250,000 where the asset is held for a brief period—e.g., *Compaq Computer* deals. See Regs. § 1.6011-4T(b). The final regulations issued on March 4, 2003, retained these six categories, but narrowed them in several significant respects, infra note 520.

[520] Prop. Regs. § 1.6664-4(c); adopted as final by TD 9109 on Dec. 29, 2003.

[521] TD 9046 issuing Regs. §§ 1.6011-4 (disclosure), 301.6111-2 (registration), and 301.6112-1 (list maintenance); also Rev. Proc. 2003-24, 2003-11 IRB 599 (exempting various nonabusive loss transactions from the reporting rules), and Rev. Proc. 2003-25, 2003-11 IRB 601 (exempting thirty book-tax disparities from the book-tax differences computation). For comment (generally favorable to this version of the regulations, though far from exultant), see supra note 505. See also Rev. Proc. 2004-45, 2004-31 IRB 140 (Aug. 8, 2004) (Disclosure Procedures for Transactions With Significant Book-Tax Difference, With New Schedule M-3 Instructions and Frequently Asked Questions (23); a targeted disclosure regime designed to elicit greater transparency). A new revised draft of 2005 Schedule M-3 was released in June 2005; see Daily Tax Rep. (BNA) No. 121 (June 24, 2005). But Notice 2006-6, 2006 IRB 385 (Jan. 31, 2006) drops the book-tax differential trigger (in view of expanded Schedule M-3 reporting).

Of special note to practitioners are the "material advisor" rules in the list maintenance regulations of § 301.6112-1(c)(2), which were "clarified" and narrowed in several respects. For comment see Rosenthal & Falstrom, "Me, A Material Adviser? What Now?"

Since filing the required disclosure statement is an official part of the corporate tax return, and is virtually an open invitation to the Service for an audit (as is the equally powerful "red flag" of registration under § 6111(d), and the related inclusion on the client "list" required to be maintained by shelter promoters),[522] corporate taxpayers that continue to invest in these high-risk transactions are clearly asking for trouble unless they are highly confident of prevailing on the merits (nondisclosure also will likely attract a penalty on top of any ultimate tax deficiency, although disclosure, unless the transaction is truly a dubious one, may at least avoid penalties). Few, if any, public corporations that the authors have dealt with have any inclination to appear on the previously mentioned billboards.

Finally, the Service has established a new "Office of Tax Shelter Analysis" to act as a clearinghouse of tax shelter activity, to review all disclosures by promoters and taxpayers, to identify new forms of shelters at an early date, and to generally serve as a central command post in the anti-shelter effort.[523] Coupled with the Service's court victories in cases such as *ACM Partnership*, *UPS, Inc.*, *Compaq Computer*, and *Winn-Dixie*,[524] it may be that the corporate tax shelter era has come to an end, or at least a near end. It may also turn out that "new" legislation is not really needed here after all—although the former Treasury remained unconvinced of this position, and reports that the Senate Finance Committee was working on a bipartisan (though limited) corporate tax shelter bill turned out to be accurate.[525] At the very least, the former Treasury

---

98 Tax Notes 1749 (Mar. 17, 2003); Doering, "The Final Disclosure and List Maintenance Tax Shelter Regulations," 81 Taxes 31 (May 2003); also supra note 505.

[522] Regs. § 301.6111-1T, TD 8896, issued on August 11, 2000, expanded the list maintenance requirement to include any noncorporate investors (although de minimis thresholds also were added here). The list maintenance regulations in § 301.6112-1T were also significantly revised and expanded by TD 9018, October 22, 2002 (effective Jan. 1, 2003); supra note 503. Especially noteworthy is the broad definition of "material advisor" in Regs. § 301.6112-1T(c); see Rojas & Stratton, "Tax Shelter Regs. Too Burdensome Practitioners Tell Government," 97 Tax Notes 1509 (Dec. 23, 2002).

[523] For description, see Stratton, "An Inside Look at the IRS OTSA," 100 Tax Notes 1246 (Sept. 8, 2003). This effort is reminiscent of the Service's earlier special task force set up in the 1980s to deal with the previous wave of tax shelters. Tightening of Circular 230 practice standards is also slated for future action. See Ann. 2000-51, 2000-22 IRB 1141 (notice of the Service plan to tighten Circular 230), which was proposed in January 2001 (see Stratton, "Treasury Proposes Tightening Tax Shelter Opinion Standards," 90 Tax Notes 284 (Jan. 15, 2001)).

[524] See supra 5.10[6][e]. Negligence penalties were imposed in two of these cases as well (*UPS* and *Compaq*). But *UPS* was reversed on appeal, 234 F3d 1014, 2001-2 USTC 50,475 (11th Cir. 2001); and so was *Compaq*, 277 F3d 778 (5th Cir. 2001). Also IES Indus., Inc. v. US, 253 F3d 350 (8th Cir. 2001) (taxpayer prevailed in *Compaq*-type transaction: had economic substance and adequate business purpose). But *Winn-Dixie* was affirmed per curiam, 254 F3d 1313, 2001-2 USTC 50,495 (11th Cir. 2001).

[525] See Daily Tax Rep. (BNA) No. 82, at G-3 (Apr. 27, 2000), and report in 87 Tax Notes 477 (Apr. 24, 2000). For a proposed draft of this legislation released by the Senate

finally recognized that it did not need new legislation to respond forcefully to the corporate tax shelter problem; it has done so on its own initiative with the temporary and now final regulations.

[c] Revision of Circular 230

As a final prong of its multifaceted attack on corporate tax shelters, the Service has proposed a major revision of the Circular 230 practice standards on January 12, 2001,[526] with a principal focus on tax shelter opinions (tightening the standards for such opinions[527] and increasing the sanctions on attorneys

---

Finance Committee on May 24, 2000, and reissued in revised form on October 5, 2000, see infra ¶ 5.10[8][a].

With the return of Democratic control of the Senate in early 2001, yet another version of the Senate Finance Committee's anti-shelter legislation was issued on August 3, 2001 (this latter version, however, is a considerably reduced proposal, with a focus primarily on taxpayer disclosure and penalties applicable to failure to adequately disclose). But revised versions issued in May, June, and July 2002 are much tougher than the 2001 model and are considered infra ¶ 5.10[8][a].

[526] Reported at Daily Tax Rep. (BNA) No. 9, at GG-1, L-1 (Jan. 12, 2001); see Stratton, "Treasury Proposes Tightening Tax Shelter Opinion Standards," 90 Tax Notes 284 (Jan. 15, 2001). The proposals are based heavily on recommendations by the ABA Tax Section, see 89 Tax Notes 147 (Oct. 2, 2000); "NYSBA Offers Suggestions on Circular 230," 92 Tax Notes 975 (Aug. 13, 2001); Shepard, "Drafting Economic Substance," 92 Tax Notes 1258, 1262 (Sept. 3, 2001); Ballard, "ABA Calls for Broad Revision to New Tax Shelter Opinion Standards," Daily Tax Rep. (BNA) No. 183, at J-1 (Sept. 24, 2001); Lavoie, "Deputizing the Tax Bar," 21 Va. Tax Rev. 43 (2001).

Portions of the Circular 230 practice standards regulations were finalized by TD 9011 on July 25, 2002, but the tax shelter opinion rules were deferred; they will be reproposed (they were reproposed on December 29, 2003 (and were not materially eased)). See comment by Sheppard, 102 Tax Notes 188 (Jan. 12, 2004); Lipton, "'Tax Shelter' and 'Tax Shelter Opinion' — IRS, in Another Try and Circular 230 Strikes Out Again," 100 J. Tax'n 134 (Mar. 2004); Mezzullo, "College of Tax Counsel Addresses Changes to Circular 230," 102 Tax Notes 1150 (Mar. 1, 2004). The revised proposals were adopted by TD 9165 on December 17, 2004 (without material change); comment by Sheppard, 106 Tax Notes 141 (Jan. 10, 2005).

For other comments, see Rabe & Rabe, "Confidence Levels, Circular 230, and Practitioner Penalties," 106 Tax Notes 187 (Jan. 10, 2005); Lipton, Walton & Dixon, "The World Changes: Broad Sweep of New Tax Shelter Rules in AJCA and Circular 230 Affect Everyone," 102 J. Tax'n 134, 145 (Mar. 2005); Giancana, "Circular 230 Decision Matrixes," 106 Tax Notes 1295 (Mar. 14, 2005); New York State Bar Ass'n, Tax Section, "Recommendations for Improving Circular 230 Regulations," 107 Tax Notes 91 (Apr. 4, 2005); Paul & Weiner, "The Final Regulations Under Circular 230," 107 Tax Notes 119 (Apr. 4, 2005); Blattmachr et al., "The Application of Circular 230 in Estate Planning," 107 Tax Notes 61 (Apr. 4, 2005); Blattmachr et al., "Circular 230 Redux," 107 Tax Notes 1533 (June 20, 2005); Baile & Macvor, "New Circular 230 Regulations Impose Strict Standards for Tax Practioners," 107 Tax Notes 939 (May 23, 2005).

[527] Thus, heightened standards of due diligence would be required, certain contingent fee arrangements would be prohibited, and the opinion must be a reasoned analysis of the

who fail to satisfy these standards).[528] Suffice it to say, the tax bar is not the least bit happy about these provisions.[529]

The new administration Treasury released its version of plans to combat abusive tax shelters, focusing primarily on increasing penalties (including strict liability for inadequate disclosures resulting in a tax deficiency) and simplifying and broadening the current disclosure regime.[530]

[8] Anti-Shelter Legislation

[a] Proposed Legislation: Senate Finance Committee Drafts

A bipartisan legislative discussion draft by the staff of the Senate Finance Committee dealing with corporate tax shelters was released on May 24, 2000, and reissued in revised form on October 5, 2000.[531] This proposal (both ver-

---

relevant facts and legal authorities (without making "unreasonable factual assumptions"). See Gould, "Giving Tax Advice—Some Ethical, Professional, and Legal Considerations," 97 Tax Notes 523 (Oct. 28, 2002).

The December regulations were modified (and eased) by TD 9201 (May 19, 2005); comment by Stratton in 107 Tax Notes 939 (May 23, 2005).

[528] Including censure or public reprimand of the offending practitioner (e.g., shaming for shoddy work). But firmwide sanctions were *not* proposed by the regulations.

[529] For uniformly hostile comments, see Raby & Raby, "Penalty Protection for the Taxpayer: Circular 230 and the Code," 107 Tax Notes 1257 (June 6, 2005); Zelesco, "TEI Suggests Changes to Circular 230 Rules," 107 Tax Notes 1183 (May 30, 2004); Bailey, "Attorney Suggests Alternatives to Improve Circular 230 Rules," 107 Tax Notes 1185 (May 30, 2005); August and Maxfield, "Attorneys Seek Delay in Implementation of Circular 230 Rules," 107 Tax Notes 1196 (May 30, 2005); Dellinger, "Circular 230: A Clarification That Muddles the Waters," 107 Tax Notes 1438 (June 3, 2005); Blattmachr et al., "Circular 230 Redux: Questions of Validity and Compliance," 107 Tax Notes 1533 (June 20, 2005); Rizzi, "A 'Sea Change' for Corporate Tax Opinions Under Circular 230," 32 Corp. Tax'n 3 (Sept. 2005); Schler, "Effects of Anti-Tax Shelter Rules on Non-Shelter Practice, 109 Tax Notes 915 (Nov. 14, 2005); Schenk, "The Circular 230 Amendments: Time to Throw the Out and Start Over," 110 Tax Notes 1311 (Mar. 20, 2006).

[530] These proposals are considered infra   5.10[8][b]. The chairman of the Ways and Means Committee also introduced anti-shelter legislation in July 2002, similarly focusing on penalties for nondisclosure, which proposals are considered infra   5.10[8][c]. The final legislation is infra   5.10[8][d].

[531] Reprinted in Tax Analyst's Highlights and Documents, Vol. 57, No. 39, at 1981 (May 25, 2000). For comments, see Donmoyer & Glenn, 87 Tax Notes 1175 (May 29, 2000); Tax Executives Institute, "Comments on Finance Committee's Corporate Tax Shelter Discussion Draft," 88 Tax Notes 695 (July 31, 2000). A newly revised draft was issued on October 5, 2000, reprinted in Daily Tax Rep. (BNA) No. 195 (Oct. 6, 2000). A revised draft was released in August 2001, infra note 531, but was considerably reduced in scope from the 2000 versions.

But new versions of this proposal were released during 2002, the Tax Shelter Transparency Act, S. 2498, and the latest version, July 2002, is a significantly different piece of

sions) was less extensive in scope than that sought by the Treasury; instead, it conformed far more closely to the Joint Committee Staff proposals of July 1999.[532] Thus, the focus here was enhanced penalties, taxpayer return disclosure, registration of shelters by promoters, and heightened practice standards (rather than enactment of substantive anti-shelter rules such as the former Treasury's proposed codification of the economic substance doctrine). The stated purpose of the Senate Finance Committee Staff proposal was a four-fold one: (1) to discourage improper tax shelter activity by large corporations through an increased penalty; (2) to require enhanced disclosure of corporate tax shelters by corporations and promoters; (3) to prohibit tax opinion writers from opining on deals in which they participate or otherwise have a financial interest and provide what must be included in a tax opinion in order for a corporation to rely on it; and (4) to expand current tax law on aiding and abetting. Yet another version of this anti-shelter legislation was proposed on August 3, 2001,[533] but the third attempt was considerably reduced in scope from the prior two versions focusing exclusively on disclosure as the touchstone for its application. The principal goal of this revised legislation was to augment the Treasury's registration, disclosure, and list maintenance regulations. Also dropped was the strict liability penalty of the October 2000 version; instead, a safe harbor was added under which taxpayers could avoid a penalty if (1) there was substantial authority for their position, (2) adequate disclosure of the transaction was made on the return, and (3) the taxpayer rea-

---

work, driven it would seem by the wave of corporate scandals that evolved during 2002. It was released in May 2002, passed the Finance Committee on June 18, 2002, and was folded into the Finance Committee's charity bill, HR 7, Title VI A, in July 2002 (and during this process it has been toughened even more along the way). Hereafter this proposal will be referred to as the July 2002 version. But this legislation failed to pass in 2002. The charity bill was introduced in 2003 as HR 476 and the tax shelter provisions are in Title VII; this bill passed the Senate on April 9, 2003, but as of April 20 no comparable provisions were pending in the House (other than the Thomas bill, see infra ¶ 5.10[8][c]). See Hariton, "How to Fix Economic Substance," 99 Tax Notes 539 (Apr. 28, 2003); Berg, "Economic Substance Codification and Legitimate Transactions," 99 Tax Notes 579 (Apr. 28, 2003); Peaslee, "More Thoughts on Proposed Economic Substance-Clarifications," 99 Tax Notes 747 (May 5, 2003); Peaslee, "Economic Substance Codification Gets Worse," 99 Tax Notes 1101 (May 19, 2003); supra ¶ 5.10[4][a].

The Senate's ultimately passed tax bill, S. 1054, May 15, 2003, was effective May 8, 2003 (a fact noted with dismay by Peaslee in his May 19, 2003, comments). This proposal did not survive in the final 2003 tax bill, however.

[532] See supra ¶ 5.10[6][c].

[533] The "Tax Shelter Disclosure Act," reprinted in Daily Tax Rep. (BNA) No. 150, at L-3 (Aug. 6, 2001). For critical comment see Sheppard, "Constructive Thinking About Tax Shelter Penalties," 92 Tax Notes 1013 (Aug. 20, 2001). For analysis of the revised Doggett tax shelter legislation, HR 2520, see Shepard, "Drafting Economic Substance," 92 Tax Notes 1258, 1260 (Sept. 3, 2001). For analysis of this version of the Finance Committee draft, see Cantley, "The Tax Shelter Disclosure Act: The Next Battle in the Tax Shelter War," 22 Va. Tax Rev. 105 (2002).

sonably believed it would more likely than not prevail on the merits.[534] The latest version, released on May 9, 2002, adopted by the Senate Finance Committee on June 18, 2002, and included in the Finance Committee's charity bill in July 2002, continued to focus on disclosure and penalties, but also returned to strict liability penalties for inadequate disclosure.[535] This version, in effect, moved more strongly to the Joint Committee Staff's earlier proposals.[536] This legislation finally passed the Senate on April 9, 2003.[537]

The central proposal in the 2000 draft legislative package (both versions) was a new increased penalty provision in proposed § 6662A for corporate tax shelter understatements of large corporations.[538] Under the May 2000 version, this enhanced penalty regime was activated if the transaction constituted a "corporate tax shelter," a term defined broadly as any "arrangement" where the corporate participant had a "significant" tax avoidance purpose for its participation. Moreover, such a tax avoidance purpose would be presumed if *one* of the following tax shelter indicators (or "badges") was present: (1) the reasonably anticipated pre-tax profit was insignificant in relation to the reasonably ex-

---

[534] Prop. IRC § 6662(i)(2); proposed § 6662(i)(3) allowed tax opinion protection only for "quality opinions" rendered by competent independent advisors (similar to the prior two versions). The July 2002 version retained this escape *only* if there was adequate disclosure; it is in § 6664(d).

[535] Tax Shelter Transparency Act, S. 2498, first reported in Daily Tax Rep. (BNA) No. 91, at L-1 (May 10, 2002), and Daily Tax Rep. (BNA) No. 92, at L-36 (May 13, 2002); it has been further folded into the Finance Committee's charity bill, HR 7, as Title VI A. See Sheppard, "Tax Shelter Opponents Turn Practical," 95 Tax Notes 1111 (May 20, 2002). The July 2002 version has also incorporated some of the Bush Treasury's proposals, see infra   5.10[6][i]. It has reversed the former trend toward increasing liberality, inspired no doubt by the Enron debacle and other recent corporate scandals. In a new feature, any penalty incurred by a public company must be reported to the SEC (i.e., public shame for shams). The proposal also denies invocation of the attorney-client privilege for tax shelter advice, § 7525(b). See New York State Bar Ass'n, Tax Section, "Comments on Pending Tax Shelter Legislation," 97 Tax Notes 115 (Oct. 7, 2002).

[536] See supra   5.10[6][c].

[537] It was moved into the Senate's tax reduction bill, S. 1054, which passed on May 15, 2003, supra note 529; but this proposal did not survive in the final 2003 tax bill of May 28, 2003. As can be seen, tracking the many versions and changes of course in this legislation has not been a fun task!

[538] The understatement penalty would be doubled, from 20 percent to 40 percent, and a "large" corporation was defined as one with annual gross receipts of at least $10 million. But the October 5, 2000, revised draft dropped the $10 million minimum. The 2002 version returned it to the disclosure penalty rules of § 6707A(b)(3)(B).

The later version also added all taxpayers, corporate or noncorporate, to its coverage. Prop. IRC §§ 6662A(c)(1), 6662(d)(2)(C)(ii). Proposed § 6662A as revised, however, imposed a 40 percent per se strict liability penalty for transactions subject to its penalty. Prop. IRC § 6664(A)(1), last sentence (with *no* escape hatches).

pected net tax benefits;[539] (2) the arrangement involved a "tax-indifferent party";[540] or (3) the transaction resulted in "significant" tax benefits for the corporation, and either involved a tax indemnity (or similar agreement), or created a permanent book-tax differential, or involved little (if any) additional economic risk to the corporation.[541] The October version dropped all of these definitions, however, and applied the § 6662A per se strict liability penalty to any "abusive tax shelter devices," a term defined by § 6662A(b)(1) as any device (broadly defined in § 6662A(b)(2)), lacking *either* a material nontax business purpose, or "economic substance" (as explicated in various court decisions). The August 2001 proposal, by contrast, dropped the strict liability proposal of § 6662A and instead merely proposed to amend the § 6662 understatement penalty provisions, adding the new § 6662(i) (an enhanced 40 percent penalty unless the disclosure safe harbor of § 6662(i)(2) was satisfied).[542] The July 2002 version, by contrast, proposed a new strict liability monetary penalty for nondisclosure in § 6707A (which was doubled for "large entities" and high net worth individuals).[543] This penalty would be triggered on failure to adequately disclose "reportable transactions" (as defined in the § 6011 regulations), or "listed transactions" (i.e., those that show up on the Service's "black list").[544] If incurred, this penalty must be reported to the SEC.[545] Unlike the August 2001 version, however, the § 6662 understatement penalty was augmented by a new special penalty provision, § 6662A, for undisclosed listed

---

[539] Prop. IRC § 6662A(c)(2)(B). This indicator was similar to the Treasury's economic substance doctrine definition.

[540] Prop. IRC § 6662A(c)(2)(C). Such parties included a tax-exempt person, a foreign corporation, or a loss corporation inserted into the arrangement in order to absorb the unfavorable tax aspects (i.e., taxable items) from the transaction.

[541] Prop. IRC § 6662A(c)(2)(D). These various tax shelter "indicators" listed in § 6662A(c)(2) were similar to those contained in both the Treasury's White Paper and the Joint Committee Staff's penalty proposals. The October revised draft dropped these "definition" provisions, however.

[542] Thus, no penalty will be imposed if the taxpayer had substantial authority for its position, adequately disclosed the transaction on its return, and reasonably believed that it more likely than not would prevail on the merits. A tax opinion by an independent advisor satisfying the quality standards of § 6662(i)(3) would supply the "reasonable belief" requirement. The July 2002 version moved this escape to §§ 6664(d)(2) and 6664(d)(3).

[543] This penalty ($50,000 for reportable transactions, $100,000 for listed transactions, both of which are doubled for large entities and high net worth individuals) will be incurred regardless of whether taxpayers prevail on the merits. There is a possibility for rescission of this penalty in § 6707A(d), but this provision is a very narrow one and is intended to be invoked only in rare and unusual cases; moreover, it does not apply to listed transactions.

[544] Prop. IRC § 6707A(c).

[545] Prop. IRC § 6707A(e), which presumably will make public the name of the offenders, an unpleasant prospect for publicly traded companies.

transactions and other undisclosed reportable tax avoidance transactions.[546] For adequately disclosed reportable and listed transactions, a stricter reasonable cause exception also was provided by § 6664(c).[547]

The May 2000 version of § 6662A(d) provided for various escapes from (or reductions of) the 40 percent penalty of § 6662A(a). Thus, no penalty would apply if the corporation reasonably believed it *should* prevail on the merits as to its tax treatment, had a material nontax business purpose for engaging in the transaction, and met the special disclosure requirements of § 6662A(d)(4).[548] The penalty could be reduced (to 20 percent) under § 6662A(d)(2) if the taxpayer reasonably believed that it "more likely than not" would prevail on the merits, had a material nontax business purpose, and met the disclosure requirements of § 6662A(d)(4), or reasonably believed that it would prevail on the merits if challenged by the Service and had a reasonable business purpose (even though no disclosure was made). Finally, the Service was prohibited by § 6662A(d)(3) from waiving the § 6662A(a) 40 percent penalty (that is, there was no discretion in the Service to abate the 40 percent penalty, other than by way of the explicit statutory escape provisions of § 6662A(d));[549] moreover, reliance on tax opinions was restricted by

---

[546] Prop. IRC § 6662A(c) (25 percent for reportable avoidance transactions and 30 percent for listed transactions). Moreover, this is a strict liability penalty as well and cannot be waived.

[547] Prop. IRC § 6664(d)(2); namely, substantial authority and a reasonable belief that the treatment is more likely than not proper. Proposed § 6664(d)(3) continues the "opinion quality" standards and "advisor independence standards of the earlier proposals."

Undisclosed nonreportable transactions continued to be subject to the general penalty rules of § 6662, but the substantial authority standard would be raised to a more likely than not belief.

[548] Such return disclosure had to be certified by the taxpayer's chief financial officer or other senior corporate officer with knowledge of the facts (under penalties of perjury). The general disclosure rule required identification of all the tax shelter indicators present in the deal and, if the expected tax benefits exceed $5 million, additional information listed in § 6662A(d)(4)(B)(ii) had to be included. In this latter case, substantial added "transparency" was required. The October revised draft added a penalty for failure to disclose in proposed § 6707A, but dropped the attestation requirement. The July 2002 proposal continues the § 6707A strict liability monetary penalty for nondisclosures (likewise without a specific attest requirement; but the committee report intends that the disclosure form require that the information is submitted under penalty of perjury). But § 6707A(d) allows for the rescission of this penalty (though only in rare and unusual cases, and only at the highest level, and only if it involves a listed transaction).

[549] Taxpayer's "reasonable belief" had to be based on the facts and law that exist at the time of the transaction and relate solely to its chances for success on the merits (rather than on the audit lottery, or settlement potential), § 6662A(d)(5)(A). The October version limited this escape to the § 6662 penalty only. IRC § 6662(d)(2)(E)(i). The August 2001 version incorporated these standards in its general safe harbor escape from the tax shelter penalty; Prop. IRC §§ 6662(i)(2), 6662(i)(3). The July 2002 version of this escape is in §§ 6664(d)(2) and 6664(d)(3).

§ 6662A(d)(5)(B) to "quality opinions" rendered by independent advisors who had no financial stake in the transaction under review.[550]

Under the October 2000 version of the § 6662A strict liability penalty, however, there was *no* escape from this penalty (not even by an amended return once the taxpayer is contacted by the Service). However, if the shelter was merely abusive (as opposed to highly abusive, and thus subject to § 6662A) the regular penalty provisions of § 6662 (and § 6664) applied, but were refined and tightened as follows:

1. This penalty could be avoided if the taxpayer had substantial authority for its position, adequately disclosed the transaction in its return, *and* reasonably believed its treatment more likely than not was correct, § 6662(d)(2)(C)(i);

2. "Reasonable belief" also was defined (and tightened) by § 6662(d)(2)(E)(i) (namely, it had to be based on the facts and law at the time of the transaction and relate solely to chances for success on the merits rather than the audit lottery on settlement potential); and

3. Only "quality opinions" by "qualified advisors" could be relied on for penalty protection purposes under § 6662(d)(2)(E)(ii) (namely, the opinion had to be rendered by an independent advisor, with no stake in the deal, § 6662(d)(2)(E)(iii); and had to be a professionally competent piece of legal work, § 6662(d)(2)(E)(iv)).

The August 2001 version dropped the special penalty of § 6662A for highly abusive transactions and incorporated the above provisions as its safe harbor escape (in proposed §§ 6662(i)(2) and 6662(i)(3)) from the new proposed 40 percent tax shelter penalty of § 6662(a)(2). The July 2002 version continued these safe harbor escape rules (in §§ 6664(d)(2) and 6664(d)(3)) from the special penalty provision of § 6662A, but they now applied only with respect to adequately disclosed listed transactions and disclosed avoidance transactions.[551]

The penalty did not apply under the May 2000 version of § 6662A to built-in losses or deductions that had been economically incurred before the

---

[550] Section 6662A(d)(5)(B)(ii) listed factors that would render the tax opinion professionally unacceptable. The October version moved this provision to the regular penalty regime of § 6662 in § 6662(d)(2)(E)(ii). The August 2001 version retains them in proposed § 6662(i)(3)(B). The July 2002 version retains them in § 6664(d)(3)(B).

[551] Understatements attributable to listed transactions and reportable tax avoidance transactions are subject to a special 20 percent strict liability penalty by § 6662A(a), augmented to 30 percent and 25 percent respectively in § 6662A(c). These penalties can be avoided only if there has been adequate disclosure and then only if the augmented reasonable cause standards of § 6664(d)(2) and 6664(d)(3) are satisfied. They are, however, subject to the potential rescindability rules of § 6707A(d) if the nondisclosure penalty is rescinded; see IRC § 6664(d)(2), last sentence.

transaction and were borne by the taxpayer;[552] but a potential penalty could not be purged by an amended return filed after the Service came knocking on the door.[553] In addition, if the corporate taxpayer incurred a penalty of $1 million or more under the May 2000 version of the legislation, proposed § 6116 required this fact to be disclosed to its shareholders, including the reasons for that penalty.[554]

The Finance Committee's May 2000 proposal did not neglect other participants in the corporate tax shelter enterprise, nor did the October 2000 revised draft proposal as well as the August 2001 and the May and July 2002 versions. Thus, the return preparer penalty of § 6694 would be raised to 50 percent of the preparer's fee in § 6694(a)(1) and the standards for escape in § 6694(a)(2) also would be tightened.[555] Similarly, the "aider and abettor" penalty of § 6701 would be raised to 50 percent of the facilitator's fee, and the standard for escape enhanced as well.[556] Moreover, the names of persons (or

---

[552] IRC § 6662A(e)(5) (this exception was similar to the one in HR 2255, the Doggett bill, supra notes 426 and 441). It was not explicitly contained in the October 2000 version; however, there are no exceptions to § 6662A under that version. It is not mentioned in the August 2001 version. Neither is it mentioned in the May or July 2002 proposals.

[553] See IRC § 6662A(e)(6) (thus, it is too late for a change of heart by the taxpayer). The October 2000 version retained this rule in § 6662A(c)(2) as well. So does the August 2001 version, in § 6662(i)(1)(c). The July 2002 version is in § 6662A(C)(3).

[554] This obviously is not the sort of "message" that corporations will enjoy reporting to their shareholders. The October 2000 version does not contain this proposal, but does provide a new penalty for taxpayer nondisclosure in § 6707A. So does the August 2001 version as well as the July 2002 version (§ 6707A(e) requires disclosures by public companies of any strict liability penalty to the SEC, however).

The October 2000 proposal does provide for public identification of penalized advisors in § 6701(c)(2), and so does the August 2001 version. The July 2002 proposal, in § 6707A(e), requires disclosure to the SEC by any publicly traded company that incurs a strict liability penalty.

[555] Thus the general standard would be "substantial authority" for the position, or a "reasonable basis" therefore (plus disclosure); for tax shelters generally, the standard is "more likely than not" (plus disclosure); for large corporate tax shelters, the standard is a reasonable belief that the taxpayer *should* prevail (plus disclosure). The October version does not contain this provision, but instead revised and tightened the aider and abettor penalty of § 6701, see infra. The August 2001 version continued the approach. The July 2002 version merely raises the standard in § 6694 and raises the monetary penalty amounts.

[556] Namely, whether a reasonable tax advisor would opine that the taxpayer should prevail (or *should* avoid a penalty). The October version also revises § 6701 to increase the penalty to 50 percent of gross proceeds (IRC § 6701(b)(3)), tightened the "escape" hatch standard in § 6701(a)(2) to "more likely than not," and added that disciplinary referral and public identification would be required for advisors who are subjected to the tax shelter advice penalty; the August 2001 version continued these proposals as well. The July 2002 version does not deal with § 6701, but provides for a new regime dealing with "material advisors" infra note 556.

firms) subjected to the § 6701 penalty would be published and the IRS Director of Practice and state licensing authorities must be notified of such violations. Finally, the tax shelter registration rules of § 6111(d) would be revised to delete the "confidentiality" requirement of current law, and by requiring registration if a significant purpose of a transaction is tax avoidance and promoter fees exceed $500,000.[557] Moreover, the penalty for "promoter's failure to maintain lists of corporate tax shelter participants" would be raised to 50 percent of the promoter's fees for each violation by an amendment to § 6708(a).

The May and July 2002 proposals both revised the tax shelter registration rules of § 6111 and the monetary penalties for failure to comply with those rules in § 6707. Not surprisingly, both of these provisions were materially enhanced in scope and potential pain, which, of course was their purpose. Revised § 6111 required each "material advisor"[558] with respect to any reportable transaction to timely file an information return spelling out the relevant details relating to that transaction as prescribed by the Service. Failure to comply with § 6111 would attract the souped-up monetary penalty of § 6707; that is, $50,000 generally or, if a listed transaction shelter is involved, the greater of $250,000 or half of the advisor's fee (increased to 75 percent in the case of an intentional failure). This penalty was subject to the rescission authority of § 6707A(d), however, unless it related to a listed transaction.[559] Finally, § 6112 (the investor list maintenance requirement) was expanded to include clients of each material advisor that was required to file the § 6111 information return and the penalty for failure to maintain this list and submit it in a timely manner to the Service was expanded in § 6708 to $10,000 per day.[560]

While passage of this legislative package remains far from certain, if enacted in its proposed form (namely, the July 2002 version) there will be a definite downside to all the players in a corporate tax shelter transaction. When

---

[557] Additional reporting would be required under amended § 6111(d)(2) for large corporate tax shelters that have any of the shelter "indicators" listed in § 6662A(c)(2). This provision is not contained in the October version, however, nor is it in any of the subsequent versions.

The 2002 versions both provide that the attorney-client privilege will not apply to any written communications in connection with the promotion of participation in any tax shelter, § 7525(b).

[558] "Material advisor" is defined by § 6111(b)(1) as any person who provides advice with respect to the reportable transaction and receives substantial compensation for that advice ($50,000 for advice to natural persons; $250,000 for advice to other advisees). See also Regs. § 301.6011-1(c) for similiar definition of "material advisor" under the list maintenance regulations.

[559] As previously noted, penalty rescissions will be a rare event, being limited to exceptional circumstances, can be invoked only at the highest levels, and are wholly discretionary with that person.

[560] This penalty, however, is subject to a reasonable cause exception.

coupled with the new temporary disclosure and registration regulations described previously,[561] very little (if any) incentive to engage in these transactions would remain. Moreover, the new Bush Treasury even entered the tax shelter assault, albeit somewhat tardily, by releasing its version of anti–tax shelter proposals on March 20, 2002, which are considered below. In the same vein, Ways and Means Committee Chairman Thomas introduced his version of anti-shelter legislation on July 11, 2002, HR 5095, the American Competitiveness Act of 2002.[562] This proposal was quite similar in many respects to the Finance Committee's July 2002 proposal, but it also differed in several significant ways and is also considered infra ¶ 5.10[8][c]. The final legislation, adopted on October 22, 2004, contained the augmented penalties and disclosure rules of these various proposals (but no substantive provisions).

[b] Current Treasury's Anti-Shelter Proposals (March 2002)

On March 20, 2002, Treasury unveiled a broad regulatory attack on abusive tax shelter transactions as well as a legislative request for enhanced penalties.[563] Treasury's regulatory initiative would focus on the disclosure rules of existing law, unifying, simplifying, and broadening the current regulations' various disclosure regimes noted above.[564] Penalty enhancement would also be a major element of the legislative package, including strict liability penalties for

---

[561] See supra ¶ 5.10[7][b]. Even with Democratic reacquisition of control in the Senate in 2001 (though it reverted to Republican control in 2002), where eventual passage has been enhanced (the proposal is a bipartisan one), its fate in the House is far more problematic. Moreover, the new Treasury's anti-shelter zeal was far less evident than its predecessors (one day before the release of the Finance Committee's draft legislation, the registration and disclosure regulations were scaled back in several significant aspects); see supra ¶ 5.10[7][g]. But see infra ¶ 5.10[8][b]. The Senate tax shelter proposals passed the Senate on April 9, 2003; but they were moved to the Senate's tax reduction bill, S. 1054, which passed on May 15, 2003, see supra notes 529 and 535, but did not survive in the final 2003 tax bill that was enacted on May 28.

[562] The anti-shelter proposals are in Title I of the bill. The Thomas bill also contains numerous other provisions as well as anti-shelter legislation. Thus it deals with expatriating corporate inversions, repeals the exclusion for extraterritorial income, and replaces that provision with a laundry list of "simplifications" of the international tax rules; these aspects are considered at the relevant points in Chapter 15.

For detailed technical explanation of this proposal, see Joint Comm. on Taxation, Technical Explanation of HR 5095 (JCX-78-02), July 19, 2002, reprinted in Daily Tax Rep. (BNA) No. 140, at L-6 (July 22, 2002). This legislation has drawn substantial criticism from a variety of sources, however, particularly the international aspects, but also with respect to some of the anti-shelter proposals, and its ultimate passage seemed uncertain.

[563] Reported in Daily Tax Rep. (BNA) No. 55, at GG-1, L-20 (Mar. 21, 2002).

[564] See supra ¶ 5.10[7][b]. These regulations were issued on October 17, 2002, as Regs. §§ 1.6011-4 and 301.6112-1T, see supra note 503. They became final in TD 9146 on March 4, 2003, see supra note 505.

tax deficiencies ensuing from transactions in which there was inadequate disclosure.[565] Finally, the practice standards of Circular 230 would be materially tightened (with the likely inclusion of penalties and fees for violations).

[c] Ways and Means Chairman's Proposal: HR 5095, Title I

Chairman Thomas of the House Ways and Means Committee joined the anti-shelter parade with the introduction of his proposed legislative draft on July 11, 2002.[566] Many features of the Thomas bill parallel those of the Senate Finance Committee's latest July 2002 legislative version (obviously the respective staffs have been talking to each other here)[567] as well as those put forward by the Treasury in its March 2002 submissions. But the Thomas bill also con-

---

[565] The strict liability penalty would preclude reliance on an opinion that the disclosure requirement was invalid. Treasury's strict liability penalty resembles the Joint Committee Staff's original anti-shelter proposal, supra 5.10[6][c] (and the earlier version of the Finance Committee legislative draft, supra 5.10[8][a]). The Finance Committee's July 2002 proposal likewise adopts this approach.

While there is not much new in the Treasury's anti-tax shelter package, other than the fact that there finally is some response from the new Treasury on these issues, the clear intent of the proposals is to build upon the disclosure cum penalty regime of current law, broaden the scope of that regime, and reduce the possibilities for escaping detection of questionable transactions. Congress also seems receptive to this effort (or at least the Senate Finance Committee did; Ways and Means and the House may be another matter). The May and July 2002 Finance Committee drafts incorporate many of these proposals as well.

Treasury also proposes two substantive legislative amendments: (1) expanding § 901(k) to deal with *Compaq*-type foreign tax credit capture devices and (2) expanding the existing income stripping rules of § 1286 (interest strips) and § 305(e) (preferred stock dividend strips) to cover a broader range of "income separation" transactions. (The Finance Committee's July 2002 proposal did not include these items, however, but the Thomas bill, supra note 560, does include them.)

All told, life will not become easier for tax shelter investors, their advisors, and promoters of tax shelter product under the various proposed regimes—which, of course, is the stated intent of the Treasury, the Senate Finance Committee, and the chairman of the Ways and Means Committee. So far, none of these legislative proposals had been enacted (as of the end of 2003). But anti-shelter legislation finally made it into law on October 22, 2004, see infra 5.10[8][d].

[566] See supra note 560. For comments, see New York State Bar Ass'n, Tax Section, "Comments on Pending Tax Shelter Legislation," 97 Tax Notes 115 (Oct. 7, 2002); Hariton, "Economic Substance Complaint No. 1: Too Vague and Too Broad," 96 Tax Notes 1893 (Sept. 30, 2002).

[567] Thus, §§ 6707A (nondisclosure penalty), 6662 (accuracy penalty for reportable transaction understatements), 6664(b) (strengthened reasonable cause exception), 7525(b) (no privilege for tax shelter advice), 6611 (advisor disclosure of reportable transactions), 6612 (material advisor list maintenance), 6707 and 6708 (penalties for violations of the registration and list maintenance requirements), and 6700 (promoter penalties) are virtually identical in most respects. Treasury's anti-shelter proposals are also quite similar to the above provisions.

tained some proposals not found in either the Finance Committee bill or the Treasury's proposals. Principal among these variances were (1) a proposed codification of the economic substance doctrine (modeled closely on earlier proposals by Representative Doggett)[568] and (2) a special strict liability penalty for transactions that result in an understatement attributable to a violation of that doctrine.[569] But the latest version of the Senate bill included these provisions as well and it passed the Senate on April 19, 2003.[570] The Thomas bill also differed from the Senate Finance Committee's version by incorporating the two substantive anti-shelter proposals contained in the Treasury's package.[571]

With the above exceptions, however, there has been a remarkable convergence between the Treasury, the Finance Committee, and the Ways and Means chairman in their respective anti-shelter legislative proposals. With these stars now relatively in alignment, ultimate passage of some significant legislative package dealing with tax shelters (both corporate and individual) has become a far more likely possibility, due in no small part to the "Enron effect." They also remain poised on the sidelines for use as revenue raising offsets for other tax reduction proposals, which is where they currently reside as of this writing (August 2004). The tax shelter disclosure and penalty package finally passed on October 22, 2004 (though without codification of economic substance).

[d] Final Legislation; The American Jobs Creation Act of 2004

After years of legislative struggle, a significant package of anti-shelter provisions (i.e., expanded disclosure and augumented penalties) was adopted on October 22, 2004.[572] It is substantially similar to the Treasury, House, and

---

[568] Prop. IRC § 7701(m); see Sheppard, "The Good and the Bad in the Thomas Bill," 96 Tax Notes 482 (July 22, 2002) (commenting principally on this aspect of the proposal). See also Hariton, supra note 510; Treasury also opposes enactment of this proposal, Daily Tax Rep. (BNA) No. 191, at J-1 (Oct. 2, 2002), interview with Assistant Treasury Secretary Olson. But the Senate bill, which passed on April 3, 2003, now also contains such a provision, HR 476, § 701, new § 7701(m). But later versions of both the Thomas bill and Senate anti-shelter legislation dropped the codification proposal, but it has returned in the Senate's most recent shelter proposals, though not in the House version.

[569] Prop. IRC § 6662B (a 40 percent strict liability nonwaivable penalty, reduced to 20 percent if the transaction was adequately disclosed).

[570] This proposal was moved into the Senate's general tax reduction bill, S. 1054, which passed the Senate on May 15, 2003 (and is effective May 8, 2003); but it did not survive in the final 2003 tax bill that passed on May 28.

[571] See supra note 563. The Thomas bill also contained a substantive provision disallowing certain partnership loss transfers; Prop. IRC § 704(c)(1)(C), amending IRC §§ 743 and 734.

[572] HR 4520, Title VIII, Subtitle B, Part I. It did not, however, codify the economic substance doctrine.

Senate proposals noted above. The final legislation evolved into a tough and, in some cases, unforgiving set of enhanced penalties and expanded disclosure rules, and the message here is clear—if you engage in listed or reportable tax reduction transactions (or "advise" persons who do) be prepared to disclose those transactions or pay a serious monetary price for the failure to do so. A principal focus of the new legislation was on "promoters" and "advisors" of tax shelter transactions, although investors were treated to some of the enhanced disclosure and penalty medicine as well. About the only good news here is that the 2004 legislation did not codify the economic substances doctrine (yet)[573] and did not adopt the Senate's expanded § 269 proposal.[574]

Heading the new penalty list in significance is new § 6707A, the promoter or advisor's penalty for failure to disclose reportable transaction information with the return as required by § 6011 (which is virtually a strict liability penalty (if applicable)).[575] Moreover, § 6707A(e) requires that any such penalty must be reported to the SEC (thus bestowing public shame on the perpetrator); and finally, § 6707A(f) provides that this penalty cumulates on top of any other penalty.[576]

New § 6662A bestows similar, though less draconian, penalty treatment for taxpayers who lose a reportable transaction case (20 percent of the understatement, raised to 30 percent, if the transaction is listed). There is, however, a "reasonable cause" escape from this penalty under § 6664(d) if the taxpayer can show good faith, the transaction was adequately disclosed, substantial authority for its position exists, and the taxpayer reasonably believed its position more likely than not to be the proper treatment.[577]

---

[573] But recent taxpayer victories in the *Black & Decker, Coltec*, and *Castle Harbour* cases may bring a renewal of interest in such a provision; see Gary & Stratton, "Economic Substance: Will Congress Have to Intercede?" 105 Tax Notes 907 (Nov. 15, 2004); supra 5.10[6][e].

[574] Nor did it adopt the CEO tax return certification proposal.

[575] Section 6707A(d) allows rescission only by the Commissioner, and prohibits judicial review as well; but for listed transactions, there is no escape.

[576] Moreover, § 6707 (the material advisor's failure penalty) likewise is virtually a strict liability penalty as well by virtue of amended § 6707(c) (similar to the § 6707A penalty; and likewise with no escape for listed transactions). For interim guidance on the new penalties, see Notices 2005-11 and 2005-12, 2005-7 IRB 493, 494.

[577] Section 6664(d)(3) refines the "reasonable belief" escape by requiring that such belief must be based on the existing facts and the law and relates solely to the merits of the position (and not the "audit lottery" or settlement potential); moreover, it must not be based on a tax opinion that is "a disqualified opinion" from a "disqualified advisor" as described in § 6664(d)(3)(B). See Lipton, "Reliance on Tax Opinions: The World Changes After LTCH and the AJTA," 101 J. Tax'n 344 (Dec. 2004); Lipton et al., "The World Changes: Broad Sweep of New Tax Shelter Rules in AJCA and Circular 230 Affect Everyone," 102 J. Tax'n 34 (Mar. 2005); McNulty & Probosco, "Tax Shelter Disclosure and Penalties: New Requirements, New Exposures," 18 J. Tax'n Fin. Insts. No. 3 (Jan. 2005); The *Long Term Capital Holdings* tax opinions would fail both of these tests. See also

Probably one of the most significant additions to the anti-shelter arsenal is the tolling of the statute of limitations for the period that required listed transactions are not reported.[578] Thus, escape through the audit lottery is no longer possible by virtue of this provision, since the statute will not begin to run again until acceptable reporting has been made.

The new law also harmonizes the material advisor disclosure, reporting, and investor list maintenance rules of §§ 6111 and 6112, creating a uniform regime as to who must disclose, what must be disclosed, and when (and to what extent) a list of shelter investors must be maintained.[579] Another notable feature of the 2004 Jobs Act is the dramatic increase in the size of penalties for violation of the disclosure and list maintenance rules;[580] these are provisions that should not be violated unless the person has very deep pockets indeed—the obvious attempt here is to redefine the risk-reward calculus for engaging in, and advising for, corporate tax shelter transactions. As such, the noose has definitely tightened around the major players in this game.

Finally, the 2004 Jobs Act[581] authorizes the IRS Director of Practice to levy monetary penalties on offending practitioners, and to set standards for tax opinions (as the Service was poised to do in the pending Circular 230 regulations, which were adopted as final regulations as this sentence was being written).[582]

[e] IRS Shelter Guidance Under the 2004 Jobs Act

The Service released the first round of guidance on the tax shelter provisions of the 2004 Jobs Act dealing with the disclosure, list maintenance, and reporting requirements applicable to "material advisors." Thus, Notice 2004-80[583] provides interim guidance on the disclosure and list maintenance require-

---

Beller, "The New Penalty Regime: Proceed With Caution," 106 Tax Notes 311 (Jan. 17, 2005).

Finally, the American Jobs Creation Act of 2004, § 838, amends § 163(n) to deny deductibility for any deficiency interest attributable to nondisclosed reportable transactions.

[578] American Jobs Creation Act of 2004, § 815, adding § 6501(c)(10) (effective Oct. 22, 2004). For guidance, see Rev. Proc. 2005-26, 2005-17 IRB 965.

[579] American Jobs Creation Act of 2004, § 815 (effective Oct. 22, 2004).

[580] American Jobs Creation Act of 2004, § 816 (§ 6707 nondisclosure penalty) and Act § 817 (§ 6708 list maintenance penalty); also Act § 817 (§ 6700 promoter penalty for abusive shelters).

[581] American Jobs Creation Act of 2004, § 822 (effective Oct. 22, 2004).

[582] December 17, 2004, TD 9165 (Dec. 20, 2004) (they continue to set rigorously high standards, especially for tax opinions); see supra note 525.

[583] Notice 2004-80, 2004-50 IRB 963 (Dec. 13, 2004). For response to the notice's request for comment, see New York State Bar Ass'n, Tax Section, "Disclosure by Material Advisers," 106 Tax Notes 1569 (Mar. 28, 2005)

ments of material advisors under §§ 6111 and 6112 (providing generally that current regulations under those sections will apply until such time as subsequent revisions are issued). Thus, the material advisor definition of Regs. § 301.6112-1(c)(2), the reportable transaction rules of Regs. § 1.6011-4(b), and the current list maintenance rules of Regs. § 301.6112-1 will continue to apply until further revisions are made to those regulations, or new regulations are issued.[584]

The Service also issued four new revenue procedures revising and expanding exceptions to the reportable transaction rules.[585] By narrowing the number of reportable transactions and expanding exceptions to those rules, the Service continues to fine tune the categories of reportable transactions. These categories are:

1. Transactions with contractual protection,[586] which exempted three common transactions from the reportable transaction rule;

2. Loss transactions,[587] further expanding the exceptions to this reporting category first announced in Revenue Procedure 2003-24;

3. Book-tax differences,[588] modifying and adding to the exceptions to the reporting requirement first promulgated in Revenue Procedure 2003-25; and

4. Brief asset holding periods,[589] listing various transactions that will not be subject to the reporting and list maintenance rules.

Thus, the first salvo of tax shelter guidance has no thunderbolts; instead it appears that the Service so far is trying to be reasonable here, though more is to come, and Revenue Procedure 2004-73[590] followed providing updated guid-

---

[584] The Service had little choice here, since the 2004 Jobs Act rules were effective October 22, 2004, leaving no time to develop new regulation projects. By continuing existing regulation rules, Notice 2004-80 thus creates no unpleasant surprises; see Notice 2005-11, 2005-7 IRB 493.

[585] Rev. Proc. 2004-65, 2004-50 IRB (Dec. 13, 2004) (contractual protection); Rev. Proc. 2004-66, 2004-50 IRB (Dec. 13, 2004) (loss transactions); Rev. Proc. 2004-67, 2004-50 IRB (Dec. 13, 2004) (book-tax differences); Rev. Proc. 2004-68, 2004-50 IRB (Dec. 13, 2004) (brief asset holding periods). All of these procedures were effective November 16, 2004, the date of their release to the public.

[586] Rev. Proc. 2004-65, 2004-50 IRB (Dec. 13, 2004).

[587] Rev. Proc. 2004-66, 2004-50 IRB (Dec. 13, 2004).

[588] Rev. Proc. 2004-67, 2004-50 IRB (Dec. 13, 2004) (the exception list now contains thirty-five items). But Notice 2006-6, 2006-5 IRB (Jan. 31, 2006) drops the book-tax trigger altogether (in view of the expanded reporting requirements on new schedule M-3).

[589] Rev. Proc. 2004-68, 2004-50 IRB (Dec. 13, 2004).

[590] Rev. Proc. 2004-73, 2004-51 IRB 999 (Dec. 20, 2004), updating Rev. Proc. 2003-77, 2003-2 CB 964. Notice 2005-75, 2005-50 IRB 113, (modifying and updating Revenue Procedure 2004-73 to reflect changes made by the 2004 Jobs Act).

ance regarding adequate disclosure to reduce penalties under §§ 6662(d) and 6694(a).

FEDERAL INCOME TAXATION OF CORPORATIONS AND SHAREHOLDERS

Seventh Edition

2007 CUMULATIVE SUPPLEMENT to
ABRIDGED STUDENT EDITION

WARREN, GORHAM & LAMONT
OF RIA

How to Use This Supplement

THIS SUPPLEMENT brings the Seventh Edition of *Federal Income Taxation of Corporations and Shareholders* up to date and serves both as a means of keeping the main volume current and as a reference to recent developments. The supplement presents relevant judicial, legislative, and administrative developments through April 2007.

Each entry in the supplement is keyed to a chapter, paragraph ( ), and specific page number in the main volume. An italicized instruction line indicates where the new material belongs in relation to text or footnotes in the main volume. To check for new developments on a point discussed in the main volume, find the corresponding paragraph number in the supplement. The sequences of the main volume and supplement are identical, and the top of each supplement page carries a paragraph reference. Cross-references marked "this Supplement" refer to new material in the supplement; all other cross-references refer to the Seventh Edition, as updated by the supplement.

To ensure easy access to new developments, this supplement contains Cumulative Tables of IRC Sections; Cases; Treasury Regulations; Revenue Rulings, Revenue Procedures, and IRS Releases; as well as a Cumulative Index; these tables and index include references to both the main volume and this supplement.

Summary of Contents

Table of Contents

4 Corporation's Capital Structure: Debt vs. Equity

A DEBT VERSUS EQUITY: PROBLEMS OF CLASSIFICATION

5   The Corporation Income Tax

6   Corporate Elections Under Subchapter S

7   Penalty Taxes on Undistributed Corporate Income

A   THE ACCUMULATED EARNINGS TAX

B   PROPERTY DISTRIBUTIONS IN KIND

C   DISTRIBUTIONS OF CORPORATION'S OWN STOCK AND STOCK RIGHTS

D   PREFERRED STOCK BAILOUTS

9   Stock Redemptions

10   Complete Liquidations and Other Taxable Dispositions of Corporate Stock and Assets in Bulk

C   TAXABLE ACQUISITIONS

11   Corporate Divisions

12   Corporate Reorganizations

A   GENERAL CONSIDERATIONS

B   "REORGANIZATION" DEFINED

13   Affiliated Corporations

A   MULTIPLE CORPORATIONS GENERALLY

B   TRANSACTIONS BETWEEN AFFILIATED CORPORATIONS: § 482 AND RELATED PROVISIONS

C   CONSOLIDATED RETURNS

14   Corporate Tax Attributes: Survival and Transfer

15   Foreign Corporations and Foreign-Source Income

A   TAXATION OF FOREIGN CORPORATIONS IN GENERAL

CHAPTER **1**

Introductory

¶ 1.01 THE CORPORATE INCOME TAX

Page 1-6:

Add text to end of ¶ 1.01.

But 2003 legislation lowering the top rate on dividends and capital gain to 15 percent effected a profound (albeit temporary) change in the corporate-shareholder relationship which resonates throughout this work.[10.1]

[10.1] The greatest impact of this change will be felt in Chapters 8, 9, 11, and 12. These cuts were extended for two years, however, by 2006 legislation.

¶ 1.02 UNDISTRIBUTED CORPORATE INCOME

Page 1-7:

Add to note 15.

But 2003 legislation, lowered the § 531 rate to 15 percent.

Add to note 16.

The 2003 Tax Act also lowered the § 541 rate to 15 percent.

Page 1-9:

Add text to end of ¶ 1.02.

Also, 2003 legislation lowered the capital gains rate to 15 percent and did the same for dividends as well (thereby preserving the 20 point rate spread between capital gain and ordinary income, but allowing dividends to individual shareholders to share in that benefit).[21.1]

[21.1] Infra   1.08[4], and   8.06.

¶ 1.03 DISTRIBUTED CORPORATE INCOME

Add to note 23.

But 2003 legislation lowered the top rate on dividends to individuals to 15 percent (and did the same for capital gain), thus materially reducing (though not entirely eliminating) the double tax effect; infra   1.08[4] and   8.06.

Page 1-11:

Add to text at end of ¶ 1.03.

Finally, 2003 legislation reduced the top rate on capital gain to 15 percent and, even more significantly, extended that treatment to dividends for individuals as well.[29.1]

[29.1] IRC § 1(h)(11) (2003); infra ¶ 1.08[4] and ¶ 8.06.

¶ 1.05 THE CORPORATION AS AN ENTITY

[1] In General

[b] Judicial Authority

Page 1-16:

Add to note 47 at the end of first paragraph.

See also Investment Research Assocs., Ltd., RIA TC Memo. ¶ 99,407 (1999) (multiple corporations disregarded as shams, assignment of income vehicles and/or § 482); fraud penalty imposed; aff'd sub nom. Kanter Estate v. CIR, 337 F3d 833, 2003-2 ¶ USTC 50,605 (7th Cir. 2003), and Ballard v. CIR, 321 F3d 1037 (11th Cir. 2003); rev'd on procedural grounds, 123 S.Ct. 1270 (2005).

For comments on the Supreme Court's *Kanter* decision, see Stratton, "Original Tax Court Report Found No Fraud by Kanter," Ballard, 107 Tax Notes 1216 (June 6, 2005); Greenhouse & Odintz, "The Status of Tax Court Special Trial Judge Reports: Where Do We Go From Here?" 102 J. Tax'n 352 (June, 2005); Tandon, "Judge's Statement on Kanter, Ballard Provoke Dismay," 108 Tax Notes 394 July 5, 2005); Stratton, "Pressure Mounts on Tax Court in Kanter, Ballard and Lisle Cases," 109 Tax Notes 1219 (Dec. 5, 2005).

[2] Broad Judicial Doctrines and Principles

[a] No Assignment of Earned Income

Page 1-20:

Add to note 65 at the end of second paragraph.

For comments, see DeHoff, "Tax Court Slams Insurance Sham: Industry Weighs Impact in UPS," 85 Tax Notes 19 (Oct. 4, 1999); Taylor & Immerman, "The Curious Role of Motive in the Tax Court's Analysis in UPS," 85 Tax Notes 1321 (Dec. 6, 1999); Stansbury, "United Parcel Service of America v. Comm'r: A New Leading Role for the Assignment of Income Doctrine in § 482 Cases?" 29 Tax Mgmt. Int'l J. 203 (Apr. 4, 2000); Cook, et al., "Tax Court Stretches Concept of Sham in *Winn-Dixie* and *UPS* Insurance Cases—Part II," (re *UPS*), 14 J. Tax'n Fin. Insts. No. 2, at 15 (Nov. 2000); "As Briefs Are Filed, Some Question *UPS* Decision," 89 Tax Notes 200 (Oct. 9, 2000). See also Investment Research Assocs., RIA TC Memo. ¶ 99,487 (1999) (assignment of income holding and fraud penalty imposed); aff'd by the 7th and 11th Circuits, infra note 70; but *UPS* was reversed, 254 F3d 1014, 2001-2 USTC ¶ 50,475 (11th Cir. 2001) (transaction had economic substance and enough business purpose to neutralize tax planning motives—business purpose standard a relatively low burden here; won't take much to meet this requirement; one dissent thought whole deal was a sham; case remanded to deal with § 482 issue). Kingson, "The Confusion Over Tax Ownership," 93 Tax Notes 409 (Oct. 15, 2001).

[b] Substance Over Form

Page 1-20:

Add to note 70.

For comments on *UPS*, see supra note 65. See also Investment Research Assocs., Ltd., RIA TC Memo. ¶ 99,407 (sham transactions and sham corporations found; fraud penalty imposed); aff'd sub nom. Kanter Estate v. CIR, 337 F3d 833, 2003-2 ¶ USTC 50,605 (7th Cir. 2003), and Ballard v. CIR, 321 F3d 1037 (11th Cir. 2003). But rev'd on procedural grounds, 123 S.Ct. 1270 (2005). See comments supra note 47. But *UPS* was reversed (2 to 1), 254 F3d 1014, 2001-2 USTC ¶ 50,475 (11th Cir. 2001) (found economic substance and enough business purpose despite heavy tax planning motives); see Kingston, supra note 65.

[c] Business Purpose

Page 1-22:

Add to note 78.

For comments on *UPS*, see supra note 65. But *UPS* was reversed, 254 F3d 1014, 2001-2 USTC ¶ 50,475 (11th Cir. 2001) (court's business purpose standard wasn't a very onerous one and should be relatively easy to meet for most corporate taxpayers). See Sheppard, "Why the IRS Should Argue the Statute First," 92 Tax Notes 465 (July 23, 2001). See also, for an extreme case (and disastrous tax results), Investment Research Assocs., Ltd., RIA TC Memo. ¶ 99,407 (1999); aff'd sub nom. Kanter Estate v. CIR, 337 F3d 833, 2003-2 ¶ USTC 50,605 (7th Cir. 2003), and Ballard v. CIR, 321 F3d 1037 (11th Cir. 2003). But rev'd on procedural grounds, 123 S.Ct. 1270 (2005); see comments supra note 47; Kingston, supra note 65.

[e] Insurance Risk (Captive Insurers)

Add to note 81.

But IRS abandoned the "economic family" theory of Rev. Rul. 77-316 in Rev. Rul. 2001-31, 2001-26 IRB 1348 (but reserved the option to attack captives in appropriate cases).

Page 1-23:

Add to note 84 following the third sentence.

For additional comments on *UPS*, see supra note 65; but *UPS* was reversed, 254 F3d 1014, 2001-2 USTC ¶ 50,475 (11th Cir. 2001) (not a sham and had enough (though relatively low) business purpose to negate tax planning motives); comment by Sheppard, 92

Tax Notes 465 (July 23, 2001). Kingson, "The Confusion Over Tax Ownership," 93 Tax Notes 409 (Oct. 15, 2001).

Add to end of first paragraph in note 86.

But Rev. Rul. 81-61 obsoleted by Rev. Rul. 2001-31, 2001-26 IRB 1348 (abandoned "economic family" theory), which ruling also modified Rev. Rul. 77-316. But see Salem & Noll, "Insuring the Risk of Brother-Sister Corporations: Think Captive," 15 J. Tax'n Fin. Insts. 5 (May 2002).

Add to text after footnote reference to note 86.

But the service finally backed off here to a considerable extent in a series of liberal rulings issued in late December 2002.[86.1] They also deleted "insurance" from the no ruling list.[86.2]

[86.1] Rev. Rul. 2002-89, 2002-52 IRB 984 (subsidiary that has more than 50 percent of business with unrelated outsiders is enough to create risk shifting and risk distribution; but if 90 percent of business came from the parent, no good); Rev. Rul. 2002-90, 2002-52 IRB 985 (domestic captive subsidiary insuring other subsidiaries of common parent can qualify if requisite risk shifting and distribution – held was here, citing *Humana* and *Kiddie* and distinguishing *Malone & Hyde*); and Rev. Rul. 2002-91, 2002-52 IRB 991 (group captive owned by multiple unrelated minority parents; created to insure risky business for which no outside insurance available).

Comments by Raby & Raby, "Captive Insurance—Some Lights in the Fog," 97 Tax Notes 1711 (Dec. 30, 2002); Hirsh & Lederman, "The Service Clarifies the Facts and Circumstances Approach to Captive Insurance Companies," 100 J. Tax'n 163 (Mar. 2004).

[86.2] Rev. Proc. 2002-75, 2002-52 IRB (deletes § 4.01(11) and § 4.01(44) from Rev. Proc. 2002-3).

[3] Broad Statutory Provisions

[a] Section 61(a)

Page 1-24:

Add to note 89.

See also UPS, Inc., RIA TC Memo. ¶ 99,268 (1999); for comments on *UPS*, see supra note 65; but UPS was reversed, 254 F3d 1014, 2001-2 USTC ¶ 50,475 (11th Cir. 2001); see also Investment Research Assocs., RIA TC Memo. ¶ 99,407 (1999).

[c] Section 482

Page 1-25:

Add to note 92.

But see UPS, Inc. v. CIR, 254 F3d 1014, 2001-2 USTC ¶ 50,475 (11th Cir. 2001) (transaction had economic substance and enough business purpose, but remanded to Tax Court to decide § 482 issue; one dissent, who thought transaction was an economic sham). The parties settled the § 482 issue, albeit at a more than significant number.

¶ 1.07 THE CORPORATION VERSUS THE PARTNERSHIP

Page 1-30:

Add to note 112.

Lee, "A Populist Perspective of the Business Entities Universe...," 78 Tex. L. Rev. 885 (2000); Goldberg, "Choice of Entity for a Venture Capital Start-Up: The Myth of Incorporation," 55 Tax Law. 923 (2002) (the LLC is it); Raby & Raby, "New Tax Laws and Choices of the Small Business Entity," 99 Tax Notes 1647 (June 16, 2003). But see Fleischer, "The Rational Exurberance of Structuring Venture Capital Start-ups," 57 Tax L. Rev. 137 (2003) (argues that C corporation structure is the better mode); Frost & Banoff, "Square Peg Meets Black Hole: Uncertain Tax Consequences of Third Generation LLEs," 100 J. Tax'n 322 (June 2004) (numerous technical tax issues created by newer types of limited liability entities).

[2] Taxability of Income

Page 1-31:

Add new note 118.1 to end of runover paragraph.

[118.1] But 2003 legislation reduced the top individual rate to 35 percent and, even more significantly, the top rate on dividends paid to individuals to 15 percent (the same rate as capital gain); § 1(h)(11), infra   1.08[4].

¶ 1.08 INTEGRATION OF CORPORATE AND INDIVIDUAL TAXES

[1] In General

Page 1-35:

Add to note 141.

Graetz & Warren, "Integration of Corporation and Individual Taxes: An Introduction," 84 Tax Notes 1767 (Sept. 27, 1999) (integration "lite").

Page 1-36:

Add to note 144.

The Bush Treasury proposal of February 2003 adopted the dividend exclusion model, infra   1.08[4].

[2] Recent Significant Integration Studies

[a] Treasury Report on Integration

Page 1-38:

Add to note 158.

The Bush dividend exclusion proposal of February 2003 adopted this approach.

Page 1-42:

Add new ¶ 1.08[4].

[4] Integration Proposal (February 2003)

The Bush administration proposed a full exclusion for dividends paid out of previously taxed corporate earnings (the exempt dividend amount, or EDA), and an alternative stock-basis step-up for the amount of accumulated previously taxed earnings.[185] While viewed in the 1992 Treasury integration study as a relatively simple model (and the preferred model there as well), the proposed 2003 version was anything but simple; indeed, it appeared in its initial version to be awesomely intricate and complex.[186] Needless to say enactment of that proposal in its initial form would have had a major impact on much of the material contained in this work (however, enactment was certainly not a forgone conclusion, and it ultimately failed to pass).[187]

Among the many ramifications of this proposal were the following (to provide only a selective listing):

1. The tax stakes between § 301 dividends and § 302(a) redemptions essentially would be reversed (the former generally would be better than the latter);[188]
2. Likewise the treatment of boot in a § 368 reorganization or § 355 spin-off would be dramatically changed;[189]

---

[185] For Treasury's description of the proposal, see Daily Tax Rep. (BNA) No. 14, at L-5 (Jan. 22, 2003); the proposal was introduced in both the House and Senate, HR 2, Title II (Feb. 27, 2003).

[186] See infra   8.06[1]; Schler, "The Administration's Dividend Exclusion Proposal," 98 Tax Notes 1895, Part I (Mar. 24, 2003); Johnson, "The Bush 35 Percent Flat Tax on Distributions From Public Corporations," 98 Tax Notes (Mar. 24, 2003).

[187] The proposal proved to be quite controversial (as well as very expensive, a fact that proved to be enough to doom it). See e.g., Ditkoff, Viewpoint, "President's Dividends Tax Relief Plan Is $364 Billion Mistake," Daily Tax Rep. (BNA) No. 9, at J-1 (Jan. 14, 2003); Analysis & Perspective, "Bush Dividend Elimination Proposal Potentially Harmful to Some States," Daily Tax Rep. (BNA) No. 10 (Jan. 15, 2003); Johnson, "The Bush 35 Percent Flat Tax on Distributions From Public Corporations," supra note 186. The final 2003 legislation did not come close to adopting the Treasury's proposal, infra note 200.

[188] See Chapters 8 and 9.

[189] See   12.44[2][d], 11.10[2]. It was unclear, however, whether § 356 boot dividends could even qualify for exclusion relief.

3. Application of the § 243 DRD similarly would be significantly altered;[190]

4. Taxability of stock dividends under § 305(b) likewise could be preferable to tax-free deferral treatment under § 305(a);[191]

5. Section 306 bail-outs would be neutralized in the case of redemptions (though not sales) of § 306 stock;[192]

6. Section 304 dividends once again would become attractive for individual shareholders;[193]

7. Repeal of the § 531 tax and the § 541 tax would not be mourned, however;[194]

8. S corporations would become less attractive viz. a viz. C corporations (reversing the relative status of these regimes under current law);[195]

9. The impact on capital structure planning (debt vs. equity, common stock vs. preferred stock, etc.) remains to be seen;[196] and

10. The foreign tax implications likewise would be considerable.[197]

This was by no means a complete list;[198] moreover, the numerous tax planning opportunities quickly began to emerge.[199]

Further complicating matters was Chairman Thomas's, of the House Ways and Means Committee, proposal to tax dividends at the same rate as

---

[190] See ¶ 5.05[9]; since corporate shareholders would qualify for exclusion benefits on their receipt of dividends, the 70 and 80 percent DRD would be phased out (though not the 100 percent DRD).

[191] See ¶ 8.41.

[192] See ¶ 8.61.

[193] See ¶ 9.09.

[194] See Chapter 7. The final legislation reduced these tax rates to 15 percent.

[195] See Chapter 6.

[196] See Chapter 4.

[197] See Chapter 15.

[198] See, e.g., Westin, "Nineteen Technical Worries About A Dividend Exclusion," 98 Tax Notes 615 (Jan. 27, 2003); Raby & Raby, "Tax Practitioners and the Dividend Exclusion," 98 Tax Notes, 553 (Jan. 23, 2003); Sheppard, "Analyzing the Dividend Exclusion," 98 Tax Notes 464 (Jan. 27, 2003); Schler, "The Administration's Dividend Exclusion Proposal," 98 Tax Notes 1895 (Mar. 24, 2003); Morrison, "Why Democrats Should Love Bush's Dividend Tax Plan," 98 Tax Notes 1602 (Mar. 10, 2003); Rizzi, "Double Taxation and Taxing Dividends: The Administration's Latest Proposal," 30 J. Corp. Tax'n 28 (Mar. 2003); Johnson, "The Bush 35 Percent Flat Tax on Distributions From Public Corporations," 98 Tax Notes 1881 (Mar. 24, 2003).

[199] See e.g., Erickson & Smith, "The President: Proposed Dividend Exclusion and Closely Held Companies," 98 Tax Notes 1244 (Feb. 24, 2003); Calegari, "Corporate Tax Minimization Strategies When Dividends Are Exempt," 98 Tax Notes 1247 (Feb. 24, 2003); Willens, "Viewpoint, Dividend Tax Relief Could Bring Greater Demand for Participating Preferred Stock," Daily Tax Rep. (BNA) No. 8, at J-1 (Jan. 13, 2003).

capital gains (and also to lower the general capital gains rate to 15 percent), a proposal that ultimately prevailed in the final legislation.[200]

---

[200] First released on May 1, 2003. The Thomas proposal would raise many of the issues noted above, but presumably would be far simpler to implement and apply since all that would be necessary here is another amendment to § 1(h). This proposal passed the House on May 9, 2003, HR 2, § 301. This was the version that ultimately prevailed in the final legislation enacted in May 2003 (and effective for all of 2003 (although it sunsets after 2008)); IRC § 1(h)(11). See   8.06[2]; but it was extened for two more years by 2006 legislation (TIPRA).

CHAPTER **2**

Definition of "Corporation"

¶ 2.01 INTRODUCTORY

[3] General Observations

Page 2-7:

Add to note 20.

The Streng portfolio was updated January 2000 as No. 700-2d. See also Lee, "Choice of Small Business Tax Entity: Facts and Fictions," 87 Tax Notes 417 (Apr. 7, 2000).

¶ 2.02 "ASSOCIATIONS" IN GENERAL

[3] Status Election for Unincorporated Business Enterprises (1997)

[a] General Background and Evolution

Page 2-13:

Add to note 45.

Miller, "The Strange Materialization of the Tax Nothing," 87 Tax Notes 685 (May 5, 2000).

Add to note 46.

The check-in-the-box regulations were held to be valid in Frank Littrielo v. United States, 2005-1 USTC ¶ 50,385 (WD Ky. 2005). Hellwig & Polsky, "The Employment Tax Challenge to the Check-the-Box Regulations," 111 Tax Notes 1039 (May 29, 2006).

Page 2-14:

Add to note 48.

Notice 2004-68, 2004-43 IRB (Oct. 25, 2004) (New European public LLCs, Societas Europea, or "SE", were classified as per se corporations). Adopted as Temp. Regs. § 301.7701-27(b)(vi), and 301.7701-27(e)(3), TD 9197 (Apr. 14, 2005); final regulations adopted by TD 9235 (Dec. 16, 2005).

[b] Check-The-Box Status Election Regime

Add to note 50.

But see Teitelbrum, "A Disregarded Entity Must Be Taken Into Account," 97 Tax Notes 1205 (Dec. 2, 2002). Rubinger, "Making Something Out of Nothing (and Vice Versa) — Inconsistent Treatment of 'Tax Nothings'," 99 J. Tax'n 288 (Nov. 2003). For planning strategies, see Steinberg & Mendelson, "Use of Partnerships and Diregarded Entities by US Corporations," 81 Taxes 261 (Mar. 2003). Hoffer, "Give Them My Regards: A Proposal For Applying the COD Rules to Disregarded Entities," 107 Tax Notes 327 (Apr. 18, 2005).

But in Prop. Regs. §301.7701-2(c)(2)(iii) (Apr. 1, 2004), a disregarded entity will be regarded as a separate entity for Federal tax liabilities incurred when it was a regarded entity, Federal tax liabilities of other entities for which it is liable, and Federal tax credits and refunds, adopted without change by TD 9183 (Feb. 25, 2005).

Moreover, proposed regulations issued on Oct. 18, 2005, also treat disregarded entities as "regarded" (namely as the taxable entity) for employment taxes and certain Federal excise taxes; Prop. Regs. §§ 301.7701-2(a)(2)(iv) and 301.7701-2(a)(2)(v) (effective Jan. 1 following the year adopted as final regulations, §§ 301.7701-2(e)(3) and 301.7701-2(e)(4). But see Hellwig & Polsky, supra note 46.

Page 2-14:

Add to note 52.

But Prop. Regs. § 301.7701-3(h) (Nov. 29, 1999), provided that IRS can disregard disregarded foreign entity status to prevent "abuse" (that is, it will be "regarded" as a foreign corporation); see Miller, "The Strange Materialization of the Tax Nothing," 87 Tax Notes 685 (May 5, 2000); Sheppard, "Putting Checks on the Check-The-Box Rules," 85 Tax Notes 1353 (Dec. 13, 1999). See   15.01[4], 15.21[1][d], 15.61[4]. But the proposed regulation was withdrawn by Notice 2003-46, 2003-28 IRB 53 (IRS will no longer deal with entity reclassification here; but "suspicious" transactions that change tax results may be challenged under other general principles—e.g., form vs. substance, step transactions, etc.). Click, "Treasury Withdraws Extraordinary Check-the-Box Regulations," 101 Tax Notes 95 (Oct. 6, 2003). For the target of this propopsed regulation, see Dover Corp., 122 TC 324 (2004).

For relief from late initial election, see Rev. Proc. 2002-59, 2002-39 IRB 615, infra note 58.1.

Page 2-15:

Add to note 53.

Bottomlee, "Application of the Check-the-Box Regulations to Financial Institutions," 15 J. Tax'n Fin. Insts. 11 (May 2002). See also four articles in 83 Taxes No. 3 (Mar. 2005), The Chicago Tax Institute Issue, at 27, 29, 35 and 43, exploring various aspects of the check-the-box regime.

Add to note 54, first paragraph.

These proposals were adopted with minor modifications and clarifications by TD 8844 on November 29, 1999 (generally effective on that date). See Pillow & Rooney, "Check-The-Box: Final Conversion Regs. Add Clarification While New Prop. Regs. Add Some Uncertainty," 92 J. Tax'n 197 (Apr. 2000).

Add to note 54, second paragraph.

Rev. Rul. 2004-85, 2004-33 IRB 189 (Aug. 16, 2004), situation 3 (transfer of LLC member interests does not change its elected C status).

Add to note 55.

Regs. §§ 301.7701-3(g)(1)(ii), 301.7701-3(g)(1)(iii), same rule (deemed transaction forms are the only routes). Prop. Regs. § 301.7701-3(g)(2)(ii) (Jan. 17, 2001) provides for a deemed § 332 plan as well, adopted by TD 8970 (Dec. 17, 2001). See also Dover Corp., 122 TC 324 (2004).

Add to note 56.

The final regulations deemed incorporation rules are in §§ 301.7701-3(g)(1)(i) and 301.7701-3(g)(1)(iv). The final regulations clarified the timing rules for § 338 elections in §§ 301.7701-3(g)(3)(ii) and 301.7701 (conversion of target status occurs on day after its acquisition date). Also § 301.7701-3(g)(3)(iii) deals with tiered entities (all deemed liquidations flow top-down unless otherwise specified).

But Rev. Rul. 2004-59, 2004-24 IRB 1050 (Rev. Rul. 84-11 principles not applicable where partnership makes a check-the-box election to corporate status; treat as deemed 351 transfer of assets by partnership and deemed liquidation distribution of stock to partners). Levi, "Exploring the Implications of State Formless Conversions After Rev. Rul. 2004-59," 82 Taxes 51 (June 2004).

Page 2-16:

Add to note 57.

These rulings are reflected in Regs. § 301.7701-3(f)(2), and they were cited with approval in TD 8844, pt. (iv).

Add text to end of ¶ 2.02[3][b].

But IRS has provided guidelines for newly formed entities to request relief for a late initial election.[58.1]

However, IRS issued temporary regulations in August of 2004[58.2] that provide a status consistency rule where business entities are organized in more than one jurisdiction; corporate status in one jurisdiction means corporate status in all. Also, if the entity is organized in both the US and a foreign country, it is domestic in all jurisdictions.[58.3] The purpose of these regulations is to block "entity shopping".

[58.1] Rev. Proc. 2002-15, 2002-6 IRB 490 (had to be filed six months prior to due date of initial election and prior to due date of entity's default status return); but superseded by Rev. Proc. 2002-59, 2002-39 IRB 615 (extended filing time to due date of entity's desired status return).

[58.2] TD 9153, issuing Regs. §§ 301.7701-2 and 301.7701-5T (effective Aug. 12, 2004). They were adopted as final regulations by TD 9246 (Jan. 30, 2006) (but are *not* retroactive).

[58.3] Regs. § 301.7701-5 (this is a separate issue and is determined after the entity status issue is decided).

¶ 2.04 PARTNERSHIPS AS "ASSOCIATIONS"

Page 2-21:

Add to note 80, first paragraph.

Rev. Rul. 2004-77, 2004-31 IRB 617 (need at least two partners to be a partnership).

¶ 2.05 SYNDICATES, JOINT VENTURES, LIMITED LIABILITY COMPANIES, AND OTHER UNINCORPORATED ENTITIES AS "ASSOCIATIONS"

[2] Limited Liability Companies

Page 2-34:

Add to note 134 after the first sentence.

The LLC Scoreboard was updated again in 93 Tax Notes 695 (Oct. 29, 2001); and again in 97 Tax Notes 1463 (Dec. 16, 2002); currently 104 Tax Notes 1059 (Sept. 6, 2004); a new update is in 106 Tax Notes Notes 1557 (Mar. 28, 2005); latest update is at 112 Tax Notes 45 (July 3, 2006).

Add to note 136.

See also Goldberg, "Choice of Entity for a Venture Capital Start-Up: The Myth of Incorporation," 55 Tax Law. 923 (2002) (the LLC is preferred here, too); but see Fleischer, "The Rational Exuberance of Structuring Venture Capital Start-ups," 57 Tax L. Rev. 137 (2003) (C corporation structure the preferred mode); Frost & Banoft, "Square Peg, Meet Black Hole; Uncertain Tax Consequences of Third Generation LLE's," 100 J. Tax'n 326 (June 2004).

CHAPTER **3**

Organization of a Corporation: Section 351 and Related Problems

¶ 3.01 INTRODUCTORY

Page 3-5:

Add to note 6.

Goldstein & Medina, "Transfers to Controlled Corporations: Section 351 Revisited—Part 1," 31 Corp. Tax"n 3 (Nov. 2004); Part 2, 32 Corp. Tax'n 3 (Jan. 2005).

¶ 3.02 TRANSFER OF PROPERTY

[2] Services and Assets Created by Services

Page 3-10:

Add to note 31.

Rizzi, "Equity and Quasi-Equity: Impact of Section 83 on Reorganization in the Technology Sector," 29 J. Corp. Tax'n 5 (Sept. 2002).

¶ 3.05 "SOLELY IN EXCHANGE": THE RECEIPT OF "BOOT"

[3] Timing and Character of Boot Recognition

Page 3-22:

Add to end of note 83.

(It should be capital gain if the net of § 1231 transactions is positive.)

[4] Debt-Like Preferred Stock as Boot

Page 3-24:

Add to note 88.

Roth, "The Disparate Treatment of Nonqualified Preferred Stock: Yet Another Tax Classification Nightmare?" 32 Cumber. L. Rev. 605 (2002) (yes).

Add to note 90.

See Prop. Regs. § 1.356-7 (Jan. 26, 2000), issuing several taxpayer-friendly rules: pre-effective date NQPS is still NQPS (so it can be swapped tax-free for new NQPS); and replacement of "clean" preferred with "substantially identical" new preferred (that is, no augmentation of rights) treated as a substitute for old preferred. These regulations became final in TD 8904 on October 2, 2000, without change. It is encouraging to note that the Service's initial regulation efforts have been taxpayer-friendly here so far.

Page 3-25:

Add to note 91 at end of first paragraph.

The 1998 temporary regulations were adopted without change by TD 8882 on May 6, 2000, Regs. § 1.356-6.

Add text to end of ¶ 3.05[4].

The American Jobs Creation Act of 2004 (the 2004 Jobs Act)[91.1] narrowed the definition of "preferred stock" in § 351(g)(3)(A) by providing that preferred stock will not be treated as participating in corporate earnings and growth (and thus will be preferred stock) unless there is a real and meaningful likelihood of actually participating in earnings and growth.[91.2]

[91.1] American Jobs Creation Act of 2004, § 899, amending § 351(g)(3)(A).

[91.2] See Willens, "Jobs Act Shores Up the Definition of Preferred Stock," 105 Tax Notes 1577 (Dec. 13, 2004).

¶ 3.06 ASSUMPTION OF LIABILITIES

[2] General Rule

Page 3-27:

Add to note 97.

Accord with Rev. Rul. 95-45 in the context of the partnership § 752 liability rules is Salina Partnership LP, RIA TC Memo.   2000-352 (short sale "obligation" held to create a
"liability"). See Sheppard, "What Is a Liability?" 89 Tax Notes 1513 (Dec. 18, 2000).
    For definition of "liability" and "obligation" in proposed regulations issued June 24,
2003, see Prop. Reg. § 1.752-1(a)(1).

Page 3-29:

Add text to end of ¶ 3.06[2].

    But proposed regulations issued in March 2005[105.1] provide that stock will
not be treated as issued for property under § 351 if either (1) the value of the
transferred property does not exceed liabilities assumed in the transaction, or
(2) the value of the transferee's assets does not exceed the amount of its liabilities immediately after the transaction (i.e., there is not an exchange of net
value).[105.2]

   [105.1] Prop. Regs. §§ 1.351-1(a)(1)(iii) (Mar. 10, 2005), and 1.351-1(a)(2), Ex. 4 (stock
not issued for property because nonrecourse debt exceeded value of transferred property.

   [105.2] This regulation was part of a proposed package imposing similar "net value exchange" requirements for § 368 reorganizations; see   12.21[2][d]. See Cummings, 103 J.
Tax'n 14 (July 2005); NYSBA Tax Section, Formations, ..., 110 Tax Notes 871 (Feb. 20,
2006).

[3] Exception for Tax-Avoidance Transactions: § 357(b)

Page 3-31:

Add to note 113.

For a revised version of this proposal, see infra   3.06[7], note 158. But see Notice 2001-
17, 2001-9 IRB 730 (IRS rejected those contingent liability transactions on multiple theories, including the application of § 357(b)). Rev. Proc. 2002-67, 2002-43 IRB 733 (guidelines and procedures for settling Notice 2001-17 contingent liability shelters), infra
   3.06[7]. Black & Decker Corp. v. US, 2004-2 USTC   50,390 (D. Md. 2004), 340 F.
Supp.2d 621. For comment on the *Black and Decker* appelate argument, see Stratton, 109
Tax Notes 595 (Oct. 31, 2005) which went very well for the taxpayer, but the case was
remanded for trial on the "sham" issue, 436 F3d 431, 2006-1 USTC   50,142 (4th Cir.
2006) (Government's motion for summary judgment denied, that is, the transaction technically worked; but taxpayer's motion was reversed and remanded for trial on the sham issue. For comments, see Willens, Viewpoint, Daily Tax Rep. (BNA) No. 28, at J-1 (Feb.
10, 2006); Lipton, "Will *Black & Decker* Turn Out to Be a Pyrrhic Victory For the IRS?"
104 J. Tax'n 200 (Apr. 2006) (the answer is yes); compare Burke, "*Black & Decker* in
the Fourth Circuit: Tax Shelters and Textualism," 111 Tax Notes 315 (Apr. 17, 2006).
Taxpayer prevailed in *Coltec Inds., Inc. v. US*, 62 Fed. Cl. (2004); but reversed on appeal
by Federal Circuit (July 12, 2006) (held a sham), 454 F3d 1340, 2006-2 USTC   50,839
(Fed. Cir. 2006); cert. denied (Feb. 20, 2007).

[4] Exception for Liabilities in Excess of Basis: § 357(c)

[b] Reducing Excess of Liabilities Over Basis

Page 3-34:

Add to note 123 at the end of the first paragraph.

Seggerman Farms, Inc., RIA TC Memo. ¶ 2001-099 (2001) (applied § 357(c)(1) even though shareholders guaranteed payment of assumed debt); Raby & Raby, "Creating Phantom Income by Incorporation," 91 Tax Notes 1129 (May 14, 2001). Tax Court aff'd in Seggerman Farms, Inc. v. CIR, 308 F3d 803 (7th Cir. 2002) (§ 357(c) applied even though transferor remainded secondarily liable on the transferred debt; *Lessinger* and *Peracchi* distinguished).

Page 3-36:

Add to note 128.

Tucker & Lipton, "Comments on Perrachi, ABA Tax Section Newsletter," Vol. 29, No. 2, at 21 (Winter 2000); Bogdanski, "Section 358 and *Crane*: A Reply to My Critics," 57 Tax Law. 905 (Sr. 2004); Lazar, Lessinger, Peracchi and the Emperor's New Clothes: Covering a § 357(c) Deficit With Invisible (or Nonexistent) Property, 58 Tax Law. 41 (Fall 2004); Blanchard, Zero Basis in the Taxpayer's Own Stock or Debt Obligations: Do These Instruments Constitute Property? 106 Tax Notes 1431 (Mar. 21, 2005).

Page 3-37:

Add to note 129.

Zimmerman, "Obtaining Basis for Promissory Notes: Is an Original Purchase Different From an Improvement?" 92 J. Tax'n 55 (Jan. 2000); Lurie, "*Crane's*, Ghost Still Spooks the Tax Law: Cf. *Owen*," 53 Tax Law. 363 (2000); Polito, "The Role of Prescription in the Interpretive Problem of Basis Determination," 53 Tax Law. 615 (2000).

[c] Deductible Liabilities of Cash Basis Taxpayers

Page 3-38:

Add to note 133.

Black & Decker Corp. v. US, 2004-2 USTC ¶ 50,359 (D. Md. 2004) (Government lost motion for summary judgment in contingent liability assumption deal); Black & Decker Corp. v. US, 2004-2 USTC ¶ 50,390 (D. Md. 2004), 340 F. Supp. 2d 621, (taxpayers won its motion); accord Coltec Inds., Inc. v. US, 2004-2 USTC ¶ 50,402, 62 Fed. Cl. 716 (Fed. Cl. 2004) (long strong opinion for taxpayer after full trial). Comment by Willens, Viewpoint, Daily Tax Rep. (BNA) No. 210, at J-1 (Nov. 17, 2004). But *Coltec* was reversed by the Federal Circuit (July 12, 2206), 454 F3d 1340, 2006-2 USTC ¶ 50,839 (Fed. Cir. 2006) (held a sham); cert. denied (Feb. 20, 2007). See also Burke, "Deconstructing Black & Decker's Contingent Liability Shelter: A Statutory Analysis," 108 Tax Notes 211 (July 11, 2005); Yale, "Reexamining Black & Decker's Contingent Liability Tax Shelter," 108 Tax Notes 223 (July 11, 2005). For comment on Black & Decker appelate argument, see Stratton, supra note 113; for remand by the Fourth Circuit, see supra note 113; for comments, see Willens, Viewpoint, Daily Tax Rep. (BNA) No. 28, at J-1 (Feb. 10, 2006); Lipton, "Will *Black & Decker* Turn Out to Be a Pyrrhic Victory For the IRS?" 104 J. Tax'n 200 (Apr. 2006); compare Burke, "*Black & Decker* in the Fourth Circuit: Tax Shelters and Textualism," 111 Tax Notes 315 (Apr. 17, 2006).

[f] New § 357(d)

Page 3-40:

Add to note 145.

Cf. Seggerman Farms, Inc., RIA TC Memo. 2001-099 (2001) (dictum that fact that transferor still liable for assumed irrelevant for § 357(d) as well, though provision not applicable to taxable year at issue).

For comments, see Banks-Golub, "Recent Amendments to Code Section 357; Congress Responds to 'Artificial Basis Creation,'" 78 Taxes 19 (May 2000); Kliegman & Martin, "Whose Liability Is It Anyway? The Impact of Recent Amendments to Section 357," 91 J. Tax'n 341 (Dec. 1999). Regs. § 1.301-1T(g) (Jan. 4, 2001) extended § 357(d) principles to § 301(b)(2) distributions as well; Shepard, "Liability Assumptions in Section 351 Transactions," 99 Tax Notes 977 (May 19, 2003) (regulation project under § 357); Burke, "Contributions, Distributions, and Assumption of Liabilities: Confronting Economic Reality," 56 Tax Law. 383 (2003). But see Black & Decker Corp. v. US, 2004-2 USTC   50,359 (D. Md. 2004) (IRS lost summary judgment motion); in the second *Black & Decker* case, 2004-2 USTC   50,390 (D. Md. 2004), taxpayer prevailed on its motion. Comment by Willens, Viewpoint, Daily Tax Rep. (BNA) No. 21, at J-1 (Nov. 11, 2004); accord with *Black & Decker* is Coltec Inds., Inc. v. US, 2004-2 USTC   50,402, 62 Fed. Cl. 716 (Fed. Cl. 2004) (after full trial), but the *Black & Decker* case was remanded for trial on the "sham" issue, 436 F3d 431, 2006-1 USTC   50,142 (4th Cir. 2006). For comments, see Willens, Viewpoint, Daily Tax Rep. (BNA) No. 28, at J-1 (Feb. 10, 2006); Lipton, "Will *Black & Decker* Turn Out to Be a Pyrrhic Victory For the IRS?" 104 J. Tax'n 200 (Apr. 2006); compare Burke, "*Black & Decker* in the Fourth Circuit: Tax Shelters and Textualism," 111 Tax Notes 315 (Apr. 17, 2006). *Coltec* was reversed by the Federal Circuit (July 12, 2206) (held a sham), 454 F3d 1340, 2006-2 USTC   50,839 (Fed. Cir. 2006); cert. denied (Feb. 20, 2007).

Add text to end of ¶ 3.06[4][f].

IRS has announced an ambitious regulations project to clarify various issues under §§ 357(d) and 362(d) (and other related provisions as well) which has all the carmarks of a major undertaking.[145.1]

[145.1] See Sheppard, supra note 145; IRS Advanced Notice of Proposed Rulemaking (REG-100818-01). Fed. Reg. (May 6, 2003).

See also Prop. Regs. § 1.358-7, proposed regulations under § 358(h) issued June 24, 2003; infra   3.06[7] and   3.10[3]; adopted as final Regs. § 1.358-7 by TD 9207 (May 26, 2005).

[7] Contingent Liabilities

Page 3-42:

In note 150, in second sentence of second paragraph replace Merkel v. CIR, __ F3d __ *with the following:*

Merkel v. CIR, 192 F3d 844 (9th Cir. 1999).

Add to note 151.

Contra to Notice 2001-17 is Black & Decker Corp. v. US 2004-2 USTC ¶ 50,390 (D. Md. 2004); also Coltec Inds. Inc. v. US, 2004-2 USTC ¶ 50,402, 62 Fed. Cl. 716 (Fed. Cl. 2004); Comment by Willens, Viewpoint, Daily Tax Rep. (BNA) No. 210, at J-1 (Nov. 11, 2004); comments supra note 133.

On appeal, denial of the Government's summary judgment motion was upheld, but grant of the taxpayer's motion was reversed and remanded for trial on the "sham" issue, Black & Decker Corp. v. US, 436 F3d 431 (4th Cir. 2006); for comments, see Willens, Viewpoint, Daily Tax Rep. (BNA) No. 28, at J-1 (Feb. 10, 2006); Lipton, "Will *Black & Decker* Turn Out to Be a Pyrrhic Victory For the IRS?" 104 J. Tax'n 200 (Apr. 2006); compare Burke, "*Black & Decker* in the Fourth Circuit: Tax Shelters and Textualism," 111 Tax Notes 315 (Apr. 17, 2006). *Coltec* also lost on appeal where the Federal Circuit held that the transaction was a sham (July 12, 2006), 454 F3d 1340, 2006-2 USTC ¶ 50,839 (Fed. Cir. 2006); cert. denied (Feb. 20, 2007).

Add to note 153.

But cf. Illinois Tool Works, Inc., 117 TC 39 (2001), aff'd, 355 F3d 997 (7th Cir. 2004) (assumed contingent liability in taxable acquisition had to be capitalized in acquired asset basis); Raby & Raby, "Contingent Liability Payments in Business Purchases," 92 Tax Notes 941 (Aug. 13, 2001); Willens, "Treatment of Contingent Liabilities in an Acquisition Setting," Daily Tax Rep. (BNA) No. 118, at J-1 (Sept. 29, 2003).

Page 3-43:

Add to note 158.

A revised version of this proposal (adopted by the Senate Finance Committee on April 4, 2000) would adopt new § 358(h)(1)—i.e., step-down basis of stock to fair market value for assumed contingent debts; thus, built-in loss would be eliminated to the extent of contingent debt assumption; two exceptions are in § 358(h)(2) if (1) liabilities are part of a related business or (2) if substantially all the related assets are transferred with the liabilities. This proposal would be effective October 19, 1999 (a retroactive look-back effect). Shepard, "What Is a Liability?" 89 Tax Notes 1513 (Dec. 18, 2000).

Proposed § 358(h) was enacted on December 21, 2000, by HR 5662, § 309 (with an effective date of October 19, 1999). See also Notice 2000-17, 2001-9 IRB 730 (contingent liability tax-shelter transactions rejected on multiple theories, including "sham" à la *ACM Partnership*; query application to cases where § 358(h)(2) exceptions apply). Rizzi, "Contingent Liabilities: The Intersection of Tax Shelters and Corporate Reorganizations," 29 J. Corp. Tax'n 25 (Jan. 2002); Leeds, "Good Reason, Bad Reason, and No Reason at All: The IRS Expands Business Purpose Requirement for Transfers to Corporations," 29 J. Corp. Tax'n 3, at 10 (Jan. 2002). For extensive analysis of § 358(h), see Jackel & Blanchard, "Reflection on Liabilities: Extension of New Law to Partnership Formations," 91 Tax Notes 1579 (May 28, 2001). See also Shepard, "Liability Assumptions in Section 351 Transactions," 99 Tax Notes 977 (May 19, 2003) (comments on IRS regulation project under § 357).

But see Black & Decker Corp. v. US, 2004-2 USTC ¶ 50,359 (D. Md. 2004) (IRS lost on its summary judgment motion); in the second *Black & Decker* decision, 2004-2 USTC ¶ 50,390 (D. Md. 2004), taxpayer won its motion. Comment by Willens, Viewpoint, Daily Tax Rep. (BNA) No. 210 (Nov. 11, 2004); accord with *Black & Decker* is Coltec Inds. Inc. v. US, 2004-2 USTC ¶ 50,402 (Fed. Cl. 2004) (full trial). See also comments supra note 133 on *Black & Decker,* but the case was remanded for trial on the "sham" issue, 436 F3d 431, 2006-1 USTC ¶ 50,142 (4th Cir. 2006); for comments, see

Willens, Viewpoint, Daily Tax Rep. (BNA) No. 28, at J-1 (Feb. 10, 2006); Lipton, "Will *Black & Decker* Turn Out to Be a Pyrrhic Victory For the IRS?" 104 J. Tax'n 200 (Apr. 2006); compare Burke, "*Black & Decker* in the Fourth Circuit: Tax Shelters and Textualism," 111 Tax Notes 315 (Apr. 17, 2006). *Coltec* also lost on appeal where the Federal Circuit held that the transaction was a sham (July 12, 2006), 454 F3d 1340, 2006-2 USTC 50,839 (Fed. Cir. 2006).

For comments on *Coltec*, see Sheppard, "A More Intelligent Economic Substance Doctrine," 112 Tax Notes 325 (July 24, 2006); compare Prusiecki; "*Coltec*: A Case of Misdirected Analysis of Economic Substance," 112 Tax Notes 524 (Aug. 7, 2006); Prusiecki, "*Coltec*: The Dialogue Continues," 112 Tax Notes 707 (Aug. 21, 2006); and Lipton, "What will be the Impact of the Government's Economic Substance Victory in *Coltec*?" 105 J. Tax'n 136 (Sept. 2006).

Add text to end of ¶ 3.06[7].

A modified version of this proposal, § 358(h), finally passed on December 21, 2000.[158.1] IRS has proposed guidelines and procedures for settling § 351 contingent liability shelter cases.[158.2] Moreover, IRS has announced a major regula-

---

[158.1] See supra note 158. This proposal was included in HR 2488, § 1512, which passed Congress on August 5, 1999, but which was vetoed in September; return of this provision in future legislation seemed likely, however, and it finally passed in late 2000. For comments see Shepard, "Tinkering With Assumption of Liabilities," 84 Tax Notes 1348 (Sept. 6, 1999); Blanchard & Hooker, "Fixing Assumption of Liabilities: The Wrong Way and the Right Way," 85 Tax Notes 933 (Nov. 15 1999); for continued attack by IRS on contingent liability tax shelter transactions, see Notice 2001-17, 2001-19 IRB 730, and comments thereon supra note 158; but contra Black & Decker Corp. v. US, supra note 158; accord with *Black & Decker* is Coltec Inds. Inc. v. US, 2004-2 USTC 50,402 (Fed. Cl. 2004) (after full trial). Lipton, "New Tax Shelter Decisions Present Further Problems For the IRS," 102 J. Tax'n 211 (comment on *Coltec* and *Black & Decker* cases). See comments supra note 133, but the case was remanded for trial on the "sham" issue, 436 F3d 431, 2006-1 USTC 50,142 (4th Cir. 2006); for comments, see Willens, Viewpoint, Daily Tax Rep. (BNA) No. 28, at J-1 (Feb. 10, 2006); Lipton, "Will *Black & Decker* Turn Out to Be a Pyrrhic Victory For the IRS?" 104 J. Tax'n 200 (Apr. 2006); compare Burke, "*Black & Decker* in the Fourth Circuit: Tax Shelters and Textualism," 111 Tax Notes 315 (Apr. 17, 2006). *Coltec* also was reversed on appeal, 454 F3d 1340, 2006-2 USTC 50,389 (Fed. Cir. 2006) (held an economic sham even though a valid business purpose and even though taxpayer correct on the technical statutory questions); cert. denied (Feb. 20, 2007). For comments on *Coltec* decision by Sheppard, Prusiecki and Lipton, see supra note 158.

[158.2] Rev. Proc. 2002-67, 2002-43 IRB 733. But see Black & Decker Corp. v. US, 2004-2 USTC 50,390 (D. Md. 2004); and supra note 158 (taxpayer prevailed here on its summary judgment motion); Coltec Inds. Inc. v. US, 2004-2 USTC 50,402, 62 Fed. Cl. 716 (Fed. Cl. 2004).

But the Fourth Circuit reversed the grant of taxpayer's summary judgment motion and remanded the case for trial on the sham issue (though it did affirm denial of the Government's motion), Black & Decker Corp. v. US, 436 F3d 431 (4th Cir. 2006); for comments, see Willens, Viewpoint, Daily Tax Rep. (BNA) No. 28, at J-1 (Feb. 10, 2006); Lipton, "Will *Black & Decker* Turn Out to Be a Pyrrhic Victory For the IRS?" 104 J. Tax'n 200 (Apr. 2006); compare Burke, "*Black & Decker* in the Fourth Circuit: Tax Shelters and Textualism," 111 Tax Notes 315 (Apr. 17, 2006). *Coltec* also lost on appeal where the Federal Circuit held that the transaction was a sham (July 12, 2006); cert. denied (Feb. 20, 2007).

tion project dealing with liabilities,[158.3] and has also issued proposed regulations under § 358(h) on June 24, 2003, which were adopted as final regulations in May of 2005.[158.4]

[158.3] See supra ¶ 3.06[4][f], note 145.1.

[158.4] Prop. Regs. § 1.358-7, infra ¶ 3.10[3]; adopted as final Regs. § 1.358-7 by TD 9207 (May 26, 2005). But the case was remanded for trial on the "sham" issue, 2006-1 USTC ¶ 50,142 (4th Cir. 2006).

¶ 3.09 CONTROL "IMMEDIATELY AFTER THE EXCHANGE"

[5] Transferred Property—Multiple Drop-Downs

Page 3-55:

Add text to end of ¶ 3.09[5].

IRS applied these multiple drop-down rulings expansively (and mercifully) in a later 2003 ruling[206.1] to save a multi-step series of transactions that technically resulted in a loss of control but could have easily been done in "double-drop" mode, so the actual method used did not violate the purposes of § 351.[206.2]

[206.1] Rev. Rul. 2003-51, 2003-21 IRB 738.

[206.2] IRS has become very user friendly in Subchapter C matters lately. See Willens, "IRS Alters the Landscape with Respect to the 351 'Control Immediately After' Requirement," 98 J. Tax'n 325 (June 2003); Rizzi, "Losing Control: IRS Accepts Successive Section 351 Transfers, 30 J. Corp. Tax'n 29 (Nov. 2003): Cummings, " Rev. Rul. 2003-51: A New Gloss on the Step Transaction Doctrine," 101 Tax Notes 1473 (Dec. 22, 2003).

¶ 3.10 TRANSFEROR'S BASIS FOR STOCK

[1] In General

Page 3-56:

Add to note 208.

But Rev. Rul. 74-503 was revoked by Rev. Rul. 2006-2, 2006-2 IRB (Jan. 9, 2006); comment by Willens, Viewpoint, Daily Tax Rep. (BNA) No. 246, at J-1 (Dec. 27, 2005); and Cummings, Viewpoint, Daily Tax Rep. (BNA) No. 4, at J-1 (Jan. 6, 2006). NYSBA Tax Section, "The Application of 'Zero Basis' in Tax-Free Reorganizations," 113 Tax Notes 761 (Nov. 20, 2006).

Page 3-58:

Add to note 215.

Prop. Regs. § 1.453-1(f)(3)(ii) allocates § 358(d) basis first to nonrecognition property (stock) up to its value; any "excess basis" is then allocated to the installment obligation; see § 1.453-1(f)(3)(iii), Exs. 1 and 2.

[3] Assumption of Liability

Page 3-60:

Add to note 223.

A revised version of this proposal (adopted by the Senate Finance Committee on April 4, 2000) would enact new § 358(h), which would step down the basis of stock to its valve to the extent of assumed contingent debts. Two exceptions would be provided: where the liabilities are part of a related business or where substantially all related assets are transferred along with the liabilities. See Shepard, "What Is a Liability?," 89 Tax Notes 1513 (Dec. 18, 2000).

This proposal was adopted on December 21, 2000, by HR 5662, § 309 (with an effective date of October 19, 1999). But see Notice 2001-17, 2001-9 IRB 730 (attacking contingent liability tax-shelter transactions on multiple grounds, apparently even those qualifying for the exceptions for § 358(h)(2)). For comments on Notice 2001-17, see Rizzi and Leeds, supra note 158. See, generally, Jackel & Blanchard, "Reflections on Liabilities: Extension of New Law to Partnership Formations," 91 Tax Notes 1579 (May 28, 2001). But see Black & Decker Corp. v. US, 2004-2 USTC   50,359 (D. Md. 2004). Black & Decker Corp. v. US, 2004-2 USTC   50,390 (D. Md. 2004) (taxpayer prevailed on its motion for summary judgment); accord, Coltec Inds. Inc. v. US, 2004-2 USTC   50,402, 62 Fed. Cl. 716 (Fed. Cl. 2004) (after a full trial; extensive opinion and taxpayer won on all points); comment by Willens, Viewpoint, Daily Tax Rep. (BNA) No. 210 (Nov. 11, 2004); Lipton, supra note 158.1 other comments supra note 133, but the *Black & Decker* case was remanded for trial on the "sham" issue, 436 F3d 431, 2006 USTC   50, 142 (4th Cir. 2006). For comments, see Willens, Viewpoint, Daily Tax Rep. (BNA) No. 28, at J-1 (Feb. 10, 2006); Lipton, "Will *Black & Decker* Turn Out to Be a Pyrrhic Victory For the IRS?" 104 J. Tax'n 200 (Apr. 2006); compare Burke, "*Black & Decker* in the Fourth Circuit: Tax Shelters and Textualism," 111 Tax Notes 315 (Apr. 17, 2006). *Coltec* also lost on appeal where the Federal Circuit held that the transaction was a sham (July 12, 2006), 454 F3d 1340, 2006-2 USTC   50,839 (Fed. Cir. 2006); cert. denied (Feb. 20, 2007). For comments, see supra notes 158 and 158.1. Court requested in *Coltec* on November 8, 2006.

For announcement of a major regulation present under §§ 357, 358 and 362, see supra   3.06[4][f], note 145.1. For proposed regulations under § 358(h); issued on June 24, 2003, see Prop. Regs. § 1.358-7; adopted as final Regs. § 1.358-7 by TD 9207 (May 26, 2005).

¶ 3.11 TRANSFEREE CORPORATION'S BASIS FOR ASSETS

[3] Corporation's Deductions for Payment of Assumed Liabilities

Page 3-65:

Add to note 236.

See also Priv. Ltr. Rul. 2000-13044 (transferee allowed deductions for assumed liabilities that could have been deducted by transferor). But see Notice 2001-17, 2001-9 IRB 730 (no deduction by transferee in contingent liability tax-shelter transaction; tax avoidance, no business purpose, and *Holdcroft*; Rev. Rul. 95-74 not applicable). But see Illinois Tool Works, Inc., 117 TC 39 (2001), aff'd, 355 F3d 997 (7th Cir. 2004) (assumed contingent liability in taxable acquisition had to be capitalized in acquired asset basis, citing *Hold-croft*); comment by Raby & Raby, "Contingent Liability Payments in Business Purchase," 92 Tax Notes 941 (Aug. 13, 2001).

Add to note 238.

But see Notice 2001-17, supra note 236.

[4] Installment Boot

Page 3-65:

Replace the text and footnotes of ¶ 3.11[4] with the following:

When a transferor receives boot in the form of transferee debt and reports gain on the installment method under § 453(f)(6),[239] the transferor's basis for trans-feree stock evidently can be increased under § 358(a) immediately by the full amount of the gain, while the transferee's basis in the acquired assets is in-creased under § 362(a) pro tanto as the gain is recognized.[240]

---

[239] See supra ¶ 3.05[3], note 83, and ¶ 3.10[1], note 215.

[240] See Prop. Regs. §§ 1.453-1(f)(3)(ii) (1984) and 1.453-1(f)(3)(iii), Exs. 1 and 2.

[5] Zero Basis Problem

Page 3-66:

Add to note 241.

Rev. Rul. 99-57, 1999-51 IRB 678 (applied Rev. Rul. 74-503 to corporation's transfer of its stock to a partnership; see infra ¶ 3.12[1] for § 1032 protection for partnership's gain recognized on use of stock to buy property or pay compensation).

But Rev. Rul. 74-503 was revoked by Rev. Rul. 2006-2, 2006-2 IRB (Jan. 9, 2006); comment by Willens, Viewpoint, Daily Tax Rep. (BNA) No. 246, at J-1 (Dec. 27, 2005); and Cummings, Viewpoint, Daily Tax Rep. (BNA) No. 4, at J-1 (Jan. 6, 2006). NYSBA Tax Section, "The Application of 'Zero Basis' in Tax-Free Reorganizations," 113 Tax Notes 761 (Nov. 20, 2006).

Add to note 243.

Regs. § 1.1032-3 was adopted in final form by TD 8883 on May 16, 2000 (effective on that date).

Add to note 244.

Rev. Rul. 80-76 was declared obsolete by TD 8883 when it adopted final Regs. § 1.1032-3 on May 16, 2000.

Add to note 245.

These proposals were adopted in final form by TD 8883 on May 16, 2000.

Add to note 246.

Final Regs. § 1.1032-3(b) is the same. See also Notice 2000-56, 2000-43 IRB 393 (application of immediacy test where contributions of parent stock to "rabbi trusts"; thus, stock not considered transferred to subsidiary until time it is issued to satisfy its deferred compensation obligations). See also Rev. Rul. 2002-1, 2002-2 IRB 268 (application in § 355 spin-offs); Cummings, "Using Compensatory NQSOs and Restricted Stock With Section 355 – New Clear Guidance From IRS," 96 J. Tax'n 71 (Feb. 2002); Rizzi, "Restricted Stock, Stock Options and Spin-Offs," 30 J. Corp. Tax'n 45 (Jan. 2003); Bennett, "Rev. Rul. 2002-1: Constructing a Bridge to Span Time," 80 Taxes 11 (Oct. 2002).

Page 3-67:

Add to note 247.

The final regulations retained the immediacy test of the proposed regulations in § 1.1032-3(c). The final regulations allow use of parent stock to acquire subsidiary debt or stock (but not parent stock). The final regulations also increased the number of examples in § 1.1032-3(e) from five to ten. See Banoff, "Partnership Use of Corporate Partner Stock and Options Easier Under 1032 Regs," 93 J. Tax'n 81 (Aug. 2000).

[7] Basis Limitation for Assumed Liabilities: § 362(d)

Page 3-67:

Add to note 249.

Burke, "Contributions, Distributions, and Assumption of Liabilities: Confronting Economic Reality," 56 Tax Law. 383 (2003).

Add to text at end of ¶ 3.11[7].

IRS announced a major regulation project to clarify various issues under §§ 357(d) and 362(d) (and other related issues as well).[249.1]

[249.1] Supra   3.06[4][f], note 145.1; Sheppard, "Liability Assumptions in Section 351 Transactions," 99 Tax Notes 977 (May 19, 2003). See also proposed regulations under § 358(h), § 1.358-7, issued June 24, 2003; adopted by TD 9207 (May 26, 2005).

Add new ¶ 3.11[8].

[8] Basis Limitation Where Transferred Property Has Net Built-In Loss: § 362(e)

The Jobs Act of 2004[249.2] adopted an anti-loss duplication rule in § 362(e)(2) where there is an aggregate net built-in loss on the transferred assets;[249.3] in such case, the basis of each loss asset is stepped-down to its share of the asset's proportionate share of the net built-in loss (allocated in proportion to each asset's built-in loss). But if both the transferor and transferee (irrevocably) elect, a basis step-down in the transferee's § 358 stock basis can be made in lieu of asset basis reduction.[249.4] Thus, it is no longer possible to duplicate losses by § 351 drop-downs, whether done domestically or cross-border.[249.5]

Proposed regulations under § 362(e)(2), the "anti-loss duplication" provision of § 362(e), were issued on October 23, 2006.[249.6] The regulations clarify that § 362(e)(2) applies separately to each transferor (and also must reflect any basis step-up as a result of recognized gain). The proposals also revise and expand Notice 2005-70[249.7] to provide more methods and time periods in which to make elections under § 362(e)(2)(C). The regulations will not apply, however, if there is no loss duplication as a result of the transaction (e.g., where the transferor distributes transferee stock under § 351(c) without recognizing gain or loss on the distribution).[249.8]

[249.2] American Jobs Creation Act of 2004, § 836, effective Oct. 22, 2004. See also ¶ 15.85[7][e] regarding § 362(e)(1) (loss import transactions blocked by similar asset basis step-down).

[249.3] Namely, aggregate asset basis in excess of aggregate fair market value.

[249.4] IRC § 362(e)(2)(C). For procedures of this election, see Notice 2005-70, 2005-41 IRB (Oct. 11, 2005).

[249.5] While loss duplication is denied by new § 362(e), net gain duplications still result in § 351 transactions. See Coven, "What Tax Shelters Can Teach Us About the Structure of Subchapter C," 105 Tax Notes 831 (Nov. 8, 2004), criticizing this new discontinuity; Avent, "Corporate Changes in the American Jobs Creation Act of 2004," 83 Taxes 103 (May 2005); Cummings & Hanson, 107 Tax Notes 1563 (June 20, 2005); Randall, et al., "Interaction of New Sections 362(e)(2) With Loss Diallowance Rules," 32 Corp. Tax'n 24 (Sept. 2005); but taxpayer won on appeal, Kohler Co. v. US,—F3d—2006-2 USTC ¶ 50,611 (7th Cir. 2006); see Raby & Raby, Taxpayer's "Untenable" Position Prevails, 113 Tax Notes 1143 (Dec. 25, 2006).

Proposed regulations under § 362(e)(2) were issued in October 2006 as Regs. § 1.362-4.

[249.6] Prop. Regs. § 1.362-4 (effective when final).

[249.7] See supra note 249.4.

[249.8] For example, the overall transaction is a Type D reorganization (infra ¶ 12.26).

¶ 3.12 CORPORATION'S GAIN, LOSS, OR DEDUCTION ON ISSUE OR SALE OF ITS STOCK

[1] Section 1032: The Basic Rule and Its Purpose

Page 3-68:

Add to note 250.

See, e.g., Rev. Rul. 99-57, 1999-51 IRB 678, where corporate partner had no gain or loss under § 1032 when partnership used its contributed stock to buy property (a taxable event to the partnership, but § 1032 for corporate partner on its share of gain). But see Notice 99-57, 1999-51 IRB 692 (IRS will deal with any basis discontinuities under §§ 705 and 743 where no § 754 election and inside gain sheltered by § 1032). These regulations were proposed on January 2, 2001, as Prop. Regs. § 1.705-2, and became Final in TD 8986 on March 29, 2002. But the 2002 regulations subsequently were revised by amended Regs. § 1.705-2, issued by TD 9049 (Mar. 18, 2003).

Add to note 253.

The protection of § 1032 was extended to gain or loss on the lapse or acquisition of a securities futures contract in December 2000. Carlisle & Lanning, "IRS's Nonrecognition Treatment For Corporations Settlement of Contract on its Stock," 106 Tax Notes 591 (Jan. 31, 2005) (comment on favorable letter ruling) vs. Sheppard, "Having It Both Ways on Feline PRIDES," 106 Tax Notes 632 (Feb. 7, 2005).

Page 3-69:

Add to note 254.

Regs. § 1.1032-3 was adopted in final form by TD 8883 on May 16, 2000. See Banoff, supra note 247.

Add to note 256.

Ruling declared obsolete in TD 8883, May 16, 2000. See also Notice 2000-56, 2000-43 IRB 393 (contributions to "rabbi trusts" and immediacy test of Regs. § 1.1032-3(c)); stock not transferred until used to satisfy subsidiary's obligations to pay deferred compensation.
  See also Rev. Rul. 2002-1, 2002-2 IRB 268 (application in § 355 spin-offs); Cummings, "Using Compensatory NQSOs and Restricted Stock With Section 355 – New Clear Guidance From IRS," 96 J. Tax'n 71 (Feb. 2002); Bennett, "Rev. Rul. 2002-1: Constructing a Bridge to Span Time," 80 Taxes 11 (Oct. 2002); Rizzi, "Restricted Stock, Stock Options and Spin-Offs," 30 J. Corp. Tax'n 45 (Jan. 2003).

[4] Exchanges Outside § 351; Cost Basis and Deductions

Page 3-72:

Add to note 272, first paragraph.

But see Bailine, "IRS Has No 'Basis' for 'Cost' Conclusion," 30 J. Corp. Tax'n 26 (May 2003).

Add to note 273.

Regs. § 1.1032-3 was adopted in final form by TD 8883 on May 16, 2000. See Banoff, supra note 247. See also Rev. Rul. 2002-1, 2002-2 IRB 268, and Cummings, supra note 256.

¶ 3.13 CONTRIBUTIONS TO CAPITAL

[1] In General: Corporate Nonrecognition of Income

Page 3-74:

Add to note 281.

Final regulations § 1.1032-3 were adopted by TD 8883 on May 16, 2000.

[b] Nonshareholder Contributions

Page 3-75:

In last sentence of note 285 change (Oct. 18, 1999) *to* (Nov. 8, 1999).

Page 3-76:

Add to note 287.

A limited return of the contribution in aid of construction exception occurred in the 1996 small business tax legislation for public water and sewer utilities; see Prop. Regs. § 1.118-2 (Dec. 17, 1999) (preamble sets out history in extensive detail).

Page 3-77:

Add to note 291, third paragraph.

But see Kohler Co. v. US, 247 F. Supp. 2d 1083, 2003-1 USTC   50,309 (DC Wisc. 2003) (summary judgment denied; material issue of fact; court rejected taxpayer's capital contribution as a matter-of-law argument); Kahn & Kahn, "Prevention of Double Deductions of a Single Loss," 26 Va. Tax Rev. (2006).

[2] Debt Forgiveness

Page 3-78:

Add to note 294.

For treatment of exempt COD income by an S Corporation, see   6.10[2][b] and Gitlitz v. CIR, 531 US 206, 121 S. Ct. 701 (2001) (shareholders got basis step up). But *Gitlitz* was overturned by legislation (which passed on Mar. 9, 2002).

[4] Treatment of Contributors

[a] Contributions by Shareholders

Page 3-81:

Add to note 306.

For impact of *Gitlitz* decision, 531 US 206, 121 S. Ct. 701 (2001), on shareholders stock basis where a capital contribution to an S Corporation, see Polsky, "Another *Gitlitz* Windfall: Double Basis Increases for S Corp. Shareholders," 92 Tax Notes 314 (July 9, 2001). But *Gitlitz* was overturned (prospectively) in the Economic Stimulus bill (which passed on Mar. 9, 2002).

Add to note 309.

For a current application of Rev. Rul. 64-155 by IRS to a series of § 351 transactions, see Priv. Ltr. Rul. 200208022.

¶ 3.15 STATUTORY EXCLUSIONS FROM § 351

[1] Transfers to Investment Companies

Page 3-87:

Add to note 328.

Jackel & Sowell, "Transfers to Investment Companies: Complexity in a Conundrum," 94 Tax Notes 1659 (Mar. 25, 2002); Sheppard, "Rationalizing the Treatment of Exchange Funds," 95 Tax Notes 152 (Apr. 8, 2002).

¶ 3.17 MIDSTREAM TRANSFERS OF POTENTIAL INCOME AND RELATED ISSUES

[6] Business Purpose, Step Transactions, and Other Principles

Page 3-96:

In first line of text, insert after the third word the:

Service has asserted that the

Add to note 366.

; currently, e.g., Notice 2001-17, 2001-9 IRB 70. See Leeds, "Good Reason, Bad Reason, and No Reason at All: The IRS Expands Business Purpose Requirement for Transfers to Corporations," 29 J. Corp. Tax'n 3 (Jan. 2002); Bowen, "Whither Business Purpose?" 80 Taxes 275, 382 (Mar. 2002).

Add to note 367.

But the issue here seems more concerned with assignment of income principles than application of § 351.

Add to note 368.

But these cases seem more concerned with application of § 368 rather than § 351 (except to the extent they involve loss of control).

¶ 3.18 COLLATERAL PROBLEMS OF INCORPORATING A GOING BUSINESS

[1] Transferors

Page 3-99:

Add to note 378.

But see Rev. Rul. 2004-59, 2004-24 IRB 1050 (Rev. Rul. 84-111 principles not applicable to case where partnership makes a check-the-box election for corporate status; treat as a deemed 351 transfer of assets by partnership and deemed liquidation distribution to partners). See Levi, "Exploring the Implications of State Formless Conversions After *Rev. Rul. 2004-59*," 82 Taxes 51 (Sept. 2004).

¶ 3.19 RELATION OF § 351 TO REORGANIZATION PROVISIONS

Page 3-103:

Add to note 401.

But see Helvering v. Cement Investors, Inc., 316 US 567 (1942) (§ 351 applied even though § 368 reorganization could not be effected).

Page 3-104:

Add to note 402.

See Ginsburg & Levin, Mergers, "Acquisitions and Buyouts" (Aspen, 2002),   902, 903.

Add to note 403.

Bailine, "Long Live the Horizontal Double Dummy!" 29 J. Corp. Tax'n 30 (Jan. 2002); Ginsburg & Levin,   9.05 (currently Aspen, 2002);   12.63[4][g]; Cummings, "Exchange Rights in Reorganizations and Section 351 Transactions," 97 Tax Notes 287 (Oct. 14, 2002).

CHAPTER **4**

Corporation's Capital Structure: Debt vs. Equity

A DEBT VERSUS EQUITY: PROBLEMS OF CLASSIFICATION

¶ 4.01 USE OF DEBT OR EQUITY: OVERVIEW

[1] In General

Page 4-5:

Add to note 1 at the end of the first paragraph.

Pratt, "The Debt-Equity Distinction in a Second-Best World," 53 Vand. L. Rev. 1055 (May 2000); Polito, "A Modest Proposal Regarding Debt-Like Preferred Stock," 20 Vir. L. Rev. 291 (2000).

Add to note 1 at the end of the second paragraph.

Pratt, "The Debt-Equity Distinction in a Second-Best World," 53 Vand. L. Rev. 1055 (May 2000); Polito, "A Modest Proposal Regarding Debt-Like Preferred Stock," 20 Vir. L. Rev. 291 (2000).

Add to end of note 1 at end of fourth paragraph.

For a recent (though not adopted) integration proposal to exempt dividends from tax at the shareholder level, see infra note 1.1.

Add to text at end of ¶ 4.01[1].

But Treasury's (rejected) proposal to exempt from tax dividends paid from previously taxed income will have a major impact on the choice of capital structure by removing, or largely neutralizing, current law's bias in favor of debt over equity (one of the major arguments for enactment);[1.1] so would the House alternative proposal to tax dividends at the same rates as capital gains, which was the proposal ultimately adopted.[1.2]

[1.1] See supra 1.08[4], and infra 8.06; proposed HR 2 and S.2 (Feb. 27, 2003).

[1.2] Supra 1.08[4], infra 8.06. This proposal was released on May 1, 2003, and passed the House on May 9, 2003; it prevailed in the final 2003 legislation.

[2] Consequences of Current Distributions

Page 4-3:

Add to note 2.

But see current proposals (Feb. 27, 2003) to exempt dividends paid from previously taxed income (or tax them at the same rate as capital gains) (the proposal ultimately adopted), supra notes 1.1, 1.2.

Page 4-8:

Add to text at end of ¶ 4.01[2].

Treasury's (rejected) proposal to exempt dividends from tax at the shareholder level would go far towards neutralizing current law's bias for debt–over–equity financing, which is one of the principal arguments asserted for this proposal,[7.1] as would the alternative House proposal (which was the one ultimately adopted) to tax dividends at the same rate as capital gains (and reduce that rate as well).[7.2]

[7.1] See supra note 1.1; ¶¶ 1.08[4], 8.06.

[7.2] See supra note 1.2. This proposal prevailed in the final 2003 legislation.

[6] Required Registration of Obligations

Page 4-11:

Add to note 28.

Land, "Bearer or Registered? Lingering Issues Under TEFRA," 58 Tax Law. 667 (2005).

¶ 4.02 DEBT OR EQUITY: CLASSIFICATION ISSUES

[2] Occasions for Dispute

Page 4-14:

Add to note 36.

ASA Investerings was affirmed, 201 F3d 505, 2000-1 USTC ¶ 50,185 (DC Cir. 2000).

[6] Classification: Question of Fact or Law?

Page 4-16:

Add to note 44.

Indmar Prods. Co. v. CIR, 444 F3d 771 (6th Cir. 2006) (majority, a question of fact; concur, question of law; dissent, question of fact.)

¶ 4.03 CLASSIFYING HYBRID SECURITIES

[2] Classification Criteria

[g] Participation in Both Corporate Gains and Corporate Losses

Page 4-30:

Add to note 90.

But § 163(l) is not working well with the new version of hybrids, infra ¶ 4.03[2][k], note 99. But the 2004 Jobs Act significantly broadened this provision; American Jobs Creation Act of 2004, § 845, effective October 3, 2004.

[k] Debt With "Equity-Dominant" Features

Page 4-32:

Add to note 99.

See also Sheppard, "The Nine Lives of Equity-Linked Securities," 92 Tax Notes 597 (Aug. 6, 2001). Sheppard, "The Second Life of Feline PRIDES," 99 Tax Notes 952 (May 19, 2003) (hybrids and § 163(l) issues, which Treasury is not applying here). But the American Jobs Creation Act of 2004, § 845, amended § 163(l) to considerably broaden its scope (effective Oct. 3, 2004).

[3] Hybrid Equity: "Tracking Stock"

Page 4-33:

Add after first sentence of note 102.

Currently Rev. Proc. 2007-3, § 3.01(63), 2007-1 IRB 108.

Add to note 103.

Dahlberg & Perry, "Tracking Stock: Virtual Equity, Virtual Entities, and Virtual Mergers and Acquisitions," 78 Taxes 18 (Mar. 2000); Rizzi, "Tracking Stock as Synthetic Spin-Offs and Contingent Consideration," 27 J. Corp. Tax'n 255 (2000); Rizzi, "Developments in Tracking Stock," 29 J. Corp. Tax'n 34 (May 2002); Bennett, Tracking Stock, Time For Round Three? 85 Taxes 15 (Feb. 2007).

[7] "Half-Breed" Hybrid Instruments (Debt and Equity)

Page 4-37:

Add to note 122.

Sheppard, "The Nine Lives of Equity-Linked Securities," 92 Tax Notes 597 (Aug. 6, 2001).

[8] "Fast-Pay Stock"

[a] In General

Page 4-39:

Add to note 131.

Miller & Stroebel, "Proposed Regulations Recharacterize 'Stepped Down Preferred' and Other 'Fast Pay' Stock," 17 J. Tax'n Invs. 122 (2000). These regulations were adopted in final form by TD 8853 on January 10, 2000 (generally effective on February 27, 1997, the date of Notice 97-21).

[b] Service Response

Page 4-40:

Add to text at end of first paragraph of ¶ 4.03[8][b].

These proposals were adopted as final regulations issued in January 2000.[134.1]

[134.1] Regs. § 1.7701(l)-3, adopted by TD 8853 on January 10, 2000 (but effective retroactively to the date of Notice 97-21). The final regulations generally retained the approach of the proposed regulations, but a § 302(d) dividend equivalent redemption will not create a fast-pay arrangement unless there is a principal purpose to achieve a fast-pay result. See Regs. §§ 1.7701(l)-3(b)(2)(ii) and 1.7701(l)-3(e), Ex. 3. The final regulations also dropped the proposed regulations' requirement that there must be two classes of stock.

Add to text in last paragraph of ¶ 4.03[8][b].

The final regulations do nothing to ease this impression.[135.1]

[135.1] Fast-pay arrangements also are included in the tax shelter tainted transactions list of Notice 2000-15, 2000-12 IRB 826; see ¶ 5.10[6][g].

¶ 4.04 CLASSIFYING SHAREHOLDER AND OTHER NON–ARM'S-LENGTH DEBT: INTENTION AND ECONOMIC REALITY

[1] In General

Page 4-42:

Add to note 141.

Raby & Raby, "Debt vs. Equity: Not Merely a Matter of Ratios," 98 Tax Notes 1707 (Mar. 17, 2003). Indmar Prods. Co. v. CIR, 444 F3d 771 (6th Cir. 2006) (reversing tax court – and penalty – applied multi-factor analysis to find valid debt); for comments see, "Shop Talk," 104 J. Tax'n 378 (June 2006); Willens, Viewpoint, Daily Tax Rep. (BNA) No. 80, at J-1 (Apr. 26, 2006).

[2] Pro Rata Holding of Stock and Debt

Page 4-44:

Add to note 147.

Cerand & Co., Inc. v. CIR, 254 F3d 258, 2001-2 USTC ¶ 50,518 (DC Cir. 2001) (review for abuse of discretion, namely, a question of fact; but Tax Court abused discretion here in finding capital contribution for open account advances to sister corporation).

[3] Excessive Debt-To-Equity Ratio ("Thin Capitalization")

Page 4-45:

Add to note 152, second paragraph.

Raby & Raby, "Debt vs. Equity: Not Merely a Matter of Ratios," 98 Tax Notes 1707 (Mar. 17, 2003).

[8] Related Tax-Exempt Payee (Interest Strips)

Page 4-50:

In second full sentence of runover paragraph change "1.158" to "1".

B DEBT VERSUS EQUITY: MAJOR INCOME TAX CONSIDERATIONS

¶ 4.22 CHARACTER OF INVESTOR'S LOSS ON SALE OR WORTHLESSNESS

[2] Noncorporate Shareholders: Loss on Stock

Page 4-60:

Replace first sentence of first complete paragraph with the following:

Liquidations are also treated as the equivalent of a sale or exchange of the stock, so that shareholders are entitled to a capital loss if they receive something for their stock (so that § 331 applies) but less than its adjusted basis.

[5] Corporate Investors: Losses on Debt and Stock

Page 4-65:

Add to note 251.

Blanchard et al., "The Deductibility of Investments in Financially Troubled Subsidiaries and Related Federal Income Tax Considerations," 80 Taxes 91 (Mar. 2002); Paul, "United Dominion: Implications for Attribute Reduction," 95 Tax Notes 262 (Apr. 8, 2002); Bennett, "Corporate Tax Watch: Code Sec. 165(g) Under the Microscope," 81 Taxes 11 (Feb. 2003); Sheppard, "When Do Subsidiary Shares Become Worthless?," 100 Tax Notes 746 (Aug. 11, 2003). See also Rev. Rul. 2003-125, 2003-52 IRB 1243; Calianno, "When Does a Conversion of a Foreign Corporation to a Foreign Branch Entitle a Domestic Parent to a

Worthless Stock Loss?" 15 J. Int'l Tax'n 22 (Apr. 2004); Bennett, "Rev. Rul. 2003-125: Worthlessness and Deemed Liquidation," 82 Taxes 17 (Apr. 2004); Cummings, "Foreign Subsidiary Losses Appear Safer," 105 Tax Notes 583 (Oct. 25, 2004); Schnee & Seago, "The Tax Result of a Subsidiary Becoming Worthless," 34 Corp. Tax'n 18 (Mar. 2007).

Add to note 252.

See Blanchard, supra note 251. Rev. Rul. 2003-125, 2003-52 IRB 1243; Blanchard and Garlock, "Worthless Stock and Debt Losses," 83 Taxes 205 (Mar. 2005).

¶ 4.25 CORPORATE DEBTOR'S GAIN ON DISCHARGE OF DEBT FOR LESS THAN FACE AMOUNT

[1] In General: Debt-Discharge Gain As Income Under § 61(a)(12)

Page 4-75:

Add to end of first paragraph of note 294.

Beer, "Unpacking the Cancellation of Indebtedness Income Doctrine: Towards Economic Reality-Based Taxation," 19 Va. Tax Rev. 457 (2000); Lashnits, "Basic Tax Issues in Insolvency and Bankruptcy," 30 J. Corp. Tax'n 26 (Jan. 2003); Cuff, "Indebtedness of a Disregarded Entity," 81 Taxes 303 (Mar. 2003); Pratt, "Corporate Cancellation of Indebtedness Income and the Debt-Equity Distinction," 24 Vir. Tax. Rev. 187 (Fall 2004).

Page 4-77:

Add to note 299 following "85 Tax Notes 77 (Oct. 4, 1999)."

But see Estate of Smith v. CIR, 198 F3d 515, 2000-1 USTC ¶ 50,147 (5th Cir. 1999) (followed *Zarin* and distinguished *Preslar*, here both existence and amount of liability contested); comment by Raby & Raby, "Valuation and Post-Death Events," 86 Tax Notes 89 (Jan. 3, 2000).

Add to end of note 299.

Merkel v. Comm'r, 192 F3d 844 (9th Cir. 1999); Lipton, "Murky Test for Insolvency in *Merkel* Continues to Cause Problems," 91 J. Tax'n 372 (Dec. 1999).

[2] Other Exceptions and Modifications to General Inclusion Rule

Page 4-78:

Add to note 306 after Gitlitz *case cite.*

Certiorari was granted in *Gitlitz* on May 1, 2000; held for the taxpayers, Gitlitz v. CIR, 531 US 206, 121 S. Ct. 701, 2001-1 USTC ¶ 50,147 (2001); but *Gitlitz* overruled by legislation enacted on March 9, 2002, the Economic Stimulus Bill.

Page 4-79:

Add ", 192 F3d 844" to note 306 following "1999-2 USTC ¶ 50,848".

Add to end of note 306.

Lipton, "Murky Test for Insolvency in *Merkel* Continues to Cause Problems," 91 J. Tax'n 372 (Dec. 1999). See also R.E. Carlson, 116 TC 87 (2001) (§ 108(d)(3) insolvency determined by including creditor exempt assets); Raby & Raby, "'Assets' for DOI and Other Tax Purposes," 90 Tax Notes 1377 (Mar. 3, 2001).

Add new item 6 to text at end of ¶ 4.25[2].

6. Temporary regulations under § 108(b) and § 1017[308.1] require attribute and basis reductions for exempt COD gain after computation of tax for the year of discharge, but before any carryovers of attributes and basis under § 381 in Type G reorganization.[308.2] Final regulations were adopted on May 11, 2004.[308.3]

[308.1] TD 9080 (July 18, 2003), Regs. §§ 1.108-7T and 1.1017-1T(b)(4). Jones & Dangelo, "Section 108 and 1017 Regulations," 31 Corp. Tax'n 3 (July 2004).

[308.2] See Regs. §§ 1.108-7T(d), Ex. 3, and 1.108-7T(d), Ex. 4. No mention was made of the *Gitlitz* decision, supra note 306, which seems contra to this sequencing order. For Type G reorganizations, see ¶ 12.30.

[308.3] TD 9127 adopting Regs. §§ 1.108-7(c) and 1.1017(b)(4) (adopting the temporary regulations).

[3] Stock-For-Debt Exchanges

[a] In General

Page 4-80:

Add to note 310.

See Willens, "Debtor Can Realize COD Income on Conversion of Trust Preferred Stock," Daily Tax Rep. (BNA) No. 48, at J-1 (Mar. 13, 2006).

[c] Section 108(e)(4): Related-Party Acquisitions

Page 4-82:

Add to note 321.

For examples of §108(e)(4), see Rev. Rul. 2004-79, 2004-31 IRB 108 (sub purchase of parent debt and distribution of debt up to parent as dividend; COD, OID, and dividend consequences illustrated).

[4] Examples

Page 4-84:

Add to text at end of Example 3.

For illustration of these principles see Rev. Rul. 2004-79.[321.1]

[321.1] 2004-31 IRB 106 (COD, OID, and dividend consequences on sub purchase of parent debt and distribution of debt up to parent as dividend); Willens, Viewpoint, Daily Tax Rep. (BNA) No. 48, J-1 (Mar. 13, 2006) (COD on conversion of debt into stock).

C   ORIGINAL ISSUE AND MARKET DISCOUNT

¶ 4.40 ORIGINAL ISSUE DISCOUNT: IN GENERAL

[4] 1982 and After

Page 4-90:

Add to end of fourth paragraph of note 343.

For invocation of the anti-abuse rule of Regs. § 1.1275-2(g) to attack the debt straddle transaction, see Rev. Rul. 2000-12, 2000-1 CB 744; Sheppard, "Corporate Tax Shelter Disclosure: But Will It Work?" 86 Tax Notes 1337 (Mar. 6, 2000).

¶ 4.41 ORIGINAL ISSUE DISCOUNT OBLIGATIONS ISSUED FOR CASH

[2] Computation of Original Issue Discount

[b] Stated Redemption Price at Maturity

Page 4-98:

Add to note 361.

Sheppard, "Can Corporate Issuers Dial Up an Overstated Interest Deduction?" 86 Tax Notes 587 (Jan. 31, 2000).

¶ 4.42 ORIGINAL ISSUE DISCOUNT OBLIGATIONS ISSUED FOR PROPERTY

[9] Debt-For-Debt Exchanges ("Premium" and "Discount")

Page 4-109:

In note 388, change ¶¶ 4.42[2] and 4.42[3] *to* ¶¶ 4.42[2][c].

In note 390, change ¶ 4.60 *to* ¶ 4.62.

In note 391, change ¶ 4.42[2] *to* ¶ 4.42[2][c].

D CONVERTIBLE DEBT AND OTHER EQUITY-FLAVORED SECURITIES

¶ 4.60 CONVERTIBLE DEBT: PREMIUM AND DISCOUNT ON ISSUE AND RETIREMENT

[1] Introductory

Page 4-115:

Add after first sentence of note 404.

For comment on contingent convertible debt, see Sheppard, "Cutting Off Excess Interest Accrual on Contingent Convertible Debt," 93 Tax Notes 737 (Nov. 5, 2001). Dixon, "Do Contingent Interest Convertible Debt Instruments Work as Advertised? Probably Not," 15 J. Tax'n Fin. Insts. 5 (Jan./Feb. 2002). But IRS accepted the hoped for tax treatment in Rev. Rul. 2002-31, 2002-22 IRB 1023

Add text to end of first paragraph.

Recent interest has focused on a hybrid version of these securities, contingent convertible debt.[405.1]

[405.1] These securities were approved by IRS in Rev. Rul. 2002-31, 2002-22 IRB 1023, and Notice 2002-36, 2002-22 IRB 1029. For comments on the Ruling and Notice, see Willens, "Viewpoint," Daily Tax Rep. (BNA) No. 89, at J-1 (May 5, 2002); Sheppard, 95 Tax Notes 961 (May 3, 2002); Kleinbard et al., "Contingent Interest Convertible Bonds and the Economic Accrual Regime," 95 Tax Notes 1949 (June 24, 2002); Trier & Farr,

"Rev. Rul. 2002-31 and the Taxation of Contingent Convertibles," Part 1, 95 Tax Notes 1963 (June 24, 2002); Part 2, 96 Tax Notes 105 (July 1, 2002); Hariton, "Conventional and Contingent Convertibles: Double or Nothing," 96 Tax Notes 123 (July 1, 2002).

Add to note 406.

As to contingent convertible debt, see Sheppard and Dixon, supra note 404; also Rev. Rul. 2002-31, 2002-22 IRB 1023; Notice 2002-36, 2002-22 IRB 1029, supra note 405.1.

[2] Issue for Cash

Page 4-117:

Add to note 413.

See also Sheppard, 93 Tax Notes 737 (Nov. 5, 2001), and Dixon, J. Tax'n Fin. Insts. 5 (Jan./Feb. 2002), discussing contingent convertible debt. But see Rev. Rul. 2002-31, 2002-22 IRB 1023; Notice 2002-36, 2002-22 IRB 1029, supra note 405.1.

[3] Retirement for Cash

Page 4-117:

Add to end of note 415.

As to contingent convertible debt, see Sheppard, 93 Tax Notes 737 (Nov. 5, 2001), and Dixon, 15 J. Tax'n Fin. Insts. 5 (Jan./Feb. 2002). But see Rev. Rul. 2002-31, 2002-22 IRB 1023; Notice 2002-36, 2002-22 IRB 1029.

¶ 4.61 CONVERTIBLE AND EXCHANGEABLE DEBT: EXERCISE OF PRIVILEGE TO CONVERT OR EXCHANGE

Page 4-121:

Add to note 429.

For tax issues created by contingent convertible debt, see Sheppard, 93 Tax Notes 737 (Nov. 5, 2001); Dixon, 15 J. Tax'n Fin. Insts. 5 (Jan. Feb. 2002). But see Rev. Rul. 2002-31, 2002-22 IRB 1023; Notice 2002-36, 2002-22 IRB 1029, supra note 405.1.

¶ 4.62 STOCK PURCHASE RIGHTS

[1] In General

Page 4-123:

Add to note 440.

Stevens, "The Tax Treatment of Contingent Options," 102 Tax Notes 525 (Jan. 26, 2004).

[3] Investment Units

Page 4-124:

Add to note 443 at the end of the first paragraph.

See, e.g., Custom Chrome, Inc. v. CIR, 217 F3d 1117 (9th Cir. 2000).

[4] Taxable Acquisition of Property for Warrants

Page 4-125:

Add to note 446.

Rizzi, "Limited Options Received in a Reorganization," 28 J. Corp. Tax'n 26 (Jan. 2001).

Page 4-126:

Add to note 450.

Adopted on May 16, 2000, by TD 8883 as Regs. § 1.1032-3(e).

[5] Issue of Warrants in Tax-Free Reorganizations

Add to note 452.

Rizzi, "Limited Options Received in a Reorganization," 28 J. Corp. Tax'n 26 (Jan. 2001).

Page 4-127:

Add to note 453.

Adopted on May 16, 2000, by TD 8883 as Regs. § 1.1032-3(e).

CHAPTER 5

The Corporation Income Tax

¶ 5.03 CORPORATE DEDUCTIONS

[10] Deduction Relating to Income Attributable to Domestic Production Activities: § 199

Page 5-22:

Add to note 76.

2006 legislation limits the wage base to wages paid to workers on the domestic production activity. Extensive regulation on the new wage limitation were proposed in October 2006.

Add to note 77.

Final regulations under § 199 were adopted by TD 9263 on May 24, 2006 (effective June 1, 2006; and for calendar year taxpayers, 2007).

¶ 5.05 DIVIDENDS-RECEIVED DEDUCTION AND RELATED PROBLEMS

[8] Basis Reduction for Extraordinary Dividends: § 1059

Page 5-59:

Add to note 220, second paragraph.

But Prop. Regs. § 1.302-5 were withdrawn for further study on April 19, 2006 (Ann. 2006-30, 2006-19 IRB 879).

¶ 5.10 CORPORATE TAX SHELTERS

[5] Targeted Anti-Abuse Proposals

[c] Offshore § 302 Basis Shifts: Seagram-DuPont Abroad

Page 5-105:

Add to note 434.

But Prop. Reg. § 1.302-5 was withdrawn for further study on April 19, 2006 (Ann. 2006-30, 2006-19 IRB 879).

Page 5-106:

Add to note 435.

But these proposals were withdrawn on April 19, 2006.

[d] Section 357 Basis Step-Up

Add to note 437, second paragraph.

Citation to *Black & Decker* is 436 F3d 431; see comments by Lipton, 104 J. Tax'n 200 (Apr. 2006), and Burke, 111 Tax Notes 315 (Apr. 17, 2006). *Coltec* was also reversed on appeal by the Fed. Cir. on July 12, 2006, 454 F3d 1340, 2006-2 USTC 850, 389; cert. denied (Feb. 20, 2007).

[6] Subsequent Developments: Treasury White Paper and Joint Committee Staff Study

[e] Case Law Developments: Post–*ACM Partnership* Decisions ("Old Wine in New Bottles")

Page 5-115:

Add to note 478, second paragraph after first sentence.

But *Castle Harbour* was reversed by the Second Circuit on August 3, 2006, 459 F3d 220, 2006-2 USTC ¶ 50,442 (2d Cir 2006) (not a valid partnership); Sheppard, "The Broad Reach of the Castle Harbour Decision," 112 Tax Notes 559 (Aug. 14, 2006).

Page 5-116:

Add to third paragraph of note 478.

Also a big win in the *Castle Harbour* reversal, supra note 478; and another in *Coltec* reversal, infra note 479.

Add to note 479, first paragraph.

But *Coltec* was reversed on appeal, 454 F3d 1340, 2006-2 USTC ¶ 50,383 (Fed. Cir, 2006); cert. denied (Feb. 20, 2007) (held no economic substance); moreover, *Castle Harbour* also was reversed by the Second Circuit on August 3, 2006, 2006-2 USTC ¶ 50,442 (not a valid partnership). For comments on *Coltec*, see Sheppard, 112 Tax Notes 325 (July 24, 2006) (thought opinion was wrong); and Prusieck: 112 Tax Notes 707 (Aug. 21, 2006); see also Lipton, 105 J. Tax'n 136 (Sept. 2006). For comment on *Castle Harbour*, see Sheppard, supra note 478. *Coltec* applied for certiorari, November 8, 2006.

Page 5-118:

Add to note 483, second paragraph.

Citation to *Dow Chemical Co.* is 435 F3d 594. Lipton, What Will Be the Long-Term Impact of the Sixth Circuit: Divided Decision in *Dow Chemical*? 104 J. Tax'n 322 (June 2006); cert. denied (Feb. 20, 2007).

Add to note 484, second paragraph.

, 435 F3d 594. See Keinan, "The COLI Cases Through the Looking Glass of the Sham Transaction Doctrine," 111 Tax Notes 327 (Apr. 17, 2006); Lipton, supra note 483; cert. applied for October 4, 2006. Keinan, "It Is Time for the Supreme Court to Voice Its Opinion on Economic Substance," 84 Taxes 27 (Dec. 2006).

Page 5-119:

Add to note 487.

But *Coltec* was reversed, 454 F3d 1340, 2006-2 USTC   50,289 (Fed. Cir. 2006); cert. denied (Feb. 20, 2007). For comment, see Sheppard, 112 Tax Notes 325 (July 24, 2006); contra is Prusiecki, 112 Tax Notes 524 (Aug. 7, 2006), and 112 Tax Notes 707 (Aug. 21, 2006). See also Lipton, 105 J. Tax'n 136 (Sept. 2006).

Page 5-120:

Add to note 488, second paragraph.

But *Castle Harbour* was reversed by the Second Circuit on August 3, 2006, 2006-2 USTC   50,442 (held not a valid partnership); comment by Sheppard, 112 Tax Notes 559 (Aug. 14, 2006). See generally Frazer, "Absurdist Humor and the Form – Substance Dialogue in Tax Law," 112 Tax Notes 707 (Aug. 21, 2006).

[8] Anti-Shelter Legislation

[e] IRS Shelter Guidance Under the 2004 Jobs Act

Page 5-144:

Add to note 583.

, and NYSB Tax Section, "Application of the Material Advisor Rules to Law and Accounting Firms," 111 Notes 929 (May 22, 2006).

Page 5-145:

Add to note 590.

See NYSB Tax Section, Application of the Material Adviser Rules..., supra note 583; Rev. Proc. 2006-48, 2006-47 IRB 934 (adequate disclosure to escape penalty; update of Rev. Proc. 2005-75).

Add to text at end of ¶ 5.10[8][e].

On November 1, 2006, the IRS released a new package of proposed regulations under §§ 6011 (reportable transactions by taxpayers), 6111 (reportable transactions by material advisers), and 6112 (investor list maintenance by material advisers).[591] These proposals update the tax shelter disclosure regulations issued in 2003[592] by incorporating the provisions of the 2004 Jobs Act and the interim guidance issued under those provisions. No fundamental shift has occurred here, but several significant changes include the following:

> 1. A new category of reportable transaction has been added to the list, "transactions of interest" to the IRS (to be identified in published

---

[591] Prop. Regs. §§ 1.6011-4 (taxpayer disclosure), 301.6111-3 (material adviser disclosure), and 301.6112-1 (investor lists).

[592] Supra   5.10[7][b].

guidance) where IRS believes there is a "potential" for tax avoidance, but needs more information to decide whether or not, to list it;[593]

2. But dropped from the filter list are book-tax differences;[594]

3. But leasing transactions are no longer to be excluded from reporting per se, although IRS believes that most customary commercial transactions will not be subject to disclosure; and

4. Transactions resulting in claimed foreign tax credits are excluded from the brief holding period rules (since foreign tax credits already are subject to a brief holding period limitation).

In other modifications, the material adviser disclosure rules were tightened, and the investor list rules will demand considerable specificity in order to meet the list maintenance rules of § 6112.[595] IRS also noted that it is concerned over the patenting of tax transactions (and may add such items to the list of reportable transactions).

The proposals generally are effective on final promulgation but warn that they will relate back to transactions effected on or after November 2, 2006.[595]

---

[593] Thus, IRS wants to look before it lists any such transaction. This provision is effective for transactions entered into on or after November 2, 2006.

[594] IRS reasoned that Schedule M-3 disclosures are enough.

[595] IRS is not happy with the "lists" it has been receiving; under the new regulations, defective lists will be ignored.

[595] For analysis, see Liptor & Walton, "Treasury Improves the Disclosure Regime by Issuing New Temporary and Proposed Regulations," 106 J. Tax'n 4 (Jan. 2007).

CHAPTER 6

Corporate Elections Under Subchapter S

¶ 6.01 INTRODUCTORY

[1] History and Purpose

Page 6-4:

Add to text at end of ¶ 6.01[1].

Treasury's proposal to exempt dividends paid by C corporations from previously taxed income[3.1] would likewise create a single tax regime, but at the corporate level rather than the shareholder level (as is the case with S corporations). But the proposal would go a long way to neutralizing one of the key advantages of the S election, viz., avoiding the classic two-tier tax regime which has historically existed under subchapter C. Thus, the S corporation

---

[3.1] See ¶ 1.08[4], ¶ 8.06. A watered-down version of this proposal passed the Senate in S. 1054 on May 15, 2003 (but sunsets in 2007). Even this version did not survive in the final legislation.

rules (though not repealed by the dividend exclusion proposal) would no longer enjoy the significant advantage that current law affords.

The Ways and Means Chair Thomas's alternative dividend relief proposal, taxing dividends at the same rates as capital gains, would not go all the way toward creating a single-tier tax regime, but it would go a long way toward that goal and would also reduce the tax advantage of S corporations under current law.[3.2] This was the proposal that ultimately prevailed in the final 2003 tax legislation.[3.3]

[3.2] See supra 1.08[4], infra 8.06. This proposal passed the House in HR 2, on May 9, 2003.

[3.3] Passed on May 28, 2003 (effective for all of 2003); § 1(h)(11), infra 8.06.

[2] Summary

Page 6-5:

In the second paragraph of note 4 change 3d ed. 1993 *to* 4th ed. 2001.

Page 6-7:

Add new ¶ 6.01[2][f] after ¶ 6.01[2][e].

[f] Additional Reform Proposals

Efforts to further reform and refine Subchapter S continue to be urged, ranging from additional liberalizations to outright repeal and replacement with a new pass-through regime.[8.1] The 2004 Jobs Act adopted some, but not much, of this liberalization agenda, however.[8.2]

[8.1] See August, "Reform or Replace Subchapter S "Small Steps Versus Radical Action," 6 Bus. Ents. (July 2004).

[8.2] E.g., increasing the number of shareholders to 100 and expanding the single shareholder pool, infra 6.02[1].

¶ 6.02 ELIGIBILITY TO ELECT UNDER SUBCHAPTER S

[1] Number of Shareholders

Page 6-7:

Add to the beginning of note 9.

The 2004 Jobs Act § 232, increased the number of shareholders to 100.

Add to note 10.

But see § 1361(c)(1) (family members treated as one shareholder); expanded again by the Jobs Act § 231 (effective 2005).

[2] Types of Shareholders

Page 6-9:

Add to end of first paragraph of note 18.

Final regulations on ESBTs were promulgated by TD 8994 on May 14, 2002, Regs. § 1.1361-1(m). See August, Huffaker & Agran, "Clarifications Made by ESBT Final Regulations Demonstrate the Need for More Statutory Changes," 97 J. Tax'n 69 (Aug. 2002).

Page 6-10:

Add to note 19.

Regs. § 1.1361-1(m) (May 14, 2002) (ESBT final regulations); see August et al., supra note 18.

Add to note 21.

As to the treatment of tax-exempt shareholders, § 512(e)(1) makes the stock a UBIT interest and all pass through items are subject to tax; § 512(e)(2) also requires all dividends to reduce stock basis. See Eustice & Kuntz, ¶ 7.13.

[6] Subsidiaries of S Corporations: 1996 Legislation

Page 6-14:

Insert the following text at the end of sentence preceding reference to note 47.

, and adopted on January 20, 2000.

Add to note 47.

TD 8869, January 20, 2000, adopted final Regs. §§ 1.1361-2 through 1.1361-6 without significant changes (effective on and after January 20, 2000; but can be elected for 2000).

Add to note 48.

The final regulations retained the deemed liquidation general timing rule in § 1.1361-4(b)(1), but added a new rule in § 1.1361-4(b)(2) for tiered subsidiaries (parent can specify order, otherwise liquidations flow bottom-up on same day). Prop. Regs. § 1.1361-4(b)(3) would add a new rule for acquired S corporations that prevents a one-day C taxable year gap; and Regs. § 1.1361-4(b)(4) adopted the § 338 coordination rule of Prop. Regs. § 1.1361-4(b)(3). See also Rev. Rul. 2004-85, 2004-33 IRB 189 (July 16, 2004) (acquisition of an S corporation and its Q-Sub by an eligible S corporation in a Type F reorganization does not terminate the Q-Sub election, which carries over under § 381 to acquiror; if acquisition is not a Type F, however, Q-Sub status terminates, but if acquiror makes Q-Sub election, the deemed 351-deemed 332 transactions are avoided and no one-day "gap" appears; but if no Q-sub election is made by acquiror, deemed 351 triggers the five-year wait in order to elect S corporation or Q-sub status).

Page 6-15:

Add to note 49.

The final regulations added new timing rules for tiered subsidiaries in §§ 1.1361-5(b)(1)(ii) and 1.1361-5(b)(3), Ex. 6 (deemed formations flow top-down on the same day). Five additional examples were added to Regs. § 1.1361-5(b)(3).

Add to note 50 at the end of the first paragraph.

Final Regs. § 1.1361-6 adopted the general effective date of January 20, 2000, but allowed an election to apply the regulations back to January 1, 2000 if all affected parties act consistently.

Add to end of note 50.

For comments on the final regulations, see Rose & Walton, The Final Q Sub Regulations—Treasury Holds Firm, 2 Bus. Enters. No. 2, at 6 (May/June 2000); Looney, "IRS Improves the Final Q Sub Regs—But Insists on Keeping the Step Transaction Doctrine," 93 J. Tax'n 276 (Nov. 2000); Lau & Soltis, "The Choice of Disregarded Entities for S Corporations," 28 J. Corp. Tax'n 13 (Jan. 2001).

Add text to end of first full sentence ending with note 50.

These regulations were adopted in final form on January 20, 2000.

Not all is sunshine here, however; as a result of the regulations' application of step transaction principles to Q-sub terminations, some tax traps have been created for unwary or ill advised taxpayers.[50.1] Moreover, proposed regulations issued in 2004[50.2] provide that a Q-Sub will be a regarded separate entity for certain purposes.[50.3]Regulations were proposed again in October 2005 to "regard" Q-Subs as a taxable entity in the case of employment taxes and certain Federal excise taxes.[50.4]

[50.1] See, e.g., Hamill, "Tax Planning for a Q-Sub Interest Transfer," 79 Taxes 43 (Sept. 2001), for some examples and alternative scenarios.

[50.2] Prop. Regs. §1.1361-4(a)(6).

[50.3] Thus, entity status is regarded for Federal tax liability incurred when it was a separate entity, for taxes of any other entity for which it is liable, and for refunds and credits of Federal tax. These proposals were adopted without change by TD 9183 (Feb. 25, 2005).

[50.4] Prop. Reg. §§ 1.1361-4(a)(7) and 1.1361-4(a)(8) (effective on Jan. 1 following the year of their adoption).

¶ 6.03 MAKING A SUBCHAPTER S ELECTION

Page 6-15:

Add to note 51, first paragraph.

Rev. Proc. 2003-43, 2003-23 IRB 998, supersedes Rev. Proc. 98-55 (but not Rev. Proc. 97-48).

Page 6-17:

Add to note 54, second paragraph.

Rev. Proc. 2004-48, 2004-32 IRB (new simplified method for requesting relief for late S elections). Rev. Proc. 2004-48, 2004-32 IRB 172 (new simplified procedures).

Add to note 55.

Rev. Proc. 2003-43, 2003-23 IRB 998 (simplified procedure for requesting relief for late S elections). Rev. Proc. 2004-48, 2004-32 IRB 172 (new procedures for requesting relief).

Add text to end of ¶ 6.03.

Temporary regulations issued in July 2004[55.1] provide that eligible entities that make a timely valid selection will also be deemed to have elected corporate status (a simplifying procedure to avoid additional paperwork).

[55.1] TD 9139 (July 20, 2004), issuing Regs. § 301.7701-3(c)(1)(v)(C).

¶ 6.04　EVENTS TERMINATING ELECTION

[3] Passive Investment Income

Page 6-19:

Add to note 59.

The proposed regulations were adopted virtually intact by TD 8869 on January 20, 2000 (except that the effective date was accelerated to January 1, 2000, if all affected parties are consistent).

[4] Inadvertent Terminations

Page 6-22:

Add to note 70.

Rev. Proc. 2003-43, 2003-23 IRB 998 (new simplified procedures for requesting relief from late filed elections, ESTB elections, QSST elections and Q-sub elections; also § 1362(f) relief for inadvertently invalid elections and terminations in lieu of private letter ruling process).

Add text to end of ¶ 6.04[4].

The 2004 Jobs Act added § 1362(f) relief for inadvertently invalid Q-Sub elections and terminations.[70.1]

[70.1] American Jobs Creation Act of 2004, § 238 (effective 2005).

[5] Short Taxable Periods

Page 6-23:

Add to note 72.

These proposals were adopted without change as temporary regulations in TD 8858 on January 5, 2000; adopted as final regulations by TD 8940 on February 13, 2001 (effective March 16, 2001).

¶ 6.06 PASS-THROUGH OF CORPORATE INCOME AND LOSSES TO SHAREHOLDERS

[1] Background

Page 6-25:

Add to note 78.

See also Catalano v. CIR, 240 F3d 842 (9th Cir. 2001) (nondeductible lease payments to sole shareholder nevertheless resulted in taxable income to shareholder-lessor).

[2] Taxation of S Corporations

[a] In General: § 1363

Page 6-26:

Add to note 81.

But Tax Court was reversed, St. Charles Inv. Co. v. CIR, 232 F3d 773, 2000-2 USTC 50,840 (10th Cir. 2000) (suspended § 469 losses do carry over from C years and are allowable in S years despite § 1371(b)(1); § 469 carryover rules trump here). Kalinka, "St. Chares Investment Company and the Carryover of PALs From C to S Years," 90 Tax Notes 1849 (Mar. 26, 2001). See also Rev. Rul. 2000-43, 2000-41 IRB 333 (S corporation not allowed to elect § 170(a)(2) accrual treatment because of § 1363(b) rule).

[c] Character Pass-Through; Conduit Treatment

Page 6-27:

Add new note 84.1 to end of first complete sentence.

[84.1] See, e.g., Catalano v. CIR, 240 F3d 842 (9th Cir. 2001) (shareholder leased an "entertainment facility" (a yacht) to his wholly owned corporation; nondeductible rent payments still resulted in taxable rental income to shareholder-lessor despite double income impact).

Change citation in next to last line of text from § 456 to § 465.

[e] Audit Procedures

Page 6-28:

In note 91, change Regs. § 1366-1(f) (1990) *to* Regs. § 1366-1(f) (1999).

[3] Pass-Through of S Corporation's Tax Items to Shareholders

Page 6-29:

Add after first sentence in note 94.

For impact of gross income on § 6501(e)(1) six-year limitations period, see Raby & Raby, "Partnership and the 25 Percent Omission Test for Limitations," 90 Tax Notes 933 (Feb. 12, 2001).

Add to note 95.

See also Gitlitz v. CIR, 182 F3d 1143 (10th Cir. 1999), infra ¶ 6.10[2][b]; the Supreme Court held for the taxpayers, 531 US 206, 121 S. Ct. 701 (2001), 2001-1 USTC ¶ 50,147, reversing the lower courts and allowing the basis step up; as a result of this decision, the regulation most likely is invalid. But *Gitlitz* reversed by legislation enacted on March 9, 2002.

Page 6-30:

Add new note 97.1 to end of second full paragraph.

[97.1] For foreign tax credit computation problems arising from S corporation subsidiaries, see Harwood, "Sourcing S Corporation Shareholder Salaries," 95 Tax Notes 1046 (May 13, 2002).

Add to text at end of ¶ 6.06[3].

If a sole shareholder contributes built-in-loss property to his S corporation (under § 351 or as a capital contribution) an amendment to § 362(e)(2) in the 2004 Jobs Act[97.2] requires the corporation to step down inside asset basis to fair market value unless an election to step-down outside stock basis is made in lieu thereof. Such an election, however, can result in total elimination of the loss, rather than merely preventing its duplication (as was the stated intent of the amendment).[97.3]

[97.2] Am. Jobs Creation Act § 836 (effective Oct. 22, 2004). See ¶ 3.11[8].

[97.3] See infra ¶ 6.06[7], Ex. 6. I am indebted to Professor Daniel Lathrope of Hastings Law School for this insight. Infra ¶ 6.06[7], Ex. 6. Prop. Regs. § 1.362-4 (Oct. 23, 2006), offer no relief from this result (yet).

[4] Adjustments to Basis of Shareholder's Investment in S Corporation's Stock and Debt

[a] Stock

Page 6-31:

Add to note 100.

For § 170 contributions of capital gain property stock basis is reduced by fair market value of contributed property, but proposed legislation would only reduce stock basis by adjusted basis of the property (in conformity to the partnership rule, Rev. Rul. 96-11, 1996-1 CB 140) infra note 105.1.

Page 6-32:

Add text to end of ¶ 6.06[4][a].

Proposed legislation (Senate Finance Committee's charity bill) would amend § 1367 to reduce stock basis only by the adjusted basis of appreciated property contributed to charity under § 170 (in conformity with the rule for partnership § 170 contributions of property).[105.1] This proposal was not adopted in the 2004 Jobs Act, however, but was finally adopted in the 2006 pension legislation[105.2]

[105.1] HR 7, § 107, CARE Act of 2002 (effective in 2003). For the partnership rule, see Rev. Rul. 96-11, 1996-1 CB 140.

[105.2] Adopted on August 17, 2006 (effective for 2006 and 2007).

[b] Debt

Page 6-33:

Add to note 107 at the end of the first paragraph.

Maloof v. CIR, 456 F3d 645, 2002-6 USTC   50,443 (6th Cir. 2006) (no basis where taxpayer mere co-obligor and guarantor on bank loan; no economic outlay here; followed numerous cases that so held). Grojean v. CIR, 248 F3d 572 (7th Cir. 2001) (shareholder's participation interest in a bank loan to the corporation held in substance to be a mere guaranty that did not augment debt basis). For comment, see Lipman, "Never-ending Limitations on S Corporation Losses: The Slippery Slope of S Corporation Debt Guarantees," 80 Taxes 29 (June 2002). But Timothy J. Miller, RIA TC Memo   2006-125 (2006) (taxpayer got basis here as in *Bolding*; restructure effective to create basis in debt because taxpayer had personal liability to outside lender and then reloaned procedes to S Corporation).

Add to end of note 107.

Fellows & Yuhas, "Tax Basis and Shareholder Guarantees of S Corporation Debt: The Economic Outlay Doctrine Revisited," 78 Taxes 17 (Nov. 2000); Lipman, "S Corporation Loss Limitation: The Tax Court Provides Potential Hope for Related-Party Debt Restructurings," 22 Va. Tax Rev. 67 (2002); Rabe and Rabe, Shareholder Loans and Basis in S Corporations, 107 Tax Notes 465 (Apr. 25, 2005); Willens, "When Can a Shareholder Deduct an S Corporation's Losses," Daily Tax Rep. (BNA) No. 137, at J-1 (July 18, 2006).

[c] Outside Basis Limitation on Amount of Pass-Through

Page 6-35:

Add to first paragraph of note 111.

Lipman, "S Corporation Loss Limitation: The Tax Court Provides Potential Hope for Re-lated-Party Debt Restructurings," 22 Va. Tax Rev. 67 (2002). Oren v. CIR, 357 F3d 854 (8th Cir. 2003) (purported back-to-back loans to and by a corporation and its controlling shareholder held to be shams and thus did not provide an outside investment basis step-up). But compare Timothy J. Miller, RIA TC Memo. ¶ 2006-125 (2006) (basis created here where taxpayer borrowed from independent lender and reloaned to his S corpora-tion); see cases supra note 107.

[5] Distributions to Shareholders

Page 6-35:

Add to note 113.

Raby & Raby, "When Is Compensation Too Low?" 86 Tax Notes 1255 (Feb. 28, 2000); Raby & Raby, "Attempting to Avoid FICA and Self-Employment Tax," 93 Tax Notes 803 (Nov. 5, 2001) (comment on Veterinary Servs. Corp., PC, 117 TC 141 (2001). Veterinary Surgical Consultants, P.C., 117 TC 141 (2001), aff'd, 54 Fed. Appx. 100, 2003-1 USTC ¶ 50,141 (3d Cir. 2002).

    Six Tax Court decisions (all by Judge Cohen) all found "employee" compensation status subject to FICA/FUTA withholding: Veterinary Surgical Consultants, P.C., RIA TC Memo. ¶ 2003-048; Mike Graham Trucking, Inc., RIA TC Memo. ¶ 2003-049; Superior Proside Inc., RIA TC Memo. ¶ 2003-050; Specialty Transport, Inc., RIA TC Memo. ¶ 2003-051; Nu-Look Design, Inc., RIA TC Memo. ¶ 2003-052; and Water-Pure Sys., Inc., RIA TC Memo. ¶ 2003-053.

    See also Carlisle, "Edwards' S Corporation Not a Tax Shelter," 104 Tax Notes 365 (July 26, 2004); for a different view, see Dellinger, 104 Tax Notes 1092 (Sept. 6, 2004). Daley, "Edward's S Corporation: Medicare Tax and Fair Share," 104 Tax Notes 1577 (Sept. 27, 2004).

[7] Examples

Page 6-37:

Add new Example 6.

> **EXAMPLE 6:** (Incorporation of built-in loss asset). *A* transfers property with a basis of 200 and a value of $120 to wholly owned *X*. *X* must step down the asset basis to $120 under § 362(e)(2) unless *A* and *X* elect to step-down stock basis in lieu thereof. But if *X* sells the asset for $120, the $80 loss passes through to *A* and also steps down stock basis (to $40) leaving *A* with a potential gain of $80 in his stock. It is unlikely that the 2004 Jobs Act intended this result.[117.1]

[117.1] Supra note 97.2. Similar loss "elimination" effect, can occur in a consolidated re-turn context, infra ¶ 13.40. Prop. Regs. § 1.362-4 offer no relief from this result so far.

¶ 6.07 CORPORATE-LEVEL TAXES ON BUILT-IN GAINS AND EXCESS NET PASSIVE INVESTMENT INCOME

[1] Tax on Built-In Gains

Page 6-38:

In note 120, change 17.06[4][j] *to* 17.06[4][k].

Page 6-39:

In the second sentence of Example delete the word all.

Page 6-41:

Add to note 134.

But Prop. Regs. §§ 1.1374-3(b) and 1.1374-3(c), Exs. 2, 3 and 4 (June 25, 2004) would fix the potential for NUBIG duplication under the current regulations (prospectively when Regs. are final); adopted as final regulations by TD 9180 (Feb. 25, 2005).

Add to note 136.

But *St. Charles* was reversed, 232 F3d 773, 2000-2 USTC ¶ 50,840 (10th Cir. 2000) (suspended § 469 losses do carry over from C-years to S-years; § 469 carryover rules trump § 1371(b)(1) rule). See Kalinka, supra note 81.

Add to note 139.

Silverman, "S Corporation Issues That Need Immediate Attention," 96 Tax Notes 739 (July 29, 2002) (interaction of §§ 1374, 332 and 337). But see proposed (and now final) regulations, supra note 134, which respond to this NUBIG duplication problem.

Add text to end of ¶ 6.07[1].

Nor does § 1374 apply to the normal operating income of the corporation,[140.1] including, according to a recent IRS ruling, income subject to "special" capital gain treatment by § 631.[140.2]

[140.1] See, e.g., Regs. § 1.1374-4(a)(3), Ex. 1; Rev. Rul. 2001-50, 2001-43 IRB 343.

[140.2] Rev. Rul. 2001-50, supra; moreover, these transactions were removed from the no ruling list by Rev. Proc. 2001-51, 2001-43 IRB 369.

[3] Recapture of Last-In, First-Out Inventory

Page 6-42:

Add to note 144.

See, e.g., Coggin Automotive Corp., 115 TC 349 (2000) (§ 1363(d) recapture trig-gered on taxpayer's conversion from C to S status even though assets held in a partner-ship); Raby & Raby,"Avoiding LIFO Recapture on S Corporation Elections," 93 Tax Notes 667 (Oct. 29, 2001). But *Coggin* was reversed in 292 F3d 1326, 2002-1 USTC ¶ 50,448 (11th Cir. 2002) (§ 1363(d) not applicable where corporation did not directly hold LIFO assets; plain meaning of statute controlled, citing *Gitlitz*; strong opinion for taxpayers here).

Add text to end of ¶ 6.07[3].

Despite its defeat in the *Coggin Auto* case, IRS has proposed new regulations on August 12, 2004,[144.1] that require recapture of indirectly owned LIFO prop-erty on the conversion from C to S status; adopted as final regulations by TD 9210 (July 12, 2005, but effective August 13, 2004).

[144.1] Prop. Regs. § 1.1362-2(b)-(g) (effective for transfers on or after Aug. 13, 2004); and these proposals were adopted in July of 2005by TD 9210 (effective Aug. 13, 2004). See LaRue, "LIFO Recapture on C-to-S Conversions," 59 Tax Law. 1 (Fall 2005).

¶ 6.08 TAXATION OF DISTRIBUTIONS

[3] S Corporations with Accumulated Earnings and Profits

[a] Tier 1

Page 6-48:

Add to note 166.

Silverman, "S Corp. Issues That Need Immediate Attention," 96 Tax Notes 739 (July 29, 2002) (AMT and AAA problem).

¶ 6.09 SUBCHAPTER C COORDINATION FOR ACQUISITIONS INVOLVING S CORPORATIONS (AND RELATED PROBLEMS)

[1] In General

Page 6-50:

In third line of first full paragraph change seventy-five *to* one hundred.

[2] Acquisitions by S Corporations

Page 6-51:

In fifth line of first paragraph change seventy-five *to* one hundred.

[3] Acquisitions of S Corporations

[a] Status Termination Aspects

Page 6-53:

Add text to end of ¶ 6.09[3][a].

In a recent ruling[191.1] IRS considered the termination of Q-Sub status when an eligible S corporation acquires an S corporation and its Q-Sub: in the first scenario, the acquisition was pursuant to a Type F reorganization and the ruling held that the Q-Sub election did not terminate because the election status carried over to the acquiror under § 381. In the second case, the Q-Sub election did terminate because the acquisition was not a Type F; but if the acquiror made an immediate Q-Sub election, the deemed § 351 drop-down and deemed § 332 liquidation transactions are ignored (and no "gap" period results; but if no Q-sub election is made, the deemed § 351 drop-down triggers the five-year waiting period before the S status (or Q-Sub status) can be elected).

[191.1] Rev. Rul. 2004-85, 2004-33 IRB 189 (July 16, 2004). Also Rev. Proc. 2004-49, 2004-33 IRB 189, (provides relief procedures to request a late Q-Sub in case two—where the target S corporation's Q-Sub election terminates).

[b] Corporate-Level Tax Aspects

Page 6-54:

Add to note 194.

For impact of 1999 repeal of § 453 for accrual-method taxpayers, see Notice 2000-26, 2000-17 IRB 954. (But allowance was retroactively reinstated by legislation enacted in December 2000).

Add to note 195.

This rule was moved to Regs. § 1.338-10T(a)(3) by TD 8858 (Jan. 5, 2000); adopted as final Regs. § 1.338-10(a)(3) on February 13, 2001.

Page 6-55:

Add to note 196.

The temporary regulations were adopted without change on February 13, 2001, by TD 8940. See Collins et al., "S Corporations in Section 338(h)(10) Transactions," 1 Bus. Enters. No. 6, at 6 (Nov./Dec. 1999);

Add to note 198.

Final Regs. § 1.1361-3, TD 8869 (Jan. 20, 2000), supra   6.02[6].

Add to note 199.

Final Regs. §§ 1.1361-4(b)(3) and 1.1361-4(d), Ex. 3, adopted by TD 8869 (Jan. 20, 2000); supra   6.02[6].

[4] Divisive Transactions

Page 6-57:

In the second sentence of note 207 replace Prop. Regs. § 1.1368-2(c)(2) *with* Prop. Regs § 1.1366-2(c)(2).

In the second sentence of note 207 replace final Regs. § 1.1368-2(c)(2) *with* final Regs. § 1.1366-2(c)(2).

[5] Liquidations

Page 6-59:

Add to note 216.

The final regulations adopted by TD 8869 on January 20, 2000, are the same.

[6] S Corporations and § 367

In note 218 replace   6.02[3] *with*   6.02[6].

¶ 6.10 FINANCIALLY DISTRESSED S CORPORATIONS

[1] Introductory

[a] Issues and Stakes

Page 6-61:

Add to note 229.

Hall, Widen & Culhane, "Financially Distressed S Corporations," 5 Bus. Ents. 4 (Jan. 2003).

[c] Transactional Patterns

Page 6-62:

In note 233, first sentence, change ¶ 12.30[5] *to* ¶ 12.30[4].

[2] Cancellation of Debt: §§ 108 and 1017 Rules Generally

[b] Insolvency and Bankruptcy Exceptions to Cancellation-of-Debt Income

Page 6-63:

In the last sentence of the first paragraph of note 237 add, "192 F3d 844," *after* "affirmed,".

In the first sentence of the last paragraph in the parenthetical phrase change the cases so far disagree *to* some, but not all, cases disagreed, but the Supreme Court held for the taxpayer on this issue. Congress ultimately overturned that decision, however, on March 9, 2002.

Page 6-64:

Add to note 239 at the end of the third paragraph.

But *Farley* was reversed, Farley v. US, 202 F3d 198 (3d Cir. 2000); and certiorari was granted in *Gitlitz* on May 1, 2000, and the Supreme Court reversed (8 to 1) on January 9, 2001, 531 US 206, 121 S. Ct. 701. Pugh v. CIR, 213 F3d 1324, 2000-1 USTC ¶ 50,514 (11th Cir. 2000) followed *Farley* (holding for the taxpayer and allowing a basis step-up); but Witzel v. CIR, 200 F3d 496 (7th Cir. 2000) followed *Gitlitz*, as did the Sixth Circuit in Guadiano v. CIR, 2000-2 USTC ¶ 50,559 (6th Cir. 2000). For comments, see Raby & Raby, 86 Tax Notes 819 (Feb. 7, 2000); Lipton, 92 J. Tax'n 207 (Apr. 2000); and Briskin, 78 Taxes 38 (May 2000).

Add to note 239 at the end of the fourth paragraph.

All of the five circuits have rejected the tax court decision that exempt COD does not pass through, differing only in the timing of the passthrough. If the Supreme Court reverses *Gitlitz* and follows *Farley*, the regulations may be vulnerable to attack. Why Congress has not intervened here remains a mystery. The Supreme Court did reverse *Gitlitz* (and followed *Farley*) in an 8 to 1 decision issued on January 9, 2001, 531 US 206 121 S. Ct. 701, 2001-1 USTC ¶ 50,147. Regs. § 1.1366-1(a)(2)(viii) likely invalidated as well.

But 2002 legislation in turn reversed the *Gitlitz* decision (and, in effect, revalidated the regulations).

Add to note 240.

Certiorari was granted in *Gitlitz* on May 1, 2000; the Court reversed (8 to 1) and held for the taxpayers, 531 US 206, 121 S. Ct. 701. This decision probably invalidated the 1999 regulations as well (although that issue was not involved in *Gitlitz*. Lipton, "Supreme Court Hands Taxpayers a Victory in *Gitlitz*, but Will Congress Take It Away?" J. Tax'n 133 (Mar. 2001). Yes; the economic stimulus bill which passed in March 2002 overturned the *Gitlitz* decision.

[3] Debt Reduction by a Transfer of Property

[a] Third-Party Transfers: Recourse Versus Nonrecourse Debt

Page 6-69:

In the first full sentence on this page change all courts *to* some, but not all courts (and the Supreme Court finally held for the taxpayers); but Congress then overturned that decision in March 2002.

¶ 6.11 COMPARISON OF C AND S CORPORATIONS AND PARTNERSHIPS

Page 6-79:

Add to note 312 at the end of the first paragraph.

Lee, "Choice of Small Business Tax Entity: Facts and Fictions," 87 Tax Notes 417 (Apr. 17, 2000).

CHAPTER **7**

Penalty Taxes on Undistributed Corporate Income

A   THE ACCUMULATED EARNINGS TAX

¶ 7.01 INTRODUCTORY

Page 7-3:

Add to note 1.

But Treasury's proposal to exempt dividends from shareholder-level taxation would neutralize this incentive and thus render § 531 irrelevant; hence, that proposal would repeal § 531 (as well as § 541, infra Part B).

Add to text at end of second full paragraph.

But Treasury's proposal to eliminate tax on dividends at the shareholder level[3.1] would render both of these provisions irrelevant and thus the proposal would repeal both of them. If enacted, the material in this *Chapter* would become matters of historical interest only. But both the House and Senate versions of the 2003 tax relief legislation[3.2] apparently do not contain such repeals (so hang onto this material). The final legislation did, however, reduce both the § 531 and § 541 rates to 15 percent.[3.3]

[3.1] See   1.08[4], 8.06. The House alternative dividend relief proposal (taxing dividends at the same rates as capital gains) say nothing about the § 531 or § 541 taxes (and presumably would retain both, so don't remove this chapter yet); but see infra note 3.2.

[3.2] The final Senate version, S. 1054, which passed on May 15, 2003, and provided for only a temporary dividend exclusion (from 2003–2006), apparently retained both the § 531 and § 541 tax regimes as well. Final 2003 legislation HR 2, § 302(e)(5) and § 302(e)(6), reduced the § 531 and § 541 tax rates to 15 percent, however, thus materially reducing the impact of the provisions.

[3.3] HR 2, §§ 302(e)(5) and 302(e)(6).

Page 7-5:

Add text to end of runover sentence.

But 2003 legislation reduced the § 531 rate to 15 percent (and also reduced the top individual rate to 35 percent).[14.1]

[14.1] HR 2, § 302(e)(5).

¶ 7.02 THE FORBIDDEN PURPOSE

[5] Relation of Tax-Avoidance Purpose to Reasonable Needs of the Business

Page 7-14:

Add to note 59.

Otto Candies, LLC v. US, 2003-1 USTC ¶ 50,516 (D. La. 2003) (textbook example of how to effectively litigate a § 531 case; easy win for taxpayers; even government's own expert supported the taxpayer).

¶ 7.03 REASONABLE NEEDS OF THE BUSINESS

[1] Introductory; Measuring the Accumulation

Page 7-16:

Add to note 67.

Otto Candies, LLC v. US, 2003-1 USTC ¶ 50,516 (D. La. 2003) (a textbook example of how to present a § 531 case).

[2] Bona Fide Expansion of Business or Replacement of Plant

Page 7-17:

Add to note 74.

For discussion of an early decision under § 531 on this issue, see Roston, "How the Board of Tax Appeals Changed Hollywood History," 55 Tax. Law. 951 (2002) (the Cecil B. de Mille case).

Page 7-18:

Add to note 76.

Otto Candies, LLC v. US, 2003-1 USTC ¶ 50,516 (DC La 2003) (taxpayer's business needs—replacement of its fleet—amply proved here).

¶ 7.04 REASONABLE NEEDS OF THE BUSINESS: ANTICIPATED NEEDS

Page 7-25:

Add to note 114.

See, e.g., Haffner's Serv. Station, Inc. v. CIR, 326 F3d 1, 2003-1 USTC 50,333 (1st Cir. 2003) (failure to meet this test fatal). Otto Candies, LLC v. US, 2003-1 USTC 50,516 (D. La. 2003) (taxpayer amply met this tests; had more than enough business needs to avoid the § 531 tax).

Add to note 116.

Haffner's Serv. Station, Inc. v. CIR, supra note 114 (alleged reasons mere afterthought here).

¶ 7.07 REASONABLE NEEDS OF THE BUSINESS: STOCK REDEMPTIONS

Page 7-31:

Add to note 145.

Otto Candies, LLC v. US, 2003-1 USTC 50,516 (DC La. 2003) (family corporate control preservation an acceptable purpose).

¶ 7.08 PRESUMPTIONS AND BURDEN-OF-PROOF PROBLEMS

[3] Presumption Applicable to Holding and Investment Companies

Page 7-36:

Add to end of note 163.

Advance Delivery & Chem. Sys. Nevada, Inc. TC Memo. 2003-250 (2003) (same).

¶ 7.09 COMPUTATION OF ACCUMULATED EARNINGS TAX

Page 7-36:

Add to note 168.

But 2003 legislation lowered this rate to 15 percent, HR 2, § 302(e)(5).

[1] Adjustments to Taxable Income

Page 7-37:

Add to note 171.

But the Tax Court rejected *Rutter Rex* in Metro Leasing & Development Corp., 119 TC 8 (2002) (reviewed) (contested taxes not accruable here even though paid); aff'd, 376 F3d 1015, 2004-2 USTC ¶ 50,308 (9th Cir. 2004). Indrees, "When Do Tax Deficiencies Accrue? Resolving the Recent Circuit Split Over the Accumulated Earnings Tax," 59 Tax Lawyer 541 (2006) (favors *Rutter* circuit view).

[2] Dividends-Paid Deduction

[a] Dividends Paid During the Taxable Year

Page 7-39:

Add to note 180.

Baneman, "Preferential Dividends in the Regulated Investment Company Context," 111 Tax Notes 49 (Apr. 3, 2006).

B   THE TAX ON PERSONAL HOLDING COMPANIES

¶ 7.20 INTRODUCTORY

Page 7-45:

Add to text at end of ¶ 7.20.

But Treasury's plan to exempt dividends paid from previously taxed corporate income also proposed to repeal the § 541 tax as well as the § 531 tax.[198.1]

[198.1] See supra ¶ 1.08[4]; infra ¶ 8.06. But see supra note 3.2 (both the final House and Senate versions of the 2003 tax bill apparently retain the §§ 531 tax and 541 tax regimes; however, the final 2003 tax bill reduced the §§ 531 and 541 tax rates to 15 percent, supra note 3.2. and 3.3; HR 2, § 302(e)(6).

¶ 7.22 DEFINITION OF "PERSONAL HOLDING COMPANY INCOME"

[2] Rents

Page 7-50:

Add to note 217.

, aff'd per curiam, 2000-2 USTC   50,827 (10th Cir. 2000); see Raby & Raby, "Due Diligence and Potential Personal Holding Companies," 89 Tax Notes 1047 (Nov. 20, 2000).

[7] Personal Service Contracts

Page 7-54:

Add to note 227.

Calypso Music, Inc., RIA TC Memo.   2000-293 (2000).

Page 7-55:

Add to note 229.

Calypso Music, Inc., supra note 227 (taxpayer designated specifically by name so held to be a PHC; but no negligence penalty because taxpayer reasonably relied on return preparer who, though unreliable, was more reliable than the shareholder). Comment by Raby & Raby, "Due Diligence and Potential Personal Holding Companies," 89 Tax Notes 1047 (Nov. 20, 2000).

Page 7-57:

Add to note 229.

But 2003 legislation lowered the § 541 rate to 15 percent (effective for 2003), HR 2, § 302(e)(6).

¶ 7.24 COMPUTATION OF PERSONAL HOLDING COMPANY TAX

[4] Planning to Avoid the Personal Holding Company Tax

Page 7-61:

Add to text at end of ¶ 7.27[4].

But if Treasury's proposal to eliminate taxation of dividends is adopted together with repeal of § 541, these (and other) planning ploys will follow the PHC tax into history.[251] The final 2003 tax bill reduced the § 541 to 15 percent, thereby greatly reducing, though not eliminating, the potential tax exposure for PHCs.

---

[251] But see supra note 3.2 (both House and Senate versions of the 2003 tax bill apparently retain the PHC tax regime), but the final legislation reduce the § 541 rate to 15 percent, a far less painful penalty.

CHAPTER 8

Dividends and Other Nonliquidating Distributions

¶ 8.00 OVERVIEW

Page 8-6:

Add text to end of ¶ 8.00.

Treasury's proposal[11.1] to allow a 100 percent exclusion for all shareholders (individual and corporate) who receive "qualified dividends" (generally dividends paid from previously taxed corporate income (the EDA)) as well as a stock-basis step-up for retained previously taxed income would have a profound effect on the above matters considered in this chapter (and in other related chapters as well).[11.2] Passage, however, was far from certain (and it ultimately foundered).

An alternative proposal released on May 1, 2003, by Ways and Means Chair Thomas would tax dividends at the same rates as capital gains (and also lower the latter rate to 15 percent).[11.3] This proposal is far simpler than Treasury's exclusion proposal, but would likewise have a profound effect on this, and other, Chapters as well. This was the proposal adopted in the final 2003 legislation.

[11.1] See infra   8.06; for comments, see supra   1.08[4], notes 198, 199.

[11.2] See, e.g., Chapters 5, 6, 7, 9, 11, 12 and 15.

[11.3] This proposal passed the House, HR 2, on May 9, 2003. The Senate adopted a temporary dividend exclusion rule (from 2003–2007) in S. 1054 on May 15, 2003. The Senate bill did not adopt Treasury's stock basis step-up for accumulated earnings, however, nor did it require corporate-level tax payments (thus, the Senate bill also was far simpler than the Treasury's dividend relief proposal). The House version prevailed in the final legislation, infra   8.06[2]; HR 2, § 302(a), adding § 1(h)(11).

A   PROPERTY DISTRIBUTIONS GENERALLY; DISTRIBUTIONS OF CASH

¶ 8.03 EARNINGS AND PROFITS

[2] Definition and Basic Approach

Page 8-22:

Add to note 78.

See also Regs. §§ 1.56(g)-1(c), 1.56(g)-1(d), and 1.56(g)-1(f) (the "adjusted current earnings" (ACE) preference rules under the AMT,   5.08[5], which regulations provide substantial guidance on what is, and what is not, included in "earnings and profits" (E&P)).

[3] Certain Items Excluded From Taxable Income Must Be Included in Computing Earnings and Profits

Page 8-23:

Add to note 82.

See also Regs. §§ 1.56(g)-1(c) (inclusion in ACE E&P) and 1.56(g)-1(d) (nondeductible items for ACE E&P).

[4] Certain Items Deducted in Computing Taxable Income May Not Be Deducted in Computing Earnings and Profits

Page 8-26:

Add to note 97.

See also Regs. § 1.56(g)-1(d) (nondeductible items for ACE E&P).

[6] Certain Items Not Deducted in Computing Taxable Income May Be Deducted in Computing Earnings and Profits

Page 8-29:

Add to note 111.

See also Regs. §§ 1.56(g)-1(c)(3) and 1.56(g)-1(d).

¶ 8.04 TAX-ACCOUNTING PRINCIPLES IN COMPUTING EARNINGS AND PROFITS AND DIVIDEND INCOME

[1] Accounting for Earnings and Profits

Page 8-34:

In second sentence of note 140, replace "Rev. Rul. 79-47" *with* "Rev. Proc. 79-47".

¶ 8.05 CONSTRUCTIVE DISTRIBUTIONS

[1] In General

Page 8-41:

Add text to end of ¶ 8.05[1].

But Treasury's proposal of February 2003 to allow a 100 percent-share-holder-level exclusion for dividends paid from previously taxed corporate income (and a stock-basis step-up for retained earnings) would have a major impact on the tax stakes and planning techniques considered in this paragraph. While this proposal failed to pass, the 2003 legislation reduced the top rate on dividends to 15 percent (the same as capital gain), and this too will have a significant impact on matters dealt with below.[175.1]

[175.1] HR 2, § 302(a), adding § 1(h)(11) (effective in 2003); infra   8.06[2].

[2] Tax Issues and Stakes

Page 8-42:

Add text to end of ¶ 8.05[2].

But Treasury's proposal to allow a 100-percent shareholder-level exclusion for dividends paid from previously taxed corporate income (and a stock-basis step-up for retained earnings) would have profound impact on the matters considered subsequently.[180.1] Certainly the tax downside will be largely eliminated, and in many cases a role reversal could arise (since dividends would be "good news" rather then the bad news that generally resulted under current law). While Treasury's version did not prevail in the final legislation (which lowered the top tax rate on dividends 15 percent, the same as capital gain),[180.2] this outcome likewise will have a major impact on the status of dividends (actual and constructive) under the new regime.

[180.1] See Infra   8.06. Ways and Means Chair Thomas's proposal to tax dividends at the same rate as capital gain also will significantly reduce the largely negative effects of dividend treatment that exist under current law. The Senate adopted a temporary version of Treasury's dividend exclusion proposal (for 2003–2006) in S. 1054, which passed on May 15, 2003; the House proposal passed on May 9, 2003, and that was the version that prevailed in the final legislation.

[180.2] HR 2, § 302(a), adding § 1(h)(11) (effective in 2003), infra   8.06[2].

[3] Excessive Salaries Paid to Shareholders or Their Relatives

Page 8-44:

Add to note 185.

Certiorari was denied in the *OCS Assoc.* case, May 1, 2000. See also Labelgraphics, Inc. v. CIR, 2000-2 USTC   50,648 (9th Cir. 2000).

Add to note 188.

E.g., Haffner's Serv. Stations, Inc. v. CIR, 326 F3d 1, 2003-1 USTC ¶ 50,333 (1st Cir. 2003) (bonuses found unreasonable and corporate § 162 deduction denied). Comment by Zelinsky, "Is Martha Stewart Overcompensated?," 99 Tax Notes 919 (May 12, 2003).

Add to note 189.

Neonatology Assocs. v. CIR, 299 F3d 221 (3d Cir. 2002) (charging excessively inflated premiums on life insurance policies for benefit of shareholder-employees of medical corporation held nondeductible constructive dividend; penalty imposed as well – taxpayers should have known deal too good to be true).

Page 8-45:

In note 190, replace Exacto Spring Corp., __ F3d __ *with* Exacto Spring Corp., 196 F3d 833.

Add the following after the second sentence of note 190.

See Raby & Raby, "Independent Investor Test for Reasonableness of Compensation," 86 Tax Notes 975 (Feb. 14, 2000). Compare Labelgraphics, Inc. v. CIR, 221 F3d 1091, 2000-2 USTC ¶ 50,648 (9th Cir. 2000) (factor analysis and taxpayer lost). Also see Eberl's Claim Serv. v. CIR, 249 F3d 994 (10th Cir. 2001) (found excessive compensation and constructive dividend; used multi-factor analysis and did not follow *Exacto Spring*); for trenchant comment on these decisions, see Zelinsky, "Eberl's Independent Investors and the Incoherence of the Reasonable Compensation Rule," 92 Tax Notes 555 (July 23, 2001); Raby & Raby, "Attempting to Avoid FICA and Self-Employment Tax," 93 Tax Notes 803 (Nov. 5, 2001) (commenting on Veterinary Servs. Corp., PC, 117 TC 141 (2001) case). Metro Leasing Corp. v. CIR, 376 F3d 1015, 2004-2 USTC ¶ 50,308 (9th Cir. 2004).

[4] Bargain Purchases or Rentals of Corporate Property by Shareholders

Add to note 192.

More currently, see Framatome Connectors USA, Inc., 118 TC 32 (2002) (various bargain transfers of assets to shareholder resulted in constructive dividends).

[6] Corporate Advances to Shareholders

Page 8-51:

Add to note 215.

See also Rountree Cotton Co., 113 TC 422 (1999), aff'd per curiam, 2001-1 USTC ¶ 50,316 (10th Cir. 2001) (§ 7872 applies to both direct and indirect loans to or for the benefit of any shareholder; not limited to cases where borrower is controlling shareholder). See Raby & Raby, "Imputing Interest in Common Transactions," 86 Tax Notes 377 (Jan. 17, 2000).

[8] Corporate Payments for Shareholders' Benefit

Page 8-52:

Add to note 222.

Lenward Hood, 115 TC 172 (2000) (corporate payment of sole shareholder's legal expenses to defend criminal charges of predecessor proprietorship held nondeductible constructive dividend to shareholders). But see Square D Co., 121 TC 168 (2003).

[10] Corporations Under Common Control: Triangular Distributions

Page 8-57:

Add to note 245 at the end of first paragraph.

Rountree Cotton Co., 113 TC 422 (1999), followed the § 7872 proposed regulation characterization method, aff'd per curiam, 2001-1 USTC   50,316 (10th Cir. 2001).

Page 8-58:

Add to note 250.

Rountree Cotton Co., 113 TC 422 (1999), followed the § 7872 proposed regulations characterization method, aff'd per curiam, 2001-1 USTC   50,316 (10th Cir. 2001).

¶ 8.06 FORMER DIVIDENDS-RECEIVED EXCLUSION FOR INDIVIDUALS—NEW LOW-RATE DIVIDENDS (2003)

Page 8-59:

Add to note 254.

For the current version of this proposal (Feb. 2003) see   1.08[4], and the discussion below. As usual, it largely foundered because of cost and complexity concerns.

Add text to end of ¶ 8.06.

[1] Treasury's Proposed Dividend Exclusion

A decade later (namely, February 2003) the dividend exclusion integration model was embraced again as the centerpiece of the President's (Bush II) proposed 2003 legislative tax agenda. While previously hailed for its simplicity in 1992, the 2003 version was not at all simple.[254.1]

[254.1] An alternative proposal released by Ways and Means on May 1, 2003, would harmonize the tax rates on dividends with those applicable to capital gains (whose top rate also would be lowered to 15 percent). This proposal passed the House in HR 2 on May 9, 2003; it prevailed in the final bill, HR 2, § 302, which passed on May 23, 2003. The

As explained briefly below, proposed § 116(a) would allow a full exclusion for all "qualified dividends" described in § 281, while § 116(b) would allow a stock-basis step-up for retained earnings to the extent provided in § 282. Moreover, the exclusion and basis adjustments would be available for all shareholders (individual or corporate). Proposed § 116(c) refers to the annual reporting requirements in amended § 6042 under which corporations would inform shareholders of the amount of their excludable dividends under § 281 and any basis allocations under § 282. Proposed § 116 was indeed simple; what follows, however, definitely was not. The basic dividend exclusion proposal will be outlined briefly below; before any more extensive discussion of this legislation is attempted, however, its passage in final form (which was by no means a sure thing) must occur (it didn't). A watered-down (and temporary) version passed the Senate on May 15, 2003 (but sunsets in 2007). The Senate version, however, was much simpler than Treasury's proposal since it merely provided for dividend exclusions. The final legislation (which passed on May 23, 2003) instead adopted a rate reduction for dividends of noncorporate shareholders (to 15 percent) but it too sunsets (in 2009). It is, however, far simpler than any of the other proposals (though it also is nearly as significant.)

[a] Excluded Dividends Amount ("EDA"): § 281

The amount of excluded dividends (or EDA) was prescribed by § 281, which was a key element in the new exclusion regime. Such amounts generally are current dividends paid from after-tax income. Thus, the purpose of the new regime is to create a single-tier tax at the corporate level for C corporations that distribute their after-tax income as dividends to their shareholders.[254.2] In its proposed version the exclusion would apply only to normal dividends (that is, those described in § 301 and § 316),[254.3] but all U.S. shareholders could qualify for the exclusion (individual and corporate).[254.4]

The dividend exclusion under § 281 had a "use-it-or-lose-it" quality since failure to distribute dividends currently would forfeit the right to exclusion; instead, retained earnings then became eligible for the stock-basis increase rules of § 282 (see below).

House version prevailed in the final legislation, § 1(h)(11) (effective for all of 2003, but sunsets in 2009) infra ¶ 8.06[2].

[254.2] Another purpose articulated by Treasury is to encourage corporations to give up tax shelters (which would serve to negatively impact shareholder exclusion amounts). The Senate exclusion provision did *not* include the corporate tax requirement; nor does the House version (or final legislation).

[254.3] Thus, § 356(a)(2) boot dividends may not be qualified but failed redemptions under § 302(d) and § 304 would (as would taxable stock dividends, and redemptions of § 306 stock).

[254.4] Corporate shareholders excluded dividends will create, or increase, their EDA account, thereby allowing pass-through exclusion when redistributed to their shareholders.

[b] Retained Earnings Basis Adjustment ("REBA"): § 282

After-tax accumulated earnings (namely, unused EDA) translated into an increase in shareholder stock basis under § 282 for excess EDA).[254.5] In effect, accumulated earnings were treated as a deemed excluded dividend followed by a deemed capital contribution back to the corporation.[254.6]

Actual distributions under § 301 from accumulated earnings which resulted in stock basis step-up for prior years,[254.7] went first to § 301(c)(2) and § 301(c)(3) to the extent of the CREBA account, and then to § 301(c)(1) and § 316 in effect reversing those previous stock basis step-ups. Thus, the "ordering regime" for § 301 distributing would be: (1) first, current dividends subject to the exclusion benefits of § 281; then (2) accumulated earnings distributions go to § 301(c)(2) and § 301(c)(3) to the extent of the corporation's CREBA account; (3) then any excess distribution went to § 301 and § 316 (to the extent of accumulated E&P); and finally (4) any additional distributions go back to § 301(c)(2) and § 301(c)(3). If this sounds like a "tracing maze," it is. The Senate dividend-exclusion regime did not include any of the above provisions and hence was a much simpler model (as is the House rate-reduction provision discussed below, which did ultimately pass in the final legislation).

[c] Other Rules

Special rules were provided in § 284 for credits and tax refunds, in § 285 for foreign corporations and foreign shareholders (who generally could not participate in the exclusion basis step-up regime), and in § 286 (dealing with application to § 302(a) redemptions, coordination with the holding period rules of § 246(c), and the debt-financed portfolio stock rules of § 246A). A massive regulations delegation was contained in § 287.[254.8]

[2] Alternative Proposal (Ways and Means Committee Chair Thomas)

[a] Alternate Proposal and Final Legislation

In lieu of Treasury's exclusion proposal, partial relief for certain dividends of noncorporate shareholders would be provided by subjecting that income to the capital gain rates (and would also lower the top rate from 20 to 15

[254.5] Regulations authority is granted by § 282(d) to allow an increase in the corporation's EDA in lieu of the stock-basis increase.

[254.6] No basis allocations can be made to § 1504(a)(4) preferred stock, however (even if it has voting rights), § 282(b)(3). The Senate dividend exclusion did not include these rules, however.

[254.7] Defined by § 283(b) as the "cumulative retained earnings basis amount" (or CREBA).

[254.8] Other collateral aspects of the proposal are considered in the relevant chapters to which they relate.

percent).[254.9] This approach (which ultimately prevailed), obviously was far simpler than the exclusion regime (and considerably less expensive as well). Even the Senate's temporary dividend exclusion was far simpler than the Treasury model since it was merely an exclusion, albeit only a temporary one. But the final bill (HR § 302, adding § 1(h)(11)) essentially adopted the House proposal.

[b] In General: Reduced Rate For Certain Dividends

New § 1(h)(11)(A) treats dividends received by individual shareholders as an addition to "net capital gain" (taxable at a top rate of 15 percent); but such dividends are not offset by any net capital loss. Only "qualified dividend income" is entitled to the new low rates, which term is defined by § 1(h)(11)(B)(i) as dividends received from domestic corporations[254.10] and certain "qualified foreign corporations."[254.11] Certain foreign corporations are excluded from qualified status by § 1(h)(11)(C)(iii), namely, § 551 FPHC, § 1246(b) foreign investment companies, and § 1291 PFICs.[254.12] But the 2004 Jobs Act repealed the FPHC and FIC provisions (effective in 2005) and also

---

[254.9] Released on May 1, 2003. This proposal passed the House in HR 2, § 302, on May 9, 2003; it prevailed in the final legislation, HR 2, § 302, adding § 1(h)(11), which passed on May 23, 2003 (but sunsets in 2009).

[254.10] But dividends, from § 501 or § 521 tax-exempt corporations, or allowed as a deduction by § 591, are not qualified dividends.

[254.11] These are defined in § 1(h)(11)(C)(i) as either foreign corporations incorporated in a possession, or in a country with an acceptable treaty (for a list of such treaties, see Notice 2003-69, 2003-2 IRB 861), or under § 1(h)(11)(C)(ii), corporations whose stock is readily tradeable on a U.S. securities market (see Notice 2003-71, 2003-43 IRB 922). For reporting procedures, see Notice 2003-79, 2003-50 IRB 1206. Notice 2004-45, 2004-45 IRB, Nov. 8, 2004, extends the simpler reporting rules in Notice 2003-79 to dividends paid in 2004.

Notice 2004-70, 2004-44 IRB, Oct. 8, 2004, gives guidance on whether distributions from various types of foreign corporations qualify for low-rate treatment (but does not reflect the 2004 Jobs Act repeal of FPHC and FIC provisions).

Legislation proposed by Sen. Baucus on July 1, 2005 (S. 1363) would add a new requirement that the publicly traded foreign corporation is created or organized under the laws of a foreign country which has a comprehensive income tax system (as determined by the Secretary).

[254.12] See Dixon, Qualified Dividend Income and Foreign Corporate Shares, 17 J. Tax'n Fin. Inst. 26 (Sept. 2003); Moritz, Dividends From Foreign Corporations Under JGTRRA, 31 J. Corp. Tax'n 19 (Sept. 2003); Rubinger, "Converting Low-Taxed Income Into Qualified Dividend Income;" 103 Tax Notes 858 (May 17, 2004). Sheppard, "Reduced Rates on Foreign Dividendi Under JGTRRA—Ambiguities and Opportunities," 15 J. Int'l Tax'n 14 (July 2004). Shepard & Harty, "Tax Treatment of Foreign Dividends Under JGTRRA: Ambiguities and Opportunities," 15 J. Int'l Tax'n 20 (Oct. 10, 2004), Part II.

Notice 2004-70, 2004-44 IRB, Oct. 8, 2004, (guidance on the QDI status of distributions by CFCs, FICs and PFICs; but does not reflect 2004 Jobs Act repeal of the first two, effective for 2005).

removed them from the disqualified foreign corporation list in § 1(h)(11)(C)(iii) (effective for 2005).

Probably the most limiting factor in obtaining qualified dividend income is the holding period limitation of § 1(h)(11)(B)(iii) (which incorporates the rules of § 246(c), but with a longer test period; that is, the stock must be held for 61 days during the 121-day period which straddles the ex-dividend date.[254.13] Moreover, the holding period also is extended for periods during which the taxpayer is in a hedged position.

[c] Technical Problems

It intially seemed that satisfaction of the drafted version of the holding period (60 out of the 120 day test period) might not be possible in cases where the dividend results from a redemption that fails to qualify for § 302(a) sale treatment for some reason (such as § 318 attribution). This may even be so where the redeeming shareholder retains some (but not enough) stock after the redemption (unless such stock is allowed to carry the post-dividend holding period which had to be at least one day). Total sales and redemptions of § 306 stock created the same problem;[254.14] even § 356(a)(2) boot dividends may not qualify since "tacking" is not permitted for this purpose.[254.15] But technical corrections added (retroactively) one day to the test period zone (raising it to 121 days), which seems to have cured these problems.

Dividends also will not qualify for capital gain rate treatment to the extent they are taken into account as investment income under § 163(d)(4)(B). Moreover, if the dividend constitutes an "extraordinary dividend" under § 1059,[254.16] any loss on a later sale of the stock is treated as a long-term capital loss to the extent of that dividend.[254.17] Finally, payments in lieu of dividends on stock that

---

[254.13] See   5.05[7][c]. The acquisition day is excluded and the disposition day is included; but § 1223 "tacking" is not allowed § 246(c)(3)(B). Paul, "Qualified Dividend Income: Issues, Problems, and Opportunities," 21 J. Tax'n Inv. 139 (Winter 2004). Technical corrections retroactively added one day to the 120 day holding period test zone (which the IRS has agreed to apply to 2003 returns in Announcement 2004-11).

[254.14] It is indeed ironic that sales of § 306 stock specifically were recharacterized as dividends, rather than ordinary gain, for purposes of § 1(h)(11) by § 306(a)(1)(D). The drafters were not thinking clearly here. See Paul, supra note 254.13, but the technical corrections bill amendment may save these transactions.

[254.15] IRC § 246(c)(3)(B); if tacking were allowed, pre-exchange holding period would add on to the new shares under § 1223(l). Reorganization boot dividends (and other dividend equivalent amounts) can be specified by regulations (but seemed likely to suffer from the same holding period problems as failed redemptions until fixed by technical corrections). See also Paul, supra note 254.13 and Willens, "Qualified Dividend Income Can Spring From Unconventional Sources," Daily Tax Rep. (BNA), at J-1 (Dec. 19, 2006) (e.g., failed § 302 redemptions, under § 302(d); taxable stock dividends under § 305(b); sales of § 306 stock under § 306(a)(1)(D); dividend boot in a spin-off under § 355(b); and boot dividends under § 356(a)(2).

[254.16] See   5.05[8].

[254.17] IRC § 1(h)(11)(D)(ii).

has been sold short will not qualify for treatment as reduced rate dividends either.

[d] Collateral Ramifications of New Low-Rate Regime

If the sun does not set on § 1(h)(11) (as it was slated to do in 2009, but it was extended through 2010 by 2006 legislation), many previous assumptions and planning principles will have to be rethought.[254.18] Among the many implications of the 2003 Act's dividend rate conformity to long-term capital gain are the following:[254.19]

1. The pain of "constructive dividend treatment"[254.20] will be greatly eased by a 15 percent, rather than 35 percent tax rate;
2. The tax stakes on a § 302(a) sale redemption versus a § 302(d)-§ 301 dividend have been reduced greatly by the new rules (basis offset and netting with capital losses are the only tax advantages now for § 302(a) sale treatment);[254.21]
3. The importance of the § 305(b) taxable stock dividend rules[254.22] has also been reduced (these "dividends" should clearly qualify for the new low rate benefits);
4. The policy of the § 306 stock bail-out provisions[254.23] has been heavily under cut as well since the new tax rate on dividends is the same as that for long-term capital gain (that is, the bail-out bucket seems to have been emptied by the new dividend rate rules);[254.24]

[254.18] For comments, see Feld, "Dividends Reconsidered," 101 Tax Notes 1117 (Dec. 2, 2003); NYSBA Tax Section Report, "Dividends Provisions of the Jobs and Growth Tax Relief Reconciliation Act of 2003," 10 Tax Notes 273 (Oct. 13, 2003); Goodman, "Choice of Entity, Stock Dividends Versus Capital Gains, and Deal Structure Remain Important Considerations Despite Changes Under Tax Act of 2003," Daily Tax Rep. (BNA) No. 202, at J-1 (Oct. 20, 2003); Calvin et al., "Jobs and Growth Tax Relief Act of 2003 Requires Planning for Rate Changes and New Dividend Rules," 17 J. Tax'n Fin. Insts. 5 (Sept. 2003); Willens, "Viewpoint, Daily Tax Rep. (BNA) No. 103, at J-1 (May 29, 2003); Willens, "Tax Relief Act Raises Issues for Unconventional Dividends Paid on Preferred Stock," Daily Tax Rep. (BNA) No. 154, at J-1 (Aug. 11, 2003); Krumwiede and Witner, "Tax Strategies for Qualified Dividends," 82 Taxes 51 (Jan. 2004). Jewett, "Characterization of Income: Compensation vs. Dividends," 103 Tax Notes 1501 (June 21, 2004); Willens, "When Will a Distribution Be a 'Dividend' and Who Will Bear the Tax Burden?" 102 J.Tax'n 345 (June 2005).

[254.19] These issues will also be considered at other points in this work.

[254.20] Supra ¶ 8.05.

[254.21] This assumes, however, that the holding period limitation does not prevent qualified dividend treatment (which could be a problem here, supra note 254.13, although technical corrections have fixed it).

[254.22] Infra ¶ 8.41.

[254.23] Infra ¶ 8.63.

[254.24] The Act even extended § 1(h)(11) dividend treatment to sales of § 306 stock in § 306(a)(1)(D) (assuming the 61-day holding period requirement can be met which, however, could be a problem for both sales and redemptions of § 306 stock supra note

5. The "boot dividend" rules of § 356(a)(2) now also seem to be completely superfluous (for individual shareholders) since both the amount of the boot dividend and its tax rate will be the same whether it is a capital gain or a dividend;[254.25]

6. Similarly, the anti-bail-out policy behind the "device" rule of § 355(a)(1)(B)[254.26] has been undermined by the new rate conformity between dividends and capital gains (where's the beef in a bail-out sale now?);

7. The pressure to issue debt in a corporate capital structure also should be reduced by the 2003 Act's significant reduction in the tax rate on dividends;[254.27]

8. The former tax advantages of S corporation status as compared to C corporations[254.28] has been narrowed by the 2003 legislation (though not eliminated, since S corporations are basically tax-exempt entities);

9. Controversies on classification of stock sales income or redemption proceeds as accrued dividend income or capital gain[254.29] should be largely eliminated; and

10. The significance of § 304 for individual shareholders[254.30] has also been significantly reduced by the new low dividend rates.[254.31]

The foregoing points are not an exhaustive list, but are indicative of the deep impact the new dividend rate provisions will have on many of the basic provisions of subchapter C (especially on matters considered in this and the ensuing chapter). What also seems likely, however, is that Wall Streets' "financial engineers" will have a field day with this regime while it lasts (which it does now until 2011).

254.14). But technical corrections add one day to the 120 day test zone, which should fix this problem (at least if the disposition spans the ex-dividend date).

[254.25] See 12.44[2][d]. The 61-day holding period could be a problem here as well since tacking of holding periods is not allowed; supra note 254.15; but techinical corrections have fixed that problem.

[254.26] See 11.06[3]; Blank, "The Device Test in a Unified Rate Regime," 102 Tax Notes 513 (Jan. 26, 2004).

[254.27] See generally Chapter 4, while interest on debt generally continues to be fully deductible, it is also fully taxable to the creditor; dividends, though not deductible, now will only be taxed at a maximum rate of 15 percent for individual shareholders. See Goodman, supra note 254.18.

[254.28] See Chapter 6.

[254.29] Considered infra 8.07[1][d].

[254.30] See 9.09[1].

[254.31] Again, however, the 61-day holding period limitation initially was a problem here as in the case of dividend equivalent stock redemptions, supra note 254.13, but it has been fixed by retroactive technical corrections.

¶ 8.07 ASSIGNMENT OF DIVIDEND INCOME AND RELATED PROBLEMS

[1] In General

[a] Gifts of Stock and/or Dividend Rights

Page 8-60:

Add to note 258.

See generally Willens, "Who 'Owns' a Dividend When Stock Is Transferred?," 98 Tax Notes 1597 (Mar. 10, 2003) (This will be an important issue if Treasury's dividend exclusion proposal is enacted, supra ¶ 8.06; it is also important under the final 2003 tax Act).

Page 8-61:

Add to note 260 at the end of the first paragraph.

But see Gerald Raeunhorst, 119 TC 157 (2002) (Government bound by *Rev. Rul. 78-197* and taxpayer's transfer satisfied the ruling so not taxed on charity's resale proceeds). Comment by Willens, Viewpoint, BNA Daily Tax Rep. No. 249, at J-1 (Dec. 30, 2002).

Add to note 260.

Haims, "Assignment of Income—Has *Ferguson* Hastened the 'Ripening' Process?" 87 Tax Notes 807 (May 8, 2000); Bernstein, "Distribution of Contingent Litigation Claims to Facilitate Mergers and Acquisitions," 30 J. Corp. Tax'n 37 (July 2003).

Add to note 261.

See also Haims, supra note 260. Compare *Gerald Raeunhorst*, supra note 260 (donor not taxed on charity resale per Rev. Rul. 78-197).

[b] Securities Loans

Add to note 262.

See Willens, "Who 'Owns' a Dividend When Stock Is Transferred?," supra note 258.

[d] Sales

Page 8-62:

Add to note 268.

Willens, "Who 'Owns' a Dividend When Stock Is Transferred?," 98 Tax Notes 1597 (Mar. 10, 2003).

Page 8-63:

Add to note 272.

See also Willens, "When the Ex-Dividend Date Falls After the Record Date," 113 Tax Notes 1023 (Dec. 11, 2006). See Willens, supra note 268.

Add to note 273.

See Willens, supra note 268.

Add text to end of ¶ 8.07[1][d].

Most of these issues should be largely neutralized for individual shareholders however, by the 2003 legislation taxing dividends received by individuals at the same low rates as capital gains (with a top rate of 15 percent).[274.1]

[274.1] IRC § 1(h)(11), supra ¶ 8.06[2].

[2] Bootstrap Sales—Taxability of Dividends Credited Against, or Used to Finance, the Purchase Price

[a] Pre-Sale Distributions (Dividend Stripping)

Page 8-65:

Add to note 279.

But see Compaq Computer Corp., 113 TC 214 (1999); compare IES Indus., Inc. v. US, 253 F3d 350 (8th Cir. 2001). *Compaq* was reversed, however, 277 F3d 778 (5th Cir. 2001).

Add to note 281.

See also Compaq Computer Corp., 113 TC 214 (1999); rev'd, 778 F3d 778 (5th Ci. 2001); compare IES Indus., Inc. v. US, 253 F3d 350 (8th Cir. 2001).

Page 8-66:

Add to note 285.

Willens, "Who 'Owns' a Dividend When Stock Is Transferred?," 98 Tax Notes 1597 (Mar. 10, 2003); Berstein, "The MC1-Verizon and AT&T-SBC Transactions (involving pre-sale dividends)," 32 Corp. Tax'n 50 (May 2005); Bernstein, "Distributions of Contingent Litigation Claims to Facilitate Mergers and Acquisitions," 30 Corp. Tax'n 37 (July 2003).

Add to end of first paragraph of note 287.

See Willens, supra note 285.

Add to note 287, first paragraph.

See Bernstein, supra note 285 (pre-sale dividend article).

Add to note 287, second paragraph.

This proposed regulation was adopted by TD 8858 on January 5, 2000, as Regs. § 1.338(h)(10)-1T (without change); and adopted as final regulation by TD 8940 on February 13, 2001 (effective March 16, 2001) (same).

Page 8-67:

In note 290, replace 113 TC No. 17 *with* 113 TC 214. But *Compaq* was reversed on appeal, 277 F3d 1278 (5th Cir. 2001).

Add to end of note 290.

But *Compaq* was reversed on appeal, 277 F3d 778 (5th Cir. 2001). Compare IES Indus., Inc. v. US, 253 F3d 350 (8th Cir. 2001) (similar transaction to *Compaq* but taxpayer won here; not a sham; had economic substance and adequate business purpose despite heavy tax planning objectives).

B PROPERTY DISTRIBUTIONS IN KIND

¶ 8.20 INTRODUCTORY

[4] Repeal of *General Utilities* Doctrine; Current Law

Page 8-73:

Add to note 319.

Bell, "*General Utilities* Repeal, Section 355(e), and the Triple Tax," 87 Tax Notes 1385 (June 5, 2000).

¶ 8.21 CORPORATE GAIN OR LOSS ON DISTRIBUTIONS OF PROPERTY

[2] Losses

Page 8-77:

Add to end of first paragraph in note 336.

But see the special loss recognition rules for consolidated return distributions in Regs. § 1.1502-13(f)(2)(iii) (loss allowed on intercompany distribution), 13.43[3][b], and Regs. § 1.1502-13(f)(6) (loss denied on dispositions of parent stock), 13.43[3][e].

¶ 8.22 TAXABILITY OF DISTRIBUTIONS TO SHAREHOLDERS

[1] Amount of Distribution and Basis Effects to Shareholders

Page 8-84:

Add to note 374.

But see Notice 99-59, 1999-52 IRB 761 (the so-called "BOSS" tax shelter transaction); see ¶ 5.10[1], note 391. See Regs. § 1.301-1T(g), issued by TD 8924 (Jan. 4, 2001), which extends § 357(d) principles to § 301(b)(2) distributions as well as pursuant to the authority in § 357(d)(3); see ¶ 3.06[4][f]. The regulations also apply retroactively to the BOSS-type transactions noted in Notice 99-59, see supra. They were adopted as final Regs. § 1.301-1(g) by TD 8964 on Sept. 27, 2001. See generally Burke, "Contributions, Distributions, and Assumptions of Liabilities: Confronting Economic Reality," 56 Tax Law. 383 (2003).

[2] Effect on Distributor's Earnings and Profits

Page 8-87:

Add new note 384.1 to end of first sentence after Example 4.

[384.1] This statement is not correct: True, § 312(c) has no role to play in the upward adjustment caused by § 311(b), but it does have a role in decreasing the downward adjustment of § 312(b); it is also needed to reduce the downward adjustment in Example 2 (built-in loss distribution case, where § 311(a) continues to apply).

C   DISTRIBUTIONS OF CORPORATION'S OWN STOCK AND STOCK RIGHTS

¶ 8.41 TAXATION OF STOCK DISTRIBUTIONS

Page 8-100:

Add to text at end of first paragraph.

But Treasury's dividend exclusion proposal of February 2003,[434.1] would materially alter the tax stakes here since taxable stock dividends can qualify for the proposed dividend exclusion benefits. Even Ways and Means Chair

---

[434.1] See supra ¶ 8.06[1].

Thomas's proposal to tax dividends at capital gains rates (which ultimately prevailed) will have a significant impact on § 305 issues.[434.2]

[434.2] Supra   8.06[2] Taxability under § 305(b) at a 15 percent rate, rather than the higher ordinary income rate, would ease the downside of a foot fault under § 305(b). There is no holding period problem for these dividends either.

[2] Exceptions to General Rule

[g] Distribution of "Tracking Stock"

Page 8-113:

Add to note 502.

See Dahlberg & Perry, "Tracking Stock: Virtual Equity, Virtual Entities, and Virtual Mergers and Acquisitions," 78 Taxes 18 (Mar. 2000); Rizzi, "Tracking Stock As Synthetic Spin-Offs and Contingent Consideration," 25 J. Corp. Tax'n 255 (2000).

[5] Treatment of Taxable Stock Distributions

Page 8-120:

Add to text after runover sentence ending with note 535.

But taxable stock dividend will be eligible for Treasury's February 2003 dividend exclusion benefits.[535.1] They also would qualify for Ways and Means Chair Thomas's alternative proposal (which ultimately prevailed here) to tax dividends at lowered capital gains rates as well.[535.2]

[535.1] See supra   8.06[1].
[535.2] See supra   8.06[2].

¶ 8.42 TAXATION OF DISTRIBUTIONS OF STOCK RIGHTS

[2] Taxable Rights

Page 8-123:

Add to text at end of first paragraph of ¶ 8.42[2].

But as a taxable dividend, such amounts can qualify for Treasury's February 2003 dividend exclusion benefit.[551.1]

[551.1] See supra   8.06. They should also qualify for Ways and Means Chair Thomas's alternative dividend relief proposal of May 1, 2003, namely, tax at capital gain rates (which would be lowered to 15 percent as well); this version prevailed in the final legislation, new § 1(h)(11) (effective January 1, 2003).

D   PREFERRED STOCK BAILOUTS

¶ 8.61 BAILOUTS UNDER CURRENT LAW

Page 8-127:

Add to text at end of ¶ 8.61.

But Treasury's February 2003 dividend exclusion proposal could significantly revive interest in classic Chamberlain–style dividend bailouts since § 306(a)(2) dividends will qualify for the proposed dividend exclusion benefits.[564.1] Moreover, under Chairman Thomas's alternative proposal (taxing dividends at capital gains rates),[564.2] the bailout ploy would no longer be necessary since regular dividends would be taxed like capital gains; this is the proposal that prevailed in the final 2003 Tax Act.[564.3]

[564.1] See supra ¶ 8.06 (but only if treated as a dividend under § 306(a)(2); § 306(a)(1) ordinary gains apparently would not qualify here (although they *would* qualify under the Senate exclusion proposal).

[564.2] The Thomas proposal to tax dividends at capital gains rates would also apparently apply only to redemptions of § 306 stock (not its sale). But the final legislation added § 306(a)(1)(D), which allows sales of § 306 stock to qualify for the reduced dividend rate as well. But query the holding period requirement of § 1(h)(11)(B)(iii), which could deny the low rate benefits to both sales and redemptions of preferred stock (but technical corrections fixed this problem retroactively by adding one day to the test period zone, raising it to 121 days).

[564.3] IRC § 1(h)(11); supra ¶ 8.06[2].

¶ 8.63 DISPOSITIONS OF SECTION 306 STOCK

Page 8-135:

Add to end of first paragraph of ¶ 8.63.

But 2003 legislation has greatly reduced that sting by taxing dividends of individual shareholders at the same low rate as long-term capital gains (a top rate of 15 percent).[599.1] The 2003 Act even extended this treatment to sales of § 306 stock for purposes of the new low rate rules in § 306(a)(1)(D).[599.2]

[599.1] IRC § 1(h)(11); supra   8.06[2]. See Willens, Viewpoint–New Tax Law Eliminates Penalty Associated With 'Section 306 Stock,' Daily Tax Rep. (BNA) No. 221, at J-1 (Nov. 7, 2003).

[599.2] Assuming the 61-day holding period limit can be met, which could be a problem here for both sales and redemptions (although this problem seems to have been eased by retroactive technical corrections legislation, adding one day to the test period zone and raising it to 121 days).

[3] Other Dispositions

[b] Charitable Contributions and Other Gifts

Page 8-139:

Add to text at end of ¶ 8.63[2][b].

But the 2003 tax Act now taxes dividends of individual shareholders at the same rate as long-term capital gain in § 1(h)(11)(A); also § 306(a)(1)(D) treats the proceeds from sales of § 306 stock as "dividends" for purposes of § 1(h)(11), so § 170(e) should no longer apply to reduce the § 170 deduction from fair market value.[617.1]

[617.1] See Willens, Viewpoint, supra note 599.1.

CHAPTER **9**

Stock Redemptions

A   SALE VERSUS § 301 DISTRIBUTION TREATMENT

¶ 9.01 BACKGROUND AND GENERAL CONCEPTS

[3] Current Law

[b] Definition of "Redemption"

Page 9-9:

Add to note 21.

See generally Rogers v. US, 281 F3d 1108, 2002-1 USTC ¶ 50,240 (10th Cir. 2002) (purported "loan" recharacterized as in substance a redemption; hence, corporate payments not deductible and bad debt loss denied).

[c] No-Ruling Areas

Page 9-11:

Add to note 31.

For current version, see Rev. Proc. 2005-3, 2005-1 IRB 118, §§ 3.01(24), 3.01(25), 3.01(26), 4.01(21).

Page 9-12:

Add new ¶ 9.01[3][d].

[d] Impact of Treasury's Dividend Exclusion Proposal [New]

Treasury's proposal to allow up to 100 percent exclusion for dividends paid out of after-tax income[36.1] would, if enacted (it wasn't), have a profound effect on the material contained in this chapter. Qualifying a redemption for sale treatment under § 302(a) would no longer be the clearly preferred tax result since the 20 percent capital gains rate would not match the zero rate on fully exempt dividends under the Treasury's proposal.[36.2] Thus, the tax-planning strategies here would likely undergo a sharp role reversal, focusing on avoiding § 302 (a) treatment in favor of § 302(d)–301 dividend equivalence.[36.3]

To the extent any ultimately enacted exclusion is less than 100 percent, however, the disparity between sale and dividend treatment will be reduced pro tanto, making the taxpayer's planning choice more difficult. But a full exclusion outcome would align the interest of noncorporate shareholders with

---

[36.1] See ¶ 8.06[1].

[36.2] The lack of stock-basis offset under § 301 as compared to § 302(a), would be a countervailing factor.

[36.3] This would especially be the case if the redeemed stock has no significant basis to offset against a redemption sale.

their corporate brethren in seeking to obtain the tax-favored dividend treatment.

The alternative proposal by Ways and Means Chair Thomas to tax dividends of individual shareholders at the same rate as capital gains would largely neutralize the present disparity between § 302 sale treatment as well (at least as far as tax rates are concerned),[36.4] and this was the version that prevailed in the final legislation.[36.5]

[36.4] See 8.06[4]. This proposal passed the House in HR 2 on May 9, 2003, and ultimately was adopted in the final Act.

[36.5] HR 2, § 302(a), adding § 1(h)(11) (effective January 1, 2003, but sunsets in 2009). This legislation also lowered the top rate on capital gains to 15 percent. See 8.06[2]. Legislation in 2006 (TIPRA) extended this provision for two more years (through 2010).

¶ 9.02 CONSTRUCTIVE OWNERSHIP OF STOCK: § 318

[1] In General

Page 9-13:

Add to note 43.

Yuhas & Fellows, "Stock Redemptions, Attribution Rules and Related Parties: The Tax Maze for Estates and Trusts," 81 Taxes 25 (Feb. 2003).

[2] Family Attribution

Page 9-15:

Add to text of last paragraph.

The Joint Committee Tax'n Staff in its April 2001 simplification report urges (as many did who have gone before) that a uniform definition of "family" should be adopted.[50.1]

[50.1] Volume II, proposal IV D, at 253.

[5] Option Attribution

Page 9-18:

Add to note 67.

Stevens, "The Tax Treatment of Contingent Options," 102 Tax Notes 525 (Jan. 26, 2004).

Add to note 71.

See Stevens, supra note 67.

¶ 9.03 SUBSTANTIALLY DISPROPORTIONATE REDEMPTIONS: § 302(b)(2)

[1] In General

Page 9-23:

Add to note 85.

But see Willens, "IRS Challenging Tax Characterization of Seagram's Dupont Stock Redemption," BNA Daily Tax Rep. No. 101, at J-1 (May 27, 2003).

[4] Disproportionate Redemptions and Corporate Shareholders

[a] General

Page 9-26:

Add to note 95.

But IRS is challenging Seagram's tax treatment of its Dupont stock redemption, supra note 85.

[b] Comments and Collateral Aspects

In note 101, delete ; see infra ¶ 9.03[4].

[c] Revised Legislative Response

Page 9-27:

Add to note 103.

Former Treasury proposals in 1999 and 2000 would extend this treatment to offshore versions of the *Seagram* failed § 302 redemption ploy, but these proposals have not been adopted, see ¶ 5.10[5][c]. But see Notice 2001-45, 2001-33 IRB 129 (attacking these transactions under current law as inappropriate basis shifting tax shelters; also added to the tax shelter blacklist, see ¶ 5.10[6][g]); Sheppard, "Dissecting the Basis Shifting Transaction," 92 Tax Notes 870 (Aug. 13, 2001). Proposed Regs. § 1.302-5 (Oct.16, 2002) deal with these basis-shifting transactions by changing the current regulations in § 1.302-2(c) to prevent creation of artificial loss deductions, infra ¶ 9.22[2]. But these regulations were withdrawn for further "study" on April 19, 2006 (Ann. 2006-30, 2006-19 IRB 879).

¶ 9.04 TERMINATION OF SHAREHOLDER'S ENTIRE INTEREST: § 302(b)(3)

[1] Introductory

Page 9-29:

Add to note 111.

For recent application of *Zenz* principles to defeat a corporate taxpayer's tax-motivated redemption plan, see Merrill Lynch & Co., 120 TC 12 (2003), aff'd, 386 F3d 464 (2d Cir.
2004). See also Richard E. Hurst, 124 TC 16 (2005) (combined sales redemption by sole
shareholder qualified for § 302(b)(3) complete termination treatment despite sale of part
of stock to son, and nonshareholder wife who continued to work for a small salary; retention of various creditor protection rights not a prohibited retained interest; lease of property at arm's-length rent not fatal either). Comment on *Hurst* by Raby & Raby, 107 Tax
Notes 152 (June 30, 2005); Willens, "Viewpoint," BNA Daily Tax Rep. No. 122, at J-1
(June 27, 2005).

[2] Waiver of Family Attribution

[a] In General

Page 9-29:

Add to note 112.

Richard E. Hurst, 124 TC 16 (2005) (redeemed shareholder's retained rights solely as a
creditor; successfully navigated § 302(b)(3) maze to get capital gain and § 453 benefits).
Comments by Raby & Willens, supra note 111.

[b] Waivers by Entities

Page 9-31:

Add to note 121.

See also Willens, "Redemptions of Stock Held by Entities," 106 Tax Notes 1585 (Mar.
28, 2005).

[c] Tainted Postredemption "Interest" in Corporation

Page 9-33:

Add to note 128.

Willens, "Viewpoint—IRS Adopts Expansive View of When Redeemed Shareholder Retains Prohibited Interest in Corporation," BNA Daily Tax Rep. No. 47, at J-4 (Mar. 11,
2002).

Add to note 129.

Richard E. Hurst, 124 TC 16 (2005) (nonshareholder wife continued to work for corporation for small salary; but not fatal); comments by Raby & Willens, supra note 111.

Add to note 130.

Richard E. Hurst, 124 TC 16 (2005) (retained rights solely those of a creditor; non-
shareholder wife's continued employment did not taint.)

Page 9-34:

Add to note 132.

Richard E. Hurst, 124 TC 16 (2005) (only retained creditor rights).

Add to note 134

See, e.g., Richard E. Hurst, 124 TC 16 (2005).

¶ 9.05 REDEMPTIONS NOT ESSENTIALLY EQUIVALENT TO DIVIDENDS: § 302(b)(1)

[1] In General

Page 9-36:

Add to note 144.

Willens, "Viewpoint, Multiple Code Considerations Come Into Play in Qualifying Stock Redemption as 'Not Essentially Equivalent to a Dividend,'" Daily Tax Rep. (BNA) No. 71, at J-1 (Apr. 14, 2003); Willens, "Considerations in Qualifying Redemptions for Sale or Exchange Treatment," Daily Tax Rep. (BNA) No. 226, at J-1 (Nov. 24, 2006).

Page 9-37:

Add to note 150.

Merrill Lynch & Co., 120 TC 12 (2003) (cross-chain stock sales integrated with planned sale of target member stock terminating taxpayer's interest in target and resulting in § 302 sale treatment rather than hoped-for dividend equivalence); *Merrill Lynch* was aff'd, 386 F3d 464 (2d Cir. 2004).

Add text to end of ¶ 9.05[1].

But if Treasury's February 2003 dividend exclusion proposal[150.1] had been enacted, qualification under § 302(a) for sale treatment would become *less* attractive, while dividend equivalency may well be the tax-preferred result. Even under Ways and Means Chair Thomas's alternative proposal to tax dividends of individual shareholders at capital gains rates, the distinction between dividend and capital gains treatment would be neutralized as to tax rates. (This was the version that ultimately prevailed in the final 2003 tax bill).[150.2] But initial holding period problems under § 1(h)(11)(B)(iii) could deny low rate benefits here (since the required 61-day and 120 day period "straddles" the redemption date; but retroactive technical connections fixed apparently this problem by raising the test period zone to 121 days).

[150.1] See   1.08[4], 8.06[1]. This legislation also lowered the top rate on capital gain to 15 percent (and apply that rate to dividends as of Jan. 1, 2003).

[150.2] IRC § 1(h)(11); see   8.06[2].

¶ 9.06 REDEMPTIONS IN CONJUNCTION WITH BOOTSTRAP ACQUISITIONS OF STOCK AND SHAREHOLDER BUY-SELL AGREEMENTS

[2] Sale-And-Seller Redemption

Page 9-45:

Add to note 190.

See also Merrill Lynch Co., 120 TC 12 (2003) (court applied *Zenz* principle to defeat tax-payer's plan to intentionally flunk § 302(b)(3), aff'd 386 F3d 464 (2d Cir. 2004).

Page 9-47:

Add to note 193.

Merrill Lynch & Co., 120 TC 12 (2003) (applied principle of Rev. Rul. 77-226 and *Zenz* to defeat taxpayer's hoped-for dividend treatment from cross-chain § 304 stock sales; re-demption integrated with planned sale of target stock so transactions resulted in § 302(b)(3) termination); *Merrill Lynch* was aff'd, 386 F3d 464 (2d Cir. 2004).

[3] Seller-Dividend-And-Sale

Page 9-48:

Add to note 200.

These regulations were adopted in temporary form (without change) by TD 8858 on Janu-ary 5, 2000, Regs. § 1.338(h)(10)-1T(e), Ex. 2; final Regs. § 1.338(h)(10)-1(e), Ex. 2 (Feb. 13, 2001), adopted by TD 8940 is the same (effective March 16, 2001).

[6] Recharacterization of Transactions

Page 9-50:

In note 214 change Arnes v. CIR *to* Arnes v. US.

Page 9-51:

Add to note 214 at end of second paragraph.

The Tax Court significantly added to the confusion here in Carol Read et al., 114 TC 14 (2000), holding that the constructive dividend standard was not applicable in divorce set-tings (here, wife's stock was redeemed on behalf of husband per divorce judgment; held wife not taxed, but husband was); *Read* followed in Craven v. US, 215 F3d 1201, 2000-2 USTC ¶ 50,541 (11th Cir. 2000) (but no mention of husband's treatment here).

Add to note 214 at end of third paragraph.

For comments on *Carol Read* decision, see Raby & Raby, "Confusion Surrounds, Stock Redemptions Incident to Divorce," 86 Tax Notes 1121 (Feb. 21, 2000); Sheppard, "How to Divorce a Millionaire, Tax Efficiently," 86 Tax Notes 1198 (Feb. 28, 2000); Lepow,

"Tales of Unrequited Love and Unexpected Taxation in the Family Corporation," 108 Tax Notes 571 (Aug. 1, 2005).

Prop. Regs. § 1.1041-2, issued August 3, 2001, would clear up the decisional mess in this area created by the *Arnes* and *Read* decisions by returning to traditional *Wall-Sullivan* constructive distribution principles (that is, whether the non-redeaming spouse is under binding obligation to purchase the transferor spouse's stock); the parties alternatively can agree in writing on which spouse will bear the tax here (a position suggested by the Joint Committee on Tax'n Staff April 2001 simplification proposals). These regulations would change the result in the Ninth Circuit *Arnes* (that is, the wife is taxable on redemption of her stock) and also *Read* (no tax to the husband; instead, the wife had taxable gain on redemption). They were adopted in final form by TD 9035 on January 13, 2003.

Page 9-52:

Add to note 218 at end of second paragraph.

But Carol Read, 114 TC 14 (2000), taxed husband because redemption effected on his behalf; primary obligation test not applicable in divorce setting said majority; multiple dissents (for comments on this unfortunate decision, see supra note 214). But Prop. Regs. §§ 1.1041-2(a)(1) and 1.1041-2(b)(1) would overrule the result in *Read* (the husband was not taxed if no binding obligation to buy wife's stock; instead, the wife was taxed on redemption gain here); these proposals were adopted by TD 9035 on January 13, 2003.

Add to note 221.

But compare Carol Read, 114 TC 14 (2000) (husband taxed on redemption of wife's stock even though not under "obligation" to buy; redemption was made on his behalf); contra John Arnes, 102 TC 522 (1994). Prop. Regs. § 1.1041-2 (Aug. 3, 2001) return to the traditional constructive distribution rules of Rev. Rul. 69-608 (that is, no constructive distribution if no discharge of binding obligation to purchase transferor spouse's stock; thus the wife, rather than the husband, would be taxed in *Read* scenario); adopted by TD 9035 on January 13, 2003.

Page 9-53:

Add to note 222.

The principles of Revenue Ruling 69-608 in effect were codified in Regs. § 1.1041-2 (2003), supra note 221, unless the parties specifically agree on a different characterization of the transaction; Regs. §§ 1.1041-2(c) and 1.1041-2(d), Exs 2 and 4. See Zipp, "Stock Redemptions in Divorce – Someone Will Have to Recognize Gain Under the Final Regs.," 99 J. Tax'n 172 (Sept. 2003); Lepow, supra note 214.

Add to note 225.

But see Carol Read, 114 TC 14 (2000) (husband had taxable constructive dividend even though not obligated to buy wife's stock). Prop. Regs. § 1.1041-2 (Aug. 3, 2001) contra to *Read*; no tax to the husband where no discharged purchase obligation; final Regs. § 1.1041-2 (Jan. 13, 2003).

Page 9-54:

Add to note 226.

But see Carol Read, 114 TC 14 (2000) (husband had taxable constructive dividend even though no primary obligation to buy wife's stock; divorce cases "different"; multiple dissents). Prop. Regs. § 1.1041-2 (Aug. 3, 2001) contra to *Read* and accord with Tax Court's

Arnes decision (where no discharge of binding obligation to buy wife's stock, no tax to husband; instead, wife taxed on sale of stock); adopted by TD 9035 on January 13, 2003.

¶ 9.07 PARTIAL LIQUIDATIONS

[1] Section 302(b)(4)

[a] In General

Page 9-55:

Add to note 231.

Willens, "The Infrequently Encountered, but Uniquely Beneficial, Partial Liquidation," BNA Daily Tax Rep. No. 217, at J-1 (Nov. 12, 2001); Haas, "Favorable Treatment for Distributions After Corporate Dispositions: Use of Partial Liquidations," 98 J. Tax'n 142 (Mar. 2003).

[3] Safe-Harbor Distributions of Qualified Active Trade or Business: § 302(e)(2)

[b] Relationship of §§ 302(e)(2) and 302(e)(3) to § 355

Page 9-67:

Add to note 296.

For a suggestion that a corporation can buy the stock of a target corporate business, liquidate it under § 332, and qualify for partial liquidation treatment under § 302(e)(2), see Willens, "Viewpoint," Daily Tax Rep. (BNA) No. 217 at J-3 (Nov. 12, 2001).

Page 9-68:

Add to text at end of runover paragraph.

While a qualified business can't be purchased in a taxable transaction within 5 years of the distribution, apparently stock of a corporation conducting such a business can be (and its business acquired via an upstream tax-free § 332 liquidation).[300.1]

[300.1] See Willens, supra note 296. Section 302(e)(3) does not contain a provision comparable to § 355(b)(2)(D).

¶ 9.08 REDEMPTIONS UNDER § 303

[1] Purpose

Page 9-69:

Add to note 305.

Willens, "Differentiating IRS's 'Active Business' Requirement for Real Estate Under Section 355 and 6166," Daily Tax Rep. (BNA) No. 156, at J-1 (Aug. 14, 2006) (recent IRS Liberalization of § 6166 in Rev. Rul. 2006-34, 2006-26 IRB 1171).

¶ 9.09 REDEMPTIONS BY AFFILIATED CORPORATIONS: § 304

[1] In General

Page 9-75:

Add text to end of ¶ 9.09[1].

But the sting of § 304 has been greatly reduced for noncorporate shareholders as a result of 2003 legislation taxing dividends at the same rate as capital gains (and reducing the top rate to 15 percent).[336.1]

[336.1] HR 2, § 302(a), adding § 1(h)(11) (effective for 2003, but sunsets in 2009; but extended for two years in 2006); see   8.06[2]. Query whether we even need § 304 any longer; corporations have largely been removed from its impact and individuals will enjoy the same low tax rate on dividends as capital gain; thus, the only remaining significance of § 304 is its effect on stock basis. This assumes that the 61-day holding period of § 1(h)(11)(B)(iii) can be met (which was, but is no longer a problem here).

[2] Application of Attribution Rules: Control

[a] Control and Attribution

Page 9-77:

Add to beginning of note 339.

See Prop. Regs. § 1.304-5(a) (Oct. 16, 2002) reflecting these rules.

Add to second paragraph of note 339.

See Willens, "Sidewise Attribution," 113 Tax Notes 685 (Nov. 13, 2006).

[3] Acquisitions by Subsidiary Corporation: § 304(a)(2) (Downstream Stock Sales)

Add to note 350.

Zhu, "The Deeming Rules: A Method to the Madness," 105 Tax Notes 1425 (Dec. 6, 2004).

Page 9-79:

Add to note 355.

But see Prop. Regs. § 1.304-2(c), Ex. 4 (Oct. 16, 2002) (unused basis preserved for later use as a loss); infra ¶ 9.22[2].

[4] Acquisitions by Related (but Nonsubsidiary) Corporations; Brother-Sister Acquisitions: § 304(a)(1) (Lateral or Cross-Chain Stock Sales)

[c] Application of § 302 in § 304(a)(1) Transactions

Page 9-82:

Add to note 370.

See also Richard E. Hurst, 124 TC 16 (2005) (court denied untimely § 304 argument — after trial — prevented taxpayer from arguing that drop from 100 to 51 percent could have satisfied § 302(b)(1) as meaningful reduction; no citation, however, to *Merrill Lynch*).

[d] Basis Results

Page 9-83:

Add to second paragraph of note 373.

See Prop. Regs. § 1.304-2(a) (Oct. 15, 2002). But this nonaggregation rule applies only for computing the deemed § 351 gain; if a dividend results under § 301(d), however, basis should continue to be aggregated under § 301(c)(2) for purposes of computing § 301(c)(3) gain. The special nonaggregation rule of § 1059(e)(1)(A)(iii) (last sentence) applies *only* to corporate shareholders; but see Prop. Regs. § 1.304-2(c), Ex. 3 (which seems wrong in this respect.) But these regulations were withdrawn on April 19, 2006, for further "study" (they should stay withdrawn), infra ¶ 9.22[2] (Ann. 2006-30, 2006-19 IRB 879).

Add to note 374.

But see Prop. Regs. § 1.304-2(c), Ex. 3 which applied the corporate shareholder § 1059 nonaggregation rule to an individual redeemed shareholder under § 301(c)(2) and § 301(c)(3) (which seems wrong); but withdrawn April 19, 2006.

Page 9-84:

Add new note 377.1 to end of second full sentence.

[377.1] But this nonaggregation rule of § 1059(e)(1)(A)(iii) applies only to corporate shareholders; individuals should still be allowed to aggregate stock basis for purposes of computing gain under §§ 301(c)(2) and 301(c)(3); but Prop. Regs. 1.304-2(c), Ex. (3) is contra on this point and seems wrong. But the proposals were withdrawn, April 19, 2006.

Add to second paragraph of note 378.

For proposed regulations explicating these 1997 amendments, see § 1.304-2(a), (c) (Oct. 16, 2002); but withdrawn April 19, 2006.

Add to note 379.

See Prop. Regs. § 1.304-2(c), Ex. 1 (2002); but withdrawn April 19, 2006.

[5] Overlap of Parent-Subsidiary and Brother-Sister Relationships

Page 9-86:

Add to second paragraph of note 383.

See Prop. Regs. § 1.304-3(a) (Oct. 16, 2002); but withdrawn April 19, 2006.

[6] Application to More Complex Transactions

[a] Overlap With § 351

Page 9-87:

Add to note 387.

See also Gary D. Combrink, 116 TC 296, withdrawn and reissued as 117 TC 82 (2001) (cancellation of shareholder debt to acquiring corporation a distribution of property for §§ 304, 302 and 301 purposes).

Add to note 388, second paragraph.

See also Gary D. Combrink, 116 TC 296, withdrawn and reissued as 117 TC 82 (2001) (transaction partially qualified for § 304(b)(3)(B) exception to extent cancelled debt was used by shareholder to acquire additional equity in transferred corporation stock).

[d] Overlap With Reorganization Provisions

Page 9-90:

Add to note 397.

But Rev. Rul. 2004-83, 2004-31 IRB 157, gives D reorganizations priority in a conflict with § 304 (e.g. parent's sale of S-1 stock to S-2 followed by integrated liquidation of S-1 into S-2 held a D reorganization).

[e] Stock Sales Within Affiliated Corporate Groups

Page 9-91:

In first line of note 399 change ¶ 9.09[4][b] to ¶ 9.09[4][d].

Add to note 400.

But this ploy was rejected in Merrill Lynch & Co., 120 TC 12 (2003) (cross-chain stock sales integrated with planned dispositions of target member stock under *Zenz* principle resulting in § 302(b)(3), § 302(a) sale treatment instead of hoped-for dividend); *Merrill Lynch* was affirmed, 386 F3d 464 (2d Cir. 2004).

Page 9-92:

Add to note 401.

But transaction rejected in Merrill Lynch & Co., 120 TC 12 (2003) (court found § 302(b)(3), 302(a) sale under *Zenz* integrated transactions principle, supra note 400); aff'd, 386 F3d 464 (2d Cir. 2004).

Add to note 405.

See Prop. Regs. § 1.304-2(a), (c) (Oct. 16, 2002).

Page 9-93:

Add after second sentence in note 406.

See also ¶¶ 13.42[2][c], 13.42[3][b].

Add to last paragraph of text in ¶ 9.09[6][e].

But if the Tax Court's decision in the *Merrill Lynch* case[406.1] stands up, all of these regulatory "fixes" may have been unnecessary.

[406.1] See supra note 400. Court denied dividend treatment for cross-chain stock sales by integrating planned sales of target member stock under *Zenz* principles, resulting in § 302(b)(3) sale treatment. Rabe & Rabe, "Section 304: A Loophole Closer, but Itself a Loophole," 98 Tax Notes 967 (Feb. 10, 2003).

[f] Foreign Corporations

Add to note 408.

See Prop. Regs. § 1.304-6(a) (Oct. 16, 2002).

Page 9-94:

Add to text at the end of ¶ 9.09[6][f].

But IRS proposed regulations issued on May 25, 2005,[410.1] to remove deemed § 351 exchanges resulting from § 304(a)(1) brother-sister transactions

---

[410.1] Prop. Regs. §§ 1.367(a)-3(a) and 1.367(b)-4(a) (effective when final). Extensive discussion for reasons in the preamble (Reg. – 127740-04).

from both §§ 367(a) and 367(b) and modified the two rulings discussed above.[410.2]

[410.2] See supra note 408. Adopted as final regulations by TD 9250 (Feb. 21, 2006) (Taxpayers can rely for all open years). Calianno, Cordonnier & Difronzo, "New Section 367 Proposed Regulations For Section 304(a)(1) Transactions: The Fiction Continues Without the Cross-Border Traps," 19 J. Int'l Tax'n 23 (Sept. 2005); also published in 32 Corp. Tax'n 19 (Nov. 2005), New 367 Regs. Provide Guidance: The Fiction Continues Without the Cross-Border Traps—New 367 Proposed Regulations Published for 304(a)(1) Transactions. But Issues Remain in Cross-Border Transactions. Calianno, Cordonnier & Difronzo, "Final Regulations: Section 367 Does Not Apply to Deemed Section 351 Exchanges in Section 304(a)(1) Transactions," 17 J. Int'l Tax'n 28 (July 2006); and 33 Corp. Tax'n 16 (Nov. 2006).

[g] Inappropriateness of § 304 Application to Corporate Shareholders

Page 9-95:

Add to text at end of subparagraph.

The Joint Committee Staff's April 2001 tax simplification report proposed to limit application of § 304 to cases resulting in dividend treatment not subject to the § 243 DRD, thus effectively removing corporate shareholders from the realm of § 304 (at last).[416.1] But noncorporate shareholders will not be very concerned with § 304 dividend treatment as a result of 2003 legislation taxing dividends at the same rate as capital gain (and lowering that rate to 15 percent).[416.2]

[416.1] Proposal IV E, at 259. Thus, § 304 would not apply if § 302 sale treatment results or if a § 302(d) dividend qualifies for the § 243 DRD deduction (§ 304 has already been removed from the consolidated return rules; see Regs. § 1.1502-80(b), supra note 404).

[416.2] HR 2, § 302(a), adding § 1(h)(11) (effective for 2003, but sunsets in 2009); see 8.06[2]. This assumes that the 61-day holding period of § 1(h)(11)(B)(iii) can be met (which was, but is no longer a problem here).

B COLLATERAL SHAREHOLDER AND CORPORATE CONSEQUENCES OF REDEMPTIONS

¶ 9.22 SHAREHOLDER TREATMENT OF REDEMPTION TREATED AS A § 301 DISTRIBUTION; MYSTERY OF THE DISAPPEARING BASIS

[1] Section 301 Distribution

Page 9-100:

Revise the sentence beginning at the bottom of the page and ending with note 441 to read as follows:

If other dividends have been distributed in the same year, they both have equal claim on current earnings and profits (and the first in time rule applies to distributions out of accumulated earnings).

Revise note 441 to read as follows:

[441] See generally ¶ 8.02[2]. For the different ordering regime where the redemption qualifies for § 302(a) sale treatment, see Rev. Rul. 74-339, 1974-2 CB 103 (regular dividends have first claim on earnings before § 302(a) redemption distributions).

[2] Basis of Stock Redeemed

Page 9-102:

Add to note 445.

But new Prop. Regs. § 1.302-5 (Oct. 16, 2002) change the basis approach here; delete Regs. § 1.302-2(c) "proper adjustment" rule and adopt a basis preservation regime for unused basis in redeemed stock (infra). Coven, "Basis Shifting: A Radical Proposal to an Intractable Problem," 105 Tax Notes 1541 (Dec. 13, 2004).

Add to note 446.

But new proposed regulations delete § 1.302-2(c), infra.

Add to note 447.

But new proposed regulations delete § 1.302-2(c), and shift to a basis preservation system, infra; thus, there is no basis shifting under the new proposals.

Add to note 449.

But new proposed regulations § 1.302-5 drop § 1.302-2(c) and replace it with a basis preservation regime (thus, no basis shifts under new proposals), infra.

Add to text after sentence ending with note 449.

Proposed regulations issued on October 16, 2002, abandon the above regime (as encouraging basis-shifting transactions), and replace it with a system that preserves unused basis in the case of redemptions taxable as a dividend;

this unused basis amount stays with the redeemed shareholder and is allowed as a loss on the occurrence of designated triggering events.[449.1] But these regulations were withdrawn for further study on April 19, 2006 (they should stay withdrawn for the many reasons set out in the cited comments).[449.2]

[449.1] Prop. Regs. § 1.302-5 (Oct. 16, 2002); the character of this deferred basis loss locks at the time of redemption. The key theme of the proposal is to deny shifting of basis. Prop. Regs. § 1.305-5(f) illustrates this new regime with eight examples (all of which involve individual shareholders). For comments, see infra note 452.1.

[449.2] See infra note 452.1; Ann. 2006-30, 2006-30, 2006-19 IRB 879 (May 8, 2006).

Add to note 450.

But Prop. Regs. §§ 1.304-2(a) and 1.304-2(c) change these rules and deny any shifting of basis; instead basis is preserved in the hands of the redeemed shareholder (and is deductible as a loss on the occurrence of designated trigger events). But these proposals were withdrawn for further study on April 19, 2006; Ann. 2006-30, 2006-19 IRB 879 (May 8, 2006).

Add to note 451.

Also Prop. Regs. §§ 1.304-2(a) and 1.304-2(c) reject the disappearing basis conclusion of the 1970 ruling. But these proposals were withdrawn April 19, 2006; Ann. 2006-30, 2006-19 IRB 879 (May 8, 2006).

Add to note 452.

See also Prop. Regs. §§ 1.304-2(a) and 1.304-2(c) implementing the 1997 amendments. But these proposals also were withdrawn for further study April 19, 2006; Ann. 2006-30, 2006-19 IRB 879 (May 8, 2006).

Add text to end of ¶ 9.22[2].

Thus, if, and when adopted in final form, the new proposed regulations will effectively block the basis-shifting transactions implicated in Notice 2001-45, which were being used to create artificial loss deductions.[452.1] By denying any shift of basis, and instead preserving unused basis following a dividend equivalent redemption for later use by the redeemed shareholder, these transac-

---

[452.1] 2001-33 IRB 129; see   5.10[5][c]. See Willens, "IRS Clamps Down on Basis-Shifting Tax Shelter Schemes With a New Approach That Defers Loss," 98 J. Tax'n 71 (Feb. 17, 2003); Feld, "Preserving Basis After Redemption," 98 Tax Notes 1143 (Feb. 17, 2003) (critique of proposed regulations as flawed); See also Coven, "Basis Shifting—A Radical Proposal to an Intractable Problem, "105 Tax Notes 154 (Dec. 13, 2004).

If Treasury's dividend exclusion proposal had been enacted, supra   8.06[1], presumably the deferred loss proposed in Regs. § 1.302-5 would be denied as a deduction under § 265 (as related to tax-exempt income). Under Ways and Means Chair Thomas's alternative proposal to tax dividends at capital gains rates (and lower that rate to 15 percent), these proposed regulations no longer seem to be needed at all; the Thomas proposal prevailed in the final 2003 tax bill; see   8.06[2].

tions will no longer be possible. But IRS withdrew the proposed regulations see further study on April 19, 2006 (and that's where they should stay).[452.2]

[452.2] Announcement 2006-30, 2006-19 IRB 879 (May 8, 2006). See Cummings, "Service's Withdrawal of Regulations Under Sections 302, 304 Highlights Confusion About Stock Redemptions," Distributions, Daily Tax Rep. No. 82, at J-1 (Apr. 28, 2006); Willens, Acquisition of Prohibited Interest After Redemption Triggers Dividend Income and Potential Basis Windfall for Related Shareholders, Daily Tax Rep. (BNA) No. 84, at J-1 (May 2, 2006).

CHAPTER 10

Complete Liquidations and Other Taxable Dispositions of Corporate Stock and Assets in Bulk

C   TAXABLE ACQUISITIONS

A GENERAL RULE: COMPLETE LIQUIDATIONS TREATED AS SALES OF LIQUIDATING CORPORATION'S STOCK AND ASSETS

¶ 10.03 SHAREHOLDER GAIN OR LOSS ON LIQUIDATING DISTRIBUTIONS

[2] Problems of Valuation and Timing

Page 10-15:

Add to note 39.

For the impact of 1999 repeal of § 453 for accrual-method taxpayers, see Notice 2000-26, 2000-17 IRB 954. But the 1999 repeal, in turn, was retroactively repealed on December 28, 2000.

Add to note 42.

But see Notice 2000-26, 2000-17 IRB 954 (only usable in rare cases).

Page 10-16:

Add to note 44.

See also Seagate Tech., Inc., RIA TC Memo. ¶ 2000-361 (2000) (assets sold for buyer's stock in "closed" transaction; gain on later sales of that stock after lapse of restrictions did not relate back to prior transaction under *Arrowsmith* principle).

Add to note 45.

Sair, Giannattasio & Perry, "Treatment of Contingent Obligations in Stock or Asset Sales Uncertain After Repeal of Installment Method of Reporting for Accrual Method Taxpayers," 27 J. Corp. Tax'n 203 (2000). But see supra note 39 for reinstatement.

But see Notice 2000-26, 2000-17 IRB 954 (accrual-method taxpayer generally cannot report liquidation on open transaction basis except in rare and extraordinary cases where value not ascertainable).

Page 10-18:

Add to note 50.

Notice 2000-26, 2000-17 IRB 954 echoes the "rarity" theme for application of *Logan* reporting.

[3] Effect of Liabilities on Shareholder's Gain or Loss

Page 10-20:

In note 57, change Peterson *to* Petersen.

Page 10-21:

Add to note 61 at end of first paragraph.

Final Regs. §§ 1.338-7(d)(1), 1.338-7(e), Ex. 1 (Feb. 13, 2001) are the same. Seagate Tech., Inc., RIA TC Memo. 2000-361 (2000) (sale of assets for buyer stock whose sale was restricted; gain on ultimate sale of that stock after lapse of restrictions did not relate back to prior transaction for *Arrowsmith* character treatment).

In note 63, change Peterson *to* Petersen.

Add to text at end of ¶ 10.03[3].

In that case, § 331 does not apply and § 165 controls the loss.[63.1]

[63.1] See 4.22[2]; see also Rev. Rul. 70-489, 1970-2 CB 53, and Rev. Rul. 56-387, 1956-2 CB 189 (former § 337 not applicable where there was no distribution to shareholders by insolvent corporation).

¶ 10.04 BASIS OF PROPERTY RECEIVED IN COMPLETE LIQUIDATION

Page 10-24:

Add to note 80.

The temporary regulations were adopted without change by TD 8940 on February 13, 2001 (effective March 16, 2001).

Page 10-25:

Add to note 82, first sentence.

Regs. § 1.1060-1(b)(3), Ex. 3 (Feb. 13, 2001) (same).

¶ 10.05 LIQUIDATING CORPORATION'S GAIN OR LOSS ON DISTRIBUTIONS OF APPRECIATED OR DEPRECIATED PROPERTY

[1] Introductory

Page 10-25:

Add to note 84 at end of second paragraph.

; Bell, "*General Utilities* Repeal, Section 355(e), and The Triple Tax," 87 Tax Notes 1385 (June 5, 2000).

Page 10-28:

Add to note 94.

Raby & Raby, "A 'Track-To-Run-On' for Built-In Gain Valuation Discounts?" 89 Tax Notes 395 (Oct. 16, 2000). But see Estate of Dunn v. CIR, 301 F3d 339 (5th Cir. 2002) (potential tax only relevant where asset-based valuation method is being applied, and extent to which that factor weighs in the process is a function of the likelihood of liquidation – to the extent this method is applied, assume all assets sold and full § 11 tax). Raby & Raby, "Reflecting Tax on Built-In Gain When Valuing Stock," 107 Tax Notes 1403 (June 13, 2005).

[2] Computation of Corporate Gain or Loss

[a] In General

Page 10-30:

Add to note 108.

Final Regs. § 1.1060-1(b)(3), Ex. 3 (Feb. 13, 2001) (effective March 16, 2001) is the same.

[c] "Deemed Liquidations"

Page 10-31:

Add to note 113.

New temporary regulations dealing with conversion from "C" to pass-through status were issued by TD 8975 on January 2, 2002; Regs. § 1.337(d)-6T (applicable to the period June 10, 1987 to January 1, 2002) and Regs. § 1.337(d)-7T (applicable on or after January 2, 2002; under this provision, § 1374 treatment is automatic unless taxpayer affirmatively elects deemed sale treatment, a change from the 2000 temporary regulations). Cummings, "New Temporary Regulations Issued on REIT and RIC Conversions by C Corporations," 96 J. Tax'n 220 (Apr. 2002). Adopted as final regulations by TD 9047 (Mar. 18, 2003).

[3] Limitations on Loss Recognition

Page 10-32:

Add to note 125.

See Randall, Spilker & Werlhof, "Interaction of New § 362(e)(2) With Loss Disallowance Rules," 32 Corp. Tax'n 24 (Sept. 2005) (for § 362(e)(2), see   3.11[8]); Kahn & Kahn, "Prevention of Double Deductions of a Single Loss: Solutions in Search of a Problem," 26 Va. Tax. Rev. 1 (2006).

[a] Losses on Distributions to Related Persons

Page 10-33:

Add to note 129.

See, e.g., Notice 2001-16, 2001-9 IRB 730 ("conduit intermediaries"); Nicole Rose Corp., 117 TC 328 (2001), aff'd 320 F3d 282 (2d Cir. 2002). See also Santa Monica Pictures, LLC, RIA TC Memo 2005-104 (2005).

[5] Prior Law

[c] Effect of Repeal on Stock Valuation

Page 10-40:

Add to note 155.

Raby & Raby, "A 'Track-To-Run-On' for Built-In Gain Valuation Discounts?" 89 Tax Notes 395 (Oct. 16, 2000). But see Estate of Dunn v. US, 301 F3d 339 (5th Cir. 2002) (no effect where valuation based on earnings potential method; only relevant where valuation based on asset valuation method and weight depends on likelihood of liquidation to extent this method is applied, assume all assets sold and full § 11 tax incurred). Raby & Raby, "Reflecting Tax on Built-In Gain When Valuing Stock," 107 Tax Notes 1403 (June 13, 2005).

     But see Estate of Kahn, 125 TC No. 11 (2005) (potential tax discount not applicable to IRAs; cases distinguished).

[6] Defenses to the Recognition Regime of § 336

Page 10-41:

Add to note 160.

New temporary regulations dealing with conversion from "C" to pass-through status were issued by TD 8975 on January 2, 2002; under § 1.337(d)-7T (applicable on or after Jan. 2, 2002), the default rule was changed from deemed sale to § 1374 treatment; taxpayer must affirmatively elect deemed sale treatment now). See Cummings, supra note 113. Adopted as final regulations by TD 9047 (Mar. 18, 2003).

Page 10-43:

Add to note 174:

See also Notice 2001-16, 2001-9 IRB 730 (IRS attack on "conduit intermediary" shelters; a listed tax shelter transaction required to be disclosed); Nicole Rose Corp., 117 TC 328 (2001), aff'd 320 F3d 282 (2d Cir. 2003).

B   SUBSIDIARY LIQUIDATIONS

¶ 10.20   INTRODUCTORY

Page 10-59:

Add to note 254.

But compare Dover Corp., 122 TC 324 (2004) (deemed liquidation under check-the-box election; parent inherited business status of its subsidiary under § 381). *Dover* opinion seemed to adopt a unitary view of parent-subsidiary liquidations.

¶ 10.21   NONRECOGNITION OF PARENT'S GAIN OR LOSS; BASIS AND OTHER CARRYOVERS

[1] In General: § 332

Page 10-63:

Add to note 265.

Final Regs. § 1.338(h)(10)-1(e), Ex. 2 (Feb. 13, 2001) (effective March 16, 2001) is the same.

[2] Insolvent Subsidiaries

Page 10-63:

Add to note 266.

But Prop. Regs. § 1.368-1(f), issued Mar. 10, 2005, requiring a "net value exchange" in order to qualify for tax-free §368 reorganization treatment; IRS will no longer follow the *Norman Scott* decision. See NYSBA Tax Section, "Formations, Reorganizations, and Liquidations Involving Insolvent Corporations," 110 Tax Notes 871 (Feb. 20, 2006); Blanchard, Hooker and Vogel, "Underwater Assets and Insolvent Corporations: Reflections on Treasury's Recently Proposed Regulations and Related Matters," 59 Tax Law. 107 (Fall 2005).

Add to note 267.

Rev. Rul. 70-489 was superceded by Rev. Rul. 2003-125, 2003-52 IRB 1243. Prop. Regs. issued Mar. 10, 2005, §§ 1.332-2(a), 1.332-2(b) and 1.332-2(e) Ex. 2, reaffirm regulations, *Spalding Bakery* and *H.K. Porter* conclusion that § 332 will not apply unless parent receives something for its common stock in the liquidation (new proposals require "net value exchange" for § 332 nonrecognition); Cummings, "New Proposed Regs. Change Rules for Transactions Where Property or Stock Lacks Net Value," 103 J. Tax'n 14 (July 2005); NYSBA Tax Section, supra note 266.

Add to note 268.

Rev. Rul. 59-296 was amplified by Rev. Rul. 2003-125, 2003-52 IRB 1243. Prop. Regs. § 1.332-2(a), 1.332-2(b) and 1.332-2(e) Ex. 2 (Mar. 10, 2005).

Page 10-64:

Add to note 269.

Blanchard et al., "The Deductibility of Investments in Financially Troubled Subsidiaries and Related Federal Income Tax Considerations," 80 Taxes 91 (Mar. 2002); Paul, *"United Dominion:* Implications For Attribute Reduction," 95 Tax Notes 262 (Apr. 8, 2001); Bennett, "Corporate Tax Watch: Code Section 165(g): Under the Microscope," 81 Taxes 11 (Feb. 2003); Shepard, "When Do Subsidiary Shares Become Worthless?" 100 Tax Notes 746 (Aug. 11, 2003). See also Rev. Rul. 2003-125, 2003-52 IRB 1243; Calianno, "When Does a Conversion of a Foreign Corporation to a Foreign Branch Entitle a Domestic Parent to a Worthless Stock Loss?" 15 J. Int'l Tax'n 22 (Apr. 2004); Bennett, "Rev. Rul. 2003-125: Worthlessness and Deemed Liquidation," 82 Taxes 17 (Apr. 2004); Rizzi, "Worthless Stock and Section 332: New Ruling Dulls the Double-Edged Sword," 31 Corp. Tax'n 24 (Mar. 2004); Cummings, "Foreign Subsidiary Losses Appear Safer," 105 Tax Notes 583 (Oct. 25, 2004); Schnee & Seago, "The Tax Result of a Subsidiary Becoming Worthless," 34 Corp. Tax'n 18 (Mar. 2007).

Add to note 273.

Final regulations adopted by TD 8940 on February 13, 2001 (effective March 16, 2001), move (but do not materially change) these rules to Regs. § 1.338-3(d). See also Rev. Rul. 2001-46, 2001-42 IRB 321 (two-step double mergers integrated into single § 368(a)(1)(A) direct merger). But new temporary regulations issued July 9, 2003, in TD 9071 modify Rev. Rul. 2001-46 and allow a § 338(h)(10) election if the first step stock acquisition is a stand-alone qualified stock purchase; Regs. §§ 1.338(h)(10)-1T, and 1.338(h)(10)-1T(e), Exs. 11–14.

Add to note 276.

Prop. Regs. § 1.332-2(b) and 1.332-2(e), Ex. 2 (Mar. 10, 2005) reaffirm these decisions. See NYSBA Tax Section report, supra note 266.

Page 10-65:

Add to text at end of last full paragraph.

A recent proposal by the NYS Bar Tax Section[281.1] would continue non-§ 332 treatment for liquidating insolvent subsidiaries, but would extend § 368 reorganization treatment to allow tax-free status for those transactions.[281.2] Proposed regulations issued on March 10, 2005, reconfirm the nonapplication of § 332 here,[281.3] but also confirm the possible application of §368(a)(1)(C) (at least if its requirements are satisfied,[281.4] in view of the repeal of the *Bausch & Lomb* case).[281.5]

[281.1] Report, "Reorganizations Involving Insolvent Subsidiaries," 101 Tax Notes 761 (Nov. 10, 2003). For such regulations, see Prop. Regs. §§ 1.332-2(a), 1.332-2(b), and 1.332-2(c), ex. 2 (Mar. 10, 2005).

[281.2] For insolvency reorganizations generally, see ¶¶ 12.30 and 12.63[1]. See also Rev. Rul. 2003-125, 2003-52 IRB 1243; comments supra note 269. See also Cummings, supra note 267, and NYSBA Tax Section, supra note 266

[281.3] Prop. Regs. §§ 1.332-2(b), and 1.332-2(e) Ex. 2.

[281.4] See ¶ 12.24 (principally the solely voting stock and substantially all requirements).

[281.5] See ¶ 12.63[5].

[3] Conditions for Qualification Under § 332

[a] Eighty Percent Stock Ownership

Page 10-67:

In fifth and sixth lines of the first paragraph change (2) at least 80 percent of the total value of shares of all other classes of stock *to* (2) at least 80 percent of the value of all other stock.

Add to note 286.

Final Regs. § 1.368-2(d)(4) were adopted without change on May 19, 2000 (effective January 1, 2000).

Page 10-68:

Add to note 291.

Final regulations adopted by TD 8940 on February 13, 2001 (effective March 16, 2001) move again (without material change) to Regs. § 1.338-3(d). See also Rev. Rul. 2001-46, 2001-42 IRB 321 (stock acquisition for 70 percent voting stock and 30 percent cash) in failed § 368(a)(2)(E) reverse merger followed by planned integrated upstream merger held

direct § 368(a)(1)(A) reorganization resulting in carryover basis; § 338 election not available here); see   12.25[3][a], 12.63[2][a].
     But new temporary regulations issued July 9, 2003, in TD 9071 modify Rev. Rul.
2001-46 and allow a § 338(h)(10) election if the first step stock acquisition is a stand-
alone qualified stock purchase; Regs. §§ 1.338(h)(10)-1T(c)(2) and 1.338(h)(10)-1T(e),
Exs. 11–14; adopted as final regulations without change on July 5, 2006.

[5] Basis and Other Carryovers

[a] Basis: § 334(b)

Page 10-74:

Add to note 325.

Can also apply where § 337(c) recognized gain results and a parent, not a direct 80-per-
cent distributee, still gets § 332 nonrecognition via consolidated return stock aggregation
rule of Regs. § 1.1502-34, infra   10.22[3].

Page 10-75:

Add to text at the end of ¶10.21[5][a].

     But the 2004 Jobs Act modified the carryover basis rule in § 334(b)(1)(B)
to prevent the import of built-in loss on the liquidation of a foreign subsidiary
into its domestic parent (basis is stepped down to fair market value at the border).[329.1]

[329.1] See   15.85[7][e].

[b] Other Carryovers: § 381

Add to note 331.

But contra to *Arco* is Dover Corp., 122 TC 324 (2004) (IRS ruling after *Arco* changed the
treatment of parent-subsidiary liquidations, as did enactment of § 381 in 1954 – transac-
tion in *Arco* preceded these events). For comments, see Sheppard, "The Undead Subpart
F," 103 Tax Notes 948 (May 24, 2004); Cummings, "Midco Transactions Resurface:
Court Holding Miscast," 103 Tax Notes 1061 (May 24, 2004). Further consideration of
Dover is in Chapter 15,   15.01[4] and 15.61[4].

Page 10-75:

Add to note 332.

     But application of § 381 to a less than 80-percent parent who is getting § 332 non-
recognition by virtue of Regs. § 1.1502-34 stock aggregation rule seems doubtful (see
"single parent" rule of § 1.381(a)-1(b)(2)(i),   14.21[2], 14.21[3][c], and 13.48[5][a]).
But see Prop. Regs. § 1.1502-80(g) (2005).

¶ 10.22 LIQUIDATING SUBSIDIARY'S RECOGNITION OF GAIN OR LOSS: § 337

[1] In General

Page 10-77:

Add to note 342.

Moreover, § 1504(a)(4) "pure preferred stock" also is disregarded for this purpose.

[4] Examples

Page 10-81:

Add new Example 6 after Example 5.

> **EXAMPLE 6:** *Alternative Structure (T-3 jointly owned by T-1 and T-2).* If T-3 liquidates up into its two co-parents, T-1 and T-2, they both receive § 332 nonrecognition via the stock aggregation rule of the consolidated return regulations;[365.1] but T-3 has taxable gain here under § 337(c), second sentence.[365.2] But if T-1 instead holds only § 1502(a)(4) "pure preferred stock" of T-3, liquidating distributions to T-2 would not trigger § 337(c) gain, though distributions to T-1 would.[365.3]

[365.1] Regs. § 1.1502-34; see infra ¶¶ 13.41[2][a] and 13.48[5][a].

[365.2] See supra ¶ 10.22[1]. Regs. § 1.381(a)-1(b)(2)(i) (the "single parent" rule) indicates no carryover here but result seems unclear at best, and no official published authority on this question to date. For the consolidated return result, see Prop. Regs. § 1.1502-80(g) (2005), ¶ 13.48[5][a].

[365.3] Such stock is "nonstock" for purposes of §§ 332 and 337 as well as § 1504 (in effect it is treated as "quasi-debt" here), supra ¶ 10.21[3][a], note 286; see also supra ¶ 10.21[2].

¶ 10.24 MINORITY SHAREHOLDERS

Page 10-84:

Add to note 383.

Adopted as final Regs. § 1.338-3(d) by TD 8940 on February 13, 2001 (effective March 16, 2001).

Page 10-85:

Add to note 385.

These proposals were adopted without change on May 19, 2000 (effective January 1, 2000).

C TAXABLE ACQUISITIONS

¶ 10.40 ASSET ACQUISITIONS: ALLOCATION OF PURCHASE PRICE IN COMPUTING BASIS AND RELATED PROBLEMS

[1] In General

Page 10-88:

Add to note 394.

But this provision in turn was retroactively repealed in December 2000; see Notice 2001-22, 2001-12 IRB 911.

Page 10-90:

Add to note 400.

The 2000 temporary regulations were adopted without change by TD 8940 on February 13, 2001 (effective March 16, 2001). All citations to the 2000 temporary regulations remain the same in this   10.40 (except the "T" should be deleted).

Add to text at end of ¶ 10.40[1].

The January 2000 temporary regulations were adopted without change on February 13, 2001 (so all citations to those regulations should delete the "T").[400.1]

[400.1] The 2000 temporary regulations were adopted without change by TD 8940 on February 13, 2001 (effective March 16, 2001). All citations to the 2000 temporary regulations remain the same in this   10.40 (except the "T" should be deleted).

[3] Allocation of Consideration Among Asset Classes

Page 10-93:

Add to text at end of ¶ 10.40[3].

These temporary regulations were adopted without change on February 13, 2001.[425.1]

[425.1] TD 8940 (effective March 16, 2001).

[4] Consideration

[a] In General

Add to note 426.

But see Bailine, IRS Has No "Basis" for "Cost" Conclusion, 30 J. Corp. Tax'n 26 (May 2003) (issues as to what is "cast"); see   3.12[4].

[b] Contingent Liabilities

Add to note 436.

Willens, "Treatment of Contingent Liabilities in an Acquisition Setting," Daily Tax Rep. (BNA) No. 188, at J-1 (Sept. 29, 2003).

Page 10-95:

Add to note 437.

Illinois Tool Works, Inc., 117 TC 39 (2001), aff'd, 355 F3d 997 (7th Cir. 2004) (assumed contingent liabilities had to be capitalized in basis of purchased assets); comment by Raby & Raby, "Contingent Liability Payments in Business Purchases," 92 Tax Notes 941 (Aug. 13, 2001); aff'd, 355 F3d 997 (7th Cir. 2004).

Add to note 438.

Notice 2000-26, 2000-17 IRB 954 repeats the "rarity" with which *Logan* open transaction treatment will be allowed.

Add to note 439.

Sair et al., "Treatment of Contingent Obligations in Stock or Asset Sales Uncertain After Repeal of Installment Method of Reporting for Accrual Method Taxpayers," 27 J. Corp. Tax'n 203 (2000); Lipton, "Installment Rule Change Creates a Multitude of Problems for Many Taxpayers," 92 J. Tax'n 134 (March 2000); Flinn, "Does Installment Sale Rule Change Make Stock Sales a More Attractive Means of Structuring Sale of Smaller C Corporations?" 78 Taxes 31 (July 2000); yes, see Notice 2000-26, 2000-17 IRB 954. But § 453 treatment was retroactively restored on December 28, 2000.

Add after first sentence of note 440.

See, e.g., Illinois Tool Works, Inc., 117 TC 39 (2001), aff'd, 355 F3d 997 (7th Cir. 2004); comment by Raby & Raby, "Contingent Liability Payments in Business Purchases," 92 Tax Notes 941 (Aug. 13, 2001).

[6] Buyer's Deductions; Amortizable Intangible Assets

Page 10-98:

Add to note 447, first paragraph.

See also Fed. Home Loan Mortgage Corp., 121 TC 129 (2003) (benefit of below-market financing created an amortizable intangible asset to be valued at fair market value on date taxpayer became a taxable entity).

Page 10-99:

In the second line of runover paragraph add new note 448.1 following "compete".

[448.1] See, e.g., Frontier Chevrolet Co., 116 TC 289 (2001) (had to use § 197 fifteen-year term for five-year noncompete covenant), aff'd, 329 F3d 1131, 2003-1 USTC ¶ 50,490 (9th Cir. 2003).

Add new note 448.2 to end of runover paragraph.

[448.2] Frontier Chevrolet Co., 116 TC 289 (2001) involved a noncompete convenant issued by majority shareholder incident to a bootstrap buy-out change of control; even though redeeming corporation acquired the covenant in connection with its own existing business, § 197 nevertheless applied. See Raby & Raby, "Section 197 Noncompete Covenants in Corporate Stock Redemptions," 91 Tax Notes 1573 (May 28, 2001). Frontier was aff'd, 329 F3d 1131, 2003-1 USTC ¶ 50,496 (9th Cir. 2003).

Add to note 451.

See, e.g., Frontier Chevrolet Co., 117 TC 289 (2001), involved a noncompete convenant issued by majority shareholder incident to a bootstrap buy-out change of control; even though redeeming corporation acquired the covenant in connection with its own existing business, § 197 nevertheless applied. See Raby & Raby, "Section 197 Noncompete Covenants in Corporate Stock Redemptions," 91 Tax Notes 1573 (May 28, 2001). Frontier was aff'd, 329 F3d 1131, 2003-1 USTC ¶ 50,496 (9th Cir. 2003).

Page 10-100:

Add to note 456.

Bryant & Foran, "Regulations Clarify Intangible Amortization and Provide Anti-Churning Rules," 78 Taxes 37 (July 2000). Cameron & Postlewaite, "Amortization of Intangible Assets Improved Under the Improved Final Regulations," 93 J. Tax'n 150 (Sept. 2000).

[7] Transactional Form Consistency Requirement: Proposed Legislation

Page 10-101:

Add to note 462.

Harris, "Should There Be a "Form Consistency" Requirement? *Danielson* Revisited," 78 Taxes 88 (Mar. 2000).

¶ 10.41 STOCK ACQUISITIONS AND TARGET ASSET BASIS: OVERVIEW

[1] *Kimbell-Diamond* Doctrine

Page 10-103:

Add to note 468.

But *Kimbell-Diamond* principle revived for two-step double mergers so long as the first step passes continuity of interest limits (as it did here), Rev. Rul. 2001-46, 2001-42 IRB 321; see   12.63[2][a]. But see Regs. § 1.338(h)(10)-1T, infra note 470.

Add to note 470.

See also Rev. Rul. 2001-46, 2001-42 IRB 321 (*Kimbell-Diamond* principle applied to turn integrated two-step double merger into direct § 368(a)(1)(A) reorganization (*P* acquired *T* stock for 70 percent *P* stock and 30 percent cash, followed by integrated upstream merger per step transaction doctrine); see   12.63[2][a]; Blanchard, "Reflections on Rev. Rul. 2001-46 and the Continued Vitality of *Kimbell-Diamond*," 93 Tax Notes 1875 (Dec. 31, 2001). Cummings, "Rev. Rul. 2001-46 Revisited," 94 Tax Notes 641 (Feb. 4, 2002); Blanchard, "Revisiting Rev. Rul. 2001-46 Once Again," 94 Tax Notes 1707 (Mar. 25, 2002).

But see Regs. § 1.338(h)(10)-1T (July 9, 2003), which modified Rev. Rul. 2001-46 by allowing a § 338(h)(10) election if the first step stock acquisition is a stand-alone qualified stock purchase. Adopted without change by TD 9271 on July 5, 2006.

[3] Section 338: 1982 to 1986

Page 10-104:

Add to note 472.

Final regulations issued by TD 8940 on February 13, 2001, moved again to § 1.338-3(d) (effective March 16, 2001). But see Rev. Rul. 2001-46, supra note 470.

[4] Section 338: Current

Page 10-108:

Add to text at end of ¶ 10.41[4].

These regulations were adopted with minor changes on February 13, 2001.[481.1]

[481.1] TD 8940 (effective March 16, 2001). MacNeal et al., "Final Regs. on Allocation of Purchase Price to Assets Affect Actual and Deemed Sales," 95 J. Tax'n 15 (July 2001).

[5] Revision of the § 338 Regulations (1999 and 2000)

[a] In General

Page 10-109:

Add to text at end of ¶ 10.41[5][a].

The final regulations adopted on February 13, 2001, made very few changes in the temporary regulations (all of which were set out in the preamble),[484.1] and these will be noted in the following pages.[484.2]

[484.1] TD 8940 (effective March 16, 2001).

[484.2] Where no changes were made in substance or location, the "T" should be removed from the 2000 temporary regulations.

[b] Restructure of the Regulations

Add to note 487.

In one of the rare substantive changes to the proposed regulations, final Regs. § 1.338-3(b)(2) dropped the "nominal payment" limitation on qualified stock purchases (can be a purchase even though nothing paid for the target stock), infra ¶ 10.42[2].

Page 10-110:

Add to note 495.

Final Regs. § 1.338(h)(10)-1 adopt these regulations without significant change.

Add to text at end of ¶ 10.42[5][b].

The final regulations adopted on February 13, 2001, retained this structure.

In heading for ¶ 10.41[5][c] replace "Assets" with "Asset".

[c] The Standard Model: Deemed Asset Sales Treated As Actual Asset Sales [Revised Heading]

Add to text at end of paragraph.

The final regulations adopted on February 13, 2001, retained this standard model as the touchstone.

[d] General "Anti-Abuse" Rule: Regulations § 1.338-1(c)

Add to text at end of paragraph.

Despite pleas for "clarification," the final regulations adopted in February 2001 retained this rule, but narrowed its scope somewhat.[497.1]

[497.1] E.g., Ex. 2 was modified slightly and regulations state that IRS adjustments should avoid duplication or omission.

Final regulations added a new rule in § 1.338-1(d) (effect of postclosing transactions under § 1.1502-76(b) allocation rules; must use next-day rule for extraordinary business transactions).

[e] Delinking of ADSP and AGUB Timing

Page 10-111:

Add to text at end of paragraph.

The final February 2001 regulations retained this approach without change.

[f] Changes to the § 338(h)(10) Regulations

Add to text at end of paragraph.

The final February 2001 regulations adopted these proposals without change.

¶ 10.42 SECTION 338: THE ELECTION AND ITS EFFECTS

[1] Effects of Election

[a] In General

Page 10-114:

Add text at end of ¶ 10.42[1][a].

The final February 2001 regulations adopted all of the previously stated temporary 2000 regulations virtually intact.[515.1]

[515.1] TD 8940, February 13, 2001 (effective March 16, 2001).

[b] Old Target's Gain or Loss

Add to note 519.

These temporary regulations were adopted in final form by TD 8940 on February 13, 2001 (effective March 16, 2001), infra   10.42[1][c].

[c] Proposed and Temporary Regulations ADSP Rule: § 1.338-4, § 1.338-4T

Page 10-117:

Add text at end of ¶ 10.42[1][c].

These temporary regulations were adopted virtually intact on February 13, 2001 (effective March 16, 2001).

[2] Qualified Stock Purchase

Add to note 531.

; but the final February 13, 2001, regulations dropped the "nominal amount" purchase price limitation of the proposed regulations and instead provide in § 1.338-3(b)(2) that no amount need be paid for the stock if the transaction otherwise qualifies as a purchase (this was one of the few substantive changes effected by the final regulations).

All other portions of the 2000 temporary regulations noted in this paragraph were adopted without change by the February 13, 2001, final regulations.

Add to note 532.

The final February 2001 regulations are the same (and so are the citations).

[3] Election

Page 10-121:

Add to note 546.

Final regulations adopted on February 13, 2001, are the same (effective March 16, 2001).

Add text to end of ¶ 10.42[3].

Later revisions of the regulations (proposed in 1999, adopted in temporary form in 2000, and finalized in 2001) continue this beneficial result.[546.1]

[546.1] Final regulations adopted on February 13, 2001, are the same (effective March 16, 2001).

[4] Consistency Requirements

[e] Comments

Page 10-126:

Add to note 567.

Final Regs. § 1.338-4(h) (effective March 16, 2001) is the same.

[5] Actual Liquidation or Reorganization of Subsidiary When § 338 Was or Could Have Been Elected

Add to note 568.

Final regulations adopted in 2001 are the same (effective March 16, 2001).

Page 10-127:

Add to note 570.

Final regulations adopted in 2001 are the same (effective March 16, 2001).

Page 10-128:

Add to note 571.

Final regulations adopted February 13, 2001, move (but do not materially change) this provision to Regs. § 1.338-3(d) (effective March 16, 2001).

Add to note 573.

Final Regs. § 1.338-3(d) (effective March 16, 2001) is virtually the same.

Add to note 574, after first sentence.

Final Regs. § 1.338-3(d) (effective March 13, 2001) (same).

Add to end of note 574.

But see Rev. Rul. 2001-46, 2001-42 IRB 321 (*P* acquired all of *T* stock for 30 percent cash and 70 percent *P* Stock, followed by planned upstream merger of *P* into *T*) held, direct § 368(a)(1)(A) reorganization and no § 338 election possible; *Kimbell-Diamond* principle redux); see 12.63[2][a]. But modified by Regs. § 1.338(h)(10)-1T (July 9, 2003) (parties can make a § 338(h)(10) election if first step qualifies as a stand-alone qualified stock purchase). Adopted without change by TD 9271 (July 5, 2006). Regs. § 1.338(h)(10)-1(c)(2).

[6] Sale of Stock Treated as Sale of Assets: § 338(h)(10)

[a] Original 1986 Temporary Regulations and Revised 1994 Regulations (Former Rules)

Page 10-128:

Add to note 575.

Final Regs. § 1.338-10(a)(1) (2001) (effective March 16, 2001) is the same. See also new Regs. § 1.338-1(d) (2001) ensuring this result in the case of "extraordinary" transactions following a qualified purchase event (and TD 8940 explanation under "Closing Date Issues").

Page 10-129:

In the first sentence of the second paragraph, insert which they did in 1994 *at the end of the parenthetical.*

Add to note 578, to the end of the first paragraph.

Seago & Barkhi, "In the Process of Preventing Triple Taxation of a Subsidiary's Income, Congress Created a Great Indoor Game," 109 Tax Notes 1081 (Nov. 21, 2005).

Page 10-132:

Add to note 595.

Illinois Tool Works, Inc. 117 TC 39 (2001) (followed *Webb* and required payment of contingent liabilities to be capitalized); Raby & Raby, "Contingent Liability Payments in Business Purchases," 92 Tax Notes 941 (Aug. 13, 2001); aff'd, 355 F3d 997 (7th Cir. 2004).

Add text at end of final full paragraph.

These temporary regulations were adopted in final form on February 13, 2001 (with a few minor modifications).[597.1]

[597.1] TD 8940 (effective March 16, 2001), infra ¶ 10.43[3].

[b] Proposed and Temporary Regulations (Current Rules)

Page 10-133:

Add to note 598.

McManus, "Prop. Regs. Shed New Light on § 338(h)(10) Transactions Involving S Corporations," 91 J. Tax'n 358 (Nov. 1999). Final regulations adopted by TD 8940 on February 23, 2001, are virtually identical to the temporary regulations (including citations).

Add to note 599.

Final regulations adopted February 13, 2001, are the same (effective March 16, 2001). See Willens, "Securing a Cost Basis at the Cost of Only a Single Level of Tax," 113 Tax Notes 183 (Oct. 9, 2006).

Add to text at end of first paragraph.

These temporary regulations were adopted without change on February 13, 2001.[599.1]

[599.1] TD 8940 (effective Mar. 13, 2001).

Page 10-134:

Add to note 603.

The final February 2001 regulations provide no special rule for this case because its assets are deemed to be owned by the S corporation so a sale of Q Sub stock is treated as a sale of its assets (see TD 8940 explanation re: "S Corporations").

Add to note 604.

For partial administrative relief, see Notice 2000-26, 2000-17 IRB 954. See generally Lipton, "Installment Rule Change Creates a Multitude of Problems for Many Taxpayers," 92 J. Tax'n 134 (Mar. 2000); Flinn, "Does Installment Sale Rule Change Make Stock Sales a More Attractive Means of Structuring Sale of Smaller C Corporations?" 78 Taxes 31 (July 2000) (yes). But § 453 treatment was retroactively restored on December 28, 2000.

¶ 10.43 ALLOCATION OF BASIS PURSUANT TO § 338 ELECTION

[2] Aggregate Basis to Be Allocated

Page 10-137:

Add to note 610.

, as are final regulations adopted by TD 8940 on February 13, 2001 (effective March 16, 2001).

[a] Grossed-Up Basis of Recently Purchased Stock

Add to note 613.

Final regulations adopted February 13, 2001, are the same (effective March 16, 2001).

Add the following text to first line of second paragraph after "temporary".

(and 2001 final)

Page 10-138:

Add to note 616.

Final Regs. § 1.338-5(b)(2) (2001).

[b] Basis of Nonrecently Purchased Stock

Add to note 619.

The February 2001 final regulations are the same (effective March 16, 2001).

Add to note 620.

The final 2001 regulations are the same (effective March 16, 2001).

[c] Target's Liabilities

Add to note 622.

Regs. §§ 1.338-5(e)(1), 1.338-5(e)(2) (2001) (same) (effective March 16, 2001).

Page 10-139:

Add to note 623.

Regs. § 1.338-5(e)(2) (2001) (same) (effective March 16, 2001).

Add to note 624.

Final Regs. § 1.338-7(d)(1) (2001) is the same. See also Illinois Tool Works, Inc., 117 TC 39 (2001) (payment of assumed contingent liabilities required to be capitalized in purchased assets); comment by Raby & Raby, 92 Tax Notes 941 (Aug. 13, 2001); aff'd, 355 F3d 997 (7th Cir. 2004).

In fourth line of text at end of parenthetical clause add "and as final regulations in 2001".

Delete citation in note 625 and replace with the following.

Prop. Regs. § 1.338-7(a) (1999) and Regs. § 1.338-7T(a) (2000). Final Regs. § 1.338-7(a) (2001) are generally the same (effective March 16, 2001), but the final regulations dropped the first-year adjustment rules of the temporary regulations (see TD 8940 explanation at "First Year Price Adjustments").

Add to note 626 at end of first paragraph.

Final Regs. § 1.338-4(d)(1) (2001) adopt the same general rule though with less specificity.

Add to note 626, second paragraph.

Final Regs. §§ 1.338-4(e) and 1.338-5(e)(3) reiterate this rule.

Page 10-140:

Add to note 627.

, as are the final regulations adopted on February 13, 2001 (effective March 16, 2001).

Add text to end of ¶ 10.43[2][c].

One of the few substantive changes made by the 2001 final regulations dropped the first-year adjustment rules of the 1999 and 2000 regulations.[627.1]

[627.1] See TD 8940, Explanation "First Year Price Adjustments." Thus, all adjustments after the acquisition date are subject to the general rule of Regs. § 1.338-7.

[d] Other Relevant Items

Add to note 629.

So do the final February 2001 regulations.

Add text to end of ¶ 10.43[2][d].

The final regulations adopted in February 2001 likewise omit these adjustments.

[3] Allocation of Adjusted Grossed-Up Basis Among Target's Assets

Add to note 630.

These regulations were adopted (with slight modifications) by TD 8940 on February 13, 2001 (effective March 16, 2001).

Page 10-142:

Add to note 633.

Final Regs. § 1.338-7 (same) (effective March 16, 2001).

Add to text after sentence ending with note 637.

These regulations were adopted as final regulations in slightly modified form on February 13, 2001.[637.1]

[637.1] TD 8940 (effective Mar. 16, 2001).

Page 10-143:

Add to note 638.

Final Regs. § 1.338-6(b)(1) (2001) is the same.

Add new note 638.1 to item 2 in text.

[638.1] Final Regs. § 1.338-6(b)(2)(ii) exclude target affiliate stock (unless traded § 1504(a)(4) stock); instead goes to class V.

Add note 638.2 to item 3 in text.

[638.2] Final Regs. § 1.338-6(b)(2)(iii) include all assets that *T* marks to market at least annually (but excludes certain debt assets that presumably fall into the general asset class V).

In text item 4, change VI to IV.

D COLLAPSIBLE CORPORATIONS

¶ 10.60 INTRODUCTORY

Page 10-147:

Add to note 679, third paragraph.

The Joint Committee Staff's April 2001 simplification report proposes that § 341 be repealed as de facto deadwood (and overly complex deadwood at that). The 2003 tax reduction bill finally repealed § 341 (effective January 1, 2003); HR 2, § 302(e)(4)(A), so the material in this Part D is now of historical interest only (and not all that interesting).

CHAPTER **11**

Corporate Divisions

¶ 11.01 GENERAL CONSIDERATIONS AND HISTORICAL BACKGROUND

[1] Introductory

[e] Form of Nontaxable Distribution

Add to text at end of item 2.

For 2006 legislation restricting (but not eliminating) "cash-rich split-offs," see infra ¶ 11.11[5].

Page 11-7:

Add to note 18 at the end of first paragraph.

Beller & Harwell, "After the Spin: Preserving Tax-Free Treatment Under Section 355," 92 Tax Notes 1587 (Sept. 17, 2001). Revenue Procedure 96-30 was revised (and scaled back for § 355 rulings) by Revenue Procedure 2003-48, 2003-29 IRB 86.

[f] Significance of Tax-Free Divisions: Tax Stakes

Page 11-8:

Add to note 20.

Beller & Harwell, "After the Spin: Preserving Tax-Free Treatment Under Section 355," 92 Tax Notes 1587 (Sept. 17, 2001).

But IRS revised Rev. Proc. 96-30 in Rev. Proc. 2003-48, 2003-29 IRB 86, and materially reduced the areas on which it would issue PLRs under § 355 (viz., will not rule on business purpose (§ 4.01), device (§ 4.02), or existence of § 355(e) "plan" (§ 4.03); it also removed App. A, the business purpose guidelines). Cummings, "Section 355 Rulings Downsized," 100 Tax Notes 405 (July 21, 2003); Rothman, "Back to the Bog: The IRS's New Policy on Spin-Off Rulings Leaves Practitioners With a Sinking Feeling," 31 J. Corp. Tax'n 3 (Sept. 2003); Bailine, "The Curtailment of Letter Rulings—A Bad Deal for All," 31 J. Corp. Tax'n 40 (Sept. 2003).

Add text to end of ¶ 11.01[1][f].

IRS is ever alert to defend the integrity of § 355's strictures: Thus, Revenue Ruling 2000-5[20.1] prohibits mergers that have a "divisive effect" as an inappropriate end around the requirements of § 355, and recent regulations deny Type A reorganization by disregarded entities.[20.2]

[20.1] 2000-5 IRB 436. See Bank, "The Runaway 'A' Train. Does the IRS Need New Breaks?" 87 Tax Notes 553 (Apr. 24, 2000); ¶ 12.22[11].

[20.2] Prop. Regs. § 1.368-2(b)(1) (May 12, 2000); ¶ 12.22[10]; Prop. Regs. § 1.368-2(b) (Nov. 15, 2001) continues this limitation, but now permits mergers into disregarded entities (unlike the first proposed regulation, which denied Type A here as well). These proposals were adopted as Temporary Regs. 1.368-2T(b)(1) by TD 9038 on Jan. 24, 2003; and became final in TD 9242 (Jan. 23, 2006).

¶ 11.02 OVERVIEW: CORPORATE DIVISIONS UNDER CURRENT LAW

[1] Roles of § 355

Page 11-13:

In note 37 change Simmons & Simmons *to* Simon & Simmons.

Add the following the end of the first sentence in note 37.

Beller & Harwell, "After the Spin: Preserving Tax-Free Treatment Under Section 355," 92 Tax Notes 1587 (Sept. 17, 2001); for reform proposals, see Schler, "Simplifying and Rationalizing the Spinoff Rules," 56 SMU L. Rev. 239 (2003); Yin, "Commentary; Taxing Corporate Divisions," 56 SMU L. Rev. 289 (2003). Canellos, "The Section 355 Edifice: Spin-offs Past, Present, and Future," 104 Tax Notes 419 (July 26, 2004).

[2] Statutory Requirements

[a] Control

Page 11-15:

Add to note 44 at the end of the first paragraph.

Currently Rev. Proc. 2003-5, § 4.01(29) (ordinarily no ruling), 2005-1 IRB 118.

[3] Other Aspects of § 355

Page 11-19:

Add to note 68.

Prop. Regs. § 1.355-6 became final on Dec. 20, 2000; the 1999 Prop. Regs. § 1.355-7 were withdrawn and reproposed on Jan. 2, 2001, and adopted as temporary Regs. § 1.355-7T on Aug. 3, 2001. These regulations were withdrawn and reissued as new temporary regulations on April 26, 2002 (and they are the most taxpayer-friendly version by far), infra   11.11[3][d]; adopted as final regulations by TD 9198 (Apr. 19, 2005) (even more liberal).

Add to text at end of ¶ 11.02[3].

For 2006 legislation dealing with a new perceived abuse, the "cash-rich split-off," see infra   11.11[5] (restricting these transactions, but *not* eliminating them).

[5] Surrogates for § 355: "Tracking Stock" and "Stapled Stock"

Page 11-20:

Add to note 74.

For the possibility of combining § 355 with a stock stapling transaction, see Dunn & Rizzi, "Spin-Off and Stapling Transactions," 25 J. Corp. Tax'n 25 (July 2001).

In note 75, change § 4.01(44) *to* § 3.01(44).

Add to end of note 75.

Currently Rev. Proc. 2005-3, § 3.01(58), 2005-1 IRB 118.

¶ 11.03 ACTIVE BUSINESS REQUIREMENT

[1] In General

Page 11-22:

Add to note 82.

Med Chem (P.R.), 116 TC 308 (2001) (failed § 936 active business requirement; extensive analysis of "active business"); aff'd, 295 F3d 118, 2002-2 USTC ¶ 50,512 (1st Cir. 2002). See also Electronic Arts, Inc., 118 TC 226 (2002).

Add to note 83.

Med Chem (P.R.), 116 TC 308 (2001) (failed § 936 active business requirement; extensive analysis of "active business"); aff'd, 295 F3d 118, 2002-2 USTC ¶ 50,512 (1st Cir. 2002).

[2] Investment Property

Page 11-24:

Add to note 93.

See also Rev. Rul. 2002-49, 2002-32 IRB 288 (managing member of LLC partnership engaged in active business). See Kalinka, "Rev. Rul. 2002-49: Corporate Spin-Offs Using LLCs," 80 Taxes 9 (Nov. 2002); Rizzi, "Active Business Expansion: Rev. Rul. 2002-49 and Conducting Businesses Through LLCs," 29 J. Corp. Tax'n 21 (Nov. 2002).

[3] Owner-Occupied Real Property

Page 11-26:

Add to note 106, first paragraph.

Rev. Rul. 2001-29, 2001-26 IRB 1348 (REIT can be in active business under current REIT rules; Rev. Rul. 73-276 obsolete); see Brandon, "The Real Spin on the New Spin-Off Ruling—Should Corporate-Owned Real Estate Be Put Into REITs?" 95 Taxes 92 (Aug. 2001); Sheppard, "Treasury Official Elaborates on REIT Ruling," 92 Tax Notes 1149 (Aug. 27, 2001); Willens, "Will IRS's Concession Regarding 'Active Business' Status Lead to a Restructuring of Corporate America?" BNA Daily Tax Rep. No. 160, at J-1 (Aug. 20, 2001); Rizzi, "The Active Trade or Business Test Shows Its Age," 28 J. Corp. Tax'n 27 (Sept. 2001); Willens & Wright, "Tax-Free Real Estate Spin-Offs: Will They Catch On?" 94 Tax Notes 619 (Feb. 4, 2002).

¶ 11.05 FIVE-YEAR PREDISTRIBUTION BUSINESS HISTORY REQUIREMENT

[1] In General

Page 11-32:

Add to note 130.

Currently Rev. Proc. 2003-3, § 4.01(30) (ordinarily no ruling), 2003-1 IRB 113. But deleted by Revenue Procedure 2003-48, § 4.07, 2003-29 IRB 86. See Beller & Harwell, "After the Spin: Preserving Tax-Free Treatment Under Section 355," 92 Tax Notes 1587 (Sept. 17, 2001); Pavin & Friedman, "Preferred Musings on the 'Active Business Requirement'," 98 Tax Notes 1133 (Feb. 17, 2003).

Page 11-33:

Add to note 131.

The Joint Committee Staff's April 2001 simplification report likewise recommends adoption of this proposal. This proposal was reintroduced by Senators Baucus & Lott in July 2005 (S. 1327). See Willens, "Attempting Once Again to Rationalize the Active Business Requirement," Daily Tax Rep. No. 132, J-1 (BNA) (July 12, 2005). It is contained in the Senate-passed 2005 tax bill, S-2020 (Nov. 18, 2005), and was adopted in the final 2005 Reconciliation Act on May 17, 2006, new § 355(b)(3), Pub. L. No. 109-222 (May 18, 2006).

For comments on the New TIPRA aggregation rule, see Bennett, "New Code § 355(b)(3): The Affiliated Group Active Trade or Business Requirement," 84 Taxes 7 (Aug. 2006). See Notice 2006-81, 2006-40 IRB [595] (Oct. 2, 2006) (procedures for electing under § 355(b)(3)(C) for corporate distributions).

Add to text at end of ¶ 11.05[1].

This proposal finally passed in the 2006 TIPRA legislation, but the new aggregation rule has turned out to cause its own set of technical difficulties.[131.1]

[131.1] See supra note 131. For the technical problems raised by § 355(b)(3), see Willens, "Holding Companies and the Active Business Test," 113 Tax Notes 87 (Oct. 2, 2006); Willens, "Positioning for a Spin-Off Through Preliminary Steps Designed to Place Corporations in 'Active Business' Positive," Daily Tax Rep. (BNA) No. 186, at J-1 (Sept. 26, 2006); Bennett, "Code Section 355(b)(3) Updated," 84 Taxes 7 (Dec. 2006).

[2] Method of Acquisition: Limitation on Taxable Acquisitions Within Five-Year Period

Add new note 131.2 to end of first sentence.

[131.2] See Pavin & Friedman, "Preferred Musings on the Active Business Requirement," 98 Tax Notes 1133 (Feb. 17, 2003).

[a] Section 355(b)(2)(C)

Page 11-33:

In fourth sentence of note 133, change "Regs. § 1.355-(d) (2000)" to "Regs. § 1.355-6(d) (2000)."

Add to note 133.

But see Rev. Rul. 2002-49, 2002-32 IRB 288 (violated § 355(b)(2)(C) even though control acquired in a tax-free § 721 exchange with appreciated asset); infra note 136.1. See Pavin & Friedman, supra note 131.1.

Page 11-34:

Add to note 135.

See Pavin & Friedman, "Preferred Musings on the 'Active Business Requirement'," 98 Tax Notes 1133 (Feb. 17, 2003).

Add to note 136.

See Pavin & Friedman, supra note 135.

Add text to end of ¶ 11.05[2][a].

Revenue Ruling 2002-49 deals with § 355(b)(2)(C) in two scenarios, one of which did not violate this provision, but the other of which did.[136.1]

[136.1] Rev. Rul. 2002-49, 2002-32 IRB 288. In the first case, the 20 percent managing member of an LLC bought out the remaining interests within the five-year period, but this did not violate § 355(b)(2)(C) even though partnership status ended and the LLC became a disregarded entity. In case two, however, acquisition of an interest in the LLC within the five-year period by exchanging appreciated assets in a tax-free § 721 exchange did violate § 355(b)(2)(C) because a direct exchange would have been taxable. See Kalinka, "Rev. Rul. 2002-49: Corporate Spin-Offs Using LLCs," 80 Taxes 9 (Nov. 2002); Rizzi, "Active Business Expansion: Rev. Rul. 2002-49 and Conducting Businesses Through LLCs," 29 J. Corp. Tax'n 21 (Nov. 2002).

[b] Section 355(b)(2)(D)

Page 11-35:

Add to note 139 after second sentence of second paragraph.

Douglas McLaulin, 115 TC 255 (2000) (followed principle of Rev. Rul. 57-144, at least where cash to fund redemption supplied by parent; taxpayers would be wise not to test the case where subsidiary has its own funds to effect the redemption), aff'd, 276 F3d 1269 (11th Cir. 2001). See Pavin & Friedman, "Preferred Musings on the 'Active Business Requirement'," 98 Tax Notes 1133 (Feb. 17, 2003).

Page 11-36:

Add to note 140, first paragraph.

Douglas McLaulin, 115 TC 255 (2000) followed Rev. Rul. 57-144, aff'd, 276 F3d 1269 (11th Cir. 2001). See Pavin & Friedman, supra note 135.

[3] Single or Multiple Businesses: What Is a Separate Business?

Add to note 144.

See also Rev. Rul. 2003-18, 2003-7 IRB 467; and Rev. Rul. 2003-38, 2003-17 IRB 811 (follow *Lockwood* and Regs. expansion exception); infra note 146.

Add to note 146, first sentence after 1957-1 CB 121.

But overruled by Rev. Rul. 2003-18, 2003-7 IRB 467 (not a separate business, citing Example 8); Willens, "Viewpoint: IRS Embraces 'Expansion' Exception to Five-Year Active Business Requirement," Daily Tax Rep. (BNA) No. 61, at J-1 (Mar. 3, 2003); see also Rev. Rul. 2003-38, 2003-17 IRB 811 (creation of internet website not a new business; instead qualified expansion of existing business).

Page 11-38:

Add to note 147.

Rizzi, "The Active Trade or Business Test Shows Its Age," 28 J. Corp. Tax'n 27, 29 (Sept. 2001). See also Rev. Rul. 2003-18, supra note 146 (qualified expansion not a new business); Willens comment, supra note 146; Rev. Rul. 2003-38, 2003-17 IRB 811 (creation of internet website a qualified expansion of existing business).

¶ 11.06 "DEVICE" RESTRICTION

[1] In General: Post-Distribution Sales As "Bailouts"

Page 11-39:

In last sentence of note 150, change Rev. Proc. 96-3 *to* Rev. Proc. 96-30.

Add to end of note 150.

But IRS will no longer rule privately on device issue, Rev. Proc. 2003-48, § 4.02, 2003-29 IRB 86; see Cummings, Rothman, and Bailine, supra note 20.

Add to note 152.

Beller & Harwell, "After the Spin: Preserving Tax-Free Treatment Under Section 355," 92 Tax Notes 1587 (Sept. 17, 2001); Willens, "Navigating the Device Test for Stock Buybacks After Spin-offs," Daily Tax Rep. (DNA) No. 182, at J-1 (Sept. 20, 2006).

Page 11-40:

Add to note 156.

Compare South Tulsa Pathology Lab., Inc., 118 TC 84 (2002) (prearranged sale of spun-off subsidiary on same day as spin-off found to be a device; no counterweights to trump either; a slam dunk for government here since if this wasn't a device, nothing is—what were these people thinking?). See Raby & Raby, "How Not to Sell a Piece of a C Corpo-

ration," 94 Tax Notes 883 (Feb. 18, 2002); Rothman, "*South Tulsa Pathology Laboratory:
A Confusing Application of Device and Business Purpose,*" 29 J. Corp. Tax'n 12 (May
2002); Willens, "The Device Test and the Business Purpose Requirements in a Spin-
Off—An Uneasy Relationship," 101 J. Tax'n 79 (Aug. 2004).

Add to note 157.

But IRS will no longer rule on business purpose, Rev. Proc. 2003-48, § 4.01, 2003-29
IRB 86.

Add to note 158.

But IRS will no longer rule on "device," Rev. Proc. 2003-48, § 4.02, 2003-29 IRB 86.

Page 11-42:

Add to note 167.

But IRS will no longer rule on "device," Rev. Proc. 2003-48, § 4.02, 2003-29 IRB 86.

Add to last sentence of ¶ 11.06[1].

(including the effect of 2003 legislation conforming the tax rates on dividends
to the capital gain rates, with a top rate of 15 percent for both).[169.1]

[169.1] Infra ¶ 11.06[7]. See IRC § 1(h)(11) (effective for 2003).

[2] Contemporaneous Tax-Free Transactions

Page 11-45:

Add to note 177.

But the 1999 proposed regulations were withdrawn and reproposed on Jan. 2, 2001 (in
considerably more lenient form), and most of these proposals were adopted as temporary
Regs. § 1.355-7T on Aug. 3, 2001. They were reissued as new temporary regulations on
April 26, 2002 (and by far the most liberal version of all); adopted as final by TD 9198
(Apr.19, 2005). Infra ¶ 11.11[3][d].

[3] Non–Pro Rata or Nondividend Distributions

Page 11-45:

Add to note 179.

See South Tulsa Pathology Lab., Inc., 118 TC 84 (2002) (no E&P does not mean a
"small" amount of E&P; also E&P was created by failed § 355 distribution); comment by
Raby & Raby, 94 Tax Notes 883 (Feb. 18, 2002).

[6] Nondevice Factors

Page 11-48:

Add to note 195.

South Tulsa Pathology Lab., Inc., 118 TC 84 (2002) (very strong device factor—prearranged prompt sale of spun-off subsidiary not trumped by any significant nondevice factors; an easy case for government). Comment by Raby & Raby, 94 Tax Notes 883 (Feb. 18, 2002).

Add new ¶ 11.06[7].

[7] Effect of 2003 Legislation Reduction of Dividend Tax Rates [New]

A substantial weakening (just short of outright repeal) of the device limitation was effected by 2003 legislation lowering the top rate on dividends for individuals to the same rate applicable to long-term capital gain (15 percent).[196.1] Certainly, at least, the tax stakes for noncorporate shareholders have been largely neutralized when admitted dividend bailouts now are taxable at the same rate as a capital gain stock sale. Thus, the device limitation is essentially a "sooner-or later" issue for individual shareholders, though corporate taxability on a failed § 355 distribution is still a potent risk.[196.2]

Odder still is IRS' recent decision not to rule on device issues;[196.3] one would have thought such rulings would be far easier to obtain in the currently rate neutral climate for dividends and capital gains.

[196.1] IRC § 1(h)(11) (effective for 2003); extended for two years by 2006 legislation (TIPRA).

[196.2] Thus, it is still unwise to ignore device implications where a current corporate tax of 35 percent could result. See Blank, "The Device Test in a Unified Rate Regime," 102 Tax Notes 513 (Jan. 26, 2004).

[196.3] Rev. Proc. 2003-48, § 4.02, 2003-29 IRB 86. See Blank, supra note 196.2 (making the same point).

¶ 11.09 NONSTATUTORY LIMITATIONS ON TAX-FREE CORPORATE DIVISIONS

[1] In General

Page 11-55:

Add new note 216.1 to end of second paragraph.

[216.1] See also Rev. Rul. 2000-5, 2000-5 IRB 436 ("divisive mergers" not valid Type A reorganization; must satisfy requirements of § 355 for tax-free treatment);   12.22[11]. See also Prop. Regs. § 1.368-2(b)(1) (May 12, 2000) (mergers into or by disregarded entities not Type A reorganizations); and Prop. Reg. § 1.368-2(b)(1) (Nov. 15, 2001);   12.22[10] (merger into disregarded entity now allowed, however); adopted as Temp.

Regs. § 1.368-2T(b)(1) by TD 9038, January 24, 2003; and adopted as final regulations by TD 9242 (Jan. 23, 2006).

[2] Independent Business Purpose

[a] Business Purpose: In General

Page 11-56:

Add to note 218 at the end of the first paragraph.

Beller & Harwell, "After the Spin: Preserving Tax-Free Treatment Under Section 355," 92 Tax Notes 1587 (Sept. 17, 2001). Coakley, "The Evolving Business Purpose Requirement for Spin-Off Transactions," 103 Tax Notes 1141 (May 31, 2004); Rizzi, "Business Purpose in Spin-Offs Involving Public Companies," 31 Corp. Tax'n 27 (Sept. 2004); Willens, "A New Era for the Business Purpose Requirement?" 111 Tax Notes 235 (Apr. 10, 2006).

Add to note 218, second paragraph.

But IRS no longer will rule on the business purpose issue, Rev. Proc. 2003-48, § 4.01, 2003-29 IRB 86 (taxpayers must proceed by representation here); see Cummings, Rothman, and Bailine, supra note 20; see also Willens, "IRS Revises Its Approach to Business Purposes Guidance Under Section 355," 99 J. Tax'n 76 (Aug. 2003).

Add to note 222.

Rev. Rul. 2003-52, 2003-22 IRB 960 (preservation of family harmony).

Page 11-57:

Add to note 223.

Rev. Rul. 2003-55, 2003-22 IRB 961 (spin-off to facilitate IPO; fact that it was cancelled due to changed circumstances *not* fatal); Comment by Willens, supra note 218.

Add to note 226.

But acquiescent in *Olson* changed to nonacquiescence in 2004; see comment by Willens, Daily Tax Rep. (BNA) No. 34, at J-1 (Feb. 23, 2004).

Add to text after item number 7.

8. Resolving market "perception" problems as to distributing corporation's two dissimilar business.[226.1]

[226.1] Rev. Rul. 2003-110, 2003-46 IRB 1083 (good business purpose to spin-off taxpayer's baby food business from its pesticide business – latter business gave off strong odor that reflected negatively on its former business and also would create positive effects for the spun-off baby food business; no other way to separate the two businesses). See also Rev. Rul. 2004-23, 2004-11 IRB 585 (value of D and C together less than value separated; another market perception problem and no other way). See Avent & Simon, "Consider Using Spin-Offs to Enhance Shareholder Value," 31 Corp. Tax'n 3 (Sept. 2004); Comment by Willens, supra note 218.

Add note 227.1 to end of last paragraph.

[227.1] Rev. Rul. 2003-55, 2003-22 IRB 961 (fact that purpose couldn't be carried out not fatal: here, purpose was to have sub do an IPO, but bad market caused cancellation).

Add text to end of last paragraph.

A recent IRS ruling also held that a strong business purpose can help to avoid a § 355(e) "plan" problem.[227.2]

[227.2] Rev. Rul. 2005-65, 2005-41 IRB (Oct. 11, 2005) (purpose of spin to eliminate competition for capital between two businesses); comment by Friedlich, IRS Reaches Common Sense Conclusion in Applying Anti-Morris Trust Rules, 33 Corp. Tax'n 45 (Mar. 2006).

Page 11-58:

Add to text at end of ¶ 11.06[2][a].

Refusal of IRS to rule on the business purpose issue has put a fog of uncertainty on whether § 355 can be relied on now.[228.1]

[228.1] Rev. Proc. 2003-48, § 4.01, 2003-29 IRB 86; see comments supra note 20. But see contrary view by Willens, supra note 218.

[b] Business Purpose for Distribution

Page 11-59:

Add to note 232.

See also Rev. Rul. 2003-110, 2003-46 IRB 1083 (no other non-taxable way to separate taxpayer's two incompatible businesses); Rev. Rul. 2004-23, 2004-11 IRB 585.

Add to note 234, first paragraph.

Rev. Rul. 2003-52, 2003-22 IRB 960 (preservation of family harmony) Rev. Rul. 2004-23, 2004-11 IRB 585 (purpose to increase values of D and C; avoid dilution on use of stock to make acquisitions and pay compensation; no other way). See Avent & Simon, "Consider Using Spin-Offs to Enhance Shareholders Value," 31 Corp. Tax'n 3 (Sept. 2004).

Add to note 234, second paragraph.

But IRS no longer will rule on business purpose, Rev. Proc. 2003-48, § 4.01, 2003-29 IRB 86.

Add to text at end of ¶ 11.06[2][b].

Satisfaction of this requirement has not been helped by IRS' recent refusal to rule on business purpose issues.[234.1]

[234.1] Rev. Proc. 2003-48, § 4.01, 2003-29 IRB 86.

[c] Shareholder-Level Versus Corporate-Level Purposes

Add to note 235.

E.g., Rev. Rul. 2003-52, 2003-22 IRB 960 (family estate planning not fatal if other good business purpose for the distribution and was here); Rev. Rul. 2004-23, 2004-11 IRB 585 (overlap of corporate and shareholder purposes not fatal).

[d] IRS Ruling Guidelines on Business Purpose: Revenue Procedure 96-30

Page 11-60:

Add to note 237.

But Rev. Proc. 96-30 was revised by Rev. Proc. 2003-48, 2003-29 IRB 86; IRS will no longer rule on business purpose, § 4.01, and Appendix A was deleted (though its memory probably will linger on; see Cummings, supra note 20.)

Add new note 237.1 to end of item 2.

[237.1] See, e.g., Rev. Rul. 2003-55, 2003-22 IRB 961 (even though planned financing cancelled due to bad markets).

Add new note 237.2 to end of item 3.

[237.2] See, e.g., Rev. Rul. 2003-75, 2003-29 IRB 79 (eliminate competition for capital funding between parent and subsidiary).

Add to note 239.

But see Rev. Rul. 2003-74, 2003-29 IRB 77 (good purpose for spin to allow parent and subsidiary to concentrate on their separate businesses). See also Rev. Rul. 2003-110, 2003-46 IRB 1083 (resolving market perception problem as to taxpayer's incompatible businesses).

Add new item to text.

   10. Resolving market perception problems as to taxpayer's incompatible businesses.[241.1]

[241.1] Rev. Rul. 2003-110, 2003-46 IRB 1083; Rev. Rul. 2004-23, 2004-11 IRB 585. See Avent & Simon, "Consider Using Spin-Offs to Enhance Shareholders Value," 31 Corp. Tax'n 3 (Sept. 2004) (comment on *Rev. Rul. 2004-23*).

Add to text at end of ¶ 11.09[2][d].

But IRS no longer will rule privately on business purpose issues (and also deleted Appendix A),[241.2] on the grounds that these issues are primarily factual in nature and also that it does not want to issue "comfort rulings." Thus, the new policy for § 355 rulings is to reduce the issuance of private rulings and increase the issuance of published guidance. In keeping with this new policy, IRS has issued a number of published rulings on common business purpose issues in order to reduce the need for individual private rulings (in each of these, IRS found the business purpose to be an acceptable one).[241.3] But the pace of published guidance has noticebly slowed in 2004, 2005, and 2006.

[241.2] Rev. Proc. 2003-48, § 4.01, 2003-29 IRB 86. See Cummings, Rothman, and Bailine, supra note 20; see also Willens, supra note 218.

[241.3] Rev. Rul. 2003-52, 2003-22 IRB 960 (preservation of family harmony); Rev. Rul. 2003-55, 2003-22 IRB 961 (facilitate a stock offering by spun-off sub; not fatal that later cancelled due to bad market); Rev. Rul. 2003-74, 2003-29 IRB 77 (spin to allow parent and sub to concentrate on their separate business); Rev. Rul. 2003-75, 2003-29 IRB 79 (spin to eliminate competition for capital funding between parent and sub). Rev. Rul. 2003-110, 2003-46 IRB 1083 (resolving market perception problem as to taxpayer's incompatible businesses); Rev. Rul. 2004-23, 2004-11 IRB 585 (market perception problem); Avent & Simon, "Consider Using Spin-offs to Enhance Shareholder Value," 31 Corp. Tax'n 3 (Sept. 2004). Rev. Rul. 2005-65, 2005-41 IRB (Oct. 11, 2005) (eliminate competition for capital between two businesses; also helped to avoid § 355(e) "plan" problem); Willens, "A New Era for the Business Purpose Requirement?" 111 Tax Notes 235 (Apr. 10, 2006) (comment on these recent rulings).

[3] Continuity of Proprietary Interest

Page 11-61:

Add to note 242.

Beller & Harwell, "After the Spin: Preserving Tax-Free Treatment Under Section 355," 92 Tax Notes 1587 (Sept. 17, 2001).

[4] Continuity of Business Enterprise

Page 11-62:

Add to note 249.

Beller & Harwell, "After the Spin: Preserving Tax-Free Treatment Under Section 355," 92 Tax Notes 1587 (Sept. 17, 2001).

¶ 11.10 "BOOT" UNDER § 355

[1] What Constitutes Boot and How Is It Allocated?

Add new heading   11.10[1][a] Definition of Boot *before first full paragraph on the page.*

[a] Definition of Boot

Page 11-63:

Add to note 252.

"Principal amount" for this purpose probably means "adjusted issue price" under the OID rules. See   12.44[1][b], note 751, and   12.44[1][f], note 756.

Page 11-64:

Add to note 257.

Note, "Section 355(a)(3)(B) After *Dunn Trust*," 19 Va. Tax Rev. 549 (2000); Willens, "Sanitizing Tainted Shaves in a Spinoff," 110 Tax Notes 899 (Feb. 20, 2006).

Page 11-65:

Add new ¶ 11.10[1][b].

[b] Allocation of Boot: Regs. § 1.356-1 [New]

On January 23, 2006, IRS promulgated regulations under § 356,[264.1] spelling out in greater detail (with four examples) how boot is to be allocated in applying the rules of § 356. The terms of the exchange will control the allocation if so specified; otherwise a pro rata portion of the boot is to be treated as received for each share surrendered based on the value of that share.[264.2] However, no loss can be recognized here by virtue of § 356(c) (even if the terms of exchange allocate all boot to a particular class of stock).[264.3]

[264.1] Regs. § 1.356-1 TD 92 44 (Jan. 23, 2006), effective on that date.

[264.2] Regs. §§ 1.356-1(b) and 1.356-1(d) Exs. 1, 3 and 4.

[264.3] Regs. § 1.356-1(d) Ex. 2; the preamble also cites Rev. Rul. 74-515 for this result (but requested comments as to whether this result should be changed).

[2] Character of Recognized Boot Gain

Page 11-65:

Add to text at end of first paragraph.

But if Treasury's dividend exclusion proposal had been enacted (it wasn't),[264.1] however, § 356(b) dividend treatment could become the preferred result, especially if that dividend qualified for a 100 percent exclusion (although it may not under that proposal as initially drafted).[264.2]

[264.1] See ¶¶ 1.08[4], 8.06[1]. The final 2003 tax bill, HR 2, reduces the top tax rate on dividends and capital gains to 15 percent (but sunsets after six years). IRC § 1(h)(11) (effective for 2003). See ¶ 8.06[2].

[264.2] Even if the dividend is only partially tax exempt, the effective tax thereon may be lower than the current 20 percent capital gains rate. The final 2003 tax bill taxes dividends at the capital gains rate (and lowers that top rate to 15 percent), supra note 264.1.

But the Treasury proposal seemed to be limited to dividends described in §§ 301 and 316, which would literally exclude boot dividends created by § 356. The final 2003 legislation also seems to be similarly so limited, although regulatory authority is granted to include § 356 (and other similar) dividends.

Page 11-66:

Add to note 267.

Willens, "Taxing 'Boot' in a Separation," 111 Tax Notes 1417 (June 19, 2006).

Add to text at end of ¶ 11.10[2].

Treasury's February 2003 dividend exclusion proposal[268.1] would have dramatically altered the tax consequences of receiving a boot dividend, especially if that dividend qualified for the 100 percent exclusion (although it may not as initially proposed).[268.2] Thus, a major role reversal could ensue here where taxpayers actively strive to obtain dividend equivalent treatment. The final legislation rejected Treasury's dividend exclusion proposal in favor of a rate reduction for qualified dividends received by non-corporate shareholders (to the same rate applicable to long-term capital gain, which was also reduced to a top rate of 15 percent).[268.3]

[268.1] See ¶¶ 1.08[4], 8.06. But the final 2003 tax bill reduces the top tax rate for dividends and capital gains to 15 percent (but sunsets after six years); see ¶ 8.06[2].

[268.2] Even if the ultimately enacted exclusion is less than 100 percent, the effective tax rate on a partially exempt dividend could be less than the present 20 percent capital gains rate. But the Treasury's proposal seemed limited to § 301/§ 316 dividends (which would exclude boot dividends created under § 356), and so does the final 2003 tax legislation (which taxes dividends the same as capital gain, with a top rate of 15 percent); see ¶ 8.06[2]. But regulation authority is granted to include § 356 boot dividends (and others as well).

[268.3] See ¶ 8.06[2]. Satisfaction of the 61-day holding period of § 1(h)(11)(B)(iii) should be possible for boot dividends in connection with a spin-off, but may cause problems in the case of a non-prorata split off since tacking of holding periods is not allowed here. But technical corrections, legislations should cure this problem (and the IRS has agreed to apply it to 2003 year's returns - see Announcement 2004-11, 2004-10 IRB 581).

¶ 11.11 DISTRIBUTING CORPORATION'S GAIN OR LOSS

[1] General Nonrecognition Rules: §§ 361 and 355(c)

[a] Introduction and Background

Page S11-67:

Add to note 269.

But *Trinova* was reversed sub nom Aeroquip-Vickers, Inc. v. CIR, 347 F3d 173 (6th Cir. 2003) (one dissent).

Page 11-68:

Add to note 272.

For application of § 83 in the context of a § 355 spin-off, see Rev. Rul. 2002-1, 2002-2 IRB (Jan. 14, 2002). Cummings, "Using Compensatory NQSOs and Restricted Stock With Section 355: New Clear Guidance From IRS," 96 J. Tax'n 71 (Feb. 2002). Rizzi, "Restricted Stock, Stock Options and Spin-Offs," 30 J. Corp. Tax'n 45 (Jan. 2003); Bennett, "Rev. Rul. 2002-1: Constructing a Bridge to Span Time," 80 Taxes 11 (Oct. 2002).

[b] Type D Reorganizations: § 361

Add text to end of first paragraph of ¶ 11.11[1][b].

But the 2004 Jobs Act[274.1] amended the boot purge rule of § 361(b)(3) to limit the amount of boot that can be purged by a distribution to creditors; only an amount up to the basis of the transferred assets is purgeable here; anything over that amount is taxed at the distributing corporate level.[274.2] The 2004 Jobs Act also limits application of § 357(c) to divisive Type D reorganizations only.[274.3]

[274.1] American Jobs Creation Act of 2004, § 898(a), effective October 22, 2002. The intent here seems to have been the creation of symmetry with § 357(c), which the American Jobs Creation Act of 2004, § 898(b) restricts solely to Type D reorganizations, § 357(c)(1)(B).

[274.2] See Barr, "Uncertainty Regarding Liabilities in Divisive Reorgs Survive AJCA," 105 Tax Notes 1125 (Nov. 22, 2004); infra   12.42[1][b] and   12.42[5], Example 12. But this "uncertainty" was cured by Rev. Rul. 2007-8, 2007-7 IRB 469.

[274.3] American Jobs Creation Act of 2004, § 898(b), amending § 357(c)(1)(B).

Page 11-68:

In the second sentence of the second paragraph of ¶ 11.11[1][b] add subsidiary *after* acquiring.

Add to note 275.

This requirement that the qualified property be received in the reorganization exchange could raise problems where the parent contributes property to an existing subsidiary in exchange for additional subsidiary stock (or without receiving any additional stock).

Page 11-69:

In fourth line of first full paragraph add and § 355(a)(1)(A)(ii) *after* § 355(c)(1) *and replace* applies *with* apply.

In last line of that paragraph, add to security holders of subsidiary stock or securities *after* distributions.

Add to beginning of note 276.

Note that "qualified property" under § 355(c)(2)(B) is narrower than the definition of such property in § 361(c)(2)(B); the former definition is limited to stock or securities in the controlled subsidiary corporation.

[d] Examples

Page 11-70:

Add text to second paragraph of Example 2.

> Boot also can be purged by a distribution to creditors under § 361(b)(3), but the 2004 Jobs Act[280.1] limits the purgeable amount to the adjusted basis of the transferred assets.

[280.1] American Jobs Creation Act of 2004, § 898(a); § 898(b) also limits § 357(c) to divisive Type D reorganizations only, § 357(c)(1)(B). See Barr, supra note 274.2; and Rev. Rul. 2007-8, 2007-7 IRB 469.

[2] Special Gain-Recognition Rule: § 355(d)

[a] In General

Page 11-71:

Add to note 287.

The proposed regulations were adopted in final form without significant change by TD 8913 on December 20, 2000 (effective on that date); most of the revisions merely clarified various aspects of the proposed regulations. Mendelson, "Section 355(d) Final Regulations Appropriately Limit Expansive Statute," 14 J. Tax'n Fin. Insts. 31 (May 2001); Hamilton

& Webster, "Actual Knowledge of Shareholders in Tax-Free Spin-Offs," 91 Tax Notes 2207 (June 25, 2001); Friedel & DeNovio, "Can Section 355(d) Be Avoided in a Cross-Border or Consolidated Spinoff?" 96 J. Tax'n 12 (Jan. 2002).

Page 11-72:

Add to note 293.

For the final regulations adopted on December 20, 2000, see infra.

Page 11-73:

Add text after first full sentence.

The final regulations adopted on December 20, 2000, are even more "taxpayer friendly."[296.1]

[296.1] See TD 8913, Explanation of Revisions and Summary of Comments. See Mendelson, "Section 355(d) Final Regulations Appropriately Limit an Expansive Statute," 14 J. Tax'n Fin. Insts. 31 (May 2001).

Add to note 297.

Final Regs. preamble, pt. 1: Regs. §§ 1.355-6(b)(3) (no violation of purpose transactions) and 1.355-6(b)(4) (anti-abuse rule).

Add to note 298.

Final Regs. §§ 1.355-6(b)(3)(ii) and 1.355-6(c).

Add to note 299.

Final Regs. § 1.355-2(d) similarly adopt the cost basis standard.

Add to note 300.

Final Regs. § 1.355-6(b)(3)(vi) increased the number of examples to ten.

Add to note 301.

The final regulations adopted similar treatment for § 351 transactions in Regs. §§ 1.355-6(d)(3) (with a few clarifications), 1.355-6(d)(4) (triangular asset reorganizations), 1.355-6(d)(5) (triangular stock reorganizations), and 1.355-6(d)(6) (affiliated group structure changes under § 1.1502-31, see infra Ch. 13). But if reverse merger overlaps with a Type B, regulations require use of the *higher* of stock or asset basis (unless a closing agreement is entered into to use one method consistently). See infra   11.11[2][b], Ex. 11.

Add to text after second sentence of first full paragraph.

Note that if a reverse subsidiary merger also overlaps with a Type B reorganization, the regulations generally require use of the *higher* of carryover stock basis or inside net asset basis (a possible pitfall here).[301.1]

[301.1] Regs. § 1.355-6(d)(5); but acquiror can agree (through a closing agreement and private ruling) to use the lower of these two amounts; see infra, Example 11.

Add to note 302.

The purging rule of the proposed regulations was replaced with Regs. § 1.355-6(b)(2)(iii) (purchase status of stock will be eliminated if and when basis in that stock is eliminated); Regs. § 1.355-6(b)(3)(vi), Exs. 7 and 8 are the same as the proposed regulations; Exs. 9 and 10 are new.

Add to note 303.

Final Regs. § 1.355-6(c)(3)(vii) retained this test (reasonable certainty of exercise); § 1.355-6(c)(3)(viii) provides two examples of this standard.

Page 11-74:

Add text after first sentence of last paragraph of ¶ 11.11[2][a].

Final Regs. § 1.355-6(b)(4)(ii) continues this lack of illumination.

Add text at end of ¶ 11.11[2][a].

  The final regulations under § 355(d) continued the taxpayer-friendly attitude of the proposed regulations; in fact, they became even a bit more friendly (hopefully a good sign for the § 355(e) regulation project, which was a taxpayer-hostile proposal in spades); it was a good omen, since the revised § 355(e) regulations are much more reasonable than their initial version. But there are some tricky parts to the § 355(d) regulations (e.g., the triangular merger basis rules) that can cause unpleasant surprises.[305.1]

[305.1] See Mendelson, "Section 355(d) Final Regulations Approximately Limit Expansive Statute," 14 J. Tax'n Fin. Inst. 31 (May 2001), Hamilton & Webster, "Actual Knowledge of Shareholders in Tax-Free Spin-Offs," 91 Tax Notes 2207 (June 25, 2001). See infra, Example 11; Friedel & DeNovio, "Can Section 355(d) Be Avoided in a Cross-Border or Consolidated Spinoff?" 96 J. Tax'n 12 (Jan. 2002).

[b] Examples

Page 11-75:

Add to note 306.

Final Regs. § 1.355-6(b)(3)(vi) (add two more examples).

Add to note 307.

Final Regs. § 1.355-6(b)(3)(vi), Exs. 1, 2, and 3.

Add to note 308.

Final Regs. § 1.355-6(e)(2).

Add to note 309.

Final Regs. §§ 1.355-6(d)(3) and 1.355-6(e)(1).

Add to note 310.

Final Regs. § 1.355-6(c)(3).

Add new Example 11 following Example 10.

> **EXAMPLE 11:** *P* acquires all the stock of *T* in a reverse triangular merger under § 368(a)(2)(E) that also qualifies as a Type B reorganization and *T* spins off a lower-tier subsidiary, *T-1*, to *P* within five years; the regulations (both the proposed and final versions)[310.1] require *P* to test for "purchased basis" in the *T* stock using the higher of *T* stock carryover basis or *T*'s inside net asset basis. As the regulations example points out,[310.2] this general rule can result in a tainted purchase for the *T* stock and hence a taxable gain to *T* on the distribution of *T-1* stock; but the second example[310.3] illustrates the letter ruling-closing agreement escape election.

[310.1] Regs. § 1.355-6(d)(5)(i); but Reg. § 1.355-6(d)(5)(ii) allows an election to use the lower of outside or inside basis if *T* obtains a closing agreement and a letter ruling from the IRS.

[310.2] Regs. § 1.355-6(d)(5)(iii), Ex. 1.

[310.3] Regs. § 1.355-6(d)(5)(iii), Ex. 2.

[3] Final 1997 Legislation ("Archer-Roth" and HR 2014): New §§ 355(e) and 355(f)

[b] Final Legislation: §§ 355(e) and 355(f)

Page 11-78:

Add to note 321.

But subsequent versions, culminating in Temp. Regs. §1.355-7T (Apr. 26, 2002), sharply reversed course on the "plan" scope issue, becoming much more reasonable in the process. Final Regs. § 1355-7 were adopted as final by TD 9198 (Apr. 19, 2005).

Page 11-79:

Add to note 322.

See, e.g., NYSB Assoc. Tax Section Report, Section 355(e) "Non Plan" Issues, 102 Tax Notes 1133 (Mar. 1, 2004).

Add new note 322.1 to end of item 1.

[322.1] For application of the "overlapping ownership" exception in § 355(e)(3)(A)(iv), see Willens, "Avoiding Application of the 'Anti–Morris Trust' Rule," 112 Tax Notes 999 (Sept. 11, 2006).

Add to note 323.

Beller & Harwell, "After the Spin: Preserving Tax-Free Treatment Under Section 355," 92 Tax Notes 1587 (Sept. 17, 2001).

Add to text after note 323.

But final regulations under § 355(e), issued as Regulations § 1.355-7 on April 19, 2005, have greatly ameliorated the scope of § 355(e).[323.1]

[323.1] See infra ¶ 11.11[3][d]. See, e.g., Rev. Rul. 2005-65, 2005-41 IRB (Oct. 11, 2005) (strong business purpose for spin overcame § 355(e) "plan" problem); comment by Friedlich, IRS Reaches Common Sense Result in Applying Anti-Morris Trust Rules, 33 Corp. Tax'n 45 (Mar. 2006).

[c] Examples

Page 11-80:

Add new note 328.1 to end of Example 4.

[328.1] But Rev. Rul. 2003-79, 2003-29 IRB 80, allowed *P* to acquire spun-off newly created *S* in a valid Type C reorganization without being subject to *Elkhorn Coal*'s wide-angle substantially all lens; but, if *P* acquires parent *T*, *Elkhorn* does apply! The ruling also seems remarkably indifferent to *S*'s status as a transitory corporation and its attendent *Gregory* problem. See infra ¶¶ 12.62[3] and 12.62[4]. See Willens, "Reverse *Morris Trust* Transactions Have Their Day in the Sun," Daily Tax Rep. (BNA) No. 169, at J-1 (Sept. 2, 2003).

Page 11-81:

Add to note 329.

The August 1999 regulations were withdrawn on December 29, 2000, and reproposed as § 1.355-7 (effective January 2, 2001), but public offerings still can cause trouble here; see Prop. Regs. § 1.355-7(m), Exs. 3 and 4. These proposals were adopted virtually intact as temporary regulations § 1.355-7T on Aug. 3, 2001, infra note 329.1. New temporary regulations were issued in TD 8988 on April 26, 2002, and they are even more liberal, surprisingly so, infra note 329.1. These regulations were adopted in final form by TD 9198 (Apr. 19, 2005).

[d] The Proposed, Temporary and Final § 355(e) Regulations

Page 11-81:

Add new note 329.1 to last sentence of first paragraph of ¶ 11.11[3][d].

[329.1] The August 1999 proposals were withdrawn on December 29, 2000, and reproposed in considerably more balanced and far less hostile form as Prop. Regs. § 1.355-7 (effective January 2, 2001). The new proposals effected a major liberalization of the withdrawn 1999 proposals and should be hailed with a collective shout of relief. These proposals were adopted as Temp. Regs. § 1.355-7T by TD 8960 on August 3, 2001 (effective at once). No changes were made in the proposed regulations (except that the risk protection rule of § 1.355-7(e)(6) and Ex. 7 of § 1.355-7(m) were reserved). New temporary regulations were issued in TD 8988 on April 26, 2002, however, which replaced the 2001 temporary regulations, substantially liberalized those regulations, and are electively effective back to the date of enactment of § 355(e) (Apr. 16, 1997) adopted as final form by TD 9198 (Apr. 19, 2005).

Page 11-82:

Add to note 331.

Silverman & Zarlenga, "Proposed Section 355(e) Regulations: Broadening the Definition of a Plan," 87 Tax Notes 117 (Apr. 3, 2000); Rizzi, "The Proposed Section 355(e) Regulations: A Parody," 27 J. Corp. Tax'n 131 (2000); Beller, "Suggestions for *Morris Trust* Regs 'Plan' Determination Rules," 87 Tax Notes 143 (Apr. 3, 2000); Calianno, "The Matrix: Prop. Regs. Provide Insight on 'Plan or Series of Related Transactions' in Section 355(e)," 10 J. Int'l Tax'n 19 (Nov. 2000); Cummings, "ABA Members Weigh in on Anti–*Morris Trust* Regs.," 86 Tax Notes 281 (Jan. 10, 1999); Bell, "*General Utilities* Repeal, Section 355(e), and the Triple Tax," 87 Tax Notes 1385 (June 5, 2000).

But the August 1999 proposals were withdrawn on December 29, 2000, and reproposed as Prop. Regs. § 1.355-7 (effective January 2, 2001). The new proposals are far less hostile, and, while still relatively tough, are a far more liberal regime than the withdrawn 1999 proposals. They were adopted in temporary form by TD 8960 on August 3, 2001. New temporary regulations were issued in TD 8988 on April 26, 2002, which replaced the 2001 regulations, substantially liberalized them, and are effective (electively) back to April 16, 1997 (the date of enactment of § 355(e)); adopted as final regulations by TD 9198 (Apr. 19, 2005).

Page 11-84:

Add text at end of ¶ 11.11[3][d].

The revised proposed regulations of January 2, 2001, while not a 180-degree about-face by IRS on the 1999 proposals, was nearly so. Thus, gone are the exclusive rebuttals and the near impossibility of avoiding a fatal "plan" when the two transactions occur within the six-month hot-zone period; also gone is the enhanced standard of proof required by the withdrawn 1999 proposals. The new proposals generally adopted a purely facts and circumstances approach in § 1.355-7(d) (which contains a nonexclusive list of factors that are to be considered in deciding whether a forbidden plan existed (these factors, moreover, are to be weighed, not merely counted). Although fact and factor analysis is not an exact science, it came in response to one of the principal criticisms of the 1999 proposals. The new proposals also embraced (or at least recognized) an exception where circumstances "unexpectedly" change following the distribution or the acquisition, see Proposed Regulations §§ 1.355-7(d)(3)(iii), 1.355-7(d)(3)(v), and 1.355-7(m), Examples (4) and (6).

Another helpful new feature of the revised proposals was their provision of six safe harbors in Regulations § 1.355-7(f) (which, if satisfied, will protect against the finding of a prohibited plan). Not surprisingly, these safe harbors, while not broad—sheltering "coves" is perhaps a more apt description—will be quite comforting in a particular case where they apply. The first four are time-sensitive: (1) no plan exists where the acquisition occurs more than six months after the distribution (and there are no "talks" during this interim period), and the distribution is motivated by a substantial non-acquisition related business purpose; (2) even if the business purpose for the distribution is acquisition-related, it will not be fatal if the intended acquisition is a relatively small one;[331.1] (3) no plan will be found where the acquisition occurs more than two years after the distributions (and no talks within the six-month post-distribution period); and (4) no plan will be found where the acquisition occurs more than two years before the distribution (and no talks about the distribution occur within six months of the acquisition). The fifth safe harbor involves trading of listed parent and distributed subsidiary stock where no five-percent shareholder is present (and no "coordinated group" acting in concert emerges).[331.2]

All told, the revised proposed regulations should be welcomed by the tax bar as the best that they had any reasonable right to expect here (at least from the former Treasury). They were certainly a vast improvement over the withdrawn 1999 proposals, a standard that would not have been difficult to meet, however.[331.3] The January 2001 proposed regulations were adopted as temporary regulations (virtually intact) on August 3, 2001.[331.4] Adoption as temporary regulations was done to give taxpayers something to rely on; indications were

---

[331.1] See, e.g., Prop. Regs. § 1.355-7(m), Ex. 4(iii)(F).

[331.2] For similar concepts under § 382(g) and its applicable regulations, see ¶¶ 14.43[2][b] and 14.43[6][a].

[331.3] See Willens, "The Reproposed 'Anti–*Morris Trust*' Regs. Are Vastly Improved, but Some Aspects Remain Vague," 94 J. Tax'n 69 (Feb. 2001); Galanis & Sobol, "IRS Reproposes Anti–Morris Trust Regulations," 3 Bus. Enterprises 4 (Jan. 2001); Rizzi, "Creating a Banker-Free Zone: The New Proposed Anti–*Morris Trust* Regulations," 28 J. Corp. Tax'n 4 (May 2001); Rizzi, "Creating a Banker-Free Zone: The New Proposed Anti–Morris Trust Regulations," 28 J. Tax'n 4 (May 2001); Willens, "IRS Letter Rulings Reveal Inconsistencies in Application of Section 355(e) to Acquisitions Preceding Spin-Offs," Daily Tax Rep. (BNA) No. 126, at J-1 (July 2, 2001); Mason, "Spinning *Morris Trust*: Interpreting 355(e) According to Its Purpose," 94 Tax Notes 1685 (Mar. 25, 2002).

[331.4] TD 8960 (effective at once). The temporary regulations are identical to the proposed regulations, except that the risk protection rule of § 1.355-7(e)(6) and Ex. 7 of § 1.355-7(m) (a controversial example involving serial acquisition) were reserved. Mom-

that final regulations might end up even more user friendly under the new Administration; and that proved to be the case.[331.5]

These predictions proved to be accurate when new even more taxpayer-friendly temporary regulations were issued on April 26, 2002, which replaced the 2001 regulations, substantially liberalized them in many respects, and even allowed an election to apply the new rules all the way back to April 16, 1997, the date of enactment of § 355(e).[331.6]

Thus, the general facts and circumstances analysis provided in Regs. § 1.353-7T(b)(1) continues to focus on all relevant facts and factors, but new § 1.355-7T(b)(2) provides that a post-distribution acquisition can be part of a plan *only* if there was an agreement, understanding or substantial negotiations regarding the acquisition (or a similar acquisition) within the 2-year period preceding the distribution. Moreover, new § 1.355-7T(h)(1) defines these terms much more narrowly than previous versions of the regulations (that is, negotiations must be with the acquirer, or a substantially similar acquirer, also a concept materially narrowed in the new regulations).[331.7] Finally the plan and non-plan "factors" in §§ 1.355-7T(b)(3) and (4) were reduced in number, focused more narrowly, and generally liberalized (e.g., "unexpected change" in circumstances now is specifically recognized in the good factor list and in Example 4).

In this same vein, the safe harbor rules in § 1.355-7T(d) were significantly eased as well: four of the six former safe harbors were revised, and liberalized (turning what formerly were mere "coves" into genuine ports), and a new seventh harbor was added (allowing stock acquisitions by qualified plans under § 401). The revised regulations also dropped the reasonable certainty rule of the former regulations as well as the substantial risk reduction rule of the 2001 proposed regulation (although they are continuing to "consider" this latter issue). About the only place that one can find a hardening of the Service's views was in the case of certain "vote-shifting" tactics.[331.8] All in all, however, taxpayers should be very pleased with the new regulation model; it seems quite generous in so many respects that it is difficult to believe there

---

brun & Thomas, "The Government Takes a Bite out of *Morris Trust*," 29 J. Corp. Tax'n 20 (May 2002).

[331.5] See Sheppard, "ABA Tax Section Meeting—Treasury Looks to Please Business on Corporate Tax Questions," 92 Tax Notes 884, at 886 (Aug. 13, 2001); Beller & Harwell, "After the Spin: Preserving Tax-Free Treatment Under Section 355," 92 Tax Notes 1587 (Sept. 17, 2001); Willens, "IRS Releases 355(e) Proposed Regulations—Be Careful What You Wish For," 95 J. Tax'n 197 (Oct. 2001); Willens, "The New Role for Spin-offs: An Effective Defense Tactic?" Daily Tax Rep. (BNA) No. 72 (Apr. 14, 2002), at J-1.

[331.6] TD 8988, April 26, 2001, promulgating Regs. § 1.355-7T, generally effective on April 27, 2002; but taxpayers can elect to apply the regulations all the way back to April 16, 1997, but not "selectively."

[331.7] See Regs. § 1.355-7T(h)(8) and § 1.355-7T(j), new Examples 6 and 7 (the result in former Example 7 is changed by the new regulations).

[331.8] See Regs. §§ 1.355-7T(d)(5)(ii)(B) and 1.355-7T(j), Example 5.

can be any further significant liberalizations of the § 355(e) "plan" rules (some may even argue that the new regulations are so generous that they have subverted the statutory mandate of § 355(e); but that "mandate," if it ever there was one, was so muddled and incoherent that it's difficult to discern what message Congress was intending to send to the regulations writers).[331.9]

While the "plan or arrangement" regulation project has finally evolved into reasonably tolerable coherence, the §355(e) regulation project still has a long way to go before it is complete, and many difficult issues remain to be dealt with.[331.10]

Final regulations under § 355(e) were adopted on April 19, 2005, by TD 9198 (effective back to the date of enactment if taxpayers so elect). Very few changes were made in the final regulation, but those that were made consisted of clarifications (and even more liberalizations). The only unfavorable change was the removal of compensatory options as an exception from option status (thereby subjecting them to the option rules of Regs. § 1.355-7(e)). Thus, the new regulations continue the trend of previous versions in providing ever greater certainty and liberalizations for taxpayers. As a result, § 355(e) and related § 355(f), have evolved into a distinctly less fearsome regime when compared to the initial 1999 proposed regulations.

The principal changes in the final regulations are the following:

1. Revision of safe harbor IV in § 1.355-7(d) to provide that an acquisition before a distribution generally is not part of a plan if it occurs to before the date of a "disclosure event" (defined in § 1.355-7(h)(5) to include communications by a person affiliated with the distributing or controlled corporation to the acquiror or to any other nonaffiliated person).
2. New safe harbor V also excludes acquisitions before a pro rata spinoff distribution if there has been a public announcement of the spinoff before the acquisition and the acquisition does not involve a public offering, but only if there have been no discussions between the distributing or controlled companies and the acquiror before the first public announcement (illustrated by Example 4 of § 1.355-7(j)).

[331.9] For comments, see Sheppard, Pre-Spin Flirting OK, But Dating is Taxable, 95 Tax Notes 639 (Apr. 29, 2002); Stratton, New Anti–*Morris Trust* Rules Are Pleasing Practitioners, 95 Tax Notes 643 (Apr. 29, 2002). Silverman & Zarlenga, "Fourth Time's a Charm: New Anti–*Morris Trust* Regs Provide Useful Guidance," 96 Tax Notes 983 (Aug. 12, 2002); Rizzi, "New Section 355(e) Regulations: A Renewed Focus on Negotiations," 29 J. Corp. Tax'n 18 (July 2002); Willens, "IRS Revises the 'Plan' Concept in the 355(e) Temp. Regs. to Infuse More Practicality," 97 J. Tax'n 6 (July 2002). Willens, "Lessons Learned From P&G/Smucker 'Reverse' *Morris Trust* Transaction," Daily Tax Rep. (BNA) No. 208, at J-1 (Oct. 28, 2002); Bernstein, "The Pfizer/Pharmacia and Procter & Gamble/Smucker *Morris Trust* Spin-Off Transactions," 29 J. Corp. Tax'n 30 (Nov. 2002); Bernstein, "Ashland-Marathon's Leveraged Morris Trust Transaction," 31 Corp. Tax'n 32 (July 2004).

[331.10] See, e.g., NYSB Assoc. Tax Section report, supra note 322.

3. New safe harbor VI also covers pre-distribution "public offerings" (defined in § 1.355-7(h)(11) as an acquisition of stock for cash where the acquirers of the stock have no opportunity to negotiate as the terms of the offering) if the offering occurs before the disclosure event in the case of the unlisted stock, or before a public announcement if the stock is listed on an established market (defined in § 1.355-7(h)(7)).

4. Three new examples are added to § 1.355-7(j) – Examples 8, 9, and 10, dealing with acquisitions involving public offerings (Examples 1-7 generally are the same as the 2002 temporary regulations).

5. The definition provisions in § 1.355-7(h) were revised and clarified at numerous points: thus, the "agreement and negotiations," rules of § 1.355-7(h)(1) were modified and clarified in several respects, as were the "discussions" provisions in § 1.355-7(h)(6); new definitions were provided for such terms as "disclosure event" in § 1.355-(h)(5), "public announcement" and "public offering" in §§ 1.355-7(h)(10), and 1.355-7(h)(11), and similar acquisitions involving a public offering in § 1.355-7(h)(13).

All in all, the final regulations have met with widespread practitioner approval (if not outright elation) as constituting "a great improvement over rules that already were very good" (see 107 Tax Notes 432, April 25, 2005). They incorporated many of the recommendations offered by the ABA Tax Section and the NYS Bar Assoc. Tax Section. Moreover, the lengthy preamble in TD 9198 is helpful in clarifying the reasons for the various changes that were made in the final regulations. It seems now to be relatively clear that the potential scope of § 355(e) has been substantially moderated by the fifth and final version of the § 355(e) regulations; what's not to like here?[331.10a]

Additional regulations under § 355(e) were proposed on November 19, 2004, dealing with whether a corporation is a predecessor or successor of the distributing or controlled corporation.[331.11] The proposed regulations provide definitions of predecessor and successor,[331.12] rules for determining whether

---

[331.10a] For comments, see Silverman and Zarlenga, "'Anti-Morris Trust Plan Regulations," 110 Tax Notes 967 (Feb. 27, 2006); Willens, "Final 'Anti-Morris Trust'' Regulations Exceedingly Taxpayer-Friendly," Daily Tax Rep. (BNA) No. 83, at J-1 (May 2, 2005). See also Rev. Rul. 2005-65, 2005-41 IRB (Oct. 11, 2005) (illustrates the liberality of the final regulations; IRS approved tax-free § 355(e) despite significant merger at the time of the spin); comment by Friedlich, "IRS Reaches Common Sense Result in Applying 'Anti-Morris Trust' Rules," 33 Corp. Tax'n 45 (Mar. 2006). Silverman and Zarlenga, "'Anti-Morris Trust' Plan Regulations: The Final Chapter in the Saga," 110 Tax Notes 967 (Feb. 27, 2006); Willens, "Realogy Corp. Deal Dispels Myth of Two-Year Rule," Daily Tax Rep. (BNA) No. 5, at J-1 (Jan. 9, 2007).

[331.11] Prop. Regs. §1.355-8 (effective when adopted in final form).

[331.12] Prop. Regs. § 1.355-8(b) (predecessors), and § 1.355-8(c) (successors); but special "deemed acquisition" rules of predecessor, distributing, and controlled corporations are provided in § 1.355-8(d).

there has been an acquisition of a distributing or controlled corporation,[331.13] and limitation on the amount of gain required to be recognized as a result of stock acquisitions aggregating a 50 percent (or more) interest in a predecessor of a distributing corporation.[331.14] Section 381 transactions generally are the key to the creation of a predecessor-successor relationship. The purpose of these proposals is to clarify the tax exposure under § 355(e) to distributing when it spins off a controlled subsidiary. The regulations provide five examples, illustrating their application.[331.15]

The proposals have been favorably reviewed by practitioners as bringing not only clarity, but also reasonable balance to a part of § 355(e) left undefined in the statute or legislative history. However, if the parent and all of its subsidiaries are members of the same affiliated group the predecessor and successor rules do not apply.[331.16]

[331.13] Prop. Regs. § 1.355-8(d).

[331.14] Prop. Regs. § 1.355-8(e).

[331.15] Prop. Regs. § 1.355-8(g).

[331.16] Prop. Regs. § 1.355-8(f). For comment, see Zarlenga & Spencer, "Who Proceeds - Who Succeeds: New Anti-*Morris Trust* Regulations, 107 Tax Notes 351 (Apr. 18, 2005); NYSBA Tax Section, Proposed Regulations on Predecessors and Successors in Distributions of Controlled Subsidiary Stock, 108 Tax Notes Notes 445 (July 25, 2005).

[4] Distribution of "Tracking Stock"

Page 11-84:

Add to note 334.

See generally Dahlberg & Perry, "Tracking Stock: Virtual Equity, Virtual Entities, and Virtual Mergers and Acquisitions," 78 Taxes 18 (Mar. 2000); Rizzi, "Tracking Stock As Synthetic Spin-offs and Contingent Considerations," 27 J. Corp. Tax'n 255 (2000).

Add to text at end of second paragraph.

But nothing seems to have come of this proposal and the new Treasury people seem far less hostile to tracking stock transactions (though IRS continues to list it as a no ruling item).[334.1]

[334.1] Rev. Proc. 2005-3, § 3.01(58), 2005-1 IRB 118.

Page 11-84:

Add new ¶ 11.11[5].

[5] Cash-Rich Split-Offs: § 355(g)

A recent development known as the "cash-rich split-off"[334.2] attracted both Treasury and Congress attention in 2005, and ultimately resulted in the enactment of § 355(g) in 2006.[334.3] If either the distributing or controlled corporation overloaded with cash (or cash-equivalent type assets)[384.4] in a non-prorata split-off exchange, the distribution is denied the application of § 355, so that the transaction is fully taxable at *both* the corporate and shareholder levels (the latter, however, should be entitled to capital gain treatment under § 302 rather than being taxed as a dividend).

The tainted asset threshold is set at a relatively high level, however, so that only "super cash-rich split-offs" need to fear this provision (it has been noted, however, that some transactions have gone as high as 90 percent, which seems to be pushing the envelope even under former law). Thus, the pigs have been reigned in by new § 355(g), but not the bulls.

[334.2] For description of one of these transactions, see Bernstien, "Janus Capital Group's Cash-Rich Split-off," 30 Corp. Tax'n 39 (Nov. 2003); see also Willens, "Does the *Tribune* Decision Endanger Cash-Rich Split-offs?"109 Tax Notes 547 (Oct. 24, 2005) (concludes no); but 2006 legislation § 355(g), does though not fatally. See Willens, "Endgame May Be in Sight for Untangling Ties of Liberty Media, News Corp.," Daily Tax Rep. (BNA) No. 194, at J-1 (Oct. 6, 2006).

[334.3] TIPRA 2005, Pub. L. No. 109-222, § 222 (May 17, 2006).

[384.4] Namely, 75 percent of its assets are "tainted" (the number drops to two thirds on May 17, 2007).

¶ 11.12 ANCILLARY MATTERS: BASIS, HOLDING PERIOD, AND EARNINGS AND PROFITS

[1] Distributees' Basis

Page 11-85:

Add to text after reference to note 340.

Proposed regulations issued on May 3, 2004[340.1] finally deal with some of these issues in a more comprehensive manner. Thus, the proposed regulations reject use of any average basis allocation method and instead require tracing of basis if it is possible to identify the particular shares;[340.2] if it is not possible to trace the particular shares, then the taxpayer is allowed to designate where the

---

[340.1] Prop. Regs. §§1.358-2(a)(2), and 1.358-2(c) (seven examples). The regulations are effective on final promulgation. The proposals remove current Regs. §§1.358-2(a)(2)-(5) and 1.358-2(c). Adopted as final regulations §§ 1.358-1 and 1.358-2 (Jan. 23, 2006).

[340.2] Prop. Regs. §§1.358-2(a)(2)(ii) and 1.358-2(c), Ex. 7. Final Regs. §§ 1.358-2(a)(2)(ii) and 1.358-2(c), Exs. 5 and 6.

§358 basis is to go.[340.3] These proposals were adopted (with modifications) in January of 2006.[340.4] The final regulations increased in complexity in a major way, however, which is not a happy result. But allowing the exchange transaction terms to specify allocations (which will control if economically reasonable) can be helpful here, as is adoption of the rule allowing shareholder designation if he or she is unable to trace basis. The basis tracing regime does not, however, apply to § 351 exchanges,[340.5] although IRS is considering expanding coverage to these transactions as well, though would not adopt it in the final regulations.

[340.3] Prop. Regs. §1.358-2(c), Ex. 7. Final Regs. §§ 1.358-2(a)(2)(ii) and 1.358-2(c), Exs. 7, 10-14.

[340.4] TD 9244 (effective Jan. 23, 2006). The number of examples was doubled (to fourteen), Regs. § 1.358-6(c).

[340.5] Regs. §§ 1.358-2(a)(2)(viii) and 1.358-2(c), Exs. 8 and 9.

[4] Earnings and Profits

Page 11-87:

Add to note 347.

For allocation of earnings (or deficits) where the divisive transaction involves a foreign corporation, see Prop. Regs. § 1.367(b)-8 (Nov. 8, 2000), discussed at   15.84[3][f]. The proposed regulations modify rules prescribed by the § 312(h) regulations (Regs. § 1.312-10) in several important respects.

Add to note 348, first paragraph.

For proposed regulations modifying Regs. § 1.312-10 in the case of foreign divisive transactions, see Prop. Regs. § 1.367(b)-8 (Nov. 8, 2000), supra note 347.

Add to last paragraph of note 348.

See also Collins, Cordonnier & Zywan, "Allocation of E & P in a Spin-off by a Consolidated Group," 28 J. Corp. Tax'n 11 (Nov. 2001).

¶ 11.13 CORPORATE DIVISIONS AND § 306

[1] In General

Page 11-89:

Add text to end of last paragraph.

But § 306 stock status (and even § 351(g) non-qualified preferred stock status) may become quite popular again if Treasury's February 2003 proposal for a

100 percent dividend exclusion is enacted in its present form.[355.1] Even if Chairman Thomas's alternative dividend relief proposal is adopted instead (and it was),[355.2] the tax bite on dividends will be materially reduced.[355.3]

[355.1] See ¶¶ 1.08[4], 8.06. Even if the exclusion is less than 100 percent, the effective tax rate on that dividend may still be lower than the current capital gains rate.

[355.2] Taxing dividends at the same rate as capital gains (and lowering the top capital gains rate to 15 percent), released on May 1, 2003, passed the House on May 9, 2003, and ultimately was adopted in the final 2003 tax legislation, § 1(h)(11) (effective Jan. 1, 2003). It was extended for two more years by 2006 legislation (TIPRA).

[355.3] Harmonizing the tax rates on dividends with those applicable to capital gains in effect largely neutralizes the tax rules applicable to redemptions of § 306 stock (though *not* those applicable to sales of that stock). The Senate's more modest dividend exclusion proposal did cover sales of § 306 stock as well, but that proposal was not the one adopted in the final legislation. It is unclear whether that legislation will apply the reduced tax rates to sales of § 306 stock (though redemptions of that stock clearly will qualify); but new § 306(a)(1)(D) does treat sales of § 306 stock as qualifying dividends for purposes of the reduced tax rates. But both sales and redemption of § 306 stock initially had trouble meeting the 61-day holding period limit of § (1)(h)(11)(B)(iii) since it "straddles" the dividend date (although technical corrections, legislations should cure this problem and IRS has agreed to apply it to 2003 returns, Supra note 268.3).

¶ 11.14 MONOPOLY OF § 355

Page 11-93:

Add to note 366 at end of first paragraph.

See Bank, "The Runaway 'A' Train. Does IRS Need New Breaks?" 87 Tax Notes 553 (Apr. 24, 2000); infra ¶ 12.22[11].

Add to note 366 at end of second paragraph.

See also supra ¶ 11.11[4].

¶ 11.16 FOREIGN CORPORATIONS

Page 11-97:

Add to note 382.

See generally Calianno, "International Aspects of Section 355 Transactions," 12 J. Int'l Tax'n 12 (Jan. 2001), reprinted in 28 J. Corp. Tax'n 13 (Mar. 2001); Bress, Anson & Dubert, "New Section 367(b)Proposed Regs.," 12 J. Int'l Tax'n 18 (July 2001).

Corporate Reorganizations

D SPECIAL PROBLEMS IN REORGANIZATIONS

A   GENERAL CONSIDERATIONS

¶ 12.01 INTRODUCTORY

[1] In General

Page 12-10:

Add to note 4.

Goodman, "Corporate and Partnership M&A Tax Law: Is It Time to Merge Subchapter C and K?" 95 Tax Notes 1497 (June 2, 2002) (not quite).

[3] General Theory for Tax-Free Reorganizations

Page 12-13:

Add to end of second paragraph in note 8.

Goodman, supra note 4 (a historical look-back at the evolution of the subchapter C and K merger rules).

[4] Statutory Structure and Stakes

Page 12-14:

Add to note 9.

The 2006 versions Rev. Proc. 2006-3, § 3.01(33) 2006-1 IRB 122. See also Rev. Proc. 2005-68, 2005-41 IRB 694 (Oct. 11, 2005) (procedures and guidelines for expedited ruling; even more significant, is IRS' retreat from its no comfort ruling policy). See Baline, "IRS Drops No Comfort Ruling Policy," 38 Corp. Tax'n 32 (Jan. 2006).

Add to note 10.

Currently Rev. Proc. 2005-3, 2005-1 IRB 118.

[5] 1985 Senate Finance Committee Staff Reform Proposals

Page 12-16:

Add to text at end of last paragraph.

But the Joint Committee Staff's April 2001 Simplification report[13.1] revived discussion of these (and other) proposals to reform the basic structure of the corporate reorganization provisions—so at least they have not been totally forgotten (though they seem to have been ignored by Congress and Treasury alike).

[13.1] Part IV A2, at 228–248.

¶ 12.04 RELATIONSHIP TO OTHER ACQUISITION TECHNIQUES

Page 12-21:

Add to end of tablenote (a) of chart.

Reorganization   *Purchase*

Pooling finally was abolished in June 2001; see Willens, "A Guide to the Tax Impact of FASB's New Rules on Accounting for Business Combinations," 96 J. Tax'n 79 (Feb. 2002); generally Ginsburg & Levin, Mergers, Acquisitions & Buyouts (Aspen, Dec. 2001),   1503.4

Page 12-22:

Add to end of tablenote (b) of chart.

Ginsburg & Levin, ¶ 1503.2.

B   "REORGANIZATION" DEFINED

¶ 12.21 CONTINUITY OF PROPRIETARY INTEREST AND PLAN OF REORGANIZATION

[1] Continuity of Interest in General

Page 12-27:

Add to note 29.

Schultz, "The Evolution of the Continuity of Interest Test, *General Utilities* Repeal and the Taxation of Corporate Acquisitions," 80 Taxes 229 (Mar. 2002).

Add to text at end of ¶ 12.21[1].

IRS also proposed regulations in August 2004 (and adopted in 2005) providing that continuity of interest (and continuity of business enterprise) principles do not apply to Type E and Type F reorganizations.[30.1]

[30.1] Prop. Regs. §§ 1.368-1(b) and 1.368-2(m) (Aug. 12, 2004); adopted as final regulations by TD 9182 (Feb. 25, 2005).

[2] Character of the Consideration

[b] Quantum of Continuity Required

Page 12-31:

Add to end of first paragraph in note 46.

The *Kass* regulation was moved again in 2001 to Regs. § 1.338-3(d) hopefully its final resting place.

Page 12-32:

Add to end of sentence in text ending with note 50.

(however, final regulations issued in August 2000 narrowed the scope of the 19 98 temporary regulations).

Add to note 50.

But final Regs. §§ 1.368-1(e)(1)(ii) and 1.368-1(e)(6), Ex. 9, adopted by TD 8898 on August 30, 2000, narrow the scope of the temporary regulations (impacts continuity only if consideration comes from acquiror corporation or would result in application of § 356 to the distribution). See Couch & Bennett, "The Effect of Target Redemptions and Distributions on Continuity of Interest," 89 Tax Notes 1301 (Dec. 4, 2000); Silverman & Weinstein, "The New Pre-Reorganization Continuity of Interest Regulations," 28 J. Corp. Tax'n 13 (Mar. 2001); reprinted in 91 Tax Notes 805 (Apr. 30, 2001).

Add to text at end of ¶ 12.21[2][b].

IRS issued very helpful proposed regulations in August 2004[50.1] dealing with the time when the value of acquiror stock is determined. The critical date for this purpose is the day before the date of a binding contract (which includes public tender offers).[50.2] If the initial agreement is modified as to the amount or type of consideration the modification date becomes the valuation date.[50.3] These proposals were adopted in revised form in September of 2005.[50.4]

The final regulations relaxed the "signing date" and contingencies rules and followed many of the commentator suggestions. Thus the final regulations (1) expanded the definition of "fixed" consideration;[50.5] (2) included non-money boot as acceptable valuation consideration;[50.6] (3) permit contingent consideration (if it only results in additional stock and continuity is otherwise

---

[50.1] Prop. Regs. §§ 1.368-1(e)(2) and redesignated 1.368-1(e)(7), Exs. 10, 11, and 12 (Aug. 10, 2004, effective when finalized). Cummings, "Three New Sets of Prop. Regs. Should Make Planning For Reorganizations Much Easier," 101 J. Tax'n 271, at 277 (Nov. 2004).

[50.2] Regs. § 1.368-1(e)(2)(ii); final Regs. § 1.368-1(e)(2)(ii).

[50.3] Prop. Regs. §§ 1.368-1(e)(2)(ii)(A) and 1.368-2(e)(7), Exs. 11 and 12; final Regs. § 1.368-2(e)(ii)(B) and 1.368-2(e)(ii)(B), Exs. 4 and 5.

[50.4] TD 9225 (Sept. 16, 2005).

[50.5] Regs. § 1.368-1(e)(2)(iii).

[50.6] Regs. §§ 1.368-1(e)(2)(iv) and 1.368-1(e)(2)(v), Ex. 6.

okay);[50.7] and sets a new (and lower) continuity line at 40 percent.[50.8] There are nine examples in the final regulations.[50.9] New temporary regulations,[50.10] revising the 2005 rules, were issued on March 20, 2007.

[50.7] Regs. § 1.368-1(e)(iii)(C).

[50.8] Regs. § 1.368-1(e)(v), Exs. 1 and 2.

[50.9] Regs. § 1.368-1(e)(v). The final regulations are effective for binding contracts after Sept. 16, 2005; Regs. § 1.368-1(e)(8), last sentence. See Willens, "New 'Continuity of Interest' Rules Will Result in 'A' Reorganization Treatment for McClatchy, Knight-Ridder Merger," Daily Tax Rep. (BNA) No. 69, at J-1 (Apr. 11, 2006).

For comments see Willens, Final Continuity of Interest Regulations Eliminate Risk That Market Fluctuations Will Deny Reorganization Treatment, BNA DTR No. 223, at J-1 (Nov. 21, 2005); Bennett, Valuing Stock For Continuity of Interest, 83 Taxes 9 (Dec. 2005).

[50.10] Regs. § 1.3681-T(e)(2), issued by TD 9316.

[c] Debt vs. Equity Aspects

Page 12-33:

Add to note 51.

See also Rev. Rul. 2003-19, 2003-7 IRB 468 (conversions of mutual insurance companies to stock insurance corporations held tax-free § 368 reorganizations (Type E and Type F; successor corporations' stock the same corporation); Rev. Rul. 2003-48, 2003-19 IRB 863 (conversions of state mutual savings banks into state stock banks in series of related steps held tax-free under § 368 (Types E, F, B and § 368(a)(2)(E) as well as global § 351).

Add to note 52, first paragraph.

See also Rev. Ruls. 2003-19, 2003-48, supra note 51.

Add new ¶ 12.21[2][d].

[d] Exchange of "Net Value" Requirement: Prop. Regs. § 1.368-1(f) [New]

Proposed regulations issued in March of 2005,[52.1] require that there must be an "exchange of net value" in order for the transaction to qualify for § 368 tax-free reorganization status. This limitation is intended to work in conjunction with general continuity of proprietary interest principles. Its purpose is to prevent transactions that economically resemble sales from qualifying as tax-free reorganizations.[52.2] As stated in the Preamble, the IRS and Treasury be-

---

[52.1] Prop. Regs. § 1.368-1(f) (effectively when finalized) similar limitations are proposed for §§ 332 and 351. See also Cummings, Net Value and Type D reorganizations, 107 Tax Notes, 249 (Apr. 11, 2005). See infra   12.65[5].

[52.2] These proposals do not apply to Type E or F reorganizations, however, because continuity of interest does not apply to them either; Regs. § 1.368-1(b)(1).

lieve that the receipt of worthless stock in exchange for assets cannot be part of a tax-free exchange for stock.

Thus, "surrender" of net value refers to assets and liabilities of the target corporation while receipt of net value is determined by assets and liabilities of the issuing corporation.[52.3]

But the net value requirement also does not apply to non-divisive Type D reorganizations since the ability to attack liquidation reincorporation transactions is governed by those provisions.[52.4] The net value exchange proposals are illustrated by ten examples in §1.368-1(f)(5).[52.5] The Preamble to these regulations is must reading (since it is longer than the regulations by many pages).

See Cummings, "New Proposed Regs. Change Rules For Transactions where Property or Stock Lacks Net Value," 103 J. Tax'n 14 (July 2005); Bennett, "Proposed Regulations on Insolvency Reorganizations, Part I," 83 Taxes 9 (Aug. 2005); Silverman, et al., "Assessing the Value of the Proposed No Net Value Regulations," 108 Tax Notes 1135 (Sept. 5, 2005). NYSBA Tax Section, "Formations, Reorganizations, and Liquidations Involving Insolvent Corporations," 110 Tax Notes 871 (Feb. 2, 2006) (opposing the § 368 proposals); Blanchard, Hooker and Vogel, "Underwater Assets and Insolvent Corporations: Reflections on Treasury's Recently Proposed Regulations and Related Matters," 59 Tax Law. 107 (Fall 2005).

[52.3] Prop. Regs. § 1.368-1(f)(2) deals with net value exchanged in asset transactions while § 1.368-1(f)(3) deals with stock transactions.

[52.4] Prop. Regs. §§ 1.368-1(f)(4) and 1.368-1(f)(5), Ex. 8; see infra ¶ 12.64; and Cummings, supra note 52.1.

[52.5] Exs. 1-7 involve asset transactions; Example 8 is a reincorporation transaction; Examples 9 and 10 involved stock transactions.

[3] Remote Continuity: *Groman* Doctrine

Page 12-35:

Add to note 56.

See also Rev. Rul. 2001-24, 2001-22 IRB 1290 (drop of subsidiary stock after forward triangular merger allowed in the "spirit" of § 368(a)(2)(C), though not its letter). Schultz, "Evolution of the Continuity of Interest Test...," 80 Taxes 229 (Mar. 2002) Prop. Regs. § 1.368-2(k) (Mar. 2, 2004) (drop after any § 368 reorganization allowed; thus; *Bashford* will be gone for good under these regulations). But the March drop-down regulations were withdrawn and reissued in revised and broadened form on Aug. 17, 2004, as § 1.368-2(k) (effective on final regulations).

Add text to end of ¶ 12.21[3].

IRS seems to have virtually (if not totally) abandoned *Groman* and *Bashford* limitations as a result of recent rulings and proposed regulations (*Bashford* is gone for good in recent proposed regulations).[56.1] The March proposed regula-

---

[56.1] Prop. Regs. § 1.368-2(k) (Mar. 2, 2004); supra note 56. Bennett, "Contributions to Controlled Corporations Following Acquisitive Code Sec. 368(a)(1)(D) Reorganizations," 82 Taxes 9 (June 2004).

tions were withdrawn and reissued in revised and broadened form on August 17, 2004[56.2] (the new proposals allow post-acquisitions push-ups as well as drop-downs).[56.3]

[56.2] Prop. Regs. §§ 1.368-1(d)(4), (5), Exs. (7), (9), (10), and (12); §§ 1.368-2(f) and 1.368-2(j)(3)(ii), (iii), (iv); and 1.368-2(k) (and drop Ex. 3 of current regulations).

[56.3] Prop. Regs. § 1.368-2(k)(3), Exs. (2) and (6). Drop-downs to COBE-qualified partnerships are allowed as well. Cummings, "Three New Sets of Prop. Regs. Should Make Planning For Reorganizations Much Easier," 101 J. Tax'n 271, at 283 (Nov. 2004).

[4] Continuity of Participation by Transferor's Historic Shareholders

Page 12-36:

Add to note 60.

Prop. Regs. § 1.368-1(e)(6) (Mar. 10, 2005) codify *Alabama Asphaltic* and its progeny principles treating creditors of an insolvent debtor corporation as holding the proprietary interest in that corporation; § 1.368-1(e)(7), Ex. 10 (though there are already earlier issued Exs. 10-12, so this example will probably become Ex. 13. These proposals adopt the continuity of interest standard for Type G reorganizations and the Senate report thereon; infra   12.30[1]. See NYSBA Tax Section Report, supra note   52.2.

Page 12-37:

Add to note 62.

But, final Regs. §§ 1.368-1(e)(1)(ii) and 1.368-1(e)(6), Ex. 9, adopted by TD 8898 on August 30, 2000, narrow the scope of the temporary regulations (distribution impacts continuity only if funds supplied by acquiror or distribution would result in application of § 356 if received in the reorganization). See Couch & Bennett, "The Effect of Target Redemptions and Distributions on Continuity of Interest," 89 Tax Notes 1301 (Dec. 4, 2000); Silverman & Weinstein, "The New Pre-Reorganization Continuity of Interest Regulations," 28 J. Corp. Tax'n 13 (Mar. 2001); reprinted in 91 Tax Notes 805 (Apr. 30, 2001); Schultz, "Evolution of the Continuity of Interest Test...," 80 Taxes 229, at 232 (Mar. 2002).

Page 12-38:

Add to sentence in text ending with note 67.

(however, final regulations issued in August 2000 narrowed the scope of the 1998 temporary regulations).

Add to note 67.

But, final Regs. §§ 1.368-1(e)(1)(ii) and 1.368-1(e)(6), Ex. 9, adopted by TD 8898 on August 30, 2000, narrowed the scope of the temporary regulations (distribution impacts continuity only if funds supplied by acquiror or distribution would result in application of § 356 if received in the reorganization). See Couch & Bennett, "The Effect of Target Redemptions and Distributions on Continuity of Interest," 89 Tax Notes 1301 (Dec. 4, 2000); Silverman & Weinstein, "The New Pre-Reorganization Continuity of Interest Regulations," 28 J. Corp. Tax'n 13 (Mar. 2001); reprinted in 91 Tax Notes 805 (Apr. 30,

2001); Schultz, "Evolution of the Continuity of Interest Test...," 80 Taxes 229, at 232 (Mar. 2002).

[5] Post-Acquisition Continuity: How Long?

Page 12-39:

Add to end of first paragraph of note 71.

But *McDonald's* step transaction doctrine followed in NovaCare, Inc. v. US, 2002-1 USTC ¶ 50,389 (Fed. Cl. 2002) (acquirer arguing failed reorganization because of target shareholders' sales of its stock; summary judgment motions denied because factual issues existed). For comments on *NovaCare*, see Raby & Raby, "Does a Sale of Stock Destroy Tax-Free Nature of a Reorganization?" 95 Tax Notes 1633 (June 10, 2002); Rizzi, "*Nova-Care* Makes Practitioners Nervous," 29 J. Corp. Tax'n 26 (July 2002).

Page 12-40:

Add to note 72.

But see NovaCare, Inc., supra note 71, and comment by Rizzi, id.

Page 12-41:

Add to note 77, first paragraph.

But, final Regs. §§ 1.368-1(e)(1)(ii) and 1.368-1(e)(6), Ex. 9, adopted by TD 8898 on August 30, 2000, narrowed the scope of the temporary regulations by focusing on whether the distribution would result in application of § 356 if received in the reorganization or whether the distribution was funded by the acquiror (in which cases continuity will be impacted). See Couch & Bennett, "The Effect of Target Redemptions and Distributions on Continuity of Interest," 89 Tax Notes 1301 (Dec. 4, 2000); Schultz, "Evolution of the Continuity of Interest Test...," 80 Taxes 229, at 232 (Mar. 2002).

Also, TD 8898 noted that Regs. § 1.368-1(e)(6), Ex. 8, is no longer necessary in view of Rev. Rul. 99-58, supra this note 77, and thus was removed.

[9] Limitations of Continuity Doctrine

Page 12-47:

Add text to end of ¶ 12.21[9].

> 5. IRS recently proposed (and adopted) regulations providing that continuity of interest (and continuity of business enterprise) do not apply to Type E and Type F reorganizations.[97.1]

[97.1] Prop. Regs. §§ 1.368-1(b), and 1.368-2(m) (Aug. 12, 2004) (effective when final). Adopted as final regulations by TD 9182 (Feb. 25, 2005).

¶ 12.22 STATUTORY MERGERS AND CONSOLIDATIONS (TYPE A REORGANIZATION)

[1] In General

Page 12-49:

Add to note 102.

As to foreign-law mergers, see Evans, "Respecting Foreign Mergers Under U.S. Tax Law," 88 Tax Notes 93 (July 3, 2000). For alternative cross-border acquisition structures, see Humphreys, "Partnership Combinations of U.S. and Non-U.S. Corporations," 92 Tax Notes 241 (July 9, 2001) (de facto mergers).Bank, "A Transcontinental 'A' Train? Foreign Mergers Under Section 368(a)(1)(A)," 54 Tax Law 555 (2001); Dolan, "Tretiak & Elman, Virtual Mergers: Is America Ready?" 80 Taxes 165 (Mar. 2002) (it better be).

Also, the preamble to the Nov. 15, 2001 revised proposed regulations on mergers involving disregarded entities, see infra   12.22[10], notes that IRS is reconsidering the foreign law issue and asks for comments. IRS officials have indicated they are working on regulations involving cross-border mergers. Proposed regulations allowing such mergers were released January 4, 2005; see Willens, Daily Tax Rep. (BNA) No. 6, at J-1 (Jan. 10, 2005); infra   12.22[12]. They were adopted as final regulations § 1.368-2(b)(1) on Jan. 23, 2006, by TD 9242 (effective on that date). See Willens, "IRS Introduces 'New and Improved' A Reorganizations," 110 Tax Notes 1235 (Mar. 13, 2006); Bennett The Final Statutory Merger Regulations, 84 Taxes 7 (Apr. 2006); Lemein et al., "New Regulations Dramatically Expand Opportunities for Taxpayers Seeking to Structure International Reorganizations," 84 Taxes 5 (May 2006).

The final regulations add five new examples to § 1.368-2(b)(1)(iii) (Exs. 13 and 14 allow "A" merger treatment under foreign law as well, both direct and triangular varients).

Page 12-51:

Add to note 108.

See also infra   12.22[11].

[3] Triangular Mergers; Subsidiary-Merger Techniques

Page 12-53:

Add to note 119.

For mergers involving "disregarded subsidiaries," see infra   12.22[10].

[9] Mergers Into Limited Liability Companies

Page 12-58:

Add to note 142.

But see a § 754 election for a possible cure. Also, the § 708 regulations dealing with § 708(b)(1)(1)(B) deemed terminations were revised on 1997 by TD 8717; Regs. § 1.708-1(b)(1) changed the sequencing rule to a § 351 model (that is, assets drop down to partnership and partnership interest are distributed up).

[10] Mergers Involving "Tax-Disregarded Entities or Subsidiaries"

[a] General

Page 12-59:

Add text to end of ¶ 12.22[10][a].

Not surprisingly, the recent proposed regulations refused to treat the merger of a disregarded entity into a regarded entity as a Type A reorganization in view of its divisive effect.[146.1] Surprisingly, however, these same proposed regulations also initially denied Type A qualification for the converse transaction involving the merger of a regarded entity into a disregarded entity.[146.2] But new proposed regulations issued on November 15, 2001 changed position on this latter issue (though not the former) and would allow mergers into, though not by, a disregarded entity to qualify under § 368(a)(1)(A).[146.3] These proposals were adopted as temporary regulations in January 2003,[146.4] which were adopted as final regulations in January 2006.[146.5]

[146.1] Prop. Regs. § 1.368-2(b)(1) (May 16, 2000); see also Rev. Rul. 2000-5, 2000-5 IRB 436; infra ¶ 12.22[11]. Prop. Regs. § 1.368-2(b)(1) (Nov. 15, 2001), Ex.1 (codifies Rev. Rul. 2000-5); final Regs. § 1.368-2(b)(1)(iii), Exs. 1 and 6 continue this treatment.

[146.2] Prop. Regs. § 1.368-2(b)(1). For comments, see Cummings & Wellen, "Merging Disregarded Entities," 87 Tax Notes 1367 (June 5, 2000); Bailine, "When Is an 'A' Not an 'A'? When It's a Fish," 28 J. Corp. Tax'n 30 (May 2001); ABA Tax Section comment, 54 Tax Law. 639 (2001).

[146.3] Prop. Regs. § 1.368-2(b)(1). The reproposed regulations flesh out the definition of "A reorganization" and add 6 examples in § 1.368-2(b)(1)(iv). See Sheppard, "Waterloo: Mergers With Disregarded Entities," 93 Tax Notes 1021 (Nov. 19, 2001); May, "Viewpoint (discussing the new proposals)," (BNA) No. 240, at J-1 (Dec. 17, 2001); Willens, Viewpoint (discussing the new proposals), Daily Tax Rep. (BNA) No. 245, at J-1 (Dec. 24, 2001); Rizzi, "Mergers Into Tax Nothings: The Service Sees the Light," 29 J. Corp. Tax'n 23 (Mar. 2002).

[146.4] TD 9038, Regs. § 1.368-2T(b)(1) (Jan. 24, 2003). The regulations have a retroactive effect as well (if all parties are consistent), Regs. § 1.368-2T(b)(1)(v). Immerman & Ashraf, "Tax-Free Corporate Mergers Have Been Redefined for the LLC Era," 30 J. Corp. Tax'n 3 (May 2003); Steinberg and Mendelson, "Use of Partnerships and Disregarded Entities by U.S Corporations," 81 Taxes 261 (Mar. 2003). Shabroody & Stalter, "Navigating a One-Way Street: Mergers With Disregarded Entities Under the New Temporary Regulations," 5 Bus. Ents. No. 3, at 4 (May/June 2003).

[146.5] TD 9242 (effective Jan. 23, 2006).

[b] Merger Into Disregarded Entity of Corporate Owner

Page 12-59:

Add to note 147, second paragraph.

But the preamble made no mention of the forward merger possibility, a curious omission. But new proposed regulations § 1.368-2(b)(1) (Nov. 15, 2001) allow direct merger treatment here under § 368(a)(1)(A); adopted as temporary regulations by TD 9038 (Jan. 24, 2003).

Add text to end of ¶ 12.22[10][b].

In denying Type A treatment, the preamble to the May 2000 proposed regulations concluded that since the acquiring corporation is not a "party" to the state law merger transaction, this technical defect prevented qualification of the transaction as a "statutory merger." In view of Treasury's numerous recent (1998) liberalizations of the § 368 regulations on continuity of interest and continuity of business enterprise,[147.1] and also their abandonment of the *Bausch & Lomb* limitation,[147.2] this rigidly narrow interpretation espoused by the proposed regulations came as an unwelcome surprise. But revised proposals issued on November 15, 2001, changed position here and permit mergers into disregarded entities to qualify under § 368(a)(1)(A) and these proposals were adopted as temporary regulations in January 2003, which in turn were adopted as final regulations in January 2006.[147.3]

[147.1] See supra   12.21.

[147.2] See infra   12.24[3][e].

[147.3] Prop. Regs. § 1.368-2(b)(1)(iii); Regs. § 1.368-2T(b)(1) (Jan. 24, 2003). The temporary regulations added new Example 8 to Regs. § 1.368-2T(b)(1)(iv) (which specifically allows pre-tailoring distributions), and new Example 3 (involving the merger of an S corporation and its Q sub into a C corporation; for Q subs generally, also a disregarded entity, see   6.02[6]. Final Regs. § 1.368(b)(1) were adopted by TD 9242 (Jan. 23, 2006). The number of examples was increased to fourteen (with five new examples), two of which permit mergers under comparable foreign law).

[c] Merger of Disregarded Entity

Page 12-60:

Add to note 148.

The revised reproposed regulations of Nov. 15, 2001, the temporary regulations of Jan. 24, 2003, and the final regulations of January 23, 2006, codify Rev. Rul. 2000-5 in Regs. § 1.368-2(b)(1)(iv), Ex. 1 and Ex. 5, and § 1.328-2T(b)(1)(iv), Ex. 1 and Ex. 6 and the final regulations are the same.

Add to note 149.

Prop. Regs. § 1.368-2(b)(1) (May 16, 2000) deny Type A treatment here on the grounds that the transaction has a divisive effect; see Rev. Rul. 2000-5 IRB 436, and infra   12.22[11]. The November 15, 2001 proposed regulations continue this limitation, denying Type A qualification here, as do the January 2003 temporary regulations and the final 2006 regulations as well.

Add new ¶ 12.22[11].

[11] Divisive Mergers

In response to recent state law developments permitting "partial mergers," IRS issued Revenue Ruling 2000-5[150.1] denying Type A qualification for such transactions on the ground the rules of § 355 constitute the exclusive route to tax-free reorganization treatment here. The ruling involved two transactional patterns, both of which had a "divisive" effect. In the first, the target transferred some of its assets (and liabilities) to the acquiring corporation, but did not liquidate as part of the transaction; in the second, the target split its assets (and liabilities) between two acquirors (and then liquidated). Both transactions were held not to qualify as Type A mergers because a merger requires, according to the ruling, that (1) *one* corporation must acquire the target's assets by operation of the corporate law merger statute and (2) the target must cease to exist.

Proposed regulations (issued in May 2000, and reissued in revised form in November 2001) involving mergers of a "disregarded entity" into a "regarded entity" likewise deny Type A treatment for this transaction in view of its divisive effect.[150.2] The 2003 temporary regulations (and the 2006 final regulations) continue this treatment.

[150.1] Rev. Rul. 2000-5, 2000-5 IRB 436. See Bank, "The Runaway 'A' Train: Does the IRS Need New Breaks?" 87 Tax Notes 553 (Apr. 24, 2000); Rocap, "More Thoughts on 'A' Reorganizations," 87 Tax Notes 856 (May 8, 2000); Bailine, "When Is an 'A' Not an 'A'? When It's a Fish," 28 J. Corp. Tax'n 30 (May 2001).

[150.2] Prop. Regs. § 1.368-2(b)(1) (May 16, 2000); Prop. Regs. § 1.368-2(b)(1) (Nov. 15, 2001); and temporary regulations § 1.368-2T(b)(1) (Jan. 24, 2003); supra ¶ 12.22[10]; final Regs. § 1.368-(2)(b)(1)(iii) Exs. 1 and 6. For treatment of divisive reorganizations, see infra ¶ 12.26 and Chapter 11.

Page 12-60:

Add new ¶ 12.22[12].

[12] Mergers Involving Foreign Corporations [New]

On January 5, 2005, the IRS released proposed regulations withdrawing long standing regulations prohibiting mergers under foreign law from qualifying as a Type A reorganization.[150.3] The proposed regulations also withdraw the exclusion of foreign disregarded entities that existed in the temporary regula-

---

[150.3] Prop. Regs. § 1.368-2(b)(1). See Tillinghast IRS Issues Guidance on International Aspects of Statutory Mergers & Securities Exchanges, 34 Tax Mgmt Int'l No. 3, at 196 Rizzi, IRS Proposes to Include Mergers In 'A' reorganizations, 32 Corp. Tax'n 40 (May 2005); Silverman, Zarlenga & Giles, "Proposed Regs. Would Permit Cross-Border 'A' Reorganizations for the First Time in 70 Years, 107 Tax Notes 881 (May 16, 2005); and Rubinger & Sherman, "Proposed Regulations on Cross-Border Mergers Will Add Much Flexibility in Planning,"102 J. Tax'n 290 (May 2005); Bress, "The New Cross-Border "A" Reorganizations," 16 J. Int'l Tax'n 14 (June 2005).

tions.[150.4] New Example 9 also expressly repudiates Rev. Rul. 57-465 (which had denied Type A treatment for the merger of two foreign corporations).[150.5]

The transaction must satisfy the regulation requirements, however, as well as more general continuity of interest, business enterprise and business purpose. But effecting the transaction under U. S. law will no longer be necessary (at least if the foreign laws are substantially similar to domestic M&A rules).

These regulations were adopted as final regulations on January 23, 2006 (effective on that date).[150.6]

[150.4] Preamble to the proposed regulations.

[150.5] IRS also released Notice 2005-6, 2005-5 IRB at the same time (dealing with exchange of securities in cross-border mergers and recapitalization).

[150.6] TD 9242 (Jan. 23, 2006, effective on that date). The final Regulations added five examples to § 1.368-2(b)(1)(iii) (the foreign law merger examples are Ex. 13 and Ex. 14). Comment by Lemein, Lipeles, et al., 84 Taxes 5 (May 2006); Bennett, 84 Taxes 7 (Apri. 2006) also Bress, 17 J. Int'l Tax'n 18 (Aug. 2006); and Requenez & Odintz, "New Flexibility Under Final Regs. Affecting Foreign-Law Mergers," 105 J. Tax'n 151 (Sept. 2006).

¶ 12.23 ACQUISITIONS OF STOCK FOR VOTING STOCK (TYPE B REORGANIZATION)

[1] In General: Solely for Voting Stock of Acquiring Corporation (or Its Parent)

Page 12-64:

Add to end of runover paragraph.

Another high profile transaction, involving the Times Mirror Corporation's disposition of its Matthew Bender subsidiary, was carefully structured to qualify as a reverse triangular merger under § 368(a)(2)(E),[163.1] and also as a triangular Type B reorganization;[163.2] instead it was held to be a taxable stock sale by the Tax Court because of various contractual rights retained by the taxpayer (principally the right to manage a substantial pot of cash deposited in an LLC of the acquiring parent corporation.[163.3] Rejecting the taxpayer's argument that these exclusive management rights were merely an attribute of the tax-

---

[163.1] Infra ¶ 12.25[3].

[163.2] Supra note 151.

[163.3] Tribune Company, 125 TC 140 (2005) (successor to the Times Mirror Company). For comments, see Lipton, "Taxable Sale or Nontaxable Reorganization? The Tax Court Draws A Line in Tribune Company," 103 J. Tax'n 261 (Nov. 2005); Willens, "Does the Tribune Decision Endanger Cash-Rich Split-Off?" 109 Tax Notes 547 (Oct. 24, 2005) (no, but pending legislation in the Senate tax bill, S.2020 does, though not fatally so); Rizzi, "Tribune Company Case and the Deconstruction of the Reorganization Rules," 33 Corp. Tax'n 23 (Mar. 2006).

payer's stock holdings, the court instead held that these rights had a separate (and substantial) value, one that far surpassed the stock portion of the consideration.[163.4] In effect the *Tribune Company* opinion bifurcated the acquisition consideration into two components: stock of the acquiring parent (which the opinion found to be negligible); and management control over the cash deposited in the LLC. While maintaining that it was not disregarding the transactional form adopted by the parties, it seems quite evident that it did just that.[163.5]

Among the many troublesome issues raised by the *Tribune* opinion, the following came to mind:

1. The consideration received by Times Mirror for its Bender stock did not differ materially from a receipt of preferred stock that is redeemable for cash after a period of time, which the Supreme Court sanctioned in its *Nelson* decision;

2. The undue weight given by the court to statements made by the taxpayer to its shareholders, regulators and the public are weak reeds upon which to base a decision;[163.6]

3. Likewise the accounting treatment for book purposes, also was given significant weight by the court in its decision, a highly questionable position as well (tax and book treatment frequently differ, as the Supreme Court noted in its *Cottage Savings* decision—that's the reason for Schedule M-3, which requires companies to reconcile such differences);

4. At bottom, the court seemed to be bothered by the high degree of tax planning evidence in the transaction; while not quite labeling it as a "tax shelter," one gets the feeling that the court wanted to treat it as such and thus prevent its effectuation;[163.7]

5. Finally, while the tax bill for the taxpayer in the Tribune case is potentially a large one (nearly one billion dollars), future revenues may suffer when acquirers start claiming a basis step-up (or estate planners begin claiming even greater discounts based on the *Tribune* case analysis).

[163.4] Though not cited in the opinion, the court's bifurcation views are reminiscent of the Supreme Court's; decision in Paulsen v. CIR, supra   4.03[2][j].

[163.5] Words like "economic substance," "constructive receipt," "in substance a sale," "objective economic realities," and "true economic effect" are frequently sprinkled throughout the opinion.

[163.6] The term "sale" is frequently used in the financial press to mean disposition (either taxable or tax-free as the case may be).

[163.7] Heavy tax planning tends to charge the atmosphere with ominous forebodings at best. Yet more often than not in many transactions under subchapter C (and elsewhere for that matter), the form is the substance; infra   12.61[1] and 12.61[3]. For an excellent articulation of this point, see Steinberg, "Form, Substance and Directionality in Subchapter C," 52 Tax Law. 457 (1999).

Add to note 166.

Thus, until such regulations are issued, the tainted stock is merely equity boot at the shareholder level (not "definitional" boot for § 368 reorganization status); see infra ¶ 12.41[5], note 652.

[3] Consideration Paid for Nonstock Interests in Target

Page 12-67:

Add to note 172.

See also TD 8898 issuing Regs. §§ 1.368-1(e)(1)(ii) and 1.368-1(e)(6), Ex. 9, on August 30, 2000, which echo this view. See Couch & Bennett, "The Effect of Target Redemptions and Distributions on Continuity of Interest," 89 Tax Notes 1301 (Dec. 4, 2000).

[5] Minority or Dissenting Shares

Page 12-69:

Change last sentence in ¶ 12.23[5] to read as follows.

Because dissenters rights arise in the reorganization, the Service will not permit the acquiror to supply the funds; only the target funds should be used here.

Add to note 184.

See also Rev. Rul. 73-54, infra note 196.

¶ 12.24 ACQUISITIONS OF PROPERTY FOR VOTING STOCK (TYPE C REORGANIZATION)

[1] In General

Page 12-76:

Add to note 212.

See also Willens, "Viewpoint: Efforts to Avoid Acquisition of Target's Liabilities Could Signal Renaissance for 'C' Reorganizations," Daily Tax Rep. (BNA) No. 155, at J-1 (Aug. 12, 2002).

[2] Acquisition of Substantially All of the Properties of Another Corporation

[c] When "Substantially All" Is Determined: Effect of Preliminary Distributions

Page 12-80:

Add to text at end of ¶ 12.24[2][c].

But in a surprising recent ruling,[225.1] IRS allowed a preliminary spin-off of a *wanted* division into a new subsidiary followed by the acquisition of its assets in a valid Type C reorganization (the *Elkhorn* limitation was not applied to this format).[225.2]

[225.1] Rev. Rul. 2003-79, 2003-29 IRB 80.

[225.2] But the Ruling would apply *Elkhorn* principles if parent had been the target company. Lack of any concern with the subsidiary's transitory existence is also surprising in light of the *Gregory* case. In any event, this Ruling goes a long way towards emasculating the substantially all requirement. See Willens, "'Reverse' *Morris Trust* Transactions Have Their Day in the Sun, Daily Tax Rep. (BNA) No. 169, at J-1 (Sept. 2, 2003); Shoji, "Revenue Ruling 2003-79, The Return of Lop-Sided Spin-Off Treatment," 31 Corp. Tax'n 10 (Mar. 2004).

[3] Consideration Paid by Acquiring Corporation

[b] Triangular Type C Reorganization

Page 12-84:

Add to end of note 236.

But when must the parent be in control of the acquiring sub (before or after the transaction)? IRS has ruled that after is allowed as well; see Baline, Section 368(c) Control: When Is It Needed? 32 Corp. Tax'n 28 (Jan. 2005), discussing a letter ruling that allowed obtaining control in the acquisition.

[c] Liabilities Assumed and Taken Subject To

Page 12-85:

Add to note 243.

But regulations proposed on March 10, 2005, drop this caveat language since these proposals will replace it by a "net value exchange" requirement in proposed § 1.368-1(f); supra   12.21[2][d], and infra   12.65[5].

[e] Other Aspects of "Solely" Limitation

Page 12-89:

Add to note 253.

These proposals were adopted without change (except for an earlier effective date) by TD 8885 on May 5, 2000, effective January 1, 2000.

[4] Requirement That Transferor Liquidate

Page 12-90:

Add to text at end of ¶ 12.24[4].

For problems where the target corporation in a C reorganization (T) receives stock of its acquiring corporation P's subsidiary (S) in an unrelated spin-off before T is able to liquidate, see the article by Robert Willens noted below.[257.1]

[257.1] Willens, "Is Price Communications (T) Affected by Verizon's (P) Proposed Spin-Off?" 113 Tax Notes 909 (Dec. 4, 2006) (yes; the subsidiary's (S) stock is not "qualified property," and thus will constitute boot to T and its shareholders when distributed in T's required liquidation). See infra ¶ 12.42[2][b].

¶ 12.25 MERGER INTO OR WITH CONTROLLED SUBSIDIARY (HYBRID TYPE A REORGANIZATION)

[1] In General

Page 12-93:

Add to note 266.

IRS has ruled that parent can acquire the necessary control of acquiror sub in the forward merger acquisition; Baline, "Section 368(c) Control: When Is It Needed, 32 Corp. Tax'n," 28 (Jan. 2005).

Add to note 269.

See also Rev. Rul. 2001-46, 2001-42 IRB 321 (failed § 368(a)(2)(E) reverse merger—30 percent of consideration paid in cash—followed by linked upstream merger of target into parent held a direct § 368(a)(1)(A) merger under Rev. Rul. 67-274, *King Enterprises* and *Seagram*). Ruling also held that first-step stock acquisition in a good § 368(a)(2)(E) reverse merger also qualified as a direct § 368(a) merger if second step upstream merger integrated with first step.Regs. § 1.338(h)(10)-1(c)(2) (2006), infra note 302.1.

See generally Willens, "Considerations in 'Electing' Reorganization Status for Mergers," Daily Tax Rep. (BNA) No. 108, at J-1 (June 6, 2006).

[2] Forward Subsidiary Mergers: § 368(a)(2)(D)

[a] In General: Relationship Between §§ 368(a)(2)(D) and 368(a)(2)(E)

Page 12-94:

Add to note 270.

Rev. Rul. 2001-24, 2001-22 IRB 1290 (forward merger not spoiled by drop-down of subsidiary's stock to another subsidiary); see Rothman, "Recent Revenue Rulings Suggest Liberal Approach to Reorganizations," 91 Tax Notes 1923 (June 11, 2001); Willens, "The Section 368 Revenue Ruling Trilogy—Below the Surface, Seismic Shifts in IRS Policy," 95 J. Tax'n 5 (July 2001).

[g] Parent As Party

Page 12-99:

Add new note 283.1 to end of second sentence in ¶ 12.25[2][g].

[283.1] But see Rev. Rul. 2001-24, 2001-1 CB 1290 (parent stock still party to forward merger even when drop-down subsidiary stock to another subsidiary); Rothman, "Recent Revenue Rulings Suggest Liberal Approach to Reorganizations," 91 Tax Notes 1923 (June 11, 2001); Willens, "The Section 368 Revenue Ruling Trilogy—Below the Surface, Seismic Shifts in IRS Policy," 95 J. Tax'n 5 (July 2001).

[3] Reverse Subsidiary Mergers: § 368(a)(2)(E)

[a] In General

Page 12-100:

Add to note 289.

See also the helpful Rev. Rul. 2001-25, 2001-22 IRB 1291 (the sale of half the target assets to unrelated buyer immediately after reverse merger did not violate substantially all limit of § 368(a)(2)(E), citing *Rev. Rul. 88-48*; thus asset replacements were not fatal as long as business continuity was satisfied and it was here); Rothman, "Recent Revenue Rulings Suggest Liberal Approach to Reorganizations," 91 Tax Notes 1923 (June 11, 2001). See also Rev. Rul. 2001-26, 2001-23 IRB 1297 (two-step acquisition of 80 percent control in single integrated transaction qualified as a good § 368(a)(2)(E) reverse merger (citing *King Enterprises* and *Seagram*); see Ginsburg & Levin, "Integrated Acquisition Reorganizations," 91 Tax Notes 1959 (June 11, 2001); Pari & Lorndale, "Two-Step Stock Acquisitions and Reverse Subsidiary Mergers," 28 J. Corp. Tax'n 3 (July 2001); Willens, "The Section 368 Revenue Ruling Trilogy," 95 J. Tax'n 5 (July 2001).

See also Rev. Rul. 2001-46, 2001-42 IRB 321 (two-step "double mergers" held to qualify as direct § 368(a)(1)(A) merger; first case involved failed § 368(a)(2)(E) reverse merger—too much cash, but not enough to kill continuity—followed by an integrated upstream merger; second case involved good § 368(a)(2)(E) followed by linked upstream A; both cases qualified as § 368(a)(1)(A) direct mergers). Regs. § 1.338(h)(10)-1T (July 9, 2003). See Swartz, Multiple - Step Acquisitions, 107 Tax Notes 609 (May 2, 2005); adopted without change by TD 9271, July 5, 2006, Regs. § 1.338(h)(10)-1(c)(2).

[b] Regulations and Comments Under § 368(a)(2)(E)

Page 12-101:

Add to note 290 after first sentence.

See also Rev. Rul. 2001-26, 2001-23 IRB 1297 (integrated two-step acquisition of 83 per-cent of *T* stock for *P* voting stock held good § 368(a)(2)(E) reverse merger); articles supra note 289; and Rev. Rul. 2001-46, 2001-42 IRB 321 (two-step "double merger" stock and asset acquisition treated as direct § 368(a)(1)(A) merger if steps integrated and continuity satisfied, and they were and it was).

Add to note 292.

Rev. Rul. 2001-25, 2001-22 IRB 1291 (but sale of half of target assets to unrelated buyer and retention of proceeds did not spoil reverse merger, citing *Rev. Rul. 88-48*; thus, asset replacements were allowed so long as business continuity was met and it was here); arti-cles supra note 289.

Page 12-104:

Add text to end of ¶ 12.25[3][b].

> 7. The scope and utility of § 368(a)(2)(E) has recently been expanded and made more user friendly by two important published rulings.[302.1]

[302.1] Rev. Rul. 2001-26, 2001-23 IRB 1297, and Rev. Rul. 2001-46, 2001-42 IRB 321. See Kohl & Storum, "Attorneys Praise IRS Ruling Collapsing Multi-Step Acquisi-tion," 93 Tax Notes 425 (Oct. 15, 2001); Brady, "Integrated Transactions: Overlap of Re-organizations With Section 338 QSPs," 93 Tax Notes 547 (Oct. 22, 2001); Fowler, "Practical Transactional Aspects of Rev. Rul. 2001-46," 93 Tax Notes 963 (Nov. 12, 2001); Ginsburg & Levin, "Integrated Acquisitions: Comments on Rev. Rul. 2001-46," 93 Tax Notes 553 (Oct. 22, 2001); Blanchard, "Reflections on Rev. Rul. 2001-46 and the Continued Vitality of *Kimball-Diamond*," 93 Tax Notes 1875 (Dec. 31, 2001); infra ¶ 12.63[2][a]; Trelease et al., "Multi-Step Acquisitions: New Solutions to Corporate and Securities Law Problems in Tax-Free Reorganizations," 29 J. Corp. Tax'n 5 (May 2002). Bernstein, "Moore Corporation Ltd.'s Two-Step Cross-Border Acquisition of Wallace Computer Services," Inc., 30 J. Corp. Tax'n 32 (May 2003); Lipeles & Nijhof, "Consoli-dating and Restructuring Global Operations," 99 Tax Notes 713 (May 5, 2003).

But Rev. Rul. 2001-46 modified by Temp. Regs. § 1.338(h)(10)-1T, TD 9071 (July 9, 2003) (a § 338(h)(10) election will be allowed if first step stock acquisition constitutes a stand-alone qualified stock purchase; e.g., case one of the Ruling). See Swartz, "Multi-ple-Step Acquistions," 107 Tax Notes 609 (May 2, 2005); adopted without change by TD 9271, July 5, 2006, Regs. § 1.338(h)(10)-1(c)(2).

[4] Overlaps

Page 12-106:

Add to note 312.

But Prop. Regs. § 1.368-2(b) (May 16, 2000) (no Type A here; only Type C or Type D possible); but the revised November 2001 proposed regulations, however, change this treatment and allow Type A here; adopted as temporary regulations, January 24, 2003; and as final regulations in January 2006 by TD 9271 (effective Jan. 23, 2006).

Add to note 313.

See also Rev. Rul. 2000-5, 2000-5 IRB 496. The November 2001 proposed regulations continue this rule, as do the January 2003 temporary regulations, and the January 2006 final regulations.

[5] Examples

Page 12-108:

Add new Example 7.

> **EXAMPLE 7:** Integrated stock-asset acquisition. IRS has recently ruled that certain integrated two-step acquisitions of stock, or of stock and assets, can qualify as either a good § 368(a)(2)(E) reverse merger,[321.1] or as a direct § 368(a)(1)(A) merger between T and P.[321.2] New regulations, however, allow a § 338(h)(10) election in Rev. Rul. 2001-46 structures if the first step stock acquisition is a stand-alone qualified stock purchase (case one of the Ruling; but not case two).[321.3]

[321.1] Rev. Rul. 2001-26, 2001-23 IRB 1297 (tender offer for part, completed as reverse merger; held, good § 368(a)(2)(E).

[321.2] Rev. Rul. 2001-46, 2001-42 IRB 1297 (failed § 68(a)(2)(E) stock acquisition (30 percent cash), followed by integrated upstream merger held good § 368(a)(1)(A) direct merger; same result even where first step a good reverse merger); see comments supra note 302.1; infra   12.63[2][a].

[321.3] Regs. § 1.338(h)(10)-1T, issued by TD 9071 on July 9, 2003; infra   12.63[2][a]. Adopted without change by TD 9271, July 5, 2006. Regs. § 1.338(h)(10)-1(c)(2) (2006).

¶ 12.26 TRANSFER OF ASSETS TO CONTROLLED CORPORATIONS (TYPE D REORGANIZATION)

[1] In General

Page 12-109:

Add to note 323.

See Schultz, "The Future of Acquisitive D Reorganizations," 84 Taxes 107 (Mar. 2006); and Temp. Regs § 1.368-2T(l) (Dec. 18, 2006), infra   12.26[3] and 12.26[6].

Page 12-110:

Add to note 328.

But the 2004 Jobs Act in § 898(b) limits application of § 357(c)(1)(B) to divisive Type D reorganizations only. The American Jobs Creation Act of 2004, § 898(a), also amends the § 361(b)(3) creditor distribution boot purge rule in divisive Type D's limiting the amount of purgeable boot to the adjusted basis of the transferred assets (creating symmetry with § 357(c)(1); but can asset basis be used twice here?). See Barr, "Uncertainty Regarding the Tax Treatment of Liabilities in Divisive Reorgs Survives the AJCA," 105 Tax Notes 1125 (Nov. 22, 2004). Technical change legislation retroactively says no.

Add to text at end of ¶ 12.26[1].

The Joint Committee Staff's April 2001 simplification report would add § 368(a)(2)(C) drop-down protection to Type D reorganizations.[328.1] But the Service jumped the gun on any legislative fix here and conferred drop-down protection under § 368(a)(2)(C) by a ruling issued in late 2002 and proposed regulations in 2004 go even further.[328.2]

[328.1] Proposal IV. F., at 261.

[328.2] Rev. Rul. 2002-85, 2002-52 IRB 986 (the Service concluded that § 369(a)(2)(C) is permissive but not exclusive or restrictive, citing Rev. Rul. 2001-24, 2001-1 CB 1290), infra ¶ 12.63[6]. Cummings, "Why Didn't Rev. Rul. 2002-85 Mention the Step Transaction Doctrine?" 98 Tax Notes 421 (Jan. 21, 2003). Bennett, "Contributions to Controlled Corporations Following Acquisitive Code Sec. 368(a)(1)(D) Reorganizations," 82 Taxes 9 (June 2004).

Prop. Regs. § 1.368-2(k) (Aug. 2004) extend drop-down protection to *all* § 368 reorganizations; see infra ¶ 12.63[6][a].

[2] Continuity-Of-Interest Aspects

Page 12-112:

Add to note 337.

Proposed Regs. §§ 1.368-1(e)(6) and 1.368-1(e)(7), Ex. 10 (Mar. 10, 2005), codify the principles of *Alabama Asphaltic* and its progeny, confirming that creditors of an insolvent debtor can succeed to the proprietary interest in the debtor in various insolvency proceedings.

Add text to end of ¶ 12.26[2].

Proposed regulations issued in March 2005 now confirm that creditors in various insolvency proceedings can succeed to the proprietary interest in the debtor corporation, adopting the principles of *Alabama Asphaltic* and its progeny.[338.1]

[338.1] Supra note 337. The preamble notes that these regulations are adopting the continuity of interest standards of the Type G reorganization, infra ¶ 12.30[1]; see also infra ¶¶ 12.65[4] and 12.65[5].

[3] Distribution Requirement

Page 12-113:

Add to end of second paragraph in item 1.

But new temporary regulations[341.2] provide that no stock of the acquiring corporation is necessary where both the transferor and transferee corporations have identical stock ownership (or a de minimis outside interest). In effect the all-cash acquisitive Type D organization has been blessed by these regulations based on cases and rulings from the liquidation-reincorporation area (infra   12.64).

[341.2] Temp. Regs. § 1.368-2T(l) (Dec. 18, 2006; effective Mar. 19, 2007), issued by TD 9303. See infra   12.26[6]. See Willens, "IRS Clarifies Contours of D Reorganization," 114 Tax Notes 217 (Jan. 15, 2007).

[5] Overlap Potential

Page 12-116:

Add to text at end of first complete paragraph.

The 2004 Jobs Act removed non-divisive D reorganizations from the application of § 357(c), but has not ended all uncertainty in cases where the transaction also overlaps with § 351.[352.1]

[352.1] See Baline, "The Trap of an Overlap," 32 Corp. Tax'n 45 (May 2005); infra 12.42[3]. But see Rev. Rul. 2007-8, 2007-7 IRB 469 (§ 351 will be trumped by § 368).

[6] Relationship of Nondivisive Type D Reorganizations to § 304: Asset and Stock Acquisition Parity

Page 12-117:

Add to note 354.

See Schultz, "The Future of Acquisitive D Reorganization," 84 Taxes 107 (Mar. 2006).

Add to item 3.

But the Joint Committee Staff's April 2001 simplification report would harmonize the § 356 boot dividend rules with the § 302 stock redemption regime.[357.1]

[357.1] Part IV H, at 267; infra   12.44[2][a] and 12.44[2][b].

Page 12-118:

Add text to end of ¶ 12.26[6].

But IRS has moved to Type D reorganization primacy in a potential conflict with § 304;[358.1] viz., parent sale of stock of Sub-1 to Sub-2 followed by integrated liquidation of Sub-1 into Sub-2 held a Type D, not § 304, under step transaction principles.

Temporary regulations issued in December of 2006[358.2] deal with the "all-cash" acquisitive Type D reorganization where stock in both the transferor and transferee corporations is held by the same shareholders in identical proportions.[358.3] In such a case, the actual issuance of additional transferor will not be required in order to find a D reorganization.[358.4] These regulations are merely interim guidance, however, and are subject to change pending the outcome of IRS's broader study of the scope of the non-divisive Type D reorganization.[358.5]

[358.1] Rev. Rul. 2004-83, 2004-32 IRB 157. See Avent, "Transfer of Asserts to Controlled Corporations: The All Cash D Reorganization," 32 Corp. Tax'n 3 (May, 2005). See also, "Attorneys Question Ruling That Transaction Wasn't a 'D' Reorg," 111 Tax Notes 241 (Apr. 10, 2006); for the numerous responses to the Attorney's letter, see Schler, More on the All-Cash D Reorg, 111 Tax Notes 383 (Apr. 17, 2006) (wasn't); Willens, "Michael Schler is correct – It's Not a D Reorg," 111 Tax Notes 491 (Apr. 24, 2006); the author of this book also agrees with Mike Schler; "Yecies, Pro-D-Reorg Signatory Responds to Schler," 111 Tax Notes 591 (May 1, 2006) (could be); Shea, "D Reorgs and Dr. Frankenstein," 111 Tax Notes 592 (May 1, 2006) (shouldn't be); and Baline, Meaningless Gesture – What Does This Mean? 33 Corp. Tax'n 36 (May 2006) (probably not); Shultz, How the Government Should Address the Acquisitive Reorg Rules, 111 Tax Notes 715 (May 8, 2006); and Feldgarden, LTR 200551018 and D Reorgs: The Debate Drags On, 111 Tax Notes 833 (May 15, 2006). See Temp. Regs. § 1.368-2T(l), infra note 358.2; the transaction is *not* a Type D under those regulations.

[358.2] TD 9303, (Dec. 18, 2006) issuing Regs. § 1.360-2T(l) (effective Mar. 19, 2007).

[358.3] De minimis holdings by outsiders will be ignored, however (Example 4 involves one percent, while Example 6 says 10 percent is too much), Regs. § 1.368-2(T)(l)(3), Exs. 4 and 6. Also disregarded is § 1504(a)(4) "pure preferred" stock (see Example 5).

[358.4] Shareholder identity, however, can be supplied by attribution; e.g., all § 318 family members are aggregated (see Example 2), and entity attribution flows "upstream through chains of subsidiaries" (see Example 3).

[358.5] These regulations do not impact the proposed regulations dealing with insolvency and the net value exchange requirement. For comments, see Willens, supra note 341.1.

[8] Examples

Page 12-120:

Add to note 364.

See Attorneys' Letter and the numerous responses, supra note 358.1.

Page 12-121:

Add to note 369.

Regs. § 1.338-2(c)(3) was moved to § 1.338-3T(c)(3) in January 2000, and was moved again to § 1.338-3(d) in final regulations issued on February 13, 2001 (effective March 16, 2001).

Add text to end of Example 2.

But IRS has ruled that the stock purchase and integrated liquidation was a Type D reorganization and trumped § 304 in such a case of clashing application.[369.1]

[369.1] Rev. Rul. 2004-83, 2004-32 IRB 157; Avent, supra 358.1.

¶ 12.27 RECAPITALIZATIONS (TYPE E REORGANIZATION)

[1] In General

Page 12-122:

Add to note 371.

See also Rev. Ruls. 2003-19, 2003-7 IRB 468, and 2003-48, 2003-19 IRB 863 (conversion of mutual insurance companies and mutual savings banks into stock insurance companies and stock savings banks recapitalization of same corporate entities).

Add to note 372.

See also Rev. Rul. 2003-19, 2003-7 IRB 468 (conversion of mutual insurance companies to stock insurance corporations tax-free § 368 recapitalization); Rev. Rul. 2003-48, 2003-19 IRB 863 (conversions of state mutual savings banks to state stock savings banks-same).

Add to note 374.

See Rev. Rul. 2003-19 and Rev. Rul. 2003-48, supra note 372.

Page 12-123:

Add to note 375.

Generally, see Willens, "The Contours of a Recapitalization," 112 Tax Notes 1079 (Sept. 18, 2006).

[2] Equity Swaps: Exchanges of Stock for Stock

[d] "Debt-Like" Preferred Stock

Page 12-127:

In note 398, change "354(a)(3)(C)(ii)" to "354(a)(2)(C)(ii)".

[3] Equity-For-Debt Swaps: Exchanges of Old Bonds for New Stock

[b] Debtor Corporation Issues (Cancellation of Debt, Original Issue Discount, and Related Problems)

Page 12-133:

Add to note 425.

Willens, "Determining Deductibility of a 'Premium' in Equity-for-Debt Exchanges," Daily Tax Rep. (BNA) No. 216, at J-1 (Nov. 18, 2006).

[4] Debt Swaps: Exchanges of Bonds for Bonds

[a] Debt Modification As "Deemed" Exchange

Page 12-136:

Add to note 436.

Peaslee, "Modifications of Nondebt Financial Instruments as Deemed Exchanges," 95 Tax Notes 737 (Apr. 29, 2002); Friedman, "Debt Exchanges After Rev. Rul. 2004-78," 105 Tax Notes 979 (Nov. 15, 2004).

Add to note 437.

The sunset date of June 30, 2000, was dropped by Rev. Proc. 2000-29, 2000-28 IRB 113.

Add to text at end of paragraph.

This procedure was modified in 2001 (and extended to electing debt holders as well).[437.1]

[437.1] Rev. Proc. 2001-21, 2001-9 IRB 742.

[6] Continuity of Interest in Recapitalizations

Page 12-150:

Add to note 494.

Regs. § 1.368-1(b), added by TD 9182 (Feb. 25, 2005), so state.

¶ 12.28 CHANGES IN IDENTITY, FORM, OR PLACE OF ORGANIZATION (TYPE F REORGANIZATION)

[1] In General

Page 12-151:

Add to note 500.

Currently, Rev. Proc. 2005-3, § 3.01(30), 2005-1 1 IRB 118.

Add to note 501.

See also Rev. Rul. 2003-19, 2003-7 IRB 468 (conversions of mutual insurance companies into stock insurance corporations; held Type E and Type F); Rev. Rul. 2003-48, 2003-19 IRB 863 (conversion of state mutual savings banks into state stock savings banks, held Type F (also Type E, Type B and global § 351).

Page 12-152:

Add to text after runover paragraph.

After remaining silent for decades, IRS has finally proposed regulations[506.1] spelling out in considerable detail the conditions for qualification as a Type F.[506.2] These same proposals also provide that continuity of interest and continuity of business enterprise do not apply to Type F reorganizations.[506.3]

[506.1] Prop. Regs. § 1.368-2(m) (Aug. 12, 2004) (effective when made final).

[506.2] See §§ 1.368-2(m)(1) (defining "mere change"), and 1.368-2(m)(5) (8 examples that are quite liberal).

[506.3] Regs. §§ 1.368-1(b) and 1.368-2(m)(2). Adopted as final regulations by TD 9182 (Feb. 25, 2005). Regs. § 1.368-2(m)(4) also states that distributions related to a Type F are not subject to the § 356 boot rules; instead they are taxed under § 301 and § 302.

See Rizzi, "Mere Transactions: Are 'F' Reorganizations Really Reorganizations?" 31 Corp. Tax'n 18 (Nov. 2004); Cummings, "Three New Sets of Prop. Regs. Make Planning For Reorgs. Much Easier," 101 J. Tax'n 271, at 283 (Nov. 2004); see Swartz, "Multiple-Step Acquistions," 107 Tax Notes 609 (May 2, 2005). Willens, "Can Post-Squeeze Out Merger Net Operating Losses Be Carried Back to Pre-Merger Years?" 103 J. Tax'n 231 (Nov. 2005) (yes, under the proposed regulations; maybe also under *Casco*, supra note 503.

Page 12-153:

Add to text at end of ¶ 12.28[1].

The Joint Committee Staff's April 2001 simplification report proposes to expand § 368(a)(2)(C) drop-down protection to Type F reorganizations as well.[508.1]

_____

[508.1] Proposal IV. F., at 261 (to eliminate the uncertainty of current law); but see Rev. Rul. 2002-85, 2002-52 IRB 986) (should cover Type F as well).Prop. Regs. § 1.368-2(k) (Mar. 2, 2004) (extends to *all* § 368 reorganizations). The March proposals were withdrawn on Aug. 17, 2004, and reissued in revised and broadened form (effective when final). The August proposals continue to allow drop-downs to controlled subsidiaries (and add partnerships that qualify under COBE Regs. § 1.368-1(d)). Moreover, the revised proposals allow push-ups of less than substantially all the target's assets or stock; § 1.368-2(k)(3), Exs. (2) and (6).

[2] Overlap Aspects

Add to note 510.

Currently Rev. Proc. 2001-3, § 3.01(29), 2001-1 IRB 111, modified by Ann. 2001-25, 2001-25 IRB 896; Rev. Proc. 2002-3, § 3.01(29), 2002-1 IRB 117 (same); Rev. Proc. 2003-3, § 3.01(29), 2003-1 IRB 113 (same); Rev. Proc. 2004-3, § 3.01(30), 2004-1 IRB 114 (same); Rev. Proc. 2005-3, § 3.01(31), 2005-1 IRB 118

Page 12-154:

Add to end of first paragraph of note 512.

See Willens, supra note 506.3

Add to note 515.

Bailine, "Section 368(a)(1)(F): The Eye of the Hurricane," 28 J. Corp. Tax'n 31 (Nov. 2001).

See also Rev. Rul. 2003-19, 1003-7 IRB 468, and Rev. Rul. 2003-48, 2003-19 IRB 863 (conversions of mutual insurance companies and mutual savings banks into stock companies held Type F).

[3] Other Special Aspects

Page 12-157:

Add to note 520.

See Willens, supra note 506.3.

¶ 12.29 TRANSACTIONS INVOLVING INVESTMENT COMPANIES

Page 12-159:

Add to end of first paragraph of note 531.

Jakel & Sowell, "Transfers to Investment Companies: Complexities in a Conundrum," 94 Tax Notes 1659 (Mar. 25, 2002); Sheppard, "Rationalizing the Treatment of Exchange Funds," 95 Tax Notes 152 (Apr. 8, 2002).

Add to note 532.

For mergers into pass-through entities (RICs and REITs), see new Temp. Regs. §§ 1.337(d)-6T and 1.337(d)-7T, issued January 2, 2002 (reversing the default rule of Regs. § 1.337(d)-5T (2000), namely, § 1374 regime applies unless taxpayer affirmatively elects deemed sale treatment). For conversion of C corporation to tax-exempt status, see Regs. § 1.337(d)-4 (Dec. 29, 1998), effective January 29, 1999. Temporary regulations were adopted as final regulations by TD 9047 (Mar. 18, 2003).

¶ 12.30 INSOLVENCY REORGANIZATIONS (TYPE G REORGANIZATION)

[1] In General

Page 12-160:

Add to note 534.

Lashnits, "Basic Tax Issues in Insolvency and Bankruptcy," 30 J. Corp. Tax'n 26 (Jan. 2003); Rizzi, "Bankruptcy Reorganizations: A Primer for the Former Bubble Economy," 24 J. Corp. Tax'n 26 (July 2003).

Page 12-161:

Add to note 535.

NYSBA Tax Section Report, "Reorganizations Involving Insolvent Subsidiaries," 101 Tax Notes 761 (Nov. 10, 2003); Rev. Rul. 2003-125, 2003-52 IRB 1243.

Add to text at end of ¶ 12.30[1].

Proposed regulations issued in March of 2005[535.1] codify the principles of *Alabama Asphaltic* (and its progeny) in applying the continuity of interest requirements of Regs. § 1.368-1(e).[535.2]

[535.1] Prop. Regs. § 1.368-1(e)(6) and § 1.368-1(e)(7), Ex. 10.

[535.2] The Preamble also states that these regulations intend to adopt the continuity of interest standards applicable to Type G reorganizations, supra note 535, and the Senate Finance Committee report on the 1980 legislation. See infra note 537.1.

[2] Type G Reorganizations Generally: Qualification and Effects

[a] Definitions

Add to note 536.

See NYSBA Tax Section Report; Rev. Rul. 2003-125, , supra note 535.

Page 12-162:

Add to text of ¶12.30[2][a].

Proposed regulations issued in March of 2005[537.1] subject various transactions involving insolvent corporations to a new limitation, viz., there must be "exchange of net value" in order for the transaction to qualify as a §368 reorganization.[537.2] This limitation is informed by continuity of interest principles and is to be applied in conjunction with those principles[537.3] Failure to surrender net value or receive net value in the transaction, in other words, will prevent qualification as a tax-free reorganization.[537.4]

[537.1] Prop. Regs. §1.368-1(b)(1) and §1.368-1(f) (Mar. 10, 2005). These same principles apply to purported §332 liquidations (see   10.21[2]) and purported §351 exchanges (see   3.06[2]).

[537.2] Excluded from this requirement are Type E and Type F reorganizations and certain nondivisive Type D reorganizations subject to the liquidation – reincorporation doctrine (see   12.64). See Cummings, No-Net Value and Type D Reorganizations, 107 Tax Notes 249 (Apr. 11, 2005). Type G reorganizations, however, are *not* excluded from these rules.

[537.3] Thus the purpose of this proposal is to prevent transactions that are economically equivalent to "sales" from obtaining tax-free treatment under §368.

[537.4] For more on these proposals, see infra   12.65[5].

[b] Results of Type G Qualification to Parties

Page 12-162:

Add to note 539.

But Regs. §§ 1.108-7T and 1.1017-1T(b)(4), added by TD 9080 on July 18, 2003, require reduction of target's tax attributes (and asset basis) *before* application of §§ 362 and 381 carryovers. Partially adopted by TD 9127 on May 11, 2004; Regs. §§ 1.108-7(c) and 1.1017(b)(4). Jones & D'Angelo, "Sections 108 and 1017 Regulations: Was It Too Much Candy for the Nickel," 31 Corp. Tax'n 3 (July 2004).

[3] Cancellation of Indebtedness

Page 12-166:

Add to note 551.

See Cecil, "Reinvigorating Chapter 11: The Case for Reinstating the Stock-For-Debt Exception in Bankruptcy," 2000 Wisc. L. Rev. 1001 (2000).

Add to note 552.

The Supreme Court held for the taxpayer in Gitlitz (8 to 1), 531 US 206, 121 S. Ct. 701 (2001) but Congress overturned *Gitlitz* in 2002 legislation.

Add to end of ¶ 12.30[3].

But temporary regulations issued on July 18, 2003, provide that § 108(b) attribute reductions (and asset basis reductions) for exempt COD gain occur *before* application of §§ 381 and 362 carryovers.[552.1]

[552.1] TD 9080, Regs. §§ 1.108-7T and 1.1017-1T(b)(4). No mention was made in the preamble to the contrary implications of *Gitlitz*, supra note 552. Part of the temporary regulations was adopted by TD 9127, May 11, 2004; Regs. §§ 1.108-7(c) and 1.1017(b)(4). Jones & D'Angelo, "Sections 108 and 1017 Regulations: Was It Really Too Much Candy for the Nickel?" 31 Corp. Tax'n 3 (July 2004).

[4] Insolvency Reorganizations of S Corporations Under § 368(a)(1)(G)

[a] Acquisitive Type G Reorganizations

Page 12-167:

Add to note 558, first paragraph.

But see Regs. § 1.108-7T (July 18, 2003) (reduce tax attributes after tax computation for year of discharge but *before* application of §§ 381 and 362 carryovers). Temp. Regs. 1.1017-1T(4)(b) applies the same ordering regime for asset basis reductions. Both of these approaches seem contrary to the *Gitlitz* decision. Partially adopted in final form by TD 9127 on May 11, 2004; Regs. §§ 1.108-7(c) and 1.1017(b)(4).

Add to note 558, second paragraph.

The Eleventh Circuit followed *Farley* in Pugh v. CIR, 213 F3d 1324, 2000-1 USTC ¶ 50,514 (11th Cir. 2000); but the Sixth Circuit followed *Gitlitz* in Guadiano v. CIR, 216 F3d 524, 2000-2 USTC ¶ 50,559 (6th Cir. 2000). *Gitlitz* was reversed, however, and the taxpayers prevailed before the Supreme Court on January 9, 2000, 531 US 206, 121 S. Ct. 701, 2001-1 USTC ¶ 50,147; but *Gitlitz* overturned by legislation on March 9, 2002, the Economic Stimulus Act.

[c] Examples

Page 12-172:

Add to note 574, second paragraph.

Certiorari was granted in *Gitlitz* on May 1, 2000; see supra note 558. The Supreme Court held for the taxpayers (8 to 1) on January 9, 2001, 531 US 206, 121 S. Ct. 701 (but reversed by legislation on Mar. 9, 2002).

Add to note 575.

See supra note 558.

Page 12-173:

Add to note 576.

Certiorari was granted in *Gitlitz* on May 1, 2000 (and the taxpayers won); see supra note 558, but overturned by legislation on March 9, 2002.

Add to note 578, second paragraph.

Certiorari was granted in *Gitlitz* on May 1, 2000 (and the taxpayers prevailed); see supra note 558, though reversed by legislation on March 9, 2002.

Page 12-174:

Add to note 581, third paragraph.

Certiorari was granted in *Gitlitz* on May 1, 2000 (and the taxpayers won, but only temporarily); see supra note 558.

[5] Collateral Aspects of Bankruptcy Tax Rules

[c] Mechanics and Operation of § 108

Page 12-176:

Add new note 586.1 to end of first paragraph.

[586.1] But temporary regulations issued by TD 9080 on July 18, 2003, Regs. §§ 1.108-7T and 1.1017-1T(b)(4), provide that attributes (and basis) are reduced after tax computation for year of discharge but *before* application of §§ 381 and 362 carryovers. See Regs. § 1.108-7T(d), Exs. 3 and 4. Partially adopted in final form by TD 9127 on May 11, 2004; Regs. §§ 1.108-7(c) and 1.1017(b)(4). See Jones & D'Angelo, "Sections 108 and 1017 Regulations: Was It Really Too Much Candy for the Nickel?," 31 Corp. Tax'n 3 (July 2004).

Page 12-177:

Add to note 587.

Rev. Rul. 2004-79, 2004-31 IRB 106 (sub purchase of parent debt and distribution of that debt up to parent as a dividend; OID, COD, dividend consequences).

Add to note 588.

For applications, see Rev. Rul. 2004-79, supra note 587.

[e] Section 1017 Basis Reduction

Page 12-179:

Add to note 595.

But see Regs. § 1.1017-1T(b)(4) (July 18, 2003) (any § 1017 basis reduction occurs after tax computation for year of discharge but *before* application of any § 362 carryover. Jones & D'Angelo, "Sections 108 and 1017 Regulations: Was It Really Too Much Candy for the Nickel?" 31 Corp. Tax'n 3 (July 2004); adopted without change by TD 9127, May 11, 2004.

C   TREATMENT OF PARTIES TO A REORGANIZATION

¶ 12.41 STOCK OR SECURITIES VERSUS BOOT: DEFINITIONS

[2] Definition of "Stock"

Page 12-188:

Add text to end of ¶ 12.41[2].

The treatment of the issuance and exchange of stock that is subject to restrictions under § 83 in corporate reorganization exchanges is unclear. Namely, is that stock issued and outstanding for purposes of § 368 qualification, or is it ignored as stock until the restrictions lapse? The NYSBA Tax Section has proposed[625.1] that the stock should be treated as issued and outstanding for purposes of determining whether the transaction qualifies as a reorganization.[625.2]

[625.1] See Daily Tax Rep. (BNA) No. 217, at G-7 (Nov. 11, 2003), reprinted in 101 Tax Notes 1031 (Nov. 24, 2003).

[625.2] Same, for purposes of continuity of interest, § 368(c) control, solely for voting stock, and non-boot status issues.

[3] Definition of "Securities"

Page 12-189:

Add to note 630, second paragraph.

Rev. Rul. 2004-78, 2004-31 IRB 108 (short-term debt issued in an acquisitive reorganization to replace target debt securities, held securities on the facts; same terms except for change in interest rates – mere substitute for target's debt so not boot); Friedman, "Debt Exchanges After Rev. Rul. 2004-78," 105 Tax Notes 979 (Nov. 15, 2004).

[4] Equity-Flavored Securities (Rights, Warrants, and Convertible Securities)

Page 12-191:

Add to note 640, first paragraph.

But modified by Rev. Rul. 98-10, 1998-1 CB 643, to reflect 1998 regulation change, supra note 638.

Add to note 640, third paragraph.

Rizzi, "Limited Options Issued in a Reorganization," 28 J. Corp. Tax'n 26 (Jan. 2001).

In note 641, replace next to last sentence with the following.

See also Ltr. Rul. 9539020 (option-for-option exchange in acquisitive reorganization held tax-free), supra note 640.

Add to note 641.

See also Levin, Rocap & Ginsburg, "Surprising Issues for Shareholder Execs Receiving Unvested Stock for Vested Stock in Reorg," 89 Tax Notes 1289 (Dec. 4, 2000); Sheppard, "The Tax Treatment of Dot-Com Brats," 89 Tax Notes 988 (Nov. 20, 2000); Starkey, "Tax Treatment of Employee Stock Options in Mergers and Acquistions," 90 Tax Notes 1231 (Feb. 26, 2001); Rizzi, "Equity and Quasi-Equity: Impact of Section 83 on Reorganizations in the Technology Sector," 29 J. Corp. Tax'n 5 (Sept. 2002).

Page 12-193:

Add to note 645.

Cummings, "Exchange Rights in Reorganizations and Section 351 Transactions," 97 Tax Notes 287 (Oct. 14, 2002).

Add to note 646 after second sentence.

Rev. Rul. 98-10, 1998-1 CB 643, modified Rev. Rul. 70-108 to reflect this change.

[5] Debt-Like Preferred Stock As Boot

Page 12-194:

Add after second sentence of note 652.

These regulations were adopted without change by TD 8882 on May 16, 2000.

Add to note 653, second paragraph.

These regulations are "taxpayer-friendly," which is encouraging. They were adopted without change by TD 8904 on October 2, 2000.

[6] "Tracking Stock": Proposed Taxability

Page 12-195:

Add to note 657, third paragraph.

Rizzi, "Tracking Stock As Synthetic Spin-Offs and Contingent Consideration," 27 J. Corp. Tax'n 255 (2000).

Add to text at end of last paragraph.

But nothing seems to have come from this proposal and the current Treasury people seem far less hostile to tracking stock (though IRS continues to list it as a no ruling item).[657.1]

[657.1] Rev. Proc. 2006-3, § 3.01(62), 2006-1 IRB 122.

¶ 12.42 TREATMENT OF CORPORATE TRANSFERORS: §§ 357, 358, AND 361

[1] Nonrecognition: § 361; General Background

[b] Receipt of Boot

Page 12-197:

Add text to end of first full paragraph.

But the 2004 Jobs Act[664.1] limits the amount of purgeable boot that can be distributed to creditors in a divisive Type D reorganization to the adjusted basis of the transferred assets, a provision seemingly intended to create symmetry with § 357(c) (which the 2004 Jobs Act also limited in § 357(c)(1)(B) to divisive D reorganizations only).[664.2]

[664.1] American Jobs Creation Act of 2004, § 898(a), amending § 361(b)(3) (effective Oct. 22, 2004). Technical corrections legislation prohibits double counting of basis, that is, basis reduced first for § 357 assumed liabilities.

[664.2] American Jobs Creation Act of 2004, § 898(b), amending § 357(c)(1)(B). See Barr, "Uncertainty Regarding the Tax Treatment of Liabilities in Divisive Reorgs Survives the AJCA," 105 Tax Notes 1125 (Nov. 22, 2004). But see Rev. Rul. 2007-8, 2007-7 IRB 469 (§ 351 will be trumped by § 368 if there is an overlap).

Page 12-198:

Add text to end of runover paragraph.

But the 2004 Jobs Act[669.1] removed non-divisive D reorganizations from the application of § 357(c) and also amended § 361(b)(3) to limit the amount of purgeable boot received by the transferor in a divisive D reorganization to the adjusted basis of the transferred assets.[669.2]

[669.1] American Jobs Creation Act of 2004, § 898(b), amending § 357(c)(1)(B).

[669.2] American Jobs Creation Act of 2004, § 898(a), amending § 361(b)(3) (the creditor distribution boot purge rule). See Barr, supra note 664.2.

[2] Nonrecognition: 1986 Revision of § 361

[b] Section 361 Redux: Current Law

Add to note 677.

Also, this rule could apply if stock of a subsidiary is received in an unrelated tax-free spin-off from the acquiring corporation after a Type C acquisition but before the target has effected its mandated liquidation; for such a case, see Willens, "Is Price Communications Affected by Verizon's Proposed Spin-Off?" 113 Tax Notes 909 (Dec. 4. 2006) (yes; price has a real problem with that stock since it's not "qualified property").

[3] Assumption of Liabilities: § 357

Page 12-202:

Add text to end of first paragraph.

But the 2004 Jobs Act[683.1] amended § 357(c)(1)(B) and § 361(b)(3) and limited § 357(c) to divisive Type D reorganizations only, but also limited the amount of purgeable boot received in a divisive D reorganization and distributed to creditors to the adjusted basis of the transferred assets (but no double counting of basis for this purpose either, that is, basis reduced first for assumed liabilities).

[683.1] American Jobs Creation Act of 2004, § 898. See Barr, supra note 664.2. But See Baline, "The Trap of an Overlap," 32 Corp. Tax'n 45 (May 2005) (continued confusion on removal of nondivisive Type D's from §357(c) where transaction also overlaps with §351). But see Rev. Rul. 2007-8, 2007-7 IRB 469 (§ 351 will be trumped by § 368 if there is an overlap).

Page 12-203:

Add to note 685, second paragraph.

But the 2004 Jobs Act, in § 898(b), amends § 357(c)(1)(B) to remove non-divisive Type D reorganizations from § 357(c) and limiting its application solely to divisive Type D reorganizations.

[5] Examples

Page 12-209:

Add new Example 12 after Example 11.

> **EXAMPLE 12:** Corporate-level boot in divisive Type D reorganization. *T* drops the *X* business assets into newly created *S* in preparation for a § 355 spin-off of *S* to *A*:
>
> a. *"Leveraged distribution"* – *S* pays $30 of borrowed cash to *T*, that *T* uses to pay off creditor *C*; under the 2004 Jobs Act, *T* is taxable on $10 of gain.[699.1]
> b. *"Excess liability assumption"* – instead, *S* assumes *T*'s debt to *C*; under § 357(c)(1)(B), *T* is also taxed on $10 of gain here.[699.2]
> c. *"Securities exchange"* – instead, *S* issues $30 of its "securities" to *T* which *T* then exchanges with *C* for the *T* debt securities; no gain or loss results to *T* in this scenario since *T* is protected by § 361(c)(3).[699.3]

All three transactions are economically the same, that is, *T*'s $30 liability is shifted to *S*; prior to the 2004 Jobs Act amendment only alternative "b" created taxable gain to *T*; now however, alternative "a" creates taxable gain to *T* as well.[699.4]

[699.1] American Jobs Creation Act of 2004, § 898(a) amending § 361(b)(3) (creditor distribution boot purge). But basis reduced first for assumed liabilities.

[699.2] No change to § 357(c)(1)(B) for divisive Type D; if the transaction instead was a non-divisive Type D, § 357(c)(1)(B) no longer would apply.

[699.3] The 2004 Jobs Act made no changes to § 361(c)(3); if the *T* debt was also a security, *C* would have § 354(a)(1) nonrecognition as well.

[699.4] See Barr, "Uncertainty Regarding Tax Treatment of Liabilities in Divisive Reorgs. Survives AJCA," 105 Tax Notes 1125 (Nov. 22, 2004); see Baline, "The Trap of an Overlap," 32 Corp. Tax'n 45 (May 2005). But see Rev. Rul. 2007-8, 2007-7 IRB 469 (§ 351 will be trumped by § 368 if there is an overlap).

¶ 12.43 TREATMENT OF CORPORATE TRANSFEREE: §§ 362 AND 1032

[1] Nonrecognition: § 1032

[c] Triangular Acquisitions

Page 12-213:

Add to note 713 at the end of the second paragraph.

But these regulations were supplanted by Regs. § 1.1032-3, infra next paragraph.

Add to note 713 at the end of the third paragraph.

Banoff, "Partnership Use of Corporate Partner Stock As Compensation Easier Under 1032 Regs," 93 J. Tax'n (Aug. 2000).

Add note to 713.

But Rev. Rul. 74-503 was revoked by Rev. Rul. 2006-2, 2006-2 IRB 261 (Jan. 9, 2006); comment by Willens, Viewpoint, Daily Tax Rep. No. 246, (BNA) at J-1 (Dec. 27, 2005); and Cummings, Viewpoint, Daily Tax Rep. No. 4, (BNA) at J-1 (Jan. 6, 2006).

Page 12-214:

Add to note 717.

These regulations were adopted by TD 8883 on May 16, 2000.

[d] Issuance of Tracking Stock: Proposed Taxation of Corporate Issuers

Page 12-214:

Add to note 721.

Rizzi, "Tracking Stock As Synthetic Spin-Offs and Contingent Consideration," 27 J. Corp. Tax'n 255 (2000).

[3] Basis of Acquired Stock: §§ 362(b) and 358(e)

Page 12-217:

Add to the first paragraph of note 732.

But Rev. Rul. 74-503 was revoked by Rev. Rul. 2006-2, 2006-2 IRB 261 (Jan. 9, 2006); comment by Willens, Viewpoint, Daily Tax Rep. No. 246, (BNA) at J-1 (Dec. 27, 2005); and Cummings, Viewpoint, Daily Tax Rep. No. 4, (BNA) at J-1 (Jan. 6, 2006); see also NYSBA, Tax Section, "The Application of 'Zero Basis' in Tax-Free Reorganizations," 113 Tax Notes 761 (Nov. 11, 2006).

Page 12-218:

Add to note 733.

See Hamilton & Webster, "Tax Basis in Stock-For-Stock Acquisitions: Billions at Stake," 87 Tax Notes 1127 (May 22, 2000). But basis sampling dropped from 2004-3 no-ruling list; Notice 2004-44, 2004-28 IRB 32 (request for comments on possible revision and relaxation of Rev. Proc. 81-17).

¶ 12.44 TREATMENT OF STOCKHOLDERS AND SECURITY HOLDERS: §§ 354, 356, AND 358

[1] Nonrecognition and Boot

[a] In General: § 354(a)

Page 12-222:

Add to note 745.

For possible application of § 83 to trump § 354, see Levin, Rocap & Ginsburg, "Surprising Issues for Shareholder Execs Receiving Unvested Stock for Vested Stock in Reorg," 89 Tax Notes 1289 (Dec. 4, 2000); Sheppard, "The Tax Treatment of Dot-Com Brats," 89 Tax Notes 988 (Nov. 20, 2000); Starkey, "Tax Treatment of Employee Stock Options in Mergers and Acquistions," 90 Tax Notes 1231 (Feb. 26, 2001). See also Rev. Rul. 2002-1, 2002-1 IRB 268 (§ 83 context of § 355 spin-off); Cummings, "Using NQ-SOs and Restricted Stock With Section 355: New Clear Guidance From IRS," 96 J. Tax'n 71 (Feb. 2002); Rizzi, "Restricted Stock, Stock Options and Spin-Offs," 30 J. Corp. Tax'n 45 (Jan. 2003); Bennett, "Rev. Rul. 2002-1: Constructing a Bridge to Span Time," 80 Taxes 11 (Oct. 2002). See also   12.41[2], notes 625.1 and 625.2.

Page 12-223:

Add to note 747.

For possible application of § 83 to exchange under § 354, see articles by Levin et al., Sheppard and Starkey, supra note 745. But see Rev. Rul. 2002-1, 2002-2 IRB 268 (Jan. 14, 2002) (application of § 83 in § 355 spin-off scenerio); Cummings, supra note 745; Rizzi, supra note 745; Bennett, supra note 745. See also   12.41[2], note 625.1.

Add to end of ¶ 12.44[1][a].

Distributions of contingent litigation claims by a target in order to facilitate a pending acquisitive reorganization raise interesting boot characterization issues, which as yet are far from clear.[750.1]

[750.1] See Bernstein, "Distribution of Contingent Litigation Claims to Facilitate Mergers and Acquisitions," 30 J. Corp. Tax'n 37 (July 2003).

[b] Boot Taxation Rules Generally: § 356

Page 12-225:

Add to note 754.

See Bernstein, supra note 750.1 (treatment of distribution of contingent value rights (CVRs), in connection with a reorganization; no § 453 if traded).

[e] "Debt-Like" Preferred Stock As Boot

Page 12-228:

Add to note 760.

It is reassuring to note that IRS is moving gingerly to exercise its regulation authority under § 351(g)(4), and even more heartening in this case where it has exercised it in a taxpayer-friendly way. Final Regs. § 1.356-7 were adopted by TD 8904 on October 2, 2000 (effective on that date).

[2] Character of Recognized Gain

[a] In General: § 356(a)(2)

Page 12-229:

Add to note 764, second paragraph.

Bernstein, supra note 750.1 (treatment of distribution of contingent value rights in connection with a reorganization).

Page 12-230:

Add to text at end of ¶ 12.44[2][a].

The Joint Committee Staff's April 2001 simplification proposal would conform the boot rules of § 356 to the redemption rules of § 302.[765.1]

But Treasury's dividend exclusion proposal of February 2003 (if applicable to § 356(a)(2) dividends[765.2]) would reverse the tax stakes here since a 100-percent exclusion (the proposed amount) would always be better than the current capital gain rate.[765.3] The final legislation (reducing the top rate on dividends to 15 percent) grants regulatory authority to include boot dividends here as well.[765.4]

[765.1] See infra ¶ 12.44[2][b].

[765.2] See ¶¶ 1.08[4], 8.06[1]. As presently drafted it was not clear whether § 356(a)(2) dividends would qualify for exclusion benefits. The final 2003 tax legislation instead reduces the top rate on dividends and capital gains, but it too is unclear as to whether it would apply to § 356(a)(2) dividends. But the final legislation gives regulatory authority to include boot dividends (as well as other similar dividend-like amounts) which authority should be forthcoming; IRC §§ 1(h)(11) and 306(a)(1)(D).

[765.3] Even if the ultimate exclusion is less than total, the effective tax rate on such dividends may still be less than that for capital gain. Also, Ways and Means Chair Thomas's alternative proposal to tax dividends at capital gain rates (which was adopted in the final tax bill) would largely eliminate the significance of the § 356(a)(2) boot dividend rules (at least with respect to tax rates); infra ¶ 12.44[2][d].

[765.4] Supra notes 765.2, 765.3.

[b] Special Features of Boot Dividend

Add new item 5 to list.

  5. Query: Will Treasury's dividend exclusion proposal apply to § 356(a)(2) boot dividends (the present draft was not at all clear that it would)? The same issue is present for the final 2003 tax Act's rate reduction benefit, but new § 306(a)(1)(D) grants regulatory authority to include boot dividends (and other similar amounts).

Add to text at end of ¶ 12.44[2][b].

  The Joint Committee Staff April 2001 simplification report[768.1] proposed to conform the boot rules of § 356 to the redemption rules of § 302 where the reorganization involves corporations under common control (that is, the Type D and F) or a single corporation (that is, a Type E).[768.2]

 [768.1] Part IV H. at 267.

 [768.2] The report also suggested that this conformity could be extended to acquisitive reorganizations (Types A and C) as well.

[c] Testing for Dividend Effect

Page 12-232:

Add to note 773, first paragraph.

The Joint Committee Staff's April 2001 simplification report proposes to conform § 356 to § 302 where the reorganization involves corporations under common control or a single corporation (or a § 355 transaction); proposal IV. H., at 267.

Page 12-233:

Add text after reference to footnote 781.

But *Clark* will turn into bad news for individual shareholders as well if Treasury's proposed 100 percent exclusion for dividends is enacted (and if that proposal applies to all such dividends).[781.1]

 [781.1] See infra 12.44[2][d]. But application of the proposal to § 356(a)(2) dividends was not at all clear under the proposal as drafted, which seemed to be limited to dividends subject to §§ 301 and 316. But if the Joint Committee Staff's boot dividend conformity proposal is adopted, supra note 768.1, such dividends clearly would qualify for exclusion benefit under the proposal. The final legislation, however, adopted a rate reduction for individual shareholders (to 15 percent), infra 12.44[2][d].

Add text to end of ¶ 12.44[2][c].

[d] Impact of Treasury's Dividend Exclusion Proposal [New]

Assuming that Treasury's February 2003 proposal to allow up to a 100 percent exclusion for qualified dividends[782.1] passes (and that it applies to § 365(a)(2) boot dividends),[782.2] boot dividend treatment under § 356(a)(2) will become the preferred tax treatment in most, if not all, cases.[782.3] While passage in its initial form (or at all, for that matter) was far from a sure thing, enactment of significant tax exemption for § 356(a)(2) dividends could spark a role reversal by taxpayers and the IRS on this issue, with taxpayers arguing for § 356(a)(2) dividend treatment and the IRS asseting capital gain status instead.[782.4] But even if Ways and Means Chair Thomas's alternative dividend relief proposal is adopted instead (and it was in the final 2003 tax Act) the tax significance of boot dividend treatment for noncorporate shareholders would be largely eliminated.[782.5]

[782.1] But this proposal failed to pass. See ¶ 8.06[2]. The final 2003 tax legislation instead adopted the House bill's rate reduction for dividends and capital gains, infra note 782.5 (though only on a temporary basis for six years).

[782.2] As presently drafted, the proposal seemed to be limited to § 301/§ 316 dividends (or their equivalent, which § 356(a)(2) dividend may not be). This same uncertainty applied to the ultimately adopted rate reduction provision. But if the Joint Committee Staff's boot dividend conformity simplification proposal, supra note 768.1, is adopted, such dividends clearly would qualify.

[782.3] Even a partial dividend exclusion could result in a lower effective tax rate than that applicable to capital gain. The final 2003 tax bill rate reduction for dividends and capital gains largely neutralizes the significance of this issue.

[782.4] This role reversal may not apply to all shareholders, however, if, for example, they want to offset capital gain with existing capital losses. See Willens, Viewpoint-Structuring Transactions to Convert 'Boot Gain' Into Dividend Income, Daily Tax Rep. (BNA) No. 15, at J-1 (Jan. 26, 2004).

[782.5] Released on May, 2003. This proposal would tax dividends at the same rate as capital gain (and also lower that rate to 15 percent). This proposal passed the House on May 9, 2003, and was adopted in the final 2003 tax bill. IRC § 1(h)(11) (effective for 2003, but sunsets in 2009). Also, § 306(a)(1)(D) extends the new low dividend rate to § 306 stock sale gain and grants regulatory authority to expand this treatment to similar amounts, e.g., § 356(a)(2) boot dividends. Moreover, shareholders should be able to satisfy the 61-day holding period limit of § 1(h)(11)(B)(iii) by way of the tacking rules of § 1223(1). But see § 246(c)(3)(B) (no tacking for this purpose). But technical corrections, retroactively fix this problem by adding one day to the 120 day test zone (viz. it is now 121 days). This provision was extended for two more years by 2006 legislation.

[3] Basis: § 358 (Outside Investment Basis)

[b] Multiple Classes of Stock or Securities Exchanged

Page 12-235:

Add to note 786.

See Kahn & Lehman, "Exchanges of Multiple Stocks and Securities in Corporate Divisions or Acquisitive Reorganizations," 104 Tax Notes 1417 (Sept. 27, 2004) (extensive analysis of various combinations of boot allocation, basis, and gain recognition).

[c] Identification: Tracing, First-In, First-Out, or Average Basis?

Page 12-236:

Add to note 788, first paragraph.

But Proposed Regs. §§ 1.358-2(a)(2) and 1.358-2(c) (May 3, 2004) reject the average basis method (and obsolete Rev. Rul. 55-355); instead, taxpayers must trace basis from the old shares if possible or, if not, designate where the basis of such shares is to be allocated among the new stock or securities. Failure to designate in such a case will preclude use of Regs. §1.1012-1(c) specific identification on later dispositions of acquiror shares; instead, FIFO rule only will apply here. These proposals were adopted as final regulations by TD 9244 on Jan. 23, 2006.

Page 12-237:

Add text to the end of runover paragraph.

But regulations proposed on May 3, 2004, and adopted on January 23, 2006,[790.1] reject the average basis method as inappropriate and instead require basis tracing if possible; if tracing is not possible, then taxpayer is allowed to designate where the § 358 basis is to be allocated among the new shares;[790.2] failure to designate the basis allocation of such a case precludes the use of specific identification on later dispositions of acquiror stock, however.[790.3] These proposals were adopted as final regulations on January 23, 2006.[790.4]

[790.1] Removing current Regs. §§ 1.358-2(a)(2)-(5) and 1.358-2(c), and proposing new §§ 1.358-2(a)(2) and 1.358-2(c) (seven examples). The proposed are effective when finalized. See NYSBA Tax Section Report, Allocation of Basis in Reorganizations and Certain Distributions of Stock on Securities, 108 Tax Notes 119 (July 4, 2005).

[790.2] Prop. Regs. §§ 1.358-2(a)(2)(i), 1.358-2(a)(2)(ii), and 1.358-2(a)(2)(iii). The new rules do not apply if the transaction overlaps with § 351; Regs. §§ 1.358-2(a)(2)(iv), and 1.358-2(c), Exs. 5 and 6.

[790.3] Instead FIFO identification is the only method allowed here under Regs. § 1.1012-1(c); Prop. Regs. § 1.358-2(a)(iii).

[790.4] TD 9244 (effective Jan. 23, 2006).

¶ 12.45 SECTION 306 STOCK RECEIVED IN CORPORATE REORGANIZATIONS

[1] In General

Page 12-239:

Add to text at end of ¶ 12.45[1].

The issuance of § 306 stock as a prelude to a later tax-exempt *dividend* bailout would be stimulated if Treasury's February 2003 proposal to allow up to a 100 percent exclusion for qualified dividends is enacted in its proposed form (it wasn't).[798.1] Only a redemption of such stock by the issuing corporation would qualify for dividend treatment, however;[798.2] resales of § 306 merely result in ordinary gain fully taxable at regular rates.

If the alternative proposal by Ways and Means Chair Thomas[798.3] is adopted instead (and it was in the final 2003 Tax Act), § 306 stock bailouts would no longer be necessary since regular dividends (including any § 306 stock redemption dividends) would be taxed at the same rates as capital gains under this proposal (which was adopted in the final legislation).[798.4]

[798.1] See supra ¶¶ 12.44[2][d], 8.06[1]. It was not adopted in the final 2003 Act.

[798.2] The proposal clearly would apply to this type of dividend, since it is taxable under §§ 301 and 316.

[798.3] Released on May 1, 2003; passed the House on May 9, 2003, and was adopted by the final legislation. See ¶ 8.06[2]. It was extended for two years by 2006 legislation (TIPRA).

[798.4] This proposal (subsequently adopted in the final Act) also lowers the top capital gains rate to 15 percent. It also covers "sale" ordinary income, § 306(a)(1)(D), and any other amounts provided by regulations, e.g., § 356(a)(2) dividends. But the holding period limit of § 1(h)(11)(B)(iii) (61-days during a 120 day period straddling the dividend date) could have denied low rate treatment for sales and redemptions of § 306 stock; since § 1(h)(11) does not allow holding period lacking for this purpose; § 246(c)(3)(B). But technical corrections retroactively fix this problem by increasing the test zone from 120 days to 121 days (and IRS agreed to apply fix to 2003 year).

D SPECIAL PROBLEMS IN REORGANIZATIONS

¶ 12.61 JUDICIAL DOCTRINES AND LIMITATIONS: BUSINESS PURPOSE, CONTINUITY OF BUSINESS ENTERPRISE, AND STEP TRANSACTIONS

[1] Business Purpose in General

Page 12-244:

Add to note 810.

See Hanna, "From Gregory to Enron: The Too Perfect Theory and Tax Law," 24 Vir. Tax Rev. 737 (2005).

Page 12-245:

Add to note 812 at the end of the first paragraph.

Hariton, "Tax Benefits, Tax Administration, and Legislative Intent," 53 Tax Law. 579 (2000).

Add to note 812 at the end of the second paragraph.

For regulations requiring registration and return disclosure for corporate tax shelter transactions, see   5.10[7][b]. For legislation proposed by the Senate Finance Committee dealing with corporate tax shelters, see   5.10[8][a]. For the final 2004 anti-tax shelter legislation, see   5.10[8][d].

Add to note 812, third paragraph.

For a considerably more relaxed view of the business purpose requirement, see UPS, Inc. v CIR, 254 F3d 1014, 2001-2 USTC   50,475 (11th Cir. 2001) (transactions had economic substance and adequate business purpose despite dominant tax planning motives); IES Indus., Inc. v. US, 253 F3d 350 (8th Cir. 2001) (same). Both decisions reversed holding of lower courts that transactions were economic shams. See also Boca Investerings Partnership, 167 F. Supp. 2d 298, 2001-2 USTC   50,690 (DDC 2001) (clone of *ACM* transaction but taxpayers prevailed on all counts; not a sham; transactions had economic substance an adequate business purpose; valid partnership existed and taxpayers were partners; but rev'd 314 F3d 625 (DC Cir. 2003) (partnership a sham); Compaq Computer Corp. v. CIR, 277 F3d 778, 2002-1 USTC   50,144 (5th Cir. 2000) (found adequate business purpose and economic substance). Klieforth & Goldman, "A Contingent Payment Installment Sale Upheld—Why Did This Transaction Pass Muster?" 96 J. Tax'n 114 (Feb. 2002) (authors attorneys in *Boca* case) (but it ultimately didn't; *Boca* was reversed by the D.C. Cir., supra, January 10, 2003); 314 F3d 625; cert denied, (Oct. 6, 2003); McMahon, "Economic Substance, Purposive Activity, and Corporate Tax Shelters," 94 Tax Notes 1017 (Feb. 25, 2002). But IRS won a major victory in Long-Term Capital Holdings v. US, 330 F. Supp 2d 122, 2004-2 USTC   50,351 (D. Conn. 2004) (lease stripping deal a sham and major penalties imposed). See   5.10[6][e].

Add to note 814, second paragraph.

Sheppard, "Borrowing Economic Substance," 91 Tax Notes 1831 (June 11, 2001); Bowen, "Whither Business Purpose?" 80 Taxes 275 (Mar. 2002). Willens, "Transactions Motivated By Tax Avoidances Can Be Respected," 109 Tax Notes 1341 (Dec. 5, 2005); Cohen, "Too Good to Be True and Too Bad to Be True," 109 Tax Notes 1437 (Dec. 12, 2005) (letter of statute vs. spirit, who should fix, Congress or the courts?); Frazer, "Absurdist Humor and the Form vs. Substance Dialectic in Tax Law," 112 Tax Notes 677 (Aug. 21, 2006).

[2] Continuity of Business Enterprise

[a] In General

Page 12-247:

Add to note 823.

But see Archie L. Honbarrier, 115 TC 300 (2000) (merger failed because no business continuity per Regs. §§ 1.368-1(b) and 1.368-1(d)); adopted as final regulations by TD 9182 (Feb. 25, 2005)

Page 12-248:

Add to note 825.

But see Archie L. Honbarrier, 115 TC 300 (2000) (merger failed because it lacked continuity of business).

[b] Continuity-Of-Business-Enterprise ("COBE") Regulations

Page 12-249:

In note 829, change see infra note 818 *to* see infra note 835.

Add to note 829.

Note that Rev. Rul. 82-34 (though unrevoked) may be of doubtful validity in view of revised COBE regulations statement in § 1.368-1(b) that COBE applies to all reorganizations (preamble makes the same statement). But Prop. Regs. § 1.368-1(b) (Aug. 12, 2004) states that COBE is not applicable to Type E and Type F reorganizations; adopted as final regulations by TD9182 (Feb. 25, 2005).

Page 12-250:

Add to note 832.

    See Archie L. Honbarrier, 115 TC 300 (2000) (failed COBE here; no continuity of historic business assets or activities; similar to Exs. 3, 4, and 5 of regulations).

[3] Step Transactions

Page 12-253:

Add to note 844, first paragraph.

But *Trinova* was reversed sub nom Aeroquip-Vickers, Inc. v. CIR, 347 F3d 173 (6th Cir. 2003) (one dissent, which had the more persuasive view here).

Page 12-254:

Add to note 845.

Bailine, "The Step Transaction Doctrine: Not Just a Matter of Time," 30 J. Corp. Tax'n 50 (Jan. 2003). Willens, "Step Transaction Doctrine Will Not Prevent Step-Up," 112 Tax Notes 371 (July 24, 2006).

Add to note 846, second paragraph.

But *Trinova* was reversed sub nom Aeroquip-Vickers, Inc. v. CIR 347 F3d 173 (6th Cir. 2003) (one dissent, which had the better view here; extensive discussion of weight to be given to a regulation versus a ruling). Willens, "The Step Transaction Doctrine Can Apply Capriciously," 111 Tax Notes 709 (July 24, 2006).

Page 12-255:

Add to note 851, first paragraph.

But *Trinova* was reversed sub nom Aeroquip-Vickers, Inc. v. CIR 347 F3d 173 (6th Cir. 2003) (one dissent, which had the more persuasive view here; extensive analysis of the weight to be given to a regulation versus a ruling).

Add to end of second paragraph of note 851.

See also NovaCare, Inc. v. US, 2002-1 USTC   50,389 (Fed. Cl. 2002); Rizzi, "*NovaCare* Makes Practitioners Nervous, 26 J. Corp. Tax 29 (July 2002).

Add to end of note 852.

Cummings, "Rev. Rul. 2003-51: A New Gloss on the Step Transaction Doctrine," 101 Tax Notes 1473 (Dec. 22, 2003). See also Kwall & Maynard, "Dethroning King Enterprises," 58 Tax Law. 1 (Fall 2004); compare Cummings, "Something Old, Something New, and Something Fairly New," 106 Tax Notes 1093, at 1095 (Feb. 28, 2005); Kwall & Maynard, "We Still Don't Like King Enterprises," 106 Tax Notes 1329 (Mar. 14, 2005).

¶ 12.62 DISPOSITION OF UNWANTED ASSETS IN CONNECTION WITH A REORGANIZATION: PRE-TAILORING TRANSACTIONS

[3] Tax-Free Spin-Off Followed by Reorganization

[a] In General

Page 12-259:

Add text to end of ¶ 12.62[3][a].

But a recent IRS ruling surprisingly refused to apply *Elkhorn* principles to a second-step Type C reorganization of a newly created spun-off subsidiary,[865.1] a result that will seriously undermine the "substantially all" limitation (if not effectively repeal it).[865.2]

[865.1] Rev. Rul. 2003-79, 2003-29 IRB 80.

[865.2] The Ruling also stated, however, that *Elkhorn* would be applied if the parent had instead been the forget, thus proving once again that form rules the roost in Subchapter C.

Also surprising is the Ruling's apparent indifference to the fact that the spun-off subsidiary was a transitory corporation (being newly created and promptly liquidated as part of a clearly integrated transaction), a formerly risky practice in light *Gregory v. Helvering*. Apparently § 355(e) was not implicated here (though it could be if there was a sufficient control shift). See Willens, "'Reverse' *Morris Trust* Transactions Have Their Day in the Sun," Daily Tax Rep. (BNA) No. 169, at J-1 (Sept. 2, 2003); Shoji, "Revenue Ruling, The Return of Lop-Sided Spin-Off Treatment," 31 Corp. Tax 'n (Mar. 2004); Baline, A Partial Epitaph for Born-to-Die Spin-offs," 32 Corp. Tax'n 25 (Mar. 2005).

[b] Section 355 Aspects

Page 12-261:

Add to text at end of full paragraph.

A surprising recent ruling allowed the acquisition of a newly created spun-off subsidiary in a valid Type C reorganization without being subjected to *Elkhorn Coal* analysis or to *Gregory* transitory existence concerns either.[872.1]

[872.1] Rev. Rul. 2003-79, 2003-29 IRB 80. Apparently § 355(e) was not implicated here (though it could be). See Willens, supra note 865.2.

[c] Transaction Structure Formats (Right Way and Wrong Way)

Page 12-263:

Add to note 874, first paragraph.

Rev. Rul. 2003-79, 2003-29 IRB 80, specifically approved this format, however, as a Type C (without *Elkhorn* exposure and also without concern about the transitory existence of the spun-off subsidiary). The Ruling also should bless forward and reverse mergers of the spun-off subsidiary as well. (i.e., no substantially all problems should arise there either). See Willens, supra note 865.2.

Add to note 875.

See also Rev. Rul. 2003-79, supra note 874, which allowed integrated acquisition of new spun-off subsidiary in a Type C (and also likely in a forward subsidiary merger) reorganization without *Elkhorn Coal* concerns and also without *Gregory* transitory existence problems. But the *Ruling* will apply *Elkhorn* if the parent is the target.

Page 12-264:

Add text to end of runover paragraph.

But a new "right way" path was blessed by a recent IRS ruling,[880.1] where a newly created subsidiary target was spun-off and then acquired in a valid Type C reorganization (despite its transitory existence and without being subjected to *Elkhorn* analysis).[880.2]

[880.1] Rev. Rul. 2003-79, 2003-29, IRB 80.

[880.2] The Ruling should also apply to forward or reverse merger acquisitions of the spun-off subsidiary as well. But *Elkhorn* will be applied if the parent is the intended target. Apparently § 355(e) was not implicated in this ruling (though it could be). See Willens, supra note 865.2.

[d] Post–April 16, 1997 *Morris Trust*–Type Transactions Under § 355(e)

Page 12-266:

Add to note 888, first paragraph.

But, the 1999 proposals were withdrawn and reproposed in far more liberal form on January 2, 2001. These proposals were adopted as temporary regulations by TD 8960 on August 3, 2001. These regulations in turn were replaced with even more liberal temporary regulations on April 26, 2002; see ¶ 11.11[3][d]; Final Regs. § 1.355-7 were adopted by TD 9198 on April 19, 2005 (and were liberalized yet again).

Add to note 888, second paragraph.

The reproposed § 355(e) regulations focus heavily on the "discussions" factor (or the lack thereof) in Prop. Regs. §§ 1.355-7(d)(2) and 1.355-7(d)(3); adopted as temporary regulations (without significant change) on August 3, 2001. These regulations, however, were replaced with an even more liberal set of temporary regulations on April 26, 2002; see

11.11[3][d]. Final Regs. § 1.355-7 were adopted by TD 9198 on April 19, 2005 (and were liberalized yet again).

Page 12-267:

Add to note 895.

But, the 1999 proposals were withdrawn and reproposed in far more liberal form on January 2, 2001. IRS has had a major change of heart here. These proposals were adopted virtually intact as temporary regulations by TD 8960 on August 3, 2001. These regulations, in turn, were replaced with even friendlier temporary regulations in TD 8988 April 26, 2002. Final Regs. § 1.355-7 were adopted by TD 9198 on April 19, 2005.

Add text at end of ¶ 12.62[3][d].

But, the 1999 proposals were withdrawn and reproposed in far more liberal form on January 2, 2001,[895.1] and they were adopted as temporary regulations on August 3, 2001. They in turn were replaced by even more liberal temporary regulations on April 26, 2002.[895.2] These regulations were adopted on April 19, 2005, and were liberalized once again.[895.3]

[895.1] Prop. Regs. § 1.355-7; TD 8960, adopting Regs. § 1.355-7T. See   11.11[3][d].

[895.2] TD 8988, Regs. § 1-355-7T. See   11.11[3][d].

[895.3] TD 9198, Regs. § 1.355-7.

[4] Examples

Page 12-268:

Add text to end of Example 1.

But IRS specifically blessed this format in a surprising recent ruling where a newly created target subsidiary was spun-off and acquired in a valid Type C reorganization without being subjected to either *Elkhorn* or *Gregory* analysis.[897.1]

[897.1] Rev. Rul. 2003-79, 2003-29 IRB 76 (the ruling will apply *Elkhorn* if the parent is the target, however). Note that *P* gets the *S* business with a clean slate of tax attributes since § 381 does not apply to *T*'s drop-down of the wanted assets to *S*. The acquisition of *S* presumably could also be done as a forward (or reverse) merger. See Willens, supra note 865.2.

Add text to end of Example 2.

Rev. Rul. 2003-79 is of no help here either because failure to liquidate is what invalidates the Type C reorganization.

Page 12-271:

Add to note 905.

Rev. Rul. 2003-79, 2003-29 IRB 80, continues to apply the *Elkhorn* substantially all test here as well where *T*, rather than *S*, is the target.

Add to note 907.

But, newly reproposed regulations on the plan linkage issue are considerably more liberal than the withdrawn 1999 proposals. See Prop. Regs. § 1.355-7 (Jan. 2, 2001), discussed at ¶ 11.11[3][d]. The new proposals even have six safe harbors in § 1.355-7(f) (not quite "harbors," but at least they are "coves"). They were adopted as temporary regulations on August 3, 2001; but replaced by new temporary regulations on April 26, 2002 (which are even more liberal); and these were adopted as final regulations by TD 9198 (Apr. 19, 2005).

¶ 12.63 AFFILIATED CORPORATIONS: SPECIAL ACQUISITION PROBLEMS AND TECHNIQUES

[1] In General

Page 12-273:

Add to note 914.

These regulations became final on May 19, 2000 (effective January 1, 2000).

Add new note 915.1 to end of runover paragraph.

[915.1] See Paul, "Triple Taxation," 56 Tax. Law 571 (2003) (intragroup restructures; up, down, sideways, etc.); see also ¶ 13.48.

Add text to end of ¶ 12.63[1].

Reorganizations involving insolvent subsidiaries continue to cause problems as to the extent to which such transactions can, or will, qualify for § 368 treatment[915.2] (they will not, however, qualify for § 332 liquidation treatment).[915.3] In March of 2005, IRS responded to the insolvent subsidiary problem with proposed regulations reconfirming the non-application of §332, but recognizing the possible application of §368 to the liquidation.[915.4] This same package of

---

[915.2] See NYSBA Tax Section Report, "Reorganizations Involving Insolvent Subsidiaries," 101 Tax Notes 761 (Nov. 10, 2003) (proposing that IRS should permit these transactions to qualify as § 368 reorganizations.) For insolvency reorganizations generally, see supra ¶ 12.30.

[915.3] Rev. Rul. 2003-125, 2003-52 IRB 1243; see ¶ 10.21[2]. See infra note 915.4

[915.4] Prop. Regs. §1.332-2(b) and §1.332-2(e), Ex. 2 (Mar. 10, 2005); see ¶ 10.21[2].

proposals, however, added a new limitation for qualifying under §368; namely, that there must be an "exchange of net value" in the transaction.[915.5]

_____

[915.5] Prop. Regs. §1.368-1(b)(1) and §1.368-1(f); see infra   12.65[5].

[2] Parent-Subsidiary Fusions

[a] Upstream Mergers of Subsidiary Into Parent

Add after end of first line in second paragraph of note 918.

, moved again to § 1.338-3(d) by TD 8940 (Feb. 13, 2001, effective March 16, 2001).

Page 12-274:

Add to end of note 918, second paragraph.

Regs. § 1.338-3(d)(4) (Feb. 13, 2001) also ignore qualified payments in applying solely test (so possible Type C here; but query § 368(a)(2)(A) rule, D trumps C where overlap).

Add to note 921.

But compare Rev. Rul. 2001-46, 2001-42 IRB 321, which distinguished Rev. Rul. 90-95 as a case where the first-step stock purchase failed continuity of interest; where continuity was satisfied, however, an integrated second step upstream merger was converted to a direct merger under § 368(a)(1)(A). But see Regs. § 1.338(h)(10)-1T, added by TD 9071 on July 9, 2003, modifying Rev. Rul. 2001-46 and allowing a § 338(h)(10) election where the first step stock acquisition is a stand-alone qualified stock purchase (case one in the ruling, but not case two); adopted without change by TD 9271, July 5, 2006.

Page 12-275:

Add to note 922.

See also Rev. Rul. 2001-26, 2001-23 IRB 1297 (two-step integrated acquisition of more than 80 percent of target stock for voting stock of acquiror held valid reverse merger under § 368(a)(2)(E), citing *King Enterprises* and *Seagram*); Ginsburg & Levin, "Integrated Acquisitive Reorganizations," 91 Tax Notes 1909 (June 11, 2001); Pari & Lorndale, "Two-Step Stock Acquisitions and Reverse Subsidiary Mergers," 28 J. Corp. Tax'n 3 (July 2001); also "Rothman Recent Revenue Rulings Suggest Liberal Approach to Reorganizations," 91 Tax Notes 1293 (June 11, 2001); Willens, "The Section 368 Revenue Rulings Trilogy—Below the Surface, Seismic Shifts in IRS Policy," 95 J. Tax'n 5 (July 2001).
    Similarly Rev. Rul. 2001-46, 2001-42 IRB 321, found a two-step stock and asset acquisition to be a direct merger under § 3689a)(1)(A); all of *T* stock acquired in a failed § 368(a)(2)(E) reverse merger (too much cash, 30 percent, but not enough to kill continuity); integrated second step upstream merger converted to direct merger between *T* and *P* citing *King Enterprises* and *Seagram*. But see Regs. §§ 1.338(h)(10)-1T(c)(2), 1.338(h)(10)-1T(e), Exs. 11-14 (July 2003) (can make a § 338(h)(10) election where, as here, first step is a stand alone qualified stock purchase), final regs. § 1.338(h)(10)-1(c)(2) (same). Willens, "Step Transaction Doctrine Will Not Prevent Step-Up," 112 Tax Notes 371 (July 24, 2006).

Add to note 923, first paragraph.

The *Bausch & Lomb* regulation became final May 19, 2000.

Page 12-276:

Add to end of note 924.

Final Regs. § 1.338-3(d) (Feb. 13, 2001).

Add to note 925.

See also Rev. Rul. 2001-26, 2001-23 IRB 1297 (two-step stock acquisition—51 percent acquired in tender offer, rest acquired via § 368(a)(2)(E) reverse merger—qualified as valid reverse merger under § 368(a)(2)(E), citing *King Enterprises*); articles supra note 922.

Revenue Ruling 2001-46, 2001-42 IRB 321 (first step failed reverse merger stock acquisition (30 percent cash), followed by integrated upstream merger of *T* into Pconverted to direct merger between *T* and *P*, citing *King Enterprises* and *Seagram*. See Kohl & Storum, "Attorneys Praise IRS Ruling Collapsing Multi-Step Acquisition," 93 Tax Notes 425 (Oct. 15, 2001); Brody, "Integrated Transactions: Overlap of Reorganizations With Section 338 QSPs," 93 Tax Notes 547 (Oct. 22, 2001); Ginsburg & Levin, "Integrated Acquisitions: Comments on Rev. Rul. 2001-46," 93 Tax Notes 553 (Oct. 22, 2001); Fowler, "Practical Transactional Aspects of Rev. Rul. 2001-46," 93 Tax Notes 963 (Nov. 12, 2001); Blanchard, "Reflections on Rev. Rul. 2001-46 and The Continued Vitality of Kimbell-Diamond," 93 Tax Notes 1875 (Dec. 31, 2001); Trelease et al., "Multi-Step Acquisitions: New Solutions to Corporate and Securities Law Problems in Tax-Free Reorganizations," 29 J. Corp. Tax'n 5 (May 2002). For use of Rev. Rul. 2001-46, structures to effect cash-rich 2-step cross-border acquisitions, see Bernstein, "Moore Corporation Ltd's Two-Step Cross Border Acquisition of Wallace Computers Services, Inc.," 30 J. Corp. Tax'n 32 (May 2003); Liples & Nijhof, "Consolidations and Restructuring Global Operations," 99 Tax Notes 703 (May 5, 2003); Swartz, "Multiple-Step Acquistions," 107 Tax Notes 609 (May 2, 2005).

But Rev. Rul. 2001-46 modified by Regs. § 1.338(h)(10)-1T (July 9, 2003) (can make § 378(h)(10) election where, as here, first step stock acquisition is a qualified stock purchase; case one of the ruling, though not case two); adopted without change by TD 9271 July 5, 2006. Willens, "Step Transaction Doctrine Will Not Prevent Step-Up," 112 Tax Notes 371 (July 24, 2006).

Add to note 926.

Rev. Rul. 2001-46, 2001-42 IRB 321, applied to taxable stock acquisition as well as tax-free initial stock acquisition step (first step taxable because too much cash for § 368(a)(2)(E), 30 percent, but not enough to kill continuity; § 338 election not possible here either). But Regs. § 1.338(h)(10)-1T (July 9, 2003) (can make a § 338(h)(10) election, where, as in the first case, initial stock acquisition is a qualified stock purchase; but not in second case where first step was tax-free); adopted without change by TD 9271 July 5, 2006. See Willens, supra note 925.

Add to note 927.

See also Rev. Rul. 2001-26, supra note 925.

Add to end of note 928.

Final Regs. § 1.338-3(d) (Feb. 13, 2001) (same).

Page 12-278:

Add to note 933.

Final Regs. § 1.338-3(d) (Feb. 13, 2001). See also Regs. § 1.338(h)(10)-1T infra note 935.3.

Page 12-279:

Add to note 934.

Accord with these authorities (both taxable *and* tax-free initial stock acquisitions followed by integrated upstream merger) is Rev. Rul. 2001-46, 2001-42 IRB 321 (held a direct merger between *T* and *P* and § 338 not available).

Add new item 6 to text after reference to note 935.

> 6. IRS has ruled that an integrated two-step acquisition of more than 80 percent of target stock for acquiror voting stock (via a first step tender offer for 51 percent followed by a reverse merger for the rest) qualified as a good § 368(a)(2)(E) reverse merger under step transaction principles.[935.1] A later ruling holds that a failed § 368(a)(2)(E) stock acquisition (30 percent cash), followed by an integrated upstream merger should be characterized as a direct § 368(a)(1)(A) merger between *T* and *P*.[935.2]
>
> 7. But new temporary regulations modify *Rev. Rul. 2001-46* where the first step stock acquisition is a stand-alone qualified stock purchase (case one of the ruling, but not case two): can elect § 338(h)(10) here and this will trump § 368 if the election is made.[935.3]

[935.1] Rev. Rul. 2001-26, 2001-23 IRB 1297 (articles supra note 922). But see Bailine, "Continental Breakfast and a History Lesson," 28 J. Corp. Tax'n 32 (Sept. 2001), for potential whipsaw opportunity here. But see Rev. Rul. 2001-46, 2001-42 IRB 321 (even though first-step stock acquisition taxable, overall transaction held to be a tax-free direct merger, so § 338 election not available). See Swartz, "Multiple-Step Acquistions," 107 Tax Notes 609 (May 2, 2005).

[935.2] Rev. Rul. 2001-46, 2001-42 IRB 321, citing *King Enterprises* and *Seagram* and distinguishing Rev. Rul. 90-95 as a case where the first step stock acquisition failed continuity of interest. For comments see articles supra note 925; Swartz, supra note 935.1.

[935.3] Regs. §§ 1.338(h)(10)-1T(c)(2) and 1.338(h)(10)-1T(e), Exs. 11-14 added by TD 9071 on July 9, 2003. In Examples 11, 12, and 13, the first step was a qualified stock purchase, but no election was made in Example 1 (so § 368 applied); the election was made in Examples 12 and 13 so § 338(h)(10) trumped § 368; Example 14 involved case two of the ruling (a tax-free first step), so § 368 applies here as in the ruling. Swartz, supra note 935.1; adopted without change by TD 9271 July 5, 2006. Willens, "Step Transaction Doctrine Will Not Prevent Step-Up," 112 Tax Notes 371 (July 24, 2006).

Add to note 936.

Final Regs. § 1.338-3(d) (Feb. 13, 2001) (same).

Add new note 936.1 to end of Example 3.

[936.1] But Rev. Rul. 2001-46, 2001-42 IRB 321 holds that it can be collapsed into a direct § 368(a)(1)(A) merger if continuity is not broken in the first step stock acquisition, as was the case in the ruling. But Regs. § 1.338(h)(10)-1T allow election of § 338(h)(10) where first step stock acquisition is a stand-alone qualified stock purchase, as here. See comments supra note 925; Final Regs. § 1.338(h)(10)-1(c)(2) (same) (but do not allow § 338(g) election).

Page 12-280:

Add to note 937.

See also Rev. Rul. 2001-26, 2001-23 IRB 1297 (two-step stock acquisition via integrated tender offer and reverse merger qualified under § 368(a)(2)(E)) and Rev. Rul. 2001-46, 2001-42 IRB 321 (two-step stock and asset acquisition characterized as direct merger between *T* and *P* where first step satisfied continuity even though it failed § 368(a)(2)(E) because too much cash was paid for the stock, 30 percent); see comments supra note 925.

Add to note 938.

See also Rev. Rul. 2001-26, 2001-23 IRB 1297 (two-step stock acquisition via integrated tender offer and reverse merger qualified under § 368(a)(2)(E)) and Rev. Rul. 2001-46, 2001-42 IRB 321 (would convert transaction to a direct merger if all steps linked into single transaction and final acquisition an upstream merger); see comments supra note 925.

Page 12-280:

Add to note 939.

Regs. § 1.338-3(d) (Feb. 13, 2001) (same). Rev. Rul. 2001-46, 2001-42 IRB 321, would convert multi-step stock and asset acquisition via upstream merger into a direct merger if all steps in the series are integrated. See comments supra note 925. But no § 338(h)(10) here, infra note 939.1.

Add to text at end of Example 5.

Revenue Ruling 2001-46 also could apply here to convert the entire transaction into a tax-free asset acquisition for everyone if all steps in the series are integrated and the final step is an upstream merger of *T* into *P* (or, in view of the repeal of *Bausch & Lomb*,[939.1] the stock acquisitions were effected solely for *P* voting stock). But § 338(h)(10) could not be elected here because the acquisition took too long (and thus did not constitute a qualified stock purchase).[939.2]

[939.1] See infra ¶ 12.63[5], Regs. § 1.368-2(d)(4).

[939.2] Regs. § 1.338(h)(10)-1T (July 9, 2003); Regs. § 1.338(h)(10)-1(c)(2) (same). But final regulations do not allow § 338(g) unilateral elections here.

[b] Downstream Mergers of Parent Into Subsidiary

Add to note 940.

Paul, "Triple Taxation," 56 Tax Law 571 (2003).

[3] Parent-Subsidiary Fission

[a] Corporate "Mitosis" Generally

Page 12-283:

Add to note 951.

See Paul, "Triple Taxation," 56 Tax Law 571 (2003).

[b] Parent-Subsidiary "Inversions"

Page 12-284:

Add to note 959.

See Sheppard, "Ingersoll Rand's Permanent Tax Holiday," 93 Tax Notes 1528 (Dec. 17, 2001) (expatriating pro rata inversion move to Bermuda); but see § 367(a) consequences for U.S. shareholders here,   15.81[3][c].

Page 12-285:

Add to text at end of ¶ 12.63[3][b].

Nothing has come of these proposals on the domestic front, but Congress and the Treasury's interest has revived in the case of expatriating inversions involving corporate migrations to tax haven jurisdictions.[961.1] But the 2004 Jobs Act[961.2] finally managed to pass legislation restricting expatriating corporate inversions in new § 7874.[961.3]

[961.1] Application of § 367(a) to outbound inversions has done little to stem these transactions due in no small part to the sharply depressed stock market. These issues are considered in Chapter 15 at   15.81[3][c], 15.82[2][c], 15.84[1][b], and 15.84[2][a].

See generally, "Treasury News Release and Preliminary Report on Tax Policy Implications of Corporate Inversion Transactions," Daily Tax Rep. (BNA) No. 97, at L-3 (May 20, 2002); Viewpoint, "NYSBA Tax Section Report Calls for Review of Law Regarding Inversion Transactions, Broader Reform," Daily Tax Rep. (BNA) No. 108, at J-1 (June 5, 2002), reprinted in 96 Tax Notes 127 (July 1, 2002) as Outbound Inversion Transactions.

[961.2] American Jobs Creation Act of 2004, § 801 (effective Mar. 5, 2003); see infra 15.82[2][c].

[961.3] The final legislation is slightly less rigorous than the original Senate Finance Committee's "REPO" proposal; but it is clearly rigorous enough to halt these transactions (which seems to have been the case even before passage of the final version).

[4] Brother-Sister Affiliated Corporation Acquisitions of Stock or Assets

[a] In General

Page 12-285:

Add to note 963.

For horizontal double-dummy acquisitions, see infra ¶ 12.63[4][g].

Page 12-286:

Add to note 964.

Regs. § 1.338-3T(c)(3) became final as § 1.338-3(d) (Feb. 2001). For horizontal double-dummy transactions, see infra ¶ 12.63[4][g].

[b] Asset Acquisitions

Add to note 967.

See Regs. § 1.368-2T(l) (Dec. 18, 2006), so holds where the issuance of additional stock would be a "meaningless gesture"; see also § 12.26[6].

Page 12-287:

Add to text at end of ¶ 12.63[4][b].

Recent temporary regulations issued in December 2006 confirm these results.[972.1]

[972.1] Regs. § 1.368-2T(l) (Dec. 18, 2006); supra ¶ 12.26[6], and infra ¶ 12.64[2][c].

Page 12-289:

Add new ¶ 12.63[4][g] following ¶ 12.63[4][f].

[g] Horizontal Double-Dummy and *National Starch* Acquisitions [New]

The horizontal double-dummy acquisition structure provides a useful acquisition technique that can, on the right facts, qualify as a reverse merger under § 368(a)(2)(E), a Type B reorganization, or a global § 351 exchange (or all three).[981.1] Inspired by the *National Starch* transaction,[981.2] a horizontal double-dummy acquisition can be effected as a wholly tax-free acquisition, as a partially taxable one, or as a fully taxable stock "purchase." In a simple version of this format, a new holding company H creates interim transitory subsidiaries, *S-1* and *S-2*; *S-1* and *S-2* then merge into *T-1* and *T-2* for voting stock of *H* (*T-1* and *T-2* survive in the merger and become subsidiaries of *H*); the shareholders at *T-1* and *T-2* become shareholders of *H*. If cash is used to any extent, however, the transaction cannot qualify as a Type B;[981.3] if more than 20 percent of non-voting stock is used it cannot qualify as a reverse merger either;[981.4] but in both these cases, it can still qualify as a global § 351 exchange (subject only to possible continuity of interest limitations).[981.5] Thus, the double dummy technique offers a highly flexible acquisition format for combining two friendly corporations on either a totally tax-free basis or in a partially (or fully) taxable transaction.[981.6]

[981.1] See Bailine, "Long Live the Horizontal Double Dummy!" 29 J. Corp. Tax'n 30 (Jan. 2002); Ginsburg & Levin, Mergers, Acquisitions and Buyouts (Aspen, Dec. 2002), 905. See also Rev. Rul. 2003-51, 2003-21 IRB 938, discussed at　3.09[5], and Willens, "IRS Alters the Landscape With Respect to the 351 'Control Immediately After' Requirement," 98 J. Tax'n 325 (June 2003).

[981.2] See　3.19 (which can also be structured as a § 338 qualified stock purchase in the *National Starch* pattern, see　10.42[2]).

[981.3] See supra　12.23[1].

[981.4] See supra　12.25[3].

[981.5] See supra　12.21.

[981.6] For more detailed analysis of *National Starch* acquisitions and the double-dummy format, see Ginsburg & Levin,　902, 903, and 904.

[5] Acquisition of Assets of Partially Controlled Subsidiary: *Bausch & Lomb* Case

[a] In General

Page 12-291:

Add to note 985.

See also Prop. Regs. §1.332-2(e), Ex. (2) (Mar. 10, 2005) (possible qualification of failed §332 subsidiary liquidation as a Type C reorganization in view of Bausch & Lomb repeal in 2000).

[b] Transactional Variations

Page 12-294:

Add to note 993.

    See also Prop. Regs. §1.332-2(e), Ex. (2) (Mar. 3, 2005) (failed §332 subsidiary liquidation can possibly qualify as a Type C in view of *Bausch & Lomb* repeal if its conditions are satisfied e.g., solely voting stock used and substantially all assets acquired).

[e] The Demise of *Bausch & Lomb*

Page 12-298:

Add to note 1011, second paragraph.

See Prop. Regs. §1.332-2(e), Ex. (2) (Mar. 10, 2004) (failed §332 subsidiary liquidation may qualify as Type C in view of Bausch & Lomb repeal if conditions of 368(a)(1)C met – i.e., solely voting stock used and substantially all assets are acquired).

[6] *Groman/Bashford* Triangular Acquisitions: Special Problems

[a] In General

Page 12-299:

Add to text at end of full paragraph.

The Joint Committee Staff's April 2001 simplification report proposes to extend § 368(a)(2)(C) drop-down protection to Type D and Type F reorganizations as well.[1017.1] The Service anticipated this legislation, however, and extended drop-down protection under § 368(a)(2)(C) to Type D reorganizations (though the ruling did not mention Type Fs).[1017.2] Proposed regulations issued in early 2004 go even further, extending drop-down protection to all acquisitions that qualify for § 368 reorganization on the first step acquisition

---

    [1017.1] Proposal IV. F., at 261. See also Rev. Rul. 2001-24, 2001-22 IRB 1290 (triangular forward merger followed by drop-down of subsidiary's stock to another subsidiary allowed by principles of § 368(a)(2)(C) rule—a liberal ruling); see Rothman, "Recent Revenue Rulings Suggest Liberal Approach to Reorganizations," 91 Tax Notes 1923 (June 11, 2001); Willens, "The Section 368 Revenue Ruling Trilogy—Below the Surface, Seismic Shifts in IRS Policy," 95 J. Tax'n 5 (July 2001).

    [1017.2] Rev. Rul. 2002-85, 2002-52 IRB 986 (although only dealing with drop-downs in Type D reorganizations, the Service's expansive interpretation of § 368(a)(2)(C) as permissive, rather than exclusive or restrictive, seems equally applicable to Type Fs; the ruling also cited Rev. Rul. 2001-24, supra note 1017.1). Cummings, "Why Didn't Rev. Rul. 2002-85 Mention the Step Transaction Doctrine?" 98 Tax Notes 421 (Jan. 21, 2003). Prop. Regs. § 1.368-2(k) (Mar. 2, 2003) will extend drop-down protection to all § 368 reorganization. Bennett, "Contributions to Controlled Corporations Following Acquisitive Sec. 368(a)(1)(D) Reorganizations," 82 Taxes 9 (June 2004). For withdrawal and reissue of the March proposals on Aug. 17, 2004, in liberal form, see infra notes 1017.3 and 1017.4.

transaction.[1017.3] The March proposals were withdrawn in August 2004 and replaced with new proposed regulations in revised and liberalized form.[1017.4] These new proposals materially facilitate group restructuring following an acquisition.

[1017.3] Prop. Regs. § 1.368-2(k) (Mar. 2, 2004) (thus *Bashford* is gone for good). NYSBA Tax Section Report, "Distributions Following Tax-Free Reorganizations," 103 Tax Notes 1267 (June 7, 2004) (proposed expanding the drop-down proposals to give parallel treatment for push-up transactions as well). Revised proposed § 1.368-2(k) (Aug. 17, 2004), adopted this proposal, infra note 1017.4.

[1017.4] Prop. Regs. § 1.368-2(k) (Aug. 17, 2004, effective when issued as final regulations. Prop. Regs. § 1.368-2(k)(3) contains eight examples; it also drops Example 3 of the current regulations. Drop-down to COBE-qualified partnerships (supra   12.61[2][b] also are allowed in addition to drops to controlled subsidiaries; finally, push-ups of less that substantially all the target's assets or stock were also added to the protected list, adopting the proposal suggested by the NYSBA Tax Section, supra note 1017.3. Cummings, "Three New Sets of Prop. Regs. Should Make Planning For Reorgs Much Easier," 101 J. Tax'n 271, at 273 (Nov. 2004); Swartz, "Multiple-Step Acquistions," 107 Tax Notes 609 (May 2, 2005).

[b] How Many Tiers Are Permitted (Remoteness Limits)?

Page 12-300:

Add to note 1018.

See also Rev. Rul. 2001-24, supra note 1017.1.

[c] Overlaps

Page 12-302:

Add to note 1030.

But the Joint Committee Staff's April 2001 simplification report proposes to add § 368(a)(2)(C) drop-down protection here; Proposal IV. F., at 261. Proposed Regulations, supra notes 1017.3 and 1017.4 go all the way, extending such protection to *all* reorganizations.

[e] Taxable Triangular Acquisitions

Page 12-303:

Add to note 1034, fourth paragraph.

These proposals were adopted by TD 8883 on May 16, 2000 (and also supplant Regs. § 1.1502-13(f)(6) noted previously). For comment, see Banoff, 93 J. Tax'n 81 (Aug. 2000).

Page 12-305:

Add to note 1042, fourth paragraph.

These proposals were adopted by TD 8883 on May 16, 2000 (and also supplant Regs. § 1.1502-13(f)(6) noted previously).

[7] Affiliated Corporations and § 355

[a] In General

Page 12-305:

Add to note 1045.

Paul, "Triple Taxation," 56 Tax L. 571 (2003).

[b] Intra-Group Divisive Type D Reorganization

Page 12-306:

Add to note 1048.

The Joint Committee Staff's April 2001 simplification report proposes to extend § 368(a)(2)(C) drop-down protection to Type D and Type F reorganizations; but see Rev. Rul. 2002-85, 2002-52 IRB 986), supra ¶ 1017.2, and Prop. Regs. § 1.368-2(k) (Aug. 2004).

[d] 1997 Legislation: §§ 355(e) and 355(f)

Page 12-308:

Add to text after last paragraph.

Five versions of regulations under the §355(e) "plan or arrangement" issue were produced during the period 1999 to 2005, all increasingly liberalized, and culminating in final regulations adopted on April 19, 2005.[1037.1]

[1037.1] See ¶ 11.11[4][d]; Regs §1.355-7, adopted by TD 9198 on Apr. 19, 2005 (the most liberal of all versions). See Willens, Viewpoint, Daily Tax Rep. (BNA) No. 83, at J-1 (May 2, 2005).

¶ 12.64 REINCORPORATIONS: LIQUIDATION VERSUS REORGANIZATION

[1] Basic Transactional Patterns and Stakes

[b] Transactional Patterns

Page 12-310:

Add to note 1065, second paragraph.

See also Bailine, "The Elucidation of the Liquidation—Reincorporation Doctrine," 30 J. Corp. Tax'n 34 (Mar. 2003) (application to various corporate restructuring transactions; analysis of two favorable private rulings). For the IRS ruling policy on the liquidation-re-organization issue, see Rev. Proc. 2005-3, § 4.01(23), 2005-1 IRB 118. See Prop. Regs. §1.368-1(f)(4) and 1.368-1(f)(5), Ex. 8 (Mar. 10, 2005) (exception to net value exchange requirement for nondivisive Type Ds); Cummings, No-Net Value and Type D Reorganizations, 107 Tax Notes 249 (Apr. 11, 2005).

[2] Legislative Evolution

[b] 1954 Code Years: 1954 to 1984

Page 12-314:

Add to note 1081.

For controversy over whether a recent private letter ruling qualified as an acquisitive Type D reorganization, see the numerous views reflected at ¶ 12.26[6], note 358.1. See, in that regard, Regs. § 1.368-2T(l) (which rejects reorganization treatment on the facts of that ruling).

Page 12-315:

Add to note 1086.

For the current IRS position on liquidation-reincorporation, see Prop. Regs. §1.368-1(f)(4) and §1.368-1(f)(5), Ex. 8 (Mar. 10, 2005) (reincorporations as an exception to net value exchange requirement); Cummings, supra note 1065.

But see Regs. § 1.368-2T(l) (Dec. 18, 2006) (the all-cash D reorganization where there is identity of shareholder ownership).

[c] Reform Proposals: 1958 Through 1986

Page 12-318:

Add to text at end of ¶ 12.64[2][c].

Recent regulations confirm that an all-cash sale of assets between related corporations will constitute a Type D reorganization (nondivisive) if the corporations are owned by the same shareholders in identical proportions (with attribution), but excluding de minimis owners and also § 1504(a)(4) pure preferred stock (this transaction is known as the all-cash Type D).[1097.1]

[1097.1] Regs. § 1.368-2T(l), issued by TD 9303 on Dec. 19, 2006, effective Mar. 19, 2006 (and expiring Dec. 18, 2009). See supra ¶ 12.26[c].

¶ 12.65 ASSUMPTION OF LIABILITIES: EFFECT ON REORGANIZATION STATUS

[2] Definition of "Liability"

[a] In General

Page 12-323:

Add to note 1111, first paragraph, after next to last sentence.

See Salina Partnership LP, RIA TC Memo   2000-352 (short sale "obligation" held to be a liability for partnership § 752 rule purposes). Sheppard, "What Is a Liability?" 89 Tax Notes 1513 (Dec. 18, 2000).

[3] Definition of "Assumption"

[a] In General

Page 12-327:

In the second paragraph of note 1125 change "Regs. § 1.368-2(j)(5)" to "Regs. § 1.368-2(j)(4)".

Add to note 1126.

But see also Regs. § 1.1001-3(e)(4)(i)(B) (not material modification if change of debtor in § 381 transaction).

[4] Continuity-of-Interest Problems

Page 12-329:

Add to note 1132.

But Prop. Regs issued on Mar. 10, 2005 would drop the liability assumption caveat on §1.368-2(d)(1), since it would be subsumed in the Prop. Regs. §1.368-1(f) "net value exchange" requirement, infra   12.65[5], supra   12.21[2][d].

Add new ¶ 12.65[5].

[5] Proposed Regulations §1.368-1(f): "Exchange of Net Value"

Proposed regulations issued in March of 2005[1136.1] require reciprocal exchanges of "net value in order for a transaction to qualify as a tax-free §368 reorganization. These provisions are intended to apply in conjunction with the continuity of interest principle and are based on the same theory and policy, viz.,

---

[1136.1] Prop. Regs. §§1.368-1(b)(1), 1.368-1(f) and 1.368-2(d)(1) issued Mar. 10, 2005.

that transactions that are the economic equivalent of "sales" should not be allowed to qualify for §368 nonrecognition treatment.[1136.2] Their principal application will involve acquisitions of "insolvent" corporations; thus, if the only consideration received in a transfer of assets or stock is the assumption (or satisfaction) of debt, it will fail to qualify as a reorganization under §368.[1136.3] Requiring some "equity" in the transaction (other than the receipt of worthless stock), will satisfy this requirement if there is both a surrender of net value and a receipt of net value in the transaction.[1136.4]

There are three "carve-outs" from the net value exchange rule:

1. The net value exchange rule is not applicable to either Type E recapitalizations or Type F reorganizations[1136.5] (because the general continuity rules do not apply to those transactions); and
2. Nondivisive Type D reorganizations where IRS wants to preserve its right to impose nonrecognition treatment under liquidation reincorporation principles.[1136.6]

The ten examples in § 1.368-1(f)(5) illustrate the application of the net value exchange limitation. All of the examples involve the acquisition of an insolvent target corporation; if qualified, the potential reorganization most likely is a Type G (supra ¶ 12.30; e.g., Examples 1,2,6 and 7; the failed transactions, Examples 3, 4 and 5 involved transfer of property solely for assumption or satisfaction of the transferors debt).[1136.7]

The proposed regulations make no attempt to define "liabilities" (though the preamble states that the term is intended to be construed broadly). Moreover, no guidance is offered as to the *amount* of any liability (i.e., face

---

[1136.2] See Preamble, Explanation of Proposals; Regs. § 1.368-1(f)(1).

[1136.3] See Preamble, Explanation of Proposals; Regs. § 1.368-1(f)(1).

[1136.4] Terms defined in Regs. §§ 1.368-1(f)(1), 1.368-1(f)(2) and 1.368-1(f)(3).

See Cummings, "New Proposed Regs. Change Rules For Transactions where Property or Stock Lacks Net Value," 103 J. Tax'n 14 (July 2005); Silverman, et al, "Assessing the Value of the Proposed No Net Value Regulations," 108 Tax Notes 1135 (Sept. 5, 2005); and critical comments, NYSBA Tax Section, "Formations, Reorganizations, Liquidations Involving Insolvent Corporations," 110 Tax Notes 871 (Feb. 20, 2006); Blanchard, Hooker and Vogel, "Underwater Assets and Insolvent Corporations: Reflections on Treasury's Recently Proposed Regulations and Related Matters," 59 Tax Law. 107 (Fall 2005).

[1136.5] Prop. Regs. §1.368-1(b)(1).

[1136.6] Prop. Regs. §1.368-1(b)(4) (the preamble cites *James Armour* and *Rev. Rul. 70-240*); Prop. Regs. §1.368-1(f)(5), Example 8.

See Cummings, No-Net Value and Type D Reorganizations, 107 Tax Notes 249 (Apr. 11, 2005); Bennett, "Proposed Regulations on Inssolvency Reorganizations—Part I," 83 Taxes 9 (Aug. 2005).

[1136.7] The example seems to be the *Norman Scott* case, 48 TC 598 (1967) (allowing a merger of an insolvent target corporation) which decision is rejected by the proposed regulations.

"value," "adjusted issue price," or some other number).[1136.8] The new proposals have placed "net value" exchange limitations not only on potential §368 transactions, but also on §332 liquidations (which already exist under current rules)[1136.9] and on §351 transfers as well.[1136.10]

[1136.8] The IRS is considering various approaches here and comments are requested; they undoubtedly will be forthcoming.

[1136.9] Prop. Regs. §1.332-2(b) and 1.332-2(e), Ex. 2, see   10.21[2].

[1136.10] Prop. Regs. §1.351-1(a)(1)(iii) and 1.351-2, Ex. 4. See   3.06[2].

¶ 12.66 CONTINGENT-CONSIDERATION ACQUISITIONS AND RELATED PROBLEMS

[1] In General

Page 12-330:

Add to note 1136.

More currently, Koenig & Boise, "Contingent Consideration: The Taxation of Earnouts and Escrows," 2 Mergers & Acquisitions 3 (July 2001) (deals only with taxable acquisitions, however). Willens, "Contingent Stock Acquisitions Should Gain Popularity in Uncertain Times," Daily Tax Rep. (BNA) No. 120, at J-1 (June 23, 2003); Walker, "Variable Stock Consideration in Corporate Reorganizations," 31 Corp. Tax'n 15 (Sept. 2004).

Page 12-331:

Add to note 1138.

Willens, supra note 1136. NYSB Assoc. Tax Section Comments (Report No. 1051) on treatment of variable stock consideration in tax-free corporate reorganization, Feb. 4, 2004 (available in BNA Tax Core); Walker, supra note 1136.

[2] Contingent Consideration Transactions

[a] In General

Add to note 1140.

Bernstein, "Distribution of Contingent Litigation Claims to Facilitate Mergers and Acquisitions," 30 J. Corp. Tax'n 37 (July 2003).

Page 12-332:

Add to note 1142.

See Willens, supra note 1136.

[3] Escrow Arrangements

[a] In General

Page 12-336:

Add to note 1153.

See Willens, supra note 1136.

[4] Back-Out Rights, Put-Back Rights, and Other Rescission Situations

[c] Taxability of Rescission Transfer

Page 12-340:

Add to note 1171.

Baline, Rescissions: "A Federal Income Tax 'Do-Over'," 32 Corp. Tax'n 32 (Nov. 2005). Bennett, "The Doctrine of Rescission," 84 Taxes 15 (June 2006); Banoff, "New IRS Rulings Approve Rescission Transactions That Change an Entities Status," 105 J. Tax'n 5 (July 2006); Willens, "Rescission Doctrine Can Make Transaction Disappear," 112 Tax Notes 801 (Aug. 24, 2006).

[5] Damages for Breach of Original Agreement

[a] Payment by Acquirer

Page 12-342:

In second paragraph of note 1179 after Tribune Publishing *cite add:*

(9th Cir. 1988)

CHAPTER **13**

Affiliated Corporations

C   CONSOLIDATED RETURNS

A   MULTIPLE CORPORATIONS GENERALLY

¶ 13.02 LIMITATIONS ON MULTIPLE TAX BENEFITS FOR MEMBERS OF CONTROLLED GROUPS OF CORPORATIONS

[1] Introductory

Page 13-14:

Add to note 14.

Raby & Raby, "Use of Multiple Corporations in 2001," 91 Tax Notes 279 (Apr. 9, 2001).

[4] "Controlled Group of Corporations": Definition

[a] In General

Page 13-17:

Add to note 23.

Notice 2003-50, 2003-32 IRB 295, modified Notice 89-94 (stapled foreign affiliate will be considered a domestic corporation for purposes of §§ 904(i) and 864(e) limitations). See Prop. Regs. § 1.269B-1 (Sept. 7, 2004), implementing Notice 2003-5 (effective when adopted as final). Adopted without change by TD 9216 (July 29, 2005).

Page 13-18:

Add to text at end of ¶ 13.02[4][a], item 2.

But the 2004 Jobs Act[25.1] materially expanded the scope of the § 1563(a)(2) brother-sister group provision by dropping the 80 percent test from the definition (leaving only the 50 percent test), though only for purposes of the § 1561 limits (the 80 percent test is retained for other provisions that incorporate the brother-sister controlled group definition).[25.2]

[25.1] American Jobs Creation Act of 2004, § 900, removing § 1563(a)(1)(A) (effective Oct. 22, 2004). Temp. Regs. § 1.563-1T, issued by TD 9341 (Dec. 22, 2006).

[25.2] New § 1563(f)(5) (retains the prior definition of § 1563(a)(2) brother-sister controlled group).

B TRANSACTIONS BETWEEN AFFILIATED CORPORATIONS: § 482 AND RELATED PROVISIONS

¶ 13.20 ALLOCATION OF INCOME AND DEDUCTIONS AMONG RELATED CORPORATIONS: § 482 GENERALLY

[1] Introductory

[a] In General

Page 13-25:

Add to note 50.

For state and local § 482-type regimes, see Brandman, Western-Overby & Shaver, "U.S. Transfer Pricing: A State by State Survey of Regulatory Regimes," BNA Daily Tax Rep. No. 170, at J-1 (Sept. 3, 2002).

Add to note 51, second paragraph.

Katz-Pearlman & Adelson, "IRS Restructuring and Transfer Pricing Enforcement," 87 Tax Notes 1375 (June 5, 2000).

[d] Contemporary § 482 Developments (An Overview)

Page 13-31:

Add to note 72, second paragraph.

Durst & Culbertson, "Clearing Away the Sand: Retrospective Methods and Prospective Documentation in Transfer Pricing Today," 57 Tax Law. 37 (Fall 2003).

Add to text at end of ¶ 13.20[1][d].

New Proposed Regs. § 1.482-9 (issued in September 2003) overhaul the services regulations in a major way.[74.1]

[74.1] Infra   13.21[3]. Adopted as temporary regulations on August 4, 2006.

[3] Common Ownership or Control

[a] In General

Page 13-34:

Add to note 84.

DHL Corp. was affirmed on the time for determining common control issue, 285 F3d 1210, 2002-1 USTC 50,354 (9th Cir. 2002) (other party not at arm's length here because tax indifferent).

[b] Mutuality of Interests

Page 13-35:

Add to note 86.

For analysis of the IRS' position in these assertions, see Levey & Garofalo, "Applying Section 482 to Third-Party Lease Strips; Has the IRS Overreached?" 12 J. Int'l Tax'n 12 (Dec. 2001). For a different approach, see Prop. Regs. § 1.7701(l)-2 (Dec. 27, 2001), based on Notice 95-53, 1995-2 CB 334. But IRS dropped the § 482 approach in the lease-stripping litigation; comment by Goulder, "IRS Chief Counsel Explains Reversal on

Lease-stripping," 98 Tax Notes 1809 (Mar. 24, 2003); Rev. Rul. 2003-96, 2003-34 IRB 246.

[4] Scope of Service's Authority: What Can and Cannot Be Done Under § 482?

[e] Diversion of "Business" Versus Diversion of "Income"

Page 13-38:

Add to note 97.

But *UPS* was reversed on appeal, 254 F3d 1014, 2001-2 USTC   50,475 (11th Cir. 2001) (not a sham; transaction had economic substance and enough business purpose despite heavy tax planning motives; but remanded for further proceedings on the § 482 issue, which was settled).

[5] Collateral Adjustments

[b] Set-Offs

Page 13-42:

Add to note 111.

See, e.g., DHL Corp. v. CIR, 285 F3d 1210, 2002-1 USTC   50,354 (9th Cir. 2002) (reversing Tax Court, held that taxpayer entitled to full set-off for foreign affiliate's assistance in developing foreign trademark intangible).

Add new note 112.1 to the end of ¶ 13.20[5][b].

112.1

112.1 See Rev. Proc. 2005-46, 2005-30 IRB 142 (new simplified and streamlined procedures for claiming set-offs against proposed § 482 adjustments).

[6] Allocation Standards and General Principles (Arm's-Length Comparability)

[c] Comparability

Page 13-46:

Add to note 125.

Durst, "The Role of Intercompany Pricing Contracts in the Transfer Pricing System," 90 Tax Notes 513 (Jan. 22, 2001).

¶ 13.21 SECTION 482: SPECIFIC SITUATIONS

[3] Services

Page 13-51:

Add to note 144.

Kenco Restaurants, Inc. v. CIR, 206 F3d 588 (6th Cir. 2000), cert. denied on October 2, 2000 (business services and taxpayer's allocation not arm's length; negligence penalty imposed); Raby & Raby, "Cost Allocation Poses Problems Beyond Multinationals," 86 Tax Notes 1411 (Mar. 6, 2000); Gaffney et al., "Taxpayers Face New Burdens in Overcoming 482 Allocations by the Service," 93 J. Tax'n 112 (Aug. 2000).

See also Zollo, Bowers & Cowan, "Transfer Pricing for Services: The Next Wave," 81 Tax Notes 117 (Mar. 2003). New regulations dealing with services were proposed on September 5, 2003, in Regs. § 1.482-9 (they are extensive, restrictive and complex), infra note 146.1.

Add text to end of ¶ 13.21[3].

But IRS warned that it was planning to revisit the service allocation regulations that are woefully out of date (having been promulgated in 1968). As discussed below they at last delivered on that warning by releasing a massive package of proposed regulations on September 5, 2003.[146.1]

A major revision of the related party services regulations has been proposed in § 1.482-9, which largely abandons the cost-based safe-harbor focus of the 1968 regulations[146.2] and shifts strongly to arm's length based principles as the near exclusive adjustment model. The preamble is must reading here (it's nearly half the length of the regulations) since the Service explains in exhaustive detail the reasons for the numerous changes in these proposed regulations. The virtual elimination of the cost allocation method for non-business services in the current regulations (as well as the complete elimination of the book allocation method) means that virtually every significant service transaction will be forced into using one of five other arm's length valuation methods set out

---

[146.1] Prop. Regs. § 1.482-9 (effective on promulgation as final regulations). For analysis of the regulations, see Kirschenbaum et al.; At Your Service(s), 14 J. Int'l Tax'n 10 (Dec. 2003); Terr, The Proposed Transfer Pricing Services Regulations, 101 Tax Notes 1439 (Dec. 22, 2003); Birnkrant, "Transfer Pricing for Services Is Broadly Affected by New Prop. Regs.," 100 J. Tax'n 8 (Jan. 2004); Zollo et al., "Transfer Pricing For Services: The Next Wave," 82 Taxes 29 (Mar. 2003); Zollo et al., "The New Wave Hits, " 82 Taxes 29 (Jan. 2004); Wolosoff et al., Proposed Section 482 Regs:..., 103 Tax Notes 589 (May 3, 2004). (All comments uniformly hostile.)

[146.2] Cost allocation lingers on in § 1.482-9(f), however, as the "simplified cost-based method" (or SCM) for certain low-margin services (e.g., routine back-office type function), which, however, is neither simple nor particularly useful since it has to be tested by arm's length valuation standards to determine its availability. It is not insignificant that nine of the 10 examples in § 1.482-9(f)(5) are not successful in applying this method (which does not appear to be a preferred method in the proposed regulations).

in the regulations (all of which require a profit factor), subject to the "best method" requirement, namely the method that is the most reliable measure of an arm's length result as to comparability and the quality of the relevant data.

The five other specified arm's length allocation methods (three of which are new, and two of which exist under the current regulations,[146.3] are direct analogs of methods provided for transfers of tangible and intangible property under Regs. § 1.482-3[146.4] and § 1.482-4[146.5] and consist of the following:

1. The comparable uncontrolled services price method;[146.6]
2. The gross services margin method;[146.7]
3. The cost of services plus method;[146.8]
4. The two existing methods in Regs. §§ 1.482-5 and 1.482-6;[146.9]
5. Unspecified methods are permitted in certain (rare) cases.[146.10]

In short, the controlled services regulations have been conformed to the basic allocation structure of the 1994 regulations applicable to transfer pricing for tangible and intangible property transfers. The intangibles rules of § 1.482-4(f) also were revised, and tightened, (but not improved as to clarity), by the September proposed regulations.[146.11]

Determination of whether a service allocation is required is found in § 1.482-9(l) which provides generally that allocation is required if a particular service provides a measurable meaningful benefit to the recipient member for which, if unrelated, it would be willing to pay (or perform itself).[146.12] Similarly to the current regulations, however, indirect or remote benefits, duplicative services benefits, stewardship or shareholder services benefits, and passive association benefits need not be paid for.[146.13] By reversing the benefit focus from the performer (current regulations, who would have charged) to the recipient (proposed regulations – who would have paid), the proposed regulations have adopted the basic OECD services guideline approach.

[146.3] Prop. Regs. § 1.482-9(e), the comparable profits method under § 1.482-5, and Prop. Regs. § 1.482-9(g), the residual profit split method under §1.482-6.

[146.4] Infra   13.21[6].

[146.5] Infra   13.21[5].

[146.6] Prop. Regs. § 1.482-9(b) (or cusp).

[146.7] Prop. Regs. § 1.482-9(c).

[146.8] Prop. Regs. § 1.482-9(d).

[146.9] Prop. Regs. §§ 1.482-9(e) and 1.482-9(g), supra note 146.3.

[146.10] Prop. Regs. § 1.482-9(h), also subject to the limitations in Regs. § 1.482-1 (e.g., the best method limitation, comparability standards, and the arm's length range rules).

[146.11] Infra   13.21[5][e], Prop. Regs. §§ 1.482-4(f)(3), 1.482-4(f)(4).

[146.12] Prop. Regs. § 1.482-9(l)(3)(i) (similar to the OECD model).

[146.13] Prop. Regs. §§ 1.482-9(l)(3)(ii), 1.482-9(l)(3)(iii), 1.482-9(l)(3)(iv) and 1.482-9(l)(3)(v). The 17 examples in § 1.482-9(l)(4) illustrate the general rule (Ex. 1), remote benefits (Exs. 2 and 3), duplicative benefits (Exs. 4, 5, and 6), stewardship (Exs. 7-14), and passive association (Exs. 15-17). See Doernberg, "Taxation Silos: Embedded Intangibles and Embedded Services," 110 Tax Notes 1189 (Mar. 13, 2006).

One will search these proposed regulations in vain, however, for clarity, bright-lines, and meaningful safe harbors. In this respect, the proposed services regulations have indeed now joined the modern world of the revised § 482 regulations.

The proposed services regulations were adopted as temporary regulations on August 4, 2006.[146.14] The principal change in this version was elimination of the heavily criticized "simplified cost basis method" (SCBM)[146.15] and adoption of a new "services cost method" (SCM) as its replacement in Treasury Regulations § 1.482-9T(b).[146.16] Under this revised method, taxpayers can charge for the costs of (1) any of the forty-eight services described in Announcement 2006-50 and a proposed revenue procedure released with the regulations (a so-called "white-list")[146.17] and (2) any service with a median comparable markup of 7 percent or less.

The regulations also deal with "shared services" arrangements[146.18] (not dealt with in the proposed regulations). The temporary regulations in § 1.482-9T(b)(6) give twenty-six examples of situations involving the new service's cost method regime, which are generally helpful in determining its scope and application. All in all, taxpayers should be at least moderately pleased, and relieved, with the new regime. The rest of the proposed regulations were adopted without significance change.

[146.14] TD 9278 (Aug. 4, 2006) (effective Jan. 1, 2007). But the IRS announced an extension for one year in December 2006 by Notice 2007-5, 2007-3 IRB (Jan. 16, 2007).

[146.15] The IRS gave many indications that SCBM would be changed, and it clearly was in the new regulations (and for the better).

[146.16] The IRS gave many indications that SCBM would be changed, and it clearly was in the new regulations (and for the better).

[146.17] Ann. 2006-50, 2006-34 IRB 321 (Aug. 21, 2006) (which can be expanded, or contracted, by future amendments). The IRS plans to expand and liberalize this list and did so in Rev. Proc. 2007-13, 2007-3 IRB (Jan. 16, 2007), to 101 items.

[146.18] Regs. §§ 1.482-9T(b)(5), and 1.482-9T(b)(6), Exs 18-23. See Nutt, "No Safety in the Harbor: New Transfer Pricing Services Regs.," 112 Tax Notes 732 (Aug. 28, 2006); "Interview-Branch 6 Chief Clarifies Application of Cost Method, Other Aspects of the New Temporary Services Regulations," Daily Tax Rep. (BNA) No. 181, at J-1 (Sept. 19, 2006); Sheppard, "Selective Issues in the New Transfer Pricing Services Regulations," 113 Tax Notes 122 (Oct. 9, 2006); Sheppard, "Practical Advice for the Section 482 Services Regs," 113 Tax Notes 1060 (Dec. 18, 2006); Wolosoff & Ryan, "Temporary Services Regs: One Step Forward, Two Steps Back?" 113 Tax Notes 71 (Oct. 2, 2006); Zolo, Cope & Blough, "Transfer Pricing for Services: The Temporary Regulations," 84 Taxes 35 (Oct. 2006); Alberal et al., "Intercompany Services and Intangible Transactions," 17 J. Int'l Tax'n 15 (Nov. 2006).

[5] Transfer or Use of Intangibles

[a] Overview

Page 13-52:

Add to end of first paragraph in note 150.

But *DHL Corp.* was reversed on appeal, 285 F3d 1210, 2002-1 USTC   50,354 (9th Cir. 2002) (allocation of deemed royalty from foreign affiliate not proper because foreign affiliate was a developer of foreign trademark intangible, or at least an "assistor" creating right to full set-off for its development expenses; penalty also reversed because taxpayer reasonably relied on its expert's opinion); Hardy, "Assignment of Corporate Opportunities—The Migration of Intangibles," 100 Tax Notes 527 (July 28, 2003).

Page 13-53:

Add to note 150.

See Hardy, supra. See also Hastbacka, "Valuation of Technology Intangibles for Transfer Pricing Time For Industry Initiatives," 101 Tax Notes 749 (Nov. 10, 2003).

[b] Super-Royalty Amendment Generally

Page 13-55:

Add to note 163.

Cope, "Limitations on Transfer Pricing Adjustments Under the Commensurate With Income Standard," 104 J. Tax'n 112 (Feb. 2006).

Add to note 164.

See Hardy, supra note 150.

[c] General Rule

Page 13-57:

Add to note 171.

Compare DHL Corp. v. CIR, 285 F3d 1210, 2002-1 USTC   50,354 (9th Cir. 2002) (taxpayer's foreign affiliate held to be "developer" of foreign trademark intangible under former regulations, or at least it was an "assister" therein creating right to full set-off). Faiferlick et al, "Planning For Transfers of U.S.-Based Intellectual Property to Related Entities," 96 J. Tax'n 359 (June 2002). Hardy, "Assignment of Corporate Opportunities—The Migration of Intangibles," 100 Tax Notes 527 (July 28, 2003).

[d] Cost-Sharing Agreements

Page 13-58:

Add to note 176.

Levey, Miesel & Garofalo, "Cost-Sharing Agreements: Buy-In/Buy Out Payments and the Valuation Problem," 11 J. Int'l Tax'n 8 (Nov. 2000)Bose, "The Effectiveness of Using Cost-Sharing Arrangements as a Mechanism to Avoid Intercompany Transfer Pricing With Respect to Intellectual Property," 21 Vis. Tax Rev. 553 (2002).

Page 13-59:

Add to text at end of runover paragraph at top.

Proposed regulations issued in July 2002 and adopted with virtually no changes on August 26, 2003 require that all equity-based compensation (e.g., stock options and the like) granted during the term of the cost-sharing agreement must be included in operating expenses if related to the development of intangibles covered by the agreement.[178.1]

[178.1] Prop. Regs. § 1.482-7(d)(2) (July 29, 2002), effective when final. Regs. § 1.482-7(d)(21) (Aug. 26, 2003), adopted by TD 9088. The regulations also prescribed rules for measuring equity-based compensation and the timing of these costs. The preamble is must reading here (it's twice as long as the Regs). See Lupi-Sher, "Reg on Compensatory Stock Options Get Mixed Reviews," 96 Tax Notes 792 (Aug. 5, 2002); Bell, "Practitioners Question Validity of Proposed Cost-Sharing Regs.," 96 Tax Notes 903 (Aug. 12, 2002). Lewis & Kochman, "Option Wars: Upping the Ante for Cost-Sharing Arrangements," 31 Tax Mgm't Int'l J. 547 (Nov. 8, 2002); Hardesty, "Stock-Based Compensation and Cost-Sharing," 98 Tax Notes 1711 (Mar. 17, 2003); Schrotenboer, "Arm's Length in Wonderland," 102 Tax Notes 265 (Jan. 12, 2004). See also Notice 2005-99, 2005-52 IRB (Dec. 27, 2005) (extends method for measuring cost-shared options to restricted shares as well; but only if related to publicly traded stock and are not subject to market conditions or significant post vesting restrictions).

But Xilinx, Inc., 125 TC 37 (2005), held for the taxpayer, rejecting IRS' attempt to allocate the parent's equity-based compensation to its R&D employees as part of the cost-sharing pool of expenses. The court held that IRS' allocations violated the basic arm's length standard of the regulations since no unrelated parties to a cost-sharing agreement would share such costs; thus, taxpayer was not required to do so in this case. The court noted the 2003 regulations adoption (but did not shed any light on whether these regulations (which were not applicable for the years involved) were valid (though the opinion's analysis and conclusions certainly cast a cloud on their validity). Sheppard, "Industry Practice as the Arm's-Length Method," 109 Tax Notes 438 (Oct. 24, 2005).

Add text to end of ¶ 13.21[5][d].

But Treasury is taking a second look at its cost-sharing regulations in view of its apparently well founded fear that the current regulations are being used (or abused) to shift intangible assets offshore.[179.1] The recently adopted amendment to the cost-sharing rules noted above is the first step in this process, with more to come. These ominous warning signals proved to be justified with the release a massive revision of the cost-sharing regulations in proposed Regulations § 1.482-7 (which are remarkable not only for their length and complexity, but also for their open hostility to these arrangements as well)[179.2a]

[179.1] Sullivan, "Will Treasury Stop the Outflow of U.S. Intellectual Property?" 97 Tax Notes 1269 (Dec. 2, 2002); Lev, "Migration of Intellectual Property: Unintended Effect of Transfer Pricing Regs," 97 Tax Notes 1345 (Dec. 9, 2002); Hardy, "Assignment of Corporate Opportunities—The Migration of Intangibles," 100 Tax Notes 527 (July 28, 2003); see also infra ¶ 13.21[5][e] (revision of intangibles regulations).

[179.2a] See Moses, "Proposed Cost-Sharing Rules Seen as Attempt to Enlarge Buy-In Payments," Daily Tax Rep. (BNA) No. 168, J-1 (Aug. 31, 2005); the proposals adopt the "investor model" as their core concept, set our various methods for valuing buy-in payments, and generally preclude taxpayers (though *not* IRS) from making periodic adjustments to reflect changed circumstances.

See also Sheppard, "Is Apportionment the Formula for Intangible Development?" 108 Tax Notes 1093 (Sept. 5, 2005); Sullivan, "Proposed IRS Rules Would Close Cost-Sharing Loophole," 108 Tax Notes 1098 (Sept. 5, 2005); Sullivan, "Half the Profits for None of the Work," 108 Tax Notes 1243 (Sept. 12, 2005). See also Reams, et al., "Proposed Cost-Sharing Regulations – Are They A Realistic Alternative?" 109 Tax Notes 239 (Oct. 10, 2005); Kirschenbaum, et al., "Proposed Cost-Sharing Regulations Introduce 'New' Standards," 16 J. Int'l Tax'n 14 (Dec. 2005); Chandler et al., "Methods in Determining Taxable Income With a Cost-Sharing Agreement: A Review and Analysis of the Proposed Cost-Sharing Regulations," 83 Taxes 19 (Dec. 2005); Moses, "Cost-Sharing Proposal Would Dictate Business Structures, Abandon Arm's-Length Standard, Taxpayer Organizations Say," Daily Tax Rep. (BNA) No. 238, at J-1 (Dec. 13, 2005); Birnkrant, "New Cost-Sharing Proposed Regulations Change the Focus of the Buy-In Analysis," 103 J. Tax'n 328 (Dec. 2005).

As the above comments indicate, there is little to like in the new proposals.

Add new ¶ 13.21[5][e].

[e] Proposed Revision of the Intangibles Regulations [New]

In connection with the Service's proposed revision of the services regulations on September 5, 2003, IRS also proposed amendments to the ownership rules of § 1.482-4(f)(3).[179.2] The principal feature of these proposals is abandonment of the "developer-assister" approach to determining the ownership of intangibles. Instead, there can be only one "owner" of a particular intangible who is either the legal (or contractual) owner, or, if none, the taxpayer who has control of the particular intangible.[179.3]

Any related member who contributes to, or enhances, the value of the owner's intangible must be appropriately compensated for that benefit. If the consideration for such contributions is embedded in the contractual terms for a controlled transaction that involves the intangible, then ordinarily no separate allocation will be made; instead, it must be accounted for in the comparability analysis.[179.4] Needless to say, this will not be a readily determinable process.[179.5]

[179.2] Prop. Regs. §§ 1.482-4(f)(3) and 1.482-4(f)(4).

[179.3] Prop. Regs. § 1.482-4(f)(3)(i)(A).

[179.4] Prop. Regs. § 1.482-4(f)(4)(i).

[179.5] Prop. Regs. § 1.482-4(f)(4)(ii), Exs. 2, 3, 5 and 6 are especially vaporous in their outcomes. See Kirschbaum et al., supra note 146.1, at 43-48 for critique. See also Lemein and McDonald, "New Order: Proposed Regulations Alter 'Developer-Assister' Regime For Ownership of Intangible Property," 82 Taxes 5 (Jan. 2004); Wolosoff et al., Proposed Section 482 Regs: Path to Uncertainty, Endless Controversy, 103 Tax Notes 589 (May 3, 2004); Moses, "Analysis & Perspective, U.S. Marketing Intangibles Stance in Glaxo: Wave of the Future," Daily Tax Rep. (BNA) No. 54, at J-1 (Mar. 29, 2004); Moses, "Glaxo Sees Global Scrutiny for Transfer Pricing of Popular Drugs," Daily Tax Rep. (BNA) No. 74, at J-1 (Apr. 19, 2004); Bell, "Glaxo Petition Raises Novel APA Issue," 103 Tax Notes 148 (Apr. 12, 2004); Sullivan, "With Billions at Stake, Glaxo Puts ADA

These regulations were adopted as temporary without significant change on August 4, 2006.[179.6]

Program on Trial," 103 Tax Notes 388 (Apr. 24, 2004); Moses, "Uphill Battle For Glaxo, Daily Tax Rep. (BNA) No. 94, at J-1 (May 7, 2004); Bell, "IRS Answers Glaxo, Sets Stage for Feud on Marketing Intangibles," 103 Tax Notes 1218 (June 7, 2004); But the *Glaxo* case settled for $3.4 billion, Daily Tax Rep. (BNA) No. 178, at G6-1 (Sept. 12, 2006); Nutt, "Glaxo, IRS Settle Dispute," 112 Tax Notes 1020 (Sept. 18, 2006); Langbein, "Transfer Pricing and the Outsourcing Problem," 106 Tax Notes 1299 (Mar. 4, 2005); Wright, "*Glaxo* Case Highlights Marketing Intangibles, Lack of U.S. Jurisprudence," Daily Tax Rep. (BNA), No. 227, at—(Nov. 27, 2006); "Taxation Silos: Embedded Intangibles and Embedded Services," 110 Tax Notes 1189 (Mar. 13, 2006); Sheppard, "Practical Advice for the Section 482 Services Regs," 113 Tax Notes 1060 (Dec. 18, 2006).

[179.6] TD 9278, Regs. § 1.482-4T(f) (effective for 2007).

[6] Intercompany Sales of Tangible Property

[b] General Rule

Page 13-62:

Add to note 190.

Meyers & Outman, "U.S. Tax and Customs Consequences of Dealing With a Related Supplier," 12 J. Int'l Tax'n 31 (Nov. 2001).

[7] The White Paper on § 482 and Implementing Regulations

[a] The White Paper on § 482

Page 13-65:

Add to note 198, second paragraph.

Hardy, "Assignment of Corporate Opportunities—The Migration of Intangibles," 100 Tax Notes 527 (July 28, 2003).

[b] The 1992 and 1993 Proposed and Temporary Regulations

Page 13-68:

Add to note 209, first paragraph.

Hardy, "Assignment of Corporate Opportunities—The Migration of Intangibles," 100 Tax Notes 527 (July 28, 2003).

[8] Advance Pricing Agreement Procedures

Page 13-70:

Add to end of third paragraph in note 212.

The third annual APA report was released on March 29, 2002, in Ann. 2002-40, 2002-15 IRB 747 (transfer pricing report on APA Program restructuring during 2001 and statistics for 2001). The APA procedures were revised once again on July 1, 2004, in Rev. Proc. 2004-40, 2004-29 IRB 50.

Add to note 213.

Wrappe & Mantegani, "APA Procedures: U.S. v. OECD," 86 Tax Notes 1751 (Mar. 20, 2000).

Page 13-71:

Add to note 217.

Bell, "Glaxo Petition Raises Novel APA Issue," 103 Tax Notes 199 (Apr. 12, 2004); Moses, "Analysis & Perspective," Daily Tax Rep. (BNA) No. 74, at J-1 (Apr. 19, 2004); Sullivan, "With Billions at Stake, Glaxo Puts APA Program on Trial," 103 Tax Notes 388 (Apr. 24, 2004); Moses, "Uphill Battle For Glaxo," Daily Tax Rep. No. 94, at J-1 (May 17, 2004). But the *Glaxo* case settled for $3.4 billion, supra note 179.5.

Add to text at end of ¶ 13.21[8].

The APA procedures were revised once again on July, 2004,[219.1] with special sections on cost-sharing agreements (a new focus by IRS) and small business taxpayers. While the new procedures are a substantial overhaul of the 1996 and 1998 procedures, no fundamental change of basic principles and procedures is intended. They were revised again (though less significantly) in January of 2006.[219.2]

[219.1] Rev. Proc. 2004-40, 2004-29 IRB 50.

[219.2] Rev. Proc. 2006-9, 2006-2 IRB 278 (Jan. 9, 2006).

[9] Allocation of Income From Global Trading of Financial Products

Page 13-72:

Add to note 222.

Sheppard, "Gremlins in the Global Dealing Regulations," 94 Tax Notes 270 (Jan. 21, 2002).

¶ 13.22 SECTION 482: COLLATERAL ASPECTS

[1] Collateral Effects of § 482 Adjustments

[b] Other Collateral Implications of § 482 Adjustments

Page 13-74:

In note 226, the citation to Rev. Proc. 99-32 should be changed to Rev. Proc. 99-32, 1999-34 IRB 296.

[3] Compliance Aspects: Legislation and Administrative Action

[b] Accuracy-Related Penalty for § 482 Violations: § 6662(e)

Page 13-78:

Add to end of first paragraph of note 242.

But *DHL Corp.* was reversed on penalty issue, 285 F3d 1210, 2002-1 USTC ¶ 50,354 (9th Cir. 2002) (§ 482 allocation improper on merits, so no penalty; Tax Court's valuation upheld, but no penalty here either because taxpayer reasonably relied on its expert's opinion as to value).

¶ 13.23 GENERAL INCOME AND DEDUCTION PRINCIPLES IN THE MULTIPLE CORPORATION CONTEXT

[1] In General

Page 13-81:

Add to note 248, first paragraph.

Investment Research Associates aff'd on fraud (and other issues) sub nom Estate of Kanter v. CIR, 337 F3d 833, 2003-2 USTC ¶ 50,605 (7th Cir. 2003), and Ballard v. CIR, 321 F3d 1037 (11th Cir. 2003). But reversed on a procedural issue by the Supreme Court in March of 2005; see ¶ 1.05[2][c].

[2] Sham Transactions

Page 13-81:

Add to note 250.

But *UPS* was reversed on appeal, 254 F3d 1014, 2001-2 USTC ¶ 50,475 (11th Cir. 2001) (not a sham; had economic substance and enough business purpose to neutralize heavy tax planning motives); see also IES Indus., Inc. v. US, 253 F3d 350 (8th Cir. 2001) (transaction had economic substance and adequate business purpose to withstand IRS attack). *Investment Research Assocs.* was aff'd by the Seventh and Eleventh Circuit, supra note 248.

Page 13-82:

Add to note 252.

But *UPS* was reversed, supra note 250; see Lupi-Sher, "Corporate Tax Shelters Regain Vitality," 92 Tax Notes 11 (July 2, 2001); Sheppard, "Why the IRS Should Argue the Statute First," 92 Tax Notes 465 (July 23, 2001); Wexler, "Notes on the Economic Substance and Business Purpose Doctrines," 92 Tax Notes 27 (July 2, 2001).

[3] Income Creation Outside of § 482

[a] Below-Market-Rate Loans: § 7872

Page 13-83:

Add to note 255.

Rountree Cotton Co., aff'd per curiam, 2001-1 USTC   50,316 (10th Cir. 2001).

[b] Other Parent-Subsidiary Bargain Dealings (Downstream and Upstream Transactions)

Page 13-84:

Add to note 257.

See e.g. Fromatome Connectors USA, Inc., 118 TC 32 (2002); aff'd, 2004-2 USTC
    50,364 (2d Cir. 2004).

Add to note 259.

See Fromatome Connectors USA, Inc., 118 TC 32 (2002), supra note 257 (bargain sales to foreign parent resulted in § 1442 withholding tax for subsidiary on constructive dividends).

[e] Premium Price Sales

Page 13-86:

In second paragraph of note 268 change 1992-1 *to* 1998-2.

In the last sentence of note 269 change 1994-34 IRB __ *to* 1994-34 IRB 296.

[5] Basic Deduction Principles: Disallowance or Deferral

[b] Expenses for the Benefit of Another Person

Page 13-88:

Add to note 273, first paragraph.

But see Square D Co., 121 TC 168 (2003) (for an exception to this general principle), and infra note 276.

Page 13-89:

Add to note 276.

See also Square D Co., 121 TC 168 (2003) (sub's reimbursement of loan-related fees and legal costs incurred by parent for benefit of sub who assumed and paid those fees held deductible amortizable loan costs).

[6] Timing Problems

[b] Section 267 Matching Rules

Page 13-93:

Add to note 289.

Tate & Lyle was also reversed by the Tax Court in Square D Co., 118 TC 299 (2002), aff'd, 438 F3d 739 (7th Cir. 2006).

C CONSOLIDATED RETURNS

¶ 13.40 INTRODUCTORY

Page 13-97:

Add to note 305.

Rite Aid Corp. v. US, 2000-1 USTC ¶ 50,429 (Fed. Cl. 2000) (validity of loss disallowance regulations upheld, infra ¶ 13.42[5][c]; significant decision re IRS regulation power here). But *Rite Aid* was reversed, 255 F3d 1357, 2001-2 USTC ¶ 50,516 (Fed. Cir. 2001) (loss duplication factor rule invalidated as arbitrary unreasonable and in conflict with specific statutory allowance, § 165); Notice 2002-11, 2002-7 IRB 536 (IRS concedes on *Rite Aid* issue and will not appeal; instead will issue revised regulations); for these "stop-gap" regulations, see Notice 2002-18, 2002-12 IRB 644, Regs. § 1.502-35T, and infra ¶ 13.42[5][c]. See also infra note 305.1 for 2004 legislative response.

Add to text after sentence ending with note 305.

Pending legislation (which finally passed on October 22, 2004) reconfirms this status for the §1502 regulations by neutralizing the court's decision in the Rite Aid case and reasserting Treasury's power to write the rules here.[305.1]

[305.1] The Senate Finance Committee charity bill, the "CARE Act of 2002," HR 7 Title VI A, § 631 (July 16, 2002) amending § 1502 (and totally retroactive as well). Identical legislation is contained in Ways & Means Chairman Thomas' proposed omnibus tax bill, HR 5095, Title I, § 123. See Lupi-Sher, "Congress Attempts to Short Circuit *Rite Aid* Decision." This provision passed on October 22, 2004, HR 4520, § 844, P.L. 108-357, the 2004 Jobs Act.

In last sentence of note 306 change But see *to* See also.

Add to end of note 306.

; Duvall et al., "Married or Just Living Together: The Consolidated vs. Seperate Choice For Affiliated Groups," 102 Tax Notes 379 (Jan. 19, 2004).

¶ 13.41 ELIGIBILITY AND ELECTION TO FILE CONSOLIDATED RETURNS

[1] Includible Corporations

Page 13-98:

Add to note 309, first paragraph.

Rev. Rul. 2001-39, 2001-33 IRB 125 (Rev. Rul. 70-379 held obsolete as of December 25, 1996, in view of change in Mexico law allowing direct foreign ownership of Mexican real estate).

Add to note 309, second paragraph.

But Notice 89-94 modified by Notice 2003-50, 2003-32 IRB 295 (stapled foreign affiliate will be treated as a domestic corporation for purposes of §§ 904(i) and 864(e) limitations). Prop. Regs. § 1.269B-1 (Sept. 7, 2004), implementing Notice 2003-50. Prop. Regs. § 1.269B-1 (Sept. 7, 2004), implementing Notice 2003-50; adopted without change by TD 9216 (July 29, 2005).

[2] Stock Ownership Threshold: § 1504(a)

[b] Voting "Power" and "Stock"

Page 13-101:

Add to end of first paragraph of note 322.

Carman, "Consolidation of SPEs in a World of Securitization: Have *INI* and *Alumax* Changed the Rules?" 97 J. Tax'n 334 (Dec. 2002).

Page 13-103:

Add to end of first pararaph of note 326.

Rev. Proc. 91-71 updated by Rev. Proc. 2002-32, 2002-20 IRB 959.

Add to text at end of ¶13.41[2][b].

    IRS has issued recent guidance dealing with inadvertent value viola-tions,[328.1] which can be corrected by the group without terminating the mem-bers affiliation status.[328.2]

    [328.1] Notice 2004-37, 2004-21 IRB 947; infra   13.41[2][d].

    [328.2] There are 2 relief exceptions to the value requirement where IRS will not chal-lenge inclusion of the member in the consolidated return; the good faith exception of § 1504(a)(5)(C), § 3.02 of the Notice; and the § 1504(a)(5)(D) inadvertence exception in § 3.03, if no designated event listed in § 3.04 has occurred (seven are listed there, which indicate lack of good faith or inadvertence).

Page 13-104:

Add new §13.41[2][d].

[d] Regulations Dealing With the Value Requirement

    Notice 2004-37 was released in May 2004,[333.1] providing interim guidance pending adoption of regulations as to when a member will be treated as satis-fying the value requirement of § 1504(a)(2)(B). If the member qualifies for one of two interim relief rules, IRS will not challenge its inclusion in the con-solidated return: these exceptions are (1) the good-faith exception of § 1504(a)(5)(C); and (2) the inadvertence exception of § 1504(a)(5)(D) (pro-vided none of the seven "designated events" listed in § 3.04 of the Notice have occurred; which indicate lack of good faith or inadvertence.

    Section 3.01 deals with the scope of the Notice (which can be relied on until replaced by regulations); § 3.02 (the good faith exception) applies where initial value was determined in good faith; § 3.03 (the inadvertence exception), occurs where values of different classes of stock change and the change is not attributable to a designated event (seven of which are listed in § 3.04).[333.2] Sec-

---

    [333.1] 2004-21 IRB 947 (May 24, 2004).

    [333.2] These events indicate lack of good faith or inadvertence.

tion 4 of the Notice requests comments on various issues being considered by IRS in drafting the regulations.[333.3]

[333.3] These are (1) how broad should the relief be; (2) what evidence of good faith or inadvertence is sufficient; (3) how far off the mark is too much; (4) must the violation be cured and if so when; (5) how should the rules be applied to other value sensitive provisions?

[4] Election to File Consolidated Return

[a] In General

Page 13-107:

Add to note 344.

See also Falconwood Corp v. US, 60 Fed. Cl. 485, 2004-1 USTC ¶ 50,242 (Ct. Fed. Cl. 2004) (taxpayer lost affiliated group status as a result of integrated restructuring transactions; fatal mistake was downstream merger of parent into its subsidiary). But *Falconwood* was reversed by the Fed. Cir., 2005-2 USTC ¶ 50,597 (Fed. Cir. 2005) (Taxpayer qualified for the exception in Regs. § 1.1502-75(d)(2)(ii) (even though affiliation existed for only three hours) and step-transaction doctrine did not apply to override that exception, which on its face has no time limit). Comment by Raby & Raby, "A Funny Thing Happened on the Way to an S Corporation," 109 Tax Notes 199 (Oct. 10, 2005).

[b] Joint Liability; Tax-Sharing Agreements

Add to note 346, first paragraph.

Raby & Raby, "Non-Tax Aspects of Tax Sharing Agreements in Affiliated Groups," 95 Tax Notes 1491 (June 3, 2002).

Page 13-108:

Add to note 347 after first sentence.

Also, Regs. § 1.1502-77T (1988) (alternative agent procedures).

Add to note 347.

For conclusion of the *Interlake* common parent "identity" litigation, see Acme Steel Co., RIA TC Memo. ¶ 2003-118 (2003). New agency procedure regulations were proposed on September 26, 2000, in Prop. Regs. § 1.1502-77 (substantially revising the agency rules), and adopted in June 2002. See infra ¶ 13.46[2][d].

Add to text at end of ¶ 13.41[4][b].

The agency regulations were extensively revised in proposed regulations issued on September 26, 2000, and were adopted as final regulations on June 26, 2002.[347.1]

[347.1] TD 9002, adopting Regs. § 1.1502-77. See also Rev. Proc. 2002-43, 2002-28 IRB 99 (procedures for determining substitute agent for the group).

¶ 13.42 COMPUTATION OF CONSOLIDATED TAXABLE INCOME AND TAX LIABILITY: GENERAL OVERVIEW

[2] Outline of Consolidated Return Regulations Structure

[b] Consolidated Tax Liability

Page 13-112:

Add to note 370.

See United Dominion Indus., Inc. v. CIR, 208 F3d 452 (4th Cir. 2000) (single entity approach not available to compute § 172(f) losses; must go member by member); contra Interment Corp. v. CIR, 209 F3d 901 (6th Cir. 2000); comment, Lupi-Sher, "Circuits Split on Application of Consolidated Return Regs," 87 Tax Notes 1199 (May 5, 2000); Hyman, "*Intermet*: IRS Note Entitled to Deterence on 10-year Carryback Issue," 88 Tax Notes 685 (July 31, 2000). Certiorari was granted in *United Dominion* on November 27, 2000; see comment by Lupi & Sher, 89 Tax Notes 1216 (Dec. 4, 2000); Axelrod & Blank, "The Supreme Court, Consolidated Returns, and 10-Year Carrybacks," 90 Tax Notes 1383 (Mar. 3, 2001); Leatherman, "*United Dominion* and the Consolidated Return Regulations," 91 Tax Notes 1391 (May 21, 2001). The Supreme Court reversed *United Dominion* and held for the taxpayer, adopting the single entity view, 121 S. Ct. 1934, 532 US 822 (2001). Comment by Lupi-Sher, "High Court Clarifies Consolidated Return Regulations," 91 Tax Notes 1961 (June 18, 2001); Paul, "*United Dominion:* Implications for Attribute Reduction," 95 Tax Notes 262 (Apr. 8, 2002); Shepherd, "Consolidated Returns: The Right Result For the Wrong Reason," 100 Tax Notes 878 (Aug. 18, 2003).

Add to note 371.

But see cases supra note 370.

Add to note 372.

As to the intersection of AMT book income preference and consolidated return regulations, § 1.1502-47 (life-nonlife insurance groups), see State Farm Ins. Co., 119 TC 342 (2002) (in computing § 56(f) book income preference by life-nonlife insurance company filing a consolidated return, use single entitiy consolidated method, see *United Dominion*, supra note 370).

[3] Intercompany Transactions: General Overview

[a] In General

Page 13-115:

Add to note 386 after second sentence.

But see Northern Telcom, Inc., RIA TC Memo. ¶ 2001-108 (2001) (similar pattern to Rev. Rul. 85-133, but held to be a deferred intercompany sale by parent to its subsidiary).

[c] Interim Revisions of the 1966 Intercompany Transaction Regulations

Page 13-122:

Add after infra in first sentence of note 409.

¶ 13.42[4][c] (notes 453, 454);

Add to note 409.

But see Merrill Lynch & Co., 120 TC 12 (2003) (found § 302(b)(3) sale for cross-chain § 304 stock sales because linked to planned sale of target member stock under *Zenz* principles; thus, regulation fixes may not have been necessary if *Merrill* decision stands up, though IRS is probably wise not to take a chance here. Merrill Lynch was aff'd, 386 F3d 464 (2d Cir. 2004).

[d] Additional Limitations Under § 267(f)

Page 13-124:

Add to note 416.

Union BanCal was affirmed (one dissent), 305 F3d 976 (9th Cir. 2002) (Temp. Regs. were valid, and prospective change in final regs no help for taxpayer; IRS did not have to change retroactively).

[4] Intercompany Distributions

[a] In General: § 301 Distributions

Page 13-127:

In second line of runover text change "deduction" to "exclusion".

In note 429 change "§ 1.1502-11(a)(1)" to "§ 1.1502-11(a)(7)".

In note 429 change "dividends-received" to "consolidated dividends-received".

In second paragraph of note 430, last sentence, change "1966" to "1986".

[c] Distributing Corporation Gain or Loss

Page 13-134:

Add to note 453, first paragraph.

But see Merrill Lynch & Co., 120 TC 12 (2003); aff'd, F3d (2d Cir. 2004).

Add to note 455.

But Merrill Lynch & Co., 120 TC 12 (2003) (denied § 304 dividend treatment on cross-chain sale of member stock because linked to planned sale of target member stock under *Zenz* principles; thus § 302(b)(3) "sale" treatment applied, rather than the hoped for dividend); Merrill Lynch was aff'd, 386 F3d 464 (2d Cir. 2004).

[5] "Mirror" Subsidiary Acquisitions

[a] In General

Page 13-137:

Add to note 467, first paragraph.

Also unclear is how § 381 applied (if at all) to these transactions in view of the "single acquiror" rule of Regs. § 1.381(a)-1(b)(2)(i); see   14.21[2] and 14.21[3][c].

[c] Stock Disposition Loss Disallowance Rule

Page 13-139:

Add to note 470.

For revival of Notice 87-14 anti-duplication approach, see Notice 2002-18, 2002-12 IRB 644 (despite its defeat in *Rite Aid* and subsequent decision not to appeal, IRS will continue to challenge loss replication transactions by consolidated groups stemming from the same property in forthcoming regulations dealing with post *Rite Aid*, infra notes 484.1, 485.2, and 485.3; these regulations will be effective March 7, 2002). Schler, "Consolidated Return Disallowance: Conceptual Issues," 95 Tax Notes 899 (May 5, 2002) (extensive analysis of entire *Rite Aid* saga and its numerous implications).

For proposed regulations issued in response to Notice 2002-18, see Prop. Regs. § 1.1502-35 (the single-loss-only requirement). These proposals are "beyond-category" complex; they make one (this one) yearn for a return to LDR. See infra, end of this   13.42[5][c]. They were adopted as temporary regulations by TD 9048 on March 14, 2003, and as final regulations by TD 9254 on March 9, 2006.

Page 13-140:

Add to beginning of note 481.

Regs. § 1.337(d)-2(c) (1991).

Add to end of note 481.

The LDR regulations were upheld in Rite Aid Corp. v. US, 2000-1 USTC ¶ 50,429 (Fed. Cl. 2000). Collins et al., "Court of Claims Upholds Validity of Loss Disallowance Rules," 28 J. Corp. Tax'n 29 (May 2001); but *Rite Aid* was reversed on appeal, 255 F3d 1357, 2001-2 USTC ¶ 50,516 (Fed. Cir. 2001) (loss duplication limitation invalid as arbitrary and in violation of a specific statutory allowance, § 165). Notice 2002-11, 2002-7 IRB 526 (IRS concedes and will rewrite regulations).

Page 13-141:

Add to note 482.

See Rite Aid Corp. v. US, supra note 481, upholding the validity of the LDR regulations;but *Rite Aid* was reversed on appeal, 255 F3d 1357 (Fed. Cir. 2001).

Add to note 484.

The duplicated loss exception to the economic loss exception (namely, the LDR rule applies) was upheld in Rite Aid Corp. v. US, supra note 481. See Sykes, "Powerful New Arguments Against the Duplicated Loss Provisions of the LDR," 91 Tax Notes 465 (Apr. 16, 2001). Sykes, "*Chevron* Deference Not Due for Overboard Loss Disallowance Rules," 92 Tax Notes 1609 (Sept. 17, 2001). Appelate court agreed, reversing the lower court and invalidating the loss duplication limitation (and arguably even the entire LDR regulation as well), 255 F3d 1357 (Fed. Cir. 2001). See Sheppard, "Federal Circuit Invalidates Loss Disallowance Rule," 92 Tax Notes 334 (July 16, 2001); Salem, "It's Time to Creatively Deconstruct LDR," 93 Tax Notes 1111 (Nov. 19, 2001). Collins & Zywan, "*Rite Aid*— The Final Word on Loss Duplication Within a Consolidated Group," 29 J. Corp. Tax'n 5 (Mar. 2002); Silverman & Zarlenga, "*Rite Aid*: A Tough Pill for the Government to Swallow," 94 Tax Notes 1343 (Mar. 11, 2002); Schler, "Consolidated Return Loss Disallowance: Conceptual Issues," 95 Tax Notes 899 (May 6, 2002).

Add to text at end of item 2.

> But the final regulations added an anti-duplication rule (namely, the disallowed amount equals (1) the excess of the subsidiary's asset bases and NOL carryovers over (2) the subsidiary's gross stock value), but this provision was struck down by the Federal Circuit decision in the Rite Aid case.[484.1]

[484.1] Supra note 484. IRS conceded defeat in Notice 2002-11, 2002-7 IRB 526 (will rewrite regulations). Temporary stop-gap regulations reflecting *Rite Aid* were issued in TD 8984 on March 7, 2002; Regs. §§ 1.337(d)-2T, 1.1502-20T(i), and 1.1502-32T(b)(4)(v); also Notice 2002-18, 2002-12 IRB 644. See Schler, "Consolidated Return Loss Disallowance: Conceptual Issues," 95 Tax Notes 899 (May 6, 2002) (major analysis of LDR, *Rite-Aid*, and ensuing temporary regulations and Notice 2002-18); see also Vogel & Hering, "New Loss Disallowance Regulations—Welcome to the Age of Tracing," 96 J. Tax'n 327 (June 2002); Gordon et al, "The Saga Continues: New Interim Loss Disallowance Regulations," 29 J. Corp. Tax'n 3 (July 2002); Axelrod & Torosyan, "Loss Disallowance After *Rite Aid*: Deconstructing—'20'," 81 Taxes 377 (Mar. 2003).

These temporary regulations were adopted as final regulations by TD 9187, Mar. 3, 2005, infra note 485.20.

Page 13-142:

Add text to end of ¶ 13.42[5][c].

Following its defeat in the *Rite Aid* litigation, the IRS conceded that it would not appeal the Federal Circuit's decision,[485.1] but instead would issue interim regulations generally adopting a tracing regime pending further regulatory action.[485.2] Temporary "stop-gap" regulations were issued on March 7, 2002,[485.3] along with Notice 2002-18[485.4] promising more extensive regulations dealing with replicated losses in the future. The temporary regulations adopt a tracing regime for prospective sales after the date of the new regulations.[485.5] For prior transactions (pre-March 7), the taxpayers are given a choice of various options.[485.6] In any event the IRS will continue to challenge duplicated losses similar to the son-of-mirror transactions challenged in Notice 87-14.[485.7] In short, the current situation is fluid, unclear, and at best highly unstable here.[485.8]The March Temporary regulations were clarified by amendments

---

[485.1] Notice 2002-11, 2002-7 IRB 536, see supra note 484.1.

[485.2] Based on Regs. § 1.337(d)-2(c) (1991); for which see Regs. § 1.337(d)-2T (applicable to transactions on or after March 7, 2002, but without the full sale requirement of the 1991 regulations). Regs. § 1.337(d)-2T(c) were amended by TD 9119 (Mar. 18, 2004), easing the application of this rule by allowing expenses attributable to the recognition of built in gain (and thereby increasing the allowable stock loss amount). See Regs. § 1.337(d)-2T(c)(2) and the examples in § 1.332(d)-2T(c)(4).

[485.3] See supra note 484.1. These regulations (as subsequently modified) were adopted as final regulations by TD 9187, Mar. 3, 2005, infra note 485.20.

[485.4] 2002-12 IRB 644; see supra note 470.

[485.5] Viz., sales on or after March 7, 2002; Regs. § 1.337(d)-2T, supra note 485.2.

[485.6] Regs. § 1.1502-20T(i): These choices are (1) follow the Regs. § 1.1502-20 LDR regulations as written (an unlikely option), (2) apply the Regs. § 1.1502-20 LDR regulations without the loss duplication factor, or (3) apply Regs. § 1.337(d)-2T (the tracing regime). Also, buyer relief is provided in Regs. § 1.1502-32T(b)(4)(v) (waiver of carryovers to avoid negative IBA hits).

[485.7] See supra note 470. See Prop. Regs. § 1.502-35 (Oct. 18, 2002), and Regs. § 1.502-35T (Mar. 14, 2003). Regs. §1.1502-35T(f) were amended by TD 9118 (Mar. 18, 2004) by revising §§ 1.1502-35T(f)(1) and 1.1502-80T(c) to ease the loss disallowance and worthless stock loss rules. They were adopted as final regulations by TD 9254 on March 3, 2006.

[485.8] For comments, see Lupi-Sher, IRS Announces Replacement for Rules Invalidated in *Rite Aid*, 94 Tax Notes 1252 (Mar. 11, 2002); Sheppard, Treasury Addresses *Rite Aid*, Nixes Bank of America's Tax Plan for Bad Loans, 94 Tax Notes 1392 (Mar. 18, 2002); Collins & Zywan, supra note 484; Silverman & Zarlenga, supra note 484; Stratton, LDR Rules in State of Flux Following *Rite Aid*, 95 Tax Notes 325 (Apr. 15, 2002); Schler, "Consolidated Return Loss Disallowance: Conceptual Issues," 95 Tax Notes 899 (May 6, 2002); Vogel & Herring, supra note 484.1; Gordon, supra note 484.1 Axelrod, supra note 484.1.

adopted in May 2002.[485.9] Moreover, Congress has proposed (and adopted) legislation that will neutralize the *Rite-Aid* decision, and retroactively at that.[485.10]

To this witch's brew of complexity was added the proposed regulations issued pursuant to Notice 2002-18 on October 18, 2002, as Regs. § 1.1502-35.[485.11] The stated purpose of this proposal is simple enough: to prevent a group from obtaining more than one tax benefit from a single economic loss. Implementation of this principle, however, is another matter since the regime proposed by these regulations defies description; we leave for others the unenviable task of extracting meaning from this Rube Goldbergian regime.[485.12] Unfortunately, they were adopted as temporary regulations on March 14, 2003 and as final regulations on March 9, 2006.[485.13]

The IRS continued to refine the post *Rite-Aid* regulations by relaxing (somewhat) the loss disallowance and worthless stock rules of the temporary regulations.[485.14] Thus, Temp. Regs. § 337(d)-2(c) were revised to allow expenses attributable to recognized built-in gain (and thereby increase the amount of allowable stock loss),[485.15] while Regs. § 1.1502-35T(f)(1) were revised to clarify that losses will be allowed where there is no risk of duplication.[485.16] Finally, Regs. § 1.1502-80T(c) allow the group to claim a worthless

---

[485.9] TD 8998 (May 31, 2002) modified the March 2002 stop-gap regulations in §§ 1.337(d)-2T(a)(4) (netting allowed), 1.337(d)-2(T)(a)(4) (netting allowed), 1.1502-20T(i)(3)(V) (items taken into account in open years effect of election), and 1.1502-20T(i)(4) (time and manner of making election).

[485.10] See supra note 305.1. The Senate Finance Committee's charity bill, HR 7, Title VI A, § 631 (July 16, 2002), and Ways and Means Chairman Thomas's proposal HR 5095, Title I, § 123 (July 11, 2002), have identical proposals to overturn the reasoning, though not the result, of *Rite Aid*. The Senate version is now in HR 476, § 721, which passed the Senate on April 9, 2003. This legislation passed on October 22, 2004. The American Jobs Creation Act, § 844, P. L. 108-357.

[485.11] See Sheppard, "Treasury Officials Discusses Bank of American Regs," 97 Tax Notes 464 (Oct. 28, 2002); Stratton, "Officials Run Through Loss Disallowance Regs," 97 Tax Notes 583 (Nov. 4, 2002) (though not very helpfully); see also Mombrun & Johnson, "Loss Disallowance Post—*Rite Aid*: The IRS and Treasury Revisit the Treatment of Subsidiary Stock Losses," 81 Taxes 21 (May 2003).

[485.12] To date, few have risen to this challenge, but see infra note 485.13. It's almost enough to wish for a judicial revisitation of *Rite Aid* (and even a return to the LDR rules of the now-departed § 1.1502-20 regulations).

[485.13] TD 9048 (Mar. 14, 2003), adopting Regs. § 1.1502-35T (and effective for 2002 returns); TD 9254, adopting final regulations (Mar. 9, 2006). See Axelrod and Gordon, "The Traps and Pitfalls of the Consolidated Duplicated Loss Rules," 30 J. Corp. Tax'n 3 (July 2003); Yeats et al., "The Final Factor—Temp. Reg. 1.1502-35T Takes a New Approach to Barring Duplicated Losses," 98 J. Tax'n 263 (May 2003), and as final regulations on March 9, 2006.

[485.14] TD 9118 (Mar. 18, 2004).

[485.15] Regs. § 1.337(d)-2T(c)(2) and 1.337(d)-2T(c)(4).

[485.16] Regs. § 1.1502-35T(f)(1).

stock deduction under § 165 at the time that such subsidiary ceases to be a member of the group.[485.17]

Matters continue to shift and evolve in LDR land, the latest extension being the release of Notice 2004-58 and associated Temporary Regulations under § 1.1502-20(i)[485.18] on August 26, 2004. The Notice deals with acceptable methods for applying the LDR limits (adding a new one, the basis disconformity method) to the tracing rules under existing regulations (and recognizing the existence of other acceptable methods as well). The Notice also states that it is working on devising a revised single set of regulations to deal with the loss disallowance issues to implement the repeal of *General Utilities* in the context of the mandate of §337(d). Thus, this project is still very much a work in process and the LDR issue is far from finally resolved.[485.19]

The 2002 stop-gap temporary regulations (as clarified by subsequent amendments noted above) were adopted as final regulations on March 3, 2005,[485.20] without significant change. The IRS essentially punted here, leaving for further amendments another day when they will be revisited in an attempt to come up with a workable regime.[485.21] Until that time, the Notice 2004-58 (the "basis disconformity method") will also be an acceptable tracing method as well.[485.22]

[485.17] Regs. § 1.1502-80T(c).

[485.18] Notice 2004-58, 2004-39 IRB 520 (Sept. 15, 2004); and Temp. Regs. § 1.1502-20T(i)(4), § 1.1502-20T(i)(6) (extending the time for taxpayers to make, amend or revoke prior elections), TD 9154 (Aug. 26, 2004). See Sheppard, "Elect Your Subsidiary Loss," 104 Tax Notes 894 (Aug. 30, 2004).

[485.19] For comments on this generally untidy scene, see Faber & Axelrod, "Interim Administrative Resolution of Loss Disallowance Issues," 104 Tax Notes 625 (Aug. 9, 2004) (proposing an amnesty from LDR for taxpayers that have held an active subsidiary's stock for 5 years before its sale); Nelson & Peabody, New Interpretational of the LDR Regime: The Basis Disconformity and Presumption Models, 104 Tax Notes 943 (Aug. 30, 2004) (a general analysis of the LDR landscape).

For comments on Notice 2004-58, see Sheppard, "IRS Defends Loss Disallowance Replacement," 105 Tax Notes 154 (Oct. 11, 2004); Sheppard, "For Better or Worse With the Loss Disallowance Replacement," 105 Tax Notes 303 (Oct. 18, 2004); Bennett, "The Loss Disallowance Rule: A Moving Target," 82 Taxes 5 (Oct. 2004); Salem, "LDR: Light at the End of the Tunnel, 105 Tax Notes (Nov. 29, 2004); but contra is Schler, "LDR: What to Do?" 105 Tax Notes 1585 (Dec. 13, 2004). For a subsequent exchange of views between Salem and Schler, see 106 Tax Notes 491 (Jan. 24, 2005).

[485.20] TD 9187, adopting Regs. §§1.337(d)-2 (loss limitation rules), 1.1502-20(i) (Disposition or disqualification of subsidiary stock), 1.1502-32(b)(4)(v) (special rule for loss carryovers of a subsidiary acquired in a transaction for which an election under §1.1502-20(i)(2) is made), and 1.1502-32(b)(4)(vii) (special rules for amending waiver of loss carryovers from separate return limitation year) (all effective Mar. 3, 2005).

[485.21] See Sheppard, Elect Your Subsidiary Loss, Part 2, 106 Tax Notes 1129 (Mar. 7, 2005) (for a helpful summary of this mess).

[485.22] Regs. §1.1502-35T (the "anti-duplication" regime) has until March 14, 2006, to be adopted, revised, or reproposed). It was adopted as Final Regs § 1.1502-35 on March 9, 2006.

The latest development in the post-*Rite-Aid* regulatory saga occurred on March 13, 2006, when IRS adopted the temporary regulations virtually intact as final regulation § 1.1503-35 (just before they were set to sunset).[485.23] Adoption of these regulations, however, is slated to be a temporary "patch," since the preamble noted that they were working on a future revision of both Regulations §§ 1.337(d)-2 (The *General Utilities* repeal protection regulations) and 1.1502-35 (the anti-loss duplication rules), and intend to combine them in a single project (coming soon – one can hardly wait for this event).[485.24]

[485.23] TD 9254 (Mar. 13, 2006).

[485.24] One can only hope that matters will be simplified, at least to some extent, but past performance is not promising on this score. Perhaps they could just bring back § 1.1502-20 (the LDR regime) now that the *Rite-Aid* decision has been overturned by the 2004 Jobs Act. See Friedel, "Final Consolidated Return Regs. Preventing Loss Duplication: Worse Than Useless?" (Part 1), 33 Corp. Tax'n 3 (July 2006); and (Part 2), 33 Corp. Tax'n 3 (Sept. 2006).

[6] Accounting Methods and Inventory

[a] In General

Page 13-144:

Add to note 496.

But see Northern Telcom, Inc., RIA TC Memo. ¶ 2001-108 (2001) (seems contrary to Rev. Rul. 85-133).

[7] Treatment of Net Operating Losses

Page 13-148:

Add to note 516.

For different "views" of how the consolidated return rules apply in computing group losses, compare Old Dominion Indus., Inc. v. CIR, 208 F3d 452 (4th Cir. 2000) (member-by-member separate entity approach), with Interment Corp. v. CIR 209 F3d 901 (6th Cir. 2000) (single entity view); supra note 370. Certiorari was granted in *United Dominion* on November 27, 2000; see comment by Lupi & Sher, 89 Tax Notes 1216 (Dec. 4, 2000). Axelrod & Blank, "The Supreme Court, Consolidated Returns, and 10-Year Carrybacks," 90 Tax Notes 1383 (Mar. 3, 2001); Leatherman, "*United Dominion* and the Consolidated Return Regulations," 91 Tax Notes 1319 (May 21, 2001). The Supreme Court reversed *United Dominion*, 121 S. Ct. 1934 (2001), adopting the single entity view and holding for the taxpayer. Comment by Lupi-Sher, "High Court Clarifies Consolidated Return Regulations," 91 Tax Notes 1961 (June 18, 2001). Gordon, "Unbaking the Consolidated Cake: Deciphering the Impact of *United Dominion*," 28 J. Corp. Tax'n 3 (Nov. 2001); Paul, "*United Dominion*: Implications for Attribute Reduction," 95 Tax Notes 262 (Apr. 8, 2002).

Add text to end of paragraph.

For computation of NOL carryback refunds, see Regulations § 1.1502-78; for timing rules in filing claims by new members, see Temporary Regulations § 1.1502-78T.[517.1]

[517.1] TD 8919 (Jan. 4, 2001) (liberalized timing rule for claiming tentative carryback adjustments by new members of consolidated group), adopted as final regulations § 1.1502-78(e) by TD 8950 on June 22, 2001.

Page 13-161:

Add new ¶ 13.42[12] to text.

[12] Consolidated § 108: Regs § 1.1502-28

[a] In General

Inspired, most likely, by the widely noted bankruptcy proceedings in WorldCom/MCI,[574.1] the Service has finally seen fit to publish regulations (in temporary form)[574.2] dealing with the application of § 108 to consolidated groups. The new regulations apply the § 108(a) exclusion qualification rules

---

[574.1] See also infra 13.47[4][b], note 901.2, for proposed legislation inspired by this proceeding.

[574.2] TD 9089 (Sept. 4, 2003), issuing Regs. § 1.1502-28T (effective for debt discharges after Aug. 29, 2003). See Daley & Friedel, "Section 108 Attribute Reduction for Consolidated Groups—Part 1," 31 J. Corp. Tax'n 3 (Jan. 2004); Part 2, 31 J. Corp. Tax'n 13 (Mar. 2004); Requenez, "The Consolidated Group Diet – Atrribute Reduction and Other Lifestyle Changes," 100 J. Tax'n 198 (Apr. 2004); Requenez, "Consolidated Attribute Reduction and COD Income Fewer Tricks and Definitely No Treats," 101 J.Tax'n

on a separate entity (member-by-member) basis,[574.3] but the attribute reduction rules of § 108(b) that are triggered in the case of tax-exempt COD may be applied on a single-entity (or modified group-wide) basis in certain cases.[574.4] Adoption by IRS of this modified single-entity approach was heavily inspired by the Supreme Court's *United Dominion* decision.[574.5]

The regulations first reduce attributes of the formal debtor member before going to group attribute reduction, however.[574.6] Moreover, asset basis reductions under §§ 108(b)(5) and 1017 are confined generally to the debtor member's properties.[574.7] Only after these adjustments have been made does the attribute reduction regime switch into group reduction mode.[574.8]

These regulations were adopted as final regulations on March 22, 2005, as Regs. § 1.1502-28.

[b] Attribute Reduction Ordering Rules

After determining whether a debtor member (or members) are entitled to exempt COD income treatment (determined on a separate entity basis), the regulations establish a priority regime for reducing tax attributes of the debtor member and the group:[574.9]

1. First, all attributes (including SRLY losses) "attributable" to the debtor member (or members)[574.10] are reduced first (unlike proposed legislation that would first reduce attributes on a group-wide basis);[574.11]

2. To the extent one of the attributes so reduced its stock of the debtor member's lower-tier subsidiary, the "look-through" rules of § 1.1502-

---

204 (Oct. 2004). These regulations were adopted in final form by TD 9192, Mar. 22, 2005, Regs. § 1.1502-28.

[574.3] Regs. § 1.1502-28T(a)(1); final Regs. § 1.1502-28(a)(1) (same).

[574.4] Regs. § 1.1502-28T(a)(4); Regs. § 1.1502-28(a)(4) (same).

[574.5] United Dominion Inds., Inc. v US, 532 US 822 (2001).

[574.6] Regs. § 1.1502-28T(a)(2) (including the look-through rules for stock of lower-tier debtor subsidiaries in § 1.1502-28T(a)(3); Regs. § 1.1502-28(a)(2) and 1.1502-28(a)(3).

[574.7] Regs. §§ 1.1502-28T(a)(3)(ii) and 1.1502-28T(b)(3); Regs. §§ 1.1502-28(a)(3)(ii), 1.1502-28(b)(2) and 1.1502-28(b)(3).

[574.8] Regs. § 1.1502-28T(a)(4). Four detailed examples illustrating the attribute reduction regime are in § 1.1502-28T(c); Regs. § 1.1502-28(a)(4); 1.1502-28(c) added 3 more.

[574.9] As noted above, § 1.1502-28T(a)(1) calculates the insolvency exception of § 108(a)(1)(B) on a separate entity basis. See generally Sheppard, Sensible Consolidated Attribute Reduction Rules, 100 Tax Notes 1235 (Sept. 8, 2003); Regs. § 1.1502-28(a)(1) (same).

[574.10] Such attribution is made under the principles of Regs. § 1.1502-21T(b)(2)(iv); and § 1.1502-21(b)(2)(iv). Multiple debtor member attributes likewise precede group-wide adjustments. But if losses are not subject to the SRLY limitation, they will be subject to group reductions as well.

[574.11] Regs. § 1.1502-28T(a)(2); Regs. § 1.1502-28(a)(2).

28T(a)(3) will cause attribute reductions by the lower-tier member in that amount (and so on down the chain of lower-tier members, proceeding top-down);[574.12]

3. After the above adjustments, Regs. § 1.1502-28T(a)(4) then requires reduction of other members' consolidated attributes outside the debtor member's chain of subsidiaries; those members in the debtor member's chain (are the only member's subjected to the look-through adjustment rules);[574.13] but

4. Asset basis reductions, however, are member specific.[574.14]

The four examples in Regs. § 1.1502-28T(c) illustrate these provisions: Example 1 provides the base case situation (debtor member first, then group attribute reductions); Examples 2 and 3 deal with the look-through tiering down of stock basis reduction (Example 2 goes one step, Example 3 goes two); Example 4 involves multiple debtor members, exempt COD (and also notes that if exempt COD exceeds reducible attributes, such excess is permanently exempt and no further adjustments need be made).

The proposed regulations were adopted as final Regs. §1.1502-28 on March 22, 2005, by TD 9192 (effective on that date). No major changes were made in the final regulations, just refinements and clarifications. The final regulations added 3 examples to §1.1502-28(c), and incorporated various modifications of the temporary regulations and corresponding amendments referred to infra ¶ 13.42[12][c] into the special rules of §1.1502-28(b)(4)-(11).

[c] Corresponding Amendments

The temporary regulations also amend the ELA regulations of § 1.1502-19T, the apportionment rules of § 1.1502-21T(b), and the IBA rules of § 1.1502-32T:[574.15] The final March 2005 regulations adopted all of these rules.

1. *The ELA rules of § 1.1502-19.* The temporary and final regulations adopt a "proportional" ELA triggering rule here (include only the

---

[574.12] Regs. §§ 1.1502-28T(b)(1)(i) and 1.1502-28T(b)(1)(ii) (multiple debtor members). But Regs. § 1.1502-28T(b)(4) (Mar. 15, 2004) prevents multiplication of § 1245 taints in subsidiary stock and assets; Regs. §§ 1.1502-28(b)(1) and 1.1502-28(b)(4).

[574.13] Regs. § 1.1502-28T(a)(4). But if losses are not subject to the SRLY limitation, those losses are subject to group reductions as well. Final Regs. § 1.1502-28(a)(4).

[574.14] Regs. § 1.1502-28T(a)(4); Regs. § 1.1502-28(a)(4).

[574.15] Regs. §§ 1502-19T(b)(2) and 1502-19T(h)(2)(ii); 1.1502-21T(b)(2)(iv), 1.1502-21T(c)(1)(vii)(6), and 1.1502-21T(c)(1)(vii)(8); and 1.1502-32T(b)(3)(ii)(C)(2), 1.1502-32T(b)(3)(ii)(A), 1.1502-32T(b)(5)(ii), Ex. 4 (revised), and 1.1502-32T(h)(7), respectively.

The final regulations are §§1.1502-19(b)(2) and 1.1502-19(h)(ii); 1.1502-21(b)(ii) and (iv); 1.1502-21(c)(2)(vii) and 1.1502-21(h)(6); 1.1502-32(b)(1)(ii), 1.1502-32(3)(ii)(C)(1), 1.1502-32(b)(3)(iii)(A), 1.1502-32(b)(5), Ex. 4, and 1.1502-32(h)(7).

amount of exempt COD income that is not absorbed by attribute re-ductions);[574.16]

2. *The IBA adjustment rules.* The temporary and regulations allow an upward basis adjustment for exempt COD income to the formal debtor member's stock regardless of the location of attribute reductions (i.e., where attributes of other members are reduced (including those attributable to the common parent).[574.17] But the temporary (and final) regulations also limit the upward basis adjustment to the amount of exempt COD that causes a reduction in tax attributes of the group.[574.18]

3. *Apportionment of NOLs to members.* The NOL apportionment rules of § 1.1502-21(b) were amended to deal with situations where consolidated NOLs apportioned to a member are absorbed and when a subsidiary leaves the group.[574.19] These rules take into account the reduction of NOLs attributable to that member that occur as a result of debt cancellation by it (or any other member).[574.20]

4. *Subsequent revisions of temporary regulations.* Regs. § 1.1502-28T was modified on March 15, 2004,[574.21] and adopted as final regulations in the following manner:

   a. Multiplication of § 1245 taints through reductions in subsidiary stock and assets (e.g., under the look through rules) are prevented by Regs. § 1.1502-28T(b)(4);

   b. Reduction of basis of intercompany obligations under the matching rules is modified by two special rules; and

   c. To the extent any ELA is required to be taken into account, Regs. § 1.1502-28T(b)(6)(ii) provides that this income is included in the year in which the subsidiary realizes the excluded COD income.[574.22]

5. *Regulations on circular stock basis adjustments when there is excluded COD income.* Proposed Regs. § 1.1502-11(c) establishes a

---

[574.16] Regs. § 1.1502-19T(b)(1)(ii); § 1.1502-19(b)(1)(ii) (thus, the ELA income is stacked at the end of the § 108(b) attribute reductions). But see Regs. § 1.1502-28T(b)(6)(i) (Mar. 15, 2004) (timing of inclusion; year of realization of excluded COD); § 1.1502-19(b)(1)(ii).

[574.17] Regs. §§ 1.1502-32T(b)(3)(iii)(A) and 1.1502-32T(b)(5)(ii), Ex. 4(b).

[574.18] Regs. §§ 1.1502-32T(b)(3)(ii)(C)(1) and 1.1502-32T(b)(5)(ii), Ex. 4(c).

[574.19] Regs. § 1.1502-21T(b)(2)(iv); Regs. 1.1502-21(b)(2)(iv).

[574.20] See Regs. § 1.1502-21T(b)(2)(iv)(B)(2). Recomputations of attributions are required after such a member leaves the group.

[574.21] TD 9117 (Mar. 15, 2004), promulgating Regs. §§ 1.1502-13T(g)(3)(ii)(B), 1.1502-28T(b)(4), 1.1502-28T(b)(5), and 1.1502-28T(b)(6)(ii) adopted by the final regulations.

[574.22] Regs. §§ 1.1502-13T(g)(3)(ii)(B)(3) and 1.1502-13T(g)(3)(ii)(B)(4); final Regs. §§ 1.1502-13(g)(3)(i)(A) and 1.1502-13(g)(3)(ii)(B).

multi-step (nine successive computations) computation regime intended to avoid circular calculations when a subsidiary's stock is disposed of when it (or any other member) realizes excluded COD income. This will *not* be a fun experience (the regulations apply when there is both an actual disposition or a deemed disposition of subsidiary stock-their message appears to be—try not to let this happen in an exempt COD income year). They were adopted in the final regulations as Regs. § 1.502-11(c) (without significant change, unfortunately).

¶ 13.43 REVISED INTERCOMPANY TRANSACTION AND DISTRIBUTION RULES

[1] Introductory

Page 13-164:

Add to note 589.

But Prop. Regs. § 1.446-1(c)(2)(iii) would overrule the *General Motors* decision (namely, the § 1.1502-13 intercompany timing rules are a method of accounting); effective prospectively on November 7, 2001; these proposals were adopted without change by TD 9025 on December 16, 2002.

[2] The Basic Intercompany Transaction Regime: Matching and Acceleration Rules

[c] Key Regulation Examples

Page 13-168:

Add to note 607.

See also Friedel, "Intercompany Sales of CFC Stock...," 92 J. Tax'n 362 (June 2000).

[3] Transactions Involving Member Stock: Regulations § 1.1502-13(f)

[c] Boot in Intragroup Reorganizations

Page 13-170:

Add to note 616.

See also Prop. Regs. § 1.1502-13(f)(7), Ex. 3(b) (Oct. 2002) (revised to reflect anti-basis-shifting proposed regulations under § 1.302-5, discussed at ¶ 9.22[2] ("unused stock basis creates deferred potential loss deduction on various triggering events). But the proposed regulations were withdrawn for further study on April 19, 2006.

[d] Other Transactions (Redemptions and Liquidations)

Add to note 618, first paragraph.

For dividend equivalent redemptions of lower-tier member stock which create an ELA in the redeemed stock, see Prop. Regs. §§ 1.1502-19(b)(5) and 1.1502-19(g), Ex. 7 (Oct. 2002) (this ELA amount is a potential ordinary income item that will be triggered under the proposed Regs. § 1.302-5 rules, 9.22[2], infra 13.44[3]). But the proposed regulations were withdrawn for further study on April 19, 2006.

Page 13-171:

Add to note 623.

See Sneet, Miniminzing Taxable Gain in Section 338(h)(10) Stock Sales (explication of the § 338(h)(10) relief rule, with examples).

Add to note 624.

See generally re these regulations, Friedel, "Whither the Group's Election? Certain Elections May Terminate When a Consolidated Group Goes out of Existence," 27 J. Corp. Tax'n 223 (2000), reprinted in 88 Tax Notes 1163 (Aug. 28, 2000); Friedel, "Intercompany Sales of CFC Stock—Where Does Reality End and Wonderland Begin?" 92 J. Tax'n 362 (June 2000).

Page 13-172:

Add text to end of ¶ 13.43[3][d].

Proposed regulations issued on February 22, 2005, modify the successor rules of §1.1502-12(j) to allow successor treatment (and hence continued deferral) for the deferred intercompany items of the liquidating member (including gain or loss generated in its liquidation) because matching can continue in the distributee members. This result will apply even if there is no 80-percent distributee.[625.1] Both proposals reflect single entity principles.[625.2]

[625.1] Prop. Regs. §§ 1.1502-13(j)(2)(ii) and 1.1502-13(j)(9), revised Exs. 6 and 7; also § 1.1502-80(g) provides a § 381-like regime for successor distributes (even though there is no 80-percent distributee member).

[625.2] See Prop. Regs. § 1.1502-13(j)(9), Ex. 7 (as revised); see also § 1.1502-80(g) (proposed carryover regime for successor member distributees.)

[e] Common Parent Stock: Regulations § 1.1502-13(f)(6)

Page 13-172:

Add to note 628.

But this exception was supplanted by Regs. § 1.1032-3, infra note 629.

Add to note 629.

Final regulations under § 1.1032-3 were adopted by TD 8883 on May 16, 2000 (and supplanted the gain nonrecognition rule of Regs. § 1.1502-13(f)(6)(ii) prospectively).

Add text to end of ¶ 13.43[3][e].

But these per se loss disallowance regulations may be vulnerable to attack under the Federal Circuit decision in *Rite Aid* which invalidated the loss disallowance regulations of § 1.1502-20.[632.1]But legislation pending in both houses of Congress proposes to neutralize the *Rite Aid* decision and this provision passed in October 2004.[632.2]

[632.1] Rite Aid Corp. v. US, 255 F3d 1357, 2001-2 USTC ¶ 50,516 (Fed. Cir. 2001); Sheppard, "Federal Circuit Invalidates Loss Disallowance Rule," 92 Tax Notes 334, at 338 (July 16, 2001); Sykes, "*Chevron*, Deference Not Due for Overboard Loss Disallowance Rules," 92 Tax Notes 1609 (Sept. 17, 2001); Salem, "Its Time to Creatively Deconstruct LDR," 93 Tax Notes 1111 (Nov. 19, 2001).

[632.2] See supra note 485.10. American Jobs Creation Act of 2004, § 844 amending § 1502; Pub. L. No. 108-357.

[4] Transactions Involving Member Debt: Regulations § 1.1502-13(g)

[b] Intercompany to Nonintercompany Status Shifts

Page 13-174:

Replace the parenthetical phrase of last sentence of first paragraph of note 637 with the following:

(which moved the "premium" alternative in the proposed regulations at Example (1)(d) of Regs. § 1.1502-13(g)(6) of the proposals to a new location without change).

[5] Other Aspects of the Regulations

[b] Miscellaneous Operating Rules: Regulations § 1.1502-13(j)

Page 13-176:

Add to note 644, second paragraph.

See generally Friedel, "Whither the Group's Election? Certain Elections May Terminate When a Group Goes out of Existence," 27 J. Corp. Tax'n 223 (2000), reprinted in 88 Tax Notes 1163 (Aug. 28, 2000).

Add to note 645.

But see Friedel, supra note 644.

Page 13-76:

Add text to end of ¶ 13.43[5][b].

Proposed regulations issued on February 22, 2005,[646.1] modify and expand the successor rules of § 1.1502-13(j) to allow successor treatment (and hence continued deferral) for deferred intercompany items of a liquidating members, (including gain or loss generated by its liquidation) because matching can continue in the distributee members. This result will apply even though there is no direct 80-percent distributee members.[646.2] Both of these proposals reflect single entity principles.

[646.1] Prop. Regs. §§ 1.1502-12(j)(2)(ii) and 1.1502-13(j)(9), revised Exs. 6 and 7; also § 1.1502-80(g) (a § 381 type carryover regime for successors).

[646.2] Prop. Regs. §§ 1.1502-13(j)(9), Ex. 7 and § 1.1502-80(g).

Add new ¶ 13.43[6].

[6] Consolidated Groups and § 265(a)(2) Interest Disallowance

In May 2004, IRS issued proposed regulations dealing with the potential disallowance of interest deductions by consolidating groups under § 265(a)(2),[647.1] and issued a Revenue Ruling[647.2] with various § 265(a)(2) scenarios. The IRS also announced a proposed regulation project under § 7701(f), the multi-party financing transaction provision, as applied to § 265(a)(2) and § 246A.[647.3]

[647.1] Prop. Regs. § 1.265-2(c) (May 7, 2004). Sheppard, "Virtual Repeal of Disallowance For Carrying Tax-Exempts," 106 Tax Notes 894 (Feb. 21, 2004).

[647.2] Rev. Rul. 2004-47, 2004-21 IRB 941; see also H. Enterprise Int'l v. CIR, 183 F3d 907 (8th Cir. 1999). Seago and Schnee, "Determining Interest Expense Incurred by Affiliated Corporations to Earn Tax-Exempt Income," 102 J.Tax'n 299 (May 2005).

[647.3] As to § 246A, see OBH, Inc. v. US, 2005-2 USTC   50,627 (DC Neb. 2005) (taxpayer prevailed on § 246A issue: loan proceeds not traceable to stock purchases; *H. Enterprises* case distinguished; big win for Warren Buffett and Berkshire Hathaway); Comments by Willens, Viewpoint, Daily Tax Rep. (BNA) No. 211, at J-1 (Nov. 12,

2005); Cummings, "IRS Tries to Apply DRD Limits to the King—and Fails," 109 Tax Notes 1191 (Nov. 28, 2005); Leeds, "Berkshire Hathaway Successfully Litigates DRD Controversy," 109 Tax Notes 1345, Dec. 12, 2005).

See generally ¶ 5.05[7][d].

¶ 13.44 REVISED INVESTMENT BASIS ADJUSTMENT SYSTEM AND RELATED PROVISIONS

[2] Investment Basis Adjustments Rules: Regulations § 1.1502-32

[a] In General

Page 13-180:

Add to note 658.

Query the impact here of the Supreme Court's decision in Gitlitz v. CIR, 531 US 206, 121 S. Ct. 701 (2001) (shareholders of S corporation allowed basis step up to their stock for tax-exempt COD corporate-level income). Regulations may be vulnerable here, since they were based on the subchapter S model. But *Gitlitz* decision overturned by legislation in March 2002. But Congress is proposing to reassert Treasury's dominance in writing § 1502 regulations, supra note 305.1 (and did so in 2004 legislation).

[3] Excess Loss Accounts: Regulations § 1.1502-19

Page 13-183:

Add to text at end of ¶ 13.44[3].

Regulations proposed in October 2002[675.1] amend the ELA regulations of § 1.1502-19 to deal with the case of lower-tier member stock redemptions (that always result in dividend equivalency because of § 318 attribution) which transaction create (or increase) an ELA in the redeemed stock. These proposals implement the anti-basis shift proposed regulations of § 1.302-5,[675.2] under which "unused basis" in the redeemed stock (in this case the newly created ELA) is deferred until a later triggering event.[675.3] The wisdom of this proposal is dubious at best. But the proposed regulations were withdrawn for further study on April 19, 2006.

[675.1] Prop. Regs. §§ 1.1502-19(b)(5) and 1.1502-19(g), Ex.7.

[675.2] See ¶ 9.22[2].

[675.3] Either on a final inclusion date (or an accelerated inclusion date). See new Example 7 in Regs. § 1.1502-19(g) (which illustrates the final inclusion date trigger).

[4] Earnings and Profits: Regulations § 1.1502-33

Page 13-184:

Add to the end of the first paragraph of note 679.

Collins, Cordonnier & Zywan, "Allocation of E&P in a Spin-Off by a Consolidated Group," 28 J. Corp. Tax'n 11 (Nov. 2001).

[5] Other Changes

Page 13-184:

Add text at end of item 1.

But proposed regulations issued in July of 2003 and adopted in April 2004, modify these regulations by allowing the parent to retain its separate cost basis for subsidiary stock acquired in a taxable transaction, thereby curing an inappropriate result that arose under the former regulations.[683.1]

[683.1] Prop. Regs. §§ 1.1502-31(c)(2), 1.1502-31(d)(2)(ii), and 1.1502-31(g), Exs. 1, 2, and 3 (in the latter example *P* retains the cost basis in *T* stock that was acquired in a taxable transaction); adopted without material change by TD 9122 on April 24, 2004.

Page 13-185:

Add to note 688.

Query the validity of these statutory "carve-outs" in Regs. § 1.1502-80 in light of Rite Aid Corp. v. US, 255 F3d 1357 (Fed. Cir. 2001), supra   13.42[5][c], which struck down portions of the loss disallowance rules in Regs. § 1.1502-20. But see pending legislation on this issue; supra notes 305.1 and 485.10, which was adopted on October 22, 2004, § 844 of the American Job Creation Act of 2004.

Add to end of item 4b.

Proposed regulations issued on November 14, 2001, amend Regs. § 1.1502-80(d) to clarify that the § 358(d)(2) exception to § 358(d)(1) basis reduction rule for § 357(c)(3) disregarded liabilities will apply here (see new Example 2); this change was needed to prevent an inappropriate double basis reduction (once on an assumption, and again when the transferee deducts it).[691.1]

[691.1] Prop. Regs. §§ 1.1502-80(d)(1) and 1.1502-80(d)(2), Ex. 2.

[7] Examples

Page 13-187:

Add to note 696.

Regs. §§ 1.1502-32(c)(5), Ex. 3(h), 1.1502-32(c)(4)(ii). Example 3(d) is the adjustment if a single-class-of-stock rule.

Page 13-189:

Add to end of first paragraph of note 701.

But Rite Aid Corp. v. US, 255 F3d 1357 (Fed. Cir. 2001), invalidated the LDR regulations' duplicated loss rule (and possibly even the entire LDR regulation); Notice 2002-11, 2002-7 IRB 526 (IRS will not appeal; will try to fix the regulations, for which see supra ¶ 13.42[5][c]). But Notice 2002-18, 2002-12 IRB 644 (will still fight son-of-mirror double losses). For "stop-gap" regulations dealing with post *Rite Aid* situations, see supra notes 485.1 and following (namely, 485.2, 485.3, 485.4, 485.5, 485.6, 485.7 and 485.8). For legislation to neutralize *Rite Aid* decision, see note 485.10. See also Prop. Regs. § 1.1502-35, implementing Notice 2002-18, supra note 485.11, adopted as Regs. § 1.1502-35T on March 14, 2003, and as Regs. § 1.1502-35 on March 9, 2006.

¶ 13.45 LIMITATIONS ON APPLICATION OF CONSOLIDATED RETURN PRINCIPLES: SEPARATE TO CONSOLIDATED RETURN AND ENTRY OF NEW MEMBERS

[4] Other Limitations on Inbound Transactions

[b] Tax Reform Act of 1986

Page 13-200:

Add the following to the end of ¶ 13.45[4][b].

IRS proposed a major overhaul of the dual consolidated loss regulations in May 2005 effecting many significant changes (largely, though not totally, for the better).[749.1] Final regulations under § 1503(d) were issued on March 16, 2007.[749.2]

[749.1] Prop. Regs. §1.1503-5 (the preamble is nearly as long as the regulations, which have 52 examples). Enlightenment on this complex subject will have to be sought elsewhere. See, e.g., Frost, "Dual Consolidated Loss Regulations—IRS Finally Updates the Rules," 103 J.Tax'n 174 (Sept. 2005); NYSBA Tax Section, "The Proposed Dual Consolidated Loss Regulations," 110 Tax Notes 369 (Jan. 23, 2006); ABA Tax Section, "Dual Consolidated Loss Regs; Suggested Modifications," 113 Tax Notes 993 (Dec. 11, 2006).

[749.2] TD 9315 (Mar. 19, 2007); for comments, see *Nadal*, 114 Tax Notes 1207 (Mar. 26, 2007).

[6] Amendments to SRLY and Built-In Loss Rules

[c] Other Modifications to SRLY Rules

Page 13-207:

Add to note 784.

Final regulations were adopted by TD 8884 on May 25, 2000 (including the overlap rule of the 1999 regulations discussed previously).

Add to note 785.

Final Regs. §§ 1.1502-3(c), 1.1502-3(d), 1.1502-4(f)(3), 1.1502-4(g)(3), 1.1502-21(c)(2), and 1.1502-55(h)(4)(iii) were adopted May 25, 2000.

Add to note 787.

Final Regs. §§ 1.1502-4(f) and 1.1502-4(g) were adopted May 25, 2000.

Page 13-208:

Add to note 793 at end of second paragraph.

For comment on the final regulations, see Brown, "Final Regs. Ease FTC Limitations for Consolidated Groups," 11 J. Int'l Tax'n 18 (Mar. 2000).

¶ 13.46 CONSOLIDATED TO SEPARATE RETURN; EXIT OF MEMBERS AND OTHER LIMITATIONS APPLICABLE TO CONSOLIDATED GROUPS

[1] Rules Applicable for Consolidated to Separate Return: Outbound Transactions

[a] In General

Page 13-211:

Add to note 801.

Query the impact of Supreme Court's decision in Gitlitz v. CIR, 531 US 206, 121 S. Ct. 701 (2001) (allowing S corporation's shareholders a stock-basis step-up for exempt COD corporate-level income). But Congress overturned this decision in March 2002.

Page 13-212:

Add to note 803.

Blanchard et al., "The Deductibility of Investment in Financially Troubled Subsidiaries and Related Federal Income Tax Considerations," 80 Taxes 91 (Mar. 2002); Paul, "*United Dominion*: Implications for Attribute Reduction," 95 Tax Notes 262 (Apr. 8, 2002) (single-entity vs. separate-entity treatment for § 108(b) adjustments); Bennett, "Corporate Tax Watch: Code Sec. 165(g): Under the Microscope," 81 Tax 11 (Feb. 2003); Sheppard, "When Do Subsidiary Shares Become Worthless?" 100 Tax Notes 746 (Aug. 11, 2003); Sheppard, "Consolidated Returns: The Right Result For the Wrong Reason," 100 Tax Notes 978 (Aug. 18, 2003); Temp. Regs § 1.1502-28T, and final Regs. § 1.1502-28, supra ¶ 13.42[12].

[2] Other Limitations on Survival of Corporate Tax Attributes Applicable to Affiliated Groups

[b] Removals From the § 1502 Regime

Page 13-217:

In second line of text after 1992 *add* (and adopted in 1994).

Add new note 828.1 to end of third line of text.

[828.1] But query the validity of these statutory removals in light of Rite Aid Corp. v. US, 255 F3d 1357 (Fed. Cir. 2001), supra ¶ 13.42[5][c]. But see pending legislation to neutralize *Rite Aid*, supra note 485.10 (which passed in 2004).

Page 13-218:

Add to note 832.

But see Rite Aid Corp. v. US, supra note 828.1.

Add new ¶ 13.46[2][d].

[d] Termination of Consolidated Group Existence [New]

A consolidated group will terminate when it no longer has a common parent or its common parent is acquired in a nonreverse acquisition transaction.[835.1] As previously noted, the regulations generally do not trigger deferred

---

[835.1] Regs. § 1.1502-75(d). Moreover, Prop. Regs. § 1.1502-77, issued on September 26, 2000, extensively revise the common parent agency rules. The current regulations were causing significant "identity" problems where the parent ceased to be the common parent of the group. Also, the proposed regulations spell out the scope of the parent's authority to act for the group. Prop. Regs. §§ 1.1502-77(d) and 1.1502-77(e) deal with common parent status changes; also, eight examples are provided in § 1.1502-77(f). These regulations became final in TD 9002, June 28, 2002. See also Rev. Proc. 2002-43, 2002-28 IRB 99 (procedures for determining substitute agent for the group).

intercompany gains or losses or excess loss accounts if there is an appropriate "successor group."[835.2] However, numerous other elections of the group may cease when the group's consolidated return existence ends (including those cases where the IRS, in its discretion, allows the filing of separate returns).[835.3]

[835.2] Regs. §§ 1.1502-13(j)(5) (see supra ¶ 13.43[5][b]), 1.1502-19(c) (see supra ¶¶ 13.42[6][b], 13.44[3]). See also Regs. § 1.1502-13(j)(6) (last "survivor" rule inherits).

[835.3] See generally Friedel, "Whither the Group's Election? Certain Elections May Terminate When a Group Goes out of Existence," 27 J. Corp. Tax'n 223 (2000), reprinted in 88 Tax Notes 1163 (Aug. 28, 2000).

See also Prop. Regs. § 1.1502-77, issued on September 26, 2000, dealing with common parent agency issues including termination of common parent status and termination of common parent existence. These regulations became final in TD 9002 on June 28, 2002. For conclusion of the *Interlake* common parent identity litigation following a corporate restructuring (where two alleged parents laid claim to the group's NOLs), see Acme Steel Co., RIA TC Memo. ¶ 2003-118 (2003).

¶ 13.47 APPLICATION OF § 382 TO CONSOLIDATED GROUPS

[1] General Overview

Page 13-221:

Add to note 848, first paragraph.

Sheppard, "When Do Subsidiary Shares Become Worthless?" 100 Tax Notes 746 (Aug. 11, 2003); ¶ 13.47[4][b], note 901.1.

[3] Special Rules: New Members, Departing Members, and Related Rules

[b] Departing Members: Regulations § 1.1502-95

Page 13-227:

In note 887, change cite from Regs. § 1.382-8(d) to 1.382-5(d).

[4] Other Aspects

[b] Insolvency Proceedings: Regulations § 1.1502-97

Page 13-230:

Add to note 900.

Paul, "*United Dominion*: Implications for Attribute Reductions," 95 Tax Notes 262 (Apr. 8, 2002) (single-entity vs. separate-entity approach).

Add to text at end of ¶ 13.47[4][b].

But proposed legislation in both the House and Senate would require that all tax attribute reductions under § 108(b) for exempt COD of a consolidated group must be netted at the consolidated corporate level.[901.1] For a similar approach see Temp. Regs. § 1.1502-28T[901.2] which, however, reduces the debtor member's attributes before turning to group attribute reductions.[901.3]

[901.1] HR 2706 and S. 1331, adding new § 108(b)(6) (effective June 25, 2003). See Sheppard, "Consolidated Returns: Right Result For the Wrong Reason," 100 Tax Notes 878 (Aug. 18, 2003). See also Regs. § 1.1502-28T (Aug. 9, 2003), issued by TD 9089 (Sept. 4, 2003) (adopting a modified single entity approach); Sheppard, "Sensible Consolidated Attribute Reductions," 100 Tax Notes 1235 (Sept. 8, 2003); supra   13.42[2].

[901.2] TD 9089 (Sept. 4, 2003, effective Aug. 29, 2003), supra   13.42[12].

[901.3] See Sheppard, "Sensible Consolidated Attribute Reduction Rules," 100 Tax Notes 1235 (Sept. 8, 2003); Sheppard, "ABA Tax Section Mulls Over Consolidated Attribute Reduction," 100 Tax Notes 1645 (Sept. 29, 2003). These temporary regulations were adopted in final form by TD 9192 on March 22, 2005); supra   13.42[12].

[5] Examples

Page 13-231:

In Example 3, parenthetical change disregarding *to which reflects.*

In note 909, change § 1.1502-96(a) to the following.

§§ 1.1502-93(a) and 1.1502-93(b).

Add to note 909.

Also include the value of member stock held by nonmembers, including § 1504(a)(4) stock; see Regs. § 1.1502-93(b)(3), Exs. 1 and 2.

¶ 13.48 REORGANIZATIONS INVOLVING CONSOLIDATED GROUPS

[1] In General

Page 13-233:

Add to note 916.

Paul, "Triple Taxation," 56 Tax Law. 571 (2003). But the Joint Committee Staff's April 2001 simplification report proposes to extend § 368(a)(2)(C) drop-down protection to Type D and Type F reorganizations; Proposal IV. F., at 261. But IRS allowed § 368(a)(2)(C) drop-down protection for Type D reorganization in Rev. Rul. 2002-85, 2002-52 IRB 986, without waiting for a statutory amendment; the reasoning of the rule seems equally applicable to Type Fs (though ruling does not mention these transactions).

Cummings, "Why Didn't Rev. Rul. 2002-85 Mention the Step Transaction Doctrine?" 98 Tax Notes 421 (Jan. 21, 2003). Bennett, "Contributions to Controlled Corporations Following Acquisitive Code Sec. 368(a)(1)(D) Reorganizations," 82 Taxes 9 (June 2004). But Prop. Regs. § 1.368-2(k) (Mar. 2, 2003) extends drop-down protection for *all* § 368 reorganizations; withdrawn and reissued Aug. 17, 2004, in revised and liberalized form (allow push-ups as well as drop-downs) (infra ¶ 13.48[3]).

[2] Intragroup Restructures—Rearrangement of Members

[a] "Downstream" Transfers

Page 13-234:

Add text to end of first paragraph of ¶ 13.48[2][a].

But the 2004 Jobs Act[919.1] now bars built-in-loss replication on § 351 drop-downs.

[919.1] American Jobs Creation Act of 2004, § 836, new § 362(e)(2) (effective Oct. 22, 2004). But the parties can elect to step-down outside stock basis in lieu of inside asset basis. See ¶¶ 3.11[8], 14.47[6][c], and 15.85[7][e].

[b] Lateral Transfers

Page 13-235:

Add to note 921.

See also Rev. Rul. 2004-83, 2004-32 IRB 921 (sale of stock to sister sub followed by integrated liquidation of target held a Type D reorganization (even where no consolidated return and § 304 overlapped—but D trumped).

Add to text at end of first paragraph.

If the assets are sold for cash (or non-security debt), new temporary regulations[922.1] provide for non-divisive Type D reorganization treatment where stock in both corporations is owned (with attribution) in identical proportions by the same shareholders. Failure to issue and distribute additional stock is ignored since to do so would be a "meaningless gesture." Reorganization treatment here apparently will trump any otherwise applicable consolidated return rules.

[922.1] Regs. § 1.368-2T(l) (Dec. 19, 2006), TD 9303, effective Mar. 19, 2007. See ¶¶ 12.26[c], 12.63[4][b]. These regulations, in effect, codify the so called all-cash D reorganization.

In third line of second paragraph of text, change Code citation to § 368(a)(2)(D).

Add to note 923.

But see Regs. § 1.368-2T(l), supra note 922.1, for the non-divisive D reorganization possibility.

Page 13-236:

Add to note 926.

Leatherman, "Should Notice 2001-45 Apply to Basis Shifts Within a Consolidated Group?" 15 J. Tax'n Fin. Insts. 9 (Mar. 2002) (argues no); but IRS says yes. see supra 13.44[3], note 675.1.

Page 13-237:

Add to note 931.

Leatherman, supra note 926.

Add text to end of ¶13.48[2][b].

IRS has recently ruled (helpfully) that a parent's sale of S-1 stock to S-2, followed by an integrated liquidation of S-1 up to S-2 is a Type D reorganization (even in a nonconsolidated return case where § 304 could apply; but § 304 trumped by the D reorganization).[931.1]

[931.1] Rev. Rul. 2004-83, 2004-39 IRB 921.

[3] Tax-Free Acquisitions of New Members

Page 13-240:

Add to note 946, first paragraph.

But the Joint Committee Staff's simplification report of April 2001 proposes to extend § 368(a)(2)(C) drop-down protection to Type D and Type F reorganizations, Proposal IV. F., at 261. IRS acted without statutory amendment, however, in Rev. Rul. 2002-85, 2002-52 IRB 986 (drop-down in Type D reorganization protected by spirit of § 368(a)(2)(C) which is permissive, rather than exclusive or restrictive; this view seems equally applicable to Type F, though not mentioned in the ruling); Cummings, supra note 916; but see Prop. Regs. § 1.368-2(k) (Mar. 2, 2004) extending drop-down protection for *all* § 368 reorganizations. But the March proposals were withdrawn on Aug. 17, 2004, and reissued in revised and liberalized form, generally adopting a NYSBA proposal that protection be extended to some push-ups as well (see infra note 950.1).

Page 13-241:

Add text to end of ¶13.48[3].

New proposed regulations issued in March and August of 2004[950.1] further expand the protective scope of § 368(a)(2)(C), even allowing post-acquisition push-ups of target assets or stock[950.2] adopting a proposal by the NYSBA to this effect.[950.3]

[950.1] Prop. Regs. § 1.368-2(k) (Aug. 17, 2004); also allow drops to COBE-qualified partnerships as well as drops to controlled subs.

[950.2] Prop. Regs. § 1.368-2(k)(3), Exs. 2 and 6.

[950.3] NYSBA Tax Section, "Distributions Following Tax-Free Reorganizations," 103 Tax Notes 1297 (June 6, 2004).

[4] Tax-Free Disposition of Existing Members

[b] *Morris Trust* Transactions

Page 13-243:

Add to note 964.

But the 1999 proposals were revised and liberalized by new proposed § 1.355-7 in January 2001, these regulations were replaced with even more liberal temporary regulations on April 26, 2002, infra; final Regs. § 1.355-7 were adopted by TD 9198 (Apr. 19, 2005).

Add text to end of ¶ 13.48[4][b].

But temporary regulations adopted in April 2002[964.1] have gone a long way to "declaw" § 355(e); while still far from harmless, the revised regulations have turned § 355(e) into a much less fearsome provision, especially when compared with the 1999 version.

[964.1] Regs. § 1.355-7T (Apr. 26, 2002) (effective retroactively as well, if all parties are consistent). They were adopted as final regulations (and liberalized yet again); TD 9195 (Apr. 19, 2005). See Willens, Daily Tax Rep. (DTR) No. 83, J-1 (May 5, 2005).

[5] Group Membership "Contractions"

[a] Upstream § 332 Liquidations: The Anti–§ 351 "Roll-Up"

Page 13-245:

Add text to end of ¶ 13.48[5][a].

Liquidation of a lower-tier member with no direct 80 percent parent nevertheless can qualify for § 332 nonrecognition by virtue of the member stock aggregation rules of the regulations,[971.1] but the liquidating subsidiary will have gain recognition under § 337(c) on its distribution of built-in gain assets to any non-80 percent shareholders.[971.2] Asset basis will carry over to those distributees (but is stepped up to fair market value by the recognized, though deferred gain).[971.3] It is unclear, however, whether other attributes of the liquidating subsidiary will carry over under § 381 (and if so, to which of the distributee members and in what amounts).[971.4] The group could switch into pure § 332-§ 337(a)-§ 381(a) mode, however, by having the appropriate members recapitalize their respective interests into "disregardable" § 1504(a)(4) preferred stock leaving only one member with the 100-percent stock interest (and thus creating single parent status).[971.5]

This area was revisited by proposed regulations under the successor rules of §1.1502-13(j) issued on February 22, 2005.[971.6] These proposals again strongly reflect single entity principles especially the member attribute carryover rules in Proposed Regs. §1.1502-80(g).[971.7]

[971.1] See Regs. § 1.1502-34, supra   13.41[2][a], infra   13.48[6], Example 6.

[971.2] Such gain is a deferred intercompany transaction, however, under Regs. § 1.1502-13(b)(2)(D), subject to the matching rules of § 1.1502-13(c) and the acceleration rules of § 1.1502-13(d). Moreover, this deferred gain carries over to the distributees under the "successor" rules of § 1.1502-13(j)(2); see § 1.1502-13(j)(9), Ex. 7. For revised Ex. 7, see infra note 971.6.

[971.3] See Regs. § 1.1502-13(j)(9), Ex. 7.

[971.4] See Regs. § 1.381(a)-1(b)(2); see   10.21[5][b], 10.22[4], Example 6, 14.21[2], and 14.21[3][c]. But for a § 380 carryover regime, see Prop. Regs. § 1.1502-80(g), infra, note 971.7.

[971.5] Targeted distributions to the preferred stock holders (e.g., of cash or high basis assets) could avoid significant impact of § 337(c); moreover, the subsidiaries tax attributes would now clearly carry over to the only remaining "parent" under § 381(a)(1). See infra 13.48[6], Example 6.

[971.6] Prop. Regs. §§1.1502-13(j)(2)(ii), and 1.1502-13(j)(9), revised Ex. 6 and Ex. 7. The new examples provide for carryover of deferred intercompany items, and also for deferred gain or loss triggered by the liquidating distribution (both for an 80-percent parent distributees member and also for a less than 80-percent parent distributee member) with continued matching at the distributee level (see revised Ex. 7). Even more significantly, Prop. Regs. §1.1502-80(g) provides for §381 type attribute carryover treatment for each distributee member (whether it is an 80-percent parent or not).

[971.7] The preamble cites single entity principles as the reason for adopting these proposals.

---

[b] "Being" or "Nothingness": The Single Member Limited Liability Company Alternative

Page 13-246:

Add to note 975.

Prop. Regs. § 1.368-2(b)(1) (May 12, 2000) say not a direct Type A, nor is it a forward triangular Type A (apparently). But Prop. Regs. § 1.368-2(b)(1) (Nov. 15, 2001) changed here and now allow direct merger status under § 368(a)(1)(A); adopted as Temp. Regs. § 1.368-2T(b)(1) by TD 9038 on January 24, 2003; adopted as final regulations by TD 9242 (Jan. 23, 2006).

Add to note 976.

See ¶ 12.22[11]; Rev. Rul. 2000-5, 2000-5 IRB 436 (not a Type A; can only be divisive Type D); Prop. Regs. § 1.368-2(b)(1) (not a Type A because of divisive effect). The November 2001 revised proposed regulations continue to deny Type A status here, however, as do the temporary regulations adopted on January 24, 2003, and the final regulations were adopted on January 23, 2006. See Steinberg & Mendelson, "The Use of Partnerships and Disregarded Entities by U.S. Corporations, 81 Taxes 261 (Mar. 2003).

[6] Examples

Downstream transfers.

Page 13-247:

Add new item c. to the end of Example 1.

> c. But new § 362(e)(2), added by the 2004 Jobs Act, halts built in loss replication on asset drop-downs.[981.1]

[981.1] American Jobs Creation Act of 2004, § 836, effective October 22, 2004. But *P* and *S-1* can elect to step-down outside stock basis in lieu of inside asset basis step-down. See ¶¶ 3.11[8], 14.47[6][c], and 15.85[7][e].

Page 13-248:

Replace note 987 with the following.

> *P*'s basis for its *H* stock would be a substitute basis under § 358 (from the *S-1* and *S-2* Stock basis), while *H* would take a § 362 carryover basis for the subsidiaries stock; the special basis rule of Regs. § 1.1502-31 would not apply in this scenario, although *H* would have to replicate *P*'s E&P account under Regs. § 1.1502-33(f)(2).

Add to end of Example 3.

> d. The problem created in part (b) could also be fixed by having *S-2* exchange its *H* common stock for § 1504(a)(4) disregarded pre-

ferred stock of *H* (a tax-free recapitalization). But redemption of *H* stock by *S-1* or *S-2* would create a dividend equivalent redemption and a potential ordinary income ELA in the redeemed stock under the proposed §§ 1.1502-19(b)(5), 1.1502-19(g), Ex. 7.[990.1]

Upstream Stock Distributions.

[990.1] See supra   13.43[3][d], 13.44[3]. But these proposed regulations were withdrawn for further study on April 19, 2006.

Page 13-249:

Add to note 993.

The initial § 355(e) regulations have been successively revised (and greatly liberalized), however, and Regs. § 1.355-7T (Apr. 26, 2002) may well not find the statutory "plan" linkage here. They were adopted as final regulations by TD 9198 (Apr. 19, 2005).

Add to note 994.

But revised (and greatly liberalized) Regs. § 1.355-7T (Apr. 26, 2002) may not find the forbidden "plan" linkage here; same for final Regs. § 1.355-7 (Apr. 2005).

Page 13-250:

Add new Example 6.

> **EXAMPLE 6:** *Lower tier subsidiary liquidation—no direct 80-percent parent.* Assume additionally that *S-3* owns 60 percent of *S-5* and *S-4* owns the other 40 percent—*S-5* liquidates up into *S-3* and *S-4* (and *S-5* assets have a value of $200 and a basis of $100).
>
>   a. The liquidation qualifies for § 332 nonrecognition under the stock aggregation rule of the regulations,[997] but *S-5* has § 337(c) gain recognition of $100.[998]
>   b. *S-5*'s gain is deferred, however, and will carry over to *S-3* and *S-4* ($40 and $60 respectively) under the successor rules of Regs. § 1.1502-13(j)(2).[999]

---

[997] Regs. § 1.1502-34; supra   13.41[2][a].

[998] The 1997 anti-mirror amendment; supra   13.42[5][b].

[999] See Regs. § 1.1502-13(j)(9), Ex. 7 (deemed reciprocal cross-chain sales of the *S-5* assets between *S-3* and *S-4*). This deferred gain will be triggered under the matching and acceleration rules of §§ 1.1502-13(c) and 1.1502-13(d). But Prop. Regs. § 1.1502-13(j), Ex. 7 changes to a pure carryover regime here.

    c. It is unclear, however, whether (and to what extent) *S-5*'s other tax attributes carry over under § 381.[1000] But, if *S-4*'s stock was § 1504(a)(4) stock (disregarded stock), all of *S-5*'s tax attributes would carryover to *S-3*.[1001]

[1000] See supra ¶ 13.48[5][a]. The § 381 regulations presumably mandate a "single parent" limitation for carryover purposes and it is unclear whether the stock aggregation rule will provide this status. But see Prop. Regs. § 1.1502-80(g) (Feb. 22, 2005), infra.

[1001] Regs. § 1.381(a)-1(b)(2)(i). See ¶ 14.21[3][c].

Add new subpart d to Example 6.

    d. But regulations issued in February 2005 provide for carryover of the liquidating subsidiary S-5's tax attributes, both those generated as a result of the liquidation as well as other deferred intercompany items of S-5.[1002]

[1002] Prop. Regs. § 1.1502-80(g) (Feb. 22, 2005), citing single entity principles for this treatment. Also Example 6 and Example 7 in the successor regulations of § 1.1502-13(j) likewise switch to a pure carryover approach (rather than the cross-chain sale method of the current regulations Example 7).

CHAPTER **14**

Corporate Tax Attributes: Survival and Transfer

B　CARRYOVER ITEMS AND COMPUTATION MECHANICS: § 381(C)

¶ 14.21　SECTION 381(a) TRANSACTIONS

[2] Liquidation of Controlled Subsidiary: § 381(a)(1)

Page 14-22:

Add to text at end of ¶ 14.21[2].

Also, identity problems arise in the application of the § 381 carry over rules to § 332 liquidations of less than 80 percent directly owned subsidiaries

under the consolidated return stock aggregation rules.[52.1] There is technically a
§ 332 liquidation here, but only so by virtue of the consolidation return regulations; moreover, those regulations are overridden by § 337(c) as to the liquidating subsidiary, which is made taxable on any built-in gains attributable to
its distributed assets.[52.2]

[52.1] Regs. § 1.1502-34 (e.g., the former mirror subsidiary liquidation transaction effectively repealed by 1987 legislation and the 1991 LDR regulations of § 1.1502-20); see
13.42[5].

[52.2] See   10.22[3] and 13.42[5][b]. See also   13.48[5][a]. Moreover, Regs.
§ 1.381(a)-1(b)(2)(i) envisions only a single acquiring corporation for § 381 attribute carryover purposes (infra note 55) which regulations could be read to bar any carryover to a
less than direct 80-percent parent. But Prop. Regs. § 1.1502-80(g) (Feb. 22, 2005) allow a
§ 381 carry-over for consolidated groups under single entity principles of the regulations.

For example, P's two controlled subsidiaries X and Y jointly own subsidiary Z (50
percent each); if Z liquidates up into X and Y, § 332 applies to the co-parents in a consolidated return, but Z is taxable on built-in gain under § 337(c); moreover, § 381 may not
apply here in view of the regulation's single parent limitation. (But will apply in consolidation under the above proposed regulations).

[3] Reorganizations: § 381(a)(2)

[a] In General

Page 14-23:

Add to note 53, first paragraph.

Temp. Regs. § 1.108-7T (July 18, 2003) require any § 108(b) attribute reduction for exempt COD gain to be made *before* application of § 381 carryovers). Partially adopted in
final form on May 11, 2004, by TD 9127; Regs. §§ 1.108-7(c) and 1.1017-1(b)(4). See
Jones & D'Angelo, "Sections 108 and 1017 Regulations: Was It Really Too Much Candy
for the Nickel?" 31 Corp. Tax'n 3 (July 2004).

[c] Acquirer Identity: Triangular Reorganizations

Page 14-24:

Add new note 55.1 to end of Example 4.

[55.1] Similar identity issues arise where § 332 nonrecognition treatment arises solely
from the consolidated return stock aggregation rules of Regs. § 1.1502-34, supra note
52.1. See also the example in note 52.2. Also,   13.48[5][a] and 13.48[6], Example 6.
But see Prop. Regs. § 1.1502-80(g) (Feb. 22, 2005), supra note 52.2.

¶ 14.23 CARRYOVER ITEMS AND COMPUTATION MECHANICS: § 381(c)

[1] Net Operating Loss Carryovers

[a] In General

Page 14-29:

Add to note 73.

See also Prop. Regs. § 1.367(b)-3(e) (Nov. 8, 2000) (same); also Prop. Regs. § 1.367(b)-3(f) purges foreign-generated E&P (or deficits) at the border.

[2] Earnings and Profits

Page 14-33:

Add to text at end of ¶ 14.23[2].

    Carryover of earnings and profits in § 381 transactions involving foreign corporations is dealt with in Chapter 15, Part E, of this work.[89.1]

    [89.1] See ¶¶ 15.83[1][b], 15.83[3], 15.84[2][f], and 15.84[3][f]. Proposed regulations issued on November 8, 2000, deal with these rules: Prop. Regs. §§ 1.367(b)-3(e) and 1.367(b)-3(f) (inbound § 332 liquidations); 1.367(b)-7 (foreign-to-foreign § 381 transactions); 1.367(b)-8 (foreign divisive transactions); and 1.367(b)-9 (foreign Type F reorganizations and similar transactions).

[3] Accounting Methods

[c] Change of Accounting Method Required

Page 14-37:

Add text to end of ¶ 14.23[3][c].

Thus, a reorganization may be an occasion for the Service to require an accounting method change that could not otherwise be required.[97.1]

    [97.1] See, e.g., Ltr. Rul. 2001-52-028.

C   LIMITATIONS ON ENJOYMENT OF CORPORATE TAX ATTRIBUTES

¶ 14.41 ACQUISITIONS TO AVOID INCOME TAX: § 269

[2] Scope and Operation

[d] Expansion of Scope for Corporate Tax Shelter Transactions

Page 14-48:

Add to note 127.

For a strong critique of this proposal (which was reproposed in February 2000), see Kleinbard, "Corporate Tax Shelters and Corporate Tax Management," 51 Tax Exec. 231 (May/June 1999). See also Trier, "Beyond the Smell Test: The Role of Substantive Anti-Avoidance Rules in Addressing the Corporate Tax Shelter Problem," 78 Taxes 62 (Mar. 2000). To date (December 2006), nothing much has become of this proposal.

[3] Section 269 Transactions

[c] Tax-Free Asset Acquisitions

Page 14-50:

In item (4) of first full paragraph of text, after word basis, *add the following.*

that is dependent for its existence on a carry over rule for its basis;

[f] Corporate Tax Avoidance Transactions

Page 14-53:

Add to note 149.

This proposal was resubmitted in February 2000; for a critique, see Kleinbard, "Corporate Tax Shelters and Corporate Tax Management," 51 Tax Exec. 231 (May/June 1999). See also Trier, "Beyond the Smell Test: The Role of Substantive Anti-Avoidance Rules in Addressing the Corporate Tax Shelter Problem," 78 Taxes 62 (Mar. 2000).

[4] Forbidden Tax-Avoidance Purpose

[d] Corporate Tax Shelters: "Tax Avoidance Transactions"

Page 14-58:

Add to note 162.

For a critique of this proposal (which was resubmitted in February 2000), see Kleinbard, "Corporate Tax Shelters and Corporate Tax Management," 51 Tax Exec. 231 (May/June 1999). See also Trier, "Beyond the Smell Test: The Role of Substantive Anti-Avoidance Rules in Addressing the Corporate Tax Shelter Problem," 78 Taxes 62 (Mar. 2000).

[6] Corporate Tax Shelter Transactions: Denial of Benefits Obtained in a "Tax Avoidance Transaction"

[a] In General

Page 14-59:

Add to note 166.

Reproposed in slightly modified form in the Treasury's February 2000 budget plan. The new Treasury, however, has not pursued this proposal.

[b] Revised § 269: A General Anti-Abuse Rule

Page 14-60:

Add to note 172.

For a critique of this proposal, see Kleinbard, "Corporate Tax Shelters and Corporate Tax Management," 51 Tax Exec. 231 (May/June 1999). See also Trier, "Beyond the Smell Test: The Role of Substantive Anti-Avoidance Rules in Addressing the Corporate Tax Shelter Problem," 78 Taxes 62 (Mar. 2000). The new Treasury has not pursued this proposal, however.

Add to text at end of ¶ 14.41[6][b].

While expansion of § 269 has not gained favor with the new Treasury (or as yet with Congress), the chairman of the House Ways and Means Committee, Representative Thomas, introduced proposed legislation on July 11, 2002,[172.1] that would attempt to codify the "economic substance" doctrine and impose a strict liability penalty for transactions that fail to satisfy this requirement. Representative Thomas's bill borrows heavily from earlier proposals by Representative Doggett,[172.2] and also closely tracks anti-shelter legislation pending in the Senate which, however, initially did not, but now also does, propose to codify economic substance.[172.3] But Congress' interest in codification of eco-

---

[172.1] HR 5095, the American Competitiveness and Corporate Accountability Act of 2002, Title I, § 101, adding § 7701(m), and § 104, adding § 6662B (the strict liability penalty). See the Joint Committee Staff Technical explanation, reprinted in Daily Tax Rep. (BNA) No. 140, L-6 (July 22, 2002), at L-7. See ¶ 5.10[8][c].

[172.2] HR 2520; see Sheppard,"The Good and the Bad in the Thomas Bill," 96 Tax Notes 482 (July 22, 2002). See McMahon, "Beyond a GAAR: Retrofitting the Code to Rein in 21st Century Tax Shelters," 98 Tax Notes 1721 (Mar. 17, 2003). Keyes & Light, "Developments in the Economic Substance Doctrine," 20 J. Tax'n Invs. 284 (2003); NYSBA Tax Section, "Economic Substance Codification," 99 Tax Notes 829 (June 23, 2003); Hyde & Kohl, "The Shelter Problem Is Too Serious Not to Change the Law," 100 Tax Notes 119 (July 7, 2003). See ¶ 5.10[4][a]; Keinan, "The Profit Motive Requirement Under the Economic Substance Doctrine," 21 J. Tax'n Invest. 81 (Fall 2003).

[172.3] See ¶ 5.10[8][b]. This provision is currently in the Senate's charity bill, HR 476, § 701, adding new § 7701(m) (Clarification of Economic Substance Doctrine; Etc.), which passed the Senate on Apr. 9, 2003). It subsequently moved into the Senate's general 2003

nomic substance seems to have waned since Chairman Thomas's current omnibus tax bill anti-shelter proposals and the Senate's energy bill anti-shelter proposals do not contain such a provision.[172.4] But the proposal has resurfaced in pending Senate legislation, though it has yet to be adopted by the full Congress.

While passage of the Thomas bill was far from certain at this point, recent taxpayer victories in several tax shelter cases[172.5] coupled with the wave of corporate scandals during the spring and summer of 2002 did not hurt its chances. But it did not survive in the final 2004 legislation adopted on October 22, 2004. The election's change in control of Congress has significantly brightened the chances for enactment of this proposal, however.

[c] Proposed Expansion of § 269 (2003)

The Joint Committee Staff's Enron Report issued in February 2003 recommended expanding § 269 in the following manner:

1. Drop the control acquisition requirement of § 269(a)(1);
2. Drop the common control exception of § 269(a)(2); and
3. Drop the "would not otherwise enjoy" language (apparently an attempt to overrule the *Cromwell* decision).[172.6]

Thus, if so revised, § 269 would apply if any person acquires stock in a corporation or any corporation acquires property of another corporation in a carryover basis transaction and the principal purpose for such acquisition is tax avoidance, then IRS can deny the acquired tax benefit.[172.7] Needless to say, such a revision would greatly expand the scope of § 269.

The Senate did pass such a revision in its version of the 2003 tax legislation, but it did not survive in the final version of that legislation. It seems likely, however, that this proposal (and other Enron-related reforms) will resurface as a convenient revenue offset to other legislation.[172.8] But it did not sur-

---

tax reduction bill, HR 2, § 301, which passed the Senate on May 15, 2003, but was not included in the final 2003 legislation.

[172.4] HR 2896 (introduced July 25, 2003); HR 6 (which passed the Senate July 31, 2003).

[172.5] See   5.10[6][e].

[172.6] Supra   14.41[5]. The check-the-box election in Dover Corp., 122 TC 324 (2004), which resulted in the avoidance of Subpart F income as a result of the sale of its subsidiary after its deemed § 332 liquidation, would be clearly vulnerable under this proposal; see Peasley, *Dover* Done in by Senate ETI Bill, 103 Tax Notes 1412 (June 12, 2004). See also Daub, "Section 269(a) Across the Border—An Appraisal," 15 J. Int'l Tax'n 22 (Sept. 2004).

[172.7] The proposal is effective Feb. 13, 2003, the date of the release of the Staff's Enron report.

[172.8] Five days after passage of the 2003 tax Act, such a proposal was made (though not, as yet, adopted). It is also contained in pending Senate legislation, See Peaslee, "Revenue Raisers in the Senate Jobs Bill," 102 Tax Notes 621 (Feb. 2, 2004), at 639. But this vive in the 2004 export repeal legislation that passed on October 22, 2004; thus, another bullet was dodged.

---

provision likewise did not survive in the final legislation adopted on October 22, 2004. For the final 2004 legislation, see ¶ 5.10[8][d].

¶ 14.43 SECTION 382: CHANGE-OF-OWNERSHIP TRIGGER

[1] General Overview

Page 14-68:

Add to note 182, third paragraph.

Avent & Simon, "Preserving Tax Benefits in Troubled Companies Navigating Mostly Uncharted Waters," 102 J. Tax'n 176 (Mar. 2005).

[2] Definitions and Special Rules

[a] "Stock"

Page 14-70:

Add to note 186.

Bennett, "Valuing Stock For Ownership Changes," 83 Taxes 7 (June 2005).

Add to note 187.

See Hoffenberg, "Owner Shifts and Fluctuations in Valve: A Theory of Relativity," 106 Tax Notes 1446 (Mar. 21, 2005).

[d] Constructive Ownership Rules Generally

Add new note 193.1 to end of third line in text, end of (1).

[193.1] See Garber Inds. Holding Co., Inc., 124 TC 1 (2005) (brothers not aggregated as one shareholder; extensive analysis of § 382 "family" definition, which didn't save taxpayers from § 382(g) owner change on these facts; stock sales between siblings trigger owner change). See Raby & Raby, "Stock Ownership Attribution and Siblings," 106 Tax Notes 675 (Feb. 1, 2005); Cummings, "Something Old, Something New and Something Fairly New," 106 Tax Notes 1093 (Feb. 28, 2005). *Garber* was aff'd, 2006-1 USTC ¶ 50,109 (5th Cir. 2006). Willens, "When Siblings Are Regarded as Strangers," 110 Tax Notes 1099 (Mar. 6, 2006).

Page 14-72:

Add text to end of ¶ 14.43[2][d].

But stock owned by § 401 trusts as not subject to outbound attribution; however, recent regulations address this problem in a generally helpful way.[194.1]

[194.1] TD 9063 (June 27, 2003), issuing Regs. § 1.382-10T (treat distributions of stock by § 401 trusts to participants as if that stock was acquired on the same date and in the same way as the trust (this rule only applies for testing date purposes).

The TD also clarifies that future regulations will provide that changes in family "composition" (e.g., birth, death, marriage divorce) will not cause a change of ownership. Adopted as Final Regs. by TD 9269 (June 23, 2006) (no change).

[3] Owner Shift Involving 5-Percent Shareholder

[c] Other Aspects of Owner-Shift Rules

Page 14-75:

Add text to end of ¶ 14.43[3][c].

Special problems stem from the fact that the § 318(a)(2) attribution rules do not apply to § 401 trusts, but recent regulations provide for special treatment here in a generally helpful way.[207.1]

[207.1] TD 9063 (June 27, 2003), Regs. § 1.382-10T, supra note 194.1.

[7] Change-Of-Ownership Regulations Under § 382(g)

[c] Testing Period and Testing Date

Page 14-83:

Add text to end of ¶ 14.43[7][c].

Recent regulations respond in a generally helpful way to distributions of stock by § 401 trusts to plan beneficiaries.[229.1]

[229.1] TD 9063 (June 27, 2003), Regs. § 1.382-10T. For testing date purposes (only), treat as if beneficiaries acquired stock on same date and in same way as acquired by trust.

[f] Attribution Rules

Page 14-85:

Add to text at end of ¶14.43[7][f].

IRS recently announced that it intends to modify the family attribution rules under § 382 to provide that changes in family "composition" (e.g., birth, death, marriage, divorce, etc.), where members join or leave the family, will not cause a change in the ultimate beneficial ownership of loss company stock.[246.1]

[246.1] TD 9063 (June 27, 2003) (will be retroactively elective as well).

¶ 14.44 OPERATION OF SECTION 382 LIMITATION

[1] In General

[c] Value Limitation "Cap"

Page 14-93:

Add to note 274.

See Peischel, "Adjustments to the Value of a Loss Corporation For Purposes of Section 382," 30 J. Corp. Tax'n 3 (Nov. 2003); Bennett, "Valuing Stock For Ownership Changes," 83 Taxes 7 (June 2005).

Page 14-94:

Add to end of note 275.

Alter, "The IRS Shrinks the Boundaries of the Section 382(e)(2) 'Corporate Contraction' Doctrine," 102 J. Tax'n 338 (June 2005).

[3] Special Modifications of the "Section 382 Limitation"

Page 14-95:

Add new note 279.1 to end of first sentence.

[279.1] See Peischel, "Adjustments to the Value of a Loss Corporation for Purposes of Section 382," 30 J. Corp. Tax'n 3 (Nov. 2003). Bennett, "Valuing Stock for Ownership Changes," 83 Taxes 7 (June 2005).

[c] Increase for Recognized Built-In Gain

Page 14-97:

Add to note 289.

See Brock, "The Forthcoming Built-In Item Regulations: Issues for the Government to Address," 95 Tax Notes 97 (Apr. 1, 2002).

Page 14-98:

Add to note 293.

See Brock, supra note 289. See also Notice 2003-65, 2003-40 IRB 747 (alternative safe harbors for identifying recognized built-in gains, infra note 295.1).

Page 14-99:

Add text to end of ¶ 14.44[3][c].

In Notice 2003-65,[295.1] IRS has provided two safe-harbors for identifying recognized built-in gains and losses, (1) the § 1374 approach,[295.2] and (2) the § 338 approach,[295.3] which can be relied on by taxpayers in determining these items until subsequent regulations are issued.[295.4]

[295.1] 2003-40 IRB 747, discussed infra   14.44[4][c].

[295.2] This safe harbor generally adopts the built-in gain taint rules of § 1374 and the relevant regulations; see   6.07[1].

[295.3] This approach generally adopts the deemed sale rules of § 338 and the applicable regulations; see   10.42 and 10.43.

[295.4] Fifteen examples illustrate the application of these rules, which are alternative approaches that can be relied on until promulgation of subsequent regulations; see infra 14.44[4][c].

[4] Limitation on Built-In Losses

[a] In General

Page 14-100:

Add to note 300, at end of first paragraph.

See Brock, "The Forthcoming Built-In Item Regulations: Issues for the Government to Address," 95 Tax Notes 97 (Apr. 1, 2002).

Change note 301 to read as follows.

[301] For similar rule in the case of § 338 elections, see former Regs. § 1.338(b)-1T, discussed at   10.42[1][b] and [c]; these rules are now discussed at   14.43[2], and the regulations have moved to new Regs. § 1.138-5.

Add text to end of ¶ 14.44[4][a].

See Notice 2003-65,[301.1] for two alternative safe harbors for identifying recognized built-in gains and losses: (1) the § 1373 method (which adopts a modified version of the § 1374 built-in gain rules;[301.2] and (2) the § 338 method, which adopts a modified version of the § 338 deemed sale rules.[301.3] These safe harbors can be relied on by taxpayers until promulgation of subsequent regulations.[301.4]

[301.1] 2003-40 IRB 747.

[301.2] See ¶ 6.07[1].

[301.3] See ¶¶ 10.42, 10.43.

[301.4] See Raby & Raby, "BIGs, BILs and Sections 1374, 338 and 382," 101 Tax Notes 621 (Nov. 3, 2003). See infra ¶ 14.44[4][c].

Page 14-101:

Add new ¶ 14.44[4][c].

[c] Identification of Recognized Built-In Loss (and Recognized Built-In Gain) [New]

The Service issued guidance in September 2003, on how to identify recognized built-in loss (RBIL) and recognized built-in gain (RBIG) for purposes of § 382(h),[306.1] which can be relied on by taxpayers in determining these items until subsequent regulations are issued. Two safe harbors were provided in the Notice: (1) the § 1374 approach,[306.2] and (2) the § 338 approach.[306.3] The basic test of the § 1374 approach is whether a particular item of income or deduction has accrued before the § 382 change date,[306.4] in which case they will be treated as built-in loss (bad) or built-in gain (good) as the case may be. The basic test of the § 338 approach is to compare the actual items of income and deduction realized during the five-year recognition period with the hypothetical amounts of such items if a § 338 deemed sale election had been made on the change date.[306.5]

[306.1] Notice 2003-65, 2003-40 IRB 747, (Built-in Gains and Losses under Section 382(h)). See Raby & Raby, BIGs, BILs, and Sections 1374, 338, and 382, 101 Tax Notes 621 (Nov. 3, 2003); Bennett, Notice 2003-65: The Safe Harbor Approaches, 83 Taxes 7 (Feb. 2005).

[306.2] Based largely on § 1374(d) and the regulations; see ¶ 6.07[1]. Note that § 1374 applies only if the S corporation has net unrealized built-in gain at the time it switches from C to S status.

[306.3] Based on the hypothetical deemed sale rules of § 338; see ¶¶ 10.42, 10.43.

[306.4] Ignoring for this purpose the economic performance rules.

[306.5] Unlike an actual § 338 election, however, the Notice requires contingent liabilities to be estimated at the change date (and no further adjustments are made once the contingency is resolved (see Example 14)).

The taxpayer is allowed to use either of these safe harbors (but may not pick and choose between parts of both) until forthcoming regulations adopt a single set of rules for identifying built-in items. Moreover, while the two methods will serve as safe harbors, they are not exclusive. Thus, taxpayers can use "other" identification methods which will be tested for accuracy on a case-by-case basis.[306.6]

[306.6] Notice 2003-65, Part V.

¶ 14.47 OTHER LIMITATIONS ON SURVIVAL OF CORPORATE TAX ATTRIBUTES

[6] Built-In Losses and Tax Attribute Imports: Fresh Start at the Border

[a] In General

Page 14-126:

Add to note 409.

It has been reproposed in February 2000. While included in the 1999 anti-tax shelter package, the February 2000 proposal was moved to the international sections (presumably because its effects can have a positive impact in some cases, e.g., basis step-up and E&P purge).

But see Prop. Regs. §§ 1.367(b)-3(e) and 1.367(b)-3(f) (Nov. 8, 2000) (no § 381 carryover of foreign generated loss carryovers or earnings and profits on inbound asset acquisitions; instead, such items are purged at the border); see   15.83[1][b] and 15.84[2][b].

[b] Mark-To-Market and Elimination of Tax Attributes

Page 14-127:

Add to text at end of ¶ 14.47[6].

A limited border purge regime has recently been proposed under the § 367(b) regulations considered in Chapter 15.[414]

---

[414] Prop. Regs. § 1.367(b)-3(e)(f) (Nov. 8, 2000) (no carryover of foreign generated losses or earnings and profits on tax-free inbound asset acquisition transactions; instead, such items are purged at the border); see   15.83[1][b] and 15.84[2][b].

Add new ¶ 14.47[6][c] after ¶ 14.47[6][b].

[c] Limitation on Loss Import Transactions: § 362(e) [New]

But the 2004 Jobs Act[415] adopted legislation designed to prevent inbound tax-free transfers of built-in loss assets, whether by inbound reorganizations,[416] inbound § 351 transactions[417] or inbound subsidiary liquidations.[418] In effect, basis of the built-in loss assets are stepped-down to fair market value at the border.[419]

---

[415] American Jobs Creation Act of 2004, § 836, adding new §§ 362(e) and 334(b)(1)(B), effective October 22, 2004.

[416] New § 362(e)(1).

[417] New § 362(e)(2) (applicable to domestic § 351 transaction as well, i.e., an anti-duplication rule, whether effected at home or abroad). The parties can elect to step down the outside stock basis in lieu of inside asset basis, however.

[418] New § 334(b)(1)(B) (last sentence).

[419] See infra ¶ 15.85[7][e].

CHAPTER **15**

Foreign Corporations and Foreign-Source Income

B DOMESTIC CORPORATIONS WITH FOREIGN-SOURCE INCOME

C   FOREIGN PERSONAL HOLDING COMPANIES AND FOREIGN INVESTMENT COMPANIES

D   CONTROLLED FOREIGN CORPORATIONS

E   Organization, Liquidation, and Reorganization of Foreign Corporations: § 367 and Related Provisions

A TAXATION OF FOREIGN CORPORATIONS IN GENERAL

¶ 15.01 INTRODUCTORY

[1] Overview

Page 15-9:

Add to note 1.

Graetz, "The David R. Tillinghast Lecture—Taxing International Income: Inadequate Principles, Outdated Concepts, and Unsatisfactory Policies," 54 Tax L. Rev. 261 (2001); Noren, Commentary—"The U.S. National Interest in International Tax Policy," 54 Tax L. Rev. 337 (2001). Other more specifically focused articles will be noted throughout this chapter.

[2] Potential Reforms

Page 15-11:

Add to note 10.

Currently, Joint Committee Staff Report (JCX −22-06) on impact of international tax reform (June 21, 2006); and ABA Tax Section Task Force Report: International Tax Reform: Objectives and Overview, 112 Tax Notes 261 (July 17, 2006); and 59 Tax Law. 649 (2006) for an expanded version.

Page 15-13:

Add text to end of ¶ 15.01[2].

Legislation introduced by Ways and Means Chairman Thomas, "The American Competitiveness and Corporate Accountability Act of 2002," HR 5095, Title III (International simplification), contained many of these proposals, and several new ones as well, some of which are fundamental changes to current law.[24.1] The most significant of the proposals were the following:

1. Repeal the CFC rules for foreign base company sales and services income;[24.2]
2. Reduce the number of § 904(d) baskets to two;[24.3]
3. Raise the § 904(c) carryover of foreign tax credits to ten years (passed);
4. Reform the § 864(e) interest allocation rules;[24.4]
5. Repeal the second-tier source rule for dividends and interest paid by foreign corporations (passed); and
6. Allow § 904(d)(3) look-through for dividends from noncontrolled § 902 subsidiaries (passed).

These (and other) proposals will be considered at the relevant points in this chapter. Many, however, have been dropped from (or been scaled back), in the Thomas Bill as it has moved through the legislative process. But all except item 1 did ultimately make it into the final 2004 tax legislation in some form, though modified to some extent.

[24.1] See Joint Committee Staff's technical explanation of these provisions, reprinted in BNA Daily Tax Rep. No. 140, at L-6, L-26 (July 22, 2002). See Lubkin, "Viewpoint: Politics and Policy; Prospects for International Tax Reform in 2003," BNA Daily Tax Rep. No. 234, at J-1 (Dec. 5, 2002). The current version is HR 2896, "The American Jobs Creation Act of 2003;" for Joint Committee Staff explanation, see BNA Daily Tax Rep. No. 157, at L-1 (Aug. 14, 2003).

[24.2] See infra ¶ 15.62[2][b], 15.62[2][c]; but this did not survive in final 2004 tax act adopted on October 22, 2004.

[24.3] See infra ¶ 15.21[4]. Passed in 2004 Tax Act (Oct. 22, 2004).

[24.4] See infra ¶ 15.02[1][g]. Passed in 2004 Tax Act.

[3] Residence: Domestic Corporations

Page 15-14:

Add text to end of ¶ 15.01[3].

But temporary regulations issued in August 2004,[27.1] provide that a business entity of any type (corporate or non-corporate) organized in both the United States and a foreign jurisdiction it is treated as a domestic entity for United States tax purposes; moreover, if it is a corporation in one jurisdiction it is a corporation in all;[27.2] the status issue is determined first (corporate or non-corporate), and the situs issue (foreign or domestic) next. These regulations were adopted as final regulations on January 30, 2006.[27.3]

[27.1] Regs. § 301.7701-5T, TD 9153 (Aug. 12, 2004) (effective at once). See May, "Important New Regulations Address Classifications of Dually Chartered Entities," 105 Tax Notes 573 (Oct. 25, 2004).

[27.2] Regs. § 301.7701-2T(b)(9).

[27.3] TD 9246 (Jan. 30, 2006); they are *not*, however, retroactive.

[4] Elective Corporate Aggregation—Consolidated Returns and Status Election Under the Check-The-Box Regulations

Page 15-14:

Add to note 30.

Prop. Regs. § 301.7701-2(b)(6) (Jan. 2, 2000) (can't disregard entity if owned by foreign government); and § 301.7701-2(c)(ii) (foreign banks engaged in U.S. business can't disregard nonbank entity). These proposed regulations became final in TD 9012 on July 31, 2002.

Page 15-15:

Add to note 32.

These temporary regulations were adopted as final regulations by TD 8889 on July 3, 2000.

Add to note 33.

Sheppard, "More Check-The-Box Fallout: Reverse Hybrids," 87 Tax Notes 1196 (May 29, 2000).

Add to note 34, second paragraph.

See also Miller, "The Strange Materialization of the Tax Nothing," 87 Tax Notes 685 (May 1, 2000); Miller, "Snake in the Box: The Hazards of Policy Making With "Anti-Abuse" Rules," 89 Tax Notes 107 (Oct. 2, 2000); Steinberg and Mendelson, "The Use of Partnerships and Disregarded Entities by U.S. Corporations," 81 Taxes 261 (Mar. 2003). But this proposed regulation was withdrawn by Notice 2003-46, 2003-28 IRB 53 (IRS will no longer deal with entity status here).

For comments on Notice 2003-46, see Click, "Treasury Withdraws Extraordinary Check-the-Box Regulations," 101 Tax Notes 95 (Oct. 6, 2003); Lemein & McDonald, "Notice 2003-46: The Extraordinary Transaction Regulations Are Withdrawn," 81 Taxes 5 (Nov. 2003); Sheppard, "Behind the Eight Ball on Check-the-Box Rules," 101 Tax Notes 437 (Oct. 27, 2003); Holland, "U.S. Check-the-box Rules in the Cross-Border Context," 108 Tax Notes 1151 (Sept. 5, 2005). See also Dover Corp., 122 TC 324 (2004) (check-and-sell plan succeeded in avoiding Subpart F income since transaction characterized as deemed § 332 liquidation and sale of assets, not stock).

Add text to end of ¶ 15.01[4].

But IRS has responded again to hybrid structure planning by issuing a status consistency requirement where a business entity is organized in more than one jurisdiction; that is, if an entity is a corporation in one jurisdiction it is a corporation in all for U.S. tax purposes; moreover, if the entity is located in the United States and another jurisdiction, it is treated as domestic in all. The status and situs issues are determined independently.[34.1]

[34.1] TD 9153 (Aug. 12, 2004), issuing Regs. §§ 301-7701-2T(b)(9) and 301.7701-5T (effective at once). Adopted as final by TD 9246 (Jan. 30, 2006) (but the final version is not retroactive to 2004).

¶ 15.02 BASIC DEFINITIONS AND CONCEPTS

[1] Source of Income and Deductions

[a] Income Source Rules: §§ 861 and 862

Page 15-16:

Add to note 35.

Shea, "Fleming & Peroni, Tillinghost Lecture: 'What's Source Got to Do With It?' Source Rules and U.S. International Taxation," 56 Tax L. Rev. 81 (2002).

Add to note 39.

The Joint Committee Staff's April 2001 simplification report proposes to eliminate the secondary withholding tax rule for dividends paid by foreign corporations; Proposal IX. H., at 436. The Thomas bill, HR 5095, § 325 would do so (effective in 2003); and this proposal passed in the 2004 Jobs Act, new § 871(i)(2)(D) (effective 2005).

Page 15-17:

Add to note 41, second paragraph.

But see Regs. § 1.881-3(e), Ex. 10 (adopts look-through treatment of Rev. Rul. 80-362; though not a conduit financing because foreign parent taxed per §§ 881 and 1441; foreign parent fixed rate license to foreign subsidiary which sublicensed at contingent rate to domestic sub-foreign subsidiary not taxed (exempt), but foreign parent was).

[b] Income Source: Special Definitional Aspects

Page 15-18:

In first paragraph of note 48, move the last three sentences to the end of the second paragraph on page 15-19.

Add to note 48 at the end of the second paragraph on page 15-19.

Extensive technical amendments to the § 1441 regulations were adopted by TD 8881 on May 22, 2000; see infra   15.03[1]; Halphen, "Revised Withholding Regulations – A Race to the Finish?" 88 Tax Notes 245 (July 10, 2000). The final § 1441 regulations (as amended in May 2000) generally retained the exception from withholding for accrued interest and OID on bonds sold between interest dates; see Regs. §§ 1.1441-2(a)(5), 1.1441-2(a)(6), and 1.1441-3(b)(2) (after flirting with a modified approach in 1997 proposed regulations, supra).

Page 15-20:

Add to note 53.

Hardin & Maloney, "Withholding in Cross-Border Securities Lending: The Ambiguity Continues," 87 Tax Notes 1533 (June 12, 2000).

Page 15-21:

Add to note 60

For sources of compensation income generally, see revised Regs. § 1.861-4, TD 9212 (July 14, 2005).

Page 15-22:

Add to note 63, first paragraph.

Hardy, "Assignment of Corporate Opportunities—The Migration of Intangibles," 100 Tax Notes 527 (July 28, 2003).

Add to note 63, second paragraph.

See also Microsoft Corp., 115 TC 228 (2000) (licensed computer software masters with right to reproduce, held not qualified export property before 1997 law change); but rev'd, 311 F3d 1178, 2002-2 USTC   50,800 (9th Cir. 2002).

Page 15-23:

Add to note 70.

See, e.g., Microsoft Corp., 115 TC 228 (2000) (status as export property for FSC benefits, infra   15.23[3][c]; licensed computer software with right to reproduce); but rev'd, 311 F3d 1178 (9th Cir. 2002); see generally Llewellyn, "U.S. Tax Regime for Taxing Foreign

Person Conducting E-Mail Operations With U.S. Customers," 30 Tax Mgmt. Int'l J. 315 (July 13, 2001); Hardy, "Migration of Intangibles," supra note 63.

[c] Personal Property: § 865

Page 15-24:

Add to note 74, third paragraph.

See generally Rubinger & Mayo, "International Tax Aspects of Cancellation of Indebtedness Income," 98 J. Tax'n 365 (June 2003).

Page 15-25:

Add to note 76.

The stock loss rules of § 1.865-2 were amended, and the general loss rules of Temp. Regs. § 1.865-1T were adopted as final regulations § 1.865-1 by TD 8973 (Dec. 28, 2001).

Page 15-26:

Add to note 78.

The Thomas bill, HR 5095, in § 301(b), treats these "round trip sales" as foreign personal holding company income in new § 954(c)(1)(H), infra ¶ 15.62[2]. But it did not pass in the 2004 Jobs Act.

Page 15-27:

Add to note 85.

The stock loss regulations in § 1.865-2 were modified slightly by TD 8973 (Dec. 28, 2001).

Add to note 86.

These temporary regulations were adopted as final regulations by TD 8973 (Dec. 28, 2001); the principal modification was an expansion of the now ubiquitous anti-abuse rules in § 1.865-1(c)(6).

Page 15-28:

Add to note 88.

Daub, "Importing and Exporting Basis and Other Tax Attributes—Do We Need a New System?" 12 J. Int'l Tax'n 15 (Nov. 2001); Katcher, "Back to Basis; Crossing the U.S. Frontier," 97 Tax Notes 547 (Oct. 28, 2002). See infra ¶ 15.85[7].

[d] Residual Source Rules: § 863

Add to note 89.

Rubinger & Mayo, "International Tax Aspects of Cancellation of Indebtedness Income," 98 J. Tax'n 365 (June 2003).

Page 15-31:

Add to note 101.

The Thomas bill, HR 5095, § 301(b), would treat "round trip" sales (i.e., U.S. origin and ultimate U.S. destination) as FPHC income under new § 954(c)(1)(H), infra   15.62[2][a]. But this provision did not survive the final 2004 Jobs Act.

In second line of second paragraph, change file *to* final.

Add to note 105 at end of second paragraph.

See Andrews, "Targeted Tax Relief for Space Commerce," 10 J. Int'l Tax'n 30, pt. 1 (Oct. 1999), 11 J. Int'l Tax'n 10, pt. 2 (Feb. 2000), and 11 J. Int'l Tax'n 34, pt. 3 (July 2000). Regulations under § 863(d) were proposed on January 17, 2001, in Prop. Regs. § 1.863-8 (they contain numerous examples in Prop. Regs. § 1.863-8(f)). For comment see Sedore, "Recently Released Regulations on Space and Ocean Income Place Heavy Burden on Insurers," 14 J. Tax'n Fin. Insts. 76 (May 2001); Nosler, et al., "If You Send It, Tax Will Come: The Section 863 Prop. Regs. Could Affect the Telecommunications Industry", 12 J. Int'l Tax'n 8 (May 2001); Littman, "Space, Ocean and Communications Income— The Final Frontier?" 30 Tax Mgmt. Int'l J. 195 (May 11, 2001); Tillinghast & Holm, "Proposed Regulations on Space and Ocean Income and International Communications Income Raise Major Issues for U.S. and Foreign Corporations," 79 Taxes 11 (June 2001).

Add to note 105, third paragraph.

Regs. under § 863(e) were proposed on January 17, 2001, in Prop. Regs. § 1.863-9 (also containing numerous examples). Cowan, "The Taxation of Space, Ocean and Communications Under the Proposal Treasury Regulations," 55 Tax Law. 133 (2001); Lainoff, "Littman, Bates & Cowan, The Proposed Taxation of Space, Ocean and Communications Activity...," 80 Taxes 185 (Mar. 2002).

Add text to end of   15.02[1][d].

But the 2001 proposed regulations on space, ocean and communications activities were withdrawn and reproposed in September of 2005.[105.1] They were scaled back in several instances to reflect concerns of the commentators noted above and also to reflect changes made by the 2004 Jobs Act.[105.2] These revised proposals were adopted as final regulations on December 27, 2006.[105.3]

[105.1] Prop. Regs. §§ 1.863-8 and 1.863-9 (Sept. 19, 2005).

[105.2] While liberalized and clarified in several respects, the basic structure and principles of the 2001 proposals continued in the revised versions. See Lebovitz & Paz, IRS Reproposes Regulations For Taxing the "Final Frontier," 84 Taxes 21 (Jan. 2006); Rubinger, "Revised Rules on Source of Income From Space, Oceans, and International Communications," 104 J. Tax'n 39 (Jan. 2006).

[105.3] TC 9305, adopting Regs. §§ 1.863-8 and 1.863-9 (generally effective for 2007, and without major change).

[e] Source of Deductions Generally

Page 15-32:

Add to note 106, second paragraph.

Dresser Indus., Inc v. US, 238 F3d 603 (5th Cir. 2000) (accord with *Bowater*). Sunoco, Inc., 118 TC 181 (2002) (interest expense allocated to § 904 numerator without netting vs. interest income; prior view in *Bowater* overruled).

Add to note 106, fourth paragraph.

But Temp. Regs. § 1.861-8T(e)(12), adopted by TD 9143 on July 28, 2004, dropped the 1991 proposals and instead allow allocation of all deductible § 170 contributions to U.S. gross income in full (a complete change of heart by IRS here); adopted as final regulations (without change) by TD 9211 (July 13, 2005).

Page 15-33:

Add to note 108.

The § 1.865-1T regulations were adopted as final regulations § 1.865-1 by TD 8973 (Dec. 28, 2001); the principal change is expansion of the anti-abuse rules in § 1.865-1(c)(6).

Add to note 109.

Daub, "Importing and Exporting Basis and Other Tax Attributes—Do We Need a New System?" 12 J. Int'l Tax'n 15 (Nov. 2001); Katcher, "Back to Basis; Crossing the U.S. Frontier," 97 Tax Notes 547 (Oct. 28, 2002).

[f] Deduction Source—Research and Development Expenses: § 864(f)

Page 15-34:

Add to note 111.

But Boeing Co. v. US, 258 F3d 958, 2001-2 USTC ¶ 50,562 (9th Cir. 2001), rejected *St. Jude* approach and upheld validity of regulation and IRS' allocation under general R&D. Reg. § 1.861-8(e)(3)—no citation to *Intel*; cert. granted May 28, 2002. Lupi-Sher, "High Court Takes on Tax Case Limited in Result and Scope," 95 Tax Notes 1565 (June 10, 2002). The Supreme Court affirmed, 537 US 437, 123 S. Ct. 1099, 2003-1 USTC ¶ 50,273 (2003) (two dissents).

[g] Affiliated Group Allocations: § 864(e)

Page 15-35:

Add to note 118, first paragraph.

Hannes & Riedy, "Time to Move to a Worldwide Group Approach for Apportioning Interest," 91 Tax Notes 1305 (May 21, 2001); Shaviro, "Does Sophisticated Mean Better? A Critique of Alternative Approaches to Sourcing the Interest Expense of U.S. Multinationals," 54 Tax L. Rev. 353 (2001). For a new proposal by Ways and Means Chairman Thomas to adopt this proposal see infra note 119.1.

Page 15-36:

Add to note 119.

TD 8916 issued final Regs. §§ 1.861-9, 1.861-11, and 1.861-14 on January 3, 2001.

Add text to end of ¶ 15.02[1][g].

Legislation proposed by the chairman of the Ways and Means Committee (Rep. Thomas) on July 11, 2002,[119.1] would amend § 864(e) to adopt the proposals first made in 1992 and 1999; they finally were adopted in the Tax Act of 2004.[119.2]

[119.1] HR 5095, § 311 (effective in 2003), that is, allow worldwide allocation and treating all foreign members (including CFCs) of an affiliated group as a single corporation.

[119.2] See supra note 118. The current version of this proposal is HR 2896, § 1111 (July 25, 2003). It was adopted in the 2004 tax legislation enacted Oct. 22, 2004. HR 4520, Act § 401 (effective in 2009), § 864(f) (election to allocate world-wide). Cunningham, "The US Worldwide Interest Apportionment Rules: Ready, Set, Wait," 111 Tax Notes 1021 (May 29, 2006).

[h] Income From a Global Securities Trading Operation

Add to note 123.

See also Sheppard, "Gremlins in the Global Dealing Regulations," 94 Tax Notes 270 (Jan. 21, 2002).

[2] Trade or Business: § 864(b) (Existence and Location)

[a] Existence Generally

Page 15-36:

Add to note 124.

Sicular & Sobel, "Selected Current Effectively Connected Income Issues For Investment Funds," 56 Tax Law. 719 (Sum. 2003) (selected current issues).

[b] Trading in Stocks, Securities, and Commodities: § 864(b)(2)

Page 15-38:

Add to note 129.

Sicular & Sobel, "Selected Current Issues," supra note 124.

Page 15-39:

Add to note 131.

Reardon, "Offshore Hedge Funds—Doing Business in the United States?" 15 J. Tax'n Fin. Insts. 19 (Sept. 2001).

[d] Location or Business Situs Generally

Page 15-43:

Add to note 143, first paragraph.

Reardon, "Offshore Hedge Funds—Doing Business in the United States?" 15 J. Tax'n Fin. Insts. 19 (Sept. 2001).

Add new note 143.1 to end of ¶ 15.02[2][d].

143.1 See generally Hannes, "Achieving Transfer Pricing Objectives Without Creating a U.S. Business for a Foreign Person," 99 Tax Notes 899 (May 12, 2003).

[e] Specific and Related Areas

Page 15-44:

Add to note 144.

See Hannes, supra note 143.1.

Add to note 145, first paragraph.

Reardon, "Offshore Hedge Funds—Doing Business in the United States?" 15 J. Tax'n Fin. Insts. 19 (Sept. 2001).

Add after first sentence of note 146.

Levine & Weintraub, "When Does E-Commerce Result in a Permanent Establishment? The OECD's Initial Response," 29 Tax Mgmt. Int'l J. 220 (Apr. 14, 2000). Doernberg, "Electronic Commerce: Changing Income Tax Treaty Principles a Bit?" 89 Tax Notes 1625 (Dec. 18, 2000). Hannes, supra note 143.1.

Page 15-45:

Add to note 147.

See Hannes, supra note 143.1.

[3] Income Effectively Connected With a U.S. Business: § 864(c)

[a] In General

Page 15-45:

Add to note 148, first paragraph.

See also Sicular & Sobel, "Selected Current Effectively Connected Issues For Investment Funds," 56 Tax Law. 719 (Sum. 2003).

[4] Bilateral Tax Treaties

[a] In General

Page 15-52:

Add to note 173.

Townsend, "Treaty Interpretation," 55 Tax Law. 219 (2001).

[d] General Categories

Page 15-54:

Add new note 177.1 in sixth line of text after United Kingdom.

[177.1] The UK Treaty, as extensively revised, was signed on July 24, 2001. See Daily Tax Rep. (BNA) No. 142, at L-3 (July 25, 2001). A main feature of the new treaty is a zero withholding rate on dividends paid by 80-percent owned subsidiaries. West, "Highlights of the New US-UK Tax Treaty," 92 Tax Notes 663 (July 30, 2001); Benett & Nickerson, "Groundbreaking Tax Treaty Between United States and United Kingdom Explained," Daily Tax Rep. (BNA) No. 150, at J-1 (Aug. 6, 2001); Sheppard, "*Nat West* Revisited in the New British Treaty," 92 Tax Notes 1516 (Sept. 17, 2001); Analysis and Perspective, Daily Tax Rep. (BNA) No. 242, at J-1 (Dec. 19, 2001).

A protocol to the U.S.-Mexican Treaty (Nov. 26, 2002) likewise follows the UK model exempting dividends paid by 80-percent-owned subsidiaries, Daily Tax Rep. (BNA) No. 229, at L-3 (Nov. 27, 2002), as does the similarly revised proposed Australian and Netherlands treaties. The new Japan treaty allows exclusion for dividends from majority owned subsidiaries. A Swedish Treaty Protocol (Sept. 30, 2005) also adopts a zero rate for dividends of 80 percent subsidiaries; so does a protocol with Denmark (May 2, 2006), Finland (May 31, 2006), and Germany (June 1, 2006).

Add to text at end of paragraph.

The Joint Committee Staff's April 2001 simplification report makes several significant proposals as to U.S. tax treaty policy (e.g., that the U.S. Model Treaty be updated and reissued every two years).[178.1]

[178.1] Proposal IX. J., at 445–447. Also Proposal IX. K., at 448–450, proposes that the status of "older treaties" (i.e., those in force at least ten years) be reported to Congress every two years. Progress on these matters has been glacial at best (and closer to nonexistent). But a new revised Model Treaty (and a Model Technical Explanation) was released in December, 2006. There were several changes here (but no zero dividend rate).

[e] Common Definitional Concepts

Page 15-55:

Add to note 179.

See also Rev. Rul. 2004-76, 2004-31 IRB 111 (Aug. 2, 2004) (corporate residence and situs for U.S. treaty purposes controlled by designated residence clause in treaty between two foreign countries of which taxpayer is a legal resident in both countries).

Add to note 181, first paragraph.

Couch & McNutt, "Permanent Establishments: Definition, Content, and Controversy: Part I," 17 J. Tax'n Fin. Insts. 32 (Sept. 2003); Part II, 17 J. Tax'n Insts. 49 (Nov. 2003).

Add to note 181 at end of second paragraph.

Levine & Weintraub, "When Does E-Commerce Result in a Permanent Establishment? The OECD's Initial Response," 29 Tax Mgmt. Int'l J. 220 (Apr. 14, 2000).

[g] General Themes of Current Treaty Policy

Page 15-57:

Add to note 185, fourth paragraph.

See Rheinhold, "What Is Treaty Abuse? (Is Treaty Shopping an Outdated Concept?)" 53 Tax Law. 663 (2000).

Page 15-58:

Add to note 187.

The temporary regulations were adopted in final (and somewhat simplified) form by TD 8889 on July 3, 2000. See Sheppard, "Hybrid Problems Continue Under Improved Treaty Regulations," 88 Tax Notes 316 (July 17, 2000).

Add new item to text.

    4. A new trend seems to be emerging following the UK Treaty's elimination of withholding for dividends from 80-percent subsidiaries; Australia, Mexico, Sweden, Denmark, the Netherlands, Finland, and Germany have followed suit and the new Japan treaty even excludes dividends from majority owned subsidiaries (the most generous of all).[188.1]

[188.1] Supra note 177.1 (but it has not been included in the new Model Income Tax Treaty).

Page 15-59:

Add to note 190.

The competent authority procedures were updated again in Rev. Proc. 2002-52, 2002-31 IRB 242. They were updated again in Rev. Proc. 2006-54, 2006-49 IRB 1035.

[h] Treaties and "Hybrid Entities"

Page 15-59:

Add to note 192.

Sheppard, "More Check-the-Box Fallout: Reverse Hybrids," 87 Tax Notes 1196 (May 5, 2000).

    Final regulations under § 1.894-1(d) were adopted by TD 8889 on July 3, 2000 (effective on June 30, 2000). The final regulations simplified, but did not basically change, the temporary regulations. The major revisions occurred in the twelve examples of Regs. § 1.894-1(d)(5), which were clarified and varied as to the situations covered. These regulations also are an important element in applying the soon to be effective § 1441 withholding regulations since they deliniate who is (and who is not) entitled to claim potential treaty benefits; see infra ¶ 15.03[1]. See Sheppard, "Hybrid Problems Continue Under Improved Treaty Regulations," 88 Tax Notes 316 (July 17, 2000); Blessing, "Final § 894(c) Regulations," 29 Tax Mgmt. Int'l J. 499 (Sept. 8, 2000); Lemein & McDonald, "Final Code Section 894 Regulations, 78 Tax 5 (Sept. 2000). See also Rev. Rul. 2000-59, 2000-52 IRB 593 (additional examples); Engle, "Special Rules for Items of Income Received by Entities Affected by a U.S. Treaty," 29 J. Corp. Tax'n 35 (Jan. 2001).

Add to text at end of ¶ 15.02[4][h].

Subsequent regulations also deal with payments by domestic reverse hybrid entities (a corporation for U.S. purposes, partnership for foreign law purposes), and these proposals were adopted with some liberalizing modifications in 2002.[192.1]

[192.1] Prop. Regs. §§ 1.894-1(d)(2)(ii), 1.894-1(d)(2)(iii) (Feb. 27, 2001), infra ¶ 15.03[7]. Final Regs. § 1.894-1(d)(2) were adopted on June 12, 2002, by TD 8999 (the final regulations narrowed the proposals somewhat, clarified various portions, and increased the examples from three to nine—but still very heavy going here). See Greenwald and Ladocsi, "Final Piece to the 894(c) Reg. Puzzle," 14 J. Int'l Tax'n 14 (Jan. 2003).

[5] Foreign Currency

[a] In General

Page 15-60:

Add to note 196.

Rubinger & Mayo, "International Tax Aspects of Cancellation of Indebtedness Income," 98 J. Tax'n 365 (June 2003).

[b] Tax Reform Act of 1986 Currency Rules

Page 15-61:

Add to note 200.

A major set of regulations under § 897 (the QBU Branch regulations) was released on September 6, 2006; Prop. Regs. §§ 1.987-1 – 1.987-11 (effective date; generally when final); the new proposals revise and tighten the current 1991 regulations which had become out of date due to numerous changes in the law. They are very long and very complicated, and will not be attempted to be summarized here due to the shortness of life. For discussion, see Greenwalk & Rubinger, "New Currency Branch Regs Shut Down Abusive Loss Recognition," 113 Tax Notes 1085 (Dec. 18, 2006).

Page 15-62:

Add to note 201, third paragraph.

See Prop. Regs. § 1.998-6 (Aug. 29, 2003); infra note 202.1.

Add to note 201, fourth paragraph.

TD 8914 (Jan. 3, 2001) issued final regulations under § 988 defining "hyperinflationary" currency.

Add to text at end of ¶ 15.02[5][b].

Proposed regulations were issued on August 29, 2003 dealing with the treatment of contingent payment foreign debt instruments.[202.1]

[202.1] Prop. Regs. § 1.988-6 (nonfunctional currency contingent payment instruments, effective when final). These proposals adopt the noncontingent bond method of the original issue discount regulations; see 4.41[2][b]. They were adopted in final form by TD 9157 on August 30, 2004.

[c] European Monetary Union Conversion to the Euro

Page 15-63:

In first sentence of note 204 change 1.1001-3T *to* 1.1001-5T.

Add text to end of ¶ 15.02[5][c].

These regulations were adopted in final form on January 11, 2001, with only minor modifications.[204.1]

[204.1] TD 8927; the final regulations added a new rule in Regs. § 1.985-8(b)(3).

¶ 15.03 FOREIGN CORPORATIONS NOT ENGAGED IN U.S. BUSINESS: § 881

[1] In General

Page 15-64:

Add to note 210 at end of first paragraph.

Numerous technical amendments to the 1997 regulations were made by TD 8881, May 22, 2000; for which, see Halphen, "Revised Withholding Regulations – A Race to the Finish?" 88 Tax Notes 245 (July 10, 2000); Shay et. al., "Qualified Intermediary Status," Act III, 29 Tax Mgmt. Int'l J. 403 (July 14, 2000). For possible exceptions to withholding, see Willens, 113 Tax Notes 1099 (Dec. 18, 2006).

Page 15-65:

Add to note 210 at end of second paragraph.

For comments on Rev. Proc. 2000-12, see Shay et al., 29 Tax Mgmt. Int'l J. 403 (July 14, 2000); Baker & McKenzie, "Nine Months of Working With the QI Agreement—What Has IRS Wrought?" 11 J. Int'l Tax'n 4 (Nov. 2000); Schneider, "Qualified Intermediaries—Caught in the Complexity of New US Withholding Requirements," 78 Taxes 15 (Dec. 2000). But for significant transition relief for the qualified intermediary rules, see Notice 2001-4, 2001-2 IRB 267. Balaban et al., (Baker & McKenzie), "A Practical Guide for New QIs," 12 J. Int'l Tax'n 12 (Apr. 2001). Notice 2001-43, 2001-30 IRB 72 (additional extension of transition relief from withholding and demands of QI agreements and issue of alternative procedures that can be applied during 2001).

Add to note 210 at end of third paragraph.

For comments on the May 2000 technical amendments to these regulations, see Halphen, supra this note 210; Shay et al., supra this note 210. For the effect of hybrid entities on these rules, see infra ¶ 15.03[7].

[2] Portfolio Interest Exemption

Page 15-65:

Add to note 211, first paragraph.

ABA Tax Section Comm., "The Need for Guidance on the Portfolio Interest Exemption," 103 Tax Notes 701 (May 10, 2004) (20 years is long enough without regulations).

Add note 211.1 in third line of second paragraph after the word shareholder.

[211.1] See Prop. Regs. § 1.871-14(g) determining who is a 10 percent shareholder for this purpose and when that determination is to be made (issued June 12, 2006, and effective when final).

Page 15-66:

Add to note 212, second paragraph.

Tate & Lyle also was overruled by the Tax Court in Square D Co., 118 TC 299 (2002); aff'd, 438 F3d 739, 2006-1 USTC ¶ 50,162 (7th Cir. 2006); Comment by Sheppard, "Do Treaty Nondiscrimination Clauses Matter?"110 Tax Notes 932 (Feb. 27, 2006).

Add to text after first full paragraph.

The American Jobs Creation Act of 2004 (2004 Jobs Act)[214.1] extended the portfolio interest exemption to payments of "interest related dividends" by RICs (and also excluded short-term capital gain dividends).[214.2]

[214.1] American Jobs Creation Act of 2004, § 411, new §§ 871(k)(1) and 881(e)(1) (effective in 2005).

[214.2] New § 871(k)(2) and § 881(e)(2).

[4] Fixed or Determinable Annual or Periodical Income

Page 15-68:

Add to note 221.

But COD income seems to be included in FDAP under Regs. § 1.1441-2(b)(1)(i) general rule which includes all § 61 gross income unless excluded by § 1.1441-2(b)(2) and COD is not mentioned there; but see Regs. § 1.1441-2(d)(2) (no withholding for COD).

Page 15-69:

Add text to last paragraph of ¶ 15.03[4].

This proposal finally passed in the 2004 Jobs Act.[227.1]

[227.1] HR 4520, American Jobs Creation Act of 2004, § 893, adding new § 332(d) (effective October 22, 2004) (serial § 332 liquidations to avoid § 881 dividend tax now are blocked).

[6] Conduit Financing Arrangements

Page 15-71:

Add to note 233 after second sentence.

Del was affirmed, Del Commercial Properties, Inc. v. CIR, 251 F3d 210 (DC Cir. 2001) (court short-circuited the devious steps to the direct end result route; also imposed negligence penalty for failure to file return and withhold tax).

[7] Payments to "Hybrid Entities"

Page 15-72:

Add to note 241.

Sheppard, "More Check-The-Box Fallout: Reverse Hybrids," 87 Tax Notes 1196 (May 29, 2000). The temporary regulations were adopted in final form without major change by TD 8889, July 3, 2000 (effective June 30, 2000). The principal revisions occurred in the twelve examples of Regs. § 1.894-1(d)(5). See Sheppard, "Hybrid Problems Continue Under Improved Treaty Regulations," 88 Tax Notes 316 (July 17, 2000); Blessing, "Final § 894(c) Regulations," 29 Tax Mgmt. Int'l J. 499 (Sept. 8, 2000); Blessing, "Final

§ 894(c) Regulations," Tax Mgmt. Int'l J. 499 (Sept. 8, 2000); Greenwald et al., "Section 894(c) Regs.," 11 J. Int'l Tax'n 28 (Dec. 2000).

Add to note 243.

See final Regs. § 1.894-1(d)(5) (2000) (the principal revisions occurred in the clarification of these twelve examples; but the final regulations "reserved" on the treatment of payments by domestic "reverse hybrids"); articles supra note 241: see also Lemein & McDonald, "Final Code Sec. 894 Regulations: Treaty Benefits for Hybrid Entity Payments," 78 Taxes 5 (Sept. 2000). See also Rev. Rul. 2000-59, 2000-52 IRB 593 (additional examples); Engle, "Special Rules for Items of Income Received by Entities Affected by a U.S. Treaty," 28 J. Corp. Tax'n 35 (Jan. 2001).

Add text to end of ¶ 15.03[7].

Additional anti-abuse regulations dealing with payments by domestic reverse hybrids (i.e., a corporation for U.S. law, but a partnership under foreign law) were proposed on February 27, 2001.[243.1] These proposals were adopted with some liberalizing modifications in June 2002.[243.2]

[243.1] Prop. Regs. § 1.894-1(d)(2)(ii) (consistency requirement to block conversion of character of U.S.-income items from high tax to low (or no) tax status), and § 1.894-1(d)(2)(iii) (examples illustrate these rules). See Sheppard, "Interest Deduction Denied by the Back Door," 90 Tax Notes 1599 (Mar. 19, 2001).

[243.2] The final regulations narrowed the proposals somewhat, clarified other portions, and increased the examples from three to nine (but still very heavy going here).

But see Sheppard, "Turbo-Charged Income Stripping," 97 Tax Notes 994 (Nov. 15, 2002) (use of "REPOs" as an alternative to avoid hybrid regs); Greenwald and Ladocsi, "Final Piece to the 894(c) Reg. Puzzle," 14 J. Int'l Tax'n 14 (Jan. 2003). Maiorano, Treadway and Zive, "Deciphering the Final Domestic Reverie Hybrid Payment Regs," 99 Tax Notes 689 (May 5, 2003).

¶ 15.04 FOREIGN CORPORATIONS ENGAGED IN U.S. BUSINESS: §§ 882 AND 884

[1] Section 882

[a] In General

Page 15-73:

Add after CB 179; in first sentence of note 244.

but Rev. Rul. 70-329 obsolete by Rev. Rul. 2001-39, 2001-33 IRB 125; as to § 1504(d), see ¶ 13.41[1], note 309.

Page 15-74:

Add to note 246, second paragraph.

Sheppard, "*Nat West* Revisited in the New British Treaty," 92 Tax Notes 1516 (Sept. 17, 2001) (adopts principle of the *Nat West* decision); Townsend, "Treaty Interpretation," 55 Tax Law. 219 (2001). Taxpayer won again in the *Nat West* litigation, Nat'l Westminster Bank PLC v. US, Fed. Cl, 2003-2 USTC   50,105 (Ct. Fed. Cl 2003) (taxpayer's allocation method was proper, that is, allocate according to properly maintained U.S. branch's books and records); Leeds, "What Does the Taxpayer Victory in *Nat West II* Mean for Foreign Bank Branches," 15 J. Int'l Tax'n 44 (July 2004). Nat West III, 2006-1 USTC   50,107 (Fed. Cl. 2006) (likewise was decided largely in the taxpayers favor).

Page 15-75:

Add to note 248.

But the IRS eased up on the 1990 waiver regulations (as too restrictive) in Temp. Regs. § 1.884-4T (Jan. 29, 2002) (inadvertent untimely filing waivable if meet various factors in § 1.884-4T(a)(3)(ii); six examples in § 1.884-4T(a)(3)(iii) illustrate the new approach; nevertheless, still a pretty tough regime), adopted by TD 9043 (Mar. 10, 2003). But the timely filing requirement was struck down in Swallows Holding Ltd, 126 TC 96 (2006) (very long majority opinion and three separate dissenting opinions). Comments by Sheppard, "Tax Court Flunks the Brand X Test," 110 Tax Notes 505 (Feb. 6, 2006) (very critical, like the three dissents); Cummings, Viewpoint, Daily Tax Rep. (BNA) No. 61, at J-1 (Mar. 30, 2006); Seago & Schnee, "The Tax Court Salvages a Foreign Corporation's Deduction *Swallows Holding*," 33 Corp. Tax'n 20 (May 2006); Friedrich, "Late Filing Corporation Does Not Forfeit Deductions: Contrary Regulation Invalidated," 33 Corp. Tax'n 44 (May 2006); Lipton, "A Divided Tax Court Rejects a Regulation and Struggles With Administrative Law – In *Swallows Holding*," 104 J. Tax'n 260 (May 2006); Daub, "Swallows-Rare Tax Court Invalidation of an International Tax Regulation," 17 J. Int'l Tax'n 26 (June 2006); Johnson, "Swallows Holding as It Is: The Distortion of NATIONAL MUFFLER," 112 Tax Notes 351 (July 24, 2006); Johnson, "Swallows as It Might Have Been: Regulations Revising Case Law," 112 Tax Notes 773 (Aug. 28, 2006).

[2] Branch Profits Tax: § 884

[c] Branch-Level Interest Tax: § 884(f)

Page 15-81:

In second sentence of note 267 change cross-reference from note 267 *to* note 268.

[d] Second-Tier Source Rules

Page 15-81:

Add to note 269.

But the Joint Committee Staff's April 2001 simplification report proposes to eliminate the second-tier source rule for dividends paid by foreign corporations; Proposal IX. H., at 436 (and so does the Thomas Bill); the final 2004 legislation adopted this proposal, American Job Creation Act of 2004, § 871(i)(2)(D) (effective in 2005).

[4] Interest-Stripping Limitations: § 163(j)

Page 15-84:

Add to text at end of ¶ 15.04[4].

Treasury, in a preliminary report on expatriating corporate inversions released on May 17, 2002,[280.1] proposed to tighten the interest-stripping rules of § 163(j) as one of several proposals to deal with these transactions.[280.2] Ways and Means Chairman Thomas has largely incorporated the Treasury interest-stripping proposal in his initial legislative proposal released on July 11, 2002.[280.3] But this proposal did not survive in the final export repeal legislation enacted on October 22, 2004.[280.4]

[280.1] Reprinted in Daily Tax Rep. (BNA) No. 97, at L-3 (May 20, 2002). For criticism of Treasury's limited approach to the inversion problem, see Sullivan Congress' Inversion Odyssey: "Oh, the Places You'll Go," 96 Tax Notes 9 (July 1, 2002); Sullivan, "Treasury's Inversion Report Rocks the Boat," 95 Tax Notes 1289 (May 27, 2002); Thompson, "Treasury's Inversion Study Misses the Mark," 95 Tax Notes 1673 (June 10, 2002); Avi-Yonah, "For Heaven's Sake: Reflections on Inversion Transactions," 95 Tax Notes 1713 (June 17, 2002); Sheppard, "Preventing Corporate Inversions," Part 3, 95 Tax Notes 1864 (June 24, 2002).

[280.2] For inversions generally, see ¶ 12.63[3][b], and infra ¶ 15.82[2][c].

[280.3] HR 5095, The American Competitiveness and Corporate Accountability Act of 2002, § 201. See Joint Comm. Staffs' Technical Explanation of HR 5095, July 19, 2002, reprinted in Daily Tax Rep. (BNA) No. 140, at L-6, L-21 (July 22, 2002). The current version of this proposal is HR 2896, § 2003 (July 25, 2003). The latest version has dropped this proposal. But this proposal did not survive in the final legislation (a mandated study only).

[280.4] American Jobs Creation Act of 2004, § 424, mandates Treasury "study" of stripping rules only.

[5] Foreign-Owned Domestic Corporations

Page 15-84:

In note 284 change ASIC *to* ASAT.

B   DOMESTIC CORPORATIONS WITH FOREIGN-SOURCE INCOME

¶ 15.20 INTRODUCTORY: TAXATION OF FOREIGN-BASED ACTIVITY

[1] In General

[b] Source-Based Tax System (How Much Special Treatment for Foreign-Source Income?)

Page 15-86:

Add to note 290.

For replacement of these rules with a partial territorial regime, see infra ¶ 15.23[4]. This provision passed on November 16, 2000, but once again has successfully been challenged by the European Union, and is slated for repeal in the Thomas bill, HR 5095, § 327 (July 11, 2002). The current version of this proposal is HR 2896, § 2001 (July 25, 2003), which was finally enacted on October 22, 2004, by the 2004 Jobs Act.

[3] General Tax Factors and Stakes as to Form of Foreign Business Structure

Page 15-89:

Add to note 300, second paragraph.

Osterberg, "International Joint Ventures: Basic Tax Goals and Structure," 91 Tax Notes 647 (Apr. 23, 2001)

Add to end of note 300.

For various planning strategies to effectively utilize foreign generated losses in the most tax efficient manner, see Brewer, "Global Tax Planning for Losses," 93 Tax Notes 1613 (Dec. 17, 2001).

¶ 15.21 FOREIGN TAX CREDIT

[1] In General

Page 15-90:

Add to end of note 301.

For reform proposals, see Peroni, Fleming & Shay, "Reformed Simplification of the U.S. Foreign Tax Credit Rules," 101 Tax Notes 103 (Oct. 6, 2003); Steines, "Foreign Tax Credit Reform: A Response to Peroni, et al," 101 Tax Notes 134 (Oct. 6, 2003). The final 2004 export repeal legislation made major changes here, though not in the direction suggested by *Peroni, et al.* See Calianno and Gotshalk, "The FTC's Changing Landscape—an Overview of the Impact of the AJCA," 103 J. Tax'n 276 (Nov. 2005).

[a] General Rules

Page 15-91:

Add to the end of the first paragraph of note 304.

Sheppard, "Banks' Foreign Tax Abritrage," 112 Tax Notes 222 (July 7, 2006).

Add to end of note 304.

Guardian Inds. v US, 65 Fed. Cl 50, 2005-1 USTC   50,263 (Ct. Fed. Cl. 2005) (sub holding company opted disregarded entity status and parent became liable for foreign taxes and thus became entitled to § 901 direct credit, rather than § 902 derivative deemed paid credit); Bennett, "Whose Tax Is It Anyway: Foreign Tax Credits in a Check-the-Box World," 83 Taxes 35 (Mar. 2005); see also NYSBA Tax Section Report, "The Allocation of Foreign Taxes Among Related Taxpayers," 107 Tax Notes 1013 (May 23, 2005); Holland, "U.S. Check-the-box Rules in the Cross-Border Context," 108 Tax Notes 1151 (Sept. 5, 2005); Sheppard, "Where Else is the Guardian Industries Result Available?" 111 Tax Notes 286 (Apr. 17, 2006). *Guardian Industries* was affirmed, 2007-1 USTC   50,281 (CA Fed. Cir. 2007) (no dissents).

Add to text after item 3.

But IRS proposed a new definition of "the taxpayer" in proposed regulations issued on August 4, 2006, amending the technical taxpayer rule of the current regulations.[304.1] The major goal of these proposals is to tie foreign tax credits to the taxpayer required to account for the associated income under foreign law.[304.2]

[304.1] Prop. Regs. § 1.901-2(f) (effective Jan. 1, 2007).

[304.2] The intent here is to prevent the separation of tax credits from the associated income (as in the *Guardian Industries* case, supra note 304), which was affirmed by the Federal Circuit on February 23, 2007.

For comments, see Gouler, 112 Tax Notes 629 (Aug. 21, 2006); Sheppard, "The Trouble With the Technical Taxpayer Rule," 112 Tax Notes 631 (Aug. 21, 2001); Calianno and Cornett, "Proposed Regs. Attack *Guardian* and Reverse Hybrids," 113 Tax Notes 491 (Oct. 30, 2006); Rollinson et al., "Foreign Tax Credit Proposed Regulations Substantially Revise the Technical Taxpayer Rule," 105 J. Tax'n 367 (Dec. 2006).

Add new note 305.1 to end of item 6 in text.

[305.1] See Regs. § 1.901-1(d) (ten years to elect either credit or deduction); Chrysler Corp., 116 TC 465 (2001) (ten-year election period runs from taxable year for which § 901 credit election made); aff'd, 436 F3d 644 (6th Cir. 2006).

[b] Creditable Taxes

Page 15-92:

Add to note 310.

See also the "in lieu" rules of §903 and Regs. § 1.903-1 for an important alternative to § 901; Sykes, The Invalidity of the 'For Everyone or No One Rule' and a Tax Recovery Strategy Suggested By the Analysis, 102 Tax Notes 1533 (Mar. 22, 2004).

Add to note 311, third paragraph, after parenthetical comment for Riggs Nat'l Corp.

and so was Bankers Trust, 225 F3d 1368, 2000-2 USTC ¶ 50,739 (Fed. Cir. 2000) (citing *Marbury v. Madison* no less; prior Court of Claims precedent trumped regulations; IRS had no power to overrule by regulation the precedent of an appellate tribunal); but *Riggs* lost again on remand, RIA TC Memo. ¶ 2001-012 (2001) (failed to prove payment); but reversed again, 295 F3d 16, 2002-USTC ¶ 50,521 (DC Cir. 2002) (taxpayer adequately proved payment here); on remand, RIA TC Memo. ¶ 2004-110 (taxpayer had to reduce credit by amount of indirect subsidy benefits paid to borrowers; thus, taxpayer got some, but not all, of its claimed § 901 credits).

[c] Holding Period Requirement: § 901(k)

Page 15-93:

In the first sentence of the third paragraph of note 315, replace 363 with 214.

Page 15-94:

Add to end of note 315.

For additional comments, see infra note 317. But contra to *Compaq* is IES Indus., Inc. v. US, 253 F3d 350 (8th Cir. 2001) (same transaction, but taxpayer got the credit here); *IES* was followed by the Fifth Circuit in *Compaq* appeal, which reversed the Tax Court and held for the taxpayer, 277 F3d 778 (5th Cir. 2001). But on remand, IES Inds, Inc. v. US, __ F. Supp. 2d __, 2002-2 USTC ¶ 50,807 (DC Iowa 2002), government was allowed a setoff against taxpayer's refunds via equitable recoupment defense. *IES* was affirmed on appeal, IES Inds., Inc. v. US, 349 F3d 574 (8th Cir. 2003); comment by Raby & Raby, "'Other' Issues When a Tax Case Goes to Court," 101 Tax Notes 1097 (Dec. 1, 2003).

Add text to end of ¶ 15.21[1][c].

The 2004 Jobs Act[316.1] added a minimum holding period requirement for withholding taxes on any item of income or gain in order to claim foreign tax credits (with the same holding period as § 901(k)). Recognizing that the reach of new § 901(l) is overly inclusive, IRS announced that it will issue regula-

---

[316.1] American Jobs Creation Act of 2004, § 832 (effective October 22, 2004), adding new § 901(l). Bogos, "A Risk-Based Analysis of Credit Derivation Under SSRP Standard (Part 1)," 112 Tax Notes 587 (Aug. 14, 2006); (Part 2), 112 Tax Notes 655 (Aug. 21, 2006); and (Part 3), 112 Tax Notes 259 (Aug. 28, 2006) (be prepared to spend some time with these pieces).

tions[316.2] exempting transactions involving back-to-back licensing of computer software to affiliates.[316.3]

[316.2] Notice 2005-90, 2005-51 IRB 1163 (Dec. 19, 2005) effective for payments accrued after Nov. 21, 2005.

[316.3] Thus § 901(l) will not be applied to deny foreign tax credits on deals where a domestic corporation licenses its software to an affiliated license which than sublicenses the material to a foreign affiliate for copying and distribution. Needless to say, the software industry is overjoyed with this result—see Daily Tax Rep. (BNA) No. 230, at 661 (Dec. 1, 2005).

[d] Abusive Foreign Tax Credit Transfers

Page 15-94:

Add after citation of Notice 98-5 in note 317.

But withdrawn by Notice 2004-19, 2004-11 IRB 606.

Add to note 317 at end of first paragraph.

Grier, "Some Thoughts on the Incidences of Foreign Taxes," 87 Tax Notes 541 (Apr. 24, 2000); Shaviro, "Economic Substance, Corporate Tax Shelters and the Compaq Case," 88 Tax Notes 221 (July 10, 2000). Kingson, "The Confusion Over Tax Ownership," 93 Tax Notes 409 (Oct. 15, 2001).

In last paragraph of note 317, replace 363 with 214.

Add to note 317 at end of second paragraph.

But contra is IES Inds., Inc. v. US, supra note 315. See Kingson, supra note 317; and *Compaq* was reversed on appeal, 277 F3d 778 (5th Cir. 2001). See Hariton, "The *Compaq* Case, Notice 98-5 and Tax Shelters: The Theory Is All Wrong," 94 Tax Notes 501 (Jan. 28, 2002); Shaviro & Weisbach, "The Fifth Circuit Got It Wrong in *Compaq v. Commissioner*," 94 Tax Notes 511 (Jan. 28, 2002); McMahon, "Economic Substance, Purposive Activity, and Corporate Tax Shelters," 94 Tax Notes 1017 (Feb. 25, 2002); Kane, "*Compaq* and *IES*: Putting the Tax Back in Taxable Income," 94 Tax Notes 1215 (Mar. 4, 2002); Goldstein, "Reflections on *Compaq* and the Sham Transaction Doctrine," 31 Tax Mgmt Int'l J. No. 4, at 145 (Apr. 12, 2002). Gunther, "Economics and *Compaq v. Commissioner*," 97 Tax Notes 555 (Oct. 28, 2002). But on remand in *IES Inds.*, government allowed set-off against taxpayer's refunds under equitable recoupment, supra note 315.

Add to note 319.

For reversal of *Compaq*, see notes 315 and 317.

Page 15-95:

Add to first paragraph of note 322.

For reversal of *Compaq* see supra notes 315 and 317.

Add to second paragraph of note 322.

But this proposed regulation was withdrawn by Notice 2003-46, 2003-28 IRB 53; supra 15.01[4], note 34.

Add to text at end of ¶ 15.21[1][d].

But the economic profit test of *Notice 98-5* was finally abandoned and Notice 98-5 was withdrawn in early 2004.[322.1]

[322.1] Notice 2004-19, 2004-11 IRB 606; but IRS will attack abusive foreign tax credit transactions by "other theories." Comment by Bell, 102 Tax Notice 1081 (Mar. 1, 2004). Engle, "IRS Revises Its Strategies For Combating Notice 98-5 Foreign Tax Credit Planning," 31 Corp. Tax'n 42 (May/June 2004); Lemein and McDonald, "Foreign Tax Credit Planning-IRS Withdraws Notice 98-5," 82 Taxes 5 (May 2004).

[2] Derivative (or Deemed-Paid) Foreign Tax Credit of § 902

[a] In General

Page 15-96:

Add to note 323, fourth paragraph.

The Joint Committee Staff's April 2001 simplification report proposes to codify the holding in Rev. Rul. 71-141 (namely, allow § 902 credit for a partner if it holds a 10-percent indirect interest in foreign corporation); Proposal IX. E., at 424. The Thomas bill, HR 5095 § 317 adopts this proposal (effective in 2003), and this provision was adopted in the final 2004 tax legislation, HR 4520, Act §§ 405, 902(c)(7); effective Oct. 22, 2004.

[c] Key Definitional Components of § 902 Credit

Page 15-99:

Add to note 330.

See generally Baline, "When Is a Dividend Not a Dividend?" 31 Corp. Tax'n 30 (Mar. 2004), commenting on later InterTAN, Inc., RIA TC Memo 2004-1 (2004) (purported dividends intended to generate a § 902 credit disregarded a sham and § 6662 penalty applied).

[f] Tax Reform Act of 1986 "Pooling" Regime

Page 15-103:

Add to note 340.

See Prop. Regs. §§ 1.367(b)-7 and 1.367(b)-9 (Nov. 8, 2000) (§ 381 carryovers of earnings and related foreign taxes in various foreign-to-foreign asset reorganizations and liquidations and application of pooling regime in that context), infra ¶¶ 15.83[3], 15.84[2][f], and 15.84[3][f]. Prop. Regs. § 1.367(b)-8 deal with foreign divisive transactions, infra ¶ 15.84[3][f]. These regulations are very heavy going.

Add to text at end of runover paragraph.

Proposed regulations were issued in January 2001 (but withdrawn in 2004) to deal with cases where qualified domestic shareholder status is interrupted;

pooling ends at that point (revert to annual peel-back method), but will restart (prospectively) if qualified shareholder status resumes.[340.1]

[340.1] Prop. Regs. §§ 1.902-1(a)(10) (pooling ends when qualified shareholder status ends), 1.902-1(a)(13) (pooling will restart, prospectively, if qualified shareholder status resumes). Fischl, "Greenwald & Suit, Foreign Tax Credit Limitations," 12 J. Int'l Tax'n 16 (Oct. 2001). But withdrawn for further study July 20, 2004.

[3] Limitations on Foreign Tax Credits: § 904 Generally

Page 15-104:

Add text to end of runover paragraph.

Taxpayers strive to maximize the size of the § 904(a) numerator; conversely, the IRS is ever alert to lower that number and thereby reduce the amount of currently usable credits.[342.1]

[342.1] The deduction allocation rules of Regs. § 1.861-8 are the prime example of this tension, supra   15.02[1][e]–15.02[1][g]. See also Harwood, "Sourcing S Corporation Salaries," 95 Tax Notes 1046 (May 13, 2002).

Add to note 343, second paragraph.

Dresser Indus., Inc. v. US, 238 F3d 603 (5th Cir. 2001) (affirmed District Court decision).

Page 15-105:

Add to text after sentence ending with note 344.

> But proposed legislation by the chair of the Ways and Means Committee[344.1] on July 11, 2002, would extend the § 904(c) carryover term to ten years, and this provision was adopted in the final 2004 tax legislation (but the carryback was shortened to one year). HR 4520, Act § 417; effective Oct. 22, 2004.

[344.1] HR 5095, § 314 (effective in 2003); the final version of this proposal is HR 4520, § 417 (effective Oct. 22, 2004).

Add to note 346.

New final and proposed regulations under § 904(d) were issued on January 1, 2001; see Fischl, "Greenwald & Suit, Foreign Tax Credit Limitations," Fischl, et al., 12 J. Int'l Tax'n 16 (Oct. 2001) (discussing these regulations).

Page 15-106:

Add to note 347.

Prop. Regs. § 1.904(b)-1 finally were issued on January 3, 2001 (they are surprisingly complex, but what wasn't in this area). They were adopted as final regulations by TD 9141 on July 20, 2004 (also applying § 904(b) limits to low-taxed dividends).

Add text to end of item 3.

The 2003 legislation reducing the top rate on dividends (and capital gain) for individuals to 15 percent[348.1] will significantly increase the importance of the § 904(b) rules since the rate differential on these items is now quite substantial.[348.2]

[348.1] IRC § 1(h)(11); see ¶ 8.06[2]. New § 1(h)(11)(iv) provides that rules "similar to the rules of § 904(b)(2)(B) will apply to the dividend rate differential as well as the newly expanded capital gain rate differential.

[348.2] Top individual rate is 35 percent while the top individual dividend rate generally is 15 percent, but can be as low as five percent (or zero in 2008).

Page 15-107:

Add to note 349.

The Thomas bill, HR 5095, § 312, reproposes the symmetry provisions of § 904(g) (effective in 2003). The current version is proposal HR 2896, § 1112 (effective in 2005), and it passed in the final 2004 Tax Act adopted on October 22nd, 2004; HR 4520, at § 402 (effective 2007). The general effect of this provision is to give back § 904(a) numerator in future years to make up for the domestic loss negative impact.

Page 15-108:

Add to text at end of ¶ 15.21[3].

Legislation introduced by the chair of Ways and Means on July 11, 2002, proposed to reduce the number of baskets in § 904(d) from nine to three, undoing much of 1986 Reform Act's multiple basket regime and effecting a major simplification of that provision.[355.1] The current version of the Thomas bill released on July 25, 2003, would reduce the number of baskets to two.[355.2] This was the version that eventually prevailed in the final 2004 Jobs Act;[355.3] a two basket regime consisting of (1) "passive category income"[355.4] and (2) "general

---

[355.1] HR 5095, § 313 (effective in 2003). See Sheppard, "The Good and the Bad in the Thomas Bill," 96 Tax Notes 482, 486 (July 22, 2002).

[355.2] HR 2896, § 1113 (effective in 2005). This proposal was adopted in the final 2004 Tax Act (but is not effective until 2007); HR 4520, Act § 404.

[355.3] American Jobs Creation Act of 2004, § 404 (but not effective until 2007).

[355.4] But revised § 904(d)(2)(B)(v) provides for "deemed" passive category income in three cases (derived from former separate baskets of still current law).

category income." While revised § 904(d) is fundamentally simplified by the 2004 revisions, the wait until 2007 will be long (and complicated).[355.5]

[355.5] During the waiting period until fully effective (in 2007) § 904(d) will continue be a truly complicated and confusing mess. But at least IRS will have sufficient time to write decent regulations explaining the new regime.

[4] Separate Basket Limitation: § 904(d)

Add to note 356.

But HR 5095 (the Thomas bill), would reduce the number of § 904(d) baskets from nine to three (effective in 2003). The current version (July 25, 2003) is HR 2896, § 1113, which reduces the number of baskets to two (effective in 2005); it was adopted Oct. 22, 2004 (but is not effective until 2007); American Jobs Creation Act of 2004, § 404.

Add to note 357.

But the Thomas bill HR 5095, goes in the opposite direction, reducing the number of § 904(d) baskets from nine to three. The current version (July 25, 2003), reduces the number of baskets to two, HR 2896, § 1113 (effective 2005). It was adopted in the final 2004 tax legislation, supra note 356.

Add to note 358.

American Air Liquide, Inc., 116 TC 23 (2001); aff'd, 2002-2 USTC   50,628 (9th Cir. 2002) (royalties received from license to foreign parent held to fall in passive income basket; look-through rule not applicable to royalties from foreign parents—only applies to royalties from CFCs). But see Prop. Regs. § 1.904-4(b)(2) (Jan. 3, 2001) (will change this result, but only prospectively); did in final Regs. § 1.904-4(b)(2), issued by TD 9141 July 20, 2004 (but prospective only).

Page 15-109:

Add to note 361, second paragraph.

Joint Committee Staff's April 2001 simplification report proposes to allow immediate look-through treatment for 10-50 basket subs regardless of year in which E&P accumulated; Proposal IX. D., at 361. The Thomas bill, HR 5095, § 316 (effective in 2003) does this as well, extending § 904(d)(4) Look-Through treatment to all noncontrolled § 902 subsidiaries. The current version is HR 2896, § 1115 (July 25, 2003), effective for 2003. This proposal passed Oct. 22, 2004. HR 4520, Act § 403 (effective for 2003).

Add to note 361, third paragraph.

Joint Committee Staff's simplification proposal also would allow immediate look-through treatment, supra this note 361, as does the Thomas bill, id. Final 2004 tax act adopted this proposal in the American Jobs Creation Act of 2004 § 403 (effective for 2003). Thus, there is now immediate look-through treatment for 10-50 sub dividends (regardless of which years is their source).

Add to text after reference to note 361.

Treasury issued important guidelines on December 20, 2002, setting out "guidelines" on regulations to be issued under the § 904(d) look-through rules

(which became effective at last in 2003) for 10/50 subsidiaries.[361.1] Temporary
regulations on the 10/50 sub-look-through rules were issued on April 20,
2006.[361.2]

[361.1] Notice 2003-5, 2003-5 IRB 294; see Klein & Felix, "Putting All Your Eggs in a
Single 10/50 Basket: Here's How," 98 Tax Notes 2015 (Mar. 31, 2003) (it won't be
easy!) Engle, "IRS Issues Guidance on 1997 Changes to Effect of 10/50 Dividends on
Foreign Tax Credit," 30 J. Corp. Tax'n 40 (May 2003). Lemein & McDonald, "Rolling
with the Changes—IRS Provides Guidance on Transition Rule For 10/50 Basket Credits,"
81 Taxes 5 (July 2003); Fissel & Collins, "10/50 Basket – Going, Going, but Not Gone,"
14 J. Int'l Tax'n 4 (Aug. 2003). How these regulations will inteface with the new two-
basket regime enacted by the 2004 Jobs Act (especially for years before 2007 when it finally becomes effective), remains to be seen.

[361.2] A huge (and complex) package of proposed and temporary regulations was released on April 20, 2006, TD 9260. They are "beyond category" difficult and cannot be
summarized in any meaningfully coherent way.

Add to note 363.

But see American Air Liquide Inc., 116 TC 23 (2001); aff'd, 2002-2 USTC ¶ 50,628 (9th
Cir. 2002) (look-through rule not applicable to converse case of royalty payments by foreign parent to domestic sub); but Prop. Regs. § 1.904-4(b)(2) (Jan. 3, 2001) will change to
allow look-through treatment here, but only prospectively. Sheppard, "Playing the Foreign
Tax Credit Basket (Ball) Game," 90 Tax Notes 1448 (Mar. 12, 2001).

Add new note 364.1 to end of item 1.

[364.1] Amendments to the separate basket rules in Regs. § 1.904-4 were proposed on
January 3, 2001, dealing with cases where intervening changes of status occur (e.g., noncontrolled, or non-§ 902) and the effect on distributions from CFCs or other look-through
corporations; Prop. Regs. §§ 1.904-4(g)(1), 1.904-4(g)(3)(i)(C), 1.904-4(g)(3)(i)(D). These
regulations relate to the § 367(b) carryover proposed regulations noted infra note 365. See
Fischl, "Greenwald & Suit, Foreign Tax Credit Limitations," 12 J. Int'l Tax'n 16 (Oct.
2001) (discussing these regulations). But these proposals were withdrawn for further study
on July 20, 2004. In view of the 2004 Jobs Act's new two-basket regime, these regulations will have to be rethought as well.

Page 15-110:

Add new note 364.2 to end of item 3.

[364.2] See Cohen & Geiger, "Timing and Base Differences Under Section 904(d), 56
Tax Law. 3 (Fall 2002).

Add to note 365.

See Prop. Regs. §§ 1.367(b)-7 and 1.367(b)-9 (Nov. 2000) (§ 381 carryovers of earnings
and related foreign taxes in various foreign-to-foreign asset reorganization § 381 transactions, infra ¶ 15.84). Prop. Regs. § 1.367(b)-8 deal with foreign divisive transactions, infra
¶ 15.84[3]. These proposals are very heavy lifting.

See Prop. Regs. §§ 1.904-4(g)(3)(i)(C), 1.904-4(g)(3)(i)(D), 1.904-4(g)(1), supra note
364.1 (intervening changes of status and effect on basket rules) relate to these proposals;
but were withdrawn for further study on July 20, 2004. The impact of the 2004 Jobs Act's
new (though long delayed) two-basket regime will be interesting as well.

[5] Special Timing and Procedural Rules: § 905

[a] Timing of Credits: § 905(a)

Page 15-110:

Add to note 367.

See also Chrysler Corp. v. CIR, 436 F3d 644 (6th Cir. 2006), affirming tax court decision, 116 TC 465 (2001).

[c] Subsequent Adjustments of Accrued Foreign Taxes: § 905(c)

Page 15-112:

Add to note 376.

See Kochman & Rosenbloom, "Deconstruction of the Foreign Tax Credit Redetermination Rules," 95 Tax Notes 1073 (May 13, 2002), infra note 384.

Page 15-113:

Add to note 384.

See Kochman & Rosenbloom, supra note 376 (analysis of 1997 legislation and development of redetermination rules).

¶ 15.22 POSSESSIONS CORPORATIONS: § 936

Page 15-114:

Add to note 389.

See Med Chem (P.R.), 116 TC 308 (2001) (taxpayer failed active business situs test; extensive analysis of active business status and location). *Med Chem* was aff'd, 295 F3d 118, 2002-2 USTC   50,512 (1st Cir. 2002). But Electronic Arts, Inc., 118 TC 226 (2002), found that taxpayer met the active business in Puerto Rico requirement under the *Med Chem* tests and also had a significant business presence there; but contract manufacturing deal did not qualify as "manufacturing" there.

Page 15-115:

In the first sentence of the Example change 75 percent *to* 80 percent *and change* 50 percent *to* 75 percent.

Page 15-116:

Add to note 394, first paragraph.

The gradual demise of § 936 mandated by § 936(j) is its most significant feature today.

¶ 15.23 FOREIGN SALES CORPORATIONS AND THEIR ANTECEDENTS

[3] Foreign Sales Corporations: §§ 921 through 927

Page 15-118:

Add to note 397.

Larkins, "WTO Appellate Body Rules Against FSCs," 11 J. Int'l Tax'n 14 (May 2000). For U.S. proposals to fix the FSC rules to conform to this decision, see Daily Tax Rep. (BNA) No. 88, at G-8 & L-10 (May 5, 2000). For new legislation replacing the FSC regime, see infra ¶ 15.23[4]. But new regime also rejected by the WTO in June 2001. Decision rejecting new regime reported at Daily Tax Rep. (BNA) No. 124, at L-1 (June 28, 2001).

[c] Export Property

Page 15-119:

Add to note 399.

But *General Electric* was reversed, General Elec. Co. v. CIR, 245 F3d 149, 2001-1 USTC ¶ 50,329 (2d Cir. 2001) (engines held to be separate qualified export property from the plane).

Add to note 400.

For prior law, see Microsoft Corp., 115 TC 228 (2000) (licensed computer softwear masters not qualified export property; regulation so stating construed and upheld as valid); but Tax Court rev'd, 311 F3d 1178, 2002-2 USTC ¶ 50,800 (9th Cir. 2002).

[f] General Tax Results of Foreign Sales Corporation Structure

Page 15-121:

Add to note 406 after second sentence.

But Dresser Indus., Inc. v. US, 238 F3d 603 (5th Cir. 2001) (holds no interest netting under later regulations).

Add to end of note 406.

But *Boeing* was reversed, Boeing Corp. v. US, 258 F3d 958, 2001-2 USTC ¶ 50,562 (9th Cir. 2001) (with no citation to *Intel*); cert. granted May 28, 2002. Lupi-Sher, "High Court Takes on Tax Case Limited in Results and Scope," 95 Tax Notes 1565 (June 10, 2002). The Supreme Court affirmed, 537 US 437, 123 S. Ct. 1099, 2003-1 USTC ¶ 50,273 (2003) (two dissents).

Page 15-122:

Add ¶ 15.23[4] following ¶ 15.23[3][f].

[4] Replacement of Foreign Sales Corporations: Partial Exclusion of "Extraterritorial Income"

[a] In General

In response to the decision by the WTO that the Foreign Sales Corporations (FSC) regime constitutes a prohibited export subsidy,[407.1] the House Ways & Means Committee approved a bipartisan proposal to replace the discredited FSC system with a "new" exclusion for "extraterritorial income" which would move the United States toward a more territorial tax system.[407.2] Dubbed the "FSC Repeal and Exclusion of Extraterritorial Income Exclusion Act of 2000," the proposal was intended to satisfy European objections to the FSC regime (it hasn't). The new legislation was effective October 1, 2000, the deadline set by the WTO for the United States to comply with its ruling?[407.3]

[407.1] See supra note 397. They think the replacement regime is also a prohibited export subsidy. The new regime was also rejected by the WTO in June 2001. Rejection decision is reported at Daily Tax Rep. (BNA) No. 121, at GG-1 (June 25, 2001) and BNA Daily Tax Rep. No. 124, at L-1 (June 28, 2001). For comments, see Pinter, "Diplomacy Along With Tax Law Change Needed to Reduce Dispute With European Union Over U.S. Export Tax Breaks," Daily Tax Rep. (BNA) No. 130 (July 9, 2001); Westin & Vasek, "The ETI Exclusion: Where Do Matters Stand Following the WTO Panel Report?" 92 Tax Notes 811 (Aug. 6, 2001). Funk, "The Thirty-Years Tax War," 93 Tax Notes 271 (Oct. 8, 2001); Lopez-Mata, "Income Taxation, International Competitiveness and the World Trade Organization's Rules on Subsidies: Lessons to the U.S. and the World From FSC Dispute," 54 Tax Law. 557 (Sept. 2001).

The WTO decision, again rejecting the new regime was upheld on appeal on January 14, 2002; reported in Daily Tax Rep. (BNA) No. 10, at 66-1, L-1 (Jan. 15, 2002). McIntyre, "How the United States Should Respond to the ET Controversy," 95 Tax Notes 1251 (May 20, 2002) (repeal this provision). HR 5095, § 327, repeals the Extraterritorial Income provisions effective in 2003. See generally Joint Comm. Tax, "Background and History of the Trade Dispute Relating to the Prior Law Foreign Sales Corporation Provisions and the Present Law Exclusion for Extraterritorial Income and a Description of These Rules," (JCX-83-02), July 26, 2002, Daily Tax Rep. (BNA) No. 145, at L-8 (July 29, 2002).

[407.2] For description of this regime, which also had Treasury support (and was developed in consultation with Senate Finance Committee staff), see Joint Comm. on Tax'n, Description of HR 4986—The "FSC Repeal and Extraterritorial Income Exclusion Act of 2000" (JCX-87-00), July 27, 2000, reprinted in Daily Tax Report (BNA) No. 146, at L-1 (July 28, 2000), and in Highlights & Documents, Vol. 58, No. 19, at 977 (July 28, 2000). Also JCX-97-00, in Daily Tax Rep. (BNA) No. 181, at L-45 (Sept. 18, 2000). See Lubkin, "Extraterritorial Exclusion: Replacing the Foreign Sales Corporation," 29 Tax Mgmt. Int'l J. 611 (Nov. 10, 2000). The export repeal legislation finally passed on October 22, 2004, HR 4520, § 101 (with grandfather and transition rules which are causing trouble once again).

[407.3] Transition rules are provided for existing FSCs, in § 5(c) of the bill. This proposal passed the House on September 13, 2000, and cleared Congress on November 14, 2000, as HR 4986, which was signed into law on November 16, 2000.

For comments, see Misey, "Planning for and Obtaining the Benefits of the Extraterritorial Increase Exclusion: From A to Z," 79 Taxes 11 (Feb. 2001); Lederman & Hirsh,

Students of the FSC provisions will find much that is familiar in the new legislation, but also some significant elements of a "new" approach; e.g., foreign taxpayers with U.S. branches also would be eligible to participate in the new regime (a key concession, it would seem, to counter the export subsidy argument; it didn't). The exclusion granted by the new legislation was only a partial one, however, but it represented a significant move by the United States to a territorial tax system (a position that historically has been opposed by U.S. tax policy). Thus, it can be viewed as a "camel's nose under the tent" in what could become a much broader approach to the taxation of foreign-source income, with a concomitant retreat from reliance on the foreign tax credit as the principal method adopted by the United States for avoiding double taxation of foreign source income.[407.4]

Accordingly, while the scope of the new legislation currently was tightly drafted, and richly encumbered with layers of complex limitations, the basic structure for a sea change in U.S. international tax policy was put in place with the adoption of this legislation. But rejection once again by the WTO[407.5] doomed this regime to a swift demise (which was pending in both the House and Senate, and passed on October 22, 2004, so you can stop reading here).[407.6]

[b] Comments

One might ask whether this new regime was significantly "different" from the FSC provisions to satisfy the European opposition to an export subsidy that caused the demise of the FSC system. There are some differences here, but they are not major ones. The replacement at heart was still essentially a partial exclusion for outbound sales and leases of U.S. property, and a transactionally elective one at that. Thus, one can call a dog's tail a fifth leg, but that still doesn't make it a five-legged dog. Although not identical twins, the new exclusion regime was sufficiently similar to a FSC to qualify as its son (or sister).[407.7]

"The Extraterritorial Income Exclusion Enhance the Tax Benefits Once Sought From FSC," 94 J. Tax'n 174 (Mar. 2001). See also Larkins, "Extraterritorial Exclusion Replaces FSC Regime: Mirror Rules, Broader Spectrum," 12 J. Int'l Tax'n 22 (May 2001); Engle, "The Tax Treatment of Foreign Income Under the EIE Act of 2000," 28 J. Corp. Tax'n 34 (Mar. 2001). For comments on new challenge by the Europeans, see Sheppard, "Eye-Poking Over the FSC Replacements," 90 Tax Notes 1288 (Mar. 5, 2001).

[407.4] Exempt extraterritorial income would be denied foreign tax credits by § 114(d); moreover, deductions attributable to such income also would be denied by § 114(c), as would deductibility of the foreign tax, § 275(a)(4)(C).

[407.5] See supra note 407.1.

[407.6] If you want to retain the more extensive explanation of this regime, save the 2004 Cumulative Supplement No. 1. HR 4520, § 101 (Oct. 22, 2004), repealed these provisions.

[407.7] See Sheppard, "An Export Subsidy Is an Export Subsidy," 88 Tax Notes 596 (July 31, 2000). Apparently the Europeans think so too: see BNA Daily Tax Rep. No. 149, at G-1 (Aug. 2, 2000). The WTO again rejected this version as an improper subsidy

Once enacted, however (the legislation was on a bipartisan fast-track and finally passed on November 16, 2000), it is important in its own right, but even more so as a first step towards a more broadly based territorial tax system, which excludes, rather than merely defers, all foreign-source income of U.S. taxpayers. Congress has been reluctant to go this route in the past (hence its resort to the targeted partial reduction schemes of DISC and FSC). A total territorial tax system would have the added benefit of eliminating the need for the foreign tax credit regime,[407.8] and also for the various anti-deferral regimes discussed later in this chapter[407.9] as well (since no credit, or deduction, would be allowed for foreign taxes imposed on exempt income, and an exclusion from tax is *always* better than a deferral of taxation).[407.10] Abandonment of these two regimes would work a huge simplification, no matter how complex the new replacement becomes. Before euphoria over this regime becomes rampant, however, the above scenario is not a likely eventuality.

More likely is simply the replacement of one complexity (the FSC rules) with another complex structure (the extraterritorial income exclusion provision), and the retention of both the foreign tax credit rules and the subpart F regime as well.[407.11] The foreign tax rules of the United States never fade away, they just keep multiplying in ever increasing convoluted legislative encrustations. But the new regime seems slated for an early demise in view of its unsurprising rejection by the WTO in 2001.[407.12] The Thomas Bill's solution to the ETI dispute was to repeal those provisions and replace them with a series of international tax breaks to benefit U.S. multinational corporations with substantial foreign operations.[407.13] An alternative proposal by Representatives Crane and Rangel[407.14] has recently emerged which would provide for a deduction reducing the effective corporate tax rate for domestic manufacturers based on the portion of a company's income attributable to U.S. manufacturing activ-

---

in June 2001, and this decision was upheld on appeal on January 14, 2002. See Sullivan, "20 Talking Points on U.S. Export Incentives," 95 Tax Notes 660 (Apr. 29, 2002); Hufbauer, "The Case of Mutating Incentives: How Will the FSC/ETI Drama End?" 95 Tax Notes 791 (Apr. 29, 2002).

[407.8] See supra ¶ 15.21.

[407.9] See infra pts. C and D.

[407.10] Subpart F's restrictions on the deferral of certain categories of CFC earnings would not be necessary if the CFC's foreign-source income is tax-exempt.

[407.11] Although the importance of these regimes abates pro tanto with any expansion of an exclusion for foreign-source income.

[407.12] Supra note 407.1. HR 5095, § 327 of the Thomas Bill proposes to repeal these provisions (effective in 2003). See Larkins, "EU 5, US 0, Game Over,"13 J. Int'l Tax'n 10 (Dec. 2002). The current version is HR 2896, § 4001 (effective 2004), introduced July 25, 2003.

[407.13] See supra note 407.25 and ¶ 15.01[2], note 24.1.

[407.14] HR 1769, introduced on Apr. 11, 2003. See Daily Tax Rep. (BNA) No. 72, at 6-5 (Apr. 15, 2003), and No. 83, at G-1 (Apr. 30, 2003); Report, 99 Tax Notes 318 (Apr. 21, 2003).

ities.[407.15] Both versions exist in pending House and Senate proposals, although the final 2004 ETI substitute deduction legislation more closely resemble the latter proposal.

[407.15] Those with long memories will recognize the ancestor in the former "Western Hemisphere Trade Corporation" deduction in what was then § 921 (repealed in 1976). HR 4520, Act § 101, adding new § 199 effective on a phased-in schedule). This provision will be a complexity nightmare, and is considered (briefly infra   15.23[5]).

Add ¶ 15.23[5] following ¶ 15.23[4].

[5] New Deduction For Income Attributable to Domestic Production Activities: § 199

[a] In General

One of the centerpieces of the 2004 Jobs Act[407.16] was the addition of new § 199, a special deduction for a percentage[407.17] of "income attributable to domestic production activities". This provision was cobbled together to placate U.S. businesses for the loss of their export tax subsidy benefits in the repealed ETI system that once again had been found to constitute a prohibited export subsidy by the Europeans. There's something in here for everyone in new § 199; the problem, of course, will be to determine just who is entitled to its benefits and, if so, in what amount. The provision does, however, apply both to corporate and noncorporate business taxpayers.

There are many regulation delegations sprinkled throughout § 199, thus assuring a period of uncertainty until such regulations are forthcoming (the provision phases in over a 5-year period)[407.18] when fully effective (in 2010) it

---

[407.16] American Jobs Creation Act of 2004, § 102, P. L. 108-357; effective for years beginning after 2004.

[407.17] Eventually nine percent (in 2010) of the deduction base (the lesser of "qualified production activities income," or taxable income for the year). For 2005 and 2006, this percentage is only three percent; for 2007–2009, it is six percent, rising to nine percent in 2010. But § 199 is no help for loss companies in view of the taxable income ceiling in § 199(a)(1)(B).

[407.18] This long phase-in should give IRS some breathing room in issuing guidance under § 199, but not much. But a massive set of proposed regulations (224 pages) was issued on Oct. 20, 2005 (and IRS tends to adopt them quickly). Regs. § 1.199-1 through 199-8, expanding in far greater detail on the interim guidance of Notice 2005-14. Needless to say they are very heavy lifting (the preamble is must reading here; it's half the length of the regulations). Final Regs. § 1.199 were adopted May 24, 2006, TD 9263 (effective June 5, 2006; for calendar year taxpayers, 2007). For comments see infra, note 407.28.

For comments, see Stratton, 109 Tax Notes 419 (Oct. 24, 2005) (can use Prop. Regs. Or Notice until final regulations); Miller, "Manousos Clarifies Thinking Behind Domestic Production Regs," 109 Tax Notes 580 (Oct. 31, 2005); Stratton, "Manousos Gives More Details on Domestic Production Guidance," 109 Tax Notes 878 (Nov. 14, 2005); Conjura et al., "Do the Section 199 Proposed Regs. Clarify or Complicate the Domestic Production

will lower the effective tax rate by approximately three points to 32 percent. No attempt will be made here to provide a detailed analysis of the scope and operation of § 199:that unhappy task will be left for others.[407.19] What follows below is a brief outline of the general contours of this provision.

Deduction: 104 J. Tax'n 9" (Jan. 2006); Sheppard, "Domestic Production Deduction: A Tax Cut for Foreign Production," 110 Tax Notes 1268 (Mar. 20, 2006). But 2006 legislation limits the deduction to wages paid to workers employed in domestic production activities (a significant cut back in the scope of § 199); proposed regulations were issued under this limitation in October 2006; temporary regulations were adopted October 19, 2006; see also Rev. Proc. 2006-47, 2006-45 IRB 869.

[407.19] For a helpful start, see Atkinson, "Assembling the Pieces of the Domestic Manufacturers' Deduction," Daily Tax Rep. (BNA) No. 215, at J-1 (Nov. 8, 2004); Notice 2005-14, 2005-7 IRB 498. Cummings and Hanson, "American Jobs Creation Act; New Section 199 Production Deduction," 16 J. Int'l Tax'n 14 (Apr. 2005); Deloitte Tax LLP, "Producing Results: An Analysis of the New Production Activities Deduction," 106 Tax Notes 961 (Feb. 21, 2005); Conjura, et al., "The Domestic Manufacturing Deduction: Treasury and IRS Fill in Some Gaps," 102 J. Tax'n 198 (Apr. 2005); Benco & Rohrs, "Domestic Production Deduction: Overview of the Interim Guidance," 106 Tax Notes 569 (Jan. 31, 2005); Reinstein, "What's In It For You? Determining Who Has Benefits and Burden of Ownership For New Code Section 199 Deduction," Daily Tax Rep. (BNA) No. 75, J-1 (Apr. 20, 2005); Kehl, "Alternative For Allocation of Costs Under Internal Revenue Code Section 199," Daily Tax Rep. (BNA) No. 23, J-1 (Feb. 4, 2005); Seago, "Who Is Worthy of the Producers' Deduction For Production Under Contract?" 107 Tax Notes 721 (May 9, 2005); Dill and Jacobs, "The Qualified Production Activities Deduction: Some Planning Tools," 108 Tax Notes 87 (July 4, 2005). Kehl, "Code Section 199 and Partnerships," 84 Taxes 21 (May 2006). Lightner, "Interpreting the Proposed Regulations: The Domestic Production Activities Deduction," 23 J. Tax'n Inv. 215 (Spring 2006).

[b] Qualified Revenues: Domestic Production Gross Receipts

One of the two key elements of the § 199 deduction base is "domestic production gross receipts," defined by § 199(c)(4)(A) ad revenues "derived from" three general sources: Gross receipts "derived from" (1) the sale, lease, etc. of "qualified production property," (a term defined by § 199(c)(5) as tangible personal property, software and sound recordings) that was manufactured or produced, etc. in the U.S.,[407.20] receipts from "qualified films",[407.21] and receipts from the production (though not the transmission) of electricity and of natural gas; (2) receipts from "construction activity" performed in the U.S.; and (3) receipts from engineering and architectural services performed for domestic construction.[407.22]

[407.20] Such "domestic" production is at the heart of § 199's basic premise for deductibility.

[407.21] Defined in § 199(c)(8) as films and video tape if at least 50 percent of the production cost, are incurred in the U.S.

[407.22] Specifically excluded from domestic production gross receipt are gross receipts from the sale at retail of food and beverages (for which see Daily Tax Rep. (BNA) No.

Many of the above terms are desperately in need of IRS guidance (which is proving to be a daunting task),[407.23] For example, what is the level at which qualified production activities income will be computed (item by item, product line by product line, entity by entity, or at the affiliated group level)? Also determining whether particular receipts are "derived from" a particular service, and the methodology fro making that determination, needs to be worked out. Moreover, defining the outer parameters of the terms "production" and "manufacturing" will be a challenging exercise as well. Disputes over these, and many other, issues seem inevitable, especially if IRS guidance is late or inconclusive.

207, at G-9 (Oct. 27, 2004), on the "Starbucks" issues), or from the transmission of electricity and natural gas, § 199(c)(4)(B).

[407.23] See Stratton, "Treasury Officials Discuss Production Deduction Guidance," 105 Tax Notes 1172 (Nov. 29, 2004) (no final decision as yet). But a huge set of proposed regulations under § 199 (224 pages were released on Oct. 20, 2005 (and IRS tends to adopt them quickly), supra note 407.18. These proposals were adopted in final form on May 24, 2006.

[c] Expenses Allocable to Production Activities

The other key element in computing the qualified production activities tax base is the proper amount of costs and expenses that are allocable to the domestic production receipts (and will therefore reduce the potentially deductible tax base). These amounts are listed in § 199(c)(1)(B) as (1) the sum of the cost of goods sold allocable to those receipts, (2) other deductions, expenses, and losses directly so allocable, and (3) a ratable portion of indirect deductions, expenses, and losses, subject to such allocation methods as are prescribed by IRS regulations under § 199(c)(2).[407.24]

Neither the statute nor the conference report shed much light on this important element in computing the § 199 deduction.[407.25] But when production activities are performed at a foreign facility a more basic issue is raised as to whether the property was produced "insignificant part" in the U.S. as required by § 199(c)(4)(A)(i). How this "significant part" threshold can be satisfied is another important issue to be resolved by IRS regulations.

[407.24] These words certainly evoke the spirit of the § 861 deduction allocation rules, supra   15.02[1][e], 15.02[1][f], and 15.02[1][g], a far from cheerful prospect.

[407.25] Section 199(c)(3) provides special rules for determining costs where the manufactured item includes imported components purchased at a less than arm's-length price. A similar adjustment is required for items exported for further manufacturing and then reimported.

[d] Limitations and Special Rules: § 199(d)

In addition to the above described conditions and limitations on the amount of the § 199(a) deduction are several other restrictions. Thus, the deduction may not exceed 50 percent of the employer's W-2 wages paid for that year (a provision that obviously discourages the use of independent contractors or "outsourced" employees). But 2006 legislation limits the deduction to wages paid to workers employed in domestic production activities. Moreover, the expanded affiliated group[407.26] rules of § 199(d)(4) treat all members of the group as a single employer – a helpful rule for purposes of the wages cap.

Section 199(d)(1) deals with the application of the § 199 deduction to pass-thru entities, which generally will apply at the entity-owner level. Qualified individual businesses use or modified AGI in lieu of taxable income as a result of § 199(d)(2). Finally, § 199(d)(7) provides a broad delegation for regulation to "carry out the purposes of this section," i.e., to prevent abuses and possibly even to fix statutory glitches.

[407.26] Using a 50 percent test and determined without application of §§ 1504(b)(2) or 1504(b)(4).

[e] Conclusions

Section 199 is a mess, (but an important mess), that largely stems from its tangled percentage.[407.27] Much will depend on IRS guidance to be issued interpreting the many uncertainties and ambiguities contained in the statute.[407.28] On the one hand, there is very little incentive for taxpayers to remain reticent in claiming the benefits of this deduction since there appears to be little serious downside (short of deficiency interest) and potentially much upside to be had from aggressive claims. On the other hand, excessive over reaching could provoke hostile responses from IRS and possibly even from Congress, though the latter is less likely to react since this provision is their creation and they are stuck with the paternity DNA test.

What is likely is the creation of a variable cottage industry of conferences, articles, lobbyists and consultants trying to wind their way through the bramble bush of what is certain to be a thicket of Notices, Rulings and Regu-

---

[407.27] It originated (and evolved) as an effort to ease the pain for domestic manufacturers from the repealed export tax relief rules.

[407.28] Every indication is that IRS will strive to make this provision reasonably administrable for both taxpayers and the government. For initial IRS guidance, see Notice 2005-14, 2005-7 IRB 498. Proposed regulations under § 199 were released on Oct. 20, 2005 (224 pages of them), supra note 407.18. Final regulations were adopted by TD 9263 (May 24, 2006, effective June 1, 2006), and in 2007 for calendar year taxpayers. They tried to be helpful and simplified as much as possible, but simple is not a word that applies to these provisions. But no more cherrypicking under the final rules.

For helpful comments on the final regulations, see Atkinson, "The Production Deduction Final Regulations: A Step Forward," Daily Tax Rep. (BNA) No. 122, at J-1 (June 26, 2006); Jenks, "Domestic Production Deduction: FAQs and a Few Answers," 112 Tax Notes 751 (Aug. 28, 2006); Conjura, Zuber & Breaks, "Practical Considerations in Implementing the Section 199 Regulations," 105 J. Tax'n 68 (Sept. 2006).

Proposed regulations under the 2006 wage limitation were issued in October 2006 (they are long and complicated as well).

lations interpreting this section. Maybe a simple three-point rate cut for domestic corporations would have been a better option; at least for the "trees" that are slated to die in the service of these matters. What seems inevitable, however, is that new § 199 is destined to create a parallel universe for domestic corporations (much on the order of the corporate AMT).

C   FOREIGN PERSONAL HOLDING COMPANIES AND FOREIGN INVESTMENT COMPANIES

¶ 15.40 INTRODUCTORY

[3] Proposed Reforms

Page 15-125:

Add to text at end of ¶ 15.40[3].

The Joint Committee Staff's April 2001 simplification report proposes to repeal the FPHC and foreign investment company provisions and to remove foreign corporations from potential coverage by the PHC rules, which occurred in the 2004 Jobs Act.[419.1]

[419.1] Proposal IX. B., at 411. The Thomas bill (July 11, 2002) HR 5095 does so in § 304(a) (effective for 2003); currently HR 2896, § 1105(a) (effective for 2005). The final 2004 tax act adopted these proposals in the 2004 Jobs Act on Oct. 22, 2004; HR 4520 § 413 (effective 2005).

¶ 15.41 FOREIGN PERSONAL HOLDING COMPANIES

[1] Definition: § 552

Page 15-127:

Add text to end of ¶ 15.41[1].

Legislation proposed by Ways and Means Chairman Thomas would simply repeal the FPHC provisions, and the 2004 Jobs Act did just that.[428.1]

[428.1] HR 2896, § 1105(a) (effective in 2005). Adopted in the final 2004 Jobs Act on Oct. 22, 2004; HR 4520, § 413 (effective 2005)

¶ 15.42 FOREIGN PERSONAL HOLDING COMPANY VERSUS U.S. PERSONAL HOLDING COMPANY

Page 15-129:

Add to the end of the first paragraph of note 438.

The Thomas bill (July 11, 2002), HR 5095, § 304(b)(1) adopts this proposal (effective in 2003). The current version is HR 2896, § 1105(b)(1) (effective 2005), which passed in the 2004 Jobs Act on Oct. 22, 2004, HR 4520, § 413 (effective in 2005).

Page 15-130:

Add to the end of the second paragraph of note 438.

The Thomas bill, HR 5095, § 304(b)(2) moves this provision to § 954(c)(1)(H) (a category of FPHC income). The current version is HR 2896, § 1105(b)(2) (effective 2005), which passed on Oct. 22, 2004.

¶ 15.44 PASSIVE FOREIGN INVESTMENT COMPANIES: §§ 1291 THROUGH 1298

[3] Taxability of U.S. Shareholders Under the Passive Foreign Investment Company Rules

Page 15-134:

Add to note 452.

Regulations under the new mark-to-market regime were proposed on July 31, 2002, infra note 453.1.

Page 15-135:

Add to note 453.

See Prop. Regs. § 1296(e)-1(b)(2) (special rule for IPOs).

Add to text at end of runover paragraph.

Regulations under the new mark-to-market regime were proposed on July 31, 2002.[453.1]

[453.1] Prop. Regs. §§ 1.1291-1(c), 1.1295-1(i), 1.1295-1(k), 1.1296-1 (basic mark-to-market regime rules), and 1.1296(e)-1(b)(2) (special rules defining marketable stock in case of an IPO).

[4] Collateral Consequences of Passive Foreign Investment Company Status

Page 15-136:

Add to note 461, first paragraph.

NYSBA Tax Section, "Proposals for PFIC Guidance," 91 Tax Notes 2211 (June 25, 2001).

D   CONTROLLED FOREIGN CORPORATIONS

¶ 15.60   INTRODUCTORY

[2] Intercompany Pricing Limits

Page 15-143:

Add to note 482, first paragraph.

But *UPS* was reversed on appeal, 254 F3d 1014, 2001-2 USTC   50,475 (11th Cir. 2001) (not a sham and not an assignment of income; transactions had economic substance and enough business purpose to negate tax planning motives; but remanded on § 482 issue); comment by Sheppard, 92 Tax Notes 465 (July 23, 2001); Lupi-Sher, 92 Tax Notes 11 (July 2, 2001); Kingson, "The Confusion Over Tax Ownership," 93 Tax Notes 409 (Oct. 15, 2001).

[3] Partial End of Deferral for Controlled Foreign Corporations (Revenue Act of 1962)

Page 15-144:

Add text to end of ¶ 15.60[3].

Legislation introduced by Ways and Means Chairman Thomas on July 11, 2002,[487.1] however, would go a long way towards eliminating the 1962 regime by repealing the CFC rules for foreign base company sales and services income, thereby confining the CFC regime to the passive income items of a controlled foreign corporation.[487.2] But these proposals did not survive in the final 2004 Jobs Act.

[487.1] HR 5095, § 301(a) (effective in 2003); infra   15.62[2][b], 15.62[2][c]. The current version is HR 2896, § 1101 (effective 2005). But this provision has been dropped in the latest (October 2003) version of the Thomas bill.

[487.2] See infra   15.62[2][a].

[4] Total Termination of Deferral? Proposed Legislation

Page 15-145:

Add to text at end of ¶ 15.60[4].

Less drastic proposals have been advanced in the former Treasury's February 2000 budget plan that would (1) require reporting disclosure for certain payments into designated tax havens (a so-called "black list") and (2) restrict tax benefits for income flowing into the U.S. from tax havens.[489.1] Treasury's long-awaited study on the future of Subpart F finally was released on December 29, 2000 (evoking a collective yawn from the international tax bar).[489.2]

[489.1] E.g., deny foreign tax credits and impose § 904(d) separate basket treatment for such income.

Representative Doggett has dutifully introduced legislation to this effect, although it appears to be languishing at this writing (July 2004).

[489.2] They want to keep Subpart F but agree that it needs significant fixing (doesn't everyone?). Treasury Department Policy Study on Deferral Income Through U.S. Controlled Foreign Corporations, BNA Daily Tax Rep. (special Supplement), Vol. 1, No. 2 (Jan. 3, 2001). For comments, see Shepard, 90 Tax Notes 149 (Jan. 8, 2001) and Sullivan, 90 Tax Notes 156 (Jan. 8, 2001); Yoder, "Planning Techniques Described in the Treasury's 'Subpart F' Study," 30 Tax Mgmt. Int'l J. 222 (May 11, 2001). NYS Bar Assoc. Tax Section's Committee on Foreign Activities of U.S. Taxpayers, "The Treasury's 'Subpart F' Study," 94 Tax Notes 629 (Feb. 4, 2002); Gomi & Lowell, "Book Review of Hanna's Treatise on Deferral," 95 Tax Notes 611 (Apr. 22, 2002); Brewer, "Treason? Or Survival of the Fittest?: Dealing With Corporate Expatriation," 95 Tax Notes 603 (Apr. 22, 2002). Rosenbloom, "Why Not Des Moines? A Fresh Entry in the Subpart F Debate," 102 Tax Notes 274 (Jan. 12, 2004).

¶ 15.61 CONTROLLED FOREIGN CORPORATIONS UNDER SUBPART F

[2] Corporations Subject to Subpart F: § 957 (the "CFC")

Page 15-147:

Add to note 494, first paragraph.

Textron, Inc. 117 TC 67 (2001) (voting trust was the § 951 shareholder (as owner of CFC stock) but trust was a grantor trust and the grantor parent taxpayer thus was taxable on the trusts § 951 income). Stevens, "A Grantor Trust Visits Subpart F: Ruminations on Textron v. Commissioner and Other Anomalies," 21 Vir. Tax Rev. 507 (2002).

Page 15-148:

Add to end of note 494.

But Notice 89-94 modified by Notice 2003-50, 2003-32 IRB 295 (will now be treated as a domestic corporation for §§ 904(i) and 864(e) rules too, a bad news result); for § 904(i), see supra note 352; for 864(e), see supra   15.02[1][g]. Prop. Regs. § 1.269B-1 (Sept. 7, 2004). Implementing Notice 2003-50 (effective when final); adopted without change by TD 9216 (July 29, 2005).

Add to note 495, second paragraph.

See also Framatome Connectors USA., 118 TC 32 (2002) (US shareholder did not have more than 50 percent of vote or value of foreign subsidiary so not a CFC; taxpayer wanted CFC status here to get § 904(d)(3) look-through benefits); aff'd, 2004-2 USTC 50,364 (2d Cir. 2004). Raby & Raby, "Substance-Over-Form in Deciding 'Control' Questions," 94 Tax Notes 611 (Feb. 4, 2002).

[3] Attribution of Income to "United States Shareholders" of Controlled Foreign Corporations: § 951

Page 15-149:

Add to beginning of note 497.

Textron, Inc., 117 TC 67 (2001) (so holds; voting trust was the § 951 taxpayer (as owner of CFC stock) and thus voting trust was the§ 951(a) U.S. income recipient, though taxpayer grantor of the trust was taxed on its § 951 CFC income); Stevens, supra note 494.

Add to note 498.

Notice 2004-70, 2004-44 IRB 724, Nov. 11, 2004, clarifies whether distributions from various foreign corporations can qualify for the § 1(h)(11) low rate treatment. Taxable distributions by CFCs generally can so qualify (at least if the CFC is a qualifying foreign corporation); see   8.06[2][b]. If § 1(h)(11) applies to a CFC; dividends, § 1248 is effectively neutered for for non-corporate shareholders since the rate on such dividends is the same as the capital gain rate (15 percent top).

Add to note 499.

A major package of proposed regulations under §§ 959 (the PTI rules) and 961 (the basis rules) was issued by IRS on Aug. 29, 2006. Their purpose is to update the existing regulations (which are old and out of date) and to clarify many of the unanswered questions under these provisions. They seem to be quite taxpayer friendly, and the preamble is must reading here.

Page 15-150:

Add to note 500.

For purposed regulations under this provision, see § 1.961-3 (Aug. 29, 2006).

Add text to end of ¶ 15.61[3].

Proposed regulations issued in August 2004[501.1] provide detailed guidance (finally) on determining the U.S. shareholders allocable share of Subpart F in-

---

[501.1] Regs. § 1.951-1(e) (Aug. 6, 2004). The regulations deal mainly with situations where the CFC has multiple classes of stock. Significantly the regulations disregard re-come (that is, the proper amount taxable to the shareholder under § 951(a)). A similar regime exists under the consolidated return investment basis adjustment rules[501.2] and this was the model used in developing the § 951 regulations. These proposals were adopted as final regulations on August 25, 2005 (which also is their effective date).[501.3] The proposed anti-abuse special rules regulations were adopted on February 22, 2006.[501.4]

---

strictions or limitations on distributions to U.S. shareholders. Leitner, Subpart F Prop. Regs. Target New Abuses Involving Investments in Structured CFC's, 101 J. Tax'n 307 (Nov. 2004).

[501.2] See ¶ 13.44[2][b].

[501.3] TD 9222 (Aug. 24, 2005); a new special rule was proposed in Prop. Regs. § 1.951-1(e) (dealing with the treatment of U.S. shareholders of a CFC possessing more than one class of stock and CFCs with cumulative preferred stock held by non-U.S. shareholders (effective for years beginning on or after Jan. 1, 2006). These are anti-abuse rules aimed at § 304 transactions, Prop. Regs. §§ 1.951-1(e)(3)(v) and 1.951-1(e)(6), Ex. 9. Ocasal & Bowler, "Final Regs. Overhaul CFC Subpart F Income Allocations Rules," 16 J. Int'l Tax'n 44 (Dec. 2005).

[501.4] TD 9251 (effective Jan. 1, 2006).

[4] CFC Hybrid Structures: Notice 98-11 and Regulations

Page 15-150:

Add to note 502.

Sheppard, "More Check-The-Box Fallout: Reverse Hybrids," 87 Tax Notes 1196 (May 29, 2000).

Page 15-151:

In note 510, last sentence, replace July 9, 1998 *with* July 13, 1999.

Page 15-152:

Add to note 513, second paragraph.

Miller, "The Strange Materialization of the Tax Nothing," 87 Tax Notes 685 (May 1, 2000); Sheppard, "Government Will Finalize Check-The-Box Anti-Abuse Rule," 88 Tax Notes 1078 (Aug. 28, 2000); Miller, Snake in the Box: The Hazards of Policy Making With "Anti-Abuse" Rules, 89 Tax Notes 107 (Oct. 2, 2000). But these proposed regulations were withdrawn by Notice 2003-46, 2003-28 IRB 53 (IRS will no longer deal with entity issues here; but warn that suspicious transactions that change tax results will be dealt with under general principles—e.g., form vs. substance, step transaction doctrine, etc.).

   For comments Notice 2003-46, see Click, "Treasury Withdraws Extraordinary Check-the-Box Regulations," 101 Tax Notes 95 (Oct. 6, 2003); Lemein & McDonald, "Notice 2003-46: The Extraordinary Transaction Regulations Are Withdrawn," 81 Taxes 5 (Nov. 2003); Sheppard, "Behind the Eight Ball on Check-the-Box Abuse," 101 Tax Notes 437 (Oct. 27, 2003).

Add to text at end of ¶ 15.61[4].

IRS tried to get at the check-and-sell transaction by litigation, but was unsuccessful in the Tax Court.[513.1]

[513.1] Dover Corp., 122 TC 324 (2004) (check-the-box election to treat sub as disregarded entity created a deemed § 332 liquidation and avoided Subpart F income on sale of subsidiary; sale of assets, not stock). See Rubinger, Tax Court Upholds 'Check and Sell' Strategy to Avoid Subpart F Income, 101 J. Tax'n 20 (July 2004): Cummings, Midco Transactions Resurface: *Court Holding* Miscast, 103 Tax Notes 1061 (May 24, 2004); Blanchard, Sheppard's Dover Discussion Dismantled, 103 Tax Notes 1297 (June 7, 2004); Bennett, *Dover Corp*: The Extraordinary Decision, 82 Taxes 23 (Aug. 2004). Kingson, Seven Lessons on Section 367, 104 Tax Notes 1014, at 1044 (Sept. 13, 2004) (Special Supplement, Appendix to Lesson 3); Holland, "U.S. Check-The-Box Rules in the Cross-Border Context," 108 Tax Notes 1151 (Sept. 5, 2005).

   Celebration may be premature if the Senate tax bill's § 269 amendments pass; see ¶ 14.41[6][c]. But that proposal didn't pass.

¶ 15.62 INCOME ATTRIBUTED TO SHAREHOLDERS OF CONTROLLED FOREIGN CORPORATIONS

Page 15-153:

Add to text at end of runover sentence.

But legislation introduced by the chairman of the Ways and Means Committee on July 11, 2002,[514.1] would contract the scope of this regime in a major way, repealing the CFC rules for foreign base company sales and services income (thereby limiting its application to the passive income items of a CFC.[514.2]

[514.1] HR 5095, § 301(a) (effective in 2003). The current version is HR 2896, § 1101 (effective 2005). But this proposal has been dropped (in October 2003), and did not survive in the final 2004 tax act.

[514.2] See infra   15.62[a] – 15.62[c].

[1] Subpart F Income Generally: § 952 and "Base Company" Concept

Add to note 515.

These regulations, proposed in 1998, withdrawn in 1999 and reproposed in 2000, were finally adopted by TD 9008 on July 23, 2002, infra notes 517, 518.

Page 15-154:

Add to note 517.

While these proposals were withdrawn on July 13, 1999, they were re-proposed on September 19, 2000. They were adopted as final regulations (except for the contract manufacturing rules) by TD 9008 on July 23, 2002, infra note 518.

Page 15-155:

Replace note 518 with the following.

[518] These proposed regulations were issued as part of the initial Notice 98-11 proposed regulations package. They were withdrawn, however, on July 13, 1999, following the prior withdrawal of other aspects of the package. See DeFronzo & Thomas, "*Brown Group* Regulations: Heads/Treasury Wins—Tails/Taxpayer Loses," 84 Tax Notes 1419 (Sept. 6, 1999). These regulations were reissued, however, on September 19, 2000 (without substantive change), as Regs. §§ 1.702-1(a)(8)(ii), 1.952-1(g), 1.954-1(g), 1.954-2(a)(5)(ii), 1.954-3(a)(6), 1.954-4(b)(2)(iii), and 1.956-2(a)(3). See DiFronzo & Thomas, "Proposed *Brown Group* Regulations—As Promised," 89 Tax Notes 669 (Oct. 30, 2000). The proposed regulations were adopted by TD 9008 on July 23, 2002, as Regs. §§ 1.702-1(a)(8)(ii), 1.952-1(g), 1.954-1(g), 1.954-2(a)(5), 1.954-3(a)(6), 1.954-4(b)(2)(iii) and 1.956-2(a)(3).

[2] Components of Foreign Base Company Income: § 954

Page 15-155:

Add to note 519.

See also Maguire & Anolik, "Subpart F and Source of Income Issues in E-Commerce," 89 Tax Notes 1767 (Dec. 27, 2000), Rubinger & Mayo, "International Tax Aspects of Cancellation of Indebtedness Income," 98 J. Tax'n 365 (June 2003).

Add to note 520.

But see HR 5095, and HR 2896, infra note 521, which would eliminate the two FBC income items of § 954(d) and § 954(e) described in ¶¶ 15.62[2][b] and 15.62[2][c].

Add to text after sentence ending with note 520.

But proposed legislation issued on July 11, 2002, and again on July 25, 2003, by the chair of the Ways and Means Committee would repeal the core of the foreign base company income rules, foreign base company sales and services income.[520.1] But these proposals were dropped in October 2003.

[520.1] HR 5095, § 301(a) (effective in 2003); HR 2896, 1101 (effective in 2006), infra ¶¶ 15.62[2][b], 15.62[2][c].

[a] Foreign Personal Holding Company Income: § 954(c)

Page 15-155:

Add to note 521, first paragraph.

See Seagate Tech., Inc., RIA TC Memo. ¶ 2000-361 (2000) (where taxpayer's CFC sold its operating assets for restricted stock of the buyer—held: no § 954(c) income on sale of assets, but gain on later sale of that stock produced § 954(c) income; later gain not characterized by prior sale transaction). Yoder & Waimon, "*Seagate*: Tax Court Holds Restricted Stock Gains Are Subpart F Income," 12 J. Int'l Tax'n 40 (Apr. 2001). Compare Dover Corp., 122 TC 324 (2004) (check-and-sell strategy avoided tainted income; sale of assets, not stock), supra note 513.1.

Page 15-156:

Add to text at end of § 15.62[2][a].

Ways and Means Chairman Thomas's proposed legislation issued on July 11, 2002,[524.1] would add two more items to the list of foreign personal holding company income: (1) income from "round trip" sales;[524.2] and (2) income from certain loaned out personal services (formerly in the slated to be repealed

---

[524.1] HR 5095 (effective in 2003); the current version is HR 2896 (effective 2005).

[524.2] HR 5095, § 301(b), adding § 954(c)(1)(H) (previous proposals had proposed to "resource" such income to the United States, supra ¶ 15.02[1][c], note 78). The current version is HR 2896, § 1101(b) (effective 2006). But it did not survive in the final 2004 Jobs Act.

FPHC income provisions).[524.3] But this proposed legislation also would liberalize the treatment of certain commodity hedging transactions,[524.4] as would similar regulations proposed in May of 2002 and adopted in January 2003.[524.5]

The new Tax Act (TIPRA 2005) added new § 954(c)(6), which provides look-through treatment for certain payments by CFCs to related CFCs, and should prove to be a useful liberalization for many taxpayers.[524.6]

[524.3] HR 5095, § 304(b)(2) (also located in proposed new § 954(c)(1)(H), which presumably would become § 954(c)(1)(I) in a technical correction bill). The current version is HR 2896, § 1105(b)(2), adding new § 954(c)(1)(I). This proposal did pass, however; 2004 Jobs Act § 413(b)(2).

[524.4] HR 5095, § 306, amending § 954(c)(1)(C) and adding new § 954(c)(6) to exempt commodity hedging transactions as defined in § 1221(b)(2) (namely, ordinary income property or business property); currently HR 2896, § 1107 (July 25, 2003) (effective 2006). This proposal also passed on October 22, 2004.

[524.5] Prop. Regs. § 1.954-2(f)(2)(V) (qualified hedges include those of producers who use the hedged commodities in the active business of producing, transporting or construction—but not to a primarily financial business); adopted by TD 9039 (Jan. 31, 2003).

[524.6] See Calianno & Collins, "The CFC Look-Through Rule: Congress Changes the Landscape," 112 Tax Notes 155 (July 10, 2006); Lemein, McDonald & Lipeles, "Looking for Opportunities in the New Look-Through Rules," 84 Taxes 5 (Sept. 2006); Palsen & Lovelace, "Factoring Transactions and CFC Look-Through Tax Treatment," 113 Tax Notes 567 (Nov. 6, 2002). Sheppard, "Looking Through the New Look-Thru Rule," 113 Tax Notes 295 (Oct. 23, 2006). For IRS guidance, see Notice 2007-9, 2007-5 IRB 401 (preview of regulations to come).

[b] Foreign Base Company Sales Income: § 954(d)

Page 15-157:

Add to note 525.

But the Thomas bill, HR 5095 (July 11, 2002) would repeal the CFC rules for foreign base company sales and services income (effective 2003); the current version is HR 2896, (July 25, 2003), § 1101 (effective 2006). But it was dropped in October 2003.

Add after first sentence of note 526.

Voce, "Foreign Base Company Income: A Primer and an Update," 53 Tax Law. 327 (2000).

Add to end of first paragraph in note 526.

These regulations became final in TD 9008 on July 23, 2002.

Page 15-158:

Add to note 527, first paragraph.

But see Electronic Arts, Inc., 118 TC 226 (2002) (contract manufacturing failed manufacturing *in* possession requirement, though it was engaged in active business there and also had substantial business presence there); MedChem (PR), Inc. v. CIR, 295 F3d 118 (1st Cir. 2002).

Add to note 527, third paragraph.

But, these proposals were withdrawn on July 13, 1999, supra notes 517, 518. When the *Brown Group* regulations were re-proposed on September 19, 2000, the proposals on contract manufacturing were not included in this package, however. Lemein & McDonald, "FSA 2002 20005: The IRS Attacks, Contract Manufacturing," 80 Taxes 5 (July 2002).

[c] Foreign Base Company Services Income: § 954(e)

Add to note 528.

But the Thomas bill (July 11, 2002), HR 5095, § 301(a), proposes to repeal the CFC rules for foreign base company services income (effective in 2003); currently HR 2896, § 1101 (July 25, 2003) (effective 2006); but it was dropped in October 2003.

Page 15-159:

In fifth line of note 530 change § 1.954-3(a)(c) *to* § 1.954-3(a)(6).

Add to note 530.

The contract manufacturing proposed regulations were withdrawn on July 13, 1999, supra notes 517, 518; but, when the *Brown Group* regulations were re-proposed on September 19, 2000, the contract manufacturing proposals were not included in this package. But see Electronic Arts, Inc., 118 TC 226 (2002) (contract manufacturing failed manufacturing in possessions test under § 954 principles, though it was held engaged in an active business there and also had substantial business presence there). Lemein and McDonald, "FSA 2002 20005: The IRS Attacks Contract Manufacturing," 80 Taxes 5 (July 2002). See generally MedChem (PR), Inc. v. CIR, 295 F3d 118 (1st Cir. 2002).

[3] Adjustments to Foreign Base Company Income: § 954(b)

Page 15-160:

Add to note 536.

The Joint Committee Staff's April 2001 simplification report proposes to raise the de minimis level to the lesser of 5 percent of gross income or $5 million; Proposal IX. C., at 419.

[4] Increase in Earnings Invested in U.S. Property

[a] In General: § 956

Page 15-161:

Add to note 538.

But Tax Court was reversed (on other grounds, that is, taxpayer entitled to "banking" exception), 286 F3d 324, 2002-1 USTC ¶ 50,353 (6th Cir. 2002). Comment by Sheppard, "Retail Tax Avoidances," 95 Tax Notes 1295 (May 27, 2002); Yoder & Christensen, "*The Limited, Inc. v. Comm'r.* Appellate Court Slams Tax Court's Narrow Interpretation of § 956 Bank Deposit Exception," 31 Tax Mgmt Int'l J. 453 (Sept. 13, 2002); Lipton, "Appellate Court Lectures Tax Court Construction in *The Limited*," 97 J. Tax'n 218 (Oct. 2002). But § 837 of the 2004 Jobs Act overruled this decision (effective Oct. 22, 2004). For extensive comment on *The Limited* decision and Congress' response, see Levy, "*The Limited* and the Congressional Response: How Well Did Congress Do?" 109 Tax Notes 983 (Oct. 24, 2005).

Page 15-162:

Add to note 540.

But *The Limited* was reversed on appeal, 286 F3d 324 (6th Cir. 2002) (held was engaged in "banking business" and CDs were "deposits" so § 956 not applicable). Ciesar and Kinster, "Section 956(c)(2)(A); A Plain-Meaning Paradigm," 13 J. Int'l Tax'n 12 (Sept. 2002). But the 2004 Jobs Act § 837 (effective Oct. 22, 2004) overruled *The Limited* decision.

Add to note 542.

Brewer, "Open Questions Regarding Pledges and Guarantees by CFCs," 94 Tax Notes 359 (Jan. 21, 2002).

Page 15-163:

Add new note 542.1 to end of ¶ 15.62[4][a].

[542.1] For CFC loans involving foreign partnership transactions, see NYSBA Tax Section Report, "Controlled Foreign Corporations and Foreign Partnership Loan Transactions," 112 Tax Notes 435 (July 31, 2006) (application of § 956 to various scenarios).

[5] Earnings Invested in Excess Passive Assets: § 956A

[c] Coordination and Ordering Rules

Page 15-166:

Add to note 554.

For a more recent explication, see Doernberg et al., "Ordering Rules Make Your Head Spin? Here's Some Aspirin," 92 Tax Notes 833 (Aug. 6, 2001) (be prepared to spend some time with this piece as well).

Add new ¶ 15.62[8] after ¶ 15.62[7].

[8] Temporary Dividends Received Deduction For Repatriated Controlled-Foreign Corporation Earnings: § 965 [New]

[a] General

One of the most significant provisions in the 2004 Jobs Act is new § 965, a "temporary" (two-year) special 85 percent dividends received deduction (DRD) for U.S. multinationals that elect to repatriate (in cash only) dividends distributed by their CFCs from previously untaxed foreign earnings (in either

2004 or 2005).[556.1] This provision was adopted as a one-shot incentive (or partial amnesty)[556.2] to encourage U.S. corporations to bring home untaxed foreign earnings that have been stored up abroad in their CFCs. The Conference Report emphasizes however, that this deduction will *not* be extended beyond its 2-year life. A key requirement for obtaining this deduction, moreover, is that the repatriated funds must stay here – that is, they must be reinvested domestically pursuant to a board-approved reinvestment "plan,"[556.3] the scope of which is far from clear at this time.

There is a pressing need for guidance on many interpretive issues that have arisen under this provision, but it is unlikely to be resolved by a traditional regulation project due to the short life of § 965, which by its terms ex-

---

[556.1] American Jobs Creation Act of 2004, § 422, adding new § 965. See Blessing, "Bringing It All Back Home: Repatriations Under the American Jobs Creation Act of 2004," 105 Tax Notes 965 (Nov. 15, 2004). Rollinson, Mundaca and Murillo, American Jobs Creation Act of 2004—Extraordinary Repatriation Incentive, 16 J. Int'l Tax'n 18 (Jan. 2005); Lederman and Hirsch, AJCA Replaces Tax Incentive for Exports With a Domestic Production Tax Break and a One-Time DRD, 102 J. Tax'n 6, at 15 (Jan. 2005). For initial interim guidance, see Notice 2005-10, 2005-6 IRB 474 (Feb. 7, 2005); Notice 2005-38, 2005-22 IRB (May 31, 2005) (second round); comment by Willens, Viewpoint Daily Tax Rep. (BNA) No. 11, at J-1; Rollinson, et al., 106 Tax Notes 444 (Jan. 24, 2005). Capital Tax Partners, "American Jobs Creation Act Repatriation Calculation Rubric," Daily Tax Rep. (BNA) No. 19, at J-1 (Jan. 31, 2005); Sheppard & Harty, The Evolving Treatment of Qualified Foreign Dividends, 16 J. Int'l Tax'n 28 (May 2005); May, "Repatriation Guidance in Notice 2005-10 a Mixed Bag For Taxpayers," Daily Tax Report (BNA) No. 29, at J-1 (Feb. 24, 2005); Sheppard, "More Bugs in the Repatriation Statute," 106 Tax Notes 1497 (Mar. 28, 2005) (focus on NYSB Tax Section report on effect of mergers, acquisitions and spin-offs on the § 965 deduction); for this NYSBA Report, see 107 Tax Notes 729 (May 9, 2005); Kaufman, "Effect of A Foreign Currency Translation on Repatriation of High-Taxed Foreign Income Under the Jobs Act," 107 Tax Notes 471 (Apr. 25, 2005).

A second round of guidance on the § 965 DRD was issued in Notice 2005-38, 2005-22 IRB (May 31, 2005), covering additional issues not addressed in the prior Notice. For comment on this Notice, see Willens, Viewpoint, Daily Tax Report (BNA) No. 93, at J-1 (May 15, 2005); Rollinson, Mundaca, Murillo & Naser, "Second Round of Guidance on Dividend Repatriation Provisions," 107 Tax Notes 988 (May 23, 2005); Giegerich, "One-time Tax Break For Repatriation of Foreign Earnings: Summary and Analysis of Guidance," 108 Tax Notes 547 (Aug. 1, 2005); Lemein & Lipeles, IRS Issues Supplement Guidance on Repatriation, 83 Taxes 39 (Sept. 2005).

A third round of guidance was issued in Notice 2005-64, 2005-36 IRB (Sept. 6, 2005). Comment by Goulder, "Practitioners Welcome Repatriation Guidance," 108 Tax Notes 975 (Aug. 29, 2005). All three Notices will be folded into ultimately issued regulations under § 965 (a dubious effort in view of the fact this provision expires on Dec. 31, 2005); see also Rollinson et al., "The Latest Guidance on Temporary Dividends Received Deduction, " 108 Tax Notes 1321 (Sept. 12, 2005).

[556.2] The 85 percent DRD translates into a 5.25 percent effective tax rate on the dividends.

[556.3] IRC § 965(b)(4). See Notice 2005-10, § 4, 2005-6 IRB 474 (as to DRIP requirements).

pires by the end of 2005 (and the Conference Report promises no extensions).[556.4]

[556.4] The most likely form of IRS guidance will be by way of Notices, Announcements, or Rulings. For which, see Notice 2005-10, 2005-6 IRB 474 (Feb. 7, 2005), answering many, though not all, of the questions as to the scope of § 965; it seems to be a reasonably liberal initial step in implementing this provision; see comments supra note 556.1. Notice 2005-38, 2005-22 IRB 1100(May 31, 2005) (second round); Notice 2005-64, 2005-36 IRB 471 (third round). See articles supra note 556.1. See also Urse, Ocasal & Lubkin, "There Is Still Time (But Not Much)—Section 965 Dividend Repatriation," Part I, 165 J. Int'l Tax'n 14 (Nov. 2005); Part 2, 16 J. Int'l Tax'n 26 (Dec. 2005); Part 3, 17 J. Int'l Tax'n 36 (Jan. 2006); Sheppard, "The Repatriation Endgame," 109 Tax Notes 1123 (Nov. 28, 2005); Lederman & Hirsh, "The Services Guidelines For Enjoying the Section 965 Foreign Earnings Holiday," 103 J. Tax'n 208 (Oct. 2005).

[b] Qualified Dividend Income: Cash Dividends From Controlled Foreign Corporations

Only cash dividends will qualify for the § 965 deduction. Moreover, such dividends generally are limited to ordinary § 301-316 dividends (although distributions that fail to satisfy §§ 302 or 304 will qualify for this purpose).[556.5] Finally the dividend must be paid to a corporate U.S. shareholder of the dividend paying CFC.[556.6] The requirement that only cash dividends can qualify raises the issue of what is "cash." Presumably cash equivalents, such as demand and time deposits should be treated as cash for this purpose (and possibly even foreign currency). Notice 2005-10, however, excludes cash equivalents (but includes foreign currency).

[556.5] Section 965(c)(3) specifically excludes deemed dividends under §§ 78, 367 or 1248; but in-bound § 332 liquidations that trigger § 367(b) actual dividend treatment will qualify to the extent the U.S. parent actually receives cash as part of the liquidation (though the Conference Report excludes check-the-box "deemed liquidations" from this treatment). Notice 2005-10, § 3.01 (cash includes foreign currency, but not cash equivalents). Also § 356(a)(2) dividends can qualify.

[556.6] However, lower-tier CFLs pass up E&P (and potential qualified dividend treatment) through higher-tier members in their chain by virtue of § 965(a)(2).

[c] Other Limitations on the § 965 Deduction

Four statutory limitations on the amount of the § 965 deductions are provided in § 965(b):

1. The general limitation of § 965(b)(1) to the greater of $500,000,000 or the amount shown on the "applicable financial statement"[556.7] as earnings permanently reinvested outside the U.S.[556.8]

[556.7] Defined in § 965(c)(1) (certified on or before June 30, 2003). See Notice 2005-38 for guidance.

[556.8] These amounts are, of course, precisely what § 965 is trying to lure home.

2. The potentially deductible repatriation dividend must be "extraordinary"; that is, they must exceed the average repatriation level over three of the five taxable years ending on or before June 30, 2003.[556.9] Thus, if the CFC has been paying up its earnings currently, it will not be able to generate a § 965 dividend for its parent (this is not the usual CFC scenario, however).

3. The U.S. shareholder (or a related party) is not permitted to fund the CFC's dividend through loans or other advances; § 965(c)(3) will reduce the potential deduction benefit by such an increase in "related party debt."[556.10]

4. Finally, the dividend reinvestment plan ("DRIP") rules of § 965(b)(4) must be satisfied; these require that the qualifying dividend must be invested in accordance with a domestic reinvestment "plan" that is timely approved (by the U.S. shareholder's CEO and its board) and provides for the reinvestment of the dividend in the U.S. (other than a payment of executive compensation). Many questions arise under this provision,[556.11] as to which early IRS guidance is especially urgent. Notice 2005-10 is the first of such guidance and answers many, though not all, questions (scope of the DRIP, good and bad investments, but no tracing or segregation of funds is required).

[556.9] The "base period years" are defined in § 965(c)(2), which looks at the five-year period 1998-2002 average dividends and drops the highest and lowest years. See Notice 2005-38 for guidance.

[556.10] The dividend paying CFC can, however, borrow from other CFCs, which, for this purpose are all treated as one CFC, thus resulting in the disregard of inter-CFC loans. Moreover, the U.S. parent apparently can guarantee third party loans to its CFC. See Notice 2005-38.

[556.11] See Blessing, supra note 556.1, at p. 972. E.g., How quickly must the funds be reinvested (and how long is the period); what happens if plans change; can plans be amended, and, if so when; most important, what are qualified reinvestments, and what are not?

See Notice 2005-10, § 5 (good investments) and § 6 (bad uses). Also § 4, dealing with the DRIP requirement, is quite flexible; but § 4.04 precludes amendment of the plan, though § 4.05 does *not* require tracing of funds or segregation.

[d] Other Consequences Under § 965: § 965(d) and § 965(e)

The collateral consequences of the § 965 deduction are contained in § 965(d)(1) which denies foreign tax credits for taxes attributable to the deductible portion of the dividend,[556.12] and § 965(d)(2), likewise denies any deduction for expenses attributable to the deductible portion of the dividend.[556.13] Finally § 965(d)(3) allows taxpayers to specifically identify dividends applied

---

[556.12] No deduction for those taxes is allowed as well.

[556.13] Apparently this disallowance rule is to be narrowly applied, see Blessing, supra note 556.1, at 975-977; Notice 2005-38 (so states).

against the base period amount (and thus treated as non-qualifying) and other dividends to be treated as qualifying; this rule is an extremely valuable one for taxpayers.

As to the nondeductible portion of the dividend (namely, the 15 percent portion that is subject to tax), § 965(e)(2)(A) provides that the entire portion of this amount is intended to be subject to tax (thus resulting in a 5.25 percent effective rate on the dividend).[556.14] While the taxable portion of the dividend is not reduced by any deductions, the tax thereon may be reduced by foreign tax credits attributable to this portion.[556.15]

There is every indication that § 965 will serve as a "super attractor" in stimulating the repatriation of embedded foreign earnings.[556.16]

[556.14] See Blessing, supra note 556.1 at 975.

[556.15] Blessing, supra note 556.1 at 977.

[556.16] See. e.g., "Willens, Viewpoint, Daily Tax Rep. (BNA) No. 198, at J-1 (Oct. 14, 2004). Moreover, the IRS' relative liberality in its initial guidance, Notice 2005-10, Notice 2005-38, and 2005-64, will encourage taxpayer hopes as well.

¶ 15.63 SALE OR LIQUIDATION OF CONTROLLED FOREIGN CORPORATIONS: § 1248

[1] In General

Page 15-167:

Add to note 557.

Friedel, "Intercompany Sales of CFC Stock—Where Does Reality End and Wonderland Begin?" 92 J. Tax'n 362 (June 2000) (very soon).

Page 15-168:

Add to note 558.

See Friedel, supra note 557. Calianno & Gregoire, "Handling Restructurings and Dispositions of a CFC," 28 J. Corp. Tax'n 3 (Sept. 2001), pointing out possible application of § 1248(f)(2) to § 355 distributions of CFC stock based on Notice 87-64, supra.

Add to note 560.

See Friedel, supra note 557.

Add to at the end of ¶ 15.63[1].

On June 1, 2006, IRS issued a substantial package of proposed regulations under § 1248[562.1] intended to clarify the calculation of deemed-dividends' E&P attributable to stock of a CFC in various nonrecognition transactions. These tracing and attribution proposals were stated to be mere "clarifications" of the current regulations which was thought to be necessary in order to resolve certain misconceptions of those rules.

Why the Service keeps tinkering with § 1248 is a mystery. This section is a virtual dead letter under current law since individuals can get the same low rate for dividends (15 percent max, the same as capital gain),[562.2] while corporate shareholders have no capital gain rate preference and thus prefer dividend treatment that can draw out foreign tax credits. It seems to be a waste of scarce resources to keep flogging § 1248; repeal seems to be a better choice here.

[562.1] Prop. Regs. § 1.248-8 (effective when final).

[562.2] IRS has ruled that § 1248 dividends can qualify for the § 1(h)(11) low rate, Notice 2004-70, 2004-49 IRB 724.

[2] Nonrecognition Transactions: § 1248(f)

[a] In General

Add § 355(c) after § 311(a) in second sentence of text.

Add to note 563, first paragraph.

But see Notice 87-64, 1987-2 CB 375 (application of § 1248(f)(2) to inbound spin-off of CFC stock stating regulations will be issued to prevent gain to distributing parent if corporate distributee does not get basis step-up; will be effective as of 1987 also). For a comparable exception in the PFIC nonrecognition proposed regulations, see Prop. Regs. § 1.1291-6(c)(iv), infra ¶ 15.85[6][a], note 1026; see also Calianno & Gregoire, supra note 558.

Add text to end of ¶ 15.63[2][a].

No regulations have been issued under § 1248(f), despite the fact that it was enacted in 1976 and the IRS promised to issue such regulations in 1987.[563.1]

[563.1] Notice 87-64, 1987-2 CB 325; Calianno & Gregoire, supra note 558.

[b] Section 1248(i)

Page 15-170:

Add to text at end of ¶ 15.63[2][b].

Despite the enactment of § 1248(i), and also despite tightening the outbound stock transfer regulations under § 367(a),[565.1] expatriating inversion
transactions have reemerged as a major issue of late, attracting the attention of
commentators, Congress, and even the Treasury.[565.2] The 2004 Jobs Act[565.3] finally responded to this situation in enacting § 7874, which repatriates pure inversion transactions, and increases the tax costs of less extreme inversion
transactions.[565.4]

[565.1] See infra   15.82[2][b].

[565.2] See infra   15.82[2][c]. See generally NYSBA Tax Section Report (calling for
review of these transactions, including legislation, and also broader reforms), reprinted in
Daily Tax Rep. (BNA) No. 108, at J-1 (June 5, 2002), and also in 96 Tax Notes 127 (July
1, 2002).

[565.3] American Jobs Creation Act of 2004, § 801, adoption of new § 7874 (effective
March 5, 2003). Kirsch, "The Congressional Response to Corporate Inversions . . .," 24
Vir. Tax Rev. 475 (Winter 2005).

[565.4] See infra   15.82[2][c].

[3] Relationship to Subpart F Rules

Add to text at end.

With the 2003 Act's enactment of § 1(h)(11), lowering the top rate on
qualified dividends to the same rate as the similiarly reduced capital gain rate
(a 15 percent top), §1248 has become virtually irrelevant for non-corporate
shareholders since IRS has ruled that CFCs can pay qualified dividends (including § 1248 dividends) if it is also a qualified foreign corporation (which it
can be).[567.1] Why the IRS continues to fight fiercely to protect the application
of § 1248 is difficult to comprehend in view of its relative insignificance. Not
only is the tax rate the same, but so is the taxable amount under § 1248 for
noncorporate taxpayers. Corporate shareholders, by contrast, prefer dividend
treatment since it can draw out foreign tax credits'; moreover, they have no
capital gain rate preference. Repeal of § 1248 for individuals as de facto
"deadwood" seems to be long overdue.[567.2]

[567.1] Notice 2004-70, 2004-49 IRB 724; see   8.06[2][b].

[567.2] See also Notice 87-64, 1987 CB 375 (suspended § 1248 in years with no rate
differential).

¶ 15.64 SCOPE OF CONTROLLED FOREIGN CORPORATION PROVISIONS

[2] Avoidance Games and Congressional Response

Page 15-172:

Add to note 571.

See generally Notice 2003-50, 2003-32 IRB 295 (stapled foreign subsidiary will be treated as a domestic § 1504(b) includible corporation for purposes of § 904(i) foreign tax credit limits and § 864(e) allocation rules). See Prop. Regs. § 1.269B-1 (Sept. 7, 2004), implementing Notice 2003-50 (effective when final); adopted without change by TD 9216 (July 29, 2005).

¶ 15.65 INTERNATIONAL ASPECTS OF § 338

[1] In General

Page 15-173:

Add to note 573.

But see Notice 2004-20, 2004-11 IRB 608 (using a US "conduit intermediary" to buy the foreign target, elect § 338, then sell its assets to the ultimate buyer and claim §§ 901 and 902 credits attacked on multiple grounds; also added to the tax shelter black list).

But see Dover Corp., 122 TC 324 (2004) (check-and-sell strategy created deemed § 332 liquidation and resulted in asset sale, not stock sale, thus avoiding Subpart F income); supra note 513.1.

Page 15-174:

Add to text at end of ¶ 15.65[1].

But nothing has come of this proposal as yet, although a variation has arisen to block so-called loss import transactions, which passed on October 22, 2004.[578.1]

[578.1] Infra   15.85[7][e]. See HR 4520, Act § 836, adding new §§ 362(e) and 334(b)(1)(B).

[4] Fresh-Start at the Border: Purge of Foreign-Generated Tax Attributes

Page 15-177:

Add to note 602.

The February 2000 budget plan moved this proposal to the more neutral international venue. It has not been reproposed by the new treasury.

Page 15-178:

Add to note 603.

For a limited attribute purge on inbound § 332 liquidations and reorganizations, see Prop. Regs. §§ 1.367(b)-3(e) and 1.367(b)-3(f) (Nov. 8, 2000), infra ¶ 15.83[1][b] (foreign-generated loss carryovers, earnings and profits (or deficits), and foreign taxes do not carryover under § 381 here).

E ORGANIZATION, LIQUIDATION, AND REORGANIZATION OF FOREIGN CORPORATIONS: § 367 AND RELATED PROVISIONS

¶ 15.80 INTRODUCTORY: BACKGROUND, EVOLUTION, AND GENERAL SCOPE OF § 367

[1] In General

Page 15-178:

Add to end of note 604.

Kingson, "Seven Lessons on Section 367," 105 Tax Notes 1015 (Sept. 13, 2004) (Special Supplement). For alternative cross-border structures that avoid implicating § 367 (e.g., partnerships), see Humphreys, "Partnership Combinations of U.S. and Non-U.S. Corporations," 92 Tax Notes 241 (July 9, 2001). Dolan, Tretiak and Elman, "Virtual Mergers: Is America Ready?" 80 Taxes 165 (Mar. 2002).

[7] Transactions Governed by § 367

[b] Uncovered Transactions

Page 15-190:

Add to note 639.

Regs. §§ 7.367(c)-1, 7.367(c)-2 (1977) repealed as deadwood by TD 8938 (Jan. 12, 2001).

Page 15-191:

Add text to end of runover paragraph.

Moreover, transfers involving noncorporate entities (e.g., partnerships) are not subject to § 367 in any meaningful way.[640.1]

[640.1] See Humphreys, "Partnership Combinations of U.S. and Non-U.S. Corporations," 92 Tax Notes 241 (July 9, 2001). Dolan, Tretiak and Elman, "Virtual Mergers: Is America Ready?" 80 Taxes 165 (Mar. 2002).

[e] Tax Avoidance Involving Imported Built-In Foreign Losses

Page 15-193:

Add text to end of ¶ 15.80[7][e].

Moreover, the 2004 Jobs Act[647.1] added new § 362(e), which prohibits the tax-free importation of built-in losses by inbound reorganizations,[647.2] § 332 liquidations, and § 351 transactions[647.3]

[647.1] American Jobs Creation Act of 2004, § 836, enacting § 362(e) and § 334(b)(1)(B) (effective October 22, 2004). See infra   15.85[7][e].

[647.2] New § 362(e)(1).

[647.3] New § 334(b)(1)(B); and § 362(e)(2) (which also applies domestically to prevent loss duplications at home or abroad). But there is an election to step-down stock basis in lieu of inside asset basis.

Add new § 15.80[7][f].

[f] Notice 2006-85: The "Killer B" [New]

On September 22, 2006, IRS announced that it intended to shut down an abusive cross-border triangular reorganization transaction known as the "Killer B."[647.4] Regulations to be issued under § 367(b) authority will provide for current taxability of the transaction despite technical arguments to the contrary.[647.5] While § 367(b) is (as will be seen) a powerful provision, it is questionable whether its scope is as broad as IRS seems to believe it is in Notice 2006-85.[647.6] Few, however, seem likely to invoke a test of strength on this issue in view of the substantial economic downside if IRS ultimately prevails here.

[647.4] Notice 2006-85, 2006-41 IRB 677 (effective Sept. 22, 2006).

[647.5] Citation of Regs. § 1.301-1(l) and *Bazley* to trump §§ 1032, 1012, and 1001, as well as § 368(a)(l)(B) seems to be a stretch here in the hope of bolstering the § 367(b) powers.

[647.6] Willens, "Service Rejects 'Killer Bees' Technique for Repatriating Earnings of Foreign Subsidiary but Courts May Reject Move for Lack of Authority," Daily Tax Rep. (BNA) No. 193, at J-1 (Oct. 5, 2006); Calianno & Petersen, "IRS Issues Notice on 'Killer B' Transactions," 18 J. Int'l Tax'n 52 (Jan. 2007).

[8] Tax Avoidance Under § 367

Page 15-195:

Add to text at end of ¶ 15.80[8].

Just when it appeared that it was safe to go back in the water, the Service released, on November 8, 2000, yet another monster package of regulations under § 367; this time dealing with the extent to which earnings and profits, deficits, and related foreign taxes carryover under § 381 in various § 367(b) transactions.[654.1] They are brutally (and needlessly) complex. In view of the 2004 tax legislation reducing the number of § 904(d) baskets from nine to two, these regulations will have to be drastically reworked (one desperately hopes). Most of these proposals (except the § 355 rules) were adopted, however, on August 8, 2006.[654.2]

[654.1] Prop. Regs. §§ 1.367(b)-3(e) and 1.367(b)-3(f) (loss carryover and earnings and profit (or deficits) on inbound asset transactions); 1.367(b)-7 (carryovers in foreign-to-foreign reorganization and § 332 liquidation transactions); and 1.367(b)-8 (allocations in various foreign divisive transactions). See infra ¶¶ 15.83[1][b], 15.83[4], 15.84[2][f], and 15.84[3][f].

[654.2] TD 9273 (effective Nov. 6, 2006).

¶ 15.81 SECTION 367: CURRENT LAW AND REGULATIONS

[1] Outbound Transfers: § 367(a)

[a] In General

Page 15-196:

Add to note 656.

See generally Med Chem (P.R.), 116 TC 308 (2001) (extensive analysis of active business status and location issues), aff'd, 295 F3d 118, 2002-2 USTC ¶ 50,512 (1st Cir. 2002).

[b] Other Assets

Page 13-197:

Add to note 660.

Hardy, "Assignment of Corporate Opportunities—The Migration of Intangibles," 100 Tax Notes 527 (July 28, 2003).

[3] Regulations Under § 367

[c] Outbound Stock Transfer Regulations

Page 15-204:

Add to note 696, first paragraph.

For current application to an expatriating inversion by Ingersoll Rand Corporation, see Sheppard, "Ingersoll Rand's Permanent Tax Holiday," 93 Tax Notes 1528 (Dec. 12, 2001). For current legislative proposals to stem these transactions, see infra   15.82[2][c] and 15.84[1][b]. The 2004 Jobs Act, § 801, adopted § 7874 (effective Mar. 5, 2003).

Page 15-205:

Add to text at end of   15.81[3][c].

A recent IRS Notice provides procedures for avoiding a GRA trigger in certain group restructures and asset reorganizations (though it is not yet applicable to divisive or triangular reorganizations).[704.1]

[704.1] Notice 2005-74, 2005-42 IRB 726. See NYSBA Tax Section comment on this Notice, 111 Tax Notes 1241 (June 12, 2006). Temporary regulations implementing this notice were issued by TD 9311 as Regs. § 1.367(a)-8T (Feb. 5, 2007).

[e] The Revised Section 367(b) Regulations

Page 15-208:

In first paragraph of ¶ 15.81[3][e], first sentence, change 1997 rules to 1977 rules.

Page 15-209:

Add to note 719, second paragraph.

For these regulations, see Prop. Regs. §§ 1.367(b)-3(e), 1.367(b)-3(f), 1.367(b)-7, 1.367(b)-8, and 1.367(b)-9 (Nov. 8, 2000), effective on final promulgation. See Connors & Voll, "Carryover of Corporate Tax Attributes in Corporate Reorganizations," 29 J. Corp. Tax'n 13 (Mar. 2002). All but § 1.367(b)-8 were adopted by TD 9273 on August 8, 2006 (effective Nov. 6, 2006).

Add to the end of note 719.

For comments on the final § 367(b) regulations, see Davis, "New Section 367(b) Regulations-Rules, Issues and Planning Opportunities," 29 Tax Mgmt. Int'l J. 230 (Apr. 14, 2000); Bress, "New Section 367(b) Regulations," 11 J. Int'l Tax'n 18 (June 2000); Lemein & McDonald, "Finally Finalized: IRS Issues Final Regulations Under Code Sec. 367(b)," 88 Taxes 10 (May 2000); Calianno, "Section 367(b)—An In-Depth Analysis," 88 Tax Notes 105 (July 3, 2000); Gosain & Jordan, "Asset and Stock Transfers Involving Foreign Corporations—Working With the 367(b) Final Regulations," 93 J. Tax'n 166

(Sept. 2000); Merrick & Munz, "IRS and Treasury Issue New Section 367(b) Regulations," 27 J. Corp. Tax'n 302 (Oct. 2000).

Page 15-210:

Add to note 725.

See Doernberg & Thompson, "Recognition of Foreign Currency Gains or Losses On Inbound Event," 98 Tax Notes 105 (Jan. 6, 2003).

Add to note 726.

See Prop. Regs. §§ 1.367(b)-3(e) and 1.367(b)-3(f) (Nov. 8, 2000) (limit carryovers of NOLs, capital losses, and E&P to items effectively connected to U.S. business (or permanent establishment); rest are purged at the border); infra ¶ 15.83[1][b].

Page 15-211:

Add to text at end of carryover paragraph.

Regulations dealing with the carryover of earnings and related foreign taxes were proposed on November 8, 2000 (and adopted in 2006), and adopted on August 8, 2006.[731.1]

[731.1] Prop. Regs. § 1.367(b)-7, infra ¶¶ 15.84[2][d] and 15.84[2][f]. Adopted by TD 9273 (effective Nov. 6, 2006).

Add to text at end of full paragraph.

Regulations dealing with allocation of earnings and profits and related foreign taxes in divisive § 367 transactions were proposed on November 8, 2000.[736.1]

[736.1] Prop. Regs. § 1.367(b)-8, infra ¶ 15.84[3][f]. These proposals, however, were not adopted with the August 2006 regulations (they will be dealt with later).

[g] Regulatory Authority to Deal With Inbound Built-In Losses

Page 15-212:

Add to note 740, second paragraph.

Prop. Regs. §§ 1.367(b)-3(e) and 1.367(b)-3(f) (Nov. 8, 2000) (carryover of NOLs, E&P (or deficit) only if ECI to U.S. business or permanent establishment; rest are purged at border).

For anti-loss import rules added by the 2004 Jobs Act in §§ 362(e) and 334(b)(1)(B), see infra ¶ 15.85[7][e].

Page 15-213:

Add new ¶ 15.81[3][h].

[h] Proposed Amendments to §367 Regulations (2005) [New]

In proposing to allow cross-border mergers to qualify as Type A reorganizations under §368(a)(1),[741.1] IRS also simultaneously released a major package of proposed regulations under §367 on January 5, 2005.[741.2] The principal purpose of these proposals (aside from recognizing Type A reorganizations as § 367 transactions) was to preserve "relevant § 1248 amounts" in certain nonrecognition exchanges of foreign corporation stock. This purpose is effected primarily by elaborate basis and holding period tracing rules in Proposed Regulations § 1.367(b)-13, which generally adopt principles similar to recent 2004 proposed regulations in §1.358-2.[741.3] This zealous defense of §1248 seems odd in view of the 2003 legislation adding § 1(h)(11), which lowers the top rate on qualified dividends (which include § 1248 dividends[741.4]) to a top rate of 15 percent (the same as for capital gain).

The proposed regulations make other significant changes to the § 367 regulations, in addition to the § 1.367(b)-13 tracing regime, of which the following are the principal ones.

1. Proposed Regulations § 1.367(b)-13(c) provides special stock basis rules for triangular reorganizations (one that does not apply the general triangular stock basis rules of Regs. § 1.358-6)[741.5], instead the basis of stock in the surviving corporation in the hands of its parent is determined by reference to the target's outside stock basis (rather

---

[741.1] Proposed Regs. § 1.368-2(b)(1) (Jan. 5, 2005); see 12.22[12].

[741.2] Proposing to amend both the § 367(a) and § 367(b) regulations. The preamble is must reading here, it is nearly as long as the regulations. See Calianno & Olin, "Cross-Border 'A' Reorganizations and the Proposed Regulations," 32 Corp. Tax'n 3 (July 2005); Bress, "The New Cross-Border 'A' Regulations," 16 J. Int'l Tax'n 14 (June 2005). Unfortunately they were adopted as final regulations by TD 9243 (effective Jan. 23, 2006). The final regulations adopted the proposals virtually intact. For comments on the final regulations, see Calianno and Olin, "Section 367 Regs. Relating to Cross-Border 'A' Reorganizations Finalized," 33 Corp. Tax'n 3 (May 2006); Lemein et al., "New Regulations Dramatically Expand Opportunities for Taxpayers Seeking to structure International Reorganizations," 84 Taxes F (May 2006). The latter article deals only with the § 368 regulations, however; Bress, "Cross-Border 'A' Final Regulations," 17 J. Int'l Tax'n 18 (Aug. 2006).

[741.3] See 12.44[3][c]; Prop. Regs. §1.367(b)-13(b) adopts the same basis and holding period principles as the § 1.358-2 proposals. Prop. Regs. §1.367(b)-13(c) also changes the triangular basis rules of § 1.358-6; 12.43[4] (infra).

[741.4] Notice 2004-70, 2004-44 IRB 724; 8.06[2]; supra note 567.1. Thus, § 1248 is largely irrelevant for non-corporate shareholders since they can obtain the same low rate for § 1248 dividends as capital gain (15 percent), while corporate shareholders prefer § 1248 dividends (that can draw out foreign tax credits under § 902) since they have no rate preference for capital gain.

[741.5] See 12.43[4] which generally adopt the "over-and-down" model in determining a parent's outside stock basis for its subsidiary after a triangular reorganization acquisition.

than, the case of the "general rule," target's inside asset basis).[741.6] This change was felt to be necessary in order to preserve the § 1248 amount in target stock. This rule applies to all triangular reorganizations where the foreign target has a § 1248 – § 367(b) shareholder.

2. Several amendments are proposed to Regs. § 1.367(a)-3(a):

    a. Type A reorganizations (direct and triangular) were added to the possible exception to the application of § 367(a),[741.7]

    b. Securities exchanges were added to the stock exchange provision; and[741.8]

    c. Transitory passage of parent's stock pursuant to the plan of a triangular reorganization will not be subject to § 367(a).[741.9]

3. The concurrent application of § 367(a) and §367(b) overlap rules of § 1.367(a)-3(b)(2) would be modified (again) to give § 367(b) priority in the case where a foreign corporation with a "§ 367(b) shareholder (that is, a 10-percent U.S. shareholder whose stock has a §1248 tainted amount) transfers its assets to a domestic acquiror in an inbound § 368 transaction that is subject to § 1.367(b)-3 and also to the indirect stock transfer rules of § 1.367(a)-3(d).[741.10] In such a case, the exchanging U.S. shareholders must include the "all earnings and profits" dividend if this amount is greater than the potential gain on its stock (and steps-up stock basis by that amount, thereby eliminating § 367(a) gain on the stock).[741.11] The current priority of § 367(a) ordering rule continues in all other cases (e.g., where the "all E&P" amount is less that potential gain on the stock.[741.12] The IRS felt that application of § 367(b) had become "elective" under the current regulations ordering regime.[741.13]

4. The indirect stock transfer regulations are revised to include triangular Type B reorganizations in which a U.S. shareholder receives stock

---

[741.6] Prop. Regs. § 1.367(b)-13(e), Exs. 2-5 illustrate the application of this rule. See Calianno & Olin, "Inbound Triangular Reorganizations – The Interaction of Sections 367(a) and (b) Under the new Proposed Regulations," 16 J. Int'l Tax'n 36 (June 2005).

[741.7] This exception applies to exempt Type E recapitalizations, and § 354 exchanges of stock for stock of a foreign corporation in asset reorganizations (Type C, D or F) that are not treated as indirect stock transfers under § 1.367(a)-3(a) and § 1.367(a)-3(d).

[741.8] As promised in Notice 2005-6, 2005-5 IRB 448.

[741.9] However, parent stock contributed to its subsidiary that is not part of the acquisition transaction is subject to § 367(a) (and thus its transfer by the subsidiary to a foreign target would be taxable to the subsidiary).

[741.10] Prop. Regs. 1.367(a)-3(b)(2)(i) See Calianno and Olin, supra note 741.6. .

[741.11] Regs. § 1.367(a)-3(b)(2)(i)(A), and § 1.367(a)-3(d), Ex. 15.

[741.12] Regs. § 1.367(a)-3(b)(2)(i)(B), and § 1.367(a)-3(d), Ex. 15.

[741.13] See Preamble, Part C (by failing to sign a gain recognition agreement (GRE), and thereby triggering tax on the § 367(a) gain, § 367(b) did not apply).

of a U.S. parent of the foreign acquiring corporation[741.14] In such case, the gain recognition agreement (GRA) maybe triggered if the U.S. parent disposes of its sub stock, or the sub disposes of its acquired stock, within 5 years of the acquisition.

5. The indirect stock transfer regulations of § 1.367(a)-3(d) are conformed to the proposed expansive changes to the § 368(a)(2)(C) dropdown regulations, § 1.368-2(k), proposed on August 16, 2004.[741.15]

6. Coordination of the indirect stock transfer rules with the asset retransfer of assets to a controlled domestic transferee (so called "round trip" transfers) that currently are excepted from the indirect stock transfer rules would be drastically tightened by the proposed regulations.[741.16] IRS stated that its was concerned that this exception could facilitate corporate inversion transactions (as well as divisive transactions).[741.17]

7. In a good news proposal, however, the proposed regulations would amend the § 1.367(b)-4 regulations to change the current regulations (which now trigger § 367(b) tax on the § 1248 amount) to allow deferral where the § 1248 taint can be preserved in a domestic corporation's stock under the basis tracing rules of § 1.367(b)-13[741.18]

8. The Preamble also notes that regulations under alternative nonrecognition regimes in § 897 (the FIRPTA Rules) and § 1291(f) (the PFIC proposed regulations) will be revised as well.[741.19]These regulations were adopted as final regulations on January 30, 2006.[741.20]

[741.14] Prop. Regs. § 1.367(a)-3(d)(1)(iii)(B), and 1.367(a)-3(d)(3) Ex. 5A.

[741.15] See   12.63[6]; also Rev. Rul. 2002-85, 2002-85, 2002-2 CB 986 (drop-down protection for drops after a Type D reorganization), and Notice 2002-77, 2002-2 CB 997 (stating that Regs. §1.367(a)-3(d) will be amended to reflect this change).

[741.16] Prop. Regs. § 1.367(a)-3(d)(2)(vi); and 1.367(a)-3(d)3, Exs. 6B, 6C, 6D, 9 and 13A.

[741.17] See Preamble, Part G.

[741.18] Prop. Regs. §1.367(b)-4(b)(1)(ii) and § 1.367(b)-4(b)(1)(iii), Ex. 3B.

[741.19] For the § 897 rules, see infra   15.85[2], 15.85[3] and 15.85[4]; For the PFIC nonrecognition proposed regulations, see infra   15.85[6]. This is not a happy prospect; the current FIRPTA regulations are a tangled out-of-date mess. For a preview of the § 897 regulations; see Notice 2006-46, infra   15.85[1][c].

[741.20] TD 9243 (Jan. 26, 2006); (they didn't improve much). For comments, see supra note 741.2.

¶ 15.82 TRANSFERS TO AND BY FOREIGN CORPORATIONS UNDER § 351

[1] Outbound Transfers of Property: General Background

Page 15-216:

Add to note 753.

See generally Med Chem (P.R.), 116 TC 308 (2001) (extensive analysis of active business status and location issues), aff'd, 295 F3d 118 (1st Cir. 2002).

[2] Outbound Property Transfer Rules of 1984

[a] In General

Page 15-219:

Add to note 762, first paragraph.

Calianno & Cornett, "Impact of the International Provisions on Outbound Section 351 Transfers," 29 J. Corp. Tax'n 16 (Jan. 2002).

[b] Outbound Stock Transfers: Revised Regulations (1991–1998)

Page 15-221:

Add to note 771, fourth paragraph.

Calianno & Cornett, supra note 762, at 22

Page 15-223:

Add new ¶ 15.82[2][c].

[c] Expatriating Corporate Inversions [New]

Despite promulgation of the tightened anti-inversion regulations in 1996, they have proved to be remarkably ineffective in stemming what has proved to be a rising tide of expatriating inversion transactions.[784.1] These regulations have proved to pose a severe burden, however, for many traditional cross-border acquisitions in which the U.S. target is larger than its foreign acquiror.[784.2] What began as a modest migration of several insurance companies to the user-

---

[784.1] See generally Crane & Workman, "Bermuda Triangle: Tax Havens, Treaties and U.S. P & C Insurance Competitiveness," 94 Tax Notes 73 (Jan. 7, 2002); Sheppard, "Would Imputed Income Prevent Escape to Bermuda?" 86 Tax Notes 1663 (Mar. 20, 2000); Gutman, "Is the United States Picking on Bermuda?" 86 Tax Notes 1669 (2000); Sheppard, "Ingersoll Rand's Permanent Tax Holiday," 93 Tax Notes 1528 (Dec. 17, 2001); Sheppard, "Preventing Corporate Inversions," 95 Tax Notes 29 (Apr. 4, 2002); Brewer, "Treason? Or Survival of the Fittest?: Dealing With Corporate Expatriation," 95 Tax Notes 603 (Apr. 22, 2002). NYSBA Tax Section, "Outbound Inversion Transactions," 96 Tax Notes 127 (July 1, 2002); also in Daily Tax Rep. (BNA) No. 108, Viewpoint, at J-1 (June 15, 2002); Hardy, "The Migration of Intangibles, 100 Tax Notes 527 (July 28, 2002).

[784.2] Thompson, Jr., "Section 367: A 'Wimp' for Inversions and a 'Bully' for Real Cross-Border Acquisitions," 94 Tax Notes 1505 (Mar. 18, 2002).

friendly climate of Bermuda, has turned into an ever increasing exodus of major domestic corporations,[784.3] even attracting notable mentions in the daily press.[784.4] Before the domestic corporate cupboard becomes completely depleted, it was not surprising to see Congress at last taking an interest an the matter (which was joined, in a limited way, by the Treasury on May 17, 2002).[784.5]

On April 11, 2002, Finance Committee members Baucus and Grassley introduced legislation prospectively targeting these expatriating inversion transactions (including partnerships).[784.6] Thus, so called "pure inversion" transactions (where the new foreign parent is essentially a paper shell) will be domesticated to U.S. corporate status, while "limited inversions" (and pre–effective date transactions)[784.7] would be subject to a strengthened § 367(a) toll charge regime, as well as tightened anti-base erosion rules in § 482 and § 163(j) (the anti–interest stripping rule).[784.8] All in all, this game will be considerably more difficult and dangerous to play if this proposed legislation is enacted.[784.9] This proposal had been attached to several different Finance Com-

---

[784.3] Articles supra note 784.1.

[784.4] David Cay Johnston, "U.S. Corporations Are Using Bermuda To Slash Tax Bills," New York Times, Feb. 18, 2002, at A1.

[784.5] Two anti-inversion bills were introduced by the House in March 2002, by Representatives Neal (HR 3883) and McInnis (HR 3857).

See generally, "Treasury Department Preliminary Report on Tax Policy Implications of Corporate Inversion Transactions," Daily Tax Rep. (BNA) No. 97, at L-3 (May 20, 2002). Sullivan, "Treasury's Inversions Report Rocks the Boat," 95 Tax Notes 1289 (May 27, 2002); Thompson, "Treasury's Inversion Study Misses the Mark," 95 Tax Notes 1673 (June 10, 2002); Avi-Yonah, "For Heaven's Sake: Reflections on Inversion Transactions," 95 Tax Notes 1793 (June 17, 2002); Sheppard, "Preventing Corporate Inversions, Part 3," 95 Tax Notes 1864 (June 24, 2002).

[784.6] S. 2119. Reversing the Expatriation of Profits Offshore Act ("REPO"), proposing new § 7874, generally effective for inversion occurring after March 20, 2002.

[784.7] Which is March 20, 2002. This legislation cleared the Finance Committee on June 18, 2002, and has been folded into the Finance Committee's charity bill as a revenue offset, HR 7, Title VI B (July 16, 2002).

[784.8] Section 7874(a) is the domestication rule for pure inversions; § 7874(c)(1) tightens the toll charge rules of § 367; § 7874(d)(1) deals with related party base erosion transactions under §§ 163(j), 267(a)(3), 482, and 845 (and requires advance IRS approval of such transactions); § 7874(d)(2) lowers the allowable § 163(j) cap from 50 to 25 percent. For the interest-stripping rules generally, see supra   15.04[4]. Treasury's principal focus is on income-stripping transactions (but also targets transfer pricing income shifting transactions and cross-border acquisitions as well).

[784.9] Hamilton, "REPO Act Targets Inversions: Are Offshore Hedge Funds Next?" 95 Tax Notes 287 (Apr. 15, 2002); Willens, "Viewpoint," Daily Tax Rep. (BNA) No. 77, at J-1 (Apr. 22, 2002). See also Treasury Preliminary Report on Corporate Inversion Transactions, supra note 784.5. For further comments on the REPO legislative proposal, see Thompson, "Non-Wimpy Grassley-Baucus Inversion Bill," 95 Tax Notes 1515 (June 3, 2002); Sheppard, "Preventing Corporate-Inversions," Part 2, 95 Tax Notes 816 (May 6, 2002); Petersen and Cohen, "Corporate Inversions: Yesterday, Today and Tomorrow," 81 Taxes 161 (Mar. 2003).

mitte bills (it was currently incorporated in the Committee's Energy Tax Incentive Act (Apr. 2003). It finally passed in slightly modified form in the 2004 Jobs Act.

Ways and Means Committee Chairman Thomas joined the anti-inversion forces with his version of proposed legislation released on July 11, 2002,[784.10] which initially was far less rigorous than the Finance Committee's REPO proposal in some respects, but more so in others;[784.11] however, it was clearly more restrictive than Treasury's proposals.[784.12] The Thomas bill also contained significant anti-shelter proposals[784.13] (and a host of international simplification provisions which have been noted throughout this Chapter). The omnibus character of this legislation has drawn criticism from both sides of the political spectrum which renders its ultimate passage somewhat doubtful. The Thomas bill was reintroduced on July 25, 2003,[784.14] and the current version is considerably more vigorous than the earlier model (the moratorium in this latest version was increased to ten years).

Responding to Treasury's June anti-inversion proposal to impose expanded 1099 reporting rules for inversion transactions, IRS did just that in temporary regulations issued on November 18, 2002.[784.15] The intent here is to "remind" shareholders involved in these taxable inversion transactions to pay attention to their obligations.

See also Sheppard Preventing Corporate Inversions, Part 4: Limitation Benefits, 105 Tax Notes 506 (Oct. 25, 2004) (discussing new Barbados Treaty and Dutch Protocol).

[784.10] HR 5095, The American Competitiveness Act of 2002, Title 2. See Joint Committee Staff Technical Explanation of HR 5095, Daily Tax Rep. (BNA) No. 140 at L-6, L-21 (July 22, 2002); Sullivan, "Thomas's Inversion Proposal: Short, Sweet, and Incomplete," 96 Tax Notes 192 (July 8, 2002); Sheppard, "The Good and the Bad in the Thomas Bill," 96 Tax Notes 482 (July 22, 2002); Thompson, "Critical Perspective on the Thomas Bill," 96 Tax Notes 581 (July 22, 2002).

[784.11] Thus, the Thomas bill proposed § 7874 provision lasts only for three years (from Mar. 20, 2002 to Mar. 20, 2005), and thus is merely a three-year moratorium; the Thomas bill's anti-stripping revisions, by contrast, is far more extensive than the Baucus-Grassley proposal. This proposal is currently in the House Energy bill which passed the House in April 11, 2003, HR 6, § 44001 (and imposes only a 22-month moratorium).

[784.12] Treasury proposes to tighten the interest-stripping rules of § 163(j) (which proposal was adopted by the Thomas bill). But also "suggests" a reworking of the § 482 regulations and the § 367 regulations; equally unpleasant prospects. Treasury also proposed expanded reporting requirements for these transactions, see infra note 784.15.

[784.13] See ¶ 5.10[6][j].

[784.14] American Jobs Creation Act of 2003, HR 2896, Title II, §§ 2001 (earnings stripping), § 2002, § 7874 (expatriated entities and their foreign parents).

[784.15] TD 9022 (Nov. 18, 2002), issuing Regs. § 1.6043-4T (for § 6043(c) information return reporting in the case acquisitions of control and substantial changes in capital structure), and § 1.6045-3T (information returns for brokers). These rules were clarified, revised and updated on December 12, 2003, by TD 9801 (Dec. 30, 2003).

New reporting regulations were issued by TD9230 on Dec. 5, under the 2004 Jobs Act provisions of § 6043A; Regs. § 1.6043-4.

But passage of some form of anti-inversion legislation in 2004 seemed increasingly likely; whether it's the Senate or the somewhat milder House version was unclear for most of 2004, but a modified version of both the House and Senate provisions finally passed on October 22, 2004.[784.16]

Responding to the criticisms noted above (that § 7874 is overly broad, and is interfering with legitimate business transactions not intended to be covered by this provision), IRS issued generally helpful temporary regulations on December 28, 2005, carving out various transactions that will not be subject to these rules.[784.17] The preamble explains Treasury's reason for relaxing the scope of § 7874, and asks for comments on eight other § 7874 issues (which no doubt will be readily forthcoming). The regulations contain numerous examples indicating their application.[784.18] But IRS also warns that it has no intention of weakening this section (and that any ensuing regulations may be retroactive).[784.19]

A second set of temporary regulations (also generally helpful) was issued on June 6, 2006,[784.20] and deal with a foreign corporation having a "substantial presence" in a foreign country and thus avoiding application of the § 7874 rules (that is, it will not be a "surrogate foreign corporation"). The regulations apply two tests for this purpose: (1) a general rule facts-and-circumstances-based test;[784.21] and (2) a safe-harbor test.[784.22] Of the two tests, the latter one is definitely to be preferred (although satisfying it will require a real presence in the foreign country). If neither test can be met, however, § 7874 will apply to

---

[784.16] HR 4520, Act § 801, new § 7874 (effective Mar. 5, 2003) without either an interest-stripping amendment or a moritorium. There is a "deemed domestication" for pure inversions (an 80 percent shareholder shift), and expanded gain recognition for more modest 60 percent inversions. New § 7874 is complicated, but its very complexity should be enough to halt most, if not all, of these transactions, which, of course, is its real purpose. For comment, see Kirsch, "The Congressional Response to Corporate Inversions: The Tension Between Symbols and Substance in the Taxation of Multinational Corporations," 24 Vir. Tax Rev. 475 (Winter, 2005); Dubert, "Accidental Inversions," 17 J. Int'l Tax'n 22 (July 2005). Dolan, et al, "What's Wrong sith the New Anti-Inversion Rules?" 19 J. Int'l Tax'n 52 (Sept. 2005).

[784.17] TD 9238 (Dec. 28, 2005, effective on the same date as § 7874, Mar. 4, 2003), issuing Regs. § 1.7874-1T. Disregard of affiliate-owned stock.

[784.18] Regs. § 1.7874-1T(e) offers eight examples: Three of which trigger the possible application of § 7874, Exs 1, 6 and 8; but five of which do not , Exs. 2, 3, 4, 5 and 7. See Sheppard, "More Questions for Inversion Regulations," 110 Tax Notes 1273 (Mar. 20 2006); Dubert, "Section 7874 Temporary Regulations: Treasury and IRS Waive Taxpayers Through the Stoplight," 17 J. Int'l Tax'n 12 (July 2006).

[784.19] Preamble.

[784.20] TD 9265 (June 6, 2006). Regs. § 1.7874-2T.

[784.21] Regs. § 1.7874-2T(d)(1); five examples applying in the general facts test are in § 1.7874-2T(d)(4) (three fail this test, two pass it).

[784.22] Regs. § 1.7874-2T(d)(2). This test will be met if the corporation (during the last twelve-month test period after the transaction) (1) has 10 percent of its employees in the foreign country (both by payroll and headcount); (2) 10 percent of its assets (by value) are located there; *and* (3) it makes 10 percent of its sales in that country.

convert the surrogate foreign corporation to domestic corporate status (but § 367 will *not* apply to tax its shareholders on the status conversion.[784.23]

[784.23] Regs. § 1.7874-2T(h). See generally, Greenwald & Kaplan, "'Substantial Business Activity' Under the Anti-Inversion Regulations," 112 Tax Notes 863 (Sept. 4, 2006).

¶ 15.83 LIQUIDATION OF CONTROLLED SUBSIDIARY UNDER § 332

[1] Inbound Repatriating Liquidations

[b] Inbound Liquidations: Revised Regulations

Page 15-225:

Add to note 792.

For interface with the consolidated return rules, see Friedel, "Intercompany Sales of CFC Stock—Where Does Reality End and Wonderland Begin?" 92 J. Tax'n 362 (June 2000); 13.43[2][a], 13.43[2][b], and 13.43[3][a].

Add to note 794.

See Doernberg & Thompson, "Recognition of Foreign Currency Gains or Losses On Inbound Event," 78 Tax Notes 105 (Jan. 6, 2003).

Add to note 795, second paragraph.

Calianno, "Section 332 Liquidation With Foreign Corporations: Always Consider Section 367," 12 J. Int'l Tax'n 36 (June 2001), reprinted in 28 J. Corp. Tax'n 13 (July 2001).

Add to text at end of ¶ 15.83[1][b].

Regulations proposed on November 8, 2000 (and adopted in 2006), only allow § 381 carryovers of losses and E&P if effectively connected to a U.S. business (or permanent establishment); the rest are purged at the border.[795.1] Thus, imports of foreign-generated losses and deficits are prohibited by the proposed regulations. More significantly, the 2004 Jobs Act[795.2] imposes a basis step-down for built-in loss assets in an inbound § 332 liquidation, thus denying

---

[795.1] Prop. Regs. §§ 1.367(b)-3(e) (loss carryovers) and 1.367(b)-3(f) (earnings or deficits), effective on final promulgation. See Bress, Anson & Dubert, "New Section 367(b) Proposed Regs. (Part 2)," 12 J. Int'l Tax'n 18 (July 2001). Daub, "Importing and Exporting Basis and Other Tax Attributes—Do We Need a New System?" 12 J. Int'l Tax'n 15 (Nov. 2001). Connors & Voll, "Carryover of Corporate Tax Attributes," 29 J. Corp. Tax'n 13 (Mar. 2002).

[795.2] American Jobs Creation Act of 2004, § 836(b), new § 334(b)(1)(B), effective October 22, 2004.

carryover asset basis in these transactions as well.[795.3] These proposals were adopted without change in August 2006.[795.4]

[795.3] See infra ¶ 15.85[7][e].

[795.4] TD 9273 (Aug. 8, 2006) (effective Nov. 6, 2006).

[2] Outbound Expatriating Liquidations

[b] Section 367(e)(2) (Added by Tax Reform Act of 1986)

Page 15-227:

Add to note 801.

Calianno, "Section 332 Liquidations With Foreign Corporations: Always Consider Section 367," 12 J. Int'l Tax'n 36 (June 2001), reprinted in 28 J. Corp. Tax'n 13 (July 2001).

[3] Foreign-to-Foreign Liquidations

Add to note 802.

Calianno, "Section 332 Liquidations With Foreign Corporations: Always Consider Section 367," 12 J. Int'l Tax'n 36 (June 2001), reprinted in 28 J. Corp. Tax'n 13 (July 2001).

Page 15-228:

Add to note 803.

But, Prop. Regs. § 1.367(b)-7 (Nov. 8, 2000) deal with § 381 carryovers of E&P and foreign taxes, see infra, ¶ 15.84[2][f]. Adopted as Final Regs. § 1.367(b)-7 by TD 9273 (effective Nov. 6, 2006).

Add to text at end of ¶ 15.83[3].

But, regulations proposed on November 8, 2000, deal with § 381 carryover of earnings and profits, deficits, and related foreign taxes in foreign-to-foreign § 332 liquidation transactions.[803.1]

[803.1] Prop. Regs. § 1.367(b)-7 (effective on final promulgation), infra ¶ 15.84[2][f]. Bress, Anson & Dubert, "New Section 367(b) Proposed Regs.—Has Treasury's Fear of Tax Attribute Trafficking Resulted in Compliance-Proof Rules? (Part 1)," 12 J. Int'l Tax'n 4 (June 2001) (yes). They were adopted as Final Regs. § 1.367(b)-7 in TD 9273 (effective Nov. 6, 2006); they are simpler, but still no walk in the park. See infra, ¶ 15.84[2][f].

[4] Regulations Under § 367(e)(2)

[a] In General

Page 15-229:

Add to note 807, second paragraph.

Calianno, "Section 332 Liquidations With Foreign Corporations Always Consider Section 367," 12 J. Int'l Tax'n 36 (June 2001), reprinted in 28 J. Corp. Tax'n 13 (July 2001).

[b] Domestic Subsidiary Liquidations

Page 15-230:

Add to note 815.

But this latter rule was dropped by TD 8834 (Mar. 3, 2001 (technical correction)).

[c] Foreign Subsidiary Liquidations

Add to note 820.

But this provision was dropped by TD 8834 (technical corrections) on March 3, 2001.

But § 836(b) of the 2004 Jobs Act adds new § 334(b)(1)(B), barring basis carryover for built-in loss assets in an inbound § 332 liquidation (effective October 22, 2004). See infra   15.85[7][e].

[e] General Anti-Abuse Rule: § 1.367(e)-2(d)

Page 15-231:

Add to text at end of ¶ 15.83[4][e].

But proposed regulations issued on November 19, 2002, would restrict this anti-abuse rule to outbound liquidations of domestic subsidiaries only.[824.1]

[824.1] Prop. Regs. § 1.367(e)-2(d) (effective Sept. 7, 1999, the date of the § 367(e)(2) regulations). The proposals also "clarify" that the liquidation may have a principal purpose of avoidance even though outweighed by other purposes taken together; adopted without change by TD 9066 on July 2, 2003.

¶ 15.84 REORGANIZATION OF FOREIGN CORPORATIONS

[1] Type B Reorganizations

[b] Current § 367 Regime for Type B Reorganizations (Outbound and Inbound)

Page 15-235:

Add to note 835, first paragraph.

See also Sheppard, "Ingersoll Rand's Permanent Tax Holiday," 93 Tax Notes 1528 (Dec. 17, 2001) (expatriating inversion move to Bermuda).

Add text to end of runover paragraph.

Expatriating inversion transactions, however, have not been deterred by the 1996 inversion regulations, though genuine cross-border acquisitions have been severely impacted by them (especially when the U.S. target is larger than its foreign acquiror).[840.1] Congress has finally begun to move against these transactions in legislation introduced in both the House and Senate in March and April of 2001.[840.2] The Senate Finance Committee proposal is more sweeping in scope than the House versions.[840.3] But Ways and Means Chairman Thomas introduced his version of anti-inversion legislation on July 11, 2002,[840.4] which falls somewhere between the Finance Committee's proposal and Treasury's far more modest proposals.[840.5] Passage of *some* form of anti-inversion legislation seemed increasingly likely, but whether it is the more rigorous Senate version or the milder House version was unclear (for most of 2004 until its eventual passage on October 22, 2004).[840.6]

[840.1] Thompson, Jr., "Section 367(a): A 'Wimp' for Inversions and a 'Bully' for Real Cross-Border Acquisitions," 94 Tax Notes 1505 (Mar. 18, 2002); supra ¶ 15.82[2][c].

[840.2] Supra ¶ 15.82[2][c], notes 784.5, 784.6, 784.14.

[840.3] Supra ¶ 15.82[2][c], note 784.6, § 2119, new § 7874 (Reversing the Expatriation of Profits Offshore Act, or REPO). This proposal has been folded into HR 7 (the Finance Committee's charity bill) as Title VI B July 16, 2002 (to serve as a revenue raises offset).

[840.4] HR 5095, The American Competitiveness Act of 2002, Title II, supra note ¶ 15.82[2][c], note 784.10; reintroduced as HR 2896, The American Jobs Creation Act of 2003, on July 25, 2003, Title II, § 2002, adding new § 7874.

[840.5] Thus, the Thomas bill initially was merely a three-year (later raised to ten years) moratorium (proposed § 7874 only lasted from Mar. 20, 2002, to Mar. 20, 2005); the current version lasts from March 4, 2003 for ten years. The Treasury's primary anti-inversion legislative proposal of June 2000 is merely to tighten the interest-stripping rules of § 163(j) (which is adopted by the Thomas bill), though Treasury also "suggests" taking another look at the § 482 regulations as they apply to intangibles and also at the § 367 regulations dealing with outbound transactions (both of these regulation regimes have undergone extensive recent—and in the case of § 367, endless revisions). Treasury also proposed expanded reporting for these transactions and IRS responded to this invitation by issuing temporary regulations on November 18, 2002, under § 6043(c); see Regs. §§ 1.6043-4T and 1.6045-3T, supra ¶ 15.82[2][c], note 784.15. These reporting rules were revised and updated by TD 9101 (Dec. 30, 2003).

[840.6] The House version is contained in its Energy bill, which passed the House on April 11, 2003, HR 6, § 44001 (only a 22-month moratorium in this legislation), but the subsequent Thomas bill of July 25, 2003; has raised it to ten years, but has dropped the interest-stripping proposals. The final legislation, HR 4520, Act § 801, new § 7874 (effective Mar. 5, 2003, has no interest-stripping changes either). For comment, see Kirsch, "The Congressional Response to Corporate Inversions: The Tension Between Symbols and

Substance in the Taxation of Multinational Corporations," 24 Vir. Tax Rev. 475 (Winter, 2005).

[2] Asset Acquisitions: Type C Reorganizations

[a] Outbound Type C Reorganizations

Page 15-244:

Add to text at end of ¶ 15.84[2][a].

In such a case, the 1996 anti-inversion regulations[878.1] can pose a significant barrier if the U.S. target is larger than the foreign acquiring corporation.[878.2]

[878.1] Regs. § 1.367(a)-3(c).

[878.2] Thompson, Jr., "Section 367: A 'Wimp' for Inversions and a 'Bully' for Real Cross-Border Acquisitions," 94 Tax Notes 1505 (Mar. 18, 2002).

[b] Inbound Type C Reorganizations

Page 15-245:

Add to note 881.

For proposed regulations dealing with § 381 carryovers of losses, earnings and profits (or deficits), see Prop. Regs. §§ 1.367(b)-3(e) and 1.367(b)-3(f) (generally purged at border unless ECI to US business (or permanent establishment)). The proposed regulations generally bar the import of foreign-generated losses. They were adopted without change by TD 9273 (effective Nov. 6, 2006).

Add text to end of ¶ 15.84[2][b].

But the 2004 Jobs Act restricts loss import transactions in new § 362(e)(1),[881.1] if aggregate asset basis exceeds aggregate asset value.

[881.1] American Jobs Creation Act of 2004, § 836, effective October 22, 2004. See infra   15.85[7][e].

[c] Foreign-To-Foreign Type C Reorganizations: Background

Page 15-246:

Add to text at end of ¶ 15.84[2][c].

Additional regulations dealing with § 381 carryovers of earnings, deficits, and related foreign taxes in foreign-to-foreign asset acquisition reorganizations were proposed on November 8, 2000 (they are very heavy going).[884.1]

[884.1] Prop. Regs. §§ 1.367(b)-7 and 1.367(b)-9 (effective on final promulgation), infra ¶ 15.84[2][f].

[d] Revised § 367(b) Regulations

Page 15-247:

Add to text at end of ¶ 15.84[2][d].

Additional regulations dealing with § 381 carryovers of earnings, deficits, and related foreign taxes in foreign-to-foreign asset acquisition reorganizations were proposed on November 8, 2000.[889.1]

[889.1] Prop. Regs. §§ 1.367(b)-7 and 1.367(b)-9, infra ¶ 15.84[2][f]. They were adopted by TD 9273 on August 8, 2006 (effective Nov. 6, 2006).

[e] Examples

Page 15-248:

Add new note 897.1 to last sentence of part 1 of Example 3.

[897.1] But, if *D* (or *S*) drops the *F* assets down into its CFC, *FS*, § 367(a)(3) (and its toll charges) would apply to that transaction. Moreover, if *D* transfers its stock to *FS* for use in payment to *FS*, Regs. § 1.367(a)-3(c) could apply (per se gain to *D*); see also Rev. Rul. 74-503, 1974-2 CB 117 (for zero basis problem). But § 1032 should protect *D* (and trump the regulation) here (one would hope).

Page 15-249:

Add to note 898, first paragraph.

For carryover of *F*'s losses, earnings, deficits, or foreign taxes under § 381, see Prop. Regs. §§ 1.367(b)-3(e) and 1.367(b)-3(f) (Nov. 8, 2000) (only carryover if ECI to US business or permanent establishment; rest are purged at the border).

Add to note 901.

For E&P (or deficit) carryover tracing rules in these transactions, see Prop. Regs. § 1.367(b)-7 (Nov. 8, 2000), infra ¶ 15.84[2][f].

Page 15-250:

Add new note 902.1 at end of second sentence of part 1 of Example 5.

[902.1] But, there are wrong ways to do this transaction in triangular mode: if *D* acquires *F* assets directly and then drops them into *S*, § 367(a)(3) applies (with its toll charges); even worse, if *D* drops its stock into *S* for its use in paying *F*, *D* may have per se gain recognition under Regs. § 1.367(a)-3(c) (and with a zero basis problem to boot under Rev. Rul. 74-503, 1974-2 CB 117, supra note 897.1); but, § 1032 should protect *D* in this latter case (and trump the regulation if it is asserted, which it shouldn't be).

Add new ¶ 15.84[2][f].

[f] Section 381 Carryover of Earnings (or Deficits) in Foreign-To-Foreign Asset Reorganizations [New]

Proposed regulations issued on November 8, 2000, provide extensive, intricate (and exceedingly complex) rules dealing with the extent to which foreign earnings (or deficits) and related foreign taxes carryover under § 381 in various foreign-to-foreign asset acquisition reorganizations.[902.2] The principal focus of the proposed regulations is identifying and preserving the identity and character of the inherited earnings for purposes of applying the foreign tax credit computation rules (viz., the § 902 "pooling" provisions and the § 904(d) separate "basket" regime).[902.3] The regulations set out an elaborate tracing regime in order to ensure that the character and identity of the corporate parties' earnings and related foreign taxes is preserved after the § 381 transaction. The stated goal here is to prevent inappropriate blending of the corporations' earnings accounts.

Thus, different rules apply depending on whether the parties are (1) a "look-through" corporation (generally a CFC), (2) a non-"look-through" [10⁄50] corporation (generally a non-CFC corporation with a § 902 shareholder), or (3) a less-than-10-percent U.S.-owned foreign corporation (viz., one with no § 902 shareholders or § 951(b) subpart F shareholders).[902.4]

Proposed Regulations § 1.367(b)-7(c) first sets out various ordering rules for post-transaction distributions by the surviving foreign corporation (which, in turn, depend on its status as a "look-through," non-"look-through" § 902, or

---

[902.2] Prop. Regs. §§ 1.367(b)-7 and 1.367(b)-9 (effective on final promulgation). For comments see Davis, "Proposed E&P Regulations Under § 367(b)," 30 Tax Mgmt. Int'l J. 67 (Feb. 9, 2001); Gosain et al., "Guidance on Tax Attributes in Section 367(b) Exchanges Will Make Planning Easier," 94 J. Tax'n 242 (Apr. 2001); DuPuy & Bower, "Layers, Pools, Credits, and Rules," 30 Tax Mgmt. Int'l J. 155 (Apr. 13, 2001); Bress, Anson & Dubert, "New Section 367(b) Proposed Regs.—Has Treasury's Fear of Tax Attribute Trafficking Resulted in Compliance-Proof Rules? (Part 1)," 12 J. Int'l Tax'n 4 (June 2001) (yes); Connors & Voll, "Carryover of Corporate Tax Attributes in Corporate Reorganizations," 29 J. Corp. Tax'n 13 (Mar. 2002).

[902.3] Supra   15.21[2][f] and 15.21[4].

[902.4] Prop. Regs. §§ 1.367(b)-7(b)(1) and 1.367(b)-7(c).

a "pure" foreign corporation).[902.5] The rest of the proposals set out the various tracing rules applicable to the earnings and related foreign taxes that are inherited by the surviving foreign corporation:

1. Proposed Regulations § 1.367(b)-7(d) involves acquisitions of one CFC by another CFC (and is generally the simplest of the transactional situations);[902.6]

2. Proposed Regulations § 1.367(b)-7(e) deals with two different acquiror identities (§ 1.367(b)-7(e)(1) involves a CFC acquiring non-look-through § 902 corporation,[902.7] while § 1.367(b)-7(e)(2) involves a non-look-through § 902 corporation acquiring either a CFC or another § 902 corporation);[902.8]

3. Proposed Regulations § 1.367(b)-7(f) involves acquisition of pre-pooling "annual layers" of earnings (viz., the pre-1986 Act § 902 rules)[902.9] by either a CFC or a § 902 corporation, § 367(b)-7(f)(1),[902.10] or by a "pure" foreign acquiring corporation, § 1.367(b)-7(f)(2);[902.11] and

4. Proposed Regulations § 1.367(b)-7(g) provides "special rules" for dealing with deficits, post-transaction status changes, and ordering rules for multiple hovering deficits.[902.12]

In sum, the proposed regulations are heavy going indeed, being driven, it would seem, by a near maniacal fear that somehow tax reduction opportunities may exist in these transactions. The real culprit, however, is the § 904(d) foreign tax credit limitation basket regime with which the elaborate tracing exer-

---

[902.5] Under these provisions, if the survivor is a "look-through" corporation (e.g., a CFC), distributions come first from the look-through pool, second from the non-look-through pool, and finally from pre-pooling annual layers under the LIFO method (the old § 902 regime, supra ¶ 15.21[2][c]). If the survivor is a non-look-through $^{10}\!/_{50}$ corporation, distributions come first from the non-look-through pool, and then from pre-pooling annual layers. If the survivor has no 10-percent U.S. shareholders, distributions follow the normal dividend ordering regime (from annual layers on a LIFO basis).

[902.6] Earnings and related foreign taxes are blended into the appropriate basket category here, Prop. Regs. § 1.367(b)-7(d)(1)(ii). The hovering deficit limitation in § 1.367(b)-7(d)(2) mirrors a similar provision in § 381(c)(2)(B). The three examples in § 1.367(b)-7(d)(3) are moderately understandable.

[902.7] Prop. Regs. § 1.367(b)-7(e)(1) (inherited earnings, deficits and foreign taxes are segregated here, viz., specific tracing is required).

[902.8] Prop. Regs. § 1.367(b)-7(e)(2) combines these earnings in a single basket, the § 904(d)(1)(E) basket.

[902.9] Supra ¶ 15.21[2][c].

[902.10] Prop. Regs. § 1.367(b)-7(f)(1) require segregation into separate categories here (specific tracing).

[902.11] Prop. Regs. § 1.367-7(f)(2) lump all these layers into a single pre-acquisition year, and require that account to be segregated.

[902.12] Prop. Regs. §§ 1.367-7(g)(1) (deficits suspended for CFC computations) and 1.367(b)-7(g)(3) (post-transaction status change will *not* restore prior status).

cise is concerned, lest earnings (and related foreign taxes) end up in the wrong limitation basket. But the 2004 Jobs Act's reduction of § 904(d) baskets from nine to two will require these proposals to be substantially reworked.[902.13]

These proposals were adopted (in significantly modified and simplified form) on August 8, 2006.[902.14] The principal changes were effected by the 2004 AJCA, which broadened the look-through rules of §§ 902 and 904(d) (retroactively) and also reduced the number of § 904(d) baskets from nine to two (in 2007).[902.15] As a result of these changes, the final regulations reduced the classification of foreign corporations involved in a § 381 transaction from three to two categories; that is, "pooling corporations" and "nonpooling corporations" as defined in § 902(c)(3)(B). Moreover, basket tracing was also reduced significantly from nine to two baskets (that is, the "general basket" earnings and associated foreign taxes, and the "passive basket" earnings and associated taxes). Consequently, the final regulations, while still daunting, have been considerably simplified in their application.

But IRS refused to drop the "hovering deficit" rules of the 2000 proposed regulations, for fear that dropping that limitation would facilitate trafficking in E&P deficits.[902.16] IRS also noted that the final regulations are also consistent with similar limitations under § 381 and the regulations thereunder.

[902.13] See   15.21[4].

[902.14] TD 9273 (Aug. 8, 2006) (effective Nov. 6, 2006), adopting final Regs. §§ 1.367(b)-3(e) and 1.367(b)-3(f) (without change) and §§ 1.367-7, 1.367(b)-9. Proposed Regs. § 1.367(b)-8 were "reserved;" so also were the rules for "PTI" carryovers (See supra   15.61[3], note 499 (for new proposed § 959 Regs.)).

[902.15] See supra   15.21[2] and 15.21[4].

[902.16] See Preamble, Summary of Comments and Changes Make, Part C, Hovering Deficits and Section 316, and Part D, Hovering Deficits and Section 902.

[3] Reincorporations and Divisions: Type D and Type F Reorganizations

[a] Nondivisive Type D (and Type F) Reorganizations

Page 15-251:

Add to note 905, first paragraph.

Prop. Regs. §§ 1.367(b)-3(e) and 1.367(b)-3(f) (Nov. 8, 2000) (foreign-generated losses, and earnings (or deficits) purged at the border; only carry over if ECI to US business or permanent establishment).

Page 15-252:

Add to note 907.

Prop. Regs. § 1.367(b)-9 (Nov. 8, 2000) (E&P or deficit carries over to survivor intact in foreign-to-foreign Type F; and hovering deficit limit not applicable here).

[b] Divisive Type D Reorganizations Generally

Page 15-252:

Add to note 908.

For allocation of E&P and foreign taxes, see Prop. Regs. §§ 1.367(b)-8(b), 1.367(b)-8(c), and 1.367(b)-9 (Nov. 8, 2000), infra ¶ 15.84[3][f].

Add new note 908.1 at end of next to last sentence of carryover paragraph.

   [908.1] See Prop. Regs. § 1.367(b)-8(d), infra ¶ 15.84[3][f].

Add new note 908.2 to last sentence of carryover paragraph.

   [908.2] See Prop. Regs. § 1.367(b)-8(e), infra ¶ 15.84[3][f].

Add to text at end of ¶ 15.84[3][b].

Proposed regulations, issued on November 8, 2000, provide for modified allocation rules under § 312(h) and Regulations § 1.312-10, reflecting different policies and concerns arising from the cross-border aspects of these transactions.[908.3]

   [908.3] Prop. Regs. § 1.367(b)-8, infra ¶ 15.84[3][f]. These proposals were not adopted in the August 2006 regulation package (they will be dealt with in a later project).

[c] Subsidiary Stock Distributions Under § 355 Generally

Page 15-253:

In first paragraph of ¶ 15.84[3][c], sentence ending with note 911, replace 1997 regulations with 1977 regulations.

[d] Revised Regulations Applicable to § 355 Distributions

Page 15-255:

Add to note 920.

See also Prop. Regs. §§ 1.367(b)-8(d)(6), Exs. 2 and 3, and 1.367(b)-8(e)(6), Exs. 1, 2, and 3.

Add to text at end of ¶ 15.84[3][d].

Proposed regulations issued on November 8, 2000, deal with allocations of earnings and profits in various divisive § 357(b) transactions.[922.1]

   [922.1] Prop. Regs. §§ 1.367(b)-8 and 1.367(b)-9 (effective on final promulgation), infra ¶ 15.84[3][f]. They are still in proposed form (they were not adopted by TD 9273 (Aug. 8, 2006); they will be dealt with in a later project.

[e] Section 1248(f)

Add to note 923.

But see Notice 87-64, 1987-2 CB 375 (stating that regulations would be issued under § 1248(f)(2) to prevent recognition of inbound spin-off of CFC stock if the distributee takes the distributing parent's carryover basis for the stock); for a comparable amnesty under the PFIC nonrecognition rules, see Prop. Regs. § 1.1291-6(c)(iv), infra 15.85[6][a], note 1026; Calianno & Gregoire, "Handling Restructures and Disposition of a CFC," 28 J. Corp. Tax'n 3, at 10 (Sept. 2001); Calianno, Gregoire & Cornett, 12 J. Int'l Tax'n 34 (Oct. 2001).

Add new paragraph ¶ 15.84[3][f].

[f] Allocation of Earnings and Profits and Foreign Taxes in Certain Divisive § 367(b) Transactions [New]

Extensive regulations dealing with E&P allocations under § 312(h) in the case of various divisive § 367(b) transactions were proposed on November 8, 2000.[923.1] The proposals build on the principles of Regulations § 1.312-10, but modify these rules in several significant ways to reflect the special policies and concerns raised by the cross-border nature of these transactions.[923.2]

Thus, Proposed Regulations § 1.367(b)-8 generally adopts the principles of the § 312(h) regulations, but modifies them as follows:

1. Allocation is made on the basis of net asset bases only;[923.3]
2. No addition is made to a stand-alone § 355 subsidiary's earnings account;[923.4]
3. There is no allocation of the parent's net deficit account to the subsidiary;[923.5]

[923.1] Prop. Regs. §§ 1.367(b)-8 and 1.367(b)-9 (effective on final promulgation); also Prop. Regs. § 1.367(b)-7 can apply in places here as well, supra 15.84[2][f]. The preamble is important for even a minimal grasp of these proposals. For comments see Davis, "Proposed E&P Regulations Under § 367(b)," 30 Tax Mgmt. Int'l J. 67 (Feb. 9, 2001); Gosain et al., "Guidance on Tax Attributes in Section 367(b) Exchanges Will Make Planning Easier," 94 J. Tax'n 242 (Apr. 2001); DuPuy & Bower, "Layers, Pools, Credits and Rules," 30 Tax Mgmt. Int'l J. 155 (Apr. 13, 2001); Bress, Anson & Dubert, "New Section 367(b) Regs. (Part 2)," 12 J. Int'l Tax'n 18 (July 2001); Connors & Voll, "Carryover of Corporate Tax Attributes in Corporate Reorganizations," 29 J. Corp. Tax'n 13 (Mar. 2002); Collins et al, "Allocation of E&P in a Spin-Off by a Consolidated Group," 28 J. Corp. Tax'n 11, at 16 (Nov. 2001).

[923.2] See preamble, pts. D of Overview and detailed description.

[923.3] Prop. Regs. § 1.367(b)-8(b)(1)(iv); the allocation method preferred in Regs. § 1.312-10(a) is relative values.

[923.4] Prop. Regs. § 1.367(b)-8(b)(1)(ii) (parent's earnings reduced without regard to § 1.312-10(b)(2), and § 1.312-10(b) does not increase subsidiary's earnings).

[923.5] Prop. Regs. § 1.367(b)-8(b)(1)(iii); for a comparable rule in the § 312(h) regulations, see § 1.312-10(c).

4. There is generally no reduction in the parent's § 884 branch profits earnings account;[923.6]
5. Allocations occur on a pro rata basis out of a cross section of the parent's earnings categories;[923.7] and
6. Allocations of the parent's foreign taxes likewise occur on a pro rata basis out of various separate categories (but *not* the § 904(c) carryover).[923.8]

The proposals go on to deal with various scenarios where the parent or its subsidiary is domestic or foreign (or both). Thus, Regulations § 1.367(b)-8(c) deals with a divisive transaction where the parent is domestic and its subsidiary is foreign (i.e., an outbound § 355 distribution);[923.9] while § 1.367(b)-8(d) deals with the converse case of a foreign parent and a domestic subsidiary (i.e., an inbound § 355 distribution).[923.10] Finally, Regulations § 1.367(b)-8(e) covers the all-foreign transaction (where both the parent and subsidiary are foreign corporations),[923.11] and Proposed Regulations § 1.367(b)-9 deals with cases where the foreign parent creates a new foreign subsidiary pursuant to an all-foreign Type D reorganization.[923.12]

Needless to say, these regulations are heavy going, like the companion proposals in § 1.367(b)-7 dealing with foreign-to-foreign asset acquisition reorganizations discussed previously.[923.13] Here, also the preamble is must reading, and the various examples, while daunting, can with effort (much effort), convey meaningful information.[923.14] Like the companion § 381 proposed regulations, these proposals will also need to be rethought in view of the 2004 Jobs Act § 904(d) basket reduction amendments. While the § 381 proposals were fi-

---

[923.6] Prop. Regs. § 1.367(b)-8(b)(1)(vi); see supra   15.04[2] and infra   15.85[5].

[923.7] Prop. Regs. § 1.367(b)-8(b)(2). The proposals rejected alternative allocation models here (e.g., an E&P tracing model, or the LIFO dividend distribution model).

[923.8] Prop. Regs. § 1.367(b)-8(b)(3).

[923.9] Prop. Regs. § 1.367(b)-8(c)(2) provides that E&P allocated from the U.S. parent retains its U.S. source; also, no foreign taxes of the parent are allocated here. The three examples in § 1.367(b)-8(c)(3) are useful.

[923.10] The inbound § 355 transaction rules of Regs. §§ 1.367(b)-3 and 1.367(b)-5 are closely related to this section of the proposals, as pointed out in the three examples in § 1.367(b)-8(d)(6).

[923.11] Prop. Regs. § 1.367(b)-8(e)(2) incorporates the foreign-to-foreign allocation rules of § 1.367(b)-7 in this situation, except that the hovering deficit rule does not apply here if the subsidiary is newly created, §§ 1.367(b)-8(e)(2)(ii) and 1.367(b)-9(b).

[923.12] The main function of this provision (which also applies to nondivisive Type D and Type Fs) is to prevent application of the hovering deficit limitation.

[923.13] Supra   15.84[2][f].

[923.14] For comments on these regulations, see Davis, Proposed E&P Regulations Under Section 367(b), 30 Tax Mgmt. Int'l J. No. 2, at 67 (Feb. 9, 2000).

nalized in August of 2006 (supra ¶ 15.84[2][f]), the proposed regulations of § 1.367(b)-8 were "reserved".[923.15]

[923.15] IRS stated in the preamble to the § 381 regulations that the § 355 regulations will be dealt with in a separate project to come.

[4] Regulations Under § 367(e)(1): Outbound § 355 Distributions

[a] General Rule

Page 15-256:

Add to note 928.

See also Prop. Regs. § 1.367(b)-8 (allocation of E&P in various foreign divisive transactions), supra ¶ 15.84[3][f].

[c] Final Regulations (1999): Per Se Gain or Nonrecognition

Page 15-259:

Add to note 945.

See also Prop. Regs. § 1.367(b)-8(c) (allocation of E&P in foreign divisive transactions). Allocate E&P only (not taxes) on outbound divisive transaction involving domestic parent and foreign subsidiary.

Page 15-260:

Add to note 946.

Cf. Prop. Regs. § 1.367(b)-8(c) (Nov. 8, 2000); but not applicable here because both parent and subsidiary are domestic; instead, general allocation rule of Regs. § 1.312-10 applies to this case.

¶ 15.85 FOREIGN INVESTMENT IN REAL PROPERTY TAX ACT AND BRANCH PROFITS TAX ASPECTS: RELATION OF §§ 897 AND 884 TO § 367

[1] In General

Page 15-262:

Change existing ¶ 15.85[1][c] to ¶ 15.85[1][d]. Add new ¶ 15.85[1][c] to precede relabeled ¶ 15.85[1][d].

[c] Revised § 897 Regulations: Notice 2006-46 [New]

As promised in the preamble to the recently revised cross-border merger regulations,[950.1] the IRS announced on May 23, 2006,[950.2] that it planned to revise the §§ 897(d) and 897(e) regulations to reflect the expanded scope of the Type A reorganization and also to revise other aspects of the current §§ 897(d) and 897(e) temporary regulations (and in the process, liberalize those provisions in several significant respects).[950.3] The notice also states that IRS will at last finalize the 1988 temporary regulations, which are definitely showing their age. These revisions will be noted at the appropriate places in   15.85[5] (they are largely good news rules as well).

[950.1] See   12.12[12].

[950.2] Notice 2006-46, 2006-24 IRB 1044 (June 12, 2006).

[950.3] The revised § 897 regulations dealing with cross-border mergers will be effective January 23, 2006 (the date of the revised merger regulations); the other portions of the §§ 897(d) and 897(e) regulations will be effective May 23, 2006 (although taxpayers can elect to apply the new rules to all open years if they do so consistently).

Also slated for revision is the look-back rule of Notice 89-95, 1989-2 CB 403 (which likewise is long overdue).

[2] Section 897 Distribution Rules

[c] Distributions of § 897 Property by a Foreign Corporation

Page 15-264:

Add to text at end of ¶ 15.85[2][c].

But Notice 2006-46 adds inbound Type A reorganizations to the type of transactions that can be effected in view of the regulatory change in 2006 allowing cross-border mergers.[966.1]

[966.1] Notice 2006-46, Parts 1 and 2; for the cross-border merger regulations, see   12.12[12].

[d] Foreign Subsidiary Liquidations

Page 15-265:

Add to note 967.

Notice 2006-46, Part 2, revises Notice 89-95 as it will be incorporated in final regulations to come.

[f] Inbound Reorganizations

Add to note 970.

But Notice 2006-46, Part 3(a), adds Type A reorganizations to the list of covered transactions.

[3] Section 897(e) Exchanges

[b] Examples Applying § 897(e)(1)

Page 15-268:

Add to note 981.

Note that this transaction also can now qualify as a Type A (including triangular variants as a result of 2006 changes in the merger regulations); see ¶ 12.12[12].

[c] Additional Nonrecognition Exceptions Under § 897(e)(2)

Page 15-268:

Add to text in fourth line after the word changes.

(basically these are "restructuring" transactions):

Add new note 982.1 to end of item 2.

982.1 Type A reorganizations can also be effected here as well; see Notice 2006-46, Part 3(a).

Add to note 983.

But Notice 2006-46, Part 3(c), modifies (and liberalizes) these transactions in three respects: (1) "all the stock of the transferee corporation" is replaced with "substantially all" thereof; (2) the same proportionate holding limit is dropped; and (3) the three-year period is reduced to one year.

Add to text after item 3.

4. Notice 2006-46, Part 3(b), adds two additional foreign-to-foreign exchange exceptions.983.1

983.1 In addition to allowing Type A foreign-to-foreign reorganizations (including triangular variants), Notice 2006-46, Part 3(b), allows an exception for cases when (1) the transferor would not be a USRPHC had it been a domestic corporation, or (2) prior to the exchange the transferor's stock is regularly traded on established market, and after the exchange the transferee corporation's stock is so traded (and where the transferor would have been a USRPHC within the five-year pre-exchange period, no foreign shareholder of the transferor owned more than 5 percent of the transferor).

Add to text at bottom of page 268 after colon:

(But Notice 2006-46, Part 3(d), drops all of these conditions as no longer necessary):

Page 15-269:

Add to text at end of ¶ 15.85[3][c].

But as a result of changes to the merger regulations in January of 2006 (allowing Type A treatment, including the triangular variants, for foreign corporation mergers), these transactions no longer need to be confined exclusively to Type C or Type D qualifications.[986.1]

[986.1] See Notice 2006-46, Part 3(a).

[d] Summary

Add to text at end.

However, in view of Notice 2006-46 and the ultimate final regulations previewed therein, life under the §§ 897(d) and 897(e) regulations will be more bearable, though far from a lovefest.

[4] Examples

Page 15-270:

Add to text at the end of first paragraph.

In the following examples, Type A mergers (including the triangular variants) are now possible as a result of the 2006 amendments to the § 368 regulations.[986.2]

[986.2] See   12.22[12] and Notice 2006-46, 2006-24 IRB [__] (June 12, 2006).

Page 15-271:

Add to note 991.

But Notice 2006-46, Part 3(d), will drop these conditions when regulations are finalized.

Page 15-273:

Add to note 1001, second paragraph.

See Notice 2006-46, Part 2, for revision of Notice 89-95 and preview of the final regulations to come under §§ 897(d) and 897(e).

Page 15-274:

Add to text at end of Example 5, item 2.

> A new problem for inbound § 332 liquidations arises if the FC sub-
> sidiary has net built-in loss assets: in such case, new § 334(b)(1)(B)[1003.1]
> steps down asset basis to fair market value in the hands of parent DC
> under the anti-loss import limitation.

[1003.1] See infra ¶ 15.85[7][e].

[5] Branch Profits Tax Aspects

[b] Branch Incorporations

Page 15-274:

Add to note 1007.

But see Prop. Regs. § 1.367(b)-8(b)(1)(vi) (Nov. 8, 2000) (no reduction of branch earnings on foreign divisive transaction); also Preamble, Details of Provisions, pt. D(2) (branch earnings stay with parent here, whether foreign or domestic).

[6] Dispositions of Passive Foreign Investment Company Stock: § 1291(f) Nonrecognition Rules

[b] Relation of Passive Foreign Investment Company Rules to Other Nonrecognition Override Regimes

Page 15-278:

Add text to end of ¶ 15.85[6][b].

The 1997 legislation effected a major reduction in the scope of the § 1.1291-6 regulations, which will need to be revisited to reflect this contraction. But pro-posed legislation (suggested by the Joint Committee Staff's February 2003 En-ron Report) would modify the overlap exception by denying its application in cases where the likelihood of § 951 income inclusion is "remote".[1031.1]

[1031.1] HR 1162, § 206, amending § 1297(e)(2) (effective Feb. 13, 2003, the date of the Staff's Enron Report). This same proposal had passed the Senate as part of its version of the 2003 tax bill, but did not survive in the final legislation.

[c] Examples From the Regulations

Page 15-279:

Add to note 1036.

Final Regs. § 1.367(b)-4(b)(1) (Jan. 21, 2000) is the same.

[7] Importation of Foreign-Generated Tax Attributes: "Fresh-Start" at the Border

[a] In General

Page 15-279:

Add to note 1038.

See also Daub, "Importing and Exporting Basis and Other Tax Attributes—Do We Need a New System?" 12 J. Int'l Tax'n (Nov. 2001).

Page 15-280:

Add to note 1039.

For these regulations, see Prop. Regs. §§ 1.367(b)-3(e) and 1.367(b)-3(f) (Nov. 8, 2000).

Add to note 1040.

The new treasury, however, has not pursued this proposal.

[d] Examples

Page 15-283:

Add to note 1053.

See Prop. Regs. §§ 1.367(b)-3(e) and 1.367(b)-3(f) (foreign-generated carryovers and earnings (or deficits) are purged at the border).

Page 15-283:

Add new ¶ 15.85[7][e].

[e] Limitation on Transfer or Importation of Built-In Losses [New]

Another Enron-related anti-abuse proposal suggested by the Joint Committee Staff's February 2003 Enron Report (and passed by the Senate in its version of the 2003 tax bill which, however, did not pass) adopts a different approach to loss import transactions; new § 362(e), a basis step-down regime for built-in loss assets acquired with a carryover basis from nontaxable transferors.[1054] This proposal passed on October 22, 2004.

This new legislation steps-down the § 362 carryover basis of built-in loss property to its fair market value "cap"[1055] in the following transactions:

[1054] S. 1162, § 201, adding §§ 362(e) and 334(b)(1)(B) (effective Feb. 13, 2003, the date of the Staff's Enron Report). The final 2004 Jobs Act, § 836, however is effective October 22, 2004, the date of enactment.

[1055] The limitation applies only to net built-in loss property (namely, the excess of aggregate basis over value).

1. Section 362(e)(1) (limitation on import of built-in losses), where the property is acquired by a taxable transferee from a nontaxable transferor;[1056]

2. Section 362(e)(2) (limitation on transfer of built-in losses in any § 351 transaction), where the net built-in loss property is acquired in a tax-free § 351 transaction;[1057] or

3. Section 334(b)(1)(B) (comparable treatment for inbound § 332 liquidations), where built-in loss property is acquired by a domestic parent in a § 332 liquidation of its foreign subsidiary.[1058]

[1056] This provision covers "loss import" transactions where the built-in loss property moves from nontaxable to taxable hands in a § 362 carryover basis transaction.

[1057] This provision also applies on an aggregate basis (where basis of all assets exceeds aggregate value of those assets). The basis reduction is allocated among assets in proportion to their respective built-in loss, § 362(e)(2)(B).

But this provision will not apply to transfers by a parent to its controlled subsidiary, § 362(e)(2)(C); instead stock received by the parent is stepped down to its fair market value, if the parties jointly so elect. See Coven, What Tax Shelters Can Teach Us About the Structure of Subchapter C, 105 Tax Notes 831 (Nov. 8, 2004).

Regulations under § 362(l)(2) were proposed in Regs. § 1.362-4 (Oct. 23, 2006).

[1058] This provision blocks the import of built-in losses by a U.S. parent from its foreign subsidiary. See HR 4520, Act § 836 (effective on date of enactment, Oct. 22, 2004).

See comments by Avent, "Corporate Provisions in the American Jobs Creation Act," 83 Taxes 103 (May, 2005); Eisenberg, "Limitations on Importation and Transfer of Built-In-Losses; Untangling the New Basis Adjustment Rules," 107 Tax Notes 869 (May 16, 2005); and NYSBA Tax Section Report, "The Importation and Duplication of Tax Losses," 110 Tax Notes 763 (Feb. 13, 2006).

Cumulative Table of IRC Sections

[Text references are to paragraphs; note references are to chapters (boldface numbers) and notes ("n."), and references to the supplement are preceded by "S."]

[Text references are to paragraphs; note references are to chapters (boldface numbers) and notes ("n."), and references to the supplement are preceded by "S."]

[Text references are to paragraphs; note references are to chapters (boldface numbers) and notes ("n."), and references to the supplement are preceded by "S."]

*[Text references are to paragraphs; note references are to chapters (boldface numbers)
and notes ("n."), and references to the supplement are preceded by "S."]*

IRC §

163(j)   4.02[8][b]; 4.04[3]; 4.04[8]; 4.24[3]; **4**
ns. 167, 172, 189, 331; 5.04[2];
10.42[7]; 14.44[7][h]; 13.23[8];
13.42[11]; 13.46[4]; **13** ns. 272, 329,
574, 840; **14** n.300; 15.04[1][a];
15.04[4]; S15.04[4]; S15.82[2][c]; **15** ns.
118, 212, 265, 280; **S15** ns. 784.8, 840.5
163(j)(2)(C) . . . . **4** n.170; 13.23[8]
163(j)(2)(C)(iii) . . . . 4.04[8]
163(j)(3) **4** n.182
163(j)(3)(B) **4** n.167
163(j)(5)(B) . . . . **4** ns. 171, 190
163(j)(6)(A) **4** n.169
163(j)(6)(A)(ii) . . . . 4.04[8]
163(j)(6)(B) . . . . 4.04[8]
163(j)(6)(D) . . . . 4.04[8]; **4** n.182
163(j)(7) . . . . 4.04[8]; 13.42[11]
163(j)(7)(B) . . . . 13.23[8]
163(k) . . . . **4** ns. 33, 79, 86, 89, 96, 122
163(*l*) . . . . . **4** ns. 33, 73, 86, 90, 98, 115, 119,
122, 123; **S4** ns. 90, 99
163(n) **5** n.575
164 . . . . 5.03[5]; 15.22
164(d) . . . . 10.07[1]; **10** n.214
164(e) . . . . 5.03[5]; **5** ns. 51, 53
165 . . . . 3.10[3]; 5.04[3]; 5.06[2][c]; **5** ns. 106,
111, 114, 115, 166, 255, 284, 287;
6.10[3][a]; **6** ns. 99, 239, 241, 291;
S10.03[3]; 12.65[3][a]; **12** n.574;
13.23[1]; 13.23[5][a]; 13.23[5][e];
S13.42[5][c]; **13** n.848; **S13** ns. 305,
481; **14** ns. 52, 406
165(a) . . . . . . 4.24[1]; 4.24[2]; 5.03[1]; **5** n.32;
12.01[1]; 13.44[3]; 13.46[1][a]; **13** n.803
165(c) . . . . 5.03[1]
165(c)(2) . . . . 4.23[3]; 4.24[1]; 4.24[2]; **4** n.241
165(e)(5) . . . . 13.46[2][b]; **15** n.212
165(f) . . . . 4.24[2]
165(g) . . . . 4.24[3]; 6.10[3][c]; 6.10[5][b]; **6** ns.
99, 310; 10.21[2]; **10** n.368; 12.30[4][a];
12.30[4][b]; 12.30[4][c]; **12** ns. 559, 575,
578, 581; 13.44[5]; 13.44[7]; 13.46[1][a];
13.46[2][b]; **13** ns. 668, 803; **14** n.406
165(g)(1) . . . 4.23[2]; 4.23[4]; 4.23[5]; 4.24[1];
4 n.232; **10** n.278
165(g)(2)(B) **4** n.232
165(g)(2)(C) . . . . 4.23[5]; **4** n.234
165(g)(3) . . . 4.23[5]; **4** n.250; **10** ns. 269, 270;
13.47[4][b]; 13.48[5][a]; **13** ns. 969, 971;
14 n.406
165(g)(3)(A) **4** n.250
165(j) **4** n.29
166 . . . . 3.10[3]; 4.23[4]; 4.24[2]; 6.10[3][a]; **6**
ns. 239, 241, 291; **13** n.281; 13.42[11]
166(a) . . . 4.23[4]; 4.23[5]; 4.24[1]; 5.03[1]; **10**
n.368
166(d) . . . . . 4.23[4]; 4.23[5]; 4.24[1]; 4.24[3];
5.03[1]; **6** n.99
166(d)(1) . . . . 4.24[1]; **4** n.238
166(d)(2) . . . . 4.23[4]
166(d)(2)(A) **4** n.239

IRC §

167 . . . . 5.03[1]; **5** n.127; 8.03[3]; 10.40[6]; **10**
n.456; 13.23[5][a]
167(a) . . . . 5.03[1]
167(f) **10** n.456
167(j) **4** n.233
168 . . . . 10.40[6]; 13.01[4][b]
168(e)(4)(D) **13** n.9
168(f)(5) . . . . 3.17[7]
168(f)(5)(A) . . . . 13.01[4][b]
168(f)(8) **13** n.529
168(g)(2) . . . . 8.03[5]
170 . . . . 5.03[1]; S6.06[4][a]; **S6** n.100;
S8.63[2][b]; **15** n.108; **S15** n.106
170(a)(1) . . . . 5.03[2]
170(a)(2) . . . . 5.03[2]; **S6** n.81
170(b)(1) . . . . **5** n.37; 6.06[3]
170(b)(2) . . . . **5** n.37; 7.09[1]; 8.03[6]
170(c)(2) **5** n.39
170(d)(1) . . . . 6.06[3]
170(d)(2) **5** n.38
170(e) . . . . S8.63[2][b]
170(e)(1)(A) . . . . 8.63[3][b]; **8** n.616
170(e)(3) **5** n.39
171 . . . . . . 4.42[1]; 4.61[2]; 4.61[5]; **4** ns. 390,
411, 419, 436; **12** ns. 426, 464
171(b)(1) **4** n.412
171(b)(1)(A) **12** n.464
171(b)(1)(B) **12** n.464
171(b)(3) . . . . 4.61[5]; **4** n.349
171(b)(4) . . . . **4** n.419; **12** ns. 426, 447
171(e) **4** n.410
172 . . . . . 1.06[4]; 4.25[4]; 5.05[7][b]; **5** n.46; **6**
n.122; 7.14[2]; 8.03[4]; 14.21[2];
14.22[2]; 14.23[1][a]; 14.42[2]; 14.42[3];
14.44[7][g]; 14.46[3]; 14.46[4]; **14** ns.
83, 133; 15.21[3]; **15** n.343
172(a) **5** n.46
172(b) **15** n.254
172(b)(1) . . . . 14.23[1][a]; **14** n.85
172(b)(1)(A) . . . . **10** n.97; 14.22[1]
172(b)(1)(E) . . . . 14.22[3]; 14.44[7][g]
172(b)(2) . . . . 14.23[1][a]; 14.23[1][b]; **14** n.85
172(c) . . . . 15.04[1][c]; **15** n.254
172(d)(2) **5** n.48
172(d)(3) **5** n.48
172(d)(4) . . . . **5** ns. 24, 48
172(d)(5) **5** n.49
172(f) **S13** n.370
172(h) . . . . . 4.26[3]; 14.22[3]; 14.44[7][g]; **13**
n.797; **14** n.82
172(h)(2) . . . . . **13** n.797; 14.22[3]; 14.44[7][g]
172(h)(3) . . . . 14.44[7][g]
172(h)(3)(B) . . . . 14.22[3]
172(h)(3)(B)(ii) **14** n.357
172(h)(3)(C) . . . . 14.22[3]
172(j) . . . . 7.03[6]; 7.04
173 . . . . 8.03[5]
174 . . . . . . **5** n.85; 8.04[1]; **10** n.202; 14.20[2]
175 . . . . 8.04[1]; **8** n.357; 14.20[2]
176 . . . . **5** n.85
179 . . . . 8.03[5]; **10** n.442; 13.02[3]

[Text references are to paragraphs; note references are to chapters (boldface numbers) and notes ("n."), and references to the supplement are preceded by "S."]

*[Text references are to paragraphs; note references are to chapters (boldface numbers)
and notes ("n."), and references to the supplement are preceded by "S."]*

[Text references are to paragraphs; note references are to chapters (boldface numbers) and notes ("n."), and references to the supplement are preceded by "S."]

[Text references are to paragraphs; note references are to chapters (boldface numbers) and notes ("n."), and references to the supplement are preceded by "S."]

[Text references are to paragraphs; note references are to chapters (boldface numbers) and notes ("n."), and references to the supplement are preceded by "S."]

[Text references are to paragraphs; note references are to chapters (boldface numbers) and notes ("n."), and references to the supplement are preceded by "S."]

IRC §

305(c) . . . . . . 4.44[2]; **4** ns. 128, 389; **5** n.193;
6.10[4]; 6.10[4][c]; 8.03[1]; 8 40[3];
8 41[7]; 8.11[2][c]; 8.41[2][e]; 8.41[3];
8.41[5]; 8.41[6]; 8.66; **8** ns. 428, 449,
457, 458, 462, 482, 521, 535;
12.27[2][c]; 12.27[2][d]; 12.27[3][b];
12.30[4][c]; **12** ns. 393, 395, 424, 458,
490, 549, 648, 794
305(c)(1) . . . . 8.41[2][c]; **8** n.459
305(c)(2) . . . . 8.41[2][c]; **8** n.463
305(c)(3) . . . . 4.01[4]; **8** ns. 453, 464
305(d) . . . 6.10[4][c]; 8.41[2][e]; **8** ns. 447, 485,
505, 545; **9** n.74
305(d)(1) . . . 8.41[3]; 8.41[6]; 8.42[1]; **8** n.553;
12 n.640
305(d)(2) . . . . 8.41[3]; 8.41[6]
305(e) . . . . . 4.44[2]; **5** n.565; 8.41[2][c]; **8** ns.
256, 276
306 . . . . . . 1.07[8]; S1.08[4]; **1** n.135; 3.05[4];
3.10[1]; **3** ns. 213, 395; 4.21; 4.22[2];
4.62[6]; **4** n.219; 5.01[5]; **5** n.16; 8.00;
S8.06[2][c]; S8.06[2][d]; 8.40[2];
8.41[1]; 8.41[2][b]; 8.41[2][e]; 8.42[4];
8.61; 8.62; 8.62[1]; 8.62[2]; 8.62[3];
8.62[4]; 8.62[5]; 8.62[5][a]; 8.62[5][b];
8.62[5][c]; 8.62[5][d]; 8.62[5][e]; 8.63;
8.63[1]; 8.63[2]; S8.63[2][b]; 8.63[3];
8.63[3][a]; 8.63[3][b]; 8.63[3][c]; 8.64;
8.64[1]; 8.64[2]; 8.64[3]; 8.64[4]; 8.65;
8.66; **8** ns. 69, 260, 446, 448, 489, 524,
561, 565, 571, 573, 579, 581, 584, 595,
598, 599, 601, 602, 616, 628, 632, 633,
637, 648; **S8** ns. 254.3, 254.14, 254.15,
254.24, 564.2; 9.08[2][b]; **9** ns. 9, 105,
140, 313, 325; 10.44; 11.02[3]; 11.06[1];
11.07[1]; 11.10[2]; 11.13; 11.13[1];
11.13[2]; 11.13[3]; 11.13[4]; **11** ns. 356,
360, 361, 364; **S11** ns. 355.1, 355.3;
12.01[4]; 12.27[2][b]; 12.27[3][a];
12.41[5]; 12.44[2][c]; 12.45; 12.45[1];
S12.45[1]; 12.45[2]; 12.45[3]; 12.45[4];
12.63[4][d]; 12.64[1][a]; **12** ns. 179, 205,
468, 774, 782, 796–799, 801–803, 807,
808; **S12** n.782.5; 13.43[3][b]
306(a) . . . . 8.63; 8.63[3]; 8.63[3][c]; 8.64;
8.64[1]; 8.64[2]; 8.64[3]; 8.64[4]; 8.66;
11.13[3]
306(a)(1) . . . . 8.63[2]; 8.63[3]; 8.63[3][a];
8.63[3][b]; **S8** n.564.1
306(a)(1)(A)(ii) . . . . 8.63[2]; **8** n.607
306(a)(1)(C) . . . . 8.63[2]
306(a)(1)(D) . . . . . . S8.63; S8.63[2][b]; **S8** ns.
254.14, 254.15, 254.24, 264.2;
S12.44[2][b]; **S12** ns. 765.2, 782.5
306(a)(2) . . . . S8.61; 8.63[1]; **S8** n.564.1;
9.08[2][b]; 12.45[2]
306(b) 8.64; 8.65

IRC §

306(b)(1)(A) . . . . . , , ,   8 64[1], 8.65, 11.13[3]
306(b)(1)(A)(ii) 8 n.621
306(b)(1)(A)(iii) 8 n.621
306(b)(1)(B) . . . . 8.64[1]; 8.65; **9** n.105
306(b)(1)(C) 8.65
306(b)(2) 8 n.626
306(b)(3) . . . . 8.63[3][c]; 8.64[3]
306(b)(4) . . . . . . 8.64[4]; **8** ns. 629, 632, 639;
11.13[3]; 12.45[3]; **12** ns. 802, 803
306(b)(4)(A) **12** n.774
306(b)(4)(B) 8 n.637
306(c) 8.62; **9** n.313
306(c)(1)(A) . . . . 8.62[1]; **8** n.565; 12.27[2][b];
12 n.807
306(c)(1)(B) . . . . **3** n.395; 8.62[2]; 8.62[4];
8.63[3][c]; 11.06[1]; 11.13[2]; 11.13[4];
12.27[2][b]; 12.45[4]
306(c)(1)(B)(ii) . . . . 12.44[2][c]
306(c)(1)(C) . . . **3** n.395; 8.62[4]; 8.63[3][c]; **8**
n.615
306(c)(2) . . . . . 8.61; 8.62[5][a]; 8.66; **8** n.586;
11.13[2]; **11** ns. 357, 359, 364; **12** n.808
306(c)(3) . . . . . **3** n.395; 8.03[1]; 8.62[3]; **8** ns.
578, 579; **12** ns. 205, 802
306(c)(4) **8** n.578; **11** n.358; **12** n.799
306(d) . . . . 8.62[5][b]
306(e) . . . . 8.62[5][e]; **8** n.599
306(e)(1) .8 n.573
306(e)(2) . . . . **12** ns. 386, 388
306(f) . . . . 15.02[1][b]
306(g) . . . . 8.62[5][c]
306(h) 8 n.561
307 . . . . 8.42[1]
307(a) . . . . 8.41[4]; 8.42[1]; 8.63[2]
307(b) . . . . 8.42[1]
311 . . . . . 3.09[4]; **3** ns. 118, 199; **4** ns. 8, 293;
6.11; 8.21[1]; 8.41[5]; **8** ns. 115, 316,
319, 328, 329, 338, 384; **S8** n.384.1;
9.01[3][b]; 9.23[1]; 9.23[2][b];
9.23[2][b]; **9** n.204; S10.03[3]; 10.05[3];
10.05[6]; 11.10[1]; 11.11[1][a];
11.11[1][c]; **11** ns. 13, 269, 270, 381;
12.42[2][b]; 12.42[5]; **12** ns. 861, 899,
996; 13.42[3][a]; 13.42[4][a];
13.43[3][b]; 13.43[3][d]; **13** ns. 387, 447,
971; **15** n.567
311(a) . . . . . 5.03[8]; 8.21[1]; 8.21[2]; 8.21[3];
8.23[2]; **8** ns. 14, 328, 330, 342, 348,
357, 360; 9.07[3][b]; 9.23[1]; **9** ns. 392,
431; 10.22[1]; **10** ns. 25, 125, 201;
11.11[1][a]; **12** ns. 699, 986; 13.43[3][b];
13 n.659; 15.63[2][a]; **15** ns. 563, 965
311(a)(1) .8 n.528
311(a)(2) . . . 4.26[1]; 8.20[2]; 8.20[3]; 8.20[4];
8.21[1]; 8.21[2]; 8.22[2]; **8** n.528; **10**
n.681; 11.15[5]; 13.42[4][c]

[Text references are to paragraphs; note references are to chapters (boldface numbers) and notes ("n."), and references to the supplement are preceded by "S."]

IRC §

311(b) . . . . . 5.08[5]; 6.08[2]; 6.10[3][b]; **6** ns. 161, 259; 8.20[4]; 8.21[1]; 8.21[3]; 8.22[1]; 8.22[2]; **8** ns. 348, 351, 357, 360, 385, 528, 553; **S8** n.384.1; 9.07[1][a]; 9.23[1]; 9.23[2][a]; 9.23[2][b]; 9.24[2]; **9** ns. 460, 473; 10.05[6]; 10.62[6]; **10** n.173; 11.11[3][a]; 11.11[4]; **11** ns. 76, 77, 311, 326; 12.41[5]; 12.42[2][a]; 12.42[2][b]; 12.43[1][d]; 12.44[1][f]; 12.62[2]; 12.66[4][c]; **12** ns. 402, 886, 947; 13.43[3][b]; 13.48[2][b]; **13** ns. 447, 448, 612, 984; 15.81[3][e]; **15** ns. 558, 948

311(b)(1) . . . . . 6.06[7]; 8.21[3]; 8.23[2]; **8** ns. 346, 528; 9.06[5]; 9.23[2][a]; 9.23[2][b]; 10.60; **10** ns. 516, 754; 11.11[1][a]; 11.11[1][b]; 11.11[2][a]; 11.11[2][b]; 11.11[3][b]; 11.15[5]; 12.30[4][b]; 12.30[5][f]; 12.62[3][b]; 12.63[7][c]; **12** ns. 573, 898, 89913.23[3][b]; 13.42[4][c]; **13** ns. 262, 263, 436, 444, 453; **15** ns. 332, 558, 948, 965

311(b)(2) . . . **3** n.119; 8.21[3]; 8.22[2]; **8** n.355
311(b)(3) . . . . 8.21[3]
311(c) **3** n.139; **10** n.100
311(d) **9** n.457
311(d)(2)(A) **12** n.986
312 . . . . . 8.22[2]; 8.41[5]; **8** n.600; 9.24[4]; **14** n.89; 15.21[2][c]; **15** n.331

312(a) . . . . . 8.02[5]; 8.03[6]; 8.22[2]; **8** ns. 60, 78, 115, 124, 148, 149; 9.24[3][a]; 9.24[3][b]; **10** n.112; **11** n.349

312(a)(2) . . . . 8.23[4]; **8** n.389
312(a)(3) . . . . 8.22[2]; **8** n.379; **9** n.479
312(b) . . . . 8.22[2]; 8.23[4]; **8** ns. 78, 115, 148, 149, 378, 383, 388; **S8** n.384.1; 9.24[2]; 9.24[3][b]; **15** 332

312(b)(1) . . . . 8.22[2]; **10** n.111; **11** n.349
312(b)(2) 8 n.379; **9** n.474
312(c) . . . . 8.22[2]
312(c)(1) **10** n.111
312(d) . . . . . 7.05; 8.22[2]; **S8** n.384.1; **8** n.128
312(d)(1) **11** n.349
312(d)(1)(B) **8** n.525
312(d)(2) **8** n.417
312(f)(1) . . . 5.08[6]; 8.03[3]; 8.03[6]; 8.04[1]; 8.22[2]; **8** ns. 88, 89, 103, 383, 385; 13.44[4]

312(f)(1)(A) **8** n.103
312(f)(1)(B) . . . . **8** ns. 38, 103
312(f)(2) . . . . **8** ns. 126, 526
312(f)(2)(A) **8** n.51
312(g) **8** n.38
312(h) . . . 11.12[4]; **S11** n.347; 12.63[7][b]; **12** ns. 570, 580; **13** n.679; 14.24; **14** ns. 44, 87, 111S15.84[3][b]; S15.84[3][f]; **S15** n.923.5

312(i) **8** n.131
312(k) . . . . . . 8.03[5]; 8.22[2]; **8** ns. 102, 383; 13.42[8][a]; **13** n.529
312(*l*) . . . . . 8.03[3]; **13** ns. 529, 549, 658, 801

IRC §

312(*l*)(2) **8** n.91
312(m) **4** n.29; **8** n.124
312(n) . . . . **5** n.353; 8.03[5]; 8.04[1]; **13** n.529
312(n)(4) **8** n.141
312(n)(5) . . . . 8.03[5]; **8** ns. 137, 143
312(n)(7)   9.24[3][b]; 9.24[4]; **9** ns. 325, 476, 478, 479; **10** ns. 112, 380; **12** n.781; **14** n.89

312(o) **8** n.401
316 . . . . 2.01[2]; 4.03[8][a]; 5.05[6]; **6** ns. 167, 168; 7.09[2][a]; 7.12[1]; 8.01; 8.02[1]; **S8.06**[1][a]; S8.06[1][b]; **S11** n.268.2; 12.44[2][b]; **12** ns. 476, 768; **S12** ns. 781.1, 782.2, 798.2; 15.02[1][b]; 15.21[2][c]; 15.62[5][b]; 15.83[1][a]; **15** n.881

316(a) . . . . . **7** n.244; 8.02[1]; 8.02[2]; 8.22[1]; 8.63[2]; **8** ns. 4, 149; 12.44[2][b]
316(a)(1) . . . . 8.02[3]; 8.02[4]
316(a)(2) . . . **7** n.244; 8.02[2]; 8.02[3]; 8.02[6]; 8.03[6]; 8.63[2]; **8** ns. 44, 369, 586
316(b)(2) **8** n.134
316(b)(2)(B) **7** n.249; **10** n.5
317 . . . . **8** ns. 216, 553
317(a) . . . . **3** n.23; 8.20[1]; 8.21[3]; 8.41[1]; **8** ns. 3, 13, 309, 346, 389, 407, 475, 528, 553; 9.01[3][b]; 9.09[3]; 9.09[6][b]; **9** ns. 20, 348; 12.63[4][d]

317(b) . . . . **5** n.129; 9.01[3][b]; 9.01[3][c]; 9.07[1][b]; 9.08[2][a]; **10** n.236
318 . . . . . . **1** n.45; 2.07[6]; **2** n.175; 3.05[4]; **5** n.220; S8.06[2][c]; 8.62[3]; 9.02; 9.02[1]; 9.02[6]; 9.02[7]; 9.03[1]; 9.04[1]; 9.04[2][a]; 9.05[2]; 9.06[1]; 9.07[1][a]; 9.09[2]; 9.09[2][a]; 9.09[2][b]; **9** ns. 38, 45, 149, 188, 315, 359, 370, 381, 396, 429; **10** ns. 318, 533; 11.11[3][b]; **11** n.358; 12.63[4][b]; 12.64[2][c]; 12.64[3]; **12** ns. 153, 323, 339, 366, 751, 771, 799, 859, 1087, 1104; **S12** n.358.4; 13.01[4][b]; 13.20[3][a]; 13.43[3][b]; **13** ns. 299, 618, 921, 925; S13.44[3]; 14.41[3][b]; 14.43[2][d]; 14.44[7][a]; **14** n.129; **15** ns. 139, 494, 981

318(a) . . . . . . 8.64[1]; **8** ns. 578, 621; 9.02[1]; 9.09[2][a]; **9** ns. 37, 39; **12** n.478; **13** n.299

318(a)(1) . . . . . 9.02[2]; 9.04[2][b]; 14.43[2][d]
318(a)(1)(A)(ii) . . . . 9.04[2][b]
318(a)(2) . . . . . . 9.02[3]; **9** n.61; S14.43[3][c]
318(a)(2)(A) **9** n.54
318(a)(2)(B) **9** n.56
318(a)(2)(B)(ii) **9** n.58
318(a)(2)(C) . . . . . . **1** n.45; **9** ns. 59, 339, 344
318(a)(3) . . . . 9.02[4]; 9.04[2][b]
318(a)(3)(A) . . . . **9** ns. 61, 62
318(a)(3)(B)(i) . . . . 9.04[2][b]; **9** n.63
318(a)(3)(B)(ii) **9** n.64
318(a)(3)(C) . . . . **1** n.45; 9.09[2][a]; 9.09[5]; **9** ns. 65, 339, 344

[Text references are to paragraphs; note references are to chapters (boldface numbers) and notes ("n."), and references to the supplement are preceded by "S."]

IRC §

318(a)(4) . . . . . . 9.02[1]; 9.02[5]; **9** ns. 69, 77
318(a)(5) **9** n.41
318(a)(5)(A) **9** n.40
318(a)(5)(B) **9** n.48
318(a)(5)(C) . . . . 9.02[1]; 9.02[7]; **9** ns. 60, 61, 66, 76
318(a)(5)(D) **9** n.75
318(b) **9** n.37; **13** n.299
318(b)(2)(C) **9** n.87
331–334(a) **6** n.182
331–338 . . . . 6.10[1][a]
331 . . . . . **4** n.229; 6.10[3][c]; 6.11; **6** n.262; **7** n.201; **8** n.9; 9.07[1][a]; 10.01; 10.02; 10.03[1]; 10.21[3][c]; 10.21[4]; 10.22[1]; **10** ns. 15, 21, 25, 28, 249, 299, 348; 12.01[4]; 12.22[9]; 12.63[5][b]; 12.64[1][b]; 12.64[3]; **12** ns. 105, 530, 665, 751, 1065, 1188; **13** ns. 441, 968; 15.02[1][a]; 15.85[2][a]
331(a) . . . . . . 10.01; 10.02; 10.03[1]; 10.03[2]; 10.03[4]; 10.04; 10.05[1]; 10.20; 10.21[3][b]; 10.24; **10** ns. 5, 19
331(a)(1) . . . . 11.15[3]
331(b) . . . . **5** n.188; 10.01; **10** ns. 5, 19
332–334(b) **12** n.988
332–334(b)(1) **14** n.110
332–337 . . . . 10.23[4]
332–338 . . . . 12.63[2][a]

IRC §

332 . . . . . 2.05[2]; **S2** n.55; 3.05[4]; 3.07[4]; **3** n.168; 5.06[1][a]; **5** ns. 251, 311, 412, 446; 6.01[2][e]; 6.07[4]; 6.09[2]; S6.09[3][a]; **6** ns. 172, 181, 182, 215; **S6** ns. 48, 139; 8.22[2]; **8** ns. 9, 133, 287, 388; 9.07[2][b]; S9.07[3][b]; **9** n.200; **S9** n.296; 10.02; 10.05[7]; 10.20; 10.21[1]; S10.21[1]; 10.21[2]; S10.21[2]; 10.21[3]; S10.21[3]; 10.21[3][a]; 10.21[3][b]; 10.21[3][c]; 10.21[4]; 10.21[5][a]; 10.22[1]; 10.22[2]; 10.22[3]; S10.22[4]; 10.23[1]; 10.23[3]; 10.23[4]; 10.24; 10.41[1]; 10.41[2]; 10.41[3]; 10.41[4]; 10.41[5][f]; 10.42[3]; 10.42[5]; S12.63[1]; 10.42[6][a]; 10.43[1]; 10.66; **10** ns. 13, 19, 147, 248, 250, 253, 254, 257, 262–265, 273, 277, 281, 287, 293, 298, 299, 305, 307, 308, 311, 321, 338, 342, 353, 375, 530, 577, 587, 599, 601; **S10** ns. 267, 325, 332, 365.3; 11.05[2][a]; **11** n.378; 12.22[4]; 12.22[9]; 12.24[3][e]; 12.26[8]; 12.30[2][a]; 12.42[5]; S12.63[1]; 12.63[2][a]; 12.63[2][b]; 12.63[4][c]; 12.63[5][a]; 12.63[5][b]; 12.63[7][a]; 12.64[3]; S12.65[5]; **12** ns. 130, 202, 365, 652, 704, 706, 785, 844, 851, 859, 917, 919, 920, 922, 923, 926, 932, 934, 984, 989, 990, 999, 1000; **S12** ns. 52.1, 537.1, 985, 993, 1011; 13.42[3][d]; 13.42[4][c]; 13.42[5][a]; 13.42[4][b]; 13.42[8][b]; 13.42[8][c]; 13.43[3][d]; 13.44[7]; 13.45[4][a]; 13.45[4][b]; 13.45[5]; 13.46[1][a]; 13.48[2][d]; 13.48[5][a]; S13.48[5][a]; 13.48[5][b]; 13.48[6]; S13.48[6]; **13** ns. 93, 439–441, 450, 556, 557, 618, 622, 703, 722, 972, 984, 988, 995; 14.03[2]; 14.20[1]; 14.21[1]; 14.21[2]; S14.21[2]; 14.23[1][b]; 14.41[1]; 14.41[3][d]; 14.41[3][e]; 14.44[7][b]; 14.44[8]; 14.45[4]; **14** ns. 13, 21, 50, 98, 208, 255, 267, 340, 385; **S14** ns. 52.2, 55.1, 89.1, 172.6; 15.04[2][b]; 15.22; 15.80[2][a]; 15.80[4][d]; 15.80[7][a]; S15.80[7][e]; 15.81[1][a]; 15.81[2]; 15.81[3][f]; 15.83[1][b]; S15.83[1][b]; 15.83[2][a]; 15.83[3]; 15.83[4][a]; S15.83[4][b]; 15.84[1][a]; 15.84[2][b]; 15.84[3][a]; 15.84[3][c]; S15.84[4]; 15.85[1][c]; 15.85[2][b]; 15.85[2][c]; 15.85[2][d]; 15.85[5][a]; 15.85[5][c]; 15.85[6][c]; 15.85[4]; 15.85[7][d]; S15.85[7][e]; **15** ns. 226, 227, 253, 563, 610, 615, 638, 655, 715, 755, 799, 808, 881, 905, 1005, 1010, 1029; **S15** ns. 34, 227.1, 513.1, 556.5, 573, 603, 820
332(b) . . . . **10** ns. 310, 381; **12** n.130
332(b)(1) . . . . **3** n.163; 10.21[3][a]; **10** ns. 286, 291, 301
332(b)(2) . . . 10.21[2]; 10.21[3][b]; 10.21[3][c]

[Text references are to paragraphs; note references are to chapters (boldface numbers) and notes ("n."), and references to the supplement are preceded by "S."]

IRC §

332(b)(3) . . . . 10.21[3][c]; **10** ns. 277, 309
332(c) . . . . **10** n.314; 12.65[3][b]; **13** n.989
332(h) . . . . 13.45[6][b]
333 . . . . **3** n.373; 10.01; 10.02; 10.05[5][a];
　　　　　　　　　10.05[5][b]; **10** ns. 151, 308
334 . . . . **10** n.202; 12.63[2][a]; **12** n.530;
　　　　　　　　　　　　　　　　　　　13.42[4][b]
334(a) . . . 6.10[3][b]; 6.10[3][c]; 6.11; **9** n.439;
　　　　　　10.03[2]; 10.04; 10.05[7]; 10.60; **10** ns.
　　　　　　46, 73, 106, 201, 263, 329, 348;
　　　　　　12.64[3]; **13** n.968; **15** n.965
334(b) . . . **6** n.215; 10.20; 10.21[2]; 10.21[5][a];
　　　　　　10.22[1]; 10.22[3]; **10** ns. 248, 316;
　　　　　　12.42[5]; 12.63[2][a]; 12.64[3]; **12** n.984;
　　　　　　13.48[5][a]; 13.48[6]; **13** ns. 450, 722;
　　　　　　15.81[3][d]; 15.83[1][a]
334(b)(1) . . . . 10.20; 10.21[1]; 10.23[2];
　　　　　　10.41[1]; 10.41[4]; 10.42[5]; **10** ns. 325,
　　　　　　326, 343; 12.63[2][a]; 12.63[4][c];
　　　　　　12.63[6][e]; **12** ns. 785, 987, 990;
　　　　　　13.42[8][b]; 13.42[8][c]; **13** n.439;
　　　　　　14.21[2]; **14** ns. 21, 50; **15** ns. 795,
　　　　　　　　　　　　　　　　　　　1033, 1053
334(b)(1)(B) . . . S10.21[5][a]; **S14** ns. 415, 418;
　　　　　　S15.84[4]; S15.85[7][e]; **S15** ns. 647.1,
　　　　　　647.3, 795.2, 820, 1064
334(b)(2) . . . . 10.41[2]; 10.41[3]; 10.42[2];
　　　　　　10.42[7]; **10** ns. 198, 200, 293, 470, 471,
　　　　　　624; 12.63[2][a]; **12** ns. 729, 919, 923,
　　　　　　944, 1188; 13.45[4][a]; **13** ns. 394, 398
　　　　　　　　　　　　　　　　450; **14** ns. 21, 50, 51
334(b)(4) **10** n.613
335(f) . . . . **13** ns. 977, 990
336–337 . . . . **15** n.965
336–338 . . . . **10** n.381; 12.42[2][b]
336 . . . 5.04[2]; 6.07[4]; 6.09[2]; 6.09[5]; 6.11;
　　　　6 ns. 183, 259; 8.20[2]; 8.20[4]; 8.22[2];
　　　　8 n.315; 10.04; 10.05[1]; 10.05[2][a];
　　　　10.05[2][c]; 10.05[5][a]; 10.05[5][b];
　　　　10.05[6]; 10.05[7]; 10.07[2]; 10.07[3];
　　　　10.08; 10.22[1]; 10.22[3]; 10.24; 10.60;
　　　　10 n.65; 11.11[1][a]; 11.11[1][c]; **11**
　　　　n.13; 12.22[9]; 12.42[5]; 12.62[2];
　　　　12.62[3][b]; 12.63[2][c]; 12.63[5][a];
　　　　12.64[1][a]; 12.64[2][c]; **12** ns. 362, 363,
　　　　665, 668, 689, 861, 905, 983, 984, 988,
　　　　1090, 1098, 1099; 13.42[3][a];
　　　　13.42[4][c]; 13.45[4][b]; **13** n.968;
　　　　15.85[2][c]; 15.85[5][d]; **15** ns. 557, 655,
　　　　　　　　　　　　　　　　799, 956
336(a) . . . 6.10[3][b]; **8** n.336; 10.01; 10.05[1];
　　　　10.05[2][a]; 10.05[3]; 10.05[4];
　　　　10.05[5][a]; 10.05[6]; 10.05[7]; 10.06[1];
　　　　10.06[2]; 10.06[3]; 10.06[4]; 10.07[1];
　　　　10.07[2]; 10.07[3]; 10.08; 10.60;
　　　　10.62[1]; 10.62[6]; **10** ns. 83, 202, 211,
　　　　214, 329, 754; 11.11[2][a]; 11.15[5];
　　　　12.30[4][b]; 12.63[5][b]; **12** ns. 573, 984;
　　　　15.85[4]; **15** ns. 948, 965

336(b) . . . **3** n.119; 6.10[3][c]; 8.21[3]; **8** n.354;
　　　　10.05[2][a]; 10.05[7]; **10** ns. 62, 100
336(c) . . . . 10.05[4]; 10.05[7]; **12** ns. 668, 699
336(d) . . . 5.04[2]; 6.07[4]; 6.09[5]; 6.10[3][b];
　　　　10.05[3][b]; **10** n.35; 11.15[5]; **12** n.573
336(d)(1) . . . 10.05[3][a]; 10.05[3][b]; 10.05[7]
336(d)(1)(B) **10** n.128
336(d)(2) . . . . 6.07[1]; 10.05[2][c]; 10.05[3][b];
　　　　10.05[7]; **10** ns. 129, 131; **13** n.472
　　　　　　　　　　　　　　n.575; **15** n.986
336(d)(2)(B) **10** n.130
336(d)(2)(C) **10** n.134
336(d)(3) . . . . . 10.22[1]; **10** ns. 329, 346, 347,
　　　　379; 12.63[5][b]; **12** ns. 984, 990
336(e) . . . . 10.42[6][a]; **10** ns. 363, 364
337 . . . . . . 3.05[4]; 6.07[4]; 6.09[2]; **6** ns. 172,
　　　　182, 215; **S6** n.139; 8.21[3]; 10.01;
　　　　10.05[1]; 10.05[5][a]; 10.05[5][b];
　　　　10.05[7]; 10.06[4]; 10.20; 10.21[2];
　　　　10.21[3][a]; 10.22; 10.22[1]; 10.22[2];
　　　　10.22[3]; 10.23[4]; 10.41[3]; 10.41[4];
　　　　10.42[5]; 10.43[1]; **10** ns. 39, 131, 146,
　　　　147, 199, 219, 233, 235, 249, 265, 304,
　　　　308, 313, 316, 320, 474, 609, 722, 737;
　　　　S10 ns. 63.1, 365.3; **11** n.136; 12.22[9];
　　　　12.26[8]; 12.42[5]; 12.63[2][a];
　　　　12.63[2][c]; 12.63[5][a]; 12.63[5][b];
　　　　12.64[1][a]; 12.64[2][c]; 12.64[3]; **12** ns.
　　　　221, 530, 665, 668, 828, 859, 919, 923,
　　　　984, 988, 1039, 1073, 1090, 1094, 1098,
　　　　1103, 1104, 1188; 14.44[7][b];
　　　　13.42[4][c]; 13.42[5][a]; 13.42[5][b];
　　　　13.45[4][b]; 13.45[4][c]; 13.48[2][d];
　　　　13.48[5][a]; 13.48[6]; **13** ns. 440, 444;
　　　　15.63[2][a]; 15.80[7][a]; 15.81[1][a];
　　　　15.83[2][b]; 15.85[2][c]; **15** ns. 557, 606,
　　　　　　　　610, 655, 799, 1033
337(a) . . . . 10.20; 10.22[1]; 10.22[3]; **10** ns. 329,
　　　　344; 12.63[5][b]; **12** n.990; S13.48[5][a];
　　　　15.83[2][a]; 15.83[2][b]; 15.85[4]
337(b)(1) . . . . . 10.23[2]; **10** ns. 326, 340, 344
337(b)(2) . . . . **10** ns. 118, 119, 343
337(b)(2)(B)(ii) **10** n.343
337(b)(3) **10** n.325
337(c) . . . 10.22[1]; 10.22[3]; S10.22[4]; **10** ns.
　　　　164, 287, 342; **S10** n.325; 12.62[5]; **12**
　　　　n.919; 13.42[5][b]; S13.48[5][a];
　　　　13.48[6]; S13.48[6]; **13** n.469; **S13**
　　　　n.971.5; S14.21[2]; **S14** n.52.2
337(d) . . . . 9.23[2][a]; 9.23[2][c]; 10.05[6]; **10**
　　　　n.161; 11.02[3]; **11** n.270; 13.42[5][c];
　　　　S13.42[5][c]; **13** n.640
337(d)(1) . . . . 10.05[2][c]; 10.05[6]; **10** n.114;
　　　　　　　　　12.29; **12** n.532
337(d)(2) **10** n.162

[Text references are to paragraphs; note references are to chapters (boldface numbers) and notes ("n."), and references to the supplement are preceded by "S."]

IRC §

338 . . . . . **S2** n.56; 3.05[4]; 3.07[4]; **3** ns. 154, 168; 5.08[5]; 5.10[5][b]; **5** n.430; 6.01[2][e]; 6.09[2]; 6.09[3][a]; 6.09[3][b]; 6.09[5]; 6.11; **6** ns. 48, 71, 72, 172, 181, 182, 215; **S6** n.48; 8.07[2][b]; 9.09[4][d]; **9** n.235; 10.05[7]; 10.20; 10.21[5][b]; 10.22[3]; 10.40[1]; 10.40[3]; 10.41[3]; S10.41[3]; 10.41[4]; S10.41[4]; 10.41[5]; 10.41[5][a]; S10.41[5][a]; 10.41[5][b]; 10.41[5][c]; 10.41[5][e]; 10.41[6]; 10.42; 10.42[1][a]; 10.42[1][b]; 10.42[1][c]; 10.42[2]; 10.42[3]; 10.42[4]; 10.42[4][a]; 10.42[4][b]; 10.42[4][e]; 10.42[5]; S10.42[5]; 10.42[6][a]; 10.42[7]; 10.43; S10.43; 10.43[1]; 10.43[2]; 10.43[2][c]; 10.43[3]; **10** ns. 61, 291, 364, 383, 386, 400, 413, 430, 436, 440, 472, 507–509, 513, 524, 530, 533, 536, 537, 543, 546, 555, 556, 572, 606, 633, 724; **S10** ns. 291, 574; 11.11[3][b]; 12.42[2][b]; 12.63[2][a]; 12.63[6][e]; 12.64[1][b]; **12** ns. 49, 61, 64, 121, 123, 369, 890, 918, 920, 922, 923, 926, 939, 944, 964, 1000, 1039; **S12** ns. 926, 934, 935.1, 981.2; 13.01[4][a]; 13.42[5][a]; 13.42[5][d]; 13.42[6][b]; 13.42[11]; 13.45[2]; 13.45[4][a]; 13.45[5]; 13.46[1][c]; **13** ns. 309, 398, 439, 450, 491, 501, 502, 722, 746, 815, 816;14.03[2]; 14.20[1]; 14.22[3]; 14.41[3][e]; 14.42[3]; 14.43[2][c]; 14.43[8]; 14.44[3][c]; S14.44[3][c]; S14.44[4][a]; S14.44[4][c]; 14.44[5]; 14.44[7][b]; 14.45[4]; 14.47[6][b]; **14** ns. 5, 21, 29, 38, 50, 113, 267, 301, 366; **S14** ns. 295.3, 301, 306.3, 306.5; 15.65[1]; 15.65[2]; 15.65[3]; 15.65[4]; 15.85[7][a]; 15.85[7][d]; **15** ns. 573, 582, 583, 590, 597, 953, 1042, 1047; **S15** n.573

338(a) . . . . 6.09[3][b]; **6** n.189; 10.42[4]; 10.42[6][a]; 10.43[1]; **10** ns. 507, 579; 15.65[2]; **15** n.581

338(a)(1) **10** n.519

338(b) . . . . 10.43[1]; 10.43[2]

338(b)(1) . . . . **10** ns. 510, 519

338(b)(1)(B) . . . . **10** ns. 542, 618

338(b)(2) . . . 10.43[2][c]; **10** ns. 519, 621, 628

338(b)(3) **10** n.619

338(b)(3)(A) **15** n.584

338(b)(4)(A) **10** n.614

338(b)(5) . . . . 10.40[1]; 10.40[3]; 10.43[3]

338(b)(6)(A) **10** n.612

338(b)(6)(B) . . . . **10** ns. 541, 618

338(c)(1) . . . 13.42[6][b]; 13.46[1][c]; **13** n.501

338(d)(3) . . . . . **3** n.163; 10.41[3]; 10.42[2]; **10** n.530; **12** n.652

338(e) . . . . 13.42[5][d]

338(e)(1) . . . . . 10.42[4]; 10.42[4][a]; **10** n.550

338(f) . . . . . . 10.42[4]; 10.42[4][b]; **10** n.557; 13.42[5][d]; 15.65[3]; **15** n.582

IRC §

338(g) . . . 10.42[3]; 10.42[6][a]; **10** n.582; **S12** ns. 936.1, 939.2; **13** n.644

338(g)(3) **10** n.544

338(h)(1) **10** n.532

338(h)(3) . . . . . 12.63[4][c]; 12.63[6][e]; **12** ns. 358, 369

338(h)(3)(A) . . . . **10** n.531; **11** n.289; 12.63[6][e]; 12.64[3]

338(h)(3)(A)(iii) . . . . 9.09[4][d]; **10** n.532

338(h)(3)(B) **10** n.539

338(h)(3)(C) . . . . **10** n.532; 12.64[3]

338(h)(4) **10** n.548

338(h)(4)(B) **14** n.343

338(h)(5) . . . . **10** ns. 534, 535

338(h)(8) . . . . **10** ns. 534, 536; 13.01[4][a]; **13** n.466

338(h)(9) . . . . **10** ns. 508, 513, 575

338(h)(10) . . . . 6.09[3][b]; 6.09[5]; **6** ns. 72, 212, 215; **8** n.287; 9.07[2][b]; 10.41[5][a]; 10.41[5][c]; 10.41[5][f]; S10.41[5][f]; 10.42[3]; 10.42[6]; 10.42[6][a]; 10.42[6][b]; 10.43[1]; 10.43[2][b]; 10.43[2][c]; **10** ns. 265, 364, 546, 557, 577, 578, 586, 587, 589, 599, 626; **S10** ns. 273, 291, 470, 574; **11** n.378; S12.25[5]; S12.63[2][a]; **12** n.859; **S12** ns. 302.1, 921, 922, 925, 926, 935.3, 936.1, 939; 13.43[3][d]; 13.44[7]; **13** ns. 474, 493, 556, 623; **S13** n.623; 14.45[4]; **14** ns. 70, 357; 15.65[3]

338(h)(11) . . . . 10.42[1][b]

338(h)(14) **10** n.724

338(h)(15) **10** n.539

338(h)(16) . . . . 15.65[3]; **15** n.601

341 . . . . 4.21; 6.11; **7** n.201; 10.00; 10.60; 10.61; 10.62[1]; 10.62[2]; 10.62[3]; 10.62[4][a]; 10.62[4][b]; 10.62[5]; 10.62[6]; 10.62[8]; 10.63; 10.64; 10.64[1]; 10.64[2]; 10.65; 10.66; **10** ns. 26, 679, 682, 686, 687, 690, 692, 696, 706, 707, 724, 734–736, 747, 758; **S10** n.679; 11.11[3][d]; **14** n.5; 15.02[1][a]; **15** n.156

341(a) . . . . 10.61; 10.64[3]; 10.66; **10** ns. 690, 737, 758

341(a)(1) 10.65

341(a)(2) **10** n.689

341(b) . . . . 10.62[1]; 10.62[3]; 10.62[4][b]; 10.62[5]; 10.64[2]; **10** ns. 704, 721

341(b)(1) . . . . 10.62[1]; 10.62[8]; **10** n.706; **13** n.766

341(b)(1)(A) . . . . . 10.62[1]; 10.62[6]; **10** n.723

341(b)(2) . . . . 10.62[8]

341(b)(2)(A) . . . . 10.62[3]

341(b)(3) . . . . 10.63; **10** ns. 706–709, 735

341(b)(3)(A) . . . . 10.62[4][b]

341(b)(3)(B) . . . . 10.62[4][b]

341(b)(3)(D) 10.65

341(b)(4) 10.66

341(c) 10.63; **10** n.735

341(c)(2) 10.63

[Text references are to paragraphs; note references are to chapters (boldface numbers) and notes ("n."), and references to the supplement are preceded by "S."]

*[Text references are to paragraphs; note references are to chapters (boldface numbers)
and notes ("n."), and references to the supplement are preceded by "S."]*

IRC §

351 .... 1.04; 2.02[3][a]; 2.02[3][b]; 2.04[4]; **2**
ns. 21, 186; **S2** n.56; 3.01; 3.02[1];
3.02[2]; 3.02[3]; 3.03[1]; 3.03[2]; 3.04;
3.05[2]; 3.05[3]; 3.05[4]; 3.06[1];
S3.06[2]; 3.06[3]; 3.06[4][a]; 3.06[4][b];
3.06[4][c]; 3.06[5]; 3.06[6]; 3.06[7];
S3.06[7]; 3.07[1]; 3.07[3]; 3.08[1];
3.08[2]; 3.09; 3.09[1]; 3.09[2]; 3.09[3];
3.09[4]; 3.09[5]; S3.09[5]; 3.09[6];
3.10[1]; 3.10[2]; 3.10[3]; 3.10[4];
3.11[1]; 3.11[2]; 3.11[3]; 3.11[4];
3.11[5]; 3.11[6]; S3.11[8]; 3.12[4];
3.12[5]; 3.13[3]; 3.13[4][a]; 3.14;
3.14[1]; 3.14[2]; 3.14[3]; 3.14[4]; 3.15;
S3.15; 3.15[1]; 3.15[2]; 3.16; 3.17[1];
3.17[2]; 3.17[3]; 3.17[4]; 3.17[5];
3.17[6]; 3.17[7]; 3.18; 3.18[1]; 3.18[2];
3.19; 3.20; 3.21; **3** ns. 3, 6, 12,
14, 16, 18, 23, 26, 27, 47, 49–51, 53,
54, 57, 58, 61, 63, 68, 70, 73, 83, 91,
97, 109, 115, 116, 118, 125, 134, 136,
162, 178, 188, 190, 198, 199, 208, 210,
211, 223, 228, 232, 250, 275, 295, 303,
310, 316, 326, 328, 329, 336, 339, 340,
344, 349, 352, 356, 364, 365, 368, 370–
373, 377, 378, 384, 390, 391, 394–396;
S3 ns. 249.5, 309, 367, 368, 378, 401;
4.02[2]; 4.03[2][a]; 4.03[2][b];
4.03[2][k]; 4.03[7]; 4.22[2]; 4.25[6];
4.25[9]; 4.61[1]; **4** ns. 26, 33, 34, 114,
219, 270, 403, 409, 453; 5.06[4]; **5** ns.
193, 412; S6.06[3]; S6.09[3][a];
6.10[4][c]; **6** ns. 13, 43, 292; **S6** n.48; **7**
n.247; **S7** n.74; 8.03[3]; 8.05[8]; 8.23[5];
8.41[2][f]; 8.62[3]; 8.62[4]; 8.62[5][a];
8.62[5][e]; 8.63[3][c]; 8.64[3]; **8** ns. 85,
133, 223, 259, 340, 573, 577, 579, 581,
585, 587; 9.06[6]; 9.09[4][d]; 9.09[6][a];
9.09[6][b]; 9.09[6][d]; S9.09[6][f]; **9** ns.
44, 373, 379, 385, 389, 393, 414, 451,
452; **S9** n.373; 10.05[1]; 10.05[3][a];
10.05[3][b]; 10.05[6]; 10.08; 10.20;
10.21[1]; 10.21[2]; 10.22[1]; 10.23[1];
10.23[4]; 10.42[2]; 10.42[5]; 10.61;
10.62[8]; 10.66; **10** ns. 138, 244, 253,
255, 284, 531, 533, 553; 11.05[2][a];
11.05[2][c]; 11.11[1][b]; 11.11[2][b];
S11.12[1]; 11.15[2]; 11.15[3]; 11.15[4];
11 ns. 258, 273, 284, 289, 368, 369; **S11**
n.301; 12.01[4]; 12.21[1]; 12.23[4];
12.23[12]; 12.24[5]; 12.25[3][b];
12.25[4]; 12.26[1]; S12.26[5]; 12.26[7];
12.26[8]; 12.27[3][a]; 12.28[2];
12.30[2][a]; 12.30[2][e]; 12.30[4][b];
12.41[2]; 12.41[5]; 12.42[1][b];
12.43[4][b]; 12.62[3][c]; 12.63[3][a];
S12.63[4][g]; 12.63[6][e]; 12.64[3];
12.65[3][b]; S12.65[5]; 12.66[2][a]; **12**
ns. 4, 9, 54, 80, 153, 179, 202, 205, 207,
258, 275, 304, 329, 347, 351, 361, 362,
366, 408, 414, 531, 569, 572, 607, 610,

IRC §

659, 683, 736, 788, 790, 802, 843, 874,
876, 877, 898, 899, 905, 954, 979, 1014,
1019, 1065, 1108, 1111, 1112, 1142;
S12 ns. 51, 52.1, 142, 352.1, 501, 537.1,
664.2, 683.1, 699.4, 790.2; 13.23[3][b];
13 n.256; 13.43[2][b]; 13.43[2][c];
13.44[7]; 13.45[3][e]; 13.48[2][a];
S13.48[2][a]; 13.48[2][b]; 13.48[3];
13.48[5][b]; 13.48[6]; **13** ns. 150, 170,
229, 325, 525, 597, 734, 889, 918, 920,
926, 928, 932, 933, 951, 980, 981, 985,
986; 14.20[3]; 14.21[3][b]; 14.21[3][d];
14.23[3][b]; 14.41[3][d]; 14.43[7][b];
S14.47[6][c]; **14** ns. 54, 60, 93, 110; **S14**
n.417; 15.04[2][b]; 15.80[2][a];
15.80[2][c]; 15.80[4][d]; 15.80[7][a];
15.80[7][b]; S15.80[7][e]; 15.81[1][a];
15.81[1][b]; 15.82[1]; 15.81[3][d];
15.82[2][a]; 15.82[3]; 15.83[2][a];
15.84[1][a]; 15.84[1][c]; 15.84[1][e];
15.84[2][a]; 15.84[3][a]; 15.84[3][b];
15.85[1][c]; 15.85[3][b]; 15.85[3][c];
15.85[4]; 15.85[5][a]; 15.85[5][b];
S15.85[7][e]; **15** ns. 266, 443, 566, 615,
627, 640, 687, 757, 785, 827, 951, 1007,
1010, 1045

351(a) . . . . . . 3.01; 3.02[2]; 3.03[1]; 3.03[2];
3.05[1]; 3.05[3]; 3.06[2]; 3.09; 3.10[1];
3.10[4]; 3.14[2]; 3.14[3]; 3.15[2]; 3.16;
3.17[1]; 3.19; **3** ns. 54, 72, 173, 190,
210, 235, 391; **4** n.272; 10.05[6];
11.11[1][d]; **11** n.254; **12** ns. 659, 669

351(b) . . . . . 3.05[1]; 3.05[3]; 3.05[4]; 3.06[2];
3.06[3]; 3.10[1]; 3.14[2]; 3.14[3]; 3.16; **3**
ns. 84–86, 99, 235, 250, 316; 9.09[6][a];
9.09[6][b]; **11** n.279; **12** n.159

351(b)(1) . . . . 3.05[2]; 3.10[1]

351(b)(2) . . . . . 3.05[1]; 3.05[2]; **3** ns. 84, 211;
11.05[2][a]

351(c) . . . . 3.09[4]; S3.11[8]; **3** n.198;
11.11[3][c]; **11** ns. 45, 323, 368, 369;
12.62[3][d]; 12.62[4]; **12** ns. 572, 874–
877, 879, 893, 896, 898–900, 902, 905

351(c)(2) . . . . 3.09[4]; **3** n.202

351(d) . . . . 3.02[1]; 3.02[2]

351(d)(1) . . . . 3.02[2]

351(d)(2) . . . 3.02[3]; 3.02[4]; **4** n.284; **6** n.292;
12.30[5][a]; **12** n.414

351(d)(3) . . . . 3.02[4]; **6** n.292; 12.30[5][a]

351(e) **3** n.329

351(e)(1) . . . . 3.15[1]; **3** ns. 329, 330, 332; **12**
n.531

351(e)(2) . . . . 3.15[2]; **3** n.54; 6.10[4][c];
12.30[2][a]; **12** ns. 569, 572

351(f) . . . . . 3.12[5]; **3** ns. 88, 275; **4** n.125; **8**
n.348; **10** n.138

351(g)   **3** ns. 88, 91, 316, 318; **4** ns. 33, 219;
5 n.171; **9** n.391; S11.13[1]; **12** n.87

351(g)(1) . . . . 9.09[6][a]

351(g)(1)(B) **3** n.91

351(g)(2) . . . . **11** n.261; **12** ns. 396, 760

[Text references are to paragraphs; note references are to chapters (boldface numbers) and notes ("n."), and references to the supplement are preceded by "S."]

IRC §

351(g)(3) **3** n.177; **12** n.396
351(g)(3)(A) . . . . S3.05[4]; **S3** n.91.1
351(g)(4) . . . . 3.05[4]; **3** n.177; **8** n.405;
    9.09[6][a]; 9.09[6][b]; **9** n.393; **12** ns.
    647, 652; **S12** n.760
351(g)(5) **3** n.148
351(h) . . . . **3** ns. 49, 57, 60
354–368 . . . . 12.01[1]
354 . . . . . . 1.04; 3.19; **3** ns. 64, 73; 4.03[2][k];
    4.03[7]; 4.61[1]; **4** ns. 114, 391, 409,
    454; 6.10[4]; 6.10[4][c]; 6.11; 8.03[3];
    8.23[5]; 8.64[3]; **8** n.10; 10.24; 10.61; **10**
    n.284; 11.02[1]; 11.14; **11** ns. 334, 366;
    12.02[1]; 12.02[2]; 12.21[2][a]; 12.21[6];
    12.21[10]; 12.22[1]; 12.23[1]; 12.24[5];
    12.25[2][g]; 12.25[3][b]; 12.26[1];
    12.26[3]; 12.26[4]; 12.26[5]; 12.27[2][a];
    12.27[3][a]; 12.27[3][b]; 12.27[5][c];
    12.27[5][e]; 12.30[2][a]; 12.30[2][b];
    12.30[2][e]; 12.30[4][a]; 12.30[4][c];
    12.40[1]; 12.40[2]; 12.41[1]; 12.41[3];
    12.41[4]; 12.42[5]; 12.44; 12.44[1][a];
    12.44[1][b]; 12.44[1][c]; 12.44[1][d];
    12.44[1][f]; 12.44[3][a]; 12.44[3][b];
    12.44[3][c]; 12.45[1]; 12.46; 12.63[2][a];
    12.63[2][b]; 12.63[4][b]; **12** ns. 174, 188,
    235, 247, 258, 279, 321, 378, 419, 472,
    480, 481, 496, 607, 622, 630, 640, 659,
    672, 710, 744, 746, 751, 798, 989, 1002,
    1026, 1125, 1135; **S12** ns. 745, 747;
    13.42[4][b]; 13.43[3][c]; 13.48[2][b];
    13.48[2][d]; 13.48[4][a]; **13** ns. 446, 952;
    15.80[2][a]; 15.80[2][c]; 15.80[7][a];
    15.80[7][d]; 15.81[1][a]; 15.81[3][d];
    15.84[2][e]; **15** ns. 709, 729, 842, 906,
    907, 976, 985; **S15** n.741.7

IRC §

354(a) . . . 6.10[4][c]; 11.14; **11** n.366; 12.21[6];
    12.25[3][b]; 12.30[2][e]; 12.42[5];
    12.44[1][a]; S12.44[1][a]; 12.44[1][b];
    12.44[5]; 12.63[4][c]; **12** ns. 173, 635,
    641, 710, 745, 794, 1152
354(a)(1) . . . . 6.10[4][c]; 12.28[1]; 12.30[4][c];
    12.42[5]; 12.44[1][a]; 12.44[1][b]; **12** ns.
    173, 174, 301, 453, 744, 745, 753, 1152,
    1181; **S12** n.699.3
354(a)(1)(A) **12** n.944
354(a)(2) . . . . **6** n.39; 12.21[4]; 12.21[6];
    12.30[2][b]; 12.41[4]; 12.44[1][a]; **12** ns.
    90, 474
354(a)(2)(A) . . . . 12.27[4][b]; 12.27[5][a];
    12.27[5][b]; 12.41[4]; 12.44[1][a]; **12** ns.
    496, 636
354(a)(2)(B) . . . . 12.27[3][a]; 12.30[4][a];
    12.44[1][a]; **12** ns. 444, 756, 783
354(a)(2)(C) **4** n.125; **12** n.87
354(a)(2)(C)(ii) **S12** n.398
354(a)(3) . . . . 12.44[1][b]
354(a)(3)(C) **12** n.783
354(a)(3)(C)(ii) **12** n.398
354(b) . . . . **10** n.135; **11** ns. 35, 365; 12.26[2];
    12.26[3]; 12.26[4]; 12.26[5]; 12.26[8];
    12.30[2][a]; 12.63[4][b]; 12.64[2][c]; **12**
    ns. 323, 340, 342, 343, 353, 744, 1080,
    1094
354(b)(1) . . . . 11.14; 12.26[8]; 12.30[2][b]; **12**
    ns. 1048, 1079; 13.48[2][b]; **14** n.53;
    15.84[3][b]
354(b)(1)(A) . . . 12.24[2][b]; 12.64[2][c]; **12** ns.
    356, 362, 944, 1080, 1094; 14.20[1]
354(b)(1)(B) . . . . 12.63[4][b]; **12** n.1080;
    14.20[1]

*[Text references are to paragraphs; note references are to chapters (boldface numbers)
and notes ("n."), and references to the supplement are preceded by "S."]*

IRC §

355 . . . S1.08[4]; 3.09[4]; 3.19; **3** n.198; **S3** ns.
246, 256; 4.03[2][k]; 4.03[3]; 4.03[7]; **4**
ns. 105, 127, 454; **5** ns. 254, 291;
6.09[4]; 6.10[4][c]; 6.11; **6** ns. 124, 129,
172, 204, 206; 7.06; **7** n.146; 8.22[2];
8.23[5]; **8** ns. 10, 449, 502, 539; 9.06[5];
9.07[3][b]; **9** ns. 205, 293–295;
10.05[4]; 10.05[6]; 10.05[7]; 10.22[4];
10.40[2]; 10.44; 10.61; **10** ns. 135, 138,
173, 238, 284, 362; 11.01[1][e];
11.01[1][f]; S11.01[1][f]; 11.01[2][a];
11.02[1]; 11.02[2]; 11.02[2][a]; 11.02[3];
11.02[4]; 11.02[5]; 11.03[1]; 11.03[2];
11.03[3]; 11.04[1]; 11.04[2]; 11.05[1];
11.05[3]; 11.05[4]; 11.06[1]; 11.06[2];
11.06[3]; S11.06[7]; 11.07[1]; 11.07[3];
11.08[1]; 11.08[2]; 11.09[1]; 11.09[2][a];
S11.09[2][a]; 11.09[2][b]; 11.09[2][d];
S11.09[2][d]; 11.09[3]; 11.09[4]; 11.10;
11.10[1]; 11.10[2]; 11.11[1][a];
11.11[1][b]; 11.11[1][c]; 11.11[1][d];
11.11[2][a]; 11.11[2][b]; 11.11[2][c];
11.11[3][a]; 11.11[3][b]; 11.11[3][c];
11.11[3][d]; S11.11[5]; 11.12[1];
11.12[2]; 11.12[4]; 11.13[1]; 11.13[2];
11.13[3]; 11.13[4]; 11.14; 11.15[1];
11.15[2]; 11.15[3]; 11.15[4]; 11.15[5];
11.16; **11** ns. 18, 20, 35, 40, 42, 44, 53,
65, 74, 77, 83, 89, 106, 137, 139, 142,
146, 171, 183, 197, 201, 214, 224, 234,
246–249, 253, 255, 260, 262, 263, 267,
269–271, 281, 311, 314, 326, 327, 328,
333, 343, 351, 360, 365, 366; **S11** ns.
20, 74, 179, 216.1, 272; 12.01[4];
12.02[1]; 12.20; 12.22[5]; 12.22[11];
S12.22[11]; 12.23[1]; 12.24[2][a];
12.24[5]; 12.26[1]; 12.26[2]; 12.26[3];
12.26[4]; 12.26[5]; 12.26[7]; 12.26[8];
12.27[5][e]; 12.30[2][a]; 12.30[2][b];
12.30[2][e]; 12.30[4][b]; 12.30[4][c];
12.41[3]; 12.42[5]; S12.42[5];
12.44[1][c]; 12.44[1][f]; 12.46;
12.61[2][c]; 12.62[1]; 12.62[3][a];
12.62[3][b]; 12.62[3][c]; 12.62[3][d];
12.62[4]; 12.62[5]; 12.63[1]; 12.63[7];
12.63[7][a]; 12.63[7][b]; 12.63[7][c];
12.63[7][d]; 12.66[4][c]; **12** ns. 108, 247,
258, 324, 329, 342, 355, 361, 511, 567,
720, 744, 818, 844, 845, 855, 866, 872–
874, 877, 883, 896, 898, 899, 902–905,
1079, 1094, 1171, 1174, 1177–1179;
S12 ns. 745, 747, 773, 872.1;
13.42[4][b]; 13.42[8][c]; 13.43[3][c];
13.43[3][d]; 13.44[3]; 13.44[7]; 13.47[5];
13.48[2][d]; 13.48[6]; **13** ns. 446, 447,
546, 556, 558, 560, 567, 617, 671, 706,
925, 940, 961, 964, 990, 991; 14.20[3];
14 ns. 54, 58, 87; 15.80[2][a];
15.80[2][c]; 15.80[6]; 15.80[7][a];

IRC §

15.80[7][d]; 15.81[1][a]; 15.81[3][d];
15.81[3][e]; 15.81[3][f]; 15.84[3][b];
15.84[3][c]; S15.84[3][c]; 15.84[3][d];
S15.84[3][d]; 15.84[3][e]; S15.84[3][f];
S15.84[4]; 15.84[4][a]; 15.84[4][b];
15.84[4][c]; 15.85[2][e]; 15.85[4]; **15** ns.
558, 638, 715, 912, 914, 916, 918, 919,
923, 933, 1026; **S15** ns. 558, 923.10
355(a) . . . . . . 11.11[1][a]; **11** n.260; 12.62[4];
12.63[7][b]; 12.63[7][c]; 12.63[7][d]; **12**
ns. 887, 896, 898, 905; 13.48[6]; **15**
n.925
355(a)(1) . . . 6.09[4]; 11.02[3]; 11.10[1]; **11** ns.
38, 253; 12.30[4][c]
355(a)(1)(A) . . . . **8** n.4; 11.07[2]; **11** n.251
355(a)(1)(A)(ii) . . . . . S11.11[1][b]; **11** ns. 278,
281; 12.30[4][c]
355(a)(1)(B) . . . 8.03[1]; S8.06[2][d]; 11.04[4];
11.05[4]; 11.06[1]; 11.06[2]; 11.06[4];
11.07[1]; 11.09[3]; 11.13[4]; **11** ns. 105,
197; 12.62[3][b]; **12** n.867; **14** n.5
355(a)(1)(D) . . . 11.07[1]; 11.07[2]; 11.11[1][d];
11 ns. 197, 207; 12.62[4]
355(a)(1)(D)(i) . . . . 11.07[2]
355(a)(1)(D)(ii) . . . . . 11.07[3]; **11** ns. 43, 203
355(a)(2)(A) . . . . 11.08[1]; 11.09[3]
355(a)(3) . . . . . . 11.06[1]; 11.07[1]; **11** n.258;
12.30[2][b]
355(a)(3)(A) **11** n.253
355(a)(3)(A)(i) **11** n.252
355(a)(3)(A)(ii) **11** n.253
355(a)(3)(B) . . . . 11.02[4]; **11** n.256
355(a)(3)(C) **11** n.259
355(a)(3)(D) **4** n.125; **11** n.260; **12** n.87
355(a)(4)(A) . . . . **11** ns. 250, 253
355(a)(4)(B) **11** n.259
355(b) . . . . . . **S8** n.254.15; 9.07[3][b]; **9** n.300;
11.02[2][b]; 11.04[2]; 11.04[4]; 11.05[1];
11 ns. 93, 106; 12.62[3][b]; 12.63[7][b];
12 n.1094; 14.44[3][b]; **14** n.5
355(b)(1) . . . . . . **10** n.362; 11.04[1]; **12** n.579
355(b)(1)(A) . . . **11** ns. 52, 55, 82; 12.62[3][b];
12.62[4]; **12** n.362
355(b)(1)(B) . . . . **11** ns. 53–55; **12** n.579
355(b)(2) . . . . **9** n.296; 11.04[1]; 11.05[2]
355(b)(2)(A) **11** n.55
355(b)(2)(B) . . . 11.02[4]; 11.05[1]; 11.05[2][c];
11.05[3]
355(b)(2)(C) . . . 11.02[4]; 11.05[2]; 11.05[2][a];
S11.05[2][a]; 11.05[2][b]; 11.05[2][c]; **11**
ns. 133, 135, 146; **S11** ns. 133, 136.1
355(b)(2)(D) . . . **S9** n.300.1; **10** n.164; 11.02[4];
11.05[2]; 11.05[2][b]; S11.05[2][b];
11.05[2][c]; **11** ns. 137, 335; 12.62[5];
13.45[4][c]; **13** n.469
355(b)(2)(D)(i) . . . . **11** ns. 137, 138
355(b)(2)(D)(ii) . . . . 11.05[2][b]; **11** n.44
355(b)(3) **S11** n.131.1
355(b)(3)(C) **S11** n.131

[Text references are to paragraphs; note references are to chapters (boldface numbers) and notes ("n."), and references to the supplement are preceded by "S."]

[Text references are to paragraphs; note references are to chapters (boldface numbers) and notes ("n."), and references to the supplement are preceded by "S."]

IRC §

356(e) . . . . . **4** ns. 33, 125; 11.10[2]; **11** n.316; 12.44[2][c]; **12** n.87
356(e)(2) . . . . **12** ns. 398, 760
356(f) **8** n.628; **12** n.744
357 . . . . . 3.06[2]; 3.06[4][f]; 3.11[7]; **3** ns. 94, 97, 99, 105, 222; **S3** ns. 145, 158, 223; 5.10[5][d]; **10** n.40; **11** n.274; 12.02[2]; 12.40[1]; 12.42; 12.42[3]; 12.43[1][b]; 12.65[2][a]; **12** ns. 189, 683, 685, 1111, 1112, 1131; **S12** n.664.1; **14** n.104; S15.84[3][d]
357(a) . . . . 3.06[1]; 3.06[2]; 3.06[3]; 3.06[4][a]; 3.06[5]; 3.06[7]; 3.10[3]; 3.11[1]; **3** ns. 97, 99, 102; 9.09[6][a]; 12.42[3]; 12.63[5][d]; 12.65[1]; 12.65[2][d]; 12.65[3][b]; **12** ns. 278, 1125, 1134, 1135; **15** n.648
357(a)(1) . . . . 3.06[4][d]
357(a)(2) **3** n.144; **12** n.228
357(b) . . . . 3.06[1]; 3.06[3]; 3.06[4][a]; 3.06[5]; 3.06[6]; 3.06[7]; 3.10[3]; 3.11[1]; 3.13[4][a]; **3** ns. 102, 110, 112, 113, 121, 148, 223, 235; 5.10[5][d]; **5** n.446; **9** n.388; 12.24[3][c]; 12.42[3]; 12.65[1]; **12** ns. 682, 683, 685, 1108, 1128
357(b)(1) . . . . 3.06[3]
357(b)(2) . . . . **3** ns. 107, 108; **S8** n.374
357(c) . . . . 3.06[4]; 3.06[4][a]; 3.06[4][b]; 3.06[4][c]; 3.06[4][d]; 3.06[4][e]; 3.06[5]; 3.06[6]; 3.06[7]; 3.10[3]; 3.11[1]; 3.11[2]; 3.13[4][a]; 3.19; **3** ns. 84, 115–117, 119–121, 123, 125–128, 135, 137, 138, 235; **S3** n.123; 5.06[4]; 5.10[5][d]; **10** n.100; 11.11[1][b]; S11.11[1][b]; **11** ns. 133, 258; **S11** ns. 274.1, 280.1; 12.25[2][h]; 12.26[1]; 12.26[5]; S12.26[5]; 12.30[2][b]; 12.30[4][a]; S12.42[1][b]; 12.42[3]; S12.42[3]; 12.43[4][b]; 12.63[7][b]; **12** ns. 350, 352, 511, 683–685, 694, 738, 1108, 1112; **S12** ns. 683.1, 685; 13.44[5]; 13.46[2][b]; 13.48[2][a]; 13.48[6]; **13** ns. 691, 831, 919, 937; **14** n.386
357(c)(1)   3.06[4][a]; 3.06[4][c]; 3.06[4][d]; **3** ns. 130, 399; **S3** n.123; 12.30[2][a]; 12.30[2][b]; 12.30[4][a]; 12.30[4][b]; **12** n.541; **S12** n.328
357(c)(1)(B) . . . . . **S11** ns. 274.1, 274.3, 280.1; S12.42[1][b]; S12.42[3]; S12.42[5]; **12** n.132; **S12** ns. 328, 664.2, 669.1, 685, 699.2
357(c)(2)(A) . . . . 3.06[4][a]
357(c)(2)(B) . . . . 12.30[2][e]; 12.30[4][a]; 12.30[4][b]; **12** ns. 538, 541, 580
357(c)(3) . . . . 3.06[4][c]; 3.06[7]; 3.10[3]; 3.11[3]; **3** ns. 130, 131, 134, 135, 153, 222, 236, 399; **12** ns. 683, 1111, 1112; S13.44[5]

357(c)(3)(A) . . . . . 3.06[4][c]; 3.06[7]; **12** n.328
357(c)(3)(A)(i) **3** n.130
357(d) . . . . . 3.06[4][f]; S3.06[4][f]; S3.11[7]; **3** ns. 105, 144; **S3** n.145; **S8** n.374
357(d)(1) . . . . 3.06[4][f]
357(d)(2) . . . . 3.06[4][f]
357(d)(3) **S8** n.374
358 . . . 3.01; 3.06[2]; 3.10[1]; 3.10[4]; S3.11[8]; 3.13[4][a]; **3** ns. 208, 222, 229; **S3** n.223; 4.25[9]; 5.06[2][d]; **10** ns. 137, 553; 11.12[1]; S11.12[1]; **11** ns. 335, 343; 12.02[2]; 12.25[3][c]; 12.40[1]; 12.42; 12.42[1][a]; 12.42[4]; 12.42[5]; 12.43[3]; 12.44; 12.44[1][d]; 12.44[3]; 12.44[3][a]; 12.44[3][c]; S12.44[3][c]; 12.64[3]; 12.65[2][a]; **12** ns. 358, 690, 729, 730, 785, 791; 13.48[2][a]; 13.48[4][a]; 13.48[6]; **13** ns. 920, 956, 987; **S13** n.987; 15.80[2][c]; 15.84[4][b]; 15.85[2][f]; **15** ns. 925, 1026
358(a) . . . . S3.11[4]; **4** n.368; 12.40[1]; 12.44[3][a]; **12** n.999
358(a)(1) . . . . . . 3.10[1]; 3.10[3]; 12.30[4][c]; 12.42[5]
358(a)(1)(A)(ii) . . . . 3.10[3]
358(a)(1)(A)(iii) **3** n.211
358(a)(1)(B)(i) . . . . 3.10[1]; **3** n.336
358(a)(1)(B)(ii) . . . . . 3.06[3]; 3.10[2]; **4** n.453
358(a)(2) . . . . . . 3.10[1]; **3** n.228; 11.12[2]; **11** n.284; 12.42[2][b]; 12.42[4]; 12.42[5]; 12.44[3][a]; **12** ns. 690, 946
358(b) . . . . 12.42[5]
358(b)(1) . . . . . . 3.10[1]; 12.42[5]; 12.44[3][b]
358(b)(2) **11** n.335
358(c) . . . . . . 11.11[2][b]; 11.12[1]; **11** n.335; 12.63[7][c]; 12.63[7][d]; **12** ns. 1049, 1051; 13.44[3]; **13** n.466
358(d) . . . . 3.06[3]; 3.06[4][a]; 3.06[4][f]; 3.06[7]; 3.10[3]; **S3** n.215; 12.42[4]; **12** n.1106
358(d)(1) . . . . 3.10[3]; **3** n.144; 12.42[5]; S13.44[5]
358(d)(2)   3.06[4][c]; 3.06[7]; **3** ns. 130, 223, 236; S13.44[5]
358(e) . . . . 3.10[1]; **3** n.208; 12.43[3]; 12.63[6][d]; **12** ns. 729, 730
358(f) . . . . 12.40[1]; 12.42[4]; **12** ns. 687, 690, 730
358(g) . . . 11.12[1]; 12.62[3][d]; 12.63[7][d]; **12** n.698; 13.44[3]; 13.44[7]; 13.48[2][d]; **13** ns. 560, 707, 964
358(h) . . . . . S3.06[7]; **S3** ns. 145.1, 158, 223, 249.1; **5** n.437
358(h)(1) **S3** n.158
358(h)(2) **S3** n.158
361–368 . . . . **12** n.658

[Text references are to paragraphs; note references are to chapters (boldface numbers) and notes ("n."), and references to the supplement are preceded by "S."]

IRC §

361. . . . . 3.19; **3** ns. 5, 134; **4** n.453; **6** n.121;
8.03[3]; 10.05[4]; 10.05[7]; 10.61; 10.66;
10 n.383; 11.05[2][a]; 11.11[1];
11.11[1][b]; **11** ns. 135, 136, 271, 275,
381; 12.02[2]; 12.21[6]; 12.21[10];
12.25[2][g]; 12.26[5]; 12.30[2][b];
12.30[2][e]; 12.40[1]; 12.40[2]; 12.41[1];
12.42; 12.42[1]; 12.42[1][a]; 12.42[1][b];
12.42[2]; 12.42[2][a]; 12.42[2][b];
12.42[3]; 12.42[4]; 12.42[5]; 12.43[1][b];
12.44[1][d]; 12.46; 12.63[2][a];
12.63[2][b]; 12.63[2][c]; 12.63[5][b];
12.63[7][b]; 12.64[3]; **12** ns. 235, 321,
347, 408, 472, 665, 668, 670, 680, 681,
699, 710, 874, 946, 990, 992, 1026,
1112, 1131; 15.80[2][a]; 15.80[2][c];
15.80[6]; 15.80[7][a]; 15.80[7][d];
15.81[1][a]; 15.81[1][b]; 15.81[3][d];
15.82[2][a]; **15** ns. 808, 907
361(a) . . . . 3.01; 4.61[1]; **4** n.409; 11.11[1][b];
11.11[1][d]; **11** ns. 273, 368; 12.21[6];
12.22[1]; 12.23[1]; 12.30[2][b];
12.30[4][a]; 12.30[4][b]; 12.30[4][c];
12.40[1]; 12.41[1]; 12.42[1][a];
12.42[1][b]; 12.42[2][a]; 12.42[3];
12.42[5]; 12.43[1][b]; 12.63[7][b]; **12** ns.
249, 636, 659, 660, 668, 689, 706, 992
361(b) . . . . **6** n.200; **11** n.280; 12.25[5];
12.30[2][b]; 12.30[4][a]; 12.42[1][b];
12.42[2][a]; 12.42[4]; **12** ns. 249, 685,
710, 725
361(b)(1) . . . . 12.42[1][b]; **12** ns. 668, 674
361(b)(1)(A) . . . . **4** n.453; 11.11[1][d];
12.42[1][b]; 12.42[3]; 12.42[5]; **12** ns.
946, 992
361(b)(1)(B) . . . 12.42[1][b]; **12** n.666; **14** n.103
361(b)(2) . . . . . 11.05[2][a]; 12.42[1][b]; **12** ns.
689, 690
361(b)(3) . . . . S11.11[1][b]; S11.11[1][d];
12.42[1][b]; S12.42[1][b]; 12.42[2][b];
12.42[3]; S12.42[3]; 12.42[5];
12.63[7][b]; **12** ns. 542, 668, 674, 693,
1131, 1135**S12** ns. 328, 664.1, 669.2,
699.1
361(c) . . . . . 6.10[4][c]; **8** n.4; 10.05[7]; **10** ns.
136, 381; 11.11[1][a]; 11.11[1][b];
11.11[1][c]; **11** ns. 39, 280; 12.22[1];
12.23[1]; 12.30[2][b]; 12.30[4][a];
12.30[4][c]; 12.40[1]; 12.42[1][a];
12.42[2][a]; 12.42[2][b]; 12.42[4];
12.42[5]; **12** ns. 249, 699, 861, 1131;
15.63[2][a]; 15.80[7][a]; **15** n.567
361(c)(1) . . . **10** n.136; 11.11[1][b]; 11.11[1][d];
11.15[5]; 12.30[4][a]; 12.30[4][b];
12.30[4][c]; 12.42[2][b]; 12.42[5];
12.63[7][b]; **12** ns. 552, 686; **15** n.1035
361(c)(2) . . . . **10** n.138; 12.42[2][b]; 12.62[2];
12.62[3][d]

IRC §

361(c)(2)(A) . . . 11.11[1][b]; 12.42[2][b]; **12** ns.
676, 677, 992
361(c)(2)(B) . . . . 6.10[4][c]; 11.11[1][b];
11.11[1][c]; **11** n.277; **S11** n.276;
12.42[2][b]; **12** n.676
361(c)(2)(B)(ii) . . . . **10** n.136; 11.11[1][d];
12.42[5]
361(c)(3) . . . 11.11[1][b]; **11** n.278; 12.30[4][b];
12.42[2][b]; 12.42[3]; 12.42[5];
S12.42[5]; **12** ns. 542, 546, 678, 693,
784, 1135**S12** n.699.3
361(c)(4) . . . . . . **8** n.348; 10.05[4]; **10** n.381;
11.15[5]; **11** n.272; 12.42[2][b];
12.42[5]; **12** n.946
362 . . . . 3.01; 3.06[4][f]; 3.11[1]; 3.12[4];
3.17[1]; **S3** n.223; **4** n.368; 8.03[3]; **10**
ns. 137, 553; **11** n.343; S12.30[3];
12.42[5]; 12.43; 12.44[1][d]; **12** ns. 304,
368; **S12** ns. 539, 558, 586.1, 595; **13**
n.920; **S13** n.987; S15.85[7][e]; **15** ns.
826, 1026; **S15** n.1066
362(a) . . . . 3.06[4][c]; 3.06[7]; 3.10[1]; 3.11[1];
3.11[2]; 3.11[3]; 3.11[4]; S3.11[4];
3.11[5]; **3** n.235; **9** n.379; 12.63[6][e];
12.64[3]; **12** n.905; 13.48[2][a]; 13.48[6]
362(a)(1) . . . . 3.06[2]; 3.13[3]; **3** n.235
362(a)(2) . . . . . 3.13[3]; **3** n.301; **9** n.373; **15**
n.329
362(b) . . . . **4** n.453; 5.06[2][d]; 11.12[3];
12.02[2]; 12.25[3][c]; 12.30[4][c];
12.40[1]; 12.40[2]; 12.42[5]; 12.43[2];
12.43[3]; 12.43[4][b]; 12.63[2][a];
12.63[4][c]; 12.63[6][d]; 12.64[3]; **12** ns.
321, 358, 705, 724, 729, 736, 919, 923,
991, 999; 13.48[2][b]; 13.48[3]; **14**
n.103; 15.80[2][c]; **15** n.1047
362(c) . . . . 3.13[3]; **3** ns. 291, 299–302
362(c)(1) . . . . 3.13[3]
362(c)(1)(B) . . . . 3.13[3]; **3** n.284
362(c)(2) . . . . 3.13[3]; **3** n.286
362(d) . . . . . . 3.06[4][f]; S3.06[4][f]; 3.11[7];
S3.11[7]**3** ns. 105, 144
362(d)(2) . . . . 3.11[7]
362(e) . . . S3.11[8]; **S3** n.249.5; **5** ns. 429, 447;
S14 n.415; S15.80[7][e]; S15.85[7][e];
S15 ns. 647.1, 1064
362(e)(1) **S3** n.249.2; **S14** n.416;
S15.84[2][b]; S15.85[7][e]; **S15** n.647.2
362(e)(2) . . . S3.11[8]; S6.06[3]; S6.06[7]; **S10**
n.125; S13.48[6]; **S13** n.919.1; **S14**
n.417; S15.85[7][e]; **S15** n.647.3
362(e)(2)(B) **S15** n.1067
362(e)(2)(C) . . . . . . S3.11[8]; **S3** n.249.4; **S15**
n.1067
362(*l*)(2) **S15** n.1057
365(a)(2) . . . . S12.44[2][d]
366(d)(3) **13** n.449

[Text references are to paragraphs; note references are to chapters (boldface numbers) and notes ("n."), and references to the supplement are preceded by "S."]

IRC §

367 . . . . 3.19; 3.21; **3** ns. 49, 51, 393; 5.10[5][b]; **5** ns. 311, 430; 6.09[6]; **6** n.220; **8** n.353; **10** ns. 239, 242; 12.40[1]; 12.46; **12** ns. 102, 179, 345; **13** n.256; **14** ns. 5, 113; 15.01[1]; 15.04[1][a]; 15.22; S15.80; 15.80[1]; 15.80[2][a]; 15.80[2][b]; 15.80[2][c]; 15.80[3]; 15.80[4][a]; 15.80[4][b]; 15.80[5]; 15.80[7][a]; 15.80[7][b]; S15.80[7][b]; 15.80[7][c]; 15.80[7][d]; 15.80[7][e]; 15.80[8]; S15.80[8]; 15.81[3]; 15.81[3][a]; 15.81[3][b]; 15.81[3][c]; 15.81[3][d]; S15.81[3][e]; 15.81[3][g]; S15.81[3][h]; 15.81[4][a]; 15.81[4][d]; 15.82[1]; 15.82[2][a]; 15.82[3]; 15.83[1][a]; 15.83[2][a]; 15.83[2][b]; 15.83[3]; 15.84[1][a]; 15.84[1][b]; 15.84[1][c]; 15.84[1][d]; 15.84[1][e]; 15.84[2][b]; 15.84[3][b]; 15.84[3][e]; S15.8515.85[1][a]; 15.85[1][c]; 15.85[5][a]; 15.85[6][b]; 15.85[7][c]; **15** ns. 252, 253, 387, 455, 605, 606, 609, 611, 620, 621, 629, 632, 639, 641, 642, 643, 651, 755, 757, 768, 791, 779, 799, 849, 861, 875, 890, 905, 906, 914, 946, 1007; **S15** ns. 556.5, 604, 784.8, 784.12, 840.5

367(a) . . . 3.21; S9.09[6][f]; **9** n.408; **10** n.165; 11.16; **S12** ns. 959, 961.1; S15.63[2][b]; 15.80[4][d]; 15.80[5]; 15.80[6]; 15.80[7][e]; 15.80[8]; 15.81[3][a]; 15.81[3][b]; 15.81[3][c]; 15.81[3][e]; S15.81[3][h]; 15.81[4][b]; 15.82[2][a]; 15.82[2][b]; S15.82[2][c]; 15.83[2][a]; 15.84[1][a]; 15.84[1][b]; 15.84[1][d]; 15.84[1][e]; 15.84[2][a]; 15.84[2][d]; 15.84[2][e]; 15.84[3][c]; 15.85[3][d]; 15.85[7][a]; **15** ns. 31, 349, 604, 613, 620, 627, 630, 638, 639, 642, 644, 648, 659, 668, 676, 681–683, 695, 698, 708, 719, 743, 748, 754, 757, 762, 796, 827, 828, 841, 846, 849, 861, 865, 867, 878, 890, 901, 904, 912, 934, 935, 936, 996, 997; **S15** ns. 741.2, 741.9, 741.13

367(a)(1)–367(a)(3) . . . . 15.84[2][a]
367(a)(1) . . . . 15.80[4][b]; 15.80[4][d]; 15.81[1][a]; 15.81[1][b]; 15.81[3][b]; 15.81[3][c]; 15.81[3][d]; 15.83[2][a]; 15.84[2][a]; **15** ns. 719, 828, 858, 896
367(a)(2) . . . . 15.80[4][b]; 15.81[1][b]
367(a)(2)(D) . . . . 13.48[2][b]
367(a)(3) . . . **11** n.83; 15.81[1][b]; 15.84[2][e]; **S15** ns. 897.1, 902.1
367(a)(3)(A) . . . . **15** ns. 753, 761, 828
367(a)(3)(B) . . . . 15.81[1][a]; 15.81[1][c]; 15.82[2][a]; 15.84[2][e]; **15** ns. 756, 797

367(a)(3)(C) . . . . 15.81[1][c]; 15.82[2][a]; 15.84[2][e]; **15** n.754
367(a)(3)(C)(i) **15** n.663
367(a)(5) . . . 15.80[6]; 15.84[2][a]; 15.84[2][e]; **15** ns. 876, 904, 908
367(a)(6) **15** n.858
367(b) . . . . . . S9.09[6][f]; 11.16; 15.80[2][b]; 15.80[2][c]; 15.80[4][c]; 15.80[4][d]; S15.80[7][f]; 15.80[8]; S15.80[8]; 15.81[2]; 15.81[3]; 15.81[3][a]; 15.81[3][c]; 15.81[3][d]; 15.81[3][e]; 15.81[3][g]; S15.81[3][h]; 15.82[2][b]; 15.82[3]; 15.83[1][a]; 15.83[1][b]; 15.83[3]; 15.84[1][a]; 15.84[1][b]; 15.84[1][c]; 15.84[1][d]; 15.84[1][e]; 15.84[2][b]; 15.84[2][c]; 15.84[2][d]; S15.84[2][d]; 15.84[2][e]; 15.84[3]; 15.84[3][a]; 15.84[3][b]; 15.84[3][c]; 15.84[3][d]; S15.84[3][f]; 15.85[6][b]; 15.85[6][c]; 15.85[7][d]; **15** ns. 31, 328, 472, 566, 622, 625, 627, 628, 629, 643, 644, 645, 647, 648, 654, 659, 664, 667, 668, 681, 682, 705, 708, 715, 719, 729, 740, 784, 785, 824, 825, 826, 827, 841, 842, 844, 846, 847, 849, 857, 861, 865, 881, 882, 884, 890, 904, 905, 906, 919, 923, 953, 1002, 1003, 1025, 1028, 1029, 1033, 1036, 1039; **S15** ns. 364.1, 556.5, 647.5, 719, 741.2, 741.13
367(b)(1) . . . 15.80[4][c]; 15.81[3][e]; 15.83[3]; 15.84[1][b]; 15.84[1][e]; 15.84[2][e]; **15** ns. 719, 743, 785
367(b)(2) . . . . 15.80[2][c]; 15.80[4][c]; 15.80[4][d]; 15.81[2]; 15.84[1][b]; 15.84[1][e]; 15.84[2][c]; **15** ns. 624, 905
367(c)(2) 3.21; **15** n.639
367(d) . . . 15.81[1][a]; 15.81[1][b]; 15.82[2][a]; **15** ns. 660, 668, 748, 751, 757, 763, 796
367(d)(2)(A) **15** n.763
367(d)(2)(C) . . . . 15.81[1][b]; 15.82[2][a]
367(d)(3) . . . . 15.81[1][b]; 15.82[2][a]
367(e) . . . . 10 n.165; 15.80[6]; 15.80[8]; 15.81[1][a]; 15.81[3][a]; **15** ns. 638, 784, 871
367(e)(1) . . . . . . 11.16; 15.80[6]; 15.80[7][a]; 15.81[3][f]; 15.84[3][e]; S15.84[4]; 15.84[4][a]; 15.84[4][b]; 15.84[4][c]; **15** ns. 638, 655, 912, 916, 919, 924, 946, 980, 993, 994
367(e)(2) . . . . **10** ns. 325, 344; 15.80[6]; 15.80[7][a]; 15.81[3][f]; 15.83[2][b]; 15.83[3]; 15.83[4][a]; 15.85[2][b]; 15.85[2][d]; **15** ns. 634, 638, 655, 671, 800, 801, 957, 960, 995, 996, 997, 1063; **S15** n.824.1
367(f)   15.80[6]; 15.82[2][a]; **15** ns. 639, 751

[Text references are to paragraphs; note references are to chapters (boldface numbers) and notes ("n."), and references to the supplement are preceded by "S."]

IRC §

368.... S1.08[4]; 3.06[4][f]; **3** ns. 91, 144; **S3** ns. 105.2, 368, 401; 4.03[3]; 4.03[7]; **4** ns. 105, 127, 419; 5.06[2][g]; **5** ns. 254, 412; 6.09[1]; 6.09[3][c]; 6.11; **6** n.277; 9.09[6][b]; 9.09[6][d]; 10.02; 10.05[4]; S10.21[2]; **10** ns. 173, 305, 375, 472, 574; **S10** n.266; 11.01[1][f]; 11.02[1]; 11.05[2][b]; 11.06[2]; 11.09[4]; 11.11[2][c]; **11** ns. 45, 260, 328, 329, 335; 12.02[1]; S12.21[2][d]; 12.21[6]; 12.22[5]; 12.22[9]; 12.22[10][a]; 12.22[10][b]; S12.22[10][b]; 12.22[10][c]; 12.23[1]; 12.25[4]; 12.26[1]; 12.26[2]; 12.26[3]; 12.26[6]; S12.21[2][d]; 12.30[4][a]; 12.30[4][b]; 12.40[1]; 12.41[1]; S12.41[2]; 12.41[5]; 12.42[3]; 12.42[5]; 12.43[1][a]; 12.44[1][d]; 12.61[1]; 12.62[4]; S12.63[1]; S12.63[2][a]; S12.63[6][a]; 12.63[6][b]; 12.63[6][c]; 12.63[6][e]; 12.64[3]; S12.65[5]; 12.67[1]; **12** ns. 121, 247, 324, 447, 530, 828, 845, 874, 876, 877, 879, 893, 898, 902, 905, 933, 934, 989, 1140; **S12** ns. 51, 52.2, 166, 328.2, 352.1, 372, 537.3, 683.1, 699.4, 915.3; 13.48[2][d]; 13.48[3]; 13.48[6]; **13** ns. 920, 925, 928, 935.3, 961, 976, 985, 990; 14.02[3]; 14.42[3]; 14.43[1]; 14.43[4]; 14.43[7][b]; 14.44[5]; **14** ns. 55, 334, 340; 15.04[2][b]; S15.81[3][h]; 15.85[1][c]; 15.85[3][c]; **15** ns. 951, 1005

368(a) ... 3.05[4]; 4.03[7]; 5.06[2][a]; **5** n.254; 11.02[1]; 12.21[10]; 12.25[1]; 12.27[5][b]; 12.40[1]; **12** ns. 247, 313, 807; **S12** n.269; 13.48[2][b]; 13.48[4][a]; 14.21[1]

368(a)(1) .... 10.21[2]; 12.01[2]; 12.01[4]; 12.02[1]; 12.02[2]; 12.20; 12.21[8]; 12.22[7]; 12.41[1]; 12.44[1][d]; 12.46; 12.64[1][c]; 15.80[2][a]; S15.81[3][h]; **15** n.715

368(a)(1)(A) ..... 6.09[2]; 10.24; **S10** ns. 273, 291, 470, 574; 11.05[2][a]; **11** n.74; 12.22[1]; 12.22[9]; S12.22[10][a]; 12.22[10][b]; S12.22[10][b]; 12.24[2][a]; 12.25[1]; 12.25[2][e]; 12.25[4]; 12.25[5]; S12.25[5]; 12.41[1]; 12.62[4]; S12.63[2][a]; 12.63[2][b]; 12.63[6][c]; 12.65[3][b]; **12** ns. 10, 148, 213; **S12** ns. 147, 269, 289. 290, 321.2, 921, 922, 936.1; **S13** n.975; 14.20[1]; 14.45[2]

368(a)(1)(B) ..... 3.03[2]; **4** n.408; 6.09[2]; **6** n.172; 12.21[8]; 12.22[1]; 12.23[1]; 12.23[2]; 12.23[7]; 12.25[3][b]; 12.43[4][b]; 12.44[1][d]; 12.62[4]; 12.63[4][d]; 12.63[6][c]; **12** ns. 151, 161, 275–277, 899; 13.48[4][a]; 15.81[3][d]; 15.84[1][c]; **S15** n.647.5

IRC §

368(a)(1)(C) ..... **4** n.408; 6.09[2]; S10.21[2]; 11.14; **11** ns. 34, 172; 12.21[8]; 12.22[1]; 12.23[7]; 12.24[1]; 12.24[2][a]; 12.24[3][b]; 12.24[3][c]; 12.24[3][e]; 12.24[5]; 12.25[2][a]; 12.25[5]; 12.26[4]; 12.26[5]; 12.41[2]; 12.62[2]; 12.62[3][a]; 12.63[4][b]; 12.63[5][a]; 12.63[5][b]; 12.65[1]; 12.65[2][a]; 12.65[2][c]; 12.65[2][d]; 12.66[4][b]; **12** ns. 10, 149, 210, 225, 227, 270, 276, 682, 1111, 1131; **S12** n.1011; 14.20[1]; 14.45[2]

368(a)(1)(D) .... 3.01; **3** ns. 190, 199; 6.06[4][c]; 6.09[4]; **6** n.172; 9.09[6][d]; 11.02[1]; 11.06[2]; 11.08[1]; 11.12[3]; 11.14; 11.15[4]; **11** ns. 33, 35, 209, 214, 329, 368; 12.24[1]; 12.24[5]; 12.26[1]; 12.26[2]; 12.26[3]; 12.26[4]; 12.26[5]; 12.26[6]; 12.26[8]; 12.62[3][a]; 12.62[3][b]; 12.62[3][c]; 12.62[4]; 12.63[4][b]; 12.63[7][b]; 12.64[2][b]; **12** ns. 258, 309, 321, 323, 340, 343, 872, 874, 900, 1080; 13.48[2][b]; 14.20[1]; 14.45[2]; **14** n.41; 15.84[3][b]

368(a)(1)(E) ..... **4** n.429; 6.10[1][a]; 6.10[4]; 9.01[3][b]; 12.27[2][a]; 12.27[3][a]; 12.27[5][b]; 12.64[2][b]; **12** n.440

368(a)(1)(F) ..... 4.25[6]; 11.15[3]; 12.26[5]; 12.28[1]; 12.28[2]; 12.28[4]; 12.64[2][b]; **12** n.204; 14.20[1]; 14.21[3][d]

368(a)(1)(G) .... 6.10[1][a]; 12.25[1]; 12.30[1]; 12.30[2][a]; 12.30[2][b]; 12.30[2][e]; 12.30[4]; 12.30[4][c]; 14.20[1]; **14** n.53

368(a)(2) 12.29

368(a)(2)(A) ...... 11.14; 12.02[1]; 12.22[7]; 12.24[5]; 12.25[3][b]; 12.26[5]; 12.63[4][b]; **12** ns. 227, 258, 321, 329, 350, 511, 694, 918; **S12** n.918; **15** n.898

368(a)(2)(B) .... 12.24[3][a]; 12.24[3][d]; 12.24[3][e]; 12.24[4]; 12.25[2][e]; 12.44[1][d]; 12.63[5][b]; 12.65[1]; 12.65[2][d]; 12.65[3][a]; **12** ns. 236, 245, 248, 249

368(a)(2)(C) ..... **3** n.204; **10** n.324; 12.22[1]; 12.22[3]; 12.24[2][d]; 12.25[1]; 12.25[3][b]; S12.26[1]; S12.28[1]; 12.30[2][c]; 12.40[2]; 12.63[6][a]; S12.63[6][a]; 12.63[6][b]; **12** ns. 30, 56, 107, 151, 156, 226, 227, 231, 242, 258, 270, 293, 329, 544, 607, 1014; **S12** ns. 56, 328.2, 1017.1, 1017.2, 1030, 1048; 13.48[3]; S13.48[3]; 13.48[6]; **S13** ns. 916, 946; S15.81[3][h]

368(a)(2)(D) .... **11** n.172; 12.22[3]; 12.22[10][b]; 12.24[5]; 12.25[1]; 12.25[2]; 12.25[2][a]; 12.25[2][b]; 12.25[2][c]; 12.25[2][e]; 12.25[2][f]; 12.25[2][g]; 12.25[4]; 12.25[5]; 12.30[2][c]; 12.40[2]; 12.66[4][b]; **12** ns. 102, 259, 270, 276, 278, 281, 321, 953, 1014, 1027, 1134, 1135, 1171; S13.48[2][b]; 14.43[8]; **15** n.875

[Text references are to paragraphs; note references are to chapters (boldface numbers) and notes ("n."), and references to the supplement are preceded by "S."]

IRC §

368(a)(2)(E) . . . . . **S10** n.291; S11.11[2][b]; **11**
n.172; 12.22[3]; S12.23[1]; 12.23[2];
12.23[12]; 12.25[1]; 12.25[2][a];
12.25[2][b]; 12.25[2][d]; 12.25[2][g];
12.25[3]; 12.25[3][a]; 12.25[3][b];
S12.25[3][b]; 12.25[3][c]; 12.25[4];
12.25[5]; S12.25[5]; 12.30[2][c];
12.30[2][e]; 12.40[2]; 12.41[1];
12.43[4][a]; S12.63[2][a]; S12.63[4][g];
12.63[6][c]; 12.66[4][b]; **12** ns. 151, 180,
206, 259, 267, 269, 272, 274, 275, 277,
288, 293, 302, 309, 315, 318, 329, 526,
730, 952, 1135, 1171; **S12** ns. 51, 269,
289, 290, 321.1, 922, 925, 926, 937,
938; 13.48[2][b]; 13.48[4][a]; **13** n.734;
14.43[8]

368(a)(2)(F) . . . **3** ns. 328, 329; 7.10; 12.29; **12**
ns. 91, 531

368(a)(2)(F)(ii) 12.29

368(a)(2)(F)(iii) 12.29

368(a)(2)(F)(iv) 12.29; **14** n.290

368(a)(2)(F)(v) 12.29

368(a)(2)(F)(vi) 12.29

368(a)(2)(G) . . . . **3** n.399; **10** ns. 23, 135;
12.62[4]; 12.63[4][b]; 12.63[5][b]; **12** ns.
249, 257, 690, 725, 727; 14.23[1][a]; **14**
n.62

368(a)(2)(G)(i) . . . 12.42[1][b]; 12.42[2][a]; **12**
n.666

368(a)(2)(H) . . . . **3** ns. 394, 396; **9** n.396;
11.11[3][c]; **11** ns. 45, 46, 171, 323;
12.26[1]; 12.62[3][d]; 12.62[4];
12.63[4][b]; **12** ns. 323, 324, 343, 351,
855, 359, 872, 874, 877, 893, 899, 1090,
1091, 1093; 13.48[6]; **13** ns. 921, 964;
15 n.981

368(a)(2)(H)(ii) . . . 11.02[2][a]; 11.11[3][c]; **11**
ns. 45, 328, 329; 12.26[1]; 12.26[2]; **12**
ns. 324, 334, 875, 876, 893, 896, 899;
13 ns. 961, 964

368(a)(3)(A) . . . . 12.30[2][a]

368(a)(3)(B) . . . . 12.30[2][a]

368(a)(3)(C) . . . . 12.30[2][a]

368(a)(3)(E) . . . . 12.30[2][c]; 12.30[2][d];
12.30[2][e]

368(a)(3)(E)(ii) **12** n.545

368(b) . . . . 12.02[2]; 12.24[3][b]; 12.25[1];
12.25[2][g]; 12.30[2][c]; 12.40[1];
12.40[2]; 12.42[1][a]; **12** ns. 107, 226,
605–607, 968

368(b)(1) . . . . **12** ns. 107, 607

368(b)(2) . . . . **12** ns. 107, 151, 203, 607

IRC §

368(c) . . . 3.01; 3.02[2]; 3.04; 3.05[4]; 3.07[1];
3.07[2]; 3.07[3]; 3.07[4]; 3.08[1];
3.09[2]; **3** ns. 161, 163, 188; 4.03[7];
11.02[2][a]; 11.02[2][d]; 11.07[1];
11.07[3]; **11** ns. 45, 140, 312; 12.22[3];
12.23[1]; 12.23[2]; 12.26[1]; 12.26[2];
12.41[4]; 12.61[2][b]; 12.62[1];
12.63[6][a]; 12.63[6][b]; **12** ns. 107, 153,
156, 230, 274, 286, 287, 290, 294, 324,
652, 834, 836, 996; **S12** n.625.2;
13.41[2][a]; 13.41[2][b]; 13.48[2][b];
13.48[3]; **13** ns. 946, 964

368(c)(2) . . . . **12** ns. 323, 1090, 1093

368(c)(2)(B) **13** n.20

371 . . . . **10** n.756; 12.30[1]

372 . . . . 12.30[1]

374(a) **10** n.756

380 . . . . **S13** n.971.4

381–382 . . . . 14.46[3]

381–384 . . . . 15.85[7][a]; **15** n.1038

381 . . . . . 2.11; 3.17[7]; 3.18[2]; 3.19; **3** n.393;
4.04[8]; S4.25[2]; 5.06[1][a]; 5.06[1][b];
5.06[2][d]; 5.10[5][b]; **5** ns. 250, 430;
6.06[4][c]; 6.09[1]; S6.09[3][a];
6.09[3][c]; 6.11; **6** ns. 165, 173, 177,
201, 202; **S6** n.48; **8** n.47; 10.20;
10.21[2]; 10.21[5][b]; 10.22[2]; 10.42[5];
10 ns. 253, 281, 509; S11.11[3][d];
11.12[5]; 11.15[3]; **11** n.346; 12.02[2];
12.04; 12.26[5]; 12.27[1]; 12.28[1];
12.30[2][e]; S12.30[3]; 12.30[5][a];
12.40[1]; 12.42[5]; 12.43[2]; 12.43[5];
12.62[3][c]; 12.63[4][c]; 12.63[7][b];
12.64[3]; 12.66[4][c]; **12** ns. 220, 242,
256, 259, 308, 353, 372, 552, 917, 920,
931, 968; 13.46[4]; 13.48[2][b];
13.48[4][a]; 13.48[5][a]; S13.48[5][a];
S13.48[6]; **S12** ns. 539, 558, 586.1,
897.1, 1126; **13** ns. 439, 502, 513, 517,
596, 644, 721, 816, 965, 995; **S13** ns.
467, 625.1, 646.1, 971.6, 1000; 14.01[1];
14.02[1]; 14.02[3]; 14.03[1]; 14.03[2];
14.03[3]; 14.20; 14.20[1]; 14.20[2];
14.20[3]; 14.21[1]; 14.21[2]; S14.21[2];
14.21[3][b]; 14.21[3][c]; 14.21[3][d];
14.22[1]; 14.22[2]; 14.23[1][a]; 14.23[2];
S14.23[2]; 14.23[3][a]; 14.23[3][b];
14.24; 14.40; 14.41[3][c]; 14.41[3][e];
14.46[2]; 14.47[3]; **14** ns. 10, 40, 51,
53–55, 60, 66, 73, 87, 88, 92, 98, 104,
106, 110, 111, 193, 255, 265; **S14** ns.
52.2, 53, 89.1, 409; 15.80[2][c];
S15.80[8]; 15.83[1][a]; 15.83[1][b];
S15.83[4][b]; S15.84[2][c]; S15.84[2][d];
S15.84[2][f]; 15.85[5][a]; **15** ns. 254,
344, 612, 825, 850; **S15** ns. 340, 365,
603, 803, 881, 898

[Text references are to paragraphs; note references are to chapters (boldface numbers) and notes ("n."), and references to the supplement are preceded by "S."]

*[Text references are to paragraphs; note references are to chapters (boldface numbers)
and notes ("n."), and references to the supplement are preceded by "S."]*

IRC §

382(b)(3) . . . . . 13.42[6][b]; 13.46[1][c]; **13** ns.
        501, 505, 815, 819;14.44[2]; 14.44[3][c]
382(b)(3)(A) . . . . 14.44[2]
382(b)(3)(B) . . . . 14.44[2]
382(c) . . . . . . **12** n.841; 13.47[2][c]; 14.42[2];
        14.44[5]; 14.44[7][b]; **14** ns. 182, 334,
                                            398
382(c)(1) . . . . . . **13** n.887;14.42[3]; 14.44[5];
        14.44[8]; **14** n.309
382(c)(2) . . . . 14.42[3]; 14.44[5]; **14** n.366
382(c)(2)(A)(ii) **10** n.509
382(d) . . . . 14.43[1]
382(d)(1) . . . . 14.43[2][c]
382(d)(1)(B) . . . . 14.44[2]
382(d)(2) . . . . 14.43[1]; 14.43[2][c]
382(e) . . . . 14.43[1]; 14.43[8]; 14.44[1][c];
        14.44[6][c]; **14** ns. 230, 275
382(e)(1) . . . . . 14.42[3]; 14.43[8]; 14.44[1][c];
        14.44[3][a]; 14.44[8]
382(e)(2) . . . . 13.47[2][c];14.42[3]; 14.44[1][c];
                                    14 ns. 261, 272, 275
382(e)(3) **14** n.272
382(f) . . . . 14.42[2]; 14.42[3]; 14.43[1];
                                            14.44[1][b]
382(g) . . . . . 11.11[3][b]; 11.11[3][d]; **11** n.329;
        S11 n.331.2; 12.62[3][d]; **12** ns. 597,
        599, 652, 889; 13.45[5]; 13.45[6][a];
        13.45[6][b]; 13.46[1][a]; 13.47[1];
        13.47[2][b]; 13.47[3][b]; 13.47[3][c];
        13.47[5]; 13.48[3]; **13** ns. 864, 881, 913,
        914; 14.43[1]; 14.43[6][d]; 14.43[7];
        14.43[7][a]; 14.46[2]; **14** n.406; **S14**
                                            n.193.1
382(g)(1) . . . . . . 11.12[5]; 14.43[1]; 14.43[5];
                                            14.46[2]
382(g)(2) . . . . 14.43[1]; 14.43[3]; 14.43[8]
382(g)(3) . . . . 14.43[1]; 14.43[4]; 14.43[8]
382(g)(3)(A) . . . . **12** n.373; 14.42[3]; 14.43[4];
                                            14 n.340
382(g)(3)(A)(ii) **12** n.511
382(g)(3)(B) . . . **12** n.1188; 14.42[3]; 14.43[4];
                                            14 n.208
382(g)(4) . . . 14.43[6]; 14.43[6][b]; 14.43[7][a];
                                            14 n.207
382(g)(4)(A) . . . . 14.42[3]; 14.43[2][b];
        14.43[3][c]; 14.43[6][a]; 14.43[6][b];
        14.43[8]; **14** n.250
382(g)(4)(B)(i) . . . 14.43[6][b]; 14.43[8]; **14** ns.
                                            215, 250
382(g)(4)(B)(ii) . . . . 14.43[6][c]; 14.43[8]
382(g)(4)(C) . . . . . 14.43[6][b]; 14.43[6][c]; **14**
                                            n.215
382(g)(4)(D) . . . **4** n.250; **10** n.270; 13.47[4][b];
        13 n.668; 14.43[3][c]; **14** ns. 52, 207,
                                            406
382(h) . . . . **6** n.124; 12.42[5]; 13.46[4]; **13** ns.
        604, 736, 777, 783; 14.42[3];
        14.44[4][a]; 14.44[4][b]; S14.44[4][c];
        14.45[2]; **14** n.362; **S14** n.306.1
382(h)(1)(A) . . . . 14.44[3][c]
382(h)(1)(B) . . . . 14.43[1]

IRC §

382(h)(1)(B)(i) . . . . 14.43[1]
382(h)(1)(C) . . . . **10** n.509; 14.44[3][c]
382(h)(2)(A) . . . . 14.44[3][c]
382(h)(2)(B) . . . . 14.44[4][a]
382(h)(3) . . . . 14.45[2]
382(h)(3)(A) . . . . 14.44[3][c]
382(h)(3)(B)(ii) **14** n.290
382(h)(4) **14** n.299
382(h)(5) . . . . 14.44[2]; 14.44[3][c]
382(h)(6) . . . **10** n.190; 14.44[4][a]; **14** ns. 289,
                                            377
382(h)(6)(A) **14** n.289
382(h)(6)(B) . . . . 14.44[7][h]; **14** n.300
382(h)(7) . . . . 14.45[2]
382(h)(7)(A) **14** n.291
382(h)(7)(B) **14** n.291
382(h)(8) . . . . 14.44[4][a]
382(i) . . . . 14.43[2][b]; 14.43[5]; 14.43[7][a];
                                            14.44[7][a]
382(j) . . . . . 14.43[1]; 14.43[2][c]; **14** n.277
382(k)(1) . . . . 14.43[1]; 14.43[2][c]
382(k)(2) . . . . 14.43[2][c]
382(k)(3) . . 14.43[1]; 14.43[2][c]; 14.44[7][b];
                                            14 n.255
382(k)(6)(A) . . . . 14.43[2][a]; 14.43[3][c];
                                            14.43[8]
382(k)(6)(B) . . . . . 14.43[2][a]; 14.43[3][c]; **14**
                                            n.273
382(k)(6)(B)(i) . . . . 6.10[4][c]
382(k)(6)(C) . . . . 14.43[2][a]; **14** n.200
382(k)(7) . . . . 14.43[2][b]; **14** n.319
382(*l*)(1) . . . 13.03[2]; 13.47[2][c]; 14.44[3][a];
                                            14.44[3][c]; 14.44[8]
382(*l*)(3)(A) . . . . . . 14.43[2][d]; 14.43[3][c];
                                            14.43[6][d]; **14** n.314
382(*l*)(3)(A)(i) . . . . 14.43[2][d]
382(*l*)(3)(A)(ii) . . . . . 14.43[2][d]; 14.43[6][d];
                                            14.43[8]; **14** n.340
382(*l*)(3)(A)(iii) . . . . 14.43[2][d]
382(*l*)(3)(A)(iv) . . . . **9** n.70; 14.43[2][e];
                                            14.43[6][d]
382(*l*)(3)(A)(v) **14** n.194
382(*l*)(3)(B) . . . . 14.42[3]; 14.43[3][a]
382(*l*)(3)(C) . . . 14.43[2][a]; 14.43[3][a]; **14** ns.
                                            199, 211
382(*l*)(4) . . . . . 14.44[3][a]; 14.44[5]; 14.44[8]
382(*l*)(4)(A) . . . . 14.42[3]; **14** n.288
382(*l*)(4)(B) **14** n.288
382(*l*)(4)(B)(ii) . . . . 14.42[3]
382(*l*)(4)(D) **14** n.284
382(*l*)(4)(E) . . . . 14.44[3][b]
382(*l*)(5) . . . . . **13** n.329;14.42[3]; 14.44[6][a];
        14.44[6][b]; 14.44[6][c]; 14.44[6][d];
        14.44[7][a]; 14.44[8]; **14** ns. 196, 207,
                                            272, 314, 324, 334
382(*l*)(5)(A)   **12** ns. 422, 543, 590, 597, 599;
                                            14.44[6][a]; **14** n.316
382(*l*)(5)(B) . . . . **12** n.597; 14.44[6][a]
382(*l*)(5)(C) . . . . 12.30[5][d]; **12** ns. 422, 590,
        597, 599; 14.44[6][a]; **14** ns. 315, 316
382(*l*)(5)(C)(ii) . . . . **12** n.597; **14** ns. 316, 369

[Text references are to paragraphs; note references are to chapters (boldface numbers) and notes ("n."), and references to the supplement are preceded by "S."]

IRC §

382(*l*)(5)(D) . . . 14.42[3]; 14.44[6][a]; 14.44[8]
382(*l*)(5)(E) . . . . **12** n.545; 14.44[6][b]; **14** ns. 113, 313
382(*l*)(5)(F) **14** n.325
382(*l*)(5)(H) . . . . 14.44[6][c]
382(*l*)(6) . . . 14.42[3]; 14.44[6][c]; 14.44[8]; **14** ns. 272, 324
382(*l*)(8) . . . 14.41[3][e]; **14** ns. 190, 193, 255, 340, 341, 371
382(m) . . . . 14.42[3]
382(m)(3) . . . . 14.43[8]; 14.44[7][e]; 14.45[4]
382(m)(4) . . . **11** n.329; 14.43[6][b]; 14.43[8]; **14** ns. 208, 272
382(m)(5)   13.03[1]; 14.44[1][c]; 14.44[3][d]; **14** n.208
383 . . . . . 1.05[1][a]; 2.11; 6.07[1]; 8.07[2][b]; 13.47[4][a]; **13** ns. 847, 899; 14.01[1]; 14.02[1]; 14.03[1]; 14.24; 14.43[1]; 14.44[1][a]; 14.44[7][a]; 14.44[7][f]; **14** ns. 10, 90, 110, 148, 181, 332, 397; **15** n.344
383(h) **14** n.345
384 . . . . . 1.05[1][a]; 5.10[5][b]; **5** n.430; **6** ns. 127, 136, 202; 8.07[2][b]; 10.05[6]; 10.06[1]; 10.42[5]; **10** ns. 183, 190, 579; 12.40[1]; **12** n.974; 13.45[1]; 13.45[3][a]; **13** ns. 339, 701, 714, 719, 725, 736; 14.01[1]; 14.02[1]; 14.02[3]; 14.03[1]; 14.03[2]; 14.44[4][b]; 14.45; 14.45[2]; 14.45[3]; 14.45[4]; 14.46[4]; 14.47[3]; 14.47[6][b]; 14.47[7]; **14** ns. 5, 10, 20, 28, 40, 46, 251, 267, 293, 365, 385, 386; **15** n.1041
384(a) . . . . 14.45[2]; **14** n.386
384(a)(1)(B) . . . . 14.45[4]; **14** n.386
384(a)(2) . . . . 14.45[4]
384(b) . . . . 14.45[2]; **14** n.305
384(c)(1) **14** n.383
384(c)(1)(B) . . . . **14** ns. 304, 377
384(c)(3) **14** n.383
384(c)(4) **14** n.383
384(c)(8) . . . . 14.45[2]; **14** n.383
384(f) . . . . 14.45[2]
384(f)(1) . . . . 14.45[4]
385 . . . . 4.02[8]; 4.02[8][a]; 4.02[8][b]; 4.03[6]; 4.26[3]; **4** ns. 30, 52, 63; **5** n.416; 6.10[4][b]; **6** n.32; **10** n.284; **12** ns. 610, 642
385(a) . . . . 4.02[5]; 4.02[8][b]; 4.03[6]; **4** n.332
385(b) . . . . 4.02[8][a]
385(b)(1) . . . . **4** ns. 58, 60
385(c) . . . . 4.02[2]; 4.02[8][b]; 4.03[2][a]; 4.03[2][i]; **4** ns. 54, 364, 443; 5.10[4][b]; **5** n.424; **7** ns. 205, 237; **10** n.461
385(c)(3) . . . . 4.02[8][b]; **4** ns. 33, 55, 124
386(d) . . . . **8**.21[3]
401 . . . . **2** n.119; **5** n.329; S14.43[2][d]; S14.43[3][c]; S14.43[7][c]; **14** n.125; **S14** n.194.1
401(a) . . . . 9.02[3]; 9.02[4]
401(a)(4) . . . . 1.05[1][a]

IRC §

404 . . . . **4** n.371; 14.23[5]
404(a)(5) **6** n.125; **10** n.429
404(k) **4** n.2
414(b) . . . . 13.01[2]; **13** n.22
414(m) **2** n.180
421–425 . . . . **4** n.438
421 . . . . **8** ns. 197, 370
424(d) **9** n.42
441 . . . . 5.07; **5** n.318; **15** n.1041
441(h) . . . . 15.23[3][a]
441(i) . . . . **2** n.181; **5** ns. 319, 320
441(i)(1) **5** n.321
442 . . . . **5** n.318
444 . . . . **2** n.181; **5** n.323; **6** n.88
444(b)(3) **5** n.325
444(c)(2) **2** n.181
446 . . . . 5.07; 5.10[6][f]; 13.23[1]; 13.42[1][b]; 13.42[6][a]; **13** n.640; 14.23[3][a]
446(a) **8** n.139
446(b) . . . 1.05[3][b]; 3.17[1]; 3.17[4]; **4** n.384; 10.06[2]; 10.07[1]; 11.12[4]; 13.23[6][d]; 14.01[1]; 14.03[1]; 14.23[3][c]; 15.60[2]; **15** n.50
446(e) **13** n.515
447 . . . . 5.09[3]; **5** n.327
448 . . . . . 5.07[2]; 5.09[3]; 13.01[4][a]; **14** n.94
448(a)(3) **5** n.326
448(b) **5** n.328
448(b)(2) **2** n.182
448(c) **5** n.328
448(d)(2) . . . . **5** ns. 2, 329
448(d)(3) **5** n.326
448(d)(4) **5** n.329
448(d)(5) **5** n.330
451 . . . . 13.23[1]
453 . . . 3.04; 3.05[3]; 3.05[4]; **3** ns. 61, 72, 80, 154; **4** ns. 427, 430; 5.01[5]; 5.08[5]; 5.08[6]; 5.09[4]; 6.07[1]; 6.09[3][b]; 6.09[5]; **6** ns. 125, 133; **S6** n.194; 8.03[5]; **8** ns. 54, 137, 160; 9.01[3][a]; 9.06[2]; 9.20; 9.21[4]; **9** ns. 359, 370; **S9** n.112; 10.05[6]; 10.41[5][f]; 10.42[6][b]; 10.44; **10** ns. 39, 506, 599, 604, 708, 744; **S10** ns. 39, 439, 604; 12.44[1][b]; **12** ns. 52, 105, 442, 481, 488, 489, 724, 754, 780, 1188; **S12** n.754; 13.01[4][b]; 13.42[3][b]; 13.43[2][a]; 13.43[2][c]; **13** ns. 406, 496; 14.23[5]; **14** ns. 292, 304, 377, 483, 490, 491; **15** ns. 61, 974
453(e) . . . . 1.05[1][a]; **9** n.434; **10** n.39; 13.01[4][b]; 13.23[1]; 13.23[4]; **13** n.291
453(e)(6)(A) **9** n.434
453(f)(3)–453(f)(5) **4** n.427
453(f)(3) **10** n.589
453(f)(4) . . . . **12** ns. 442, 481
453(f)(4)(A) **9** n.435
453(f)(4)(B) **5** n.399
453(f)(5) . . . . . **2** n.116; **12** ns. 442, 481, 1147
453(f)(6) . . . . 3.05[3]; 3.11[4]; **6** n.203; **12** ns. 442, 754
453(g) . . . . 1.05[1][a]; **3** n.85; 5.04[2]

[Text references are to paragraphs; note references are to chapters (boldface numbers) and notes ("n."), and references to the supplement are preceded by "S."]

IRC §

453(g)(1) . . . . 13.23[4]
453(g)(1)(B)(ii) . . . . 13.23[4]
453(g)(2) . . . . 13.23[4]
453(h) . . . 6.08[2]; 6.09[3][b]; 6.09[5]; **6** n.194;
    10 ns. 39, 83; **12** ns. 105, 1188
453(h)(2) **6** n.214; **10** n.39
453(i) **10** n.394; **13** n.406
453(k)(2) **2** n.116; **4** n.427; **5** n.398
453(k)(2)(A) . . . . **9** n.436; **12** ns. 442, 481, 754
453(*l*) . . . . 6.09[5]
453A . . . 5.08[5]; 6.09[5]; **12** n.754; **13** n.406
453B **3** n.265; 4.45; **8** n.357; **10** n.39;
    12.27[3][a]; **12** ns. 408, 442; **13** n.270
453B(a) **10** n.83
453B(d) **10** n.341
453B(h) . . . 6.09[3][b]; 6.09[5]; **6** ns. 163, 194,
    211; **10** n.83
456 . . . . 6.06[2][c]; **S6** n.84.1
460 . . . . 5.08[3]; 5.09[3]; 13.01[4][a]
460(e) **5** n.391
461 . . . . **4** n.384; 13.23[1]; 15.21[5][a]
461(f) **7** n.171; **8** n.147
461(h) . . . . 3.06[4][c]; 10.07[2]; 10.41[5][e]; **10**
    ns. 429, 617, 623
461(i)(3) **5** n.326
464 . . . . 5.03[8]
465 . . . . . **1** n.126; **4** n.188; 5.03[6]; 5.09[3]; **6**
    n.85; **S6** n.84.1; 7.10; 7.14[3]
465(a)(1)(B) . . . . **5** ns. 55, 392
465(b)(3)(C) **5** n.139
465(b)(6)(B) **5** n.54
465(c)(4)(A) **11** n.83
465(c)(7) **11** n.83
467 . . . . **4** n.371; 13.21[2]
469 . . . . **1** n.126; 2.04[3]; **4** ns. 188, 267;
    5.03[6]; 5.09[3]; 5.10[1]; 5.10[5][e];
    6.06[2][c]; **6** ns. 81, 136; **S6** ns. 81, 136;
    7.10; **11** n.187; **13** n.350; 15.46[4]; **15**
    ns. 74, 221
469(a)(2) **5** n.394
469(e)(2) **2** n.179
469(g)(1)(A) . . . . . . 3.18[1]; **3** n.380; **10** n.228
469(h)(4)(B) **11** n.83
469(j)(2) **5** n.56
469(k) **2** n.115; **10** n.169
471 . . . . **10** n.676
472–473 . . . . **10** n.676
474 . . . . 5.09[3]
474(c) **5** n.395
475 . . . . . **4** n.193; **8** n.410; **12** n.1; 13.43[2][c];
    13 n.605
481 . . . . 3.17[4]; 3.17[7]; **3** ns. 360, 372; **6**
    n.125; **8** n.140; 14.23[3][a]; 14.23[3][c];
    14 n.92

IRC §

482 . . . . 1.02; 1.05[3][c]; **1** n.90; **S1** ns. 47, 65,
    92; 2.07[3]; 2.07[4]; 2.07[6]; **2** ns. 155,
    158, 159, 168–170; 3.17[1]; 3.18[1]; **3**
    ns. 352, 355, 356; **4** n.84; 5.04[2];
    5.10[2][a]; 5.10[6][f]; **5** ns. 12, 411, 416,
    479; 7.12[7]; **7** ns. 175, 189; 207;
    8.05[10]; 8.21[3]; **8** ns. 212, 250, 251,
    358; 10.06[2]; 10.07[1]; 10.41[5][d]; **10**
    ns. 129, 196, 353, 391, 677; 11.04[4];
    11.12[4]; **11** n.106; 13.01[3][a];
    13.01[3][b]; 13.01[3][c]; 13.01[4][b];
    13.20[1][a]; 13.20[1][b]; 13.20[1][c];
    13.20[1][d]; 13.20[2][a]; 13.20[2][b];
    13.20[3][a]; 13.20[3][b]; 13.20[4][a];
    13.20[4][b]; 13.20[4][d]; 13.20[4][e];
    13.20[4][f]; 13.20[4][g]; 13.20[4][h];
    13.20[4][i]; 13.20[5][a]; 13.20[5][d];
    13.20[5][e]; 13.20[6][a]; 13.20[6][d];
    13.20[6][e]; 13.21[1]; 13.21[2];
    S13.21[3]; 13.21[4]; 13.21[5][a];
    13.21[5][b]; 13.21[5][c]; 13.21[5][d];
    13.21[6][a]; 13.21[6][b]; 13.21[7][a];
    13.21[7][b]; 13.21[7][c]; 13.21[9];
    S13.22[1]; 13.22[1][a]; 13.22[1][b];
    S13.22[1][b]; 13.22[2]; S13.22[3];
    13.22[3][b]; 13.23[1]; 13.23[3][a];
    13.23[3][b]; 13.23[3][c]; 13.23[3][d];
    13.23[5][b]; 13.23[5][c]; 13.23[5][e];
    13.23[6][d]; 13.23[7]; 13.40; 13.46[2][a];
    13 ns. 51, 57, 60, 61, 63, 76, 79, 81, 86,
    93, 96, 118, 145, 151, 170, 182, 186,
    192, 196, 197, 199, 201, 220, 224, 228–
    231, 233, 239–242, 245, 247, 254, 256,
    269, 272, 277, 279, 288, 309, 388, 504,
    515, 640, 818; **S13** ns. 50, 86, 97, 112.1,
    242; 14.01[1]; 14.02[1]; 14.03[1];
    14.23[3][a]; 14.47[4]; **14** ns. 21, 401;
    15.01[1]; 15.02[1][d]; 15.02[2][b];
    15.02[3][d]; 15.02[1][h]; 15.04[1][d];
    15.04[5]; 15.23[3][f]; 15.60[2]; 15.62[1];
    15.80[3]; 15.80[7][e]; S15.82[2][c]; **15**
    ns. 78, 94, 103, 108, 161, 208, 244, 247,
    257, 283, 288, 333, 390, 482, 484, 604,
    648; **S15** ns. 482, 784.8, 784.12, 840.5
482(b) . . . . . 13.20[4][i]; **13** n.105; 15.04[5]; **15**
    ns. 16, 285
482A . . . . 13.20[2][b]
483 . . . . 3.12[1]; 3.12[4]; 3.17[3]; 4.43[1];
    4.43[3]; 4.43[5]; 4.43[6]; **4** ns. 383–385,
    427; 7.12[11]; **9** n.107; **10** n.49;
    12.23[10]; 12.27[5][d]; 12.41[3];
    12.66[2][b]; 12.66[3][a]; **12** ns. 197, 444,
    481, 485, 621, 756, 1113, 1148–1151,
    1154, 1179; 13.21[2]; 13.23[4]; **13**
    n.254; 15.02[1][b]
483(d)(1) . . . . 4.43[6]; **12** n.1151
483(e) . . . . 4.43[4]
483(f) **12** n.1151
501 . . . . 5.05[7][a]; **5** n.196; **S8** n.254.10;
    13.02[5]; 13.41[1]; 14.47[6][a]; **15**
    n.1043

[Text references are to paragraphs; note references are to chapters (boldface numbers) and notes ("n."), and references to the supplement are preceded by "S."]

IRC §

501(a) . . . . 1.06[8]; 6.02[2]
501(c) . . . . 1.06[8]
501(c)(3) . . . . . . 6.02[2]; 8.63[3][b]; 10.05[6]
502 . . . . 1.06[8]
503 . . . . 1.06[8]
511 . . . . 1.06[8]; **5** n.5; 10.05[2][c]; 15.02[3][b]
512(b)(1) **1** n.108
512(b)(13) **1** n.108
512(c)(1) **1** n.107
512(e)(1) **S6** n.21
512(e)(2) **S6** n.21
521 . . . . . 5.05[7][a]; **5** n.196; **S8** n.254.10; **13**
                                                    n.215
527 . . . . 1.06[9]
531 . . . . . . 1.02; 1.05[1][a]; S1.08[4]; **S1** n.15;
          2.06; **3** n.111; 5.08[5]; 5.09[1]; 5.09[2];
          5 ns. 9, 10, 377, 385; 6.11; **6** n.80; 7.01;
          S7.01; 7.02; 7.02[1]; 7.02[2]; 7.02[4];
          7.02[5]; 7.03[6]; 7.05; 7.07; 7.08[1];
          7.08[3]; 7.09; 7.09[3]; 7.10; S7.20;
          S7.24[4]; **7** ns. 7, 13, 14, 25, 26, 30, 51,
          55, 74, 87, 105, 108, 111, 124, 145, 146,
          156, 163, 168, 171, 179, 197; **S7** ns. 1,
          3.1, 3.2, 59, 67, 114, 198.1; **8** n.277; **11**
          n.187; 12.64[1][a]; 13.22[1][a];
          13.42[2][b]; 13.42[9]; **13** ns. 301, 563;
          14 n.5; 15.02[3][b]; 15.04[1][a];
          15.21[1][a]; 15.41[1]; 15.40[4];
          15.41[2][b]; 15.45[1]; 15.45[2]; 15.45[3];
          15.62[5][a]; **15** ns. 335, 387, 388, 413,
          418, 428, 462, 464, 467, 648
531(a) 7.08
532 . . . . 7.02[2]; **7** n.7
532(a) . . . . 7.02[1]; 7.02[2]; **7** n.31
532(b) . . . . 7.08[3]; **7** n.18
532(b)(1) . . . . 7.08[3]; **7** n.194
532(b)(2) . . . . 7.08[3]
532(b)(4) . . . . 7.08[3]; 15.44[4]
532(c) . . . . . . 5.09[2]; 7.02[1]; 7.08[3]; **7** n.26
533 . . . . 7.05
533(a) . . . **3** n.108; 7.02[5]; 7.03[1]; 7.06; 7.07;
          7.08[1]; 7.08[2]; 7.08[3]; **7** ns. 9, 62; **14**
                                                    n.155
533(b) . . . . 7.08[3]; **7** n.8
534 . . . 7.08[1]; 7.08[2]; 7.08[3]; **7** ns. 12, 157,
                                                    158
534(a)(1) . . . . 7.08[2]
534(a)(2) . . . . 7.08[2]; **7** n.160
534(b) **7** n.157
534(c) . . . . 7.08[2]; **7** n.158
535 . . . . 6.11; 7.03[1]; 7.09; **7** ns. 13, 62, 171,
          175; **8** ns. 107, 147; 15.22; 15.45[1]
535(a) **7** n.176
535(b) . . . . 13.42[9]
535(b)(1) **7** n.171
535(b)(2) **7** n.172
535(b)(3) **7** n.173
535(b)(4) **7** n.173
535(b)(5) **7** n.172
535(b)(6) **7** n.174
535(b)(7)(B) **7** n.173

IRC §

535(b)(8) **7** n.175
535(c) . . . . 7.03[1]; 7.09; 7.09[3]; **7** n.15
535(c)(1) . . . . 7.02[5]; 7.06; 7.08[2]; **7** ns. 87,
                                                    187
535(c)(2) . . . . . . **2** n.179; **7** n.186; 14.41[2][b]
535(c)(2)(B) . . . . 7.09[3]; **7** n.186; **13** n.17
535(c)(3) . . . . 7.09[3]
535(d) . . . . 15.45[2]
537 . . . . 7.04; **7** n.112
537(a) 7.04
537(a)(1) **7** n.10
537(a)(2) **9** n.302
537(b) 7.04
537(b)(1)–537(b)(3) **7** n.139
537(b)(4) **7** n.98; 15.22
541 . . . . . 1.02; 1.05[1][a]; S1.08[4]; **S1** n.16; **3**
          n.111; 5.08[5]; 5.09[1]; 5.09[2]; **5** ns. 10,
          377, 385; 6.11; **6** n.80; 7.01; S7.01;
          7.10; 7.14; 7.14[2]; S7.20; S7.24[4]; **7**
          ns. 193, 197; **S7** ns. 1, 3.1, 3.2, 198.1,
          229; **8** n.277; **10** n.43; 13.42[2][b];
          13.42[9]; **13** n.301; **14** n.5; 15.04[1][a];
          15.21[1][a]; 15.40[4]; 15.41[2][b]; 15.42;
          15.44[4]; **15** ns. 335, 388, 413, 418, 428,
          437, 438, 439, 467
542(a) 7.10
542(a)(1) 7.11; **7** n.200
542(a)(2) . . . . . 5.03[6]; 5.09[3]; **5** ns. 56, 392;
                                                    7.11; 7.13
542(b) . . . . . **7** n.200; **8** n.301; **13** ns. 565, 566
542(b)(1) **7** n.200; **13** n.565
542(b)(2) **13** n.565
542(b)(4) . . . . **7** n.200; **13** ns. 566, 430
542(c) **7** n.193
542(c)(2) . . . . **7** n.209; 15.41[1]; **15** n.437
542(c)(6) **7** n.209
542(c)(7) . . . . 15.04[1][a]; 15.41[1]; 15.42; **15**
                                                    n.130
542(c)(8) **7** n.209
542(c)(10) . . . . 15.44[4]
542(d) . . . . **7** ns. 193, 209
543(a) 7.12
543(a)(1) . . . . . 7.12[1]; 7.12[6]; **7** ns. 204, 208
543(a)(2) . . . . 7.12[1]; 7.12[2]; **7** n.214
543(a)(3) 7 n.218; **15** n.438
543(a)(4) **7** n.219
543(a)(5) **7** n.221
543(a)(6) . . . . 7.12[2]; 7.12[6]
543(a)(6)(A) . . . . 7.12[6]; **7** n.223
543(a)(6)(B) . . . . 7.12[6]; **7** n.225
543(a)(7) . . . . . . 7.12[7]; 7.14[1]; 15.42
543(a)(8) **7** n.236
543(b) 7.11
543(b)(1)(C) **15** n.130
543(b)(2)(B) . . . . 7.12[3]; **7** n.218
543(b)(2)(C) . . . . 7.12[1]
543(b)(3) . . . . . . 7.12[2]; **7** ns. 213, 216, 217
543(b)(4) **7** n.218
543(d) . . . . 7.12[1]
544 . . . 5.09[3]; 7.13; **9** ns. 38, 42; **10** n.738; **15**
                                      n.426; **15** n.438

[Text references are to paragraphs; note references are to chapters (boldface numbers) and notes ("n."), and references to the supplement are preceded by "S."]

[Text references are to paragraphs; note references are to chapters (boldface numbers) and notes ("n."), and references to the supplement are preceded by "S."]

[Text references are to paragraphs; note references are to chapters (boldface numbers) and notes ("n."), and references to the supplement are preceded by "S."]

IRC §

877 . . . . **15** n.1037
881 . . . . **5** ns. 11, 181; **9** ns. 409, 410; **14** n.73;
15.01[1]; 15.02[3][a]; 15.03[1]; 15.03[4];
15.03[5]; 15.03[7]; 15.04[1][a];
15.04[1][c]; 15.04[5]; 15.40[4]; 15.60[1];
15.83[2][a]; 15.84[2][e]; **15** ns. 206, 208,
212, 221, 223, 224, 229, 254, 574, 861;
S15 ns. 41, 227.1
881(a) . . . . 5.04[2]; **6** n.80; 15.02[3][b];
15.02[3][c]; 15.04[2][c]; 15.03[5]; **15**
n.218
881(a)(1) . . . . 15.03[3]; 15.03[4]
881(a)(3) **15** n.46
881(a)(3)(A) **15** n.228
881(a)(3)(B) **15** n.229
881(a)(4) . . . . **15** ns. 62, 230, 231
881(c) **4** n.7
881(c) . . . . **15** ns. 211, 214
881(c)(1) . . . . 15.03[2]
881(c)(2) . . . . 15.03[2]
881(c)(3) . . . . 15.03[2]
881(c)(4) . . . . 15.03[2]
881(d) . . . . . 15.02[1][a]; 15.03[2]; 15.03[3]; **15**
n.220
881(e)(1) **S15** n.214.1
881(e)(2) **S15** n.214.2
882 . . . . **5** n.11; **13** n.108; **14** n.73; 15.02[3][a];
15.02[3][b]; 15.02[3][c]; 15.02[3][d];
15.02[3][e]; 15.04[1][a]; 15.04[1][b];
15.04[1][c]; 15.04[2][f]; 15.04[3];
15.04[5]; 15.40[4]; 15.60[1]; 15.83[2][a];
15.84[2][e]; 15.85[5][d]; 15.85[7][d]; **15**
ns. 223, 246, 254, 267, 288, 574, 795
882(a) . . . . 15.04[1][a]
882(c) **5** n.181
882(c)(1) . . . . 15.04[1][a]
882(c)(2) . . . . **13** n.109; 15.04[1][a]
882(c)(3) . . . . 15.04[1][a]
882(d) . . . 15.02[2][c]; 15.04[1][a]; 15.04[1][b];
15 ns. 250, 254
883(a) **15** n.105
884 . . . . **5** n.11; 15.02[1][a]; 15.04[2][a];
15.04[2][b]; 15.04[2][e]; 15.04[3];
15.84[2][e]; S15.84[3][f]; 15.85[1][c];
15.85[5][a]; 15.85[5][b]; 15.85[5][c];
15.85[5][d]; **15** ns. 255, 261, 266, 268,
269, 788, 951, 987, 998, 1007, 1008,
1010, 1012, 1013
884(a) . . . . 15.04[2][d]
884(b) . . . . 15.04[2][a]
884(b)(1) **15** n.788
884(d) . . . . 15.04[2][a]
884(e) . . . . 15.85[3][c]; **15** n.261
884(e)(1) . . . . 15.04[2][a]
884(e)(3)(A) . . . . 15.04[2][d]
884(e)(3)(B) . . . . 15.04[2][c]
884(e)(4) . . . . **15** ns. 179, 185
884(e)(4)(A)(i) . . . . 15.04[2][a]
884(e)(4)(A)(ii) . . . . 15.04[2][a]
884(f)　　 15.04[2][e]; 15.04[4]; 15.04[5]; **15** ns.
37, 261, 267, 268, 279
884(f)(1) . . . . 15.04[2][c]
884(f)(1)(A) **15** n.268
884(f)(1)(B) . . . . . 15.04[2][c]; **15** ns. 267, 268
884(f)(3) . . . . **15** ns. 179, 185, 267
884(g) **15** n.951
885(g)(2) **15** n.75
887 . . . . **15** n.105
891(i) **15** n.967
894 . . . . 15.82[3]; **15** n.221
894(a) . . . . **15** ns. 174, 175
894(b) . . . . 15.03[1]; **15** n.149
894(c) . . . 15.02[4][g]; 15.03[7]; **15** ns. 16, 32,
186, 187, 191, 240
894(c)(1) . . . . . 15.02[4][h]; 15.03[7]; **15** n.242
894(c)(2) . . . 15.02[4][h]; 15.03[7]; **15** ns. 186,
242
894(e)(4) **15** n.186
897 . . . . 12.40[1]; **12** n.604; 15.02[2][c];
S15.81[3][h]; 15.82[3]; S15.85;
15.85[1][a]; 15.85[1][b]; 15.85[2][a];
15.85[2][b]; 15.85[2][d]; 15.85[2][f];
15.85[3][a]; 15.85[3][c]; 15.85[3][d];
15.85[4]; 15.85[5][a]; 15.85[5][d]; **15** ns.
136, 150, 252, 254, 798, 800, 801, 929,
949, 960, 963, 957, 967, 971, 976, 979,
980, 985, 988, 994, 995, 996, 998, 1001,
1007**S15** n.741.19
897(a) . . . . 15.85[2][a]
897(a)(1) . . . 15.02[2][c]; 15.85[1][a]; **15** n.948
897(a)(1)(B) . . . . 15.04[1][b]
897(c) . . . 15.85[1][a]; 15.85[2][a]; 15.02[2][c];
15 n.814
897(c)(1)(A)(ii) . . . . . . 15.85[2][a]; **15** n.948
897(c)(1)(B) . . . 15.85[2][a]; 15.85[4]; **15** n.948
897(c)(2) . . . . 15.02[2][c]
897(d) . . . . . . **8** n.357; 15.85[1][a]; 15.85[2][a];
15.85[2][c]; 15.85[3][d]; 15.85[4];
15.85[6][a]; 15.85[7][a]; **15** ns. 253, 949
897(d)(1) . . . . 15.85[1][a]; 15.85[2][c];
15.85[2][f]; 15.85[4]; **15** ns. 253, 905,
948, 961
897(d)(2) . . . . 15.85[1][a]; 15.85[2][d];
15.85[2][f]; 15.85[4]; **15** ns. 962, 975,
1001
897(d)(2)(A) . . . . . 15.85[2][d]; 15.85[2][f]; **15**
n.1026
897(e) . . . 15.85[1][a]; 15.85[2][a]; 15.85[3][a];
15.85[3][c]; 15.85[3][d]; 15.85[4];
15.85[6][a]; 15.85[7][a]; **15** ns. 253, 929,
949, 971
897(d)(2)(A)(ii) . . . . 15.85[4]; **15** n.988
897(e)(1) . . . . 15.85[2][b]; 15.85[2][f];
15.85[3][a]; 15.85[3][b]; 15.85[4]; **15** ns.
787, 798, 929, 960, 975, 997, 1025
897(e)(2) . . . 15.85[1][a]; 15.85[3][c]; 15.85[4]
897(f) . . . . **8** ns. 357, 376; **15** n.948
897(i) . . . 15.85[2][b]; 15.85[2][f]; 15.85[3][b];
15.85[3][c]; 15.85[4]; **15** ns. 948, 967,
980, 996, 1003
898 . . . . 15.61[1]; **15** n.492

[Text references are to paragraphs; note references are to chapters (boldface numbers) and notes ("n."), and references to the supplement are preceded by "S."]

IRC §

899 . . . . 15.02[2][c]; **15** ns. 16, 140, 138, 225, 253, 798
899(b) **15** n.139
899(d) **15** n.139
899(e) . . . . **15** ns. 139, 225
901–904 . . . . 15.20[2][a]
901–906 . . . . 5.05[4][b]
901–908 . . . . 15.21[1]
901 . . . . 6.06[2][b]; 6.06[3]; 15.21[1][a]; 15.21[1][b]; **15** ns. 306, 309, 311, 312; **S15** ns. 304, 305.1, 310, 311, 573
901(b) **15** n.302
901(b)(1) . . . . 15.04[1][a]
901(b)(4) . . . . 15.04[1][a]
901(f) **15** n.303
901(g) **15** n.391
901(i) . . . . . . 15.21[3]; **15** ns. 303, 311, 355
901(j) . . . . 15.21[3]; **15** n.303
901(j)(2)(C) **15** n.355
901(k) . . . . 5.10[6][e]; **5** ns. 481, 565; S15.21[1][c]; 15.21[1][d]; **15** ns. 315, 338
901(k)(2) **15** n.323
901(*l*) . . . . S15.21[1][c]; **S15** ns. 316.1, 316.3
902 . . . 5.05[4][b]; **5** n.192; **9** n.408; **12** n.1019; **13** n.233; 15.01[2]; S15.01[2]; 15.20[2][b]; S15.21[2]; 15.21[2][a]; 15.21[2][b]; 15.21[2][c]; 15.21[2][e]; 15.21[2][f]; 15.21[2][g]; 15.21[5][c]; 15.22; 15.60[1]; 15.61[3]; 15.63[1]; S15.84[2][f]; 15.85[7][d]; **15** ns. 323–327, 329, 332, 333, 337–341, 345, 361, 364.1, 372, 378, 387, 429, 481, 560, 1043, 1044; **S15** ns. 304, 323, 330, 361, 364.1, 573, 741.4, 902.5
902(a)(1) . . . . . **8** n.79; 15.21[2][e]; **15** n.337
902(b) . . . . 15.21[2][b]; **15** ns. 326, 451
902(b)(3) . . . . **12** n.1019; 15.21[2][b]
902(c)(1) **15** n.331
902(c)(1)(B) **15** n.332
902(c)(3)(A) **15** n.323
903 . . . 15.21[1][a]; 15.21[2][f]; 15.21[3]; 15.22; **S15** n.310**15** ns. 106, 118, 342
904 . . . . **14** n.110; **S15** n.106
904(a) . . . . **5** n.335; 15.21[3]; S15.21[3]; 15.21[4]; **15** ns. 342, 349, 366; **S15** n.349
904(b) . . . . S15.21[3]; **S15** n.347
904(b)(2) . . . . 15.21[3]
904(b)(2)(A) **15** n.347
904(b)(2)(B) **15** n.347; **S15** n.348.1
904(b)(3) . . . . 15.21[3]
904(b)(3)(E) **15** n.347
904(b)(4) . . . . 15.21[3]; 15.22
904(c) . . . . . . 15.01[2]; S15.01[2]; 15.20[2][b]; 15.21[3]; S15.84[3][f]; **15** ns. 13, 296, 343, 358, 366,

IRC §

904(d) . . . . 14.20[2]; **14** n.110; 15.01[2]; S15.01[2]; 15.20[2][b]; 15.21[3]; S15.21[3]; 15.21[4]; S15.21[4]; 15.44[1]; S15.80[8]; S15.84[2][f]; **15** ns. 76, 352, 357, 361, 364, 365; **S15** ns. 346, 355.5, 356, 357, 364.1, 489.1
904(d)(1) . . . . 15.21[4]; **15** n.345
904(d)(1)(E) **S15** n.902.8
904(d)(2) . . . . 15.21[4]
904(d)(2)(A) . . . . . **11** n.83; 15.21[4]; **15** n.345
904(d)(2)(B) . . . . 15.21[4]; **15** n.345
904(d)(2)(B)(v) **S15** n.355.4
904(d)(2)(C) . . . . 15.21[4]
904(d)(2)(C)(ii) **15** n.360
904(d)(2)(E) . . . . 15.21[4]
904(d)(2)(F) . . . . 15.21[4]
904(d)(3) . . . . S15.01[2]; 15.21[3]; 15.21[4]; **15** ns. 13, 296, 352, 361; **S15** n.495
904(d)(4) **S15** n.361
904(f) . . . . . 13.45[6][c]; **13** n.793; 15.21[3]; 15.80[5]; **15** n.349
904(f)(3) . . . . 15.21[3]; 15.81[1][c]
904(g) . . . 15.21[3]; **15** ns. 349, 352; **S15** n.349
904(i) . . . . **13** n.329; **S13** ns. 23, 309; **15** ns. 118, 352; **S15** ns. 494, 571
905 . . . . 15.21[1][a]; 15.21[5]; **15** n.306
905(a) . . . . 15.21[5][a]
905(b) . . . . 15.21[5][b]
905(c) . . . . 15.21[5][c]; **15** ns. 377, 381
906 . . . . 15.04[1][a]
907 . . . . 15.21[3]; **15** ns. 211, 357
907(a) . . . . 15.21[3]
907(b) . . . . 15.21[3]
908 . . . . 15.21[3]; 15.24; **15** n.353
911 . . . . **6** n.42
911(d)(3) **15** n.179
921–927 . . . . 15.23[1]; **15** n.290
921 . . . . . . 15.04[1][a]; **15** n.561; **S15** n.407.15
921(a) . . . . 15.23[3][f]
921(b) . . . . 15.23[3][e]; 15.23[3][f]
921(c) . . . . 15.23[3][e]; 15.23[3][f]
921(d) . . . . 15.23[3][f]
921(d)(1)(B) . . . . 15.23[3][f]
922 . . . . **15** n.561
922(a) . . . . 15.23[3][a]
922(b) . . . . 15.23[3][b]
923 . . . . 15.23[3][e]; 15.23[3][f]
924(a) . . . . 15.23[3][d]
924(a)(5) **15** n.401
924(b)(2) . . . . 15.23[3][b]; **15** n.402
924(c) . . . . 15.23[3][d]; **15** n.403
924(d) . . . . 15.23[3][d]; **15** n.404
924(e) . . . . **15** ns. 404, 405
925 . . . . . . 15.23[3][e]; 15.23[3][f]; **15** n.407
925(a) **15** n.405
926(a) . . . . 15.23[3][f]
926(b) . . . . 15.23[3][f]
927(a) . . . . 15.23[3][c]
927(a)(2) . . . . 15.23[3][c]; **15** n.400
927(c)(2) 15.24
927(e)(1) **15** n.405

[Text references are to paragraphs; note references are to chapters (boldface numbers) and notes ("n."), and references to the supplement are preceded by "S."]

IRC §

927(e)(3) **15** n.398
931 . . . . 15.22; **15** ns. 385, 387
936 . . . . . . 6.02[5]; **S11** ns. 82, 83; 13.41[1];
15.20[1][a]; 15.21[3]; 15.22; **15** ns. 39,
385, 391; **S15** n.394
936(a) 15.22
936(a)(1) **13** n.310
936(a)(2) 15.22
936(a)(2)(B) **11** n.83
936(a)(3) **15** n.388
936(b) **15** n.389
936(c) 15.22
936(d)(2) 15.22
936(e) 15.22
936(g)(1) 15.22
936(g)(2) 15.22
936(h) 15.22; **15** n.390
936(h)(3)(B) . . . . 13.21[5][b]
936(j) **15** n.394; **S15** n.394
951–964 . . . . **6** n.7; 15.64[2]; **15** n.490
951 . . . . . 13.01[3][c]; 15.02[3][e]; 15.21[2][e];
15.40[4]; 15.41[2][b]; 15.61[2]; 15.61[3];
S15.61[3]; 15.63[1]; 15.63[3]; 15.65[2];
15.65[3]; 15.80[4][c]; S15.85[6][b]; **15**
ns. 212, 328, 336, 416, 418, 492, 541,
581, 643, 791; **S15** ns. 494, 497
951(a) . . . . S15.61[3]; 15.62[6]; 15.64[1]
951(a)(1) . . . . 15.62; 15.64[1]
951(a)(1)(A) . . . . 15.62[5][c]; **15** n.553
951(b) . . . . . 15.61[2]; 15.81[3][e]; **15** ns. 457,
881; **S15** n.497
951(c)(1)(A) **15** n.497
951(d) . . . 15.41[2][b]; S15.84[2][f]; **15** ns. 436,
541
952 . . . . S15.62[1]
953(d)(3) . . . . 1.05[2][e]
951(f) . . . . 15.44[4]
952–954 . . . . **15** ns. 14, 297
952 . . . . 15.62[1]; **15** ns. 14, 297, 488, 526
952(a)(3) 15.24
952(a)(4) . . . . 15.62[1]
952(c)(2) **15** n.497
952(d) **15** n.537
953 . . . . 15.62[1]
954 . . . . 13.01[3][c]; 15.62[1]; 15.62[2];
15.62[2][a]; 15.62[2][d]; 15.62[5][a];
15.62[5][c]; **15** ns. 515, 519, 526, 533,
553; **S15** n.530
954(b) **15** n.522
954(b)(3) . . . . 15.62[3]; 15.64[1]; **15** n.536
954(c) . . . . S15.62[2][a]; **S15** n.521
954(c)(2)(A) **11** n.83
954(b)(4) . . . . . 15.62[3]; 15.64[1]; **15** ns. 473,
534, 535, 535
954(c) . . . . **15** ns. 345, 521, 522, 532
954(c)(1) . . . . 15.62[2][a]
954(c)(1)(C) **S15** n.524.4
954(c)(1)(F) . . . . **15** ns. 521, 524, 532
954(c)(1)(G) . . . . **15** ns. 521, 532
954(c)(1)(H) . . . . . **S15** ns. 78, 101, 438, 524.2,
524.3

954(c)(1)(I) **S15** n.524.3
954(c)(6) **S15** n.524.4
954(d) . . . . . . **15** ns. 74, 527, 529; **S15** n.520
954(d)(2) . . . 15.62[2][b]; **15** ns. 262, 527, 556
954(d)(3) . . . . **15** ns. 217, 525, 526
954(d)(5) **15** n.926
954(e) . . . . . S15.62[2][c]; **15** n.529; **S15** n.520
954(f) . . . . 15.62[2][d]; **15** n.531
954(g) . . . . 15.62[2][d]
954(h) . . . . 15.62[2][a]; **15** ns. 523, 551
956 . . . . . 5.10[6][e]; 15.62[4][a]; S15.62[4][a];
15.62[5][a]; 15.62[5][b]; 15.62[5][c]; **15**
ns. 212, 538–543, 546, 553
956(c)(2)(F) **15** n.540
956(c)(2)(G) **15** n.540
956(c)(2)(H) **15** n.540
956(c)(2)(K) **15** n.540
956A . . . . . 15.45[3]; 15.62[5][a]; 15.62[5][b];
15.62[5][c]; **15** ns. 21, 514, 544, 553
956A(b) . . . . 15.62[5][b]
956A(c)(1) **15** n.545
956A(c)(1)(B) . . . . 15.62[5][b]
956A(c)(2)(A) **15** n.546
956A(c)(2)(B) **15** n.546
957 . . . . 15.61[2]; **15** n.496
957(a) . . . . 15.61[2]; **15** n.493
958 . . . . 15.61[2]; **15** ns. 689, 771, 830
958A(c) . . . . 15.62[5][b]
959 . . . . . 15.61[3]; 15.62[5][a]; **15** ns. 543, 553
959(a) . . . . 15.62[4][b]
959(a)(2) **15** n.543
959(e) . . . . **15** ns. 543, 560
959A . . . . 15.62[5][b]
960 . . . . 15.61[3]
961 . . . . 15.61[3]
961(c) . . . . 15.61[3]
962 . . . . 15.61[3]; 15.62[6]; 15.64[1]
963 . . . . **15** ns. 14, 297, 488
964 . . . . 15.21[2][f]
964(a) . . . . **8** n.124; **15** ns. 331, 491
964(c) **15** n.605
965 . . . . S15.62[8]; S15.62[8][a]; S15.62[8][b];
S15.62[8][c]; S15.62[8][d]; **S15** ns.
556.1, 556.4, 556.8
965(a)(2) **S15** n.556.6
965(b) . . . . S15.62[8][c]
965(b)(1) . . . . S15.62[8][c]
965(b)(4) **S15** n.556.3
965(c)(1) **S15** n.556.7
965(c)(2) **S15** n.556.9
965(c)(3) . . . . S15.62[8][c]; **S15** n.556.5
965(d) . . . . S15.62[8][d]
965(d)(1) . . . . S15.62[8][d]
965(d)(2) . . . . S15.62[8][d]
965(d)(3) . . . . S15.62[8][d]
965(e) . . . . S15.62[8][d]
965(e)(2)(A) . . . . S15.62[8][d]
982 . . . . **15** n.190
985–989 . . . . **15** n.196
985 . . . . 15.02[5][b]; **15** n.196
986 . . . . 15.02[5][b]; **15** n.327

[Text references are to paragraphs; note references are to chapters (boldface numbers) and notes ("n."), and references to the supplement are preceded by "S."]

*[Text references are to paragraphs; note references are to chapters (boldface numbers)
and notes ("n."), and references to the supplement are preceded by "S."]*

IRC §

1059(c)(4) **5** n.227
1059(d)(3) **5** n.216
1059(d)(5) **5** n.216
1059(d)(6) **5** n.217; **9** n.443
1059(e) **5** n.213; **9** n.443
1059(e)(1) . . . . . 5.05[8]; **5** ns. 217, 220, 222;
       9.03[4][a]; 9.09[4][d]; **9** ns. 103, 443
1059(e)(1)(A) **5** n.220; **9** n.237
1059(e)(1)(A)(iii) . . . . 9.09[4][d]; 9.09[6][g]; **9**
                   n.405**S9** ns. 373, 377.1
1059(e)(1)(A)(iii)(II) **9** n.405
1059(e)(1)(B) **5** n.222; **8** n.521
1059(e)(2) **5** n.218; **8** n.297
1059(e)(2)(B)(ii) **8** n.297
1059(e)(3) **5** n.219
1059(f) . . . . 4.03[8][a]; **5** n.221
1059(g) . . . . **5** ns. 221, 225; **5** n.225
1059A . . . . 13.21[6][b]
1060 . . . **3** ns. 154, 233; 5.06[2][c]; 5.10[4][b];
        5 ns. 283, 424; 10.04; 10.05[2][a];
     10.40[1]; 10.40[2]; 10.40[3]; 10.40[4][a];
     10.40[4][b]; 10.40[5]; 10.41[5][a];
     10.43[2][c]; 10.43[3]; **10** ns. 80, 82, 393,
        395, 397, 400, 436, 448, 461
1060(a) **3** n.79; **10** n.393
1060(c)(2) **10** n.105
1060(e) . . . . 10.40[5]
1071 . . . . 12.05[2]; **13** n.546
1081–1083 . . . . 12.05[2]
1087 . . . . **13** n.10
1091 . . . . . 8.03[3]; **8** n.88; 12.27[4][b]; **12** n.3
1092 . . . . 13.43[2][c]; **13** n.605
1102 . . . . **15** n.384
1105 . . . . **15** n.361
1123 . . . . **15** n.445
1131(b)(2) **15** n.637
1141–1145 . . . . **15** n.751
1162 . . . . **15** n.130
1171 . . . . **15** n.400
1201(a) . . . . . 5.01[2]; **5** n.5; **10** n.8; **12** n.1090
1202 . . . . 1.06[4]; **1** n.101; **5** n.6; **12** ns. 1090,
                                1098
1202(a) **15** n.340
1211 . . . . **4** n.192; 6.09[5]; 7.09[1]; 8.03[6]; **10**
                   n.229; **15** n.254
1211(a) . . . . . 5.01[2]; **5** n.41; **8** n.53; **10** n.96
1211(b) **1** n.21; **5** n.41; **10** n.7
1211(d) **15** n.77
1212 . . . 6.09[5]; **6** n.122; 8.03[4]; 15.21[3]; **15**
                                n.254
1212(a) . . . . 5.01[2]; **5** n.42; 14.21[2]
1212(a)(1) **10** n.97
1212(b) **10** n.7
1221 . . . . 4.21; **4** n.226; **5** n.19; 6.11; 10.03[1];
             13 n.393; **14** ns. 150, 232
1221(1) . . . . . 4.21; **4** n.201; **5** n.43; **10** ns. 69,
                                709
1221(2) **15** n.156
1221(4) **3** n.52; 4.21
1221(a)–1222(4) **15** n.156
1221(b)(2) **S15** n.524.4

IRC §

1222 . . . . . 3.03[1]; **3** n.57; 4.21; 4.22[1]; **4** ns.
       209, 222, 223, 232; 8.22[1]; **8** n.351;
       10.03[1]; 10.03[2]; 10.04; **15** n.156
1222(3) . . . . **4** ns. 224, 226
1222(10) **5** n.42
1223 . . . . 8.41[5]; **S8** n.254.13; 9.25; **10** n.708
1223(1) . . . . 3.10[4]; **3** ns. 227, 248; **S8**
             n.254.15; 11.12[2]; **S12** n.782.5
1223(2) . . . . 3.11[6]; **3** n.248; **10** n.330;
                   11.12[3]; **12** n.724
1223(5) . . . . 8.41[4]; 8.42[1]
1231 . . . . . **3** ns. 84, 137, 227, 248; **S3** n.83;
       6.09[5]; **7** n.201; 10.62[4][a]; **10** n.97;
     13.42[1][b]; 13.42[2][b]; **13** ns. 393, 785;
                14.41[2][b]; **15** ns. 76, 156
1235(a) **15** n.62
1231(a)(2) **3** n.84
1231(b) . . . . . 3.10[4]; 7.11; 10.62[4][a]; 10.65
1231(c) **7** n.201
1232 . . . . 12.27[4][b]
1232(b) **12** n.448
1232(b)(4) . . . . **12** ns. 448, 456
1232A . . . . 12.27[4][b]
1234 . . . . **3** n.253; 4.62[3]; 4.62[4]; **4** n.439; **5**
             n.183; **7** n.201; **8** n.196; 12.66[6]
1234(a) **4** n.442
1234(b) **12** n.1186
1235 . . . . **3** n.57
1235(a) . . . . 4.43[4]
1236 . . . . 4.21; **4** n.193
1239 . . . 1.05[1][a]; 3.05[3]; **3** ns. 84, 85, 137;
       5.04[2]; 6.06[7]; **7** n.201; **8** n.352; **10** ns.
       97, 677; 13.01[4][b]; 13.23[1]; 13.23[4]
1241 . . . . **7** n.201; **15** n.156
1242 . . . . 1.06[4]
1243 . . . . 1.06[4]
1244 . . . . . 1.06[4]; 1.07[3]; **1** n.102; 3.18[1]; **3**
       n.306; 4.01[4]; 4.21; 4.23[2]; 4.25;
       4.25[1]; 4.25[2]; 4.25[3]; 4.25[4];
       4.25[5]; 4.25[6]; 4.25[7]; 4.25[8];
     4.25[9]; **4** ns. 242, 270, 273, 275, 277,
             282, 287, 289; 5.09[1]; 6.09[3][b];
     6.09[5]; 6.10[3][c]; **6** ns. 241, 267, 271,
             311; 12.30[4][a]; **12** n.575
1244(a) . . . . 4.25[7]
1244(b) . . . . 4.25[8]
1244(c)(1) **4** n.279
1244(c)(1)(A) **4** n.273
1244(c)(1)(B) . . . . 4.25[6]
1244(c)(1)(C) . . . . 4.25[4]
1244(c)(2)(C) **4** n.278
1244(c)(3) **4** n.275
1244(c)(3)(A) . . . . 4.25[9]
1244(c)(3)(B) **4** n.274
1244(d)(1) **4** n.279
1244(d)(1)(A) . . . . 4.25[9]
1244(d)(1)(B) . . . . 4.25[9]
1244(d)(2) . . . . 4.25[6]; **12** n.511
1244(d)(3) . . . . 4.25[8]
1244(d)(4) . . . . 4.25[2]

[Text references are to paragraphs; note references are to chapters (boldface numbers) and notes ("n."), and references to the supplement are preceded by "S."]

IRC §

1245 . . . . 3.05[3]; **3** ns. 86, 137, 227, 364;
5.03[7]; **7** n.201; **8** n.357; **10** ns. 97,
675; 12.30[5][c]; 12.30[5][e]; 12.40[1];
12.46; S13.42[12][c]; **S13** n.574.12; **15**
ns. 156, 560
1245(b) 4.45
1245(b)(3) **3** n.371; **12** n.603
1246 . . . . . **7** n.201; 15.40[4]; 15.43; 15.44[4];
15.46[1]; **15** n.418
1246(a)(3) 15.43
1246(b) . . . . S8.06[2][b]; **15** ns. 442, 791
1246(c) **15** n.443
1246(e) . . . . 15.44[3]; **15** n.443
1247 . . . . 15.43; 15.46[1]
1248 . . . . . . **8** ns. 351, 357; **10** n.5; 12.46; **13**
n.607; 15.40[4]; 15.60[3]; 15.63[1];
15.63[2][a]; 15.63[2][b]; 15.63[3];
S15.63[3]; 15.64[2]; 15.65[1]; 15.65[2];
15.80[4][c]; 15.81[3][d]; 15.81[3][e];
S15.81[3][h]; 15.82[2][b]; 15.82[3];
15.84[1][a]; 15.84[1][b]; 15.84[1][c];
15.84[1][d]; 15.84[1][e]; 15.84[2][b];
15.84[2][c]; 15.84[2][d]; 15.84[2][e];
15.84[3][a]; 15.84[3][c]; 15.84[3][d];
15.84[3][e]; **15** ns. 328, 543, 558, 559,
560, 561, 563, 566, 583, 628, 648, 724,
729, 733, 734, 761; 825, 826, 830, 942,
857, 879, 882, 885, 898, 914, 918, 922,
1026; **S15** ns. 498, 556.5, 567.2, 741.4
1248(a) **7** n.204; **15** n.563
1248(b) . . . . 15.63[1]; **15** n.561
1248(c) . . . . 15.83[1][a]
1248(d) . . . . 15.83[1][a]
1248(e) . . . . 1.07[8]; **10** n.672; **15** n.567
1248(f) . . . . 15.63[2][b]; 15.64[2]; 15.84[3][e];
15 n.567
1248(f)(1) . . . . 15.63[2][a]; **15** n.918
1248(f)(2) . . . . S15.63[2][a]; **15** ns. 563, 1026;
S15 ns. 558, 563, 923
1248(i) . . . . **9** ns. 392, 464; **12** n.956;
15.63[2][b]; S15.63[2][b]; 15.64[2]
1249 . . . . 12.46
1250 . . . . 3.05[3]; **3** ns. 137, 227, 364; 5.03[7];
7 n.201; **8** n.357; **10** ns. 97, 675;
12.30[5][c]; 12.30[5][e]; 12.40[1]; 12.46;
15 n.156
1250(d)(3) **12** n.603
1252 . . . . **8** n.357
1253 . . . . **7** n.211; **10** ns. 443, 675; **15** ns. 62,
63
1253(d) **10** n.443
1253(d)(1) . . . . 10.40[6]; **10** n.443
1254 . . . . **8** n.357
1256 . . . . **8** n.410; **12** n.1
1259 . . . . **12** n.72
1261 . . . . **15** n.196
1271–1275 . . . . . . 4.21; **4** n.352; 12.27[4][b]
1271 . . . **3** n.72; **4** ns. 128, 232; 12.27[5][a]; **12**
n.756; **15** n.156

IRC §

1271(a)(1) . . . . **3** ns. 55, 61, 72; 4.22[1]; **4** ns.
11, 209, 210, 416; **7** n.208; 8.23[3]; **10**
n.47
1271(a)(2) . . . . **4** ns. 212, 366
1271(b) **4** n.207
1271(c)(1) **4** n.12
1271(c)(2) **4** n.12
1272–1274 . . . . 4.43[6]
1272–1275 . . . . 7.12[1]; **12** n.443
1272 . . . 4.26[3][d]; 4.41[4]; 4.42[2]; 4.42[2][a];
4.42[4]; 4.43[2]; 4.43[3]; 4.43[6]; 4.45;
4.61[2]; 4.61[5]; 4.61[6]; **4** n.349;
6.10[4][c]; **6** ns. 251, 284; 8.41[2][c];
12.27[5][d]; 12.41[3]; 12.41[4]; 12.41[5];
12.66[2][b]; **12** ns. 412, 756; 15.02[1][b]
1272(a) . . . . 4.42[1]; 4.62[3]; 8.41[2][c]
1272(a)(1) **8** n.401
1272(a)(2)(C) **4** n.376
1272(a)(3) . . . . 4.42[1]; 4.42[3]
1272(a)(3)(A) . . . . 4.42[3]
1272(a)(4) **4** n.388
1272(a)(7) 4.42[4]; **4** ns. 368, 419; **12** n.447
1272(b) **4** n.345
1272(c) **4** n.419; **12** n.447
1272(c)(1) . . . . 4.42[4]; **4** n.368
1272(d)(1) **4** n.376
1272(d)(2) . . . . 4.42[3]
1273–1274 . . . . **4** n.419
1273 . . . . . . 4.26[1]; 4.43[3]; 4.43[7]; 4.61[4];
5.09[4]; 6.10[4][b]; 12.27[4][b];
12.27[4][c]; 12.66[2][b]; **12** n.481
1273(a) **4** n.352
1273(a)(1) **8** n.401
1273(a)(2) . . . . 4.42[2][b]; **4** n.353
1273(a)(3) . . . . . **4** n.352; 8.41[2][c]; **8** n.459
1273(b) **4** n.371
1273(b)(1) . . . . 4.42[2][c]; 4.43[3][b]
1273(b)(2) . . . . 4.42[2][c]; 4.62[3]
1273(b)(3) . . . . . . **2** n.116; 4.43[2]; 4.43[3][b];
4.43[4]; 4.43[7]; **8** n.401; **12** ns. 450,
460, 728, 756
1273(b)(4) **8** n.402; **12** n.463
1273(b)(5) **4** n.371
1273(c)(2) . . . . . 4.42[2][c]; 4.43[3][b]; 4.62[3]
1274 . . . . **3** ns. 210, 269; 4.26[1]; 4.43[3];
4.43[3][b]; 4.43[4]; 4.43[5]; 4.43[6];
4.43[7]; 4.61[4]; 4.61[5]; **4** ns. 362, 371,
375, 376, 383, 385, 427; 5.09[4];
6.10[4][b]; **9** n.107; **10** n.49; 12.23[10];
12.27[4][b]; 12.27[4][c]; **12** ns. 444, 451,
457, 463, 481, 485, 756, 1113, 1150,
1151; 13.21[2]; 13.23[4]; **13** ns. 254,
288
1274(a)(2) . . . . . 4.43[3]; 4.43[3][b]; **12** n.483
1274(a)(4) **12** n.483
1274(b)(3) . . . . 4.43[3][b]; **4** ns. 373, 381, 383;
6.10[4][b]; **6** n.285; **12** ns. 457, 484
1274(c) . . . . 4.43[3]; 4.43[3][b]
1274(c)(1)(B) **4** n.376
1274(c)(2) . . . . 6.10[4][b]
1274(c)(3) . . . . 4.43[4]

[Text references are to paragraphs; note references are to chapters (boldface numbers) and notes ("n."), and references to the supplement are preceded by "S."]

IRC §

1274(c)(4) **4** n.376
1274(c)(4)(C) **4** n.427
1274(d) . . . . 8.05[6]; **8** n.212; 14.42[2];
14.44[1][b]
1274(e) **4** n.376
1274(e)(3)(D) **4** n.382
1274A . . . . 4.43[3][a]; 4.43[5]
1274A(a) **4** n.383
1274A(b) . . . . 4.43[6]; **4** ns. 379, 383
1274A(c)(4) **4** n.383
1274A(d)(1) . . . . 4.43[3][a]
1275 . . . . **12** n.1150
1275(a) . . . . 4.03[5]
1275(a)(1) . . . 4.22[1]; 4.42[2]; 12.66[2][b]; **12**
n.1112
1275(a)(4) . . . . . . 4.43[7]; **4** n.387; **8** n.401;
12.27[4][b]; 12.27[4][c]; 12.28[1]; **12** ns.
452, 456, 457, 459, 756
1275(d) **12** n.1151
1276 . . . . 4.22[1]; 4.41[4]; 4.45; **4** ns. 12, 197,
352; **10** n.49; **12** n.748; 15.02[1][b]; **15**
n.229
1276(a)(1) . . . . **4** n.403; **12** ns. 413, 756
1276(a)(2) 4.45
1276(a)(3) **12** n.413
1276(a)(4) . . . . **7** ns. 201, 208; **12** n.756; **15** n.47
1276(b)(1) **12** n.412
1276(c) **4** n.403
1276(c)(2) **12** n.748
1276(c)(2)(A) **12** n.445
1276(c)(2)(B) . . . . 6.10[4][c]; **12** n.413
1276(d)(1) . . . . **4** n.403; 6.10[4][c]
1276(d)(1)(A) 4.45
1276(d)(1)(B) . . . 12.27[4][b]; **12** ns. 413, 445,
748
1276(d)(1)(C) . . . . **3** ns. 53, 364, 371; **4** n.403
1277 . . . . **4** n.401
1278 . . . . 4.45
1278(a)(1)(C) **11** n.335
1278(a)(1)(C)(i) **3** n.210
1278(a)(1)(C)(ii)(I) **8** n.402
1278(a)(1)(D) **4** n.402
1278(a)(2)(A) **11** n.335
1278(a)(2)(B) 4.45
1278(b) **4** n.401
1281 . . . . **4** ns. 396, 397
1283(a)(1)(A) **4** n.396
1286 . . . . . . **4**.21; 4.44[1]; 4.44[2]; **5** n.565; **8**
n.255
1286(a) . . . . 4.44[1]; **4** ns. 397, 398
1286(b) . . . . 4.44[1]
1286(e) . . . . 4.44[1]
1286(e)(2) **4** n.196
1286(e)(3) **4** n.196
1287 . . . . 4.21
1287(a) **4** n.29
1291–1297 . . . . . 15.46[1]; 15.44[4]; **15** n.411

IRC §

1291 . . . . S8.06[2][b]; 15.40[4]; 15.44[3];
15.45[3]; 15.46[1]; 15.46[3][b];
15.46[3][c]; 15.85[6][b]; 15.85[6][c]; **15**
ns. 417, 418, 449, 472, 477, 1023, 1028,
1029, 1033
1291(a) . . . . 15.46[3][b]
1291(c) **15** n.476
1291(d) **15** n.476
1291(e) . . . . 15.44[3]
1291(f) . . . S15.81[3][h]; 15.85[1][c]; S15.85[6];
15.85[6][a]; 15.85[6][b]; 15.85[6][c];
15.85[7][a]; **15** ns. 1023, 1036
1292 . . . . 15.46[3][c]
1292(a) . . . . 15.46[3][a]
1292(b) . . . . 15.46[3][a]; **15** n.468
1292(b)(1) . . . . 15.46[3][a]
1292(b)(3) . . . . 15.46[3][a]; **15** n.473
1293 . . . . 15.44[3]; 15.46[3][c]; 15.85[6][b]; **15**
ns. 328, 477, 1023
1294 . . . . **15** n.477
1295 . . . . 15.44[3]; 15.44[4]; 15.85[6][b]
1296 . . . . 15.44[2]; 15.44[3]; 15.46[2];
15.62[5][b]; **15** ns. 446, 452, 547; **S15**
n.476
1296(a) . . . . 15.44[1]; **15** n.445
1296(a)(3) . . . . 15.46[2]
1296(b) . . . . 15.62[5][a]
1296(b)(1) . . . . 15.44[1]
1296(b)(2) . . . . 15.44[1]
1297 . . . . 15.44[2]; **15** ns. 446, 452
1297(b)(6) **15** n.542
1297(b)(7) . . . . 15.44[4]
1297(c) . . . . 15.46[3][b]
1297(e) . . . **15** ns. 446, 457, 1023, 1031, 1036
1297(e)(2) **S15** n.1031.1
1297(f) . . . . 15.46[3][b]; **15** n.445
1297(f)(1) . . . . 15.46[2]
1297(f)(2) **15** n.472
1297(i) **15** n.448
1298 . . . . **15** n.452
1311–1314 . . . . . 2.01[4]; 3.10[2]; **3** n.219; **4**
n.37; **8** n.211
1311 . . . . **8** n.244; **10** n.73
1312(7) **3** n.219
1312(7)(B) **3** n.219
1341 . . . . . **5** n.157; **8** n.180; **10** n.61; **13** n.267
1361–1379 . . . . 6.01[1]
1361 . . . . . **14** ns. 5, 113; 15.41[2][b]; **15** n.335
1361(a) **6** n.5
1361(b) . . . . . . 5.04[7]; **5** n.147; 6.02; 6.04[2]
1361(b)(1) . . . . 6.01[2][a]; 6.02[2]
1361(b)(1)(B) . . . . 6.02[1]
1361(b)(1)(D) . . . . 6.02[3]; 6.10[4][c]
1361(b)(2) . . . . 6.01[2][a]
1361(b)(2)(A) . . . **6** ns. 43, 180; 13.01[4][b]; **13**
n.8
1361(b)(2)(B)–1361(b)(2)(E) **6** n.45
1361(b)(3) . . . 6.02[6]; **6** ns. 50, 148; **12** n.144
1361(b)(3)(A) **13** n.972
1361(c)(1) **6** n.10; **S6** n.10
1361(c)(2) . . . . 6.02[2]

[Text references are to paragraphs; note references are to chapters (boldface numbers) and notes ("n."), and references to the supplement are preceded by "S."]

IRC §

1361(c)(2)(A) **6** n.17
1361(c)(2)(B) . . . . 6.02[2]
1361(c)(3) **6** n.230
1361(c)(4) . . . . 6.02[3]; **6** n.288
1361(c)(5) . . . . 6.02[3]; 6.10[4][b]
1361(c)(5)(B) **4** n.58
1361(c)(5)(B)(i) **6** n.40
1361(c)(5)(B)(iii) **6** n.32
1361(c)(6) . . . . 6.02[2]
1361(d) **6** n.18
1361(d)(3) . . . . 6.02[2]
1361(e) . . . . 6.02[2]
1362(a) 6.03
1362(a)(2) 6.03
1362(b) 6.03; 6.05
1362(d) 6.05; **6** n.143; **12** n.553
1362(d)(1) . . . . 6.04[2]
1362(d)(2) . . . . 6.04[2]; 6.04[4]; 12.22[8];
                                          12.30[4][a]
1362(d)(2)(B) **6** n.242
1362(d)(3) . . . 6.04[3]; 6.04[4]; 6.07[2]; **8** n.68
1362(d)(3)(A) . . . . 6.04[3]
1362(d)(3)(C) **6** n.63
1362(d)(3)(D) . . . . 6.04[3]
1362(d)(3)(D)(i) **6** n.235
1362(d)(3)(E) . . . . **6** ns. 59, 64
1362(e) . . . . . 6.04[5]; 6.10[2][b]; 13.42[6][b];
                          13.46[1][c]; **13** ns. 501, 815
1362(e)(1)(A) . . . . 6.04[5]
1362(e)(1)(B) . . . . 6.04[5]
1362(e)(2) . . . . 6.04[5]
1362(e)(3) . . . . 6.04[5]
1362(e)(5) . . . . 6.04[5]
1362(e)(6)(A) . . . . 6.04[5]
1362(e)(6)(B) . . . . 6.04[5]
1362(e)(6)(C) . . . . . . 6.09[3][b]; **6** ns. 72, 189
1362(e)(6)(D) . . . . **6** ns. 72, 190
1362(f) . . . . 6.02[3]; 6.03; 6.04[4]; S6.04[4]; **6**
                                          n.70; **S6** n.70
1362(g) . . . . . 6.05; **6** n.73; 12.22[8]; **12** n.553
1363 . . . . 6.06[2][a]; S6.06[2][a]
1363(a) . . . . . . 6.06[2][a]; 6.09[3][b]; 6.10[3];
                          6.10[3][b]; 6.10[3][c]; 6.10[5][a]; **6** ns.
                          80, 235; **7** ns. 7, 19, 193; 12.30[4][b];
                                          12.30[4][c]; **15** n.663
1363(b) . . . 6.06[2][a]; 6.11; **S6** n.81; **15** n.663
1363(c) 6.11
1363(c)(1) **6** n.83
1363(c)(2) **6** n.84
1363(d) . . . . . 6.07[3]; 6.11; **6** n.144; **S6** n.144
1363(d)(1) **6** n.126
1366 . . . . 6.06[1]; 6.09[3][b]; 6.09[5]; 6.10[3];
                          6.10[3][b]; 6.10[3][c]; 6.10[5][a]; **6** ns.
                          80, 160, 173; 10.06[3]; 12.30[4][a];
                          12.30[4][b]; **12** ns. 559, 574; **15** n.663
1366(a) . . . . 6.06[3]; 6.06[7]
1366(a)(1) **6** n.94
1366(b) . . . **5** n.35; 6.06[2][c]; 6.06[7]; 6.09[5];
                                          6.11; **6** n.194
1366(d) . . . . 6.06[4][c]; **6** n.110

1366(d)(1) . . . . 6.06[4][c]; 6.06[7]; 6.10[2][b];
                          6.10[3][c]; 6.10[5][b]; **6** ns. 99, 266
1366(d)(1)(A) . . . . **6** ns. 268, 310
1366(d)(1)(B) **6** n.310
1366(d)(2) . . . . . . 6.06[4][c]; 6.06[7]; 6.09[5];
                          6.10[3][c]; **6** ns. 167, 240; **12** n.559
1366(d)(3) . . . . 6.06[4][c]; 6.10[2][b]; 12.30[4][a]
1366(d)(3)(D) **6** n.85
1366(e) . . . . **1** n.130; 2.07[4]; **2** n.168; 6.06[6]
1366(f)(2) **6** n.162
1367 . . . . . . 6.06[4][a]; S6.06[4][a]; 6.06[4][b];
                          6.08[3][a]; 6.08[3][c]; 6.09[5]; 6.10[3];
                          6.10[3][c]; **6** ns. 160, 239, 267, 268,
                          310; **12** ns. 559, 574–576; 13.44[1]
1367(a) . . . 6.06[4][a]; 6.06[7]; 12.30[4][b]; **12**
                                          ns. 559, 574
1367(a)(1) . . . 6.06[4][a]; 6.10[2][a]; 6.10[3][a];
                          6.10[3][b]; 6.10[3][c]; **6** ns. 239, 240,
                          257, 268, 310; 12.30[4][a]; 12.30[4][c]
1367(a)(1)(A) . . . . 6.10[2][b]
1367(a)(2) . . . 6.06[4][b]; 6.10[3][b]; **6** ns. 167,
                                          278
1367(a)(2)(A) . . . . 6.06[4][a]
1367(a)(2)(B) . . . . 6.06[4][a]
1367(a)(2)(C) . . . . 6.06[4][a]
1367(b)(1) . . . . 6.06[4][a]
1367(b)(2) . . . **3** n.292; 6.06[4][b]; 6.10[2][c]; **6**
                                          ns. 106, 241
1367(b)(2)(A) . . . . 6.10[3][b]
1367(b)(2)(B) . . . . 6.06[7]; 6.10[3][b]; **6** n.108
1367(b)(3) . . . . 6.10[3][a]; 6.10[3][c]; **6** ns. 99,
                          239, 241, 310; **12** ns. 559, 574, 581
1367(d)(1) **6** n.238
1368 . . . 6.06[7]; 6.08[1]; 6.08[3][c]; 6.09[3][c];
                          6.10[1][a]; 6.10[3][b]; **6** ns. 155, 167,
                          261; **12** n.560; 14.24
1368(b) . . . . 6.06[7]; 6.08[2]; 6.08[3][a];
                          6.08[3][c]; 6.10[3][c]; **6** n.160; **8** n.55
1368(b)(2) **6** n.262
1368(c) . . . . 6.08[3]; 6.08[3][b]; **8** n.68
1368(e)(1) . . . . 6.08[3]; 6.08[3][a]
1368(e)(1)(A) . . . . 6.10[2][a]; 6.10[2][b];
                                          6.10[3][a]; **6** n.160
1368(e)(3) **6** n.164
1371 . . . . **6** n.9; **8** n.291
1371(a) . . . . 6.09[1]; **6** n.8
1371(a)(1) . . . . 6.08[1]
1371(a)(2) . . . . . 6.01[2][e]; 6.09[1]; **6** ns. 127,
                          172, 182; 10.42[3]; **10** ns. 295, 296;
                          12.30[4][b]; 12.30[4][c]; **12** n.566
1371(b) . . . . 6.09[1]; **6** n.96
1371(b)(1) . . . . . **6** ns. 81, 136; **S6** ns. 81, 136
1371(c)(1) . . . . . 6.06[7]; 6.08[1]; 6.10[3][c]; **8**
                                          n.68
1371(c)(2) . . . . 6.08[1]; 6.08[2]; 6.09[1]; **6** ns.
                                          177, 201
1371(d)(2) . . . . 6.06[2][e]; **6** n.80
1371(e) . . . . 6.08[3][a]; 6.09[3][a]; 12.30[4][a];
                                          12 ns. 134, 559
1371(e)(1) **6** n.165
1372 . . . . **6** n.86

[Text references are to paragraphs; note references are to chapters (boldface numbers) and notes ("n."), and references to the supplement are preceded by "S."]

[Text references are to paragraphs; note references are to chapters (boldface numbers) and notes ("n."), and references to the supplement are preceded by "S."]

IRC §

1504(a)(4) . . . . . 3.07[4]; **5** n.171; **S8** n.254.6; 10.21[2]; **10** n.286; **S10** ns. 342, 638.1; **11** n.50; 12.23[1]; 12.23[2]; 12.63[6][b]; S12.64[2][c]; **12** ns. 119, 230, 274, 287, 327, 336; **S12** n.358.3; 13.41[2][a]; 13.41[2][b]; 13.42[2][c]; 13.46[3]; S13.48[5][a]; S13.48[6]; **13** ns. 324, 325, 359, 838, 946; **S13** n.909; 14.43[2][a]; 14.43[7][d]
1504(a)(4)(C) . . . . 13.41[2][b]
1504(a)(5) . . . **11** n.50; 13.41[2][b]; **13** ns. 322, 327, 328
1504(a)(5)(A) . . . . 6.10[4][c]; **12** n.640; 13.41[2][c]
1504(a)(5)(C) . . . . . S13.41[2][d]; **S13** n.328.2
1504(a)(5)(D) . . . . S13.41[2][d]; **S13** n.328.2**13** n.358
1504(b) . . . . **6** n.43; **9** n.462; **10** n.534; 12.63[7][d]; 13.41[1]; **14** n.375; **S15** n.571
1504(b)(2) **S15** n.407.26
1504(b)(3) . . . . **5** n.178; 15.04[1][a]
1504(b)(4) 15.22; **S15** n.407.26
1504(b)(8) **13** n.311
1504(c) . . . . 13.41[1]
1504(d) . . . 13.41[1]; **13** n.309; 15.04[1][a]; **15** ns. 244, 625, 904, 905, 906; S15 n.244
1504(e) . . . . 13.41[1]
1551 . . . **7** n.185; **11** n.4; 14.02[1]; 13.01[3][d]; 13.02[1]; 13.02[6]; **13** ns. 14, 35, 36; 14.03[1]; **14** n.5; **15** n.648
1551(a) **3** n.108
1551(b) . . . . 13.02[6]
1551(b)(1) . . . . 13.02[6]
1551(c) **13** n.35
1552 . . . . 13.41[4][b]; **13** n.346
1561–1563 . . . . 5.09[2]
1561 . . . . . . **1** n.13; **11** n.4; 14.03[1]; 13.01[2]; 13.01[3][a]; 13.01[3][d]; 13.01[3][e]; 13.01[3][f]; 13.01[4][b]; 13.02[2]; 13.02[3]; S13.02[4][a]; 13.02[6]; 13.02[7]; 13.20[1][c]; 13.42[1][b]; **13** n.15; **14** ns. 5, 135
1561(a) . . . . **7** n.185; 13.02[5]
1561(a)(1) **13** n.16
1561(a)(2) . . . . **13** ns. 1, 17
1561(a)(3) **13** n.18
1561(a)(4) **13** n.16
1562(a) **13** n.21
1563 . . . . . . 5.04[2]; **9** ns. 45, 73; 13.01[3][b]; 13.02[6]; 13.02[7]; 14.44[1][c]; 14.44[3][d]; 14.45[2]
1563(a) . . . . 13.01[4][a]; 13.02[3]; 13.02[4][a]; 13.03[1]
1563(a)(1)(A) **S13** n.25.1
1563(a)(2) . . . . S13.02[4][a]; **S13** n.25.2
1563(b) . . . . 13.02[5]
1563(b)(2) . . . . 13.02[5]; 13.02[6]
1563(b)(3) . . . . 13.02[5]; 13.02[6]
1563(b)(4) . . . . 13.02[5]
1563(c)(1) **13** n.26

IRC §

1563(c)(2)(A) **13** n.27
1563(c)(2)(B) **13** n.28
1563(d)(1)(B) **13** n.30
1563(e) . . . . **9** ns. 38, 42; 13.02[4][c]
1563(e)(4) **1** n.45
1563(f)(2) . . . . 13.02[4][c]
1563(f)(3) . . . . 13.02[4][c]
1563(f)(3)(C) . . . . **13** ns. 27, 28
1563(f)(4) . . . . 13.02[5]
1563(f)(5) **S13** n.25.2
1601 . . . . **15** n.394
2035(d)(3)(A) . . . . 9.08[2][c]
2053–2054 . . . . 9.08[2][c]
2105(b) **15** n.214
2205–2207 . . . . 9.08[2][d]
2205 . . . . **9** n.321
2207A . . . . 9.08[2][d]
2207B . . . . 9.08[2][d]
2245 . . . . **15** n.39
2501 . . . . 3.08[2]; **12** n.744
2701–2704 . . . 8.65; **8** ns. 516, 641; **12** n.379
3121 . . . . 1.07[2]
3321(d) **S15** n.227.1
4701(a) **4** n.29
4982 . . . . **1** n.96
4999 . . . . 5.04[7]
5881 . . . . 9.25
5881(b) **9** n.488
5881(b)(3) **9** n.493
5881(c)(1) **9** n.491
5881(c)(2) **9** n.490
5881(d) **9** n.492
6011 . . . . S5.10[8][e]
6013(e) **13** n.345
6037 . . . . 6.06[2][a]
6037(c) **6** n.91
6038 . . . . **15** n.605
6038A . . . 13.20[1][d]; 13.20[4][h]; 13.22[3][a]; **13** ns. 103, 239, 240; 15.04[1][d]; 15.04[5]; **15** ns. 142, 190, 224, 259
6038A(e) . . . . 13.20[4][h]; **13** ns. 203, 239; **15** n.259
6038A(e)(3) **13** n.239
6038B . . . . . 15.81[4][b]; **15** ns. 611, 621, 748, 751
6038C . . . . 13.20[1][d]; 13.22[3][a]; **13** ns. 81, 103; 15.04[1][d]; **15** ns. 94, 127, 142
6042 . . . . S8.06[1]; **8** n.161
6042(a) **8** n.156
6043(a) **10** n.12;
6043(c) . . . . 4.26[3]; **4** n.334; **12** n.370; **S15** ns. 784.14, 840.5
6043A **S15** n.784.15
6046 . . . . **15** n.605
6050P **4** n.296
6103(e)(1)(C) **1** n.120
6103(e)(1)(D)(iii) **1** n.120
6103(e)(1)(D)(v) **1** n.120
6111 . . . . . 5.10[8][d]; 5.10[8][e]; S5.10[8][e]
6111(b)(1) **5** n.556
6111(d) . . . . . . 5.10[7][b]; 5.10[8][a]; **5** n.496

[Text references are to paragraphs; note references are to chapters (boldface numbers) and notes ("n."), and references to the supplement are preceded by "S."]

IRC §

6111(d)(2) **5** n.555
6112 . . . . 5.10[8][a]; 5.10[8][d]; 5.10[8][e];
                                        S5.10[8][e]
6114 . . . . **15** n.175
6116 . . . . 5.10[8][a]
6166 . . . **6** n.15; 9.08[1]; 9.08[2][e]; **9** ns. 305,
                                        323; **S9** n.305
6241–6245 . . . . 6.06[2][e]
6241 . . . . **6** ns. 99, 115
6501(c)(8) . . . . 15.81[4][b]
6501(c)(10) **5** n.576
6501(e)(1) **S6** n.94
6501(e)(1)(A)(i) **7** n.202
6501(f) **7** n.239
6511–6515 . . . . 15.21[5][c]
6511(d)(1) **4** n.227
6511(d)(3) **15** n.367
6511(g) **15** n.373
6601(b)(4) **7** n.168
6601(d)(2) **15** n.343
6611 . . . . **5** n.565
6612 . . . . **5** n.565
6621(c) **5** n.18
6653 . . . . **13** n.345; **15** n.611
6653(b)(1)(A) **13** n.345
6655(g)(4) **6** n.118
6662 . . . . **4** ns. 343, 376; 5.10[3][a]; 5.10[7][c];
        5.10[8][a]; **5** ns. 547, 549, 550, 567;
        13.22[3][b]; **13** n.241; 14.41[4][d]; **S15**
                                        n.330
6662(a)(2) . . . . 5.10[8][a]
6662(d) . . . . 5.10[8][e]
6662(d)(2) . . . . 5.10[8][a]
6662(d)(2)(C)(i) . . . . 5.10[8][a]
6662(d)(2)(C)(ii) **5** n.536
6662(d)(2)(E)(i) . . . . 5.10[8][a]; **5** n.549
6662(d)(2)(E)(ii) . . . . 5.10[8][a]; **5** n.550
6662(d)(2)(E)(iii) . . . . 5.10[8][a]
6662(d)(2)(E)(iv) . . . . 5.10[8][a]
6662(d)(3) . . . . 5.10[8][a]
6662(e)   13.20[1][d]; 13.20[6][d]; 13.20[7][c];
        13.22[3][b]; **13** ns. 70, 151, 168, 192,
                                207, 227, 243
6662(e)(3)(B)(i) **13** n.242
6662(e)(3)(B)(ii) **13** n.242
6662(i) . . . . 5.10[8][a]
6662(i)(1)(C) **5** n.553
6662(i)(2) . . . . 5.10[8][a]; **5** ns. 534, 549
6662(i)(3) . . . . 5.10[8][a]; **5** ns. 534, 542, 549
6662(i)(3)(B) **5** n.550
6662A   5.10[8][a]; 5.10[8][d]; **5** ns. 417, 538,
                                        552
6662A(a) . . . . 5.10[8][a]; **5** n.550
6662A(b)(1) . . . . 5.10[8][a]
6662A(b)(2) . . . . 5.10[8][a]
6662A(c) **5** n.550
6662A(c)(1) **5** n.538
6662A(c)(2) . . . . **5** ns. 541, 553, 557
6662A(c)(2)(B) **5** n.539
6662A(c)(2)(C) **5** n.540
6662A(c)(2)(D) **5** n.541

IRC §

6662A(c)(3) **5** n.553
6662A(d) . . . . 5.10[8][a]
6662A(d)(2) . . . . 5.10[8][a]
6662A(d)(3) . . . . 5.10[8][a]
6662A(d)(4) . . . . 5.10[8][a]
6662A(d)(4)(B)(ii) **5** n.548
6662A(d)(5)(A) **5** n.549
6662A(d)(5)(B) . . . . 5.10[8][a]
6662A(d)(5)(B)(ii) **5** n.548
6662A(e)(5) **5** n.550
6662A(e)(6) **5** n.551
6662B **5** n.567; **S13** n.172.1
6664 . . . . 5.10[8][a]
6664(a)(1) **5** n.538
6664(b) **5** n.567
6664(c) . . . . 5.10[3][a]; 5.10[8][a]
6664(d) . . . . 5.10[8][d]; **5** n.534
6664(d)(2) . . . . **5** ns. 542, 547, 551
6664(d)(3) . . . . **5** ns. 542, 547, 551, 577
6664(d)(3)(B) . . . . **5** ns. 550, 577
6672 . . . . **5** n.18
6689 . . . . 15.21[5][c]
6694 . . . . 5.10[8][a]; **5** n.555
6694(a) . . . . 5.10[8][e]
6694(a)(1) . . . . 5.10[8][a]
6694(a)(2) . . . . 5.10[8][a]
6700 . . . . **5** ns. 567, 580
6701 . . . . 5.10[8][a]; **5** ns. 555, 556
6701(a)(2) **5** n.556
6701(b)(3) **5** n.556
6701(c)(2) **5** n.554
6707 . . . . 5.10[8][a]; **5** ns. 567, 576, 580
6707(c) **5** n.576
6707A   5.10[8][a]; 5.10[8][d]; **5** ns. 548, 554,
                                        567, 576
6707A(b)(3)(B) **5** n.538
6707A(c) **5** n.544
6707A(c)(25) **5** n.546
6707A(d) . . . . . 5.10[8][a]; **5** ns. 543, 548, 551,
                                        575
6707A(e) . . . . 5.10[8][d]; **5** ns. 545, 554
6707A(f) . . . . 5.10[8][d]
6708 . . . . 5.10[8][a]; **5** ns. 567, 580
6708(a) . . . . 5.10[8][a]
6712 . . . . **15** n.175
6901 . . . . **10** n.54
6901(a)(2) **12** n.24
7201 . . . . **13** n.839
7206 . . . . **8** n.242
7421 . . . . **15** n.174
7477 . . . . 15.80[5]; 15.81[4][b]; 15.82[2][a]; **15**
                                ns. 611, 621, 631
7482 . . . . **4** n.45
7491 . . . . **3** n.107; 7.08
7491(a)(1)(C) **7** n.150
7491(a)(3) **7** n.150
7503 . . . . **9** n.113
7519 . . . . **5** n.324; **6** n.88
7525(b) . . . . **5** ns. 535, 557, 567
7701 . . . . 5.10[6][b]
7701(a)(1) . . . . **11** n.288; 14.41[1]

[Text references are to paragraphs; note references are to chapters (boldface numbers) and notes ("n."), and references to the supplement are preceded by "S."]

IRC §

7701(a)(3) . . . . 1.01; 2.01; 2.02[1]
7701(a)(4) . . . . 15.01[3]; **15** n.206
7701(a)(5) **15** n.206
7701(a)(14) . . . . 6.06[2][a]
7701(a)(30) . . . . 15.61[2]
7701(a)(43) . . . . 10.05[4]
7701(a)(44) . . . . 10.05[4]
7701(b) . . . . 15.01[3]; **15** n.179,
7701(f) . . . . **5** ns. 204, 208; 13.01[4][b];
          13.23[1]; S13.43[6]; **13** ns. 272, 281,
          825
7701(g) . . . 3.06[4][f]; **3** ns. 119, 123; **6** n.255;
          8 ns. 355, 613; 10.03[3]; 10.42[1][b]; **10**
          ns. 78, 98, 432
7701(*l*) . . . 4.03[8][b]; 4.04[8]; **4** ns. 182, 264;
          5.10[6][f]; 15.03[6]; **15** ns. 185, 190,
          213, 233, 280
7701(m) . . . . . 5.10[6][b]; **5** ns. 421, 568; **S13**
          n.172.1; **S14** n.172.3
7704 . . . . . . 1.08[3]; 2.04[1]; 2.04[4]; **2** ns. 43,
          113, 114, 140; 10.05[6]
7704(a) . . . . 2.04[4]
7704(b) . . . . 2.04[4]
7704(c) . . . . 2.04[4]

IRC §

7704(f) . . . . 2.04[4]; **3** n.378
7704(g) **2** n.114
7805 . . . . **9** n.394
7805(a) . . . . 2.01[3]
7805(e) . . . . 15.81[3][f]; **15** ns. 376, 491, 493,
          496, 522, 538, 710, 801, 804, 949
7806(b) **5** n.95
7852(d) . . . . **15** ns. 174, 175
7872 . . . . . . 1.05[1][a]; 4.42[5]; **4** ns. 84, 385;
          7.12[1]; 8.05[6]; **8** ns. 215, 250; **S8** ns.
          215, 250; 12.27[5][d]; **12** n.485;
          13.21[2]; S13.22[3][a]; 13.23[1];
          13.23[3][a]; **13** ns. 254, 255, 288; **15**
          n.208
7872(b) . . . . 4.42[5]
7872(c)(3) . . . . 8.05[6]
7874 . . . . S12.63[3][b]; S15.63[2][b];
          S15.82[2][c]; **S15** ns. 565.3, 696, 784.6,
          784.11, 784.16–784.18, 840.3–840.5
7874(a) **S15** n.784.8
7874(c)(1) **S15** n.784.8
7874(d)(1) **S15** n.784.8
7874(d)(2) **S15** n.784.8

Cumulative Table of Treasury Regulations

[Text references are to paragraphs; note references are to chapters (boldface numbers) and notes ("n."), and references to the supplement are preceded by "S."]

[Text references are to paragraphs; note references are to chapters (boldface numbers)
and notes ("n."), and references to the supplement are preceded by "S."]

Reg. §

1.118-1 . . . . **3** ns. 283, 289, 306
1.138-5 . . . . **S14** n.301
1.162-1(a) . . . . . **5** ns. 81, 154; **8** ns. 122, 124
1.162-6 . . . . **3** n.364
1.162-8 . . . . **8** ns. 188, 189
1.162-15(b) **3** n.311
1.162-27 . . . . **5** ns. 69, 403
1.162-27(e) . . . . **5** ns. 69, 403
1.162(j)-5(b)(6)(i) **13** n.573
1.162(j)-5(b)(6)(ii) **13** n.574
1.162(j)-5(d) **13** n.571
1.162(j)-5(e) **13** n.572
1.162(j)-6 . . . . **13** n.574
1.163-3 . . . . **4** n.443
1.163-3(c) **4** n.415
1.163-4 . . . . **4** n.443
1.163-4(c) **12** n.462
1.163-5(a)(3) **13** n.299
1.163-7(b)(1) **4** n.352
1.163-7(b)(2) **4** n.352
1.163-7(c) . . . . **4** ns. 394, 406, 415, 416, 419,
                    426; **12** ns. 426, 461–463
1.163-12 . . . **13** ns. 289, 295; **15** ns. 211, 212,
                    224
1.163-13 . . . . . . **4** ns. 394, 411, 420, 425, 426
1.163-13(c) **4** n.421
1.163(j)-5 . . . . **13** ns. 297, 569
1.163(j)-5(b) . . . . 13.23[8]
1.163(j)-5(b)(2) **13** n.670
1.163(j)-5(b)(3) **13** n.570
1.163(j)-5(b)(4) **13** n.570
1.163(j)-5(c) . . . . 13.23[8]
1.163(j)-5(c)(2) **13** n.300
1.163(j)-5(c)(3) **13** n.300
1.163(j)-5(d) . . . . 13.23[8]
1.163(j)-6 . . . . **13** n.840
1.163(j)-6(a)(3) **13** n.842
1.163(j)-6(b)(1) **13** n.841
1.163(j)-6(b)(2) **13** n.841
1.164-7 . . . . **5** n.52
1.165-4(a) **10** n.278
1.165-5(i) **4** n.250
1.166-9 . . . . **4** n.254
1.166-9(a) **4** n.235; **5** n.23
1.166-9(b) **4** n.235
1.166-9(c) **3** n.280
1.167(a)-3 . . . . **10** n.446
1.167(g)-1 . . . . **3** n.231
1.170A-4(b)(1) **8** n.616
1.171-1 – 1.171-5 . . . . **4** ns. 394, 420
1.171-1(a) **4** n.410
1.171-1(e)(1)(ii) **4** n.421
1.171-1(f) **4** n.421
1.171-2 . . . . **4** n.410
1.197-1T **10** n.455
1.197-2(b) . . . . 10.40[6]
1.197-2(c) . . . . 10.40[6]
1.197-2(d) . . . . 10.40[6]
1.197-2(f) . . . . 10.40[6]
1.197-2(f)(3)(iii) **10** n.456
1.197-2(g) . . . . 10.40[6]

Reg. §

1.197-2(h) . . . . 10.40[6]
1.197-2(h) . . . . 10.40[6]
1.197-2(k) . . . . 10.40[6]; **10** n.456
1.199 . . . . **S15** n.407.18
1.212-1(k) . . . . **5** ns. 98, 120
1.212-1(n) **5** n.98
1.243-1(a)(3) **5** n.185
1.243-4 . . . . **5** n.176
1.243-4(c) **5** n.174
1.243-5 . . . . **5** n.174
1.246-2(b) **5** n.197
1.246-3(c)(3) **5** n.202
1.246-5 . . . . **5** n.205
1.248-1(a)(1) **5** n.245
1.248-1(a)(2) **5** n.246
1.248-1(a)(3) **5** n.233
1.248-1(b)(2) **5** n.234
1.248-1(b)(3) **5** n.161
1.248-1(b)(3)(i) **5** n.235
1.248-1(b)(4) . . . . **5** ns. 277, 278
1.248-1(c) **5** n.244
1.263(a)-2(a) **5** n.98
1.263(a)-2(c) **5** n.98
1.263(a)-2(e) . . . . **5** ns. 98, 101
1.263(a)-2(f) **3** n.306; **5** n.306
1.263(a)-2T . . . . . . **13** ns. 283, 288, 294, 416
1.263(a)-4 . . . . **5** n.113
1.263(a)-5 . . . . **5** ns. 113, 255, 256, 259, 260,
                    284, 287
1.267(a)-3 . . . . **5** n.96; **13** ns. 289, 295; **15** ns.
                    211, 212, 224
1.267(f)-1 . . . . **13** ns. 283, 284, 294, 295, 416,
                    418, 419, 587
1.267(f)-1(c)(1) **8** n.117
1.267(f)-1(h) . . . . 13.43[5][a]; **14** n.113
1.267(f)-1T . . . . . . **13** ns. 283, 294, 416, 419
1.267(f)-2T . . . **13** ns. 283, 284, 416, 417. 419
1.267(f)-2T(g) **13** n.418
1.267(f)-2T(j) **13** n.418
1.269-1(a) **14** n.117
1.269-2(b) . . . . **14** ns. 115, 153
1.269-3(b) **14** n.131
1.269-3(b)(1) **14** n.144
1.269-3(c)(2) . . . . **14** ns. 118, 139
1.269-3(d) . . . . **14** ns. 314, 334
1.269-3(e) . . . . **14** ns. 314, 335
1.269-5(b) **14** n.336
1.269-6 . . . . **14** n.139
1.269-7 . . . . **10** n.569; **14** ns. 148, 333
1.279-5(e)(1) **12** n.1112
1.280G-1 . . . . **5** n.140
1.280H-1T **5** n.325
1.301-1(b) . . . . . . 8.04[2]; **8** ns. 151, 154, 158
1.301-1(c) . . . . **8** ns. 14, 165, 432
1.301-1(d) **8** n.529
1.301-1(d)(1)(ii) . . . . **8** ns. 389, 395
1.301-1(f) . . . . **8** ns. 16, 38, 48
1.301-1(g) **S8** n.374
1.301-1(h)(2)(i) **8** n.389
1.301-1(j) . . . **3** n.337; **8** ns. 192, 329, 387, 434;
                    13 ns. 230, 257

[Text references are to paragraphs; note references are to chapters (boldface numbers) and notes ("n."), and references to the supplement are preceded by "S."]

Reg. §

1.301-1(*l*)   **3** n.405; **8** ns. 14, 389, 397, 399; **10** n.245; **11** n.375; 12.27[5][b]; 12.64[1][c]; 12.64[2][b]; **12** ns. 112, 750; **S15** n.647.5
1.301-1(m) . . . . **4** n.295; **6** n.234; **8** ns. 13, 210
1.301-1T(g) **S3** n.145; **S8** n.374
1.302-1(a) **9** n.39
1.302-2(a) **9** n.160
1.302-2(b) . . . .**9** ns. 147, 148, 162
1.302-2(c)   **9** ns. 445–447, 448; **S9** ns. 445–447, 449
1.302-3(a) . . . . **9** ns. 68, 88
1.302-3(a)(3) **3** n.164; **9** n.86
1.302-3(b) **9** n.90
1.302-4(a) **9** n.114
1.302-4(a)(2) **9** n.114
1.302-4(c) **9** n.115
1.302-4(d) . . . . **9** ns. 34, 133
1.302-4(e) **9** n.133
1.302-4(f) **9** n.117
1.302-4(g) **9** n.139
1.302-5 . . . **S9** n.452.1; **S13**.44[3]; **S13** ns. 616, 618
1.303-2(d) . . . . **9** ns. 311, 314
1.303-2(f) . . . . **9** ns. 328, 329
1.303-2(g) . . . . **9** ns. 307, 327
1.303-2(g)(2) **9** n.303
1.304-2(a)   **9** ns. 93, 363, 373, 374, 380, 442
1.304-2(b) **9** n.362
1.304-2(c) . . . . **9** ns. 172, 335, 345, 356, 379, 382, 450
1.304-3(a) . . . . **9** ns. 354, 450
1.304-3(b) . . . . **9** ns. 345, 359
1.304-4T **9** n.394
1.304-5 . . . . **9** ns. 363, 365
1.304-5(b) . . . . **9** ns. 360, 381
1.304-5(b)(1) **9** n.361
1.304-5(b)(2) **9** n.361
1.305-1(a) **8** n.433
1.305-1(b) **8** n.529
1.305-1(b)(1) . . . . **8** ns. 434, 535
1.305-1(b)(3) **8** n.535
1.305-1(c) **8** n.494; **12** n.209
1.305-2(a)(5) **8** n.421
1.305-2(b) . . . .**8** ns. 445, 529, 531
1.305-3(b) **8** n.478
1.305-3(b)(2) **8** n.479
1.305-3(b)(3)   **8** ns. 480, 481, 483, 521, 542; **9** n.185
1.305-3(b)(4) **8** n.479
1.305-3(b)(5) **8** n.505
1.305-3(b)(6) **8** n.486
1.305-3(c) **8** n.495; **12** n.186
1.305-3(d) . . . .**8** ns. 449, 492, 509
1.305-3(d)(2) **8** n.509
1.305-3(e) . . . . **8** ns. 425, 451, 464, 477, 480, 481, 483, 488, 490–493, 504, 509–511, 516, 518, 520–522, 535, 540, 542; **12** ns. 392, 393, 494
1.305-4(b) **8** n.446

1.305-5(a) . . . . **8** ns. 448, 449, 509, 598; **12** n.797; **13** n.324
1.305-5(b) **8** n.451
1.305-5(b)(1) **8** n.460; **12** n.794
1.305-5(b)(2) . . . .**8** ns. 455, 464, 468
1.305-5(b)(3) **8** n.464
1.305-5(b)(3)(i) . . . .**8** ns. 462, 469
1.305-5(d) . . . . **8** ns. 448, 450, 453, 455, 461, 464, 513, 516, 521, 540; **12** ns. 409, 411, 794; **13** n.324
1.305-5(e) **8** n.461
1.305-6(a)(2) . . . .**8** ns. 471, 472
1.305-6(b) . . . .**8** ns. 471, 472
1.305-7(a) . . . .**8** ns. 503, 507, 513, 514, 521
1.305-7(b) . . . .**8** ns. 449, 492, 508, 509
1.305-7(b)(1) . . . .**8** ns. 493, 510
1.305-7(c) . . . . .**8** n.514; **12** ns. 394, 409, 411
1.305-7(c)(1) **8** n.515
1.305-7(c)(1)(ii) **8** n.450; **12** n.391
1.305-8 . . . .**8** n.426
1.306-1(b)(1) . . . .**8** ns. 608, 611
1.306-1(b)(2) . . .**8** ns. 586, 603, 605, 606, 609
1.306-2(a) . . . .**8** ns. 622, 624
1.306-2(b)(3) . . . .**8** ns. 632, 636
1.306-3(a) **8** n.586
1.306-3(b) **8** n.590
1.306-3(c) **8** n.565
1.306-3(d) . . . . **8** ns. 569, 570, 573, 620; **11** n.360; **12** ns. 800, 803, 808
1.306-3(e) . . . .**8** ns. 582, 584, 620, 628
1.306-3(f) . . . .**8** ns. 573, 599
1.306-3(g) **8** n.592
1.307-1 . . . .**8** n.523
1.307-1(a) . . . .**8** ns. 546, 547
1.307-1(b) . . . .**8** ns. 546, 547
1.307-2 . . . .**8** n.548
1.312-1(d) **8** n.531
1.312-1(e) . . . .**8** ns. 69, 608
1.312-3 . . . .**8** n.384
1.312-4 . . . .**8** n.384
1.312-6 . . . .**7** n.68
1.312-6(a) . . . .**8** ns. 77, 135, 137
1.312-6(b) . . . . . . 8.03[3]; **8** ns. 74, 79, 80
1.312-6(c) **8** n.98
1.312-6(d) **8** n.59
1.312-7(b)(1) . . . .**8** ns. 87, 111, 117, 138
1.312-7(c)(1) **8** n.103
1.312-7(c)(2) **8** n.103
1.312-9(b)(2) **8** n.38
1.312-10 . . . . . **11** n.348; **S11** ns. 347, 348; **13** n.529; **14** ns. 44, 53; **S15**.84[3][b]; **S15**.84[3][f]; **S15** n.946
1.312-10(a) . . .**12** n.1050; **14** ns. 87, 111; **S15** n.923.3
1.312-10(b) **11** n.348; **12** n.1051; **S15** n.923.4
1.312-10(b)(1) **11** n.346
1.312-10(b)(2) **S15** n.923.4
1.312-10(c) **S15** n.923.5
1.312-11 . . . . 14.24; **14** n.53
1.312-11(a) . . . .**8** n.133; **11** ns. 368, 370, 380

[Text references are to paragraphs; note references are to chapters (boldface numbers) and notes ("n."), and references to the supplement are preceded by "S."]

[Text references are to paragraphs; note references are to chapters (boldface numbers) and notes ("n."), and references to the supplement are preceded by "S."]

[Text references are to paragraphs; note references are to chapters (boldface numbers) and notes ("n."), and references to the supplement are preceded by "S."]

[Text references are to paragraphs; note references are to chapters (boldface numbers) and notes ("n."), and references to the supplement are preceded by "S."]

[Text references are to paragraphs; note references are to chapters (boldface numbers) and notes ("n."), and references to the supplement are preceded by "S."]

Reg. §

[Text references are to paragraphs; note references are to chapters (boldface numbers) and notes ("n."), and references to the supplement are preceded by "S."]

[Text references are to paragraphs; note references are to chapters (boldface numbers) and notes ("n."), and references to the supplement are preceded by "S."]

Reg. §

1.367(b)-5(f)	**15** n.736
1.367(b)-5(g)	**15** ns. 920, 921
1.367(b)-6	**15** n.722
1.367(b)-6(b)	**15** n.722
1.367(b)-6(c)	**15** n.722
1.367(b)-7(c)(1)	**15** n.857
1.367(b)-7(c)(1)(ii)	**15** n.850
1.367(b)-7(c)(1)(iii)	**15** ns. 825, 850
1.367(b)-9(b)(4)	**15** ns. 825, 850
1.367(b)-13	15.81[3][d]; **15** n.628
1.367(d)-1T	**15** ns. 660, 668, 757, 763, 796
1.367(e)-1	**15** ns. 633, 912, 916, 924, 980, 993
1.367(e)-1T	**15** ns. 633, 924, 912, 927, 944
1.367(e)-1(b)	**15** n.980
1.367(e)-1(b)(1)	**15** ns. 925, 928, 931, 945, 993
1.367(e)-1(b)(2)	**15** n.925
1.367(e)-1(b)(3)	**15** n.926
1.367(e)-1T(b)(3)	**15** n.932
1.367(e)-1(b)(4)	**15** ns. 925, 932
1.367(e)-1(b)(6)	**14** n.113
1.367(e)-1(c)	**15** ns. 928, 929, 930, 934, 946, 980, 994
1.367(e)-1(c)(1)	**15** n.929
1.367(e)-1(c)(2)	**15** n.931
1.367(e)-1(c)(3)	**15** n.930
1.367(e)-1T(c)(3)	15.84[4][b]
1.367(e)-1T(c)(3)(i)	**15** n.942
1.367(e)-1T(c)(3)(i)(B)	**15** ns. 940, 941
1.367(e)-1T(c)(3)(ii)(B)	**15** n.939
1.367(e)-1T(c)(3)(ii)(C)	**15** n.938
1.367(e)-1T(c)(3)(ii)(E)	**15** n.939
1.367(e)-1T(c)(3)(ii)(F)	**15** n.938
1.367(e)-1T(c)(3)(iii)	**15** n.939
1.367(e)-1T(c)(3)(vi)	**15** n.942
1.367(e)-1T(c)(3)(vi)(G)	**15** n.943
1.367(e)-1(c)(3)(vii)	**15** n.936
1.367(e)-1T(c)(3)(vii)	**15** n.944
1.367(e)-1T(c)(3)(vii)(A)	**15** n.938
1.367(e)-1T(c)(3)(vii)(B)	**15** n.936
1.367(e)-1(c)(3)(viii)	**15** n.936
1.367(e)-1T(c)(3)(viii)	**15** ns. 936, 942
1.367(e)-1(d)	15.84[4][c]; **15** n.925
1.367(e)-1(d)(1)	**15** n.932
1.367(e)-1(d)(3)	**15** n.923
1.367(e)-1T(d)(4)	**15** n.939
1.367(e)-1(e)	**15** ns. 929, 930, 931, 932, 936
1.367(e)-1T(e)	**15** ns. 936, 937, 941, 942, 943
1.367(e)-2	**15** ns. 634, 806, 957, 960, 996
1.367(e)-2T	**15** n.634
1.367(e)-2(b)	**15** ns. 800, 801
1.367(e)-2(b)(1)(ii)(B)	**15** n.808
1.367(e)-2(b)(1)(ii)(C)	**15** n.808
1.367(e)-2(b)(1)(iii)	**15** n.809
1.367(e)-2(b)(2)(i)(E)	**15** n.811
1.367(e)-2(b)(2)(i)(A)	**15** n.811
1.367(e)-2(b)(2)(i)(B)	**15** n.811
1.367(e)-2(b)(2)(i)(C)	**15** n.811
1.367(e)-2(b)(2)(i)(D)	**15** n.811

Reg. §

1.367(e)-2(b)(2)(iii)(A)	**15** n.814
1.367(e)-2(b)(2)(iii)(B)	**15** n.814
1.367(e)-2(b)(2)(iii)(C)	**15** n.814
1.367(e)-2(b)(2)(iii)(D)	**15** n.814
1.367(e)-2(b)(3)	**15** n.815
1.367(e)-2(b)(3)(i)	**15** n.815
1.367(e)-2(b)(ii)	**15** n.995
1.367(e)-2(c)	**15** n.967
1.367(e)-2(c)(1)	**15** n.816
1.367(e)-2(c)(2)	**15** ns. 806, 817
1.367(e)-2(c)(2)(i)	**15** n.818
1.367(e)-2(c)(2)(ii)	**15** n.819
1.367(e)-2(c)(3)	**15** n.420
1.367(e)-2(d)	**15** ns. 227, 822, 806, 1051, 1053
1.368-1(b)	**10** n.387; **11** n.209; 12.03; 12.21[2][a]; 12.61[1]; **12** ns. 44, 90, 329, 816, 820, 1068; **S12** ns. 494, 823, 829; **14** n.40
1.368-1(c)	12.21[2][a]; 12.61[1]; **12** n.816
1.368-1(d)	12.63[6][b]; **12** ns. 231, 531, 827, 1015, 1017; **S12** ns. 823, 1082, 1088, 1167, 1168; 14.44[5]; **14** n.398
1.368-1(d)(1)(iii)	**12** n.99
1.368-1(d)(4)	**12** ns. 30, 115, 156, 229, 829, 831, 833, 838, 1022; **13** n.947
1.368-1(d)(4)(ii)	**12** ns. 230, 834
1.368-1(d)(4)(iii)	**12** ns. 231, 835
1.368-1(d)(4)(iv)	**12** n.839
1.368-1(d)(5)	12.61[2][b]; **12** ns. 115, 156, 229, 231, 833, 838, 1022, 1023; **S12** n.832; **13** n.947
1.368-1(e)	**11** n.247; 12.21[2][a]; S12.30[1]; **12** ns. 30, 44, 62, 75, 922
1.368-1T(e)	**12** ns. 30, 50, 61, 62
1.368-1(e)(1)	**12** ns. 46, 47, 49, 61, 65, 122, 927, 937, 1000
1.368-1(e)(1)(i)	**12** ns. 934, 964
1.368-1(e)(1)(ii)	**S12** n.50; **S12** ns. 62, 67, 77, 172
1.368-1T(e)(1)(ii)	**12** ns. 67, 77
1.368-1(e)(2)	**12** ns. 47, 1005
1.368-1T(e)(2)	**12** n.1005; **S12** n.50.10
1.368-1T(e)(2)(i)	**12** n.77
1.368-1(e)(2)(i)	**S12** n.50.2
1.368-1T(e)(2)(ii)	**12** ns. 67, 77
1.368-1(e)(2)(iii)	**S12** n.50.5
1.368-1(e)(2)(iii)(C)	**S12** n.50.7
1.368-1(e)(2)(iv)	**S12** n.50.6
1.368-1(e)(2)(v)	**S12** n.50.9
1.368-1(e)(2)(v), Ex. 1	**S12** n.50.8
1.368-1(e)(2)(v), Ex. 2	**S12** n.50.8
1.368-1(e)(2)(v), Ex. 6	**S12** n.50.6
1.368-1(e)(3)	**12** n.77
1.368-1(e)(6)	**12** ns. 49, 65–67, 74, 76; **S12** ns. 62, 67, 77, 172, 1000, 1005
1.368-1(e)(6), Ex. 9	**S12** n.50
1.368-1(e)(8)	**S12** n.50.9
1.368-1(g)	**12** n.662
1.368-1(j)(5)	**12** n.279
1.368-2(b)	**12** n.102; **15** n.875

[Text references are to paragraphs; note references are to chapters (boldface numbers) and notes ("n."), and references to the supplement are preceded by "S."]

[Text references are to paragraphs; note references are to chapters (boldface numbers) and notes ("n."), and references to the supplement are preceded by "S."]

Reg. §

1.382-2T(a)(2)(i) . . . . . 14.43[7][c]; **14** ns. 183, 209, 217	
1.382-2T(b) . . . . 14.43[7][a]	
1.382-2T(c) . . . . 14.43[7][a]	
1.382-2T(c)(1) . . . 14.43[7][c]; **14** ns. 210, 229	
1.382-2T(c)(3) . . . . 14.43[7][c]	
1.382-2T(c)(4) . . . . **14** ns. 210, 229	
1.382-2T(d) . . . . 14.43[7][a]; **14** n.228	
1.382-2T(e) . . . . 14.43[7][a]; 14.43[7][b]	
1.382-2T(e)(1) **14** n.200	
1.382-2T(e)(1)(i) . . . . 14.43[7][b]	
1.382-2T(e)(1)(iii) . . . . **14** ns. 218, 259	
1.382-2T(e)(2) **14** n.207	
1.382-2T(e)(2)(iii) . . . . **14** ns. 183, 209	
1.382-2T(e)(2)(iv) . . . . **14** ns. 250, 254	
1.382-2T(f) . . . . 14.43[7][a]	
1.382-2T(f)(1)–1.382-2T(f)(5) **14** n.190	
1.382-2T(f)(1)(ii) **14** n.193	
1.382-2T(f)(1)(iv) **14** n.193	
1.382-2T(f)(3) . . . . **14** ns. 147, 255	
1.382-2T(f)(4) **14** n.193	
1.382-2T(f)(5) **14** n.193	
1.382-2T(f)(18) . . . . 14.43[7][d]; **14** n.185	
1.382-2T(f)(18)(i) **14** n.186	
1.382-2T(f)(18)(iii) **14** n.193	
1.382-2T(f)(19) **14** n.192	
1.382-2T(f)(22) **14** n.191	
1.382-2T(g) . . . . 14.43[7][a]; **14** ns. 188, 212, 214	
1.382-2T(g)(1) . . . . 14.43[7][e]	
1.382-2T(g)(2) . . . . 14.43[7][f]; **14** n.237	
1.382-2T(g)(3) **14** n.237	
1.382-2T(g)(4) . . . . **14** ns. 188, 214	
1.382-2T(g)(5) **14** n.237	
1.382-2T(h) . . . . 14.43[7][a]; **14** n.234	
1.382-2T(h)(1)–1.382-2T(h)(3) **14** n.194	
1.382-2T(h)(2) . . . . 14.43[7][f]	
1.382-2T(h)(2)(ii) **14** n.238	
1.382-2T(h)(4) . . . . 14.43[7][f]; **14** n.195	
1.382-2T(h)(4)(ii) **14** n.239	
1.382-2T(h)(4)(iii) **14** n.240	
1.382-2T(h)(4)(v) **14** n.240	
1.382-2T(h)(4)(vi) **14** n.240	
1.382-2T(h)(4)(vii) **14** n.242	
1.382-2T(h)(4)(viii) **14** n.241	
1.382-2T(h)(4)(x) . . . . 14.43[7][f]	
1.382-2T(h)(6) **14** n.194	
1.382-2T(j) . . . . 14.43[7][a]	
1.382-2T(j)(1) . . . 14.43[7][g]; **14** ns. 188, 212, 214, 231, 232, 235	
1.382-2T(j)(1)(vi) **13** n.912; **14** ns. 188, 214, 264	
1.382-2T(j)(2) . . . 14.43[7][h]; **14** ns. 215, 217, 233, 236	
1.382-2T(j)(2)(iii)(B) **14** n.218	
1.382-2T(j)(2)(iii)(B)(1) **14** n.259	
1.382-2T(j)(2)(iii)(B)(2) **14** n.259	
1.382-2T(j)(3) . . . 14.43[7][h]; **14** ns. 215, 233, 236	
1.382-2T(k) . . . . 14.43[7][a]	
1.382-2T(k)(1) **14** n.237	

1.382-2T(k)(3) **14** n.237	
1.382-3(a)(1) **13** n.895; **14** n.331	
1.382-3(a)(1)(i) . . . . **14** ns. 212, 268	
1.382-3(a)(1)(ii) . . . . **14** ns. 212, 268	
1.382-3(e) **14** n.314	
1.382-3(j) . . . . **14** ns. 218, 219, 222, 237, 249, 262	
1.382-3(j)(2) **14** n.219	
1.382-3(j)(3) . . . . **14** ns. 247, 260	
1.382-3(j)(5)(i) **14** n.260	
1.382-3(j)(6) **14** n.219	
1.382-3(j)(13) . . . . **14** ns. 219, 260	
1.382-3(j)(14) **14** n.219	
1.382-3(m) **14** n.334	
1.382-4(d) . . . . **6** n.302; **13** n.894; **14** ns. 197, 224, 246	
1.382-4(d)(2)(B) **14** n.198	
1.382-4(d)(4)(i) **14** n.113	
1.382-4(d)(6) **14** n.198	
1.382-4(d)(7) **14** n.198	
1.382-4(d)(9)(ii) . . . . **14** ns. 185, 195	
1.382-5 . . . . **13** n.40	
1.382-5(c) **14** n.278	
1.382-5(d) . . . **13** ns. 881, 892, 893; **S13** n.887	
1.382-5T **14** n.297	
1.382-5T(c) **14** n.278	
1.382-5T(d) **14** n.270	
1.382-6 . . . . **13** ns. 505, 819; **14** n.279	
1.382-6(d) **14** n.279	
1.382-6(d)(3) **14** n.279	
1.382-8 . . . . . **13** ns. 49, 871; **14** ns. 271, 276, 283, 297	
1.382-8T **13** n.40; **14** n.182	
1.382-8(a) . . . . 13.03[2]	
1.382-8(b) **13** n.45	
1.382-8(b)(2) **13** n.49	
1.382-8(c) . . . . 13.03[2]	
1.382-8(c)(2) **13** n.44	
1.382-8(c)(3) **13** n.44	
1.382-8(d) . . . . **13** ns. 46, 887	
1.382-8(f) . . . . 13.03[2]; **13** n.47	
1.382-8(g) . . . . **13** ns. 44, 45, 47	
1.382-9(d) . . . . **14** ns. 313, 318	
1.382-9(d)(2)(iv) **14** n.320	
1.382-9(d)(3) **14** n.319	
1.382-9(d)(3)(i) **14** n.321	
1.382-9(e) . . . . **14** ns. 196, 314	
1.382-9(i)–1.382-9(p) **14** n.324	
1.382-9(m) **14** n.334	
1.382-10T . . . . . **S14** ns. 194.1, 207.1, 229.1	
1.383-1T **14** n.354	
1.383-1T(c)(6) . . . . 14.44[7][f]	
1.383-1T(d)(2) . . . . 14.44[7][f]	
1.383-1T(e) . . . . 14.44[7][f]	
1.383-1T(f) . . . . 14.44[7][f]	
1.383-3(b)(1) **14** n.107	
1.383-3A(c)(3) **12** n.99	
1.388(b)-3T(b)(2)(ii) **3** n.154	
1.421-6 . . . . **4** n.438	
1.441-1T(b)(2) **3** n.382; **5** n.318	
1.441-4T(c) **5** n.321	

[Text references are to paragraphs; note references are to chapters (boldface numbers) and notes ("n."), and references to the supplement are preceded by "S."]

Reg. §

1.441-4T(d)	**5** n.320
1.441-4T(d)(1)(i)	**5** n.319
1.442-1(a)(1)	**3** n.382
1.444-1T	**5** n.323
1.444-2T	**5** n.323
1.444-3T	**5** n.323
1.446-1(d)	**14** n.94
1.446-1(e)(1)	**3** n.383
1.446-4(e)(9)	**13** n.576
1.448-1T(b)(3)	**5** n.326
1.448-1T(e)	**5** n.2
1.451-2(b)	**8** n.156
1.482-9T(b)	S13.21[3]
1.482-9T(b)(5)	**S13** n.146.17
1.482-9T(b)(6) Exs. 1–26	S13.21[3]
1.482-9T(b)(6) Exs. 18–23	**S13** n.146.17
15A.453-1(b)(3)(i)	**3** n.83
15A.453-1(c)	**10** n.439
15A.453-1(c)(4)	**3** n.154
15A.453-1(d)(2)(iii)	**10** ns. 50, 438
15A.453-1(e)(4)	**2** n.116
15A.453-1(e)(5)	**2** n.116
1.453-6(b)	**12** n.1176
1.453-9(c)(2)	**12** n.408
1.453-11	**10** n.39
1.461-1(a)(2)	**3** n.136
1.461-4(d)(5)	**10** n.230
1.471-2(c)	**8** n.75
1.482	**13** n.160
1.482-1	13.20[6][e]; **13** ns. 68, 138, 162, 193; **S13** n.146.10
1.482-1(a)(1)	**13** n.53
1.482-1(a)(2)	**13** n.88
1.482-1(a)(3)	**13** ns. 101, 115
1.482-1(b)	**13** n.54
1.482-1(b)(1)	**13** ns. 121, 124
1.482-1T	**13** ns. 66, 207
1.482-1T(a)(2)	**13** n.88
1.482-1T(a)(3)	**13** n.101
1.482-1T(b)	**13** ns. 54, 119
1.482-1(b)(1)	**2** n.166
1.482-1T(b)(2)	13.20[6][b]
1.482-1T(b)(2)(iii)(A)	**13** n.122
1.482-1(c)	**13** n.122
1.482-1T(c)	**13** ns. 120, 124
1.482-1(c)(2)	**13** n.123
1.482-1T(c)(2)(i)	**13** n.124
1.482-1T(c)(2)(ii)	**13** n.145
1.482-1T(c)(3)	**13** n.125
1.482-1T(c)(4)	**13** n.126
1.482-1T(c)(5)(i)	**13** n.112
1.482-1(d)	**13** ns. 121, 124
1.482-1T(d)(1)(ii)	**13** n.89
1.482-1T(d)(1)(iii)	**13** n.92
1.482-1T(d)(1)(iv)	**13** n.94
1.482-1(d)(2)	**13** ns. 124, 125, 145
1.482-1(d)(3)	**13** n.125
1.482-1T(d)(3)(i)	**13** n.119
1.482-1(d)(4)(i)	**13** n.126
1.482-1(d)(4)(ii)	**13** n.126
1.482-1(d)(4)(ii)(C)	**13** n.185

1.482-1(d)(4)(iii)	**13** n.126
1.482-1(d)(4)(iii)(A)	**13** n.124
1.482-1(e)	**13** n.121
1.482-1T(e)(2)	**13** n.114
1.482-1T(e)(2)(ii)	**13** n.114
1.482-1T(e)(2)(iv)	**13** n.114
1.482-1T(e)(3)	**13** n.109
1.482-1T(e)(3)(i)	**13** n.110
1.482-1T(e)(3)(iv)	**13** n.109
1.482-1T(e)(4)	**13** ns. 116, 224
1.482-1T(e)(5)	**13** n.111
1.482-1T(e)(5)(i)	**13** n.111
1.482-1(f)	**13** n.87
1.482-1T(f)(1)	**13** n.201
1.482-1(f)(1)(ii)	**13** n.89
1.482-1(f)(1)(iii)	**3** n.352; **13** n.92
1.482-1(f)(1)(iv)	**13** ns. 50, 94
1.482-1(f)(2)	**13** n.56
1.482-1(g)	**13** n.114
1.482-1T(g)(1)–1.482-1T(g)(3)	**13** n.75
1.482-1(g)(2)	**13** n.109
1.482-1(g)(2)(i)	**13** n.110
1.482-1(g)(2)(iv)	**13** n.109
1.482-1(g)(3)	**13** ns. 116, 224
1.482-1(g)(4)	**13** n.111
1.482-1T(g)(4)	**13** n.85
1.482-1(g)(4)(ii)	**13** n.112
1.482-1T(g)(5)	**13** n.81
1.482-1T(h)	**13** n.67
1.482-1(h)(1)	**13** n.201
1.482-1(h)(2)	**13** ns. 100, 132
1.482-1(i)(1)	**13** n.75
1.482-1(i)(2)	**13** n.75
1.482-1(i)(4)	**13** ns. 85, 86
1.482-1(i)(5)	**13** n.81
1.482-1(i)(9)	**13** n.56
1.482-1(j)(1)	**13** ns. 68, 162
1.482-1(j)(2)	**13** n.68
1.482-1A(a)(1)	**13** n.75
1.482-1A(a)(3)	**13** n.85
1.482-1A(b)(2)	**13** n.75
1.482-1A(b)(3)	**13** ns. 94, 101
1.482-1A(d)(1)	**13** n.88
1.482-1A(d)(3)	**13** n.113
1.482-1A(d)(4)	**13** n.89
1.482-1A(d)(5)	**3** n.352; **13** n.92
1.482-1A(d)(6)	**13** n.99
1.482-2	13.20[6][e]; **13** n.68
1.482-2(a)–1.482-2(c)	**13** n.138
1.482-2(a)(1)	**13** n.139
1.482-2(a)(1)(iii)(B)	**13** n.140
1.482-2(a)(1)(iii)(C)	**13** n.140
1.482-2(a)(2)(iii)(D)	**13** n.141
1.482-2(a)(2)(iii)(E)	**13** n.141
1.482-2(a)(3)	**13** n.142
1.482-2(a)(3)(ii)	**13** n.254
1.482-2(a)(4)	**13** n.254
1.482-2(b)	**13** n.143
1.482-2(b)(3)	**2** n.166; **13** n.144
1.482-2(c)	**13** n.147
1.482-2(c)(2)	**13** n.149

[Text references are to paragraphs; note references are to chapters (boldface numbers) and notes ("n."), and references to the supplement are preceded by "S."]

*[Text references are to paragraphs; note references are to chapters (boldface numbers)
and notes ("n."), and references to the supplement are preceded by "S."]*

Reg. §

1.861-18(b)(1)	**15** n.65
1.861-18(b)(2)	**15** n.65
1.861-18(c)(2)	**15** n.66
1.861-18(c)(3)	**15** n.67
1.861-18(d)	**15** n.68
1.861-18(f)	**15** n.67
1.861-18(f)(1)	**15** n.66
1.861-18(f)(2)	**15** n.67
1.861-18(g)	**15** n.67
1.861-18(h)	**15** ns. 67, 68, 69
1.861-2(a)(4)	**15** n.45
1.861-2(a)(5)	**15** n.49
1.861-3(a)(1)	15.02[1][b]; **15** n.54
1.861-4	**S15** n.60
1.861-7(c)	**15** n.72
1.861-8	**15** ns. 106, 119, 482, 483
1.861-8T – 1.861-12T	**15** n.119
1.861-8(a)	15.02[1][e]
1.861-8(e)(2)	**15** ns. 106, 108
1.861-8(e)(2)(v)	**15** n.106
1.861-8(e)(3)	15.02[1][f]; **S15** n.111
1.861-8(e)(6)	**15** ns. 106, 108
1.861-8(e)(7)	**15** ns. 76, 84
1.861-8T(e)(12)	**S15** n.106
1.861-8(g)	**15** ns. 106, 108
1.861-9	**S15** n.119
1.861-11	**S15** n.119
1.861-14	**S15** n.119
1.862-3(c)(2)	**15** n.92
1.863-1(b)	15.02[1][d]; **15** n.91
1.863-1(d)	**15** n.89
1.863-2	**15** n.98
1.863-3	**15** ns. 98, 482
1.863-3(b)	**15** ns. 94, 95
1.863-3(b)	**15** n.99
1.863-3(b)(1)	**15** n.92
1.863-3(b)(2)	**15** ns. 90, 94
1.863-3(c)	**15** n.94
1.863-3(c)(1)	**15** n.99
1.863-3(c)(1)(iii)	**15** n.102
1.863-3(c)(1)(iv)	**15** n.102
1.863-3(c)(2)	**15** ns. 78, 101
1.863-3(e)(1)	**15** ns. 94, 99
1.863-3(f)	**15** n.104
1.863-3 – 1.863-5	15.02[1][d]
1.863-3(h)(v)	**15** n.134
1.863-3T	**15** n.119
1.863-7	**15** ns. 50, 89
1.863-8	**S15** ns. 105, 105.3
1.863-8(f)	**S15** n.105
1.863-9	**S15** ns. 105, 105.3
1.864-2(c)	**15** n.128
1.864-2(c)(2)(iii)	15.02[2][e]; **15** n.130
1.864-2(d)	**15** n.128
1.864-2(d)(3)	**15** n.132
1.864-3	**15** n.157
1.864-3(b)	**15** n.169
1.864-4(b)	**15** n.157
1.864-4(c)	**15** n.151
1.864-4(c)(2)(iii)(a)	**15** n.152
1.864-4(c)(5)(i)	**15** n.156

Reg. §

1.864-4(c)(6)(i)	**15** n.154
1.864-4(c)(ii)	**15** n.152
1.864-4(c)(iv)	**15** n.152
1.864-5	**15** n.159
1.864-6	**15** ns. 150, 162
1.864-6(b)(2)(i)	**15** n.163
1.864-6(b)(3)(i)	**15** n.165
1.864-7	**15** ns. 150, 160
1.864-7(d)	**15** n.144
1.864-7(e)	**15** n.145
1.865-1	**S15** ns. 76, 108
1.865-1T	**15** ns. 84, 86, 108; **S15** ns. 76, 108
1.865-1(c)(1)(iv)	**S15** ns. 86, 108
1.865-2	**15** ns. 76, 84, 85, 108; **S15** ns. 76, 85
1.865-2T	**15** ns. 84, 108
1.865-2T(4)(iii)	**15** n.85
1.865-2T(4)(iv)	**15** n.85
1.865-2(c)(2)	**15** n.108
1.705-2	**S3** n.250
1.871-8(c)(2)	**15** n.169
1.871.11	**15** n.231
1.871-11(c)	**15** ns. 62, 67
1.881-3	**4** ns. 182, 184, 264; **15** ns. 233, 236
1.881-3(a)(2)(ii)(A)(2)	**15** n.237
1.881-3(a)(2)(iii)(B)	**15** n.237
1.881-3(e)	**15** n.238
1.881-3(e), Ex. 10	**S15** n.41
1.881-3(f)	**15** n.239
1.881-4	**15** ns. 224, 236
1.882-4	**15** n.248
1.882-5	**15** n.246
1.884-0	**15** n.261
1.884-0T	**15** n.261
1.884.1	15.04[2][e]; **15** n.261
1.884-1T	**15** n.261
1.884-1(b)	**15** n.263
1.884-1(c)	**15** n.263
1.884-1(d)	**15** ns. 263, 271
1.884-1(e)	**15** ns. 263, 271
1.884-1(f)	**15** n.271
1.884-1(g)	**15** n.264
1.884-2T	15.04[2][e]; **15** ns. 261, 266, 270, 951, 1004
1.884-2T(a)	**15** ns. 266, 998, 1014
1.884-2T(b)	**15** n.1015
1.884-2T(c)	**15** ns. 266, 1005, 1011
1.884-2T(c)(4)	**15** n.1012
1.884-2T(c)(6)	**15** n.1013
1.884-2(d)	**15** n.266
1.884-2T(d)	**15** ns. 987, 1005, 1006, 1010
1.884-2T(d)(6)	**15** n.1010
1.884-2T(e)	**15** n.1005
1.884-2T(e)(5)	**15** n.1012
1.884-3T	**15** n.269
1.884-4	15.04[2][e]; **15** ns. 261, 267
1.884-4T	**S15** n.248
1.884-4T(a)(3)(ii)	**S15** n.248
1.884-4T(a)(3)(iii)	**S15** n.248

[Text references are to paragraphs; note references are to chapters (boldface numbers) and notes ("n."), and references to the supplement are preceded by "S."]

[Text references are to paragraphs; note references are to chapters (boldface numbers) and notes ("n."), and references to the supplement are preceded by "S."]

[Text references are to paragraphs; note references are to chapters (boldface numbers) and notes ("n."), and references to the supplement are preceded by "S."]

[Text references are to paragraphs; note references are to chapters (boldface numbers) and notes ("n."), and references to the supplement are preceded by "S."]

[Text references are to paragraphs; note references are to chapters (boldface numbers) and notes ("n."), and references to the supplement are preceded by "S."]

[Text references are to paragraphs; note references are to chapters (boldface numbers) and notes ("n."), and references to the supplement are preceded by "S."]

[Text references are to paragraphs; note references are to chapters (boldface numbers) and notes ("n."), and references to the supplement are preceded by "S."]

Reg. §

1.1502-17(e) **13** n.514	
1.1502-18 . . . . **13** n.511	
1.1502-19 . . . S13.44[3]; **13** ns. 354, 364, 395, 534, 550, 916	
1.1502-19T . . . . S13.42[12][c]	
1.1502-19(a) **13** n.553	
1.1502-19(a)(2)(i)(B) **13** n.554	
1.1502-19(a)(2)(ii) . . . . **13** ns. 540, 666	
1.1502-19(a)(3) **13** n.543	
1.1502-19(a)(6) . . . . **13** ns. 382, 550	
1.1502-19(b) **13** n.549	
1.1502-19(b)(1) **13** n.549	
1.1502-19T(b)(1)(ii) **S13** n.574.16	
1.1502-19(b)(2) . . . . **13** ns. 413, 544; **S13** n.574.15	
1.1502-19(b)(2)(i) **13** ns. 545, 546, 556, 557, 705, 937, 981	
1.1502-19(b)(2)(ii) . . . . **13** ns. 548, 556, 702, 709, 804, 807, 955, 981	
1.1502-19(b)(3) **13** n.702	
1.1502-19(b)(4) **13** n.549	
1.1502-19(c) . . . . **13** ns. 540, 542; **S13** n.835.2	
1.1502-19(c)(1) **13** n.826	
1.1502-19(c)(1)(i) . . . . **13** ns. 543, 544	
1.1502-19(c)(1)(i)(A) **13** n.955	
1.1502-19(c)(1)(ii) . . . . **13** ns. 548, 556	
1.1502-19(c)(1)(ii)(B) **13** n.546	
1.1502-19(c)(1)(ii) . . . . . **13** ns. 702, 801, 803, 804, 805, 807, 955	
1.1502-19(c)(1)(iii) **4** n.251; **13** ns. 541, 667, 689, 708, 969	
1.1502-19(c)(1)(iii)(A) **13** n.848	
1.1502-19(c)(1)(iii)(C) **13** n.667	
1.1502-19(c)(2) **13** n.826	
1.1502-19(c)(2)(iii)(A) **13** n.901	
1.1502-19(c)(3) **13** n.709	
1.1502-19(d) . . . . **13** ns. 561, 669	
1.1502-19(e) . . . . **13** ns. 669, 803, 805	
1.1502-19(f) **13** n.669	
1.1502-19(g) . . . **4** n.251; **13** ns. 545, 546, 548, 556, 557, 559, 560, 561, 667, 671, 702, 703, 705, 708, 804, 807, 941, 966, 981, 983, 991, 995	
1.1502-19(h) **13** n.669	
1.1502-19(h)(1) **13** n.552	
1.1502-19T(h)(2)(ii) **S13** n.574.15	
1.1502-20 . . . . **10** n.257; 13.43[3][e]; S13.43[3][e]; **13** ns. 355, 364, 469, 482, 659, 694, 700, 701, 747; **S13** ns. 485.6, 485.12, 485.24, 688; **S14** n.52.1	
1.1502-20T . . . . **13** ns. 471, 475, 476	
1.1502-20(a) . . . . 13.42[5][c]; **13** n.959	
1.1502-20(a)(3) **13** n.483	
1.1502-20(a)(4) **13** n.483	
1.1502-20(b) . . . . 13.42[5][c]	
1.1502-20(b)(4) **13** n.483	
1.1502-20(c) . . . . 13.42[5][c]	
1.1502-20(c)(2)(i) **13** n.484	
1.1502-20(c)(2)(vi) **13** n.484	
1.1502-20(d) . . . . 13.42[5][c]; **13** n.958	
1.1502-20(e) . . . . 13.42[5][c]	

Reg. §

1.1502-20(e)(3) **13** n.490	
1.1502-20(f) . . . . 13.42[5][c]	
1.1502-20(g) . . . . 13.42[5][c]; **13** n.959	
1.1502-20(g)(2) **13** n.485	
1.1502-20(i) **S13** n.485.20	
1.1502-20T(i) . . . . S13.42[5][c]; **S13** ns. 484.1, 485.6	
1.1502-20(i)(2) **S13** n.485.20	
1.1502-20T(i)(3)(v) **S13** n.485.9	
1.1502-20T(i)(4) . . . . . **S13** ns. 485.9, 485.18	
1.1502-20T(i)(6) **S13** n.485.18	
1.1502-21 – 1.1502-27 . . . . **13** n.365	
1.1502-21 . . . . **13** ns. 41, 365, 516, 719	
1.1502-21T . . . . . **13** ns. 710, 719, 760, 771	
1.1502-21(b) . . . **13** ns. 796, 798, 884, 885, 913, 915, 916, 953	
1.1502-21T(b) . . . . . S13.42[12][c]; **13** ns. 794– 796, 798	
1.1502-21(b)(2)(ii)(B) . . . **13** ns. 796, 798, 810, 812	
1.1502-21T(b)(2)(iv) **S13** ns. 574.10, 574.15, 574.19	
1.1502-21T(b)(2)(iv)(B)(2) **S13** n.574.20	
1.1502-21(b)(2)(v) **13** n.796	
1.1502-21(b)(3)(i) **13** n.517	
1.1502-21(b)(3)(ii)(B) **13** n.517	
1.1502-21(b)(3)(iii) **13** n.517	
1.1502-21(c) – 1.1502-21(h) **13** n.772	
1.1502-21(c) . . . . . . **13** ns. 710, 720, 721, 916	
1.1502-21T(c)(1)(iii) **13** n.785	
1.1502-21T(c)(1)(vii)(6) **S13** n.574.15	
1.1502-21T(c)(1)(vii)(8) **S13** n.574.15	
1.1502-21(c)(2) **S13** n.785	
1.1502-21(c)(2)(vii) **S13** n.574.15	
1.1502-21(c)(3) **14** n.26	
1.1502-21(d) . . . . **13** ns. 712, 727, 739	
1.1502-21(e) . . . . **13** ns. 730, 770	
1.1502-21(g) . . . . **13** ns. 723, 757, 773	
1.1502-21(g)(2)(ii) **13** n.774	
1.1502-21(g)(4) **13** n.775	
1.1502-21(c)(2)(vii) **S13** n.574.15	
1.1502-22(c) **13** n.710	
1.1502-22(d) **13** n.712	
1.1502-23T(b) **13** n.785	
1.1502-26(b) **5** n.211; **13** n.429	
1.1502-28 S13.42[12][a]; S13.42[12][b]; **S13** ns. 574.2, 803	
1.1502-28T . . . . . . S13.42[12]; S13.42[12][c]; S13.47[4][b]; **S13** ns. 574.2, 901.1	
1.1502-28(a)(1) . . . . **S13** ns. 574.3, 574.9	
1.1502-28T(a)(1) . . . . **S13** ns. 574.3, 574.9	
1.1502-28(a)(2) . . . . **S13** ns. 574.6, 574.11	
1.1502-28T(a)(2) . . . . . . **S13** ns. 574.6, 574.11	
1.1502-28(a)(3) **S13** n.574.6	
1.1502-28T(a)(3) . . . S13.42[12][b]; **S13** n.574.6	
1.1502-28(a)(3)(ii) **S13** n.574.7	
1.1502-28T(a)(3)(ii) **S13** n.574.7	
1.1502-28(a)(4) . . . . **S13** ns. 574.4, 574.8, 574.13, 574.14	
1.1502-28T(a)(4) . . . . S13.42[12][c]; **S13** n.574.13	

[Text references are to paragraphs; note references are to chapters (boldface numbers) and notes ("n."), and references to the supplement are preceded by "S."]

[Text references are to paragraphs; note references are to chapters (boldface numbers) and notes ("n."), and references to the supplement are preceded by "S."]

[Text references are to paragraphs; note references are to chapters (boldface numbers) and notes ("n."), and references to the supplement are preceded by "S."]

[Text references are to paragraphs; note references are to chapters (boldface numbers) and notes ("n."), and references to the supplement are preceded by "S."]

Reg. §

7.367(b)-3 . . . . 15.81[3][d]
7.367(b)-4 . . . . 15.81[3][d]
7.367(b)-4(b) . . . 15.81[3][d]; **15** ns. 708, 715, 827, 844, 845, 848, 868
7.367(b)-4(c) . . . . **15** ns. 639, 906
7.367(b)-4(d) . . . . **15** ns. 882, 903, 904
7.367(b)-5 . . . . 15.81[3][d]
7.367(b)-5(c) **15** n.643
7.367(b)-7 – 7.367(b)-12 . . . . 15.81[3][d]
7.367(b)-7 . . . . 15.81[3][d]; 15.84[1][c]; **15** ns. 847, 869, 882, 883
7.367(b)-7(a) . . . . **15** ns. 882, 903
7.367(b)-7(b) . . . . **15** ns. 866, 907
7.367(b)-7(c) **15** n.711
7.367(b)-7(c)(1) . . . **15** ns. 825, 841, 862, 881
7.367(b)-7(c)(1)(ii) . . . . . . **15** ns. 710, 825, 850
7.367(b)-7(c)(2) . . . . **15** ns. 880, 905
7.367(b)-8 . . . . **15** n.785
7.367(b)-9 . . . . 15.81[3][d]; 15.84[1][c]; **15** ns. 866, 870, 871, 882, 883, 907
7.367(b)-9(b)(4) . . . . **15** ns. 710, 850
7.367(b)-9(c) **15** n.713
7.367(b)-9(d) **15** n.713
7.367(b)-9(e) **15** n.714
7.367(b)-9(f) **15** n.714
7.367(b)-10 . . . . 15.81[3][d]; **15** n.915
7.367(b)-10(b) **15** n.923
7.367(b)-10(i) **15** n.910
7.367(b)-11 . . . . 15.81[3][d]
7.367(b)-12 . . . . 15.81[3][d]
7.367(b)-13 . . . . **15** ns. 715, 848, 871
7.637(b)-10(j) **15** n.911
25.2511-1(h)(1) . . . . **3** ns. 177, 302
156.5881-1(a) **9** n.492
156.5881-1(b)(2) **9** n.490
301.6011-1(c) **5** n.558
301.6111-1T **5** n.522
301.6111-2 . . . . **5** ns. 506, 521
301.6111-2(b)(3) . . . . **5** ns. 507, 509
301.6111-2T(b)(3) . . . . **5** ns. 507, 508
301.6111-2(b)(3)(i) **5** n.509
301.6111-2(b)(3)(ii) **5** n.509
301.6111-2T(b)(3)(ii) **5** n.507
301.6111-2T(b)(4) . . . . **5** ns. 507, 509
301.6111-2(b)(4)(i) **5** n.507
301.6111-2T(b)(4)(i) **5** n.507
301.6111-2(b)(4)(ii) **5** n.507
301.6111-2(b)(4)(iii) **5** n.507
301.6111-2T(b)(5) **5** n.507
301.6111-2T(b)(6) **5** n.507
301.6111-2(f) **5** n.511
301.6111-2T(f) **5** n.511
301.6111-2(g) **5** n.511
301.6111-2T(g) **5** n.511
301.6111-3 . . . . **S5** n.591
301.6112-1 . . . . . 5.10[8][e]; **5** ns. 506, 521; **S5** n.591
301.6112-1T . . . . . . **5** ns. 497, 504, 522, 564
301.6112-1T(c) **5** n.522
301.6112-1(c)(2) . . . . 5.10[8][e]; **5** n.521
301.6112-2T **5** n.497

Reg. §

301.6117-1 . . . . **15** n.175
301.6712-1 . . . . **15** n.175
301.6901-1(b) **12** n.24
301.7701 . . . . **S2** n.56
301.7701-1 . . . . **2** ns. 45, 80
301.7701-1(a) **2** n.47
301.7701-1(a)(1) **2** n.4
301.7701-1(b) . . . . **2** ns. 47, 113, 125
301.7701-1(c) **2** n.47
301.7701-1(f) **2** n.53
301.7701-2 . . . 2.02[2]; **2** ns. 5, 45, 80; **15** n.27
301.7701-2T **S2** n.58.2
301.7701-2(a)(1) **2** n.42; **5** n.22
301.7701-2(a)(2) . . . . . . **2** ns. 29–32, 42, 80
301.7701-2(a)(3) . . . . . . **2** ns. 28, 29, 42, 80
301.7701-2(b)–301.7701-2(g) **2** n.33
301.7701-2(b) . . . . 2.02[3][a]; **2** n.60
301.7701-2(b)(1)–301.7701-2(b)(7) . . . **2** ns. 6, 7
301.7701-2(b)(1) **2** n.35
301.7701-2(b)(2) . . . . **2** ns. 34, 35
301.7701-2(b)(3) . . . . **2** ns. 35, 83
301.7701-2(b)(7) **2** n.113
301.7701-2(b)(8) **2** n.48; **15** n.29
301.7701-2T(b)(9) . . . . . **S15** ns. 27.2, 34.1
301.7701-2(c) . . . . **2** ns. 36, 49
301.7701-2(c)(4) . . . . **2** ns. 83, 93
301.7701-2(d) . . . . **2** ns. 38, 48, 53
301.7701-2(d)(1) . . . . **2** ns. 39, 83
301.7701-2(e) . . . . **2** ns. 40, 53
301.7701-2(e)(2) **2** n.41
301.7701-2(e)(3) **S2** n.50
301.7701-2(e)(4) **S2** n.50
301.7701-3 . . . . . 2.02[3][a]; **2** ns. 5, 45, 80; **15** n.27
301.7701-3T . . . . **15** ns. 33, 507
301.7701-3(a) . . . . **2** ns. 5, 49
301.7701-3(b) . . . . 2.02[3][b]
301.7701-3(b)(1) **2** n.50
301.7701-3(b)(2) . . . **2** ns. 5, 51; **15** ns. 27, 30
301.7701-3(b)(2)(ii) **2** n.4
301.7701-3(b)(3) . . . . **2** ns. 51, 53
301.7701-3(c) . . . . **2** ns. 52, 84
301.7701-3(c)(1)(v)(C) **S6** n.55.1
301.7701-3(e) **13** n.176
301.7701-3(e)(1) **2** n.53
301.7701-3(f)(2) . . . . . . **2** ns. 51, 53; **S2** n.57
301.7701-3(g)(1)(i) **S2** n.56
301.7701-3(g)(1)(ii) **S2** n.55
301.7701-3(g)(1)(iii) **S2** n.55
301.7701-3(g)(1)(iv) **S2** n.56
301.7701-3(g)(3)(ii) **S2** n.56
301.7701-4(a) . . . . **2** ns. 61, 62
301.7701-4(b) . . . . 1 n.95; **2** ns. 63, 69
301.7701-4(c) . . . 2.03[2]; **2** ns. 72, 75; **4** n.108
301.7701-4(c)(2) **2** n.75
301.7701-4(d) . . . . **2** ns. 76, 78, 200
301.7701-5T   **S2** ns. 58.2, 58.3; **S15** ns. 27.1, 34.1
301.7701-27(b)(6) **S2** n.48
301.7701-27(e)(3) **S2** n.48

[Text references are to paragraphs; note references are to chapters (boldface numbers) and notes ("n."), and references to the supplement are preceded by "S."]

[Text references are to paragraphs; note references are to chapters (boldface numbers) and notes ("n."), and references to the supplement are preceded by "S."]

Prop. Reg. §

1.338-3(b)(4) **10** n.539
1.338-3(b)(5) **10** n.538
1.338-3(c)(1) . . . . . . **10** ns. 545, 568, 570
1.338-3(c)(3) . . . . **10** ns. 291, 383, 472, 571, 573, 574
1.338-3(d)(1) . . . . **10** ns. 520, 522
1.338-3(d)(2) **10** n.522
1.338-4 . . . . 10.42[1][c]; **10** ns. 525, 549, 554, 583
1.338-4(b)(1) **10** n.522
1.338-4(c)(1)(i) **10** n.506
1.338-4(d) **10** n.627
1.338-4(d)(1) . . . . **10** ns. 527, 626
1.338-4(d)(3) **10** n.626
1.338-4(e)(2) **10** n.554
1.338-4(h) . . . . . . **10** n.567; **15** ns. 588, 594
1.338-5 . . . . **10** n.525
1.338-5(b)(1) . . . . **10** ns. 522, 613
1.338-5(d) **15** n.586
1.338-5(d)(3)(i) **10** n.619
1.338-5(d)(3)(iii) **10** n.619
1.338-5(e) **10** n.627
1.338-5(e)(1) **10** n.622
1.338-5(e)(2) . . . . **10** ns. 622, 623
1.338-6 . . . . **10** n.596
1.338-6(b)(1) **10** n.638
1.338-7 . . . . **10** n.525
1.338-7(a) **S10** n.625
1.338-(7)(d)(1) . . . . **10** ns. 624, 625
1.338-8 . . . . **10** n.480
1.338-10(a)(1) . . . . **10** ns. 508, 512, 575
1.338-10(a)(2)(i) **10** n.513
1.338-10(a)(2)(iii) **10** n.509
1.338(h)(10)-1 . . . . **10** n.578
1.338(h)(10)-1(c) **10** n.582
1.338(h)(10)-1(c)(2) . . . . **6** ns. 72, 197
1.338(h)(10)-1(d)(1) **10** n.620
1.338(h)(10)-1(d)(2) . . . . . . **10** ns. 588, 627
1.338(h)(10)-1(d)(3) **10** n.627
1.338(h)(10)-1(d)(3)(i) . . . **6** ns. 72, 196; **10** ns. 591, 593
1.338(h)(10)-1(d)(4)(i) . . . . **6** ns. 72, 196
1.338(h)(10)-1(d)(5) . . . . **6** ns. 72, 196
1.338(h)(10)-1(d)(5)(iii) **10** n.585
1.338(h)(10)-1(d)(8) . . . . . . **10** ns. 589, 604
1.338(h)(10)-1(e) . . . . **8** n.287; **9** n.200; **10** ns. 265, 581, 587, 604
1.338(h)(10)-1(e)(3) **10** n.577
1.338(i)-1 . . . . **10** n.479
1.338(i)-1(a) **10** n.549
1.341-4(c)(4) **10** n.740
1.351-1(a)(1)(iii) . . . **S3** n.105.1; **S12** n.1136.10
1.351-1(a)(2), Ex. 4 . . . . **S3** n.105.1; **S12** n.1136.10
1.351-1(c) . . . . **12** ns. 531, 632
1.354-1(e) . . . **3** ns. 64, 68, 73; **4** n.453; **12** ns. 622, 632, 638
1.355 . . . . **11** ns. 116, 117
1.355-1(c) . . . . **4** n.453; **11** n.255; **12** ns. 632, 638
1.355-2(b)(1) **11** n.234

Prop. Reg. §

1.355-2(c)(2) **11** n.155
1.355-2(c)(4) **11** n.155
1.355-2(d) **11** n.205
1.355-6 . . . **11** ns. 68, 270, 287, 296; **S11** n.68
1.355-6(b)(3) **11** n.297
1.355-6(b)(3)(i) **11** n.300
1.355-6(b)(3)(ii) **11** n.298
1.355-6(b)(3)(iv) **11** n.302
1.355-6(b)(3)(v) . . . **11** ns. 300, 302, 306, 307
1.355-6(b)(4) . . . . 11.11[2][a]; **11** n.297
1.355-6(c) . . . . 11.11[2][a]; **11** n.298
1.355-6(c)(3) . . . . 11.11[2][a]; **11** n.310
1.355-6(c)(3)(vii) **11** n.303
1.355-6(d) . . . . . 11.11[2][a]; **11** ns. 133, 299
1.355-6(d)(1) **11** n.301
1.355-6(d)(3) . . . . **10** n.531; **11** ns. 301, 309
1.355-6(d)(4) **11** n.301
1.355-6(d)(5) **11** n.301
1.355-6(e) . . . . 11.11[2][a]
1.355-6(e)(1) **11** n.309
1.355-6(e)(2) . . . . 11.11[2][a]; **11** n.308
1.355-6(e)(3) . . . . 11.11[2][a]
1.355-7 . . . **11** ns. 68, 177, 270, 305, 321, 325; **S11** ns. 68, 329, 329.1, 331; **12** ns. 127, 888, 893, 895, 1057; **S12** ns. 895.1, 907; **S13** n.964
1.355-7(a) **10** n.714
1.355-7(a)(2)(iii)(D) **12** n.894
1.355-7(a)(5) . . . . 11.11[3][d]
1.355-7(a)(6) . . . . 11.11[3][d]
1.355-7(a)(8) . . . . 11.11[3][d]; **11** n.329
1.355-7(d) . . . . **S11**.11[3][d]
1.355-7(d)(2) **S12** n.888
1.355-7(d)(3) **S12** n.888
1.355-7(d)(3)(iii) . . . . **S11**.11[3][d]
1.355-7(d)(3)(v) . . . . **S11**.11[3][d]
1.355-7(f) . . . . **S11**.11[3][d]; **S12** n.907
1.355-7(m) . . . . **S11**.11[3][d]; **S11** n.329
1.355-7(m)(4)(iii)(F) **S11** n.331.1
1.355-8 . . . . **S11** n.331.11
1.355-8(b) **S11** n.331.12
1.355-8(c) **S11** n.331.12
1.355-8(d) . . . . **S11** ns. 331.12, 331.13
1.355-8(e) **S11** n.331.14
1.355-8(f) **S11** n.331.16
1.355-8(g) **S11** n.331.15
1.356-3(b) . . . . **3** n.64; **4** n.453; **11** n.255; **12** ns. 622, 632, 638
1.356-7 . . . **S3** n.90; **11** n.261; **12** ns. 653, 760
1.358-2(a)(2) . . . . . **S11** n.340.1; **S12** ns. 788, 790.1
1.358-2(a)(2)(i) **S12** n.790.2
1.358-2(a)(2)(ii) **S11** n.340.2; **S12** n.790.2
1.358-2(a)(2)(iii) . . . . **S12** ns. 790.2, 790.3
1.358-2(c) . . . **S11** n.340.1; **S12** ns. 788, 790.1
1.358-2(c) Ex. 7 . . . . **S11** ns. 340.2, 340.3
1.368-2(k) . . . . **S12** ns. 56.1, 1017.3
1.358-6 . . . . **12** ns. 734, 1039, 1040
1.358-6(a) **12** n.734
1.358-6(a)(3) **12** n.738
1.358-6(b) **12** n.734

[Text references are to paragraphs; note references are to chapters (boldface numbers) and notes ("n."), and references to the supplement are preceded by "S."]

Prop. Reg. §

1.358-6(b)(3) **12** n.738
1.358-6(c) . . . . **12** ns. 303, 304, 734, 736
1.358-6(c)(2) **12** n.730
1.358-6(c)(2)(ii) **12** n.737
1.358-6(c)(2)(iii) . . . . . . **12** ns. 304, 736, 737
1.358-6(c)(3) **12** n.738
1.358-6(c)(4) **12** n.737
1.358-6(c)(5) **12** n.730, 737
1.358-6(d) **12** n.303
1.358-7 . . . . . . **S3** ns. 145.1, 158.4, 223, 249.1
1.362-4 . . . . . . **S3** n.249.6; **S6** ns. 97.3, 117.1
1.367-2(k) . . . . **S15**.81[3][h]
1.367(a)-3 . . . . **15** ns. 658, 659, 668, 676, 677,
            686, 708, 761, 769, 829, 859, 860, 872
1.367(a)-3(a) . . . . **S9** n.410.1; **15** ns. 683, 846,
                                            864, 867, 889
1.367(a)-3(b) . . . . **15** ns. 683, 771
1.367(a)-3(b)(1) **15** n.876
1.367(a)-3(b)(2) **15** n.684
1.367(a)-3(b)(2)(i) **S15** n.741.10
1.367(a)-3(b)(3) . . . . **15** ns. 772, 896
1.367(a)-3(c) **15** n.829
1.367(a)-3(d) . . . 15.81[3][c]; **15** ns. 854, 875,
                                                     888
1.367(a)-3(d)(1) . . . . **15** ns. 687, 774
1.367(a)-3(d)(1)(iii)(B) **S15** n.741.14
1.367(a)-3(d)(2)(vi) **S15** n.741.16
1.367(a)-3(d)(3) . . . . . **15** ns. 772, 891, 892, 893
1.367(a)-3(d)(3), Ex. 5A **S15** n.741.14
1.367(a)-3(d)(3), Ex. 6B **S15** n.741.16
1.367(a)-3(d)(3), Ex. 6C **S15** n.741.16
1.367(a)-3(d)(3), Ex. 6D **S15** n.741.16
1.367(a)-3(d)(3), Ex. 9 . . . . . . **S15** n.741.16
1.367(a)-3(d)(3), Ex. 13A **S15** n.741.16
1.367(a)-3(f) **15** n.689
1.367(a)-8 . . . . **15** ns. 659, 668, 761, 829
1.367(b) **15** n.686
1.367(b)-1 – 1.367(b)-6   **15** ns. 625, 664, 628,
                                                     629
1.367(b)-1 . . . . **15** n.716
1.367(b)-1(a) . . . . . **15** ns. 643, 686, 846, 889
1.367(b)-1(b) . . . . . **15** ns. 639, 641, 785, 786,
                                            826, 842, 857, 897
1.367(b)-2 . . . . **15** n.716
1.367(b)-2(c) **15** n.707
1.367(b)-2(d) **15** n.707
1.367(b)-2(f) . . . . **15** ns. 639, 904, 906
1.367(b)-2(g) . . . . **15** ns. 639, 905
1.367(b)-3 . . . . **15** ns. 716, 720, 792, 881
1.367(b)-3(a) **15** n.639
1.367(b)-3(b)(2) **15** n.881
1.367(b)-3(b)(2)(i)(A) **15** n.856
1.367(b)-3(b)(2)(ii) **15** n.725
1.367(b)-3(b)(2)(ii)(A) **15** n.794
1.367(b)-3(b)(2)(iii)(A) . . . **15** ns. 726, 793, 795
1.367(b)-3(b)(2)(iii)(A)(1) **15** n.254
1.367(b)-3(c) . . . . **15** ns. 727, 881
1.367(b)-3(e) . . . . **S14** ns. 73, 89.1, 409, 414;
            S15 ns. 603, 654.1, 719, 726, 740,
                 795.1, 881, 898, 905, 1039, 1053

Prop. Reg. §

1.367(b)-3(f) . . . . **S14** ns. 73, 89.1, 409, 414;
            S15 ns. 603, 654.1, 719, 726, 740,
                 795.1, 881, 898, 905, 1039, 1053
1.367(b)-3(j) **15** n.905
1.367(b)-3T(b)(4)(i)(B)(1) **15** n.254
1.367(b)-4 . . . . **15** ns. 710, 716, 721, 850, 851,
                                                825, 884
1.367(b)-4(a) **S9** n.410.1; **15** n.639
1.367(b)-4(b)(1) . . . **15** ns. 728, 729, 826, 842,
            852, 857, 863, 866, 874, 885, 900, 1036
1.367(b)-4(b)(1)(ii) **S15** n.741.18
1.367(b)-4(b)(1)(iii), Ex. 3B **S15** n.741.18
1.367(b)-4(b)(2) . . . **15** ns. 730, 731, 853, 887
1.367(b)-4(b)(3) **15** n.731
1.367(b)-4(c) . . . . **15** ns. 729, 856
1.367(b)-4(e) . . . . . **15** ns. 846, 855, 856, 865,
                                     867, 874, 887, 889
1.367(b)-5 . . . . **15** ns. 716, 722, 732
1.367(b)-5(b)(1) **15** n.733
1.367(b)-5(c) **15** n.734
1.367(b)-5(d) **15** n.735
1.367(b)-5(f)(1) **15** n.736
1.367(b)-6 . . . . **15** ns. 716, 722
1.367(b)-7   **S14** n.89.1; **S15**.84[3][f]; **S15** ns.
            340, 365, 654.1, 719, 731.1, 803, 803.1,
            884.1, 889.1, 901, 902.2, 923.1, 923.11
1.367(b)-7(b)(1) **S15** n.902.4
1.367(b)-7(c) . . . . **S15**.84[2][f]; **S15** n.902.4
1.367(b)-7(d) . . . . **S15**.84[2][f]
1.367(b)-7(d)(1)(ii) **S15** n.902.6
1.367(b)-7(d)(2) **S15** n.902.6
1.367(b)-7(d)(3) **S15** n.902.6
1.367(b)-7(e) . . . . **S15**.84[2][f]
1.367(b)-7(e)(1) . . . . **S15**.84[2][f]; **S15** n.902.7
1.367(b)-7(e)(2) . . . . **S15**.84[2][f]; **S15** n.902.8
1.367(b)-7(f) . . . . **S15**.84[2][f]
1.367(b)-7(f)(1) . . . . **S15**.84[2][f]; **S15** n.902.10
1.367(b)-7(f)(2) . . . . **S15**.84[2][f]; **S15** n.902.11
1.367(b)-7(g) . . . . **S15**.84[2][f]
1.367(b)-7(g)(1) **S15** n.902.12
1.367(b)-7(g)(3) **S15** n.902.12
1.367(b)-8 . . . . . **S11** ns. 347, 348; **S14** n.89.1;
            S15.84[3][f]; **S15** ns. 340, 365, 654.1,
            719, 736.1, 908.3, 922.1, 923.1, 928
1.367(b)-8(b) **S15** n.908
1.367(b)-8(b)(1)(ii) **S15** n.923.4
1.367(b)-8(b)(1)(iii) **S15** n.923.5
1.367(b)-8(b)(1)(iv) **S15** n.923.3
1.367(b)-8(b)(1)(vi) . . . . **S15** ns. 923.6, 1007
1.367(b)-8(b)(2) **S15** n.923.7
1.367(b)-8(b)(3) **S15** n.923.8
1.367(b)-8(c)   **S15**.84[3][f]; **S15** ns. 908, 945,
                                                     946
1.367(b)-8(c)(2) **S15** n.923.9
1.367(b)-8(c)(3) **S15** n.923.9
1.367(b)-8(d) . . . . . . **S15**.84[3][f]; **S15** n.908.1
1.367(b)-8(d)(6) . . . . **S15** ns. 920, 923.10
1.367(b)-8(e) . . . . . . **S15**.84[3][f]; **S15** n.908.2
1.367(b)-8(e)(2) **S15** n.923.11
1.367(b)-8(e)(2)(ii) **S15** n.923.11
1.367(b)-8(e)(6) **S15** n.920

*[Text references are to paragraphs; note references are to chapters (boldface numbers)
and notes ("n."), and references to the supplement are preceded by "S."]*

Prop. Reg. §

1.367(b)-9   **S14** n.89.1; S15.84[3][f]; **S15** ns. 340, 365, 719, 884.1, 889.1, 902.2, 907, 908, 922.1, 923.1
1.367(b)-9(b) **S15** n.923.11
1.367(b)-13 . . . . S15.81[3][h]
1.367(b)-13(b) **S15** n.741.3
1.367(b)-13(c) . . . . . S15.81[3][h]; **S15** n.741.3
1.367(b)-13(e), Exs. 2–5 . . . . **S15** n.741.6
1.368-1(b)(1) . . . .
1.367(e)-2(b) **15** n.801
1.367(e)-2(b)(1) **15** n.808
1.367(e)-2(b)(2) **15** n.810
1.367(e)-2(b)(2)(i)(A) **15** n.811
1.367(e)-2(b)(2)(i)(B) **15** n.811
1.367(e)-2(b)(2)(i)(C) **15** n.811
1.367(e)-2(b)(2)(ii) **15** n.812
1.367(e)-2(b)(2)(iii) **15** n.813
1.367(e)-2(b)(2)(iii) . . . . **15** ns. 805, 808
1.367(e)-2(b)(4) **15** n.821
1.367(e)-2(c)(2) **15** n.806
1.367(e)-2(c)(4) **15** n.821
1.367(e)-2(d) **15** n.808; **S15** n.824.1
1.367(e)-2T **15** n.804
1.368-1(b) . . . . **S12** ns. 30.1, 97.1, 506.3, 829
1.368-1(b)(1) . . . . . **S12** ns. 52.2, 537.1, 915.5, 1136.1, 1136.5
1.368-1(b)(4) **S12** n.1136.6
1.368-1(d) **S12** n.508.1
1.368-1(d)(4) **S12** n.56.2
1.368-1(d)(5)   **12** ns. 56, 115, 156, 229, 829, 833, 1015, 1022
1.368-1(d)(5), Ex. (7) **S12** n.56.2
1.368-1(d)(5), Ex. (9) **S12** n.56.2
1.368-1(d)(5), Ex. (10) **S12** n.56.2
1.368-1(d)(5), Ex. (12) **S12** n.56.2
1.368-1(d)(5)(iii) **12** n.834
1.368-1(d)(5)(v) **12** n.835
1.368-1(d)(6) . . . . 12.61[2][b]; **12** ns. 56, 115, 156, 229, 833, 1015, 1016, 1022
1.368-1(e) **12** n.73
1.368-1(e)(2) **S12** n.50.1
1.368-1(e)(2)(ii) **S12** n.50.2
1.368-1(e)(2)(ii)(A) **S12** n.50.3
1.368-1(e)(3) . . . . **12** ns. 74, 76
1.368-1(e)(6) . . . . . . **S12** ns. 60, 337, 535.1
1.368-1(e)(7), Exs. 10–12 . . . . **S12** n.60
1.368-1(e)(7), Ex. 10 . . . **S12** ns. 50.1, 60, 337, 535.1
1.368-1(e)(7), Ex. 11 . . . . **S12** n.50.1
1.368-1(e)(7), Ex. 12 . . . . **S12** n.50.1
1.368-1(e)(7), Ex. 13 . . . . **S12** n.60
1.368-1(f) . . . . **S10** n.266; S12.21[2][d]; S12.65[5]; **12** ns. 56, 115, 156, 229, 1015, 1022; **S12** ns. 52.1, 243, 537.1, 915.5, 1132, 1136.1
1.368-1(f)(1) . . . . **S12** ns. 1136.2–1136.4
1.368-1(f)(2) . . . . . **12** ns. 836, 1016, 1023; **S12** ns. 52.3, 1136.4
1.368-1(f)(3) . . . . **S12** ns. 52.3, 1136.4
1.368-1(f)(4) . . . . . . **S12** ns. 52.4, 1065, 1086
1.368-1(f)(5) . . . . S12.21[2][d]; S12.65[5]

Prop. Reg. §

1.368-1(f)(5), Exs. 1–7 . . . . **S12** n.52.5
1.368-1(f)(5), Exs. 1–10 . . . . S12.65[5]
1.368-1(f)(5), Ex. 1 . . . . S12.65[5]
1.368-1(f)(5), Ex. 2 . . . . S12.65[5]
1.368-1(f)(5), Ex. 3 . . . . S12.65[5]
1.368-1(f)(5), Ex. 4 . . . . S12.65[5]
1.368-1(f)(5), Ex. 5 . . . . S12.65[5]
1.368-1(f)(5), Ex. 6 . . . . S12.65[5]
1.368-1(f)(5), Ex. 7 . . . . S12.65[5]
1.368-1(f)(5), Ex. 8 . . . . . . **S12** ns. 52.4, 52.5, 1065, 1086, 1136.6
1.368-1(f)(5), Ex. 9 . . . . **S12** n.52.5
1.368-2(b) **S11** n.20.2; **S12** n.312
1.368-2(b)(1) . . . . . . **S11** n.216.1; **12** n.150.2; 150.3; **S12** ns. 146.1, 146.2, 146.3, 147, 149, 150.2; **S13** n.975; **S15** n.741.1
1.368-2(b)(1)(iii) **S12** n.147.3
1.368-2(b)(1)(iv), Exs. 1–6 . . . . . . **S12** n.146.3
1.368-2(b)(1)(iv), Ex. 1 . . . . **S12** n.148
1.368-2(b)(1)(iv), Ex. 5 . . . . **S12** n.148
1.368-2(d)(1) . . . . **S12** ns. 1132, 1136.1
1.368-2(d)(4) . . . . **10** ns. 286, 385; **12** ns. 253, 914, 985, 997, 1006, 1011, 1131
1.368-2(d)(4)(i) **12** n.993
1.368-2(d)(4)(ii) . . . . **12** ns. 1005, 1012
1.368-2(e)(7), Ex. 11 . . . . **S12** n.50.3
1.368-2(e)(7), Ex. 12 . . . . **S12** n.50.3
1.368-2(f) **S12** n.56.2
1.368-2(j)(3)(ii) **S12** n.56.2
1.368-2(j)(3)(iii) **S12** n.56.2
1.368-2(j)(3)(iv) **S12** n.56.2
1.368-2(k) . . . **S12** ns. 56, 56.2, 328.2, 1017.3, 1017.4; **S13** n.950.1
1.368-2(k)(3), Exs. 1–8 . . . . **S12** n.1017.4
1.368-2(k)(3), Ex. (2) . . . . **S12** ns. 56.3, 508.1; **S13** n.950.2
1.368-2(k)(3), Ex. (6) . . . . **S12** ns. 56.3, 508.1; **S13** n.950.2
1.368-2(m) . . . . **S12** ns. 30.1, 97.1, 506.1
1.368-2(m)(1) **S12** n.506.2
1.368-2(m)(2) **S12** n.506.3
1.368-2(m)(4) **S12** n.506.3
1.368-2(m)(5), Exs. 1–8 . . . . **S12** n.506.2
1.368-4 . . . . **12** n.531
1.368-4(d)(5) **12** n.528
1.368-4(g) **12** n.530
1.376(b)-4(e) **15** n.853
1.382-2(a)(3)(ii) **14** n.197
1.382-2T(f)(1)(iv) . . . . **14** ns. 250, 255
1.382-2T(f)(1)(v) . . . . **14** ns. 193, 255
1.382-2T(f)(4) . . . . **14** ns. 193, 255
1.382-2T(f)(18)(i)   **14** ns. 201, 211, 230, 251
1.382-3(i) **14** n.324
1.382-3(j) **14** n.324
1.382-3(k) **14** n.324
1.382-3(k)(6) **14** n.337
1.382-3(*l*) **14** n.324
1.382-3(*l*)(4) **14** n.337
1.382-3(m)(2) **14** n.324
1.382-3(n) **14** n.324
1.382-3T(c) **14** n.314

[Text references are to paragraphs; note references are to chapters (boldface numbers) and notes ("n."), and references to the supplement are preceded by "S."]

Prop. Reg. §

1.382-4(d) **14** n.197
1.382-4(d)(1) **14** n.197
1.382-4(d)(2) **14** n.197
1.382-4(d)(2)(ii)(B) **14** n.197
1.382-4(d)(2)(iii)(B) **14** n.245
1.382-4(d)(3)(ii) **14** n.197
1.382-5 . . . . **14** n.297
1.382-6 . . . . **14** n.279
1.382-9(d) . . . . **14** ns. 313, 318
1.382-9(d)(3) **14** n.313
1.382-9(d)(3)(ii)(A) **14** n.337
1.382-9(d)(5) **14** n.322
1.382-9(d)(5)(iii) **14** n.337
1.446-1(c)(2)(iii) **S13** n.589
1.446-1(h) **12** n.1151
1.446-2(b) **12** n.621
1.446-2(h) . . . . **12** ns. 1149, 1151
1.446-3 . . . . **15** n.50
1.453-1(f)(2) **12** n.754
1.453-1(f)(2)(a)(i) **6** n.203; **12** n.754
1.453-1(f)(2)(a)(iv) **12** n.755
1.453-1(f)(3) **3** n.215
1.453-1(f)(3)(ii) . . . . **3** ns. 83, 240; **S3** ns. 215,
240; **12** n.724
1.453-1(f)(3)(iii), Ex. 1 . . . . . . **S3** ns. 215, 240
1.453-1(f)(3)(iii), Ex. 2 . . . . . . **S3** ns. 215, 240
1.453-1(f)(4) **9** n.434
1.453-2 . . . . **10** n.39
1.453-2(e) **6** n.214
1.453-11 . . . . **10** n.39
1.482-1(b)(1) . . . . **13** ns. 119, 152
1.482-1T(f)(2) . . . . . . **13** ns. 66, 99, 129, 207
1.482-1T(f)(2)(ii) **13** n.99
1.482-2(c)(1) **13** n.152
1.482-2(c)(2)(ii) **13** n.152
1.482-2(d) . . . . **13** ns. 152, 153, 198
1.482-2(d)(3) . . . . **13** ns. 153, 206
1.482-2(d)(4) **13** n.153
1.482-2(d)(5) **13** n.153
1.482-2(d)(6) **13** n.153
1.482-2(d)(8) **13** n.153
1.482-2(f) . . . . **13** ns. 152, 153, 154, 181
1.482-2(f)(11) **13** n.154
1.482-2(g) . . . . **13** ns. 152, 155, 174
1.482-2(g)(2) **13** n.155
1.482-2(g)(3) **13** n.155
1.482-2(g)(4) **13** n.155
1.482-2(g)(6) **13** n.155
1.482-4(f)(3) . . . . **S13.21[5][e]; S13** ns. 146.11,
179.2
1.482-4(f)(3)(i)(A) **S13** n.179.3
1.482-4(f)(4) . . . . **S13** ns. 146.11, 179.2
1.482-4(f)(4)(i) **S13** n.179.4
1.482-4(f)(4)(ii), Ex. 2 . . . . **S13** n.179.5
1.482-4(f)(4)(ii), Ex. 3 . . . . **S13** n.179.5
1.482-4(f)(4)(ii), Ex. 5 . . . . **S13** n.179.5
1.482-4(f)(4)(ii), Ex. 6 . . . . **S13** n.179.5
1.482-6T . . . . **13** ns. 66, 128, 207
1.482-7 . . . . **S13.21[5][d]
1.482-7(d)(2) **S13** n.178.1

Prop. Reg. §

1.482-8 . . . . . 13.21[9]; **13** ns. 82, 220; **15** ns.
120, 121, 134
1.482-9 . . . . . . **S13.20[1][d]; S13.21[3]; S13**
n.146.1
1.482-9(b) **S13** n.146.6
1.482-9(c) **S13** n.146.7
1.482-9(d) **S13** n.146.8
1.482-9(e) . . . . **S13** ns. 146.3, 146.9
1.482-9(f) **S13** n.146.2
1.482-9(f)(5), Exs. **S13** n.146.2
1.482-9(g) . . . . **S13** ns. 146.3, 146.9
1.482-9(h) **S13** n.146.10
1.482-9(*l*) . . . . **S13.21[3]
1.482-9(*l*)(3)(i) **S13** n.146.12
1.482-9(*l*)(3)(ii) **S13** n.146.13
1.482-9(*l*)(3)(iii) **S13** n.146.13
1.482-9(*l*)(3)(iv) **S13** n.146.13
1.482-9(*l*)(3)(v) **S13** n.146.13
1.482-9(*l*)(4), Ex. 1 . . . . **S13** n.146.13
1.482-9(*l*)(4), Ex. 2 . . . . **S13** n.146.13
1.482-9(*l*)(4), Ex. 3 . . . . **S13** n.146.13
1.482-9(*l*)(4), Ex. 4 . . . . **S13** n.146.13
1.482-9(*l*)(4), Ex. 5 . . . . **S13** n.146.13
1.482-9(*l*)(4), Ex. 6 . . . . **S13** n.146.13
1.482-9(*l*)(4), Exs. 7–14 . . . . . . **S13** n.146.13
1.482-9(*l*)(4), Exs. 15–17 . . . . . . **S13** n.146.13
1.483-4(b) . . . . **12** ns. 1149, 1151
1.483-5(b)(1) **12** n.1149
1.702-1(a)(8)(ii) **15** n.517
1.705-2 . . . . **S3** n.250
1.752-1(a)(1) **S3** n.97
1.861-2(a)(7) **15** n.48
1.861-3(a)(6) **15** n.53
1.861-4 . . . . **15** n.40
1.861-8(e)(12) . . . . **15** ns. 106, 108
1.861-8(g) . . . . **15** ns. 106, 108
1.861-9–1.861-11 . . . . **15** n.119
1.861-10(e) **15** n.119
1.861-18 . . . . **15** n.64
1.861-18(h) **15** n.67
1.863-3(a) **15** n.92
1.863-3(b) **15** n.94
1.863-3(b)(2) **15** n.94
1.863-3(c)(1) **15** n.99
1.863-3(d)(1) **15** n.94
1.863-3(f) **15** n.104
1.863-3(g) **15** n.100
1.863-3(h) . . . . . **13** ns. 82, 220, 221; **15** n.120
1.863-3(h)(3) . . . . **15** ns. 122, 134
1.863-3(h)(3)(iv) **15** n.145
1.863-3(h)(3)(v) **15** n.145
1.863-8 . . . . **S15** n.105.1
1.863-9 . . . . **S15** n.105.1
1.864-4(c)(2)(v) **15** n.172
1.864-4(c)(3)(ii) **15** n.172
1.864-4(c)(5)(vi)(a) **15** n.172
1.864-6(b)(2)(ii)(d)(3) **15** n.172
1.864-6(b)(3)(i) **15** n.172
1.864-6(b)(3)(ii)(c) **15** n.172
1.864-8(e)(3) **15** n.113
1.864-8(g) **15** n.113

[Text references are to paragraphs; note references are to chapters (boldface numbers) and notes ("n."), and references to the supplement are preceded by "S."]

Prop. Reg. §

1.864(b)-1 . . . . **15** ns. 132, 133
1.865-1 . . . . **15** ns. 76, 84
1.865-1(c)(6) **S15** n.86
1.865-2 . . . . **15** ns. 76, 84
1.865-2(a) . . . . **15** ns. 84, 108
1.865-2(b) **15** n.84
1.871-14(g) **S15** n.211.1
1.881-2(b)(2) **15** n.213
1.881-3 . . . . 15.03[6]; **15** n.232
1.881-3(g) **15** n.234
1.881-4(e) **15** n.234
1.894-1(d) **15** n.146
1.894-1(d)(2)(ii) . . . . . . **S15** ns. 192.1, 243.1
1.894-1(d)(2)(iii) . . . . . . **S15** ns. 192.1, 243.1
1.898-1–1.898-4 . . . . **15** ns. 410, 492
1.898-1 . . . . **15** n.492
1.898-2 . . . . **15** n.492
1.898-3 . . . . **15** n.492
1.898-4 . . . . **15** n.492
1.901-2(f) **S15** n.304.1
1.902-1(a)(1) **15** n.323
1.902-1(a)(10) **S15** n.340.1
1.902-1(a)(13) **S15** n.340.1
1.904-4(b)(2) . . . . **S15** ns. 358, 363
1.904-4(g)(1) . . . . **S15** ns. 364.1, 365
1.904-4(g)(3)(i)(C) . . . . . . **S15** ns. 364.1, 365
1.904-4(g)(3)(i)(D) . . . . . . **S15** ns. 364.1, 365
1.904(b)-1 . . . . **S15** n.347
1.905-2(a)(2) **15** n.371
1.905-2(b)(3) **15** n.371
1.951-1(e) **S15** n.501.3
1.951-1(e)(3)(v) **S15** n.501.3
1.951-1(e)(6), Ex. 9 . . . . **S15** n.501.3
1.952-1(b)(1) **15** n.517
1.952-1(e) **15** n.497
1.952-1(f) **15** n.497
1.954-1(g) **15** n.517
1.954-2(a)(5)(ii) **15** n.517
1.954-2(f)(2)(v) **S15** n.524.5
1.954-3(a)(4) . . . . **15** ns. 527, 530
1.954-3(a)(4)(i) **15** n.517
1.954-3(a)(4)(ii) **15** n.517
1.954-3(a)(6) . . . . **15** ns. 517, 527
1.954-3(a)(c) **15** n.530
1.954-4(b)(2)(iii) **15** n.517
1.956-2(a)(3) . . . . **15** ns. 517, 542
1.960-1(i) **15** n.501
1.963-3(h)(3)(iv) **15** n.134
1.964-1(c)(1) **15** n.491
1.987-1–1.987-11 . . . . **S15** n.200
1.988-6 . . . . **S15** ns. 201, 202.1
1.1001-3(c) **12** n.430
1.1001-3(d) **12** n.430
1.1001-3(e) **12** n.431
1.1001-3(g) **12** n.431
1.1012-2 . . . . **13** ns. 260, 265
1.1012-2(a) . . . . **13** ns. 258, 267, 268
1.1012-2(c) . . . . **13** ns. 258, 267, 268
1.1032-2 . . . . **12** ns. 240, 305, 711, 713, 1039, 1040
1.1032-2(b) **12** n.711

Prop. Reg. §

1.1032-2(c) **12** n.711
1.1032-2(d) **12** n.711
1.1032-2(e) **4** n.453; **12** n.717
1.1032-3 . . . 3.11[5]; **3** ns. 243, 254, 256, 273, 281; **4** n.450; **12** ns. 713, 1034, 1042, 1043; **13** ns. 629, 632
1.1032-3(b) **3** n.246; **S3** n.246
1.1032-3(c) . . . . . . 3.11[5]; **S3** n.256; **4** n.451
1.1032-3(d) **4** n.451
1.1032-3(e) **3** n.247
1.1041-2 . . . . **S9** ns. 214, 221, 225, 226
1.1041-2(a)(1) **S9** n.218
1.1041-2(b)(1) **S9** n.218
1.1059(e)-1(a) . . . . **5** ns. 218, 222
1.1060-1 . . . . **10** n.400
1.1060-1(b)(1) **10** n.402
1.1060-1(b)(2)(iii) **10** n.404
1.1060-1(b)(3) . . . . **10** ns. 82, 108
1.1060-1(b)(4) **10** n.406
1.1060-1(b)(5) **10** n.407
1.1060-1(b)(6) **10** n.408
1.1060-1(b)(7) **10** n.409
1.1060-1(b)(8) **10** n.401
1.1060-1(c)(1) . . . . **10** ns. 426, 428
1.1060-1(c)(2) . . . . . **10** ns. 413, 421, 425, 436, 440
1.1060-1(c)(4) . . . . **10** ns. 393, 430
1.1060-1(d) **10** n.401
1.1060-1(e)(1) **10** n.441
1.1253-1 . . . . **10** n.443
1.1253-2 . . . . **10** n.443
1.1253-3 . . . . **10** n.443
1.1274-2(e) . . . . **10** ns. 438, 439
1.1274-4(e)(1) **12** n.1149
1.1274-4(g)(2)(iv) **6** n.285
1.1275-2(a) . . . .
1.1275-1(b)(1) **12** n.1151
1.1275-1(d) **12** n.1151
1.1275-4 . . . **4** ns. 356, 356, 357, 419, 444; **12** n.1151
1.1275-4(b) **4** n.358
1.1275-4(c) **4** n.359
1.1275-4(f) **4** n.357
1.1275-5(a)(1) **4** n.354
1.1275-5(c)(1)(i) **4** n.354
1.1275-5(d) **4** n.354
1.1275-6 . . . . **4** ns. 356, 360
1.1291-1–1.1291-10 . . . . **15** n.455
1.1291-1(c) **S15** n.453.1
1.1291-2 . . . . **15** n.449
1.1291-2(c)(1) **15** n.449
1.1291-2(e)(2) **15** n.1028
1.1291-3 . . . . **15** n.1028
1.1291-6 . . . . **15** ns. 455, 1021
1.1291-6(a)(2) **15** n.1023
1.1291-6(a)(3) . . . . **15** ns. 1023, 1030
1.1291-6(b)(1) . . . . **15** ns. 1023, 1028
1.1291-6(b)(2) . . . . **15** ns. 1027, 1028
1.1291-6(b)(4) **15** n.1029
1.1291-6(b)(4)(i) **15** n.1029
1.1291-6(b)(4)(iv) . . . . **15** ns. 1033, 1029

[Text references are to paragraphs; note references are to chapters (boldface numbers) and notes ("n."), and references to the supplement are preceded by "S."]

Prop. Reg. §

1.1291-6(c)	**15** n.1024
1.1291-6(c)(1)	**15** ns. 1025, 1032, 1034
1.1291-6(c)(2)	**15** n.1026
1.1291-6(c)(2)(ii)	**15** n.1035
1.1291-6(c)(2)(iv)	**11** n.343; **15** n.1025; **S15** ns. 563, 923
1.1291-6(d)(1)	**15** n.1028
1.1291-6(d)(1)(ii)	**15** n.1036
1.1291-6(e)	**15** n.1028
1.1291-6(f)	15.85[6][c]
1.1291-8	**15** ns. 468, 475
1.1291-9	**15** ns. 468, 473
1.1295-1(i)	**S15** n.453.1
1.1295-1(k)	**S15** n.453.1
1.1296-1	**S15** n.453.1
1.1296-4	**15** n.447
1.1296-6	**15** n.447
1.1296(e)-1	**15** n.453
1.1296(e)-1(b)(2)	**S15** ns. 453, 453.1
1.1361-2	**6** n.47
1.1361-3	**6** ns. 47, 198
1.1361-4	**6** n.47
1.1361-4(a)	**6** ns. 48, 216
1.1361-4(a)(6)	**S6** n.50.2
1.1361-4(a)(7)	**S6** n.50.4
1.1361-4(a)(8)	**S6** n.50.4
1.1361-4(b)(1)	**6** n.48
1.1361-4(b)(2)	**6** n.48
1.1361-4(b)(3)	**6** ns. 48, 199, 216; **S6** n.48
1.1361-4(d)	**6** ns. 199, 216
1.1361-5	**6** n.47
1.1361-5(a)	**6** n.49
1.1361-5(b)	**6** n.49
1.1361-6	**6** ns. 47, 50
1.1362-2(b)-1.1362-2(g)	**S6** n.144.1
1.1362-8	**6** n.59
1.1366-1(a)	**6** ns. 80, 94
1.1366-1(a)(2)(viii)	**6** n.95; **8** n.95
1.1366-1(b)	**6** n.80
1.1366-1(c)	**6** n.80
1.1366-1(c)(1)	**6** n.94
1.1366-1(e)	**6** ns. 80, 94
1.1366-1(f)	**6** n.91
1.1366-2(a)	**6** n.110
1.1366-2(a)(6)	**6** n.99
1.1366-2(b)	**6** n.110
1.1366-2(c)(1)	**6** n.201; **12** n.562
1.1366-2(c)(2)	**S6** n.207; **12** n.570
1.1366-3	**6** n.115
1.1366-4(b)	**6** n.160
1.1367-1(f)	**6** n.117
1.1368-1(e)	**6** n.155
1.1368-1(e)(2)	**6** n.117
1.1368-2(a)(3)(ii)	**6** n.155
1.1368-2(a)(5)	**6** ns. 155, 169
1.1368-2(c)(2)	**6** n.207
1.1368-2(d)(2)	**12** n.561
1.1368-2(d)(3)	**11** n.346; **12** ns. 570, 580
1.1368-3	**6** ns. 155, 169
1.1374-3(b)	**S6** n.134
1.1374-3(c), Ex. 2	**S6** n.134

Prop. Reg. §

1.1374-3(c), Ex. 3	**S6** n.134
1.1374-3(c), Ex. 4	**S6** n.134
1.1402-11(b)	**13** n.524
1.1402-13	**13** n.575
1.1402-21	**13** n.710
1.1441-1 – 1.1441-9	**15** n.209
1.1441-2(b)(1)(i)	**S15** n.221
1.1441-2(b)(2)	**S15** n.221
1.1441-3(b)(2)(i)	**15** n.48
1.1441-6	**15** n.189
1.1502-3	**13** n.567
1.1502-9	**13** ns. 568, 793
1.1502-11(b)	**13** n.648
1.1502-11(c)	S13.42[12][c]
1.1502-13	**13** ns. 379, 460
1.1502-13(a)(2)	**13** ns. 390, 393
1.1502-13(a)(4)	**13** n.589
1.1502-13(c)	**13** n.395
1.1502-13(c)(1)(i)	**13** n.393
1.1502-13(c)(4)(i)	**13** n.393
1.1502-13(c)(4)(ii)	13.43[2][c]; **13** ns. 440, 596, 606, 925; **15** ns. 90, 97, 560
1.1502-13(d)	**13** n.395
1.1502-13(e)(1)	**13** n.511
1.1502-13(f)(2)(iv)	**13** n.434
1.1502-13(f)(4)	**13** n.443
1.1502-13(f)(6)	**13** n.443
1.1502-13(f)(7), Ex. 3(b)	**S13** n.616
1.1502-13(g)(2)(i)(A)	**12** n.1110
1.1502-13(h)	**13** n.584
1.1502-13(j)(2)(ii)	**S13** ns. 625.1, 646.1, 971.6
1.1502-13(j)(6)	**13** ns. 440, 449, 596
1.1502-13(j)(9), Ex. 6	**S13** ns. 625.1, 646.1, 971.6, 1002
1.1502-13(j)(9), Ex. 7	**S13** ns. 625.1, 625.2, 646.1, 646.2, 971.6, 999, 1002
1.1502-15	**13** ns. 741, 758
1.1502-15(b)(1)	**13** n.778
1.1502-15(b)(2)	**13** n.780
1.1502-15(b)(2)(ii)	**13** n.778
1.1502-15(c)	**13** n.779
1.1502-15(d)	**13** ns. 778, 779
1.1502-17(c)	**13** n.512
1.1502-19	**13** n.648
1.1502-19(b)(5)	S13.48[6]; **S13** ns. 618, 675.1
1.1502-19(g), Ex. 7	S13.48[6]; **S13** ns. 618, 675.1, 675.3
1.1502-19(g)(1)	**13** n.692
1.1502-20	**13** ns. 475, 477, 478
1.1502-20(c)	**13** ns. 479, 480
1.1502-21	**13** ns. 719, 758
1.1502-21(b)	**13** ns. 794, 796
1.1502-21(b)(2)	**13** ns. 795, 809
1.1502-21(b)(2)(ii)(B)	**13** ns. 796, 798, 810
1.1502-21(b)(2)(v)	**13** ns. 795, 798
1.1502-21(b)(3)	**13** n.517
1.1502-21(b)(3)(ii)	**13** n.517
1.1502-21(b)(4)	**13** n.517
1.1502-21(c)(1)(i)	**13** n.765

[Text references are to paragraphs; note references are to chapters (boldface numbers) and notes ("n."), and references to the supplement are preceded by "S."]

Prop. Reg. §

1.1502-21(c)(1)(iii) **13** n.770	
1.1502-21(c)(2)(i) . . . . **13** ns. 766, 767	
1.1502-21(c)(2)(iii) **13** n.770	
1.1502-21(c)(2)(iv) **13** n.766	
1.1502-21(c)(3) **13** n.719	
1.1502-21(c)(4) **13** n.719	
1.1502-21(g) **13** n.517	
1.1502-22(b)(3) **13** n.809	
1.1502-30 . . . . **12** n.303	
1.1502-31 . . . . **13** n.648	
1.1502-31(c)(2) **S13** n.683.1	
1.1502-31(d)(2)(ii) **S13** n.683.1	
1.1502-31(g), Exs. 1–3 . . . . **S13** n.683.1	
1.1502-32 . . . . **13** ns. 534, 536, 648	
1.1502-32(b)(4)(iv) **13** n.434	
1.1502-32(e)(1) **13** n.654	
1.1502-32(e)(4) **13** n.654	
1.1502-32(g) **13** n.665	
1.1502-32(h) **13** n.648	
1.1502-32(h)(1) **13** n.692	
1.1502-33 . . . . **13** ns. 536, 648	
1.1502-33(d) **13** n.346	
1.1502-33(j)(1) **13** n.692	
1.1502-35 . . . . **S13**.42[5][c]; **S13** ns. 470, 701	
1.1502-55 . . . . **13** ns. 350, 367, 372	
1.1502-75(d)(4) **13** n.734	
1.1502-76(b) . . . . **13** ns. 510, 648, 824	
1.1502-76(b)(4)(ii) . . . . **13** ns. 508, 822	
1.1502-76(b)(5) **13** n.824	
1.1502-77 . . . . . . **S13** ns. 347, 835.1, 835.3	
1.1502-77(d) **S13** n.835.1	
1.1502-77(e) **S13** n.835.1	
1.1502-77(f) **S13** n.835.1	
1.1502-80(c) **13** n.648	
1.1502-80(d) **13** n.830	
1.1502-80(d)(1) **S13** n.691.1	
1.1502-80(d)(2), Ex. 2 . . . . **S13** n.691.1	
1.1502-80(e) **13** n.648	
1.1502-80(g) . . . . **S10** ns. 332, 365.2;	
S13.48[5][a]; **S13** ns. 625.1, 625.2,	
646.1, 646.2, 971.4, 971.6, 1000, 1002;	
S14 n.52.2	
1.1502-90–1.1502-99 . . . . **13** n.843	
1.1502-99(a) **13** n.902	
1.1502-99(c) **13** n.903	
1.1441-7(g) **4** n.134	
1.1502-13(c)(4)(ii) **14** n.291	
1.1502-15 . . . . **14** n.345	
1.1502-76(b) **6** n.71	
1.1502-76(b)(1) **10** n.513	
1.1502-92 . . . . **14** n.227	
1.1502-96(c) **14** n.270	
1.1503-5 . . . . **S13** n.749.1	

Prop. Reg. §

1.6038C-1 . . . . **13** n.240; **15** n.142	
1.6043-4 . . . . **4** n.334	
1.6662-3(a) **5** n.505	
1.6662-3(b)(2) **5** n.505	
1.6662-3(c)(1) **5** n.505	
1.6662-5 . . . . **13** ns. 207, 243	
1.6664-4(c) . . . . **5** ns. 505, 512, 520	
1.6664-4(d) **13** n.243	
1.7701(*l*)-2 . . . . **5** n.406; **S13** n.86	
1.7701(*l*)-3 . . . . . . 4.03[8][b]; **4** ns. 129, 131; **5** n.406	
1.7701(*l*)-3(b)(2) . . . . 4.03[8][b]	
1.7701(*l*)-3(c)(1) **4** n.135	
1.7701(*l*)-3(c)(2) **4** n.133	
1.7701(*l*)-3(c)(3)(i) **4** n.133	
1.7701(*l*)-3(d) **4** n.135	
1.7701(*l*)-3(f) **4** n.134	
1.7704-1 . . . . **2** n.117	
1.7704-1(d)(1) **2** n.119	
1.7704-1(d)(2) **2** n.119	
1.7704-1(g) **2** n.118	
1.7704-1(h) **2** n.120	
1.7872-1(a)(2)(iii) **13** n.142	
1.7872-2(a)(2)(ii) **12** n.485	
1.7872-2(a)(2)(iii) . . . **8** ns. 212, 250; **13** n.254	
1.7872-4(d) **12** n.485	
1.7872-4(d)(1) . . . . **8** ns. 212, 214	
1.7872-4(g)(1) . . **8** ns. 245, 250, 252; **13** n.255	
1.7872-7(a)(1) **8** n.214	
1.7872-7(a)(3)(ii) **8** n.214	
7.367(c)-1 . . . . **S15** n.639	
7.367(c)-2 . . . . **S15** n.639	
7.367(e)-2(c) **15** n.802	
301.7701-1 . . . . **2** n.45	
301.7701-2 . . . . **2** n.45	
301.7701-2(a)(2)(iv) **S2** n.50	
301.7701-2(a)(2)(v) **S2** n.50	
301.7701-2(b)(6) **S15** n.30	
301.7701-2(c)(ii) **S15** n.30	
301.7701-2(c)(2)(iii) **S2** n.50	
301.7701-3 . . . . **2** n.45	
301.7701-3(f) **2** n.54	
301.7701-3(g) **2** n.54	
301.7701-3(g)(1)(i) **2** n.56	
301.7701-3(g)(1)(ii) **2** n.55	
301.7701-3(g)(1)(iii) **2** n.56	
301.7701-3(g)(1)(iv) **2** n.55	
301.7701-3(g)(2)(ii) **S2** n.55	
301.7701-3(g)(3) **2** n.56	
301.7701-3(h) . . . . **S2** n.52; **15** ns. 28, 34, 322, 513	
301.7701(b)-7(a)(4) **6** n.42	
301.7701(b)-7(a)(4)(iv) **6** n.42	

Cumulative Table of Revenue Rulings, Revenue Procedures, and Other IRS Releases

[Text references are to paragraphs; note references are to chapters (boldface numbers) and notes ("n."), and references to the supplement are preceded by "S."]

*[Text references are to paragraphs; note references are to chapters (boldface numbers)
and notes ("n."), and references to the supplement are preceded by "S."]*

Rev. Rul.

57-328	. . . . **8** n.614
57-332	. . . . **8** ns. 123, 146
57-387	. . . . **9** ns. 128, 429
57-465	. . . S12.22[12]; 12.63[2][b]; **12** ns. 102, 259, 345, 944
57-491	. . . . **10** n.744
57-492	. . . .**11** n.92
57-502	. . . . **5** n.81
57-518	. . . . 12.24[2][b]; **12** ns. 216, 219, 221, 222, 224
57-535	. . . . **12** n.384
57-575	. . . . **10** n.721
58-1	. . . . **8** n.198
58-55	. . . . **15** ns. 306, 367
58-68	. . . . 12.62[4]; **12** ns. 862, 871, 903
58-79	. . . . **9** n.339; **10** n.533
58-93	. . . . **12** ns. 227, 1000
58-164	. . . . **11** n.106
58-234	. . . . **4** n.439
58-391	. . . . **10** n.302
58-402	. . . . **10** ns. 43, 50
58-471	. . . . **13** n.343
58-479	. . . . **15** n.221
58-546	. . . . **8** n.96; **12** n.419
58-603	. . . . **14** ns. 33, 40, 391
58-614	. . . .**9** n.424
59-84	. . . . **12** n.799
59-97	. . . .**9** ns. 332, 357, 428
59-98	. . . . **12** ns. 409, 630
59-119	. . . .**9** n.125
59-184	. . . . **8** n.234
59-197	. . . . **11** n.169
59-222	. . . **12** ns. 83, 187, 188, 322, 419, 630
59-228	. . . . **10** ns. 56, 59
59-259	. . . . **3** n.166
59-296	. . . . . . **10** ns. 268, 368; **S10** n.268; **12** n.322
59-387	. . . . **5** ns. 165, 296, 298
59-400	. . . . **11** n.148
60-1	. . . . **12** n.803
60-18	. . . . **9** n.53; **10** n.744
60-37	. . . . **4** n.434; **12** n.446
60-48	. . . .**4** n.254
60-50	. . . . **10** ns. 244, 300
60-68	. . . . **10** n.708
60-177	. . . . **8** n.262
60-192	. . . . **15** n.441
60-232	. . . .**9** n.281
60-302	. . . . **3** ns. 84, 137
60-322	. . . .**9** n.269
60-331	. . . . **3** n.367; **7** n.247; **8** n.258
61-18	. . . . **3** n.268; **12** n.613
61-97	. . . . **12** n.789
61-112	. . . . **6** n.66
61-134	. . . . **8** n.235
61-156	12.64[1][c]; 12.64[2][b]; **12** ns. 1071, 1085
61-175	. . . . **2** ns. 65, 73
61-191	. . . . **2** n.197; **14** ns. 404, 405
62-31	. . . . **15** ns. 142, 145
62-42	. . . . **5** n.204

Rev. Rul.

62-45	. . . . **10** n.213
62-131	. . . . **8** ns. 50, 152
62-138	. . . . **3** n.198
62-217	. . . . **3** n.255
63-6	. . . . 15.83[1][a]; **15** ns. 331, 790
63-29	. . . . **12** ns. 826, 828
63-40	**14** ns. 25, 26, 28, 164, 267, 306, 365, 374
63-51	. . . . **15** n.304
63-63	. . . . **8** n.113
63-107	. . . . **2** n.25; **10** n.15
63-113	. . . . **15** n.142
63-125	. . . . **10** n.737
63-225	. . . . **4** n.439
63-226	. . . . **3** n.165
63-228	. . . . **2** n.77
63-259	. . . . **5** n.240
63-260	. . . . **11** n.44
64-51	. . . . **15** n.221
64-56	. . . **3** ns. 36, 50, 58; **7** n.211; **15** ns. 59, 757
64-73	. . . . . 12.63[6][b]; **12** ns. 227, 236, 237, 1018, 1133
64-102	. . . . **11** n.149
64-125	. . . . **10** n.704
64-146	. . . . **8** ns. 100, 147
64-147	. . . . **11** n.114
64-155	. . . **3** n.309; **S3** n.309; **13** ns. 229, 256
64-157	. . . . **15** n.643
64-177	. . . . **15** ns. 610, 620
64-220	. . . . **2** n.73
64-232	. . . . **6** n.66
64-235	. . . . **13** n.170
64-236	. . . . **5** n.108
64-290	. . . . **8** n.156
65-261	. . . . **13** n.170
65-23	. . . . **8** ns. 153, 155, 156
65-31	. . . . **4** n.439
65-68	. . . .**7** n.124
65-80	. . . .**9** n.248
65-83	. . . . **6** n.66
65-91	. . . . **6** n.66
65-155	. . . . **12** n.754
65-184	. . . . **10** n.743
65-235	. . . . **10** n.304
65-256	. . . . **8** ns. 264, 423
65-261	. . . . **3** n.49
65-263	. . . . **15** n.142
65-289	. . . .**9** n.324
66-23	. . . 12.21[5]; 12.66[4][b]; **12** ns. 57, 68, 1163
66-81	. . . . **10** n.41
66-112	. . . . . . **3** ns. 67, 68; **12** ns. 619, 1141
66-116	. . . . **6** n.53
66-142	. . . . **3** n.142
66-204	. . . . **11** n.89
66-214	. . . . 14.03[2]
66-224	. . . . **12** n.43
66-284	. . . . **14** n.58; **12** n.503
66-293	. . . . **4** n.290
66-332	. . . . **12** n.796

[Text references are to paragraphs; note references are to chapters (boldface numbers) and notes ("n."), and references to the supplement are preceded by "S."]

Rev. Rul.

66-336	**8** n.113
66-339	**3** ns. 66, 163; **12** n.154
66-345	**14** n.103
66-353	**8** n.93
66-365	**12** ns. 186, 774
67-1	**5** n.109
67-15	**5** n.232
67-16	**9** n.273
67-24	**9** n.61
67-64	**7** n.76
67-90	**12** ns. 620, 1141, 1143
67-103	**14** n.92
67-125	**5** ns. 106, 129, 161, 166, 268
67-189	**13** n.498
67-192	**3** n.79; **15** n.607
67-202	**14** n.140
67-269	**9** n.64; **12** n.640
67-274	**12** ns. 124, 202, 260, 270, 926, 934; **S12** n.269; **14** n.140
67-275	**12** n.195
67-279	**6** n.37
67-309	**3** n.248
67-326	12.22[3]; **12** ns. 116, 132, 259, 265, 275, 298, 307, 319, 1026
67-376	**12** n.503
67-382	**6** n.73
67-402	**8** n.432
67-411	**3** n.306; **5** n.306; **10** n.239
67-412	**13** n.394
67-423	**7** n.215
67-425	**9** ns. 307, 324
67-448	12.25[1]; **12** ns. 117, 151, 152, 268, 275, 298, 307, 315, 730, 737, 1028, 1190
68-13	**3** n.80
68-21	**9** n.17
68-22	12.66[4][b]; **12** ns. 69, 613, 1164
68-23	**12** ns. 753, 791
68-43	**3** n.2; **15** n.641
68-55	**3** ns. 78–80, 84, 86
68-128	**15** n.304
68-261	**12** ns. 107, 226
68-284	**11** n.89
68-285	**12** n.181
68-288	**4** n.417
68-298	**3** n.198
68-333	**15** n.46
68-344	**2** n.127
68-348	**9** ns. 426, 428; **10** ns. 30, 31
68-349	**3** ns. 18, 326, 373, 400; **12** n.513
68-350	**14** ns. 90, 110, 395
68-357	12.24[5]; **12** n.263
68-358	**12** n.256
68-359	**10** ns. 268, 272
68-364	**6** n.69
68-388	**9** ns. 24, 120
68-407	**11** n.84
68-409	**7** n.181
68-435	**12** n.199
68-443	**15** n.41
68-473	**12** n.747

Rev. Rul.

68-526	**12** n.994
68-527	**14** n.92
68-558	**3** n.291
68-562	**12** n.181
68-601	**9** ns. 69–71, 73, 74
68-602	**10** ns. 272, 280
68-603	**11** n.174; 12.62[4]; **12** ns. 872, 904; **14** n.52
68-623	**13** n.317
68-629	**3** n.127
68-631	**7** n.171
68-632	**7** n.171
68-637	**12** n.1111
68-658	**8** n.229
68-662	**5** n.153
68-674	**4** n.433
69-3	**12** n.51
69-6	**10** ns. 180, 387, 543; **12** ns. 51, 139, 530, 665, 751, 1188
69-34	**12** n.774
69-48	**12** ns. 252, 1005
69-75	**3** n.273
69-91	**4** n.404; **12** ns. 154, 173
69-115	**8** n.180
69-117	**3** n.230
69-126	**3** n.163; **13** ns. 322, 324
69-130	**8** n.273; **9** n.420
69-131	**8** ns. 273, 450; **9** n.420
69-135	**4** ns. 428, 436; **12** n.389
69-142	**12** ns. 173, 188, 301
69-156	**3** n.57
69-172	**10** n.265
69-182	**15** n.244
69-185	12.28[4]; **12** ns. 517, 976
69-227	**5** n.125
69-235	**15** n.58
69-244	**15** n.221
69-261	**9** ns. 350, 353
69-264	**12** n.635
69-265	**4** n.428; 12.41[4]; 12.66[4][b]; **12** ns. 70, 389, 645, 1014, 1162
69-293	**11** n.246
69-294	**12** n.999
69-299	**7** n.229
69-330	**5** n.163
69-334	**10** n.38
69-378	**10** n.703
69-379	**10** n.260
69-407	**11** n.44
69-413	**12** ns. 607, 968, 1014
69-415	**12** n.1030
69-440	**8** n.41
69-443	**12** n.199
69-447	**8** ns. 39, 44
69-460	**11** ns. 221, 230, 236
69-461	**11** ns. 134, 135
69-491	**5** ns. 123, 156
69-516	**12** n.515
69-562	**9** n.77
69-566	**6** n.176
69-585	**12** ns. 170, 999

[Text references are to paragraphs; note references are to chapters (boldface numbers) and notes ("n."), and references to the supplement are preceded by "S."]

Rev. Rul.

69-591	. . . . **2** n.186; **6** n.54; **13** n.317
69-594	. . . . **9** n.315
69-608	**8** ns. 228, 289; **9** ns. 218, 221–226, 229; **S9** ns. 221, 222
69-615	. . . . **5** n.164
69-617	. . . . **10** ns. 273, 324; **12** ns. 931, 989, 1000
69-630	. . . . **13** n.228
70-18	. . . . **11** n.44
70-27	. . . . **14** n.61
70-41	. . . . **12** ns. 173, 188, 301
70-45	. . . . **3** n.49
70-65	. . . . **12** ns. 190, 203
70-83	. . . . **14** n.90
70-101	. . . . **2** ns. 25, 142, 143
70-104	. . . . **9** n.128
70-106	. . . . **10** ns. 293, 304
70-107	. . . . **12** ns. 242, 1134
70-108	**4** n.110; **12** ns. 154, 646; **S12** n.646
70-111	. . . . **9** n.370
70-120	. . . . **12** ns. 621, 1154
70-128	. . . . **14** n.92
70-140	**3** ns. 187, 326, 368; **12** ns. 207, 858, 897, 899
70-141	. . . . **13** n.440
70-153	. . . . **7** n.210
70-172	. . . . **12** ns. 199, 862, 871
70-199	. . . . **12** n.801
70-223	**12** ns. 96, 121, 940, 944; **14** ns. 124, 125, 165
70-224	. . . . **12** ns. 227, 242, 1134
70-225	. . . . **11** ns. 171, 328; 12.62[3][c]; 12.62[4]; **12** ns. 207, 874, 876, 879, 898, 899, 901; **13** n.961
70-238	. . . . **14** n.124
70-239	. . . . **3** ns. 47, 378
70-240	. . . . . **12** ns. 339, 341, 767, 1086; **S12** n.1136.6
70-241	. . . . **5** ns. 239, 250, 272, 278; **14** n.90
70-269	. . . . **12** ns. 174, 1111
70-271	. . . . **8** n.330; **10** ns. 56, 369; **11** n.276; 12.44[3][a]; **12** ns. 419, 665, 678, 692, 745, 753, 784, 1131
70-290	. . . . **15** n.306
70-297	. . . . **9** n.329
70-298	. . . . **12** ns. 51, 280
70-300	. . . . **12** ns. 621, 1148
70-301	. . . . **7** n.105; **12** n.1111
70-304	. . . . **15** n.74
70-305	. . . . **3** n.242; **12** n.713
70-329	. . . . **S15** n.244
70-353	. . . . **5** n.165
70-357	. . . . **10** n.263
70-359	. . . . **5** ns. 134, 165
70-360	. . . . **5** ns. 134, 165
70-368	. . . . **4** n.417
70-377	. . . . **15** n.49
70-378	. . . . **13** n.498
70-379	. . . . **S13** n.309; **15** n.244
70-433	**3** n.398; **12** ns. 179, 205, 954; **15** ns. 640, 786, 844

Rev. Rul.

70-434	**11** n.171; **12** ns. 207, 871, 874, 878, 902, 903
70-469	. . . . **13** n.317
70-489	. . . **10** ns. 267, 368; **S10** ns. 63.1, 267
70-496	9.09[6][e]; **9** ns. 355, 368, 370, 375, 377, 399, 451; **13** n.826
70-497	. . . . **7** n.175
70-521	. . . . . **4** n.439; 8.05[4]; **8** ns. 197, 328, 346, 407; **11** n.285
70-522	. . . . **3** n.187
70-531	. . . . **9** n.476
70-540	. . . . **15** n.46
70-609	. . . . **8** n.144
70-639	. . . . **9** n.106
71-65	. . . . **15** ns. 332, 327
71-83	. . . . **12** n.154; **13** n.324
71-141	. . . . **15** n.323; **S15** n.323
71-165	. . . . **8** n.264
71-165	. . . . **8** n.114
71-211	. . . . **9** n.57
71-250	. . . . **9** ns. 250, 279
71-261	. . . . **9** ns. 149, 326
71-277	. . . . **2** n.142
71-326	. . . . **10** n.307
71-336	. . . . **11** n.214
71-350	. . . . **8** n.523
71-364	. . . . **12** n.701; **14** n.89
71-372	. . . . **7** n.230
71-383	. . . . **11** ns. 149, 183; **12** n.1177
71-384	. . . . **11** n.183
71-426	. . . . **9** n.126
71-427	. . . . **12** ns. 442, 756
71-433	. . . . **15** n.607
71-434	. . . . **2** ns. 84, 142
71-455	. . . . **6** n.69
71-473	. . . . **9** ns. 286, 295
71-496	. . . . **14** n.100
71-523	. . . . **13** n.309; **15** n.244
71-527	. . . . **9** ns. 333, 372
71-533	. . . . **15** n.343
71-534	. . . . **15** n.343
71-562	. . . . **4** n.244; **9** ns. 113, 124
71-563	. . . . **9** ns. 359, 373, 374
71-564	. . . . . . **3** ns. 49, 58; **7** n.211; **15** n.59
71-569	. . . . **3** n.364
71-593	. . . . **11** ns. 44, 183
72-30	. . . . **13** n.735
72-57	. . . . **12** n.382
72-71	. . . . **8** n.545
72-72	. . . . **12** n.154
72-75	. . . . **2** n.64
72-87	. . . . **15** n.56
72-120	. . . . **2** n.64
72-121	. . . . **2** n.64
72-122	. . . . **2** n.141
72-137	. . . . **2** n.76; **10** ns. 37, 56, 61
72-148	. . . . **7** n.218
72-151	. . . . **3** n.77
72-152	. . . . **7** ns. 181, 245
72-198	. . . . **4** ns. 442, 446; **12** ns. 1185–1187
72-199	. . . . **12** n.381

[Text references are to paragraphs; note references are to chapters (boldface numbers) and notes ("n."), and references to the supplement are preceded by "S."]

Rev. Rul.

72-206 . . . . **12** ns. 378, 503
72-264 . . . . **4** n.430; **12** n.408
72-265 . . . . **4** n.428; **6** n.275; **12** ns. 384, 407
72-274 . . . . **12** n.954
72-281 . . . . **15** n.399
72-306 . . . . **7** ns. 171, 242
72-320 . . . **3** n.377; **6** ns. 13, 16, 43, 182, 204;
          13 n.430
72-321 . . . . **13** n.395
72-322 . . . . **13** n.735
72-327 . . . **12** ns. 703, 726, 732, 768, 991; **14**
          n.89
72-343 . . . . **12** ns. 175, 248, 1122, 1131
72-348 . . . . **4** n.433
72-354 . . . . **12** ns. 170, 252, 1006
72-380 . . . . **9** n.127
72-405 . . . . **12** n.270
72-420 . . . . **12** n.511; **15** n.906
72-421 . . . . **14** n.73; **15** ns. 254, 795
72-422 . . . . **10** n.704
72-452 . . . . **14** n.110
72-453 . . . . **14** n.110
72-457 . . . . **6** n.64
72-464 . . . . **10** ns. 366, 372; **12** ns. 683, 703–
          705, 726, 1009, 1010, 1131
72-472 . . . . **9** n.122
72-498 . . . . **13** n.433
72-530 . . . . **12** n.877
72-576 . . . . **12** ns. 270, 1014
72-578 . . . . **14** n.92
73-2 . . . . **9** n.385
73-16 . . . . **12** n.151
73-28 . . . . **12** ns. 154, 999
73-33 . . . . **12** n.620
73-42 . . . . **5** n.53
73-44 . . . . **11** ns. 130, 139, 186
73-54 . . . . . **12** ns. 189, 190, 196, 1119; **S12**
          n.184
73-73 . . . . **13** n.546
73-102 . . . . **12** ns. 184, 189, 245, 248, 1116,
          1120
73-177 . . . . **9** n.314
73-139 . . . . **7** n.187
73-160 . . . . **6** n.275
73-205 . . . . **12** ns. 620, 1141
73-226 . . . . **5** n.90
73-227 . . . . **15** n.166
73-233 . . . . **3** ns. 178, 306; **12** n.744
73-234 . . . . **11** n.106
73-236 . . . . **11** n.106
73-237 . . . . **11** n.106
73-254 . . . . **2** n.5
73-257 . . . . **12** ns. 228, 242, 278, 1134
73-276 . . . . **S11** n.106
73-298 . . . . **12** n.1149
73-303 . . . . **13** n.735
73-360 . . . . **11** n.93
73-378 . . . . **10** n.691
73-423 . . . . **3** n.265; **12** n.408
73-427 . . . . **5** n.132; **9** n.25; **12** ns. 269, 311,
          714, 1039, 1190, 1191

Rev. Rul.

73-463 . . . . **5** n.161
73-472 . . . . **3** ns. 71, 173
73-473 . . . . **3** ns. 71, 160, 173
73-496 . . . . **6** ns. 43, 181, 182
73-498 . . . . **13** n.310
73-522 . . . . **15** n.251
73-552 . . . . **12** ns. 256, 745
73-572 . . . . **15.21[3]**; **15** n.348
73-580 . . . . **5** ns. 100, 106, 166, 255
73-583 . . . . **3** n.273
73-605 . . . . **13** n.346
73-611 . . . . **3** n.165
74-5 . . . . **11** ns. 137, 138, 170, 335
74-27 . . . . **8** n.263
74-35 . . . . **12** ns. 202, 999
74-36 . . . . **12** n.774
74-54 . . . . **10** ns. 260, 373; **12** n.706
74-59 . . . . **15** n.429
74-63 . . . . **15** n.207
74-79 . . . . **11** ns. 55, 130, 186
74-106 . . . . **15** n.563
74-108 . . . . **15** n.61
74-131 . . . . **7** n.200
74-164 . . . . **8** ns. 40, 62
74-210 . . . . **4** n.415; **5** n.298
74-269 . . . . **12** ns. 378, 744
74-296 . . . . **9** ns. 269, 272
74-297 . . . . **12** ns. 102, 281; **15** n.875
74-329 . . . . **3** n.302
74-338 . . . . **8** n.43
74-339 . . . . **8** n.43; **9** n.441; **S9** n.441
74-382 . . . . **11** n.55
74-387 . . . . **15** n.329
74-396 . . . . **10** n.198
74-406 . . . . **11** n.171
74-432 . . . . **7** n.200
74-436 . . . . **15** n.542
74-457 . . . . **12** n.225
74-462 . . . . **14** n.405
74-477 . . . . **3** n.97
74-501 . . . . **8** n.549
74-502 . . . . **3** n.62; **12** n.954
74-503   **3** ns. 26, 27, 208, 214, 241, 255; **S3**
          ns. 208, 241; **12** ns. 239, 689, 713, 732,
          1040; **S12** ns. 713, 732; **S15** ns. 897.1,
          902.1
74-515 . . . . **9** n.166; **S11** n.264.3; **12** ns. 753,
          771
74-516 . . . . **11** n.267; **12** ns. 771, 775
74-525 . . . . **15** n.304
74-544 . . . . **9** n.425
74-545 . . . . **12** ns. 258, 351, 968
74-550 . . . . **15** n.332
74-555 . . . . **15** n.221
74-562 . . . . **8** n.258
74-564 . . . . **12** ns. 151, 269, 275, 277, 1019,
          1020, 1029
74-565 . . . . **12** ns. 151, 269, 275, 277, 1019,
          1020, 1029
74-585 . . . . **13** ns. 497, 503
74-589 . . . . **13** n.388

[Text references are to paragraphs; note references are to chapters (boldface numbers) and notes ("n."), and references to the supplement are preceded by "S."]

Rev. Rul.

74-598	**13** n.440
74-605	**9** ns. 336, 367; **13** n.618
74-607	**15** n.46
74-610	**13** ns. 796, 798
75-2	**9** ns. 127, 128
75-3	**9** n.280
75-7	**15** n.527
75-19	**2** n.86
75-23	**15** ns. 126, 142, 251
75-31	**1** n.52
75-33	**4** n.110; **12** ns. 154, 620, 646
75-54	**13** n.796
75-67	**7** n.230
75-83	**12** ns. 770, 771
75-93	**8** n.516; **12** n.392
75-94	**12** ns. 745, 1152, 1181
75-95	**12** n.43
75-117	**4** n.372
75-123	**12** ns. 158, 180
75-139	**7** n.179
75-143	**15** n.556
75-144	**6** n.107
75-153	**8** n.113
75-160	**11** n.115
75-161	**12** ns. 132, 348, 683, 945, 1108
75-174	**9** n.370
75-179	**8** n.455; **12** ns. 392, 794
75-186	**4** n.250
75-192	**2** n.74
75-202	**7** n.211
75-222	**8** n.598; **12** n.797
75-223	**9** ns. 274–276; **11** n.378
75-236	**8** ns. 448, 597; **12** n.797
75-237	**12** n.1152
75-247	**8** n.637
75-249	**7** n.230
75-250	**7** n.230
75-253	**15** n.166
75-263	**15** n.74
75-292	**3** ns. 326, 373
75-300	**3** n.291
75-320	**8** ns. 273, 450; **9** n.420
75-321	**11** ns. 207, 219
75-337	**11** ns. 221, 236
75-348	**3** n.273
75-349	**6** n.66
75-360	**9** n.192; **12** ns. 172, 200
75-371	**3** n.291
75-378	**13** n.721
75-383	**12** ns. 345, 968; **13** n.440; **15** n.905
75-406	**11** ns. 171, 174; 12.62[3][d]; **12** ns. 871, 872, 877, 899; **13** ns. 961, 962
75-421	**8** n.222; **12** n.194
75-433	**9** n.33
75-447	**9** ns. 92, 111, 190–192
75-450	**12** ns. 665, 1131
75-456	**12** n.1152
75-468	**8** ns. 453, 455, 459; **12** n.794
75-469	**11** n.207
75-493	**8** ns. 286, 289
75-502	**9** n.170

Rev. Rul.

75-512	**9** n.174
75-513	**8** n.504
75-514	**3** n.85
75-515	**8** ns. 91, 115
75-521	**10** n.293
75-522	**12** n.175
75-557	**8** n.93
75-561	12.28[4]; **12** ns. 503, 517–520, 932, 976; **14** ns. 58, 66; **15** n.882
76-12	**8** n.102
76-13	**15** n.914
76-14	**12** n.782
76-15	**12** n.782
76-23	**6** n.15
76-26	**1** n.52
76-42	**12** ns. 1160, 1161
76-48	**6** n.66
76-53	**8** ns. 444, 524, 529, 532
76-54	**11** n.139
76-88	**13** n.279
76-90	**15** ns. 610, 620, 799
76-107	**8** n.456
76-108	**12** n.322
76-123	**12** ns. 202, 264
76-125	**15** n.542
76-164	**13** n.735
76-175	**11** n.276
76-186	**8** ns. 504, 531, 535
76-187	**11** n.224
76-188	**3** ns. 117, 399; **12** ns. 254, 258, 351, 683, 968, 1108; **14** n.60
76-192	**15** n.542
76-223	**12** n.153
76-258	**8** ns. 438, 439, 457
76-277	**5** ns. 123, 156
76-279	**9** n.279
76-283	**15** n.221
76-289	**9** n.280
76-320	**7** n.200
76-333	**15** n.607
76-334	**12** ns. 1160, 1179, 1183
76-363	**14** n.125
76-364	**9** n.173
76-365	**12** ns. 194, 196, 245, 1116, 1117, 1119
76-385	**9** n.177
76-386	**8** n.595
76-387	**8** ns. 448, 594
76-396	**8** n.616
76-429	**9** n.284; **10** ns. 244, 319, 320; **12** n.1073
76-454	**3** n.178
76-462	**2** n.193
76-469	**6** n.66
76-496	**9** n.115
76-508	**15** n.333
76-520	**10** n.437
76-524	**9** n.106
76-525	**10** n.298
76-526	**9** n.272
76-527	**11** n.223

*[Text references are to paragraphs; note references are to chapters (boldface numbers)
and notes ("n."), and references to the supplement are preceded by "S."]*

Rev. Rul.

76-528	**11** n.246
76-538	**15** n.543
77-11	**3** ns. 198, 396; **11** n.214
77-19	**8** n.521; **12** ns. 751, 794, 1188
77-20	**11** n.65
77-22	**11** n.223
77-31	**2** n.142
77-37	**8** n.449
77-81	**3** n.61
77-83	**8** n.358
77-108	**8** ns. 581, 587
77-133	**11** n.351; **14** ns. 54, 58, 265
77-149	**8** ns. 444, 529
77-150	**10** n.313
77-155	**6** n.76
77-191	**12** n.1079
77-204	**5** ns. 254, 296, 299, 300, 311; **10** n.233
77-214	**2** ns. 32, 85
77-218	**9** ns. 149, 167, 169
77-220	**6** n.9
77-226	**9** ns. 192, 193; **S9** n.193
77-237	**9** ns. 88, 92
77-238	**12** n.383
77-245	**9** n.425
77-256	**8** ns. 330, 332
77-271	**12** n.192
77-293	**9** n.140
77-306	**10** n.703
77-307	**12** n.273
77-316	**1** ns. 81, 86; **S1** ns. 81, 86
77-335	**11** ns. 360, 361
77-336	**7** n.189
77-360	**8** ns. 217, 400; **9** ns. 214, 387
77-375	**9** ns. 274, 276, 288
77-376	**9** ns. 274, 276, 277
77-377	**11** n.183
77-415	**12** ns. 90, 331, 440, 453, 480, 497, 751
77-426	**9** n.161
77-427	**9** ns. 339, 370, 379; **10** n.533
77-428	**12** ns. 276, 277, 953, 954
77-437	**4** n.404; **12** n.464
77-442	**8** n.124
77-449	3.09[5]; **3** n.205; **12** ns. 54, 329, 1014, 1019
77-455	**8** ns. 632, 637; **9** n.140
77-467	**9** ns. 34, 134
77-468	**9** n.250
77-479	**12** ns. 70, 90, 497
77-483	**15** n.327
78-25	**10** n.61
78-47	12.63[2][b]; **12** ns. 224, 943–945, 1001, 1082
78-55	**9** ns. 264, 272
78-60	**8** ns. 482, 522; **9** n.175
78-83	**8** n.248
78-115	**8** n.521
78-117	**8** n.158
78-119	**12** ns. 1174, 1177; **13** n.322
78-123	**8** n.115

Rev. Rul.

78-130	**12** ns. 258, 351, 968, 1030; **15** n.981
78-142	**4** n.110; 12.66[4][b]; **12** ns. 69, 620, 646, 1165
78-182	**4** n.439
78-197	**8** ns. 260, 649; **S8** ns. 260, 261
78-201	15.81[1][c]; 15.82[2][a]; **15** ns. 650, 754, 764
78-210	**5** n.122
78-250	**5** n.132; **9** n.25; **12** ns. 97, 109, 311, 1190, 1192
78-251	**11** n.174; **12** ns. 872, 874, 899, 902, 903
78-278	**10** ns. 200, 353
78-280	**3** n.365
78-286	**12** n.51
78-287	**12** ns. 517, 519, 944; **14** n.66
78-289	**12** n.1108
78-294	**3** ns. 188, 193; **14** n.217
78-330	**3** n.121; **10** n.280; **12** ns. 683, 1108
78-338	**1** n.86
78-351	**12** n.382
78-371	**2** n.68
78-375	**8** ns. 444, 522, 529
78-376	**12** ns. 1157, 1160
78-381	**15** n.906
78-383	**11** ns. 149, 226; **15** n.914
78-397	**12** ns. 276, 953
78-401	**9** n.169
78-408	**12** ns. 174, 640
78-422	**8** n.216; **9** ns. 374, 385–388
78-430	**7** n.175
78-441	**12** n.519
78-442	**11** ns. 133, 258
79-2	**5** ns. 101, 166
79-4	**12** n.190
79-9	**5** n.40; **8** n.229
79-10	**10** n.32
79-20	**8** n.102
79-21	**13** n.324
79-42	**8** n.444
79-47	**8** n.140
79-50	**8** n.232
79-52	**6** n.179
79-59	**7** n.242
79-60	**7** n.200
79-67	**9** ns. 24, 120, 140
79-68	**8** n.142
79-69	**8** ns. 140, 144
79-70	**3** n.183
79-71	**12** n.520
79-77	**2** n.68
79-89	**12** n.190
79-100	**12** n.181
79-106	**2** ns. 30, 43, 91, 94, 95, 107
79-150	**15** n.709
79-155	**4** n.428; **6** n.275; **12** ns. 2, 280, 283, 389, 428, 747, 1125, 1126
79-163	**8** ns. 448, 594, 596, 597
79-184	**9** ns. 274, 275; **11** n.378
79-194	**3** ns. 35, 175, 182, 183
79-235	**10** n.744

[Text references are to paragraphs; note references are to chapters (boldface numbers) and notes ("n."), and references to the supplement are preceded by "S."]

Rev. Rul.

79-250	**12** ns. 515, 845
79-252	**9** n.319
79-258	**3** ns. 110, 112
79-273	**11** n.248; **12** ns. 269, 311, 859, 1039, 1190, 1192
79-274	**8** ns. 579, 585, 586; **12** ns. 179, 205, 802
79-275	**9** ns. 272, 291
79-279	**13** n.736
79-287	**12** n.799
79-288	**3** n.49; **15** n.757
79-289	**12** ns. 352, 511, 683; **14** n.386
79-314	**12** n.986
79-334	**9** n.127
79-347	**5** n.198
79-376	**9** n.476
79-394	**11** n.106
79-401	**9** n.318
79-433	**12** ns. 826, 828
79-434	**12** n.828
80-26	**9** n.49
80-33	**8** n.632
80-46	**14** n.129
80-58	**12** n.1171
80-76	**3** ns. 244, 256, 281; **S3** n.244; **12** n.713
80-79	**13** n.796
80-101	**10** n.25; **12** n.986
80-105	**12** ns. 51, 501
80-119	**5** ns. 99, 155
80-134	**4** ns. 442, 446; **12** n.1186
80-143	**4** n.212
80-144	**14** ns. 90, 107, 110, 396; **15** n.344
80-150	**2** n.77
80-154	**8** n.438
80-169	**6** n.180; **13** n.320
80-177	**10** n.36
80-181	**11** n.106
80-189	**3** n.242; **9** ns. 350, 352, 353, 384, 485; **12** ns. 239, 713, 1035
80-198	**3** ns. 236, 238, 349, 355
80-211	**5** n.158
80-221	**9** n.27
80-228	**3** n.76
80-231	**13** n.233; **15** n.333
80-238	**5** n.205
80-239	**3** n.339
80-240	**3** n.97; **9** ns. 219, 388; **12** n.1128
80-362	**15** n.41
80-283	**3** ns. 118, 139; **8** n.356; **10** n.100
80-284	**3** n.402
80-358	**10** n.533
80-362	**S15** n.41
81-3	**9** n.245
81-4	**15** ns. 650, 755
81-25	**12** ns. 826, 828; **14** ns. 310, 311
81-41	**9** n.89
81-61	**S1** n.86
81-78	**15** ns. 156, 181, 223, 254
81-81	**12** ns. 774, 782
81-84	**13** ns. 395, 542, 546

Rev. Rul.

81-91	**8** ns. 593, 598; **12** n.796
81-92	**12** n.829
81-169	**12** n.5
81-186	**12** n.801
81-187	**6** n.111
81-190	**8** ns. 453, 455, 459; **12** n.794
81-197	**6** n.66
81-233	**9** n.126
81-247	**12** ns. 226, 270, 829; **14** n.310
81-256	**9** n.319
81-289	**9** ns. 149, 156, 178
82-11	**5** ns. 186, 201; **8** ns. 268, 272, 276
82-20	**13** ns. 398, 567
82-34	**12** ns. 374, 497, 829; **S12** n.829; **14** ns. 310, 311
82-45	**13** n.98
82-72	**9** ns. 325, 478
82-80	**13** ns. 224, 269
82-112	**15** n.743
82-118	**12** n.799
82-129	**9** n.137
82-130	**11** ns. 223, 231
82-131	**11** ns. 226, 231
82-150	**3** ns. 64, 207; **9** n.41; **14** n.185
82-152	**13** ns. 344, 734
82-158	**8** ns. 433, 494; **12** n.209
82-187	**9** n.278
82-191	**8** n.594; **12** n.799
82-219	**11** n.81
83-14	**13** n.738
83-23	**11** n.219; **15** n.914
83-34	**3** n.205; **12** ns. 54, 1014, 1019, 1021
83-38	**8** n.327; **9** n.27
83-42	**8** n.449
83-61	**9** n.278; **10** n.347
83-68	**8** ns. 439, 442
83-73	**3** n.306; **12** ns. 1159, 1182; **14** ns. 91, 100
83-98	**4** ns. 84, 86
83-114	**11** ns. 149, 174, 223, 258; **12** n.903
83-116	**9** n.113
83-119	**8** ns. 453–455; **12** ns. 378, 392, 393
83-120	**12** n.378
83-142	**11** n.40; **12** n.845
83-155	**3** n.236
83-156	3.09[5]; **3** n.206
84-2	**10** n.323
84-6	**15** n.323
84-10	**2** ns. 65, 74
84-11	**S2** n.56; **S3** n.378
84-17	**15** ns. 156, 181, 254
84-30	**12** ns. 54, 258, 351, 1014, 1019; **15** n.981
84-33	**13** n.728
84-44	**3** n.171
84-68	**3** n.305; **5** n.85
84-71	**3** ns. 63, 402, 403
84-76	**9** n.317
84-79	**13** n.317
84-101	**7** n.186
84-104	**12** n.272

[Text references are to paragraphs; note references are to chapters (boldface numbers) and notes ("n."), and references to the supplement are preceded by "S."]

Rev. Rul.

84-111	. . . . . **2** n.123; **3** ns. 47, 378; **12** n.140
84-114	. . . . **9** n.173; **12** ns. 378, 771
84-125	. . . . **15** ns. 306, 367
84-134	. . . . **12** n.594
84-135	. . . .**9** n.128
84-137	. . . .**7** n.226
84-138	. . . . **5** n.79
84-141	. . . .**8** n.447
84-152	. . . . **4** ns. 183, 264; **15** ns. 185, 190
84-153	. . . . **4** ns. 183, 264; **15** n.185
84-154	. . . .**5** n.175
85-3	. . . . **15** n.323
85-14	. . . . **9** n.94
85-19	. . . .**9** n.141
85-48	. . . . **9** n.426; **10** ns. 31, 38
85-106	. . . . **9** ns. 157, 161, 165, 176
85-107	. . . . **12** ns. 1000, 1007, 1010
85-119	. . . . **4** ns. 83, 88; **14** n.243
85-122	. . . . **11** n.223
85-127	. . . . **11** ns. 221, 229
85-133	. . . . **13** ns. 385, 496; **S13** ns. 386, 496
85-134	. . . .**3** n.372
85-138	. . . . **12** ns. 252, 1005
85-139	. . . . **12** ns. 181, 1005
85-140	. . . . **7** n.193; **15** ns. 438, 439
85-144	. . . .**5** n.175
85-164	. . . . . . **3** ns. 79, 229; **12** ns. 788, 790
85-186	. . . . **10** n.202
85-197	. . . . . . **12** ns. 826, 829; **14** n.310
85-198	. . . . . **12** ns. 826, 829, 831; **14** n.310
86-4	. . . . **11** ns. 149, 185, 258
86-9	. . . . **4** ns. 442, 446
86-25	. . . .**8** n.446
86-27	. . . .**7** n.246
86-54	. . . .**9** n.323
86-67	. . . .**5** n.165; **10** n.227
86-104	. . . .**7** n.247
86-110	. . . . **6** n.70
86-125	. . . . **11** ns. 98, 106
86-126	. . . . **11** ns. 98, 106
86-141	. . . .**6** ns. 51, 73
86-154	. . . . **15** n.151
86-156	. . . .**15** n.41
87-5	. . . . **15** ns. 181, 201
87-9	. . . .**3** n.330; **12** n.527
87-14	. . . . **15** ns. 304, 327
87-19	. . . . **12** n.2
87-27	. . . . **12** ns. 352, 501, 511; **13** n.749; **14** n.386; **15** ns. 904, 906
87-47	. . . .**8** n.351; **15** n.558
87-57	. . . .**5** n.321
87-60	. . . . **13** ns. 388, 396
87-64	. . . . **15** n.106
87-65	. . . . **15** n.106
87-66	. . . . . **12** ns. 352, 501, 511; **15** ns. 136, 253, 905, 949, 950, 970, 973, 991
87-72	. . . . **15** ns. 331, 332
87-75	. . . . **7** n.200; **13** ns. 430, 566
87-76	. . . . **12** n.831
87-80	. . . . **15** ns. 251, 126
87-88	. . . . **9** n.87

Rev. Rul.

87-89	. . . **4** ns. 183, 264; **15** ns. 185, 213, 542
87-90	. . . . **15** n.445
87-96	. . . . **8** n.351; **13** n.447; **15** n.558
87-110	. . . . **12** n.658
87-132	. . . . **8** n.439; **9** n.312
88-3	. . . . **15** n.125
88-8	. . . . **2** n.5
88-19	. . . . **9** n.300; **11** ns. 84, 106, 336
88-25	. . . **12** ns. 501, 511; **15** ns. 206, 905, 949, 950
88-31	. . . . **3** n.253; **4** ns. 440, 442, 446
88-32	. . . .**3** n.330
88-33	. . . . **11** n.219
88-34	. . . . **11** ns. 221, 233
88-38	. . . .**2** n.171
88-41	. . . .**7** n.193
88-48	. . . **12** ns. 216, 223, 858, 860, 862; **S12** ns. 289, 292
88-49	. . . .**5** n.227
88-55	. . . .**9** n.124
88-66	. . . .**5** n.208
88-72	. . . . **1** n.86
88-73	. . . .**15** n.94
88-76	. . . .**2** n.132
88-77	. . . . **3** n.130; **12** n.1111
88-79	. . . . **2** ns. 64, 88
88-100	. . . . . . **8** n.570; **12** ns. 799, 803, 808
89-3	. . . . **12** n.378
89-18	. . . . **11** n.269
89-20	. . . . **7** n.238; **9** n.42
89-27	. . . . **11** n.106
89-37	. . . . **11** ns. 138, 170, 335
89-46	. . . . **3** n.162; **10** n.287; **12** ns. 347, 351, 979; **13** ns. 440, 618, 918, 926, 985
89-57	. . . .**9** n.338
89-61	. . . . **1** n.86
89-63	. . . **8** ns. 633, 634, 639; **12** ns. 801, 803, 804
89-64	. . . . **9** ns. 69, 72, 85
89-72	. . . . **15** ns. 515, 526
89-73	. . . . **15** n.538
89-80	. . . . **13** n.797
89-85	. . . . **13** ns. 396, 405
89-98	. . . . **10** n.587; **13** n.556
89-101	. . . . **11** n.224
89-102	. . . . **13** ns. 253, 279
89-103	. . . . **12** ns. 501, 511; **15** ns. 639, 905, 949, 950, 970, 973
89-121	. . . .**12** n.22
89-122	. . . . **6** n.275; **12** n.2
89-123	. . . . **2** n.89
89-124	. . . . **2** n.73
90-11	. . . **4** n.110; **6** n.304; **8** ns. 31, 373, 555; **14** ns. 195, 239, 240, 243
90-13	. . . .**9** ns. 245, 246, 425
90-15	. . . . **6** n.302; **14** ns. 195, 218, 240, 259
90-16	. . . 6.10[3][b]; 6.10[3][c]; **6** ns. 256, 265
90-27	. . . . **4** ns. 63, 85, 92; **5** ns. 193, 205; **8** n.448
90-31	. . . . **15** ns. 543, 560
90-76	. . . . **15** n.967

[Text references are to paragraphs; note references are to chapters (boldface numbers) and notes ("n."), and references to the supplement are preceded by "S."]

Rev. Rul.

90-80 . . . . **11** n.93; **15** ns. 127, 142, 146
90-87 . . . . **4** n.314; **6** ns. 299, 307; **8** ns. 453, 470; **12** ns. 418, 424, 549, 577, 591, 592, 598, 599; **14** n.327
90-95 . . . . **10** ns. 472, 573; 12.63[2][a]; **12** ns. 369, 918, 919, 921, 923, 926, 933, 936; **S12** ns. 921, 935.2
90-98 . . . . **8** n.443
90-112 . . . . **15** n.542
91-5 . . . . . **9** n.408; **15** ns. 323, 325, 329, 606, 639, 642, 762
91-26 . . . . **6** n.86
91-30 . . . . **5** ns. 320, 329, 387
91-31 . . . . **4** n.302; **6** ns. 245, 255, 256
91-32 . . . . **11** n.93; **15** ns. 127, 142, 151
91-47 . . . . **4** n.317; **12** n.587
91-58 . . . . **6** n.42
91-70 . . . . **13** n.326
92-17 . . . . **11** ns. 93, 106
92-32 . . . . **2** n.75
92-53 . . . . **4** n.302; **6** ns. 245, 255, 256
92-65 . . . . **5** ns. 320, 329, 387
92-74 . . . . **15** ns. 250, 254
92-75 . . . . **15** n.333
92-85 . . . . **9** n.409; **15** n.221
92-86 . . . . . **3** n.408; **9** n.408; **15** ns. 323, 325, 329, 606, 639, 642, 762
92-92 . . . . **4** n.301; **15** ns. 74, 221
92-93 . . . . **1** n.86
92-99 . . . . **4** n.301; **6** n.245
93-4 . . . . **2** n.87
93-6 . . . . **2** ns. 92, 132, 138
93-16 . . . . **3** n.286
93-38 . . . . **2** ns. 135, 138
93-61 . . . . **12** ns. 771, 775, 801
93-62 . . . . . . **11** n.267; **12** ns. 771, 775, 801
93-68 . . . . **4** n.244
93-79 . . . . **6** n.52
94-28 . . . . **4** n.81; **5** n.205
94-43 . . . . **6** n.9
95-2 . . . . **2** n.97
95-14 . . . . **6** n.167
95-45 . . . . **3** ns. 97, 135, 222; **S3** n.97; **12** ns. 1111, 1112
95-69 . . . . **12** n.54
95-71 . . . . . **3** n.165; **6** n.37; **8** ns. 216, 327; **9** ns. 17, 27, 70, 325, 374, 385, 387, 388, 476, 478; **10** ns. 41, 302, 737; **12** ns. 256, 745
95-74 . . . . **3** ns. 130, 133, 135, 136, 151, 153, 157, 220, 222, 223, 236, 238; **12** n.1111
96-11 . . . . **S6** ns. 100, 105.1
96-29 . . . . **12** ns. 515, 845
96-30 . . . . . **11** ns. 171, 176, 328; **12** ns. 845, 871, 872, 877, 899; **13** ns. 961, 962
97-48 . . . . **15** ns. 527, 530
98-10 . . . **12** ns. 173, 174, 188, 279, 297, 301, 302; **S12** ns. 640, 646

Rev. Rul.

98-27 . . . **3** n.202; **11** ns. 44, 45, 48, 139, 140, 171, 328; **12** ns. 326, 845, 871, 872, 874–877, 879, 896, 898, 899, 901, 902, 905; **13** n.961
98-37 . . . . **2** n.97
98-44 . . . **11** ns. 171, 328; **12** ns. 874, 876, 879, 898, 899, 901; **13** n.961
99-5 . . . . **2** n.57
99-6 . . . . **2** n.57; **10** n.406
99-14 . . . . **5** ns. 58, 406, 502
99-23 . . . . **5** ns. 107, 241
99-57 . . . . **S3** ns. 241, 250
99-58 . . . . **12** n.77; **S12** n.77
2000-5 . . . . **S11.01[1][f]**; **11** ns. 74, 366; **S11** n.216.1; 12.22[11]; **S12.22[11]**; **12** ns. 108, 126, 132, 148, 150.1, 213, 857, 897; **S12** ns. 146.1, 148, 149, 150.1, 313, 437; **S13** n.976
2000-12 . . . . . . **S4** n.343; **5** ns. 407, 497, 503
2000-43 . . . . **S6** n.81
2000-59 . . . . **S15** ns. 192, 243
2001-24 . . . . . . **S12** ns. 56, 270, 283.1, 328.2, 1017.1, 1017.2, 1018
2001-25 . . . . **S12** ns. 289, 292
2001-26 . . . . **S1** n.86; **S12** ns. 289, 290, 303.1, 321.1, 922, 925, 927, 935.1, 937, 938
2001-29 . . . . **S11** n.106
2001-31 . . . . **S1** n.81
2001-39 . . . . **S13** n.309; **S15** n.244
2001-46 . . . **S10** ns. 273, 291, 468, 470, 472, 574; S12.25[5]; S12.63[2][a]; **S12** ns. 269, 289, 290, 302.1, 303.1, 321.2, 921, 922, 925, 926, 934, 935.1, 935.2, 936.1, 937, 938, 939
2001-50 . . . . **S6** ns. 140.1, 140.2
2001-51 . . . . **S6** n.140.2
2002-1 . . . . **S3** ns. 246, 256, 273; **S11** n.272; **S12** ns. 745, 747
2002-31 . . . . **S4** n.405.1
2002-49 . . . . . . S11.05[2][a]; **S11** ns. 93, 133, 136.1
2002-85 . . . **S12** ns. 328.2, 1017.2; **S13** ns. 916, 946; **S15** n.741.15
2002-89 . . . . **S1** n.86.1
2002-90 . . . . **S1** n.86.1
2002-91 . . . . **S1** n.86.1
2003-18 . . . . **S11** ns. 144, 146, 147
2003-19 . . . **S12** ns. 51, 52, 371, 372, 374, 501, 515
2003-38 . . . . **S11** ns. 144, 146, 147
2003-48 . . . **S12** ns. 51, 52, 371, 372, 374, 501, 515
2003-51 . . . . **S3** n.206.1; **S12** n.981.1
2003-79 . . . . . . **S12** ns. 865.2, 872.1, 874, 875, 880.1, 905
2003-96 . . . . **S13** n.86
2003-110 . . . . . **S11** ns. 226.1, 232, 239, 241.1, 241.3
2003-125 . . . **S10** ns. 267–269, 281.2; **S12** ns. 535, 536, 915.3

[Text references are to paragraphs; note references are to chapters (boldface numbers)
and notes ("n."), and references to the supplement are preceded by "S."]

Rev. Rul.

2004-23 . . . . **S11** ns. 226.1, 232, 234, 235, 241.1, 241.3
2004-47 . . . . **S13** n.647.2
2004-59 . . . . **S2** n.56; **S3** n.378
2004-76 . . . . **S15** n.179
2004-77 . . . . **S2** n.80
2004-78 . . . . **S12** n.630
2004-79 . . . . . **S4**.25[4]; **S4** ns. 321, 321.1; **S12** ns. 587, 588
2004-83 . . . . . **S9** n.397; **S12** ns. 358.1, 369.1; **S13** ns. 921, 931.1
2004-85 . . . . **S2** n.54; **S6** ns. 48, 191.1
2004-87 . . . . **5** n.151
2005-39 . . . . **5** n.145
2005-65 . . . . **S11** ns. 227.2, 241.3, 323.1, 331.10a
2006-2 . . . . **S3** ns. 208, 241; **S12** ns. 713, 732
2006-34 . . . . **S9** n.305
2007-8 . . . . . **S11** ns. 274.2, 280.1; **S12** ns. 352.1, 664.2, 683.1, 699.4

REVENUE PROCEDURES

Rev. Proc.

65-17	13.21[8]; 13.22[1][b]; **13** ns. 212, 224, 228, 233, 235, 269
65-27	. . . . **2** n.25
65-29	. . . . **4** n.439
67-14	. . . . **8** n.266
68-23	. . . 15.80[2][c]; 15.80[3]; 15.81[3][b]; **15** ns. 612, 614, 625, 672
69-19	. . . . . **3** n.51; **13** n.170; **15** ns. 59, 575
70-4	. . . . **13** ns. 342, 343
70-8	. . . . **13** n.113
70-18	. . . . **13** n.233
72-13	. . . . **2** n.103
74-36	. . . . **3** n.51; **15** n.59
74-47	. . . . **2** n.103
75-17	. . . . **8** ns. 64, 163
75-29	. . . . **15** ns. 614, 882
76-4	. . . . **15** ns. 614, 882
76-20	. . . . **15** ns. 614, 882
76-24	. . . . **15** ns. 614, 882
76-44	. . . . **15** ns. 614, 882
77-5	. . . . **15** ns. 621, 629, 672
77-9	. . . . **15** n.408
77-17	. . . . **15** n.614
77-37	. . . . . **3** ns. 35, 175; **8** ns. 634, 638; **11** n.55; 12.24[2][e]; 12.42[5]; 12.63[2][a]; 12.66[3][a]; **12** ns. 10, 11, 43, 44, 58, 88, 96, 217, 222, 225, 232, 257, 270, 330, 345, 620, 691, 783, 802, 803, 862, 1142, 1145, 1153, 1155
79-47	. . . . **S8** n.140
79-68	. . . . **12** n.828
80-14	. . . . **15** n.762
81-17	. . . . **S12** n.733
81-42	. . . . **9** ns. 231, 271
81-60	. . . . **12** n.374

Rev. Proc.

81-70	. . . . **12** n.733
82-58	. . . . **2** n.76
83-16	. . . . **2** n.113
83-59	. . . . **3** ns. 6, 51, 109
84-42	. . . . . . **12** ns. 88, 620, 1142, 1153
86-9	. . . . **12** n.1185
86-18	. . . . **9** n.9
86-42	. . . . **12** ns. 10, 11, 43, 44, 61, 72, 330
87-22	. . . . **9** n.24
87-32	. . . . **5** n.321
87-33	. . . . **5** n.227
87-59	. . . . **8** n.430
89-12	. . . . . . **2** ns. 20, 92, 98, 100, 105, 132
89-28	. . . . **11** ns. 204, 207
89-30	. . . **8** ns. 634, 638, 639; **12** ns. 801–804
89-39	. . . . **11** n.224
89-50	. . . . **12** ns. 257, 341
89-56	. . . . **13** n.497
90-19	. . . . **15** ns. 967, 996, 1001, 1003
90-39	. . . . **13** n.346
90-52	. . . **10** ns. 248, 275, 286, 299, 300, 321, 322, 354
90-53	. . . . **13** n.326
90-56	. . . . **12** n.9
91-11	. . . . **13** ns. 342, 475
91-13	. . . . **2** ns. 20, 105
91-15	. . . . **2** n.76
91-22	. . . . . . 13.21[8]; **13** ns. 104, 212–215
91-23	. . . . **13** ns. 104, 212, 224, 232, 233; **15** n.190
91-24	. . . **13** ns. 104, 212, 224, 232, 233, 235; **15** n.190
91-26	. . . . **13** ns. 212, 232, 233; **15** n.190
91-54	. . . . **12** n.9
91-62	. . . . **11** ns. 204, 207
91-63	. . . . **11** ns. 150, 167
91-71	. . . . **13** n.326; **S13** n.326
92-9	. . . . **2** n.85
92-13	. . . . **5** n.318
92-33	. . . . **2** ns. 40, 100
92-35	. . . . **2** n.98
92-56	. . . . **15** ns. 111, 112
92-88	. . . . **2** n.105
93-3	. . . **2** ns. 20, 85, 132; **10** n.321; **11** n.366
93-7	. . . . **2** n.132
93-44	. . . . **2** ns. 87, 132
94-26	. . . . **4** n.313
94-45	. . . . **2** ns. 78, 132
94-46	. . . . **2** n.98
94-67	. . . . **13** ns. 217, 237, 247
95-3	. . . . **12** n.943
95-10	. . . . **2** n.132
95-11	. . . . **13** ns. 343, 650, 694
96-3	. . . . **12** n.943
96-13	. . . . **15** n.190
96-14	. . . . **13** ns. 224, 233, 235
96-21	. . . . **13** n.576
96-22	. . . . **12** n.943
96-30	. . . 11.09[2][d]; **11** ns. 20, 42, 150, 158, 167, 204, 207, 218, 234, 237, 320; **S11** ns. 20, 237

[Text references arc to paragraphs; note references are to chapters (boldface numbers)
and notes ("n."), and references to the supplement are preceded by "S."]

Rev. Proc.

96-39   **11** ns. 171, 176; **12** ns. 872, 877, 899;
                      13 ns. 343, 420, 575
96-43 . . . . **11** n.130
96-53 . . . . 13.21[8]; **13** ns. 104, 212, 218
97-3 . . . . **11** ns. 44, 171; **12** ns. 872, 877, 899;
                      13 n.962
97-40 . . . . **6** n.54
97-48 . . . . **6** n.54; **S6** n.51
97-49 . . . . **13** n.576
97-53 . . . **11** n.171; **12** ns. 872, 899; **13** n.962
98-3 . . . . **11** ns. 44, 171; **12** n.943
98-21 . . . . **15** n.190
98-23 . . . . **6** ns. 18, 19
98-27 . . . . **15** n.210
98-55 . . . . **6** ns. 19, 50, 51, 54; **S6** n.51
99-1 . . . . **9** n.24
99-3 . . . . **2** n.113; 3.15[1]; **3** ns. 6, 331, 391; **4**
              ns. 43, 102, 109; **8** ns. 64, 107, 430,
              630; **9** ns. 31, 246, 271, 283, 425; **10** ns.
              21, 318, 321, 704, 719; **11** ns. 44, 75,
              130, 366; **12** ns. 872, 943
99-18 . . . . **12** n.437
99-32 . . . . . 13.22[1][b]; 13.22[2]; **13** ns. 226,
              269; **S13** n.226
2000-3 . . . . **12** ns. 9–11, 275, 374, 401, 500,
              510, 733, 877
2000-12 . . . . **15** n.210; **S15** n.210
2001-3 . . . . **S4** n.102; **S12** ns. 500, 510
2001-21 . . . . **S12** n.437.1
2002-3   **S1** n.86.2; **S4** n.102; **S11** ns. 44, 75,
              130, 334.1; **S12** ns. 500, 510
2002-11 . . . . **S13** ns. 481, 484.1
2002-13 . . . . **5** n.140
2002-15 . . . . **S2** n.58.1
2002-18 . . . . **S13** n.484.1
2002-32 . . . . **S13** n.326
2002-43 . . . . **S13** ns. 347.1, 835.1
2002-45 . . . . **5** n.140
2002-52 . . . . **S15** n.190
2002-59 . . . . **S2** ns. 52, 58.1
2002-67 . . . . **S3** ns. 113, 158.2
2002-75 . . . . **S1** n.86.2
2003-5 . . . . **S12** ns. 510, 657.1
2003-24 . . . . . . 5.10[8][e]; **5** ns. 506, 512, 521
2003-25 . . . . . . 5.10[8][e]; **5** ns. 506, 512, 521
2003-43 . . . . **S6** ns. 51, 55, 70
2003-48 . . . . . **S11** n.20; **S11** ns. 130, 150, 157,
              158, 167, 196.3, 218, 228.1, 234, 234.1,
              237, 241.2
2003-52 . . . . **S11** ns. 222, 234, 235, 241.3
2003-55 . . . . . **S11** ns. 223, 227.1, 237.1, 241.3
2003-68 . . . . **5** n.140
2003-74 . . . . **S11** ns. 239, 241.3
2003-75 . . . . **S11** ns. 237.2, 241.3
2003-77 . . . . **5** n.590
2003-79 . . . . . **S11** n.328.1; **S12**.62[4]; **S12** ns.
              225.1, 897.1
2004-3 . . . . **S9** n. 31
2004-40 . . . . **S13** ns. 212, 219.1
2004-45 . . . . **5** n.521
2004-48 . . . . **S6** ns. 54, 55

Rev. Proc.

2004-49 . . . . **S6** n.191.1
2004-65 . . . . **5** ns. 585, 586
2004-66 . . . . **5** ns. 585, 587
2004-67 . . . . **5** ns. 585, 588
2004-68 . . . . **5** ns. 585, 589
2004-73 . . . . 5.10[8][e]; **5** n.590
2005-3 . . . **S11** ns. 75, 334.1; **S12** ns. 10, 500,
              510, 1065
2005-26 . . . . **5** n.577
2005-46 . . . . **S13** n.112.1
2005-68 . . . . **S12** n.9
2006-3 . . . . **S12** ns. 9, 657.1
2006-9 . . . . **S13** n.219.2
2006-47 . . . . **S15** n.407.18
2006-48 . . . . **S5** n.590
2006-54 . . . . **S15** n.190
2007-3 . . . . **S4** n.102; **S13** n.146.17

LETTER RULINGS

Ltr. Rul.

7946008 . . . . **13** n.529
8022010 . . . . **8** n.31
8027017 . . . . **12** n.828
8052018 . . . . **12** n.426
8305036 . . . . **15** ns. 648, 757
8512071 . . . . **3** n.234
8516031 . . . . **3** n.234
8517040 . . . . **3** n.234
8532053 . . . . **8** n.457
8540058 . . . . **3** n.234
8550037 . . . . **3** n.234
8645041 . . . . **10** n.572
8748049 . . . . **8** n.197
8750015 . . . . **13** n.734
8753046 . . . . **6** ns. 43, 127
8801026 . . . . **6** ns. 43, 127
8802042 . . . . **12** n.71
8806031 . . . . **6** ns. 43, 127
8806074 . . . . **12** n.940
8806081 . . . . **12** n.341
8808015 . . . . **15** n.211
8809081 . . . . **14** n.217
8818049 . . . . **6** n.182
8819075 . . . . **11** n.226
8821001 . . . . **12** n.877
8821002 . . . . **7** n.106
8822062 . . . . **3** n.403
8825048 . . . . **12** n.929
8825085 . . . . **11** n.224
8826030 . . . . **11** n.224
8826041 . . . . **11** n.224
8827041 . . . . **9** ns. 367, 385
8829023 . . . . **8** n.197
8830006 . . . . **12** n.341
8833046 . . . . **11** n.226
8836046 . . . . **11** n.207
8847067 . . . . **14** n.278
8847084 . . . . **6** n.52

[Text references are to paragraphs; note references are to chapters (boldface numbers) and notes ("n."), and references to the supplement are preceded by "S."]

Ltr. Rul.

8849017	**10** n.573
8903073	**7** n.180
8906059	**8** n.388
8910040	**11** n.65; **12** ns. 1171, 1179
8922080	**12** n.587
8923052	**12** n.1179
8928032	**12** n.944
8930005	**11** n.226
8933001	**12** n.443
9007036	**9** n.275; **11** n.378
9008041	**6** n.179
9010027	**2** n.133
9010042	**3** n.377; **4** n.270; **6** ns. 13, 16, 43
9012030	**12** n.944
9017057	**6** n.13
9024076	**9** n.57
9036001	**13** ns. 344, 734, 796
9044063	**8** n.287; **9** n.200; **10** ns. 265, 587; **12** n.859
9046036	**6** n.179
9102040	**12** n.944
9104043	**14** n.187
9111055	**12** n.339
9113009	**8** n.218
9214018	**12** n.529
9229025	**7** n.29
9237015	**8** n.338
9245004	**10** ns. 296, 546
9245027	**10** n.161
9253011	**12** n.442
9253027	**10** n.321
9317011	**12** n.964
9320019	**2** n.137
9333048	**4** n.309; **12** ns. 426, 542, 550, 590
9343011	**3** n.153
9409014	**12** n.141
9409016	**12** n.141
9437004	**9** ns. 368, 399
9516025	**4** n.309; **12** ns. 542, 550, 590
9539020	**12** ns. 640, 641; **S12** n.641
9615036	**12** n.293
9729011	**15** n.74
9743010	**12** ns. 202, 926, 934
9804038	**12** ns. 926, 934
9832003	**6** n.18
9835011	**8** n.438
9836027	**9** n.275
9836032	**12** n.926
9838007	**12** n.1152
9849014	**15** ns. 698, 780
9910038	**12** n.926
199903048	**15** ns. 698, 780
199929039	**15** ns. 698, 780
200013044	**S3** n.236

ANNOUNCEMENTS

Ann.

85-95	**15** n.627

Ann.

86-128	**14** n.293
87-57	**15** n.201
88-118	**2** ns. 30, 106, 107
95-9	**13** ns. 224, 233; **15** n.190
95-49	**13** n.212
96-124	**13** ns. 212, 218
97-4	**6** ns. 54, 70
99-1	13.22[1][b]; **13** n.225
99-76	**15** n.201
2000-12	**5** n.498
2000-51	**5** n.523
2001-25	**S12** ns. 500, 510
2002-40	**S13** n.212
2002-63	**5** ns. 501, 517
2006-30	**S5** ns. 220, 434; **S9** ns. 103, 373, 449.2, 450–452, 452.2
2006-50	**S13**.21[3]; **S13** n.146.16

GENERAL COUNSEL'S MEMORANDA

GCM

35824	**8** n.457
38798	**12** n.587
39264	**11** n.139
39404	**12** ns. 929, 1000
39768	**6** ns. 43, 127, 172, 182, 200, 204, 206

INCOME TAX UNIT REGULATIONS

IT

3119	**15** ns. 74, 221
3543	**8** n.137
3757	**14** n.124
3781	**15** n.221
3930	2.05[1]; **2** n.130
3948	**2** n.130
4007	**8** n.258
4109	**10** n.371

NOTICES

Notice

86-17	**15** ns. 266, 788, 951, 987
87-4	**15** ns. 48, 201
87-5	**15** ns. 638, 800, 802, 805
87-6	**15** n.340
87-14	**S13**.42[5][c]; **13** ns. 469, 470, 473; **S13** n.470
87-54	**15** n.339
87-56	**15** n.264
87-63	**10** n.287; **13** n.327

*[Text references are to paragraphs; note references are to chapters (boldface numbers)
and notes ("n."), and references to the supplement are preceded by "S."]*

Notice

87-64 .... **15** ns. 558, 567; **S15** ns. 558, 563,
563.1, 567.2, 923
87-66 .... **15** ns. 800, 802, 805
87-79 .... 14.44[2]; **14** n.278
87-82 .... **3** n.287
87-85 ... 15.81[3][c]; 15.84[1][b]; **15** ns. 658,
659, 676, 683, 684, 689, 761, 770, 829,
840
88-10 .... **6** n.88
88-19 .... **6** n.127; **10** ns. 113, 160; **12** n.532
88-22 .... **15** n.447
88-36 .... **6** n.88
88-50 .... **12** n.501; **15** n.905
88-65 .... **15** ns. 314, 370
88-67 .... **14** ns. 185, 195, 197
88-70 .... **15** n.339
88-71 .... **15** ns. 339, 364, 543
88-75 .... 2.04[4]; **2** ns. 115, 117, 122
88-96 .... **6** n.127; **10** ns. 113, 160; **12** n.532
88-123 .... **13** ns. 52, 194; **15** ns. 482, 484
88-129 .... **3** n.287
89-3 .... **15** n.349
89-21 .... **15** ns. 50, 201
89-30 .... **15** ns. 710, 825, 850
89-37 ..... **8** n.360; 9.23[2][a]; 9.23[2][b]; **9**
n.459; **10** n.170
89-58 .... **15** n.76
89-64 .... **15** ns. 963, 979, 996, 1001
89-80 .... **15** n.267
89-81 .... **15** n.447
89-84 ..... **5** n.96; **13** n.289; **15** ns. 211, 212
89-85 ... **15** ns. 949, 967, 971, 973, 988, 996,
1001, 1003
89-90 .... **15** n.521
89-94 .... **13** ns. 23, 309; **S13** ns. 23, 309; **15**
n.494; **S15** n.494
90-26 .... **15** n.378
90-27 .... **6** n.125; **14** ns. 292, 304, 377
91-27 .... **13** n.902
92-59 .... **13** ns. 509, 823
93-2 .... **9** ns. 461, 462; **10** n.170
94-46 ..... **12** n.957; 15.81[3][b]; 15.81[3][c];
15.82[2][b]; **15** ns. 659, 678, 689, 691,
761, 771, 772, 830, 832, 860, 867, 872,
878, 896
94-47 .... **4** ns. 63, 75, 78, 84, 88
94-48 .... **4** n.63; **8** n.31
94-49 .... **13** n.578
94-85 .... **15** n.185
94-89 .... **4** n.287
94-93 .... 9.23[2][c]; **9** ns. 460, 467;
12.63[3][b]; **12** ns. 957, 958; **13** n.935
95-13 .... **15** n.410
95-14 .... 2.02[3][a]; **2** ns. 5, 44, 80
95-53 .... **5** ns. 406, 503, 517; **S13** n.86
96-6 .... **12** n.943
96-39 .... 15.62[1]; **15** ns. 515, 526
97-3 .... **6** n.88
97-4 .... **6** n.50
97-18 .... **15** ns. 746, 748
97-20 .... **6** n.88

Notice

97-21   4.03[8][a]; 4.03[8][b]; **4** ns. 129, 130;
S4 ns. 131, 134.1; **5** n.406
97-40 .... **15** n.516
97-42 .... **15** ns. 746, 748
97-66 .... **15** n.210
98-5 .... **5** ns. 423, 481, 503; 15.21[1][d];
S15.21[1][d]; 15.61[4]; **15** ns. 317, 506
98-10 .... 13.21[8]; **13** n.219
98-11 .... **5** ns. 423, 487; 15.61[4]; **15** ns. 33,
502, 507, 510, 518; **S15** n.518
98-16 .... **15** ns. 48, 210
98-35 ..... **5** n.423; 15.61[4]; **15** ns. 33, 510,
511, 512
98-38 .... 13.45[6][c]; **13** ns. 773, 789
98-40 .... **13** n.791
98-65 .... **13** n.219
99-6 .... **2** n.50; **6** n.47
99-8 .... **15** n.210
99-25 .... **15** ns. 48, 210
99-43 .... **15** ns. 976, 985
99-57 .... **S3** n.250
99-59 .... **5** ns. 407, 503; **S8** n.374
2000-1 .... **12** n.1011
2000-15 .... 5.10[7][b]; **5** ns. 497, 503
2000-18 .... **5** n.515
2000-26 .... **S6** n.194; **S10** ns. 39, 42, 45, 50,
438, 439, 604
2000-44 .... **5** ns. 406, 503
2000-56 .... **S3** ns. 246, 256
2000-59 .... **S15** n.243
2000-60 .... **5** ns. 406, 502
2000-61 .... **5** ns. 406, 502
2001-4 .... **S15** n.210
2001-15 .... **5** n.502
2001-16 .... **5** ns. 407, 503; **S10** ns. 129, 174
2001-17 ... **S3** ns. 113, 158, 158.1, 223, 366; **5**
ns. 406, 437, 503
2001-22 .... **S10** n.394
2001-43 .... **S15** n.210
2001-45 ..... 5.10[5][c]; **5** ns. 220, 406, 434,
503; S9.22[2]; **S9** n.103
2001-51 .... **5** ns. 497, 503
2002-11 .... **S13** ns. 485.1, 701
2002-18 ...... S13.42[5][c]; **S13** ns. 305, 470,
484.1, 485.4, 701
2002-36 ..... **S4** ns. 405.1, 406, 413, 415, 429
2002-77 .... **S15** n.741.15
2003-5 .... **S13** n.23; **S15** n.361.1
2003-46 .... **S2** n.52; **S15** ns. 34, 322, 513
2003-50 .... **S13** ns. 23, 309; **S15** ns. 494, 571
2003-65 ... S14.44[3][c]; S14.44[4][a]; **S14** ns.
293, 295.1, 301.1, 306.1, 306.6
2003-69 .... **S8** n.254.11
2003-71 .... **S8** n.254.11
2003-76 .... **5** ns. 407, 497, 503
2003-79 .... **S8** n.254.11
2004-19 .... **S15** ns. 317, 322.1
2004-20 .... **S15** n.573
2004-37 .... S13.41[2][d]; **S13** ns. 328.1, 333.1
2004-38 ... **S15** ns. 556.1, 556.4, 556.7, 556.9,
556.10, 556.13

*[Text references are to paragraphs; note references are to chapters (boldface numbers)
and notes ("n."), and references to the supplement are preceded by "S."]*

Notice

2004-44	**S12** n.733
2004-45	**S8** n.254.11
2004-58	S13.42[5][c]; **S13** n.485.18
2004-67	5.10[7][b]; **5** ns. 407, 497, 503
2004-68	**S2** n.48
2004-70	**S8** ns. 254.11, 254.12; **S15** ns. 498, 667.1, 741.4
2004-80	5.10[8][e]; **5** ns. 583, 584
2005-6	**S12** n.150.5; **S15** ns. 556.3, 741.8
2005-10	S15.62[8][b]; S15.62[8][c]; **S15** ns. 556.3–556.5, 556.11, 556.16
2005-11	**5** ns. 576, 584
2005-12	**5** n.576
2005-14	**5** ns. 73, 77; **S15** ns. 407.18, 407.19, 407.28
2005-38	**S15** n.556.16
2005-64	**S15** ns. 556.1, 556.4
2005-70	S3.11[8]; **S3** n.249.4
2005-74	**S15** n.704.1
2005-75	**5** n.589
2005-90	**S15** n.316.2
2005-99	**S13** n.178.1
2006-6	**5** n.587
2006-81	**S11** n.131
2006-85	S15.80[7][f]; **S15** n.647.4
2007-5	**S13** n.146.14

OFFICE DECISIONS

OD

735	**8** n.523

SOLICITOR'S MEMORANDA

SM

3710	**12** n.370

TECHNICAL ADVICE MEMORANDA

TAM

7946005	**12** n.788
8430002	**8** n.457
8741001	**10** n.623
8930001	**8** n.616
8939001	**4** n.250
9003003	**8** n.298; **9** n.202
9144042	**5** n.114
9215005	**12** n.227
9245004	**6** ns. 43, 172, 181, 182
9326001	**5** n.260
9329002	**13** n.435
9342005	**5** ns. 128, 133; **12** n.1192

TAM

9403003	**6** n.107
9423003	**6** n.239
9647004	**15** n.743
9714002	**13** n.322
9716001	**3** n.236
9743001	**12** ns. 202, 926, 934
9748003	**9** n.373
9822005	**4** n.309
9830002	**3** n.292; **4** ns. 303, 309
199929038	**13** n.215

TECHNICAL INFORMATION RELEASES

TIR

113	**6** n.20
1160	**12** ns. 729, 732

TREASURY DECISIONS

TD

4603	**4** n.433
6378	**7** n.52
6476	**8** n.423
6990	**8** n.424
7004	**8** n.424
7422	**12** ns. 271, 732
7467	**15** n.408
7889	**2** n.95
7918	**15** n.310
7920	**4** n.50
7954	**15** n.675
7965	**15** n.213
7967	**15** n.213
7991	**13** n.416
8149	**14** ns. 225, 227
8178	**15** n.451
8198	**15** n.949
8209	**9** n.394
8210	**15** n.376
8214	**15** n.364
8216	**15** n.496
8223	**15** ns. 261, 270
8226	**13** n.521
8228	**15** n.119
8238	**11** ns. 18, 67, 117, 154
8243	**15** ns. 707, 710
8263	**15** n.197
8279	**15** n.197
8280	**15** ns. 804, 912, 924
8283	**15** n.491
8307	**5** n.352
8319	**13** n.475
8340	**5** n.352
8352	**14** n.193

[Text references are to paragraphs; note references are to chapters (boldface numbers) and notes ("n."), and references to the supplement are preceded by "S."]

[Text references are to paragraphs; note references are to chapters (boldface numbers) and notes ("n."), and references to the supplement are preceded by "S."]

TD

8856 . . . . **15** n.210
8858　　**S6** ns. 72, 195; **S8** n.287; **S9** n.200; **10** n.598; **15** ns. 579, 580, 582, 587, 591, 592, 593, 594, 596, 597, 598, 600, 645, 647, 654, 664, 670, 716, 721, 785, 792, 824, 842, 846, 857, 884, 953, 1039
8863 . . . . **15** ns. 724, 793
8864 . . . . **15** ns. 802, 852
8865 . . . . **10** n.456
8867 . . . . **15** n.453
8868 . . . . **15** n.394
8869 . . . . **S6** ns. 47, 59, 198, 199, 216
8870 . . . . **15** n.829
8872 . . . . **10** ns. 113, 160
8875 . . . . **5** n.497
8876 . . . . **5** n.497
8877 . . . . **5** ns. 497, 512
8881 . . . . **S15** ns. 48, 210
8882 . . . . **S3** n.91; **12** n.647; **S12** n.652
8883 . . . **S3** ns. 243–245, 254, 256, 273, 281**S4** ns. 450, 453; **12** ns. 713, 1043; **S12** ns. 717, 1034, 1042; **S13** n.629
8884 . . . . **S13** n.784
8885 . . . . **12** n.985; **S12** n.253
8889 . . . . **S15** ns. 32, 187, 192, 241
8896 . . . .**5** ns. 497, 512, 522
8898 . . . . . . **S12** ns. 50, 62, 67, 77, 172
8904 . . . . **S3** n.90; **S12** ns. 653, 760
8913 . . . . **S11** ns. 287, 296.1
8914 . . . . **S15** n.201
8916 . . . . **S15** n.119
8919 . . . . **S13** n.517.1
8924 . . . . **S8** n.374
8927 . . . . **S15** n.204.1
8940 . . . **S6** n.196; S10.21[2]; **S10** ns. 80, 291, 383, 400, 401.1, 425.1, 472, 484.1, 515.1, 519, 575, 596.1, 598, 599.1, 603, 610, 625, 627.1, 637.1; **S12** n.918
8944 . . . . **S10** n.481.1
8950 . . . . **S13** n.517.1
8960 . . . . . **S11** ns. 329.1, 331, 331.4; **S12** ns. 888, 895, 895.1
8961 . . . . . **5** ns. 497, 507, 508, 512, 515, 516
8964 . . . . **S8** n.374
8970 . . . . **S2** n.55
8973 . . . . **S15** ns. 76, 85, 86, 108
8975 . . . . **10** ns. 113, 160
8986 . . . . **S3** n.250
8988 . . . . **S11** ns. 329, 329.1, 331, 331.6
8994 . . . . **S6** n.18
8998 . . . . **S13** n.485.9
8999 . . . . **S15** n.192.1
9000 . . . . **5** ns. 497, 502, 512, 516, 517
9002 . . . . **S13** ns. 347.1, 835.1, 835.3
9008 . . . . . . **S15** ns. 515, 517, 518, 526
9011 . . . . **5** n.527
9012 . . . . **S15** n.30
9017 . . . . **5** ns. 497, 504, 512, 518
9018 . . . . **5** ns. 504, 512
9022 . . . . **S15** n.784.14
9025 . . . . **S13** n.589

TD

9035 . . . . **S9** ns. 214, 218, 221, 226
9038 . . . . **S11** n.20.2
9046 . . . .**5** ns. 497, 506, 521
9047 . . . . **S10** n.113; **S12** n.532
9049 . . . . **S3** n.250
9063 . . . . **S14** ns. 194.1, 207.1, 229.1, 246.1
9071 . . . **S10** ns. 273, 291; **S12** ns. 321.3, 921, 935.3
9080 . . . . **S4** n.308.1; **S12** ns. 539, 552.1
9083 . . . .**5** n.140
9088 . . . . **S13** n.178.1
9089 . . . . **S13** ns. 574.2, 901.1, 901.2
9101 . . . . **S15** ns. 784.15, 840.5
9107 . . . .**5** n.113
9108 . . . .**5** n.510
9109 . . . . **5** ns. 505, 520
9117 . . . . **S13** n.574.20
9118 . . . . **S13** ns. 485.7, 485.14
9119 . . . . **S13** n.485.2
9127 . . . . **S4** n.308.3; **S12** ns. 539, 552.1, 558, 586.1; **S14** n.53
9139 . . . . **S6** n.55.1
9141 . . . . **S15** ns. 347, 358
9143 . . . . **S15** n.106
9146 . . . .**5** n.564
9153 . . . . . **S2** n.58.2; **S15** ns. 27.1, 34.1
9154 . . . . **S13** n.485.18
9157 . . . . **S15** n.202.1
9165 . . . . **5** ns. 526, 582
9182 . . . . **S12** n.494
9183 . . . . **S2** n.50
9187 . . . . . . **S13** ns. 484.1, 485.3, 485.20
9192 . . . S13.42[12][b]; **S13** ns. 574.2, 901.3
9195 . . . . **S13** n.964.1
9197 . . . . **S2** n.48
9198 . . . S11.11[3][d]; **S11** ns. 329, 329.1, 331; **S12** ns. 888, 895, 895.3, 907, 1037; **S13** n.964
9201 . . . . **5** n.527
9207 . . . . **S3** n.249.1; **5** n.437
9210 . . . . **S6** n.144.1
9211 . . . . **S15** n.106
9212 . . . . **S15** n.60
9222 . . . . **S15** n.501.3
9230 . . . . **S15** n.784.15
9235 . . . . **S2** n.48
9242 . . . . **S12** ns. 102, 150.6
9243 . . . . **S15** n.741.2
9244 . . . . **S11** n.264.1; **S12** n.790.4
9246 . . . . **S2** n.58.2; **S15** n.27.3
9251 . . . . **S15** n.501.4
9254 . . . . **S13** n.485.23
9260 . . . . **S15** n.361.2
9263 . . . . **S5** n.77; **S15** ns. 407.18, 407.28
9269 . . . . **S14** n.194.1
9271 . . . . **S10** n.574
9278 . . . . **S13** ns. 146.14, 179.6
9303 . . . . . . **S12** ns. 341.2, 358.2, 1097.1; **S13** n.922.1
9305 . . . . **S15** n.105.3
9316 . . . . **S12** n.50.10

Cumulative Table
of Cases

*[Text references are to paragraphs; note references are to chapters (boldface numbers)
and notes ("n."), and references to the supplement are preceded by "S."]*

A

A.A. Lewis & Co. v. CIR **2** n.32
Abatti v. CIR **13** n.102
Abbott v. CIR **10** n.703
Abdalla v. CIR . . . . **10** ns. 57, 58, 60
Abegg v. CIR . . . . **12** n.345; **13** n.256; **15** ns.
    127, 639, 642
Abegg, Werner v. CIR **3** n.309
Abraham v. US **2** n.77
Ach v. CIR . . . . **13** ns. 79, 83; **14** n.399
Achiro, Silvano v. CIR . . . . **1** n.89; **2** ns. 154,
    155, 166, 173; **13** n.102; **14** ns. 125, 165
Acme Steel Co. . . . . **S13** ns. 347, 835.3
ACM Partnership v. CIR **1** n.78;
    5.10[6][b]; 5.10[6][e]; 5.10[7][b]; **5** ns.
    407, 414, 477, 478, 487, 490, 502; **10**
    n.439; **12** n.812; **S12** n.812; **14** ns. 6,
    149, 161, 167, 170; **13** n.250
Acro Mfg. Co. v. CIR   **10** ns. 76, 263, 331;
    S10 n.331
Action Distrib. Co. v. CIR **10** n.221
Adams, Robert W. **3** n.316
Adams v. CIR **9** n.203
Adda, Fernand . . . . . 15.02[2][b]; **15** ns. 126,
    127, 129
Addison Intl, Inc. v. CIR   **1** ns. 52, 65, 78;
    15 n.396
Adelson v. US **4** n.247
Ades, Albert . . . . **4** ns. 432, 434
Adkins-Phelps, Inc., US v. . . . . **12** ns. 45, 59,
    69, 823
Adobe Resources Corp. v. US . . . **13** ns. 735,
    797
Adolph Coors Co. **7** n.122
A.D. Saenger, Inc. v. CIR **8** n.157
Advance Delivery & Chem. Sys. Nev., Inc.
    . . . . **S7** n.163
Aeroquip-Vickers, Inc. v. CIR   **S11** n.269;
    S12 ns. 844, 846, 851
A.E. Staley Mfg. Co. v. CIR . . . . . **5** ns. 106,
    111, 114, 115, 166, 275, 284, 287

Aetna Casualty & Sur. Co. v. US . . . **12** ns.
    90, 259, 269, 308, 505, 518, 931, 968,
    1014
Affiliated Capital Corp. . . . . . **5** ns. 163, 164
Affiliated Gov't Employees' Distrib. Co. v.
    CIR **3** n.262
Agway, Inc. v. US **9** n.166
Ahles Realty Corp. v. CIR **12** n.503
Aidoo, Joe Richard **5** n.85
Aiken Indus., Inc. v. CIR . . . .
    . . . . **1** n.47; **15** n.185
Ajax Eng'g Corp. **2** n.185
Alabama Asphaltic Limestone Co., Helvering
    v. . . . . . . **10** n.277; 12.21[4]; 12.21[6];
    12.26[2]; S12.26[2]; S12.30[1]; **12** ns.
    60, 83, 222, 337, 415; **S12** ns. 60, 337;
    14 n.336
Alabama By-Prods. Corp. v. US **8** n.90
Aladdin Indus., Inc. **13** n.91
Alan v. CIR **12** n.1111
Albany Car Wheel Co. v. CIR   **3** n.149; **10**
    n.595
Albers v. CIR . . . . **9** ns. 154, 157
Alcazar Hotel Co. **12** n.1112
Alcorn Wholesale Co. **14** n.151
Alderman, Velma W. . . . . **3** ns. 84, 127, 137;
    12 n.689
Alderson v. Healy **2** n.24; **8** n.65
Aldon Homes, Inc. **13** n.14
Alexander, Morris **10** n.27
Alex Brown, Inc. **7** n.167
Alleghany Corp. . . . . **5** ns. 108, 307
Allen, Horace E. **10** n.33
Allen, Ivan, Co. v. US . . . . **7** ns. 70, 85
Allen, Norma F., Estate of **4** n.244
Allen Mach. Corp. **7** n.233
Allied Chem. Corp. v. US **5** n.105; **10**
    n.241
Alma Piston Co. . . . . **7** ns. 95, 105
Alprosa Watch Corp. . . . . 14.02[2]; **14** ns. 16,
    119
Altama Delta Corp. . . . **13** ns. 139, 142, 185,
    186, 231
Alterman Foods, Inc. **8** n.205
Alterman Foods, Inc. v. US **8** n.208

[Text references are to paragraphs; note references are to chapters (boldface numbers) and notes ("n."), and references to the supplement are preceded by "S."]

[Text references are to paragraphs; note references are to chapters (boldface numbers) and notes ("n."), and references to the supplement are preceded by "S."]

[Text references are to paragraphs; note references are to chapters (boldface numbers) and notes ("n."), and references to the supplement are preceded by "S."]

Behrend v. US **8** n.615
Bell, John L., Estate of **12** n.767
Bell, William H. **2** n.155; **13** n.228
Benak, Henry J. . . . . . . **4** ns. 242, 247, 254
Bender, American Compress & Warehouse
 Co. v. **3** n.17
Benedek v. CIR **10** n.743
Benedict Oil Co. v. US **10** n.235
Benjamin, Blanche S. . . . . **9** ns. 150, 157
Bennet v. Helvering **3** n.218
Bennett v. US **11** n.348
Bentsen v. Phinney **12** n.826
Bercy Indus., Inc. v. CIR . . . 12.28[4]; **12** ns.
 204, 505, 512, 517, 526, 931; **14** ns. 64,
 67
Berenbaum, CIR v. **9** n.163
Beretta v. CIR **9** n.247
Berg v. US **10** n.81
Berger, Ernest H. . . . . **8** ns. 173, 179
Berger Mach. Prods., Inc. . . . **12** ns. 503, 517,
 518
Bergersen v. CIR **8** n.209
Berghash, CIR v. . . . 12.64[3]; **12** ns. 45, 859,
 1087, 1103, 1104
Bergman v. US **4** n.261; **6** n.111
Bergstrom v. US **10** n.78
Berlands, Inc. **14** n.151
Berlin, Irving, Music Corp. v. US . . . . **7** ns.
 212, 220
Berner v. US **12** n.473
Bernstein, Estate of **12** n.409
Bernstein v. US **8** n.123
Berry Petroleum Co. (9th Cir.) . . . **5** ns. 104,
 121, 276; **12** ns. 664, 723
Berry Petroleum Co. (TC)   **14** ns. 271, 274,
 275, 288, 309
Bhada, R. K. . . . . . . **8** n.407; 9.09[6][b]; **9** ns.
 349, 389, 392; **12** n.975
Bhada v. CIR . . . . . . **8** n.407; 9.09[6][b]; **9** ns.
 349, 389, 392; **12** n.975
Bialo, Walter . . . . **8** ns. 616, 632
Bianchi, Angelo J. **2** n.146
Bickmeyer, Henry C., Estate of **8** n.261
Biddle v. CIR **15** n.304
Biernbaum, Ralph **4** n.242
Bijou Park Properties, Inc. **10** n.533
Bilar Tool & Dye Corp. v. CIR . . . **5** ns. 254,
 291; **10** n.238
Bird Management, Inc. **10** n.199
Birmingham, Bartels v. **1** n.72
Birren, P.A., & Son v. CIR **3** n.233
Bishop v. Shaughnessy **8** n.259
Black & Decker Corp. (3d Cir.) . . . **15** n.108
Black & Decker Corp. v. US (4th Cir.)   **S3**
 ns. 113, 145, 151, 158, 158.1, 158.2,
 223; **5** ns. 437, 479, 488, 573; **S5** n.437
Black & Decker Corp. v. US (D. Md. 2004,
 2004-2 USTC ¶ 50,390) . . . **S3** ns. 113,
 133, 145, 151, 158, 158.1, 158.2, 223; **5**
 ns. 437, 479, 488, 573
Black & Decker Corp. v. US (D. Md. 2004,
 2004-2 USTC ¶ 50,359) . . . **S3** ns. 133,
 145, 158, 158.1, 223; **5** n.437

Black Dome Corp. **5** n.26
Black Gold Energy Corp. **4** n.255
Black Hills Corp. **1** n.85
Blaffer, R.L., & Co. **7** n.55
Blake v. CIR . . . **8** ns. 260, 289, 649; **12** n.843
Blanco v. US **9** n.29
Blaschka v. US . . . . **9** ns. 249, 299, 371
Blass, Gus, Co. **7** n.141
Blatt, Gloria . . . . **9** ns. 214, 218
Blauvelt, Ernest E. **8** n.52
Bleily & Collishaw, Inc. **9** n.190
Blenheim Co. v. CIR **15** n.247
Bliss Dairy, Inc., US v. **10** n.201
Bloch v. CIR **12** n.788
Bloch v. US . . . . **9** ns. 68, 172
Bloomfield Ranch v. CIR **2** n.126
Bloomington Transmission Serv., Inc. **2**
 n.196
Blount v. CIR **9** n.150
Blumeyer, Arthur R., III **4** n.254
Bobsee Corp. v. US **14** n.135
Boca Investerings Partnership v. US (DC
 Cir.) . . . **5** ns. 407, 479, 488; **S12** n.812
Boca Investerings Partnership v. US (DDC)
 5 ns. 407, 478, 479, 488; **S12** n.812
Boecking, H.E., Jr. **8** n.205; **10** n.60
Boehm, Robert **5** n.92
Boehm v. CIR **4** n.228
Boeing Corp. v. US (9th Cir.)   **S15** ns. 111,
 406
Boeing Corp. v. US (WD Wash.) . . . **15** n.406
Boettger, Lloyd . . . . **11** ns. 146, 147
Bolding v. CIR **6** n.107; **S6** n.107
Bolker v. CIR **3** n.373
Bollinger, CIR v.
 . . . . 2.10; **2** ns. 203, 205–209
Bolnick v. CIR **4** n.212
Bondy v. CIR **11** n.30
Bone, Thos. E. **6** n.54
Bonsall v. CIR . . . . **11** ns. 105, 236
Book Prod. Indus., Inc.
 . . . . **12** n.615; **13** n.336
Booth, Earnest, M.D., P.C. **7** n.108
Bordo Prods. Co. v. US **4** n.165
Borg, Joe E. **6** n.106
Borg & Beck Co. **5** n.240
Borge, Victor v. CIR . . . **2** n.169; **14** ns. 123,
 402; **13** n.79
Bothin Real Estate Co. v. CIR **3** n.302
Boulex, Pierre **15** n.62
Bowater, Inc. v. CIR . . . **15** n.106; **S15** n.106
Bowers v. CIR **4** n.246
Boyer, Robert A. **2** n.204; **13** n.147
Braddock Land Co. **10** n.28
Bradford, James C., Jr. **5** n.104
Bradford-Robinson Printing Co. v. US **7**
 n.103
Bradshaw v. US . . . . . . **3** ns. 72, 314, 317; **4**
 n.152; **6** n.64
Bramblett, Richard H. v. CIR **2** n.208; **3**
 n.314
Brams, Stanley H. v. CIR . . . .
 . . . . **3** n.161; **8** n.160

[Text references are to paragraphs; note references are to chapters (boldface numbers) and notes ("n."), and references to the supplement are preceded by "S."]

[Text references are to paragraphs; note references are to chapters (boldface numbers) and notes ("n."), and references to the supplement are preceded by "S."]

Carter, Susan J. 10 n.194; 13 n.292
Carter, CIR v. 10 n.43
Caruth v. US . . . 3 ns. 14, 349, 370; 8 n.259
Caruth Corp. v. US 8 n.259
Casco Bank & Trust Co. v. US 4 n.261
Casco Prods. Corp. . . . . . 9 n.24; 12 ns. 503,
   505, 512, 931; S12 n.506.3
Case v. CIR . . . . 11 ns. 32, 208
Casey v. CIR . . . . 7.02[2]; 7 ns. 31, 39, 101
Casner v. CIR . . . . 8 ns. 30, 286
Castle Harbour . . . .
   . . . . See TIFD III-E, Inc. v. US
Castner Garage, Ltd. 8 n.82
Catalano v. CIR . . . . S6 ns. 78, 84.1
Catalano, Eduardo 2 n.146
Cataphote Corp. of Miss. v. US . . . . 7 ns. 45,
   48, 52, 111
CCA, Inc. . . . . 15 ns. 495, 496
C.E. Hooper, Inc. v. US 7 n.90
Celanese Corp. v. US 4 n.257
Cement Investors, Inc., Helvering v. S3
   n.401
Cenex, Inc. v. US . . . 4 n.201; 5 n.44; 10 n.70
Centel Communications Co. v. CIR 4
   n.438; 8 ns. 182, 432, 544, 551
Centeral de Gas de Chihuahua S.A. 15
   n.208
Centennial Sav. Bank, FSB, US v.   4 n.295;
   6 n.234; 12 n.2
Central Bank of S. v. US 13 n.90
Central Cuba Sugar Co. v. CIR   3 ns. 355,
   358
Central de Gas de Chihuahua S.A. 13
   n.147
Central Foundry Co. 5 n.110
Central Motor Co. v. US . . . . . . .7 ns. 90, 95
Cerand & Co., Inc. v. CIR S4 n.147
Cerone, Michael N. . . . . 9 ns. 49, 129
C.F. Mueller Co. v. CIR . . . 5 n.40; 13 n.278
Challenge Mfg. Co. 8 n.199
Challenger, Inc. . . . . . . 13.23[3][d]; 13 ns. 36,
   265, 277, 285; 14 n.128
Chamberlin v. CIR (6th Cir.) . . . 8.60; 8.62;
   8.62[1]; 8.62[3]; 8.63[2]; 8.64[4]; 8.66; 8
   ns. 561, 645, 646; 11.13[4]; 11 n.363; 12
   n.468
Chamberlin v. CIR (7th Cir.) 10 n.44
Champion, CIR v. 9 n.259
Champion Int'l Corp. . . . . . . 15 ns. 331, 332
Chandler, Estate of 9 n.262
Chaney & Hope, Inc. . . . . 7 ns. 115, 138
Chapman v. CIR . . . . .12 ns. 89, 158, 160
Char-Lil Corp. (10th Cir.) S7 n.217
Char-Lil Corp. (TCM) 7 n.216
Charles Town, Inc. v. CIR 13 n.83
Chase, Ransom W. 8 n.202; 13 n.278
Chase Nat'l Bank, CIR v. 2 n.72
Cherry v. US 14 n.165
Cherry-Burrell Corp. v. US 10 n.308
Chertkof v. CIR . . . . 9 ns. 129, 130
Chesapeake Corp. of Va. 5 n.164
Chesterton, A.W. Chesterton Co., Inc. v.   6
   ns. 58, 74

Chesterton, A.W., Co., Inc. v. Chesterton . . .
   . . . . .6 ns. 58, 74
Cheyenne Newspapers, Inc. v. CIR . . . 7 ns.
   92, 116
Chevron Corp. (1995) . . . . . . 13 n.209; 15 ns.
   108, 482
Chicago, B. & Q. R.R., US v. . . . . 3 ns. 286,
   290
Chicago, Board of Trade of 3 n.291
Chicago, Milwaukee, St. Paul & Pac. R.R.
   Co. v. US 4 n.433; 5 n.165
Chicago & W. Ind. R.R. v. CIR . . . 13 n.273
Chicago N. Shore & Milwaukee R.R. Co. v.
   US 4 n.433
Chicago Stadium Corp. 12 n.60
Chicago Stock Yards Co., Helvering v. 7
   n.123
Chism, Estate of, v. CIR 8 n.173
Choate v. CIR . . . 8.42[2]; 8 ns. 256, 552, 553
Chock Full O'Nuts Corp. v. US 4 n.413
Christie v. CIR 4 n.152
Chrome Plate v. US 10 n.536
Chrysler Corp. (6th Cir.) . . . . S15 ns. 305.1,
   367
Chrysler Corp. (BTA) 4 n.441
Ciaio, Frank 9 n.219
Ciba-Geigy Corp. . . . . 13 ns. 146, 148
CIR (Commissioner of Internal Revenue) . . .
   . . . . See individual taxpayer
Circle K Corp. v. US 4 n.201; 5 n.44; 10
   n.70
Cities Serv. Co. v. US 12 n.455
Citizens & S. Corp. 10 n.447
Citizens Bank & Trust Co. v. US   8 n.168;
   9 ns. 228, 388, 482
Citizens Nat'l Bank v. US 3 n.228
Citizens Trust Co. . . . . 5 ns. 251, 253
Civic Center Fin. Co. v. Kuhl 12 n.222,
   1132
Claggett, S.O. 7 n.228
Clark, Donald . . . . 12 ns. 163, 770
Clark v. CIR . . . . . . 8 n.572; 11 ns. 175, 267;
   12.44[2][c]; S12.44[2][c]; 12.45[3]; 12
   ns. 357, 770, 773, 775, 777, 779, 781,
   801; 13 n.616; 14 n.89
Clark, US v. 4 n.243
Clark Equip. Corp. v. US . . . . 4 ns. 415, 435
Clarksdale Rubber Co. 14 n.30
Clauson, Dunton v. 9 n.260
Claussen's, Inc. v. US 12 n.483
Cleveland v. CIR 9 n.270
Cleveland Trust Co. v. CIR 2 n.73
Clifford, Helvering v. . . . . . 1.05[3][a]; 1 n.88
Climaco v. US 15 n.208
Cline v. CIR 5 n.150
Clougherty Packing Co. v. CIR 1 n.83
Cloutier, Harry H. 8 n.366
C.M. Gooch Lumber Sales Co. . . . 4 ns. 144,
   147
CM Holdings, Inc., IRS v. . . . 5 ns. 483, 484
C.M. Thibodaux Co. v. CIR . . . .
   . . . . 8 ns. 170, 310
CMI Int'l, Inc. 15 n.641

[Text references are to paragraphs; note references are to chapters (boldface numbers) and notes ("n."), and references to the supplement are preceded by "S."]

[Text references are to paragraphs; note references are to chapters (boldface numbers) and notes ("n."), and references to the supplement are preceded by "S."]

[Text references are to paragraphs; note references are to chapters (boldface numbers) and notes ("n."), and references to the supplement are preceded by "S."]

*[Text references are to paragraphs; note references are to chapters (boldface numbers)
and notes ("n."), and references to the supplement are preceded by "S."]*

[Text references are to paragraphs; note references are to chapters (boldface numbers) and notes ("n."), and references to the supplement are preceded by "S."]

[Text references are to paragraphs; note references are to chapters (boldface numbers) and notes ("n."), and references to the supplement are preceded by "S."]

General Indus. Corp. **13** n.282
General Ins. Agency, Inc., ... **10** n.52
General Management Corp. v. CIR **7** n.233
General Motors Corp. v. US   **5** n.51; **13** ns. 388, 589; **S13** n.589
General Utilities . . . . 13.42[4][c]; 13.42[5][a]; 13.42[5][b]; 13.42[5][c]; 13.42[5][d]; 13.43[3][e]; 13.45[4][b]; 13.48[2][c]; **13** ns. 444, 449; 15.65[3]; 15.80[6]; **15** n.800
General Utils. & Operating Co. v. Helvering . . . . **2** n.111; **3** n.275; 8.20[2]; 8.20[3]; 8.20[4]; S8.20[4]; 8.21[1]; 8.21[2]; 8.21[3]; 8.21[4]; 8.22[2]; 8.41[2][g]; **8** ns. 311–314, 321, 332, 334, 384; 9.07[1][a]; 9.23[1]; 9.23[2][a]; 9.23[2][c]; **9** n.455; 10.05[1]; 10.05[2][c]; 10.05[3][a]; 10.05[5][a]; 10.05[5][c]; 10.05[6]; 10.06[1]; 10.07[1]; 10.07[2]; 10.20; 10.22[2]; 10.41[1]; 10.41[3]; 10.41[4]; 10.42[1][b]; 10.42[4]; 10.42[4][e]; 10.43[1]; 10.60; 10.62[1]; 10.66; **10** ns. 39, 84, 89, 139, 156, 357, 475, 609, 679, 681; 11.01[1][d]; 11.01[1][f]; 11.02[1]; 11.02[2]; 11.02[3]; 11.03[2]; 11.06[1]; 11.11[2][a]; 11.11[3][a]; 11.11[3][d]; 11.11[4]; **11** ns. 39, 76, 152, 270, 271, 314; 12.26[7]; 12.30[4][b]; 12.41[6]; 12.62[5]; 12.63[3][b]; **12** ns. 402, 719, 947, 961, 996; S13.42[5][c]; 14.45[1]; 14.47[6][b]; **14** n.372
Generes, US v. . . . . **2** n.172; 4.23[4]; **4** n.247
George, James M. v. CIR (5th Cir. 1988) . . . . **2** ns. 206, 209
George, James M. v. CIR (5th Cir. 1986) **2** n.209
George, William H. **12** n.210
George L. Riggs, Inc. . . . . . . **10** ns. 293, 304
Georgia-Pacific Corp. **4** n.145; **13** n.551
Georgia-Pacific Corp. v. US **12** n.729
Georgia R.R. & Banking Co., US v. **5** n.189; **8** n.256
Gerald D. Roberts Consultants, Inc. **7** n.231
Gerli & Co. . . . **5** n.311; **10** ns. 239, 242; **15** ns. 611, 621, 755, 791
Gershkowitz v. CIR **6** n.255
Giant Auto Parts, Ltd. **2** n.84
Gibson Prods. Co. **5** n.28
Gidwitz, Victor E., Family Trust . . . **8** n.273; **12** n.1179
Gilbert, Gilbert L. . . . . **8** ns. 245, 251
Gilbert v. CIR (2d Cir. 1977) **8** n.208
Gilbert v. CIR (2d Cir. 1957) . . . . 4.04[5]; **4** ns. 31, 58, 142, 159
Gilmore, Estate of, CIR v. **12** n.941
Gilmore, Merrill C. **8** n.282
Giovanini v. US **14** n.106
Gitlitz v. CIR (US) . . . . . **S3** ns. 294, 306; **S4** 306, 308.2; **S6** ns. 95, 144, 239, 240;

S12 ns. 558, 574–576, 578; **S13** ns. 658, 801
Gitlitz v. CIR (10th Cir.) . . . . . . **4** n.306; **S4** n.306; **6** ns. 239, 240, 267, 268, 310; **S6** ns. 239, 240; **12** ns. 552, 558, 559, 574, 581; **S12** ns. 552, 552.1, 558, 574, 576, 578, 581
Given v. CIR **1** n.52
Glacier State Elec. Supply Co. . . . . . **9** ns. 94, 219; **12** n.847
Gladstone Co. **15** n.247
Glaxo . . . . **S13** ns. 179.5, 217
Glen Raven Mills, Inc. **14** n.155
Glensder Textile Co. . . . . . . **2** ns. 35, 91, 96
Glickman v. CIR . . . . **10** ns. 699, 718
G.M. Trading Corp. **3** n.291
Golconda Mining Corp. v. CIR . . . . **7** ns. 25, 163
Golden v. CIR **8** n.83
Golden Nugget, Inc. . . . . **12** ns. 90, 370, 453, 480, 497
Gold Kist, Inc. . . . . . **8** ns. 14, 327, 328, 357, 359, 360; **10** ns. 201, 202
Goldstein v. CIR . . . . 5.10[6][e]; **8** n.202; **12** n.812; **13** ns. 250, 252
Goldstein, Estate of, CIR v. **10** n.73
Goldwyn, CIR v. **8** n.152
Golsen **9** n.214
Gooch, C.M., Lumber Sales Co.   **4** ns. 144, 147
Goodall, Estate of v. CIR . . . . **7** ns. 111, 171
Gooding v. US **3** n.219
Gooding Amusement Co. . . . 4.04[5]; **4** n.157
Gooding Amusement Co. v. CIR   4.04[5]; **4** ns. 142, 151, 158
Goodyear Tire & Rubber Co. v. US **15** n.331
Gordon v. CIR (US) **11** n.366
Gordon v. CIR (2d Cir.) . . . . **9** ns. 246, 291; **11** ns. 40, 201, 366; 12.41[4]; **12** ns. 511, 613, 635
Gordon, CIR v. . . . . **8** n.195; **11** ns. 40, 135, 367; **12** ns. 101, 848
Gordon Lubricating Co. **4** n.166
Gorton, E.W. **10** n.201
Gottesman & Co. **13** n.563
Gould, James O. . . . **2** n.172; **4** n.244; **5** n.84
Gowran, Helvering v. . . . . . . 8.40[1]; **8** n.412
GPD, Inc. v. CIR . . . **7** ns. 4, 56, 68, 144, 169, 180
Grabowski Trust **9** n.157
Gracey, CIR v. **3** n.248
Graham v. CIR . . . . **5** ns. 108, 118
Graham, George **12** n.823
Granite Trust Co. v. US **10** n.290
Gravois Planing Mill Co. v. CIR . . . **5** n.296; **10** n.238
Gray v. CIR **10** n.71
Gray, John D. **15** n.430
Great W. Power **12** n.462
Grede Foundries, Inc. v. US . . . . **12** ns. 251, 983
Green v. US . . . . **8** ns. 177, 192, 265

[Text references are to paragraphs; note references are to chapters (boldface numbers) and notes ("n."), and references to the supplement are preceded by "S."]

H

Hedberg-Freidheim Contracting Co. v. CIR
. . . . **7** ns. 24, 39, 146
Hedden v. CIR **12** n.54
Heger, John H. **4** n.273
Helgerson v. US **5** n.101
Heller, Walter S. **12** n.1078
Helvering, Commissioner of Internal Revenue
(CIR) . . . . *See* individual taxpayer
Helvering, Gregory v. . . . . 13.23[2]; **13** n.249
Heminway, Willard S. **8** n.256
Hempt Bros., Inc. v. US . . . . 3.17[2]; **3** n.350
Henderson, US v. **4** n.152
Hendler, US v. . . . 3.06[1]; 3.06[2]; **3** ns. 93,
94; 12.21[2][a]; 12.23[7]; 12.65[1]; **12**
ns. 39, 242, 1105
Hendricksen, Washmont Corp. v. . . . **7** n.237
Henry Beck Builders, Inc. **13** n.394
Henry C. Beck Co. . . . . **8** ns. 73, 95
Henry Schwartz Corp. **7** n.246
Henry, T.J., Assocs., Inc. . . . . . . **6** ns. 58, 74
Henry Van Hummell, Inc. v. CIR . . . . **7** ns.
43, 53, 76, 87
H. Enters. Int'l, Inc. v. CIR **5** n.208; **13**
ns. 272, 281, 825; **S13** ns. 647.2, 647.3
Herbert v. Riddell **10** n.684
Herbert, Elizabeth **15** n.126
Hercules Powder Co. v. US **3** n.252
Herculite Protective Fabrics Corp. v. CIR
. . . . **14** n.159
Hermes Consol., Inc. v. US **3** n.163; **13**
n.322; **14** ns. 128, 129, 187, 211
Hershey Foods Corp. . . . . . . **15** ns. 611, 621
Hershey Mfg. Co. v. CIR **5** n.252; **10**
n.225
Hersloff, Sigurd N. **2** n.200
Hersloff, Sigurd N. v. US **2** n.199
Herzog Miniature Lamp Works, Inc. v. CIR
. . . . **7** ns. 119, 158
Hewett, Walton O. . . . . **5** ns. 82, 161
Heyward, T.C., & Co. v. US . . . **7** ns. 32, 111
H. Group Holdings, Inc. . . . . . **13** ns. 144, 145,
146, 151
H.H. King Flour Mills Co. v. US **7** n.180
Hiawatha Home Builders, Inc. **13** n.36
Hickman, William P. **9** n.42
Hickock, Alan O. . . . . . . 12.27[6]; **12** ns. 478,
495–497
Higgins, De Guire v. **8** n.280
Higgins v. Smith . . . . 1.05[1][b]; **1** ns. 46, 50,
71; **3** n.312; 9.21[3]; **9** n.431; 13.23[2];
13 n.250
Higginson v. US **8** n.52
Hill, R.G. **4** n.282
Hill v. US **5** n.339
Hilldun Corp. v. CIR **7** n.215
Hillsboro Nat'l Bank v. CIR **3** n.362; **5**
n.51; **10** ns. 201, 202
Hillsborough Holdings Corp. v. US **5**
n.100
Hilton Hotels Corp., US v. . . . . 5.04[3];
5.04[5]; 5.06[1][a]; 5.06[2][c];
5.06[2][d]; **5** ns. 99, 104, 121, 124, 127,

239, 291; 10.07[3]; 12.66[5][a]; **12**
n.1180
Himmel v. CIR . . . . . 9.05[3][a]; 9.05[3][c];
9.05[3][d]; **9** ns. 155, 163
Hinds, Houck v. **3** n.316
Hitchins, F. Howard **6** n.107
Hitchon, Estate of **3** n.302
H.K. Porter Co. . . . **10** ns. 254, 276, 285; **S10**
n.267
Hoboken Land & Improvement Co. v. CIR
. . . . **12** n.181
Hochschild v. CIR **5** n.118
Hodgkins, Estate of **8** n.265
Hoey, National Investors Corp. v. **1** n.51
Hoffman, Alfred N. **9** n.32
Holdcroft Transp. Co. v. CIR . . . **3** n.236; **10**
n.437
Hollenbeck v. CIR **4** n.282
Hollywood Baseball Ass'n **3** n.274; **5**
n.252; **10** n.225
Holsey v. CIR **9** n.225
Holstein, George M. **3** n.24
Home Constr. Corp. v. US . . . . . **12** ns. 518,
525, 976
Homecrest Tract, US v. **2** n.64
Home Sav. & Loan Ass'n v. US . . . **12** ns. 52,
1188
Homes Beautiful, Inc. **5** n.93
Honbarrier, Archie L. . . . **S12** ns. 823, 8254,
832
Honeywell, Inc. . . . . . **4** ns. 413, 419, 436; **12**
n.426
Honigman v. CIR . . . . **8** ns. 192, 329
Hood, Lenward **S8** n.222
Hooper, C.E., Inc. v. US **7** n.90
Hoover v. US **15** n.561
Hopkins, Burk-Waggoner Oil Ass'n v. . . . . . .
. . . . 2.01[1]; **2** n.3
Horn, Louis G. III . . . **2** ns. 156, 173; **6** n.115
Hornby, Lynch v. . . . . **8** ns. 48, 66
Horne, Estate of **8** n.235
Horne v. CIR **4** n.254
Horst, Helvering v. . . . . 1.05[2][a]; **1** n.64;
3.17[2]; **3** n.345; **8** n.256
Horton Dairy, Inc. v. US **1** n.60
Hospital Corp. of Am. . . . . **1** n.84; **13** ns. 88,
96, 144, 170, 180; **15** ns. 59, 642, 757
Hospital Corp. of Am. v. CIR . . . . . **1** ns. 52,
65, 89; **3** n.49
Houck v. Hinds **3** n.316
House v. CIR **6** n.66
Houston Natural Gas Corp. **10** n.369
Houston Oil & Minerals Corp. **8** n.319
Houston Pipeline Co., US v. **5** n.127
Howard v. CIR . . . . . 12.44[1][d]; **12** ns. 181,
757
Howard, Charles B. v. US . . . . . **2** ns. 63, 64
Hoyt, Elton 2d **8** n.75
Huber Homes, Inc. . . . . **13** ns. 229, 256
Hudspeth v. CIR **6** n.99
Hudspeth v. US **10** n.33
Hughes, Inc. . . . . **7** ns. 59, 63, 70, 78, 85, 87,
93, 101, 130, 158, 160, 187

[Text references are to paragraphs; note references are to chapters (boldface numbers) and notes ("n."), and references to the supplement are preceded by "S."]

[Text references are to paragraphs; note references are to chapters (boldface numbers) and notes ("n."), and references to the supplement are preceded by "S."]

[Text references are to paragraphs; note references are to chapters (boldface numbers) and notes ("n."), and references to the supplement are preceded by "S."]

L

*[Text references are to paragraphs; note references are to chapters (boldface numbers)
and notes ("n."), and references to the supplement are preceded by "S."]*

M

[Text references are to paragraphs; note references are to chapters (boldface numbers) and notes ("n."), and references to the supplement are preceded by "S."]

[Text references are to paragraphs; note references are to chapters (boldface numbers) and notes ("n."), and references to the supplement are preceded by "S."]

[Text references are to paragraphs; note references are to chapters (boldface numbers) and notes ("n."), and references to the supplement are preceded by "S."]

[Text references are to paragraphs; note references are to chapters (boldface numbers) and notes ("n."), and references to the supplement are preceded by "S."]

O

Oakes, Alden B. 8 n.204
Oakland Hills Country Club . . . . . 3 ns. 268, 282
OBH, Inc. v. US 5 n.207; S13 n.647.3
O'Brien, Joseph L., Co. v. CIR 8 n.282
O'Brien, Pat . . . . . . 10 ns. 44, 189, 683, 684
O'Brion, Clarence R. 9 n.260
O'Bryan, Dennis M. 2 n.184
Ocean Drilling & Exploration Co. v. US . . . 1 n.85
Of Course, Inc. v. CIR 10 n.235
Offutt, CIR v. 13 n.282
Ogilvie v. CIR 4 n.210
Ogiony v. CIR 1 n.52
OKC Corp. 4 n.295; 6 n.234
Old Colony Trust Co. v. CIR . . . . 8.05[8]; 8 n.220; 10 n.626
Old Dominion Plywood Corp. 4 n.136
Old Va. Brick Co. v. CIR 6 n.15
Olin Corp. v. CIR 7 n.137
Ollendorff, Morton 10 n.81
Olmsted, Joseph . . . . 10 ns. 14, 19, 22
Olson, Sidney L. 11 n.226; S11 n.226
Olton Feed Yard, Inc. v. US 8 n.181
Oman Constr. Co. . . . . 7 ns. 87, 145
O'Mealia Research & Dev., Inc. . . . 14 n.137
Omholt, Ray E. . . . . 8 ns. 202, 391
O'Neal v. US 8 n.244
O'Neill, Hugh A. v. US 2 n.8
Opine Timber Co. 6 n.69
Oren v. CIR S6 n.111
Orr, William P. 3 n.130
O.S.C. Assocs. v. CIR 8 n.185; S8 n.185
Osenbach v. CIR 10 n.43
Osrow, Leonard . . . . 3 n.229; 12 ns. 788, 790
Osteopathic Med. Oncology & Hematology P.C. 15 n.59
Ostrom, C.A. 5 n.159
O'Sullivan Rubber Co. v. CIR 7 n.197
Oswald, Vincent E. . . . 5 ns. 143, 150; 8.05[2]; 8 n.180
OTM Corp. v. US . . . . . 13 ns. 101, 118, 277
Otto Candies, LLC v. US . . . . S7 ns. 59, 67, 76, 114, 145
Outlaw v. US 2 n.64
Overton v. CIR 8 n.256
Owen v. US 3 n.129
Owen, William F., Jr. v. CIR . . . . 3 ns. 119, 123
Owens v. CIR 1 n.57; 10 n.71
Owens Mach. Co. 8 n.328
Owensby & Kritikos, Inc. v. CIR . . . . 8 ns. 185, 189

P

P.A. Birren & Son v. CIR 3 n.233
Pabst Brewing Co. . . . . 9 ns. 204, 210
Pacific Coast Biscuit Co. . . . 5 n.161; 10 n.232

Pacific Coast Music Jobbers, Inc. v. CIR 8 n.291
Pacific Transp. Co. v. CIR . . . . 10 ns. 437, 595, 624; 14 n.51
Pacific Vegetable Oil Corp. v. CIR 9 n.13
Page v. CIR 10 n.235
Pahl v. CIR (9th Cir.) 6 n.12
Pahl v. CIR (TC) 8 n.180
PAL Int'l Corp. 5 n.26
Palmer v. CIR . . . 8.05[4]; 8 ns. 167, 168, 194
Palmer v. US 10 n.51
Palmer, Alden C. v. CIR 3 n.360
Panhandle E. Pipeline Co. v. US . . . 12 n.594
Paper Co. v. US 13 n.599
Paramount-Richards Theaters, Inc. v. CIR . . . . 8 ns. 174, 232
Parker, US v. 3 n.85
Parshelsky, Estate of v. CIR . . . . . 11 ns. 30, 236; 12.61[1]; 12 ns. 818, 819
Patten Fine Papers, Inc. v. CIR . . . 14 ns. 13, 48
Patterson, Ingalls v. 5 n.118
Patterson, Ingalls Iron Works v. 5 n.117
Patterson, Pizitz v. 8 n.416
Patterson, Henry T., Trust v. US . . . 9 ns. 74, 151, 168
Paulsen v. CIR . . . 4.03[2][j]; 4 ns. 41, 95; 12 ns. 52, 154, 613, 616; S12 n.163.4
Paymer v. CIR . . . . 1.05[1][b]; 1 n.53
Payne v. CIR . . . . 10 ns. 718, 724, 731, 733, 743
Peabody Hotel Co. 12 n.1112
Peacock v. CIR 8 n.198
Pebble Springs Distilling Co. v. CIR 12 n.826
Pechiney Ugine Kuhlmann Corp. . . . . 13 ns. 278, 282
Peck v. CIR . . . . . . 3 n.351; 13 ns. 147, 277
Peck, Donald A. (9th Cir. 1990) 13 n.147
Peerless Inv. Co. 10 n.256
Pelton Steel Casting Co. v. CIR . . . . 7 ns. 37, 146
Penfield, Davis v. . . . . 12 ns. 473, 496
Penn-Dixie Steel Corp. 3 n.207
Penn Needle Art Co. 7 n.145
Pennroad Corp. 5 n.119
Penn-Texas Corp. v. US 3 n.252
Penrod, Robert A. . . . . 12 ns. 71, 846
PEPI, Inc. 14 n.152
Peracchi, Donald 3 n.128; S3 n.123
Peracchi v. CIR . . . . 3 ns. 125, 126, 128
Perfection Foods, Inc. 13 n.36
Performance Sys., Inc. v. US . . . . 12 ns. 518, 525, 932
Perkin-Elmer Corp. . . . . . 13.21[8]; 13 ns. 180, 186, 188; 15 n.111
Perlman, Leo 3 n.306
Perma-Rock Prods., Inc. v. CIR 9 n.282
Perry, Thomas L. 8 n.285
Perry v. CIR 6 n.107
Perryman, Lawrence . . . . 3 ns. 357, 358, 369
Pescosolido, Carl A. . . . . 8 ns. 616, 632

[Text references are to paragraphs; note references are to chapters (boldface numbers) and notes ("n."), and references to the supplement are preceded by "S."]

[Text references are to paragraphs; note references are to chapters (boldface numbers) and notes ("n."), and references to the supplement are preceded by "S."]

S

[Text references are to paragraphs; note references are to chapters (boldface numbers) and notes ("n."), and references to the supplement are preceded by "S."]

Silco, Inc. v. US . . . . 5 ns. 186, 201; 8 n.268; 11 n.336

Silverman, Mose, Estate of . . . . 12 ns. 52, 1188

Silverstein v. US 6 n.111

Simmonds Precision Prods., Inc. . . . 3 n.273; 4 ns. 447–449; 12 n.728

Simon v. CIR 12 n.100; 13 n.256

Simon J. Murphy Co. v. CIR 1 n.92; 10 n.216

Simons-Eastern Co. v. US . . . 7 ns. 30, 74, 90, 103

Simpson, W.H.B. . . . . 3 ns. 111, 121

Sincoff, Jacob, Inc. v. CIR 7 n.134

Singleton v. CIR 8 n.168

Singleton (5th Cir. 1978) v. CIR . . . 13 n.318

Singleton, Jr., Marvin E. 13 n.346

Siple, J. Meredith 4 n.258

Six Seam Co. v. US 3 n.315

S.K. Ames, Inc. . . . . 9 ns. 225, 226

Skaggs Cos. 5 n.161

Skarda v. CIR 2 n.186

Skenandoa Rayon Corp. v. CIR . . . 12 n.391

Sleiman v. CIR 6 n.107

Slocomb, J.T., Co. v. CIR . . . 14 ns. 123, 160

Smalley, Eleanor H. 3 n.370

Smartt, Billie H. 4 n.245

Smith, Arthur C., Jr. 9 n.226

Smith-Bridgman & Co. 13 n.90

Smith, Charles A., Estate of . . . . 12 ns. 635, 753

Smith, David N. 9 n.29

Smith, Milton 12 n.216

Smith, Oddee . . . . 4 ns. 245, 247

Smith, R.M., Inc. v. CIR 10 n.633

Smith, Tempel 5 n.31

Smith, Higgins v. . . . . 1.05[1][b]; 1 ns. 46, 50, 71; 3 n.312; 9.21[3]; 9 n.431

Smith & Wiggins Gin, Inc. 2 n.184

Smith, Estate of v. CIR (3d Cir.) . . . 7 n.247; 8 n.259

Smith, Estate of v. CIR (5th Cir.) S4 n.299

Smith, Estate of v. CIR (8th Cir.) . . . 2 n.35

Smith, George F., Jr. 3 n.123

Smith, Jon P. 6 n.51

Smith, Philip K., US v. . . . . . . 8 ns. 171, 223

Smith, Raymond I., Inc. v. CIR . . . . 7 ns. 48, 134

Smokeless Fuel Co. 7 n.101

Smoot Sand & Gravel Corp. v. CIR (4th Cir. 1960) . . . . . 7 ns. 33, 65, 76, 82, 101

Smoot Sand & Gravel Corp. v. CIR (4th Cir. 1957) . . . 7 ns. 87, 115, 116, 123, 126

Smothers v. US . . . . . . 12 ns. 224, 345, 1082

Smyers, J. Paul . . . . 4 ns. 261, 282

Snap-Drape, Inc. v. CIR 5 n.354

Snider, US v. . . . . 14.23[2]; 14 n.15

Snite, CIR v. 9 n.423

Snively, H.B. . . . . 10 ns. 64, 65

Snow Mfg. Co. . . . . 7 ns. 48, 52, 69, 89, 95, 116, 187

Snyder, Elizabeth W. 8 n.542; 12 n.378

Snyder Bros. Co., US v. 4 n.44

Soeder v. US 2 n.185

Sol C. Siegel Prod., Inc. 10 n.192; 13 n.292

Sol Lessinger 13 n.229

Solow v. CIR 10 n.717

Sorem v. CIR . . . . 9 ns. 69, 74

South Atl. S.S. Line v. CIR 12 n.391

South Bay Corp. v. CIR . . . 12 ns. 202, 729

South Carolina v. Baker 1 n.5; 4 n.28; 8 n.81

Southeastern Canteen Co. v. CIR 13 n.277

Southern Bancorp. 8 n.358

Southern Bancorp., Inc. v. CIR 10 n.447

Southern Col. Sav. & Loan Ass'n . . . 13 ns. 305, 498

Southern Pac. Co. v. Edwards 3 n.297

South Lake Farms, Inc., CIR v. . . . 10 n.201

Southland Corp. v. Campbell . . . 14 ns. 141, 142

Southland Ice Co. . . . 12 ns. 221, 1117, 1125

South Tex. Lumber Co., CIR v. 8 n.137

South Tex. Rice Warehouse Co. v. CIR 13 n.83

South Tulsa Pathology Lab, Inc. . . . . S11 ns. 156, 179, 195

Southwest Consol. Corp., Helvering v. . . . . 3.03[2]; 3 n.65; 12.21[8]; 12.23[1]; 12.26[2]; 12.28[1]; 12.41[2]; 12.41[4]; 12.65[2][c]; 12 ns. 59, 89, 154, 157, 234, 245, 247, 338, 370, 502, 623, 634, 635, 1116; 14 n.336

Southwest Natural Gas Co. v. CIR . . . . 12.21[2][a]; 12.21[2][b]; 12 ns. 40, 106

Southwest Properties, Inc. 10 n.721

Spangler, Chester E. 11 n.32

Spangler v. CIR . . . . 10 ns. 732, 743

Sparks Farm, Inc. 2 n.208

Sparks Farm, Inc. v. CIR . . . . . . 1 ns. 48, 78

Sparks Nugget, Inc. v. CIR 8 n.246; 13 n.277

Spaulding Bakeries, Inc., CIR v. . . . . 10.21[2]; 10 ns. 276, 281; S10 n.267

Specialty Transport, Inc. S6 n.113

Spector v. CIR 1 n.71

Spencer, Bill L. . . . . 6 ns. 107, 111

Spencer, Maloney v. 4 n.246

Spermacet Whaling & Shipping Co., CIR v. 15 n.142

Spicer Accounting Inc. v. US 6 n.113

Spreckels 13 n.828

Sprint Corp. . . . . 10 n.444; 15 ns. 63, 80

Sproul Realty Co. 10 n.722

Sprouse, Helvering v. . . . 8.40[1]; 8 ns. 414, 415

Square D. Co. (7th Cir.) S13 n.289; S15 n.212

Square D Co. (TC) . . . . . 5 ns. 88, 128, 138, 143, 144, 165; S8 n.222; S13 ns. 273, 276

Squier, Arthur H., Estate of 9 n.49

[Text references are to paragraphs; note references are to chapters (boldface numbers) and notes ("n."), and references to the supplement are preceded by "S."]

[Text references are to paragraphs; note references are to chapters (boldface numbers) and notes ("n."), and references to the supplement are preceded by "S."]

Temple Square Mfg. Co. **14** n.160

Tennessee-Carolina Transp. Inc. v. CIR **10** n.198

Tennessee Life Ins. Co. v. Phinney **10** n.215

Tennessee Sec., Inc. v. CIR **8** n.222

Texaco, Inc. v. CIR **13** n.98

Texas Farm Bureau v. US . . . . **4** ns. 45, 160

Texasgulf, Inc. v. US (1999) **15** n.311

Texasgulf, Inc. v. US (1996) **15** n.311

Textron, Inc. . . . . **S15** ns. 494, 497

Textron, Inc. v. US . . . . . **4** n.250; **10** n.270; 14.43[3][c]; **14** ns. 52, 206, 406

TFI Cos. v. US . . . . **12** ns. 518, 976

The Limited, Inc. . . . . . . **15** ns. 538, 540, 542

Thibodaux, C.M., Co. v. CIR . . . . **8** ns. 170, 310

Third Nat'l Bank in Nashville v. US   **5** ns. 101, 306

Thomas, Calvin A. . . . . **10** ns. 704, 707

Thomas P. Byrnes, Inc. **7** n.229

Thompson, John D. **6** n.64

Thompson v. Campbell **3** n.108

Thompson v. US **8** n.145

Thompson Eng'g Co. v. CIR . . . **7** ns. 42, 63, 92, 104

320 E. 4th St. Corp. v. CIR **7** n.197

Tibbals v. US **10** n.718

TIFD III-E, Inc. v. US (Castle Harbour— GE) (2d Cir.) . . . . **S5** ns. 478, 479, 488

TIFD III-E, Inc. v. US (Castle Harbour— GE) (D. Conn.) . . . . . **S5** ns. 478, 479, 488, 573

Tilford v. CIR . . . . **3** ns. 281, 306

Title Guarantee & Trust Co., US v. . . . . **4** ns. 32, 61

T.J. Henry Assocs., Inc. . . . . **6** ns. 58, 74

Toledo Blade Co. **8** n.392

Tolzman, Alfred H. . . . . **4** ns. 242, 244, 247, 254

Tomerlin, James O. Trust **7** n.211; **15** n.62

Tomlinson, Tyler v. . . . . . **4** ns. 65, 140, 152

Tourtelot v. CIR **8** n.416

Tower Bldg. Corp. **12** n.419

Towne v. Eisner . . . . **8.40[1]**; **8** n.408

Towne Square, Inc. **4** n.163

Townshend v. US **4** n.243

Toyota Motor Sales, USA, Inc. **13** n.139

Transamerica Corp. v. US **10** n.444

Transamerica Corp., US v. **5** n.293; **10** n.238

Trent v. CIR **4** n.244

Trianon Hotel Co. **9** n.332

Tribune Co. . . . . **S12**.23[1]; **S12** n.163.3

Tribune Publishing Co. **13** n.29

Tribune Publishing Co. v. US . . . **12** ns. 745, 768, 1148, 1179; **S12** n.1179

Trico Prods. Corp. **7** n.30

Trico Prods. Corp. v. CIR . . . . . **7** ns. 25, 37

Trico Prods. Corp., Mahler v. **7** n.25

Trico Prods. Corp. v. McGowan **7** n.25

Trico Sec. Corp. **7** n.55

Tri-Lakes S.S. Co. v. CIR **10** n.260

Trinova Corp. . . . . **11** n.269; **S11** n.269; **12** ns. 844, 846, 851; **S12** ns. 844, 846, 851; **13** ns. 398, 567, 546, 617, 940; **15** ns. 106, 108

T.R. Miller Mill Co., CIR v. **8** n.392

Trotz, Harry **3** n.85

Truck Terminals, Inc. v. CIR . . . **3** n.232; **12** n.724

True v. US . . . . **12** ns. 843, 844, 851

Truesdell, James v. . . . . **8** ns. 242, 243

Truschel, W.H. . . . **12** ns. 92, 105, 615, 1122

TSN Liquidating Corp. v. US **8** n.287

Tufts, CIR v. . . . **3** n.119; **6**.10[3]; **6** n.255; **10** ns. 78, 99; **12** n.1111

Tulia Feedlot, Inc. v. US . . . . . **8** ns. 181, 218

Turnbow v. CIR . . . . **12**.44[1][d]; **12** ns. 157, 758

Turner Advertising of Ky., Inc. **12** n.322

Turner Broad. Sys., Inc. . . . **1** n.74; **3** n.85; **5** ns. 93, 94; **8** n.342; **9** ns. 192, 196, 204, 213, 429, 457; **12** n.844; **13** ns. 416, 417

Turner Constr. Co. v. US . . . **3** n.219; **12** ns. 322, 630

Tyler v. Tomlinson . . . . . **4** ns. 65, 140, 152

U

Underhill, Wingate E. **10** n.52

Underwood v. CIR **6** n.111

Uneco, Inc. v. US . . . . **4** ns. 145, 161

Ungar, J., Inc. v. CIR . . . **2** n.193; **10** n.192

Unger, Robert v. CIR . . . . . **15** ns. 127, 146, 151, 181

UnionBanCal Corp. **5** n.94; **S13** n.416

Union Oil Co. of Cal. **13** n.347

UnionbanCal Corp. . . . . **13** ns. 284, 416, 417

Union Pac. R.R. Co. v. CIR **5** n.165

Union Pac. R.R. Co. v. US **8** n.65

Uniroyal, Inc. . . . . . **8** n.287; **12** ns. 844, 847, 851

Unisys Corp. v. US **15** n.537

United Cancer Council, Inc. **8** n.190

United Contractors, Inc., CIR v. **13** n.394

United Dairy Farmers, Inc. v. US . . . **5** n.287

United Dominion Indus., Inc. v. CIR . . . **S13** ns. 370, 372, 516

United Dominion Indus., Inc. v. US . . . . **S13**.42[12][a]; **S13** n.574.5

United Gas Improvement Co. v. CIR **12** n.370

United Grocers, Ltd. v. US **3** n.291

United Mercantile Agencies **10** n.44

United Nat'l Corp. v. CIR **8** n.89

United States (US) . . . *See* specific party name

United States Padding Corp. **13** n.309; **15** n.244

United States Steel Corp. v. CIR . . . . **13** ns. 180, 124, 145

United States Steel Corp. v. US . . . **4** n.296; **6** ns. 283, 294; **12** ns. 455, 464, 484

[Text references are to paragraphs; note references are to chapters (boldface numbers) and notes ("n."), and references to the supplement are preceded by "S."]

Universal Castings Corp. **4** n.83
Universal Leaf Tobacco Co., CIR v. **8**
　　n.95; **10** n.259
Universal Mfg. Co. . . . . **8** ns. 190, 205
Upham, Samuel A. **9** n.259
UPS, Inc. v. Cir. . . . **1** ns. 65, 70, 78, 84, 89;
　　S1 ns. 65, 70, 78, 84, 89, 92, 488;
　　5.10[6][e]; 5.10[7][b]; **5** ns. 479, 480,
　　488, 491, 524; **S12** n.812; **13** ns. 97,
　　252; **S13** ns. 97, 250, 252; **15** n.482;
　　S15 n.482
Uri v. CIR **6** n.107
Uris, Estate of v. CIR **9** n.476
US General Bancshares Corp. **10** n.238
U.S. Gypsum v. US **5** n.304
U.S. Holding Co. **12** n.791
U.S. Shelter Corp. v. US . . . **14** ns. 150, 153–
　　155, 158
Utley v. CIR . . . . **3** ns. 265, 371

V

Vahlsing Christina Corp. **9** n.192
Van Cleave v. US **8** n.180
Van Dale Corp. **13** n.83
Van Heusden, Estate of v. CIR　　**10** ns. 707,
　　731
Van Hummell, Henry, Inc. v. CIR . . . . **7** ns.
　　43, 53, 76, 87
Van Keuren **5** n.161
Van Suetendael v. CIR **4** n.193
Vaughn, In re . . . . **4** ns. 256, 257
VCA Corp. v. US . . . . **12** n.1115; **14** ns. 91,
　　100
Velvet O'Donnell Corp. **13** n.456
Vermont Hydro-Electric Corp. **13** n.323
Versitron, Inc. v. US **6** n.73
Vesper Co. v. CIR **12** n.766
Vest, Earl **3** n.326
Veterans Found. v. CIR **3** n.302
Veterinary Servs. Corp. **S6** n.113
Veterinary Surgical Consultants, P.C. . . . **S6**
　　n.113
Vetco, Inc. . . . . **15** ns. 262, 527
VGS Corp. . . . . **14** ns. 150, 153
V. H. Monette & Co. **13** n.36
Victory Mkts., Inc. . . . . **5** ns. 115, 259
Viereck v. US . . . . **9** n.270; **12** ns. 774, 1082
Vinnell, Allan S. **8** n.391
Virginia Nat'l Bank v. CIR **5** n.53
Virginia State Lottery, International Lotto
　　Fund v. **15** n.174
Vogel Fertilizer Co., US v.　　**9** n.361; **13** ns.
　　15, 25, 34
VSC, PC **S8** n.190
Vulcan Materials Co. v. US **5** n.253; **14**
　　n.120
Vulcan Materials Co. **15** n.327
Vulcan Steam Forging Co. **7** n.121
Vuono-Lione, Inc. . . . . . **7** ns. 42, 59, 87, 104

W

Wachner, Linda **10** n.28
W.A. Drake, Inc. v. CIR **5** n.93; **9** n.429
WAGE, Inc. **14** n.151
Wagner, William . . . .**5** ns. 101, 104, 155
Wagner Elec. Co. v. US **4** n.145
Walker v. CIR (7th Cir.) **8** n.201
Walker v. CIR (9th Cir.) **8** n.283
Wall v. US　　9.06[6]; **9** ns. 20, 214, 215, 218,
　　228; **S9** n.214
Wallace, Gerald, Estate of . . . **8** ns. 183, 190
Wallace v. US **10** n.25
Walt Disney, Inc. . . . **12** ns. 844, 851, 874; **13**
　　ns. 398, 567
Walt Disney Productions v. US **15** n.163
Wanamaker, John Rodman, Trustee, CIR v.
　　. **9** n.332
Ward v. US **6** n.42
Waring, Fred M. v. CIR . . . . . **10** ns. 44, 53
Warren v. CIR **10** n.51
Warren, William K. v. US **10** n.53
Warren Jones Co. v. CIR **10** n.52
Warsaw Photographic Assocs., Inc. . . . **5** ns.
　　237, 245; **12** ns. 45, 339, 1081
Washburne, Elihu B. **3** n.45
Washburn, Helvering v. **2** n.77
Washington Athletic Club v. US **3** n.282
Washmont Corp. v. Hendricksen . . . **7** n.237
Waterman S.S. Corp. v. CIR . . . . 8.07[2][a];
　　8.07[2][b]; **8** ns. 285–287; **9** n.13
Water-Pure Sys., Inc. **S6** n.113
Water Resource Control **2** n.67
Watts, Helvering v.
　　. . . . . 12.21[6]; **12** ns. 38, 79
Waxenberg, Maynard **15** n.311
Webb, David R., Co. v. CIR . . . . **10** ns. 595,
　　624
Webb, Helen M. **9** n.350
Webb, William C. **8** n.144
Webbe, Peter J. **5** n.122
Webber, Estate of v. US **9** n.53
Webster, Estate of, CIR v. **12** n.941
Weddle v. CIR **4** n.244
W.E. Gabriel Fabrication Co. **11** n.142
Weidenhoff, Joseph, Inc. . . . . . **14** ns. 25, 405
Weigl, Louis A. . . . . **8** ns. 197, 370
Weikel, Maurice . . . **3** ns. 326, 370; **12** n.207
Weil v. CIR **10** n.701
Weil, Lawrence M., Estate of **4** n.246
Weinberg, Adolph **3** n.347
Weir v. CIR **8** n.241
Weis, Thomas J. **4** n.384
Weiskopf, Edwin C., Estate of . . . **15** ns. 495,
　　566
Weiskopf, Estate of (2d Cir.) **10** n.71
Weiskopf, Estate of (TC) **9** n.53
Weiss, Joseph J. **10** n.52
Wekesser, Robert A. **8** n.260
Welch v. Helvering **5** n.111
Welch, Schaefer v. **10** n.25

[Text references are to paragraphs; note references are to chapters (boldface numbers) and notes ("n."), and references to the supplement are preceded by "S."]

[Text references are to paragraphs; note references are to chapters (boldface numbers) and notes ("n."), and references to the supplement are preceded by "S."]

Cumulative Index

*[References are to paragraphs;
references to the supplement are preceded by "S."]*

Legislative issues — Cont'd